Collins
World Atlas

Title	Scale	Page
Map Symbols and Time Zones		2
National Statistics		3–5

World

World Countries		6–7
World Landscapes		8–9

Europe

Northern Europe	1:10 000 000	10–11
Western Russian Federation	1:7.5 000 000	12–13
Scandinavia and the Baltic States	1:5 000 000	14–15
Inset: Iceland	1:6 000 000	
Inset: Faroe Islands	1:5 000 000	
Northwest Europe	1:5 000 000	16–17
England and Wales	1:2 000 000	18–19
Scotland	1:2 000 000	20
Inset: Shetland Islands	1:2 000 000	
Ireland	1:2 000 000	21
Southern Europe and the Mediterranean	1:10 000 000	22–23
France	1:5 000 000	24
Spain and Portugal	1:5 000 000	25
Italy and the Balkans	1:5 000 000	26–27

Asia

Northern Asia	1:20 000 000	28–29
Central and Southern Asia	1:20 000 000	30–31
Southwest Asia	1:13 000 000	32–33
Eastern Mediterranean, the Caucasus and Iraq	1:7 000 000	34–35
Northern India, Nepal, Bhutan and Bangladesh	1:7 000 000	36–37
Southern India and Sri Lanka	1:7 000 000	38
Middle East	1:3 000 000	39
Eastern and Southeast Asia	1:20 000 000	40–41
Eastern Asia	1:15 000 000	42–43
Japan, North Korea and South Korea	1:7 000 000	44–45

Africa

Northern Africa	1:16 000 000	46–47
Inset: Cape Verde	1:16 000 000	
Central and Southern Africa	1:16 000 000	48–49
Republic of South Africa	1:5 000 000	50–51

Oceania

Australia, New Zealand and Southwest Pacific	1:20 000 000	52–53
Western Australia	1:8 000 000	54–55
Eastern Australia	1:8 000 000	56–57
Inset: Tasmania	1:8 000 000	
Southeast Australia	1:5 000 000	58
New Zealand	1:5 250 000	59

North America

Canada	1:16 000 000	60–61
United States of America	1:12 000 000	62–63
Inset: Hawaii	1:12 000 000	
Northeast United States	1:3 500 000	64
Southwest United States	1:3 500 000	65
Central America and the Caribbean	1:14 000 000	66–67

South America

Northern South America	1:14 000 000	68–69
Inset: Galapagos Islands	1:14 000 000	
Southern South America	1:14 000 000	70
Southeast Brazil	1:7 000 000	71

Oceans and Poles

Atlantic Ocean, Indian Ocean	1:50 000 000	72–73
Pacific Ocean	1:50 000 000	74–75
Antarctica	1:26 000 000	76
The Arctic	1:26 000 000	77

Index		78–127

Collins

Settlements

Population	National capital	Administrative capital	Other city or town
over 10 million	**BEIJING** ⊛	**Karachi** ◉	**New York** ◉
5 million to 10 million	**JAKARTA** ✪	**Tianjin** ◉	**Nova Iguaçu** ◉
1 million to 5 million	**KĀBUL** ✪	**Sydney** ◉	**Kaohsiung** ◉
500 000 to 1 million	**BANGUI** ✪	**Trujillo** ◎	**Jeddah** ◎
100 000 to 500 000	WELLINGTON ✪	Mansa ◎	Apucarana ◎
50 000 to 100 000	PORT OF SPAIN ✪	Potenza ◎	Arecibo ◎
10 000 to 50 000	MALABO ✿	Chinhoyi ◦	Ceres ◦
under 10 000	VALLETTA ✿	Ati ◦	Venta ◦

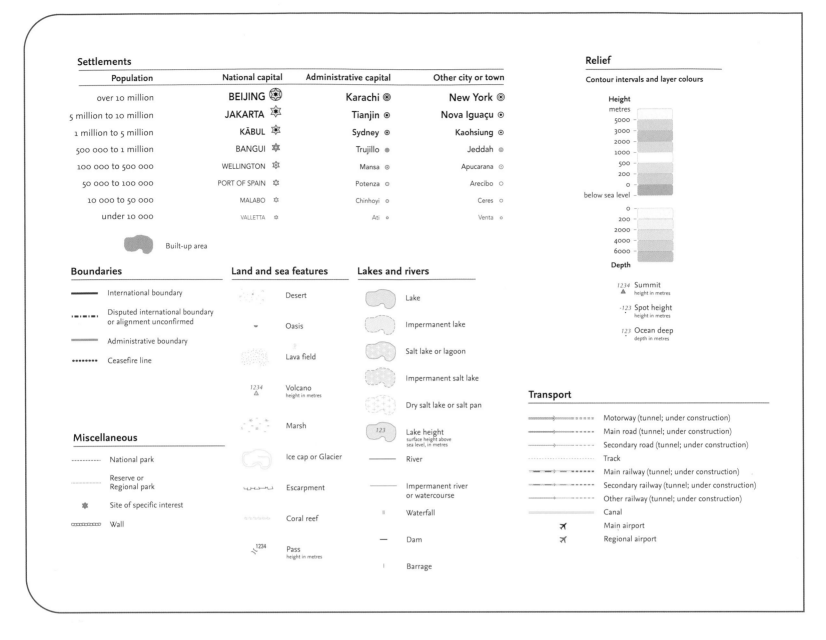

Built-up area

Boundaries

——	International boundary
─·─·─	Disputed international boundary or alignment unconfirmed
——	Administrative boundary
········	Ceasefire line

Miscellaneous

----------	National park
············	Reserve or Regional park
✸	Site of specific interest
⬡⬡⬡⬡	Wall

Land and sea features

⛱	Desert
⬮	Oasis
⣿	Lava field
1234 △	Volcano height in metres
⣿	Marsh
⬭	Ice cap or Glacier
⤳	Escarpment
⣿	Coral reef
)(1234	Pass height in metres

Lakes and rivers

⬬	Lake
⬬	Impermanent lake
⬬	Salt lake or lagoon
⬬	Impermanent salt lake
⬬	Dry salt lake or salt pan
123	Lake height surface height above sea level, in metres
——	River
——	Impermanent river or watercourse
‖	Waterfall
—	Dam
¦	Barrage

Transport

⟶ ----	Motorway (tunnel; under construction)
⟶ ----	Main road (tunnel; under construction)
⟶ ----	Secondary road (tunnel; under construction)
········	Track
┼┼┼ ----	Main railway (tunnel; under construction)
┼┼┼ ----	Secondary railway (tunnel; under construction)
┼┼┼ ----	Other railway (tunnel; under construction)
——	Canal
✈	Main airport
✈	Regional airport

Relief

Contour intervals and layer colours

Height
metres
5000
3000
2000
1000
500
200
0
below sea level
0
200
2000
4000
6000
Depth

1234 Summit height in metres

-123 Spot height height in metres

123 Ocean deep depth in metres

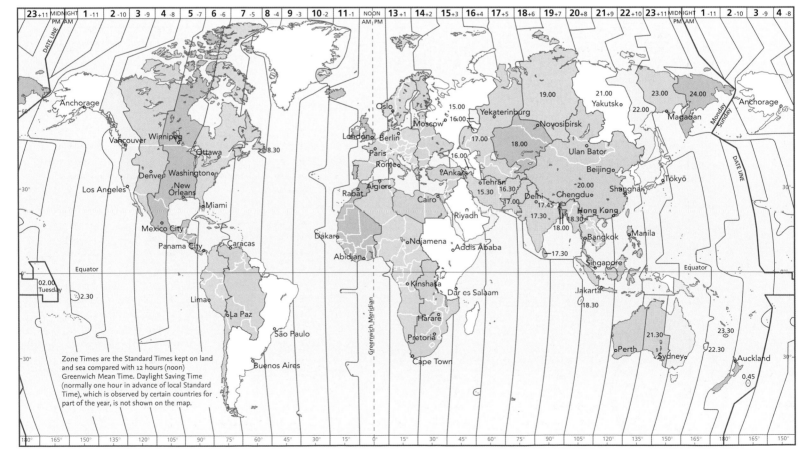

Zone Times are the Standard Times kept on land and sea compared with 12 hours (noon) Greenwich Mean Time. Daylight Saving Time (normally one hour in advance of local Standard Time), which is observed by certain countries for part of the year, is not shown on the map.

Map Symbols and Time Zones

Europe

Europe		Area sq km	Area sq miles	Population	Capital	Languages	Religions	Currency	Internet link
ALBANIA		28 748	11 100	3 130 000	Tirana	Albanian, Greek	Sunni Muslim, Albanian Orthodox, Roman Catholic	Lek	www.km.gov.al
ANDORRA		465	180	67 000	Andorra la Vella	Spanish, Catalan, French	Roman Catholic	Euro	www.andorra.ad
AUSTRIA		83 855	32 377	8 189 000	Vienna	German, Croatian, Turkish	Roman Catholic, Protestant	Euro	www.oesterreich.at
BELARUS		207 600	80 155	9 755 000	Minsk	Belorussian, Russian	Belorussian Orthodox, Roman Catholic	Belarus rouble	www.government.by
BELGIUM		30 520	11 784	10 419 000	Brussels	Dutch (Flemish), French (Walloon), German	Roman Catholic, Protestant	Euro	www.belgium.be
BOSNIA-HERZEGOVINA		51 130	19 741	3 907 000	Sarajevo	Bosnian, Serbian, Croatian	Sunni Muslim, Serbian Orthodox, Roman Catholic, Protestant	Marka	www.fbihvlada.gov.ba
BULGARIA		110 994	42 855	7 726 000	Sofia	Bulgarian, Turkish, Romany, Macedonian	Bulgarian Orthodox, Sunni Muslim	Lev	www.government.bg
CROATIA		56 538	21 829	4 551 000	Zagreb	Croatian, Serbian	Roman Catholic, Serbian Orthodox, Sunni Muslim	Kuna	www.vlada.hr
CZECH REPUBLIC		78 864	30 450	10 220 000	Prague	Czech, Moravian, Slovak	Roman Catholic, Protestant	Czech koruna	www.czechcentrum.cz
DENMARK		43 075	16 631	5 431 000	Copenhagen	Danish	Protestant	Danish krone	www.denmark.dk
ESTONIA		45 200	17 452	1 330 000	Tallinn	Estonian, Russian	Protestant, Estonian and Russian Orthodox	Kroon	www.valitsus.ee
FINLAND		338 145	130 559	5 249 000	Helsinki	Finnish, Swedish	Protestant, Greek Orthodox	Euro	www.valtioneuvosto.fi
FRANCE		543 965	210 026	60 496 000	Paris	French, Arabic	Roman Catholic, Protestant, Sunni Muslim	Euro	www.premier-ministre.gouv.fr
GERMANY		357 022	137 849	82 689 000	Berlin	German, Turkish	Protestant, Roman Catholic	Euro	www.bundesregierung.de
GREECE		131 957	50 949	11 120 000	Athens	Greek	Greek Orthodox, Sunni Muslim	Euro	www.greece.gov.gr
HUNGARY		93 030	35 919	10 098 000	Budapest	Hungarian	Roman Catholic, Protestant	Forint	www.magyarorszag.hu
ICELAND		102 820	39 699	295 000	Reykjavík	Icelandic	Protestant	Icelandic króna	www.iceland.is
IRELAND		70 282	27 136	4 148 000	Dublin	English, Irish	Roman Catholic, Protestant	Euro	www.irlgov.ie
ITALY		301 245	116 311	58 093 000	Rome	Italian	Roman Catholic	Euro	www.governo.it
LATVIA		63 700	24 595	2 307 000	Rīga	Latvian, Russian	Protestant, Roman Catholic, Russian Orthodox	Lats	www.saeima.lv
LIECHTENSTEIN		160	62	35 000	Vaduz	German	Roman Catholic, Protestant	Swiss franc	www.liechtenstein.li
LITHUANIA		65 200	25 174	3 431 000	Vilnius	Lithuanian, Russian, Polish	Roman Catholic, Protestant, Russian Orthodox	Litas	www.lrv.lt
LUXEMBOURG		2 586	998	465 000	Luxembourg	Letzeburgish, German, French	Roman Catholic	Euro	www.gouvernement.lu
MACEDONIA (F.Y.R.O.M.)		25 713	9 928	2 034 000	Skopje	Macedonian, Albanian, Turkish	Macedonian Orthodox, Sunni Muslim	Macedonian denar	www.vlada.mk
MALTA		316	122	402 000	Valletta	Maltese, English	Roman Catholic	Maltese lira	www.gov.mt
MOLDOVA		33 700	13 012	4 206 000	Chişinău	Romanian, Ukrainian, Gagauz, Russian	Romanian Orthodox, Russian Orthodox	Moldovan leu	www.moldova.md
MONACO		2	1	35 000	Monaco-Ville	French, Monegasque, Italian	Roman Catholic	Euro	www.monaco.gouv.mc
MONTENEGRO		13 812	5 333	620 145	Podgorica	Serbian (Montenegrin), Albanian	Montenegrin Orthodox, Sunni Muslim	Euro	www.montenegro.yu
NETHERLANDS		41 526	16 033	16 299 000	Amsterdam/The Hague	Dutch, Frisian	Roman Catholic, Protestant, Sunni Muslim	Euro	www.overheid.nl
NORWAY		323 878	125 050	4 620 000	Oslo	Norwegian	Protestant, Roman Catholic	Norwegian krone	www.norway.no
POLAND		312 683	120 728	38 530 000	Warsaw	Polish, German	Roman Catholic, Polish Orthodox	Złoty	www.poland.gov.pl
PORTUGAL		88 940	34 340	10 495 000	Lisbon	Portuguese	Roman Catholic, Protestant	Euro	www.portugal.gov.pt
ROMANIA		237 500	91 699	21 711 000	Bucharest	Romanian, Hungarian	Romanian Orthodox, Protestant, Roman Catholic	Romanian leu	www.guv.ro
RUSSIAN FEDERATION		17 075 400	6 592 849	143 202 000	Moscow	Russian, Tatar, Ukrainian, local languages	Russian Orthodox, Sunni Muslim, Protestant	Russian rouble	www.gov.ru
SAN MARINO		61	24	28 000	San Marino	Italian	Roman Catholic	Euro	www.consigliograndeegenerale.sm
SERBIA		88 361	34 116	9 379 000	Belgrade	Serbian, Albanian, Hungarian	Serbian Orthodox, Sunni Muslim	Serbian dinar, Euro	www.srbija.sr.gov.yu
SLOVAKIA		49 035	18 933	5 401 000	Bratislava	Slovak, Hungarian, Czech	Roman Catholic, Protestant, Orthodox	Slovakian koruna	www.government.gov.sk
SLOVENIA		20 251	7 819	1 967 000	Ljubljana	Slovene, Croatian, Serbian	Roman Catholic, Protestant	Tólar	www.sigov.si
SPAIN		504 782	194 897	43 064 000	Madrid	Castilian, Catalan, Galician, Basque	Roman Catholic	Euro	www.la-moncloa.es
SWEDEN		449 964	173 732	9 041 000	Stockholm	Swedish	Protestant, Roman Catholic	Swedish krona	www.sweden.se
SWITZERLAND		41 293	15 943	7 252 000	Bern	German, French, Italian, Romansch	Roman Catholic, Protestant	Swiss franc	www.admin.ch
UKRAINE		603 700	233 090	46 481 000	Kiev	Ukrainian, Russian	Ukrainian Orthodox, Ukrainian Catholic, Roman Catholic	Hryvnia	www.kmu.gov.ua
UNITED KINGDOM		243 609	94 058	59 668 000	London	English, Welsh, Gaelic	Protestant, Roman Catholic, Muslim	Pound sterling	www.direct.gov.uk
VATICAN CITY		0.5	0.2	552	Vatican City	Italian	Roman Catholic	Euro	www.vatican.va

Asia

Asia		Area sq km	Area sq miles	Population	Capital	Languages	Religions	Currency	Internet link
AFGHANISTAN		652 225	251 825	29 863 000	Kābul	Dari, Pushtu, Uzbek, Turkmen	Sunni Muslim, Shi'a Muslim	Afghani	www.afghanistan-mfa.net
ARMENIA		29 800	11 506	3 016 000	Yerevan	Armenian, Azeri	Armenian Orthodox	Dram	www.gov.am
AZERBAIJAN		86 600	33 436	8 411 000	Baku	Azeri, Armenian, Russian, Lezgian	Shi'a Muslim, Sunni Muslim, Russian and Armenian Orthodox	Azerbaijani manat	www.president.az
BAHRAIN		691	267	727 000	Manama	Arabic, English	Shi'a Muslim, Sunni Muslim, Christian	Bahrain dinar	www.bahrain.gov.bh
BANGLADESH		143 998	55 598	141 822 000	Dhaka	Bengali, English	Sunni Muslim, Hindu	Taka	www.bangladesh.gov.bd
BHUTAN		46 620	18 000	2 163 000	Thimphu	Dzongkha, Nepali, Assamese	Buddhist, Hindu	Ngultrum, Indian rupee	www.bhutan.gov.bt
BRUNEI		5 765	2 226	374 000	Bandar Seri Begawan	Malay, English, Chinese	Sunni Muslim, Buddhist, Christian	Brunei dollar	www.brunei.gov.bn
CAMBODIA		181 035	69 884	14 071 000	Phnom Penh	Khmer, Vietnamese	Buddhist, Roman Catholic, Sunni Muslim	Riel	www.cambodia.gov.kh
CHINA		9 584 492	3 700 593	1 323 345 000	Beijing	Mandarin, Wu, Cantonese, Hsiang, regional languages	Confucian, Taoist, Buddhist, Christian, Sunni Muslim	Yuan, HK dollar*, Macao pataca	www.china.org.cn
CYPRUS		9 251	3 572	835 000	Nicosia	Greek, Turkish, English	Greek Orthodox, Sunni Muslim	Cyprus pound	www.cyprus.gov.cy
EAST TIMOR		14 874	5 743	947 000	Dili	Portuguese, Tetun, English	Roman Catholic	United States dollar	www.timor-leste.gov.tl
GEORGIA		69 700	26 911	4 474 000	T'bilisi	Georgian, Russian, Armenian, Azeri, Ossetian, Abkhaz	Georgian Orthodox, Russian Orthodox, Sunni Muslim	Lari	www.parliament.ge
INDIA		3 064 898	1 183 364	1 103 371 000	New Delhi	Hindi, English, many regional languages	Hindu, Sunni Muslim, Shi'a Muslim, Sikh, Christian	Indian rupee	www.india.gov.in
INDONESIA		1 919 445	741 102	222 781 000	Jakarta	Indonesian, local languages	Sunni Muslim, Protestant, Roman Catholic, Hindu, Buddhist	Rupiah	www.indonesia.go.id
IRAN		1 648 000	636 296	69 515 000	Tehrān	Farsi, Azeri, Kurdish, regional languages	Shi'a Muslim, Sunni Muslim	Iranian rial	www.president.ir
IRAQ		438 317	169 235	28 807 000	Baghdād	Arabic, Kurdish, Turkmen	Shi'a Muslim, Sunni Muslim, Christian	Iraqi dinar	www.iraqigovernment.org
ISRAEL		20 770	8 019	6 725 000	Jerusalem (Yerushalayim) (El Quds)**	Hebrew, Arabic	Jewish, Sunni Muslim, Christian, Druze	Shekel	www.gov.il
JAPAN		377 727	145 841	128 085 000	Tōkyō	Japanese	Shintoist, Buddhist, Christian	Yen	web-japan.org
JORDAN		89 206	34 443	5 703 000	'Ammān	Arabic	Sunni Muslim, Christian	Jordanian dinar	www.jordan.jo
KAZAKHSTAN		2 717 300	1 049 155	14 825 000	Astana	Kazakh, Russian, Ukrainian, German, Uzbek, Tatar	Sunni Muslim, Russian Orthodox, Protestant	Tenge	www.government.kz
KUWAIT		17 818	6 880	2 687 000	Kuwait	Arabic	Sunni Muslim, Shi'a Muslim, Christian, Hindu	Kuwaiti dinar	www.e.gov.kw
KYRGYZSTAN		198 500	76 641	5 264 000	Bishkek	Kyrgyz, Russian, Uzbek	Sunni Muslim, Russian Orthodox	Kyrgyz som	www.gov.kg
LAOS		236 800	91 429	5 924 000	Vientiane	Lao, local languages	Buddhist, traditional beliefs	Kip	www.un.int/lao
LEBANON		10 452	4 036	3 577 000	Beirut	Arabic, Armenian, French	Shi'a Muslim, Sunni Muslim, Christian	Lebanese pound	www.presidency.gov.lb
MALAYSIA		332 965	128 559	25 347 000	Kuala Lumpur/Putrajaya	Malay, English, Chinese, Tamil, local languages	Sunni Muslim, Buddhist, Hindu, Christian, traditional beliefs	Ringgit	www.gov.my
MALDIVES		298	115	329 000	Male	Divehi (Maldivian)	Sunni Muslim	Rufiyaa	www.maldivesinfo.gov.mv

**De facto capital. Disputed   *Hong Kong dollar

National Statistics   3

Asia continued

		Area sq km	Area sq miles	Population	Capital	Languages	Religions	Currency	Internet link
MONGOLIA		1 565 000	604 250	2 646 000	Ulan Bator	Khalka (Mongolian), Kazakh, local languages	Buddhist, Sunni Muslim	Tugrik (tögrög)	www.pmis.gov.mn
MYANMAR (BURMA)		676 577	261 228	50 519 000	Rangoon/Naypyidaw	Burmese, Shan, Karen, local languages	Buddhist, Christian, Sunni Muslim	Kyat	www.myanmar.com
NEPAL		147 181	56 827	27 133 000	Kathmandu	Nepali, Maithili, Bhojpuri, English, local languages	Hindu, Buddhist, Sunni Muslim	Nepalese rupee	www.nepalhmg.gov.np
NORTH KOREA		120 538	46 540	22 488 000	P'yŏngyang	Korean	Traditional beliefs, Chondoist, Buddhist	North Korean won	www.korea-dpr.com
OMAN		309 500	119 499	2 567 000	Muscat	Arabic, Baluchi, Indian languages	Ibadhi Muslim, Sunni Muslim	Omani riyal	www.omanet.om
PAKISTAN		803 940	310 403	157 935 000	Islamabad	Urdu, Punjabi, Sindhi, Pushtu, English	Sunni Muslim, Shi'a Muslim, Christian, Hindu	Pakistani rupee	www.infopak.gov.pk
PALAU		497	192	20 000	Melekeok	Palauan, English	Roman Catholic, Protestant, traditional beliefs	United States dollar	www.palauembassy.sc
PHILIPPINES		300 000	115 831	83 054 000	Manila	English, Pilipino, Cebuano, local languages	Roman Catholic, Protestant, Sunni Muslim, Aglipayan	Philippine peso	www.gov.ph
QATAR		11 437	4 416	813 000	Doha	Arabic	Sunni Muslim	Qatari riyal	www.mofa.gov.qa
RUSSIAN FEDERATION		17 075 400	6 592 849	143 202 000	Moscow	Russian, Tatar, Ukrainian, local languages	Russian Orthodox, Sunni Muslim, Protestant	Russian rouble	www.gov.ru
SAUDI ARABIA		2 200 000	849 425	24 573 000	Riyadh	Arabic	Sunni Muslim, Shi'a Muslim	Saudi Arabian riyal	www.saudinf.com
SINGAPORE		639	247	4 326 000	Singapore	Chinese, English, Malay, Tamil	Buddhist, Taoist, Sunni Muslim, Christian, Hindu	Singapore dollar	www.gov.sg
SOUTH KOREA		99 274	38 330	47 817 000	Seoul	Korean	Buddhist, Protestant, Roman Catholic	South Korean won	www.korea.net
SRI LANKA		65 610	25 332	20 743 000	Sri Jayewardenepura Kotte	Sinhalese, Tamil, English	Buddhist, Hindu, Sunni Muslim, Roman Catholic	Sri Lankan rupee	www.priu.gov.lk
SYRIA		185 180	71 498	19 043 000	Damascus	Arabic, Kurdish, Armenian	Sunni Muslim, Shi'a Muslim, Christian	Syrian pound	www.moi-syria.com
TAIWAN		36 179	13 969	22 858 000	T'aipei	Mandarin, Min, Hakka, local languages	Buddhist, Taoist, Confucian, Christian	Taiwan dollar	www.gov.tw
TAJIKISTAN		143 100	55 251	6 507 000	Dushanbe	Tajik, Uzbek, Russian	Sunni Muslim	Somoni	www.tjus.org
THAILAND		513 115	198 115	64 233 000	Bangkok	Thai, Lao, Chinese, Malay, Mon-Khmer languages	Buddhist, Sunni Muslim	Baht	www.thaigov.go.th
TURKEY		779 452	300 948	73 193 000	Ankara	Turkish, Kurdish	Sunni Muslim, Shi'a Muslim	Turkish lira	www.mfa.gov.tr
TURKMENISTAN		488 100	188 456	4 833 000	Aşgabat	Turkmen, Uzbek, Russian	Sunni Muslim, Russian Orthodox	Turkmen manat	www.turkmenistanembassy.org
UNITED ARAB EMIRATES		77 700	30 000	4 496 000	Abu Dhabi	Arabic, English	Sunni Muslim, Shi'a Muslim	United Arab Emirates dirham	www.uae.gov.ae
UZBEKISTAN		447 400	172 742	26 593 000	Toshkent	Uzbek, Russian, Tajik, Kazakh	Sunni Muslim, Russian Orthodox	Uzbek som	www.gov.uz
VIETNAM		329 565	127 246	84 238 000	Ha Nôi	Vietnamese, Thai, Khmer, Chinese, local languages	Buddhist, Taoist, Roman Catholic, Cao Dai, Hoa Hao	Dong	www.na.gov.vn
YEMEN		527 968	203 850	20 975 000	Şan'ā'	Arabic	Sunni Muslim, Shi'a Muslim	Yemeni rial	www.nic.gov.ye

Africa

		Area sq km	Area sq miles	Population	Capital	Languages	Religions	Currency	Internet link
ALGERIA		2 381 741	919 595	32 854 000	Algiers	Arabic, French, Berber	Sunni Muslim	Algerian dinar	www.el-mouradia.dz
ANGOLA		1 246 700	481 354	15 941 000	Luanda	Portuguese, Bantu, local languages	Roman Catholic, Protestant, traditional beliefs	Kwanza	www.angola.org
BENIN		112 620	43 483	8 439 000	Porto-Novo	French, Fon, Yoruba, Adja, local languages	Traditional beliefs, Roman Catholic, Sunni Muslim	CFA franc*	www.gouv.bj/en/index.php
BOTSWANA		581 370	224 468	1 765 000	Gaborone	English, Setswana, Shona, local languages	Traditional beliefs, Protestant, Roman Catholic	Pula	www.gov.bw
BURKINA		274 200	105 869	13 228 000	Ouagadougou	French, Moore (Mossi), Fulani, local languages	Sunni Muslim, traditional beliefs, Roman Catholic	CFA franc*	www.primature.gov.bf
BURUNDI		27 835	10 747	7 548 000	Bujumbura	Kirundi (Hutu, Tutsi), French	Roman Catholic, traditional beliefs, Protestant	Burundian franc	www.burundi.gov.bi
CAMEROON		475 442	183 569	16 322 000	Yaoundé	French, English, Fang, Bamileke, local languages	Roman Catholic, traditional beliefs, Sunni Muslim, Protestant	CFA franc*	www.spm.gov.cm
CAPE VERDE		4 033	1 557	507 000	Praia	Portuguese, creole	Roman Catholic, Protestant	Cape Verde escudo	www.governo.cv
CENTRAL AFRICAN REPUBLIC		622 436	240 324	4 038 000	Bangui	French, Sango, Banda, Baya, local languages	Protestant, Roman Catholic, traditional beliefs, Sunni Muslim	CFA franc*	www.rca-gouv.org
CHAD		1 284 000	495 755	9 749 000	Ndjamena	Arabic, French, Sara, local languages	Sunni Muslim, Roman Catholic, Protestant, traditional beliefs	CFA franc*	www.primature-tchad.org
COMOROS		1 862	719	798 000	Moroni	Comorian, French, Arabic	Sunni Muslim, Roman Catholic	Comoros franc	www.beit-salam.km
CONGO		342 000	132 047	3 999 000	Brazzaville	French, Kongo, Monokutuba, local languages	Roman Catholic, Protestant, traditional beliefs, Sunni Muslim	CFA franc*	www.congo-site.com
CONGO, DEM. REP. OF THE		2 345 410	905 568	57 549 000	Kinshasa	French, Lingala, Swahili, Kongo, local languages	Christian, Sunni Muslim	Congolese franc	www.un.int/drcongo
CÔTE D'IVOIRE (IVORY COAST)		322 463	124 504	18 154 000	Yamoussoukro	French, creole, Akan, local languages	Sunni Muslim, Roman Catholic, traditional beliefs, Protestant	CFA franc*	www.presidence.ci
DJIBOUTI		23 200	8 958	793 000	Djibouti	Somali, Afar, French, Arabic	Sunni Muslim, Christian	Djibouti franc	www.presidence.dj
EGYPT		1 000 250	386 199	74 033 000	Cairo	Arabic	Sunni Muslim, Coptic Christian	Egyptian pound	www.sis.gov.eg
EQUATORIAL GUINEA		28 051	10 831	504 000	Malabo	Spanish, French, Fang	Roman Catholic, traditional beliefs	CFA franc*	www.ceiba-equatorial-guinea.org
ERITREA		117 400	45 328	4 401 000	Asmara	Tigrinya, Tigre	Sunni Muslim, Coptic Christian	Nakfa	www.shabait.com
ETHIOPIA		1 133 880	437 794	77 431 000	Addis Ababa	Oromo, Amharic, Tigrinya, local languages	Ethiopian Orthodox, Sunni Muslim, traditional beliefs	Birr	www.ethiopar.net
GABON		267 667	103 347	1 384 000	Libreville	French, Fang, local languages	Roman Catholic, Protestant, traditional beliefs	CFA franc*	www.legabon.org
THE GAMBIA		11 295	4 361	1 517 000	Banjul	English, Malinke, Fulani, Wolof	Sunni Muslim, Protestant	Dalasi	www.statehouse.gm
GHANA		238 537	92 100	22 113 000	Accra	English, Hausa, Akan, local languages	Christian, Sunni Muslim, traditional beliefs	Cedi	www.ghana.gov.gh
GUINEA		245 857	94 926	9 402 000	Conakry	French, Fulani, Malinke, local languages	Sunni Muslim, traditional beliefs, Christian	Guinea franc	www.guinee.gov.gn
GUINEA-BISSAU		36 125	13 948	1 586 000	Bissau	Portuguese, crioulo, local languages	Traditional beliefs, Sunni Muslim, Christian	CFA franc*	www.republica-da-guine-bissau.org
KENYA		582 646	224 961	34 256 000	Nairobi	Swahili, English, local languages	Christian, traditional beliefs	Kenyan shilling	www.kenya.go.ke
LESOTHO		30 355	11 720	1 795 000	Maseru	Sesotho, English, Zulu	Christian, traditional beliefs	Loti, S. African rand	www.lesotho.gov.ls
LIBERIA		111 369	43 000	3 283 000	Monrovia	English, creole, local languages	Traditional beliefs, Christian, Sunni Muslim	Liberian dollar	www.micat.gov.lr
LIBYA		1 759 540	679 362	5 853 000	Tripoli	Arabic, Berber	Sunni Muslim	Libyan dinar	www.libya-un.org
MADAGASCAR		587 041	226 658	18 606 000	Antananarivo	Malagasy, French	Traditional beliefs, Christian, Sunni Muslim	Malagasy Ariary, Malagasy franc	www.madagascar.gov.mg
MALAWI		118 484	45 747	12 884 000	Lilongwe	Chichewa, English, local languages	Christian, traditional beliefs, Sunni Muslim	Malawian kwacha	www.malawi.gov.mw
MALI		1 240 140	478 821	13 518 000	Bamako	French, Bambara, local languages	Sunni Muslim, traditional beliefs, Christian	CFA franc*	www.maliensdelexterieur.gov.ml
MAURITANIA		1 030 700	397 955	3 069 000	Nouakchott	Arabic, French, local languages	Sunni Muslim	Ouguiya	www.mauritania.mr
MAURITIUS		2 040	788	1 245 000	Port Louis	English, creole, Hindi, Bhojpurī, French	Hindu, Roman Catholic, Sunni Muslim	Mauritius rupee	www.gov.mu
MOROCCO		446 550	172 414	31 478 000	Rabat	Arabic, Berber, French	Sunni Muslim	Moroccan dirham	www.maroc.ma
MOZAMBIQUE		799 380	308 642	19 792 000	Maputo	Portuguese, Makua, Tsonga, local languages	Traditional beliefs, Roman Catholic, Sunni Muslim	Metical	www.mozambique.mz
NAMIBIA		824 292	318 261	2 031 000	Windhoek	English, Afrikaans, German, Ovambo, local languages	Protestant, Roman Catholic	Namibian dollar	www.grnnet.gov.na
NIGER		1 267 000	489 191	13 957 000	Niamey	French, Hausa, Fulani, local languages	Sunni Muslim, traditional beliefs	CFA franc*	www.delgi.ne/presidence
NIGERIA		923 768	356 669	131 530 000	Abuja	English, Hausa, Yoruba, Ibo, Fulani, local languages	Sunni Muslim, Christian, traditional beliefs	Naira	www.nigeria.gov.ng
RWANDA		26 338	10 169	9 038 000	Kigali	Kinyarwanda, French, English	Roman Catholic, traditional beliefs, Protestant	Rwandan franc	www.gov.rw
SÃO TOMÉ AND PRÍNCIPE		964	372	157 000	São Tomé	Portuguese, creole	Roman Catholic, Protestant	Dobra	www.parlamento.st
SENEGAL		196 720	75 954	11 658 000	Dakar	French, Wolof, Fulani, local languages	Sunni Muslim, Roman Catholic, traditional beliefs	CFA franc*	www.gouv.sn
SEYCHELLES		455	176	81 000	Victoria	English, French, creole	Roman Catholic, Protestant	Seychelles rupee	www.virtualseychelles.sc

*Communauté Financière Africaine franc

4

Africa continued

		Area sq km	Area sq miles	Population	Capital	Languages	Religions	Currency	Internet link
SIERRA LEONE		71 740	27 699	5 525 000	Freetown	English, creole, Mende, Temne, local languages	Sunni Muslim, traditional beliefs	Leone	www.statehouse-sl.org
SOMALIA		637 657	246 201	8 228 000	Mogadishu	Somali, Arabic	Sunni Muslim	Somali shilling	www.somali-gov.info
SOUTH AFRICA, REPUBLIC OF		1 219 090	470 693	47 432 000	Pretoria/Cape Town	Afrikaans, English, nine official local languages	Protestant, Roman Catholic, Sunni Muslim, Hindu	Rand	www.gov.za
SUDAN		2 505 813	967 500	36 233 000	Khartoum	Arabic, Dinka, Nubian, Beja, Nuer, local languages	Sunni Muslim, traditional beliefs, Christian	Sudanese dinar	www.sudan.gov.sd
SWAZILAND		17 364	6 704	1 032 000	Mbabane	Swazi, English	Christian, traditional beliefs	Emalangeni, South African rand	www.gov.sz
TANZANIA		945 087	364 900	38 329 000	Dodoma	Swahili, English, Nyamwezi, local languages	Shi'a Muslim, Sunni Muslim, traditional beliefs, Christian	Tanzanian shilling	www.tanzania.go.tz
TOGO		56 785	21 925	6 145 000	Lomé	French, Ewe, Kabre, local languages	Traditional beliefs, Christian, Sunni Muslim	CFA franc*	www.republicoftogo.com
TUNISIA		164 150	63 379	10 102 000	Tunis	Arabic, French	Sunni Muslim	Tunisian dinar	www.tunisiaonline.com
UGANDA		241 038	93 065	28 816 000	Kampala	English, Swahili, Luganda, local languages	Roman Catholic, Protestant, Sunni Muslim, traditional beliefs	Ugandan shilling	www.mofa.go.ug
ZAMBIA		752 614	290 586	11 668 000	Lusaka	English, Bemba, Nyanja, Tonga, local languages	Christian, traditional beliefs	Zambian kwacha	www.statehouse.gov.zm
ZIMBABWE		390 759	150 873	13 010 000	Harare	English, Shona, Ndebele	Christian, traditional beliefs	Zimbabwean dollar	www.zim.gov.zw

*Communauté Financière Africaine franc

Oceania

		Area sq km	Area sq miles	Population	Capital	Languages	Religions	Currency	Internet link
AUSTRALIA		7 692 024	2 969 907	20 155 000	Canberra	English, Italian, Greek	Protestant, Roman Catholic, Orthodox	Australian dollar	www.gov.au
FIJI		18 330	7 077	848 000	Suva	English, Fijian, Hindi	Christian, Hindu, Sunni Muslim	Fiji dollar	www.fiji.gov.fj
KIRIBATI		717	277	99 000	Bairiki	Gilbertese, English	Roman Catholic, Protestant	Australian dollar	
MARSHALL ISLANDS		181	70	62 000	Delap-Uliga-Djarrit	English, Marshallese	Protestant, Roman Catholic	United States dollar	www.rmiembassyus.org
MICRONESIA, FEDERATED STATES OF		701	271	110 000	Palikir	English, Chuukese, Pohnpeian, local languages	Roman Catholic, Protestant	United States dollar	www.fsmgov.org
NAURU		21	8	14 000	Yaren	Nauruan, English	Protestant, Roman Catholic	Australian dollar	www.un.int/nauru
NEW ZEALAND		270 534	104 454	4 028 000	Wellington	English, Maori	Protestant, Roman Catholic	New Zealand dollar	www.govt.nz
PAPUA NEW GUINEA		462 840	178 704	5 887 000	Port Moresby	English, Tok Pisin (creole), local languages	Protestant, Roman Catholic, traditional beliefs	Kina	www.pngonline.gov.pg
SAMOA		2 831	1 093	185 000	Apia	Samoan, English	Protestant, Roman Catholic	Tala	www.govt.ws
SOLOMON ISLANDS		28 370	10 954	478 000	Honiara	English, creole, local languages	Protestant, Roman Catholic	Solomon Islands dollar	www.commerce.gov.sb
TONGA		748	289	102 000	Nuku'alofa	Tongan, English	Protestant, Roman Catholic	Pa'anga	www.pmo.gov.to
TUVALU		25	10	10 000	Vaiaku	Tuvaluan, English	Protestant	Australian dollar	www.timelesstuvalu.com
VANUATU		12 190	4 707	211 000	Port Vila	English, Bislama (creole), French	Protestant, Roman Catholic, traditional beliefs	Vatu	www.vanuatugovernment.gov.vu

North America

		Area sq km	Area sq miles	Population	Capital	Languages	Religions	Currency	Internet link
ANTIGUA AND BARBUDA		442	171	81 000	St John's	English, creole	Protestant, Roman Catholic	East Caribbean dollar	www.ab.gov.ag
THE BAHAMAS		13 939	5 382	323 000	Nassau	English, creole	Protestant, Roman Catholic	Bahamian dollar	www.bahamas.gov.bs
BARBADOS		430	166	270 000	Bridgetown	English, creole	Protestant, Roman Catholic	Barbados dollar	www.barbados.gov.bb
BELIZE		22 965	8 867	270 000	Belmopan	English, Spanish, Mayan, creole	Roman Catholic, Protestant	Belize dollar	www.belize.gov.bz
CANADA		9 984 670	3 855 103	32 268 000	Ottawa	English, French, local languages	Roman Catholic, Protestant, Eastern Orthodox, Jewish	Canadian dollar	canada.gc.ca
COSTA RICA		51 100	19 730	4 327 000	San José	Spanish	Roman Catholic, Protestant	Costa Rican colón	www.casapres.go.cr
CUBA		110 860	42 803	11 269 000	Havana	Spanish	Roman Catholic, Protestant	Cuban peso	www.cubagob.gov.cu
DOMINICA		750	290	79 000	Roseau	English, creole	Roman Catholic, Protestant	East Caribbean dollar	www.ndcdominica.dm
DOMINICAN REPUBLIC		48 442	18 704	8 895 000	Santo Domingo	Spanish, creole	Roman Catholic, Protestant	Dominican peso	www.cig.gov.do
EL SALVADOR		21 041	8 124	6 881 000	San Salvador	Spanish	Roman Catholic, Protestant	El Salvador colón, United States dollar	www.casapres.gob.sv
GRENADA		378	146	103 000	St George's	English, creole	Roman Catholic, Protestant	East Caribbean dollar	www.gnv.grd
GUATEMALA		108 890	42 043	12 599 000	Guatemala City	Spanish, Mayan languages	Roman Catholic, Protestant	Quetzal, United States dollar	www.congreso.gob.gt
HAITI		27 750	10 714	8 528 000	Port-au-Prince	French, creole	Roman Catholic, Protestant, Voodoo	Gourde	www.haiti.org
HONDURAS		112 088	43 277	7 205 000	Tegucigalpa	Spanish, Amerindian languages	Roman Catholic, Protestant	Lempira	www.congreso.gob.hn
JAMAICA		10 991	4 244	2 651 000	Kingston	English, creole	Protestant, Roman Catholic	Jamaican dollar	www.jis.gov.jm
MEXICO		1 972 545	761 604	107 029 000	Mexico City	Spanish, Amerindian languages	Roman Catholic, Protestant	Mexican peso	www.gob.mx
NICARAGUA		130 000	50 193	5 487 000	Managua	Spanish, Amerindian languages	Roman Catholic, Protestant	Córdoba	www.asamblea.gob.ni
PANAMA		77 082	29 762	3 232 000	Panama City	Spanish, English, Amerindian languages	Roman Catholic, Protestant, Sunni Muslim	Balboa	www.pa
ST KITTS AND NEVIS		261	101	43 000	Basseterre	English, creole	Protestant, Roman Catholic	East Caribbean dollar	www.gov.kn
ST LUCIA		616	238	161 000	Castries	English, creole	Roman Catholic, Protestant	East Caribbean dollar	www.stlucia.gov.lc
ST VINCENT AND THE GRENADINES		389	150	119 000	Kingstown	English, creole	Protestant, Roman Catholic	East Caribbean dollar	www.svgtourism.com
TRINIDAD AND TOBAGO		5 130	1 981	1 305 000	Port of Spain	English, creole, Hindi	Roman Catholic, Hindu, Protestant, Sunni Muslim	Trinidad and Tobago dollar	www.gov.tt
UNITED STATES OF AMERICA		9 826 635	3 794 085	298 213 000	Washington D.C.	English, Spanish	Protestant, Roman Catholic, Sunni Muslim, Jewish	United States dollar	www.firstgov.gov

South America

		Area sq km	Area sq miles	Population	Capital	Languages	Religions	Currency	Internet link
ARGENTINA		2 766 889	1 068 302	38 747 000	Buenos Aires	Spanish, Italian, Amerindian languages	Roman Catholic, Protestant	Argentinian peso	www.info.gov.ar
BOLIVIA		1 098 581	424 164	9 182 000	La Paz/Sucre	Spanish, Quechua, Aymara	Roman Catholic, Protestant, Baha'i	Boliviano	www.bolivia.gov.bo
BRAZIL		8 514 879	3 287 613	186 405 000	Brasília	Portuguese	Roman Catholic, Protestant	Real	www.brazil.gov.br
CHILE		756 945	292 258	16 295 000	Santiago	Spanish, Amerindian languages	Roman Catholic, Protestant	Chilean peso	www.gobiernodechile.cl
COLOMBIA		1 141 748	440 831	45 600 000	Bogotá	Spanish, Amerindian languages	Roman Catholic, Protestant	Colombian peso	www.gobiernoenlinea.gov.co
ECUADOR		272 045	105 037	13 228 000	Quito	Spanish, Quechua, other Amerindian languages	Roman Catholic	US dollar	www.ec-gov.net
GUYANA		214 969	83 000	751 000	Georgetown	English, creole, Amerindian languages	Protestant, Hindu, Roman Catholic, Sunni Muslim	Guyana dollar	www.gina.gov.gy
PARAGUAY		406 752	157 048	6 158 000	Asunción	Spanish, Guaraní	Roman Catholic, Protestant	Guaraní	www.presidencia.gov.py
PERU		1 285 216	496 225	27 968 000	Lima	Spanish, Quechua, Aymara	Roman Catholic, Protestant	Sol	www.peru.gob.pe
SURINAME		163 820	63 251	449 000	Paramaribo	Dutch, Surinamese, English, Hindi	Hindu, Roman Catholic, Protestant, Sunni Muslim	Suriname guilder	www.kabinet.sr.org
URUGUAY		176 215	68 037	3 463 000	Montevideo	Spanish	Roman Catholic, Protestant, Jewish	Uruguayan peso	www.presidencia.gub.uy
VENEZUELA		912 050	352 144	26 749 000	Caracas	Spanish, Amerindian languages	Roman Catholic, Protestant	Bolívar	www.gobiernoenlinea.ve

Countries

The current pattern of the world's countries and territories is a result of a long history of exploration, colonialism, conflict and politics. The fact that there are currently 194 independent countries in the world – the most recent, Montenegro, only being created in June 2006 – illustrates the significant political changes which have occurred since 1950 when there were only eighty two. There has been a steady progression away from colonial influences over the last fifty years, although many dependent overseas territories remain.

The shapes of countries and the pattern of international boundaries reflect both physical and political processes. Some borders follow natural features – rivers, mountain ranges, etc – others are defined according to political agreement or as a result of war. Some are still subject to dispute between two or more countries, and many remain undefined on the ground.

Facts

● The longest single continuous land border stretches for 6 416 kilometres between Canada and the USA

● Both China and the Russian Federation have borders with 14 different countries

● Vatican City, the smallest independent country, was created in 1929 as an enclave within Rome, the capital of Italy

● All countries of the world are members of the United Nations except Taiwan and Vatican City

Internet Links

● United Nations	www.un.org
● Foreign and Commonwealth Office	www.fco.gov.uk
● International Boundaries Research Unit	www.ibru.dur.ac.uk
● Permanent Committee on Geographic Names	www.pcgn.org.uk
● United States Board on Geographic Names	geonames.usgs.gov

Abbreviation Key

A.	ANDORRA	**HUN.**	HUNGARY	**R.F.**	RUSSIAN FEDERATION
AL.	ALBANIA	**ISR.**	ISRAEL	**ROM.**	ROMANIA
ARM.	ARMENIA	**JOR.**	JORDAN	**S.**	SERBIA
AUST.	AUSTRIA	**L.**	LUXEMBOURG	**SL.**	SLOVENIA
AZER.	AZERBAIJAN	**LAT.**	LATVIA	**SLA.**	SLOVAKIA
B.	BURUNDI	**LEB.**	LEBANON	**SUR.**	SURINAME
BEL.	BELGIUM	**LITH.**	LITHUANIA	**SW.**	SWITZERLAND
B.H.	BOSNIA-HERZEGOVINA	**M.**	MACEDONIA	**TAJIK.**	TAJIKISTAN
BULG.	BULGARIA	**MO.**	MONTENEGRO	**TURKM.**	TURKMENISTAN
CR.	CROATIA	**MOL.**	MOLDOVA	**U.A.E.**	UNITED ARAB EMIRATES
CZ.R.	CZECH REPUBLIC	**NETH.**	NETHERLANDS	**U.K.**	UNITED KINGDOM
EST.	ESTONIA	**N.Z.**	NEW ZEALAND	**U.S.A.**	UNITED STATES OF AMERICA
GEOR.	GEORGIA	**R.**	RWANDA	**UZBEK.**	UZBEKISTAN

High-resolution satellite image of **Vatican City**, the world's smallest country by both population and area.

World extremes

Countries			
Largest country (area)	**Russian Federation**	17 075 400 sq km	6 592 849 sq miles
Smallest country (area)	**Vatican City**	0.5 sq km	0.2 sq miles
Largest country (population)	**China**	1 323 345 000	
Smallest country (population)	**Vatican City**	552	
Most densely populated country	**Monaco**	17 500 per sq km	35 000 per sq mile
Least densely populated country	**Mongolia**	2 per sq km	4 per sq mile
Capitals			
Largest national capital (population)	**Tōkyō, Japan**	35 327 000	
Smallest national capital (population)	**Melekeok, Palau**	391	
Most northerly national capital	**Reykjavík, Iceland**	64° 08'N	
Most southerly national capital	**Wellington, New Zealand**	41° 18'S	
Highest national capital	**La Paz, Bolivia**	3 630 m	11 909 ft

Landscapes

The earth's physical features, both on land and on the sea bed, closely reflect its geological structure. The current shapes of the continents and oceans have evolved over millions of years. Movements of the tectonic plates which make up the earth's crust have created some of the best-known and most spectacular features. The processes which have shaped the earth continue today with earthquakes, volcanoes, erosion, climatic variations and man's activities all affecting the earth's landscapes.

The total topographic range of the earth's surface is nearly 20 000 metres, from the highest point Mount Everest, to the lowest point in the Mariana Trench. Major mountain ranges include the Himalaya, the Andes and the Rocky Mountains, each of which give rise to some of the world's greatest rivers. In contrast, the deserts of the Sahara, Australia, the Arabian Peninsula and the Gobi cover vast areas and each provide unique landscapes.

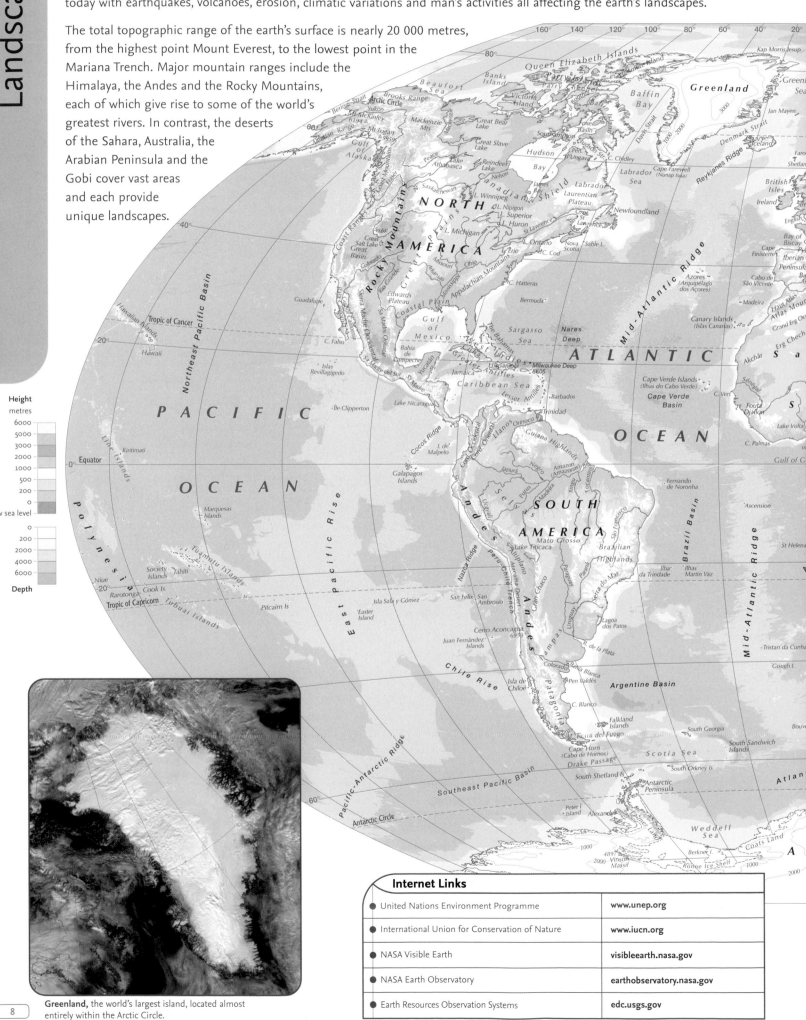

Height
metres
6000
5000
3000
2000
1000
500
200
0
below sea level
0
200
2000
4000
6000
Depth

Greenland, the world's largest island, located almost entirely within the Arctic Circle.

Internet Links	
● United Nations Environment Programme	**www.unep.org**
● International Union for Conservation of Nature	**www.iucn.org**
● NASA Visible Earth	**visibleearth.nasa.gov**
● NASA Earth Observatory	**earthobservatory.nasa.gov**
● Earth Resources Observation Systems	**edc.usgs.gov**

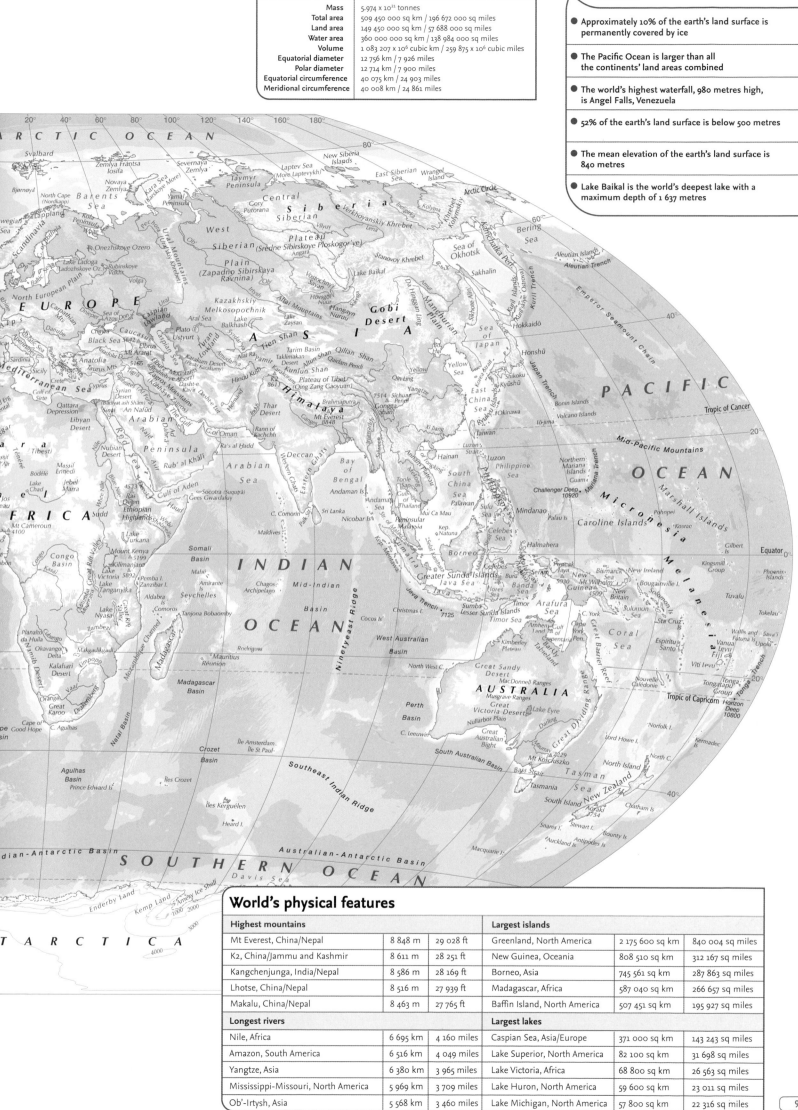

Earth's dimensions

Mass	5.974 x 10²¹ tonnes
Total area	509 450 000 sq km / 196 672 000 sq miles
Land area	149 450 000 sq km / 57 688 000 sq miles
Water area	360 000 000 sq km / 138 984 000 sq miles
Volume	1 083 207 x 10⁶ cubic km / 259 875 x 10⁶ cubic miles
Equatorial diameter	12 756 km / 7 926 miles
Polar diameter	12 714 km / 7 900 miles
Equatorial circumference	40 075 km / 24 903 miles
Meridional circumference	40 008 km / 24 861 miles

(Mass value written as 5.974×10^{21} tonnes; Volume as $1\,083\,207 \times 10^{6}$ cubic km / $259\,875 \times 10^{6}$ cubic miles)

Facts

- Approximately 10% of the earth's land surface is permanently covered by ice
- The Pacific Ocean is larger than all the continents' land areas combined
- The world's highest waterfall, 980 metres high, is Angel Falls, Venezuela
- 52% of the earth's land surface is below 500 metres
- The mean elevation of the earth's land surface is 840 metres
- Lake Baikal is the world's deepest lake with a maximum depth of 1 637 metres

World's physical features

Highest mountains			Largest islands		
Mt Everest, China/Nepal	8 848 m	29 028 ft	Greenland, North America	2 175 600 sq km	840 004 sq miles
K2, China/Jammu and Kashmir	8 611 m	28 251 ft	New Guinea, Oceania	808 510 sq km	312 167 sq miles
Kangchenjunga, India/Nepal	8 586 m	28 169 ft	Borneo, Asia	745 561 sq km	287 863 sq miles
Lhotse, China/Nepal	8 516 m	27 939 ft	Madagascar, Africa	587 040 sq km	266 657 sq miles
Makalu, China/Nepal	8 463 m	27 765 ft	Baffin Island, North America	507 451 sq km	195 927 sq miles
Longest rivers			**Largest lakes**		
Nile, Africa	6 695 km	4 160 miles	Caspian Sea, Asia/Europe	371 000 sq km	143 243 sq miles
Amazon, South America	6 516 km	4 049 miles	Lake Superior, North America	82 100 sq km	31 698 sq miles
Yangtze, Asia	6 380 km	3 965 miles	Lake Victoria, Africa	68 800 sq km	26 563 sq miles
Mississippi-Missouri, North America	5 969 km	3 709 miles	Lake Huron, North America	59 600 sq km	23 011 sq miles
Ob'-Irtysh, Asia	5 568 km	3 460 miles	Lake Michigan, North America	57 800 sq km	22 316 sq miles

Conic Equidistant Projection

1:10 000 000

| 0 | | 100 | | 200 | | 300 | | 400 miles |
| 0 | 100 | 200 | 300 | 400 | 500 | 600 | km |

Europe
Northern Europe

Europe
Western Russian Federation

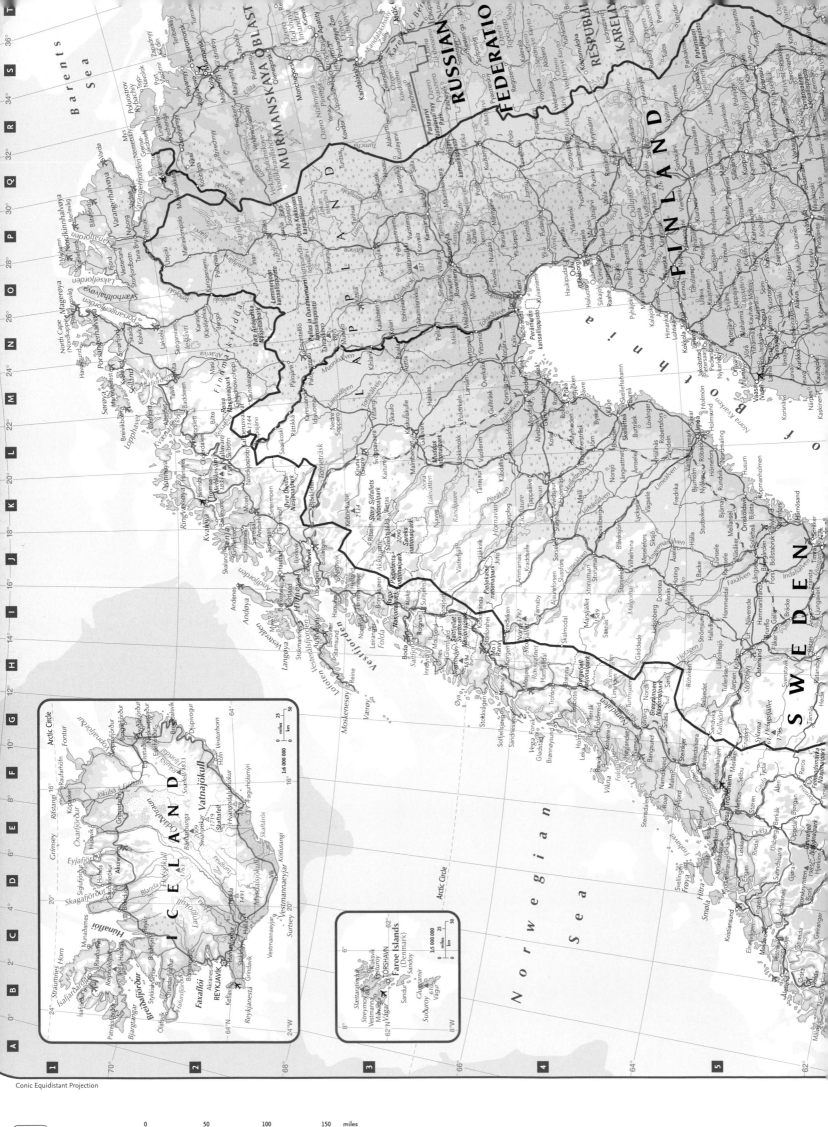

Conic Equidistant Projection

1:5 000 000

Europe
Scandinavia and the Baltic States

ATLANTIC
OCEAN

North

Sea

UNITED
KINGDOM

IRELAND

CONNAUGHT

LEINSTER

MUNSTER

Great   Britain

Irish
Sea

Isle
of Man
(U.K.)

Celtic
Sea

St George's Channel

Cardigan Bay

Bristol Channel

English Channel
(La Manche)

Channel Islands
(Îles Normandes)

Guernsey
(U.K.)

Jersey
(U.K.)

Golfe
de
St-Malo

NORMANDY

BRITTANY

ANJOU

POITOU

FRANCE

BELGIUM

NETH

AMSTERDAM

THE HAGUE
('s-Gravenhage)

Rotterda

BRUSSELS
(Bruxelles)

ARTOIS

PICARDY

PARIS

LONDON

Strait of Dover
(Pas de Calais)

1:5 000 000

0   50   100   150 miles
0   50 100 150 200 250 km

Europe
Northwest Europe

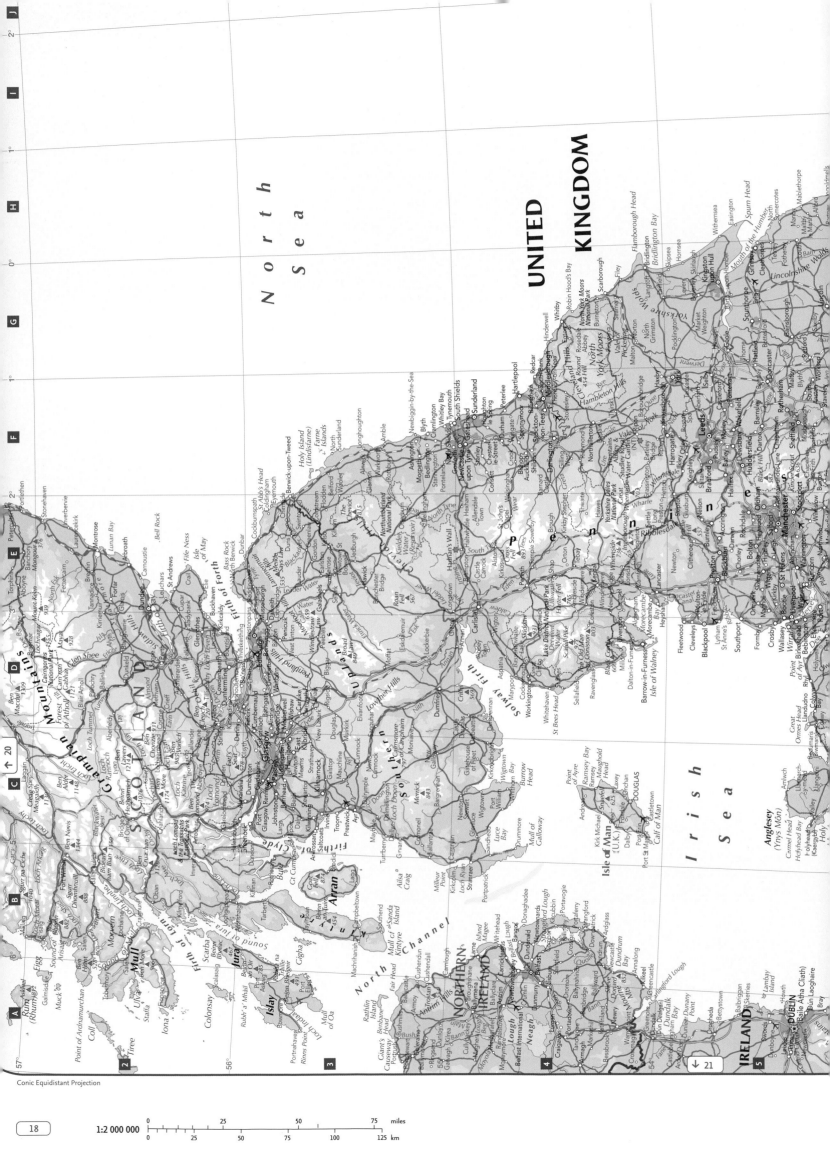

UNITED

KINGDOM

North Sea

SCOTLAND

Grampian Mountains

NORTHERN IRELAND

IRELAND

Irish Sea

North Channel

Isle of Man (U.K.)

Anglesey (Ynys Môn)

Pennines

Southern Uplands

DUBLIN
Dún Laoghaire

Conic Equidistant Projection

1:2 000 000

| 0 | 25 | 50 | 75 | miles |
| 0 | 25 | 50 | 75 | 100 | 125 | km |

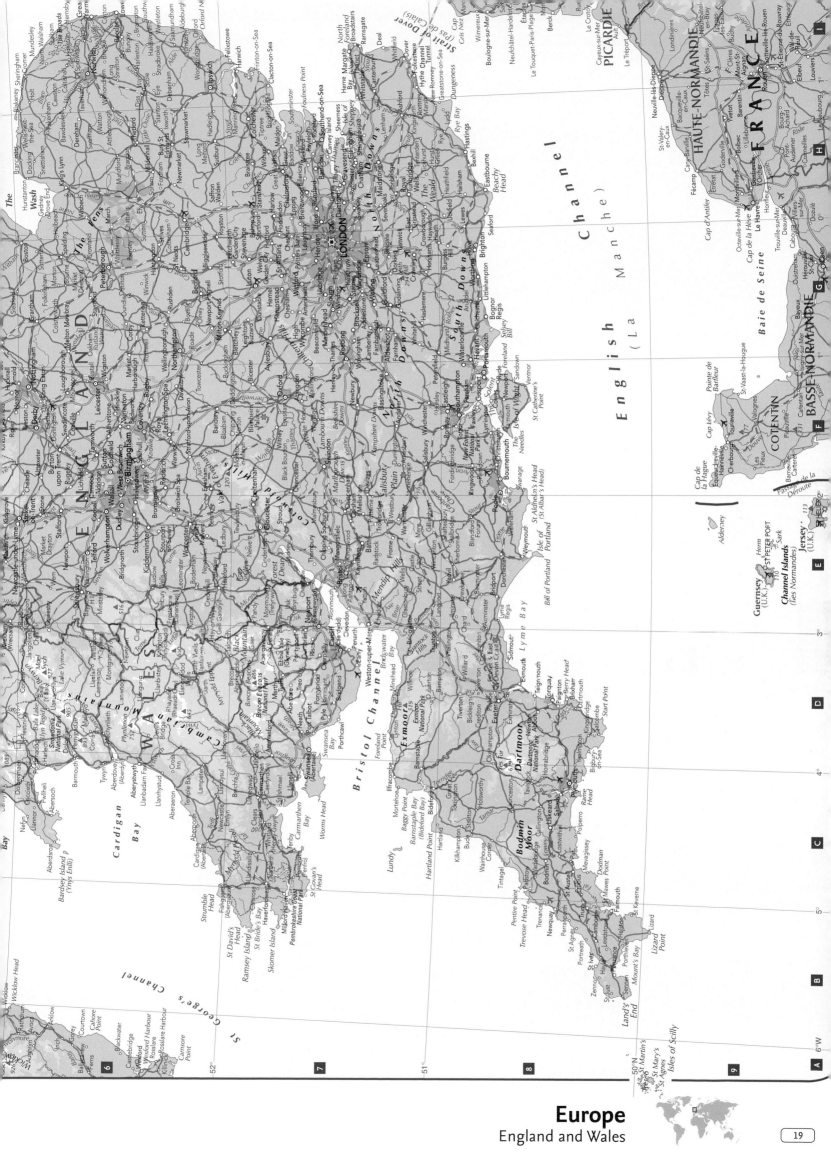

Europe

England and Wales

Europe
Scotland

1:2 000 000

ATLANTIC

OCEAN

SCOTLAND

UNITED

KINGDOM

ULSTER

NORTHERN IRELAND

CONNAUGHT

IRELAND

LEINSTER

MUNSTER

DUBLIN
(Baile Átha Cliath)

Irish

Sea

Isle of Man
(U.K.)

WALES

St George's

Channel

Conic Equidistant Projection

1:2 000 000

0   25   50   75 miles
0   25   50   75   100   125 km

Europe
Ireland

21

1:10 000 000

Conic Equidistant Projection

| 0 | 100 | 200 | 300 | 400 miles |

| 0 | 100 | 200 | 300 | 400 | 500 | 600 | km |

Europe

Southern Europe and the Mediterranean

23

Conic Equidistant Projection

Europe
France

1:5 000 000

0   50   100   150 miles
0   50   100   150   200   250 km

Conic Equidistant Projection

1:5 000 000

0   50   100   150   miles

0   50   100   150   200   250   km

Europe
Spain and Portugal

25

Conic Equidistant Projection

1:5 000 000

Europe

Italy and the Balkans

Conic Equidistant Projection

1:20 000 000

| | 200 | 400 | 600 | miles |
| 0 | 200 | 400 | 600 | 800 | 1000 | km |

Asia
Northern Asia

Albers Conic Equal Area Projection

1:20 000 000

| | 0 | 200 | 400 | 600 | miles |
| | 0 | 200 400 600 800 | 1000 km |

Asia

Central and Southern Asia

Albers Conic Equal Area Projection

1:13 000 000

| 0 | 100 | 200 | 300 | 400 | 500 miles |
| 0 | 100 | 200 | 300 | 400 | 500 | 600 | 700 | 800 km |

Asia
Southwest Asia

Administrative divisions in Russian Federation
numbered on the map:

1. RESPUBLIKA KALMYKIYA - KHALM'G-TANGCH (G1)
2. RESPUBLIKA DAGESTAN (G2)
3. CHECHENSKAYA RESPUBLIKA (G2)
4. RESPUBLIKA INGUSHETIYA (G2)
5. RESPUBLIKA SEVERNAYA OSETIYA - ALANIYA (G2)
6. KABARDINO-BALKARSKAYA RESPUBLIKA (F2)
7. KARACHAYEVO-CHERKESSKAYA RESPUBLIKA (F2)
8. RESPUBLIKA ADYGEYA (F1)

Conic Equidistant Projection

34   1:7 000 000

0   100   200   miles

0   100   200   300   400   km

Asia

Eastern Mediterranean, the Caucasus and Iraq

Conic Equidistant Projection

Administrative divisions in India
numbered on the map:

1. DADRA AND NAGAR HAVELI (C5)
2. DAMAN AND DIU (B5, C5)

1:7 000 000

miles
0   100   200

km
0   100   200   300   400

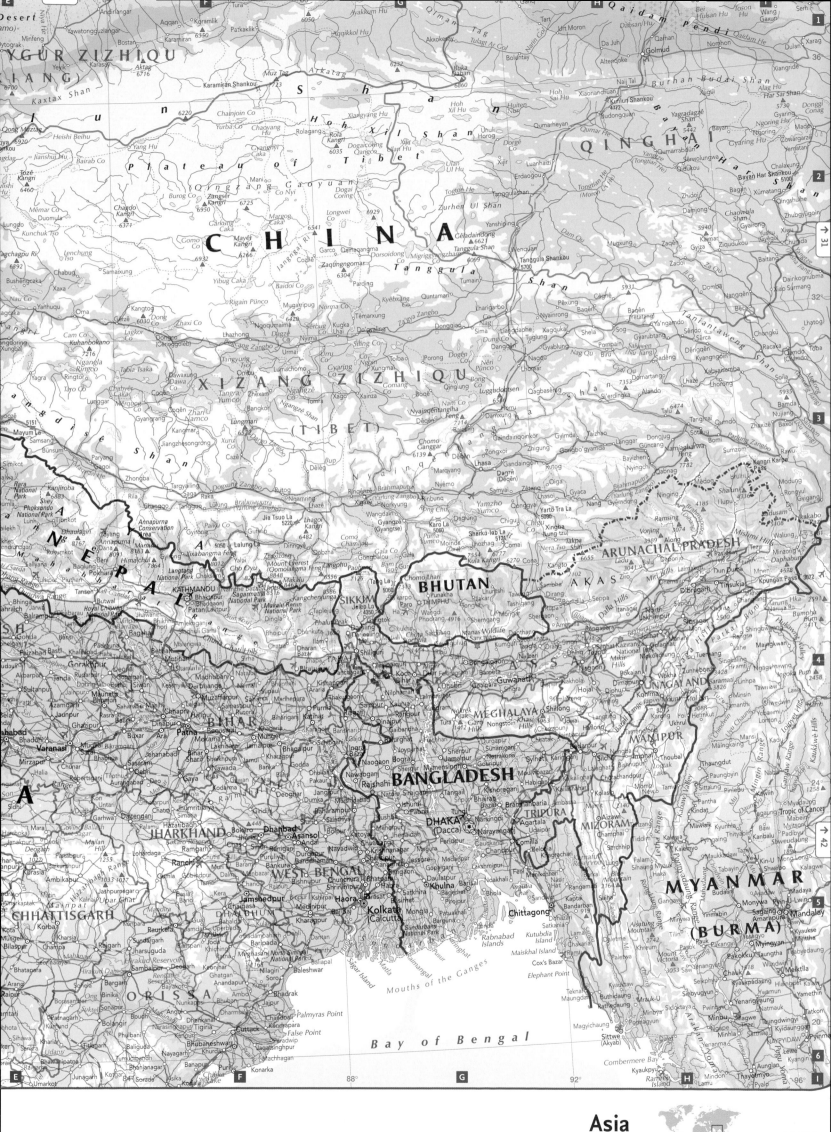

Asia

Northern India, Nepal, Bhutan and Bangladesh

Asia
Southern India and Sri Lanka

1:7 000 000

Conic Equidistant Projection

0   100   200 miles
0 100 200 300 400 km

Administrative divisions in India
numbered on the map:

1. DADRA AND NAGAR HAVELI (B1)
2. DAMAN AND DIU (A1, B1)
3. PUDUCHERRY (C4)

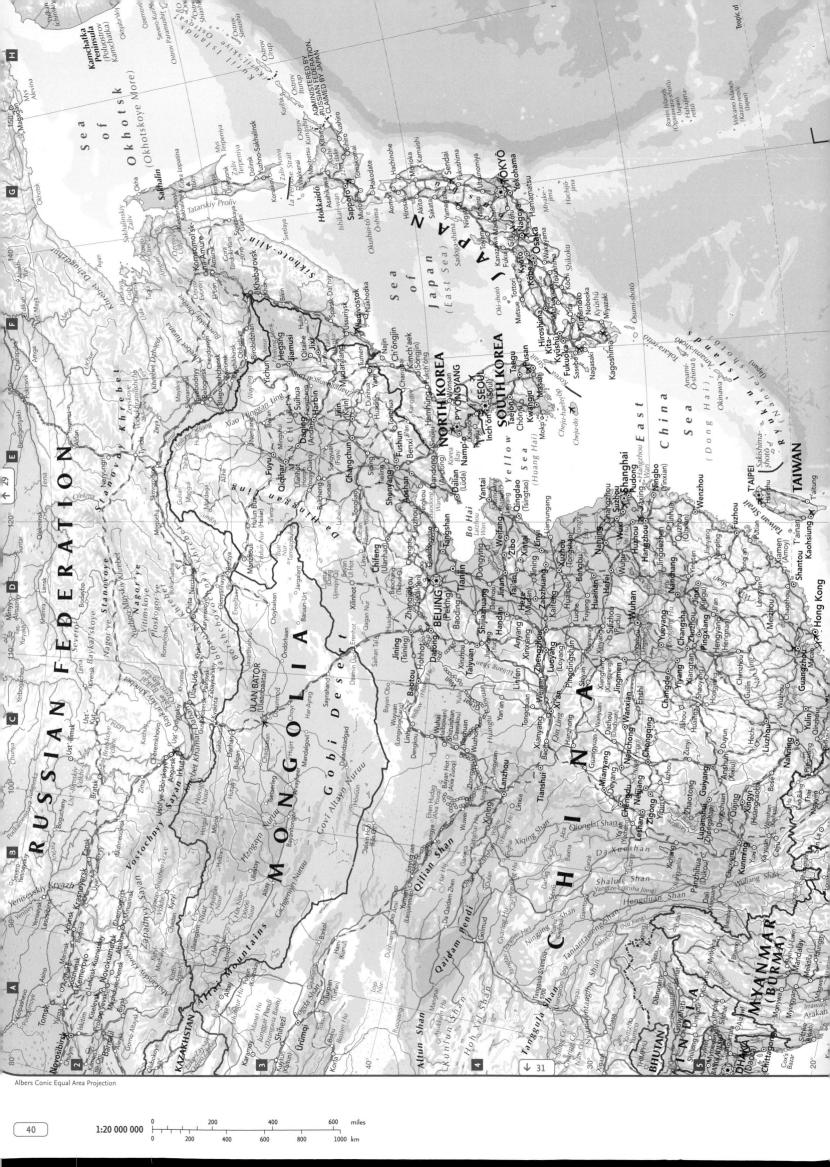

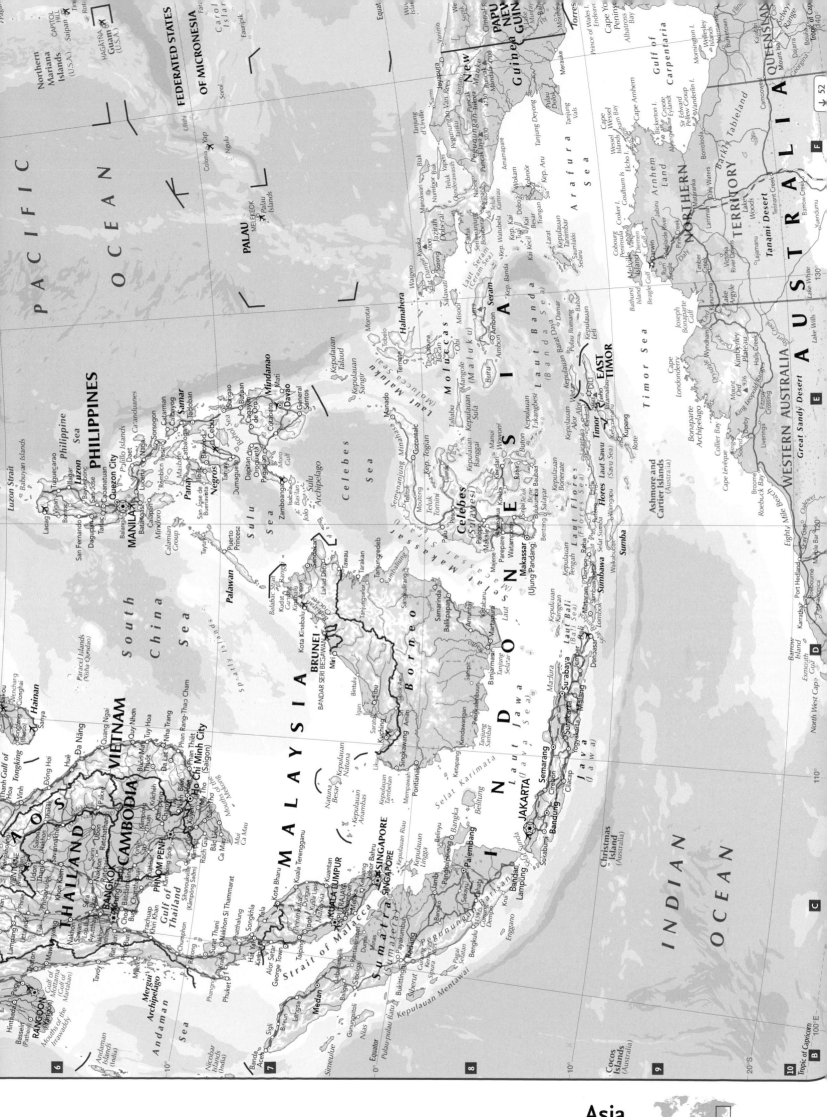

Asia

Eastern and Southeast Asia

Albers Conic Equal Area Projection

1:15 000 000

Asia
Eastern Asia

Conic Equidistant Projection

1:7 000 000

| 0 | 100 | 200 | miles |
| 0 | 100 | 200 | 300 | 400 | km |

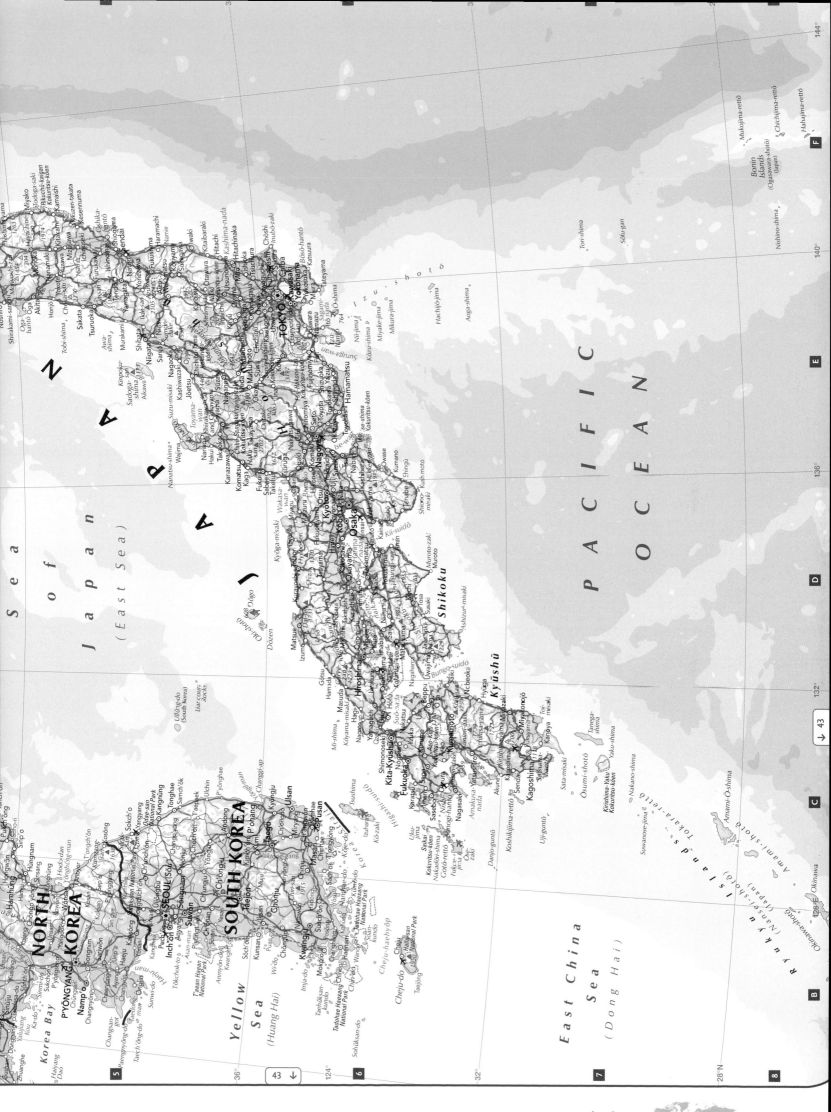

Asia

Japan, North Korea and South Korea

Lambert Azimuthal Equal Area Projection

1:16 000 000

Africa
Central and Southern Africa

Lambert Azimuthal Equal Area Projection

1:5 000 000

| 0 | 100 | 200 | 300 | miles |
| 0 | 100 | 200 | 300 | 400 | 500 | km |

Africa
Republic of South Africa

Sea
Tanjungredeb
Sambaliung
Manado
Semenanjung Minahasa
Tolitoli
Ternate Halmahera
Waigeo
Tanjung d'Urville
Manokwari
Biak
Numfoor
Wuvulu Island
Hermit Islands
St Matthias Group
Mussau Island
Admiralty Islands
Manus Island
New Hanover
Tabar Island
Lihir Group
Lyra Reef

Borneo
Sangkulirang
Samarinda
Balikpapan
Kotabaru
Laut
Majene
Makassar (Ujung Pandang)
Bontosunggu
Salayar

INDONESIA

I N D O N E S I A

PAPUA
NEW GUINEA

New Guinea

PORT MORESBY

**INDIAN
OCEAN**

Ashmore and Cartier Islands (Australia)

Darwin
Arnhem Land
Gulf of Carpentaria
Cape York Peninsula

**NORTHERN
TERRITORY**
Tanami Desert
Tennant Creek

Kimberley Plateau

Great Sandy Desert

**WESTERN

AUSTRALIA**

Gibson Desert

Alice Springs
Macdonnell Ranges

QUEENSLAND

Mount Isa

Great Sandy Desert

Simpson Desert

**SOUTH
AUSTRALIA**

Great Victoria Desert

NEW SOUTH WALES

Nullarbor Plain

Kalgoorlie

Broken Hill

Newcastle
Sydney
Wollongong
CANBERRA
A.C.T.

Perth
Fremantle

Great Australian Bight

Adelaide

VICTORIA
Melbourne

Bass Strait

TASMANIA
Hobart

**Coral Sea
Islands
Territory
(Australia)**

Cairns

Townsville

Rockhampton

Brisbane

Lambert Azimuthal Equal Area Projection

1:20 000 000

0   200   400   600 miles

0   200   400   600   800   1000 km

NAURU

YAREN
Nauru

Aranuka

Howland Island (U.S.A.)

Baker Island (U.S.A.)

0°
1

Banaba
(Ocean Island)

Nonouti

K I R I B A T I

Tabiteuea
Onotoa   Kingsmill Group
Tamana   Arorae

Beru   Nikunau

Phoenix
Islands   Kanton

McKean   Rawaki

Nikumaroro   Orona   Manra

2

Takuu
Islands

Nukumanu
Islands

Nanumea
Nanumanga

Niutao

TUVALU   Funafuti
VAIAKU

Nui   Vaitupu

Nukufetau

Swains Island

Tokelau
(New Zealand)

Atafu

Nukunonu

Fakaofo

Pukapuka
(Danger Islands)   Nassau

10°

Ontong
Java Atoll

SOLOMON
ISLANDS

Roncador
Reef

Choiseul

Santa
Isabel

Buala

Malu'u

Stewart
Islands

Nukulaelae

Niulakita

New Georgia Sound
New
Georgia
Islands

Florida
Islands

Malaita

Maramasike
Ulawa Island

Duff
Islands

Nupani   Swallow Islands

Rotuma
(Fiji)

Wallis and
Futuna Islands
(France)

Îles
Wallis

MATĀ'UTU

SAMOA

American
Samoa
(U.S.A.)

Suwarrow

Guadalcanal

Kirakira

Santa
Ana

Ndeni

Santa Cruz Islands
(Solomon Islands)

Mitre
Island

Îles de Hoorn

Savai'i   APIA

'Upolu

Manu'a
Islands

Cook Islands
(New Zealand)

San Cristobal
(Makira)

Utupua

Tutuila   FAGATOGO
Rose
Island

Rennell

Indispensable
Reefs

Vanikoro
Islands

Cherry
Island

Tikopia

Niuafo'ou
210

Tafahi
Niuatoputapu

Palmerston

al Sea

Torres Islands

Uréparapara

Great Sea Reef   Vanua Levu

Yasawa
Group   Bligh
Water   Labasa
(Lembasa)

Vava'u
Group

ALOFI   Niue
(New Zealand)

Espíritu Santo

Banks
Islands

Vanua Lava
Santa María Island

VANUATU

Mount
Tabwémasana
1879

Maéwo

Aoba

Pentecost Island

Northern
Lau Group

Tonga
Group

Lautoka

Tomanivi
Mt Victoria
Koro

Taveuni

Viti Levu

Koro
Sea

Doi   Ono-i-Lau

TONGA

Southern
Lau Group

Tofua
500

Ha'apai
Group

Norsup

Ambrym

Malakula

Epi

Émaé

FIJI

SUVA

Gau

Lakeba

Kabara

Shepherd
Islands

Kadavu Passage

Moala

Vatoa

Matuku

NUKU'ALOFA

Tongatapu
Group

PORT VILA   Éfaté

Kadavu

Ata

Erromango

Ceva-i-Ra
(Conway Reef)

Minerva Reefs

Îles Chesterfield
(France)

Récifs
d'Entrecasteaux

Grand Passage

Tanna
361

Anatom
(Aneityum)

Futuna

Grand Récif
de Cook

Îles Belep

New Caledonia
(France)

Récif des
Français

Koumac

Nouvelle Calédonie

Ouvéa

Lifou

Îles Loyauté
(France)

Tadine

Maré

Tropic of Capricorn
160°

Hunter
Island
100

Bourail

Yaté

NOUMÉA

Île des Pins

P A C I F I C   O C E A N

Grand Récif
du Sud

Norfolk Island
(Australia)

KINGSTON

4

Lord Howe Island
(Australia)

Raoul Island

Kermadec Islands
(New Zealand)

Macauley Island
Curtis Island

Havre Rock
L'Espérance Rock

30°

Three Kings
Islands

North
Cape

Cape
Maria van Diemen

Awanui

North Island

Great Barrier Island

an Sea

Whangarei

Takapuna   Auckland
Manukau

East Cape

NEW
ZEALAND

Hamilton
Tokoroa

Tauranga   Whakatane

Gisborne

New
Plymouth

Te Kuiti   Taupo

Mount   Wairoa
Ruapehu

Mahia Peninsula

Mount Taranaki
(Mount Egmont)

Hawera   Napier

Wanganui   Hastings

Cape Farewell   Tasman
Bay

Palmerston North

Masterton

5

South
Island

Nelson

Blenheim

Lower Hutt

WELLINGTON

Westport

Cook Strait

Hokitika

Greymouth

Aoraki
(Mount Cook)

Christchurch

Banks Peninsula

Chatham Islands
(New Zealand)

Southern Alps

Mount
Aspiring
3030

Ashburton

Timaru

Chatham Island

Mount
Christina
502

Queenstown

Oamaru

Waitangi

Pitt Island

Cape Providence

Gore

Foveaux Strait
Invercargill

Dunedin

40°

Stewart Island
South West Cape

Snares
Islands

Bounty Islands
(New Zealand)

6

Auckland Islands
(New Zealand)

Antipodes Islands
(New Zealand)

160°   G   170°   H   180°   I   170°   J   160°   K   150°W   L

Oceania
Australia, New Zealand and Southwest Pacific

53

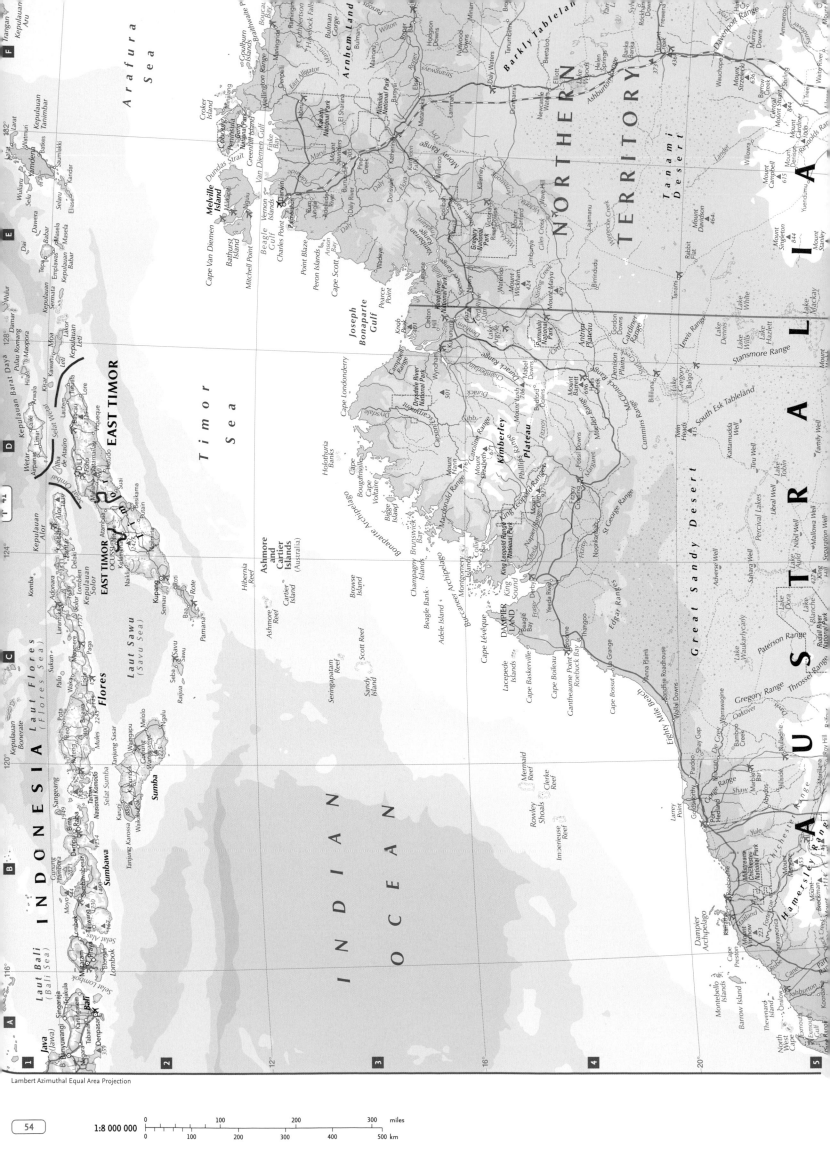

Lambert Azimuthal Equal Area Projection

1:8 000 000

0   100   200   300   miles
0   100   200   300   400   500 km

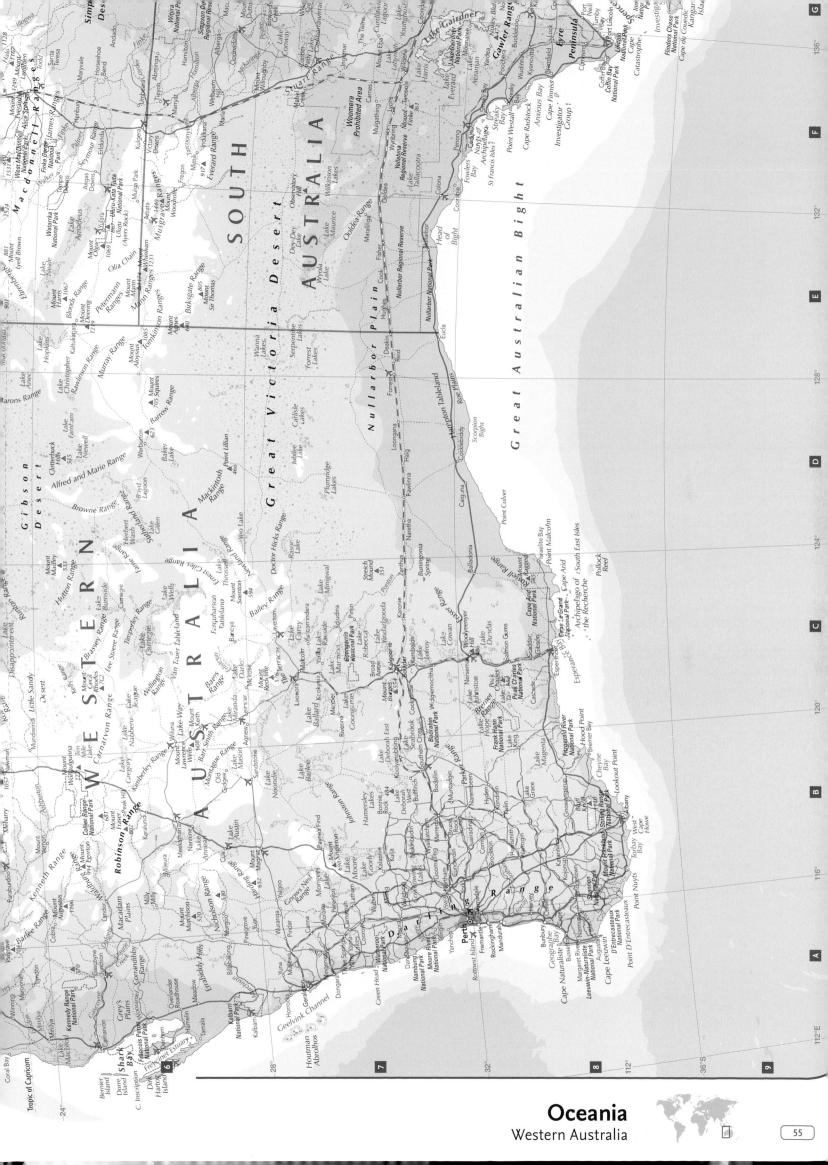

Oceania
Western Australia

Lambert Azimuthal Equal Area Projection

1:8 000 000

0   100   200   300 miles

0   100   200   300   400   500 km

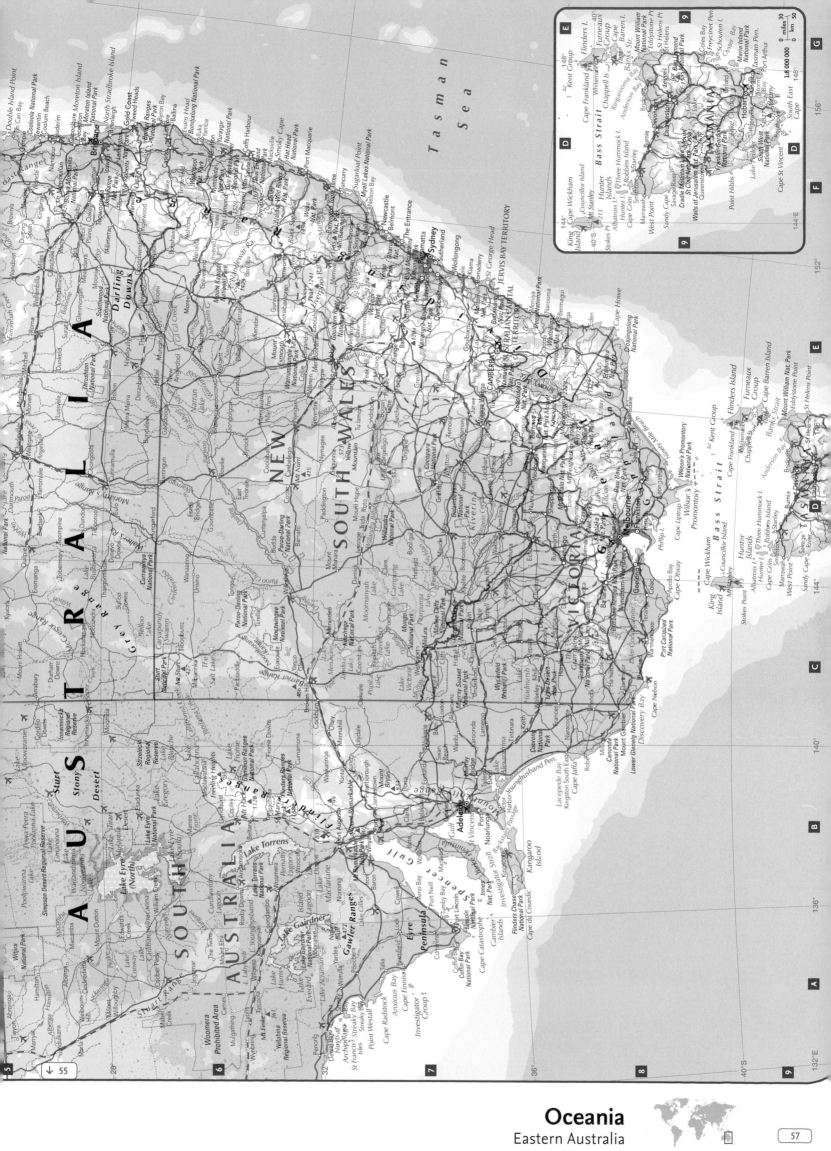

Oceania
Eastern Australia

Oceania
Southeast Australia

Three Kings Islands

Cape Maria
van Diemen
North Cape
Te Paki

T a s m a n

S e a

North Island

NEW

ZEALAND

Cape Farewell
Farewell Spit

Cook Strait

South Island

P A C I F I C

O C E A N

Stewart Island

onic Equidistant Projection

Lambert Conformal Conic Projection

1:16 000 000

↓ 62

North America
Canada

Lambert Conformal Conic Projection

1:12 000 000

| miles | 0 | 100 | 200 | 300 | 400 |
| km | 0 | 100 | 200 | 300 | 400 | 500 | 600 | 700 |

North America

United States of America

North America
Northeast United States

1:3 500 000

Lambert Conformal Conic Projection

North America
Southwest United States

3 500 000

ambert Conformal Conic Projection

Lambert Conformal Conic Projection

1:14 000 000

| 0 | | 200 | | 400 | | miles |
| 0 | 200 | 400 | 600 | 800 | km |

North America
Central America and the Caribbean

PACIFIC

OCEAN

Galapagos Islands
(Islas Galápagos)
(Ecuador)

Equator

Isla Fernandina
Isla Isabela

Isla
San Salvador
Isla
Santa Cruz
Puerto
Baquerizo Moreno
Isla
Santa María
Isla
San Cristóbal

1:14 000 000

0   miles   100
0   km   150

Lambert Azimuthal Equal Area Projection

1:14 000 000

0   200   400   miles
0   200   400   600   800 km

10°

5°

Equator

5°

10°

15°

20°

ATLANTIC

OCEAN

GEORGETOWN
New Amsterdam
PARAMARIBO
UYANA
SURINAME
French
Guiana

BRAZIL

Fortaleza
(Ceará)

Teresina

Natal

João Pessoa

Recife
(Pernambuco)

Maceió

Salvador
(Bahia)

Vitória
Vila Velha

Belo
Horizonte

BRASÍLIA

Goiânia

Campo
Grande

São Paulo
Campinas
Rio de
Janeiro
Nova
Iguaçu

ARAGUAY

South America
Southern South America

1:14 000 000

Lambert Azimuthal Equal Area Projection

| miles |
| 0 | 200 | 400 |
| 0 | 200 | 400 | 600 | 800 km |

South America
Southeast Brazil

1:7 000 000

ATLANTIC

OCEAN

Lambert Azimuthal Equal Area Projection

Atlantic Ocean
Indian Ocean

73

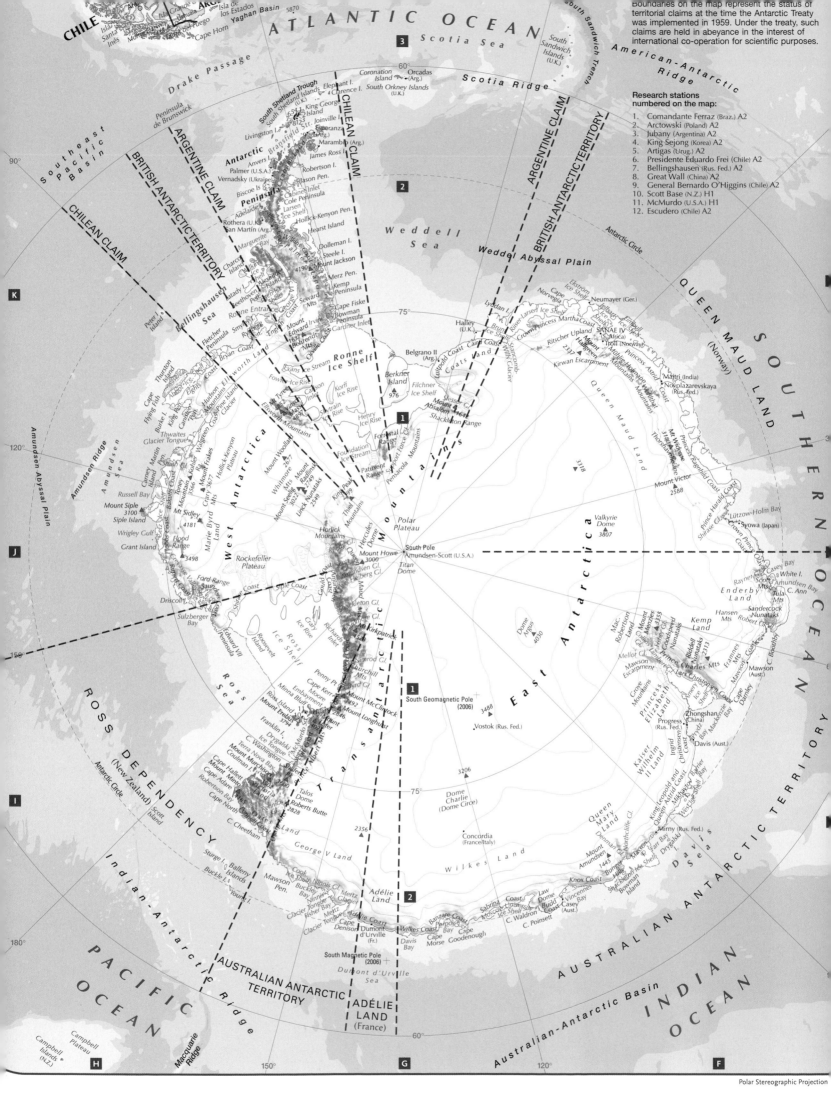

Research stations numbered on the map:

1. Comandante Ferraz (Braz.) A2
2. Arctowski (Poland) A2
3. Jubany (Argentina) A2
4. King Sejong (Korea) A2
5. Artigas (Urug.) A2
6. Presidente Eduardo Frei (Chile) A2
7. Bellingshausen (Rus. Fed.) A2
8. Great Wall (China) A2
9. General Bernardo O'Higgins (Chile) A2
10. Scott Base (N.Z.) H1
11. McMurdo (U.S.A.) H1
12. Escudero (Chile) A2

Antarctica

Polar Stereographic Projection

1:26 000 000

| 0 | 200 | 400 | 600 | 800 | 1000 miles |

| 0 | 200 | 400 | 600 | 800 | 1000 | 1200 | 1400 | 1600 km |

Introduction to the index

The index includes all names shown on the reference maps in the atlas. Each entry includes the country or geographical area in which the feature is located, a page number and an alphanumeric reference. Additional entry details and aspects of the index are explained below.

Name forms

The names policy in this atlas is generally to use local name forms which are officially recognized by the governments of the countries concerned. Rules established by the Permanent Committee on Geographical Names for British Official Use (PCGN) are applied to the conversion of non-roman alphabet names, for example in the Russian Federation, into the roman alphabet used in English.

However, English conventional name forms are used for the most well-known places for which such a form is in common use. In these cases, the local form is included in brackets on the map and appears as a cross-reference in the index. Other alternative names, such as well-known historical names or those in other languages, may also be included in brackets on the map and as cross-references in the index. All country names and those for international physical features appear in their English forms. Names appear in full in the index, although they may appear in abbreviated form on the maps.

Referencing

Names are referenced by page number and by grid reference. The grid reference relates to the alphanumeric values which appear on the edges of each map. These reflect the graticule on the map – the letter relates to longitude divisions, the number to latitude divisions. Names are generally referenced to the largest scale map page on which they appear. For large geographical features, including countries, the reference is to the largest scale map on which the feature appears in its entirety, or on which the majority of it appears.

Rivers are referenced to their lowest downstream point – either their mouth or their confluence with another river. The river name will generally be positioned as close to this point as possible.

Alternative names

Alternative names appear as cross-references and refer the user to the index entry for the form of the name used on the map.

For rivers with multiple names - for example those which flow through several countries - all alternative name forms are included within the main index entries, with details of the countries in which each form applies.

Administrative qualifiers

Administrative divisions are included in entries to differentiate duplicate names - entries of exactly the same name and feature type within the one country - where these division names are shown on the maps. In such cases, duplicate names are alphabetized in the order of the administrative division names.

Additional qualifiers are included for names within selected geographical areas, to indicate more clearly their location.

Descriptors

Entries, other than those for towns and cities, include a descriptor indicating the type of geographical feature. Descriptors are not included where the type of feature is implicit in the name itself, unless there is a town or city of exactly the same name.

Insets

Where relevant, the index clearly indicates [inset] if a feature appears on an inset map.

Alphabetical order

The Icelandic characters Þ and þ are transliterated and alphabetized as 'Th' and 'th'. The German character ß is alphabetized as 'ss'. Names beginning with Mac or Mc are alphabetized exactly as they appear. The terms Saint, Sainte, etc, are abbreviated to St, Ste, etc, but alphabetized as if in the full form.

Numerical entries

Entries beginning with numerals appear at the beginning of the index, in numerical order. Elsewhere, numerals are alphabetized before 'a'.

Permuted terms

Names beginning with generic geographical terms are permuted - the descriptive term is placed after, and the index alphabetized by, the main part of the name. For example, Mount Everest is indexed as Everest, Mount; Lake Superior as Superior, Lake. This policy is applied to all languages. Permuting has not been applied to names of towns, cities or administrative divisions beginning with such geographical terms. These remain in their full form, for example, Lake Isabella, USA.

Gazetteer entries and connections

Selected entries have been extended to include gazetteer-style information. Important geographical facts which relate specifically to the entry are included within the entry in coloured type.

Entries for features which also appear on, or which have a topical link to, the thematic pages of the atlas include a reference to those pages.

Abbreviations

admin. dist.	administrative district	IL	Illinois	plat.	plateau
admin. div.	administrative division	imp. l.	impermanent lake	P.N.G.	Papua New Guinea
admin. reg.	administrative region	IN	Indiana	Port.	Portugal
Afgh.	Afghanistan	Indon.	Indonesia	pref.	prefecture
AK	Alaska	Kazakh.	Kazakhstan	prov.	province
AL	Alabama	KS	Kansas	pt	point
Alg.	Algeria	KY	Kentucky	Qld	Queensland
AR	Arkansas	Kyrg.	Kyrgyzstan	Que.	Québec
Arg.	Argentina	l.	lake	r.	river
aut. comm.	autonomous community	LA	Louisiana	reg.	region
aut. reg.	autonomous region	lag.	lagoon	res.	reserve
aut. rep.	autonomous republic	Lith.	Lithuania	resr	reservoir
AZ	Arizona	Lux.	Luxembourg	RI	Rhode Island
Azer.	Azerbaijan	MA	Massachusetts	Rus. Fed.	Russian Federation
b.	bay	Madag.	Madagascar	S.	South, Southern
Bangl.	Bangladesh	Man.	Manitoba	S.A.	South Australia
B.C.	British Columbia	MD	Maryland	salt l.	salt lake
Bol.	Bolivia	ME	Maine	Sask.	Saskatchewan
Bos.-Herz.	Bosnia-Herzegovina	Mex.	Mexico	SC	South Carolina
Bulg.	Bulgaria	MI	Michigan	SD	South Dakota
c.	cape	MN	Minnesota	sea chan.	sea channel
CA	California	MO	Missouri	Sing.	Singapore
Cent. Afr. Rep.	Central African Republic	Moz.	Mozambique	Switz.	Switzerland
CO	Colorado	MS	Mississippi	Tajik.	Tajikistan
Col.	Colombia	MT	Montana	Tanz.	Tanzania
CT	Connecticut	mt.	mountain	Tas.	Tasmania
Czech Rep.	Czech Republic	mts	mountains	terr.	territory
DC	District of Columbia	N.	North, Northern	Thai.	Thailand
DE	Delaware	nat. park	national park	TN	Tennessee
Dem. Rep. Congo	Democratic Republic of the Congo	N.B.	New Brunswick	Trin. and Tob.	Trinidad and Tobago
depr.	depression	NC	North Carolina	Turkm.	Turkmenistan
des.	desert	ND	North Dakota	TX	Texas
Dom. Rep.	Dominican Republic	NE	Nebraska	U.A.E.	United Arab Emirates
E.	East, Eastern	Neth.	Netherlands	U.K.	United Kingdom
Equat. Guinea	Equatorial Guinea	NH	New Hampshire	Ukr.	Ukraine
esc.	escarpment	NJ	New Jersey	U.S.A.	United States of America
est.	estuary	NM	New Mexico	UT	Utah
Eth.	Ethiopia	N.S.	Nova Scotia	Uzbek.	Uzbekistan
Fin.	Finland	N.S.W.	New South Wales	VA	Virginia
FL	Florida	N.T.	Northern Territory	Venez.	Venezuela
for.	forest	NV	Nevada	Vic.	Victoria
Fr. Guiana	French Guiana	N.W.T.	Northwest Territories	vol.	volcano
F.Y.R.O.M.	Former Yugoslav Republic of Macedonia	NY	New York	vol. crater	volcanic crater
g.	gulf	N.Z.	New Zealand	VT	Vermont
GA	Georgia	OH	Ohio	W.	West, Western
Guat.	Guatemala	OK	Oklahoma	WA	Washington
HI	Hawaii	OR	Oregon	W.A.	Western Australia
H.K.	Hong Kong	PA	Pennsylvania	WI	Wisconsin
Hond.	Honduras	Para.	Paraguay	WV	West Virginia
i.	island	P.E.I.	Prince Edward Island	WY	Wyoming
IA	Iowa	pen.	peninsula	Y.T.	Yukon Territory
ID	Idaho	Phil.	Philippines		

1

3-y Severnyy Rus. Fed. 11 S3
5 de Outubro Angola see Xá-Muteba
9 de Julio Arg. 70 D5
25 de Mayo Buenos Aires Arg. 70 D5
25 de Mayo La Pampa Arg. 70 C5
100 Mile House Canada 62 C1

A

Aabenraa Denmark 15 F9
Aachen Germany 17 K5
Aalborg Denmark 15 F8
Aalborg Bugt b. Denmark 15 G8
Aalen Germany 17 M6
Aaley Lebanon see Aley
Aanaar Fin. see Inari
Aarhus Denmark see Århus
Aarlen Belgium see Arlon
Aars Denmark 15 F8
Aasiaat Greenland 61 M3
Aba China 42 I6
Aba Nigeria 46 D4
Aba Dem. Rep. Congo 48 D3
Abacaxis r. Brazil 69 G4
Ābādān Iran 35 H5
Abadan Turkm. 33 I2
Ābādeh Iran 35 I5
Ābādeh Tashk Iran 35 I5
Abadla Alg. 22 D5
Abaeté Brazil 71 B2
Abaetetuba Brazil 69 I4
Abagnar Qi China see Xilinhot
Abaiang atoll Kiribati 74 H5
Abakaliki Nigeria 46 D4
Abakan Rus. Fed. 42 G2
Abakanskiy Khrebet mts Rus. Fed. 42 F2
Abalak Niger 46 D3
Abana Turkey 34 D2
Abancay Peru 68 D6
Abariringa atoll Kiribati see Kanton
Abarkūh Iran 35 I5
Abarkūh, Kavīr-e des. Iran 35 I5
Abarqū Iran 35 I5
Abashar Iran see Neyshābūr
Abashiri Japan 44 G3
Abashiri-wan b. Japan 44 G3
Abava r. Latvia 15 L8
Abay P.N.G. 56 E1
Abaya Häyk' l. Eth. see Abaya, Lake
Abaya, Lake Eth. 48 D3
Abay Wenz r. Eth. see Blue Nile
Abay Wenz r. Eth. 48 D2 see Blue Nile
Abaza Rus. Fed. 42 G2
Abba Cent. Afr. Rep. 48 B3
Abbasabad Iran 35 I4
Abbasanta Sardinia Italy 26 C4
Abbatis Villa France see Abbeville
Abbe, Lake Djibouti/Eth. 32 F7
Abbeville France 24 E1
Abbeville LA U.S.A. 63 I6
Abbeville SC U.S.A. 63 D5
Abbeyfeale Ireland 21 C5
Abbey Town U.K. 18 D4
Abborrträsk Sweden 14 K4
Abbot, Mount Australia 56 D4
Abbot Ice Shelf Antarctica 76 K2
Abbott VA U.S.A. 64 D4
Abbottabad Pak. 33 L3
'Abd al 'Azīz, Jabal hill Syria 35 F3
'Abd al Kūrī i. Yemen 32 H7
'Abd Allah, Khawr sea chan. Iraq/Kuwait 35 H5
Abdānān Iran 35 G4
Abdollāhābād Iran 35 I4
Abdulino Rus. Fed. 11 Q5
Abéché Chad 47 F3
Abellinum Italy see Avellino
Abel Tasman National Park N.Z. 59 D5
Abengourou Côte d'Ivoire 46 C4
Åbenrå Denmark see Aabenraa
Abeokuta Nigeria 46 D4
Aberaeron U.K. 19 C6
Aberchirder U.K. 20 G3
Abercorn Zambia see Mbala
Abercrombie r. Australia 58 D4
Aberdare U.K. 19 D7
Aberdaugleddau U.K. see Milford Haven
Aberdeen Australia 58 E4
Aberdeen S. Africa 50 E7
Aberdeen U.K. 20 G3
Aberdeen U.S.A. 62 H2
Aberdeen Lake Canada 61 I3
Aberdovey U.K. 19 C6
Aberfeldy U.K. 20 F4
Aberford U.K. 18 F5
Aberfoyle U.K. 20 E4
Abergavenny U.K. 19 D7
Abergwaun U.K. see Fishguard
Aberhonddu U.K. see Brecon
Abermaw U.K. see Barmouth
Aberporth U.K. 19 C6
Abersoch U.K. 19 C5
Abertawe U.K. see Swansea
Aberteifi U.K. see Cardigan
Aberystwyth U.K. 19 C6
Abeshr Chad see Abéché
Abez' Rus. Fed. 11 S2
Abhā Saudi Arabia 32 F6
Abhar Iran 35 H3
Abiad, Bahr el r. Sudan/Uganda 32 D6 see White Nile
Abidjan Côte d'Ivoire 46 C4
Abijatta-Shalla National Park Eth. 48 D3
Abilene TX U.S.A. 62 H5
Abingdon U.K. 19 F7
Abington Reef Australia 56 E3
Abinsk Rus. Fed. 34 E1
Abitibi, Lake Canada 63 K2
Abminga Australia 55 F6
Abnūb Egypt 34 C5
Åbo Fin. see Turku
Abohar India 36 C3
Aboisso Côte d'Ivoire 46 C4
Abomey Benin 46 D4
Abong Mbang Cameroon 46 E4
Abou Déia Chad 47 F3
Abovyan Armenia 35 G2
Aboyne U.K. 20 G3
Abqaiq Saudi Arabia 48 E1
Abramov, Mys pt Rus. Fed. 12 I2
Abrantes Port. 25 B4
Abra Pampa Arg. 70 C2
Abri Sudan 32 D5
Abrolhos Bank sea feature S. Atlantic Ocean 72 F7
Abruzzo, Parco Nazionale d' nat. park Italy 26 E4
Absalom, Mount Antarctica 76 B1
Absaroka Range mts U.S.A. 62 E3
Abtar, Jabal al hills Syria 39 C2
Abū aḍ Ḍuhūr Syria 39 C2
Abū al Ḥusayn, Qā' imp. l. Jordan 39 D3
Abū 'Alī i. Saudi Arabia 35 H6
Abū 'Āmūd, Wādī watercourse Jordan 39 C4

2

Abū 'Arīsh Saudi Arabia 32 F6
Abū 'Aweigîla well Egypt see Abū 'Uwayqilah
Abu Deleiq Sudan 32 D6
Abu Dhabi U.A.E. 33 H5
Abū Du'ān Syria 39 D1
Abū Ḥafnah, Wādī watercourse Jordan 39 D3
Abu Haggag Egypt see Ra's al Ḩikmah
Abū Ḥallūfah, Jabal hill Jordan 39 C4
Abu Hamed Sudan 32 D6
Abuja Nigeria 46 D4
Abū Jurdhān Jordan 39 B4
Abu Kamāl Syria 35 F4
Abu Matariq Sudan 47 F3
Abumombazi Dem. Rep. Congo 48 C3
Abunā r. Bol. 68 E5
Abunã Brazil 68 E5
Ābune Yosēf mt. Eth. 32 E7
Abū Nujaym Libya 47 E1
Abū Qa'ţūr Syria 39 C2
Abu Rawthah, Jabal mt. Egypt 39 B5
Aburo mt. Dem. Rep. Congo 48 D3
Abu Road India 31 G4
Abū Rujmayn, Jabal mts Syria 39 D2
Abū Rūtha, Gebel mt. Egypt see Abū Rawthah, Jabal
Abū Simbil Egypt see Abū Sunbul
Abū Sunbul Egypt 32 D5
Abū Ţarfā', Wādī watercourse Egypt 39 A5
Abū 'Uwayqilah well Egypt 39 B4
Abu Zabad Sudan 32 C7
Abū Ẓabī U.A.E. see Abu Dhabi
Abu Zanîmah Egypt 34 D5
Abu Zenîma Egypt see Abū Zanīmah
Abyad Sudan 32 C7
Abyaḍ, Jabal al mts Syria 39 C2
Abyār al Ḩakim well Libya 34 A5
Abydos Australia 54 B5
Abyei Sudan 32 C8
Abyssinia country Africa see Ethiopia
Academician Vernadsky research station Antarctica see Vernadsky
Academy Bay Rus. Fed. see Akademii, Zaliv
Acadia prov. Canada see Nova Scotia
Açailândia Brazil 69 I5
Acamarachi mt. Chile see Pili, Cerro
Acampamento de Caça do Mucusso Angola 49 C5
Acandí Col. 66 E7
A Cañiza Spain 25 B2
Acaponeta Mex. 66 E4
Acapulco Mex. 66 E5
Acapulco de Juárez Mex. see Acapulco
Acará Brazil 69 I4
Acarai Mountains hills Brazil/Guyana 69 G3
Acaraú Brazil 69 J4
Acaray, Represa de resr Para. 70 E3
Acarigua Venez. 68 E2
Acatlan Mex. 66 E5
Accho Israel see 'Akko
Accomac VA U.S.A. 64 D4
Accra Ghana 46 C4
Accrington U.K. 18 E5
Acebuches Mex. 67 G2
Achacachi Bol. 68 E7
Achaguas Venez. 68 E2
Achalpur India 36 D5
Achampet India 38 C2
Achan Rus. Fed. 44 E2
Achayvayam Rus. Fed. 29 S3
Acheng China 44 B3
Achhota India 38 D1
Achill Ireland 21 C4
Achillbeg Island Ireland 21 B4
Achill Island Ireland 21 B4
Achiltibuie U.K. 20 D2
Achinsk Rus. Fed. 28 K4
Achit Rus. Fed. 11 R1
Achit Nuur l. Mongolia 42 G3
Achkhoy-Martan Rus. Fed. 35 G2
Achna Cyprus 39 A2
Achnasheen U.K. 20 D3
Achuev Rus. Fed. 12 I2
Acıpayam Turkey 34 E3
Acireale Sicily Italy 26 F6
Acklins Island Bahamas 67 J4
Acle U.K. 19 I6
Aconcagua, Cerro mt. Arg. 70 B4
Açores terr. N. Atlantic Ocean see Azores
Açores, Arquipélago dos terr. N. Atlantic Ocean see Azores
A Coruña Spain 25 B2
Acqui Terme Italy 26 C2
Acra NY U.S.A. 64 D1
Acragas Sicily Italy see Agrigento
Acraman, Lake salt flat Australia 57 A7
Acre r. Brazil 68 E6
Acre Israel see 'Akko
Acre, Bay of Israel see Haifa, Bay of
Acri Italy 26 G5
Ács Hungary 17 Q7
Actaeon Group is Fr. Polynesia see Actéon, Groupe
Actéon, Groupe is Fr. Polynesia 75 K7
Acton Ont. Canada 64 A1
Acton CA U.S.A. 65 C4
Acungui Brazil 71 A4
Acunum Acusio France see Montélimar
Ada OK U.S.A. 63 H5
Adaja r. Spain 25 D3
Adalia Turkey see Antalya
Adam Oman 33 I5
Adam, Mount hill Falkland Is 70 E8
Adamantina Brazil 71 A3
Adams MA U.S.A. 64 I2
Adam's Peak Sri Lanka 38 D5
Adamstown Pitcairn Is 75 L7
'Adan Yemen see Aden
Adana Turkey 39 B1
Adana prov. Turkey 39 B1
Adana Yemen see Aden
Adapazarı Turkey 27 N4
Adare Ireland 21 D5
Adare, Cape Antarctica 76 H2
Adavale Australia 57 C5
Ad Dabbah Sudan see Ed Debba
Ad Dafinah Saudi Arabia 32 F5
Ad Dahnā' des. Saudi Arabia 35 G5
Ad Dakhla W. Sahara 46 B2
Ad Damir Sudan see Ed Damer
Ad Dammām Saudi Arabia see Dammam
Addanki India 38 C3
Ad Dār al Ḩamrā' Saudi Arabia 32 E4
Ad Darb Saudi Arabia 32 F6
Ad Dawādimī Saudi Arabia 32 F5
Ad Dawḥah Qatar see Doha
Ad Dawr Iraq 35 F4
Ad Dayr Iraq 35 G5
Ad Dibdibah plain Saudi Arabia 35 G6
Aḍ Ḍiffah plat. Egypt/Libya see Libyan Plateau
Addis Ababa Eth. 48 D3
Addison NY U.S.A. 64 C1
Addlestone U.K. 19 G7
Addo Elephant National Park S. Africa 51 G7

3

Ad Duwayd well Saudi Arabia 35 F5
Ad Duwaym Sudan see Ed Dueim
Adegaon India 36 D5
Adelaide Australia 57 B7
Adelaide i. Australia 54 E3
Adelaide River Australia 54 F3
Adele Island Australia 54 C3
Adélie Coast Antarctica 76 G2
Adélie Land reg. Antarctica 76 G2
Adelong Australia 58 D5
Aden Yemen 32 F7
Aden, Gulf of Somalia/Yemen 32 G7
Adena OH U.S.A. 64 A2
Aderbissinat Niger 46 D3
Aderno Sicily Italy see Adrano
Adesar India 36 B5
Adh Dhāyūf well Saudi Arabia 35 G6
'Adhfā' well Saudi Arabia 35 F5
'Ādhirīyāt, Jibāl al mts Jordan 39 C4
Adi i. Indon. 41 I8
'Adi Ārk'ay Eth. 32 E7
Adige r. Italy 26 E2
Ādigrat Eth. 32 E7
Adilabad India 38 C2
Adilcevaz Turkey 35 F3
Adīrī Libya 47 E2
Adirondack Mountains NY U.S.A. 64 D1
Ādīs Ābeba Eth. see Addis Ababa
Adi Ugri Eritrea see Mendefera
Adıyaman Turkey 34 E3
Adjud Romania 27 L1
Admiralty Island Canada 61 H3
Admiralty Island National Monument-Kootznoowoo Wilderness nat. park U.S.A. 60 E4
Admiralty Islands P.N.G. 52 E2
Ado-Ekiti Nigeria 46 D4
Adok Sudan 32 D8
Adonara i. Indon. 54 C2
Adoni India 38 C3
Ado-Tymovo Rus. Fed. 44 F2
Adour r. France 24 D5
Adra Spain 25 E5
Adramyttium Turkey see Edremit
Adramyttium, Gulf of Turkey see Edremit Körfezi
Adrano Sicily Italy 26 F6
Adrar Alg. 46 C2
Adrar hills Mali see Ifôghas, Adrar des
Adré Chad 47 F3
Adria Italy 26 E2
Adrian TX U.S.A. 62 G4
Adrianople Turkey see Edirne
Adrianopolis Turkey see Edirne
Adriatic Sea Europe 26 E3
Adua Indon. 41 H7
Adua Eth. see Ādwa
Adunara i. Indon. see Adonara
Adusa Dem. Rep. Congo 48 C3
Aduwa Eth. see Ādwa
Adverse Well Australia 54 C5
Ādwa Eth. 48 D2
Adycha r. Rus. Fed. 29 O3
Adyk Rus. Fed. 13 J7
Adzopé Côte d'Ivoire 46 C4
Aegean Sea Greece/Turkey 27 K5
Aegina i. Greece see Aigina
Aegyptus country Africa see Egypt
Aela Jordan see Al 'Aqabah
Aelana Jordan see Al 'Aqabah
Aelia Capitolina Israel/West Bank see Jerusalem
Aelönlaplap atoll Marshall Is see Ailinglaplap
Aenus Turkey see Enez
Aesernia Italy see Isernia
A Estrada Spain 25 B2
Afabet Eritrea 32 E6
Afanas'yevo Rus. Fed. 12 L4
Affreville Alg. see Khemis Miliana
Afghānestān country Asia see Afghanistan
Afghanistan country Asia 33 K3
Afgooye Somalia 48 E3
'Afīf Saudi Arabia 32 F5
Afiun Karahissar Turkey see Afyon
Afjord Norway 14 G5
Aflou Alg. 22 D5
Afmadow Somalia 48 E3
Afogados da Ingazoira Brazil 69 K5
A Fonsagrada Spain 25 C2
Afonso Cláudio Brazil 71 C3
Afrēra Terara vol. Eth. 32 F7
Africa Nova country Africa see Tunisia
'Afrīn Syria 39 C1
'Afrīn, Nahr r. Syria/Turkey 39 C1
Afşin Turkey 34 E3
Afuá Brazil 69 H4
'Afula Israel 39 B3
Afyon Turkey 27 N5
Afyonkarahisar Turkey see Afyon
Agadès Niger see Agadez
Agadez Niger 46 D3
Agadir Morocco 46 C1
Agalega Islands Mauritius 73 L6
Agan r. Rus. Fed. 11 Q3
Agapa Russia 76 E2
Agara Georgia 35 F2
Agartala India 37 G5
Agashi India 38 B2
Agashi Iraq 35 G4
Agate Fossil Beds National Monument NY U.S.A. see 'Agra
Agattu i. U.S.A. see Attu
Agboville Côte d'Ivoire 46 C4
Ağcabadi Azer. 35 G2
Ağdam Azer. 35 G3
Ağdaş Azer. 35 G2
Agde France 24 F5
Agdzhabedi Azer. see Ağcabadi
Agedabia Libya see Ajdābiyā
Agen France 24 E4
Aggeneys S. Africa 50 D5
Agfa r. Australia 54 B5
Agghierid nat. park Hungary 17 R6
Aghil Pass China/Jammu and Kashmir 36 D1
Ağın Turkey 34 E3
Aginskoye Rus. Fed. 42 G1
Aginum France see Agen
Agios Dimitrios Greece 27 J6
Agios Efstratios i. Greece 27 K5
Agios Georgios i. Greece 27 J6
Agios Nikolaos Greece 27 K7
Agios Theodoros Cyprus 39 B2
Agiou Orous, Kolpos b. Greece 27 J4
Agirwat Hills Sudan 32 E6
Agisanang S. Africa 51 G4
Agnes, Mount hill Australia 55 E6
Agnew Australia 55 C6
Agnibilékrou Côte d'Ivoire 46 C4
Agnita Romania 27 K2
Agniye-Afanas'yevsk Rus. Fed. 44 E2
Agra India 36 D4
Agrakhanskiy Poluostrov pen. Rus. Fed. 35 G2
Agram Croatia see Zagreb
Agri Turkey 35 F3
Agria Gramvousa i. Greece 27 J7
Agrigento Sicily Italy 26 E6
Agrigentum Sicily Italy see Agrigento
Agrinio Greece 27 I5
Agropoli Italy 26 F4
Ağrız Rus. Fed. 11 Q4
Ağsu Azer. 35 H2

4

Agua, Volcán de vol. Guat. 66 F6
Agua Clara Brazil 70 F2
Aguadilla Puerto Rico 67 K5
Agua Escondida Arg. 70 C5
Aguanga CA U.S.A. 65 D4
Aguapeí r. Brazil 71 A3
Agua Prieta Mex. 66 C2
Aguaro-Guariquito, Parque Nacional nat. park Venez. 68 E2
Aguascalientes Mex. 66 D4
Agudos Brazil 71 A3
Águeda Port. 25 B3
Aguemour reg. Alg. 46 D2
Aguié Niger 46 D3
Aguijan i. N. Mariana Is 41 L3
Aguilar de Campóo Spain 25 D2
Aguilas Spain 25 F5
Agulhas, Cape S. Africa 50 E8
Agulhas Bay sea feature Southern Ocean 73 J9
Agulhas Negras mt. Brazil 71 B3
Agulhas Plateau sea feature Southern Ocean 73 J8
Agulhas Ridge sea feature S. Atlantic Ocean 72 I8
Ahaggar plat. Alg. see Hoggar
Ahar Iran 35 H3
Ahaura N.Z. 59 C6
Ahipara Bay N.Z. 59 D2
Ahiri India 38 D2
Ahklun Mountains U.S.A. 60 B4
Ahmadabad India 36 C5
Aḥmad al Bāqir, Jabal mt. Jordan 39 B5
Ahmadnagar India 38 B2
Ahmadpur East Pak. 33 L4
Ahmar mts Eth. 48 E3
Ahmar Mountains Eth. see Ahmar
Ahmedabad India see Ahmadabad
Ahmednagar India see Ahmadnagar
Ahram Iran 35 H5
Āhtāri Fin. 14 N5
Āhū Iran 35 H5
Ahun France 24 F3
Ahvāz Iran 35 H4
Ahwa India 38 B1
Ahwāz Iran see Ahvāz
Ai-Ais Namibia 50 C4
Ai-Ais Hot Springs and Fish River Canyon Park nature res. Namibia 50 C4
Aichwara India 36 D4
Aigialousa Cyprus 39 B2
Aigina i. Greece 27 J6
Aigio Greece 27 J5
Aigle de Chambeyron mt. France 24 H4
Aigües Tortes i Estany de Sant Maurici, Parc Nacional d' nat. park Spain 25 G2
Ai He r. China 44 B4
Aihui China 42 D4
Aijal India see Aizawl
Aikawa Japan 45 E5
Aiken U.S.A. 63 K5
Aileron Australia 54 F5
Ailinglabelab atoll Marshall Is see Ailinglaplap
Ailinglaplap atoll Marshall Is 74 H5
Ailsa Craig Ont. Canada 64 A1
Ailsa Craig i. U.K. 20 D5
Aimangala India 38 C3
Almorés, Serra dos hills Brazil 71 C2
Aïn Beïda Alg. 26 B7
'Aïn Ben Tili Mauritania 46 C2
'Aïn Dâlla spring Egypt see 'Ayn Dāllah
Aïn Defla Alg. 25 G5
Aïn Deheb Alg. 25 G6
Aïn el Hadjel Alg. 25 H6
'Aïn el Maqfi spring Egypt see 'Ayn al Maqfī
Aïn el Melh Alg. 25 H6
Aïn-M'Lila Alg. 26 B7
Aïn Oussera Alg. 25 H6
Aïn Salah Alg. see In Salah
Aïn Sefra Alg. 22 D5
Aïn Taya Alg. 25 H5
Aïn Tédélès Alg. 25 G5
Aïn Temouchent Alg. 22 D5
'Aïn Tibaghbagh spring Egypt see 'Ayn Tabaghbagh
'Aïn Tîmeïra spring Egypt see 'Ayn Tumayrah
'Aïn Zeïtûn Egypt see 'Ayn Zaytūn
Aiquile Bol. 68 E7
Airdric Canada 62 C1
Airdrie U.K. 20 F5
Aire-sur-l'Adour France 24 D5
Air Force Island Canada 61 K3
Airpanas Indon. 54 D1
Aisne r. France 24 F2
Aïssa, Djebel mt. Alg. 22 D5
Aitamännikkö Fin. 14 N3
Aitana mt. Spain 25 F4
Aït Benhaddou tourist site Morocco 22 C5
Aiud Romania 27 J1
Aix France see Aix-en-Provence
Aix-en-Provence France 24 G5
Aix-la-Chapelle Germany see Aachen
Aix-les-Bains France 24 G4
Aíyina i. Greece see Aigina
Aíyion Greece see Aigio
Aizawl India 37 H5
Aizkraukle Latvia 15 N8
Aizpute Latvia 15 L8
Aizu-Wakamatsu Japan 45 E5
Ajaccio Corsica France 24 I6
Ajanta India 38 B1
Ajanta Range hills India see Sahyadriparvat Range
Ajayameru India see Ajmer
Aj Bogd Uul mt. Mongolia 42 H4
Ajdābiyā Libya 47 F1
a-Jiddet plain Oman see Ḩarāsīs, Jiddat al
'Ajlūn Jordan 39 B3
Ajmer India 36 C4
Ajmer-Merwara India see Ajmer
Ajnala India 36 C3
Ajo AZ U.S.A. 65 F4
Ajrestan Afgh. 36 H2
Ajyyap Turkm. 35 I3
Akademii, Zaliv b. Rus. Fed. 44 E1
Akagera National Park Rwanda 48 D4
Akalkot India 38 C2
Akama, Akra c. Cyprus see Arnauti, Cape
Akamagaseki Japan see Shimonoseki
Akan Kokuritsu-kōen Japan 44 G4
Akaroa N.Z. 59 D6
Akāshat Iraq 35 E4
Akbarābād Iran 35 I5
Akbarpur Uttar Prad. India 36 E4
Akbarpur Uttar Prad. India 37 E4
Akbez Turkey 35 F3
Akçadağ Turkey 34 E3
Akçakale Turkey 27 N4
Akçakoca Turkey 27 N4
Akçaova Dağları mts Turkey 27 M5
Akçaköyunlu Turkey 39 C1
Akçalı Dağları mts Turkey 39 A1
Akchâr reg. Mauritania 46 B3

5

Akdağlar mts Turkey 27 M6
Akdağmadeni Turkey 34 D3
Akdere Turkey 39 A1
Åkersberga Sweden 15 K7
Aketi Dem. Rep. Congo 48 C3
Akgyr Erezi hills Turkm. 35 I2
Akhali-Afoni Georgia see Akhali Ap'oni
Akhali Ap'oni Georgia 35 F2
Akhḍar, Al Jabal al mts Libya 47 F1
Akhḍar, Jabal mts Oman 33 I5
Akhisar Turkey 27 L5
Akhnoor Jammu and Kashmir 36 C2
Akhsu Azer. see Ağsu
Akhta Armenia see Hrazdan
Akhtarin Syria 39 C1
Akhtubinsk Rus. Fed. 13 J6
Akhty Rus. Fed. 35 G2
Akhtyrka Ukr. see Okhtyrka
Aki Japan 45 D6
Akiéni Gabon 48 B4
Akimiski Island Canada 63 K1
Akishma r. Rus. Fed. 44 D1
Akita Japan 45 F5
Akjoujt Mauritania 46 B3
Akkajaure l. Sweden 14 J3
Akkerman Ukr. see Bilhorod-Dnistrovs'kyy
'Akko Israel 39 B3
Akkol' Akmolinskaya Oblast' Kazakh. 28 I4
Akkol' Atyrauskaya Oblast' Kazakh. 13 K7
Akku Kazakh. 42 D2
Akkul' Kazakh. see Akkol'
Akkuş Turkey 34 E2
Akkyr, Gory hills Turkm. see Akgyr Erezi
Aklavik Canada 60 E3
Aklera India 36 D4
Ak-Mechet Kazakh. see Kyzylorda
Akmenrags pt Latvia 15 L8
Akmeqit China 36 D3
Akmola Kazakh. see Astana
Akmolinsk Kazakh. see Astana
Akobo Sudan 47 G4
Akobo Wenz r. Eth./Sudan 48 D3
Akokan Niger 46 D3
Akola India 38 C1
Akom II Cameroon 46 E4
Akonolinga Cameroon 46 E4
Akordat Eritrea 32 E6
Akot India 36 D5
Akpatok Island Canada 61 L3
Akqi China 42 D4
Akra, Jabal mt. Syria/Turkey see Aqra', Jabal al
Akranes Iceland 14 [inset]
Akrehamn Norway 15 D7
Akrérèb Niger 46 D3
Akron OH U.S.A. 64 A2
Akron PA U.S.A. 64 C2
Akron NY U.S.A. 64 B1
Akrotiri Bay Cyprus 39 A2
Akrotiri Bay Cyprus see Akrotiri Bay
Akrotiriou, Kolpos b. Cyprus see Akrotiri Bay
Akrotiri Sovereign Base Area military base Cyprus 39 A2
Aksai Chin terr. Asia 36 D2
Aksaray Turkey 34 D3
Aksay China 42 G5
Aksay Kazakh. 11 Q5
Ak-Say r. Kyrg. 33 M1
Aksay Rus. Fed. 13 H7
Akşehir Turkey 27 N5
Akşehir Gölü l. Turkey 27 N5
Akseki Turkey 34 C3
Aksha Rus. Fed. 43 K2
Akshiganak Kazakh. 42 A3
Akshukur Kazakh. 35 H2
Aksu China 42 E4
Aksu Kazakh. 42 D2
Aksu r. Turkey 27 N6
Aksual Kazakh. 42 B1
Aksu-Ayuly Kazakh. 42 C3
Aksubayevo Rus. Fed. 13 K5
Āksum Eth. 32 E7
Aktag mt. China 37 G1
Aktaş Dağı mt. Turkey 35 G3
Aktau Kazakh. 30 E2
Aktobe Kazakh. 30 E1
Aktogay Karagandinskaya Oblast' Kazakh. 42 D3
Aktogay Vostochnyy Kazakhstan Kazakh. 42 D3
Aktsyabrski Belarus 13 F5
Aktyubinsk Kazakh. see Aktobe
Akulivik Canada 61 K2
Akune Japan 45 C6
Akure Nigeria 46 D4
Akureyri Iceland 14 [inset]
Akusha Rus. Fed. 13 G2
Akwanga Nigeria 46 D4
Akxokesay China 37 G1
Akyab Myanmar see Sittwe
Akyatan Gölü salt l. Turkey 39 B1
Akyazı Turkey 27 N4
Akzhaykyn, Ozero salt l. Kazakh. 42 B4
Ål Norway 15 F6
'Alā, Jabal al hills Syria 39 C2
Alabama state U.S.A. 63 J5
Alabama r. U.S.A. 63 J6
Alabat i. Phil. 41 G4
Alaca Turkey 34 D2
Alacahan Turkey 34 E3
Alaçam Turkey 34 D2
Alaçam Dağları mts Turkey 27 M5
Alacant Valencia Spain see Alicante
Alaçatı Turkey 27 L5
Aladağ Turkey 34 D3
Ala Dağı mt. Turkey 35 F3
Ala Dağları mts Turkey 34 D3
'Alā' al Dīn Libya 34 A5
'Alam Libya see Al 'Adam
Ala'er China 42 E4
Alag Hu l. China 37 I2
Alagir Rus. Fed. 35 G2
Alagoinhas Brazil 71 D1
Alahärmä Fin. 14 M5
Al Aḩmadī Kuwait 35 H5
Alai Range mts Asia 33 L2
Ajnala India 36 C3
Alajärvi Fin. 14 M5
Ajo AZ U.S.A. 65 F4
Al 'Ajrūd well Egypt 39 B4
Alakanuk U.S.A. 60 B3
Al Akhḍar Saudi Arabia 32 E4
Alakol', Ozero salt l. Kazakh. 28 J5
Ala Kul salt l. Kazakh. see Alakol', Ozero
Alakurtti Rus. Fed. 14 Q3
Al 'Alamayn Egypt 34 C5
Al 'Alayyah Saudi Arabia 32 F6
Alama Somalia 48 E3
Alāmarvdasht watercourse Iran 35 I5
Alameda CA U.S.A. 65 B3
'Alam el Rūm, Rās pt Egypt see 'Alam ar Rūm, Ra's
Al Amghar waterhole Iraq 35 G5
Al 'Āmirīyah Egypt 34 C5
Alamo NV U.S.A. 65 D3
Alamo Dam AZ U.S.A. 65 F3
Alamogordo U.S.A. 62 F5

6

Alamos Sonora Mex. 66 B3
Alamos Sonora Mex. 66 C3
Alamos r. Mex. 62 G6
Alamosa U.S.A. 62 F4
Alampur India 38 C3
Alan Myanmar see Aunglan
Alanäs Sweden 14 I4
Åland is Fin. see Åland Islands
Aland India 38 C2
Al Andarin Syria 39 C2
Åland Islands Fin. 15 K6
Alando China 37 H3
Alandur India 38 D3
Alanya Turkey 34 D3
Alaplı Turkey 27 N4
Alappuzha India see Alleppey
Alapuzha India see Alleppey
Al 'Aqabah Jordan 39 B5
Al 'Aqīq Saudi Arabia 32 F5
Al 'Arabīyah as Sa'ūdīyah country Asia see Saudi Arabia
Alarcón, Embalse de resr Spain 25 E4
Al 'Arīsh Egypt 39 A4
Arṭāwīyah Saudi Arabia 32 G4
Alas, Selat sea chan. Indon. 54 B2
Alaşehir Turkey 27 M5
Alashiya country Asia see Cyprus
Al Ashmūnayn Egypt 34 C6
Alaska state U.S.A. 60 D3
Alaska, Gulf of U.S.A. 60 D4
Alaska Peninsula U.S.A. 60 B4
Alaska Range mts U.S.A. 60 D3
Ālāt Azer. 35 H3
Alatyr' Rus. Fed. 13 J5
Alatyr' r. Rus. Fed. 13 J5
Alausí Ecuador 68 C4
Alaverdi Armenia 35 G2
'Alavī Iran 35 H4
Alavieska Fin. 14 N4
Alavus Fin. 14 M5
Alawoona Australia 57 C7
Alay Kyrka Toosu mts Asia see Alai Range
Alayskiy Khrebet mts Asia see Alai Range
Al 'Azīzīyah Iraq 35 G4
Al 'Azīzīyah Libya 23 G5
Al Azraq al Janūbī Jordan 39 C4
Alba Italy 26 C2
Albacete Spain 25 F4
Al Bādiyah al Janūbīyah hill Iraq 35 G5
Al Bahrayn country Asia see Bahrain
Alba Iulia Romania 27 J1
Albājī Iran 35 H5
Albania country Europe 27 H4
Albany Australia 55 B8
Albany r. Canada 63 K1
Albany GA U.S.A. 63 K5
Albany NY U.S.A. 64 I1
Albany OR U.S.A. 62 C3
Albany Downs Australia 58 D1
Albardão do João Maria coastal area Brazil 70 F4
Al Bardī Libya 34 B5
Al Bāridah hills Saudi Arabia 39 C5
Al Baṣrah Iraq see Basra
Al Baṭḥa' marsh Iraq 35 G5
Albatross Bay Australia 56 C2
Albatross Island Australia 57 [inset]
Al Bawītī Egypt 34 C5
Al Bayḍā' Libya 32 K3
Al Bayḍā' Yemen 32 G7
Albemarle Island Galápagos Ecuador see Isabela, Isla
Albenga Italy 26 C2
Alberche r. Spain 25 D4
Alberga Australia 54 F5
Alberga watercourse Australia 57 A5
Albergaria-a-Velha Port. 25 B3
Albert Australia 58 C4
Albert France 24 F2
Albert, Lake Dem. Rep. Congo/Uganda 48 D3
Albert, Parc National nat. park Dem. Rep. Congo see Virunga, Parc National des
Alberta prov. Canada 62 E1
Alberta U.S.A. 64 C4
Albert Lea U.S.A. 63 I3
Albert Nile r. Sudan/Uganda 47 G4
Alberto de Agostini, Parque Nacional nat. park Chile 70 B8
Alberton S. Africa 51 I4
Albertville Dem. Rep. Congo see Kalemie
Albertville France 24 H4
Albi France 24 F5
Albina Suriname 69 H2
Albino Italy 26 C2
Albion NY U.S.A. 64 B1
Albion PA U.S.A. 64 A2
Al Biqā' valley Lebanon see El Béqaa
Al Bi'r Saudi Arabia 34 E5
Al Birk Saudi Arabia 32 F6
Al Biyāḍh reg. Saudi Arabia 32 G5
Alborán, Isla de i. Spain 25 E6
Ålborg Denmark see Aalborg
Ålborg Bugt b. Denmark see Aalborg Bugt
Al Buḩayrāt al Murrah lakes Egypt see Bitter Lakes
Albuquerque U.S.A. 62 F4
Al Burayj Syria 39 C2
Al Buraymī Oman 33 I5
Al Burj Jordan 39 B4
Alburquerque Spain 25 C4
Albury Australia 58 C6
Al Buşayrah Syria 39 D2
Al Buşayţā' plain Saudi Arabia 39 D4
Al Bushūk well Saudi Arabia 35 G5
Alcácer do Sal Port. 25 B4
Alcalá de Henares Spain 25 E3
Alcalá la Real Spain 25 E5
Alcamo Sicily Italy 26 E6
Alcañiz Spain 25 F3
Alcántara Spain 25 C4
Alcaraz Spain 25 E4
Alcázar de San Juan Spain 25 E4
Alcazarquivir Morocco see Ksar el Kebir
Alchevs'k Ukr. 13 H6
Alcobaça Brazil 71 D2
Alcoi Spain see Alcoy-Alcoi
Alcoota Australia 54 F5
Alcoy Spain see Alcoy-Alcoi
Alcoy-Alcoi Spain 25 F4
Alcúdia Spain 25 H4
Aldabra Islands Seychelles 49 E4
Aldan Rus. Fed. 29 N4
Aldan r. Rus. Fed. 29 N3
Alde r. U.K. 19 I6
Aldeburgh U.K. 19 I6
Alder Creek NY U.S.A. 64 D1
Alderney i. Channel Is 19 E9
Alder Peak CA U.S.A. 65 B3
Aldershot U.K. 19 G7
Aldingham U.K. 18 D4
Aldridge U.K. 19 F6
Aleg Mauritania 46 B3
Alegre Espírito Santo Brazil 71 C3
Alegre Minas Gerais Brazil 71 B2
Alegrete Brazil 70 E3

Aleksandra, Mys hd Rus. Fed. 44 E1
Aleksandriya Ukr. see Oleksandriya
Aleksandro-Nevskiy Rus. Fed. 13 I5
Aleksandropol Armenia see Gyumri
Aleksandrov Rus. Fed. 12 H4
Aleksandrov Gay Rus. Fed. 13 K6
Aleksandrovsk Rus. Fed. 11 R4
Aleksandrovskiy Rus. Fed. see
   Aleksandrovsk
Aleksandrovskoye Rus. Fed. 35 F1
Aleksandrovsk-Sakhalinskiy Rus. Fed.
   44 F2
Aleksandry, Zemlya i. Rus. Fed. 28 F1
Alekseyevka Akmolinskaya Oblast' Kazakh.
   see Akkol'
Alekseyevka Vostochnyy Kazakhstan Kazakh.
   see Terekty
Alekseyevka Amurskaya Oblast' Rus. Fed.
   44 B1
Alekseyevka Belgorodskaya Oblast'
   Rus. Fed. 13 H6
Alekseyevka Belgorodskaya Oblast'
   Rus. Fed. 13 H6
Alekseyevskaya Rus. Fed. 13 I6
Alekseyevskoye Rus. Fed. 12 K5
Aleksin Rus. Fed. 13 H5
Aleksinac Serbia 27 I3
Alèmbé Gabon 24 E2
Ålen Norway 14 G5
Alençon France 24 E2
Alenquer Brazil 69 H4
'Alenuihāhā Channel U.S.A. 62 [inset]
Alep Syria see Aleppo
Aleppo Syria 39 C1
Alert Canada 61 L1
Alerta Peru 68 D6
Alès France 24 G4
Aleşd Romania 27 J1
Aleshki Ukr. see Tsyurupyns'k
Aleşkirt Turkey see Eleşkirt
Alessandria Italy 26 C2
Alessio Albania see Lezhë
Ålesund Norway 14 F5
Aleutian Basin sea feature Bering Sea
   74 H2
Aleutian Islands U.S.A. 60 A4
Aleutian Range mts U.S.A. 60 C4
Aleutian Trench sea feature
   N. Pacific Ocean 74 I2
Alevina, Mys c. Rus. Fed. 29 Q4
Alevişik Turkey see Samandağı
Alexander, Kap c. Greenland see Ullersuaq
Alexander, Mount hill Australia 56 B2
Alexander Archipelago is U.S.A. 60 E4
Alexander Bay b. Namibia/S. Africa 50 C5
Alexander Bay S. Africa 50 C5
Alexander Island Antarctica 76 L2
Alexandra Australia 58 B6
Alexandra N.Z. 59 B7
Alexandra, Cape S. Georgia 70 I8
Alexandra Land i. Rus. Fed. see
   Aleksandry, Zemlya
Alexandreia Greece 27 J4
Alexandretta Turkey see Iskenderun
Alexandria Afgh. see Ghazni
Alexandria Egypt 34 C5
Alexandria Romania 27 K3
Alexandria S. Africa 51 H7
Alexandria Turkm. see Mary
Alexandria U.K. 20 E5
Alexandria LA U.S.A. 63 I5
Alexandria U.K. 18 I5
Alexandria VA U.S.A. 64 C3
Alexandria Arachoton Afgh. see Kandahār
Alexandria Prophthasia Afgh. see Farāh
Alexandrina, Lake Australia 57 B7
Alexandroupoli Greece 27 K4
Alexis Creek Canada 62 C1
Aley Lebanon 39 B3
Aleysk Rus. Fed. 42 E2
Al Farwānīyah Kuwait 35 G5
Al Fas Morocco see Fès
Al Fatḩah Syria 35 F4
Al Fāw Iraq 35 H5
Al Fayyūm Egypt 34 C5
Alfenas Brazil 71 B3
Alford U.K. 18 H5
Alfred ME U.S.A. 64 F1
Alfred NY U.S.A. 64 C1
Alfred and Marie Range hills Australia
   55 D6
Al Fujayrah U.A.E. see Fujairah
Al Fuqahā' Libya 47 E2
Al Furāt r. Iraq/Syria see Euphrates
Al Furāt r. Iraq/Syria 39 D2 see Euphrates
Ålgård Norway 15 D7
Algarrobo del Aguila Arg. 70 C5
Algarve reg. Port. 25 B5
Algeciras Spain 25 D5
Algemesí Spain 25 F4
Algena Eritrea 32 E6
Alger Alg. see Algiers
Algeria country Africa 46 C2
Algérie country Africa see Algeria
Al Ghammās Iraq 35 G5
Al Ghardaqah Egypt see Al Ghurdaqah
Al Ghawr plain Jordan/West Bank 39 B4
Al Ghaydah Yemen 32 H6
Alghero Sardinia Italy 26 C4
Al Ghurdaqah Egypt 32 D4
Algiers Alg. 25 H5
Algoa Bay S. Africa 51 G7
Algona U.S.A. 63 I3
Algorta Spain 25 E2
Algueirao Moz. see Hacufera
Al Ḩabakah Saudi Arabia 35 F5
Al Ḩabbānīyah Iraq 35 F4
Al Ḩadaqah well Saudi Arabia 35 G5
Al Ḩadhālīl plat. Saudi Arabia 35 F5
Al Ḩadīdīyah Syria 39 C2
Al Ḩadīthah Saudi Arabia 39 C4
Al Ḩadīthah Iraq 35 F4
Al Ḩaḍr Iraq see Hatra
Al Ḩafar well Saudi Arabia 35 F5
Al Ḩaffah Syria 39 C2
Al Ḩaggounia W. Sahara 46 B2
Al Ḩamād plain Asia 35 E4
Al Ḩamādah al Ḩamra' plat. Libya 46 E2
Alhama de Murcia Spain 25 F5
Al Ḩamīdīyah Syria 39 B2
Al Ḩammām Egypt 34 C5
Al Ḩanākīyah Saudi Arabia 32 F5
Al Ḩaniyah esc. Iraq 35 G5
Al Ḩarūj al Aswad hills Libya 47 E2
Al Ḩasakah Syria 35 F3
Al Ḩawi salt pan Saudi Arabia 39 D5
Al Ḩawjā' Saudi Arabia 34 C5
Al Ḩayy Iraq 35 G4
Al Ḩayz Egypt 34 C5
Al Ḩazm Saudi Arabia 34 E5
Al Ḩazm al Jawf Yemen 32 F6
Al Ḩibāk des. Saudi Arabia 33 H6
Al Ḩijānah Syria 39 C3
Al Ḩillah Iraq see Hillah
Al Ḩillah Saudi Arabia 48 E1
Al Ḩinnāh Saudi Arabia 48 E1
Al Ḩinw mt. Saudi Arabia 39 D4

Al Ḩīshah Syria 39 D1
Al Ḩismā plain Saudi Arabia 34 D5
Al Ḩişn Jordan 39 B3
Al Hoceima Morocco 25 E6
Al Ḩudaydah Yemen see Hodeidah
Al Ḩufrah reg. Saudi Arabia 34 E5
Al Ḩufūf Saudi Arabia 32 G4
Al Ḩüj hills Saudi Arabia 34 E5
Ali China 36 D2
'Alīābād Golestān Iran 35 I3
'Alīābād Hormozgan Iran 33 I4
'Alīābād Kordestān Iran 35 I3
Alīābād, Kūh-e mt. Iran 35 H4
Aliağa Turkey 27 L5
Aliakmonas r. Greece 27 J4
Alibag India 38 B2
Āli Bayramli Azer. 35 H3
Alicante Spain 25 F4
Alice r. Australia 56 C2
Alice watercourse Australia 56 D5
Alice U.S.A. 62 H3
Alice, Punta pt Italy 26 G5
Alice Springs Australia 55 F5
Alichur Tajik. 33 L2
Alick Creek r. Australia 56 C4
Aliganj India 36 D3
Aligarh Rajasthan India 36 C4
Aligarh Uttar Prad. India 36 D4
Aligüdarz Iran 35 H4
Alihe China 44 A2
Alijūq, Kūh-e mt. Iran 35 H5
'Alī Kheyl Afgh. 36 B2
Al Imārāt al 'Arabīyah at Muttaḩidah
   country Asia see United Arab Emirates
Alimia i. Greece 27 L6
Alindao Cent. Afr. Rep. 48 C3
Alingsås Sweden 15 H8
Alipura India 36 D4
Alipur Duar India 37 G4
Aliquippa PA U.S.A. 64 A2
Alirajpur India 36 C5
Al 'Irāq country Asia see Iraq
Al 'Īsāwīyah Saudi Arabia 39 C4
Al Iskandarīyah Egypt see Alexandria
Al Iskandarīyah Iraq 35 G4
Al Ismā'īlīyah Egypt 34 D5
Al Ismā'īlīyah governorate Egypt 39 A4
Aliveri Greece 27 K5
Aliwal North S. Africa 51 H6
Al Jafr Jordan 39 C4
Al Jaghbūb Libya 34 B5
Al Jahrah Kuwait 35 G5
Al Jamalīyah Qatar 32 H4
Al Jarāwī well Saudi Arabia 39 D4
Al Jauf Saudi Arabia see Dumat al Jandal
Al Jawf Libya 47 F2
Al Jawsh Libya 47 E1
Al Jaza'ir country Africa see Algeria
Al Jaza'ir Alg. see Algiers
Aljezur Port. 25 B5
Al Jīl well Iraq 35 G5
Al Jithāmīyah Saudi Arabia 35 F6
Al Jīzah Egypt see Giza
Al Jīzah Jordan 39 B4
Al Jufrah Libya 47 E2
Al Julayqah well Saudi Arabia 35 H6
Aljustrel Port. 25 B5
Al Juwayf depr. Syria 39 C3
Al Juwayr well Saudi Arabia 32 F4
Al Kahfah Al Qaşīm Saudi Arabia 32 F4
Al Kahfah Ash Sharqīyah Saudi Arabia
   35 H6
Al Karak Jordan 39 B4
Al Kāzimīyah Iraq 35 G4
Al Khalīl West Bank see Hebron
Al Khāliş Iraq 35 G4
Al Khārijah Egypt 32 D4
Al Kharrūbah Egypt 39 A4
Al Khaṣab Oman 33 I4
Al Khawkhah Yemen 32 F7
Al Khawr Qatar 32 H4
Al Khums Libya 47 E1
Al Khunfah sand area Saudi Arabia 34 E5
Al Khunn Saudi Arabia 48 E1
Al Kifl Iraq 35 G4
Al Kiswah Syria 39 C3
Al Kūbrī Egypt 39 A4
Al Kūfah Iraq 35 G4
Al Kumayt Iraq 35 G4
Al Kuntillah Egypt 39 B5
Al Kusūr hills Saudi Arabia 39 D4
Al Kūt Iraq 35 G4
Al Kuwayt country Asia see Kuwait
Al Kuwayt Kuwait see Kuwait
Al Labbah plain Saudi Arabia 35 F5
Al Lādhiqīyah Syria see Latakia
Allagadda India 38 C3
Allahabad India 37 E4
Al Lajā lava field Syria 39 C3
Allakaket U.S.A. 60 C3
Allakh-Yun' Rus. Fed. 29 O3
Allanmyo Myanmar see Aunglan
Allanridge S. Africa 51 H4
Allapalli India 38 D2
'Allāqī, Wādī al watercourse Egypt 32 D5
'Allāqī, Wādī al watercourse Egypt see
   'Allāqī, Wādī al
Alldays S. Africa 51 I2
Allegheny r. PA U.S.A. 64 B2
Allegheny Mountains U.S.A. 64 A4
Allegheny Reservoir PA U.S.A. 64 B2
Allen, Lough l. Ireland 21 D3
Allendale Town U.K. 18 E4
Allende Coahuila Mex. 62 F6
Allentown PA U.S.A. 64 D2
Alleppey India 38 C4
Aller r. Germany 17 L4
Alliance NE U.S.A. 62 G3
Alliance OH U.S.A. 64 A2
Allier r. France 24 F3
Al Lihābah well Saudi Arabia 35 G6
Allinge-Sandvig Denmark 15 I9
Al Lişāfah well Saudi Arabia 35 G6
Al Lisān pen. Jordan 39 B4
Al Lith Saudi Arabia 32 F5
Alloa U.K. 20 F4
Allora Australia 58 F2
Allur India 38 D3
Alluru Kottapatnam India 38 D3
Alma Canada 63 M2
Alma U.S.A. 63 J3
Al Ma'āniyah well Saudi Arabia 35 F5
Alma-Ata Kazakh. see Almaty
Almada Port. 25 B4
Al Madāfi' plat. Saudi Arabia 34 D5
Almaden Australia 56 D3
Almadén Spain 25 D4
Al Madīnah Saudi Arabia see Medina
Al Mafraq Jordan 39 C3
Al Mahdum Syria 39 C1
Al Maḩia depr. Saudi Arabia 34 E6
Al Manāmah Bahrain see Manama
Almansa Spain 25 F4
Al Manşūrah Egypt 34 C5
Almanzor mt. Spain 25 D3

Al Mariyyah U.A.E. 33 H5
Al Marj Libya 47 F1
Almas, Rio das r. Brazil 71 A1
Al Maţariyah Egypt 34 D5
Almaty Kazakh. 42 D4
Al Mawşil Iraq see Mosul
Al Mayādīn Syria 35 F4
Al Mazār Egypt 39 A4
Almazny Rus. Fed. 29 M3
Almeirim Brazil 69 H4
Almeirim Port. 25 B4
Almelo Neth. 17 K4
Almenara Brazil 71 C2
Almendra, Embalse de resr Spain 25 C3
Almendralejo Spain 25 C4
Almería Spain 25 E5
Almería, Golfo de b. Spain 25 E5
Almetievsk Rus. Fed. see Al'met'yevsk
Al'met'yevsk Rus. Fed. 11 Q5
Älmhult Sweden 15 I8
Almina, Punta pt Spain 25 D6
Al Mindak Saudi Arabia 32 F5
Al Minyā Egypt 34 C5
Almirós Greece see Almyros
Al Mish'āb Saudi Arabia 35 H5
Almodôvar Port. 25 B5
Almond r. U.K. 20 F4
Almonte Spain 25 C5
Almora India 36 D3
Al Mu'ayzilah hill Saudi Arabia 39 D5
Al Mubarrez Saudi Arabia 32 G4
Al Mudaibī Oman 33 I5
Al Mukallā Yemen see Mukalla
Al Mukhā Yemen see Mocha
Al Mukhaylī Libya 32 B3
Almuñécar Spain 25 E5
Al Muqdādīyah Iraq 35 G4
Al Mūrītānīyah country Africa see
   Mauritania
Al Murūt well Saudi Arabia 35 E5
Almus Turkey 34 E2
Al Musannāh ridge Saudi Arabia 35 G5
Al Muwaqqar Jordan 39 C4
Almyros Greece 27 J5
Almyrou, Ormos b. Greece 27 K7
Alnwick U.K. 18 F3
Alofi Niue 53 J3
Aloja Latvia 15 N8
Along India 37 H3
Alongshan China 44 A2
Alonnisos i. Greece 27 J5
Alor i. Indon. 41 E8
Alor, Kepulauan is Indon. 41 E8
Alor Setar Malaysia 41 C7
Alor Star Malaysia see Alor Setar
Aloost Belgium see Aalst
Aloysius, Mount Australia 55 E6
Alozero Rus. Fed. 14 Q4
Alpena U.S.A. 63 K2
Alpercatas, Serra das hills Brazil 69 J5
Alpha Australia 56 D4
Alpha Ridge sea feature Arctic Ocean 77 A1
Alpine NY U.S.A. 64 C1
Alpine TX U.S.A. 62 G5
Alpine National Park Australia 58 C6
Alps mts Europe 24 H4
Al Qa'āmīyāt reg. Saudi Arabia 32 G6
Al Qaddāḩīyah Libya 47 E1
Al Qadmūs Syria 39 C2
Al Qāhirah Egypt see Cairo
Al Qā'īyah Saudi Arabia 32 F5
Al Qalībah Saudi Arabia 34 E5
Al Qāmishlī Syria 35 F3
Qar'ah Libya 34 B5
Al Qar'ah lava field Syria 39 C3
Al Qardāḩah Syria 39 C2
Al Qarqar Saudi Arabia 39 C4
Al Qaryatayn Syria 39 C2
Al Qaṭn Yemen 32 G6
Al Qaţrānah Jordan 39 C4
Al Qaṭrūn Libya 47 E2
Al Qāysūmah well Saudi Arabia 35 G5
Al Qumur country Africa see Comoros
Al Qunayţirah Syria 39 B3
Al Qunfidhah Saudi Arabia 32 F6
Al Qurayyāt Saudi Arabia 39 C4
Al Qurnah Iraq 35 G5
Al Quşaymah Egypt 39 B4
Al Quşayr Egypt 32 D4
Al Quşayr Syria 39 C2
Al Qūşīyah Egypt 34 C6
Al Quṭayfah Syria 39 C3
Al Quwayīyah Saudi Arabia 32 G5
Al Quwayrah Jordan 39 B5
Alroy Downs Australia 56 B3
Alsace reg. France 24 H2
Al Samīt well Iraq 35 F5
Alsager U.K. 19 E5
Alsatia reg. France see Alsace
Alston U.K. 18 E4
Alstonville Australia 58 F2
Alsunga Latvia 15 L8
Alta Norway 14 M2
Alta, Mount N.Z. 59 B7
Altaelva r. Norway 14 M2
Altafjorden sea chan. Norway 14 M1
Alta Floresta Brazil 69 G5
Altai Mountains Asia 42 F3
Altamaha r. U.S.A. 63 K6
Altamira Brazil 69 H4
Altamura Italy 26 G4
Altan Shiret China see Altan Shiret
Alta Paraíso de Goiás Brazil 71 B1
Altavista VA U.S.A. 64 B4
Altay China 42 F3
Altay Mongolia 42 I3
Altaysky Khrebet mts Asia see
   Altai Mountains
Altdorf Switz. 24 I3
Altea Spain 25 F4
Alteidet Norway 14 M1
Altenqoke China 37 H1
Altin Köprü Iraq 35 G4
Altinoluk Turkey 27 L5
Altınözü Turkey 39 C1
Altıntaş Turkey 27 N5
Altiplano plain Bol. 68 E7
Altmühl r. Germany 17 M6
Alto, Monte hill Italy 26 D2
Alto Chicapa Angola 49 B5
Alto del Moncayo mt. Spain 25 F3
Alto de Pencoso hills Arg. 70 C4
Alto Garças Brazil 69 H7
Alto Madidi, Parque Nacional nat. park Bol.
   68 E6
Alton NH U.S.A. 64 F1
Altoona PA U.S.A. 64 B2
Alto Parnaíba Brazil 69 I5
Alto Taquarí Mato Grosso Brazil 69 H7
Altötting Germany 17 N6
Altrincham U.K. 18 E5
Altún Kübrī Iraq see Altin Köprü
Altun Shan mts China 42 F4
Alturas U.S.A. 62 C3
Altus U.S.A. 62 H5
Al Ubaylah Saudi Arabia 48 F1
Alucra Turkey 34 E2
Alūksne Latvia 15 O8
Alūm Iran 35 H4
Alum Bridge WV U.S.A. 64 A3

Al 'Uqaylah Libya 47 E1
Al 'Uqaylah Saudi Arabia see An Nabk
Al Uqsur Egypt see Luxor
Alur India 38 C3
Al Urayq des. Saudi Arabia 34 E5
Al 'Urdun country Asia see Jordan
Alur Setar Malaysia see Alor Setar
'Alūt Iran 35 G4
Aluva India see Alwaye
Al 'Uwaynāt Libya 32 B5
Al 'Uwayqīlah Saudi Arabia 35 F5
Al 'Uzayr Iraq 35 G5
Alva U.S.A. 62 H4
Alvand, Kūh-e mt. Iran 35 H4
Alvarães Brazil 68 F4
Alvdal Norway 14 G5
Älvdalen Sweden 15 H6
Alvesta Sweden 15 I8
Ålvik Norway 15 E6
Alvik Sweden 14 J5
Alvin U.S.A. 63 H6
Alvorada do Norte Brazil 71 B1
Älvsbyn Sweden 14 L4
Al Wafrah Kuwait 35 G5
Al Wajh Saudi Arabia 32 E5
Al Waqbá well Saudi Arabia 35 G5
Alwar India 36 D4
Al Wari'ah Saudi Arabia 35 G5
Al Waţiyah well Egypt 34 B5
Alwaye India 38 C4
Al Widyān plat. Iraq/Saudi Arabia 35 F4
Al Wusayt well Saudi Arabia 35 G5
Alxa Youqi China see Ehen Hudag
Alxa Zuoqi China see Bayan Hot
Al Yaman country Asia see Yemen
Alyangula Australia 56 B2
Alyth U.K. 20 F4
Alytus Lith. 15 N9
Alzada U.S.A. 62 G3
Amacayacu, Parque Nacional nat. park
   Col. 68 D4
Amadeus, Lake salt flat Australia 55 E6
Amadjuak Lake Canada 61 K3
Amadora Port. 25 B4
Amakusa-nada b. Japan 45 C6
Åmål Sweden 15 H7
Amalia S. Africa 51 G4
Amaliada Greece 27 I6
Amalner India 36 C5
Amamapare Indon. 41 F8
Amambaí Brazil 70 E2
Amambaí, Serra de hills Brazil/Para. 70 E2
Amami-Ō-shima i. Japan 45 C7
Amami-shotō is Japan 45 C7
Amamula Dem. Rep. Congo 48 C4
Amantea Italy 26 G5
Amanzimtoti S. Africa 51 J6
Amapá Brazil 69 H3
Amarante Brazil 69 J5
Amarapura Myanmar 37 I5
Amareleja Port. 25 C4
Amargosa Brazil 71 D1
Amargosa watercourse CA U.S.A. 65 D2
Amargosa Desert NV U.S.A. 65 D2
Amargosa Range mts CA U.S.A. 65 D2
Amargosa Valley NV U.S.A. 65 D2
Amarillo U.S.A. 62 G4
Amarillo, Cerro mt. Arg. 70 C4
Amarkantak India 37 E5
Amarpur Madh. Prad. India 36 E5
Amasia Turkey see Amasya
Amasine W. Sahara 46 B2
Amasra Turkey 34 D2
Amasya Turkey 34 D2
Amata Australia 55 E6
Amatulla hill P.N.G. 56 E1
Amau P.N.G. 56 E1
Amazar Rus. Fed. 44 A1
Amazar r. Rus. Fed. 44 A1
Amazon r. S. America 68 F4
Amazonas r. S. America see Amazon
Amazon Cone sea feature S. Atlantic Ocean
   72 E5
Amazónia, Parque Nacional nat. park
   Brazil 69 G4
Ambajogai India 38 C2
Ambala India 36 D3
Ambalangoda Sri Lanka 38 D5
Ambalavao Madag. 49 E6
Ambam Cameroon 48 B3
Ambanja Madag. 49 E5
Ambarchik Rus. Fed. 29 R3
Ambarnyy Rus. Fed. 14 R4
Ambasa India see Ambassa
Ambasamudram India 38 C4
Ambassa India 37 G5
Ambathala Australia 57 D5
Ambato Ecuador 68 C4
Ambato Boeny Madag. 49 E5
Ambato Finandrahana Madag. 49 E6
Ambatolampy Madag. 49 E5
Ambatomainty Madag. 49 E5
Ambatondrazaka Madag. 49 E5
Ambejogai India see Ambajogai
Amberg Germany 17 M6
Ambergris Cay i. Belize 66 G5
Ambérieu-en-Bugey France 24 G4
Ambgaon India 37 H5
Ambianum France see Amiens
Ambikapur India 37 E5
Ambilobe Madag. 49 E5
Amble U.K. 18 F3
Ambler U.S.A. 60 C3
Ambleside U.K. 18 E4
Ambo India 37 F5
Amboasary Madag. 49 E6
Ambodifotatra Madag. 49 E5
Ambohimahasoa Madag. 49 E6
Ambohitra mt. Madag. 49 E5
Amboina Indon. see Ambon
Ambon Indon. 41 E8
Ambon i. Indon. 41 E8
Amboró, Parque Nacional nat. park Bol.
   68 F7
Ambositra Madag. 49 E6
Ambovombe Madag. 49 E6
Amboy CA U.S.A. 65 E3
Ambre, Cap d' c. Madag. see
   Bobaomby, Tanjona
Ambrim i. Vanuatu see Ambrym
Ambriz Angola 49 B4
Ambrizete Angola see N'zeto
Ambrym i. Vanuatu 53 G3
Am-Dam Chad 47 F3
Amded, Oued watercourse Alg. 46 D2
Amdo China see Lharigarbo
Amelia Court House VA U.S.A. 64 C4
Amenia NY U.S.A. 64 E2
Amer, Erg d' des. Alg. 48 A1
Amereli India see Amreli
American, North Fork r. CA U.S.A. 65 B1
Americana Brazil 71 B3
American Falls U.S.A. 62 E3
American Falls Reservoir U.S.A. 62 E3
American Fork U.S.A. 62 F4
American Samoa terr. S. Pacific Ocean
   53 J3
Americus U.S.A. 63 K5
Amersfoort Neth. 16 J4

Amersfoort S. Africa 51 I4
Amersham U.K. 19 G7
Amery Ice Shelf Antarctica 76 E2
Ames U.S.A. 63 I3
Amesbury U.K. 19 F7
Amesbury MA U.S.A. 64 F1
Amet India 36 C4
Amethi India 37 E4
Amfissa Greece 27 J5
Amga Rus. Fed. 29 O3
Amgalang China 43 L3
Amguid Alg. 46 D2
Amgu Rus. Fed. 44 E3
Amgun' r. Rus. Fed. 44 E1
Amherst MA U.S.A. 64 E1
Amherst U.K. 19 F7
Amherst NY U.S.A. 64 B1
Amida Turkey see Diyarbakır
Amiens France 24 E2
'Amij, Wādī watercourse Iraq 35 F4
Amik Ovası marsh Turkey 39 C1
'Amīnābād Iran 35 I5
Amindivi atoll Saudi Arabia 34 E5
Amindivi Islands India 38 B4
Amini atoll India 38 B4
Amino Eth. 48 E3
Aminuis Namibia 50 D2
Amīrābād Iran 35 G4
Amirante Islands Seychelles 73 L6
Amirante Trench sea feature Indian Ocean
   73 L6
Amisk Lake Canada 62 G1
Amistad, Represa de resr Mex./U.S.A. see
   Amistad Reservoir
Amistad Reservoir Mex./U.S.A. 62 G6
Amisus Turkey see Samsun
Amity Point Australia 58 F1
Amla India 36 D5
Amlapura Indon. see Karangasem
Amlash Iran 35 H3
Amlekhganj Nepal 37 F4
Åmli Norway 15 F7
Amlia Island U.S.A. 60 A4
Amlwch U.K. 18 C5
'Ammān Jordan 39 B4
Ammanazar Turkm. 35 I3
Ammanford U.K. 19 D7
Ämmänsaari Fin. 14 P4
'Ammār, Tall hill Syria 39 C3
Ammarnäs Sweden 14 J4
Ammaroo Australia 56 B4
Ammassalik Greenland 77 J2
Ammochostos Cyprus see Famagusta
Ammochostos Bay Cyprus 39 B2
Am Nābiyah Yemen 32 F7
Amne Machin Range mts China see
   A'nyêmaqên Shan
Amnok-kang r. China/N. Korea see
   Yalu Jiang
Amol Iran 35 I3
Amorgos i. Greece 27 K6
Amory U.S.A. 63 J5
Amos Canada 63 L2
Amoy China see Xiamen
Ampani India 38 D2
Amparai Sri Lanka 38 D5
Amparo Brazil 71 B3
Ampasimanolotra Madag. 49 E5
Amphitheatre Australia 58 A6
Amraoti India see Amravati
Amravati India 38 C1
Amrawad India 36 D5
Amreli India 36 B5
Amri Pak. 36 B4
Amring India 37 H4
Amritsar India 36 C3
Amroha India 36 D3
Amsele Sweden 14 K4
Amstelveen Neth. 16 I4
Amsterdam Neth. 16 I4
Amsterdam NY U.S.A. 64 D1
Amsterdam, Île i. Indian Ocean 73 N8
Amstetten Austria 17 O6
Am Timan Chad 47 F3
Amudar'ya r. Asia see Amudar'ya
Amudaryo r. Asia see Amudar'ya
Amund Ringnes Island Canada 61 I2
Amundsen, Mount Antarctica 76 F2
Amundsen Abyssal Plain sea feature
   Southern Ocean 76 J2
Amundsen Basin sea feature Arctic Ocean
   77 H1
Amundsen Bay Antarctica 76 D2
Amundsen Coast Antarctica 76 J1
Amundsen Glacier Antarctica 76 I1
Amundsen Gulf Canada 60 F2
Amundsen Ridges sea feature
   Southern Ocean 76 J2
Amundsen-Scott research station
   Antarctica 76 C1
Amundsen Sea Antarctica 76 K2
Amuntai Indon. 41 D8
Amur r. China 40 F3
Amur r. Rus. Fed. 44 F1
Amurdaryo r. Asia see Amudar'ya
Amur Oblast admin. div. Rus. Fed.
   Amurskaya Oblast'
Amursk Rus. Fed. 44 E2
Amurskaya Oblast' admin. div. Rus. Fed.
   44 C1
Amurskiy Liman strait Rus. Fed. 44 F1
Amurzet Rus. Fed. 44 C3
Amvrosiyivka Ukr. 13 H7
Amyderya r. Asia see Amudar'ya
Am-Zoer Chad 47 F3
Anaa atoll Fr. Polynesia 75 K7
Anabanua Indon. 41 A8
Anabar r. Rus. Fed. 29 M2
Anaco Venez. 68 F2
Anaconda U.S.A. 62 E2
Anacortes U.S.A. 62 C2
Anacuya Islands CA U.S.A. 65 C3
Anadolu Dağları mts Turkey 34 E2
Anadyr' Rus. Fed. 29 S3
Anadyr' r. Rus. Fed. see
   Anadyrskiy Zaliv
Anadyrskiy Liman strait Rus. Fed. 44 F1
Anadyrskiy Zaliv b. Rus. Fed. 29 T3
Anafi i. Greece 27 K6
Anage Brazil 71 C1
'Ānah Iraq 35 F4
Anaheim CA U.S.A. 65 D4
Anaimalai Hills India 38 C4
Anaiteum i. Vanuatu see Anatom
Anajás Brazil 69 I4
Anakie Australia 56 D4
Analalava Madag. 49 E5
Anama Brazil 68 F4
Anambas, Kepulauan is Indon. 41 C7
Anamur Turkey 39 A1
Anan Japan 45 D6
Anand India 36 C5
Anandapur India 37 F5
Anantapur India see Anantapur
Anantnag India 36 C2
Anant Peth India 36 D4
Anantapur India see Anantapur
Ananyev Ukr. see Anan'yiv
Anan'yiv Ukr. 13 F7

Anapa Rus. Fed. 34 E1
Anápolis Brazil 71 A2
Anár Iran see Anar
Anār Iran 35 I5
Anatolia reg. Turkey 34 D3
Anatom i. Vanuatu 53 G4
Añatuya Arg. 70 D3
Anaypazari Turkey see Gülnar
Anbyon N. Korea 45 B5
Ancenis France 24 D3
Anchorage U.S.A. 60 D3
Anchorage Island atoll Cook Is see
   Suwarrow
Anchuthengu India see Anjengo
Anci China see Langfang
An Cóbh Ireland see Cobh
Ancona Italy 26 E3
Ancud Chile 70 B6
Ancud, Golfo de g. Chile 70 B6
Ancyra Turkey see Ankara
Anda Heilong. China 44 B3
Anda Heilong. China see Daqing
Andacollo Chile 70 B4
Andado Australia 56 A5
Andahuaylas Peru 68 D6
Andal India 37 F5
Åndalsnes Norway 14 E5
Andalucía aut. comm. Spain 25 D5
Andalusia aut. comm. Spain see Andalucía
Andaman Basin sea feature Indian Ocean
   73 O5
Andaman Islands India 31 I5
Andaman Sea Indian Ocean 41 B6
Andamooka Australia 57 B6
Andapa Madag. 49 E5
Andegavum France see Angers
Andelle r. France 19 I9
Andenes Norway 14 J2
Andenne Belgium 16 J5
Andéramboukane Mali 46 D3
Andermatt Switz. 24 I3
Andernos-les-Bains France 24 D4
Anderson r. Canada 60 F3
Anderson AK U.S.A. 60 D3
Anderson IN U.S.A. 63 J3
Anderson SC U.S.A. 63 K5
Anderson Bay Australia 57 [inset]
Andes mts S. America 70 C4
Andfjorden sea chan. Norway 14 J2
Andhíparos i. Greece see Antiparos
Andhra Lake India 38 B2
Andhra Pradesh state India 38 C2
Andijon Uzbek. 33 L1
Andijon Uzbek. see Andijon
Andikithira i. Greece see Antikythira
Andilamena Madag. 49 E5
Andilanatoby Madag. 49 E5
Andimeshk Iran 35 H4
Andímilos i. Greece see Antimilos
Andípsara i. Greece see Antipsara
Andırın Turkey 34 E3
Andirlangar China 37 G1
Andkhvoy Afgh. 36 A1
Andoany Madag. 49 E5
Andoas Peru 68 C4
Andogskaya Gryada hills Rus. Fed. 12 H4
Andol India 38 C2
Andong China see Dandong
Andong S. Korea 45 C5
Andoom Australia 56 C2
Andorra country Europe 25 G2
Andorra la Vella Andorra 25 G2
Andorra la Vieja Andorra see
   Andorra la Vella
Andover U.K. 19 F7
Andover NY U.S.A. 64 C1
Andover OH U.S.A. 64 A2
Andøya i. Norway 14 I2
Andrade CA U.S.A. 65 E4
Andradina Brazil 71 A3
Andranomavo Madag. 49 E5
Andranopasy Madag. 49 E6
Andreanof Islands U.S.A. 74 I2
Andreapol' Rus. Fed. 12 G4
Andreas Isle of Man 18 C4
André Félix, Parc National de nat. park
   Cent. Afr. Rep. 48 C3
Andrelândia Brazil 71 B3
Andrews TX U.S.A. 62 G5
Andria Italy 26 G4
Androka Madag. 49 E6
Andropov Rus. Fed. see Rybinsk
Andros i. Bahamas 67 I4
Andros i. Greece 27 K6
Andros Town Bahamas 67 I4
Andrott i. India 38 B4
Andselv Norway 14 K2
Andújar Spain 25 D4
Andulo Angola 49 B5
Anec, Lake salt flat Australia 55 E5
Åneen-Kio terr. N. Pacific Ocean see
   Wake Island
Anéfis Mali 46 D3
Anegada, Bahía b. Arg. 70 D6
Anegada Passage Virgin Is (U.K.) 67 L5
Aného Togo 46 D4
Aneityum i. Vanuatu see Anatom
'Aneiza, Jabal hill Iraq see 'Unayzah, Jabal
Anemourion tourist site Turkey 39 A1
Anetchom, Île i. Vanuatu see Anatom
Aneto mt. Spain 25 G2
Ånewetak atoll Marshall Is see Enewetak
Aney Niger 46 E3
Aneytioum, Île i. Vanuatu see Anatom
Angalarri r. Australia 54 E3
Angamos, Punta pt Chile 70 B2
Ang'angxi China 44 A3
Angara r. Rus. Fed. 42 G1
Angarsk Rus. Fed. 42 I2
Angas Downs Australia 55 F6
Angatuba Brazil 71 A3
Ånge Sweden 14 I5
Angel, Salto waterfall Venez. see Angel Falls
Ángel de la Guarda, Isla i. Mex. 66 B3
Angel Falls waterfall Venez. 68 F2
Ängelholm Sweden 15 H8
Angellala Creek r. Australia 58 C1
Angels Camp CA U.S.A. 65 C2
Ångermanälven r. Sweden 14 J5
Angers France 24 D3
Angikuni Lake Canada 61 I3
Angistri i. Greece see Angkistri
Anglem, Mount hill N.Z. 59 A8
Anglesea Australia 58 B7
Anglesey i. U.K. 18 C5
Anglo-Egyptian Sudan country Africa see
   Sudan
Angmagssalik Greenland see Ammassalik
Ango Dem. Rep. Congo 48 C3
Angoche Moz. 49 D5
Angol Chile 70 B5
Angola country Africa 49 B5
Angola NY U.S.A. 64 B1
Angola Basin sea feature S. Atlantic Ocean
   72 H7
Angora Turkey see Ankara
Angoulême France 24 E4
Angra dos Reis Brazil 71 B3
Angren Uzbek. 33 L1
Anguang China 44 A3
Anguilla terr. West Indies 67 L5
Angul India 38 E1

Angutia Char i. Bangl. 37 G5
Anholt i. Denmark 15 G8
Anhui prov. China 43 L6
Anhumas Brazil 69 H7
Anhwei prov. China see Anhui
Aniak U.S.A. 60 C3
Aniakchak National Monument and Preserve nat. park U.S.A. 60 C4
Anitápolis Brazil 71 A4
Anıtlı Turkey 39 A1
Aniva Rus. Fed. 44 F3
Aniva, Mys c. Rus. Fed. 44 F3
Aniva, Zaliv b. Rus. Fed. 44 F3
Anjadip i. India 38 B3
Anjalankoski Fin. 15 O6
Anjengo India 38 C4
Anjir Avand Iran 35 I4
Anjou reg. France 24 D3
Anjouan i. Comoros see Nzwani
Anjozorobe Madag. 49 E5
Anjuthengu India see Anjengo
Ankang China 43 J6
Ankara Turkey 34 D3
Ankaratra mt. Madag. 49 E5
Ankazoabo Madag. 49 E6
Ankleshwar India 36 C5
Anklesvar India see Ankleshwar
Ankola India 38 B3
Anlu China 43 K6
Anmoore WV U.S.A. 64 A3
An Muileann gCearr Ireland see Mullingar
Anmyŏn-do i. S. Korea 45 B5
Ann, Cape Antarctica 76 D2
Ann, Cape MA U.S.A. 64 F1
Anna Rus. Fed. 13 I6
Anna, Lake VA U.S.A. 64 C3
Annaba Alg. 26 B6
An Nabk Saudi Arabia 39 C4
An Nabk Syria 39 C2
An Nafūd des. Saudi Arabia 35 F5
An Najaf Iraq 35 G5
Annalee r. Ireland 21 E3
Annalong U.K. 21 G3
Annan U.K. 20 F6
Annan r. U.K. 20 F6
'Annān, Wādī al watercourse Syria 39 D2
Annandale VA U.S.A. 64 C3
Anna Plains Australia 54 C4
Annapolis MD U.S.A. 64 C3
Annapurna Conservation Area nature res. Nepal 37 F3
Annapurna I mt. Nepal 37 E3
Ann Arbor U.S.A. 63 K3
Anna Regina Guyana 69 G2
An Nás Ireland see Naas
An Nāṣirīyah Iraq 35 G5
An Naṣrānī, Jabal mts Syria 39 C3
Annean, Lake salt flat Australia 55 B6
Annecy France 24 H4
An Nimārah Syria 39 C3
An Nimāṣ Saudi Arabia 32 F6
Anniston U.S.A. 63 J5
Annobón i. Equat. Guinea 46 D5
Annonay France 24 G4
An Nu'mānīyah Iraq 35 G4
An Nuṣayrīyah, Jabal mts Syria 39 C2
Anoón de Sardinas, Bahía de b. Col. 68 C3
Anorontany, Tanjona hd Madag. 49 E5
Anqing China 43 L6
Ansbach Germany 17 M6
Anser Group is Australia 58 C7
Anshan China 44 A4
Anshun China 42 J7
Anshunchang China 42 I7
An Sirhān, Wādī watercourse Saudi Arabia 34 E5
Anson Bay Australia 54 E3
Ansongo Mali 46 D3
Ansted WV U.S.A. 64 A3
Antabamba Peru 68 D6
Antakya Turkey 39 C1
Antalaha Madag. 49 F5
Antalya Turkey 27 N6
Antalya prov. Turkey 39 A1
Antalya Körfezi g. Turkey 27 N6
Antananarivo Madag. 49 E5
An tAonach Ireland see Nenagh
Antarctica 76
Antarctic Peninsula Antarctica 76 L2
Antas r. Brazil 71 A5
An Teallach mt. U.K. 20 D3
Antelope Range mts NV U.S.A. 65 D1
Antequera Spain 25 D5
Anthony Lagoon Australia 56 A3
Anti Atlas mts Morocco 22 C6
Antibes France 24 H5
Anticosti, Île d' i. Canada 61 L5
Anticosti Island Canada see Anticosti, Île d'
Antifer, Cap d' c. France 19 H9
Antigua i. Antigua and Barbuda 67 L5
Antigua country West Indies see Antigua and Barbuda
Antigua and Barbuda country West Indies 67 L5
Antikythira i. Greece 27 J7
Antikythiro, Steno sea chan. Greece 27 J7
Anti Lebanon mts Lebanon/Syria see Sharqī, Jabal ash
Antimilos i. Greece 27 K6
An tInbhear Mór Ireland see Arklow
Antioch Turkey see Antakya
Antioch CA U.S.A. 65 B1
Antiocheia ad Cragum tourist site Turkey 39 A1
Antiochia Turkey see Antakya
Antiparos i. Greece 27 K6
Antipodes Islands N.Z. 53 H6
Antipsara i. Greece 27 K5
Antium Italy see Anzio
Antofagasta Chile 70 B2
Antofagasta de la Sierra Arg. 70 C3
Antofalla, Volcán vol. Arg. 70 C3
António Enes Moz. see Angoche
Antri India 36 D4
Antrim U.K. 21 F3
Antrim Hills U.K. 21 F2
Antrim Plateau Australia 54 E4
Antropovo Rus. Fed. 12 I4
Antsalova Madag. 49 E5
Antseranana Madag. see Antsirañana
Antsirabe Madag. 49 E5
Antsirañana Madag. 49 E5
Antsla Estonia 15 O8
Antsohihy Madag. 49 E5
Anttis Sweden 14 M3
Anttola Fin. 15 O6
Antwerp Belgium 16 J5
Antwerpen Belgium see Antwerp
An Uaimh Ireland see Navan
Anuchino Rus. Fed. 44 D4
Anugul India see Angul
Anupgarh India 36 C3
Anuradhapura Sri Lanka 38 D4
Anveh Iran 35 I6
Anvers Island Antarctica 76 L2
Anvik U.S.A. 60 B3
Anxi Gansu China 42 H4
Anxious Bay Australia 55 F8
Anyang Henan China 43 K5
Anyang S. Korea 45 B5
A'nyêmaqên Shan mts China 42 H6
Anyuy r. Rus. Fed. 44 E2
Anyuysk Rus. Fed. 29 R3
Anzhero-Sudzhensk Rus. Fed. 28 J4
Anzi Dem. Rep. Congo 48 C4
Anzio Italy 26 E4
Aoba i. Vanuatu 53 G3
Aoga-shima i. Japan 45 E6
Aomen China see Macao
Aomori Japan 44 F4
Aoraki mt. N.Z. 59 C6
Aoraki/Mount Cook National Park N.Z. 59 C6
Aorangi mt. N.Z. see Aoraki
Aosta Italy 26 B2
Aotearoa country Oceania see New Zealand
Aouk, Bahr r. Cent. Afr. Rep./Chad 47 E4
Aoukâr reg. Mali/Mauritania 46 C2
Aoulef Alg. 46 D2
Aozou Chad 47 E2
Apa r. Brazil 70 E2
Apaiang atoll Kiribati see Abaiang
Apalachee Bay U.S.A. 63 K6
Apalachin NY U.S.A. 64 C1
Apamea Turkey see Dinar
Apaporis r. Col. 68 E4
Aparecida do Tabuado Brazil 71 A3
Aparima N.Z. see Riverton
Aparri Phil. 74 E4
Apatity Rus. Fed. 14 R3
Apatzingán Mex. 66 D5
Ape Latvia 15 O8
Apeldoorn Neth. 17 J4
Apennines mts Italy 26 C2
Api mt. Nepal 36 E3
Api i. Vanuatu see Epi
Apia atoll Kiribati see Abaiang
Apia Samoa 53 I3
Apiacas, Serra dos hills Brazil 69 G6
Apiaí Brazil 71 A4
Apiti N.Z. 59 E4
Aplao Peru 68 D7
Apoera Suriname 69 G2
Apollo Bay Australia 58 A7
Apollonia Bulg. see Sozopol
Apolo Bol. 68 E6
Aporé Brazil 71 A2
Aporé r. Brazil 71 A2
Apostolens Tommelfinger mt. Greenland 61 N3
Apostolos Andreas, Cape Cyprus 39 B2
Apoteri Guyana 69 G3
Apozai Pak. 36 B3
Appalachian Mountains U.S.A. 63 K4
Appalla i. Fiji see Kabara
Appennino mts Italy see Apennines
Appennino Abruzzese mts Italy 26 E3
Appennino Tosco-Emiliano mts Italy 26 D3
Appennino Umbro-Marchigiano mts Italy 26 E3
Applecross U.K. 20 D3
Appleton WI U.S.A. 63 J3
Apple Valley CA U.S.A. 65 D3
Appomattox VA U.S.A. 64 B4
Aprilia Italy 26 E4
Apsheronsk Rus. Fed. 13 H7
Apsheronskaya Rus. Fed. see Apsheronsk
Apt France 24 G5
Apucarana Brazil 71 A3
Apucarana, Serra da hills Brazil 71 A3
Apulum Romania see Alba Iulia
Aq"a Georgia see Sokhumi
'Aqaba Jordan see Al 'Aqabah
'Aqaba, Gulf of Asia 34 D5
'Aqaba, Wādī el watercourse Egypt see 'Aqabah, Wādī al
'Aqabah, Wādī al watercourse Egypt 39 A4
Aqadyr Kazakh. see Agadyr'
Aqdoghmish r. Iran 35 G3
Aqköl Akmolinskaya Oblast' Kazakh. see Akkol'
Aqköl Atyrauskaya Oblast' Kazakh. see Akkol'
Aqmola Kazakh. see Astana
Aqqan China 37 F1
Aqqikkol Hu salt l. China 37 G1
Aqra', Jabal al mt. Syria/Turkey 39 B2
'Aqran hill Saudi Arabia 39 D4
Aqsay Kazakh. see Aksay
Aqsayqin Hit terr. Asia see Aksai Chin
Aqshuqyr Kazakh. see Akshukur
Aqsū Kazakh. see Aksu
Aqsūat Kazakh. see Aksuat
Aqsū-Ayuly Kazakh. see Aksu-Ayuly
Aqtaū Kazakh. see Aktau
Aqtöbe Kazakh. see Aktobe
Aqtoghay Kazakh. see Aktogay
Aquae Grani Germany see Aachen
Aquae Gratianae France see Aix-les-Bains
Aquae Sextiae France see Aix-en-Provence
Aquae Statiellae Italy see Acqui Terme
Aquarius Mountains AZ U.S.A. 65 F3
Aquaviva delle Fonti Italy 26 G4
Aquidauana Brazil 70 E2
Aquincum Hungary see Budapest
Aquiry r. Brazil see Acre
Aquisgranum Germany see Aachen
Aquitaine reg. France 24 D5
Aquitania reg. France see Aquitaine
Aqzhayqyn Köli salt l. Kazakh. see Akzhaykyn, Ozero
Ara India 37 F4
Āra Ārba Eth. 48 E3
Arab, Bahr el watercourse Sudan 47 F4
'Arab, Khalīg el b. Egypt see 'Arab, Khalīj al
'Arab, Khalīj al b. Egypt 34 C5
'Arabah, Wādī al watercourse Israel/Jordan 39 B5
Arabian Basin sea feature Indian Ocean 73 M5
Arabian Gulf Asia see The Gulf
Arabian Peninsula Asia 32 G5
Arabian Sea Indian Ocean 33 K6
Araç Turkey 34 D2
Araça r. Brazil 68 F4
Aracaju Brazil 69 K6
Aracati Brazil 69 K4
Aracatu Brazil 71 C1
Araçatuba Brazil 71 A3
Aracena Spain 25 C5
Aracruz Brazil 71 C2
Araçuaí Brazil 71 C2
Araçuaí r. Brazil 71 C2
'Arad Israel 39 B4
Arad Romania 27 I1
Arafura Sea Australia/Indon. 52 D2
Arafura Shelf sea feature Australia/Indon. 74 E6
Aragarças Brazil 69 H7
Aragón r. Spain 25 F2
Araguaçu Brazil 71 A1
Araguaia r. Brazil 71 A1
Araguaia, Parque Nacional de nat. park Brazil 69 H6
Araguaiana Brazil 71 A1
Araguaína Brazil 69 I5
Araguari Brazil 71 A2
Araguari r. Brazil 69 H3
Araguatins Brazil 69 I5
Arai Brazil 71 B1
'Arâif el Naga, Gebel hill Egypt see 'Urayf an Nāqah, Jabal
Araiosos Brazil 69 J4
Arak Alg. 46 D2
Arāk Iran 35 H4
Arak Syria 39 D2
Arakan Yoma mts Myanmar 37 H5
Arakkonam India 38 C3
Araks r. Armenia see Araz
Araku India 38 D2
Aral Kazakh. see Aral'sk
Aral Tajik. see Vose
Aral Sea salt l. Kazakh./Uzbek. 30 F2
Aral'sk Kazakh. 28 H5
Aral'skoye More salt l. Kazakh./Uzbek. see Aral Sea
Aralsor, Ozero l. Kazakh. 13 K6
Aral Tengizi salt l. Kazakh./Uzbek. see Aral Sea
Aramac Australia 56 D4
Aramac Creek watercourse Australia 56 D4
Aran r. India 38 C2
Aranda de Duero Spain 25 E3
Aranđelovac Serbia 27 I2
Arandis Namibia 50 B2
Arang India 37 E5
Arani India 38 C3
Aran Island Ireland 21 D3
Aran Islands Ireland 21 C4
Aranjuez Spain 25 E3
Aranos Namibia 50 D3
Aransas Pass U.S.A. 63 H6
Arantangi India 38 C4
Aranuka atoll Kiribati 53 H1
Arao Japan 45 C6
Araouane Mali 46 C3
Arapgir Turkey 34 E3
Arapiraca Brazil 69 K5
Arapis, Akrotirio pt Greece 27 K4
Arapkir Turkey see Arapgir
Arapongas Brazil 71 A3
Araquari Brazil 71 A4
'Ar'ar Saudi Arabia 35 F5
Araracuara Col. 68 D4
Araranguá Brazil 71 A5
Araraquara Brazil 71 A3
Araras Brazil 69 H5
Ararat Armenia 35 G3
Ararat Australia 58 A6
Ararat, Mount Turkey 35 G3
Araria India 37 F4
Araripina Brazil 69 J5
Aras Turkey 35 F3
Aras r. Turkey see Araz
Arataca Brazil 71 D1
Arauca Col. 68 D2
Arauca r. Venez. 68 E2
Aravalli Range mts India 36 C4
Aravete Estonia 15 N7
Arawa P.N.G. 52 F2
Araxá Brazil 71 B2
Araxes r. Asia see Araz
Arayıt Dağı mt. Turkey 27 N5
Araz r. Azer. 35 H2
Arbailu Iraq see Arbīl
Arbat Iraq 35 G4
Arbela Iraq see Arbīl
Arberth U.K. see Narberth
Arbīl Iraq 35 G3
Arboga Sweden 15 I7
Arbroath U.K. 20 G4
Arbuckle CA U.S.A. 65 A1
Arbu Lut, Dasht-e des. Afgh. 33 J4
Arcachon France 24 D4
Arcade NY U.S.A. 64 B1
Arcadia FL U.S.A. 63 K6
Arc Dome mt. NV U.S.A. 65 D1
Arcelia Mex. 66 D5
Archangel Rus. Fed. 12 I2
Archer r. Australia 41 G9
Archer Bend National Park Australia 56 C2
Archipiélago Los Roques nat. park Venez. 68 E1
Ärçivan Azer. 35 H3
Arckaringa watercourse Australia 57 A6
Arco U.S.A. 62 E3
Arcos Brazil 71 B3
Arcos de la Frontera Spain 25 D5
Arctic Bay Canada 61 J2
Arctic Institute Islands Rus. Fed. see Arkticheskogo Instituta, Ostrova
Arctic Mid-Ocean Ridge sea feature Arctic Ocean 77 H1
Arctic Ocean 77 B1
Arctic Red r. Canada 60 E3
Arctowski research station Antarctica 76 A2
Arda r. Bulg. 27 L4
Ardabīl Iran 35 H3
Ardahan Turkey 35 F2
Ardakān Iran 35 I4
Årdalstangen Norway 15 E6
Ardara Ireland 21 D3
Ardas r. Bulg. see Arda
Ard aş Şawwān plain Jordan 39 C4
Ardatov Nizhegorodskaya Oblast' Rus. Fed. 13 I5
Ardatov Respublika Mordoviya Rus. Fed. 13 J5
Ardee Ireland 21 F4
Ardennes plat. Belgium 16 J6
Arden Town CA U.S.A. 65 B1
Arderin hill Ireland 21 E4
Ardestān Iran 35 I4
Ardglass U.K. 21 G3
Ardila r. Port. 25 C4
Ardlethan Australia 58 C5
Ardmore U.S.A. 63 H5
Ardnamurchan, Point of U.K. 20 C4
Ardon Rus. Fed. 35 G2
Ardrishaig U.K. 20 D4
Ardrossan U.K. 20 E5
Ardvasar U.K. 20 D3
Areia Branca Brazil 69 K4
Arel Belgium see Arlon
Arelas France see Arles
Arelate France see Arles
Arena, Point U.S.A. 62 C4
Arenas de San Pedro Spain 25 D3
Arendal Norway 15 F7
Areopoli Greece 27 J6
Arequipa Peru 68 D7
Arere Brazil 69 H4
Arévalo Spain 25 D3
Arezzo Italy 26 D3
'Arfajah well Saudi Arabia 39 D4
Argadargada Australia 56 B4
Arganda del Rey Spain 25 E3
Argel Alg. see Algiers
Argentan France 24 D2
Argentario, Monte hill Italy 26 D3
Argentera, Cima dell' mt. Italy 26 B2
Argentina country S. America 70 C5
Argentine Abyssal Plain sea feature S. Atlantic Ocean 72 E9
Argentine Basin sea feature S. Atlantic Ocean 72 F8
Argentine Republic country S. America see Argentina
Argentine Rise sea feature S. Atlantic Ocean 72 E8
Argentino, Lago l. Arg. 70 B8
Argenton-sur-Creuse France 24 E3
Argentoratum France see Strasbourg
Argeş r. Romania 27 L2
Arghandab r. Afgh. 36 A3
Argi r. Rus. Fed. 44 C1
Argolikos Kolpos b. Greece 27 J6
Argos Greece 27 J6
Argostoli Greece 27 I5
Arguís Spain 25 F2
Argun' r. China/Rus. Fed. 43 M2
Argun Rus. Fed. 35 G2
Argungu Nigeria 46 D3
Argus Range mts CA U.S.A. 65 D3
Argyle, Lake Australia 54 E4
Argyrokastron Albania see Gjirokastër
Ar Horqin Qi China see Tianshan
Århus Denmark 15 G8
Ariah Park Australia 58 C5
Ariamsvlei Namibia 50 D5
Ariana Tunisia see L'Ariana
Ariano Irpino Italy 26 F4
Aribinda Burkina 46 C3
Arica Chile 68 D7
Arid, Cape Australia 55 C8
Arīḩā Syria 39 C2
Arīḩā West Bank see Jericho
Arima Trin. and Tob. 67 L6
Ariminum Italy see Rimini
Arinos Brazil 71 B1
Aripuanã Brazil 69 G6
Aripuanã r. Brazil 68 F5
Ariquemes Brazil 68 F5
Aris Namibia 50 C2
Arisaig U.K. 20 D4
Arisaig, Sound of sea chan. U.K. 20 D4
'Arīsh, Wādī al watercourse Egypt 39 A4
Arixang China see Wenquan
Ariyalur India 38 C4
Arizaro, Salar de salt flat Arg. 70 C2
Arizona Arg. 70 C5
Arizona state U.S.A. 62 E5
Arizpe Mex. 62 E5
'Arjah Saudi Arabia 32 F5
Arjeplog Sweden 14 J3
Arjuni Chhattisgarh India 38 D1
Arjuni India 36 E5
Arkadak Rus. Fed. 13 I6
Arkadelphia U.S.A. 63 I5
Arkaig, Loch l. U.K. 20 D4
Arkalyk Kazakh. 42 B2
Arkansas r. U.S.A. 63 I5
Arkansas state U.S.A. 63 I4
Arkansas City KS U.S.A. 63 H4
Arkatag Shan mts China 37 G1
Arkenu, Jabal mt. Libya 32 B5
Arkhangel'sk Rus. Fed. see Archangel
Arkhara Rus. Fed. 44 C2
Arkhipovka Rus. Fed. 44 D4
Árki i. Greece see Arkoi
Arklow Ireland 21 F5
Arkoi i. Greece 27 L6
Arkona Ont. Canada 64 A1
Arkona, Kap c. Germany 17 N3
Arkonam India see Arakkonam
Arkport NY U.S.A. 64 C1
Arkticheskogo Instituta, Ostrova is Rus. Fed. 28 J2
Arkul' Rus. Fed. 12 K4
Arlandag mt. Turkm. 35 I3
Arles France 24 G5
Arlington S. Africa 51 H5
Arlington NY U.S.A. 64 E2
Arlington VA U.S.A. 64 C3
Arlit Niger 46 D3
Arlon Belgium 17 J6
Armadale Australia 55 A8
Armagh U.K. 21 F3
Armant Egypt 32 D4
Armavir Armenia 35 G2
Armavir Rus. Fed. 13 I7
Armenia country Asia 35 G2
Armenia Col. 68 C3
Armenopolis Romania see Gherla
Armeria Mex. 66 D5
Armidale Australia 58 E3
Armori India 38 D1
Armoy U.K. 21 F2
Armstrong r. Australia 54 E4
Armstrong Island Cook Is see Rarotonga
Armu r. Rus. Fed. 44 E3
Armur India 38 C2
Armutçuk Dağı mts Turkey 27 L5
Armyanskaya S.S.R. country Asia see Armenia
Arnaoutis, Cape Cyprus see Arnauti, Cape
Arnauti, Cape Cyprus 39 A2
Årnes Norway 15 G6
Arnhem Neth. 17 J5
Arnhem, Cape Australia 56 B2
Arnhem Land reg. Australia 54 F3
Arno r. Italy 26 D3
Arno Bay Australia 57 B7
Arnold U.K. 19 F5
Arnon r. Jordan see Mawjib, Wādī al
Arnprior Canada 63 L2
Arnsberg Germany 17 L5
Aroab Namibia 50 D4
Aroma Sudan 32 E6
Arona Italy 26 C2
Arorae i. Kiribati 53 H2
Arore i. Kiribati see Arorae
Aros r. Mex. 62 F6
Arossi i. Solomon Is see San Cristobal
Arqalyq Kazakh. see Arkalyk
Arquipélago da Madeira aut. reg. Port. 46 B1
Arrabury Australia 57 C5
Arrah India see Ara
Arraias Brazil 71 B1
Arraias, Serra de hills Brazil 71 B1
Ar Ramādī Iraq 35 F4
Ar Ramlah Jordan 39 B5
Ar Ramthā Jordan 39 C3
Arran i. U.K. 20 D5
Ar Raqqah Syria 39 D2
Arras France 24 F1
Ar Rass Saudi Arabia 32 F4
Ar Rastān Syria 39 C2
Ar Rayyān Qatar 32 H4
Arrecife Canary Is 46 B2
Arretium Italy see Arezzo
Arriagá Mex. 66 F5
Ar Rifā'ī Iraq 35 G5
Ar Rihāb salt flat Iraq 35 G5
Ar Rimāl reg. Saudi Arabia 48 F1
Arrington VA U.S.A. 64 B4
Ar Riyāḍ Saudi Arabia see Riyadh
Arrochar U.K. 20 E4
Arrojado r. Brazil 71 B1
Arrow, Lough l. Ireland 21 D3
Arrowsmith, Mount N.Z. 59 C6
Arroyo Grande CA U.S.A. 65 B3
Ar Rummān Jordan 39 B3
Ar Ruq'ī well Saudi Arabia 35 G5
Ar Ruṣāfah Syria 39 D2
Ar Ruṣayfah Jordan 39 C3
Ar Rustāq Oman 33 I5
Ar Ruṭbah Iraq 35 F4
Ar Ruwayḍah Syria 39 C2
Års Denmark see Aars
Ars Iran 35 G3
Arsen'yev Rus. Fed. 44 D3
Arsk Rus. Fed. 12 K4
Arta Greece 27 I5
Artem Rus. Fed. 44 D4
Artemivs'k Ukr. 13 H6
Artemovsk Ukr. see Artemivs'k
Artenay France 24 E2
Artesia NM U.S.A. 62 G5
Arthur, Lake PA U.S.A. 64 A2
Arthur's Pass National Park N.Z. 59 C6
Arti Rus. Fed. 11 R4
Artigas research station Antarctica 76 A2
Artigas Uruguay 70 E4
Art'ik Armenia 35 F2
Artillery Lake Canada 60 H3
Artisia Botswana 51 H3
Artois reg. France 24 E1
Artos Dağı mt. Turkey 35 F3
Artova Turkey 34 E2
Artsakh aut. reg. Azer. see Dağlıq Qarabağ
Artsiz Ukr. see Artsyz
Artsyz Ukr. 27 M2
Artur de Paiva Angola see Kuvango
Artux China 42 D5
Artvin Turkey 35 F2
Aru, Kepulauan is Indon. 41 F8
Arua Uganda 48 D3
Aruanã Brazil 71 A1
Aruba terr. West Indies 67 K6
Arumã Brazil 68 F4
Arunachal Pradesh state India 37 H4
Arundel U.K. 19 G8
Arun Gol r. China 44 B3
Arun He r. China see Arun Gol
Arun Qi China see Naji
Aruppukkottai India 38 C4
Arusha Tanz. 48 D4
Aruwimi r. Dem. Rep. Congo 48 C3
Arvagh Ireland 21 E4
Arvayheer Mongolia 42 I3
Arviat Canada 61 I3
Arvidsjaur Sweden 14 K4
Arvika Sweden 15 H7
Arvonia VA U.S.A. 64 B4
Arwād i. Syria 39 B2
Arwala Indon. 54 D1
Arxan China 43 L3
Aryanah Tunisia see L'Ariana
Arys' Kazakh. 42 B4
Arzamas Rus. Fed. 13 I5
Arzew Alg. 25 F6
Arzgir Rus. Fed. 35 G1
Arzila Morocco see Asilah
Asaba Nigeria 46 D4
Asad, Buḩayrat al resr Syria 39 D1
Asadābād Afgh. 36 B2
Asadābād Iran 35 H4
Asahi-dake vol. Japan 44 F4
Asahikawa Japan 44 F4
'Asal Egypt 39 A5
Āsalē l. Eth. 48 E2
Asālem Iran 35 H3
'Asalūyeh Iran 35 I6
Asan-man b. S. Korea 45 B5
Asansol India 37 F5
Āsayita Eth. 48 E2
Asbestos Mountains S. Africa 50 F5
Asbury Park NJ U.S.A. 64 D2
Ascalon Israel see Ashqelon
Ascea Italy 26 F4
Ascensión Bol. 68 F7
Ascension atoll Micronesia see Pohnpei
Ascension i. S. Atlantic Ocean 72 H6
Aschaffenburg Germany 17 L6
Ascoli Piceno Italy 26 E3
Asculum Italy see Ascoli Piceno
Asculum Picenum Italy see Ascoli Piceno
Ascutney VT U.S.A. 64 E1
Āseb Eritrea see Assab
Åseda Sweden 15 I8
Åsele Sweden 14 J4
Asenovgrad Bulg. 27 K3
Aşfar, Jabal al mt. Jordan 39 C3
Aşfar, Tall al hill Syria 39 C3
Aşgabat Turkm. 30 E3
Aşgabat Turkm. see Aşgabat
Asha Rus. Fed. 11 R5
Ashburton watercourse Australia 54 A5
Ashburton N.Z. 59 C6
Ashburton Range hills Australia 54 F4
Ashdod Israel 39 B4
Asheville U.S.A. 63 K4
Ashford Australia 58 E2
Ashford U.K. 19 H7
Ashibetsu Japan 44 F4
Ashikaga Japan 45 E5
Ashington U.K. 18 F3
Ashizuri-misaki pt Japan 45 D6
Ashkelon Israel see Ashqelon
Ashkhabad Turkm. see Aşgabat
Ashland OR U.S.A. 62 C3
Ashland VA U.S.A. 64 C4
Ashland WI U.S.A. 63 I2
Ashley Australia 58 D2
Ashmore and Cartier Islands terr. Australia 54 C3
Ashmore Reef Australia 54 C3
Ashmore Reefs Australia 56 D1
Ashmyany Belarus 15 N9
Ashqelon Israel 39 B4
Ash Shabakah Iraq 35 F5
Ash Shaddādah Syria 35 F3
Ash Shallūfah Egypt 39 A4
Ash Sham Syria see Damascus
Ash Shanāfīyah Iraq 35 G5
Ash Shaqīq well Saudi Arabia 35 F5
Ash Sharāh mts Jordan 39 B4
Ash Sharawrah Saudi Arabia 32 G6
Ash Shāriqah U.A.E. see Sharjah
Ash Sharqāṭ Iraq 35 F4
Ash Shaṭrah Iraq 35 G5
Ash Shaṭṭ Egypt 39 A5
Ash Shawbak Jordan 39 B4
Ash Shaybānī well Saudi Arabia 35 F5
Ash Shaykh Ibrāhīm Syria 39 D2
Ash Shiblīyāt hill Saudi Arabia 39 C5
Ash Shiḩr Yemen 32 G7
Ash Shu'aybah Saudi Arabia 35 F6
Ash Shu'bah Saudi Arabia 32 F4
Ash Shurayf Saudi Arabia see Khaybar
Ashta India 36 D5
Ashtabula OH U.S.A. 64 A2
Ashtarak Armenia 35 G2
Ashti Mahar. India 36 D5
Ashti Mahar. India 38 B2
Ashti Mahar. India 38 C2
Ashtiān Iran 35 H4
Ashton S. Africa 50 E7
Ashton-under-Lyne U.K. 18 E5
Ashuanipi Lake Canada 61 L4
Ashur Iraq see Ash Sharqāṭ
Asi r. Asia 34 E3 see 'Āṣī, Nahr al
'Āṣī r. Lebanon/Syria see Orontes
'Āṣī, Nahr al r. Asia 34 E3
Āsīā Bak Iran 35 H4
Asifabad India 38 C2
Asika India 38 E2
Asilah Morocco 25 C6
Asinara, Golfo dell' b. Sardinia Italy 26 C4
Asino Rus. Fed. 28 J4
Asipovichy Belarus 13 F5
Asīr Iran 35 I6
'Asīr reg. Saudi Arabia 32 F5
Asisium Italy see Assisi
Askale Jammu and Kashmir 36 C2
Aşkale Turkey 35 F3
Asker Norway 15 G7
Askersund Sweden 15 I7
Askim Norway 15 G7
Askī Mawşil Iraq 35 F3
Askino Rus. Fed. 11 R4
Askival hill U.K. 20 C4
Asl Egypt see 'Asal
Aslanköy r. Turkey 39 B1
Asmara Eritrea 32 E6
Āsmera Eritrea see Asmara
Åsnen l. Sweden 15 I8
Aso-Kuju Kokuritsu-kōen Japan 45 C6
Asop India 36 C4
Āsosa Eth. 48 D2
Aspang-Markt Austria 17 P7
Aspatria U.K. 18 D4
Aspen U.S.A. 62 F4
Aspiring, Mount N.Z. 59 B7
Aspro, Cape Cyprus 39 A2
Aspromonte, Parco Nazionale dell' nat. park Italy 26 F5
Aspron, Cape Cyprus see Aspro, Cape
As Sa'an Syria 39 C2
Assab Eritrea 32 F7
Assad, Lake resr Syria see Asad, Buḩayrat al
Aş Şafā lava field Syria 39 C3
Aş Şafāqis Tunisia see Sfax
Aş Şaff Egypt 34 C5
As Safīrah Syria 39 C1
Aş Şaḩrā' al Gharbīyah des. Egypt see Western Desert
Aş Şaḩrā' ash Sharqīyah des. Egypt see Eastern Desert
Aş Şaḩrā' ash Sharqīyah des. Egypt see Eastern Desert
Assake-Audan, Vpadina depr. Kazakh./Uzbek. 35 J2
'Assal, Lac l. Djibouti see Assal, Lake
Assal, Lake Djibouti 32 F7
Aş Şāliḩīyah Syria 35 F4
As Sallūm Egypt 34 B5
As Salmān Iraq 35 G5
As Salṭ Jordan 39 B3
Assam state India 37 G4
Assamakka Niger 46 D3
As Samāwah Iraq 35 G5
As Samrā' Jordan 39 C3
Aş Şanām reg. Saudi Arabia 32 H5
As Sarīr reg. Libya 47 F2
Assateague Island MD U.S.A. 64 D3
Assayeta Eth. see Āsayita
Assen Neth. 17 K4
As Sidrah Libya 47 E1
Assiniboia Canada 62 F2
Assiniboine r. Canada 62 H2
Assiniboine, Mount Canada 60 G4
Assis Brazil 71 A3
Assisi Italy 26 E3
Aş Şubayḩīyah Kuwait 35 G5
Aş Şufayrī well Saudi Arabia 35 G5
As Sukhnah Syria 39 D2
As Sulaymānīyah Iraq 35 G4
As Sulaymī Saudi Arabia 32 F4
As Sūq Saudi Arabia 32 F5
As Sūrīyah country Asia see Syria
Aş Şuwar Syria 35 F4
As Suwaydā' Syria 39 C3
As Suways Egypt see Suez
As Suways governorate Egypt 39 A4
Assynt, Loch l. U.K. 20 D2
Astacus Kocaeli Turkey see İzmit
Astakida i. Greece 27 L7
Astakos Greece 27 I5
Astana Kazakh. 42 C2
Astaneh Iran 35 H3
Astara Azer. 35 H3
Āstārā Iran 32 G2
Asterabad Iran see Gorgān
Asti Italy 26 C2
Astillero Peru 68 E6
Astin Tag mts China see Altun Shan
Astipálaia i. Greece see Astypalaia
Astor r. Pak. 36 C2
Astorga Spain 25 C2
Astoria U.S.A. 62 C2
Åstorp Sweden 15 H8
Astrabad Iran see Gorgān
Astrakhan' Rus. Fed. 13 K7
Astrakhan' Bazar Azer. see Cəlilabad
Astravyets Belarus 15 N9
Astrida Rwanda see Butare
Asturias aut. comm. Spain 25 C2
Asturias, Principado de aut. comm. Spain see Asturias
Asturica Augusta Spain see Astorga
Astypalaia i. Greece 27 L6
Asunción Para. 70 E3
Aswān Egypt 32 D5
Aswân Egypt see Aswān
Asyūṭ Egypt 34 C6
Asyût Egypt see Asyūṭ
Ata i. Tonga 53 I4
Atacama, Desierto de des. Chile see Atacama Desert
Atacama, Salar de salt flat Chile 70 C2
Atacama Desert Chile 70 C3
Atafu atoll Tokelau 53 I2
Atafu i. Tokelau 74 I6
'Aṭā'iṭah, Jabal al mt. Jordan 39 B4
Atakent Turkey 39 B1
Atakpamé Togo 46 D4
Atalándi Greece see Atalanti
Atalanti Greece 27 J5
Atalaya Peru 68 D6
Ataléia Brazil 71 C2
Atambua Indon. 54 D2
Atamyrat Turkm. 30 F3
Ataniya Turkey see Adana
'Ataq Yemen 32 G7
Atâr Mauritania 46 B2
Atari Pak. 36 C3
Atascadero CA U.S.A. 65 B3
Atasu Kazakh. 42 C3
Ataúro, Ilha de i. East Timor 54 D2
Atáviros mt. Greece see Attavyros
Atayurt Turkey 39 A1
Atbara Sudan 32 D6
Atbara r. Sudan 32 D6
Atbasar Kazakh. 28 H4
Atchison U.S.A. 63 H4
Atebubu Ghana 46 C4
Ateransk Kazakh. see Atyrau
Āteshān Iran 35 I4
Atessa Italy 26 F3
Athabasca r. Canada 60 G4
Athabasca, Lake Canada 60 H4
Atharan Hazari Pak. 36 C3
Athboy Ireland 21 F4
Athenae Greece see Athens
Athenry Ireland 21 D4
Athens Greece 27 J6
Athens GA U.S.A. 63 K5
Athens OH U.S.A. 63 K4
Athens PA U.S.A. 64 C2
Athens TN U.S.A. 63 K4
Atherstone U.K. 19 F6
Atherton Australia 56 D3
Athina Greece see Athens
Athínai Greece see Athens

Athleague Ireland 21 D4
Athlone Ireland 21 E4
Athnā', Wādī al watercourse Jordan 39 D3
Athni India 38 B2
Athol N.Z. 59 B7
Athol MA U.S.A. 64 E1
Atholl, Forest of reg. U.K. 20 E4
Athos mt. Greece 27 K4
Ath Thamad Egypt 39 B5
Ath Thāyat mt. Saudi Arabia 39 C5
Ath Thumāmī well Saudi Arabia 35 G6
Athy Ireland 21 F5
Ati Chad 47 E3
Atico Peru 68 D7
Atikokan Canada 61 I5
Atka Rus. Fed. 29 Q3
Atka Island U.S.A. 60 A4
Atkarsk Rus. Fed. 13 J6
Atlanta GA U.S.A. 63 K5
Atlantic IA U.S.A. 63 H3
Atlantic City NJ U.S.A. 64 D3
Atlantic-Indian-Antarctic Basin sea feature S. Atlantic Ocean 72 H10
Atlantic-Indian Ridge sea feature Southern Ocean 72 H9
Atlantic Ocean 72
Atlantis S. Africa 50 D7
Atlas Méditerranéen mts Alg. see Atlas Tellien
Atlas Mountains Africa 22 C5
Atlas Saharien mts Alg. 22 E5
Atlas Tellien mts Alg. 25 H6
Atmakur India 38 C3
Atmore U.S.A. 63 J5
Atnur India 38 C2
Atocha Bol. 68 E8
Atouila, Erg des. Mali 46 C2
Atqan China see Aqqan
Atrak r. Iran/Turkm. see Atrek
Atrato r. Col. 68 C2
Atrek r. Iran/Turkm. 33 H2
Atrek r. Iran/Turkm. 33 I2
Atropatene country Asia see Azerbaijan
Atsonupuri vol. Rus. Fed. 44 G3
Aţ Ţafīlah Jordan 39 B4
Aţ Ţā'if Saudi Arabia 32 F5
Attalea Turkey see Antalya
Attalia Turkey see Antalya
At Tamīmī Libya 34 A4
Attavyros mt. Greece 27 L6
Attawapiskat Canada 63 K1
Attawapiskat r. Canada 63 K1
Attawapiskat Lake Canada 63 J1
Aţ Ţawīl mts Saudi Arabia 35 E5
At Taysīyah plat. Saudi Arabia 35 F5
Attersee l. Austria 17 N7
Attila Line Cyprus 39 A2
Attleborough U.K. 19 I6
Attu Greenland 61 M3
Aţ Ţubayq reg. Saudi Arabia 39 C5
Attu Island U.S.A. 29 S4
At Tūnisīyah country Africa see Tunisia
Aţ Ţūr Egypt 34 D5
Attur India 38 C4
Aţ Ţuwayyah well Saudi Arabia 35 F6
Atuk Mountain hill U.S.A. 60 A3
Åtvidaberg Sweden 15 I7
Atwater CA U.S.A. 65 B2
Atyashevo Rus. Fed. 13 J5
Atyrau Kazakh. 30 E2
Atyraū admin. div. Kazakh. see Atyrauskaya Oblast'
Atyrau Oblast admin. div. Kazakh. see Atyrauskaya Oblast'
Atyrauskaya Oblast' admin. div. Kazakh. 11 Q6
Aubagne France 24 G5
Aubenas France 24 G4
Aubrey Cliffs mts AZ U.S.A. 65 F3
Aubry Lake Canada 60 F3
Auburn r. Australia 57 E5
Auburn CA U.S.A. 65 B1
Auburn NE U.S.A. 63 H3
Auburn NY U.S.A. 64 C1
Auburn Range hills Australia 56 E5
Aubusson France 24 F4
Auch France 24 E5
Auchterarder U.K. 20 F4
Auckland N.Z. 59 E3
Auckland Islands N.Z. 53 G7
Audo mts Eth. 48 E3
Audo Range mts Eth. see Audo
Augathella Australia 57 D5
Augher U.K. 21 E3
Aughnacloy U.K. 21 F3
Aughrim Ireland 21 F5
Augrabies S. Africa 50 E5
Augrabies Falls S. Africa 50 E5
Augrabies Falls National Park S. Africa 50 E5
Augsburg Germany 17 M6
Augusta Australia 55 A8
Augusta Sicily Italy 26 F6
Augusta GA U.S.A. 63 K5
Augusta ME U.S.A. 63 N3
Augusta Auscorum France see Auch
Augusta Taurinorum Italy see Turin
Augusta Treverorum Germany see Trier
Augusta Vindelicorum Germany see Augsburg
Augusto de Lima Brazil 71 B2
Augustus, Mount Australia 55 B6
Aukštaitijos nacionalinis parkas nat. park Lith. 15 O9
Aulavik National Park Canada 60 G2
Auld, Lake salt flat Australia 54 C5
Auliye Ata Kazakh. see Taraz
Aulon Albania see Vlorë
Ault France 19 I8
Aumale Alg. see Sour el Ghozlane
Aundh India 38 B2
Aundhi India 38 D1
Aunglan Myanmar 37 H6
Aunglan Myanmar see Aunglan
Auob watercourse Namibia/S. Africa 50 E4
Aura Fin. 15 M6
Auraiya India 36 D4
Aurangabad Bihar India 37 F4
Aurangabad Mahar. India 38 B2
Aure r. France 19 F9
Aurich Germany 17 K4
Aurigny i. Channel Is see Alderney
Aurilândia Brazil 71 A2
Aurillac France 24 F4
Aurora CO U.S.A. 62 G4
Aurora IL U.S.A. 63 J3
Aurora Island Vanuatu see Maéwo
Aurukun Australia 56 C2
Aus Namibia 50 C4
Auskerry i. U.K. 20 G1
Austin MN U.S.A. 63 I3
Austin NV U.S.A. 62 D4
Austin TX U.S.A. 62 H5
Austin, Lake salt flat Australia 55 B6
Austintown OH U.S.A. 64 A2
Austral Downs Australia 56 B4
Australes, Îles is Fr. Polynesia see Tubuai Islands
Australia country Oceania 52 C4
Australian-Antarctic Basin sea feature S. Atlantic Ocean 74 C9
Australian Antarctic Territory reg. Antarctica 76 G2
Australian Capital Territory admin. div. Australia 58 D5
Austria country Europe 17 N7
Austvågøy i. Norway 14 I2
Autazes Brazil 69 G4
Autesiodorum France see Auxerre
Autti Fin. 14 O3
Auvergne reg. France 24 F4
Auvergne, Monts d' mts France 24 F4
Auxerre France 24 F3
Auxonne France 24 G3
Auyuittuq National Park Canada 61 L3
Auzangate, Nevado mt. Peru 68 D6
Ava NY U.S.A. 64 D1
Avallon France 24 F3
Avalon CA U.S.A. 65 C4
Avalon Peninsula Canada 61 M5
Avān Iran 35 G3
Avarau atoll Cook Is see Palmerston
Avaré Brazil 71 A3
Avaricum France see Bourges
Avarua Cook Is 75 J7
Aveiro Port. 25 B3
Aveiro, Ria de est. Port. 25 B3
Āvej Iran 35 H4
Avellino Italy 26 F4
Avenal CA U.S.A. 65 B2
Avenio France see Avignon
Aversa Italy 26 F4
Avesta Sweden 15 J6
Aveyron r. France 24 E4
Avezzano Italy 26 E3
Aviemore U.K. 20 F3
Avignon France 24 G5
Ávila Spain 25 D3
Avilés Spain 25 D2
Avis PA U.S.A. 64 C2
Avlama Dağı mt. Turkey 39 A1
Avlama Dağı mt. Turkey 39 A1
Avlona Albania see Vlorë
Avnyugskiy Rus. Fed. 12 J3
Avoca Australia 58 A6
Avoca r. Australia 58 A5
Avoca Ireland 21 F5
Avoca NY U.S.A. 64 C1
Avola Sicily Italy 26 F6
Avon r. England U.K. 19 E6
Avon r. England U.K. 19 E7
Avon r. England U.K. 19 F8
Avon r. Scotland U.K. 20 F3
Avon NY U.S.A. 64 C1
Avonmore r. Ireland 21 F5
Avonmore PA U.S.A. 64 B2
Avonmouth U.K. 19 E7
Avranches France 24 D2
Avsuyu Turkey 39 C1
Avuavu Solomon Is 53 G2
Avveel Fin. see Ivalo
Avvil Fin. see Ivalo
A'waj r. Syria 39 B3
Awakino N.Z. 59 E4
Awanui N.Z. 59 D2
Āwarē Eth. 48 E3
'Awārid, Wādī al watercourse Syria 39 D2
Awarua Point N.Z. 59 B7
Āwash Eth. 48 E3
Āwash r. Eth. 48 E2
Awa-shima i. Japan 45 E5
Āwash National Park Eth. 48 D3
Awasib Mountains Namibia 50 B3
Awat China 42 E4
Awatere r. N.Z. 59 E5
Awbārī Libya 46 E2
Awbeg r. Ireland 21 D5
'Awdah, Hawr al imp. l. Iraq 35 G5
Aw Dheegle Somalia 47 H4
Awe, Loch l. U.K. 20 D4
Aweil Sudan 47 F4
Awka Nigeria 46 D4
Awserd W. Sahara 46 B2
Axe r. England U.K. 19 D8
Axe r. England U.K. 19 E7
Axedale Australia 58 B6
Axel Heiberg Glacier Antarctica 76 I1
Axel Heiberg Island Canada 61 I2
Axim Ghana 46 C4
Axminster U.K. 19 E8
Axum Eth. see Āksum
Ayachi, Jbel mt. Morocco 22 D5
Ayacucho Arg. 70 E5
Ayacucho Peru 68 D6
Ayadaw Myanmar 37 H5
Ayagoz Kazakh. 42 E3
Ayaguz Kazakh. see Ayagoz
Ayakkum Hu salt l. China 37 G1
Ayaköz Kazakh. see Ayagoz
Ayan Rus. Fed. 29 O4
Ayancık Turkey 34 D2
Ayang N. Korea 45 B5
Ayaş Turkey 34 D2
Āybak Afgh. 36 B1
Aybas Kazakh. 13 K7
Aydar r. Ukr. 13 H6
Aydarko'l ko'li l. Uzbek. 33 K1
Aydın Turkey 27 L6
Aydıncık Turkey 39 A1
Aydın Dağları mts Turkey 27 L5
Āydyň Turkm. 35 I3
Āyelu Terara vol. Eth. 32 F7
Ayer MA U.S.A. 64 F1
Ayers Rock hill Australia see Uluru
Ayeyarwady r. Myanmar see Irrawaddy
Ayila Ri'gyü mts China 36 D2
Áyios Dhimítrios Greece see Agios Dimitrios
Áyios Evstrátios i. Greece see Agios Efstratios
Áyios Nikólaos Greece see Agios Nikolaos
Áyios Yeóryios i. Greece see Agios Georgios
Aylesbury N.Z. 59 D6
Aylesbury U.K. 19 G7
Aylett VA U.S.A. 64 C4
Ayllón Spain 25 E3
Aylmer Ont. Canada 64 A1
Aylmer Lake Canada 60 H3
'Ayn al 'Abd well Saudi Arabia 35 H5
'Ayn al Baidā' Saudi Arabia 39 C4
'Ayn al Bayḍā' well Syria 39 C2
'Ayn al Ghazalah well Libya 34 A4
'Ayn al Maqfī spring Egypt 34 C6
'Ayn Dāllah spring Egypt 34 B6
'Ayn 'Īsá Syria 39 D1
'Ayn Tabaghbugh spring Egypt 34 B5
'Ayn Tumayrah spring Egypt 34 B5
'Ayn Zaytūn Egypt 34 B5
Ayod Sudan 32 D8
Ayon, Ostrov i. Rus. Fed. 29 R3
'Ayoûn el 'Atroûs Mauritania 46 C3
Ayr Australia 56 D3
Ayr U.K. 20 E5
Ayr r. U.K. 20 E5
Ayr, Point of U.K. 18 D5
Ayrancı Turkey 34 D3
Ayre, Point of Isle of Man 18 C4
Aytos Bulg. 27 L3
Ayutthia Thai. see Ayutthaya
Ayutthaya Thai. 31 J5
Ayvacık Turkey 27 L5
Ayvalı Turkey 34 E3
Ayvalık Turkey 27 L5
Azak Rus. Fed. see Azov
Azamgarh India 37 E4
Azaouâd reg. Mali 46 C3
Azaouagh, Vallée de watercourse Mali/Niger 46 D3
Azaran Iran see Hashtrud
Azärbaycan country Asia see Azerbaijan
Azärbayjan country Asia see Azerbaijan
Azare Nigeria 46 E3
A'zāz Syria 39 C1
Azbine mts Niger see L'Aïr, Massif de
Azdavay Turkey 34 D2
Azerbaijan country Asia 35 G2
Azerbaydzhanskaya S.S.R. country Asia see Azerbaijan
Azhikal India 38 B4
Aziziye Turkey see Pınarbaşı
Azogues Ecuador 68 C4
Azores terr. N. Atlantic Ocean 72 G3
Azores-Biscay Rise sea feature N. Atlantic Ocean 72 G3
Azotus Israel see Ashdod
Azov Rus. Fed. 13 H7
Azov, Sea of Rus. Fed./Ukr. 13 H7
Azovs'ke More sea Rus. Fed./Ukr. see Azov, Sea of
Azovskoye More sea Rus. Fed./Ukr. see Azov, Sea of
Azraq, Bahr el r. Sudan 32 D6 see Blue Nile
Azraq ash Shīshān Jordan 39 C4
Azrou Morocco 22 C5
Azuaga Spain 25 D4
Azuero, Península de pen. Panama 67 H7
Azul, Cordillera mts Peru 68 C5
Azuma-san vol. Japan 45 F5
'Azza Gaza see Gaza
Azzaba Alg. 26 B6
Az Zahrān Saudi Arabia see Dhahran
Az Zaqāzīq Egypt 34 C5
Az Zarbah Syria 39 C1
Az Zarqā' Jordan 39 C3
Az Zawr, Ra's pt Saudi Arabia 35 H6
Azzeffāl hills Mauritania/W. Sahara 46 B2
Az Zubayr Iraq 35 G5
Az Zuqur i. Yemen 32 F7

B

Baa Indon. 54 C2
Baabda Lebanon 39 B3
Ba'albek Lebanon 39 C2
Ba'al Hazor mt. West Bank 39 B4
Baan Baa Australia 58 D3
Baardheere Somalia 48 E3
Bab India 36 D4
Bābā, Kūh-e mts Afgh. 36 B2
Baba Burnu pt Turkey 27 L5
Babadağ mt. Azer. 35 H2
Babadag Romania 27 M2
Babaeski Turkey 27 L4
Babahoyo Ecuador 68 C4
Babai India 36 D5
Babai r. Nepal 37 E3
Bābā Kalān Iran 35 H5
Bāb al Mandab strait Africa/Asia 32 F7
Babanusa Sudan 32 C7
Babar i. Indon. 41 E8
Babar, Kepulauan is Indon. 54 E1
Babati Tanz. 49 D4
Babayevo Rus. Fed. 12 G4
Babayurt Rus. Fed. 13 J8
B'abdâ Lebanon see Baabda
Bab el Mandeb, Straits of Africa/Asia see Bāb al Mandab
Babine Lake Canada 60 F4
Bābol Iran 35 I3
Bābol Sar Iran 35 I3
Babongo Cameroon 47 E4
Baboon Point S. Africa 50 D7
Baboua Cent. Afr. Rep. 48 B3
Babruysk Belarus 13 F5
Babstovo Rus. Fed. 44 D2
Babu China see Hezhou
Babuhri India 36 B4
Babusar Pass Pak. 36 C2
Babuyan i. Phil. 43 M9
Babuyan Channel Phil. 43 M9
Babuyan Islands Phil. 41 E6
Bacaadweyn Somalia 48 E3
Bacabal Brazil 69 J4
Bacan i. Indon. 41 E8
Bacău Romania 27 L1
Bacha China 44 D2
Bach Ice Shelf Antarctica 76 L2
Bachu China 42 D5
Back r. Australia 56 C3
Back r. Canada 61 I3
Bačka Palanka Serbia 27 H2
Backbone Mountain MD U.S.A. 64 B3
Backe Sweden 14 J5
Backstairs Passage Australia 57 B7
Băc Liêu Vietnam 31 J6
Bacolod Phil. 41 E6
Bacqueville-en-Caux France 19 H9
Bād Iran 35 I4
Bada mt. Eth. 48 D3
Badagara India 38 B4
Badain Jaran Shamo des. China 42 I4
Badajoz Spain 25 C4
Badami India 38 B3
Badampaharh India 37 F5
Badanah Saudi Arabia 35 F5
Badanjilin Shamo des. China see Badain Jaran Shamo
Badaojiang China see Baishan
Badarpur India 37 H4
Badaun India see Budaun
Badderen Norway 14 M2
Bademli Turkey see Aladağ
Bademli Geçidi pass Turkey 34 C3
Baden Austria 17 P6
Baden Switz. 24 I3
Baden-Baden Germany 17 L6
Bad Hersfeld Germany 17 L5
Bad Hofgastein Austria 17 N7
Badia Polesine Italy 26 D2
Badin Pak. 33 K5
Bad Ischl Austria 17 N7
Bādiyat ash Shām des. Asia see Syrian Desert
Bad Kissingen Germany 17 M5
Bad Königsdorff Poland see Jastrzębie-Zdrój
Badnawar India 36 C5
Badnera India 38 C1
Badnor India 36 C4
Badou Togo 46 D4
Badrah Iraq 35 G4
Bad Reichenhall Germany 17 N7
Badr Ḥunayn Saudi Arabia 32 E5
Bad Salzungen Germany 17 M5
Bad Schwartau Germany 17 M4
Bad Segeberg Germany 17 M4
Badu Island Australia 56 C1
Badulla Sri Lanka 38 D5
Badzhal Rus. Fed. 44 D2
Badzhal'skiy Khrebet mts Rus. Fed. 44 D2
Bae Colwyn U.K. see Colwyn Bay
Baeza Spain 25 E5
Bafatá Guinea-Bissau 46 B3
Baffa Pak. 36 C2
Baffin Bay sea Canada/Greenland 61 L2
Baffin Island Canada 61 L3
Bafia Cameroon 46 E4
Bafilo Togo 46 D4
Bafing r. Africa 46 B3
Bafoulabé Mali 46 B3
Bafoussam Cameroon 46 E4
Bāfq Iran 35 I5
Bafra Turkey 34 D2
Bafra Burnu pt Turkey 34 D2
Bāft Iran 33 I4
Bafwaboli Dem. Rep. Congo 48 C3
Bafwasende Dem. Rep. Congo 48 C3
Bagaha India 37 F4
Bagalkot India 38 B2
Bagalkote India see Bagalkot
Bagamoyo Tanz. 49 D4
Bagan China 37 I2
Bagata Dem. Rep. Congo 48 B4
Bagdad AZ U.S.A. 65 F3
Bagdarin Rus. Fed. 43 K2
Bagé Brazil 70 F4
Bagerhat Bangl. 37 G5
Bageshwar India 36 D3
Baggy Point U.K. 19 C7
Bagh India 36 C5
Bàgh a' Chaisteil U.K. see Castlebay
Baghak Pak. 36 A3
Baghdād Iraq 35 G4
Bāgh-e Malek Iran 35 H5
Bagherhat Bangl. see Bagerhat
Baghlān Afgh. 36 B1
Baghrān Afgh. 36 A2
Bağırsak r. Turkey 39 C1
Bağırsak Deresi r. Syria/Turkey see Sājūr, Nahr
Baglung Nepal 37 E3
Bagnères-de-Luchon France 24 E5
Bago Myanmar see Pegu
Bagrationovsk Rus. Fed. 15 L9
Bagrax China see Bohu
Bagrax Hu l. China see Bosten Hu
Bagur, Cabo c. Spain see Begur, Cap de
Bagzane, Monts mts Niger 46 D3
Bahalda India 37 F5
Bahāmabād Iran see Rafsanjān
Bahara Pak. 36 A4
Baharampur India 37 G4
Bahardipur Pak. 36 B4
Bahariya Oasis oasis Egypt see Baḥrīyah, Wāḥāt al
Bahawalnagar Pak. 36 C3
Bahawalpur Pak. 33 L4
Bahçe Adana Turkey 39 B1
Bahçe Osmaniye Turkey 34 E3
Baher Dar Eth. see Bahir Dar
Baheri India 36 D3
Bahia Brazil see Salvador
Bahia state Brazil 71 C1
Bahía Blanca Arg. 70 D5
Bahía Laura Arg. 70 C7
Bahía Negra Para. 70 E2
Bahía Tortugas Mex. 66 B3
Bahir Dar Eth. 48 D2
Bahl India 36 C3
Bahlā Oman 33 I5
Bahraich India 37 E4
Bahrain country Asia 32 H4
Bahrām Beyg Iran 35 H3
Baḥrīyah, Wāḥāt al oasis Egypt 34 C6
Bahuaja-Sonene, Parque Nacional nat. park Peru 68 E6
Baia Mare Romania 27 J1
Baiazeh Iran 35 I4
Baicang China 37 G3
Baicheng Jilin China 44 A3
Baicheng Xinjiang China 42 E4
Baidoa Somalia see Baydhabo
Baidoi Co l. China 37 F2
Baie-aux-Feuilles Canada see Tasiujaq
Baie-Comeau Canada 63 N2
Baie-du-Poste Canada see Mistissini
Baie-St-Paul Canada 63 M2
Baihar India 36 E5
Baihe Jilin China 44 C4
Baiji Iraq see Bayjī
Baikal, Lake Rus. Fed. 42 J2
Baikunthpur India 37 E5
Baile Átha Cliath Ireland see Dublin
Baile Átha Luain Ireland see Athlone
Baile Mhartainn U.K. 20 B3
Băileşti Romania 27 J2
Bailey Range hills Australia 55 C7
Bailieborough Ireland 21 F4
Baima Qinghai China 42 I6
Baima Xizang China see Baxoi
Bain r. U.K. 18 G5
Bainang China see Norkyung
Bainbridge GA U.S.A. 63 K5
Bainbridge NY U.S.A. 64 D1
Bainduru India 38 B3
Baingoin China see Porong
Baiona Spain 25 B2
Baiquan China 44 B3
Bā'ir Jordan 39 C4
Bā'ir, Wādī watercourse Jordan/Saudi Arabia 39 C4
Bairab Co l. China 37 E2
Bairat India 36 D4
Baird Mountains U.S.A. 60 C3
Bairiki Kiribati 74 H5
Bairin Youqi China see Daban
Bairnsdale Australia 58 C6
Baishan Jilin China 44 B4
Baishan Jilin China see Baishanzhen
Baishanzhen China 44 B4
Baisogala Lith. 15 M9
Baitadi Nepal 36 E3
Baitang China 37 I2
Baiyin China 42 I5
Baiyuda Desert Sudan 32 D6
Baja Hungary 26 H1
Baja California pen. Mex. 66 A2
Bajawa Indon. 54 C2
Baj Baj India 37 G5
Bājil Yemen 32 F7
Bajo Caracoles Arg. 70 B7
Bajoga Nigeria 46 E3
Bajrakot India 37 F5
Bakala Cent. Afr. Rep. 47 F4
Bakanas Kazakh. 42 D4
Bakar Pak. 36 B4
Bakel Senegal 46 B3
Baker CA U.S.A. 65 D3
Baker MT U.S.A. 62 G2
Baker NV U.S.A. 65 E1
Baker OR U.S.A. 62 D3
Baker WV U.S.A. 64 B3
Baker, Mount vol. U.S.A. 62 C2
Baker Island terr. N. Pacific Ocean 53 I1
Baker Lake salt flat Australia 55 D6
Baker Lake Canada 61 I3
Baker Lake Canada 61 I3
Bakersfield CA U.S.A. 65 C3
Bakhardok Turkm. see Bokurdak
Bakhasar India 36 B4
Bakhirevo Rus. Fed. 44 C2
Bakhmach Ukr. 13 G6
Bakhma Dam Iraq see Bēkma, Sadd
Bakhmut Ukr. see Artemivs'k
Bākhtarān Iran see Kermānshāh
Bakhtegan, Daryācheh-ye l. Iran 35 I5
Bakı Azer. see Baku
Baki Somalia 48 E2
Bakırköy Turkey 27 M4
Bakkejord Norway 14 K2
Bakloh India 36 C2
Bako Eth. 48 D3
Bakouma Cent. Afr. Rep. 48 C3
Baksan Rus. Fed. 35 F2
Baku Azer. 35 H2
Baku Dem. Rep. Congo 48 D3
Bakutis Coast Antarctica 76 J2
Baky Azer. see Baku
Balâ Turkey 34 D3
Bala U.K. 19 D6
Bala, Cerros de mts Bol. 68 E6
Balabac Strait Malaysia/Phil. 41 D7
Baladeh Māzandarān Iran 35 H3
Baladeh Māzandarān Iran 35 H3
Baladek Rus. Fed. 44 D1
Balaghat India 36 E5
Balaghat Range hills India 38 B2
Balaka Malawi 49 D5
Balakän Azer. 35 G2
Balakhna Rus. Fed. 12 I4
Balakhta Rus. Fed. 42 G1
Balaklava Australia 57 B7
Balaklava Ukr. 34 D1
Balakleya Ukr. see Balakliya
Balakliya Ukr. 13 H6
Balakovo Rus. Fed. 13 J5
Bala Lake l. U.K. 19 D6
Balaman India 36 E4
Balan India 36 B4
Balanda Rus. Fed. see Kalininsk
Balanda r. Rus. Fed. 13 J6
Balan Dağı hill Turkey 27 M6
Balanga Phil. 41 E6
Balangir India see Bolangir
Balaözen r. Kazakh./Rus. Fed. see Malyy Uzen'
Balarampur India see Balrampur
Balashov Rus. Fed. 13 I6
Balasore India see Baleshwar
Balaton, Lake Hungary 26 G1
Balatonboglár Hungary 26 G1
Balatonfüred Hungary 26 G1
Balbina Brazil 69 G4
Balbina, Represa de resr Brazil 69 G4
Balbriggan Ireland 21 F4
Balchik Bulg. 27 M3
Balclutha N.Z. 59 B8
Bald Mountain NV U.S.A. 65 E2
Baldwin PA U.S.A. 64 B2
Baldy Mountain hill Canada 62 G1
Baldy Peak U.S.A. 62 F5
Bâle Switz. see Basel
Baléa Mali 46 B3
Baleares is Spain see Balearic Islands
Baleares, Islas is Spain see Balearic Islands
Baleares Insulae is Spain see Balearic Islands
Balearic Islands is Spain 25 G4
Balears is Spain see Balearic Islands
Balears, Illes is Spain see Balearic Islands
Baleia, Ponta da pt Brazil 71 D2
Bale Mountains National Park Eth. 48 D3
Baleshwar India 37 F5
Balestrand Norway 15 E6
Baléyara Niger 46 D3
Balezino Rus. Fed. 11 Q4
Balfe's Creek Australia 56 D4
Balfour Downs Australia 54 C5
Balgo Australia 54 D5
Balguntay China 42 F4
Bali India 36 C4
Bali i. Indon. 41 D8
Bali, Laut sea Indon. 41 D8
Balia India see Ballia
Baliapal India 37 F5
Balige Indon. 41 B7
Baliguda India 38 D1
Balıkesir Turkey 27 L5
Balīkh r. Syria/Turkey 39 D2
Balikpapan Indon. 41 D8
Balimila Reservoir India 38 D2
Balimo P.N.G. 52 E2
Balin China 44 A2
Balingen Germany 17 L6
Balintore U.K. 20 F3
Balkanabat Turkm. 35 I3
Balkan Mountains Bulg./Serbia 27 J3
Balkassar Pak. 36 C2
Balkhash Kazakh. 42 C3
Balkhash, Lake Kazakh. 42 C3
Balkhash, Ozero l. Kazakh. see Balkhash, Lake
Balkuduk Kazakh. 13 J7
Ballachulish U.K. 20 D4
Balladonia Australia 55 C8
Balladoran Australia 58 D3
Ballaghaderreen Ireland 21 D4
Ballan Australia 58 B6
Ballangen Norway 14 J2
Ballantrae U.K. 20 E5
Ballarat Australia 58 A6
Ballard, Lake salt flat Australia 55 C7
Ballarpur India 38 C2
Ballater U.K. 20 F3
Ballé Mali 46 C3
Ballena, Punta pt Chile 70 B3
Balleny Islands Antarctica 76 H2
Ballia India 37 F4
Ballina Australia 58 F2
Ballina Ireland 21 C3
Ballinafad Ireland 21 D3
Ballinalack Ireland 21 E4
Ballinamore Ireland 21 E3
Ballinasloe Ireland 21 D4
Ballindine Ireland 21 D4
Ballinger U.S.A. 62 H5
Ballinluig U.K. 20 F4
Ballinrobe Ireland 21 C4
Ballston Spa NY U.S.A. 64 E1
Ballybay Ireland 21 F3
Ballybrack Ireland 21 B6
Ballybunnion Ireland 21 C5
Ballycanew Ireland 21 F5
Ballycastle Ireland 21 C3
Ballycastle U.K. 21 F2
Ballyclare U.K. 21 G3
Ballyconnell Ireland 21 E3
Ballygar Ireland 21 D4
Ballygawley U.K. 21 E3
Ballygorman Ireland 21 E2
Ballyhaunis Ireland 21 D4
Ballyheigue Ireland 21 C5
Ballykelly U.K. 21 E2
Ballylynan Ireland 21 E5
Ballymacmague Ireland 21 E5
Ballymahon Ireland 21 E4
Ballymena U.K. 21 F3
Ballymoney U.K. 21 F2
Ballymote Ireland 21 D3
Ballynahinch U.K. 21 G3
Ballyshannon Ireland 21 D3
Ballyteige Bay Ireland 21 F5
Ballyvaughan Ireland 21 C4
Ballyward U.K. 21 F3
Balmartin U.K. see Baile Mhartainn
Balmer India see Barmer
Balochistan prov. Pak. 36 A3
Balombo Angola 49 B5
Balonne r. Australia 58 D2
Balotra India 36 C4
Balqash Kazakh. see Balkhash
Balqash Köli l. Kazakh. see Balkhash, Lake
Balrampur India 37 E4
Balranald Australia 58 A5
Balş Romania 27 K2
Balsas Brazil 69 I5
Balta Ukr. 13 F7
Baltasound U.K. 20 [inset]
Baltay Rus. Fed. 13 J5
Bălţi Moldova 13 E7
Baltic Sea g. Europe 15 J9
Balţīm Egypt 34 C5
Balţîm Egypt see Balţīm
Baltimore S. Africa 51 I2
Baltimore MD U.S.A. 64 C3
Baltinglass Ireland 21 F5
Baltistan reg. Jammu and Kashmir 36 C2
Baltiysk Rus. Fed. 12 C5
Balurghat India 37 G4
Balvi Latvia 15 O8
Balya Turkey 27 L5
Balykchy Kyrg. 42 D4
Balykshi Kazakh. 30 E2
Balyqshy Kazakh. see Balykshi
Bam Iran 33 I4
Bamako Mali 46 C3
Bamba Mali 46 C3
Bambari Cent. Afr. Rep. 48 C3
Bamberg Germany 17 M6
Bambili Dem. Rep. Congo 48 C3
Bambio Cent. Afr. Rep. 48 B3
Bamboesberg mts S. Africa 51 H6
Bamboo Creek Australia 54 C5
Bambouti Cent. Afr. Rep. 48 C3
Bambuí Brazil 71 B3
Bamda China 37 I3
Bamenda Cameroon 46 E4
Bāmīān Afgh. 36 A2
Bamiantong China see Muling
Bamingui Cent. Afr. Rep. 48 C3
Bamingui-Bangoran, Parc National du nat. park Cent. Afr. Rep. 48 B3
Bamor India 36 D4
Bamori India 38 C1
Bam Posht, Kūh-e mts Iran 33 J4
Bampton U.K. 19 D8
Bamrūd Iran 33 J3
Bam Tso l. China 37 G3
Bamyili Australia 54 F3
Banaba i. Kiribati 53 G2
Banabuiu, Açude resr Brazil 69 K5
Bañados del Izozog swamp Bol. 68 F7
Banagher Ireland 21 E4
Banalia Dem. Rep. Congo 48 C3
Banamana, Lagoa l. Moz. 51 K2
Banamba Mali 46 C3
Banana Australia 56 E5
Bananal, Ilha do i. Brazil 69 H6
Banapur India 38 E2
Banas r. India 36 D4
Banaz Turkey 27 M5
Ban Ban Laos 42 I9
Banbar China see Domartang
Banbridge U.K. 21 F3
Banbury U.K. 19 F6
Ban Cang Vietnam 42 I8
Banc d'Arguin, Parc National du nat. park Mauritania 46 B2
Banchory U.K. 20 G3
Bancroft Zambia see Chililabombwe
Banda Dem. Rep. Congo 48 C3
Banda India 36 E4
Banda, Kepulauan is Indon. 41 E8
Banda, Laut sea Indon. 41 F8
Banda Aceh Indon. 41 B7
Banda Banda, Mount Australia 58 F3
Banda Daud Shah Pak. 36 B2
Bandama r. Côte d'Ivoire 46 C4
Bandar India see Machilipatnam
Bandar Moz. 49 D5
Bandar Abbas Iran see Bandar-e 'Abbās
Bandarban Bangl. 37 H5
Bandar-e 'Abbās Iran 33 I4
Bandar-e Anzalī Iran 35 H3
Bandar-e Deylam Iran 35 H5
Bandar-e Emām Khomeynī Iran 35 H5
Bandar-e Lengeh Iran 33 H4
Bandar-e Ma'shur Iran 35 H5
Bandar-e Nakhīlū Iran 35 I6
Bandar-e Pahlavī Iran see Bandar-e Anzalī
Bandar-e Shāh Iran see Bandar-e Torkeman
Bandar-e Shāhpūr Iran see Bandar-e Emām Khomeynī
Bandar-e Shīū' Iran 35 I6
Bandar-e Torkeman Iran 35 I3
Bandar Lampung Indon. 41 C8
Bandarpunch mt. India 36 D3
Bandar Seri Begawan Brunei 41 D7
Banda Sea sea Indon. see Banda, Laut
Band-e Amīr r. Afgh. 36 A2
Band-e Amīr, Daryā-ye r. Afgh. 36 A1
Bandeira Brazil 71 C1
Bandeirante Brazil 71 A1
Bandeiras, Pico de mt. Brazil 71 C3
Bandelierkop S. Africa 51 I2
Banderas, Bahía de b. Mex. 66 C4
Band-e Sar Qom Iran 35 I4
Band-e Torkestān mts Afgh. 36 A2
Bandhi Pak. 36 B4
Bandhogarh India 36 E5
Bandi r. India 36 C4
Bandiagara Mali 46 C3
Bandikui India 36 D4
Bandipur National Park India 38 C4
Bandırma Turkey 27 L4
Bandjarmasin Indon. see Banjarmasin
Bandon Ireland 21 D6
Bandon r. Ireland 21 D6
Ban Don Thai. see Surat Thani
Band Qīr Iran 35 H5
Bandra India 38 B2
Bandundu Dem. Rep. Congo 48 B4
Bandung Indon. 41 C8
Bandya Australia 55 C6
Bāneh Iran 35 G4
Banera India 36 C4
Banes Cuba 67 I4
Banff Canada 62 D1
Banff U.K. 20 G3
Banfora Burkina 46 C3
Banga Dem. Rep. Congo 49 C4
Bangalore India 38 C3
Bangalow Australia 58 F2
Bangaon India 37 G5
Bangassou Cent. Afr. Rep. 48 C3
Bangdag Co salt l. China 37 E2
Banggai Indon. 52 C2
Banggai, Kepulauan is Indon. 41 E8
Banggi i. Malaysia 41 D7
Banghāzī Libya see Benghazi
Bangka i. Indon. 41 C8
Bangko Indon. 41 C8
Bangkok Thai. 31 J5
Bangkor China 37 F3

Bangla state India see West Bengal
Bangladesh country Asia 37 G4
Bangolo Côte d'Ivoire 46 C4
Bangong Co salt l. China/Jammu and Kashmir 36 D2
Bangor Northern Ireland U.K. 21 G3
Bangor Wales U.K. 18 C5
Bangor ME U.S.A. 63 N3
Bangor PA U.S.A. 64 D2
Bangor Erris Ireland 21 C3
Bangs, Mount AZ U.S.A. 65 F2
Bangsund Norway 14 G4
Bangued Phil. 43 M9
Bangui Cent. Afr. Rep. 48 B3
Bangweulu, Lake Zambia 49 C5
Banhā Egypt 34 C5
Banhine, Parque Nacional de nat. park Moz. 51 K2
Ban Houei Sai Laos see Huayxay
Bani, Jbel ridge Morocco 22 C6
Bania Cent. Afr. Rep. 48 B3
Bani-Bangou Niger 46 D3
Banifing r. Mali 46 C3
Banihal Pass and Tunnel Jammu and Kashmir 36 C2
Banister r. VA U.S.A. 64 B4
Banī Suwayf Egypt 34 C5
Banī Walīd Libya 47 E1
Bāniyās Al Qunayṭirah Syria 39 B3
Bāniyās Ṭarṭūs Syria 39 B2
Banja Luka Bos.-Herz. 26 G2
Banjarmasin Indon. 41 D8
Banjes, Liqeni i resr Albania 27 I4
Banjul Gambia 46 B3
Banka India 37 F4
Banka Banka Australia 54 F4
Bankapur India 38 B3
Bankass Mali 46 C3
Bankilaré Niger 46 D3
Banks Island N.W.T. Canada 60 F2
Banks Islands Vanuatu 53 G3
Banks Peninsula N.Z. 59 D6
Banks Strait Australia 57 [inset]
Bankura India 37 F5
Banmaw Myanmar see Bhamo
Banmo Myanmar see Bhamo
Bann r. Ireland 21 F5
Bann r. U.K. 21 F2
Banning CA U.S.A. 65 D4
Banningville Dem. Rep. Congo see Bandundu
Bannu Pak. 36 B2
Bano India 37 F5
Bañolas Spain see Banyoles
Bansi Bihar India 37 F4
Bansi Rajasthan India 36 C4
Bansi Uttar Prad. India 36 D4
Bansi Uttar Prad. India 37 E4
Bansihari India 37 G4
Banská Bystrica Slovakia 17 Q6
Banspani India 37 F5
Bansur India 36 D4
Banswara India 36 C5
Banteer Ireland 21 D5
Bantry Ireland 21 C6
Bantry Bay Ireland 21 C6
Bantval India 38 B3
Banyo Cameroon 46 E4
Banyoles Spain 25 H2
Banyuwangi Indon. 54 A2
Banzare Coast Antarctica 76 G2
Banzare Seamount sea feature Indian Ocean 73 N9
Banzart Tunisia see Bizerte
Banzyville Dem. Rep. Congo see Mobayi-Mbongo
Bao'an China see Shenzhen
Baochang China 43 L4
Baoding China 43 L5
Baoji Shaanxi China 42 J6
Baokang Nei Mongol China 44 A3
Baolin China 44 C3
Baoqing China 44 D3
Baoro Cent. Afr. Rep. 48 B3
Baoshan China 42 H7
Baotou China 43 K4
Baotou Shan mt. China/N. Korea 44 C4
Baoulé r. Mali 46 C3
Bap India 36 C4
Bapatla India 38 D3
Baq'ā' oasis Saudi Arabia 35 F6
Baqbaq Egypt see Buqbuq
Baqên Xizang China 37 H2
Baqên Xizang China 37 H3
Ba'qūbah Iraq 35 G4
Bar Montenegro 27 H3
Bara Sudan 32 D7
Baraawe Somalia 48 E3
Barabanki India 36 E4
Bara Banki India see Barabanki
Baracaju r. Brazil 71 A1
Baracaldo Spain see Barakaldo
Baracoa Cuba 67 J4
Baradā, Nahr r. Syria 39 C3
Baradine Australia 58 D3
Baradine r. Australia 58 D3
Baragarh India see Bargarh
Barahona Dom. Rep. 67 J5
Barail Range mts India 37 H4
Baraka watercourse Eritrea/Sudan 47 G3
Barakaldo Spain 25 E2
Barakī Barak Afgh. 36 B2
Baralaba Australia 56 E5
Bara Lacha Pass India 36 D2
Baram India 37 F5
Baramati India 38 B2
Baramula India see Baramulla
Baramulla India 36 C2
Baran India 36 D4
Baran r. Pak. 36 B4
Baranavichy Belarus 15 O10
Baranikha Rus. Fed. 29 R3
Baranīs Egypt 32 E5
Baranīs Egypt see Baranīs
Barannda India 36 E4
Baranof Island U.S.A. 60 E4
Baranovichi Belarus see Baranavichy
Baranowicze Belarus see Baranavichy
Baraouéli Mali 46 C3
Barasat India 37 G5
Barat Daya, Kepulauan is Indon. 41 E8
Baraut India 36 D3
Barbacena Brazil 71 C3
Barbados country West Indies 67 M6
Barbar, Gebel el mt. Egypt see Barbar, Jabal
Barbar, Jabal mt. Egypt 39 A5
Barbastro Spain 25 G2
Barbate de Franco Spain 25 D5
Barberton S. Africa 51 J3
Barbezieux-St-Hilaire France 24 D4
Barbuda i. Antigua and Barbuda 67 L5
Barcaldine Australia 56 D4
Barce Libya see Al Marj
Barcelona Spain 25 H3
Barcelona Venez. 68 F1
Barcelonnette France 24 H4
Barcelos Brazil 68 F4
Barcino Spain see Barcelona
Barclay de Tolly atoll Fr. Polynesia see Raroia
Barclayville Liberia 46 C4
Barcoo watercourse Australia 56 C5
Barcoo Creek watercourse Australia see Cooper Creek
Barcoo National Park Australia see Welford National Park
Barcs Hungary 26 G2
Bärdä Azer. 35 G2
Bárðarbunga mt. Iceland 14 [inset]
Bardawīl, Khabrat al salt pan Saudi Arabia 39 D4
Bardawīl, Sabkhat al lag. Egypt 39 A4
Barddhaman India 37 F5
Bardejov Slovakia 13 D6
Bardera Somalia see Baardheere
Bardhaman India see Barddhaman
Bardsey Island U.K. 19 C6
Bardsīr Iran 33 I4
Barðsneshorn pt Iceland 10 D2
Barduli Italy see Barletta
Bareilly India 36 D3
Barellan Australia 58 C5
Barentin France 19 H9
Barentsburg Svalbard 28 C2
Barents Sea Arctic Ocean 12 I1
Barentu Eritrea 32 E6
Barfleur, Pointe de pt France 19 F9
Bargarh India 37 E5
Bargrennan U.K. 20 E5
Barguna Bangl. 37 G5
Barhaj India 37 E4
Barham Australia 58 B5
Bari Italy 26 G4
Bari Doab lowland Pak. 33 L3
Barika Alg. 22 F4
Barinas Venez. 68 D2
Baripada India 37 F5
Bariri Brazil 71 A3
Bari Sadri India 36 C4
Barisal Bangl. 37 G5
Barisan, Pegunungan mts Indon. 41 C8
Barito r. Indon. 41 D8
Barium Italy see Bari
Barkal Bangl. 37 H5
Barkam China 42 I6
Barkan, Ra's-e pt Iran 35 H5
Barkava Latvia 15 O8
Barkly East S. Africa 51 H6
Barkly Homestead Australia 56 A3
Barkly-Oos S. Africa see Barkly East
Barkly Tableland reg. Australia 56 A3
Barkly-Wes S. Africa see Barkly West
Barkly West S. Africa 50 G5
Barkol China 42 G4
Barla Turkey 27 N5
Bârlad Romania 27 L1
Bar-le-Duc France 24 G2
Barlee, Lake salt flat Australia 55 B7
Barlee Range hills Australia 55 A5
Barletta Italy 26 G4
Barlow Canada 60 E3
Barmah Forest Australia 58 B5
Barmedman Australia 58 C5
Barmen-Elberfeld Germany see Wuppertal
Barmer India 36 B4
Barm Fīrūz, Kūh-e mt. Iran 35 H5
Barmouth U.K. 19 C6
Barnala India 36 C3
Barnard Castle U.K. 18 F4
Barnato Australia 58 B3
Barnaul Rus. Fed. 42 E2
Barnegat Bay NJ U.S.A. 64 D3
Barnes Icecap Canada 61 K2
Barneville-Carteret France 19 F9
Barneys Lake imp. l. Australia 58 B4
Barnsley U.K. 18 F5
Barnstable MA U.S.A. 64 F2
Barnstaple U.K. 19 C7
Barnstaple Bay U.K. 19 C7
Baro Nigeria 46 D4
Baroda Gujarat India see Vadodara
Baroda Madh. Prad. India 36 D4
Barons Range hills Australia 55 D6
Barowghīl, Kowtal-e Afgh. 36 C1
Barpeta India 37 G4
Bar Pla Soi Thai. see Chon Buri
Barquisimeto Venez. 68 E1
Barra Brazil 69 J6
Barra i. U.K. 20 B4
Barra, Ponta da pt Moz. 51 L2
Barra, Sound of sea chan. U.K. 20 B3
Barraba Australia 58 E3
Barra Bonita Brazil 71 A3
Barracão do Barreto Brazil 69 G5
Barra do Bugres Brazil 69 G7
Barra do Corda Brazil 69 I5
Barra do Cuieté Brazil 71 C2
Barra do Garças Brazil 69 H7
Barra do Piraí Brazil 71 C3
Barra do São Manuel Brazil 69 G5
Barra do Turvo Brazil 71 A4
Barra Falsa, Ponta da pt Moz. 51 L2
Barraigh i. U.K. see Barra
Barra Mansa Brazil 71 B3
Barrana Pak. 36 C3
Barranca Peru 68 C4
Barranqueras Arg. 70 E3
Barranquilla Col. 68 D1
Barre MA U.S.A. 64 E1
Barre des Ecrins mt. France 24 H4
Barreiras Brazil 69 J6
Barreirinha Brazil 69 G4
Barreirinhas Brazil 69 J4
Barreiro Port. 25 B4
Barreiros Brazil 69 K5
Barren Island Kiribati see Starbuck Island
Barretos Brazil 71 A3
Barrett, Mount hill Australia 54 D4
Barrhead U.K. 20 E5
Barrier Bay Antarctica 76 E2
Barrière Canada 62 C1
Barrier Range hills Australia 57 C6
Barrington, Mount Australia 58 E4
Barrington Tops National Park Australia 58 E4
Barringun Australia 58 B2
Barro Alto Brazil 71 A1
Barrocão Brazil 71 C2
Barron U.S.A. 63 I2
Barrow r. Ireland 21 F5
Barrow U.S.A. 60 C2
Barrow, Point U.S.A. 60 C2
Barrow Creek Australia 54 F5
Barrow-in-Furness U.K. 18 D4
Barrow Island Australia 54 A5
Barrow Range hills Australia 55 D6
Barrow Strait Canada 61 I2
Barr Smith Range hills Australia 55 C6
Barry U.K. 19 D7
Barrydale S. Africa 50 E7
Barry Mountains Australia 58 C6
Barryville NY U.S.A. 64 D2
Barsalpur India 36 C3
Barshatas Kazakh. 42 D3
Barshi India see Barsi
Barsi India 38 B2
Barstow CA U.S.A. 65 D3
Barsur India 38 D2
Bar-sur-Aube France 24 G2
Barth Germany 17 N3
Bartica Guyana 69 G2
Bartın Turkey 34 D2
Bartle Frere, Mount Australia 56 D3
Barton-upon-Humber U.K. 18 G5
Bartoszyce Poland 17 R3
Barú, Volcán vol. Panama 67 H7
Barunga Australia see Bamyili
Barun-Torey, Ozero l. Rus. Fed. 43 L2
Baruunturuun Mongolia 42 G3
Baruun-Urt Mongolia 43 K3
Baruva India 38 E2
Barwani India 36 C5
Barwéli Mali see Baraouéli
Barwon r. Australia 58 C3
Barygaza India see Bharuch
Barysaw Belarus 15 P9
Barysh Rus. Fed. 13 J5
Basalt r. Australia 56 D3
Basankusu Dem. Rep. Congo 48 B3
Basar India 38 C2
Basarabi Romania 27 M2
Basargechar Armenia see Vardenis
Bascuñán, Cabo c. Chile 70 B3
Basel Switz. 24 H3
Bashanta Rus. Fed. see Gorodovikovsk
Bashee r. S. Africa 51 I7
Bāshī Iran 35 H5
Bashi Channel Phil./Taiwan 43 M8
Bashmakovo Rus. Fed. 13 I5
Bāsht Iran 35 H5
Bashtanka Ukr. 13 G7
Basi Punjab India 36 D3
Basi Rajasthan India 36 D4
Basia India 37 F5
Basilan i. Phil. 41 E7
Basildon U.K. 19 H7
Basile, Pico mt. Equat. Guinea 46 D4
Basingstoke U.K. 19 F7
Basirhat India 37 G5
Basīṭ, Ra's al pt Syria 39 B2
Başkale Turkey 35 G3
Baskatong, Réservoir resr Canada 63 L2
Baskerville, Cape Australia 54 C4
Başkomutan Tarıhı Milli Parkı nat. park Turkey 27 N5
Başköy Turkey 39 A1
Baskunchak, Ozero l. Rus. Fed. 13 J6
Basle Switz. see Basel
Basmat India 38 C2
Basoko Dem. Rep. Congo 48 C3
Basra Iraq 35 G5
Bassano Canada 62 E1
Bassano del Grappa Italy 26 D2
Bassar Togo 46 D4
Bassas da India reef Indian Ocean 49 D6
Bassas de Pedro Padua Bank sea feature India 38 B3
Bassein Myanmar 42 G9
Basse-Normandie admin. reg. France 19 F9
Bassenthwaite Lake U.K. 18 D4
Basse Santa Su Gambia 46 B3
Basse-Terre Guadeloupe 67 L5
Basseterre St Kitts and Nevis 67 L5
Bassikounou Mauritania 46 C3
Bass Rock i. U.K. 20 G4
Bass Strait Australia 57 D8
Båstad Sweden 15 H8
Bastanābād Iran 35 G3
Basti India 37 E4
Bastia Corsica France 24 I5
Bastioes r. Brazil 69 K5
Bastogne Belgium 17 J5
Bastrop LA U.S.A. 63 I5
Basuo China see Dongfang
Basutoland country Africa see Lesotho
Başyayla Turkey 39 A1
Bata Equat. Guinea 46 D4
Batabanó, Golfo de b. Cuba 67 H4
Batagay Rus. Fed. 29 O3
Batala India 36 C3
Batalha Port. 25 B4
Batamay Rus. Fed. 29 N3
Batan i. Phil. 43 M8
Batangafo Cent. Afr. Rep. 48 B3
Batangas Phil. 41 E6
Batan Islands Phil. 41 E5
Batavia Indon. see Jakarta
Batavia NY U.S.A. 64 B1
Bataysk Rus. Fed. 13 H7
Batchawana Mountain hill Canada 63 K2
Bătdâmbâng Cambodia 31 J5
Batéké, Plateaux Congo 48 B4
Batemans Bay Australia 58 E5
Bates Range hills Australia 55 C6
Batesville AR U.S.A. 63 I4
Batetskiy Rus. Fed. 12 F4
Bath U.K. 19 E7
Bath NY U.S.A. 64 C1
Batha watercourse Chad 47 E3
Bathgate U.K. 20 F5
Bathinda India 36 C3
Bathurst Australia 58 D4
Bathurst Canada 63 N2
Bathurst Gambia see Banjul
Bathurst S. Africa 51 H7
Bathurst, Cape Canada 60 F2
Bathurst, Lake Australia 58 D5
Bathurst Inlet Canada 60 H3
Bathurst Inlet inlet Canada 60 H3
Bathurst Island Australia 54 E2
Bathurst Island Canada 61 I2
Batié Burkina 46 C4
Batı Menteşe Dağları mts Turkey 27 L6
Batı Toroslar mts Turkey 27 N6
Batken Kyrg. 42 C5
Batkes Indon. 54 D2
Bāṭlāq-e Gavkhūnī marsh Iran 35 I4
Batley U.K. 18 F5
Batlow Australia 58 D5
Batman Turkey 35 F3
Batna Alg. 22 F4
Baton Rouge U.S.A. 63 I5
Batouri Cameroon 47 E4
Batrā' tourist site Jordan see Petra
Batrā', Jabal al mt. Jordan 39 B5
Batroûn Lebanon 39 B2
Båtsfjord Norway 14 P1
Battambang Cambodia see Bătdâmbâng
Batticaloa Sri Lanka 38 D5
Battipaglia Italy 26 F4
Battle r. Canada 62 F1
Battle Creek U.S.A. 63 J3
Battle Mountain U.S.A. 62 D3
Battura Glacier Jammu and Kashmir 36 C1
Batu mt. Eth. 48 D3
Batu, Pulau-pulau is Indon. 41 B8
Batum Georgia see Bat'umi
Bat'umi Georgia 35 F2
Baturité Brazil 69 K4
Batyrevo Rus. Fed. 13 J5
Batys Qazaqstan admin. div. Kazakh. see Zapadnyy Kazakhstan
Baubau Indon. 41 E8
Baucau East Timor 54 D2
Bauchi Nigeria 46 D3
Bauda India see Boudh
Baudh India see Boudh
Baugé France 24 D3
Bauhinia Australia 56 E5
Baukau East Timor see Baucau
Baume-les-Dames France 24 H3
Baundal India 36 C2
Baura Bangl. 37 G4
Bauru Brazil 71 A3
Bauska Latvia 15 N8
Bautino Kazakh. 35 H1
Bautzen Germany 17 O5
Bavānāt Iran 35 I5
Bavaria reg. Germany 17 M6
Bavda India 38 B2
Baviaanskloofberge mts S. Africa 50 F7
Bavla India 36 C5
Bavly Rus. Fed. 11 Q5
Baw Myanmar 37 H5
Bawal India 36 D3
Baw Baw National Park Australia 58 C6
Bawdeswell U.K. 19 I6
Baxoi China 42 H6
Bay China see Baicheng
Bayamo Cuba 67 I4
Bayan Heilong. China 44 B3
Bayan Qinghai China 37 I2
Bayan Mongolia 43 K3
Bayana India 36 D4
Bayanaul Kazakh. 42 D2
Bayanbulag Mongolia 42 H3
Bayanbulak China 42 E4
Bayanday Rus. Fed. 42 J2
Bayan Gol China see Dengkou
Bayan Har Shan mts China 42 G5
Bayan Har Shankou pass China 37 I2
Bayanhongor Mongolia 42 I3
Bayan Hot China 42 J5
Bayan Mod China 42 I4
Bayan Obo China 43 J4
Bayan-Ovoo Mongolia 42 G4
Bayan Ul Hot China 43 L4
Bayasgalant Mongolia 43 K3
Bayat Turkey 27 N5
Bayburt Turkey 35 F2
Bay City MI U.S.A. 63 K3
Bay City TX U.S.A. 63 H6
Baydaratskaya Guba Rus. Fed. 28 H3
Baydhabo Somalia 48 E3
Bayerischer Wald mts Germany 17 N6
Bayerischer Wald nat. park Germany 17 N6
Bayer Wald, Nationalpark nat. park Germany 17 N6
Bayeux France 19 G9
Bayfield Ont. Canada 64 A1
Bayındır Turkey 27 L5
Bay Islands is Hond. see La Bahía, Islas de
Bayizhen China 37 H3
Bayjī Iraq 35 F4
Baykal, Ozero l. Rus. Fed. see Baikal, Lake
Baykal-Amur Magistral Rus. Fed. 44 C1
Baykal Range mts Rus. Fed. see Baykal'skiy Khrebet
Baykal'skiy Khrebet mts Rus. Fed. 43 J2
Baykan Turkey 35 F3
Bay-Khaak Rus. Fed. 42 G2
Baykibashevo Rus. Fed. 11 R4
Baykonur Kazakh. see Baykonyr
Baykonyr Kazakh. 42 A3
Baymak Rus. Fed. 28 G4
Bayombong Phil. 41 E6
Bayona Spain see Baiona
Bayonne France 24 D5
Bayonne NJ U.S.A. 64 D2
Bayqongyr Kazakh. see Baykonyr
Bayram-Ali Turkm. see Bayramaly
Bayramaly Turkm. 33 J2
Bayramiç Turkey 27 L5
Bayreuth Germany 17 M6
Bayrūt Lebanon see Beirut
Bay Shore NY U.S.A. 64 E2
Bayston Hill U.K. 19 E6
Bayt Lahm West Bank see Bethlehem
Bay View N.Z. 59 F4
Bayy al Kabīr, Wādī watercourse Libya 47 E1
Baza Spain 25 E5
Baza, Sierra de mts Spain 25 E5
Bazardüzü Dağı mt. Azer./Rus. Fed. see Bazardyuzyu, Gora
Bazardyuzyu, Gora mt. Azer./Rus. Fed. 35 G2
Bāzār-e Māsāl Iran 35 H3
Bazarnyy Karabulak Rus. Fed. 13 J5
Bazaruto, Ilha do i. Moz. 49 D6
Bazdar Pak. 33 K4
Bazhong China 42 J6
Bazhou China see Bazhong
Bazmān Iran 33 J4
Bazmān, Kūh-e mt. Iran 33 J4
Bcharré Lebanon 39 C2
Beachy Head hd U.K. 19 H8
Beacon NY U.S.A. 64 E2
Beacon Bay S. Africa 51 H7
Beaconsfield U.K. 19 G7
Beagle, Canal sea chan. Arg. 70 C8
Beagle Bank reef Australia 54 C3
Beagle Bay Australia 54 C4
Beagle Gulf Australia 54 E3
Bealanana Madag. 49 E5
Béal an Átha Ireland see Ballina
Béal Átha na Sluaighe Ireland see Ballinasloe
Beale, Lake India 38 B2
Beaminster U.K. 19 E8
Bearalváhki Norway see Berlevåg
Beardmore Glacier Antarctica 76 H1
Bear Island Arctic Ocean see Bjørnøya
Bear Island Ireland 21 C6
Bearma r. India 36 D4
Bearnaraigh i. U.K. see Berneray
Bear Paw Mountain U.S.A. 62 F2
Bearpaw Mountains U.S.A. 62 F2
Beas Dam India 36 C3
Beata, Cabo c. Dom. Rep. 67 J5
Beatrice U.S.A. 63 H3
Beatrice, Cape Australia 56 B2
Beatty NV U.S.A. 65 D2
Beaucaire France 24 G5
Beauchene Island Falkland Is 70 E8
Beaufort Australia 58 A6
Beaufort Sea Canada/U.S.A. 60 D2
Beaufort West S. Africa 50 F7
Beauly U.K. 20 E3
Beauly r. U.K. 20 E3
Beaumaris U.K. 18 C5
Beaumont N.Z. 59 B7
Beaumont TX U.S.A. 63 I5
Beaune France 24 G3
Beaupréau France 24 D3
Beauséjour Canada 63 H1
Beauvais France 24 F2
Beaver r. Alberta/Saskatchewan Canada 60 H4
Beaver PA U.S.A. 64 A2
Beaver UT U.S.A. 65 F1
Beaver r. UT U.S.A. 65 F1
Beaver Creek Canada 77 A2
Beaver Falls PA U.S.A. 64 A2
Beaver Hill Lake Canada 63 H1
Beaver Island U.S.A. 63 J2
Beawar India 36 C4
Beazley Arg. 70 C4
Bebedouro Brazil 71 A3
Bebington U.K. 18 D5
Bêca China 37 I3
Beccles U.K. 19 I6
Bečej Serbia 27 I2
Becerreá Spain 25 C2
Béchar Alg. 22 D5
Bechuanaland country Africa see Botswana
Beckley WV U.S.A. 64 A4
Bedale U.K. 18 F4
Bedelē Eth. 48 D3
Bedford E. Cape S. Africa 51 H7
Bedford Kwazulu-Natal S. Africa 51 J5
Bedford U.K. 19 G6
Bedford IN U.S.A. 63 J4
Bedford PA U.S.A. 64 B2
Bedford VA U.S.A. 64 B4
Bedford, Cape Australia 56 D2
Bedford Downs Australia 54 D4
Bedgerebong Australia 58 C4
Bedi India 36 B5
Bedla India 36 C4
Bedlington U.K. 18 F3
Bedourie Australia 56 B5
Bedworth U.K. 19 F6
Beechworth Australia 58 C6
Beecroft Peninsula Australia 58 E5
Beed India see Bid
Beenleigh Australia 58 F1
Beersheba Israel 39 B4
Be'ér Sheva' Israel see Beersheba
Be'ér Sheva' watercourse Israel 39 B4
Beervlei Dam S. Africa 50 F7
Beerwah Australia 58 F1
Beetaloo Australia 54 F4
Beethoven Peninsula Antarctica 76 L2
Beeville U.S.A. 62 H6
Befori Dem. Rep. Congo 48 C3
Beg, Lough l. U.K. 21 F3
Bega Australia 58 D6
Begari r. Pak. 36 B3
Begicheva, Ostrov i. Rus. Fed. see Bol'shoy Begichev, Ostrov
Begur, Cap de c. Spain 25 H3
Begusarai India 37 F4
Béhague, Pointe pt Fr. Guiana 69 H3
Behbehān Iran 35 H5
Behrendt Mountains Antarctica 76 L2
Behrūsī Iran 35 I5
Behshahr Iran 35 I3
Behsūd Afgh. 36 A2
Bei'an China 44 B2
Beida Libya see Al Bayḍā'
Beiguan China see Anyang
Beihai China 43 J8
Bei Hulsan Hu salt l. China 37 H1
Beijing China 43 L5
Beijing municipality China 43 L4
Beik Myanmar see Myeik
Beinn an Oir hill U.K. 20 D5
Beinn an Tuirc hill U.K. 20 D5
Beinn Bheigeir hill U.K. 20 C5
Beinn Bhreac hill U.K. 20 D4
Beinn Dearg mt. U.K. 20 E3
Beinn Heasgarnich mt. U.K. 20 E4
Beinn Mholach hill U.K. 20 C2
Beinn Mhòr hill U.K. 20 B3
Beinn na Faoghlia i. U.K. see Benbecula
Beipiao China 43 M4
Beira Moz. 49 D5
Beirut Lebanon 39 B3
Bei Shan mts China 42 H4
Beitbridge Zimbabwe 49 C6
Beith U.K. 20 E5
Beit Jālā West Bank 39 B4
Beja Port. 25 C4
Béja Tunisia 26 C6
Bejaïa Alg. 25 I5
Béjar Spain 25 D3
Bekaa valley Lebanon see El Béqaa
Békés Hungary 27 I1
Békéscsaba Hungary 27 I1
Bekily Madag. 49 E6
Bekkai Japan 44 G4
Bēkma, Sadd dam Iraq 35 G3
Bekovo Rus. Fed. 13 I5
Bekwai Ghana 46 C4
Bela India 37 E4
Bela Pak. 33 K4
Belab r. Pak. 36 B3
Bela-Bela S. Africa 51 I3
Bélabo Cameroon 46 E4
Bela Crkva Serbia 27 I2
Bel Air MD U.S.A. 64 C3
Belalcázar Spain 25 D4
Belapur India 38 B2
Belarus country Europe 13 E5
Belau country N. Pacific Ocean see Palau
Bela Vista Brazil 70 E2
Bela Vista Moz. 51 K4
Bela Vista de Goiás Brazil 71 A2
Belaya r. Rus. Fed. 29 S3
Belaya Glina Rus. Fed. 13 I7
Belaya Kalitva Rus. Fed. 13 I6
Belaya Kholunitsa Rus. Fed. 12 K4
Belaya Tserkva Ukr. see Bila Tserkva
Belbédji Niger 46 D3
Bełchatów Poland 17 Q5
Belcher Islands Canada 61 K4
Belcoo U.K. 21 E3
Beleapani reef India see Cherbaniani Reef
Belebey Rus. Fed. 11 Q5
Beledweyne Somalia 48 E3
Belém Brazil 69 I4
Belém Novo Brazil 71 A5
Belén Arg. 70 C3
Belen Antalya Turkey 39 A1
Belen Hatay Turkey 39 C1
Belen U.S.A. 62 F5
Belep, Îles is New Caledonia 53 G3
Belev Rus. Fed. 13 H5
Belfast S. Africa 51 J3
Belfast U.K. 21 G3
Belfast U.S.A. 63 N3
Belfast Lough inlet U.K. 21 G3
Bēlfodiyo Eth. 48 D2
Belford U.K. 18 F3
Belfort France 24 H3
Belgaum India 38 B3
Belgian Congo country Africa see Congo, Democratic Republic of the
België country Europe see Belgium
Belgique country Europe see Belgium
Belgium country Europe 16 J5
Belgorod Rus. Fed. 13 H6
Belgorod-Dnestrovskyy Ukr. see Bilhorod-Dnistrovs'kyy
Belgrade Serbia 27 I2
Belgrano II research station Antarctica 76 A1
Belice r. Sicily Italy 26 E6
Belinskiy Rus. Fed. 13 I5
Belinyu Indon. 41 C8
Belitung i. Indon. 41 C8
Belize Angola 49 B4
Belize Belize 66 G5
Belize country Central America 66 G5
Beljak Austria see Villach
Belkina, Mys pt Rus. Fed. 44 E3
Bel'kovskiy, Ostrov i. Rus. Fed. 29 O2
Bell Australia 58 E1
Bell r. Australia 58 D4
Bellac France 24 E3
Bellary India 38 C3
Bellata Australia 58 D2
Bella Unión Uruguay 70 E4
Bellbrook Australia 58 F3
Bell Cay reef Australia 56 E4
Belledonne mts France 24 G4
Bellefonte PA U.S.A. 64 C2
Belle Fourche U.S.A. 62 G3
Belle Fourche r. U.S.A. 62 G3
Belle Glade U.S.A. 63 K6
Belle-Île i. France 24 C3
Belle Isle i. Canada 61 M4
Belle Isle, Strait of Canada 61 M4
Belleville IL U.S.A. 63 J4
Bellevue WA U.S.A. 62 C2
Bellin Canada see Kangirsuk
Bellingham U.K. 18 E3
Bellingham U.S.A. 62 C2
Bellingshausen research station Antarctica 76 A2
Bellingshausen Sea Antarctica 76 L2
Bellinzona Switz. 24 I3
Bellows Falls VT U.S.A. 64 E1
Bellpat Pak. 36 B3
Belluno Italy 26 E1
Belluru India 38 C3
Bell Ville Arg. 70 D4
Bellville S. Africa 50 D7
Belmont Australia 58 E4
Belmont U.K. 20 [inset]
Belmont NY U.S.A. 64 B1
Belmonte Brazil 71 D1
Belmopan Belize 66 G5
Belmore, Mount hill Australia 58 F2
Belmullet Ireland 21 C3
Belo Madag. 49 E6
Belo Campo Brazil 71 C1
Belogorsk Rus. Fed. 44 C2
Belogorsk Ukr. see Bilohirs'k
Beloha Madag. 49 E6
Belo Horizonte Brazil 71 C2
Beloit WI U.S.A. 63 J3
Belokurikha Rus. Fed. 42 E2
Belo Monte Brazil 69 H4
Belomorsk Rus. Fed. 12 G2
Belonia India 37 G5
Belorechensk Rus. Fed. 35 E1
Belorechenskaya Rus. Fed. see Belorechensk
Belören Turkey 34 D3
Beloretsk Rus. Fed. 28 G4
Belorussia country Europe see Belarus
Belorusskaya S.S.R. country Europe see Belarus
Belostok Poland see Białystok
Belot, Lac l. Canada 60 F3
Belo Tsiribihina Madag. 49 E5
Belovo Rus. Fed. 42 F2
Beloyarskiy Rus. Fed. 11 T3
Beloye, Ozero l. Rus. Fed. 12 H3
Beloye More sea Rus. Fed. see White Sea
Belozersk Rus. Fed. 12 H3
Belpre OH U.S.A. 64 A3
Beltana Australia 57 B6
Belted Range mts NV U.S.A. 65 D2
Bel'ts' Moldova see Bălţi
Bel'tsy Moldova see Bălţi
Belukha, Gora mt. Kazakh./Rus. Fed. 42 F3
Belush'ye Rus. Fed. 12 J2
Belvidere NJ U.S.A. 64 D2
Belyando r. Australia 56 D4
Belyayevka Ukr. see Bilyayivka
Belyy Rus. Fed. 12 G5
Belyy, Ostrov i. Rus. Fed. 28 I2
Bemaraha, Plateau du Madag. 49 E5
Bembe Angola 49 B4
Bemidji U.S.A. 63 I2
Béna Burkina 46 C3
Bena Dibele Dem. Rep. Congo 48 C4
Ben Alder mt. U.K. 20 E4
Benalla Australia 58 B6
Benares India see Varanasi
Ben Arous Tunisia 26 D6
Benavente Spain 25 D2
Ben Avon mt. U.K. 20 F3
Benbane Head hd U.K. 21 F2
Benbecula i. U.K. 20 B3
Ben Boyd National Park Australia 58 E6
Benburb U.K. 21 F3
Ben Chonzie hill U.K. 20 F4
Ben Cleuch hill U.K. 20 F4
Ben Cruachan mt. U.K. 20 D4
Bend U.S.A. 62 C3
Bendearg mt. S. Africa 51 H6
Bender Moldova see Tighina
Bender-Bayla Somalia 48 F3
Bendery Moldova see Tighina
Bendigo Australia 58 B6
Bendoc Australia 58 D6
Bene Moz. 49 D5
Benenitra Madag. 49 E6
Benešov Czech Rep. 17 O6
Benevento Italy 26 F4
Beneventum Italy see Benevento
Benezette PA U.S.A. 64 B2
Bengal, Bay of sea Indian Ocean 31 H5
Bengamisa Dem. Rep. Congo 48 C3
Bengbu China 43 L6
Benghazi Libya 47 F1
Bengkulu Indon. 41 C8
Bengtsfors Sweden 15 H7
Benguela Angola 49 B5
Benha Egypt see Banhā
Ben Hiant hill U.K. 20 C4
Ben Hope hill U.K. 20 E2
Ben Horn hill U.K. 20 E2
Beni r. Bol. 68 E6
Beni Dem. Rep. Congo 48 C3
Beni Nepal 37 E3
Beni-Abbès Alg. 22 D5
Benidorm Spain 25 F4
Beni Mellal Morocco 22 C5
Benin country Africa 46 D4
Benin, Bight of g. Africa 46 D4
Benin City Nigeria 46 D4
Beni-Saf Alg. 25 F6
Beni Snassen, Monts des mts Morocco 25 E6
Beni Suef Egypt see Banī Suwayf
Benito Juárez Arg. 70 E5
Benito Juárez Baja California Mex. 65 E4
Benjamim Constant Brazil 68 E4
Benjamín Hill Mex. 66 B2
Benjina Indon. 52 D2
Ben Klibreck hill U.K. 20 E2
Ben Lavin Nature Reserve S. Africa 51 I2
Ben Lawers mt. U.K. 20 E4
Ben Lomond mt. Australia 58 E3
Ben Lomond hill U.K. 20 E4
Ben Lomond National Park Australia 57 [inset]
Ben Macdui mt. U.K. 20 F3
Benmara Australia 56 B3
Ben More hill U.K. 20 C4
Ben More mt. U.K. 20 E4
Benmore, Lake N.Z. 59 C7
Ben More Assynt hill U.K. 20 E2
Bennetta, Ostrov i. Rus. Fed. 29 P2
Bennett Island Rus. Fed. see Bennetta, Ostrov
Ben Nevis mt. U.K. 20 D4
Bennington NH U.S.A. 64 F1
Bennington VT U.S.A. 64 E1
Benoni S. Africa 51 I4
Ben Rinnes hill U.K. 20 F3
Benson AZ U.S.A. 62 E5
Benteng Indon. 41 E8
Bentiu Sudan 32 C8

Bent Jbaïl Lebanon 39 B3
Bentley U.K. 18 F5
Benton Gonçalves Brazil 71 A5
Benton CA U.S.A. 65 C2
Benton Harbor U.S.A. 63 J3
Bentonville U.S.A. 63 I4
Benue r. Nigeria 46 D4
Benwee Head hd Ireland 21 C3
Benwood WV U.S.A. 64 A2
Ben Wyvis mt. U.K. 20 E3
Benxi Liaoning China 44 A4
Benxi Liaoning China 44 A4
Beograd Serbia see Belgrade
Béoumi Côte d'Ivoire 46 C4
Beppu Japan 45 C6
Béqaa valley Lebanon see El Béqaa
Berach r. India 36 C4
Beraketa Madag. 49 E6
Berasia India 36 D5
Berat Albania 27 H4
Beravina Madag. 49 E5
Berber Sudan 32 D6
Berbera Somalia 48 E2
Berbérati Cent. Afr. Rep. 48 B3
Berchtesgaden, Nationalpark nat. park
    Germany 17 N7
Berck France 24 E1
Berdichev Ukr. see Berdychiv
Berdigestyakh Rus. Fed. 29 N3
Berdyans'k Ukr. 13 H7
Berdychiv Ukr. 13 F6
Beregovo Ukr. see Berehove
Beregovoy Rus. Fed. 44 B1
Berehove Ukr. 13 D6
Bereina P.N.G. 52 E2
Bereket Turkm. 35 I3
Berekum Ghana 46 C4
Berenice Egypt see Baranis
Berenice Libya see Benghazi
Berens River Canada 63 H1
Bereza Belarus see Byaroza
Berezino Belarus see Byerazino
Berezivka Ukr. 13 F6
Berezne Ukr. 13 E6
Bereznik Rus. Fed. 12 I3
Berezniki Rus. Fed. 11 R4
Berezov Rus. Fed. see Berezovo
Berezovka Rus. Fed. 44 B2
Berezovka Ukr. see Berezivka
Berezovo Rus. Fed. 11 T3
Berezovyy Rus. Fed. 44 D2
Berga Spain 25 G2
Bergama Turkey 27 L5
Bergamo Italy 26 C2
Bergby Sweden 15 J6
Bergen Mecklenburg-Vorpommern
    Germany 17 N3
Bergen Norway 15 D6
Bergen NY U.S.A. 64 C1
Bergerac France 24 E4
Bergheim (Erft) Germany 17 K5
Bergland Namibia 50 C2
Bergoo U.S.A. see Bergamo
Bergsjö Sweden 15 J6
Bergsviken Sweden 14 L4
Bergville S. Africa 51 I5
Berhampur India see Baharampur
Beringa, Ostrov i. Rus. Fed. 29 R4
Beringovskiy Rus. Fed. 29 S3
Bering Sea N. Pacific Ocean 29 S4
Bering Strait Rus. Fed./U.S.A. 29 U3
Berislav Ukr. see Beryslav
Berkåk Norway 14 G5
Berkane Morocco 25 E6
Berkeley CA U.S.A. 65 B3
Berkeley Springs WV U.S.A. 64 B3
Berkner Island Antarctica 76 A1
Berkovitsa Bulg. 27 J3
Berkshire Downs hills U.K. 19 F7
Berkshire Hills MA U.S.A. 64 E1
Berlevåg Norway 14 P1
Berlin Germany 17 N4
Berlin MD U.S.A. 64 D3
Berlin PA U.S.A. 64 B3
Berlin OH U.S.A. 64 A2
Berlin Lake OH U.S.A. 64 A2
Bermagui Australia 58 E6
Bermejo r. Arg./Bol. 70 E3
Bermejo Bol. 68 F8
Bermen, Lac l. Canada 61 L4
Bermuda terr. N. Atlantic Ocean 67 L2
Bermuda Rise sea feature N. Atlantic Ocean
    72 D4
Bern Switz. 24 H3
Bernardino de Campos Brazil 71 A3
Bernardo O'Higgins, Parque Nacional
    nat. park Chile 70 B7
Bernasconi Arg. 70 D5
Berne Switz. see Bern
Berner Alpen mts Switz. 24 H3
Berneray i. Scotland U.K. 20 B4
Berneray i. Scotland U.K. 20 B4
Bernier Island Australia 55 A6
Bernina Pass Switz. 24 J3
Beroea Greece see Veroia
Beroea Syria see Aleppo
Bororoha Madag. 49 E6
Beroun r. Czech Rep. 17 O6
Berounka r. Czech Rep. 17 O6
Berovina Madag. see Beravina
Berri Australia 57 C7
Berriane Alg. 22 E5
Berridale Australia 58 D6
Berriedale U.K. 20 F2
Berrigan Australia 58 B5
Berrima Australia 58 E5
Berrouaghia Alg. 25 H5
Berry Australia 58 E5
Berryessa, Lake CA U.S.A. 65 A1
Berry Head hd U.K. 19 D8
Berry Islands Bahamas 67 I3
Berryville VA U.S.A. 64 C3
Berseba Namibia 50 C4
Berté, Lac l. Canada 63 N1
Bertolinía Brazil 69 J5
Bertoua Cameroon 46 E4
Bertraghboy Bay Ireland 21 C4
Beru atoll Kiribati 53 H2
Beruri Brazil 68 F4
Beruwala Sri Lanka 38 C5
Berwick Australia 58 B7
Berwick-upon-Tweed U.K. 18 E3
Berwyn hills U.K. 19 D6
Beryslav Ukr. 27 O1
Berytus Lebanon see Beirut
Besalampy Madag. 49 E5
Besançon France 24 H3
Beshneh Iran 35 I5
Besikama Indon. 54 D2
Beskra Alg. see Biskra
Beslan Rus. Fed. 35 G2
Besni Turkey 34 E3
Besoa watercourse Israel 39 B4
Beşparmak Dağları mts Cyprus see
    Pentadaktylos Range
Bessbrook U.K. 21 F3
Bessemer U.S.A. 63 J5

Besshoky, Gora hill Kazakh. 35 I1
Besskorbnaya Rus. Fed. 13 I7
Bessonovka Rus. Fed. 13 J5
Betanzos Spain 25 B2
Bethal S. Africa 51 I4
Bethanie Namibia 50 C4
Bethel Park U.S.A. 64 A2
Bethel U.K. 18 C5
Bethesda MD U.S.A. 64 C3
Bethesda OH U.S.A. 64 A2
Bethesda U.K. 18 C5
Bethlehem S. Africa 51 I5
Bethlehem PA U.S.A. 64 D2
Bethlehem West Bank 39 B4
Bethulie S. Africa 51 G6
Beti Pak. 36 B3
Betim Brazil 71 B2
Bet Lehem West Bank see Bethlehem
Betma India 36 C5
Betoota Australia 56 C5
Betpak-Dala plain Kazakh. 42 C3
Betroka Madag. 49 E6
Bié Angola see Kuito
Bet She'an Israel 39 B3
Betsiamites Canada 63 N2
Bettiah India 37 E4
Bettyhill U.K. 20 E2
Bettystown Ireland 21 F4
Betul India 36 D5
Betwa r. India 36 D4
Betws-y-coed U.K. 19 D5
Beulah Australia 57 C7
Beult r. U.K. 19 H7
Beuthen Poland see Bytom
Beverley U.K. 18 G5
Beverly MA U.S.A. 64 F1
Beverly Hills CA U.S.A. 65 C3
Bexhill U.K. 19 H8
Bexley, Cape Canada 60 G3
Beyānlü Iran 35 G4
Beyce Turkey see Orhaneli
Bey Dağları mts Turkey 27 N6
Beykoz Turkey 27 M4
Beyla Guinea 46 C4
Beylagan Azer. see Beyläqan
Beyläqan Azer. 35 G3
Beyneu Kazakh. 30 E2
Beypazarı Turkey 27 N4
Beypınarı Turkey 34 E3
Beypore India 38 B4
Beyrouth Lebanon see Beirut
Beyşehir Turkey 34 C3
Beyşehir Gölü l. Turkey 34 C3
Beytonovo Rus. Fed. 44 B1
Beytüşşebap Turkey 35 F3
Bezbozhnik Rus. Fed. 12 K4
Bezhanitsy Rus. Fed. 12 F4
Bezhetsk Rus. Fed. 12 H4
Béziers France 24 F5
Bezmein Turkm. see Abadan
Bezwada India see Vijayawada
Bhabha India see Bhabhua
Bhabhar India 36 B4
Bhabhua India 37 E4
Bhabua India see Bhabhua
Bhachau India 36 B5
Bhachbhar India 36 B4
Bhadgaon Nepal see Bhaktapur
Bhadohi India 37 E4
Bhadra India 36 C3
Bhadrachalam Road Station India see
    Kottagudem
Bhadrak India 37 F5
Bhadrakh India see Bhadrak
Bhadravati India 38 B3
Bhag Pak. 36 A3
Bhagalpur India 37 F4
Bhainsa India 38 C2
Bhainsdehi India 36 D5
Bhairab Bazar Bangl. 37 G4
Bhaktapur Nepal 37 F4
Bhalki India 38 C2
Bhamo Myanmar 42 H8
Bhamragarh India 38 D2
Bhandara India 36 D5
Bhanjanagar India 38 E2
Bhanrer Range hills India 36 D5
Bharatpur India 36 D4
Bhareli r. India 37 H4
Bharuch India 36 C5
Bhatapara India 37 E5
Bhatarsaigh i. U.K. see Vatersay
Bhatghar Lake India 38 B2
Bhatinda India see Bathinda
Bhatnair India see Hanumangarh
Bhatpara India 37 G5
Bhaunagar India see Bhavnagar
Bhavani r. India 38 C4
Bhavani Sagar l. India 38 C4
Bhavnagar India 36 C5
Bhawana Pak. 36 C3
Bhawanipatna India 38 D2
Bheanraigh, Eilean i. U.K. see Berneray
Bheemavaram India see Bhimavaram
Bhekuzulu S. Africa 51 J4
Bhera Pak. 36 C2
Bhigvan India 38 B2
Bhikhna Thori Nepal 37 F4
Bhilai India 38 E5
Bhildi India 36 C4
Bhilwara India 36 C4
Bhima r. India 38 C2
Bhimar India 36 B4
Bhimavaram India 38 D2
Bhimlath India 38 E5
Bhind India 36 D4
Bhinga India 37 E4
Bhiwandi India 38 B2
Bhiwani India 36 D3
Bhogaipur India 36 D4
Bhojpur Nepal 37 F4
Bhola Bangl. 37 G5
Bhongweni S. Africa 51 I6
Bhopal India 36 D5
Bhopalpatnam India 38 D2
Bhrigukaccha India see Bharuch
Bhubaan Bhutan 37 G4
Bhubaneshwar India 38 E1
Bhubaneswar India see Bhubaneshwar
Bhuj India 36 B5
Bhusawal India 36 C5
Bhutan country Asia 37 G4
Bhuttewala India 36 B4
Bia r. Ghana 46 C4
Bia, Phou mt. Laos 42 I9
Biafo Glacier Jammu and Kashmir 36 C2
Biafra, Bight of g. Africa see Benin, Bight of
Biak Indon. 41 F8
Biak i. Indon. 41 F8
Biała Podlaska Poland 13 D5
Białogard Poland 17 O4
Białystok Poland 13 D5
Bianco, Monte mt. France/Italy see
    Blanc, Mont
Bianzhao China 44 A3
Biaora India 36 D4
Biarritz France 24 D5
Bibai Japan 44 F4
Bibbenluke Australia 58 D6
Bibbiena Italy 26 D3
Biberach an der Riß Germany 17 L6

Bibile Sri Lanka 38 D5
Biblos Lebanon see Jbail
Bicas Brazil 71 C3
Biçer Turkey 27 N5
Bicester U.K. 19 F7
Bichabhera India 36 C4
Bichevaya Rus. Fed. 44 D3
Bichi r. Rus. Fed. 44 E1
Bickerton Island Australia 56 B2
Bickleigh U.K. 19 D8
Bicuari, Parque Nacional do nat. park
    Angola 49 B5
Bid India 38 B2
Bida Nigeria 46 D4
Bidar India 38 C2
Biddeford ME U.S.A. 64 F1
Bidean nam Bian mt. U.K. 20 D4
Bideford U.K. 19 C7
Bideford Bay U.K. see Barnstaple Bay
Bidzhan Rus. Fed. 44 C3
Bié, Planalto do Angola 49 B5
Biebrzański Park Narodowy nat. park
    Poland 15 M10
Biel Switz. 24 H3
Bielawa Poland 17 P5
Bielefeld Germany 17 L4
Bielitz Poland see Bielsko-Biała
Biella Italy 26 C2
Bielsko-Biała Poland 17 Q6
Biên Hoa Vietnam 41 J5
Bienne Switz. see Biel
Bienville, Lac l. Canada 61 K4
Bierbank Australia 58 B1
Biesiesvlei S. Africa 51 G4
Bifoun Gabon 48 B4
Biga Turkey 27 L4
Bigadiç Turkey 27 M5
Biga Yarımadası pen. Turkey 27 L5
Big Bear Lake CA U.S.A. 65 D3
Big Bend Swaziland 51 J4
Bigbury-on-Sea U.K. 19 D8
Biger Nuur salt l. Mongolia 42 H3
Biggar Canada 62 I1
Biggar U.K. 20 F5
Bigge Island Australia 54 D3
Biggenden Australia 57 F5
Biggleswade U.K. 19 G6
Big Hole r. U.S.A. 62 E2
Bighorn r. U.S.A. 62 F2
Bighorn Mountains U.S.A. 62 F3
Big Island Nunavut Canada 61 K3
Bircot Eth. 48 E3
Big Lake U.S.A. 62 G5
Bignona Senegal 46 B3
Big Pine CA U.S.A. 65 C2
Big Pine Peak CA U.S.A. 65 C3
Big Rapids U.S.A. 63 J3
Big River Canada 62 I1
Big Smokey Valley valley NV U.S.A. 65 D1
Big Spring U.S.A. 62 G5
Bigstone Lake Canada 63 H1
Big Timber U.S.A. 62 F2
Big Trout Lake Canada 63 J1
Big Trout Lake Canada 63 I1
Bihać Bos.-Herz. 26 F2
Bihar state India 37 F4
Bihar India see Bihar Sharif
Bihariganj India 37 F4
Bihar Sharif India 37 F4
Bihor, Vârful mt. Romania 27 J1
Bihoro Japan 44 G4
Bijagós, Arquipélago dos is
    Guinea-Bissau 46 B3
Bijaipur India 36 D4
Bijapur India 38 B3
Bijār Iran 35 G4
Bijbehara Jammu and Kashmir 36 C2
Bijeljina Bos.-Herz. 27 H2
Bijelo Polje Montenegro 27 H3
Bijeraghogarh India 36 E5
Bijie China 42 J7
Bijji India 38 D2
Bijnor India 36 D3
Bijnore India see Bijnor
Bikampur India 36 C4
Bikaner India 36 C3
Bikin Rus. Fed. 44 D3
Bikin r. Rus. Fed. 44 D3
Bikini atoll Marshall Is 74 H5
Bikori Sudan 32 D7
Bikoro Dem. Rep. Congo 48 B4
Bikou China 42 J6
Bikramganj India 37 E4
Biläd Banī Bū 'Alī Oman 33 I5
Bilaigarh India 38 D1
Bilara India 36 C4
Bilaspur Chhattisgarh India 37 E5
Bilaspur Hima. Prad. India 36 D3
Biläsuvar Azer. 35 H3
Bila Tserkva Ukr. 13 F6
Bilauktaung Range mts Thai./Myanmar see
    Tenasserim
Bilbao Spain 25 E2
Bilbays Egypt see Bilbeis
Bilbe Spain see Bilbao
Bilecik Turkey 27 M4
Biłgoraj Poland 13 D6
Bilharamulo Tanz. 48 D4
Bilhaur India 36 E4
Bilhorod-Dnistrovs'kyy Ukr. 27 N1
Bili Dem. Rep. Congo 48 C3
Bilibino Rus. Fed. 29 R3
Billabalong Australia 55 A6
Billabong Creek r. Australia see
    Moulamein Creek
Billericay U.K. 19 H7
Billiluna Australia 54 D4
Billingham U.K. 18 F4
Billings U.S.A. 62 F2
Billiton i. Indon. see Belitung
Bill of Portland hd U.K. 19 E8
Bill Williams r. AZ U.S.A. 65 E3
Bilma Niger 46 E3
Bilo r. Rus. Fed. see Belaya
Biloela Australia 57 E5
Bilohirs'k Ukr. 34 D1
Bilohir"ya Ukr. 13 E6
Biloku Guyana 69 G3
Biloli India 38 C2
Bilovods'k Ukr. 13 H6
Biloxi U.S.A. 63 I5
Bilpa Morea Claypan salt flat Australia 56 B5
Bilston U.K. 20 F5
Bilto Norway 14 L2
Bilyayivka Ukr. 27 N1
Bima Indon. 54 B2
Bimberi, Mount Australia 58 D5
Bimbo Cent. Afr. Rep. 48 B4
Bimini Islands Bahamas 67 I3
Binäb Iran 35 H3
Bina-Etawa India 36 D4
Binaija, Gunung mt. Indon. 41 E8
Binboğa Dağı mt. Turkey 34 E3
Bincheng China see Binzhou
Bindebango Australia 58 C1
Bindki India 38 E4
Bindu Dem. Rep. Congo 49 B4
Bindura Zimbabwe 49 C5
Binefar Spain 25 F3
Binga Zimbabwe 49 C5
Binga, Monte mt. Moz. 49 D5

Bingara Australia 58 B2
Bingaram i. India 38 B4
Bing Bong Australia 56 B2
Binghamton NY U.S.A. 64 D1
Bingöl Turkey 35 F3
Bingöl Dağı mt. Turkey 35 F3
Binika India 37 E5
Binjai Indon. 41 B7
Binnaway Australia 58 D3
Binpur India 37 F5
Bint Jbeil Lebanon see Bent Jbaïl
Bintulu Sarawak Malaysia 41 D7
Binxian Heilong. China 44 B3
Binxian Shaanxi China 43 J6
Binya Australia 58 C5
Bin-Yauri Nigeria 46 D3
Binzhou Heilong. China see Binxian
Binzhou Shandong China 43 L5
Bioco i. Equat. Guinea 46 D4
Biograd na Moru Croatia 26 F3
Bioko i. Equat. Guinea see Bioco
Biokovo mts Croatia 26 G3
Biquinhas Brazil 71 B2
Bir India see Bid
Bira Rus. Fed. 44 D2
Bīr Abū Jady oasis Syria 39 D1
Birak Libya 47 E2
Birakan Rus. Fed. 44 C2
Bi'r al 'Abd Egypt 39 A4
Bi'r al Ḥalbā well Syria 39 D2
Bi'r al Jifjāfah well Egypt 39 A4
Bi'r al Khamsah well Egypt 39 A5
Bi'r al Māliḥah well Egypt 39 A5
Bi'r al Mulūsī Iraq 35 F4
Bi'r al Munbaţiḥ well Syria 39 D2
Bi'r al Qaţrānī well Egypt 34 B5
Bi'r al Ubbayid well Egypt 34 B6
Bi'r an Nuṣf well Egypt 39 A4
Bi'r an Nuṣṣ well Egypt 39 A4
Bir Anzarane W. Sahara 46 B2
Birao Cent. Afr. Rep. 48 C2
Bi'r ar Rābiyah well Egypt 34 B5
Bi'r aţ Ţarfāwī well Libya 34 A5
Bi'r Bayḍā' well Egypt 39 B4
Bi'r Beida well Egypt see Bi'r Bayḍā'
Bi'r Buţaymān Syria 35 E3
Birch Mountains Canada 60 G4
Birch River WV U.S.A. 64 A3
Bi'r Dignāsh well Egypt see Bi'r Diqnāsh
Bi'r Diqnāsh well Egypt 34 B5
Birdsville Australia 57 B5
Birecik Turkey 34 E3
Bi'r el 'Abd Egypt see Bi'r al 'Abd
Bir el Arbi well Alg. 25 I6
Bi'r el Istabl well Egypt see Bi'r Istabl
Bi'r el Khamsa well Egypt see
    Bi'r al Khamsah
Bi'r el Nuṣṣ well Egypt see Bi'r an Nuṣṣ
Bi'r el Obeiyid well Egypt see
    Bi'r al Obbayid
Bi'r el Qaţrāni well Egypt see Bi'r al Qaţrānī
Bi'r el Rābia well Egypt see Bi'r ar Rābiyah
Bir en Natrûn well Sudan 32 C6
Bi'r Fajr well Saudi Arabia 34 E5
Bi'r Fu'ad well Egypt 34 B5
Bi'r Gifqāfa well Egypt see Bi'r al Jifjāfah
Bi'r Ḥajal well Syria 39 D2
Birhan mt. Eth. 48 D2
Bi'r Ḥasanah well Egypt 39 A4
Bi'r Ḥayzān well Saudi Arabia 35 E5
Bi'r Ibn Hirmās Saudi Arabia see Al Bi'r
Birigüi Brazil 71 A3
Birin Syria 39 C2
Birini well Egypt 39 B4
Birjand Iran 33 I3
Bi'r Jubnī well Libya 34 B5
Birkat Hamad well Iraq 35 G5
Birkenhead U.K. 18 D5
Birkirkara Malta 26 F7
Birksgate Range hills Australia 55 E6
Bîrlad Romania see Bârlad
Bi'r Lahfān well Egypt 39 A4
Birlik Kazakh. 42 C4
Birmingham U.K. 19 F6
Birmingham U.S.A. 63 J5
Bîr Mogreïn Mauritania 46 B2
Bi'r Muḥaymid al Wazwaz well Syria 39 D2
Bi'r Nāhid oasis Egypt 34 C5
Birnin-Gwari Nigeria 46 D3
Birni-Kebbi Nigeria 46 D3
Birnin Konni Niger 46 D3
Birobidzhan Rus. Fed. 44 D2
Bi'r Qaşir as Sirr well Egypt 34 B5
Birr Ireland 21 E4
Bi'r Rawḍ Sālim well Egypt 39 A4
Birrie r. Australia 58 C2
Birrindudu Australia 54 E4
Bi'r Rōd Sālim well Egypt see
    Bi'r Rawḍ Sālim
Birsay U.K. 20 F1
Birsk Rus. Fed. 11 R4
Birstall U.K. 19 F6
Birthday Mountain hill Australia 56 C2
Biru China 37 H3
Birur India 38 B3
Biruxiong China see Biru
Biržai Lith. 15 N8
Bisalpur India 36 D3
Bisau India 36 C3
Bisbee U.S.A. 62 F5
Biscay, Bay of sea France/Spain 24 B4
Biscay Abyssal Plain sea feature
    N. Atlantic Ocean 72 H3
Biscoe Islands Antarctica 76 L2
Biscotasi Lake Canada 63 K2
Bishkek Kyrg. see Bishkek
Bishenpur India see Bishnupur
Bishkek Kyrg. 42 C4
Bishnupur Manipur India 37 H4
Bishnupur W. Bengal India 37 F5
Bisho S. Africa 51 H7
Bishop CA U.S.A. 65 C2
Bishop Auckland U.K. 18 F4
Bishop's Stortford U.K. 19 H7
Bishri, Jabal hills Syria 39 D2
Bishui Heilong. China 44 A1
Bisisthal Switz. 42 H4
Biskra Alg. 22 F5
Bismarck U.S.A. 62 G2
Bismarck Archipelago is P.N.G. 52 E2
Bismarck Range mts P.N.G. 52 E2
Bismarck Sea P.N.G. 52 E2
Bismil Turkey 35 F3
Bismo Norway 14 F6
Bispgården Sweden 14 J5
Bissa, Djebel mt. Alg. 25 G5
Bissamcuttak India 38 D2
Bissau Guinea-Bissau 46 B3
Bissaula Nigeria 46 E4
Bissett Canada 63 J2
Bistcho Lake Canada 60 G3
Bistriţa Romania 27 K1
Bistriţa r. Romania 27 L1
Bitburg Germany 17 K6

Bitche France 24 H2
Blue Stack hill Ireland 21 D3
Blue Stack Mts hills Ireland 21 D3
Bluestone Lake WV U.S.A. 64 A4
Bluff N.Z. 59 B8
Bluff Knoll mt. Australia 55 B8
Blumenau Brazil 71 A4
Blyde River Canyon Nature Reserve
    S. Africa 51 J3
Blyth England U.K. 18 F3
Blyth England U.K. 18 F3
Blythe CA U.S.A. 65 E4
Blytheville U.S.A. 63 J4
Bø Norway 15 F7
Bo Sierra Leone 46 B4
Boa Esperança Brazil 71 B3
Boali Cent. Afr. Rep. 48 B3
Boane Moz. 51 K4
Boa Nova Brazil 71 C1
Boatlaname Botswana 51 G2
Boa Viagem Brazil 69 K5
Boa Vista Brazil 68 F3
Boa Vista i. Cape Verde 46 [inset]
Bobadah Australia 58 C4
Bobai China 43 K4
Bobaomby, Tanjona c. Madag. 49 E5
Bobbili India 38 D2
Bobo-Dioulasso Burkina 46 C3
Bobotov Kuk mt. Montenegro see Durmitor
Bobriki Rus. Fed. see Novomoskovsk
Bobrinets Ukr. see Bobrynets'
Bobrov Rus. Fed. 13 I6
Bobrovitsa Ukr. see Bobrovytsya
Bobrovytsya Ukr. 13 F6
Bobruysk Belarus see Babruysk
Bobynets' Ukr. 13 G6
Bobuk Sudan 32 D7
Bobures Venez. 68 D2
Boby mt. Madag. 49 E6
Boca de Macareo Venez. 68 F2
Boca do Acre Brazil 68 E5
Boca do Jari Brazil 69 H4
Bocaiúva Brazil 71 C2
Bocaranga Cent. Afr. Rep. 48 B3
Bocas del Toro Panama 67 H7
Bochnia Poland 17 R6
Bochum Germany 17 K5
Bochum S. Africa 51 I2
Bocoio Angola 49 B5
Boda Cent. Afr. Rep. 48 B3
Bodalla Australia 58 E6
Bodallin Australia 55 B7
Bodaybo Rus. Fed. 29 M4
Boddam U.K. 20 I4
Bodega Head CA U.S.A. 65 A1
Bodélé reg. Chad 47 E3
Boden Sweden 14 L4
Bodenham U.K. 19 E6
Bodensee l. Germany/Switz. see
    Constance, Lake
Bodie CA U.S.A. 65 C1
Bodinayakkanur India 38 C4
Bodmin U.K. 19 C8
Bodmin Moor moorland U.K. 19 C8
Bodø Norway 14 I3
Bodoquena Brazil 69 G7
Bodoquena, Serra da hills Brazil 70 E2
Bodrum Turkey 27 L6
Bodträskfors Sweden 14 L3
Boende Dem. Rep. Congo 47 F5
Boffa Guinea 46 B3
Bogalusa U.S.A. 63 J5
Bogan r. Australia 58 C4
Bogandé Burkina 46 C3
Bogan Gate Australia 58 C4
Boğazlıyan Turkey 34 D3
Bogcang Zangbo r. China 37 F3
Bogda Shan mts China 42 F4
Boggabilla Australia 58 E2
Boggabri Australia 58 E3
Boggeragh Mts hills Ireland 21 C5
Boghar Alg. 25 H6
Boghari Alg. see Ksar el Boukhari
Bognor Regis U.K. 19 G8
Bogodukhov Ukr. see Bohodukhiv
Bog of Allen reg. Ireland 21 E4
Bogong, Mount Australia 58 C6
Bogopol' Rus. Fed. 44 D3
Bogoroditsk Rus. Fed. 13 H5
Bogorodsk Rus. Fed. 12 I4
Bogorodskoye Khabarovskiy Kray
    Rus. Fed. 44 E1
Bogorodskoye Kirovskaya Oblast'
    Rus. Fed. 12 K4
Bogotá Col. 68 D3
Bogotol Rus. Fed. 28 J4
Bogoyavlenskoye Rus. Fed. see
    Pervomayskiy
Bogra Bangl. 37 G4
Boguchany Rus. Fed. 29 K4
Boguchar Rus. Fed. 13 I6
Bogué Mauritania 46 B3
Bo Hai g. China 43 L5
Bohai Wan b. China 40 D4
Bohemia reg. Czech Rep. 17 N6
Bohemian Forest mts Germany see
    Böhmer Wald
Bohlokong S. Africa 51 I5
Böhmer Wald mts Germany 17 N6
Bohodukhiv Ukr. 13 G6
Bohol Sea Phil. 41 H5
Böhöt Mongolia 43 J3
Bohu China 42 F4
Boiaçu Brazil 68 F4
Boichoko S. Africa 50 F5
Boikhutso S. Africa 51 H4
Boileau, Cape Australia 54 C4
Boim Brazil 69 G4
Boipeba, Ilha i. Brazil 71 D1
Bois r. Brazil 71 A2
Boise U.S.A. 62 D3
Boise City U.S.A. 62 G4
Boitumelong S. Africa 51 G4
Bojnürd Iran 33 I2
Bokaak atoll Marshall Is see Taongi
Bokajan India 37 H4
Bokaro India 37 F5
Bokaro Reservoir India 37 F5
Bokatola Dem. Rep. Congo 48 B4
Boké Guinea 46 B3
Bokele Dem. Rep. Congo 48 C4
Bokhara r. Australia 58 C2
Bokhara India see Bukhara
Boknafjorden sea chan. Norway 15 D7
Bokoro Chad 47 E3
Bokovskaya Rus. Fed. 13 I6
Bokspits S. Africa 50 E4
Boktor Rus. Fed. 44 E2
Bokurdak Turkm. 33 I2
Bol Chad 47 E3
Bolaiti Dem. Rep. Congo 48 C4
Bolama Guinea-Bissau 46 B3
Bolangir India 38 D1
Bolan Pass Pak. 36 A3
Bolbec France 24 E2
Bole China 42 E4
Bole Ghana 46 C4
Boleko Dem. Rep. Congo 48 B4
Bolen Rus. Fed. 44 D2
Bolgar Rus. Fed. 13 K5
Bolgatanga Ghana 46 C3

Bolgrad Ukr. see Bolhrad
Bolhrad Ukr. 27 M2
Boli China 44 C3
Bolia Dem. Rep. Congo 48 B4
Boliden Sweden 14 L4
Bolintin-Vale Romania 27 K2
Bolívar Peru 68 C5
Bolivar NY U.S.A. 64 B1
Bolívar, Pico mt. Venez. 68 D2
Bolivia country S. America 68 E7
Bolkhov Rus. Fed. 13 H5
Bollène France 24 G4
Bollnäs Sweden 15 J6
Bollon Australia 58 C2
Bollstabruk Sweden 14 J5
Bolmen l. Sweden 15 H8
Bolobo Dem. Rep. Congo 48 B4
Bologna Italy 26 D2
Bolognesi Peru 68 D5
Bologoye Rus. Fed. 12 G4
Bolokanang S. Africa 51 G5
Bolomba Dem. Rep. Congo 48 B3
Bolon' Rus. Fed. see Achan
Bolpur India 37 F5
Bolsena, Lago di l. Italy 26 D3
Bol'shakovo Rus. Fed. 15 L9
Bol'shaya Chernigovka Rus. Fed. 11 Q5
Bol'shaya Glushitsa Rus. Fed. 13 K5
Bol'shaya Imandra, Ozero l. Rus. Fed. 14 R3
Bol'shaya Martinovka Rus. Fed. 13 I7
Bol'shaya Tsarevshchina Rus. Fed. see Volzhskiy
Bol'shenarymskoye Kazakh. 42 E3
Bol'shevik, Ostrov i. Rus. Fed. 29 L2
Bol'shezemel'skaya Tundra lowland Rus. Fed. 12 L2
Bol'shiye Chirki Rus. Fed. 12 J3
Bol'shiye Kozly Rus. Fed. 12 H2
Bol'shoy Aluy r. Rus. Fed. 29 Q3
Bol'shoy Begichev, Ostrov i. Rus. Fed. 77 E2
Bol'shoye Murashkino Rus. Fed. 12 J5
Bol'shoy Irgiz r. Rus. Fed. 13 J6
Bol'shoy Kamen' Rus. Fed. 44 D4
Bol'shoy Kavkaz mts Asia/Europe see Caucasus
Bol'shoy Kundysh r. Rus. Fed. 12 J4
Bol'shoy Lyakhovskiy, Ostrov i. Rus. Fed. 29 P2
Bol'shoy Tokmak Kyrg. see Tokmok
Bol'shoy Tokmak Ukr. see Tokmak
Bolton U.K. 18 E5
Bolu Turkey 27 N4
Boluntay China 37 H1
Bolus Head hd Ireland 21 B6
Bolvadin Turkey 27 N5
Bolzano Italy 26 D1
Boma Dem. Rep. Congo 49 B4
Bomaderry Australia 58 E5
Bombala Australia 58 D6
Bombay India see Mumbai
Bombay Beach CA U.S.A. 65 E4
Bomberai, Semenanjung pen. Indon. 41 F8
Bomboma Dem. Rep. Congo 48 B3
Bom Comércio Brazil 68 E5
Bomdila India 37 H4
Bomi China 42 H7
Bomili Dem. Rep. Congo 48 C3
Bom Jardim Brazil 71 D1
Bom Jardim de Goiás Brazil 71 A2
Bom Jesus Brazil 71 A5
Bom Jesus da Gurgueia, Serra do hills Brazil 69 J5
Bom Jesus da Lapa Brazil 71 C1
Bom Jesus do Norte Brazil 71 C3
Bømlo i. Norway 15 D7
Bomokandi r. Dem. Rep. Congo 48 C3
Bom Retiro Brazil 71 A4
Bom Sucesso Brazil 71 B3
Bon, Cap c. Tunisia 26 D6
Bona Alg. see Annaba
Bonāb Iran 35 G3
Bon Air VA U.S.A. 64 C4
Bonaire i. Neth. Antilles 67 K6
Bonaparte Archipelago is Australia 54 D3
Bonar Bridge U.K. 20 E3
Bonavista Bay Canada 61 M5
Bonchester Bridge U.K. 20 G5
Bondo Dem. Rep. Congo 48 C3
Bondoukou Côte d'Ivoire 46 C4
Bondyuzhskiy Rus. Fed. see Mendeleyevsk
Bône Alg. see Annaba
Bone, Teluk b. Indon. 41 E8
Bonerate, Kepulauan is Indon. 41 E8
Bo'ness U.K. 20 F4
Bonete, Cerro mt. Arg. 70 C3
Bonga Eth. 48 D3
Bongaigaon India 37 G4
Bongandanga Dem. Rep. Congo 48 C3
Bongani S. Africa 50 F5
Bongba China 36 E2
Bong Co l. China 37 G3
Bongo, Massif des mts Cent. Afr. Rep. 48 C3
Bongo, Serra do mts Angola 49 B4
Bongolava mts Madag. 49 E5
Bongor Chad 47 E3
Boni Mali 46 C3
Bonifacio Corsica France 24 I6
Bonifacio, Bocche di strait France/Italy see Bonifacio, Strait of
Bonifacio, Bouches de strait France/Italy see Bonifacio, Strait of
Bonifacio, Strait of France/Italy 24 I6
Bonin Islands Japan 45 F8
Bonn Germany 17 K5
Bonna Germany see Bonn
Bonnåsjøen Norway 14 I3
Bonners Ferry U.S.A. 62 D2
Bonneville France 24 H3
Bonnie Rock Australia 55 B7
Bonnyrigg U.K. 20 F5
Bonnyville Canada 62 E1
Bononia Italy see Bologna
Bonorva Sardinia Italy 26 C4
Bonshaw Australia 58 E2
Bontebok National Park S. Africa 50 E8
Bonthe Sierra Leone 46 B4
Bontoc Phil. 41 E6
Bontosunggu Indon. 52 B2
Bontrug S. Africa 51 G7
Bonvouloir Islands P.N.G. 56 E1
Bonwapitse Botswana 51 H2
Boolba Australia 58 D2
Booligal Australia 58 B4
Boomer WV U.S.A. 64 A3
Boomi Australia 58 D2
Boonah Australia 58 F1
Boones Mill VA U.S.A. 64 B4
Booneville MS U.S.A. 63 J5
Böön Tsagaan Nuur salt l. Mongolia 42 H3
Boonville CA U.S.A. 65 A1
Boonville NY U.S.A. 64 D1
Boorabin National Park Australia 55 C7
Booroma Somalia 48 E3
Booroorban Australia 58 B5
Boorowa Australia 58 D5
Boort Australia 58 A6
Boothby, Cape Antarctica 76 D2
Boothia, Gulf of Canada 61 J3
Boothia Peninsula Canada 61 I2
Bootle U.K. 18 E5
Booué Gabon 48 B4
Boqê China 37 G3
Boqueirão, Serra do hills Brazil 69 J6
Bor Rus. Fed. 12 J4
Bor Serbia 27 J2
Bor Sudan 47 G4
Bor Turkey 34 D3
Boraha, Nosy i. Madag. 49 F5
Borai India 38 D1
Borakalalo Nature Reserve S. Africa 51 H3
Boran Kazakh. see Buran
Borås Sweden 15 H8
Borasambar India 38 D1
Borāzjān Iran 35 H5
Borba Brazil 69 G4
Borborema, Planalto da plat. Brazil 69 K5
Borçka Turkey 35 F2
Bor Dağı mt. Turkey 27 M6
Bordeaux France 24 D4
Borden Island Canada 61 G2
Borden Peninsula Canada 61 J2
Border Ranges National Park Australia 58 F2
Borðeyri Iceland 14 [inset]
Bordj Bou Arréridj Alg. 25 I5
Bordj Bounaama Alg. 25 G6
Bordj Flye Ste-Marie Alg. 46 C2
Bordj Messaouda Alg. 22 F5
Bordj Mokhtar Alg. 46 D2
Bordj Omar Driss Alg. see Bordj Omer Driss
Bordj Omer Driss Alg. 46 D2
Boreas Abyssal Plain sea feature Arctic Ocean 77 H1
Borgå Fin. see Porvoo
Borgarfjörður Iceland 14 [inset]
Borgarnes Iceland 14 [inset]
Børgefjell Nasjonalpark nat. park Norway 14 H4
Borgholm Sweden 15 J8
Borgo San Lorenzo Italy 26 D3
Bori India 38 C1
Bori r. India 36 C5
Borislav Ukr. see Boryslav
Borisoglebsk Rus. Fed. 13 I6
Borisov Belarus see Barysaw
Borisovka Rus. Fed. 13 H6
Borispol' Ukr. see Boryspil'
Bo River Post Sudan 47 F4
Borja Peru 68 C4
Borkenes Norway 14 J2
Borkovskaya Rus. Fed. 12 K2
Borlänge Sweden 15 I6
Borlaug Norway 15 E6
Borlu Turkey 27 M5
Borneo i. Asia 41 D7
Bornholm county Denmark 77 H3
Bornholm i. Denmark 15 I9
Bornova Turkey 27 L5
Borodino Rus. Fed. 28 J3
Borodinskoye Rus. Fed. 15 P6
Borogontsy Rus. Fed. 29 O3
Borohoro Shan mts China 42 E4
Borok-Sulezhskiy Rus. Fed. 12 H4
Boromo Burkina 46 C3
Boron CA U.S.A. 65 D3
Borondi India 38 D2
Boroughbridge U.K. 18 F4
Borovichi Rus. Fed. 12 G4
Borovoy Kirovskaya Oblast' Rus. Fed. 12 K4
Borovoy Respublika Kareliya Rus. Fed. 14 R4
Borovoy Respublika Komi Rus. Fed. 12 L3
Borpeta India see Barpeta
Borrisokane Ireland 21 D5
Borroloola Australia 56 B3
Børsa Norway 14 G5
Borşa Romania 13 E7
Borsakelmas sho'rxogi salt marsh Uzbek. 35 J2
Borshchiv Ukr. 13 E6
Borshchovochnyy Khrebet mts Rus. Fed. 43 J3
Bortala China see Bole
Borūjen Iran 35 H5
Borūjerd Iran 35 H4
Borve U.K. 20 C3
Boryslav Ukr. 13 D6
Boryspil' Ukr. 13 F6
Borzna Ukr. 13 G6
Borzya Rus. Fed. 43 L2
Bosanska Dubica Bos.-Herz. 26 G2
Bosanska Gradiška Bos.-Herz. 26 G2
Bosanska Krupa Bos.-Herz. 26 G2
Bosanski Novi Bos.-Herz. 26 G2
Bosansko Grahovo Bos.-Herz. 26 G2
Boscawen Island Tonga see Niuatoputopu
Bose China 42 J8
Boshof S. Africa 51 G5
Bosna i Hercegovina country Europe see Bosnia-Herzegovina
Bosna Saray Bos.-Herz. see Sarajevo
Bosnia-Herzegovina country Europe 26 G2
Bosobogolo Pan salt pan Botswana 50 F3
Bosobolo Dem. Rep. Congo 48 B3
Bōsō-hantō pen. Japan 45 F6
Bosporus strait Turkey 27 M4
Bossangoa Cent. Afr. Rep. 48 B3
Bossembélé Cent. Afr. Rep. 48 B3
Bossiesvlei Namibia 50 C3
Bossut, Cape Australia 54 C4
Bostan China 37 F1
Bostān Iran 35 G5
Bostan Pak. 36 A3
Bosten Hu l. China 42 F4
Boston U.K. 19 G6
Boston MA U.S.A. 64 F1
Boston Mountains U.S.A. 63 I4
Boston Spa U.K. 18 F5
Botad India 36 B5
Botany Bay Australia 58 E4
Botev mt. Bulg. 27 K3
Botevgrad Bulg. 27 J3
Bothaville S. Africa 51 H4
Bothnia, Gulf of Fin./Sweden 15 K6
Botlikh Rus. Fed. 35 G2
Botoşani Romania 13 E7
Botou China 43 L5
Botshabelo S. Africa 51 H5
Botswana country Africa 49 C6
Botte Donato, Monte mt. Italy 26 G5
Bottesford U.K. 18 G5
Bottrop Germany 17 K5
Botucatu Brazil 71 A3
Botuporã Brazil 71 C1
Bouaflé Côte d'Ivoire 46 C4
Bouaké Côte d'Ivoire 46 C4
Bouar Cent. Afr. Rep. 48 B3
Bouârfa Morocco 22 D5
Bouba Ndjida, Parc National de nat. park Cameroon 47 E4
Bouca Cent. Afr. Rep. 48 B3
Boucaut Bay Australia 54 F3
Boudh India 38 E1
Bougaa Alg. 25 I5
Bougainville, Cape Australia 54 D3
Bougainville Island P.N.G. 52 F2
Bougainville Reef Australia 56 D2
Boughessa Mali 46 D3
Bougie Alg. see Bejaïa
Bougouni Mali 46 C3
Bougtob Alg. 22 E5
Bouillon Belgium 16 J6
Bouira Alg. 25 H5
Bou Izakarn Morocco 46 C2
Boujdour W. Sahara 46 B2
Boulder Australia 55 C7
Boulder CO U.S.A. 62 F3
Boulder Canyon gorge NV U.S.A. 65 E2
Boulder City NV U.S.A. 65 E3
Boulevard CA U.S.A. 65 D4
Boulia Australia 56 B4
Boulogne France see Boulogne-sur-Mer
Boulogne-Billancourt France 24 F2
Boulogne-sur-Mer France 24 E1
Boumerdes Alg. 25 H5
Bouna Côte d'Ivoire 46 C4
Bou Naceur, Jbel mt. Morocco 22 D5
Boû Nâga Mauritania 46 B3
Boundary Peak NV U.S.A. 65 C2
Boundiali Côte d'Ivoire 46 C4
Boundji Congo 48 B4
Bounty Islands N.Z. 53 H6
Bounty Trough sea feature S. Pacific Ocean 74 H9
Bourail New Caledonia 53 G4
Bourbon reg. France see Bourbonnais
Bourbon terr. Indian Ocean see Réunion
Bourbonnais reg. France 24 F3
Bourem Mali 46 C3
Bouressa Mali see Boughessa
Bourg-Achard France 19 H9
Bourganeuf France 24 E4
Bourg-en-Bresse France 24 G3
Bourges France 24 F3
Bourgogne reg. France see Burgundy
Bourgogne, Canal de France 24 G3
Bourke Australia 58 B3
Bourne U.K. 19 G6
Bournemouth U.K. 19 F8
Bourtoutou Chad 47 F3
Bou Saâda Alg. 25 I6
Bou Salem Tunisia 26 C6
Bouse AZ U.S.A. 65 E4
Bouse Wash watercourse AZ U.S.A. 65 E3
Boutilimit Mauritania 46 B3
Bouvet Island terr. S. Atlantic Ocean see Bouvetøya
Bouvetøya terr. S. Atlantic Ocean 72 I9
Bova Marina Italy 26 F6
Bow r. Alta Canada 62 E2
Bowa China see Muli
Bowden WV U.S.A. 64 B3
Bowditch atoll Tokelau see Fakaofo
Bowen Australia 56 E4
Bowen, Mount Australia 58 D6
Bowenville Australia 58 E1
Bowers Ridge sea feature Bering Sea 74 H2
Bowie Australia 56 D4
Bow Island Canada 62 E2
Bowling Green KY U.S.A. 63 J4
Bowling Green OH U.S.A. 63 K3
Bowling Green VA U.S.A. 64 C3
Bowling Green Bay National Park Australia 56 D3
Bowman U.S.A. 62 G2
Bowman Island Antarctica 76 F2
Bowman Peninsula Antarctica 76 L2
Bowmore U.K. 20 C5
Bowo China see Bomi
Bowral Australia 58 E5
Boyabat Turkey 34 D2
Boyana tourist site Bulg. 27 J3
Boyd r. Australia 58 F2
Boyd Lagoon salt flat Australia 55 D6
Boyers PA U.S.A. 64 B2
Boyle Ireland 21 D4
Boyne r. Ireland 21 F4
Boysun Uzbek. 33 K2
Boysun Uzbek. see Boysun
Boyuibe Bol. 68 F8
Böyük Qafqaz mts Asia/Europe see Caucasus
Bozcaada i. Turkey 27 L5
Bozdağ mt. Turkey 27 L5
Bozdağ mt. Turkey 39 C1
Boz Dağları mts Turkey 27 L5
Bozdoğan Turkey 27 M6
Bozeat U.K. 19 G6
Bozeman U.S.A. 62 E2
Bozen Italy see Bolzano
Bozoum Cent. Afr. Rep. 48 B3
Bozova Turkey 34 E3
Bozqūsh, Kūh-e mts Iran 35 G3
Bozüyük Turkey 27 N5
Bozyazı Turkey 39 A1
Bra Italy 26 B2
Brač i. Croatia 26 G3
Bracadale U.K. 20 C3
Bracadale, Loch b. U.K. 20 C3
Bracara Port. see Braga
Bracciano, Lago di l. Italy 26 E3
Bracebridge Canada 63 L2
Brachet, Lac au l. Canada 63 N2
Bräcke Sweden 14 I5
Bracknell U.K. 19 G7
Bradano r. Italy 26 G4
Bradenton U.S.A. 63 K6
Brades Montserrat 67 L5
Bradford U.K. 18 F5
Bradford PA U.S.A. 64 B2
Brady U.S.A. 62 H5
Brae U.K. 20 [inset]
Braemar U.K. 20 F3
Braga Port. 25 B3
Bragado Arg. 70 D5
Bragança Brazil 69 I4
Bragança Port. 25 C3
Bragança Paulista Brazil 71 B3
Brahin Belarus 13 F6
Brahmanbaria Bangl. 37 G5
Brahmapur India 38 E2
Brahmaputra r. Asia 37 H4
Brahmaputra r. China 42 F7
Brahmaputra r. China/India 40 B5
Brahmaur India 36 D2
Brăila Romania 27 L2
Brainerd U.S.A. 63 I2
Braintree U.K. 19 H7
Braithwaite Point Australia 54 F2
Brak r. S. Africa 51 I2
Brakwater Namibia 50 C2
Bramfield Australia 55 F8
Bramming Denmark 15 F9
Brämön i. Sweden 14 J5
Brampton England U.K. 18 E4
Brampton England U.K. 19 I6
Bramwell Australia 56 C2
Brancaster U.K. 19 H6
Branco r. Brazil 68 F4
Brandberg mt. Namibia 49 B6
Brandbu Norway 15 G6
Brande Denmark 15 F9
Brandenburg Germany 17 N4
Brandfort S. Africa 51 H5
Brandon Canada 62 H2
Brandon U.K. 19 H6
Brandon Head hd Ireland 21 B5
Brandon Mountain hill Ireland 21 B5
Brandvlei S. Africa 50 E6
Braniewo Poland 17 Q3
Bransfield Strait Antarctica 76 L2
Brantford Ont. Canada 64 A1
Branxton Australia 58 E4
Brasil country S. America see Brazil
Brasil, Planalto do plat. Brazil 69 J7
Brasileia Brazil 68 E6
Brasília Brazil 71 B1
Brasília de Minas Brazil 71 B2
Braslav Belarus see Braslaw
Braslaw Belarus 15 O9
Braşov Romania 27 K2
Brassey, Mount Australia 55 F5
Brassey Range hills Australia 55 C6
Bratislava Slovakia 17 P6
Bratsk Rus. Fed. 42 I1
Bratskoye Vodokhranilishche resr Rus. Fed. 42 I1
Brattleboro VT U.S.A. 64 E1
Braunau am Inn Austria 17 N6
Braunschweig Germany 17 M4
Brava i. Cape Verde 46 [inset]
Brave PA U.S.A. 64 A3
Bråviken inlet Sweden 15 J7
Bravo, Cerro mt. Bol. 68 F7
Bravo del Norte, Río r. Mex. 62 H6
Bravo del Norte, Río r. Mex./U.S.A. see Rio Grande
Brawley CA U.S.A. 65 E4
Bray Ireland 21 F4
Bray Island Canada 61 K3
Brazil country S. America 69 G5
Brazil Basin sea feature S. Atlantic Ocean 72 G7
Brazos r. U.S.A. 63 H6
Brazzaville Congo 49 B4
Brčko Bos.-Herz. 26 H2
Bré Ireland see Bray
Breadalbane Australia 56 B4
Breaksea Sound inlet N.Z. 59 A7
Bream Bay N.Z. 59 E2
Brechfa U.K. 19 C7
Brechin U.K. 20 G4
Břeclav Czech Rep. 17 P6
Brecon U.K. 19 D7
Brecon Beacons reg. U.K. 19 D7
Brecon Beacons National Park U.K. 19 D7
Breda Neth. 16 J5
Bredasdorp S. Africa 50 E8
Bredbo Australia 58 D5
Bredviken Sweden 14 I3
Bregenz Austria 17 L7
Breiðafjörður b. Iceland 14 [inset]
Breiðdalsvík Iceland 14 [inset]
Breivikbotn Norway 14 M1
Breizh reg. France see Brittany
Brejo Velho Brazil 71 C1
Brekstad Norway 14 F5
Bremen Germany 17 L4
Bremer Bay Australia 55 B8
Bremerhaven Germany 17 L4
Bremer Range hills Australia 55 C8
Bremersdorp Swaziland see Manzini
Brenham U.S.A. 63 H5
Brenna Norway 14 H4
Brennero, Passo di pass Austria/Italy see Brenner Pass
Brenner Pass Austria/Italy 26 D1
Brennerpaß pass Austria/Italy see Brenner Pass
Brentwood U.K. 19 H7
Brescia Italy 26 D2
Breslau Poland see Wrocław
Bresle r. France 19 I8
Bressanone Italy 26 D1
Bressay i. U.K. 20 [inset]
Bressuire France 24 D3
Brest Belarus 15 M10
Brest France 24 B2
Brest-Litovsk Belarus see Brest
Bretagne reg. France see Brittany
Breton Sound b. U.S.A. 63 J6
Brett, Cape N.Z. 59 E2
Bretton U.K. 18 E5
Breves Brazil 69 H4
Brewarrina Australia 58 C2
Brewster OH U.S.A. 64 A2
Brewster, Kap c. Greenland see Kangikajik
Brewster, Lake imp. l. Australia 58 B4
Breyten S. Africa 51 I4
Breytovo Rus. Fed. 12 H4
Brezhnev Rus. Fed. see Naberezhnyye Chelny
Brezno Slovakia 17 Q6
Brezovo Bulg. 27 K3
Brezovo Polje hill Croatia 26 G2
Bria Cent. Afr. Rep. 48 C3
Briançon France 24 H4
Brian Head mt. UT U.S.A. 65 F2
Bribbaree Australia 58 C5
Bribie Island Australia 58 F1
Briceni Moldova 13 E6
Brichany Moldova see Briceni
Brichen' Moldova see Briceni
Bridgend U.K. 19 D7
Bridge of Orchy U.K. 20 E4
Bridgeport CA U.S.A. 65 C1
Bridgeport CT U.S.A. 64 E2
Bridgeport NE U.S.A. 62 G3
Bridgeton NJ U.S.A. 64 D3
Bridgetown Australia 55 B8
Bridgetown Barbados 67 M6
Bridgeville DE U.S.A. 64 D3
Bridgewater Canada 63 O3
Bridgewater NY U.S.A. 64 D1
Bridgnorth U.K. 19 E6
Bridgwater U.K. 19 D7
Bridgwater Bay U.K. 19 D7
Bridlington U.K. 18 G4
Bridlington Bay U.K. 18 G4
Bridport Australia 57 [inset]
Bridport U.K. 19 E8
Brie reg. France 24 F2
Brieg Poland see Brzeg
Briery Knob mt. WV U.S.A. 64 A3
Brig Switz. 24 H3
Brigg U.K. 18 G5
Brigham City U.S.A. 62 E3
Brightlingsea U.K. 19 I7
Brighton U.K. 19 G8
Brighton NY U.S.A. 64 C1
Brignoles France 24 H5
Brikama Gambia 46 B3
Brindisi Italy 26 G4
Brioude France 24 F4
Brisbane Australia 58 F1
Brisbane Ranges National Park Australia 58 B6
Bristol U.K. 19 E7
Bristol CT U.S.A. 64 E2
Bristol NH U.S.A. 64 F1
Bristol RI U.S.A. 64 F2
Bristol TN U.S.A. 63 K4
Bristol Bay U.S.A. 60 B4
Bristol Channel est. U.K. 19 C7
Bristol Lake CA U.S.A. 65 E3
Britannia Island New Caledonia see Maré
British Antarctic Territory reg. Antarctica 76 L2
British Columbia prov. Canada 62 C1
British Empire Range mts Canada 61 J1
British Guiana country S. America see Guyana
British Honduras country Central America see Belize
British Indian Ocean Territory terr. Indian Ocean 73 M6
British Solomon Islands country S. Pacific Ocean see Solomon Islands
Brito Godins Angola see Kiwaba N'zogi
Brits S. Africa 51 H3
Britstown S. Africa 50 F6
Brittany reg. France 24 C2
Brive-la-Gaillarde France 24 E4
Briviesca Spain 25 E2
Brixham U.K. 19 D8
Brixia Italy see Brescia
Brlik Kazakh. see Birlik
Brno Czech Rep. 17 P6
Broach India see Bharuch
Broad r. U.S.A. 63 K5
Broadalbin NY U.S.A. 64 D1
Broad Arrow Australia 55 C7
Broadback r. Canada 63 L1
Broad Bay U.K. see Tuath, Loch a'
Broadford Australia 58 B6
Broadford Ireland 21 D5
Broadford U.K. 20 D3
Broad Law hill U.K. 20 F5
Broadmere Australia 56 A3
Broad Sound sea chan. Australia 56 E4
Broadstairs U.K. 19 I7
Broadus U.S.A. 62 F2
Broadway VA U.S.A. 64 B3
Broadwood N.Z. 59 D2
Brochet Canada 77 L3
Brochet, Lac l. Canada 61 H4
Brockman, Mount Australia 54 B5
Brockton MA U.S.A. 64 F1
Brockway PA U.S.A. 64 B2
Brodeur Peninsula Canada 61 J2
Brodick U.K. 20 D5
Brodnica Poland 17 Q4
Brody Ukr. 13 E6
Broken Arrow U.S.A. 63 H4
Broken Bay Australia 58 E4
Broken Hill Australia 57 C6
Broken Hill Zambia see Kabwe
Broken Plateau sea feature Indian Ocean 73 O8
Brokopondo Suriname 69 G2
Brokopondo Stuwmeer resr Suriname see Professor van Blommestein Meer
Bromberg Poland see Bydgoszcz
Bromsgrove U.K. 19 E6
Brønderslev Denmark 15 F8
Brønnøysund Norway 14 H4
Brooke U.K. 19 I6
Brookhaven U.S.A. 63 I5
Brookings OR U.S.A. 62 C3
Brookings SD U.S.A. 63 H3
Brookline MA U.S.A. 64 F1
Brookneal VA U.S.A. 64 B4
Brooks Canada 62 E1
Brooks Range mts U.S.A. 60 D3
Brookton Australia 55 B8
Brookville PA U.S.A. 64 B2
Broom, Loch inlet U.K. 20 D3
Broome Australia 54 C4
Brora U.K. 20 F2
Brora r. U.K. 20 F2
Brösarp Sweden 15 I9
Brosna r. Ireland 21 E4
Brough U.K. 18 E4
Brough Ness pt U.K. 20 G2
Broughshane U.K. 21 F3
Broughton Island Canada see Qikiqtarjuaq
Broughton Islands Australia 58 F4
Brovary Ukr. 13 F6
Brovinia Australia 57 E5
Brovst Denmark 15 F8
Browne Range hills Australia 55 D6
Brownfield U.S.A. 62 G5
Brown Mountain CA U.S.A. 65 D3
Brownsville PA U.S.A. 64 B2
Brownsville TN U.S.A. 63 J4
Brownsville TX U.S.A. 63 H6
Brownwood U.S.A. 62 H5
Browse Island Australia 54 C3
Bruay-la-Bussière France 24 F1
Bruce Rock Australia 55 B7
Bruck an der Mur Austria 17 O7
Brue r. U.K. 19 E7
Bruges Belgium see Brugge
Brugge Belgium 16 I5
Bruin PA U.S.A. 64 B2
Brulnt India 37 I3
Brûk, Wâdi el watercourse Egypt see Burūk, Wādī al
Brukkaros Namibia 50 D3
Brûlé Canada 62 D1
Brumado Brazil 71 C1
Brumunddal Norway 15 G6
Brundisium Italy see Brindisi
Brunei country Asia 41 D7
Brunei Brunei see Bandar Seri Begawan
Brunette Downs Australia 56 A3
Brunflo Sweden 14 I5
Brunico Italy 26 D1
Brünn Czech Rep. see Brno
Brunner, Lake N.Z. 59 C6
Brunswick Germany see Braunschweig
Brunswick GA U.S.A. 63 K5
Brunswick MD U.S.A. 64 C3
Brunswick ME U.S.A. 63 N3
Brunswick, Península de pen. Chile 70 B8
Brunswick Bay Australia 54 D3
Bruntál Czech Rep. 17 P6
Brunt Ice Shelf Antarctica 76 B2
Bruntville S. Africa 51 J5
Bruny Island Australia 57 [inset]
Brusa Turkey see Bursa
Brusenets Rus. Fed. 12 I3
Brusque Brazil 71 A4
Brussel Belgium see Brussels
Brussels Belgium 16 J5
Bruthen Australia 58 C6
Bruxelles Belgium see Brussels
Bruzual Venez. 68 E2
Bryan TX U.S.A. 63 H5
Bryan, Mount hill Australia 57 B7
Bryan Coast Antarctica 76 L2
Bryansk Rus. Fed. 13 G5
Bryanskoye Rus. Fed. 35 G1
Brynbuga U.K. see Usk
Bryne Norway 15 D7
Bryukhovetskaya Rus. Fed. 13 H7
Brzeg Poland 17 P5
Brześć nad Bugiem Belarus see Brest
Bua r. Malawi 49 D5
Bu'aale Somalia 48 E3
Buala Solomon Is 53 F2
Būbiyān, Jazīrat Kuwait 35 H5
Bucak Turkey 27 N6
Bucaramanga Col. 68 D2
Buccaneer Archipelago is Australia 54 C4
Buchanan Liberia 46 B4
Buchanan VA U.S.A. 64 B4
Buchanan, Lake salt flat Australia 56 D4
Buchan Gulf Canada 61 K2
Bucharest Romania 27 L2
Buchon, Point CA U.S.A. 65 B3
Buchy France 19 I9
Bucin, Pasul pass Romania 27 K1
Buckambool Mountain hill Australia 58 B3
Buckeye U.S.A. 62 E5
Buckhannon WV U.S.A. 64 A3
Buckhaven U.K. 20 F4
Buckie U.K. 20 G3
Buckingham U.K. 19 G6
Buckingham VA U.S.A. 64 B4
Buckingham Bay Australia 41 F9
Buckland Tableland reg. Australia 56 E5
Buckleboo Australia 55 G8
Buckle Island Antarctica 76 H2
Buckley watercourse Australia 56 B4
Buckley Bay Antarctica 76 G2
Buckskin Mountains AZ U.S.A. 65 F3
București Romania see Bucharest
Budalin Myanmar 37 H5
Budapest Hungary 27 H1
Budaun India 36 D3
Budawang National Park Australia 58 E5
Budda Australia 58 B3
Budd Coast Antarctica 76 F2
Buddusò Sardinia Italy 26 C4
Bude U.K. 19 C8
Budennovsk Rus. Fed. 13 J7
Buderim Australia 58 F1
Budīyah, Jabal hills Egypt 39 A5
Budongquan China 37 H2
Budoni Sardinia Italy 26 C4
Budweis Czech Rep. see České Budějovice
Buenaventura Col. 68 C3
Buena Vista i. N. Mariana Is see Tinian
Buena Vista VA U.S.A. 64 B4
Buendia, Embalse de resr Spain 25 E3
Buenos Aires Arg. 70 E4
Buenos Aires, Lago l. Arg./Chile 70 B7
Buerarema Brazil 71 D1
Buffalo NY U.S.A. 64 B1
Buffalo SD U.S.A. 62 G2
Buffalo WY U.S.A. 62 F3
Buffalo Narrows Canada 77 L3
Buffels watercourse S. Africa 50 C5
Buffels Drift S. Africa 51 H2
Buftea Romania 27 K2
Bug r. Poland 17 S5
Buga Col. 68 C3
Bugaldie Australia 58 D3
Bugdaýly Turkm. 35 I3
Bugojno Bos.-Herz. 26 G2
Bugrino Rus. Fed. 12 K1
Bugt China 44 A2
Bugul'ma Rus. Fed. 11 Q5
Bügür China see Luntai
Buguruslan Rus. Fed. 11 Q5
Buhera Zimbabwe 49 D5
Buhuşi Romania 27 L1
Builth Wells U.K. 19 D6
Bui National Park Ghana 46 C4
Buinsk Rus. Fed. 13 K5
Bu'īn Zahrā Iran 35 H4
Buir Nur l. Mongolia 43 L3
Buitepos Namibia 50 D2
Bujanovac Serbia 27 I3
Bujumbura Burundi 48 C4
Bukachacha Rus. Fed. 43 L2
Buka Daban mt. China 37 G1
Buka Island P.N.G. 52 F2
Būkān Iran 35 G3
Būkand Iran 35 I5
Bukavu Dem. Rep. Congo 48 C4
Bukhoro Uzbek. see Buxoro
Bukittinggi Indon. 41 C8
Bukkapatnam India 38 C3
Bukoba Tanz. 48 D4
Bükreş Romania see Bucharest
Būl, Kūh-e mt. Iran 35 I5
Bülach Switz. 24 I3
Bulancak Turkey 34 E2
Bulandshahr India 36 D3
Bulanık Turkey 35 F3
Bulava Rus. Fed. 44 F2
Bulawayo Zimbabwe 49 C6
Buldan Turkey 27 M5
Buldana India see Buldhana
Buldhana India 38 C1
Bulembu Swaziland 51 J3
Bulgan Bulgan Mongolia 42 I3
Bulgan Hovd Mongolia see Bürenhayrhan
Bulgar Rus. Fed. see Bolgar
Bulgaria country Europe 27 K3
Bŭlgariya country Europe see Bulgaria
Bullawarra, Lake salt flat Australia 58 A1
Buller r. N.Z. 59 C5
Buller, Mount Australia 58 C6
Bulleringa National Park Australia 56 C3
Bullfinch Australia 55 B7
Bullhead City AZ U.S.A. 65 E3
Bulli Australia 58 E5
Bullion Mountains CA U.S.A. 65 D3
Bullo r. Australia 54 E3
Bulloo Downs Australia 57 C6
Bulloo Lake salt flat Australia 57 C6
Büllsport Namibia 50 C3
Bulman Australia 54 F3
Bulman Gorge Australia 54 F3
Buloke, Lake dry lake Australia 58 A6
Bulsar India see Valsad
Bultfontein S. Africa 51 H5
Bulukumba Indon. 41 E8
Bulun Rus. Fed. 29 N2
Bulungu Dem. Rep. Congo 49 C4
Bulung'ur Uzbek. 42 B5
Bumba Dem. Rep. Congo 48 C3
Būmbah Libya 34 A4
Bumbah, Khalīj b. Libya 34 A4
Bumpha Bum mt. Myanmar 37 I4
Buna Dem. Rep. Congo 48 B4
Buna Kenya 48 D3
Bunazi Tanz. 48 D4
Bunbeg Ireland 21 D2
Bunbury Australia 55 A8
Bunclody Ireland 21 F5
Buncrana Ireland 21 E2
Bunda Tanz. 48 D4
Bundaberg Australia 56 F5
Bundaleer Australia 58 C2
Bundarra Australia 58 E3
Bundi India 36 C4
Bundjalung National Park Australia 58 F2
Bundoran Ireland 21 D3
Bunduqiya Sudan 47 G4
Bungay U.K. 19 I6
Bungendore Australia 58 D5
Bunger Hills Antarctica 76 F2
Bungle Bungle National Park Australia see Purnululu National Park
Bungo-suidō sea chan. Japan 45 D6
Bunguran, Kepulauan is Indon. see Natuna, Kepulauan
Bunguran, Pulau i. Indon. see Natuna Besar
Bunia Dem. Rep. Congo 48 D3
Bunianga Dem. Rep. Congo 48 C4
Buningonia well Australia 55 C7
Bunji Jammu and Kashmir 36 C2
Bunker Group atolls Australia 56 F4
Bunkeya Dem. Rep. Congo 49 C5
Bünsum China 37 E3
Bunya Mountains National Park Australia 58 E1
Bünyan Turkey 34 D3

Buôn Ma Thuôt Vietnam 31 J5
Buorkhaya, Guba b. Rus. Fed. 29 O2
Bup r. China 37 F3
Buqayq Saudi Arabia see Abqaiq
Buqbuq Egypt 34 B5
Bura Kenya 48 D4
Buraan Somalia 48 E2
Buram Sudan 47 F3
Buran Kazakh. 42 F3
Buranhaém Brazil 71 C2
Buranhaém r. Brazil 71 D2
Burāq Syria 39 C3
Buray r. India 36 C5
Buraydah Saudi Arabia 32 F4
Burbank CA U.S.A. 65 C3
Burcher Australia 58 C4
Burco Somalia 48 E3
Burdigala France see Bordeaux
Burdur Turkey 27 N6
Burdur Gölü l. Turkey 27 N6
Burdwan India see Barddhaman
Burē Eth. 48 D2
Bure r. U.K. 19 I6
Bureå Sweden 14 L4
Bureinskiy Khrebet mts Rus. Fed. 44 D2
Bürenhayrhan Mongolia 42 G3
Bureya r. Rus. Fed. 44 C2
Bureya Range mts Rus. Fed. see Bureinskiy Khrebet
Bureyinski Zapovednik nature res. Rus. Fed. 44 D2
Burford Ont. Canada 64 A1
Burgas Bulg. 27 L3
Burgeo Canada 61 M5
Burgersdorp S. Africa 51 H6
Burgersfort S. Africa 51 J3
Burges, Mount hill Australia 55 C7
Burgess Hill U.K. 19 G8
Burghausen Germany 17 N6
Burghead U.K. 20 F3
Burgio, Serra di hill Sicily Italy 26 F6
Burgos Mex. 62 H7
Burgos Spain 25 E2
Burgsvik Sweden 15 K8
Burgundy reg. France 24 G3
Burhan Budai Shan mts China 42 G5
Burhaniye Turkey 27 L5
Burhanpur India 36 D5
Burhar-Dhanpuri India 37 E5
Buri Brazil 71 A3
Buritama Brazil 71 A3
Buriti Alegre Brazil 71 A2
Buriti Bravo Brazil 69 J5
Buritirama Brazil 69 J6
Buritis Brazil 71 B1
Burj Aziz Khan Pak. 36 A3
Burke Island Antarctica 76 K2
Burke Pass N.Z. see Burkes Pass
Burkes Pass N.Z. 59 C7
Burketown Australia 56 B3
Burkeville VA U.S.A. 64 B4
Burkina country Africa 46 C3
Burkina Faso country Africa see Burkina
Burley U.S.A. 62 E3
Burlington Ont. Canada 64 B1
Burlington CO U.S.A. 62 G4
Burlington IA U.S.A. 63 I3
Burlington VT U.S.A. 63 M3
Burma country Asia see Myanmar
Burmantovo Rus. Fed. 11 S3
Burney, Monte vol. Chile 70 B8
Burnie Australia 57 [inset]
Burniston U.K. 18 G4
Burnley U.K. 18 E5
Burns U.S.A. 62 D3
Burnside r. Canada 60 H3
Burnside, Lake salt flat Australia 55 C6
Burns Lake Canada 60 F4
Burntisland U.K. 20 F4
Burntwood r. Canada 61 I4
Burog Co l. China 37 F2
Burqin China 42 F3
Burqu' Jordan 39 D3
Burra Australia 57 B7
Burra i. U.K. 20 [inset]
Burravoe U.K. 20 [inset]
Burrel Albania 27 I4
Burrel CA U.S.A. 65 C2
Burren reg. Ireland 21 C4
Burrendong, Lake Australia 58 D4
Burren Junction Australia 58 D3
Burrewarra Point Australia 58 E5
Burrinjuck Australia 58 D5
Burrinjuck Reservoir Australia 58 D5
Burro, Serranías del mts Mex. 66 D3
Burro Creek watercourse AZ U.S.A. 65 F3
Burrowa Pine Mountain National Park Australia 58 C6
Burrow Head hd U.K. 20 E6
Burrundie Australia 54 E3
Bursa Turkey 27 M4
Bûr Safâga Egypt see Būr Safājah
Būr Safājah Egypt 32 D4
Būr Sa'īd Egypt see Port Said
Bûr Sa'îd Egypt see Port Said
Bûr Sa'îd governorate Egypt 39 A4
Bûr Sa'îd governorate Egypt see Būr Sa'īd
Bursinskoye Vodokhranilishche resr Rus. Fed. 44 C2
Būr Sudan Sudan see Port Sudan
Burtonport Ireland 21 D3
Burton upon Trent U.K. 19 F6
Burträsk Sweden 14 L4
Burt Well Australia 55 F5
Buru i. Indon. 41 E8
Buruk, Wadi al watercourse Egypt 39 A4
Burullus, Baḥra el lag. Egypt see Burullus, Lake
Burullus, Buḥayrat al lag. Egypt see Burullus, Lake
Burullus, Lake lag. Egypt 34 C5
Burultokay China see Fuhai
Burūn, Ra's pt Egypt 39 A4
Burundi country Africa 48 C4
Burunniy Rus. Fed. see Tsagan Aman
Bururi Burundi 48 C4
Burwash Landing Canada 60 E3
Burwick U.K. 20 G2
Buryn' Ukr. 13 G6
Bury St Edmunds U.K. 19 H6
Burzil Pass Jammu and Kashmir 36 C2
Busan S. Korea see Pusan
Busanga Dem. Rep. Congo 48 C4
Buseire Syria see Al Buşayrah
Bush r. U.K. 21 F2
Büshehr Iran 35 H5
Bushêngcaka China 37 E2
Bushenyi Uganda 48 D4
Bushire Iran see Büshehr
Bushmills U.K. 21 F2
Businga Dem. Rep. Congo 48 C3
Buşrá ash Shām Syria 39 C3
Busse Rus. Fed. 44 B2
Busselton Australia 55 A8
Busto Arsizio Italy 26 C2
Buta Dem. Rep. Congo 48 C3
Butare Rwanda 48 C4
Butaritari atoll Kiribati 74 H5
Bute Australia 57 B7
Bute i. U.K. 20 D5
Butha Buthe Lesotho 51 I5
Butha Qi China see Zalantun
Buthidaung Myanmar 37 H5
Butler PA U.S.A. 64 B2
Butlers Bridge Ireland 21 E3
Buton i. Indon. 41 E8
Butte MT U.S.A. 62 E2
Butterworth S. Africa 51 I7
Buttevant Ireland 21 D5
Butt of Lewis hd U.K. 20 C2
Button Bay Canada 61 I4
Butuan Phil. 41 E7
Buturlinovka Rus. Fed. 13 I6
Butwal Nepal 37 E4
Buulobarde Somalia 48 E3
Buur Gaabo Somalia 48 E4
Buurhabaka Somalia 48 E3
Buxar India 37 F4
Buxoro Uzbek. 33 J2
Buxton U.K. 18 F5
Buy Rus. Fed. 12 I4
Buyant Mongolia 42 H3
Buynaksk Rus. Fed. 13 J8
Büyükçekmece Turkey 34 C2
Büyük Egri Dağ mt. Turkey 39 A1
Büyükmenderes r. Turkey 27 L6
Buzău Romania 27 L2
Buzdyak Rus. Fed. 11 Q5
Búzi Moz. 49 D5
Büzmeÿin Turkm. see Abadan
Buzuluk Rus. Fed. 11 Q5
Buzuluk r. Rus. Fed. 13 I6
Buzzards Bay MA U.S.A. 64 F2
Byakar Bhutan see Jakar
Byala Bulg. 27 K3
Byala Slatina Bulg. 27 J3
Byalynichy Belarus 13 F5
Byarezina r. Belarus 13 F5
Byaroza Belarus 15 N10
Byblos tourist site Lebanon 39 B2
Bydgoszcz Poland 17 Q4
Byelorussia country Europe see Belarus
Byerazino Belarus 13 F5
Byeshankovichy Belarus 13 F5
Byesville OH U.S.A. 64 A3
Bygland Norway 15 E7
Bykhaw Belarus 13 F5
Bykhov Belarus see Bykhaw
Bykle Norway 15 E7
Bykovo Rus. Fed. 13 J6
Bylot Island Canada 61 K2
Byramgore Reef India 38 A4
Byrd Glacier Antarctica 76 H1
Byrkjelo Norway 15 E6
Byrock Australia 58 C3
Byron, Cape Australia 58 F2
Byron Bay Australia 58 F2
Byron Island Kiribati see Nikunau
Byrranga, Gory mts Rus. Fed. 29 K2
Byske Sweden 14 L4
Byssa Rus. Fed. 44 C1
Byssa r. Rus. Fed. 44 C1
Bytom Poland 17 Q5
Bytów Poland 17 P3
Byurgyutli Turkm. 35 I3
Byzantium Turkey see İstanbul

C

Caacupé Para. 70 E3
Caatinga Brazil 71 B2
Caazapá Para. 70 E3
Caballas Peru 68 C6
Caballococha Peru 68 D4
Caballos Mesteños, Llano de los plain Mex. 66 D3
Cabanaconde Peru 68 D7
Cabanatuan Phil. 41 E6
Cabdul Qaadir Somalia 48 E2
Cabeceira Rio Manso Brazil 69 G7
Cabeceiras Brazil 71 B1
Cabeza del Buey Spain 25 D4
Cabezas Bol. 68 F7
Cabimas Venez. 68 D1
Cabinda Angola 49 B4
Cabinda prov. Angola 49 B5
Cabinet Inlet Antarctica 76 L2
Cabistra Turkey see Ereğli
Cabo Frio Brazil 71 C3
Cabo Frio, Ilha do i. Brazil 71 C3
Cabonga, Réservoir resr Canada 63 L2
Caboolture Australia 58 F1
Cabo Orange, Parque Nacional de nat. park Brazil 69 H3
Cabo Pantoja Peru 68 C4
Cabora Bassa, Lake resr Moz. 49 D5
Cabo Raso Arg. 70 C6
Caborca Mex. 66 B2
Cabot Strait Canada 61 L5
Cabourg France 19 G9
Cabo Verde country N. Atlantic Ocean see Cape Verde
Cabo Verde, Ilhas do is N. Atlantic Ocean 46 [inset]
Cabo Yubi Morocco see Tarfaya
Cabral, Serra do mts Brazil 71 B2
Cäbrayıl Azer. 35 G3
Cabrera, Illa de i. Spain 25 H4
Çaçador Brazil 71 A4
Čačak Serbia 27 I3
Caccia, Capo c. Sardinia Italy 26 C4
Cacequi Brazil 70 F3
Cáceres Brazil 69 G7
Cáceres Spain 25 C4
Cache Creek Canada 62 C1
Cacheu Guinea-Bissau 46 B3
Cachi, Nevados de mts Arg. 70 C2
Cachimbo, Serra do hills Brazil 69 H5
Cachoeira Brazil 71 D1
Cachoeira Alta Brazil 71 A2
Cachoeira de Goiás Brazil 71 A2
Cachoeira do Arari Brazil 69 I4
Cachoeiro de Itapemirim Brazil 71 C3
Cacine Guinea-Bissau 46 B3
Caciporé, Cabo c. Brazil 69 H3
Cacolo Angola 49 B5
Cacongo Angola 49 B4
Caçu Brazil 71 A2
Caculé Brazil 71 C1
Čadca Slovakia 17 Q6
Cadereyta Mex. 62 G6
Cadibarrawirracanna, Lake salt flat Australia 57 A6
Cadillac U.S.A. 63 J3
Cádiz Spain 25 C5
Cadiz OH U.S.A. 64 A2
Cádiz, Golfo de g. Spain 25 C5
Cadiz Lake CA U.S.A. 65 E3
Cadotte Lake Canada 60 G4
Caen France 24 D2
Caerdydd U.K. see Cardiff
Caerffili U.K. see Caerphilly
Caerfyrddin U.K. see Carmarthen
Caergybi U.K. see Holyhead
Caernarfon U.K. 19 C5
Caernarfon Bay U.K. 19 C5
Caernarvon U.K. see Caernarfon
Caerphilly U.K. 19 D7
Caesaraugusta Spain see Zaragoza
Caesarea Alg. see Cherchell
Caesarea Cappadociae Turkey see Kayseri
Caesarea Philippi Syria see Bāniyās
Caesarodunum France see Tours
Caesaromagus U.K. see Chelmsford
Caetité Brazil 71 C1
Cafayate Arg. 70 C3
Cafelândia Brazil 71 A3
Caffa Ukr. see Feodosiya
Cagayan de Oro Phil. 41 E7
Cagli Italy 26 E3
Cagliari Sardinia Italy 26 C5
Cagliari, Golfo di b. Sardinia Italy 26 C5
Çagyl Turkm. 35 I2
Cahama Angola 49 B5
Caha Mts hills Ireland 21 C6
Cahermore Ireland 21 B6
Cahersiveen Ireland see Cahirciveen
Cahir Ireland 21 E5
Cahirciveen Ireland 21 B6
Cahora Bassa, Lago de resr Moz. see Cabora Bassa, Lake
Cahore Point Ireland 21 F5
Cahors France 24 E4
Cahuapanas Peru 68 C5
Cahul Moldova 27 M2
Caia Moz. 49 D5
Caiabis, Serra dos hills Brazil 69 G6
Caianda Angola 49 C5
Caiapó r. Brazil 71 A1
Caiapó, Serra do mts Brazil 71 A2
Caiapônia Brazil 71 A2
Caicara Venez. 68 E2
Caicos Islands Turks and Caicos Is 67 J4
Caicos Passage Bahamas/Turks and Caicos Is 67 J4
Caiguna Australia 55 D8
Caimodorro mt. Spain 25 F3
Caipe Arg. 70 C2
Caird Coast Antarctica 76 B1
Cairngorm Mountains U.K. 20 F3
Cairnryan U.K. 20 D6
Cairns Australia 56 D3
Cairnsmore of Carsphairn hill U.K. 20 E5
Cairo Egypt 34 C5
Caisleán an Bharraigh Ireland see Castlebar
Caiundo Angola 49 B5
Caiwarro Australia 58 B2
Cajamarca Peru 68 C5
Cajati Brazil 71 A4
Cajuru Brazil 71 B3
Čakovec Croatia 26 G1
Çal Denizli Turkey 27 M5
Cala S. Africa 51 H6
Calabar Nigeria 46 D4
Calabria, Parco Nazionale della nat. park Italy 26 G5
Calafat Romania 27 J3
Calagurris Spain see Calahorra
Calahorra Spain 25 F2
Calai Angola 49 B5
Calais France 24 E1
Calais U.S.A. 63 N2
Calalasteo, Sierra de mts Arg. 70 C3
Calama Brazil 68 F5
Calama Chile 70 C2
Calamar Col. 68 D1
Calamian Group is Phil. 41 D6
Calamocha Spain 25 F3
Calandula Angola 49 B4
Calapan Phil. 41 E6
Călărași Romania 27 L2
Calatayud Spain 25 F3
Calayan i. Phil. 43 M9
Calbayog Phil. 41 E6
Calçoene Brazil 69 H3
Calcutta India see Kolkata
Caldas da Rainha Port. 25 B4
Caldas Novas Brazil 69 I7
Caldera Chile 70 B3
Caldervale Australia 56 D5
Caldew r. U.K. 18 E4
Caldwell ID U.S.A. 62 D3
Caldwell OH U.S.A. 64 A3
Caledon r. Lesotho/S. Africa 51 H6
Caledon S. Africa 50 D8
Caledon Bay Australia 56 B2
Caledonia Ont. Canada 64 B1
Caledonia admin. div. U.K. see Scotland
Caleta el Cobre Chile 70 B2
Calexico CA U.S.A. 65 E4
Calf of Man i. Isle of Man 18 C4
Calgary Canada 62 E1
Cali Col. 68 C3
Calicut India 38 B4
Caliente NV U.S.A. 65 E2
California PA U.S.A. 64 B2
California state U.S.A. 62 C3
California, Golfo de g. Mex. see California, Gulf of
California, Gulf of Mex. 66 B2
California Aqueduct canal CA U.S.A. 65 B2
Cälilabad Azer. 35 H3
Calingasta Arg. 70 C4
Calipatria CA U.S.A. 65 E4
Calistoga CA U.S.A. 65 A1
Calkiní Mex. 66 F4
Callabonna, Lake salt flat Australia 57 C6
Callabonna Creek watercourse Australia 57 C6
Callan Ireland 21 E5
Callan r. U.K. 21 F3
Callander U.K. 20 E4
Callao Peru 68 C6
Callicoon NY U.S.A. 64 D2
Callington U.K. 19 C8
Calliope Australia 56 E5
Callipolis Turkey see Gallipoli
Caloundra Australia 58 F1
Caltagirone Sicily Italy 26 F6
Caltanissetta Sicily Italy 26 F6
Calucinga Angola 49 B5
Calulo Angola 49 B4
Calunga Angola 49 B5
Caluquembe Angola 49 B5
Caluula Somalia 48 F2
Caluula, Raas pt Somalia 48 F2
Calvert Hills Australia 56 B3
Calvi Corsica France 24 I5
Calvià Spain 25 H4
Calvinia S. Africa 50 D6
Calvo, Monte mt. Italy 26 F4
Cam r. U.K. 19 H6
Camaçari Brazil 71 D1
Camache Reservoir CA U.S.A. 65 B1
Camacho Mex. 66 D4
Camacuio Angola 49 B5
Camacupa Angola 49 B5
Camagüey Cuba 67 I4
Camagüey, Archipiélago de is Cuba 67 I4
Camamu Brazil 71 D1
Camana Peru 68 D7
Camanongue Angola 49 C5
Camapuã Brazil 69 H7
Camaquã Brazil 70 F4
Çamardı Turkey 34 D3
Camargo Bol. 68 E8
Camargue reg. France 24 G5
Camarillo CA U.S.A. 65 C3
Camarones Arg. 70 C6
Camarones, Bahía b. Arg. 70 C6
Ca Mau Vietnam 31 J6
Cambay India see Khambhat
Cambay, Gulf of India see Khambhat, Gulf of
Camberley U.K. 19 G7
Cambodia country Asia 31 J5
Camboriú Brazil 71 A4
Camborne U.K. 19 B8
Cambrai France 24 F1
Cambria admin. div. U.K. see Wales
Cambrian Mountains hills U.K. 19 D6
Cambridge Ont. Canada 64 A1
Cambridge N.Z. 59 E3
Cambridge U.K. 19 H6
Cambridge MA U.S.A. 64 F1
Cambridge MD U.S.A. 64 C3
Cambridge MN U.S.A. 63 I2
Cambridge NY U.S.A. 64 E1
Cambridge OH U.S.A. 63 K3
Cambridge Bay Canada 61 H3
Cambrien, Lac l. Canada 61 L4
Cambulo Angola 49 C4
Cambundi-Catembo Angola 49 B5
Cambuquira Brazil 71 B3
Cam Co l. China 37 E2
Camden AR U.S.A. 63 I5
Camden NJ U.S.A. 64 D3
Camden NY U.S.A. 64 D1
Cameia Angola 49 C5
Cameia, Parque Nacional da nat. park Angola 49 C5
Cameron Island Canada 61 H2
Cameron Park CA U.S.A. 65 B1
Cameroon country Africa 46 E4
Cameroon, Mount vol. Cameroon see Cameroun, Mont
Cameroon Highlands slope Cameroon/Nigeria 46 E4
Caméroun country Africa see Cameroon
Cameroun, Mont vol. Cameroon 46 D4
Cametá Brazil 69 I4
Camiña Chile 68 E7
Camiri Bol. 68 F8
Camisea Peru 68 D6
Camocim Brazil 69 J4
Camooweal Australia 56 B3
Camooweal Caves National Park Australia 56 B4
Campana, Isla i. Chile 70 A7
Campbell S. Africa 50 F5
Campbell, Cape N.Z. 59 E5
Campbell, Mount hill Australia 54 E5
Campbell Island N.Z. 74 H9
Campbell Plateau sea feature S. Pacific Ocean 74 H9
Campbell Range hills Australia 54 D3
Campbell River Canada 62 B1
Campbellton Canada 63 N2
Campbelltown Australia 58 E5
Campbeltown U.K. 20 D5
Campeche Mex. 66 F5
Campeche, Bahía de g. Mex. 66 F5
Camperdown Australia 58 A7
Câmpina Romania 27 K2
Campina Grande Brazil 69 K5
Campinas Brazil 71 B3
Campina Verde Brazil 71 A2
Campo Cameroon 46 D4
Campobasso Italy 26 F4
Campo Belo Brazil 71 B3
Campo Belo do Sul Brazil 71 A4
Campo de Diauarum Brazil 69 H6
Campo Florido Brazil 71 A2
Campo Gallo Arg. 70 D3
Campo Grande Brazil 70 F2
Campo Largo Brazil 71 A4
Campo Maior Brazil 69 J4
Campo Maior Port. 25 C4
Campo Mourão Brazil 70 F2
Campos Brazil 71 C3
Campos Altos Brazil 71 B2
Campos Novos Brazil 71 A4
Campos Sales Brazil 69 J5
Câmpulung Romania 27 K2
Câmpulung Moldovenesc Romania 27 K1
Camrose Canada 62 E1
Camrose U.K. 19 B7
Camsell Portage Canada 60 H4
Camulodunum U.K. see Colchester
Çan Turkey 27 L4
Canaan CT U.S.A. 64 E1
Canabrava Brazil 71 B2
Canacona India 38 B3
Canada country N. America 60 H4
Canada Basin sea feature Arctic Ocean 77 A1
Canadian U.S.A. 62 G4
Canadian r. U.S.A. 62 H4
Canadian Abyssal Plain sea feature Arctic Ocean 77 A1
Cañadon Grande, Sierra mts Arg. 70 C7
Canaima, Parque Nacional nat. park Venez. 68 F2
Çanakkale Turkey 27 L4
Çanakkale Boğazı strait Turkey see Dardanelles
Canalejas Arg. 70 C5
Cañamares Spain 25 E3
Canandaigua NY U.S.A. 64 C1
Cananea Mex. 66 B2
Cananéia Brazil 71 B4
Canápolis Brazil 71 A2
Cañar Ecuador 68 C4
Canarias terr. N. Atlantic Ocean see Canary Islands
Canárias, Ilha das i. Brazil 69 J4
Canarias, Islas terr. N. Atlantic Ocean see Canary Islands
Canary Islands terr. N. Atlantic Ocean 46 B2
Canastota NY U.S.A. 64 D1
Canastra, Serra da mts Brazil 71 B2
Canastra, Serra da mts Brazil 71 A1
Canatiba Brazil 71 C1
Canatlán Mex. 66 D4
Canaveral, Cape FL U.S.A. 63 K6
Cañaveras Spain 25 E3
Canavieiras Brazil 71 D1
Canbelego Australia 58 C3
Canberra Australia 58 D5
Cancún Mex. 67 G4
Çandar Turkey see Kastamonu
Çandarlı Turkey 27 L5
Candia Greece see Iraklion
Cândido de Abreu Brazil 71 A4
Çandır Turkey 34 D2
Candle Lake Canada 62 F1
Candlewood, Lake CT U.S.A. 64 E2
Cane r. Australia 54 A5
Canea Greece see Chania
Canela Brazil 71 A5
Canelones Uruguay 70 E4
Cangallo Peru 68 D6
Cangamba Angola 49 B5
Cangandala, Parque Nacional de nat. park Angola 49 B4
Cangbu r. China see Brahmaputra
Cango Caves S. Africa 50 F7
Cangola Angola 49 B4
Canguaretama Brazil 69 K5
Canguçu Brazil 70 F4
Canguçu, Serra do hills Brazil 70 F4
Cangzhou China 43 L5
Caniapiscau Canada 61 L4
Caniapiscau r. Canada 61 L4
Caniapiscau, Lac l. Canada 61 K4
Caniçado Moz. see Guija
Canicattì Sicily Italy 26 E6
Canindé Brazil 69 K4
Canisteo r. NY U.S.A. 64 C1
Canisteo Peninsula Antarctica 76 K2
Çankırı Turkey 34 D2
Canna Australia 55 A7
Canna i. U.K. 20 C3
Cannanore India 38 B4
Cannanore Islands India 38 B4
Cannes France 24 H5
Cannock U.K. 19 E6
Cann River Australia 58 D6
Canoas Brazil 71 A5
Canõas, Rio das r. Brazil 71 A4
Canoeiros Brazil 71 B2
Canoinhas Brazil 71 A4
Canoona Australia 56 E4
Canora Canada 62 G1
Canowindra Australia 58 D4
Cantabrian Mountains Spain see Cantábrica, Cordillera
Cantábrica, Cordillera mts Spain 25 D2
Cantábrico, Mar sea Spain 25 C2
Canterbury U.K. 19 I7
Canterbury Bight b. N.Z. 59 C7
Canterbury Plains N.Z. 59 C6
Cân Thơ Vietnam 31 J5
Cantil CA U.S.A. 65 D3
Canton MS U.S.A. 63 J5
Canton OH U.S.A. 64 A2
Canton PA U.S.A. 64 C2
Canton Island atoll Kiribati see Kanton
Cantuaria U.K. see Canterbury
Canunda National Park Australia 57 C8
Canutama Brazil 68 F5
Canvey Island U.K. 19 H7
Cany-Barville France 19 H9
Canyon U.S.A. 62 G4
Canyon Ferry Lake U.S.A. 62 E2
Cao Bằng Vietnam 31 J4
Caohu China 42 E4
Caoshi China 44 B4
Caozhou China see Heze
Çapakçur Turkey see Bingöl
Capanaparo r. Venez. 68 E2
Capanema Brazil 69 I4
Capão Bonito Brazil 71 A4
Caparaó, Serra do mts Brazil 71 C3
Cape r. Australia 56 D4
Cape Arid National Park Australia 55 C8
Cape Barren Island Australia 57 [inset]
Cape Basin sea feature S. Atlantic Ocean 72 I8
Cape Breton Island Canada 61 L5
Cape Charles VA U.S.A. 64 C4
Cape Coast Ghana 46 C4
Cape Coast Castle Ghana see Cape Coast
Cape Cod Bay MA U.S.A. 64 F2
Cape Cod National Seashore nature res. MA U.S.A. 64 G2
Cape Crawford Australia 56 A3
Cape Dorset Canada 61 K3
Cape Girardeau U.S.A. 63 J4
Cape Johnson Depth sea feature N. Pacific Ocean 74 E5
Cape Juby Morocco see Tarfaya
Cape Krusenstern National Monument nat. park U.S.A. 60 B3
Capel Australia 55 A8
Cape Le Grand National Park Australia 55 C8
Capelinha Brazil 71 C2
Capella Australia 56 E4
Capelongo Angola see Kuvango
Cape May NJ U.S.A. 64 D3
Cape May Court House NJ U.S.A. 64 D3
Cape May Point NJ U.S.A. 64 D3
Cape Melville National Park Australia 56 D2
Capenda-Camulemba Angola 49 B4
Cape of Good Hope Nature Reserve S. Africa 50 D8
Cape Palmerston National Park Australia 56 E4
Cape Range National Park Australia 54 A5
Cape Town S. Africa 50 D7
Cape Tribulation National Park Australia 56 D2
Cape Upstart National Park Australia 56 D3
Cape Verde country N. Atlantic Ocean 46 [inset]
Cape Verde Basin sea feature N. Atlantic Ocean 72 F5
Cape Verde Plateau sea feature N. Atlantic Ocean 72 F4
Cape York Peninsula Australia 56 C2
Cap-Haïtien Haiti 67 J5
Capim r. Brazil 69 I4
Capitán Arturo Prat research station Antarctica 76 A2
Capivara, Represa resr Brazil 71 A3
Čapljina Bos.-Herz. 26 G3
Cappoquin Ireland 21 E5
Capraia, Isola di i. Italy 26 C3
Caprara, Punta pt Sardinia Italy 26 C4
Capri, Isola di i. Italy 26 F4
Capricorn Channel Australia 56 E4
Capricorn Group atolls Australia 56 F4
Caprivi Strip reg. Namibia 49 C5
Capsa Tunisia see Gafsa
Captain Cook U.S.A. 62 [inset]
Captina r. OH U.S.A. 64 A3
Capuava Brazil 71 B4
Caquetá r. Col. 68 E4
Caracal Romania 27 K2
Caracas Venez. 68 E1
Caraguatatuba Brazil 71 B3
Caraí Brazil 71 C2
Carajás Brazil 69 H5
Carajás, Serra dos hills Brazil 69 H5
Carales Sardinia Italy see Cagliari
Caralis Sardinia Italy see Cagliari
Carandaí Brazil 71 C3
Caransebeş Romania 27 J2
Caraquet Canada 63 N2
Caratasca, Laguna de lag. Hond. 67 H5
Caratinga Brazil 71 C2
Carauari Brazil 68 E4
Caravaca de la Cruz Spain 25 F4
Caravelas Brazil 71 D2
Carbó Mex. 66 B3
Carbonara, Capo c. Sardinia Italy 26 C5
Carbondale PA U.S.A. 64 D2
Carbonia Sardinia Italy 26 C5
Carbonita Brazil 71 C2
Carcaixent Spain 25 F4
Carcassonne France 24 F5
Cardamom Hills India 38 C4
Cárdenas Cuba 67 H4
Cárdenas Mex. 66 E4
Cardenyabba watercourse Australia 58 A2
Çardi Turkey see Harmancık
Cardiel, Lago l. Arg. 70 B7
Cardiff U.K. 19 D7
Cardiff MD U.S.A. 64 C3
Cardigan U.K. 19 C6
Cardigan Bay U.K. 19 C6
Cardoso Brazil 71 A3
Cardoso, Ilha do i. Brazil 71 B4
Carei Romania 27 J1
Carentan France 24 D2
Carey, Lake salt flat Australia 55 C7
Cargados Carajos Islands Mauritius 73 L7
Carhaix-Plouguer France 24 C2
Cariacica Brazil 71 C3
Cariamanga Ecuador 68 C4
Caribbean Sea N. Atlantic Ocean 67 H5
Caribou U.S.A. 63 N2
Caribou Lake Canada 61 J4
Caribou Mountains Canada 60 G4
Carinda Australia 58 C3
Cariñena Spain 25 F3
Carinhanha r. Brazil 71 C1
Carlabhagh U.K. see Carloway
Carletonville S. Africa 51 H4
Carlingford Lough inlet Ireland/U.K. 21 F3
Carlisle U.K. 18 E4
Carlisle NY U.S.A. 64 D1
Carlisle PA U.S.A. 64 C2
Carlisle Lakes salt flat Australia 55 D7
Carlit, Pic mt. France 24 E5
Carlos Chagas Brazil 71 C2
Carlow Ireland 21 F5
Carloway U.K. 20 C2
Carlsbad Czech Rep. see Karlovy Vary
Carlsbad CA U.S.A. 65 D4
Carlsbad NM U.S.A. 62 G5
Carlsberg Ridge sea feature Indian Ocean 73 L5
Carlson Inlet Antarctica 76 L1
Carlton Hill Australia 54 E3
Carluke U.K. 20 F5
Carlyle Canada 62 G2
Carmacks Canada 60 E3
Carmagnola Italy 26 B2
Carman Canada 62 H2
Carmana Iran see Kermān
Carmarthen U.K. 19 C7
Carmarthen Bay U.K. 19 C7
Carmaux France 24 F4
Carmel NY U.S.A. 64 E2
Carmel, Mount hill Israel 39 B3
Carmel Head hd U.K. 18 C5
Carmel Valley CA U.S.A. 65 B2
Carmen, Isla i. Mex. 66 B3
Carmen de Patagones Arg. 70 D6
Carmichael CA U.S.A. 65 B1
Carmo da Cachoeira Brazil 71 B3
Carmo do Paranaíba Brazil 71 B2
Carmona Angola see Uíge
Carmona Spain 25 D5
Carnac France 24 C3
Carnamah Australia 55 A7
Carnarvon Australia 55 A6
Carnarvon S. Africa 50 F6
Carnarvon National Park Australia 56 D5
Carnarvon Range hills Australia 55 C6
Carnarvon Range mts Australia 56 E5
Carn Dearg hill U.K. 20 E3
Carndonagh Ireland 21 E2
Carnegie Australia 55 C6
Carnegie, Lake salt flat Australia 55 C6
Carn Eige mt. U.K. 20 D3
Carnes Australia 55 F7
Carney Island Antarctica 76 J2
Carnforth U.K. 18 E4
Carn Glas-choire hill U.K. 20 F3
Carnlough U.K. 21 G3
Carn nan Gabhar mt. U.K. 20 F4
Carn Odhar hill U.K. 20 E3
Carnot Cent. Afr. Rep. 48 B3
Carnoustie U.K. 20 G4
Carnsore Point Ireland 21 F5
Carnwath U.K. 20 F5
Carola Cay reef Australia 56 F3
Carolina Brazil 69 I5
Carolina S. Africa 51 J4
Caroline Island atoll Kiribati 75 J6
Caroline Islands N. Pacific Ocean 41 G7
Caroline Peak N.Z. 59 A7
Caroline Range hills Australia 54 D4
Caroní r. Venez. 68 F2
Carpathian Mountains Europe 13 C6
Carpaţii mts Europe see Carpathian Mountains
Carpaţii Meridionali mts Romania see Transylvanian Alps
Carpaţii Occidentali mts Romania 27 J2
Carpentaria, Gulf of Australia 56 B2
Carpentras France 24 G4
Carpi Italy 26 D2
Carpinteria CA U.S.A. 65 C3
Carra, Lough l. Ireland 21 C4
Carraig na Siuire Ireland see Carrick-on-Suir
Carrantuohill mt. Ireland 21 C6
Carrara Italy 26 D2
Carrasco, Parque Nacional nat. park Bol. 68 F7
Carrathool Australia 58 B5
Carrhae Turkey see Harran
Carrickfergus U.K. 21 G3
Carrickmacross Ireland 21 F4
Carrick-on-Shannon Ireland 21 D4
Carrick-on-Suir Ireland 21 E5
Carrigallen Ireland 21 E4
Carrigtwohill Ireland 21 D6
Carrington U.S.A. 62 H2
Carrizal Bajo Chile 70 B3
Carrizo Springs U.S.A. 62 H6
Carrizozo U.S.A. 62 F5
Carroll U.S.A. 63 I3
Carrollton GA U.S.A. 63 J5
Carrollton OH U.S.A. 64 A2
Carrolltown PA U.S.A. 64 B2
Carron r. U.K. 20 E3
Carrowmore Lake Ireland 21 C3
Çarşamba Turkey 34 E2
Carson City NV U.S.A. 65 C1
Carson Escarpment Australia 54 D3
Carson Lake NV U.S.A. 65 C1
Carstensz Pyramid mt. Indon. see Jaya, Puncak
Carstensz-top mt. Indon. see Jaya, Puncak
Cartagena Col. 68 C1
Cartagena Spain 25 F5
Carteret Group is P.N.G. see Kilinailau Islands
Carteret Island Solomon Is see Malaita
Carthage tourist site Tunisia 26 D6
Carthage MO U.S.A. 63 I4
Carthago tourist site Tunisia see Carthage
Carthago Nova Spain see Cartagena
Cartier Island Australia 54 C3
Cartmel U.K. 18 E4
Cartwright Nfld. and Lab. Canada 61 M4
Caruarú Brazil 69 K5
Carúpano Venez. 68 F1
Caryapundy Swamp Australia 57 C6
Casablanca Morocco 22 C5
Casa Branca Brazil 71 B3
Casa de Piedra, Embalse resr Arg. 70 C5
Casa Grande U.S.A. 62 E5
Casale Monferrato Italy 26 C2
Casalmaggiore Italy 26 D2
Casca Brazil 71 A5

Cascade Australia 55 C8
Cascade r. N.Z. 59 B7
Cascade Point N.Z. 59 B7
Cascade Range mts Canada/U.S.A. 60 F5
Cascais Port. 25 B4
Cascavel Brazil 70 F2
Caserta Italy 26 F4
Casey research station Antarctica 76 F2
Casey Bay Antarctica 76 D2
Caseyr, Raas c. Somalia see Gwardafuy, Gees
Cashel Ireland 21 E5
Cashmere Australia 58 D1
Casino Australia 58 F2
Casiquiare, Canal r. Venez. 68 E3
Casnewydd U.K. see Newport
Caspe Spain 25 F3
Casper U.S.A. 62 F3
Caspian Lowland Kazakh./Rus. Fed. 30 D2
Caspian Sea l. Asia/Europe 35 H1
Cass r. WV U.S.A. 64 E4
Cassacatiza Moz. 49 D5
Cassadaga NY U.S.A. 64 F1
Cassaigne Alg. see Sidi Ali
Cassamba Angola 49 C5
Cássia Brazil 71 B3
Cassilândia Brazil 71 A2
Cassilis Australia 58 D4
Cassino Italy 26 E4
Cassley r. U.K. 20 E3
Cassongue Angola 49 B5
Castanhal Brazil 69 I4
Castano r. Arg. 70 C4
Castaños Mex. 66 D3
Castelfranco Veneto Italy 26 D2
Castell-nedd U.K. see Neath
Castell Newydd Emlyn U.K. see
   Newcastle Emlyn
Castellón Spain see Castellón de la Plana
Castellón de la Plana Spain 25 F4
Castelo Branco Port. 25 C4
Castelo de Vide Port. 25 C4
Casteltermini Sicily Italy 26 E6
Castelvetrano Sicily Italy 26 E6
Castiglione della Pescaia Italy 26 D3
Castilla y León reg. Spain 24 B6
Castlebar Ireland 21 C4
Castlebay U.K. 20 B4
Castlebellingham Ireland 21 F4
Castleblayney Ireland 21 F3
Castlebridge Ireland 21 F5
Castle Carrock U.K. 18 E4
Castlederg U.K. 21 E3
Castledermot Ireland 21 F5
Castle Dome Mountains AZ U.S.A. 65 F4
Castle Donington U.K. 19 F6
Castle Douglas U.K. 20 F6
Castleford U.K. 18 F5
Castlegar Canada 60 F5
Castlegregory Ireland 21 B5
Castleisland Ireland 21 C5
Castlemaine Australia 58 B6
Castlemaine Ireland 21 C5
Castlemartyr Ireland 21 D6
Castle Mountain CA U.S.A. 65 B3
Castlepoint N.Z. 59 F5
Castlepollard Ireland 21 E4
Castlerea Ireland 21 D4
Castlereagh r. Australia 58 C3
Castle Rock U.S.A. 62 G4
Castletown Ireland 21 E5
Castletown Isle of Man 18 C4
Castra Regina Germany see Regensburg
Castres France 24 F5
Castries St Lucia 67 L6
Castro Brazil 71 A4
Castro Chile 70 B6
Castro Alves Brazil 71 D1
Castro Verde Port. 25 B5
Castrovillari Italy 26 G5
Castroville CA U.S.A. 65 B3
Catacaos Peru 68 B5
Cataguases Brazil 71 C3
Çatak Turkey 35 F3
Catalão Brazil 71 B2
Çatalca Yarımadası pen. Turkey 27 M4
Catalonia aut. comm. Spain see Cataluña
Cataluña aut. comm. Spain 25 G3
Catalunya aut. comm. Spain see Cataluña
Catamarca Arg. 70 C3
Catana Sicily Italy see Catania
Catanduanes i. Phil. 41 E6
Catanduva Brazil 71 A3
Catania Sicily Italy 26 F6
Catanzaro Italy 26 G5
Catarman Phil. 41 E6
Cataxa Moz. 49 D5
Catbalogan Phil. 41 E6
Catembe Moz. 51 K4
Catengue Angola 49 B5
Catete Angola 49 B4
Cathcart Australia 58 D6
Cathcart S. Africa 51 H7
Cathedral Peak S. Africa 51 I5
Cathedral Rock National Park Australia
   58 F3
Catherdaniel Ireland 21 B6
Catheys Valley CA U.S.A. 65 B2
Catió Guinea-Bissau 46 B3
Catisimiña Venez. 68 F3
Cat Island Bahamas 67 F4
Cat Lake Canada 63 I1
Catoche, Cabo c. Mex. 67 G4
Cato Island and Bank reef Australia 56 F4
Catrilo Arg. 70 D5
Catskill NY U.S.A. 64 E1
Catskill Mountains NY U.S.A. 64 D1
Catuane Moz. 51 K4
Caubvick, Mount Canada 61 L4
Cauca r. Col. 67 J7
Caucaia Brazil 69 K4
Caucasia Col. 68 C2
Caucasus mts Asia/Europe 35 F2
Câu Giat Vietnam 42 J9
Caulonia Italy 26 G5
Caungula Angola 49 B4
Cauquenes Chile 70 B5
Cavaglià Italy 26 C2
Cavalcante, Serra do hills Brazil 71 B1
Cavan Ireland 21 E4
Çavdır Turkey 27 M6
Caveira r. Brazil 71 C1
Caviana, Ilha i. Brazil 69 H3
Cawdor U.K. 20 F3
Cawnpore India see Kanpur
Cawston U.K. 19 I6
Caxias Brazil 69 J4
Caxias do Sul Brazil 71 A5
Caxito Angola 49 B4
Çay Turkey 27 N5
Çaya Turkey 35 I5
Cayambe, Volcán vol. Ecuador 68 C3
Çaybaşı Turkey see Çayeli
Çaycuma Turkey 27 O4
Çayeli Turkey 35 F2
Çayırhan Turkey 27 N4
Cayenne Fr. Guiana 69 H3
Cayeux-sur-Mer France 19 I8
Cayman Brac i. Cayman Is 67 I5
Cayman Islands terr. West Indies 67 H5

Cayman Trench sea feature Caribbean Sea
   72 C4
Caynabo Somalia 48 E3
Cayucos CA U.S.A. 65 B3
Cayuga Ont. Canada 64 F2
Cayuga Lake NY U.S.A. 64 C1
Cazê China 37 F3
Cazenovia NY U.S.A. 64 D1
Cazombo Angola 49 C5
Ceadâr-Lunga Moldova see Ciadîr-Lunga
Ceanannus Mór Ireland see Kells
Ceann a Deas na Hearadh pen. U.K. see
   South Harris
Ceará Brazil see Fortaleza
Ceara Abyssal Plain sea feature
   S. Atlantic Ocean 72 F6
Ceatharlach Ireland see Carlow
Ceballos Mex. 66 D3
Cebu Phil. 41 E6
Cecil Plains Australia 58 E1
Cecil Rhodes, Mount hill Australia 55 C6
Cecina Italy 26 D3
Cedar City UT U.S.A. 65 F2
Cedar Island VA U.S.A. 64 D4
Cedar Lake Canada 62 G1
Cedar Rapids Canada 60 E3
Cedar Run NJ U.S.A. 64 D3
Cedarville U.S.A. 62 D3
Cedros, Isla i. Mex. 66 A3
Ceduna Australia 55 F8
Ceelbuur Somalia 48 E3
Ceeldheere Somalia 48 E3
Ceerigaabo Somalia 48 E2
Cefalù Sicily Italy 26 F5
Cegléd Hungary 27 H1
Cêgnê China 37 H2
Çekerek Turkey 34 D2
Celaya Mex. 66 D4
Celbridge Ireland 21 F4
Celebes i. Indon. 41 E8
Celebes Basin sea feature Pacific Ocean
   74 E5
Celebes Sea Indon./Phil. 41 E7
Celestún Mex. 66 D3
Celje Slovenia 26 F1
Celle Germany 17 M4
Celovec Austria see Klagenfurt
Celtic Sea Ireland/U.K. 16 B5
Celtic Shelf sea feature N. Atlantic Ocean
   72 H7
Cenderawasih, Teluk b. Indon. 41 F8
Çendir r. Turkm. 35 I3
Centane S. Africa see Kentani
Centenary Zimbabwe 49 D5
Centereach NY U.S.A. 64 E2
Centerville U.S.A. 62 E3
Centrafricaine, République country Africa
   see Central African Republic
Central admin. dist. Botswana 51 H2
Central, Cordillera mts Col. 68 C3
Central, Cordillera mts Peru 68 C6
Central African Empire country Africa see
   Central African Republic
Central African Republic country Africa
   48 B3
Central Brahui Range mts Pak. 33 K4
Central City U.S.A. 62 H3
Central Kalahari Game Reserve nature res.
   Botswana 50 G2
Central Kara Rise sea feature Arctic Ocean
   77 F1
Central Makran Range mts Pak. 33 J4
Central Mount Stuart hill Australia 54 F5
Central Pacific Basin sea feature
   Pacific Ocean 74 H5
Central Provinces state India see
   Madhya Pradesh
Central Range mts P.N.G. 52 E2
Central Russian Upland hills Rus. Fed.
   13 H5
Central Siberian Plateau Rus. Fed. 29 M3
Central Square NY U.S.A. 64 C1
Centreville MD U.S.A. 64 D4
Ceos i. Greece see Tzia
Cephaloedium Sicily Italy see Cefalù
Cephalonia i. Greece 27 I5
Ceram i. Indon. see Seram
Cerbat Mountains AZ U.S.A. 65 E4
Ceres Arg. 70 D3
Ceres Brazil 71 A1
Ceres S. Africa 50 D7
Ceres CA U.S.A. 65 B3
Céret France 24 F5
Cerezo de Abajo Spain 25 E3
Cerignola Italy 26 F4
Cêringgolêb China see Dongco
Çerkeş Turkey 34 D2
Çerkeşli Turkey 27 M4
Çermik Turkey 35 F3
Cernăuţi Ukr. see Chernivtsi
Cernavodă Romania 27 M2
Cerralvo, Isla i. Mex. 66 C4
Cêrrik Albania 27 H4
Cerritos Mex. 66 D4
Cerro Azul Brazil 71 A4
Cerro de Pasco Peru 68 C6
Cerros Colorados, Embalse resr Arg. 70 C5
Cervantes, Cerro mt. Arg. 70 B8
Cervati, Monte mt. Italy 26 F4
Cervione Corsica France 24 I5
Cervo Spain 25 C2
Cesena Italy 26 E2
Cēsis Latvia 15 N8
Česká Republika country Europe see
   Czech Republic
České Budějovice Czech Rep. 17 O6
Českomoravská vysočina hills Czech Rep.
   17 O6
Český Krumlov Czech Rep. 17 O6
Český les mts Czech Rep./Germany 17 N6
Çeşme Turkey 27 L5
Cessnock Australia 58 E4
Cetatea Albă Ukr. see
   Bilhorod-Dnistrovs'kyy
Cetinje Montenegro 26 H3
Cetraro Italy 26 F5
Ceuta N. Africa 25 D6
Ceva-i-Ra reef Fiji 53 H4
Cévennes mts France 24 F5
Cévennes, Parc National des nat. park
   France 24 F4
Cevizli Turkey 39 C1
Cevizlik Turkey 34 A3
Ceyhan Turkey 34 D3
Ceyhan r. Turkey 39 B1
Ceyhan Boğazı r. mouth Turkey 39 B1
Ceylanpınar Turkey 35 F3
Ceylon country Asia see Sri Lanka
Chābahār Iran 33 J4
Chabrol i. New Caledonia see Lifou
Chabug China 43 H7
Chabyêr Caka salt l. China 37 F3
Chachapoyas Peru 68 C5
Chacharan Pak. 36 B3
Chachoengsao Thai. 31 [unreadable]
Chaco Boreal reg. Para. 70 E2
Chad country Africa 47 E3
Chad, Lake Africa 47 E3
Chadaasan Mongolia 42 I3
Chadan Rus. Fed. 42 H1
Chadibe Botswana 51 H2

Chadron U.S.A. 62 G3
Chadyr-Lunga Moldova see Ciadîr-Lunga
Chaeryŏng N. Korea 45 B5
Chagai Pak. 33 J4
Chagda Kangri mt. China 37 F2
Chaghā Khūr mt. Iran 35 H5
Chaghcharān Afgh. 36 A2
Chagny France 24 G3
Chagoda Rus. Fed. 12 G4
Chagos Archipelago is B.I.O.T. 73 M6
Chagos-Laccadive Ridge sea feature
   Indian Ocean 73 M6
Chagos Trench sea feature Indian Ocean
   73 M6
Chagoyan Rus. Fed. 44 C1
Chahbounia Alg. 25 H6
Chāh-e Bāgh well Iran 35 I5
Chāh-e Bāzargānī well Iran 35 I4
Chāh-e Gonbad well Iran 35 I4
Chāh-e Khorāsān well Iran 35 I4
Chāh-e Malek well Iran 35 I4
Chāh-e Mūjān well Iran 35 I4
Chāh-e Qobād well Iran 35 I4
Chāh-e Shūr well Iran 35 I4
Chāh Kūh Iran 35 I5
Chah Pas well Iran 35 I4
Chaibasa India 37 F5
Chainjoin Co l. China 37 F2
Chaiten Chile 70 B6
Chajari Arg. 70 E4
Chak Amru Pak. 36 C2
Chakar r. Pak. 36 B3
Chakaria Bangl. 37 H5
Chakdarra Pak. 36 C2
Chakku Pak. 36 B4
Chakonipau, Lac l. Canada 61 L4
Chakoria Bangl. see Chakaria
Ch'ak'vi Georgia 35 F2
Chala Peru 68 D7
Chalatenango El Salvador 66 G6
Chalaua Moz. 49 D5
Chalaxung China 37 I2
Chalcedon Turkey see Kadıköy
Chalengkou China 42 I5
Chaleur Bay inlet Canada 63 N2
Chaleurs, Baie des inlet Canada see
   Chaleur Bay
Chalisgaon India 38 B1
Chalki i. Greece 27 L6
Chalkida Greece 27 J5
Challakere India 38 C3
Challans France 24 D3
Challapata Bol. 68 E7
Challenger Deep sea feature
   N. Pacific Ocean 74 F5
Challenger Fracture Zone sea feature
   S. Pacific Ocean 74 M8
Challis U.S.A. 62 E3
Châlons-en-Champagne France 24 G2
Châlons-sur-Marne France see
   Châlons-en-Champagne
Chalon-sur-Saône France 24 G3
Chaltan Pass Azer. 35 H2
Chālūs Iran 35 H3
Cham, Kūh-e hill Iran 35 H4
Chamaico Arg. 70 D5
Chamais Bay Namibia 50 B4
Chaman Pak. 30 F3
Chaman Bid Iran 35 J3
Chamba India 36 D2
Chamba Tanz. 49 D5
Chambal r. India 36 D4
Chamberlain r. Australia 54 D4
Chamberlain U.S.A. 62 H3
Chambersburg PA U.S.A. 64 C3
Chambéry France 24 G4
Chambeshi r. Zambia 49 C5
Chambi, Jebel mt. Tunisia 26 C7
Chamdo China see Qamdo
Chamechaude mt. France 24 G4
Chamoli India see Gopeshwar
Chamonix-Mont-Blanc France 24 H4
Champa India 37 E5
Champagne Castle mt. S. Africa 51 I5
Champagne Humide reg. France 24 G2
Champagne Pouilleuse reg. France 24 F2
Champagnole France 24 G3
Champagny Islands Australia 54 D3
Champaign U.S.A. 63 J3
Champhai India 37 H5
Champlain VA U.S.A. 64 C3
Champlain, Lake Canada/U.S.A. 61 K5
Champotón Mex. 66 F5
Chamrajnagar India 38 C4
Chamzinka Rus. Fed. 13 J5
Chanak Turkey see Çanakkale
Chañaral Chile 70 B3
Chanda India see Chandrapur
Chandalar r. U.S.A. 60 D3
Chandausi India 36 D3
Chandbali India 37 F5
Chanderi India 36 D4
Chandil India 37 F5
Chandler AZ U.S.A. 65 E5
Chandod India 36 C5
Chandpur India 36 D3
Chandpur Bangl. 37 G5
Chandragiri India 38 C3
Chandrapur India 38 C2
Chandvad India 38 B1
Changane r. Moz. 51 K3
Changbai China 44 B4
Changbai Shan mts China/N. Korea 44 B4
Chang Cheng research station Antarctica see
   Great Wall
Changchow Fujian China see Zhangzhou
Changchow Jiangsu China see Changzhou
Changchun China 44 B4
Changchunling China 44 B3
Changde China 43 K7
Changgi-ap pt S. Korea 45 C5
Changgo China 37 F3
Changhua Taiwan 43 M8
Changhŭng S. Korea 45 B6
Changhwa Taiwan see Changhua
Changi China 42 F4
Changji China 42 F4
Chang Jiang r. China see Yangtze
Changjin-ho resr N. Korea 45 B4
Changkiang China see Zhanjiang
Changling China 44 B3
Changlun Jammu and Kashmir 33 M3
Changma China 42 H5
Changnyon N. Korea 45 B5
Ch'ang-pai Shan mts China/N. Korea see
   Changbai Shan
Changp'yŏng S. Korea 45 C5
Changsan-got pt N. Korea 45 B5
Changsha China 43 K7
Changshu China see Changde
Changtang Heilong. China 44 C3
Changting Heilong. China 44 C3
Ch'angwŏn S. Korea 45 C6
Changyŏn N. Korea 45 C6
Changzhi China 43 K5
Changzhou China 43 L6
Chanhi Nevado del mt. Arg. 70 C2
Chania Greece 27 K7
Chanion, Kolpos b. Greece 27 J7
Channapatna India 38 C3

Channel Islands English Chan. 19 E9
Channel Islands CA U.S.A. 65 C4
Channel Islands National Park CA U.S.A.
   65 C3
Channel-Port-aux-Basques Canada 61 M5
Channel Tunnel France/U.K. 19 I7
Chantada Spain 25 C2
Chanthaburi Thai. 31 J5
Chantilly France 24 F2
Chanumla India 38 C3
Chany, Ozero salt l. Rus. Fed. 28 I4
Chaor He r. China see Qulin Gol
Chaouen Morocco 25 D6
Chaowula Shan mts China 37 I2
Chaoyang Heilong. China see Jiayin
Chaoyang Liaoning China 43 M4
Chaoyangcun China 44 B2
Chaoyang Hu l. China 37 F2
Chaozhong China 44 A2
Chaozhou China 43 L8
Chapada Diamantina, Parque Nacional
   nat. park Brazil 71 C1
Chapada dos Veadeiros, Parque Nacional
   da nat. park Brazil 71 B1
Chapak Guzar Afgh. 36 A1
Chāpala, Laguna de l. Mex. 66 D4
Chāpārī, Kowtal-e Afgh. 36 A2
Chapayev Kazakh. 30 L1
Chapayevo Kazakh. see Chapayev
Chapayevsk Rus. Fed. 13 K5
Chapecó Brazil 70 F3
Chapecó r. Brazil 70 F3
Chapel-en-le-Frith U.K. 18 F5
Chapel Hill U.S.A. 63 J5
Chapeltown U.K. 18 F5
Chapleau Canada 63 K2
Chaplygin Rus. Fed. 13 H5
Chapra Bihar India see Chhapra
Chapra Jharkhand India see Chatra
Charagua Bol. 68 F7
Charcas Mex. 66 D4
Charcot Island Antarctica 76 L2
Chard U.K. 19 E8
Chardara Kazakh. see Shardara
Chardara, Step' plain Kazakh. 42 B4
Chardon U.S.A. 64 E2
Chardzhev Turkm. see Türkmenabat
Chardzhou Turkm. see Türkmenabat
Charef Alg. 25 H6
Charef, Oued watercourse Morocco 22 D5
Charente r. France 24 D4
Chari r. Cameroon/Chad 47 E3
Chārīkār Afgh. 36 B2
Chārjew Turkm. see Türkmenabat
Charkayuvom Rus. Fed. 12 L2
Chār Kent Afgh. 36 A1
Charkhlik China see Ruoqiang
Charleroi Belgium 21 I5
Charles, Cape VA U.S.A. 64 D4
Charles City IA U.S.A. 63 I3
Charles City VA U.S.A. 64 C4
Charles Hill Botswana 50 E2
Charles Island Galápagos Ecuador see
   Santa María, Isla
Charles Point Australia 54 E3
Charleston N.Z. 59 C5
Charleston SC U.S.A. 63 L5
Charleston WV U.S.A. 63 K4
Charleston Peak NV U.S.A. 65 E2
Charlestown Ireland 21 D4
Charlestown NH U.S.A. 64 E1
Charlestown RI U.S.A. 64 F2
Charles Town WV U.S.A. 64 C3
Charleville Australia 57 D5
Charleville Ireland see Rathluirc
Charleville-Mézières France 24 G2
Charlotte NC U.S.A. 63 K4
Charlotte Amalie Virgin Is (U.S.A.) 67 L5
Charlotte Harbor b. U.S.A. 63 K6
Charlottesville VA U.S.A. 64 B3
Charlottetown Canada 61 L5
Charlton Australia 58 A6
Charlton Island Canada 63 L1
Charsadda Pak. 36 B2
Charshangngy Turkm. see Köytendag
Charters Towers Australia 56 D4
Chartres France 24 E2
Chas India 37 F5
Chase Canada 62 D1
Chashmeh-ye Palasi Iran 35 I4
Chashmeh-ye Shotoran well Iran 35 I4
Chashniki Belarus 13 F5
Chaslands Mistake c. N.Z. 59 B8
Chasong N. Korea 44 B4
Chasseral mt. Switz. 19 H7
Chassiron, Pointe de pt France 24 D3
Chastab, Kūh-e mts Iran 35 I4
Chāt Iran 35 I3
Chatanika U.S.A. 60 D3
Château-du-Loir France 24 E3
Châteaubriant France 24 D3
Châteaudun France 24 E2
Châteaulin France 24 B2
Châteaumeillant France 24 F3
Châteauneuf-sur-Loire France 24 F2
Châteauroux France 24 E3
Château-Thierry France 24 F2
Châtellerault France 24 E3
Chatham U.K. 19 H7
Chatham MA U.S.A. 64 G2
Chatham NY U.S.A. 64 E1
Chatham PA U.S.A. 64 D3
Chatham VA U.S.A. 64 C4
Chatham, Isla i. Chile 70 B8
Chatham Island Galápagos Ecuador see
   San Cristóbal, Isla
Chatham Island Samoa see Savai'i
Chatham Islands N.Z. 53 I6
Chatham Islands N.Z. 53 I6
Chatham Rise sea feature S. Pacific Ocean
   74 I8
Châtillon-sur-Seine France 24 G3
Chatkal Range mts Kyrg./Uzbek. 33 L1
Chatra India 37 F4
Chatra Nepal 37 F4
Chatsworth NJ U.S.A. 64 D3
Chattagam Bangl. see Chittagong
Chattanooga U.S.A. 63 J4
Chattarpur India see Chhatarpur
Chatteris U.K. 19 H6
Chattisgarh state India see Chhattisgarh
Chatyr-Tash Kyrg. 33 M1
Chauhtan India 36 B4
Chauk Myanmar 37 H5
Chaumont France 24 G2
Chaunskaya Guba b. Rus. Fed. 29 R3
Chauny France 24 F2
Chausy Belarus see Chavusy
Chautauqua, Lake NY U.S.A. 64 B1
Chauter Afgh. 36 A3
Chavakachcheri Sri Lanka 38 D4
Chaves Port. 25 C3
Chavuma Zambia 49 C5
Chavusy Belarus 13 F5
Chayatyn, Khrebet ridge Rus. Fed. 44 E1
Chayevo Rus. Fed. 12 H4
Chaykovskiy Rus. Fed. 11 Q4
Chazhegovo Rus. Fed. 12 L3
Cheadle U.K. 19 F6
Cheat r. WV U.S.A. 64 B3
Cheb Czech Rep. 17 N5
Chebba Tunisia 26 D7

Cheboksarskoye Vodokhranilishche resr
   Rus. Fed. 12 J5
Cheboksary Rus. Fed. 12 J4
Cheboygan U.S.A. 63 K2
Chech'ŏn S. Korea 45 C5
Cheddar U.K. 19 E7
Cheektowaga NY U.S.A. 64 B1
Cheepie Australia 58 B1
Cheetham, Cape Antarctica 76 H2
Chefoo China see Yantai
Chefornak U.S.A. 60 B3
Chegdomyn Rus. Fed. 44 D2
Chegga Mauritania 46 C2
Chegutu Zimbabwe 49 D5
Chehalis U.S.A. 62 C2
Chehel Chashmeh, Kūh-e hill Iran 35 G4
Cheju S. Korea 45 B6
Cheju-do i. S. Korea 45 B6
Cheju-haehyŏp sea chan. S. Korea 45 B6
Chekhov Sakhalinskaya Oblast' Rus. Fed.
   44 F3
Chekhov Moskovskaya Oblast' Rus. Fed.
   13 H5
Chekiang prov. China see Zhejiang
Chekichler Turkm. see Çekiçler
Chekunda Rus. Fed. 44 D2
Chela, Serra da mts Angola 49 B5
Chelan, Lake U.S.A. 62 C2
Cheleken Turkm. see Hazar
Chélif, Oued r. Alg. 25 G5
Cheline Moz. 51 L2
Chelkar Kazakh. see Shalkar
Chełm Poland 13 D6
Chelmer r. U.K. 19 H7
Chełmno Poland 17 Q4
Chelmsford U.K. 19 H7
Cheltenham U.K. 19 E7
Chelva Spain 25 F4
Chelyabinsk Rus. Fed. 28 H4
Chelyuskin Rus. Fed. 77 E1
Chemba Moz. 49 D5
Chêm Co l. China 36 D2
Chemnitz Germany 17 N5
Chemulpo S. Korea see Inch'ŏn
Chenab r. India/Pak. 36 B3
Chenachane, Oued watercourse Alg. 46 C2
Chendir r. Turkm. see Çendir
Chengalpattu India see Chengalpattu
Chengde China 43 L4
Chengdu China 42 I6
Chengjiang China see Taihe
Chengtu China see Chengdu
Chengxian China 43 J6
Chenkaladi Sri Lanka 38 D4
Chennai India 38 D3
Chenqing China see Chenqing
Chenqingqiao China see Chenqing
Chentejn Nuruu mts Mongolia 43 J3
Chenzhou China 43 K7
Chepén Peru 68 C5
Chepes Arg. 70 C4
Chepo Panama 67 I7
Chepstow U.K. 19 E7
Cheptsa r. Rus. Fed. 12 K4
Chera state India see Kerala
Cherbaniani Reef India 38 A3
Cherbourg France 24 D2
Cherchell Alg. 25 H5
Cherchen China see Qiemo
Cherdakly Rus. Fed. 13 K5
Cherdyn' Rus. Fed. 11 R3
Chereapani reef India see Byramgore Reef
Cheremkhovo Rus. Fed. 42 I2
Cheremshany Rus. Fed. 44 D3
Cheremukhovka Rus. Fed. 12 K4
Cherepanovo Rus. Fed. 28 J4
Cherepovets Rus. Fed. 12 H4
Cherevkovo Rus. Fed. 12 J3
Chergui, Chott ech imp. l. Alg. 22 D5
Chéria Alg. 26 B7
Cheriton VA U.S.A. 64 D4
Cheriyam atoll India 38 B4
Cherkasy Ukr. 13 G6
Cherkessk Rus. Fed. 13 I7
Cherla India 38 D2
Chernaya Rus. Fed. 12 M1
Chernava Rus. Fed. 13 H6
Chernigov Ukr. see Chernihiv
Chernihivka Rus. Fed. 44 D3
Chernihiv Ukr. 13 F6
Cherninivka Ukr. 13 H7
Chernobyl' Ukr. see Chornobyl'
Chernogorsk Rus. Fed. 42 G2
Chernovtsy Ukr. see Chernivtsi
Chernoye More sea Asia/Europe see
   Black Sea
Chernushka Rus. Fed. 11 R4
Chernyakhiv Ukr. 13 F6
Chernyakhovsk Rus. Fed. 15 L9
Chernyanka Rus. Fed. 13 H6
Chernyayeve Rus. Fed. 44 B1
Chernyshevsk Rus. Fed. 43 L2
Chernyshevskiy Rus. Fed. 29 M3
Chernyshkovskiy Rus. Fed. 13 I6
Chernyye Zemli reg. Rus. Fed. 13 J7
Chernyy Irtysh r. China/Kazakh. see
   Ertix He
Chernyy Porog Rus. Fed. 12 G3
Chernyy Yar Rus. Fed. 13 J6
Cherrapunji India 37 G4
Cherry Hill NJ U.S.A. 64 D3
Cherry Island Solomon Is 53 G3
Cherry Lake CA U.S.A. 65 C1
Cherskiy Rus. Fed. 77 C2
Cherskiy Range mts Rus. Fed. see
   Cherskogo, Khrebet
Cherskogo, Khrebet mts Rus. Fed. 29 P3
Cherskogo, Khrebet mts Rus. Fed. 43 K2
Chertkov Ukr. see Chortkiv
Chertkovo Rus. Fed. 13 I6
Cherven Bryag Bulg. 27 K3
Chervonoarmeyskoye Ukr. see
   Vil'nyans'k
Chervonoarmiys'k Donets'ka Oblast' Ukr.
   see Krasnoarmiys'k
Chervonoarmiys'k Rivnens'ka Oblast' Ukr.
   see Radyvyliv
Chervonograd Ukr. see Chervonohrad
Chervonohrad Ukr. 13 E6
Chervyen' Belarus 13 F5
Cherwell r. U.K. 19 F7
Cherykaw Belarus 13 F5
Chesapeake VA U.S.A. 64 D4
Chesapeake Bay Maryland/Virginia U.S.A.
   64 C3
Chesham U.K. 19 G7
Cheshire Plain U.K. 18 E5
Cheshskaya Guba b. Rus. Fed. 12 J2
Cheshunt U.K. 19 H7
Chesnokovka Rus. Fed. see Novoaltaysk
Chester U.K. 18 E5
Chester SC U.S.A. 63 K5
Chester r. MD U.S.A. 64 D3
Chester CA U.S.A. 62 C4
Chesterfield U.K. 18 F5

Chesterfield VA U.S.A. 64 C4
Chesterfield, Îles is New Caledonia 53 F3
Chesterfield Inlet Canada 61 I3
Chesterfield Inlet Canada 61 I3
Chester-le-Street U.K. 18 F4
Chestertown MD U.S.A. 64 C3
Chestertown NY U.S.A. 64 E1
Chestnut Ridge PA U.S.A. 64 B2
Chesuncook Lake U.S.A. 63 N2
Chetaïbi Alg. 26 B6
Chetlat i. India 38 B4
Chetumal Mex. 66 F5
Chetwynd Canada 60 F4
Cheviot N.Z. 59 D6
Cheviot Hills U.K. 18 E3
Cheviot Range hills Australia 56 C5
Cheyenne WY U.S.A. 62 G3
Cheyenne r. U.S.A. 62 G3
Cheyenne Wells U.S.A. 62 G4
Cheyne Bay Australia 55 B8
Cheyur India 38 D3
Chhapra India 37 F4
Chhata India 36 D4
Chhatak Bangl. 37 G4
Chhatarpur Jharkhand India 37 F4
Chhatarpur Madh. Prad. India 36 D4
Chhatr Pak. 36 B3
Chhatrapur India see Chatrapur
Chhattisgarh state India 37 E5
Chhindwara India 36 D5
Chhitkul India 36 D3
Chhukha Bhutan 37 G4
Chiai Taiwan 43 M8
Chiamboni Somalia 48 E4
Chiange Angola 49 B5
Chiang Mai Thai. 31 I5
Chiang Rai Thai. 31 I5
Chiari Italy 26 C2
Chiavenna Italy 26 C1
Chiayi Taiwan see Chiai
Chiba Japan 45 F6
Chibi China 43 K7
Chibia Angola 49 B5
Chibizovka Rus. Fed. see Zherdevka
Chiboma Moz. 49 D6
Chibougamau Canada 63 M2
Chibu-Sangaku National Park Japan 45 E5
Chibuto Moz. 51 K3
Chicacole India see Srikakulam
Chicago U.S.A. 63 J3
Chichagof Island U.S.A. 60 E4
Chichaoua Morocco 22 C5
Chichatka Rus. Fed. 44 A1
Chichester U.K. 19 G8
Chichester Range mts Australia 54 B5
Chichgarh India 38 D1
Chichibu Japan 45 E6
Chichibu-Tama Kokuritsu-kōen Japan
   45 E6
Chichijima-rettō is Japan 45 F8
Chickasha U.S.A. 62 H4
Chiclana de la Frontera Spain 25 C5
Chiclayo Peru 68 C5
Chico r. Arg. 70 C6
Chico r. Arg. 70 C7
Chico CA U.S.A. 62 C4
Chicomo Moz. 51 L3
Chicopee MA U.S.A. 64 E1
Chicoutimi Canada 61 K5
Chicualacuala Moz. 51 J2
Chidambaram India 38 C4
Chidenguele Moz. 51 L3
Chidley, Cape Canada 61 L3
Chido China see Sêndo
Chido S. Korea 45 B6
Chiducuane Moz. 51 L3
Chiemsee l. Germany 17 N7
Chiengmai Thai. see Chiang Mai
Chieti Italy 26 F3
Chifeng China 43 L4
Chifre, Serra do mts Brazil 71 C2
Chiganak Kazakh. 42 C3
Chiginagak Volcano, Mount U.S.A. 60 C4
Chigu China 37 G3
Chigubo Moz. 51 L2
Chigu Co l. China 37 G3
Chihli, Gulf of China see Bo Hai
Chihuahua Mex. 66 C3
Chili Kazakh. 42 C3
Chikalda India 36 D5
Chikhali Kalan Parasia India 36 D5
Chikhli India 38 C1
Chikishlyar Turkm. see Çekiçler
Chikodi India 38 B2
Chikmagalur India 38 B3
Chilako r. Canada 62 C1
Chilas Jammu and Kashmir 36 C1
Chilaw Sri Lanka 38 C5
Childers Australia 56 F5
Childress U.S.A. 62 G5
Chile country S. America 70 B4
Chile Basin sea feature S. Pacific Ocean
   75 O8
Chile Chico Chile 70 B7
Chile Rise sea feature S. Pacific Ocean 75 O8
Chilgir Rus. Fed. 13 J7
Chilia-Nouă Ukr. see Kiliya
Chilika Lake India 38 E2
Chililabombwe Zambia 49 C5
Chilko Lake Canada 62 C1
Chillán Chile 70 B5
Chillicothe MO U.S.A. 63 I4
Chillicothe OH U.S.A. 63 K4
Chilliwack Canada 62 C1
Chilo India 36 C4
Chiloé, Isla de i. Chile 70 B6
Chiloé, Isla Grande de i. Chile see
   Chiloé, Isla de
Chilpancingo Mex. 66 E5
Chilpancingo de los Bravos Mex. see
   Chilpancingo
Chilpi Jammu and Kashmir 36 C1
Chiltern Hills U.K. 19 G7
Chiluage Angola 49 C4
Chilubi Zambia 49 C5
Chilung Taiwan 43 M7
Chilwa, Lake Malawi 49 D5
Chimala Tanz. 49 D4
Chimaltenango Guat. 66 F6
Chimbas Arg. 70 C4
Chimborazo mt. Ecuador 68 C4
Chimbote Peru 68 C5
Chimboy Uzbek. 35 J2
Chimboy Uzbek. see Chimboy
Chimian Pak. 36 C3
Chimishliya Moldova see Cimişlia
Chimkent Kazakh. see Shymkent
Chimoio Moz. 49 D5
Chimtargha, Qullai mt. Tajik. 33 K2
Chimtorga, Gora mt. Tajik. see
   Chimtargha, Qullai
China country Asia 42 H5
China, Republic of country Asia see Taiwan
China Lake CA U.S.A. 65 D3
Chinandega Nicaragua 66 G6
China Point CA U.S.A. 65 C4
Chincha Alta Peru 68 C6
Chinchaga r. Canada 60 G4
Chinchilla Australia 58 E1
Chincholi India 38 C2
Chinchorro, Banco sea feature Mex. 67 G5

Chincoteague Bay *Maryland/Virginia* U.S.A. 64 D4
Chinde Moz. 49 D5
Chindo S. Korea 45 B6
Chin-do i. S. Korea 45 B6
Chindwin r. Myanmar 37 H5
Chinese Turkestan *aut. reg.* China see Xinjiang Uygur Zizhiqu
Chinghai *prov.* China see Qinghai
Chingiz-Tau, Khrebet *mts* Kazakh. 42 D3
Chingleput India see Chengalpattu
Chingola Zambia 49 C5
Chinguar Angola 49 B5
Chinguetti Mauritania 46 B2
Chinhae S. Korea 45 C6
Chinhoyi Zimbabwe 49 D5
Chini India see Kalpa
Chining China see Jining
Chiniot Pak. 38 L3
Chinju S. Korea 45 C6
Chinle U.S.A. 62 F4
Chinnamp'o N. Korea see Namp'o
Chinnur India 38 C2
Chino Creek *watercourse* AZ U.S.A. 65 F3
Chinon France 24 E3
Chinook Trough *sea feature* N. Pacific Ocean 74 I3
Chino Valley U.S.A. 62 E5
Chintamani India 38 C3
Chioggia Italy 26 E2
Chios Greece 27 L5
Chios i. Greece 27 K5
Chipata Zambia 49 D5
Chipchihua, Sierra de *mts* Arg. 70 C6
Chipindo Angola 49 B5
Chipinga Zimbabwe see Chipinge
Chipinge Zimbabwe 49 D6
Chippenham U.K. 19 E7
Chipping Norton U.K. 19 F7
Chipping Sodbury U.K. 19 E7
Chipurupalle *Andhra Prad.* India 38 D2
Chipurupalle *Andhra Prad.* India 38 D2
Chiquinquira Col. 68 D2
Chir r. Rus. Fed. 13 I6
Chirada India 38 D3
Chirala India 38 D3
Chiras Afgh. 36 I4
Chirchiq Uzbek. 33 K1
Chiredzi Zimbabwe 49 D6
Chirfa Niger 46 E2
Chiricahua Peak U.S.A. 62 F5
Chirikof Island U.S.A. 60 C4
Chiriquí, Golfo de b. Panama 67 H7
Chiriquí, Volcán de vol. Panama see Barú, Volcán
Chiri-san *mt.* S. Korea 45 B6
Chirk U.K. 19 D6
Chirnside U.K. 20 G5
Chirripo *mt.* Costa Rica 67 H7
Chisamba Zambia 49 C5
Chisasibi Canada 61 K4
Chishima-retto is Rus. Fed. see Kuril Islands
Chishtian Mandi Pak. 33 L4
Chishui China 42 J7
Chisimaio Somalia see Kismaayo
Chişinău Moldova 27 M1
Chistopol' Rus. Fed. 12 K5
Chita Rus. Fed. 43 K2
Chitado Angola 49 B5
Chitaldrug India see Chitradurga
Chitalwana India 36 B4
Chitambo Zambia 49 C5
Chita Oblast' *admin. div.* Rus. Fed. see Chitinskaya Oblast'
Chitato Angola 49 C4
Chitembo Angola 49 B5
Chitina U.S.A. 60 D3
Chitinskaya Oblast' *admin. div.* Rus. Fed. 44 I1
Chitipa Malawi 49 D4
Chitkul India see Chhitkul
Chitobe Moz. 49 D6
Chitoor India see Chittoor
Chitor India see Chittaurgarh
Chitose Japan 44 F4
Chitradurga India 38 C3
Chitrakoot India 36 E4
Chitrakut India see Chitrakoot
Chitral Pak. 38 L2
Chitral r. Pak. 36 B2
Chitravati r. India 38 C3
Chitrod India 38 D3
Chitré Panama 67 H7
Chittagong Bangl. 37 G5
Chittaurgarh India 38 C4
Chittoor India 38 C3
Chittor India see Chittoor
Chittorgarh India see Chittaurgarh
Chittur India 38 C4
Chitungwiza Zimbabwe 49 D5
Chiu Lung H.K. China see Kowloon
Chiume Angola 49 C5
Chivasso Italy 26 B2
Chivhu Zimbabwe 49 D5
Chivilcoy Arg. 70 D4
Chizarira National Park Zimbabwe 49 C5
Chizha Vtoraya Kazakh. 13 K6
Chizu Japan 45 D6
Chkalov Rus. Fed. see Orenburg
Chkalovsk Rus. Fed. 12 I4
Chkalovskoye Rus. Fed. 44 D3
Chlef Alg. 25 G5
Chloride AZ U.S.A. 65 E3
Chlya, Ozero l. Rus. Fed. 44 F1
Chobe National Park Botswana 49 C5
Choele Choel Arg. 70 C5
Chogar r. Rus. Fed. 44 D1
Chogori Feng *mt.* China/Jammu and Kashmir see K2
Chograyskoye Vodokhranilishche *resr* Rus. Fed. 13 J7
Choiseul i. Solomon Is 53 F2
Choix Mex. 66 C3
Chojnice Poland 17 P4
Chōkai-san vol. Japan 45 F5
Ch'ok'ē mts Eth. 48 D2
Ch'ok'ē Range Mountains Eth. see Ch'ok'ē
Chokola *mt.* China 38 E3
Chokue Moz. see Chókwé
Chokurdakh Rus. Fed. 29 P2
Chókwé Moz. 51 K3
Cholame U.S.A. 65 B3
Cholet France 24 D3
Choluteca Hond. 67 G6
Choma Zambia 49 C5
Chomo Ganggar *mt.* China 37 G3
Chomo Lhari *mt.* China/Bhutan 37 G4
Chomutov Czech Rep. 17 N5
Ch'ŏnan S. Korea 45 B5
Chon Buri Thai. 31 J5
Ch'ŏnch'ŏn N. Korea 44 B4
Chone Ecuador 68 B4
Ch'ŏngch'ŏn-gang r. N. Korea 45 B5
Ch'ŏngdo S. Korea 45 C6
Chonggye China see Qonggyai
Ch'ŏngjin N. Korea 44 C4
Ch'ŏngju S. Korea 45 B5
Chongkü China 37 I3
Chongming Dao i. China 43 M6
Chongoroi Angola 49 B5

Chŏngp'yŏng N. Korea 45 B5
Chongqing China 42 J7
Chongqing *municipality* China 42 J6
Chonguene Moz. 51 K3
Ch'ŏngŭp S. Korea 45 B6
Chŏnju S. Korea 45 B6
Chonogol Mongolia 43 L3
Chopda India 36 B4
Chor Pak. 36 B4
Chora Sfakion Greece 27 K7
Chorley U.K. 18 E5
Chornobyl' Ukr. 13 F6
Chornomors'ke Ukr. 27 O2
Chortkiv Ukr. 13 E6
Chōshi Japan 45 F6
Chosŏn *country* Asia see South Korea
Chosŏn-minjujuǔi-inmin-konghwaguk *country* Asia see North Korea
Choszczno Poland 17 O4
Chota Peru 68 C5
Chota Sinchula *hill* India 37 G4
Choti Pak. 36 B3
Choûm Mauritania 46 B2
Chowchilla CA U.S.A. 65 B2
Chowghat India see Chavakkad
Choybalsan Mongolia 43 K3
Choyr Mongolia 43 J3
Chřiby *hills* Czech Rep. 17 P6
Chrissiesmeer S. Africa 51 J4
Christchurch N.Z. 59 D6
Christchurch U.K. 19 F8
Christian, Cape Canada 61 L2
Christiana S. Africa 51 G4
Christiana Norway see Oslo
Christiansburg VA U.S.A. 64 A4
Christiansdhåb Greenland see Qasigiannguit
Christina, Mount N.Z. 59 B7
Christmas Island *terr.* Indian Ocean 41 C9
Christopher, Lake *salt flat* Australia 55 D6
Chrysochou Bay Cyprus see Chrysochou Bay
Chrysochous, Kolpos b. Cyprus see Chrysochou Bay
Chu Kazakh. see Shu
Chu r. Kazakh./Kyrg. 42 B4
Chuadanga Bangl. 37 G5
Chuali, Lago l. Moz. 51 K3
Chuanhui China see Zhoukou
Chubarovka Ukr. see Polohy
Chubartau Kazakh. see Barshatas
Chuchkovo Rus. Fed. 13 I5
Chudniv Ukr. 13 F6
Chudovo Rus. Fed. 12 F4
Chudskoye, Ozero l. Estonia/Rus. Fed. see Peipus, Lake
Chugach Mountains U.S.A. 60 D3
Chūgoku-sanchi *mts* Japan 45 D6
Chugqênsumdo China see Jigzhi
Chuguchak China see Tacheng
Chuguyev Ukr. see Chuhuyiv
Chuguyevka Rus. Fed. 44 D3
Chuhuyiv Ukr. 13 H6
Chu-Iliyskiye Gory *mts* Kazakh. 42 C4
Chujiang China see Shimen
Chukchagirskoye, Ozero l. Rus. Fed. 44 E1
Chukchi Abyssal Plain *sea feature* Arctic Ocean 77 B1
Chukchi Peninsula Rus. Fed. see Chukotskiy Poluostrov
Chukchi Plateau *sea feature* Arctic Ocean 77 B1
Chukchi Sea Rus. Fed./U.S.A. 29 T3
Chukhloma Rus. Fed. 12 I4
Chukotskiy, Mys c. Rus. Fed. 60 A3
Chukotskiy Poluostrov *pen.* Rus. Fed. 29 T3
Chulakkurgan Kazakh. see Sholakkorgan
Chulaktau Kazakh. see Karatau
Chula Vista CA U.S.A. 65 D4
Chulucanas Peru 68 B5
Chulung Pass Pak. 36 D2
Chulym r. Rus. Fed. 28 J4
Chumar Jammu and Kashmir 36 D2
Chumbicha Arg. 70 C4
Chumda China 37 I2
Chumikan Rus. Fed. 29 O4
Chumphon Thai. 31 I5
Chunar India 37 E4
Ch'unch'ŏn S. Korea 45 B5
Chunchura India 37 G5
Chundzha Kazakh. 42 E4
Chunga Zambia 49 C5
Chung-hua Jen-min Kung-ho-kuo *country* Asia see China
Chung-hua Min-kuo *country* Asia see Taiwan
Ch'ungju S. Korea 45 B5
Chungking China see Chongqing
Ch'ungmu S. Korea see T'ongyŏng
Chŭngsan N. Korea 45 B5
Chunskiy Rus. Fed. 42 H1
Chunya r. Rus. Fed. 29 K3
Chupa Rus. Fed. 14 Q4
Chūplū Iran 35 G3
Chuquicamata Chile 70 C2
Chur Switz. 24 I3
Churachandpur India 37 H4
Churapcha Rus. Fed. 29 O3
Churchill r. Man. Canada 61 I4
Churchill r. Nfld. and Lab. Canada 61 L4
Churchill, Cape Canada 61 I4
Churchill Mountains Antarctica 76 H1
Churchville VA U.S.A. 64 A3
Churia Ghati Hills Nepal 37 F4
Churu India 37 H3
Churún-Merú *waterfall* Venez. see Angel Falls
Chushul Jammu and Kashmir 36 D2
Chusovaya r. Rus. Fed. 11 R4
Chusovoy Rus. Fed. 11 R4
Chust Ukr. see Khust
Chute-des-Passes Canada 63 M2
Chutia Assam India 37 H4
Chutia *Jharkhand* India 37 F5
Chuuk is Micronesia 74 G5
Chuxiong China 42 I7
Chüy r. Kazakh./Kyrg. see Chu
Chymyshliya Moldova see Cimişlia
Chyulu Hills National Park Kenya 48 D4
Ciadâr-Lunga Moldova see Ciadir-Lunga
Ciadir-Lunga Moldova 27 M1
Cianorte Brazil 70 F2
Čičarija *mts* Croatia 26 E2
Cide Turkey 34 D2
Ciechanów Poland 17 R4
Ciego de Ávila Cuba 67 I4
Ciénaga Col. 68 D1
Cienfuegos Cuba 67 H4
Cieza Spain 25 F4
Çiftlik Turkey see Kelkit
Cifuentes Spain 25 E3
Cigüela r. Spain 25 E4
Cihanbeyli Turkey 34 D3
Cijara, Embalse de *resr* Spain 25 D4
Cilacap Indon. 41 C8
Çıldır Turkey 35 F2
Çıldır Gölü l. Turkey 35 F2
Çıldıroba Turkey 39 C1

Cilento e del Vallo di Diano, Parco Nazionale del *nat. park* Italy 26 F4
Cilician Gates *pass* Turkey see Gülek Boğazı
Cill Airne Ireland see Killarney
Cill Chainnigh Ireland see Kilkenny
Cill Mhantáin Ireland see Wicklow
Çilmämmetgum *des.* Turkm. 35 I2
Cilo Daği *mt.* Turkey 35 G3
Çiloy Adası i. Azer. 35 H2
Cimarron r. U.S.A. 62 H4
Cimişlia Moldova 27 M1
Cimone, Monte mt. Italy 26 D2
Cîmpina Romania see Câmpina
Cîmpulung Romania see Câmpulung
Cîmpulung Moldovenesc Romania see Câmpulung Moldovenesc
Çınar Turkey 35 F3
Cinaruco-Capanaparo, Parque Nacional *nat. park* Venez. 68 E2
Cinca r. Spain 25 G3
Cinco de Outubro Angola see Xá-Muteba
Cinderford U.K. 19 E7
Çine Turkey 27 M6
Cintalapa Mex. 66 F5
Cinto, Monte *mt.* France 24 I5
Circeo, Parco Nazionale del *nat. park* Italy 26 E4
Circle AK U.S.A. 60 D3
Cirebon Indon. 41 C8
Cirencester U.K. 19 F7
Cirò Marina Italy 26 G5
Cirta Alg. see Constantine
Citlaltépetl vol. Mex. see Orizaba, Pico de
Çitluk Bos.-Herz. 26 G3
Citrus Heights CA U.S.A. 65 B1
Città di Castello Italy 26 E3
Ciucaş, Vârful mt. Romania 27 K2
Ciudad Acuña Mex. 62 G6
Ciudad Altamirano Mex. 66 D5
Ciudad Bolívar Venez. 68 F2
Ciudad Camargo Mex. 66 C3
Ciudad Constitución Mex. 66 B3
Ciudad del Carmen Mex. 66 F5
Ciudad de Panamá Panama see Panama City
Ciudad de Valles Mex. 66 E4
Ciudad Flores Guat. see Flores
Ciudad Guayana Venez. 68 F2
Ciudad Guzmán Mex. 66 D5
Ciudad Juárez Mex. 66 C2
Ciudad Mante Mex. 66 E4
Ciudad Obregón Mex. 66 C3
Ciudad Real Spain 25 E4
Ciudad Río Bravo Mex. 62 H6
Ciudad Rodrigo Spain 25 C3
Ciudad Trujillo Dom. Rep. see Santo Domingo
Ciudad Victoria Mex. 66 E4
Ciutadella Spain 25 H3
Civa Burnu pt Turkey 34 E2
Cividale del Friuli Italy 26 E1
Civitanova Marche Italy 26 E3
Civitavecchia Italy 26 D3
Çivril Turkey 35 F3
Cizre Turkey 35 F3
Clacton-on-Sea U.K. 19 I7
Clady U.K. 21 I3
Claire, Lake Canada 60 G4
Clairfontaine Alg. see El Aouinet
Clamecy France 24 F3
Clane Ireland 21 F4
Clanwilliam Dam S. Africa 50 D7
Clara Ireland 21 E4
Claraville Australia 56 C3
Clare N.S.W. Australia 58 A4
Clare S.A. Australia 57 B7
Clare r. Ireland 21 C4
Clarecastle Ireland 21 D5
Clare Island Ireland 21 B4
Claremont NH U.S.A. 64 E1
Claremorris Ireland 21 D4
Clarence r. Australia 58 F2
Clarence N.Z. 59 D6
Clarence r. N.Z. 59 D6
Clarence Island Antarctica 76 A2
Clarence Town Bahamas 63 M7
Clarendon PA U.S.A. 64 B2
Clarenville Canada 61 M5
Claresholm Canada 62 E1
Clarie Coast Antarctica see Wilkes Coast
Clarington OH U.S.A. 64 A3
Clarion PA U.S.A. 64 B2
Clarion r. PA U.S.A. 64 B2
Clarión, Isla i. Mex. 66 B5
Clarkebury S. Africa 51 I6
Clarke Range Australia 56 D4
Clarke River Australia 56 D3
Clark Mountain CA U.S.A. 65 E3
Clarksburg WV U.S.A. 64 A4
Clarksdale U.S.A. 63 I5
Clarksville AR U.S.A. 63 I4
Clarksville TN U.S.A. 63 J4
Claro r. Goiás Brazil 71 A2
Claro r. Mato Grosso Brazil 71 A1
Clashmore Ireland 21 E5
Claudy U.K. 21 E3
Clay U.K. see Cley
Clay WV U.S.A. 64 A4
Clayhole Wash *watercourse* AZ U.S.A. 65 F2
Clayton DE U.S.A. 64 D4
Clayton NM U.S.A. 62 G4
Claytor Lake VA U.S.A. 64 A4
Clear, Cape Ireland 21 C6
Clearco WV U.S.A. 64 A4
Clear Creek Ont. Canada 64 A1
Cleare, Cape U.S.A. 60 D4
Clearfield PA U.S.A. 64 B2
Clear Island Ireland 21 C6
Clear Lake IA U.S.A. 63 I3
Clear Lake CA U.S.A. 65 A1
Clear Lake UT U.S.A. 65 F1
Clearwater r. Alberta/Saskatchewan Canada 60 G4
Clearwater U.S.A. 63 K6
Cleburne U.S.A. 63 H5
Cleethorpes U.K. 18 G5
Clendenin WV U.S.A. 64 A4
Clendening Lake OH U.S.A. 64 A3
Clères France 19 I9
Clerke Reef Australia 56 B4
Clermont Australia 56 D4
Clermont-Ferrand France 24 F4
Cles Italy 26 D1
Clevedon U.K. 19 E7
Cleveland MS U.S.A. 63 I5
Cleveland OH U.S.A. 64 A3
Cleveland TN U.S.A. 63 K4
Cleveland, Cape Australia 56 D3
Cleveland, Mount U.S.A. 62 E2
Cleveland Heights OH U.S.A. 64 A3
Cleveland Hills U.K. 18 F4
Cleveleys U.K. 18 D5
Clew Bay Ireland 21 C4
Clifden Ireland 21 B4
Cliffoney Ireland 21 D3
Clifford U.K. 19 E6
Clifton Australia 58 E1
Clifton U.S.A. 62 F5
Clifton Beach Australia 56 D3
Clifton Forge VA U.S.A. 64 B4
Clifton Park NY U.S.A. 64 E1

Clinton Ont. Canada 64 A1
Clinton IA U.S.A. 63 I3
Clinton OK U.S.A. 62 H4
Clipperton, Île *terr.* N. Pacific Ocean 75 M5
Clisham hill U.K. 20 C3
Clitheroe U.K. 18 E5
Cliza Bol. 68 E7
Clocolan S. Africa 51 H5
Cloghan Ireland 21 E4
Clonakilty Ireland 21 D6
Clonbern Ireland 21 D4
Cloncurry Australia 56 C4
Cloncurry r. Australia 56 C3
Clones Ireland 21 E3
Clonmel Ireland 21 E5
Clonygowan Ireland 21 E4
Cloonbannin Ireland 21 C5
Cloonboo Ireland 21 C4
Clooney Ireland 21 D3
Cloppenburg Germany 17 I2
Cloud Peak WY U.S.A. 62 F3
Cloverdale CA U.S.A. 65 A1
Clovis CA U.S.A. 65 C2
Clovis NM U.S.A. 62 G5
Cluain Meala Ireland see Clonmel
Cluanie, Loch l. U.K. 20 D3
Cluff Lake Mine Canada 61 H3
Cluj-Napoca Romania 27 J1
Clun U.K. 19 D6
Clunes Australia 58 A6
Cluny France 24 F3
Cluses France 24 H3
Clutterbuck Hills hill Australia 55 D6
Clwydian Range hills U.K. 18 D5
Clyde r. U.K. 20 E5
Clyde NY U.S.A. 64 C1
Clyde, Firth of est. U.K. 20 E5
Clydebank U.K. 20 E5
Clyde River Canada 61 M2
Côa r. Port. 25 C3
Coachella CA U.S.A. 65 D4
Coaldale NV U.S.A. 65 D2
Coalinga CA U.S.A. 65 B2
Coalport PA U.S.A. 64 B2
Coal River Canada 60 E3
Coal Valley valley NV U.S.A. 65 E2
Coalville U.K. 19 F6
Coari Brazil 68 F4
Coari r. Brazil 68 F4
Coarsegold CA U.S.A. 65 C2
Coast Mountains Canada 60 F4
Coast Range hills Australia 57 E5
Coast Ranges mts CA U.S.A. 65 B2
Coatbridge U.K. 20 E5
Coatesville PA U.S.A. 64 D3
Coats Island Canada 61 J3
Coats Land reg. Antarctica 76 A1
Coatzacoalcos Mex. 66 F5
Cobar Australia 58 B3
Cobargo Australia 58 D6
Cobden Australia 58 A7
Cobden Ont. Canada 63 K2
Cobh Ireland 21 D6
Cobija Bol. 68 E6
Coblence Germany see Koblenz
Cobleskill NY U.S.A. 64 E1
Cobourg Peninsula Australia 54 F2
Cobram Australia 58 B5
Coburg Germany 17 M5
Coburg Island Canada 61 K2
Coca Ecuador 68 C4
Coca Spain 25 D3
Cocalinho Brazil 71 A1
Cocanada India see Kakinada
Cochabamba Bol. 68 E7
Cochin India 38 C4
Cochrane Alta Canada 62 E1
Cochrane Ont. Canada 63 K2
Cockburn Australia 57 C7
Cockburn, Mount U.S.A. 65 C7
Cockburnspath U.K. 20 G5
Cockburn Town Turks and Caicos Is see Grand Turk
Cockermouth U.K. 18 D4
Cockatoo Australia 55 D8
Cockscomb *mt.* S. Africa 50 G7
Coco r. Hond./Nicaragua 67 H6
Coco, Isla de i. N. Pacific Ocean 67 G7
Cocobeach Gabon 48 A3
Coconino Plateau AZ U.S.A. 65 F3
Cocopara National Park Australia 58 C5
Cocos Basin *sea feature* Indian Ocean 73 O5
Cocos Islands *terr.* Indian Ocean 41 B9
Cocos Ridge *sea feature* N. Pacific Ocean 75 O5
Cocuy, Sierra Nevada del *mt.* Col. 68 D2
Cod, Cape MA U.S.A. 64 F2
Codajás Brazil 68 F4
Codfish Island N.Z. 59 A8
Codigoro Italy 26 E2
Cod Island Canada 61 L4
Codlea Romania 27 K2
Codó Brazil 69 J4
Codsall U.K. 19 E6
Cod's Head hd Ireland 21 B6
Cody U.S.A. 62 F3
Coen Australia 56 C2
Coeur d'Alene U.S.A. 62 D2
Coffee Bay S. Africa 51 I6
Coffeyville U.S.A. 63 H4
Coffin Bay Australia 57 A7
Coffin Bay National Park Australia 57 A7
Coffs Harbour Australia 58 F3
Cofimvaba S. Africa 51 H6
Cognac France 24 D4
Cogo Equat. Guinea 46 D4
Coguno Moz. 51 L3
Cohoes NY U.S.A. 64 E1
Coiba, Isla de i. Panama 67 H7
Coigeach, Rubha c. U.K. 20 D2
Coihaique Chile 70 B7
Coimbatore India 38 C4
Coimbra Port. 25 B3
Coipasa, Salar de salt flat Bol. 68 E7
Coire Switz. see Chur
Colac Australia 58 A7
Colair Lake India see Kolleru Lake
Colatina Brazil 71 D2
Colby U.S.A. 62 G4
Colchester U.K. 19 H7
Colchester CT U.S.A. 64 E2
Cold Lake Canada 61 H4
Coldingham U.K. 20 G5
Coldstream U.K. 20 G5
Coleambally Australia 58 B5
Coleman r. Australia 56 C2
Coleman U.S.A. 62 H5
Colenso S. Africa 51 I5
Coleraine S. Africa 51 I5
Coleraine U.K. 21 F2
Coles, Punta de pt Peru 68 D7
Coles Bay Australia 57 [inset]
Colesberg S. Africa 51 G6
Colfax U.S.A. 62 F5
Coligny S. Africa 51 H4
Colima Mex. 66 D5
Colima, Nevado de vol. Mex. 66 D5

Coll i. U.K. 20 C4
Collado Villalba Spain 25 E3
Collarenebri Australia 58 D2
Collecchio Italy 26 D2
Collerina Australia 58 C2
Collie N.S.W. Australia 58 D3
Collie W.A. Australia 55 B8
Collier Bay Australia 54 D4
Collier Range National Park Australia 55 B6
Collingwood N.Z. 59 D5
Collins Glacier Antarctica 76 E2
Collinson Peninsula Canada 61 H2
Collipulli Chile 70 B5
Collooney Ireland 21 D3
Colmar France 24 H2
Colmenar Viejo Spain 25 E3
Colmonell U.K. 20 E5
Colne U.K. 18 E5
Cologne Germany 17 K5
Colomb-Béchar Alg. see Béchar
Colômbia Brazil 71 A3
Colombia country S. America 68 D3
Colombian Basin *sea feature* S. Atlantic Ocean 72 C5
Colombo Sri Lanka 38 C5
Colomiers France 24 E5
Colón Buenos Aires Arg. 70 D4
Colón Entre Ríos Arg. 70 E4
Colón Panama 67 I7
Colón, Archipiélago de is Ecuador see Galapagos Islands
Colona Australia 55 F7
Colonelganj India 37 E4
Colônia r. Brazil 71 D1
Colonia Agrippina Germany see Cologne
Colonia Julia Fenestris Italy see Fano
Colonial Heights VA U.S.A. 64 C4
Colonsay i. U.K. 20 C4
Colorado r. Arg. 70 D5
Colorado r. Mex./U.S.A. 65 E4
Colorado r. U.S.A. 62 H6
Colorado state U.S.A. 62 F4
Colorado City AZ U.S.A. 65 F2
Colorado Desert CA U.S.A. 65 D4
Colorado Plateau U.S.A. 62 F4
Colorado River Aqueduct *canal* CA U.S.A. 65 E3
Colorado Springs U.S.A. 62 G4
Colossae Turkey see Honaz
Colotlán Mex. 66 D4
Colquiri Bol. 68 E7
Colsterworth U.K. 19 G6
Colstrip U.S.A. 62 F2
Coltishall U.K. 19 I6
Colton CA U.S.A. 65 D3
Columbia MD U.S.A. 64 C3
Columbia MO U.S.A. 63 I4
Columbia PA U.S.A. 64 C2
Columbia SC U.S.A. 63 K5
Columbia TN U.S.A. 63 J4
Columbia r. U.S.A. 62 C2
Columbia, District of admin. dist. U.S.A. 64 C3
Columbia, Mount Canada 62 D1
Columbia Mountains Canada 62 C1
Columbia Plateau U.S.A. 62 D2
Columbine, Cape S. Africa 50 C7
Columbus U.S.A. 63 K5
Columbus IN U.S.A. 63 J4
Columbus MS U.S.A. 63 J5
Columbus NE U.S.A. 63 H3
Columbus NM U.S.A. 62 F5
Columbus OH U.S.A. 64 A3
Columbus Salt Marsh NV U.S.A. 65 C1
Colusa CA U.S.A. 65 B1
Colville r. U.S.A. 60 C2
Colville N.Z. 59 E3
Colville Channel N.Z. 59 E3
Colville Lake Canada 60 F3
Colwyn Bay U.K. 18 D5
Comacchio Italy 26 E2
Comacchio, Valli di lag. Italy 26 E2
Comai China 37 G3
Comalcalco Mex. 66 F5
Comandante Ferraz *research station* Antarctica 76 A2
Comandante Salas Arg. 70 C4
Comănești Romania 27 L1
Combarbalá Chile 70 B4
Comber U.K. 21 G3
Combermere Bay Myanmar 37 H5
Combomune Moz. 51 K2
Comboyne Australia 58 F3
Comencho, Lac l. Canada 63 L1
Comendador Dom. Rep. see Elías Piña
Comendador Gomes Brazil 71 A2
Comercinho Brazil 71 C2
Cometela Moz. 51 L1
Comilla Bangl. 37 G5
Comino, Capo c. Sardinia Italy 26 C4
Comitán de Domínguez Mex. 66 F5
Commentry France 24 F3
Committee Bay Canada 61 J3
Commonwealth Territory admin. div. Australia see Jervis Bay Territory
Como Italy 26 C2
Como, Lago di Italy see Como, Lake
Como, Lake Italy 26 C2
Como Chamling l. China 37 G3
Comodoro Rivadavia Arg. 70 C7
Comores country Africa see Comoros
Comorin, Cape India 38 C4
Comoro Islands country Africa see Comoros
Comoros country Africa 49 E5
Compiègne France 24 F2
Comprida, Ilha i. Brazil 71 B4
Comrat Moldova 27 M1
Comrie U.K. 20 F4
Cona China 37 G4
Cona Niyeo Arg. 70 C6
Conakry Guinea 46 B4
Conceição r. Brazil 71 D1
Conceição da Barra Brazil 71 D2
Conceição do Araguaia Brazil 69 I5
Conceição do Mato Dentro Brazil 71 C2
Concepción Chile 70 B5
Concepción Para. 70 E2
Concepción de la Vega Dom. Rep. see La Vega
Conception, Point CA U.S.A. 65 B3
Conchos r. Nuevo León/Tamaulipas Mex. 66 E4
Conchos r. Mex. 66 D3
Concord CA U.S.A. 65 A2
Concord NH U.S.A. 64 E1
Concórdia Arg. 70 E4
Concordia Peru 68 D4
Concordia KS U.S.A. 62 H4
Concordia S. Africa 50 C5
Concordia KS U.S.A. 62 H4
Concord Peak Afgh. 36 C1
Condamine Australia 58 E1
Condamine r. Australia 58 D1
Condega Nic. 66 [inset] I6
Condobolin Australia 58 C4
Condom France 24 E5

Condor, Cordillera del *mts* Ecuador/Peru 68 C4
Conegliano Italy 26 E2
Conemaugh r. PA U.S.A. 64 B2
Conesus Lake NY U.S.A. 64 C1
Conflict Group is P.N.G. 56 E1
Confoederatio Helvetica country Europe see Switzerland
Confusion Range mts UT U.S.A. 65 F1
Congdü China 37 F3
Congleton U.K. 18 E5
Congo country Africa 48 B4
Congo r. Congo/Dem. Rep. Congo 48 B4
Congo (Brazzaville) country Africa see Congo
Congo (Kinshasa) country Africa see Congo, Democratic Republic of the
Congo, Democratic Republic of the country Africa 48 C4
Congo, Republic of country Africa see Congo
Congo Basin Dem. Rep. Congo 48 C4
Congo Cone sea feature S. Atlantic Ocean 72 I6
Congo Free State country Africa see Congo, Democratic Republic of the
Congonhas Brazil 71 C3
Congress AZ U.S.A. 65 F3
Conimbla National Park Australia 58 D4
Coningsby U.K. 19 G5
Coniston U.K. 18 D4
Conjuboy Australia 56 D3
Conn, Lough l. Ireland 21 C3
Connacht reg. Ireland see Connaught
Connaught reg. Ireland 21 C4
Conneaut OH U.S.A. 64 A2
Connecticut state U.S.A. 64 E2
Connellsville PA U.S.A. 64 B2
Connemara reg. Ireland 21 C4
Connemara National Park Ireland 21 C4
Connors Range hills Australia 56 E4
Conoble Australia 58 B4
Conquista Brazil 71 B2
Conrad U.S.A. 62 E2
Conselheiro Lafaiete Brazil 71 C3
Consett U.K. 18 F4
Constance Germany see Konstanz
Constance, Lake Germany/Switz. 17 L7
Constância dos Baetas Brazil 68 F5
Constanța Romania 27 M2
Constantia tourist site Cyprus see Salamis
Constantine Alg. 24 F4
Constantine, Cape U.S.A. 60 C4
Constantinople Turkey see Istanbul
Contagalo Brazil 71 C3
Contamana Peru 68 C5
Contas r. Brazil 71 D1
Contria Brazil 71 B2
Contwoyto Lake Canada 60 G3
Convención Col. 68 D2
Conway AR U.S.A. 63 I4
Conway, Cape Australia 56 E4
Conway, Lake salt flat Australia 57 A6
Conway National Park Australia 56 E4
Conway Reef Fiji see Ceva-i-Ra
Conwy U.K. 18 D5
Conwy r. U.K. 18 D5
Coober Pedy Australia 55 F7
Cooch Behar India see Koch Bihar
Coochbehar India see Koch Bihar
Cook Australia 55 E7
Cook, Grand Récif de reef New Caledonia 53 G3
Cook, Mount N.Z. see Aoraki
Cookhouse S. Africa 51 G7
Cook Ice Shelf Antarctica 76 H2
Cook Inlet sea chan. U.S.A. 60 C3
Cook Islands terr. S. Pacific Ocean 74 J7
Cooksburg NY U.S.A. 64 D1
Cookstown S. Africa 51 G7
Cookstown U.K. 21 F3
Cooktown Australia 56 D2
Coolabah Australia 58 C3
Cooladdi Australia 57 C5
Coolah Australia 58 D3
Coolamon Australia 58 C5
Coolgardie Australia 55 C7
Coolibah Australia 54 E3
Cooloola National Park Australia 57 F5
Coolum Beach Australia 57 F5
Cooma Australia 58 D6
Coombah Australia 57 C7
Coonabarabran Australia 58 D3
Coonamble Australia 58 D3
Coondambo Australia 57 A6
Coondapoor India see Kundapura
Coongoola Australia 58 B1
Cooper Creek watercourse Australia 57 B6
Coopernook Australia 58 F3
Cooperstown NY U.S.A. 64 D1
Coopracambra National Park Australia 58 D6
Coorabie Australia 55 F7
Coorong National Park Australia 57 B8
Coorow Australia 55 B7
Coos Bay U.S.A. 62 B3
Cootamundra Australia 58 C5
Cootehill Ireland 21 E3
Cooyar Australia 58 E1
Copala Mex. 66 E5
Copenhagen Denmark 15 H9
Copertino Italy 26 H4
Copeton Reservoir Australia 58 E2
Copiapó Chile 70 B3
Copley Australia 57 B6
Copparo Italy 26 D2
Coppermine Canada see Kugluktuk
Coppermine r. Canada 77 L2
Copperton S. Africa 50 F5
Coqên China 37 F3
Coqên Xizang China 37 F3
Coquilhatville Dem. Rep. Congo see Mbandaka
Coquille i. Micronesia see Pikelot
Coquimbo Chile 70 B3
Corabia Romania 27 K3
Coração de Jesus Brazil 71 B2
Coracesium Turkey see Alanya
Coraki Australia 58 F2
Coral Bay Australia 55 A5
Coral Harbour Canada 61 J3
Coral Sea S. Pacific Ocean 52 F3
Coral Sea Basin S. Pacific Ocean 74 G6
Coral Sea Islands Territory terr. Australia 52 F3
Corangamite, Lake Australia 58 A7
Corat Azer. 35 H2
Corbett National Park India 36 D3
Corby U.K. 19 G6
Corcaigh Ireland see Cork
Corcoran CA U.S.A. 65 C2
Corcovado, Golfo de sea chan. Chile 70 B6
Corcyra i. Greece see Corfu
Cordele U.S.A. 63 K5

Cordelia CA U.S.A. 65 A1
Cordilheiras, Serra das hills Brazil 69 I5
Cordillera Azul, Parque Nacional nat. park Peru 68 C5
Cordillera de los Picachos, Parque Nacional nat. park Col. 68 D2
Cordillo Downs Australia 57 C5
Cordisburgo Brazil 71 B2
Córdoba Arg. 70 D4
Córdoba Veracruz Mex. 66 E5
Córdoba Spain 25 D5
Córdoba, Sierras de mts Arg. 70 D4
Cordova Spain see Córdoba
Cordova U.S.A. 60 D3
Corduba Spain see Córdoba
Corfu i. Greece 27 H5
Coria Spain 25 C4
Coribe Brazil 71 B1
Coricudgy mt. Australia 58 E4
Corigliano Calabro Italy 26 G5
Coringa Islands Australia 56 E3
Corinium U.K. see Cirencester
Corinth Greece 27 J6
Corinth MS U.S.A. 63 J5
Corinth NY U.S.A. 64 E1
Corinth, Gulf of sea chan. Greece 27 J5
Corinthus Greece see Corinth
Corinto Brazil 71 B2
Corleone Sicily Italy 26 E6
Cormeilles France 19 H9
Cornelia S. Africa 51 I4
Cornélio Procópio Brazil 71 A3
Cornélios Brazil 71 A5
Corner Brook Canada 61 M5
Corner Inlet b. Australia 58 C7
Corner Seamounts sea feature N. Atlantic Ocean 72 E3
Corneto Italy see Tarquinia
Corning NY U.S.A. 64 C1
Cornish watercourse Australia 56 D4
Corn Islands is Nicaragua see Maíz, Islas del
Corno, Monte mt. Italy 26 E3
Corno di Campo mt. Italy/Switz. 24 J3
Cornwall Canada 63 M2
Cornwallis Island Canada 61 I2
Cornwall Island Canada 61 I2
Coro Venez. 68 E1
Coroaci Brazil 71 C2
Coroatá Brazil 69 J4
Corofin Ireland 21 C5
Coromandel Brazil 71 B2
Coromandel Coast India 38 D4
Coromandel Peninsula N.Z. 59 E3
Coromandel Range hills N.Z. 59 E3
Corona CA U.S.A. 65 D4
Coronado, Bahía de b. Costa Rica 67 H7
Coronation Gulf Canada 60 G3
Coronation Island S. Atlantic Ocean 76 A2
Coronda Arg. 70 D4
Coronel Fabriciano Brazil 71 C2
Coronel Oviedo Para. 70 E3
Coronel Pringles Arg. 70 D5
Coronel Suárez Arg. 70 D5
Corovodë Albania 27 I4
Corowa Australia 58 C5
Corpus Christi U.S.A. 63 H6
Corque Bol. 68 E7
Corral de Cantos mt. Spain 25 D4
Corrandibby Range hills Australia 55 A6
Corrente Brazil 69 J6
Corrente r. Bahia Brazil 71 C1
Corrente r. Minas Gerais Brazil 71 A2
Correntes Brazil 69 H7
Correntina Brazil 71 B1
Correntina r. Brazil see Éguas
Corrib, Lough l. Ireland 21 C4
Corrientes Arg. 70 E3
Corrientes, Cabo c. Col. 68 C2
Corrientes, Cabo c. Mex. 66 C4
Corrigin Australia 55 B8
Corris U.K. 19 D6
Corry PA U.S.A. 64 B2
Corse i. France see Corsica
Corse, Cap c. Corsica France 24 I5
Corsham U.K. 19 F7
Corsica i. France 24 I5
Corsicana U.S.A. 63 H5
Corte Corsica France 24 I5
Cortegana Spain 25 C5
Cortes, Sea of g. Mex. see California, Gulf of
Cortez U.S.A. 62 F4
Cortina d'Ampezzo Italy 26 E1
Cortland NY U.S.A. 64 C1
Corton U.K. 19 I6
Cortona Italy 26 D3
Coruche Port. 25 B4
Çoruh Turkey see Artvin
Çoruh r. Turkey 35 F2
Çorum Turkey 34 D2
Corumbá Brazil 69 G7
Corumbá r. Brazil 71 A2
Corumbá de Goiás Brazil 71 A1
Corumbaíba Brazil 71 A2
Corumbaú, Ponta pt Brazil 71 D2
Corunna Spain see A Coruña
Corvallis U.S.A. 62 C3
Corwen U.K. 19 D6
Coryville PA U.S.A. 64 B2
Cos i. Greece see Kos
Cosalá Mex. 66 C4
Cosenza Italy 26 G5
Cosne-Cours-sur-Loire France 24 F3
Costa Blanca coastal area Spain 25 F4
Costa Brava coastal area Spain 25 H3
Costa de la Luz coastal area Spain 25 C5
Costa del Sol coastal area Spain 25 D5
Costa de Miskitos coastal area Nicaragua see Costa de Mosquitos
Costa de Mosquitos coastal area Nicaragua 67 H6
Costa Marques Brazil 68 F6
Costa Rica Brazil 69 H7
Costa Rica country Central America 67 H6
Costa Rica Mex. 66 C4
Costa Verde coastal area Spain 25 C2
Costermansville Dem. Rep. Congo see Bukavu
Costeşti Romania 27 K2
Cotabato Phil. 41 E7
Cotagaita Bol. 68 E8
Cotahuasi Peru 68 D7
Côte d'Azur coastal area France 24 H5
Côte d'Ivoire country Africa 46 C4
Côte Française de Somalis country Africa see Djibouti
Cotentin pen. France 19 F9
Cothi r. U.K. 19 C7
Cotiaeum Turkey see Kütahya
Cotiella mt. Spain 25 G2
Cotonou Benin 46 D4
Cotopaxi, Volcán vol. Ecuador 68 C4
Cotswold Hills U.K. 19 E7
Cottage Grove U.S.A. 62 C3
Cottbus Germany 17 O5
Cottenham U.K. 19 H6
Cottian Alps mts France/Italy 24 H4

Cottica Suriname 69 H3
Cottiennes, Alpes mts France/Italy see Cottian Alps
Coudersport PA U.S.A. 64 B2
Couedic, Cape du Australia 57 B8
Coulman Island Antarctica 76 H2
Coulterville CA U.S.A. 65 B3
Council Bluffs U.S.A. 63 H3
Councillor Island Canada 57 [inset]
Courland Lagoon b. Lith./Rus. Fed. 15 L9
Courtenay Canada 62 C2
Courtmacsherry Ireland 21 D6
Courtmacsherry Bay Ireland 21 D6
Courtown Ireland 21 F5
Courtrai Belgium see Kortrijk
Coutances France 24 D2
Cove Fort UT U.S.A. 65 F1
Cove Mountains hills PA U.S.A. 64 B3
Coventry U.K. 19 F6
Covesville VA U.S.A. 64 B4
Covilhã Port. 25 C3
Covington VA U.S.A. 64 A4
Cowal, Lake dry lake Australia 58 C4
Cowan, Lake salt flat Australia 55 C7
Cowangarzê China 37 I2
Cowcowing Lakes salt flat Australia 55 B7
Cowdenbeath U.K. 20 F4
Cowell Australia 57 B7
Cowes U.K. 19 F8
Cowley Australia 58 B1
Cowper Point Canada 61 G2
Cowra Australia 58 D4
Cox r. Australia 56 A2
Coxá r. Brazil 71 B1
Coxen Hole Hond. see Roatán
Coxilha de Santana hills Brazil/Uruguay 70 E4
Coxilha Grande hills Brazil 70 F3
Coxim Brazil 69 H7
Cox's Bazar Bangl. 37 G5
Coyhaique Chile see Coihaique
Coyote Lake CA U.S.A. 65 D3
Coyote Peak hill AZ U.S.A. 65 E4
Cozhê China 37 F2
Cozie, Alpi mts France/Italy see Cottian Alps
Cozumel Mex. 67 G4
Cozumel, Isla de i. Mex. 67 G4
Craboon Australia 58 D4
Cracovia Poland see Kraków
Cracow Australia 56 E5
Cracow Poland see Kraków
Cradle Mountain Lake St Clair National Park Australia 57 [inset]
Cradock S. Africa 51 G7
Craig U.K. 20 D3
Craig CO U.S.A. 62 F3
Craigavon U.K. 21 F3
Craigieburn Australia 58 B6
Craignure U.K. 20 D4
Craigsville WV U.S.A. 64 A3
Crail U.K. 20 G4
Crailsheim Germany 17 M6
Craiova Romania 27 J2
Cramlington U.K. 18 F3
Cranberry Portage Canada 62 G1
Cranborne Chase for. U.K. 19 E8
Cranbourne Australia 58 B7
Cranbrook Canada 62 D2
Cranston RI U.S.A. 64 F2
Cranz Rus. Fed. see Zelenogradsk
Crary Ice Rise Antarctica 76 I1
Crary Mountains Antarctica 76 J1
Crateús Brazil 69 J5
Crato Brazil 69 K5
Crawley U.K. 19 G7
Creag Meagaidh mt. U.K. 20 E4
Credenhill U.K. 19 E6
Crediton U.K. 19 D8
Creel Mex. 66 C3
Cree Lake Canada 60 H4
Crema Italy 26 C2
Cremona Italy 26 D2
Crépy-en-Valois France 24 F2
Cres i. Croatia 26 F2
Crescent City CA U.S.A. 62 C3
Crescent Head Australia 58 F3
Cressy Australia 58 A7
Creston Canada 62 D2
Creston IA U.S.A. 63 I3
Crestview U.S.A. 63 J5
Creswick Australia 58 A6
Creta i. Greece see Crete
Crete U.K. 19 G8
Creus, Cap de i. Spain 25 H2
Creuse r. France 24 E3
Crevasse Valley Glacier Antarctica 76 J1
Crewe U.K. 19 E5
Crewe VA U.S.A. 64 B4
Crewkerne U.K. 19 E8
Crianlarich U.K. 20 E4
Criccieth U.K. 19 C6
Criciúma Brazil 71 A5
Criel U.K. 20 F4
Criffel hill U.K. 20 F6
Criffell hill U.K. see Criffel
Crikvenica Croatia 26 F2
Crimea pen. Ukr. 34 D1
Crimond U.K. 20 H3
Crisfield MD U.S.A. 64 D4
Cristalândia Brazil 69 I6
Cristalina Brazil 71 B2
Cristalino r. Brazil see Mariembero
Cristóbal Colón, Pico mt. Col. 68 D1
Crixás Brazil 71 A1
Crixás Açu r. Brazil 71 A1
Crixás Mirim r. Brazil 71 A1
Crni Vrh mt. Serbia 27 J2
Črnomelj Slovenia 26 F2
Croagh Patrick hill Ireland 21 C4
Croajingolong National Park Australia 58 D6
Croatia country Europe 26 G2
Crocker, Banjaran mts Malaysia 41 D7
Croker Island Australia 54 F2
Cromarty U.K. 20 E3
Cromarty Firth est. U.K. 20 E3
Cromer U.K. 19 I6
Crook U.K. 18 F4
Crooked Island Bahamas 67 J4
Crooked Island Passage Bahamas 67 J4
Crookston U.S.A. 63 H2
Crookwell Australia 58 D5
Croom Ireland 21 D5
Croppa Creek Australia 58 E2
Crosby U.K. 18 D5
Crosby ND U.S.A. 62 F1
Cross City U.S.A. 63 K6
Cross Fell hill U.K. 18 E4
Crossgar U.K. 21 G3
Crosshaven Ireland 21 D6
Cross Inn U.K. 19 C6
Cross Lake Canada 61 I4
Cross Lake NY U.S.A. 64 C1
Crossmaglen U.K. 21 F3
Crossman Peak AZ U.S.A. 65 E3
Croton Italy see Crotone
Crotone Italy 26 G5
Crouch r. U.K. 19 H7
Crowal watercourse Australia 58 C3
Crowborough U.K. 19 H7

Crowdy Bay National Park Australia 58 F3
Crowland U.K. 19 G6
Crowley, Lake CA U.S.A. 65 C2
Crown Prince Olav Coast Antarctica 76 D2
Crown Princess Martha Coast Antarctica 76 B1
Crows Nest Australia 58 F1
Croydon Australia 56 C3
Crozet VA U.S.A. 64 B3
Crozet, Îles is Indian Ocean 73 L9
Crozet Basin sea feature Indian Ocean 73 M8
Crozet Plateau sea feature Indian Ocean 73 K8
Crozon France 24 B2
Cruden Bay U.K. 20 H3
Crumlin U.K. 21 F3
Crusheen Ireland 21 D5
Cruz Alta Brazil 70 F3
Cruz del Eje Arg. 70 D4
Cruzeiro Brazil 71 B3
Cruzeiro do Sul Brazil 68 D5
Crystal City U.S.A. 62 H6
Crystal Falls U.S.A. 63 J2
Csongrád Hungary 27 I1
Cuamba Moz. 49 D5
Cuando r. Angola/Zambia 49 C5
Cuangar Angola 49 B5
Cuango Angola 49 B4
Cuanza r. Angola 49 B4
Cuatro Ciénegas Mex. 66 D3
Cuauhtémoc Mex. 62 F6
Cuba NY U.S.A. 64 C1
Cuba country West Indies 67 H4
Cubal Angola 49 B5
Cubango r. Angola/Namibia 49 C5
Cubatão Brazil 71 B3
Çubuk Turkey 34 D2
Cuchi r. Angola 49 B5
Cuchilla Grande hills Uruguay 70 E4
Cucuí Brazil 68 E3
Cúcuta Col. 68 D2
Cudal Australia 58 D4
Cuddalore India 38 C4
Cuddapah India 38 C3
Cuddeback Lake CA U.S.A. 65 D3
Cue Australia 55 B6
Cuéllar Spain 25 D3
Cuemba Angola 49 B5
Cuenca Ecuador 68 C4
Cuenca Spain 25 E3
Cuenca, Serranía de mts Spain 25 E3
Cuernavaca Mex. 66 E5
Cuervos Baja California Mex. 65 E4
Cugir Romania 27 J2
Cuiabá Amazonas Brazil 69 G6
Cuiabá Mato Grosso Brazil 69 G7
Cuiabá r. Brazil 69 G7
Cuilcagh hill Ireland/U.K. 21 E3
Cuillin Hills U.K. 20 C3
Cuillin Sound sea chan. U.K. 20 C3
Cuilo Angola 49 B4
Cuiluan China 44 C3
Cuité r. Brazil 71 C2
Cuito r. Angola 49 C5
Cuito Cuanavale Angola 49 B5
Çukurova plat. Turkey 39 B1
Culcairn Australia 58 C5
Culfa Azer. 35 G3
Culgoa r. Australia 58 C2
Culiacán Mex. 66 C4
Culiacán Rosales Mex. see Culiacán
Cullen U.K. 20 G3
Cullen Point Australia 56 C1
Cullera Spain 25 F4
Cullivoe U.K. 20 [inset]
Cullman U.S.A. 63 J5
Cullybackey U.K. 21 F3
Cul Mòr hill U.K. 20 D2
Culpeper VA U.S.A. 64 C3
Culuene r. Brazil 69 H6
Culver, Point Australia 55 D8
Culverden N.Z. 59 D6
Cumaná Venez. 68 F1
Cumari Brazil 71 A2
Cumbal, Nevado de vol. Col. 68 C3
Cumberland MD U.S.A. 64 B3
Cumberland VA U.S.A. 64 B4
Cumberland Lake Canada 62 G1
Cumberland Peninsula Canada 61 L3
Cumberland Plateau U.S.A. 63 J4
Cumberland Sound sea chan. Canada 61 L3
Cumbernauld U.K. 20 F5
Cumbum India 38 C3
Cummins Australia 57 A7
Cummins Range hills Australia 54 D4
Cumnock Australia 58 D4
Cumnock U.K. 20 E5
Çumra Turkey 34 D3
Cumuruxatiba Brazil 71 D2
Cunderdin Australia 55 B7
Cunene r. Angola 49 B5
Cuneo Italy 26 B2
Cunnamulla Australia 58 B2
Cunningsburgh U.K. 20 [inset]
Cupar U.K. 20 F4
Cupica, Golfo de b. Col. 68 C2
Curaçá Brazil 69 K5
Curaçá r. Brazil 68 E4
Curaçao i. Neth. Antilles 67 K6
Curaray r. Ecuador 68 C4
Curdlawidny Lagoon salt flat Australia 57 B6
Curia Switz. see Chur
Curicó Chile 70 B4
Curitiba Brazil 71 A4
Curitibanos Brazil 71 A4
Curlewis Australia 58 E3
Curnamona Australia 57 B6
Currabubula Australia 58 E3
Currais Novos Brazil 69 K5
Currane, Lough l. Ireland 21 B6
Currant NV U.S.A. 65 E1
Curranyalpa Australia 58 B3
Currawilla Australia 56 C5
Currawinya National Park Australia 58 B2
Currie Australia 52 E5
Currockbilly, Mount Australia 58 E5
Curtis Channel Australia 56 E4
Curtis Island Australia 56 E4
Curtis Island N.Z. 53 I5
Curuá r. Brazil 69 G6
Curupira, Serra mts Brazil/Venez. 68 F3
Cururupu Brazil 69 J4
Curvelo Brazil 71 B2
Cusco Peru 68 D6
Cusco Peru see Cusco
Cushendall U.K. 21 F2
Cushendun U.K. 21 F2
Cut Bank U.S.A. 62 E2
Cuttaburra Creek r. Australia 58 B2
Cuttack India 38 E1
Cuvelai Angola 49 B5
Cuxhaven Germany 17 L4
Cuya Chile 68 D7
Cuyahoga Falls OH U.S.A. 64 A2
Cuyama r. CA U.S.A. 65 C3
Cuyuni r. Guyana 69 G2
Cuzco Peru see Cusco
Cwmbrân U.K. 19 D7

Cyangugu Rwanda 48 C4
Cyclades is Greece 27 K6
Cydonia Greece see Chania
Cymru admin. div. U.K. see Wales
Cypress Hills Canada 62 E2
Cyprus country Asia 39 A2
Cythera i. Greece see Kythira
Czechia country Europe see Czech Republic
Czech Republic country Europe 17 O6
Czernowitz Ukr. see Chernivtsi
Czersk Poland 17 P3
Częstochowa Poland 17 Q5

D

Đa, Sông r. Vietnam see Black
Da'an China 44 B3
Dâb̧ab, Jabal al mt. Jordan 39 B4
Dabakala Côte d'Ivoire 46 C4
Daban China see Bairin Zuoqi
Daba Shan mts China 43 J6
Dabhoi India 36 B5
Dabie China 43 L4
Dabola Guinea 46 B3
Dabqig China 43 J5
Dąbrowa Górnicza Poland 17 Q5
Dabsan Hu salt l. China 39 H1
Dabus Nur l. China see Dabs Nur
Dacca Bangl. see Dhaka
Dachau Germany 17 M6
Dachuan China see Dazhou
Daday China 34 D2
Dadeldhura Nepal 36 D3
Dadra India 36 B5
Dadu Pak. 33 K4
Daegu S. Korea see Taegu
Daejŏn S. Korea see Taejŏn
Daet Phil. 41 E6
Dafang China 44 B4
Dafla Hills India 37 H4
Dagana Senegal 46 B3
Dagcagolin China see Zoigê
Dagê China 43 J5
Daglung China 37 G3
Dago i. Estonia see Hiiumaa
Dagon Myanmar see Rangoon
Daguokui Shan hill China 44 C3
Dagupan Phil. 41 E6
Dagzê China 37 G3
Dagzê Co salt l. China 37 F3
Dahabān Saudi Arabia 32 E5
Dahei Shan mts China 44 B4
Dahezhen China 44 C3
Da Hinggan Ling mts China 44 A2
Dahlak Archipelago is Eritrea 32 F6
Dahlak Marine National Park Eritrea 32 F6
Dahm, Ramlat des. Saudi Arabia/Yemen 32 G6
Dahmani Tunisia 26 C7
Dahod India 36 C5
Dahomey country Africa see Benin
Dahongliutan Aksai Chin 36 D2
Dahra Senegal see Dara
Dahūk Iraq 35 F3
Dai i. Indon. 54 E1
Daïkeni Nepal 37 E3
Dailly U.K. 20 E5
Daimiel Spain 25 E4
Dainkognubma China 37 I2
Daintree National Park Australia 56 D3
Dairen China see Dalian
Dai-sen vol. Japan 45 D6
Daisetsu-zan Kokuritsu-kōen Japan 44 F4
Daiyun Shan mts China 43 L7
Dajarra Australia 56 B4
Da Juh China 37 H1
Dakar Senegal 46 B3
Dākhilah, Wāḩāt ad oasis Egypt 32 C4
Dakhla W. Sahara see Ad Dakhla
Dakhla Oasis oasis Egypt see Dākhilah, Wāḩāt ad
Dakol'ka r. Belarus 13 F5
Dakor India 36 C5
Dakoro Niger 46 D3
Dakovica Serbia 27 I3
Đakovo Croatia 26 H2
Daktuy Rus. Fed. 44 B1
Dala Angola 49 C5
Dalaba Guinea 46 B3
Dalai China see Da'an
Dalain Hob China 42 I4
Dālakī Iran 35 H5
Dalālven r. Sweden 15 J6
Dalaman Turkey 27 M6
Dalandzadgad Mongolia 42 I4
Dalap-Uliga-Darrit Marshall Is see Delap-Uliga-Djarrit
Đa Lat Vietnam 31 J5
Dalatando Angola see N'dalatando
Dalaud India 36 C5
Dalauda India 36 C5
Dalbandin Pak. 33 J4
Dalbeattie U.K. 20 F6
Dalbeg Australia 56 D4
Dalby Australia 58 E1
Dalby Isle of Man 18 C4
Dale Hordaland Norway 15 D6
Dale Sogn og Fjordane Norway 15 D6
Dale City VA U.S.A. 64 C3
Dale Hollow Lake U.S.A. 63 J4
Dalet Myanmar 37 H5
Daletme Myanmar 37 H5
Dalfors Sweden 15 I6
Dalgety Australia 58 D6
Dalgety r. Australia 55 A6
Dalhart U.S.A. 62 G4
Dalhousie, Cape Canada 60 F2
Dali Yunnan China 42 I7
Dalian China 43 M5
Dalin China 44 A4
Dalizi China 44 B4
Dalkeith U.K. 20 F5
Dallas TX U.S.A. 63 H5
Dalles City U.S.A. see The Dalles
Dall Island U.S.A. 60 E4
Dalmacija reg. Bos.-Herz./Croatia see Dalmatia
Dalmatia reg. Bos.-Herz./Croatia 30 A2
Dalmau India 36 D4
Dalmellington U.K. 20 E5
Dalmi India 37 F5
Dal'negorsk Rus. Fed. 44 D3
Dal'nerechensk Rus. Fed. 44 D3
Dalny China see Dalian
Daloa Côte d'Ivoire 46 C4
Dalol Eth. 32 F7
Daloloia Group is P.N.G. 56 E1
Dalry U.K. 20 E5
Dalrymple, Lake Australia 56 D4
Dalrymple, Mount Australia 56 D4

Dalton S. Africa 51 J5
Dalton GA U.S.A. 63 K5
Dalton MA U.S.A. 64 E1
Dalton U.S.A. 64 D2
Dalton-in-Furness U.K. 18 D4
Daly r. Australia 54 E3
Daly City CA U.S.A. 65 B3
Daly River Australia 54 E3
Daly Waters Australia 54 F3
Daman India 38 B1
Daman and Diu union terr. India 38 A1
Damanhur Egypt 34 D5
Damanhûr Egypt see Damanhur
Damão India see Daman
Damar i. Indon. 41 E8
Damara Cent. Afr. Rep. 48 B3
Damaraland reg. Namibia 49 B6
Damas Syria see Damascus
Damascus Syria 39 C3
Damaturu Nigeria 46 E3
Damāvand Iran 35 I4
Damāvand, Qolleh-ye mt. Iran 35 I4
Dambulla Sri Lanka 38 D5
Damghan Iran 35 I3
Damianópolis Brazil 71 B1
Damietta Egypt see Dumyât
Damiyā Jordan 39 B3
Damjong China 43 J5
Damlasu Turkey 39 D1
Dammam Saudi Arabia 32 H4
Damoh India 36 D5
Damour Lebanon 39 B3
Dampier Archipelago is Australia 54 B5
Dampier Island P.N.G. see Karkar Island
Dampier Land reg. Australia 54 C4
Dampier Strait P.N.G. 52 E2
Dampir, Selat sea chan. Indon. 41 F8
Damqoq Zangbo r. China see Maquan He
Dam Qu r. China 37 H2
Damxoi China see Comai
Damxung China 37 G3
Dana Nepal 37 E3
Danakil reg. Africa see Denakil
Danané Côte d'Ivoire 46 C4
Đa Nang Vietnam 31 J5
Danba China 43 H2
Danbury CT U.S.A. 64 E2
Danby VT U.S.A. 64 E1
Danby Lake CA U.S.A. 65 E3
Dandaragan Australia 55 A7
Dande r. China 44 B3
Dandeldhura Nepal 36 D3
Dandeli India 38 B3
Dandong China 45 B4
Dandot Pak. 36 C2
Dane r. U.K. 18 E5
Daneborg Greenland 77 I2
Danese WV U.S.A. 64 A4
Dangara Tajik. see Danghara
Dangbizhen Rus. Fed. 44 C3
Dangchengwan China see Subei
Danger Islands atoll Cook Is see Pukapuka
Danger Point S. Africa 50 D8
Danghara Tajik. 33 K2
Danghe Nanshan mts China 42 G5
Dang La pass China see Tanggula Shankou
Dangla Shan mts China see Tanggula Shan
Dangqên China 37 G3
Dangriga Belize 66 G5
Dangshan China 43 L5
Danglu-guntō is Japan 45 C6
Dankhar India 36 D2
Dankov Rus. Fed. 13 H5
Danlí Hond. 67 G6
Danmark country Europe see Denmark
Dannebrog Ø i. Greenland see Qillak
Dannevirke N.Z. 59 F5
Dannhauser S. Africa 51 J5
Dano Burkina 46 C3
Dansville NY U.S.A. 64 C1
Dantan India 37 F5
Dantewada India see Dantewara
Dantewara India 38 D2
Danube r. Austria/Germany 24 I2
Danube r. Bulg./Croatia/Serbia 13 F7
Danube r. Europe 17 P6
Danube r. Hungary 17 P8
Danube Delta Romania/Ukr. 27 M2
Danville IL U.S.A. 63 J3
Danville PA U.S.A. 64 C2
Danville VA U.S.A. 64 B5
Danzig Poland see Gdańsk
Danzig, Gulf of Poland/Rus. Fed. see Gdańsk, Gulf of
Dao Tay Sa i. S. China Sea see Paracel Islands
Daoud Alg. see Aïn Beïda
Daoukro Côte d'Ivoire 46 C4
Dapaong Togo 46 D3
Daphabum mt. India 37 I4
Dapitan Phil. 41 E7
Daporijo India 37 H4
Da Qaidam Zhen China 42 H5
Daqing China 44 B3
Daqq-e Sorkh, Kavir-e salt flat Iran 35 I4
Dara Senegal 46 B3
Dar'ā Syria 39 C3
Dâra, Gebel mt. Egypt see Dārah, Jabal
Darabani Romania 13 F6
Daraj Libya 46 E1
Daraj r. China 37 H4
Darah, Jabal mt. Egypt 34 D6
Daraj Libya see Daraj
Dārākūyeh Iran 35 I5
Dārān Iran 35 H4
Darazo Nigeria 46 E3
Darbhanga India 37 F4
Dardanelles strait Turkey 27 L4
Dardania prov. Serbia see Kosovo
Dardo China see Kangding
Dar el Beida Morocco see Casablanca
Darende Turkey 34 E3
Dar es Salaam Tanz. 49 D4
Darfo Boario Terme Italy 26 D2
Dargai Pak. 36 B2
Darganata Turkm. 33 J1
Dargaville N.Z. 59 D2
Dargo Burkina 46 C3
Dargo Zangbo r. China 37 F3
Darhan Mongolia 42 J3
Darién, Golfo del g. Col. 68 C2
Darién, Parque Nacional de nat. park Panama 67 I7
Darjeeling India see Darjiling
Darjiling India 37 G4
Darkhazineh Iran 35 H5
Darlag China 42 H6
Darling r. Australia 58 A3
Darling Downs hills Australia 58 D1
Darling Range hills Australia 55 A8
Darlington U.K. 18 F4
Darlington Point Australia 58 C5
Darlot, Lake salt flat Australia 55 C6

Darłowo Poland 17 P3
Darma Pass China/India 36 E3
Darmstadt Germany 17 L6
Darnah Libya 34 A4
Darnall S. Africa 51 J5
Darnick Australia 58 A4
Darnley, Cape Antarctica 76 E2
Daroca Spain 25 F3
Darovskoy Rus. Fed. 12 J4
Darr watercourse Australia 56 C4
Darreh-ye Bāhābād Iran 35 I5
Darreh-ye Shahr Iran 35 G4
Darsi India 38 C3
Dart r. U.K. 19 D8
Dartang China see Baqên
Dartford U.K. 19 H7
Dartmoor Australia 57 C8
Dartmoor hills U.K. 19 C8
Dartmoor National Park U.K. 19 D8
Dartmouth Canada 63 O3
Dartmouth U.K. 19 D8
Dartmouth, Lake salt flat Australia 57 C5
Darton U.K. 18 F5
Daru P.N.G. 52 E2
Daru Sierra Leone 46 B4
Darwazgai Afgh. 36 A3
Darwen U.K. 18 E5
Darwin Australia 54 E3
Darwin, Monte mt. Chile 70 C8
Daryācheh-ye Orūmīyeh salt l. Iran see Urmia, Lake
Dar'yalyktakyr, Ravnina plain Kazakh. 42 A3
Dar'yoi Amu r. Asia see Amudar'ya
Dasada India 36 B5
Dashhowuz Turkm. see Daşoguz
Dashkesan Azer. see Daşkäsän
Dashkhovuz Turkm. see Daşoguz
Dashköpri Turkm. see Daşköpri
Dasht Iran 35 J3
Daska Pak. 36 C2
Daşkäsän Azer. 35 G2
Daşköpri Turkm. 33 J3
Daşoguz Turkm. 30 E2
Daşoguz Turkm. see Daşoguz
Daspar mt. Pak. 36 C1
Datça Turkey 27 L6
Date Japan 44 F4
Date Creek watercourse AZ U.S.A. 65 F3
Dateland AZ U.S.A. 65 F4
Datha India 36 C5
Datia India 36 D4
Datong Heilong. China 44 B3
Datong Shanxi China 43 K4
Datong He r. China 42 I5
Dattapur India 38 C1
Daudkandi Bangl. 37 G5
Daugava r. Latvia 15 N8
Daugavpils Latvia 15 O9
Daulatabad India 38 B2
Daulatabad Iran see Malāyer
Daulatpur Bangl. 37 G5
Daungyu r. Myanmar 37 H5
Dauphin Canada 62 G1
Dauphiné reg. France 24 G4
Dauphiné, Alpes du mts France 24 G4
Dauphin Lake Canada 62 H1
Daurie Creek r. Australia 55 A6
Dausa India 36 D4
Dava U.K. 20 F3
Dāvāçi Azer. 35 H2
Davanagere India see Davangere
Davangere India 38 B3
Davao Phil. 41 E7
Davel S. Africa 51 I4
Davenport IA U.S.A. 63 I3
Davenport Downs Australia 56 C5
Davenport Range hills Australia 54 F5
Daventry U.K. 19 F6
Daveyton S. Africa 51 I4
David Panama 67 H7
Davidson Canada 62 F1
Davidson, Mount hill Australia 54 E5
Davis r. Australia 54 E5
Davis research station Antarctica 76 E2
Davis CA U.S.A. 65 B1
Davis WV U.S.A. 64 B3
Davis, Mount hill PA U.S.A. 64 D3
Davis Bay Antarctica 76 G2
Davis Dam AZ U.S.A. 65 E3
Davis Inlet Canada 61 L4
Davis Sea Antarctica 76 H2
Davis Strait Canada/Greenland 61 M3
Davlekanovo Rus. Fed. 11 Q5
Davos Switz. 24 I3
Dawa Co l. China 37 F3
Dawa Wenz r. Eth. 48 E3
Dawaxung China 37 F3
Dawei Myanmar see Tavoy
Dawera i. Indon. 54 E1
Dawo China see Maqên
Dawqah Oman 33 H6
Dawson r. Australia 56 D4
Dawson Canada 60 B2
Dawson Creek Canada 60 F4
Dawsons Landing Canada 62 D2
Dawu Qinghai China see Maqên
Dawukou China see Shizuishan
Dax France 24 D5
Daxian China see Dazhou
Daxing'an Ling mts China see Da Hinggan Ling
Da Xueshan mts China 31 J3
Dayan China see Lijiang
Dayangshu China 44 B2
Dayao China 42 I7
Daykundi Afgh. 36 A2
Daylesford Australia 58 B6
Daylight Pass NV U.S.A. 65 D2
Dayong China see Zhangjiajie
Dayr Abū Sa'īd Jordan 39 B3
Dayr az Zawr Syria 35 F4
Dayr Ḩāfir Syria 39 C1
Dayton OH U.S.A. 63 K4
Dayton VA U.S.A. 64 B3
Daytona Beach U.S.A. 63 K6
Dayyer Iran 35 H6
Dazhou China 42 I6
Daz Aar S. Africa 50 G6
Dead r. Ireland 21 D5
Deadman Lake CA U.S.A. 65 D3
Dead Mountains NV U.S.A. 65 E3
Dead Sea salt l. Asia 38 B4
Deakin Australia 55 E7
Dealesville S. Africa 51 G5
Dean, Forest of U.K. 19 E7
Deán Funes Arg. 70 D4
Deanuvuotna inlet Norway see Tanafjorden
Dearne r. U.K. 18 F5
Dease Lake Canada 60 F4
Dease Strait Canada 60 H3
Death Valley depr. CA U.S.A. 65 D2
Death Valley Junction CA U.S.A. 65 D2
Death Valley National Park CA U.S.A. 65 D2
Deauville France 24 E2
De Baai S. Africa see Port Elizabeth
Debar Macedonia 27 I4
Debenham U.K. 19 I6
Débo, Lac l. Mali 46 C3
Deborah East, Lake salt flat Australia 55 B7

Deborah West, Lake salt flat Australia 55 B7
Debrecen Hungary 27 I1
Debre Markos Eth. 32 E7
Debre Tabor Eth. 32 E7
Debre Zeyit Eth. 48 D3
Decatur IL U.S.A. 63 I5
Decatur IL U.S.A. 63 J4
Deccan plat. India 34 E5
Deception Bay Australia 58 F1
Děčín Czech Rep. 17 O5
Decorah U.S.A. 63 I3
Deddington U.K. 19 F7
Dedegöl Dağları mts Turkey 27 N6
Dedo de Deus mt. Brazil 71 B4
Dedovichi Rus. Fed. 13 P4
Dedu China see Wudalianchi
Dee r. India 37 F4
Dee est. U.K. 18 D5
Dee r. England/Wales U.K. 19 D5
Dee r. Scotland U.K. 20 G3
Deel r. Ireland 21 F4
Deel r. Ireland 21 F4
Deep Creek Lake MD U.S.A. 64 B3
Deepwater Australia 58 E2
Deeri Somalia 48 E2
Deering U.S.A. 60 B3
Deering, Mount Australia 55 E6
Deer Island U.S.A. 60 B4
Deer Lodge U.S.A. 62 E2
Deesa India see Disa
Defensores del Chaco, Parque Nacional nat. park Para. 70 D2
Degana India 36 C4
Degeh Bur Eth. 48 E3
Degema Nigeria 46 D4
Deggendorf Germany 17 N6
Degh r. Pak. 36 C3
De Grey r. Australia 54 B5
Degtevo Rus. Fed. 13 I6
Dehaj India 36 C5
Dehej India 36 H4
Dehe Golän Iran 35 G4
Dehi Afgh. 36 C3
Dehiwala-Mount Lavinia Sri Lanka see Mount Lavinia
Dehlorän Iran 35 G4
De Hoop Nature Reserve S. Africa 50 E8
Dehra Dun India 36 D3
Dehradun India see Dehra Dun
Dehri India 37 F4
Deim Zubeir Sudan 47 F4
Deir-ez-Zor Syria see Dayr az Zawr
Dej Romania 27 J1
Deji China see Rinbung
Dejiang China 43 J7
De Kalb IL U.S.A. 63 J3
De-Kastri Rus. Fed. 44 F2
Dekemhare Eritrea 32 E6
Dekina Nigeria 46 D4
Dékoa Cent. Afr. Rep. 48 B3
Delaki Indon. 54 D2
Delamar Lake NV U.S.A. 65 E2
Delano CA U.S.A. 65 C3
Delano Peak UT U.S.A. 65 F1
Delap-Uliga-Djarrit Marshall Is 74 H5
Deläräm Afgh. 33 J3
Delareyville S. Africa 51 G4
Delaronde Lake Canada 62 F1
Delaware r. New Jersey/Pennsylvania U.S.A. 64 D3
Delaware state U.S.A. 64 D3
Delaware, East Branch r. NY U.S.A. 64 D2
Delaware Bay Delaware/New Jersey U.S.A. 64 D3
Delaware Water Gap National Recreational Area park New Jersey/Pennsylvania U.S.A. 64 D2
Dêlêg China 37 F3
Delegate Australia 58 D6
Delémont Switz. 24 H3
Delfinópolis Brazil 71 B3
Delft Neth. 16 J4
Delfzijl Neth. 15 E10
Delgado, Cabo c. Moz. 49 E5
Delhi Ont. Canada 64 A1
Delhi China 42 H5
Delhi India 36 D3
Delhi NY U.S.A. 64 D1
Delice Turkey 34 D3
Delice r. Turkey 34 D2
Delijän Iran 35 H4
Déline Canada 60 F3
Delingha China see Delhi
Dellys Alg. 25 H5
Del Mar CA U.S.A. 65 D4
Delmenhorst Germany 17 L4
Delnice Croatia 26 F2
De-Longa, Ostrova is Rus. Fed. 29 Q2
De Long Islands Rus. Fed. see De-Longa, Ostrova
De Long Mountains U.S.A. 60 B3
De Long Strait Rus. Fed. see Longa, Proliv
Deloraine Canada 62 F1
Delportshoop S. Africa 50 G5
Del Rio U.S.A. 62 F6
Delsbo Sweden 15 J6
Delta CO U.S.A. 62 F4
Delta UT U.S.A. 62 E4
Delta Downs Australia 56 C3
Delta Junction U.S.A. 60 D3
Delungra Australia 58 E2
Delvin Ireland 21 E4
Delvinë Albania 27 I5
Delwara India 36 C4
Demavend mt. Iran see Damävand, Qolleh-ye
Demba Dem. Rep. Congo 49 C4
Dembï Dolo Eth. 32 E8
Demchok Jammu and Kashmir see Dêmqog
Demerara Guyana see Georgetown
Demerara Abyssal Plain sea feature S. Atlantic Ocean 72 E5
Demidov Rus. Fed. 13 P5
Deming U.S.A. 62 F5
Demirci Turkey 27 M5
Demirköy Turkey 27 L4
Demirtaş Turkey 39 A1
Dempo, Gunung vol. Indon. 41 C8
Dêmqog Jammu and Kashmir 36 D2
Dem'yanovo Rus. Fed. 12 J3
De Naawte S. Africa 50 D5
Denakil reg. Africa 48 E2
Denali U.S.A. see McKinley, Mount
Denali National Park and Preserve U.S.A. 60 C3
Denan Eth. 48 E3
Denbigh U.K. 18 D5
Den Bosch Neth. see 's-Hertogenbosch
Dendi mt. Eth. 48 D3
Dendron S. Africa see Mogwadi
Denezhkin Kamen', Gora mt. Rus. Fed. 11 R3
Dêngka China see Têwo
Dengkagoin China see Têwo
Dengkou China 42 J4
Dêngqên China 37 G3
Den Haag Neth. see The Hague
Denham Australia 55 A6

Denham r. Australia 54 E3
Denham Range mts Australia 56 E4
Den Helder Neth. 16 J4
Denia Spain 25 G4
Denial Bay Australia 57 A7
Deniliquin Australia 58 B5
Denison IA U.S.A. 63 H3
Denison, Cape Antarctica 76 G2
Denison Plains Australia 54 E4
Deniyaya Sri Lanka 38 D5
Denizli Turkey 27 M6
Denman Australia 58 E4
Denman Glacier Antarctica 76 F2
Denmark Australia 52 B3
Denmark country Europe 15 G8
Denmark Strait Greenland/Iceland 10 A2
Dennis, Lake salt flat Australia 54 E5
Denny U.K. 20 F4
Denpasar Indon. 41 D8
Denton MD U.S.A. 64 D3
Denton TX U.S.A. 63 H5
D'Entrecasteaux, Point Australia 55 A8
D'Entrecasteaux, Récifs reef New Caledonia 53 G3
D'Entrecasteaux Islands P.N.G. 52 F2
D'Entrecasteaux National Park Australia 55 A8
Denver CO U.S.A. 62 F4
Denver PA U.S.A. 64 C2
Deo India 37 F4
Deoband India 36 D3
Deogarh Jharkhand India see Deoghar
Deogarh Orissa India 37 F5
Deogarh Rajasthan India 36 C4
Deogarh Uttar Prad. India 36 D4
Deogarh mt. India 37 E5
Deoghar India 37 F4
Deolali India 38 B2
Deoli India 37 F5
Deori Madh. Prad. India 36 D5
Deoria India 37 F4
Deosil India 37 E5
Deosai, Plains of Jammu and Kashmir 36 C2
Deothang Bhutan 37 G4
Deposit NY U.S.A. 64 D2
Depsang Point hill Aksai Chin 36 D2
Deputatskiy Rus. Fed. 29 O3
Dêqên Xizang China see Dagzê
Dêqên Xizang China 37 G3
Dêqên Xizang China 37 G3
De Queen U.S.A. 63 I5
Dera Ghazi Khan Pak. 33 L3
Dera Ismail Khan Pak. 33 L3
Derawar Fort Pak. 36 B3
Derbent Rus. Fed. 35 H2
Derbesiye Turkey see Şenyurt
Derbur China 44 A2
Derby Australia 54 C4
Derby U.K. 19 F6
Derby CT U.S.A. 64 E3
Derby NY U.S.A. 64 B1
Dereham U.K. 19 H6
Derg r. Ireland/U.K. 21 E3
Derg, Lough l. Ireland 21 D5
Dergachi Rus. Fed. 13 K6
Dergachi Ukr. see Derhachi
Derhachi Ukr. 13 H6
De Ridder U.S.A. 63 I6
Derik Turkey 35 F3
Derm Namibia 50 D2
Derna Libya see Darnah
Dernberg, Cape Namibia 50 B4
Dêrong China 42 H7
Derravaragh, Lough l. Ireland 21 E4
Derry U.K. see Londonderry
Derry NH U.S.A. 64 F2
Derryveagh Mts hills Ireland 21 D3
Dêrub China 36 D2
Derudeb Sudan 32 E6
De Rust S. Africa 50 F7
Derventa Bos.-Herz. 26 G2
Derwent r. England U.K. 18 F6
Derwent r. England U.K. 18 G5
Derwent Water l. U.K. 18 D4
Derzhavinsk Kazakh. 28 H4
Derzhavinskiy Kazakh. see Derzhavinsk
Desaguadero r. Arg. 70 C4
Désappointement, Îles du is Fr. Polynesia 75 K6
Desë Eth. 48 D2
Deseado Arg. 70 C7
Deseado r. Arg. 70 C7
Desengaño, Punta pt Arg. 70 C7
Desert Canal Pak. 36 B3
Desert Center CA U.S.A. 65 E4
Desert Lake NV U.S.A. 65 E2
Des Moines IA U.S.A. 63 H3
Des Moines r. U.S.A. 63 I3
Desna r. Rus. Fed./Ukr. 13 F6
Desnogorsk Rus. Fed. 13 G5
Desolación, Isla i. Chile 70 B8
Dessau Germany 17 N5
Dessye Eth. see Desë
Destruction Bay Canada 77 A2
Dete Zimbabwe 49 C5
Detmold Germany 17 L5
Detroit U.S.A. 63 K3
Detroit Lakes U.S.A. 63 H2
Dett Zimbabwe see Dete
Deua National Park Australia 58 D5
Deutschland country Europe see Germany
Deutschlandsberg Austria 17 O7
Deva Romania 27 J2
Deva U.K. see Chester
Devana U.K. see Aberdeen
Devangere India see Davangere
Devanhalli India 38 C3
Deve Bair pass Bulg./Macedonia see Velbüzhdki Prokhod
Develi Turkey 34 D3
Deventer Neth. 17 K4
Deveron r. U.K. 20 G3
Devět Skal hill Czech Rep. 17 P6
Devgarh India 38 B2
Devghar India see Deoghar
Devikot India 36 B4
Devil's Bridge U.K. 19 D6
Devil's Gate pass CA U.S.A. 65 C1
Devil's Lake U.S.A. 62 H2
Devil's Paw mt. U.S.A. 60 E4
Devil's Peak CA U.S.A. 65 C2
Devizes U.K. 19 F7
Devli India 36 C4
Devnya Bulg. 27 L3
Devon r. U.K. 20 F4
Devon U.K. 20 F4
Devon Island Canada 61 I2
Devonport Australia 57 [inset]
Devrek r. U.K. 17 N4
Devrukh India 38 B2
Dewas India 36 D5
Dewetsdorp S. Africa 51 H5
Dewsbury U.K. 18 F5
Dexter MO U.S.A. 63 J4
Deyang China 42 I6
Dey-Dey Lake salt flat Australia 55 E7
Deyhuk Iran 35 I3
Deyong, Tanjung pt Indon. 41 F8
Dez r. Iran 32 G3
Dezful Iran 35 H4
Dezhneva, Mys c. Rus. Fed. 29 T3

Dezhou Shandong China 43 L5
Dezh Shähpür Iran see Marïvän
Dhabarau India 37 H4
Dhahab, Wädï adh r. Syria 39 D3
Dhähiriya West Bank 39 B4
Dhahran Saudi Arabia 30 C4
Dhaka Bangl. 37 G5
Dhalbhum reg. India 37 F5
Dhalgaon India 38 B2
Dhamär Yemen 32 F7
Dhamoni India 36 D4
Dhamtari India 38 D1
Dhana India 36 B3
Dhana Sar Pak. 36 B3
Dhanbad India 37 F5
Dhanera India 36 C4
Dhang Range mts Nepal 37 E3
Dhankuta Nepal 37 F4
Dhansia India 36 C3
Dhar India 36 C5
Dhar Adrar hills Mauritania 46 B3
Dharampur India 38 B1
Dharan Bazar Nepal 37 F4
Dharashiv India see Osmanabad
Dhari India 36 B5
Dharmapuri India 38 C3
Dharmavaram India 38 C3
Dharmsala Hima. Prad. India see Dharmshala
Dharmsala Orissa India 37 F5
Dharmshala India 36 D2
Dharnaoda India 36 D4
Dhar Oualâta hills Mauritania 46 C3
Dhar Tîchît hills Mauritania 46 C3
Dharug National Park Australia 58 E4
Dharur India 38 C2
Dharwad India 38 B3
Dharwar India see Dharwad
Dharwas India 36 D2
Dhasan r. India 36 D4
Dhät al Hajj Saudi Arabia 34 E5
Dhaulagiri mt. Nepal 37 E3
Dhaulpur India see Dholpur
Dhaura India 36 D4
Dhaurahra India 36 E4
Dhawlagiri mt. Nepal see Dhaulagiri
Dhebar Lake India see Jaisamand Lake
Dhekianal India 38 E1
Dhekelia Sovereign Base Area military base Cyprus 39 A2
Dhemaji India 37 H4
Dhenkanal India 38 E1
Dhîbän Jordan 39 B4
Dhidhimótikhon Greece see Didymoteicho
Dhing India 37 H4
Dhirwah, Wädï adh watercourse Jordan 39 C4
Dhodhekánisos is Greece see Dodecanese
Dhola India 36 B5
Dholera India 36 C5
Dholpur India 36 D4
Dhomokós Greece see Domokos
Dhone India 38 C3
Dhoraji India 36 B5
Dhori India 36 B5
Dhrangadhra India 36 B5
Dhubab Yemen 32 F7
Dhubri India 37 G4
Dhuburi India see Dhubri
Dhudial Pak. 36 C2
Dhule India 38 B1
Dhulia India see Dhule
Dhulian India 37 F4
Dhulian Pak. 36 C2
Dhuma India 36 D5
Dhund r. India 36 D4
Dhurwai India 36 D4
Dhuusa Marreeb Somalia 48 E3
Dia i. Greece 27 K7
Diablo, Mount CA U.S.A. 65 B2
Diablo, Picacho del mt. Mex. 66 A2
Diablo Range mts CA U.S.A. 65 B2
Diagbe Dem. Rep. Congo 48 C3
Diamante Arg. 70 D4
Diamantina watercourse Australia 56 B5
Diamantina Brazil 71 C2
Diamantina, Chapada plat. Brazil 71 C1
Diamantina Deep sea feature Indian Ocean 73 O8
Diamantina Gates National Park Australia 56 C4
Diamantino Brazil 69 G6
Diamond Islets Australia 56 E3
Dian Chi l. China 42 I8
Diandioumé Mali 46 C3
Diane Bank sea feature Australia 56 E3
Dianópolis Brazil 69 I6
Diaobingshan China 44 A4
Diaoling China 44 C3
Diapaga Burkina 46 D3
Diarizos r. Cyprus 39 A2
Diaz Point Namibia 50 B4
Dibaya Dem. Rep. Congo 49 C4
Dibella well Niger 46 E3
Dibeng S. Africa 50 F4
Dibete Botswana 51 H2
Dibrugarh India 37 H4
Dibse Syria see Dibsī
Dibsī Syria 39 D2

Dillwyn VA U.S.A. 64 B4
Dilolo Dem. Rep. Congo 49 C5
Dimapur India 37 H4
Dimashq Syria see Damascus
Dimbokro Côte d'Ivoire 46 C4
Dimboola Australia 57 C8
Dimitrov Ukr. see Dymytrov
Dimitrovgrad Bulg. 27 K3
Dimitrovgrad Rus. Fed. 13 K5
Dimitrovo Bulg. see Pernik
Dîmona Israel 39 B4
Dimpho Pan salt pan Botswana 50 E3
Dinajpur Bangl. 37 G4
Dinan France 24 C2
Dinant Belgium 16 J5
Dinapur India 37 F4
Dinar Turkey 27 N5
Dinar, Küh-e mt. Iran 35 H5
Dinara Planina mts Bos.-Herz./Croatia see Dinaric Alps
Dinaric Alps mts Bos.-Herz./Croatia 26 G2
Dinbych U.K. see Denbigh
Dinbych-y-pysgod U.K. see Tenby
Dinder National Park Sudan 47 G3
Dindi r. India 38 C2
Dindigul India 38 C4
Dindima Nigeria 46 E3
Dindori India 36 E5
Dingla Nepal 37 F4
Dingle Ireland 21 B5
Dingle Bay Ireland 21 B5
Dingnan China 43 L8
Dingo Australia 56 E4
Dinguiraye Guinea 46 B3
Dingwall U.K. 20 E3
Dingxi China 42 I5
Dinnyê China 37 H3
Dinokwe Botswana 51 H2
Dinosaur CO U.S.A. 62 G3
Dinuba CA U.S.A. 65 C3
Dinwiddie VA U.S.A. 64 C4
Dioïla Mali 46 C3
Dionísio Cerqueira Brazil 70 F3
Diorama Brazil 71 A2
Dioscurias Georgia see Sokhumi
Dioulolou Senegal 46 B3
Diourbel Senegal 46 B3
Dipayal Nepal 36 E3
Diphu India 37 H4
Dipkarpaz Cyprus see Rizokarpason
Diplo Pak. 36 B4
Dipperu National Park Australia 56 E4
Dirang India 37 H4
Diré Mali 46 C3
Dire Dawa Eth. 48 E3
Dirico Angola 49 C5
Dirk Hartog Island Australia 55 A6
Dirranbandi Australia 58 D2
Dirs Saudi Arabia 48 E2
Dirschau Poland see Tczew
Disa India 36 C4
Disang r. India 37 H4
Disappointment, Cape S. Georgia 70 I8
Disappointment, Lake salt flat Australia 55 C5
Disappointment Islands Fr. Polynesia see Désappointement, Îles du
Disaster Bay Australia 58 D6
Discovery Bay Australia 57 C8
Disko i. Greenland see Qeqertarsuaq
Disko Bugt b. Greenland see Qeqertarsuup Tunua
Dispur India 37 G4
Disputanta VA U.S.A. 64 C4
Disüq Egypt 34 C5
Ditloung S. Africa 50 F5
Dittaino r. Sicily Italy 26 F6
Diu India 38 B1
Divehi country Indian Ocean see Maldives
Divi, Point India 38 D3
Divichi Azer. see Däviçi
Divinópolis Brazil 71 B3
Divnoye Rus. Fed. 13 I7
Divo Côte d'Ivoire 46 C4
Divriği Turkey 34 E3
Diwana Pak. 36 A4
Diwaniyah Iraq see Ad Dīwānīyah
Dixon CA U.S.A. 65 B1
Dixon IL U.S.A. 63 J3
Dixon Entrance sea chan. Canada/U.S.A. 60 E4
Diyadin Turkey 35 F3
Diyarbakır Turkey 35 F3
Diz Chah Iran 35 I4
Dize Turkey see Yüksekova
Djado Niger 46 E2
Djado, Plateau du Niger 46 E2
Djaja, Puntjak mt. Indon. see Jaya, Puncak
Djakarta Indon. see Jakarta
Djakovica Serbia see Đakovica
Djakovo Croatia see Đakovo
Djambala Congo 48 B4
Djanet Alg. 46 D2
Djejma Cent. Afr. Rep. 48 C3
Djenné Mali 46 C3
Djerdap nat. park Serbia 27 J2
Djibo Burkina 46 C3
Djibouti country Africa 32 F7
Djibouti Djibouti 32 F7
Djidjelli Alg. see Jijel
Djougou Benin 46 D4
Djoum Cameroon 46 E4
Djourab, Erg du des. Chad 47 E3
Djúpivogur Iceland 14 [inset]
Djurås Sweden 15 I6
Djurdjura, Parc National du Alg. 25 I5
Dmitriyevka, Proliv sea chan. Rus. Fed. 29 P2
Dmitriyev-L'govskiy Rus. Fed. 13 G5
Dmitriyevsk Ukr. see Makiyivka
Dmitrov Rus. Fed. 12 H4
Dmytriyevs'k Ukr. see Makiyivka
Dnepr r. Ukr. see Dnieper
Dneprodzerzhinsk Ukr. see Dniprodzerzhyns'k
Dnepropetrovsk Ukr. see Dnipropetrovs'k
Dnieper r. Europe 13 G7
Dnieper r. Europe 13 G7
Dniester r. Moldova 13 F7
Dniester r. Ukr. 13 F6 see Dniester
Dnipro r. Ukr. see Dnieper
Dnipro r. Ukr. 13 G7 see Dnieper
Dniprodzerzhyns'k Ukr. 13 G6
Dnipropetrovs'k Ukr. 13 G6
Dnister r. Ukr. 13 F6 see Dniester
Dno Rus. Fed. 13 P4
Dnyapro r. Belarus 13 F6 see Dnieper
Dnyapro r. Belarus see Dnieper
Doäb Afgh. 36 A2
Doaba Pak. 36 B3
Doaktown Canada 61 I5
Doba Chad 47 E4
Doba China see Toiba
Dobele Latvia 15 M8
Doberai, Jazirah pen. Indon. 41 F8

Doberai Peninsula Indon. see Doberai, Jazirah
Dobo Indon. 41 F8
Doboj Bos.-Herz. 26 H2
Dobrich Bulg. 27 L3
Dobrinka Rus. Fed. 13 I5
Dobroye Rus. Fed. 13 H5
Dobruja reg. Romania 27 L3
Dobrush Belarus 13 F5
Dobryanka Rus. Fed. 11 R4
Dobzha China 37 G3
Doce r. Brazil 71 D2
Dochart r. U.K. 20 E4
Do China Qala Afgh. 36 B3
Docking U.K. 19 H6
Doctor Hicks Range hills Australia 55 D7
Doctor Pedro P. Peña Para. 70 D2
Doda India 36 C2
Doda Betta mt. India 38 C4
Dod Ballapur India 38 C3
Dodecanese is Greece 27 L7
Dodekanisos is Greece see Dodecanese
Dodge City U.S.A. 62 G4
Dodman Point U.K. 19 C8
Dodoma Tanz. 49 D4
Dogai Coring salt l. China 37 G2
Dogaicoring Qangco salt l. China 37 G2
Doğanşehir Turkey 34 E3
Dogên Co l. Xizang China 37 G3
Dogên Co l. Xizang China see Bam Tso
Dôgo i. Japan 45 D5
Dogondoutchi Niger 46 D3
Doğubeyazıt Turkey 35 G3
Doğu Menteşe Dağları mts Turkey 27 M6
Dogxung Zangbo r. China 37 F3
Do'gyaling China 37 F3
Doha Qatar 32 H4
Dohad India see Dahod
Dohazari Bangl. 37 H5
Dohrighat India 37 E4
Doi i. Fiji 53 I4
Doire U.K. see Londonderry
Dois Irmãos, Serra dos hills Brazil 69 J5
Dokan, Sadd Iraq 35 G4
Dok-do i. N. Pacific Ocean see Liancourt Rocks
Dokhara, Dunes de des. Alg. 22 F5
Dokka Norway 15 G6
Dokkum Neth. 17 J4
Dokri Pak. 36 B4
Dokshukino Rus. Fed. see Nartkala
Dokshytsy Belarus 15 O9
Dokuchayeva, Mys c. Rus. Fed. 44 G3
Dokuchayevs'k Ukr. 13 H7
Dolbenmaen U.K. 19 C6
Dol-de-Bretagne France 24 D2
Dole France 24 G3
Dolgellau U.K. 19 D6
Dolgiy, Ostrov i. Rus. Fed. 12 L1
Dolgorukovo Rus. Fed. 13 H5
Dolinsk Rus. Fed. 44 F3
Dolisie Congo see Loubomo
Dolleman Island Antarctica 76 L2
Dolok, Pulau i. Indon. 41 F8
Dolomites mts Italy 26 D2
Dolomiti mts Italy see Dolomites
Dolomiti Bellunesi, Parco Nazionale delle nat. park Italy 26 D2
Dolomitiche, Alpi mts Italy see Dolomites
Dolonnur China 43 L4
Dolo Odo Eth. 48 E3
Dolores Arg. 70 E5
Dolores Uruguay 70 E4
Dolores r. CO U.S.A. 65 I2
Dolphin and Union Strait Canada 60 G3
Dolphin Head hd Namibia 50 B3
Dolyna Ukr. 13 D6
Domaila India 36 D3
Domanič Turkey 27 M5
Domar China 43 I4
Domartang China 42 G6
Domažlice Czech Rep. 17 N6
Domba China 37 F3
Dom Bäkh Iran 35 H4
Dombås Norway 14 F5
Dombóvár Hungary 26 H1
Dombrau Poland see Dąbrowa Górnicza
Dombrowa Poland see Dąbrowa Górnicza
Domda China see Qingshuihe
Dome Argus ice feature Antarctica 76 E1
Dome Charlie ice feature Antarctica 76 F2
Dome Creek Canada 60 F4
Dome Rock Mountains AZ U.S.A. 65 E4
Domeyko Chile 70 B3
Domfront France 24 D2
Dominica country West Indies 67 L5
Dominican Republic country West Indies 67 J5
Dominion, Cape Canada 61 K3
Dominique i. Fr. Polynesia see Hiva Oa
Dom Joaquim Brazil 71 C2
Domo Eth. 48 F3
Domokos Greece 27 J5
Dompu Indon. 41 D8
Domula China see Duomula
Domuyo, Volcán vol. Arg. 70 B5
Domville, Mount hill Australia 58 E2
Don r. U.K. see Donetsk
Don r. U.K. 20 G3
Don r. U.K. 20 G3
Donaghadee U.K. 21 G3
Donaghmore U.K. 21 F3
Donald Australia 58 A6
Doñana, Parque Nacional de nat. park Spain 25 C5
Donau r. Austria/Germany 17 P6 see Danube
Donau r. Austria/Germany see Danube
Donauwörth Germany 17 M6
Don Benito Spain 25 D4
Doncaster U.K. 18 F5
Dondo Angola 49 B5
Dondo Moz. 49 D5
Dondra Head hd Sri Lanka 38 D5
Donegal Ireland 21 D3
Donegal Bay Ireland 21 D3
Donetsk Ukr. 13 H7
Donetsko-Amvrosiyevka Ukr. see Amvrosiyivka
Donets'kyy Kryazh hills Rus. Fed./Ukr. 13 H6
Donga r. Cameroon/Nigeria 46 D4
Dongan, Lagoa lag. Moz. 51 L3
Dongara Australia 55 A7
Dongbo China see Mêdog
Dongchuan Yunnan China 42 I7
Dongco China 37 F2
Dong Co l. China 37 F2
Dongfanghong China 44 D3
Dongfang China 43 L5
Donggala Indon. 41 G7
Donggang Shandong China 43 L5
Donggi Conag l. China 37 F2
Dongguan China see Donggang
Dong Hai sea N. Pacific Ocean see East China Sea
Đông Hới Vietnam 31 J5

Dongjug China 37 H3
Dongliao He r. China 44 A4
Dongminzhutun China 44 A3
Dongning China 44 C3
Dongo Angola 49 B5
Dongo Dem. Rep. Congo 48 B3
Dongola Sudan 32 D6
Dongou Congo 48 B3
Dongqiao China 37 G3
Dongtai China 43 M6
Dongting Hu l. China 43 K7
Dong Ujimqin Qi China see Uliastai
Dongxing Heilong. China 44 C3
Dongying China 43 L5
Donnellys Crossing N.Z. 59 D2
Donner Pass U.S.A. 62 C4
Donostia-San Sebastián Spain 25 F2
Donousa i. Greece 27 K6
Donskoye Rus. Fed. 13 I7
Dooagh Ireland 21 B4
Doomadgee Australia 56 B3
Doon r. U.K. 20 E5
Doon, Loch l. U.K. 20 E5
Doonbeg r. Ireland 21 C5
Dooxo Nugaaleed valley Somalia 48 E3
Dor Israel 39 B3
Dora, Lake salt flat Australia 54 C5
Dorah Pass Afgh. 36 B1
Dorbiljin China see Emin
Dorbod China see Taikang
Dorbod Qi China see Ulan Hua
Dorchester U.K. 19 E8
Dordabis Namibia 50 C2
Dordogne r. France 24 D4
Dordrecht Neth. 16 J5
Dordrecht S. Africa 51 H6
Doreenville Namibia 50 D2
Doré Lake Canada 60 H4
Dores do Indaiá Brazil 71 B2
Dorgê Co l. China 37 H3
Dori r. Afgh. 36 A3
Dori Burkina 46 C3
Doring r. S. Africa 50 D6
Dorisvale Australia 54 E3
Dorking U.K. 19 G7
Dormidontovka Rus. Fed. 44 D3
Dornoch U.K. 20 E3
Dornoch Firth est. U.K. 20 E3
Doro Mali 46 C3
Dorogobuzh Rus. Fed. 13 G5
Dorogorskoye Rus. Fed. 12 J2
Dorohoi Romania 13 E7
Döröö Nuur salt l. Mongolia 42 G3
Dorostol Bulg. see Silistra
Dorotea Sweden 14 J4
Dorpat Estonia see Tartu
Dorre Island Australia 55 A6
Dorrigo Australia 58 F3
Dorsoidong Co l. China 37 G2
Dortmund Germany 17 K5
Dörtyol Turkey 39 C1
Doruma Dem. Rep. Congo 48 C3
Dorylaeum Turkey see Eskişehir
Dos Bahías, Cabo c. Arg. 70 C6
Dos de Mayo Peru 68 C5
Dos Palos CA U.S.A. 65 C3
Dosso Niger 46 D3
Dothan U.S.A. 63 C6
Douai France 24 F1
Douala Cameroon 46 D4
Douarnenez France 24 B2
Double Island Point Australia 57 F5
Double Peak CA U.S.A. 65 C3
Double Point Australia 56 D3
Doubs r. France/Switz. 24 G3
Doubtful Sound inlet N.Z. 59 A7
Doubtless Bay N.Z. 59 D2
Douentza Mali 46 C3
Dougga tourist site Tunisia 26 C6
Douglas Isle of Man 18 C4
Douglas S. Africa 50 F5
Douglas U.K. 20 F5
Douglas AZ U.S.A. 62 F5
Douglas GA U.S.A. 63 K5
Douglas WY U.S.A. 62 F3
Douglas Reef i. Japan see Okino-Tori-shima
Doulatpur Bangl. see Daulatpur
Doullens France 24 F1
Douna Mali 46 C3
Doune U.K. 20 E4
Dourada, Serra hills Brazil 71 A1
Dourada, Serra mts Brazil 71 A1
Dourados Brazil 70 F2
Douro r. Port. 25 B3
Douve r. France 19 F9
Dove r. U.K. 19 F6
Dover DE U.S.A. 64 D3
Dover NH U.S.A. 64 F1
Dover NJ U.S.A. 64 D2
Dover OH U.S.A. 64 A2
Dover, Strait of France/U.K. 24 E1
Dover-Foxcroft U.S.A. 63 N2
Dovey r. U.K. 19 D6
Dovrefjell Nasjonalpark nat. park Norway 14 F5
Dowlaiswaram India 38 D2
Dowlatäbäd Färs Iran 35 H5
Dowlatäbäd Färs Iran 35 I5
Dowl at Yär Afgh. 36 A2
Downpatrick U.K. 21 G3
Downsville NY U.S.A. 64 D2
Dow Rud Iran 35 H4
Doylestown PA U.S.A. 64 D2
Dözen is Japan 45 D5
Dozulé France 17 [inset]
Dracena Brazil 71 A3
Drachten Neth. 17 K4
Drägäneşti-Olt Romania 27 K2
Drägäşani Romania 27 K2
Dragonera, Isla i. Spain see Sa Dragonera
Dragsfjärd Fin. 15 M6
Draguignan France 24 H5
Drahichyn Belarus 15 N10
Drake Australia 58 F2
Drakensberg mts S. Africa 51 I6
Drake Passage S. Atlantic Ocean 72 D9
Drakes Bay CA U.S.A. 65 A2
Drama Greece 27 K4
Drammen Norway 15 G7
Drangedal Norway 15 F7
Draperstown U.K. 21 F3
Drapsaca Afgh. see Kunduz
Dras Jammu and Kashmir 36 C2
Drasan Pak. 36 C1
Drau r. Austria 17 O7 see Drava
Dráva r. Hungary see Drava
Drave r. Slovenia/Croatia see Drava
Drayton Valley Canada 62 E1
Drazinda Pak. 36 B3
Dréan Alg. 26 B6
Dresden Germany 17 N5
Dreux France 24 E2
Drevsjø Norway 15 H6
Dri China 37 I3
Driffield U.K. 18 G4
Driftwood PA U.S.A. 64 B2
Drillham Australia 58 E1
Drimoleague Ireland 21 C6

Drina r. Bos.-Herz./Serbia 27 H2
Driscoll Island Antarctica 76 J1
Drissa Belarus see Vyerkhnyadzvinsk
Drniš Croatia 26 G3
Drobeta-Turnu Severin Romania 27 J2
Drogheda Ireland 21 F4
Drogichin Belarus see Drahichyn
Drogobych Ukr. see Drohobych
Drohobych Ukr. 13 D6
Droichead Átha Ireland see Drogheda
Droichead Nua Ireland see Newbridge
Droitwich U.K. see Droitwich Spa
Droitwich Spa U.K. 19 E6
Dromedary, Cape Australia 58 E6
Dromod Ireland 21 E4
Dromore Northern Ireland U.K. 21 E3
Dromore Northern Ireland U.K. 21 F3
Dronfield U.K. 18 F5
Dronning Louise Land reg. Greenland 77 I1
Dronning Maud Land reg. Antarctica see Queen Maud Land
Druk-Yul country Asia see Bhutan
Drumheller Canada 62 E1
Drummond atoll Kiribati see Tabiteuea
Drummond Island Kiribati see McKean
Drummond Range hills Australia 56 D5
Drummondville Canada 63 M2
Drummore U.K. 20 E6
Druskieniki Lith. see Druskininkai
Druskininkai Lith. 15 N10
Druzhina Rus. Fed. 29 P3
Druzhnaya Gorka Rus. Fed. 15 Q7
Dry r. Australia 54 F3
Dryanovo Bulg. 27 K3
Dryden Canada 63 I2
Dryden NY U.S.A. 64 C1
Drygalski Ice Tongue Antarctica 76 H1
Drygalski Island Antarctica 76 F2
Dry Lake NV U.S.A. 65 E2
Drymen U.K. 20 E4
Drysdale r. Australia 54 D3
Drysdale River National Park Australia 54 D3
Duaringa Australia 56 E4
Duarte, Pico mt. Dom. Rep. 67 J5
Duartina Brazil 71 A3
Ḍubā Saudi Arabia 32 E4
Dubai U.A.E. 33 I4
Dubawnt Lake Canada 61 H3
Dubayy U.A.E. see Dubai
Dubbo Australia 58 D4
Dublin Ireland 21 F4
Dublin U.S.A. 63 K5
Dubna Rus. Fed. 12 H4
Dubno Ukr. 13 E6
Du Bois PA U.S.A. 64 B2
Dubovka Rus. Fed. 13 J6
Dubovskoye Rus. Fed. 13 I7
Dubréka Guinea 46 B4
Dubris U.K. see Dover
Dubrovnik Croatia 26 H3
Dubrovytsya Ukr. 13 E6
Dubuque U.S.A. 63 I3
Dubysa r. Lith. 15 M9
Duc de Gloucester, Îles du is Fr. Polynesia 75 K7
Duchess Australia 56 B4
Ducie Island atoll Pitcairn Is 75 L7
Duck Bay Canada 62 G1
Duck Creek r. Australia 54 B5
Duckwater Peak NV U.S.A. 65 E1
Dudhi India 37 E4
Dudhwa India 36 E3
Dudinka Rus. Fed. 28 J3
Dudley U.K. 19 E6
Dudna r. India 38 C2
Dudu India 36 C4
Duékoué Côte d'Ivoire 46 C4
Duero r. Spain 25 C3
Duff Islands Solomon Is 53 G2
Dufferboy, Lac l. Canada 61 K4
Dufftown U.K. 20 F3
Dufourspitze mt. Italy/Switz. 24 H4
Dugi Otok i. Croatia 26 F2
Dugi Rat Croatia 26 G3
Duida-Marahuaca, Parque Nacional nat. park Venez. 68 E3
Duisburg Germany 17 K5
Duiwelskloof S. Africa 51 J2
Dukathole S. Africa 51 H6
Duke of Clarence atoll Tokelau see Nukunonu
Duke of Gloucester Islands Fr. Polynesia see Duc de Gloucester, Îles du
Duke of York atoll Tokelau see Atafu
Duk Fadiat Sudan 47 G4
Dukhovnitskoye Rus. Fed. 13 K5
Duki Pak. 36 B3
Duki Rus. Fed. 44 D2
Duki r. Rus. Fed. 44 D2
Dukou China see Panzhihua
Dūkštas Lith. 15 O9
Dulan China 42 H5
Dulce r. Arg. 70 D4
Dul'durga Rus. Fed. 43 K2
Dulhunty r. Australia 56 C1
Dulishi Hu salt l. China 37 E2
Dullewala Pak. 36 B3
Dullstroom S. Africa 51 J3
Dulmera India 36 C3
Dulovo Bulg. 27 L3
Duluth U.S.A. 63 I2
Dulverton U.K. 19 D7
Dūmā Syria 39 C3
Dumaguete Phil. 41 E7
Dumai Indon. 41 C7
Dumaresq r. Australia 58 E2
Dumas U.S.A. 62 G4
Dumat al Jandal Saudi Arabia 35 E5
Dumayr Syria 39 C3
Dumayr, Jabal mts Syria 39 C3
Dumbakh Iran see Dom Bākh
Dumbarton U.K. 20 E5
Dumbe S. Africa 51 J4
Ďumbier mt. Slovakia 17 Q6
Dumchele Jammu and Kashmir 36 D2
Dum Duma India 37 H4
Dumfries U.K. 20 F5
Dumka India 37 F4
Dumont d'Urville research station Antarctica 76 G2
Dumont d'Urville Sea Antarctica 76 G2
Dumyāṭ Egypt 34 C5
Dumyât Egypt see Dumyāṭ
Duna r. Hungary see Danube
Duna r. Hungary 26 H2 see Danube
Dünaburg Latvia see Daugavpils
Dunaj r. Slovakia see Danube
Dunajská Streda Slovakia 17 P7
Dunakeszi Hungary 27 H1
Dunany Point Ireland 21 F4
Dunărea r. Romania see Danube
Dunării, Delta Romania/Ukr. see Danube Delta
Dunaújváros Hungary 26 H1
Dunav r. Bulg./Croatia/Serbia see Danube
Dunav r. Bulg./Croatia/Serbia 26 L2 see Danube
Dunay r. Ukr. see Danube
Dunayivtsi Ukr. 13 E6
Dunbar Australia 56 C3
Dunbar U.K. 20 G4
Dunblane U.K. 20 F4
Dunboyne Ireland 21 F4
Duncan OK U.S.A. 62 H5
Duncansby Head hd U.K. 20 F2
Duncormick Ireland 21 F5
Dundaga Latvia 15 M8
Dundalk Ireland 21 F3
Dundalk MD U.S.A. 64 C3
Dundalk Bay Ireland 21 F4
Dundas Ont. Canada 64 B1
Dundas Greenland 61 L2
Dundas, Lake salt flat Australia 55 C8
Dundas Strait Australia 54 E2
Dún Dealgan Ireland see Dundalk
Dundee S. Africa 51 J5
Dundee U.K. 20 G4
Dundee NY U.S.A. 64 C1
Dundonald U.K. 21 G3
Dundoo Australia 58 B1
Dundrennan U.K. 20 F6
Dundrum U.K. 21 G3
Dundrum Bay U.K. 21 G3
Dundwa Range mts India/Nepal 37 E4
Dunedin N.Z. 59 C7
Dunfermline U.K. 20 F4
Dungannon U.K. 21 F3
Dún Garbhán Ireland see Dungarvan
Dungarpur India 36 C5
Dungarvan Ireland 21 E5
Dung Co l. China 37 G3
Dungeness hd U.K. 19 H8
Dungeness, Punta pt Arg. 70 C8
Dungiven U.K. 21 F3
Dungloe Ireland 21 D3
Dungog Australia 58 E4
Dungu Dem. Rep. Congo 48 C3
Dungun Malaysia 41 C7
Dungunab Sudan 32 E5
Dunhua China 44 C4
Dunhuang China 42 G4
Dunkeld Australia 58 D1
Dunkeld U.K. 20 F4
Dunkellin r. Ireland 21 D4
Dunkerque France see Dunkirk
Dunkery Hill hill U.K. 19 D7
Dunkirk France 24 F1
Dunkirk NY U.S.A. 64 B1
Dún Laoghaire Ireland 21 F4
Dunlavin Ireland 21 F4
Dunleer Ireland 21 F4
Dunloy U.K. 21 F2
Dunmanway Ireland 21 C6
Dunmarra Australia 54 F4
Dunmore Ireland 21 D4
Dunmore PA U.S.A. 64 D2
Dunmurry U.K. 21 G3
Dunnet Head hd U.K. 20 F2
Dunnigan CA U.S.A. 65 B1
Dunnville Ont. Canada 64 B1
Dunolly Australia 58 A6
Dunoon U.K. 20 E5
Duns U.K. 20 G5
Dunstable U.K. 19 G7
Dunstan Mountains N.Z. 59 B7
Duntroon N.Z. 59 C7
Dunyapur Pak. 36 B3
Duolun Nei Mongol China see Dolonnur
Duomula China 37 E2
Dupang Ling mts China 43 K7
Duperré Alg. see Aïn Defla
Dupnitsa Bulg. 27 J3
Duque de Bragança Angola see Calandula
Dūrā West Bank 39 B4
Durack r. Australia 54 D3
Durack Range hills Australia 54 D4
Dura Europos Syria see Aş Şālihīyah
Durağan Turkey 34 D2
Durance r. France 24 G5
Durango Mex. 66 D4
Durango Spain 25 E2
Durango U.S.A. 62 F4
Durant U.S.A. 63 H5
Durazno Uruguay 70 E4
Durazzo Albania see Durrës
Durban S. Africa 51 J5
Durban-Corbières France 24 F5
Durbanville S. Africa 50 D7
Durbin WV U.S.A. 64 B3
Durg India 36 E5
Durgapur Bangl. 37 G4
Durgapur India 37 F5
Durham U.K. 18 F4
Durham U.S.A. 63 L4
Durham Downs Australia 57 C5
Durlas Ireland see Thurles
Durleşti Moldova 27 M1
Durmitor mt. Montenegro 27 H3
Durmitor nat. park Montenegro 26 H3
Durness U.K. 20 E2
Durocortorum France see Reims
Durong South Australia 57 E5
Durostorum Bulg. see Silistra
Durovernum U.K. see Canterbury
Durrës Albania 27 H4
Durrie Australia 56 C5
Durrington U.K. 19 F7
Dursey Island Ireland 21 B6
Dursunbey Turkey 27 M5
Durukhsi Somalia 48 E3
Durusu Gölü l. Turkey 27 M4
Durūz, Jabal ad mt. Syria 39 C3
D'Urville, Tanjung pt Indon. 41 F8
D'Urville Island N.Z. 59 D5
Durzab Afgh. 36 A2
Duşak Turkm. 33 I2
Dushai Pak. 36 A3
Dushanbe Tajik. 33 K2
Dushet'i Georgia 35 G2
Dushore PA U.S.A. 64 C2
Dusse-Alin', Khrebet mts Rus. Fed. 44 D2
Düsseldorf Germany 17 K5
Dutch East Indies country Asia see Indonesia
Dutch Guiana country S. America see Suriname
Dutch West Indies terr. West Indies see Netherlands Antilles
Dutlwe Botswana 50 F2
Dutse Nigeria 46 D3
Dutsin-Ma Nigeria 46 D3
Dutton r. Australia 56 C4
Dutton Ont. Canada 64 A1
Dutton, Lake salt flat Australia 57 B6
Duvno Bos.-Herz. see Tomislavgrad
Duwin Iraq 35 G3
Düxanbibazar China 36 E1
Duyun China 43 J7
Düzce Turkey 27 N4
Duzdab Iran see Zāhedān
Dvina r. Europe see Zapadnaya Dvina
Dvina r. Rus. Fed. see Severnaya Dvina
Dvinsk Latvia see Daugavpils
Dvinskaya Guba g. Rus. Fed. 12 H2
Dwarka India 36 B5
Dwarsberg S. Africa 51 H3
Dwyka S. Africa 50 E7
Dyat'kovo Rus. Fed. 13 G5
Dyce U.K. 20 G3
Dyer, Cape Canada 61 L3
Dyersburg U.S.A. 63 J4
Dyffryn U.K. see Valley
Dyfi r. U.K. see Dovey
Dyfrdwy r. U.K. see Dee
Dyje r. Austria/Czech Rep. 17 P6
Dyke U.K. 20 F3
Dykh-Tau, Gora mt. Rus. Fed. 35 F2
Dylewska Góra hill Poland 17 Q4
Dymytrov Ukr. 13 H6
Dynevor Downs Australia 58 B2
Dyoki S. Africa 51 I6
Dyrrhachium Albania see Durrës
Dysart Australia 56 E4
Dysselsdorp S. Africa 50 F7
Dyurtyuli Rus. Fed. 11 Q4
Dzamïn Üüd Mongolia 43 K4
Dzanga-Ndoki, Parc National de nat. park Cent. Afr. Rep. 48 B3
Dzaoudzi Mayotte 49 E5
Dzaudzhikau Rus. Fed. see Vladikavkaz
Dzerzhinsk Belarus see Dzyarzhynsk
Dzerzhinsk Rus. Fed. 12 I4
Dzhagdy, Khrebet mts Rus. Fed. 44 C1
Dzhaki-Unakhta Yakbyyana, Khrebet mts Rus. Fed. 44 D2
Dzhalalabad Azer. see Cälilabad
Dzhalal-Abad Kyrg. see Jalal-Abad
Dzhalil' Rus. Fed. 11 Q4
Dzhalinda Rus. Fed. 44 A1
Dzhaltyr Kazakh. see Zhaltyr
Dzhambeyty Kazakh. see Zhympity
Dzhambul Kazakh. see Taraz
Dzhangala Kazakh. 11 Q6
Dzhankoy Ukr. 13 G7
Dzhanybek Kazakh. see Zhanibek
Dzharkent Kazakh. see Zharkent
Dzhava Georgia see Java
Dzhetygara Kazakh. see Zhitikara
Dzhezkazgan Kazakh. see Zhezkazgan
Dzhidinskiy, Khrebet mts Mongolia/Rus. Fed. 42 I2
Dzhokhar Ghala Rus. Fed. see Groznyy
Dzhubga Rus. Fed. 34 E1
Dzhugdzhur, Khrebet mts Rus. Fed. 29 O4
Dzhul'fa Azer. see Culfa
Dzhungarskiy Alatau, Khrebet mts China/Kazakh. 42 D4
Dzhusaly Kazakh. 42 A3
Działdowo Poland 17 R4
Dzūkija nat. park Lith. 15 N9
Dzungarian Basin China see Junggar Pendi
Dzur Mongolia 42 H3
Dzüünharaa Mongolia 42 J3
Dzuunmod Mongolia 42 J3
Dzyaniskavichy Belarus 15 O10
Dzyarzhynsk Belarus 15 O10
Dzyatlavichy Belarus 15 O10

E

Eagle AK U.S.A. 60 D3
Eagle Cap mt. U.S.A. 62 D2
Eagle Crags mt. CA U.S.A. 65 D3
Eagle Lake Canada 63 I2
Eagle Lake CA U.S.A. 62 C3
Eagle Mountain CA U.S.A. 65 E4
Eagle Pass U.S.A. 62 G6
Eagle Plain Canada 60 E3
Eagle Rock VA U.S.A. 64 B4
Eap i. Micronesia see Yap
Ear Falls Canada 63 I1
Earlimart CA U.S.A. 65 C3
Earl's Seat hill U.K. 20 E4
Earlston U.K. 20 G5
Earn r. U.K. 20 F4
Earn, Loch l. U.K. 20 E4
Earp CA U.S.A. 65 E3
Easington U.K. 18 H5
East Alligator r. Australia 54 F3
East Antarctica reg. Antarctica 76 F1
East Ararat PA U.S.A. 64 D2
East Aurora NY U.S.A. 64 B1
East Bengal country Asia see Bangladesh
Eastbourne U.K. 19 H8
East Branch Clarion River Reservoir PA U.S.A. 64 B2
East Cape N.Z. 59 G3
East Caroline Basin sea feature N. Pacific Ocean 74 F5
East China Sea N. Pacific Ocean 43 N6
East Coast Bays N.Z. 59 E3
Eastend Canada 62 F2
Easter Island S. Pacific Ocean 75 M7
Eastern Cape prov. S. Africa 51 H6
Eastern Desert Egypt 32 D4
Eastern Desert Egypt 32 D4
Eastern Fields reef Australia 56 D1
Eastern Ghats mts India 38 C4
Eastern Island U.S.A. 74 I4
Eastern Nara canal Pak. 36 B4
Eastern Samoa terr. S. Pacific Ocean see American Samoa
Eastern Sayan Mountains Rus. Fed. see Vostochnyy Sayan
Eastern Taurus plat. Turkey see Güneydoğu Toroslar
Eastern Transvaal prov. S. Africa see Mpumalanga
Easterville Canada 62 H1
East Falkland i. Falkland Is 70 E8
East Falmouth MA U.S.A. 64 F2
East Frisian Islands Germany 17 K4
East Greenwich RI U.S.A. 64 F2
East Grinstead U.K. 19 G7
Easthampton MA U.S.A. 64 E1
East Hampton NY U.S.A. 64 E2
East Hartford CT U.S.A. 64 E2
East Indiaman Ridge sea feature Indian Ocean 73 O7
East Kilbride U.K. 20 E5
Eastlake OH U.S.A. 64 A2
Eastleigh U.K. 19 F8
East Liverpool OH U.S.A. 64 A2
East London S. Africa 51 H7
Eastmain Canada 63 L1
Eastmain r. Canada 63 L1
East Mariana Basin sea feature N. Pacific Ocean 74 G5
Eastmere Australia 56 D4
Easton MD U.S.A. 64 C3
Easton PA U.S.A. 64 D2
East Orange NJ U.S.A. 64 D2
East Pacific Rise sea feature N. Pacific Ocean 75 M4
East Pakistan country Asia see Bangladesh
East Palestine OH U.S.A. 64 A2
East Providence RI U.S.A. 64 F2
East Retford U.K. see Retford
East Sea N. Pacific Ocean see Japan, Sea of
East Siberian Sea Rus. Fed. 29 P2
East Side Canal r. CA U.S.A. 65 C3
East Stroudsburg PA U.S.A. 64 D2
East Timor country Asia 54 D2
East Toorale Australia 58 B3
Eastville VA U.S.A. 64 D4
East York Ont. Canada 64 B1
Eau Claire U.S.A. 63 I3
Eauripik atoll Micronesia 41 G7
Eauripik Rise-New Guinea Rise sea feature N. Pacific Ocean 74 F5
Eaurypyg atoll Micronesia see Eauripik
Ebbw Vale U.K. 19 D7
Ebebiyin Equat. Guinea 46 E4
Ebenerde Namibia 50 C3
Ebensburg PA U.S.A. 64 B2
Eber Gölü l. Turkey 27 N5
Eberswalde-Finow Germany 17 N4
Ebetsu Japan 44 F4
Ebi Nor salt l. China see Ebinur Hu
Ebinur Hu salt l. China 42 E4
Eboli Italy 26 F4
Ebolowa Cameroon 46 E4
Ebony Namibia 50 B2
Ebre r. Spain see Ebro
Ebro r. Spain 25 G3
Eburacum U.K. see York
Ebusus i. Spain see Ibiza
Ecbatana Iran see Hamadān
Eceabat Turkey 27 L4
Ech Chélif Alg. see Chlef
Echegárate, Puerto pass Spain 25 E2
Echeng China see Ezhou
Echeverria, Pico mt. Mex. 66 B3
Echmiadzin Armenia see Ejmiatsin
Echuca Australia 58 B6
Écija Spain 25 D5
Eckernförde Germany 17 L3
Eclipse Sound sea chan. Canada 61 J2
Écrins, Parc National des nat. park France 24 H4
Ecuador country S. America 68 C4
Ed Eritrea 32 F7
Ed Sweden 15 G7
Eday i. U.K. 20 G1
Ed Da'ein Sudan 47 F3
Ed Dair, Jebel mt. Sudan 32 D7
Ed Damazin Sudan 32 D7
Ed Damer Sudan 32 D6
Ed Debba Sudan 32 D6
Ed Dueim Sudan 32 D7
Eddystone Point Australia 57 [inset]
Edéa Cameroon 46 E4
Edéia Brazil 71 A2
Eden Australia 58 D6
Eden r. U.K. 18 D4
Edenburg S. Africa 51 G5
Edendale N.Z. 59 B8
Edenderry Ireland 21 E4
Edenville S. Africa 51 H4
Edessa Greece 27 J4
Edessa Turkey see Şanlıurfa
Edfu Egypt see Idfū
Edgar Ranges hills Australia 54 C4
Edgartown MA U.S.A. 64 F2
Edgecumbe Island Solomon Is see Utupua
Edge Island Svalbard see Edgeøya
Edgeøya i. Svalbard 28 D2
Edgeworthstown Ireland 21 E4
Édhessa Greece see Edessa
Edinboro PA U.S.A. 64 A2
Edinburg TX U.S.A. 62 H6
Edinburg VA U.S.A. 64 B3
Edinburgh U.K. 20 F5
Edirne Turkey 27 L4
Edith Ronne Land ice feature Antarctica see Ronne Ice Shelf
Edjeleh Libya 46 D2
Edjudina Australia 55 C7
Edku Egypt see Idkū
Edmonton Canada 62 E1
Edmundston Canada 63 N2
Edo Japan see Tōkyō
Edom reg. Israel/Jordan 39 B4
Édouard, Lac l. Dem. Rep. Congo/Uganda see Edward, Lake
Edremit Turkey 27 L5
Edremit Körfezi b. Turkey 27 L5
Edrengiyn Nuruu mts Mongolia 42 H4
Edsbyn Sweden 15 I6
Edson Canada 60 G4
Edward r. N.S.W. Australia 58 B5
Edward r. Qld Australia 56 C2
Edward, Lake Dem. Rep. Congo/Uganda 48 C4
Edward, Mount Antarctica 76 L1
Edwardesabad Pak. see Bannu
Edward's Creek Australia 57 A6
Edwards Plateau U.S.A. 62 G5
Edward VII Peninsula Antarctica 76 I1
Edzo Canada see Rae-Edzo
Eenzamheid Pan salt pan S. Africa 50 E4
Eesti country Europe see Estonia
Éfaté i. Vanuatu 53 G3
Effingham U.S.A. 63 J4
Efsus Turkey see Afşin
Egadi, Isole is Sicily Italy 26 D5
Egedesminde Greenland see Aasiaat
Eger Hungary 17 R7
Egersund Norway 15 E7
Egerton, Mount hill Australia 55 B6
Egilsstaðir Iceland 14 [inset]
Eğin Turkey see Kemaliye
Eğirdir Turkey 27 N6
Eğirdir Gölü l. Turkey 27 N6
Eglinton U.K. 21 E2
Egmont, Cape N.Z. 59 D4
Egmont, Mount vol. N.Z. see Taranaki, Mount
Egmont National Park N.Z. 59 E4
eGoli S. Africa see Johannesburg
Eğrigöz Dağı mts Turkey 27 M5
Egton U.K. 18 G4
Éguas r. Brazil 71 B1
Egvekinot Rus. Fed. 29 T3
Egypt country Africa 32 C4
Ehden Lebanon 39 B2
Ehen Hudag China 42 I5
Ehingen (Donau) Germany 17 L6
Ehrenberg AZ U.S.A. 65 E4
Ehrenberg Range hills Australia 55 E5
Eidfjord Norway 15 E6
Eidsvold Australia 56 E5
Eidsvoll Norway 15 G6
Eifel hills Germany 17 K5
Eigg i. U.K. 20 C4
Eight Degree Channel India/Maldives 38 B5
Eights Coast Antarctica 76 K2
Eighty Mile Beach Australia 54 C4
Eilat Israel 39 B5
Eildon Australia 58 B6
Eildon, Lake Australia 58 C6
Einasleigh Australia 56 D3
Einasleigh r. Australia 56 C3
Eindhoven Neth. 16 J5
Einsiedeln Switz. 24 I3
Ein Yahav Israel 39 B4
Eirik Ridge sea feature N. Atlantic Ocean 72 F2
Eiriosgaigh i. U.K. see Eriskay
Eirunepé Brazil 68 E5
Eiseb watercourse Namibia 49 C5
Eisenach Germany 17 M5
Eisenhüttenstadt Germany 17 O4
Eisenstadt Austria 17 P7
Eite, Loch inlet U.K. see Etive, Loch
Eivissa Spain see Ibiza
Eivissa i. Spain see Ibiza
Ejea de los Caballeros Spain 25 F2
Ejeda Madag. 49 E6
Ejin Horo Qi China see Altan Shiret
Ejin Qi China see Dalain Hob
Ejmiadzin Armenia see Ejmiatsin
Ejmiatsin Armenia 35 G2
Ekenäs Fin. 15 M7
Ekerem Turkm. 35 I3
Eketahuna N.Z. 59 E5
Ekibastuz Kazakh. 42 D2
Ekimchan Rus. Fed. 44 D1
Ekinyazı Turkey 39 D1
Ekonda Rus. Fed. 29 L3
Ekostrovskaya Imandra, Ozero l. Rus. Fed. 12 G2
Ekshärad Sweden 15 H6
Eksjö Sweden 15 I8
Eksteenfontein S. Africa 50 C5
Ekström Ice Shelf Antarctica 76 B2
Ekwan r. Canada 63 K1
El Aaiún W. Sahara see Laâyoune
Elafonisou, Steno sea chan. Greece 27 J6
El 'Agrûd well Egypt see Al 'Ajrūd
Elaia, Cape Cyprus 39 B2
El 'Alamein Egypt see Al 'Alamayn
El 'Âmirîya Egypt see Al 'Āmirīyah
Elands r. S. Africa 51 I3
Elandsdoorn S. Africa 51 I3
El Aouinet Alg. 26 B7
Elar Armenia see Abovyan
El Araïche Morocco see Larache
El Ariana Tunisia see L'Ariana
El Aricha Alg. 22 D5
El 'Arîsh Egypt see Al 'Arīsh
El Arrouch Alg. 26 B6
El Ashmûnein Egypt see Al Ashmūnayn
El Asnam Alg. see Chlef
Elassona Greece 27 J5
Elat Israel see Eilat
Elazığ Turkey 35 E3
Elba, Isola d' i. Italy 26 D3
El'ban Rus. Fed. 44 E2
El Barco de Valdeorras Spain see O Barco
Elbasan Albania 27 I4
El Batroun Lebanon see Batroûn
El Baúl Venez. 68 E2
El Bawîti Egypt see Al Bawīṭī
El Bayadh Alg. 22 E5
Elbe r. Germany 17 L4
El Béqaa valley Lebanon 39 C2
Elbert, Mount U.S.A. 62 F4
Elbeuf France 24 E2
Elbeyli Turkey 39 C1
Elbing Poland see Elbląg
Elbistan Turkey 34 E3
Elbląg Poland 17 Q3
El Bouláida Alg. see Blida
El'brus mt. Rus. Fed. 35 F2
El Burgo de Osma Spain 25 E3
Elburz Mountains Iran 35 H3
El Cajon CA U.S.A. 65 D4
El Callao Venez. 68 F2
El Campo U.S.A. 63 H6
El Centro CA U.S.A. 65 E4
El Cerro Bol. 68 F7
Elche Spain see Elche-Elx
Elche-Elx Spain 25 F4
Elcho Island Australia 56 A1
El Coca Ecuador see Coca
El Cocuy, Parque Nacional nat. park Col. 68 D2
Elda Spain 25 F4
El'dikan Rus. Fed. 29 O3
El Djezair country Africa see Algeria
El Djezair Alg. see Algiers
Eldorado Arg. 70 F3
Eldorado Brazil 71 A4
El Dorado Col. 68 D3
El Dorado Mex. 62 F7
El Dorado AR U.S.A. 63 I5
El Dorado KS U.S.A. 63 H4
Eldorado Venez. 68 F2
Eldorado Mountains NV U.S.A. 65 E3
Eldoret Kenya 48 D3
Elea, Cape Cyprus see Elaia, Cape
Elefantes r. Moz. see Olifants
El Eglab plat. Alg. 46 C2
El Ejido Spain 25 E5
Elemi Triangle terr. Africa 48 D3
El Encanto Col. 68 D4
Elephanta Caves tourist site India 38 B2
Elephant Island Antarctica 76 A2
Elephant Pass Sri Lanka 38 D4
Elephant Point Bangl. 37 H5
Eleşkirt Turkey 35 F3
El Eulma Alg. 22 F4
Eleuthera i. Bahamas 67 I3
El Fahs Tunisia 26 C6
El Faiyûm Egypt see Al Fayyūm
El Fasher Sudan 47 F3
El Ferrol Spain see Ferrol
El Ferrol del Caudillo Spain see Ferrol
El Fud Eth. 48 E3
El Fuerte Mex. 66 C3
El Gara Egypt see Qārah
El Geneina Sudan 47 F3
El Geteina Sudan 32 D7
El Ghardaqa Egypt see Al Ghurdaqah
El Ghor plain Jordan/West Bank see Al Ghawr
Elgin U.K. 20 F3
Elgin IL U.S.A. 63 J3
Elgin NV U.S.A. 65 E2
El'ginskiy Rus. Fed. 29 P3
El Gîza Egypt see Giza
El Goléa Alg. 22 E5
El Golfo de Santa Clara Mex. 62 E5
Elgon, Mount Kenya/Uganda 30 C6
El Hadjar Alg. 26 B6
El Ḥammâm Egypt see Al Ḥammām
El Hammâmi reg. Mauritania 46 B2
El Hank esc. Mali/Mauritania 46 C2
El Ḥarra Egypt see Al Ḥarrah
El Hazim Jordan see Al Ḥazīm
El Heiz Egypt see Al Ḥayz
El Hierro i. Canary Is 46 B2
El Homr Alg. 22 E6
El Homra Sudan 32 D7
Eliase Indon. 54 E2
Elías Piña Dom. Rep. 67 J5
Elichpur India see Achalpur
Elie U.K. 20 G4
Elila r. Dem. Rep. Congo 48 C4
Elim U.S.A. 60 B3
Elimberrum France see Auch
Elingampangu Dem. Rep. Congo 48 C4
Élisabethville Dem. Rep. Congo see Lubumbashi
Eliseu Martins Brazil 69 J5
El Iskandarîya Egypt see Alexandria
Elista Rus. Fed. 13 J7
Elizabeth NJ U.S.A. 64 D2
Elizabeth WV U.S.A. 64 A3
Elizabeth, Mount hill Australia 54 D4
Elizabeth Bay Namibia 50 B4
Elizabeth City U.S.A. 63 L4
Elizabeth Island Pitcairn Is see Henderson Island
Elizabeth Point Namibia 50 B4
Elizabethtown KY U.S.A. 63 J4
El Jadida Morocco 22 C5
El Jem Tunisia 26 D7
Ełk Poland 17 S4
Elk r. MD U.S.A. 64 D3
El Kaa Lebanon see Qaa
El Kab Sudan 32 D6
El Kala Alg. 26 C6
Elk City U.S.A. 62 H4
Elkedra Australia 56 A4
Elkedra watercourse Australia 56 B4
El Kef Tunisia see Le Kef
El Kelaâ des Srarhna Morocco 22 C5
Elkford Canada 62 E1
Elk Grove CA U.S.A. 65 B1
El Khalil West Bank see Hebron
El Khandaq Sudan 32 D6
El Khârga Egypt see Al Khārijah
El Kharrûba Egypt see Al Kharrūbah
Elkhart IN U.S.A. 63 J3
El Khartûm Sudan see Khartoum
El Khenachich esc. Mali see El Khnâchîch
El Khnâchîch esc. Mali 46 C2
Elkhovo Bulg. 27 L3
Elki Turkey see Beytüşşebap
Elkins WV U.S.A. 64 B3
Elkland PA U.S.A. 64 C2
Elko Canada 62 D2
Elko U.S.A. 62 D3
Elkton MD U.S.A. 64 D3
Elkton VA U.S.A. 64 B3
El Kûbri Egypt see Al Kubrī
El Kuntilla Egypt see Al Kuntillah
Elkview WV U.S.A. 64 A3
Ellas country Europe see Greece
Ellef Ringnes Island Canada 61 H2
Ellendale U.S.A. 62 H2
Ellensburg U.S.A. 62 C2
Ellenville NY U.S.A. 64 D2
Ellesmere, Lake N.Z. 59 D6
Ellesmere Island Canada 61 J2
Ellesmere Island National Park Reserve Canada see Quttinirpaaq National Park
Ellesmere Port U.K. 18 E5
Ellice r. Canada 61 H3
Ellice Island atoll Tuvalu see Funafuti
Ellice Islands country S. Pacific Ocean see Tuvalu
Ellicott City MD U.S.A. 64 C3
Elliot S. Africa 51 H6
Elliot, Mount Australia 56 D3
Elliotdale S. Africa 51 I6
Elliot Knob mt. VA U.S.A. 64 B3
Elliott Australia 54 F4
Elliston VA U.S.A. 64 A4
Ellon U.K. 20 G3
Ellora Caves tourist site India 38 B1
Ellsworth ME U.S.A. 63 N3
Ellsworth Land reg. Antarctica 76 K1
Ellsworth Mountains Antarctica 76 L1
El Maghreb country Africa see Morocco
Elmakuz Dağı mt. Turkey 39 A1
Elmalı Turkey 27 M6
El Manṣûra Egypt see Al Manṣūrah
El Maṭarîya Egypt see Al Maṭarīyah
El Mazâr Egypt see Al Mazār
El Meghaïer Alg. 22 F5
El Milia Alg. 22 F4
El Minya Egypt see Al Minyā
Elmira Ont. Canada 64 A1
Elmira NY U.S.A. 64 C1
El Moral Spain 25 E5
Elmore Australia 58 B6
El Mreyyé reg. Mauritania 46 C3
Elmshorn Germany 17 L4
El Muglad Sudan 32 C7
Elnesvågen Norway 14 E5
El Nevado, Cerro mt. Col. 68 D3
El Oasis Baja California Mex. 65 E4
El Obeid Sudan 32 D7
El Odaiya Sudan 32 C7
El Oro Mex. 62 G6
Elorza Venez. 68 E2
El Oued Alg. 22 F5
El Paso TX U.S.A. 62 F5
Elphin U.K. 20 D2
El Portal CA U.S.A. 65 C2
El Porvenir Mex. 66 C2
El Porvenir Panama 67 I7
El Prat de Llobregat Spain 25 H3
El Progreso Hond. 66 G5
El Puerto de Santa María Spain 25 C5
El Qâhira Egypt see Cairo
El Qasimiye r. Lebanon 39 B3
El Quds Israel/West Bank see Jerusalem
El Quseima Egypt see Al Quṣaymah
El Quṣeir Egypt see Al Quṣayr
El Qûṣîya Egypt see Al Qūṣīyah
El Reno U.S.A. 62 H4
Elsa Canada 60 E3
El Ṣaff Egypt see Aṣ Ṣaff
El Sahuaro Mex. 65 F5
El Salado Mex. 66 D4
El Salto Mex. 66 C4
El Salvador country Central America 66 G6
El Salvador Chile 70 C3
El Salvador Mex. 62 G7
Elsass reg. France see Alsace
El Sellûm Egypt see As Sallūm
Elsey Australia 54 F3
El Shallûfa Egypt see Ash Shallūfah
El Sharana Australia 54 F3
El Shaṭṭ Egypt see Ash Shaṭṭ
Elsinore Denmark see Helsingør
Elsinore CA U.S.A. 65 D4
Elsinore Lake CA U.S.A. 65 D4
El Suweis Egypt see Suez
El Suweis governorate Egypt see As Suways
El Tama, Parque Nacional nat. park Venez. 68 D2
El Tarf Alg. 26 C6
El Teleno mt. Spain 25 C2
El Temascal Mex. 66 E4
El Ter r. Spain 25 H2
El Thamad Egypt see Ath Thamad
El Tigre Venez. 68 F2
El'ton Rus. Fed. 13 J6
El'ton, Ozero l. Rus. Fed. 13 J6
El Tuparro, Parque Nacional nat. park Col. 68 E2
El Ṭûr Egypt see Aṭ Ṭūr
El Turbio Chile 70 B8
El Uqṣur Egypt see Luxor
Eluru India 38 D2
Elva Estonia 15 O7
Elvanfoot U.K. 20 F5
Elvas Port. 25 C4
Elverum Norway 15 G6
Elvira Brazil 68 D5
El Wak Kenya 48 E3
El Wâṭya well Egypt see Al Wāṭiyah
El Wuz Sudan 32 D7
Elx Spain see Elche-Elx
Ely U.K. 19 H6
Ely MN U.S.A. 63 I2
Ely NV U.S.A. 65 E1
Elyria U.S.A. 63 K3
El Zagâzîg Egypt see Az Zaqāzīq
Émaé i. Vanuatu 53 G3
Emāmrūd Iran 35 I3
Emām Ṣaḥeb Afgh. 36 B1
Emån r. Sweden 15 J8
Emas, Parque Nacional das nat. park Brazil 69 H7

Emba Kazakh. 28 G5
Embalenhle S. Africa 51 I4
Embarcación Arg. 70 D2
Embi Kazakh. see Emba
Embira r. Brazil see Envira
Emborcação, Represa de resr Brazil 71 B2
Embu Kenya 48 D4
Emden Germany 17 K4
Emden Deep sea feature N. Pacific Ocean see Cape Johnson Depth
Emerald Australia 56 E4
Emerita Augusta Spain see Mérida
Emerson Canada 63 H2
Emesa Syria see Homs
Emet Turkey 27 M5
eMgwenya S. Africa 51 J3
Emigrant Valley valley NV U.S.A. 65 E2
Emi Koussi mt. Chad 47 E3
Emiliano Zapata Mex. 66 F5
Emin China 42 E3
Emine, Nos pt Bulg. 27 L3
Eminska Planina hills Bulg. 27 L3
Emirdağ Turkey 27 N5
Emir Dağı mt. Turkey 27 N5
Emir Dağları mts Turkey 27 N5
eMjindini S. Africa 51 J3
Emmaboda Sweden 15 I8
Emmaste Estonia 15 M7
Emmaus PA U.S.A. 64 D2
Emmaville Australia 58 E2
Emmen Neth. 17 K4
Emmen Switz. 24 I3
Emmet Australia 56 D5
Emmiganuru India 38 C3
Emona Slovenia see Ljubljana
Emory Peak U.S.A. 62 G6
Empangeni S. Africa 51 J5
Emperor Seamount Chain sea feature N. Pacific Ocean 74 H2
Emperor Trough sea feature N. Pacific Ocean 74 H2
Empingham Reservoir U.K. see Rutland Water
Emplawas Indon. 54 E2
Empoli Italy 26 D3
Emporia KS U.S.A. 63 H4
Emporia VA U.S.A. 63 L4
Emporium PA U.S.A. 64 B2
Empty Quarter des. Saudi Arabia see Rub' al Khālī
Ems r. Germany 17 K4
eMzinoni S. Africa 51 I4
Enafors Sweden 14 H5
Encantadas, Serra das hills Brazil 70 F4
Encarnación Para. 70 E3
Enchi Ghana 46 C4
Encinitas CA U.S.A. 65 D4
Encruzilhada Brazil 71 C1
Ende Indon. 41 E8
Endeavour Strait Australia 56 C1
Endeh Indon. see Ende
Enderby Land reg. Antarctica 76 D2
Endicott NY U.S.A. 64 C1
Endicott Mountains U.S.A. 60 C3
EnenKio terr. N. Pacific Ocean see Wake Island
Energodar Ukr. see Enerhodar
Enerhodar Ukr. 13 G7
Enewetak atoll Marshall Is 74 G5
Enez Turkey 27 L4
Enfe Lebanon 39 B2
Enfião, Ponta do pt Angola 49 B5
Enfidaville Tunisia 26 D6
Engan Norway 14 F5
Engaru Japan 44 F3
Engcobo S. Africa 51 H6
En Gedi Israel 39 B4
Engel's Rus. Fed. 13 J6
Enggano i. Indon. 41 C8
England admin. div. U.K. 19 E6
English Bazar India see Ingraj Bazar
English Channel France/U.K. 19 F9
English Coast Antarctica 76 L2
Engozero Rus. Fed. 12 G2
Enhlalakahle S. Africa 51 J5
Enid U.S.A. 62 H4
Eniwa Japan 44 F4
Eniwetok atoll Marshall Is see Enewetak
Enkeldoorn Zimbabwe see Chivhu
Enköping Sweden 15 J7
Enna Sicily Italy 26 F6
Ennadai Lake Canada 61 H3
En Nahud Sudan 32 C7
Ennedi, Massif mts Chad 47 F3
Ennell, Lough l. Ireland 21 E4
Enngonia Australia 58 B2
Ennis Ireland 21 D5
Ennis TX U.S.A. 63 H5
Enniscorthy Ireland 21 F5
Enniskillen U.K. 21 E3
Ennistymon Ireland 21 C5
Enn Nâqoûra Lebanon 39 B3
Enns r. Austria 17 O6
Eno Fin. 14 Q5
Enoch UT U.S.A. 65 F2
Enontekiö Fin. 14 M2
Ensay Australia 58 C6
Enschede Neth. 17 K4
Ensenada Mex. 66 A2
Enshi China 43 J6
Entebbe Uganda 48 D3
Enterprise Canada 60 G3
Enterprise UT U.S.A. 65 F2
Entre Ríos Bol. 68 F8
Entre Rios Brazil 69 H5
Entre Rios de Minas Brazil 71 B3
Entroncamento Port. 25 B4
Enugu Nigeria 46 D4
Enurmino Rus. Fed. 29 T3
Envira Brazil 68 D5
Envira r. Brazil 68 D5
Enyamba Dem. Rep. Congo 48 C4
Eochaill Ireland see Youghal
Epéna Congo 48 B3
Ephrata PA U.S.A. 64 C2
Epi i. Vanuatu 53 G3
Epidamnus Albania see Durrës
Épinal France 24 H2
Episkopi Bay Cyprus 39 A2
Episkopis, Kolpos b. Cyprus see Episkopi Bay
ePitoli S. Africa see Pretoria
Epomeo, Monte hill Italy 26 E4
Epping U.K. 19 H7
Epping Forest National Park Australia 56 D4
Eppynt, Mynydd hills U.K. 19 D6
Epsom U.K. 19 G7
Eqlīd Iran 35 I5
Equatorial Guinea country Africa 46 D4
Équeurdreville-Hainneville France 19 F9
Erac Creek watercourse Australia 58 B1
Erandol India 38 B1
Erawadi r. Myanmar see Irrawaddy
Erbaa Turkey 34 E2
Erbeskopf hill Germany 17 K6
Ercan airport Cyprus 39 A2
Erciş Turkey 35 F3
Erciyes Dağı mt. Turkey 34 D3
Érd Hungary 26 H1
Erdaobaihe China see Baihe
Erdaogou China 37 H2
Erdao Jiang r. China 44 B4
Erdek Turkey 27 L4
Erdemli Turkey 39 B1
Erdenet Mongolia 42 I3
Erdi reg. Chad 47 F3
Erdniyevskiy Rus. Fed. 13 J7
Erebus, Mount vol. Antarctica 76 H1
Erechim Brazil 70 F3
Ereentsav Mongolia 43 L3
Ereğli Konya Turkey 34 D3
Ereğli Zonguldak Turkey 27 N4
Erego Moz. see Errego
Erei, Monti mts Sicily Italy 26 F6
Erementaū Kazakh. see Yereymentau
Erenhot China 43 K4
Erepucu, Lago de l. Brazil 69 G4
Erevan Armenia see Yerevan
Erfurt Germany 17 M5
Ergani Turkey 35 E3
'Erg Chech des. Alg./Mali 46 C2
Ergel Mongolia 43 J4
Ergene r. Turkey 27 L4
Ērgļi Latvia 15 N8
Ergu China 44 C3
Ergun China 43 M2
Ergun He r. China/Rus. Fed. see Argun'
Ergun Youqi China see Ergun
Ergun Zuoqi China see Genhe
Erhulai China 44 B4
Eriboll, Loch inlet U.K. 20 E2
Ericht r. U.K. 20 F4
Ericht, Loch l. U.K. 20 E4
Erie PA U.S.A. 64 A1
Erie, Lake Canada/U.S.A. 64 A1
'Erîgât des. Mali 46 C3
Erik Eriksenstretet sea chan. Svalbard 28 D2
Erimo-misaki c. Japan 44 F4
Erinpura Road India 36 C4
Eriskay i. U.K. 20 B3
Eritrea country Africa 32 E6
Erlangen Germany 17 M6
Erldunda Australia 55 F6
Erlistoun watercourse Australia 55 C6
Erlong Shan mt. China 44 C4
Erlongshan Shuiku resr China 44 B4
Ermak Kazakh. see Aksu
Ermelo S. Africa 51 I4
Ermenek Turkey 39 A1
Ermenek r. Turkey 39 A1
Ermont Egypt see Armant
Ermoupoli Greece 27 K6
Ernakulam India 38 C4
Erne r. Ireland/U.K. 21 D3
Ernest Giles Range hills Australia 55 C6
Erode India 38 C4
Eromanga Australia 57 C5
Erongo admin. reg. Namibia 50 B1
Errabiddy Hills Australia 55 A6
Er Rachidia Morocco 22 D5
Er Raoui des. Alg. 22 D6
Errego Moz. 49 D5
Er Remla Tunisia 26 D7
Er Renk Sudan 32 D7
Errigal hill Ireland 21 D2
Errinundra National Park Australia 58 D6
Erris Head hd Ireland 21 B3
Erromango i. Vanuatu 53 G3
Erronan i. Vanuatu see Futuna
Erseka Albania see Ersekë
Ersekë Albania 27 I4
Ersmark Sweden 14 L5
Ertai China 42 G3
Ertil' Rus. Fed. 13 I6
Ertis r. Kazakh./Rus. Fed. see Irtysh
Ertix He r. China/Kazakh. 42 F3
Ērtra country Africa see Eritrea
Eruh Turkey 35 F3
Eryuan China 42 H7
Erzerum Turkey see Erzurum
Erzgebirge mts Czech Rep./Germany 17 N5
Erzhan China 44 B2
Erzin Turkey 39 C1
Erzincan Turkey 35 E3
Erzurum Turkey 35 F3
Esa-ala P.N.G. 56 E1
Esan-misaki pt Japan 44 F4
Esashi Japan 44 F3
Esbjerg Denmark 15 F9
Esbo Fin. see Espoo
Escalante Desert UT U.S.A. 65 F2
Escalón Mex. 66 D3
Escanaba U.S.A. 63 J2
Escárcega Mex. 66 F5
Escatrón Spain 25 F3
Eschscholtz atoll Marshall Is see Bikini
Eschwege Germany 17 M5
Escondido CA U.S.A. 65 D4
Escuinapa Mex. 66 C4
Escuintla Guat. 66 F6
Eséka Cameroon 46 E4
Eşen Turkey 27 M6
Esenguly Turkm. 35 I3
Esenguly Döwlet Gorugy nature res. Turkm. 35 I3
Eşfahān Iran 35 H4
Eshkamesh Afgh. 36 B1
Eshkanān Iran 35 I6
Eshowe S. Africa 51 J5
Esikhawini S. Africa 51 K5
Esil Kazakh. see Yesil'
Esil r. Kazakh./Rus. Fed. see Ishim
Esk Australia 58 F1
Esk r. Australia 57 [inset]
Esk r. U.K. 18 D4
Eskdalemuir U.K. 20 F5
Esker Canada 61 L4
Eskifjörður Iceland 14 [inset]
Eski Gediz Turkey 27 M5
Eskilstuna Sweden 15 J7
Eskimo Lakes Canada 60 E3
Eskimo Point Canada see Arviat
Eskipazar Turkey 34 D2
Eskişehir Turkey 27 N5
Esla r. Spain 25 C3
Eslāmābād-e Gharb Iran 35 G4
Esler Dağı mt. Turkey 27 M6
Eslöv Sweden 15 H9
Eşme Turkey 27 M5
Esmeraldas Ecuador 68 C3
Esmont VA U.S.A. 64 B4
Espakeh Iran 33 J4
Espalion France 24 F4
España country Europe see Spain
Espanola Canada 63 K2
Esperance Australia 55 C8
Esperance Bay Australia 55 C8
Esperanza research station Antarctica 76 A2
Esperanza Arg. 70 B8
Esperanza Mex. 62 F6
Espichel, Cabo c. Port. 25 B4
Espigão, Serra do mts Brazil 71 A4
Espigüete mt. Spain 25 D2
Espinhaço, Serra do mts Brazil 71 C2
Espinosa Brazil 71 C1
Espírito Santo Brazil see Vila Velha
Espírito Santo state Brazil 71 C2
Espíritu Santo i. Vanuatu 53 G3
Espíritu Santo, Isla i. Mex. 62 E7
Espoo Fin. 15 N6
Espuña mt. Spain 25 F5
Esquel Arg. 70 B6
Essaouira Morocco 46 C1
Es Semara W. Sahara 46 B2
Essen Germany 17 K5
Essequibo r. Guyana 69 G2
Essex CA U.S.A. 65 E3
Essex MD U.S.A. 64 C3
Esso Rus. Fed. 29 Q4
Essoyla Rus. Fed. 12 G3
Eşţahbān Iran 35 I5
Estância Brazil 69 K6
Estats, Pic d' mt. France/Spain 24 E5
Estcourt S. Africa 51 I5
Estelí Nicaragua 67 G6
Estella Spain 25 E2
Estepa Spain 25 D5
Estepona Spain 25 D5
Esteras de Medinaceli Spain 25 E3
Esterhazy Canada 62 G1
Estero Bay CA U.S.A. 65 B3
Esteros Para. 70 D2
Estevan Canada 62 G2
Estherville U.S.A. 63 I3
Eston Canada 62 F1
Estonia country Europe 15 N7
Estonskaya S.S.R. country Europe see Estonia
Estrela Brazil 71 A5
Estrela, Serra da mts Port. 25 C3
Estrela do Sul Brazil 71 B2
Estrella mt. Spain 25 E4
Estremoz Port. 25 C4
Estrondo, Serra hills Brazil 69 I5
Etadunna Australia 57 B6
Etah India 36 D4
Étampes France 24 F2
Étaples France 24 E1
Etawah Rajasthan India 36 D4
Etawah Uttar Prad. India 36 D4
Ethandakukhanya S. Africa 51 J4
Ethel Creek Australia 55 C5
E'Thembini S. Africa 50 F5
Ethiopia country Africa 48 D3
Etimesğut Turkey 34 D3
Etive, Loch inlet U.K. 20 D4
Etna, Mount vol. Sicily Italy 26 F6
Etne Norway 15 D7
Etobicoke Ont. Canada 64 B1
Etolin Strait U.S.A. 60 B3
Etorofu-tō i. Rus. Fed. see Iturup, Ostrov
Etosha National Park Namibia 49 B5
Etosha Pan salt pan Namibia 49 B5
Etoumbi Congo 48 B3
Etrek r. Iran/Turkm. see Atrek
Etrek Turkm. 35 I3
Étrépagny France 19 I9
Étretat France 19 H9
Ettelbruck Lux. 17 K6
Ettrick Water r. U.K. 20 F5
Euabalong Australia 58 C4
Euboea i. Greece see Evvoia
Eucla Australia 55 E7
Euclid OH U.S.A. 64 A2
Euclides da Cunha Brazil 69 K6
Eucumbene, Lake Australia 58 D6
Eudunda Australia 57 B7
Eufaula Lake resr U.S.A. 63 H4
Eugene U.S.A. 62 C3
Eugenia, Punta pt Mex. 66 A3
Eugowra Australia 58 D4
Eulo Australia 58 B2
Eumungerie Australia 58 D3
Eungella Australia 56 E4
Eungella National Park Australia 56 E4
Euphrates r. Asia 35 G5
Euphrates r. Iraq/Syria 32 F3
Euphrates r. Turkey 23 L4
Eura Fin. 15 M6
Eureka CA U.S.A. 62 C3
Eureka MT U.S.A. 62 D2
Eureka NV U.S.A. 62 D4
Eureka Sound sea chan. Canada 61 J2
Eureka Valley valley CA U.S.A. 65 D2
Euriowie Australia 57 C6
Euroa Australia 58 B6
Eurombah Australia 57 E5
Eurombah Creek r. Australia 57 E5
Europa, Île i. Indian Ocean 49 E6
Europa, Punta de pt Gibraltar see Europa Point
Europa Point Gibraltar 25 D5
Eva Downs Australia 54 F4
Evans, Lac l. Canada 63 L1
Evans City PA U.S.A. 64 A2
Evans Head Australia 58 F2
Evans Head hd Australia 58 F2
Evans Ice Stream Antarctica 76 L1
Evanston WY U.S.A. 62 E3
Evansville IN U.S.A. 63 J4
Eva Perón Arg. see La Plata
Evaton S. Africa 51 H4
Evaz Iran 35 I6
Evensk Rus. Fed. 29 Q3
Everard, Lake salt flat Australia 57 A6
Everard, Mount Australia 55 F5
Everard Range hills Australia 55 F6
Everek Turkey see Develi
Everest, Mount China/Nepal 37 F4
Everett PA U.S.A. 64 B2
Everett WA U.S.A. 62 C2
Everglades swamp U.S.A. 63 K6
Evesham Australia 56 C4
Evesham U.K. 19 F6
Evesham, Vale of valley U.K. 19 F6
Evijärvi Fin. 14 M5
Evje Norway 15 E7
Évora Port. 25 C4
Evoron, Ozero l. Rus. Fed. 44 E2
Évreux France 24 E2
Evros r. Bulg. see Meriç
Evros r. Turkey see Maritsa
Evrotas r. Greece 27 J6
Evrychou Cyprus 39 A2
Evrykhou Cyprus see Evrychou
Evvoia i. Greece 27 K5
Ewan Australia 56 D3
Ewaso Ngiro r. Kenya 48 E3
Ewe, Loch b. U.K. 20 D3
Ewo Congo 48 B4
Exaltación Bol. 68 E6
Excelsior S. Africa 51 H5
Excelsior Mountain CA U.S.A. 65 C1
Excelsior Mountains NV U.S.A. 65 C1
Exe r. U.K. 19 D8
Exeter Australia 58 E5
Exeter Ont. Canada 64 A1
Exeter U.K. 19 D8
Exeter CA U.S.A. 65 C2
Exeter NH U.S.A. 64 F1
Exminster U.K. 19 D8
Exmoor hills U.K. 19 D7
Exmoor National Park U.K. 19 D7
Exmore VA U.S.A. 64 D4
Exmouth Australia 54 A5
Exmouth U.K. 19 D8
Exmouth, Mount Australia 58 D3
Exmouth Gulf Australia 54 A5
Exmouth Plateau sea feature Indian Ocean 73 P7
Expedition National Park Australia 56 E5
Expedition Range mts Australia 56 E5
Exton PA U.S.A. 64 D2
Extremadura aut. comm. Spain 25 D4
Exuma Cays is Bahamas 67 I4
Eyasi, Lake salt l. Tanz. 48 D4
Eyawadi r. Myanmar see Irrawaddy
Eye U.K. 19 I6
Eyelenoborsk Rus. Fed. 11 S3
Eyemouth U.K. 20 G5
Eyjafjörður inlet Iceland 14 [inset]
Eyl Somalia 48 E3
Eylau Rus. Fed. see Bagrationovsk
Eynsham U.K. 19 F7
Eyre (North), Lake Australia 57 B6
Eyre (South), Lake Australia 57 B6
Eyre, Lake Australia 57 B6
Eyre Creek watercourse Australia 56 B5
Eyre Mountains N.Z. 59 B7
Eyre Peninsula Australia 57 A7
Eysturoy i. Faroe Is 14 [inset]
Ezakheni S. Africa 51 J5
Ezenzeleni S. Africa 51 I4
Ezequiel Ramos Mexía, Embalse resr Arg. 70 C5
Ezhou China 43 K6
Ezhva Rus. Fed. 12 K3
Ezine Turkey 27 L5
Ezo i. Japan see Hokkaidō
Ezousa r. Cyprus 39 A2

F

Faaborg Denmark 15 G9
Faadhippolhu Atoll Maldives 38 B5
Faafxadhuun Somalia 48 E3
Fåborg Denmark see Faaborg
Fabriano Italy 26 E3
Fachi Niger 46 E3
Fada Chad 47 F3
Fada-N'Gourma Burkina 46 D3
Fadghāmī Syria 35 F4
Fadiffolu Atoll Maldives see Faadhippolhu Atoll
Fadippolu Atoll Maldives see Faadhippolhu Atoll
Faenza Italy 26 D2
Færoerne terr. N. Atlantic Ocean see Faroe Islands
Faeroes terr. N. Atlantic Ocean see Faroe Islands
Făgăraş Romania 27 K2
Fagatogo American Samoa 53 I3
Fagersta Sweden 15 I7
Fagurhólsmýri Iceland 14 [inset]
Fagwir Sudan 32 D8
Fahraj Iran 35 I5
Fā'id Egypt 34 D5
Fairbanks U.S.A. 60 D3
Fairchance PA U.S.A. 64 B3
Fairfax VA U.S.A. 64 C3
Fairfield CA U.S.A. 65 A1
Fair Haven VT U.S.A. 64 E1
Fair Head hd U.K. 21 F2
Fair Isle i. U.K. 20 H1
Fairmont MN U.S.A. 63 I3
Fairmont WV U.S.A. 64 A3
Fairview Australia 56 D2
Fairview PA U.S.A. 64 A1
Fairweather, Mount Canada/U.S.A. 60 E4
Faisalabad Pak. 33 L3
Faith U.S.A. 62 G2
Faizabad Afgh. see Feyzābād
Faizabad India 37 E4
Fakaofo atoll Tokelau 53 I2
Fakaofu atoll Tokelau see Fakaofo
Fakenham U.K. 19 H6
Fåker Sweden 14 I5
Fakfak Indon. 41 F8
Fakhrabad Iran 35 I5
Fakiragram India 37 G4
Fako vol. Cameroon see Cameroun, Mont
Fal r. U.K. 19 C8
Falaba Sierra Leone 46 B4
Falam Myanmar 37 H5
Falavarjan Iran 35 H4
Falenki Rus. Fed. 12 K4
Falkenberg Sweden 15 H8
Falkirk U.K. 20 F5
Falkland U.K. 20 F4
Falkland Escarpment sea feature S. Atlantic Ocean 72 E9
Falkland Islands terr. S. Atlantic Ocean 70 E8
Falkland Plateau sea feature S. Atlantic Ocean 72 E9
Falkland Sound sea chan. Falkland Is 70 D8
Falköping Sweden 15 H7
Fallbrook CA U.S.A. 65 D4
Fallieres Coast Antarctica 76 L2
Fallon U.S.A. 62 D4
Fall River MA U.S.A. 64 F2
Fall River Pass U.S.A. 62 F3
Falmouth U.K. 19 B8
Falmouth VA U.S.A. 64 C3
False Bay S. Africa 50 D8
False Point India 37 F5
Falster i. Denmark 15 G9
Fălticeni Romania 13 E7
Falun Sweden 15 I6
Famagusta Cyprus 39 A2
Famagusta Bay Cyprus see Ammochostos Bay
Famenin Iran 35 H4
Fame Range hills Australia 55 C6
Family Well Australia 54 D5
Fāmūr, Daryācheh-ye l. Iran 35 H5
Fana Mali 46 C3
Fanad Head hd Ireland 21 E2
Fandriana Madag. 49 E6
Fane r. Ireland 21 F4
Fangxian China 43 K6
Fangzheng China 44 C3
Fannūj Iran 33 I4
Fano Italy 26 E3
Fanum Fortunae Italy see Fano
Faqīh Aḩmadān Iran 35 H5
Faraba Mali 46 B3
Faradofay Madag. see Tôlañaro
Farafangana Madag. 49 E6
Farāfirah, Wāḩāt al oasis Egypt 32 C4
Farafra Oasis oasis Egypt see Farāfirah, Wāḩāt al
Farāh Afgh. 33 J3
Farahābād Iran see Khezerābād
Farallones de Cali, Parque Nacional nat. park Col. 68 C3
Faranah Guinea 46 B3
Fararah Oman 33 I6
Farasān, Jazā'ir is Saudi Arabia 32 F6
Faraulep atoll Micronesia 41 G7
Fareham U.K. 19 F8
Farewell, Cape Greenland 61 N3
Farewell, Cape N.Z. 59 D5
Farewell Spit N.Z. 59 D5
Färgelanda Sweden 15 H7
Farghona Uzbek. see Farg'ona
Fargo U.S.A. 63 H2
Farg'ona Uzbek. 33 L1
Faribault U.S.A. 63 I3
Faribault, Lac l. Canada 61 K4
Faridabad India 36 D3
Faridkot India 36 C3
Faridpur Bangl. 37 G5
Farīmān Iran 33 I2
Farkhar Afgh. see Farkhato
Farkhato Afgh. 36 B1
Farmahin Iran 35 H4
Farmington ME U.S.A. 63 M3
Farmington NH U.S.A. 64 F1
Farmington NM U.S.A. 62 F4
Farmville VA U.S.A. 64 B4
Farnborough U.K. 19 G7
Farne Islands U.K. 18 F3
Farnham U.K. 19 G7
Farnham, Lake salt flat Australia 55 D6
Farnham, Mount Canada 62 D1
Faro Brazil 69 G4
Faro Port. 25 C5
Fårö i. Sweden 15 K8
Faroe - Iceland Ridge sea feature Arctic Ocean 77 I2
Faroe Islands terr. N. Atlantic Ocean 14 [inset]
Fårösund Sweden 15 K8
Farquhar Group is Seychelles 49 F5
Farquhar Islands hills Australia 55 C6
Farrāshband Iran 35 I5
Farr Bay Antarctica 76 F2
Farrukhabad India see Fatehgarh
Farsund Norway 15 E7
Farwell TX U.S.A. 62 G5
Fasā Iran 35 I5
Fasano Italy 26 G4
Faşikan Geçidi pass Turkey 39 A1
Fastiv Ukr. 13 F6
Fastov Ukr. see Fastiv
Fatehabad India 36 C3
Fatehgarh India 36 D4
Fatehpur Rajasthan India 36 C4
Fatehpur Uttar Prad. India 36 E4
Fatick Senegal 46 B3
Fattoilep atoll Micronesia see Faraulep
Faughan r. U.K. 21 E2
Fauresmith S. Africa 51 G5
Fauske Norway 14 I3
Fawley U.K. 19 F8
Faxaflói b. Iceland 14 [inset]
Faxälven r. Sweden 14 J5
Faya Chad 47 E3
Fayetteville AR U.S.A. 63 I4
Fayetteville NC U.S.A. 63 L4
Fayetteville WV U.S.A. 64 A3
Fâyid Egypt see Fā'id
Faylakah i. Kuwait 35 H5
Fazao Malfakassa, Parc National de nat. park Togo 46 D4
Fazilka India 36 C3
Fdérik Mauritania 46 B2
Fead Group is P.N.G. see Nuguria Islands
Feale r. Ireland 21 C5
Fear, Cape U.S.A. 63 L5
Featherston N.Z. 59 E5
Feathertop, Mount Australia 58 C6
Fécamp France 24 E2
Federal District admin. dist. Brazil see Distrito Federal
Federalsburg MD U.S.A. 64 D3
Federated Malay States country Asia see Malaysia
Fedusar India 36 C4
Fehmarn i. Germany 17 M3
Feia, Lagoa lag. Brazil 71 C3
Feijó Brazil 68 D5
Feilding N.Z. 59 E5
Feio r. Brazil see Aguapeí
Feira de Santana Brazil 71 D1
Fejd-el-Abiod pass Alg. 26 B6
Feke Turkey 34 D3
Felanitx Spain 25 H4
Feldberg mt. Germany 17 L7
Feldkirch Austria 17 L7
Feldkirchen in Kärnten Austria 17 O7
Felipe C. Puerto Mex. 66 G5
Felixlândia Brazil 71 B2
Felixstowe U.K. 19 I7
Felixton S. Africa 51 J5
Fellowsville WV U.S.A. 64 B3
Felsina Italy see Bologna
Felton DE U.S.A. 64 D3
Feltre Italy 26 D1
Femunden l. Norway 14 G5
Femundsmarka Nasjonalpark nat. park Norway 14 H5
Fenaio, Punta del pt Italy 26 D3
Fener Burnu hd Turkey 39 B1
Fénérive Madag. see Fenoarivo Atsinanana
Fengari mt. Greece 27 K4
Fengguang China 44 B3
Fengshui Shan mt. China 44 A1
Fengxian China 42 J6
Fengxiang Heilong. China see Luobei
Fengxiang Yunnan China see Lincang
Fengyüan Taiwan 43 M8
Fengzhen China 43 K4
Feni Bangl. 37 G5
Feni Islands P.N.G. 52 F2
Feno, Capo di c. Corsica France 24 I6
Fenoarivo Atsinanana Madag. 49 E5
Fenua Ura atoll Fr. Polynesia see Manuae
Feodosiya Ukr. 34 D1
Fer, Cap de c. Alg. 26 B6
Férai Greece see Feres
Ferdows Iran 33 I3
Feres Greece 27 L4
Fergus Falls U.S.A. 63 H2
Fergusson Island P.N.G. 52 F2
Fériana Tunisia 26 C7
Ferijaz Serbia see Uroševac
Ferkessédougou Côte d'Ivoire 46 C4
Fermo Italy 26 E3
Fermont Canada 61 L4
Fermoselle Spain 25 C3
Fermoy Ireland 21 D5
Fernandina, Isla i. Galápagos Ecuador 68 [inset]
Fernandina Beach U.S.A. 63 K5
Fernando de Magallanes, Parque Nacional nat. park Chile 70 B8
Fernando de Noronha i. Brazil 72 F6
Fernandópolis Brazil 71 A3
Fernando Poó i. Equat. Guinea see Bioco
Fernão Dias Brazil 71 B2
Ferndown U.K. 19 F8
Fernlee Australia 58 C2
Ferns Ireland 21 F5
Ferozepore India see Firozpur
Ferrara Italy 26 D2
Ferreira-Gomes Brazil 69 H3
Ferro, Capo c. Sardinia Italy 26 C4
Ferrol Spain 25 B2
Ferros Brazil 71 C2
Ferryville Tunisia see Menzel Bourguiba
Fertő-tavi nat. park Hungary 26 G1
Fès Morocco 22 D5
Feshi Dem. Rep. Congo 49 B4
Fété Bowé Senegal 46 B3
Fethard Ireland 21 E5
Fethiye Malatya Turkey see Yazıhan
Fethiye Muğla Turkey 27 M6
Fethiye Körfezi b. Turkey 27 M6
Fetisovo Kazakh. 35 I2
Fetlar i. U.K. 20 [inset]
Fettercairn U.K. 20 G4
Feuilles, Rivière aux r. Canada 61 K4
Fevral'sk Rus. Fed. 44 C1
Fevzipaşa Turkey 34 E3
Feyzābād Afgh. 36 B1
Fez Morocco see Fès
Ffestiniog U.K. 19 D6
Fianarantsoa Madag. 49 E6
Fichē Eth. 48 D3
Fier Albania 27 H4
Fiery Creek r. Australia 56 B3
Fife Ness pt U.K. 20 G4
Fifield Australia 58 C4
Figeac France 24 F4
Figueira da Foz Port. 25 B3
Figueras Spain see Figueres
Figueres Spain 25 H2
Figuig Morocco 22 D5
Figuil Cameroon 47 E4
Fiji country S. Pacific Ocean 53 H3
Fīk' Eth. 48 E3
Filadelfia Para. 70 D2
Filchner Ice Shelf Antarctica 76 A1
Filey U.K. 18 G4
Filibe Bulg. see Plovdiv
Filingué Niger 46 D3
Filipinas country Asia see Philippines
Filippiada Greece 27 I5
Filipstad Sweden 15 I7
Fillan Norway 14 F5
Fillmore CA U.S.A. 65 C3
Fillmore UT U.S.A. 65 F1
Fīltu Eth. 48 E3
Fimbull Ice Shelf Antarctica 76 C2
Fin Iran 35 H4
Findhorn r. U.K. 20 F3
Findlay U.S.A. 63 K3
Finger Lakes NY U.S.A. 64 C1
Finike Turkey 27 N6
Finike Körfezi b. Turkey 27 N6
Finisterre Spain see Fisterra
Finisterre, Cabo c. Spain see Finisterre, Cape
Finisterre, Cape Spain 25 B2
Finke watercourse Australia 56 A5
Finke, Mount hill Australia 55 F7
Finke Bay Australia 54 E3
Finke Gorge National Park Australia 55 F6
Finland country Europe 14 O5
Finland, Gulf of Europe 15 M7
Finlay r. Canada 60 F4
Finn r. Ireland 21 E3
Finnigan, Mount Australia 56 D2
Finniss, Cape Australia 55 F8
Finnmarksvidda reg. Norway 14 H2
Finnsnes Norway 14 J2
Finspång Sweden 15 I7
Fintona U.K. 21 E3
Fintown Ireland 21 D3
Finucane Range hills Australia 56 C4
Fionn Loch l. U.K. 20 D3
Fionnphort U.K. 20 C4
Fiordland National Park N.Z. 59 A7
Fırat r. Turkey see Euphrates
Fırat r. Turkey 34 E3 see Euphrates
Firebaugh CA U.S.A. 65 B2
Firenze Italy see Florence
Firk, Sha'īb watercourse Iraq 35 G5
Firmat Arg. 70 D4
Firminy France 24 G4
Firmum Italy see Fermo
Firmum Picenum Italy see Fermo
Firovo Rus. Fed. 12 G4
Firozabad India 36 D4
Firozpur India 36 C3
First Three Mile Opening sea chan. Australia 56 D2
Fīrūzābād Iran 35 I5
Fīrūzkūh Iran 35 I4
Fischersbrunn Namibia 50 B3
Fish watercourse Namibia 50 C5
Fisher Australia 55 E7
Fisher Bay Antarctica 76 G2
Fisher Glacier Antarctica 76 E2
Fishers Island NY U.S.A. 64 F2
Fisher Strait Canada 61 J3
Fishguard U.K. 19 C7
Fishing Creek MD U.S.A. 64 C3
Fiske, Cape Antarctica 76 L2
Fiskenæsset Greenland see Qeqertarsuatsiaat
Fismes France 24 F2
Fisterra Spain 25 B2
Fisterra, Cabo c. Spain see Finisterre, Cape
Fitri, Lac l. Chad 47 E3
Fitzgerald River National Park Australia 55 B8
Fitz Roy Arg. 70 C7
Fitzroy r. Australia 54 C4
Fitz Roy, Cerro mt. Arg. 70 B7
Fitzroy Crossing Australia 54 D4
Fiume Croatia see Rijeka
Fivemiletown U.K. 21 E3
Five Points CA U.S.A. 65 B2
Fizi Dem. Rep. Congo 49 C4
Fizuli Azer. see Füzuli
Flå Norway 15 F6
Flagstaff S. Africa 51 I6
Flagstaff U.S.A. 62 E4
Flamborough Head hd U.K. 18 G4
Flamingsvlei salt pan S. Africa 50 E6
Flannan Isles U.K. 20 B2
Flåsjön l. Sweden 14 I4
Flathead r. U.S.A. 62 E2
Flathead Lake U.S.A. 62 E2
Flattery, Cape Australia 56 D2
Flattery, Cape U.S.A. 62 C2
Fleetwood Australia 56 D4
Fleetwood U.K. 18 D5
Fleetwood PA U.S.A. 64 D2
Flekkefjord Norway 15 E7
Flemington NJ U.S.A. 64 D2
Flen Sweden 15 J7
Flensburg Germany 17 L3
Flers France 24 D2
Fletcher Peninsula Antarctica 76 L2
Flinders r. Australia 56 C3
Flinders Chase National Park Australia 57 B7
Flinders Group National Park Australia 56 D2
Flinders Island Australia 57 [inset]
Flinders Passage Australia 56 E3
Flinders Ranges mts Australia 57 B7
Flinders Ranges National Park Australia 57 B6
Flinders Reefs Australia 56 E3
Flin Flon Canada 62 G1
Flint U.K. 18 D5
Flint U.S.A. 63 K3
Flint Island Kiribati 75 J6
Flinton Australia 58 D1
Flisa Norway 15 H6
Flissingskiy, Mys c. Rus. Fed. 28 H2
Flodden U.K. 18 E3
Flood Range mts Antarctica 76 J1

Flora r. Australia 54 E3
Florac France 24 F4
Flora Reef Australia 56 D3
Florence Italy 26 D3
Florence AL U.S.A. 63 J5
Florence AZ U.S.A. 62 E5
Florence SC U.S.A. 63 L5
Florencia Col. 68 C3
Florentia Italy see Florence
Florentino Ameghino, Embalse resr Arg. 70 C6
Flores r. Arg. 70 E5
Flores Guat. 66 G5
Flores i. Indon. 41 E8
Flores, Laut sea Indon. 41 D8
Floresta Brazil 69 K5
Floriano Brazil 69 J5
Florianópolis Brazil 71 A4
Florida Uruguay 70 E4
Florida state U.S.A. 63 K5
Florida, Straits of Bahamas/U.S.A. 67 H4
Florida Islands Solomon Is 53 G2
Florida Keys is U.S.A. 63 K7
Florin CA U.S.A. 65 B1
Florina Greece 27 I4
Florø Norway 15 D6
Floyd VA U.S.A. 64 A4
Floyd, Mount AZ U.S.A. 65 F3
Flushing Neth. see Vlissingen
Fly r. P.N.G. 52 E2
Flying Fish, Cape Antarctica 76 K2
Foam Lake Canada 62 G1
Foča Bos.-Herz. 26 H3
Foça Turkey 27 L5
Fochabers U.K. 20 F3
Focşani Romania 27 L2
Foggia Italy 26 F4
Fogo i. Cape Verde 46 [inset]
Foinaven hill U.K. 20 E2
Foix France 24 E5
Folda sea chan. Norway 14 I3
Foldereid Norway 14 H4
Foldfjorden sea chan. Norway 14 G4
Folegandros i. Greece 27 K6
Foleyet Canada 63 K2
Foley Island Canada 61 K3
Foligno Italy 26 E3
Folkestone U.K. 19 I7
Folkingham U.K. 19 G6
Folkston U.S.A. 63 K5
Folldal Norway 14 G5
Follonica Italy 26 D3
Folsom Lake CA U.S.A. 65 B1
Fomboni Comoros 49 E5
Fomin Rus. Fed. 13 I7
Fominskaya Rus. Fed. 12 K2
Fominskoye Rus. Fed. 12 I4
Fonda NY U.S.A. 64 D1
Fond-du-Lac Canada 60 H4
Fond du Lac U.S.A. 63 J3
Fondevila Spain 25 B3
Fondi Italy 26 E4
Fonni Sardinia Italy 26 C4
Fonsagrada Spain see A Fonsagrada
Fonseca, Golfo do b. Central America 66 G6
Fonte Boa Brazil 68 E4
Fontur pt Iceland 14 [inset]
Foochow China see Fuzhou
Foraker, Mount U.S.A. 60 C3
Foraulep atoll Micronesia see Faraulep
Forbes Australia 58 D4
Forchheim Germany 17 M6
Ford City CA U.S.A. 65 C3
Førde Norway 15 D6
Fordham U.K. 19 H6
Fordingbridge U.K. 19 F8
Ford Range mts Antarctica 76 J1
Fords Bridge Australia 58 B2
Forécariah Guinea 46 B4
Forel, Mont mt. Greenland 61 O3
Foreland hd U.K. 19 F8
Foreland Point U.K. 19 D7
Forest MS U.S.A. 63 J5
Forest Creek r. Australia 56 C3
Forest Hill Australia 58 C5
Forestville CA U.S.A. 65 A1
Forfar U.K. 20 G4
Forges-les-Eaux France 19 I9
Forked River NJ U.S.A. 64 D3
Fork Union VA U.S.A. 64 B4
Forlì Italy 26 E2
Formby U.K. 18 D5
Formentera i. Spain 25 G4
Formentor, Cap de c. Spain 25 H4
Former Yugoslav Republic of Macedonia country Europe see Macedonia
Formiga Brazil 71 B3
Formosa Arg. 70 E3
Formosa country Asia see Taiwan
Formosa Brazil 71 B1
Formosa, Serra hills Brazil 69 G6
Formosa Bay Kenya see Ungwana Bay
Formosa Strait China/Taiwan see Taiwan Strait
Formoso r. Bahia Brazil 71 B1
Formoso r. Tocantins Brazil 71 A1
Fornos Moz. 51 L2
Forres U.K. 20 F3
Forrest Vic. Australia 58 A7
Forrest W.A. Australia 55 E7
Forrestal Range mts Antarctica 76 A1
Forrest City U.S.A. 63 I4
Forrest Lakes salt flat Australia 55 E7
Fors Sweden 14 J5
Forsayth Australia 56 C3
Forsnäs Sweden 14 M3
Forssa Fin. 15 M6
Forster Australia 58 F4
Forsyth MT U.S.A. 62 F2
Forsyth Range hills Australia 56 C4
Fort Abbas Pak. 36 C3
Fort Albany Canada 63 K1
Fortaleza Brazil 69 K4
Fort Archambault Chad see Sarh
Fort Ashby WV U.S.A. 64 B3
Fort Augustus U.K. 20 E3
Fort Beaufort S. Africa 51 H7
Fort Benton U.S.A. 62 E2
Fort Brabant Canada see Tuktoyaktuk
Fort Bragg U.S.A. 62 C4
Fort Charlet Alg. see Djanet
Fort Chimo Canada see Kuujjuaq
Fort Chipewyan Canada 60 G4
Fort Crampel Cent. Afr. Rep. see Kaga Bandoro
Fort-Dauphin Madag. see Tôlañaro
Fort-de-France Martinique 67 L6
Fort de Kock Indon. see Bukittinggi
Fort de Polignac Alg. see Illizi
Fort Dodge U.S.A. 63 I3
Fort Edward NY U.S.A. 64 E1
Fortescue r. Australia 54 B5
Forte Veneza Brazil 69 H5
Fort Flatters Alg. see Bordj Omer Driss
Fort Foureau Cameroon see Kousséri
Fort Franklin Canada see Déline
Fort Gardel Alg. see Zaouatallaz
Fort George Canada see Chisasibi
Fort Good Hope Canada 60 F3
Fort Gouraud Mauritania see Fdérik
Forth r. U.K. 20 F4
Forth, Firth of est. U.K. 20 F4
Fort Hertz Myanmar see Putao
Fortification Range mts NV U.S.A. 65 E1
Fortín General Mendoza Para. 70 D2
Fortín Leonida Escobar Para. 70 D2
Fortín Madrejón Para. 70 E2
Fortín Pilcomayo Arg. 70 D2
Fortín Ravelo Bol. 68 F7
Fortín Sargento Primero Leyes Arg. 70 E2
Fortín Suárez Arana Bol. 68 F7
Fortín Teniente Juan Echauri López Para. 70 D2
Fort Jameson Zambia see Chipata
Fort Johnston Malawi see Mangochi
Fort Lamy Chad see Ndjamena
Fort Laperrine Alg. see Tamanrasset
Fort Lauderdale U.S.A. 63 K6
Fort Liard Canada 60 F3
Fort Macleod Canada 62 E2
Fort Manning Malawi see Mchinji
Fort McMurray Canada 60 G4
Fort McPherson Canada 60 E3
Fort Munro Pak. 36 B3
Fort Myers U.S.A. 63 K6
Fort Nelson Canada 60 F4
Fort Payne U.S.A. 63 J5
Fort Peck Reservoir U.S.A. 62 F2
Fort Pierce U.S.A. 63 K6
Fort Portal Uganda 48 D3
Fort Providence Canada 60 G3
Fort Randall U.S.A. see Cold Bay
Fort Resolution Canada 60 G3
Fortrose N.Z. 59 B8
Fortrose U.K. 20 E3
Fort Rosebery Zambia see Mansa
Fort Rousset Congo see Owando
Fort Rupert Canada see Waskaganish
Fort Sandeman Pak. see Zhob
Fort Saskatchewan Canada 62 E1
Fort Scott U.S.A. 63 I4
Fort Severn Canada 61 J4
Fort-Shevchenko Kazakh. 30 E2
Fort Simpson Canada 60 F3
Fort Smith Canada 60 G3
Fort Smith U.S.A. 63 I4
Fort Stockton U.S.A. 62 G5
Fort Sumner U.S.A. 62 G5
Fort Trinquet Mauritania see Bîr Mogreïn
Fort Vermilion Canada 77 L3
Fort Victoria Zimbabwe see Masvingo
Fort Ware Canada see Ware
Fort Wayne U.S.A. 63 J3
Fort William U.K. 20 D4
Fort Worth U.S.A. 63 H5
Fort Yukon U.S.A. 60 D3
Forum Iulii France see Fréjus
Forvik Norway 14 H4
Fossano Italy 26 B2
Fossil Downs Australia 54 D4
Foster Australia 58 C7
Fotadrevo Madag. 49 E6
Fotherby U.K. 18 G5
Fotokol Cameroon 47 E3
Fotuna i. Vanuatu see Futuna
Fougères France 24 D2
Foula i. U.K. 20 [inset]
Foulness Point U.K. 19 H7
Foul Point Sri Lanka 38 D4
Foumban Cameroon 46 E4
Foundation Ice Stream glacier Antarctica 76 L1
Fountains Abbey and Royal Water Garden (NT) tourist site U.K. 18 F4
Fourches, Mont des hill France 24 G2
Four Corners CA U.S.A. 65 D3
Fouriesburg S. Africa 51 I5
Fournoi i. Greece 27 L6
Fourpeaked Mountain U.S.A. 60 C4
Fouta Djallon reg. Guinea 46 B3
Foveaux Strait N.Z. 59 A8
Fowey r. U.K. 19 C8
Fowler CO U.S.A. 62 G4
Fowler Ice Rise Antarctica 76 L1
Fowlers Bay Australia 52 D5
Fowlers Bay b. Australia 55 F8
Fox Creek Canada 60 G4
Foxdale Isle of Man 18 C4
Foxe Basin g. Canada 61 K3
Foxe Channel Canada 61 J3
Foxe Peninsula Canada 61 K3
Fox Glacier N.Z. 59 C6
Fox Islands U.S.A. 60 B4
Fox Mountain Canada 60 E3
Fox Valley Canada 62 F1
Foyers U.K. 20 E3
Foyle r. Ireland/U.K. 21 E3
Foyle, Lough b. Ireland/U.K. 21 E2
Foynes Ireland 21 C5
Foz de Areia, Represa de resr Brazil 71 A4
Foz do Cunene Angola 49 B5
Foz do Iguaçu Brazil 70 F3
Fraga Spain 25 G3
Frakes, Mount Antarctica 76 K1
Framingham MA U.S.A. 64 F1
Framnes Mountains Antarctica 76 E2
Franca Brazil 71 B3
Français, Récif des reef New Caledonia 53 G3
Francavilla Fontana Italy 26 G4
France country Europe 24 F3
Frances Australia 57 C8
Franceville Gabon 48 B4
Francis atoll Kiribati see Beru
Francisco de Orellana Ecuador see Coca
Francistown Botswana 49 C6
Francois Peron National Park Australia 55 A6
Frankenhöhe hills Germany 17 M6
Frankfort KY U.S.A. 63 K4
Frankfurt Germany see Frankfurt am Main
Frankfurt am Main Germany 17 L5
Frankfurt an der Oder Germany 17 O4
Frank Hann National Park Australia 55 C8
Fränkische Alb hills Germany 17 M6
Fränkische Schweiz reg. Germany 17 M6
Frankland, Cape Australia 57 [inset]
Franklin MA U.S.A. 64 F1
Franklin NH U.S.A. 64 F1
Franklin PA U.S.A. 64 B2
Franklin Bay Canada 77 A2
Franklin D. Roosevelt Lake resr U.S.A. 62 D2
Franklin-Gordon National Park Australia 57 [inset]
Franklin Island Antarctica 76 H1
Franklin Mountains Canada 60 F3
Franklin Strait Canada 61 I2
Franklinville NY U.S.A. 64 B1
Frankston Australia 58 B7
Fränsta Sweden 14 J5
Frantsa-Iosifa, Zemlya is Rus. Fed. 28 G2
Franz Josef Glacier N.Z. 59 C6
Frasca, Capo della c. Sardinia Italy 26 C5
Frascati Italy 26 E4
Fraser r. Australia 54 C4
Fraser r. B.C. Canada 62 C2
Fraser r. Nfld. and Lab. Canada 61 L4
Fraser, Mount hill Australia 55 B6
Fraserburg S. Africa 50 E6
Fraserburgh U.K. 20 G3
Fraserdale Canada 63 K2
Fraser Island Australia 56 F5
Fraser Island National Park Australia 56 F5
Fraser National Park Australia 58 B6
Fraser Range hills Australia 55 C8
Frauenfeld Switz. 24 I3
Fray Bentos Uruguay 70 E4
Freckleton U.K. 18 E5
Frederica DE U.S.A. 64 D3
Fredericia Denmark 15 F9
Frederick MD U.S.A. 64 C3
Frederick Reef Australia 56 F4
Fredericksburg TX U.S.A. 62 H5
Fredericksburg VA U.S.A. 64 C3
Fredericton Canada 61 L5
Frederikshåb Greenland see Paamiut
Frederikshavn Denmark 15 G8
Frederiksværk Denmark 15 H9
Fredonia AZ U.S.A. 65 F2
Fredonia NY U.S.A. 64 B1
Fredrika Sweden 14 K4
Fredrikshamn Fin. see Hamina
Fredrikstad Norway 15 G7
Freehold NJ U.S.A. 64 D2
Freeland PA U.S.A. 64 D2
Freeling Heights hill Australia 57 B6
Freel Peak CA U.S.A. 65 C1
Freeport TX U.S.A. 63 H6
Freeport City Bahamas 67 I3
Free State prov. S. Africa 51 H5
Freetown Sierra Leone 46 B4
Fregenal de la Sierra Spain 25 C4
Fregon Australia 55 F6
Fréhel, Cap c. France 24 C2
Freiburg Switz. see Fribourg
Freiburg im Breisgau Germany 17 K6
Freising Germany 17 M6
Freistadt Austria 17 O6
Fréjus France 24 H5
Fremantle Australia 55 A8
Fremont CA U.S.A. 65 B2
Fremont NE U.S.A. 63 H3
French Congo country Africa see Congo
French Guiana terr. S. America 69 H3
French Guinea country Africa see Guinea
French Island Australia 58 B7
Frenchman r. U.S.A. 62 F2
Frenchman Lake NV U.S.A. 65 E2
Frenchpark Ireland 21 D4
French Pass N.Z. 59 D5
French Polynesia terr. S. Pacific Ocean 75 K7
French Somaliland country Africa see Djibouti
French Southern and Antarctic Lands terr. Indian Ocean 73 M8
French Sudan country Africa see Mali
French Territory of the Afars and Issas country Africa see Djibouti
Frenda Alg. 25 G6
Fresco r. Brazil 69 H5
Freshford Ireland 21 E5
Fresnillo Mex. 66 D4
Fresno CA U.S.A. 65 C2
Fresno r. CA U.S.A. 65 B2
Freu, Cap des c. Spain 25 H4
Freudenstadt Germany 17 L6
Frew watercourse Australia 56 A4
Frewena Australia 56 A3
Freycinet Estuary inlet Australia 55 A6
Freycinet Peninsula Australia 57 [inset]
Freyming-Merlebach France 24 H2
Fria Guinea 46 B3
Fria, Cape Namibia 49 B5
Friant CA U.S.A. 65 C2
Frias Arg. 70 C3
Fribourg Switz. 24 H3
Friedens PA U.S.A. 64 B2
Friedland Rus. Fed. see Pravdinsk
Friedrichshafen Germany 17 L7
Friendly Islands country S. Pacific Ocean see Tonga
Frinton-on-Sea U.K. 19 I7
Frisco Mountain UT U.S.A. 65 F1
Frissell, Mount hill CT U.S.A. 64 E1
Frobisher Bay Canada see Iqaluit
Frobisher Bay b. Canada 61 L3
Frohavet b. Norway 14 F5
Frolovo Rus. Fed. 13 I6
Frome watercourse Australia 57 B6
Frome U.K. 19 E7
Frome r. U.K. 19 E8
Frome, Lake salt flat Australia 57 B6
Frome Downs Australia 57 B6
Frontera Tabasco Mex. 66 F5
Fronteras Mex. 66 C2
Front Royal VA U.S.A. 64 B3
Frosinone Italy 26 E4
Frostburg MD U.S.A. 64 B3
Frøya i. Norway 14 F5
Frunze Kyrg. see Bishkek
Frusino Italy see Frosinone
Fruška Gora nat. park Serbia 27 H2
Frýdek-Místek Czech Rep. 17 Q6
Fucheng Shaanxi China see Fuxian
Fuding China 43 M7
Fuenlabrada Spain 25 E3
Fuerte Olimpo Para. 70 E2
Fuerteventura i. Canary Is 46 B2
Fuga i. Phil. 43 M9
Fuhai China 42 F3
Fuḩaymī Iraq 35 F4
Fujairah U.A.E. 33 I4
Fujeira U.A.E. see Fujairah
Fuji Japan 45 E6
Fujian prov. China 43 L7
Fuji-Hakone-Izu Kokuritsu-kōen Japan 45 E6
Fujin China 44 C3
Fujinomiya Japan 45 E6
Fuji-san vol. Japan 45 E6
Fujiyoshida Japan 45 E6
Fûka Egypt see Fūkah
Fūkah Egypt 34 B5
Fukien prov. China see Fujian
Fukuchiyama Japan 45 D6
Fukue-jima i. Japan 45 C6
Fukui Japan 45 E5
Fukuoka Japan 45 C6
Fukushima Japan 45 F5
Fukuyama Japan 45 C7
Fül, Gebel hill Egypt see Fūl, Jabal
Fūl, Jabal hill Egypt 39 A5
Fulchhari Bangl. 37 G4
Fulda Germany 17 L5
Fulda r. Germany 17 L5
Fulham U.K. 19 G7
Fuli China see Jixian
Fulitun China see Jixian
Fullerton CA U.S.A. 65 D4
Fulton MO U.S.A. 63 I4
Fulton NY U.S.A. 64 C1
Fumane Moz. 51 K3
Fumay France 24 G2
Funabashi Japan 45 F6
Funafuti atoll Tuvalu 53 H2
Funchal Madeira 46 B1
Fundão Brazil 71 C2
Fundão Port. 25 C3
Fundi Italy see Fondi
Fundy, Bay of g. Canada 61 L5
Fünen i. Denmark see Fyn
Funeral Peak CA U.S.A. 65 D2
Fünfkirchen Hungary see Pécs
Funhalouro Moz. 51 L2
Funing Yunnan China 42 J8
Funtua Nigeria 46 D3
Funzie U.K. 20 [inset]
Fürgun, Kūh-e mt. Iran 33 I4
Furmanov Rus. Fed. 12 I4
Furmanovka Kazakh. see Moyynkum
Furmanovo Kazakh. see Zhalpaktal
Furnás hill Spain 25 G4
Furnas, Represa resr Brazil 71 B3
Furneaux Group is Australia 57 [inset]
Fürstenwalde Germany 17 O4
Fürth Germany 17 M6
Furukawa Japan 45 F5
Fury and Hecla Strait Canada 61 J3
Fusan S. Korea see Pusan
Fushun China 44 A4
Fushuncheng China see Shuncheng
Fusong China 44 B4
Futuna i. Vanuatu 53 H3
Futuna Islands Wallis and Futuna Is see Hoorn, Îles de
Fuxian Liaoning China see Wafangdian
Fuxian Shaanxi China 43 J5
Fuxin China 43 M4
Fuxing China see Wangmo
Fuxinzhen China see Fuxin
Fuyang Anhui China 43 L6
Fuyu Heilong. China 44 B3
Fuyu Jilin China see Songyuan
Fuyu Jilin China 44 B3
Fuyuan Heilong. China 44 D2
Fuyun China 42 F3
Fuzhou Fujian China 43 L7
Fuzhou Jiangxi China 31 K4
Füzuli Azer. 35 G3
Fyn i. Denmark 15 G9
Fyne, Loch inlet U.K. 20 D5

G

Gaâfour Tunisia 26 C6
Gaalkacyo Somalia 48 E3
Gabakly Turkm. 33 J2
Gabakly Turkm. see Gabakly
Gabbs NV U.S.A. 65 D1
Gabbs Valley Range mts NV U.S.A. 65 C1
Gabela Angola 49 B5
Gaberones Botswana see Gaborone
Gabès Tunisia 22 G5
Gabès, Golfe de g. Tunisia 22 G5
Gabo Island Australia 58 D6
Gabon country Africa 48 B4
Gaborone Botswana 51 G3
Gabrovo Bulg. 27 K3
Gabú Guinea-Bissau 46 B3
Gadag India 38 B3
Gadaisu P.N.G. 56 E1
Gadchiroli India 38 D1
Gäddede Sweden 14 I4
Gades Spain see Cádiz
Gadhap Pak. 36 A4
Gadhra India 36 B5
Gadra Pak. 36 B4
Gadsden U.S.A. 63 J5
Gadwal India 38 C2
Gadyach Ukr. see Hadyach
Gaer U.K. 19 D7
Găeşti Romania 27 K2
Gaeta Italy 26 E4
Gaeta, Golfo di g. Italy 26 E4
Gaferut i. Micronesia 74 F5
Gafsa Tunisia 26 C7
Gagarin Rus. Fed. 13 G5
Gagnoa Côte d'Ivoire 46 C4
Gagnon Canada 63 N1
Gago Coutinho Angola see Lumbala N'guimbo
Gagra Georgia 13 I8
Gaiab watercourse Namibia 50 D5
Gaibanda Bangl. see Gaibandha
Gaibandha Bangl. 37 G4
Gaïdouronisi i. Greece 27 K7
Gaifi, Wâdi el watercourse Egypt see Jayfī, Wādī al
Gaillac France 24 E5
Gaillimh Ireland see Galway
Gaindainqoinkor China 37 G3
Gainesville FL U.S.A. 63 K6
Gainesville GA U.S.A. 63 K5
Gainesville TX U.S.A. 63 H5
Gainsborough U.K. 18 G5
Gairdner, Lake salt flat Australia 57 A6
Gairloch U.K. 20 D3
Gair Loch b. U.K. 20 D3
Gajipur India see Ghazipur
Gajol India 37 G4
Gakarosa mt. S. Africa 50 F4
Gala China 37 G3
Gala Co l. China 37 G3
Galâla el Baḥarîya, Gebel el plat. Egypt see Jalālah al Baḩrīyah, Jabal
Galana r. Kenya 48 E4
Galanta Slovakia 17 P6
Galapagos Islands is Ecuador 75 O6
Galapagos Rise sea feature Pacific Ocean 75 N6
Galashiels U.K. 20 G5
Galaţi Romania 27 M2
Galatina Italy 26 H4
Gala Water r. U.K. 20 G5
Galaýmor Turkm. 33 J2
Galaymor Turkm. see Galaýmor
Galbally Ireland 21 D5
Galdhøpiggen mt. Norway 15 F6
Galeana Nuevo León Mex. 66 D4
Galena AK U.S.A. 60 C3
Galena MD U.S.A. 64 D3
Galera, Punta pt Chile 70 B6
Galesburg IL U.S.A. 63 I3
Galeshewe S. Africa 50 G5
Galeton PA U.S.A. 64 C2
Galey r. Ireland 21 C5
Galheirão r. Brazil 71 B1
Galich Rus. Fed. 12 I4
Galichskaya Vozvyshennost' hills Rus. Fed. 12 I4
Galicia aut. comm. Spain 25 C2
Galičica nat. park Macedonia 27 I4
Galilee, Lake salt flat Australia 56 D4
Galilee, Sea of l. Israel 39 B3
Galizia aut. comm. Spain see Galicia
Gallabat Sudan 32 E7
Gallatin TN U.S.A. 63 J4
Galle Sri Lanka 38 D5
Gallego Rise sea feature Pacific Ocean 75 M6
Gallegos r. Arg. 70 C8
Gallia country Europe see France
Gallinas, Punta pt Col. 68 D1
Gallipoli Italy 26 H4
Gallipoli Turkey 27 L4
Gällivare Sweden 14 L3
Gällö Sweden 14 I5
Gallup U.S.A. 62 F4
Galmisdale U.K. 20 C4
Galong Australia 58 D5
Galoya Sri Lanka 38 D4
Gal Oya National Park Sri Lanka 38 D5
Galston U.K. 20 E5
Galt CA U.S.A. 65 B1
Galtat Zemmour W. Sahara 46 B2
Galtee Mountains hills Ireland 21 D5
Galtymore hill Ireland 16 C4
Galveston TX U.S.A. 63 I6
Galveston Bay U.S.A. 63 I6
Galwa Nepal 37 E3
Galway Ireland 21 C4
Galway Bay Ireland 21 C4
Gamalakhe S. Africa 51 J6
Gamba China see Gongbalou
Gamba Gabon 48 A4
Gambēla Eth. 48 D3
Gambēla National Park Eth. 48 D3
Gambell U.S.A. 60 A3
Gambella Eth. see Gambēla
Gambia, The country Africa 46 B3
Gambier, Îles is Fr. Polynesia 75 L7
Gambier Islands Australia 57 B7
Gambier Islands Fr. Polynesia see Gambier, Îles
Gamboma Congo 48 B4
Gamboola Australia 56 C3
Gamboula Cent. Afr. Rep. 48 B3
Gamda China see Zamtang
Gamlakarleby Fin. see Kokkola
Gamleby Sweden 15 J8
Gammelstaden Sweden 14 M4
Gammon Ranges National Park Australia 57 B6
Gamova, Mys pt Rus. Fed. 44 C4
Gamtog China 42 H6
Gamud mt. Eth. 48 D3
Ganado U.S.A. 62 F4
Gäncä Azer. 35 G2
Ganda Angola 49 B5
Gandaingoin China 37 G3
Gandajika Dem. Rep. Congo 49 C4
Gandak Barrage Nepal 37 E4
Gandari Mountain Pak. 36 B3
Gandava Pak. 33 K4
Gander Canada 61 M5
Gandesa Spain 25 G3
Gandhidham India 36 B5
Gandhinagar India 36 C5
Gandhi Sagar resr India 36 C4
Gandía Spain 25 F4
Gandzha Azer. see Gäncä
Ganga r. Bangl./India 37 G5 see Ganges
Ganga Cone sea feature Indian Ocean see Ganges Cone
Gangán Arg. 70 C6
Ganganagar India 36 C3
Gangapur India 36 D4
Ganga Sera India 36 B4
Gangaw Myanmar 37 H5
Gangawati India 38 C3
Gangaw Range mts Myanmar 37 I5
Gangca China 42 I5
Gangdisê Shan mts China 37 E3
Ganges r. Bangl./India 37 G5
Ganges France 24 F5
Ganges, Mouths of the Bangl./India 37 G5
Ganges Cone sea feature Indian Ocean 73 N4
Gangouyi China 42 J5
Gangra Turkey see Çankırı
Gangtok India 37 G4
Ganjig China 43 M4
Ganmain Australia 58 C5
Gannan China 44 A3
Gannat France 24 F3
Gannett Peak U.S.A. 60 H5
Ganq China 42 G5
Gansu prov. China 42 H4
Gantheaume Point Australia 54 C4
Gantsevichi Belarus see Hantsavichy
Ganye Nigeria 46 E4
Ganyushkino Kazakh. 11 P6
Ganzhou China 43 K7
Ganzi Sudan 47 G4
Gao Mali 46 C3
Gaocheng China see Litang
Gaoleshan China see Xianfeng
Gaotai China 42 H5
Gaoua Burkina 46 C3
Gaoual Guinea 46 B3
Gaoxiong Taiwan see Kaohsiung
Gaoyao China see Zhaoqing
Gaoyou Hu l. China 43 L6
Gap France 24 H4
Gap Carbon hd Alg. 25 F6
Gapuwiyak Australia 56 A2
Gaqoi China 37 E3
Gar China 36 E2
Gar' r. Rus. Fed. 44 C1
Gara, Lough l. Ireland 21 D4
Garabekewül Turkm. 33 J2
Garabekewyul Turkm. see Garabekewül
Garabil Belentligi hills Turkm. 33 J2
Garabil Belentligi hills Turkm. see Garabil Belentligi
Garabogaz Turkm. 35 I2
Garabogaz Aylagy b. Turkm. see Garabogazköl Aýlagy
Garabogazköl Aýlagy b. Turkm. 35 I2
Garabogazköl Aylagy b. Turkm. see Garabogazköl Aýlagy
Garabogazköl Bogazy sea chan. Turkm. 35 I2
Garagum des. Turkm. see Karakum Desert
Garagum Kanaly canal Turkm. 33 J2
Garagum Kanaly canal Turkm. see Garagum Kanaly
Garah Australia 58 D2
Garalo Mali 46 C3
Garamba r. Dem. Rep. Congo 48 C3
Garanhuns Brazil 69 K5
Ga-Rankuwa S. Africa 51 H3
Garapuava Brazil 71 B2
Gărasavvon Sweden see Karesuando
Garautha India 36 D4
Garba China see Jiulong
Garbahaarrey Somalia 48 E3
Garba Tula Kenya 48 D3
Garbo China see Lhozhag
Garbsen Germany 17 L4
Garça Brazil 71 A3
Garco China 37 G2
Garda, Lago di Italy see Garda, Lake
Garda, Lake Italy 26 D2
Garde, Cap de c. Alg. 26 B6
Garden City U.S.A. 62 G4
Garden Hill Canada 63 I1
Garden Mountain VA U.S.A. 64 A4
Gardeyz Afgh. see Gardēz
Gardēz Afgh. 36 B2
Gardinas Belarus see Hrodna
Gardiner, Mount Australia 54 F5
Gardiner Range hills Australia 54 E4
Gardiners Island NY U.S.A. 64 E2
Gardīz Afgh. see Gardēz
Gardner atoll Micronesia see Faraulep
Gardner MA U.S.A. 64 F1
Gardner Inlet Antarctica 76 L1
Gardner Island atoll Kiribati see Nikumaroro
Gardner Pinnacles is U.S.A. 74 I4
Gáregasnjárga Fin. see Karigasniemi
Garelochhead U.K. 20 E4
Garet El Djenoun mt. Alg. 46 D2
Gargano, Parco Nazionale del nat. park Italy 26 F4
Gargunsa China see Gar
Gargždai Lith. 15 L9
Garhchiroli India see Gadchiroli
Garhi Madh. Prad. India 38 C1
Garhi Rajasthan India 36 C5
Garhi Khairo Pak. 36 A3
Garhwa India 37 E4
Gari Rus. Fed. 11 S4
Gariep Dam resr S. Africa 51 G6
Garies S. Africa 50 C6
Garigliano r. Italy 26 E4
Garissa Kenya 48 D4
Garkalne Latvia 15 N8
Garkung Caka l. China 37 F2
Garm Tajik. see Gharm
Garmī Iran 35 H3
Garmsar Iran 35 I4
Garnpung Lake imp. l. Australia 58 A4
Garo Hills India 37 G4
Garonne r. France 24 D4
Garoowe Somalia 48 E3
Garopaba Brazil 71 A5
Garoua Cameroon 46 E4
Garoua Boulai Cameroon 47 E4
Garqêntang China see Sog
Garré Arg. 70 D5
Garruk Pak. 36 A3
Garry r. U.K. 20 E3
Garry Lake Canada 61 H3
Garrynahine U.K. 20 C2
Garsen Kenya 48 E4
Garshy Turkm. see Garşy
Garsila Sudan 47 F3
Garşy Turkm. 35 I2
Garth U.K. 19 D6
Gartok China see Garyarsa
Garub Namibia 50 C4
Garvagh U.K. 21 F3
Garve U.K. 20 E3
Garwa India see Garhwa
Garwha India see Garhwa
Gar Xincun China 36 E2
Gary IN U.S.A. 63 J3
Gary WV U.S.A. 64 A4
Garyarsa China 36 E3
Garyū-zan mt. Japan 45 D6
Garza García Mex. 66 D3
Garzê China 42 H6
Gasan-Kuli Turkm. see Esenguly
Gascogne reg. France see Gascony
Gascogne, Golfe de g. France see Gascony, Gulf of
Gascony reg. France 24 D5
Gascony, Gulf of France 24 C5
Gascoyne r. Australia 55 A6
Gascoyne Junction Australia 55 A6
Gasherbrum I mt. China/Jammu and Kashmir 36 D2
Gashua Nigeria 46 E3
Gaspé Canada 63 O2
Gaspé, Péninsule de pen. Canada 63 N2
Gassan vol. Japan 45 F5
Gassaway WV U.S.A. 64 A3
Gasteiz Spain see Vitoria-Gasteiz
Gastello Rus. Fed. 44 F2
Gastonia U.S.A. 63 K4
Gata, Cabo de c. Spain 25 E5
Gata, Cape Cyprus 39 A2
Gata, Sierra de mts Spain 25 C3
Gatas, Akra c. Cyprus see Gata, Cape
Gatchina Rus. Fed. 12 F4
Gatehouse of Fleet U.K. 20 E6
Gateshead U.K. 18 F4
Gates of the Arctic National Park and Preserve U.S.A. 60 C3
Gatesville U.S.A. 62 H5
Gatineau r. Canada 63 L2
Gatong China see Jomda
Gatooma Zimbabwe see Kadoma
Gatton Australia 58 F1
Gatvand Iran 35 H3
Gatyana S. Africa see Willowvale
Gau i. Fiji 53 H3
Gauhati India see Guwahati
Gaujas nacionālais parks nat. park Latvia 15 N8
Gaul country Europe see France
Gaula r. Norway 14 G5
Gaurama Brazil 71 A4
Gauribidanur India 38 C3
Gauteng prov. S. Africa 51 I4
Gavarr Armenia 35 G2
Gāvbandī Iran 35 I6
Gāvbūs, Kūh-e mts Iran 35 I6
Gavdos i. Greece 27 K7
Gavião r. Brazil 71 C1
Gavīleh Iran 35 G4
Gav Khūnī Iran 35 I4
Gävle Sweden 15 J6
Gavrilovka Vtoraya Rus. Fed. 13 I5
Gavrilov-Yam Rus. Fed. 12 H4
Gawachab Namibia 50 C4
Gawan India 37 F4
Gawilgarh Hills India 36 D5
Gawler Australia 57 B7
Gawler Ranges hills Australia 57 A7
Gaxun Nur salt l. China 42 I4
Gaya India 37 F4
Gaya Niger 46 D3
Gaya He r. China 44 C4
Gayéri Burkina 46 D3
Gaylord U.S.A. 63 K2
Gayndah Australia 57 E5
Gayny Rus. Fed. 12 L3
Gaysin Ukr. see Haysyn
Gayutino Rus. Fed. 12 H4
Gaz Iran 35 H4
Gaza terr. Asia 39 B4
Gaza Gaza 39 B4
Gaza prov. Moz. 51 K2
Gazan Pak. 36 A3
Gazanjyk Turkm. see Bereket
Gaza Strip terr. Asia see Gaza
Gaziantep Turkey 34 E3
Gaziantep prov. Turkey 39 C1
Gazibenli Turkey see Yahyalı
Gazimağusa Cyprus see Famagusta
Gazimurskiy Khrebet mts Rus. Fed. 43 L2
Gazimurskiy Zavod Rus. Fed. 43 L2
Gazipaşa Turkey 39 A1
Gazli Uzbek. 33 J1
Gbarnga Liberia 46 C4
Gboko Nigeria 46 D4
Gcuwa S. Africa see Butterworth
Gdańsk Poland 17 Q3
Gdańsk, Gulf of Poland/Rus. Fed. 17 Q3
Gdańska, Zatoka g. Poland/Rus. Fed. see Gdańsk, Gulf of
Gdingen Poland see Gdynia
Gdov Rus. Fed. 12 E4
Gdynia Poland 17 Q3
Geaidnovuohppi Norway 14 M2
Gearraidh na h-Aibhne U.K. see Garrynahine
Geçitkale Cyprus see Lefkonikon

Gedaref Sudan 32 E7
Gediz r. Turkey 27 L5
Gedney Drove End U.K. 19 H6
Gedser Denmark 15 G9
Geelong Australia 58 B7
Geelvink Channel Australia 55 A7
Geel Vloer salt pan S. Africa 50 E5
Gees Gwardafuy, Cape c. Somalia see
   Gwardafuy, Gees
Geidam Nigeria 46 E3
Geikie r. Canada 60 H4
Geilo Norway 15 F6
Geiranger Norway 14 E5
Geisûm, Gezā'ir is Egypt see
   Qaysûm, Juzur
Geita Tanz. 48 D4
Gejiu China 42 I8
Gela Sicily Italy 26 F6
Gêladaindong mt. China 37 G2
Geladī Eth. 48 E3
Gelendzhik Rus. Fed. 34 E1
Gelibolu Turkey see Gallipoli
Gelidonya Burnu pt Turkey see
   Yardımcı Burnu
Gelincik Dağı r. Turkey 27 N5
Gemena Dem. Rep. Congo 48 B3
Geminokağı Cyprus see Karavostasi
Gemlik Turkey 27 M4
Gemona del Friuli Italy 26 E1
Gemsa Egypt see Jamsah
Gemsbok National Park Botswana 50 E3
Gemsbokplein well S. Africa 50 E4
Genalē Wenz r. Eth. 48 E3
Genāveh Iran 35 H5
General Acha Arg. 70 D5
General Alvear Arg. 70 C5
General Belgrano II research station
   Antarctica see Belgrano II
General Bernardo O'Higgins
   research station Antarctica 76 A2
General Carrera, Lago l. Arg./Chile 70 B7
General Conesa Arg. 70 D6
General Freire Angola see Muxaluando
General Juan Madariaga Arg. 70 D5
General La Madrid Arg. 70 D5
General Machado Angola see Camacupa
General Pico Arg. 70 D3
General Pinedo Arg. 70 D3
General Roca Arg. 70 C5
General Salgado Brazil 71 A3
General San Martín research station
   Antarctica see San Martín
General Santos Phil. 41 E7
General Villegas Arg. 70 D5
Genesee PA U.S.A. 64 C2
Geneseo NY U.S.A. 64 C1
Geneva S. Africa 51 H4
Geneva Switz. 24 H3
Geneva NY U.S.A. 64 C1
Geneva OH U.S.A. 64 E1
Geneva, Lake France/Switz. 24 H3
Genève Switz. see Geneva
Genf Switz. see Geneva
Genhe China 44 A2
Genichesk Ukr. see Heniches'k
Genji India 36 C5
Genk Belgium 17 J5
Genoa Australia 58 D6
Genoa Italy 26 C2
Genoa, Gulf of Italy 26 C2
Genova Italy see Genoa
Genova, Golfo di Italy see Genoa, Gulf of
Gent Belgium see Ghent
Gentioux, Plateau de France 24 F4
Genua Italy see Genoa
Geographe Bay Australia 55 A8
Geographical Society Ø i. Greenland 61 P2
Georga, Zemlya i. Rus. Fed. 28 F1
George r. Canada 61 L4
George S. Africa 50 F7
George, Lake Australia 58 D5
George, Lake NY U.S.A. 64 L1
George Land r. Rus. Fed. see
   Georga, Zemlya
Georges Mills NH U.S.A. 64 E1
George Sound inlet N.Z. 59 A7
Georgetown Australia 56 C3
George Town Cayman Is 67 H5
Georgetown Gambia 46 B3
Georgetown Guyana 69 G2
George Town Malaysia 41 C7
Georgetown DE U.S.A. 64 D3
Georgetown SC U.S.A. 63 L5
Georgetown TX U.S.A. 62 H6
George VI Sound sea chan. Antarctica 76 L2
George V Land reg. Antarctica 76 G2
Georgia country Asia 35 F2
Georgia state U.S.A. 63 K5
Georgian Bay Canada 63 K2
Georgienne, Baie b. Canada see
   Georgian Bay
Georgina watercourse Australia 56 B5
Georgiu-Dezh Rus. Fed. see Liski
Georgiyevka Vostochnyy Kazakhstan Kazakh.
   42 E3
Georgiyevka Zhambylskaya Oblast' Kazakh.
   see Korday
Georgiyevsk Rus. Fed. 13 J7
Georgiyevskoye Rus. Fed. 12 J4
Georg von Neumayer research station
   Antarctica see Neumayer
Gera Germany 17 N5
Geral, Serra mts Brazil 71 A4
Geral de Goiás, Serra hills Brazil 71 B1
Geraldine N.Z. 59 C7
Geral do Paraná, Serra hills Brazil 71 B1
Geraldton Australia 55 A7
Gerar watercourse Israel 39 B4
Gerçüş Turkey 35 F3
Gerede Turkey 34 D2
Gereshk Afgh. 33 J3
Gerlachovský štít mt. Slovakia 17 R6
Germania country Europe see Germany
Germanicea Turkey see Kahramanmaraş
German South-West Africa country Africa
   see Namibia
Germany country Europe 17 L5
Germersheim Germany 17 L6
Gerona Spain see Girona
Gerrit Denys is P.N.G. see Lihir Group
Gers r. France 24 E4
Géryville Alg. see El Bayadh
Gêrzê China 37 F2
Gerze Turkey 34 D2
Gesoriacum France see Boulogne-sur-Mer
Gettysburg PA U.S.A. 64 C3
Gettysburg SD U.S.A. 62 H2
Gettysburg National Military Park nat. park
   PA U.S.A. 64 C3
Getz Ice Shelf Antarctica 76 J2
Geurie Australia 58 D4
Gevaş Turkey 35 F3
Gevgelija Macedonia 27 J4
Gexto Spain see Algorta
Gey Iran see Nikshahr
Geyikli Turkey 27 L5
Geyserville CA U.S.A. 65 A1
Geyve Turkey 27 N4

Ghaap Plateau S. Africa 50 F4
Ghāb, Wādī al r. Syria 39 C2
Ghabāghib Syria 39 C3
Ghabeish Sudan 32 C7
Ghadaf, Wādī al watercourse Jordan 39 C4
Ghadāmis Libya 46 D1
Ghaem Shahr Iran 35 I3
Ghaghara r. India 37 F4
Ghaibi Dero Pak. 36 A4
Ghalkarteniz, Solonchak salt marsh
   Kazakh. 42 A3
Ghana country Africa 46 C4
Ghantila India 36 B5
Ghanwā Saudi Arabia 32 G4
Ghanzi Botswana 49 C6
Ghanzi admin. dist. Botswana 50 F2
Ghap'an Armenia see Kapan
Ghardaïa Alg. 46 C1
Gharghoda India 38 D1
Ghârib, Gebel mt. Egypt see Ghârib, Jabal
Ghārib, Jabal mt. Egypt 34 D5
Gharm Tajik. 33 I2
Gharwa India see Garhwa
Gharyān Libya 47 E1
Ghāt Libya 46 E2
Ghatol India 36 C5
Ghawdex i. Malta see Gozo
Ghazal, Bahr el watercourse Chad 47 E3
Ghazaouet Alg. 25 F6
Ghaziabad India 36 D3
Ghazi Ghat Pak. 36 B3
Ghazipur India 37 E4
Ghaznī Afgh. see Ghazni
Ghazni Afgh. 36 A2
Ghazoor Afgh. 36 A2
Ghazzah Gaza see Gaza
Ghent Belgium 16 I5
Gheorghe Gheorghiu-Dej Romania see
   Oneşti
Gheorgheni Romania 27 K1
Gherla Romania 27 J1
Ghijduwon Uzbek. see G'ijduvon
Ghinah, Wādī al watercourse Saudi Arabia
   39 D4
Ghisonaccia Corsica France 24 I5
Ghotaru India 36 B4
Ghotki Pak. 33 K4
Ghudamis Libya see Ghadāmis
Ghugri r. India 37 F4
Ghurayfah hill Saudi Arabia 39 C4
Ghūrī Iran 35 I5
Ghurian Afgh. 33 J3
Ghuzor Uzbek. see G'uzor
Giaginskaya Rus. Fed. 35 F1
Gialias r. Cyprus 39 A2
Gianisada i. Greece 27 L7
Giannitsa Greece 27 J4
Giant's Castle mt. S. Africa 51 I5
Giant's Causeway lava field U.K. 21 F2
Giarre Sicily Italy 26 F6
Gibb r. Australia 54 D3
Gibeon Namibia 50 C3
Gibraltar terr. Europe 25 D5
Gibraltar Gibraltar 72 H3
Gibraltar, Strait of Morocco/Spain 25 C6
Gibraltar Range National Park Australia
   58 F2
Gibson Australia 55 C8
Gibson Desert Australia 55 C6
Gichgeniyn Nuruu mts Mongolia 42 G3
Giddalur India 38 C3
Giddi, Gebel el hill Egypt see Jiddī, Jabal al
Gidolē Eth. 47 G4
Gien France 24 F3
Gießen Germany 17 L5
Gifford r. Canada 61 J2
Gifu Japan 45 E6
Gigha i. U.K. 20 D5
Gigiga Eth. see Jijiga
G'ijduvon Uzbek. 33 J1
Gijón Spain see Gijón-Xixón
Gijón-Xixón Spain 25 D2
Gila r. AZ U.S.A. 65 E4
Gila Bend AZ U.S.A. 65 F4
Gila Bend Mountains AZ U.S.A. 65 F4
Gīlān-e Gharb Iran 35 G4
Gilbert r. Australia 56 C3
Gilbert Islands Kiribati 74 H5
Gilbert Islands country Pacific Ocean see
   Kiribati
Gilbert Ridge sea feature Pacific Ocean
   74 H2
Gilbert River Australia 56 C3
Gilbués Brazil 69 I5
Gil Chashmeh Iran 35 I4
Gilé Moz. 49 D5
Giles Creek r. Australia 54 E4
Gilgai Australia 58 E2
Gilgandra Australia 58 D3
Gil Gil Creek r. Australia 58 D2
Gilgit Jammu and Kashmir 36 C2
Gilgit r. Jammu and Kashmir 33 L2
Gilgunnia Australia 58 C4
Gilindire Turkey see Aydıncık
Gillam Canada 61 I4
Gillen, Lake salt flat Australia 55 D6
Gilles, Lake salt flat Australia 57 B7
Gillett PA U.S.A. 64 C2
Gillette U.S.A. 62 F3
Gilliat Australia 56 C4
Gillingham England U.K. 19 E7
Gillingham England U.K. 19 H7
Gilling West U.K. 18 F4
Gilmour Island Canada 61 K4
Gilroy CA U.S.A. 65 C3
Gīmbī Eth. 48 D3
Gimhae S. Korea see Kimhae
Gimli Canada 63 H1
Gimol'skoye, Ozero l. Rus. Fed. 12 G3
Ginebra, Laguna l. Bol. 68 E6
Gineifa Egypt see Junayfah
Gin Gin Australia 56 E5
Gingin Australia 55 A7
Ginginда Namibia 50 D2
Ginir Eth. 48 E3
Ginosa Italy 26 G4
Ginzo de Limia Spain see Xinzo de Limia
Gioia del Colle Italy 26 G4
Gioia Tauro Italy 26 F5
Gippsland reg. Australia 58 B7
Girā, Wādī watercourse Egypt see Jirā', Wādī
Girard U.S.A. 64 A1
Giresun Turkey 34 E2
Girgenti Sicily Italy see Agrigento
Giridih India see Giridih
Giridih India 37 F4
Girilambone Australia 58 C3
Girna r. India 36 C5
Gir National Park India 36 B5
Girne Cyprus see Kyrenia
Girón Ecuador 68 C4
Giron Sweden see Kiruna
Girona Spain 25 H3
Gironde est. France 24 D4
Girot Pak. 36 C2
Girral Australia 58 C4
Girraween National Park Australia 58 E2
Girvan U.K. 20 E5
Girvas Rus. Fed. 12 G3

Gisborne N.Z. 59 G4
Gislaved Sweden 15 H8
Gissar Range mts Tajik./Uzbek. 33 K2
Gissarskiy Khrebet mts Tajik./Uzbek. see
   Gissar Range
Gitarama Rwanda 48 C4
Gitega Burundi 48 C4
Giuba r. Somalia see Jubba
Giulianova Italy 26 E3
Giurgiu Romania 27 K3
Giuvala, Pasul pass Romania 27 K2
Givar Iran 35 J3
Givors France 24 G4
Giyani S. Africa 51 J2
Giza Egypt 34 C5
Gizhiga Rus. Fed. 29 R3
Gjakovë Serbia see Đakovica
Gjilan Serbia see Gnjilane
Gjirokastër Albania 27 I4
Gjirokastra Albania see Gjirokastër
Gjoa Haven Canada 61 I3
Gjøra Norway 14 F5
Gjøvik Norway 15 G6
Gkinas, Akrotirio pt Greece 27 M6
Glace Bay Canada 61 M5
Glacier Bay National Park and Preserve
   U.S.A. 60 E4
Glacier Peak vol. U.S.A. 62 C2
Gladstad Norway 14 G4
Gladstone Australia 56 E4
Gladstone U.S.A. 64 B1
Gladys VA U.S.A. 64 B4
Glamis U.K. 20 F4
Glamis CA U.S.A. 65 F4
Glamoč Bos.-Herz. 26 G2
Glanton U.K. 18 F3
Glasgow U.K. 20 E5
Glasgow KY U.S.A. 63 J4
Glasgow MT U.S.A. 62 F2
Glasgow VA U.S.A. 64 B4
Glass, Loch l. U.K. 20 E3
Glass Mountain CA U.S.A. 65 C2
Glastonbury U.K. 19 E7
Glazov Rus. Fed. 12 L4
Gleiwitz Poland see Gliwice
Glen Allen VA U.S.A. 64 C4
Glen Alpine Dam S. Africa 51 I2
Glenamaddy Ireland 21 D4
Glenamoy r. Ireland 21 C3
Glenbawn, Lake Australia 58 E4
Glencoe Ont. Canada 64 A1
Glencoe S. Africa 51 J5
Glendale AZ U.S.A. 62 E5
Glendale CA U.S.A. 65 C3
Glendale UT U.S.A. 65 F2
Glendale Lake PA U.S.A. 64 B2
Glen Davis Australia 58 E4
Glenden Australia 56 E4
Glendive U.S.A. 62 G2
Glenfield NY U.S.A. 64 D1
Glengavlen Ireland 21 D3
Glengyle Australia 56 B5
Glen Innes Australia 58 E2
Glenluce U.K. 20 E6
Glen More valley U.K. 20 E4
Glenmorgan Australia 58 D1
Glennallen U.S.A. 60 D3
Glenore Australia 56 C3
Glenormiston Australia 56 B4
Glenreagh Australia 58 F3
Glenrothes U.K. 20 F4
Glens Falls NY U.S.A. 64 E1
Glen Shee valley U.K. 20 F4
Glenties Ireland 21 D3
Glenville WV U.S.A. 64 A3
Glenwood Springs U.S.A. 62 F4
Glevum U.K. see Gloucester
Glittertinden mt. Norway 15 F6
Gliwice Poland 17 Q5
Globe U.S.A. 62 E5
Glogau Poland see Głogów
Głogów Poland 17 P5
Glomfjord Norway 14 H3
Glomma r. Norway 14 G7
Glommersträsk Sweden 14 K4
Glorieuses, Îles is Indian Ocean 49 E5
Glorioso Islands Indian Ocean see
   Glorieuses, Îles
Gloucester Australia 58 E3
Gloucester U.K. 19 E7
Gloucester MA U.S.A. 64 F1
Gloucester VA U.S.A. 64 C4
Gloversville NY U.S.A. 64 D1
Glubinnoye Rus. Fed. 44 D4
Glubokiy Krasnoyarskiy Kray Rus. Fed.
   42 H2
Glubokiy Rostovskaya Oblast' Rus. Fed.
   13 I6
Gluboksóye Belarus see Hlybokaye
Glubokoye Kazakh. 42 F2
Glukhov Ukr. see Hlukhiv
Glusburn U.K. 18 F5
Glynebwy U.K. see Ebbw Vale
Gmelinka Rus. Fed. 13 J6
Gmünd Austria 17 O6
Gmunden Austria 17 N7
Gnarp Sweden 15 J5
Gnesen Poland see Gniezno
Gniezno Poland 17 P4
Gnjilane Serbia 27 I3
Gnowangerup Australia 55 B8
Gnows Nest Range hills Australia 55 B7
Goa India 38 B3
Goa state India 38 B3
Goageb Namibia 50 C4
Goalen Head hd Australia 58 E6
Goalpara India 37 G4
Goat Fell hill U.K. 20 D5
Goba Eth. 48 E3
Gobabis Namibia 50 D2
Gobannium U.K. see Abergavenny
Gobas Namibia 50 D3
Gobi Desert des. China/Mongolia 42 J4
Gobindpur India 37 F5
Gobō Japan 45 D6
Gochas Namibia 50 D3
Godalming U.K. 19 G7
Godavari r. India 38 D2
Godavari, Cape India 38 D2
Godē Eth. 48 E3
Godere Eth. 48 E3
Godē Eth. 48 E3
Goderich Canada 63 K3
Goderville France 19 H9
Godhra India 36 C5
Gods r. Canada 61 I4
Gods Lake Canada 63 I1
Godthåb Greenland see Nuuk
Godwin-Austen, Mount
   China/Jammu and Kashmir see K2
Goedgegun Swaziland see Nhlangano
Goegap Nature Reserve S. Africa 50 D5
Goélands, Lac aux l. Canada 61 L4
Gogra r. India see Ghaghara
Goiana Brazil 69 L5
Goiandira Brazil 71 A2
Goiânia Brazil 71 A2
Goiás Brazil 71 A1

Goiás state Brazil 71 A2
Goio-Erê Brazil 70 F2
Gojra Pak. 36 C3
Gokak India 38 B2
Gokarn India 38 B3
Gök Çay r. Turkey 39 A1
Gökçeada i. Turkey 27 K4
Gökdere r. Turkey 39 A1
Goklenkuy, Solonchak salt l. Turkm. 35 I2
Gökova, Körfezi b. Turkey 27 L6
Göksun Turkey 34 E3
Goksu Parkı r. Turkey 39 A1
Gol Norway 15 F6
Golaghat India 37 H4
Gölbaşı Turkey 34 E3
Gölcük Turkey 27 M4
Gold PA U.S.A. 64 C2
Gołdap Poland 17 S3
Gold Coast Australia 58 F2
Gold Coast country Africa see Ghana
Gold Coast Australia 58 F2
Golden Hinde mt. Canada 62 B2
Golden Bay N.Z. 59 D5
Golden Gate Highlands National Park
   S. Africa 51 I5
Goldfield NV U.S.A. 65 D2
Goldsboro U.S.A. 63 L4
Goldstone Lake CA U.S.A. 65 D3
Goldsworthy Australia 54 B5
Goldvein VA U.S.A. 64 C3
Göle Turkey 35 F2
Goleta CA U.S.A. 65 C3
Golets-Davydov, Gora mt. Rus. Fed. 43 J2
Golfo di Orosei Gennargentu e Asinara,
   Parco Nazionale del nat. park Sardinia
   Italy 26 C4
Gölgeli Dağları mts Turkey 27 M6
Golingka China see Gongbo'gyamda
Gölköy Turkey 34 E2
Gollel Swaziland see Lavumisa
Golmud China 42 G5
Golovnino Rus. Fed. 44 G4
Golpäyegän Iran 35 H4
Gölpazarı Turkey 27 N4
Golspie U.K. 20 F3
Golyama Syutkya mt. Bulg. 27 K4
Golyam Persenk mt. Bulg. 27 K4
Golyshi Rus. Fed. see Vetluzhskiy
Goma Dem. Rep. Congo 48 C4
Gomang Co salt l. China 37 F2
Gomati r. India 37 E4
Gombe Nigeria 46 E3
Gombe r. Tanz. 49 D4
Gombi Nigeria 46 E3
Gombroon Iran see Bandar-e 'Abbās
Gomel' Belarus see Homyel'
Gómez Palacio Mex. 66 D3
Gomishān Iran 35 I3
Gomo Co salt l. China 37 F2
Gonaïves Haiti 67 J5
Gonarezhou National Park Zimbabwe
   49 D6
Gonbad-e Kavus Iran 35 I3
Gonda India 37 E4
Gondal India 36 B5
Gondar Eth. see Gonder
Gonder Eth. 48 D2
Gondia India 36 E1
Gondiya India see Gondia
Gönen Turkey 27 L4
Gonfreville-l'Orcher France 19 H9
Gongbalou China 37 G3
Gongbo'gyamda China 37 H3
Gongchang China see Longxi
Gongga Shan mt. China 42 I7
Gonghe China Qinghai China 42 I5
Gongogi r. Brazil 71 D1
Gongolgon Australia 58 C3
Gongtang China see Damxung
Gonjo China see Coqên
Gonzales CA U.S.A. 65 B2
Gonzales TX U.S.A. 63 H6
Gonzha Rus. Fed. 44 B1
Goochland VA U.S.A. 64 C4
Gowan Range hills Australia 56 D5
Gowārān Afgh. 36 A3
Gowd-e Mokh l. Iran 35 I5
Gowd-e Zereh plain Afgh. 33 J4
Gowmal Kalay Afgh. 36 B2
Gowna, Lough l. Ireland 21 E4
Goya Arg. 70 E3
Göyçay Azer. 35 G2
Goyder watercourse Australia 55 F6
Goýmatdag hills Turkm. see Goýmatdag
Goýmatdag hills Turkm. see Goýmatdag
Göynük Turkey 27 N4
Goyoum Cameroon 46 E4
Goz-Beïda Chad 47 F3
Gozha Co salt l. China 36 E2
Gözkaya Turkey 39 C1
Gozo i. Malta 26 F6
Graaff-Reinet S. Africa 50 G7
Grabo Côte d'Ivoire 46 C4
Grabouw S. Africa 50 D8
Gračac Croatia 26 F2
Gradaús, Serra dos hills Brazil 69 H5
Gradiška Bos.-Herz. see Bosanska Gradiška
Grafton Australia 58 F2
Grafton WV U.S.A. 64 A3
Grafton, Cape Australia 56 D3
Grafton, Mount NV U.S.A. 65 E2
Grafton Passage Australia 56 D3
Graham TX U.S.A. 62 H5
Graham Bell Island Rus. Fed. see
   Greem-Bell, Ostrov
Graham Island B.C. Canada 62 B3
Graham Island Nunavut Canada 61 I2
Graham Land reg. Antarctica 76 L2
Grahamstown S. Africa 51 H7
Grahovo Bos.-Herz. see Bosansko Grahovo
Graigue Ireland 21 F5
Grajaú Brazil 69 I5
Grajaú r. Brazil 69 J4
Grammos mt. Greece 27 I4
Grampian Mountains U.K. 20 E4
Grampians National Park Australia 57 C8
Granada Nicaragua 67 G6
Granada Spain 25 E5
Granard Ireland 21 E4
Granby Canada 61 F5
Gran Canaria i. Canary Is 46 B2
Gran Chaco reg. Arg./Para. 70 D3
Grand r. MO U.S.A. 62 I3
Grand Ballon mt. France 17 K7
Grand Bank Canada 61 M5
Grand Banks of Newfoundland sea feature
   N. Atlantic Ocean 72 F3
Grand Bend Ont. Canada 64 A1
Grand Canal China 42 L5
Grand Canary i. Canary Is see Gran Canaria
Grand Canyon AZ U.S.A. 65 F2
Grand Canyon gorge AZ U.S.A. 65 F2
Grand Canyon National Park AZ U.S.A.
   65 F2
Grand Cayman i. Cayman Is 67 H5
Grand Drumont mt. France 17 K7
Grande r. Bahia Brazil 71 B1
Grande r. São Paulo Brazil 71 A3
Grande r. Nicaragua 67 H6

Grande, Bahía b. Arg. 70 C8
Grande, Ilha i. Brazil 71 B3
Grande Comore i. Comoros see Njazidja
Grande Prairie Canada 60 G4
Grand Erg de Bilma des. Niger 46 E3
Grand Erg Occidental des. Alg. 22 D5
Grand Erg Oriental des. Alg. 22 F6
Grande-Rivière Canada 63 O2
Grandes, Salinas salt marsh Arg. 70 C4
Grand Falls N.B. Canada 63 N2
Grand Falls-Windsor Nfld. and Lab.
   Canada 61 M5
Grand Forks U.S.A. 63 H2
Grand Gorge NY U.S.A. 64 D1
Grandioznyy, Pik mt. Rus. Fed. 42 H2
Grand Island U.S.A. 62 H3
Grand Isle U.S.A. 63 I6
Grand Junction U.S.A. 62 F4
Grand-Lahou Côte d'Ivoire 46 C4
Grand Lake N.B. Canada 63 N2
Grand Manan Island Canada 63 N3
Grand Marais MN U.S.A. 63 I2
Grândola Port. 25 B4
Grand Passage New Caledonia 53 G3
Grand Rapids Canada 62 H1
Grand Rapids MI U.S.A. 63 J3
Grand Rapids MN U.S.A. 63 I2
Grand-Sault Canada see Grand Falls
Grand-St-Bernard, Col du pass Italy/Switz.
   see Great St Bernard Pass
Grand Teton mt. U.S.A. 62 E3
Grand Turk Turks and Caicos Is 67 J4
Grand Wash Cliffs AZ U.S.A. 65 E3
Grange Ireland 21 E6
Grängesberg Sweden 15 I6
Grangeville U.S.A. 62 D2
Granite Mountains CA U.S.A. 65 E3
Granite Mountains CA U.S.A. 65 E4
Granite Peak MT U.S.A. 62 F2
Granitola, Capo c. Sicily Italy 26 E6
Granja Brazil 69 J4
Gran Laguna Salada l. Arg. 70 C6
Gränna Sweden 15 I7
Gran Paradiso mt. Italy 26 B2
Gran Paradiso, Parco Nazionale del
   nat. park Italy 26 B2
Gran Pilastro mt. Austria/Italy 17 M7
Gran San Bernardo, Colle del pass
   Italy/Switz. see Great St Bernard Pass
Gran Sasso e Monti della Laga, Parco
   Nazionale del nat. park Italy 26 E3
Grantham U.K. 19 G6
Grant Island Antarctica 76 J2
Grantown-on-Spey U.K. 20 F3
Grant Range mts NV U.S.A. 65 E1
Grants U.S.A. 62 F4
Grants Pass U.S.A. 62 C3
Grantsville WV U.S.A. 64 A3
Grantville PA U.S.A. 64 C2
Granville France 24 D2
Granville NY U.S.A. 64 E1
Granville Lake Canada 61 H4
Grão Mogol Brazil 71 C2
Grapevine Mountains NV U.S.A. 65 D2
Graskop S. Africa 51 J3
Grasplatz Namibia 50 B4
Grasse France 24 H5
Grassflat PA U.S.A. 64 B2
Grassington U.K. 18 F4
Grass Valley CA U.S.A. 65 B1
Grästorp Sweden 15 H7
Graudenz Poland see Grudziądz
Graus Spain 25 G2
Gravataí Brazil 71 A5
Grave, Pointe de pt France 24 D4
Gravelotte S. Africa 51 J2
Gravesend Australia 58 E2
Gravesend U.K. 19 H7
Gravina in Puglia Italy 26 G4
Gray France 24 G3
Grays U.K. 19 H7
Graz Austria 17 O7
Great Abaco i. Bahamas 67 I3
Great Australian Bight g. Australia 55 E8
Great Baddow U.K. 19 H7
Great Bahama Bank sea feature Bahamas
   67 I3
Great Barrier Island N.Z. 59 E3
Great Barrier Reef Australia 56 D1
Great Barrier Reef Marine Park (Cairns
   Section) Australia 56 D3
Great Barrier Reef Marine Park (Capricorn
   Section) Australia 56 E4
Great Barrier Reef Marine Park (Central
   Section) Australia 56 D3
Great Barrier Reef Marine Park (Far North
   Section) Australia 56 D2
Great Barrington MA U.S.A. 64 E1
Great Basalt Wall National Park Australia
   56 D3
Great Basin U.S.A. 62 D4
Great Basin National Park NV U.S.A. 65 E1
Great Bear Lake Canada 60 G3
Great Belt sea chan. Denmark 15 G9
Great Bend U.S.A. 62 H4
Great Bitter Lake Egypt 39 A4
Great Blasket Island Ireland 21 B5
Great Britain i. U.K. 16 G4
Great Clifton U.K. 18 D4
Great Cumbrae i. U.K. 20 E5
Great Dividing Range mts Australia 58 D3
Great Eastern Erg des. Alg. see
   Grand Erg Oriental
Greater Antarctica reg. Antarctica see
   East Antarctica
Greater Antilles is Caribbean Sea 67 H4
Greater Khingan Mountains China see
   Da Hinggan Ling
Greater St Lucia Wetland Park nature res.
   S. Africa 51 K4
Great Exuma i. Bahamas 67 I4
Great Falls U.S.A. 62 E2
Great Fish r. S. Africa 51 H7
Great Fish Point S. Africa 51 H7
Great Fish River Reserve Complex
   nature res. S. Africa 51 H7
Great Gandak r. India 37 F4
Great Ganges atoll Cook Is see Manihiki
Great Inagua i. Bahamas 67 J4
Great Karoo plat. S. Africa 50 F7
Great Kei r. S. Africa 51 H7
Great Lake Australia 57 [inset]
Great Malvern U.K. 19 E6
Great Meteor Tablemount sea feature
   N. Atlantic Ocean 72 G4
Great Namaqualand reg. Namibia 50 C4
Great Nicobar i. India 31 I6
Great Ormes Head U.K. 18 D5
Great Ouse r. U.K. 19 H6
Great Oyster Bay Australia 57 [inset]
Great Palm Islands Australia 56 D3
Great Plain of the Koukdjuak Canada
   61 K3
Great Point MA U.S.A. 64 F2
Great Rift Valley Africa 48 D4
Great Ruaha r. Tanz. 49 D4
Great Sacandaga Lake NY U.S.A. 64 E1
Great Salt Lake U.S.A. 62 E3
Great Salt Lake Desert U.S.A. 62 E4
Great Sand Sea des. Egypt/Libya 34 B5
Great Sandy Desert Australia 54 C5

Great Sandy Island Australia see Fraser Island
Great Sea Reef Fiji 53 H3
Great Slave Lake Canada 60 G3
Great St Bernard Pass Italy/Switz. 26 B2
Greatstone-on-Sea U.K. 19 H8
Great Stour r. U.K. 19 I7
Great Torrington U.K. 19 C8
Great Victoria Desert Australia 55 E7
Great Wall research station Antarctica 76 A2
Great Wall tourist site China 43 L4
Great Waltham U.K. 19 H7
Great Western Erg des. Alg. see Grand Erg Occidental
Great Whernside hill U.K. 18 F4
Great Yarmouth U.K. 19 I6
Grebenkovskiy Ukr. see Hrebinka
Grebyonka Ukr. see Hrebinka
Greco, Cape Cyprus see Greko, Cape
Gredos, Sierra de mts Spain 25 D3
Greece country Europe 27 I5
Greece NY U.S.A. 64 C1
Greeley U.S.A. 62 G3
Greem-Bell, Ostrov i. Rus. Fed. 28 H1
Green r. WY U.S.A. 62 F4
Green Bay U.S.A. 63 J3
Green Bay U.S.A. 63 J2
Greenbrier r. WV U.S.A. 64 A4
Green Cape Australia 58 E6
Greencastle U.K. 21 F3
Greene NY U.S.A. 64 D1
Greeneville U.S.A. 63 K4
Greenfield CA U.S.A. 65 B2
Greenfield MA U.S.A. 64 E1
Green Head hd Australia 55 A7
Greenhill Island Australia 54 F2
Green Lake Canada 62 F1
Greenland terr. N. America 61 N3
Greenland Basin sea feature Arctic Ocean 77 I2
Greenland Fracture Zone sea feature Arctic Ocean 77 I1
Greenland Sea Greenland/Svalbard 28 A2
Greenlaw U.K. 20 G5
Greenock U.K. 20 E5
Greenore Ireland 21 F3
Greenport NY U.S.A. 64 E2
Green River WY U.S.A. 62 F3
Greensburg PA U.S.A. 64 B2
Greenstone Point U.K. 20 D3
Greenville Liberia 46 C4
Greenville AL U.S.A. 63 J5
Greenville MS U.S.A. 63 I5
Greenville NH U.S.A. 64 F1
Greenville PA U.S.A. 64 A2
Greenville SC U.S.A. 63 K5
Greenville TX U.S.A. 63 H5
Greenwich atoll Micronesia see Kapingamarangi
Greenwich CT U.S.A. 64 E2
Greenwood SC U.S.A. 63 K5
Gregory r. Australia 56 B3
Gregory, Lake salt flat S.A. Australia 57 B6
Gregory, Lake salt flat W.A. Australia 54 D5
Gregory, Lake salt flat W.A. Australia 55 B6
Gregory Downs Australia 56 B3
Gregory National Park Australia 54 E4
Gregory Range hills Qld Australia 56 C3
Gregory Range hills W.A. Australia 54 C5
Greifswald Germany 17 N3
Greko, Cape Cyprus 39 B2
Gremikha Rus. Fed. 77 G2
Gremyachinsk Rus. Fed. 11 R4
Grenå Denmark 15 G8
Grenaa Denmark see Grenå
Grenada U.S.A. 63 J5
Grenada country West Indies 67 L6
Grenade France 24 E5
Grenen spit Denmark 15 G8
Grenfell Australia 58 D4
Grenfell Canada 62 G1
Grenoble France 24 G4
Grense-Jakobselv Norway 14 Q2
Grenville, Cape Australia 56 C1
Grenville Island Fiji see Rotuma
Greshak Pak. 36 A4
Gressåmoen Nasjonalpark nat. park Norway 14 H4
Greta r. U.K. 18 E4
Gretna U.K. 20 F6
Gretna VA U.S.A. 64 B4
Grevena Greece 27 I4
Grevesmühlen Germany 17 M4
Grey, Cape Australia 56 B2
Greybull U.S.A. 62 F3
Grey Hunter Peak Canada 60 E3
Greylock, Mount MA U.S.A. 64 E1
Greymouth N.Z. 59 C6
Grey Range hills Australia 58 A2
Grey's Plains Australia 55 A6
Greytown S. Africa 51 J5
Gribanovskiy Rus. Fed. 13 I6
Griffin U.S.A. 63 K5
Griffith Australia 58 C5
Grim, Cape Australia 57 [inset]
Grimari Cent. Afr. Rep. 48 C3
Grimmen Germany 17 N3
Grimsby U.K. 18 G5
Grímsey i. Iceland 14 [inset]
Grimshaw Canada 60 G4
Grímsstaðir Iceland 14 [inset]
Grimstad Norway 15 F7
Grindavík Iceland 14 [inset]
Grindsted Denmark 15 F9
Grindul Chituc spit Romania 27 M2
Grinnell Peninsula Canada 61 I2
Griqualand East reg. S. Africa 51 I6
Griqualand West reg. S. Africa 50 F5
Griquatown S. Africa 50 F5
Grise Fiord Canada 61 J2
Grishino Ukr. see Krasnoarmiys'k
Gris Nez, Cap c. France 19 I8
Gritley U.K. 20 G2
Grmeč mts Bos.-Herz. 26 G2
Groblersdal S. Africa 51 I3
Groblershoop S. Africa 50 F5
Grodno Belarus see Hrodna
Groen watercourse S. Africa 50 F6
Groen watercourse S. Africa 50 C6
Groix, Île de i. France 24 C3
Grombalia Tunisia 26 D6
Grong Norway 14 H4
Groningen Neth. 17 K4
Grønland terr. N. America see Greenland
Groom Lake NV U.S.A. 65 E2
Groot-Aar Pan salt pan S. Africa 50 E4
Groot Berg r. S. Africa 50 D7
Groot Brakrivier S. Africa 50 F8
Grootdraaidam dam S. Africa 51 I4
Grootdrink S. Africa 50 E5
Groote Eylandt i. Australia 56 B2
Grootfontein Namibia 49 B5
Groot Karas Berg plat. Namibia 50 D4
Groot Letaba r. S. Africa 51 J2
Groot Marico S. Africa 51 H3
Groot Swartberge mts S. Africa 50 E7
Grootvloer salt pan S. Africa 50 E5
Groot Winterberg mt. S. Africa 51 H7
Gross Barmen Namibia 50 C2
Großer Rachel mt. Germany 17 N6
Grosser Speikkogel mt. Austria 17 O7
Grosseto Italy 26 D3
Grossevichi Rus. Fed. 44 E3
Groß-Gerau Germany 17 L6
Großglockner mt. Austria 17 N7
Gross Ums Namibia 50 D2
Großvenediger mt. Austria 17 N7
Grottoes VA U.S.A. 64 B3
Groundhog r. Canada 63 K2
Grove Mountains Antarctica 76 E2
Grover Beach CA U.S.A. 65 B3
Growler Mountains AZ U.S.A. 65 F4
Groznyy Rus. Fed. 13 J8
Grubišno Polje Croatia 26 G2
Grudovo Bulg. see Sredets
Grudziądz Poland 17 Q4
Grünau Namibia 50 D4
Grünberg Poland see Zielona Góra
Grundarfjörður Iceland 14 [inset]
Gruzinskaya S.S.R. country Asia see Georgia
Gryazi Rus. Fed. 13 H5
Gryazovets Rus. Fed. 12 I4
Gryfice Poland 17 O4
Gryfino Poland 17 O4
Gryfów Śląski Poland 17 O5
Gryllefjord Norway 14 J2
Grytviken S. Georgia 70 I8
Gua India 37 F5
Guacanayabo, Golfo de b. Cuba 67 I4
Guadajoz r. Spain 25 D5
Guadalajara Mex. 66 D4
Guadalajara Spain 25 E3
Guadalcanal i. Solomon Is 53 G2
Guadalete r. Spain 25 C5
Guadalope r. Spain 25 F3
Guadalquivir r. Spain 25 C5
Guadalupe i. Mex. 66 A3
Guadalupe CA U.S.A. 65 B3
Guadalupe, Sierra de mts Spain 25 D4
Guadalupe Peak U.S.A. 62 G5
Guadalupe Victoria Durango Mex. 62 G7
Guadarrama, Sierra de mts Spain 25 D3
Guadeloupe terr. West Indies 67 L5
Guadeloupe Passage Caribbean Sea 67 L5
Guadiana r. Port./Spain 25 C5
Guadix Spain 25 E5
Guafo, Isla i. Chile 70 B6
Guaíba Brazil 71 A5
Guaiçuí Brazil 71 B2
Guaíra Brazil 70 F2
Gualala CA U.S.A. 65 A1
Gualeguay Arg. 70 E4
Gualeguaychu Arg. 70 E4
Gualicho, Salina salt flat Arg. 70 C6
Guam terr. N. Pacific Ocean 41 G6
Guamblin, Isla i. Chile 70 A6
Guampí, Sierra de mts Venez. 68 E2
Guamúchil Mex. 66 C3
Guanajuato Mex. 66 D4
Guanambi Brazil 71 C1
Guanare Venez. 68 E2
Guane Cuba 67 H4
Guangdong prov. China 43 K8
Guanghua China see Laohekou
Guangxi aut. reg. China see Guangxi Zhuangzu Zizhiqu
Guangxi Zhuangzu Zizhiqu aut. reg. China 43 J8
Guangyuan China 42 J6
Guangzhou China 43 K8
Guanhães Brazil 71 C2
Guanipa r. Venez. 68 F2
Guanshui China 44 B4
Guantánamo Cuba 67 I4
Guapé Brazil 71 B3
Guapí Col. 68 C3
Guaporé r. Bol./Brazil 68 E6
Guaporé Brazil 71 A5
Guaqui Bol. 68 E7
Guará r. Brazil 71 B1
Guarabira Brazil 69 K5
Guaranda Ecuador 68 C4
Guarapari Brazil 71 C3
Guarapuava Brazil 71 A4
Guararapes Brazil 71 A3
Guaratinguetá Brazil 71 B3
Guaratuba Brazil 71 A4
Guaratuba, Baía de b. Brazil 71 A4
Guarda Port. 25 C3
Guardafui, Cape Somalia see Gwardafuy, Gees
Guardiagrele Italy 26 F3
Guardo Spain 25 D2
Guárico, del Embalse resr Venez. 68 E2
Guarujá Brazil 71 B3
Guasave Mex. 62 F6
Guasdualito Venez. 68 D2
Guatemala country Central America 66 F5
Guatemala Guat. see Guatemala City
Guatemala City Guat. 66 F6
Guaviare r. Col. 68 E3
Guaxupé Brazil 71 B3
Guayaquil Ecuador 68 C4
Guayaquil, Golfo de g. Ecuador 68 B4
Guaymas Mex. 66 B3
Guba Eth. 48 D2
Gubakha Rus. Fed. 11 R4
Gubbi India 38 C3
Gubio Nigeria 46 E3
Gubkin Rus. Fed. 13 H6
Gucheng China 43 K6
Gudari India 38 D2
Gudbrandsdalen valley Norway 15 F6
Gudermes Rus. Fed. 13 J8
Gudivada India 38 D2
Gudiyattam India 38 C3
Gudur Andhra Prad. India 38 C3
Gudur Andhra Prad. India 38 C3
Gudvangen Norway 15 E6
Gudzhal r. Rus. Fed. 44 D2
Guecho Spain see Algorta
Guéckédou Guinea 46 B4
Guelma Alg. 26 B6
Guelmine Morocco 46 B2
Guelph Ont. Canada 64 A1
Guerara Alg. 22 E5
Guercif Morocco 22 D5
Guéret France 24 E3
Guernsey terr. Channel Is 19 E9
Guérou Mauritania 46 B3
Guerrah Et-Tarf salt pan Alg. 26 B7
Guerrero Negro Mex. 62 E6
Guers, Lac l. Canada 61 L4
Gueugnon France 24 G3
Gugē mt. Eth. 48 D3
Gügerd, Küh-e mts Iran 35 I4
Guiana Basin sea feature N. Atlantic Ocean 72 E5
Guiana Highlands mts S. America 68 E2
Guidan-Roumji Niger 46 D3
Guider Cameroon 47 E4
Guidonia-Montecelio Italy 26 E4
Guigang China 43 J8
Guiglo Côte d'Ivoire 46 C4
Guija Moz. 51 K3
Guildford U.K. 19 G7
Guilherme Capelo Angola see Cacongo
Guilin China 43 K7
Guillaume-Delisle, Lac l. Canada 61 K4
Guimarães Brazil 69 J4
Guimarães Port. 25 B3
Guinea country Africa 46 B3
Guinea, Gulf of Africa 46 D4
Guinea Basin sea feature N. Atlantic Ocean 72 H5
Guinea-Bissau country Africa 46 B3
Guinea-Conakry country Africa see Guinea
Guinea Ecuatorial country Africa see Equatorial Guinea
Guiné-Bissau country Africa see Guinea-Bissau
Guinée country Africa see Guinea
Güines Cuba 67 H4
Guingamp France 24 C2
Guipavas France 24 B2
Guiratinga Brazil 69 H7
Guiyang Guizhou China 42 J7
Guizhou prov. China 42 J7
Gujarat state India 36 C5
Gujar Khan Pak. 36 C2
Gujerat state India see Gujarat
Gujranwala Pak. 33 L3
Gujrat Pak. 33 L3
Gukovo Rus. Fed. 13 H6
Gulabgarh Jammu and Kashmir 36 D2
Gulbarga India 38 C2
Gulbene Latvia 15 O8
Gul'cha Kyrg. see Gülchö
Gülchö Kyrg. 42 C4
Gülcihan Turkey 39 B1
Gülek Boğazı pass Turkey 34 D3
Gulfport U.S.A. 63 J5
Gulian China 44 A1
Guliston Uzbek. 33 K1
Guliston Uzbek. see Guliston
Guliya Shan mt. China 44 A2
Gulja China see Yining
Gul Kach Pak. 36 B3
Gul'kevichi Rus. Fed. 35 F1
Gull Lake Canada 62 F1
Gullträsk Sweden 14 L3
Güllük Körfezi b. Turkey 27 L6
Gülnar Turkey 39 A1
Gulu Uganda 48 D3
Guluwuru Island Australia 56 B1
Gulyayevskiye Koshki, Ostrova is Rus. Fed. 12 L1
Guma China see Pishan
Gumal r. Pak. 33 L3
Gumare Botswana 49 C5
Gumbaz Pak. 36 B3
Gumbinnen Rus. Fed. see Gusev
Gumdag Turkm. 35 I3
Gumel Nigeria 46 D3
Gümgüm Turkey see Varto
Gumla India 37 F5
Gümüşhacıköy Turkey 34 D2
Gümüşhane Turkey 35 E2
Guna India 36 D4
Guna Terara mt. Eth. 32 E7
Gunbar Australia 58 B5
Gunbower Australia 58 B5
Güncang China 37 H3
Gundagai Australia 58 D5
Güney Turkey 27 M5
Güneydoğu Toroslar plat. Turkey 34 F3
Gungu Dem. Rep. Congo 49 B4
Gunib Rus. Fed. 35 G2
Gunnaur India 36 D3
Gunnbjørn Fjeld nunatak Greenland 61 P3
Gunnedah Australia 58 E3
Gunning Australia 58 D5
Gunnison U.S.A. 62 F4
Güns Hungary see Kőszeg
Guntakal India 38 C3
Guntur India 38 D2
Gunungsitoli Indon. 41 B7
Günyüzü Turkey 34 C3
Gunza Angola see Porto Amboim
Günzburg Germany 17 M6
Guovdageaidnu Norway see Kautokeino
Gupis Jammu and Kashmir 36 C1
Gurbantünggüt Shamo des. China 42 F4
Gurdaspur India 36 C2
Gurdzhaani Georgia see Gurjaani
Güre Turkey 27 M5
Gurgan Iran see Gorgān
Gurgaon India 36 D3
Gurgei, Jebel mt. Sudan 47 F3
Gurha India 36 B4
Guri, Embalse de resr Venez. 68 F2
Gurig National Park Australia 54 F2
Gurinhatã Brazil 71 A2
Gurjaani Georgia 35 G2
Guro Moz. 49 D5
Guru China 37 G3
Gürün Turkey 34 E3
Gurupá Brazil 69 H4
Gurupi Brazil 69 I6
Gurupi r. Brazil 69 I4
Gurupi, Serra do hills Brazil 69 I4
Guru Sikhar mt. India 36 C4
Guruzala India 38 C2
Gur'yev Kazakh. see Atyrau
Gur'yevsk Rus. Fed. 15 L9
Gur'yevskaya Oblast' admin. div. Kazakh. see Atyrauskaya Oblast'
Gusau Nigeria 46 D3
Gusev Rus. Fed. 15 M9
Gushan China 45 A5
Gusino Rus. Fed. 13 F5
Gusinoozersk Rus. Fed. 42 J2
Gus'-Khrustal'nyy Rus. Fed. 12 I5
Guspini Sardinia Italy 26 C5
Gustav Holm, Kap c. Greenland see Tasiilap Karra
Gustine CA U.S.A. 65 B2
Güstrow Germany 17 N4
Gütersloh Germany 17 L5
Gutsuo China 37 F3
Guwahati India 37 G4
Guwēr Iraq 35 F3
Guwlumaýak Turkm. 35 I2
Guwlumayak Turkm. see Guwlumaýak
Guyana country S. America 69 G2
Guyane Française terr. S. America see French Guiana
Guyang Nei Mongol China 43 K4
Guyenne reg. France 24 D4
Guy Fawkes River National Park Australia 58 F3
Guymon U.S.A. 62 G4
Guyra Australia 58 E3
Guyuan Hebei China 43 L4
Guyuan Ningxia China 42 J5
Güzeloluk Turkey 39 B1
Güzelyurt Cyprus see Morfou
Guzmán Mex. 66 C2
Guzmán, Lago de l. Mex. 66 C2
G'uzor Uzbek. 33 K2
Gvardeysk Rus. Fed. 15 L9
Gvasyugi Rus. Fed. 44 E3
Gwa Myanmar 42 G9
Gwabegar Australia 58 D3
Gwaii Haanas National Park Reserve Canada 60 E4
Gwal Haidarzai Pak. 36 B3
Gwalior India 36 D4
Gwanda Zimbabwe 49 C6
Gwane Dem. Rep. Congo 48 C3
Gwardafuy, Gees c. Somalia 48 F2
Gweebarra Bay Ireland 21 D3
Gweedore Ireland 21 D2
Gwelo Zimbabwe see Gweru
Gweru Zimbabwe 49 C5
Gweta Botswana 49 C6
Gwoza Nigeria 46 E3
Gwydir r. Australia 58 D2
Gyablung China 37 H3
Gyaca China 37 H3
Gya'gya China see Saga
Gyaijêpozhanggê China see Zhidoi
Gyai Qu r. China 37 H3
Gyairong China 37 I2
Gyaisi China see Jiulong
Gyali i. Greece 27 L6
Gyamotang China see Dêngqên
Gyamug China 36 E2
Gyandzha Azer. see Gäncä
Gyangkar China see Dinngyê
Gyangnyi Caka salt l. China 37 F2
Gyangrang China 37 F3
Gyangtse China see Gyangzê
Gyangzê China 37 G3
Gyaring China 37 I2
Gyaring Co l. China 37 G3
Gyaring Hu l. China 42 H6
Gyaros i. Greece 27 K6
Gyarubtang China 42 G6
Gydan, Khrebet mts Rus. Fed. see Kolymskiy, Khrebet
Gydan Peninsula Rus. Fed. 28 I2
Gydanskiy Poluostrov pen. Rus. Fed. see Gydan Peninsula
Gyêgu China see Yushu
Gyêmdong China 37 H3
Gyigang China 42 H7
Gyimda China 37 H3
Gyirong Xizang China 37 F3
Gyirong Xizang China 37 F3
Gyiza China 37 H2
Gyldenløve Fjord inlet Greenland see Umiiviip Kangertiva
Gympie Australia 57 F5
Gyöngyös Hungary 17 Q7
Győr Hungary 26 G1
Gypsumville Canada 62 H1
Gyrfalcon Islands Canada 61 L4
Gytheio Greece 27 J6
Gyula Hungary 27 I1
Gyulafehérvár Romania see Alba Iulia
Gyümai China see Darlag
Gyumri Armenia 35 F2
Gzhatsk Rus. Fed. see Gagarin

H

Ha Bhutan 37 G4
Haa-Alif Atoll Maldives see Ihavandhippolhu Atoll
Ha'apai Group is Tonga 53 I3
Haapajärvi Fin. 14 N5
Haapavesi Fin. 14 N4
Haapsalu Estonia 15 M7
Ha 'Arava watercourse Israel/Jordan see 'Arabah, Wādī al
Ha'Arava, Naḥal watercourse Israel/Jordan see Jayb, Wādī al
Haarlem Neth. 16 J4
Haarlem S. Africa 50 F7
Hab r. Pak. 36 A4
Habahe China 42 F3
Habana Cuba see Havana
Habarane Sri Lanka 38 D4
Habaswein Kenya 48 D3
Habbān Yemen 32 G7
Ḥabbānīyah, Hawr al l. Iraq 35 F4
Hab Chauki Pak. 36 A4
Habiganj Bangl. 37 G4
Habra India 37 G5
Hachijō-jima i. Japan 45 E6
Hachinohe Japan 44 F4
Hacıköy Turkey see Çekerek
Hack, Mount Australia 57 B6
Hackberry AZ U.S.A. 65 F3
Hackensack NJ U.S.A. 64 D2
Hacufera Moz. 49 D6
Ḥadabat al Jilf al Kabīr plat. Egypt see Jilf al Kabīr, Haḍabat al
Hadagalli India 38 B3
Hada Mountains Afgh. 36 A3
Hadayang China 44 B2
Ḥadd, Ra's al pt Oman 33 I5
Haddington U.K. 20 G5
Hadejia Nigeria 46 E3
Hadera Israel 39 B3
Hadera r. Israel 39 B3
Haderslev Denmark 15 F9
Hadhramaut reg. Yemen see Ḥaḍramawt
Ḥādī, Jabal al mts Jordan 39 C4
Hadım Turkey 34 D3
Hadleigh U.K. 19 H6
Hadong S. Korea 45 B6
Ḥaḍraj, Wādī watercourse Saudi Arabia 39 C4
Ḥaḍramawt reg. Yemen 48 E2
Hadranum Sicily Italy see Adrano
Hadrian's Wall tourist site U.K. 18 E3
Hadrumetum Tunisia see Sousse
Hadsund Denmark 15 G8
Hadyach Ukr. 13 G6
Haeju N. Korea 45 B5
Haeju-man b. N. Korea 45 B5
Haenam S. Korea 45 B6
Haenertsburg S. Africa 51 I2
Ha'erbin China see Harbin
Ḥafar al Bāṭin Saudi Arabia 32 G4
Hafik Turkey 34 E3
Ḥafīrah, Qā' al salt pan Jordan 39 C4
Hafizabad Pak. 36 C2
Haflong India 37 H4
Hafnarfjörður Iceland 14 [inset]
Hafren r. U.K. see Severn
Haft Gel Iran 35 H5
Hafursfjörður b. Iceland 14 [inset]
Haga Myanmar see Haka
Hagar Nish Plateau Eritrea 32 E6
Hagåtña Guam 41 G6
Hagen Germany 17 K5
Hagerstown MD U.S.A. 64 C3
Hagfors Sweden 15 H6
Hagi Japan 45 C6
Ha Giang Vietnam 31 J4
Hagley U.K. 19 E6
Hag's Head hd Ireland 21 C5
Haguenau France 24 H2
Hahajima-rettō is Japan 45 F8
Hai Tanz. 47 G5
Haib watercourse Namibia 50 C5
Haibowan China see Wuhai
Haicheng Liaoning China 43 M4
Haifa Israel 39 B3
Haifa, Bay of Israel 39 B3
Haig Australia 55 D7
Haikakan country Asia see Armenia
Haikou China 43 K8
Ḥā'il Saudi Arabia 35 F6
Ḥā'il, Wādī watercourse Saudi Arabia 35 F6
Hailin China 44 C3
Hailong China see Meihekou
Hailsham U.K. 19 H8
Hailun China 44 B3
Hailuoto Fin. 14 N4
Hainan i. China 43 K9
Hainan prov. China 43 J9
Hainan Strait China 43 J9
Haines U.S.A. 60 E4
Haines Junction Canada 60 E3
Hai Phong Vietnam 31 J4
Haiphong Vietnam see Hai Phong
Haiqing China 44 D3
Haitan Dao i. China 43 L7
Haiti country West Indies 67 J5
Haiwee Reservoir CA U.S.A. 65 D2
Haiya Sudan 32 E6
Haiyan Qinghai China 42 I5
Haiyang Dao i. China 45 A5
Haizhou Wan b. China 43 L6
Hāj Ali Qoli, Kavīr-e salt l. Iran 35 I4
Hajdúböszörmény Hungary 27 I1
Hajeb El Ayoun Tunisia 26 C7
Ḥajhir mt. Yemen 33 H7
Haji Mahesar Pak. 36 A3
Hajipur India 37 F4
Ḥajjah Yemen 32 F6
Ḥajjīābād Fārs Iran 35 I5
Ḥajjīābād Iran 35 I4
Haka Myanmar 37 H5
Hakha Myanmar see Haka
Hakkâri Turkey 35 F3
Hakkas Sweden 14 L3
Hakken-zan mt. Japan 45 D6
Hako-dake mt. Japan 44 F3
Hakodate Japan 44 F4
Hakos Mountains Namibia 50 C2
Hakseen Pan salt pan S. Africa 50 E4
Hakui Japan 45 E5
Haku-san vol. Japan 45 E5
Hala Pak. 36 B4
Ḥalab Syria see Aleppo
Ḥalabja Iraq 35 G4
Halaç Turkm. 33 J2
Halac Turkm. see Halaç
Halaha China 44 B3
Halahai China 44 B3
Halaib Sudan 32 E5
Halaib Triangle terr. Egypt/Sudan 32 E5
Halâl, Gebel hill Egypt see Hilāl, Jabal
Ḥalāniyāt, Juzur al is Oman 33 I6
Hālawa U.S.A. 62 [inset]
Halba Lebanon 39 C2
Halban Mongolia 42 H3
Halberstadt Germany 17 M5
Halden Norway 15 G7
Haldensleben Germany 17 M4
Haldwani India 36 D3
Hale watercourse Australia 56 A5
Hāleh Iran 35 I6
Haleparki Deresi r. Syria/Turkey see Quwayq, Nahr
Halesowen U.K. 19 E6
Halesworth U.K. 19 I6
Half Assini Ghana 46 C4
Halfmoon Bay N.Z. 59 B8
Halfway Ireland 21 D6
Halhgol Mongolia 43 L3
Halia India 37 E4
Ḥalībīyah Syria 35 E4
Halicarnassus Turkey see Bodrum
Halifax Canada 61 L5
Halifax U.K. 18 F5
Halifax, Mount Australia 56 D3
Ḥalīmah mt. Lebanon/Syria 39 C2
Halkirk U.K. 20 F2
Halla Sweden 14 J5
Halladale r. U.K. 20 F2
Halla-san National Park S. Korea 45 B6
Hall Beach Canada 61 J3
Halle (Saale) Germany 17 M5
Hällefors Sweden 15 I7
Hallein Austria 17 N7
Hallett, Cape Antarctica 76 H2
Halley research station Antarctica 76 B1
Hallgreen, Mount Antarctica 76 B2
Hall Islands Micronesia 74 G5
Hallnäs Sweden 14 K4
Hallock U.S.A. 63 H2
Hall Peninsula Canada 61 L3
Hallsberg Sweden 15 I7
Halls Creek Australia 54 D4
Hallstead PA U.S.A. 64 D2
Hallviken Sweden 14 I5
Halmahera i. Indon. 41 E7
Halmstad Sweden 15 H8
Hals Denmark 15 G8
Hälsingborg Sweden see Helsingborg
Halsua Fin. 14 N5
Haltwhistle U.K. 18 E4
Haly, Mount hill Australia 58 E1
Hamada Japan 45 D6
Hamâda El Ḥaricha des. Mali 46 C2
Hamadān Iran 35 H4
Ḥamādat Murzuq plat. Libya 48 B1
Ḥamāh Syria 39 C2
Hamam Turkey 39 C1
Hamamatsu Japan 45 E6
Hamar Norway 15 G6
Hamarøy Norway 14 I2
Ḥamâṭa, Gebel mt. Egypt see Ḥamāṭah, Jabal
Ḥamāṭah, Jabal mt. Egypt 32 D5
Hamatonbetsu Japan 44 F3
Hambantota Sri Lanka 38 D5
Hambleton Hills U.K. 18 F4
Hamburg Germany 17 L4
Hamburg S. Africa 51 H7
Hamburg NY U.S.A. 64 B1
Hamburgisches Wattenmeer, Nationalpark nat. park Germany 17 L4
Ḥamḍ, Wādī al watercourse Saudi Arabia 32 E4
Hamden CT U.S.A. 64 E2
Hämeenlinna Fin. 15 N6
HaMelah, Yam salt l. Asia see Dead Sea
Hamelin Australia 55 A6
Hameln Germany 17 L4
Hamersley Lakes salt flat Australia 55 B7
Hamersley Range mts Australia 54 B5
Hamhŭng N. Korea 45 B5
Hami China 42 G4
Hamid Sudan 32 D5
Hamilton Qld Australia 56 C4
Hamilton S.A. Australia 57 A5
Hamilton Vic. Australia 57 C8
Hamilton watercourse Qld Australia 56 B4
Hamilton watercourse S.A. Australia 57 A5
Hamilton Bermuda 67 L2
Hamilton Ont. Canada 64 B1
Hamilton r. Canada see Churchill
Hamilton N.Z. 59 E3
Hamilton U.K. 20 E5
Hamilton MT U.S.A. 62 E2
Hamilton NY U.S.A. 64 D1
Hamilton OH U.S.A. 63 K4
Hamilton, Mount CA U.S.A. 65 B2
Hamilton, Mount NV U.S.A. 65 E1
Hamilton Mountain hill NY U.S.A. 64 D1
Hamīm, Wādī al watercourse Libya 23 I5
Hamina Fin. 15 O6
Hamirpur Hima. Prad. India 36 D3
Hamirpur Uttar Prad. India 36 E4
Hamitabat Turkey see Isparta
Hamju N. Korea 45 B5
Hamm Germany 17 K5
Hammada du Drâa plat. Alg. 22 C6
Ḥammām al 'Alīl Iraq 35 F3
Hammam Boughrara Alg. 25 F6
Hammamet Tunisia 26 D6
Hammamet, Golfe de g. Tunisia 26 D6
Ḥammār, Hawr al imp. l. Iraq 35 G5
Hammarstrand Sweden 14 J5
Hammerdal Sweden 14 I5
Hammerfest Norway 14 M1
Hammonton NJ U.S.A. 64 D3
Hampden Sydney VA U.S.A. 64 B4
Hampshire Downs hills U.K. 19 F7
Hampton NH U.S.A. 64 F1
Hampton VA U.S.A. 64 C4
Hampton Tableland reg. Australia 55 D8
Ḥamrā, Birkat al well Saudi Arabia 35 F5
Hamra, Vâdii watercourse Syria/Turkey see Ḥimār, Wādī al
Hamrat esh Sheikh Sudan 32 C7
Hamta Pass India 36 D2
Hāmūn-e Jaz Mūrīān salt marsh Iran 33 I4
Hāmūn-e Lowrah dry lake Afgh./Pak. see Hamun-i-Lora
Hamun-i-Lora dry lake Afgh./Pak. 33 K4
Hamun-i-Mashkel salt flat Pak. 33 J4
Hamur Turkey 35 F3
Hamwic U.K. see Southampton
Hanahai watercourse Botswana/Namibia 50 F2
Ḥanak Saudi Arabia 32 E4
Hanakpınar Turkey see Çınar
Hanalei U.S.A. 62 [inset]
Hanamaki Japan 45 F5
Hanang mt. Tanz. 49 D4
Hanbin China see Ankang
Hancheng China 43 K5
Hancock MD U.S.A. 64 B3
Hancock NY U.S.A. 64 D2
Handa Island U.K. 20 D2
Handan China 43 K5
Handeni Tanz. 49 D4
HaNegev des. Israel see Negev
Haneqarot watercourse Israel 39 B4
Hanford CA U.S.A. 65 C2
Hangayn Nuruu mts Mongolia 42 H3
Hangchow China see Hangzhou
Hangö Fin. see Hanko
Hangu China 43 L5
Hangya China 42 H5
Hangzhou China 43 M6
Hangzhou Wan b. China 43 M6
Hani Turkey 35 F3
Hanish Kabir i. Yemen see Suyūl Ḥanīsh
Hankey S. Africa 50 G7
Hanko Fin. 15 M7
Hanle Jammu and Kashmir 36 D2
Hann, Mount hill Australia 54 D3
Hanna Canada 62 E1
Hannibal MO U.S.A. 63 I4
Hannibal NY U.S.A. 64 C1
Hannover Germany 17 L4
Hann Range mts Australia 55 F5
Hanöbukten b. Sweden 15 I9
Ha Nôi Vietnam 31 J4
Hanoi Vietnam see Ha Nôi
Hanover Germany see Hannover
Hanover S. Africa 50 G6
Hanover PA U.S.A. 64 C3
Hanover VA U.S.A. 64 C4
Hansen Mountains Antarctica 76 D2
Hansi India 36 D3
Hansnes Norway 14 K2
Hanstholm Denmark 15 F8
Hantsavichy Belarus 15 O10
Hanumangarh India 36 C3
Hanwood Australia 58 C5
Hanzhong China 42 J6
Hao atoll Fr. Polynesia 75 K7
Haora India 37 G5
Haparanda Sweden 14 N4
Happy Valley-Goose Bay Canada 61 L4
Ḥaql Saudi Arabia 39 B5
Ḥarad, Jabal al mt. Jordan 39 B5
Ḥaradh Saudi Arabia 32 G5
Haradok Belarus 13 F5
Haramachi Japan 45 F5
Haramukh mt. Jammu and Kashmir 36 C2
Haran Turkey see Harran
Harappa Road Pak. 36 C3
Harar Eth. see Hārer
Harare Zimbabwe 49 D5
Ḥarāsīs, Jiddat al des. Oman 33 I6
Harat Iran 35 I5
Har-Ayrag Mongolia 43 J3
Haraze-Mangueigne Chad 47 F3
Harb, Jabal mt. Saudi Arabia 34 D6
Harbin China 44 B3
Harboi Hills Pak. 36 A3
Harchoka India 37 E5
Harda India 36 D5
Harda Khas India see Harda
Hardangerfjorden sea chan. Norway 15 D7
Hardangervidda plat. Norway 15 E6
Hardangervidda Nasjonalpark nat. park Norway 15 E6
Hardap admin. reg. Namibia 50 C3
Hardap nature res. Namibia 50 C3
Hardap Dam Namibia 50 C3
Hardeveld mts S. Africa 50 D6
Hardin U.S.A. 62 F2
Harding S. Africa 51 I6
Harding Range hills Australia 55 B6
Hardoi India 36 E4
Hardwar India see Haridwar
Hareidīn, Wādī watercourse Egypt see Ḥuraydīn, Wādī
Hārer Eth. 48 E3
Harf el Mreffi mt. Lebanon 39 B3
Hargeisa Somalia see Hargeysa
Hargele Eth. 48 E3
Hargeysa Somalia 48 E3
Harghita-Mădăraş, Vârful mt. Romania 27 K1
Harhorin Mongolia 42 I3
Har Hu l. China 42 H5
Haridwar India 36 D3
Ḥarif, Har mt. Israel 39 B4
Harihar India 38 B3
Harihari N.Z. 59 C6
Hariharpur India 38 B3
Ḥārim Syria 39 C1
Harima-nada b. Japan 45 D6
Haringhat r. Bangl. 37 G5
Ḥarīr, Wādī adh r. Syria 39 C3
Hari Rūd r. Afgh./Iran 33 J2
Harjavalta Fin. 15 M6
Harlech U.K. 19 C6
Harleston U.K. 19 I6
Harlow U.K. 19 H7
Harlowton U.S.A. 62 F2
Harman WV U.S.A. 64 B3
Harmancık Turkey 27 M5
Harnai India 38 B2
Harnai Pak. 36 A3
Harney Basin U.S.A. 62 C3
Härnösand Sweden 14 J5
Har Nuur l. Mongolia 42 G3
Haroldswick U.K. 20 [inset]
Harper Liberia 46 C4

Harper, Mount U.S.A. 60 D3
Harper Lake CA U.S.A. 65 D3
Harrai India 36 D5
Harran Turkey 39 D1
Harricanaw r. Canada 63 L1
Harrington Australia 58 F3
Harrington DE U.S.A. 64 D3
Harris, Lake salt flat Australia 57 A6
Harris, Mount Australia 55 E6
Harrisburg PA U.S.A. 64 C2
Harrismith Australia 55 B8
Harrison AR U.S.A. 63 I4
Harrison Bay U.S.A. 60 C2
Harrison, Cape Canada 61 M4
Harrisonburg VA U.S.A. 64 B3
Harrisonville U.S.A. 63 I4
Harrisville PA U.S.A. 64 A2
Harrogate U.K. 18 F5
Hørrodsville N.Z. see Otorohanga
Harsin Iran 35 G4
Harşit r. Turkey 34 E2
Hârșova Romania 27 L2
Harstad Norway 14 J2
Harsud India 36 D5
Hart r. Canada 60 E3
Hartbees watercourse S. Africa 50 E5
Hartberg Austria 17 O7
Harteigan mt. Norway 15 E6
Harter Fell hill U.K. 18 E4
Hartford CT U.S.A. 64 E2
Hartland U.K. 19 C8
Hartland Point U.K. 19 C7
Hartlepool U.K. 18 F4
Hartley Zimbabwe see Chegutu
Hartley Bay Canada 60 D4
Hartola Fin. 15 O6
Harts r. S. Africa 51 G5
Härtsfeld hills Germany 17 M6
Harts Range mts Australia 55 F5
Hartswater S. Africa 50 G4
Har Us Nuur l. Mongolia 42 G3
Harvey Australia 55 A8
Harvey U.S.A. 62 G2
Harwich U.K. 19 I7
Haryana state India 36 D3
Harz hills Germany 17 M5
Har Zin Israel 39 B4
Hasa, Wādī al watercourse Jordan 39 B4
Hasah, Wādī al watercourse Jordan/Saudi Arabia 39 C4
Hasanah, Wādī al watercourse Egypt 39 A4
Hasan Dağı mts Turkey 34 D3
Hasan Guli Turkm. see Esenguly
Hasankeyf Turkey 35 F3
Hasanur India 38 C4
Hasardag mt. Turkm. 35 J3
Hasbaïya Lebanon 39 B3
Hasbaya Lebanon see Hasbaïya
HaSharon plain Israel 39 B3
Hashtgerd Iran 35 H4
Hashtpar Iran 35 H3
Hashtrud Iran 35 G3
Haslemere U.K. 19 G7
Häşmaşul Mare mt. Romania 27 K1
Haşş, Jabal al hills Syria 39 C1
Hasselt Belgium 16 J5
Hassan India 38 C3
Hassi Bel Guebbour Alg. 46 D2
Hassi Messaoud Alg. 22 F5
Hässleholm Sweden 15 H8
Hastings Australia 58 B7
Hastings r. Australia 58 F3
Hastings N.Z. 59 F4
Hastings U.K. 19 H8
Hastings MN U.S.A. 63 I3
Hastings NE U.S.A. 62 H3
Hata India 37 E4
Hatay Turkey see Antakya
Hatay prov. Turkey 39 C1
Hatch UT U.S.A. 65 F2
Hatches Creek Australia 56 A4
Hatfield Australia 58 A4
Hatfield U.K. 18 G5
Hatgal Mongolia 42 I2
Hath India 38 D1
Hat Head National Park Australia 58 F3
Hathras India 36 D4
Hatisar Bhutan see Geylegphug
Hatod India 36 C5
Hato Hud East Timor see Hatudo
Hatra Iraq 35 F4
Hattah Australia 57 C7
Hatteras, Cape U.S.A. 63 L4
Hatteras Abyssal Plain sea feature S. Atlantic Ocean 72 D4
Hattfjelldal Norway 14 H4
Hattiesburg U.S.A. 63 J5
Hatudo East Timor 54 D2
Hat Yai Thai. 31 J6
Haud reg. Eth. 48 E3
Hauge Norway 15 E7
Haugesund Norway 15 D7
Haukeligrend Norway 15 E7
Haukipudas Fin. 14 N4
Haukivesi l. Fin. 14 P5
Hauraki Gulf N.Z. 59 E3
Haut Atlas mts Morocco 22 C5
Haute-Normandie admin. reg. France 19 I9
Haute-Volta country Africa see Burkina
Haut-Folin hill France 24 G3
Hauts Plateaux Alg. 22 D5
Havana Cuba 67 H4
Havant U.K. 19 G8
Havasu, Lake Arizona/California U.S.A. 65 E3
Havel r. Germany 17 M4
Haveli Pak. 36 C3
Havelock Swaziland see Bulembu
Havelock Falls Australia 54 F3
Havelock N.Z. 59 D5
Havelock North N.Z. 59 F4
Haverfordwest U.K. 19 C7
Haverhill MA U.S.A. 64 F1
Haveri India 38 B3
Havlíčkův Brod Czech Rep. 17 O6
Havøysund Norway 14 N1
Havran Turkey 27 L5
Havre U.S.A. 62 F2
Havre Rock i. Kermadec Is 53 I5
Havre-St-Pierre Canada 63 O1
Havza Turkey 34 D2
Hawai'i i. U.S.A. 62 [inset]
Hawaiian Islands N. Pacific Ocean 74 I4
Hawaiian Ridge sea feature N. Pacific Ocean 74 I4
Hawallī Kuwait 35 H5
Hawarden U.K. 18 D5
Hawea, Lake N.Z. 59 B7
Hawera N.Z. 59 E4
Hawes U.K. 18 E4
Hāwī U.S.A. 62 [inset]
Hawick U.K. 20 G5
Ḥawīzah, Hawr al imp. l. Iraq 35 G5
Hawkdun Range mts N.Z. 59 B7
Hawke Bay N.Z. 59 F4
Hawkes Peak UT U.S.A. 65 F2
Hawler Iraq see Arbīl
Hawley PA U.S.A. 64 D2
Ḥawrān, Wādī watercourse Iraq 35 F4
Hawston S. Africa 50 D8

Hawthorne NV U.S.A. 65 C1
Haxat China 44 B3
Haxby U.K. 18 F4
Hay Australia 58 B5
Hay watercourse Australia 56 B5
Hay r. Canada 60 G3
Hayachine-san mt. Japan 45 F5
Haydān, Wādī al r. Jordan 39 B4
Hayes r. Nunavut Canada 61 I3
Hayes Halvø pen. Greenland 61 L2
Hayfield Reservoir U.S.A. 65 E4
Hayl, Wādī watercourse Syria 39 D1
Hayl, Wādī al watercourse Syria 39 D2
Hayle U.K. 19 B8
Haymana Turkey 34 D3
Haymarket VA U.S.A. 64 C3
Hay-on-Wye U.K. 19 D6
Hayrabolu Turkey 27 L4
Hay River Canada 60 G3
Hays KS U.S.A. 62 H4
Hays Yemen 32 F7
Ḥaytān, Jabal hill Egypt 39 A4
Haysyn Ukr. 13 F6
Hayward CA U.S.A. 65 A2
Haywards Heath U.K. 19 G8
Hazar Turkm. 35 I3
Hazaribag India see Hazaribagh
Hazaribagh India 37 F5
Hazaribagh Range mts India 37 E5
Hazār Masjed, Kūh-e mts Iran 33 I2
Hazelton Canada 60 E4
Hazelton PA U.S.A. 64 D2
Hazlett, Lake salt flat Australia 54 E5
Hazrat Sultan Afgh. 36 H2
H. Bouchard Arg. 70 D4
Headford Ireland 21 C4
Headingly Australia 56 B4
Head of Bight b. Australia 55 E7
Healdsburg CA U.S.A. 65 A1
Healesville Australia 58 B6
Healy U.S.A. 60 D3
Heanor U.K. 19 F5
Heard and McDonald Islands terr. Indian Ocean 73 M9
Heard Island Indian Ocean 73 M9
Hearst Canada 63 K2
Hearst Island Antarctica 76 L2
Heart of Neolithic Orkney tourist site U.K. 20 F1
Heathcote Australia 58 B6
Heathfield U.K. 19 H8
Heathsville VA U.S.A. 64 C4
Hebei prov. China 43 L5
Hebel Australia 58 C2
Heber City U.S.A. 62 E3
Hebi China 43 K5
Hebron Canada 61 L4
Hebron West Bank 39 B4
Hecate Strait Canada 60 E4
Hechi China 43 J8
Hede Sweden 14 H5
Hedemora Sweden 15 I6
Hefa Israel see Haifa
Hefa, Mifraz Israel see Haifa, Bay of
Hefei China 43 L6
Hegang China 44 C3
Heidan r. Jordan see Haydān, Wādī al
Heide Germany 17 L3
Heide Namibia 50 C2
Heidelberg Germany 17 L6
Heidelberg S. Africa 51 I4
Heihe China 44 B2
Heilbron S. Africa 51 H4
Heilbronn Germany 17 L6
Heiligenhafen Germany 17 M3
Heilong Jiang r. Rus. Fed. see Amur
Heilongjiang prov. China 44 C3
Heilungkiang prov. China see Heilongjiang
Heinola Fin. 15 O6
Heirnkut Myanmar 37 H4
Heishi Beihu l. China 37 E2
Heisker Islands U.K. see Monach Islands
Heiţān, Gebel hill Egypt see Ḥaytān, Jabal
Hejaz reg. Saudi Arabia see Hijaz
Hekimhan Turkey 34 E3
Hekla vol. Iceland 14 [inset]
Hekou Gansu China 44 I5
Helagsfjället mt. Sweden 14 H5
Helan Shan mts China 42 J5
Helena MT U.S.A. 62 E2
Helensburgh U.K. 20 E4
Helen Springs Australia 54 F4
Helez Israel 39 B4
Helgoland i. Germany 17 K3
Helgoländer Bucht g. Germany 17 L3
Heligoland i. Germany see Helgoland
Heligoland Bight g. Germany see Helgoländer Bucht
Heliopolis Lebanon see Ba'albek
Helixi China see Ningguo
Hella Iceland 14 [inset]
Helland Norway 14 J2
Hellas country Europe see Greece
Helleh r. Iran 35 H5
Hellespont strait Turkey see Dardanelles
Hellhole Gorge National Park Australia 56 D5
Hellín Spain 25 F4
Hellinikon tourist site Greece 34 A3
Hell-Ville Madag. see Andoany
Helmand r. Afgh. 36 A2
Helmantica Spain see Salamanca
Helmeringhausen Namibia 50 C3
Helmond Neth. 17 J5
Helmsdale U.K. 20 F2
Helmsdale r. U.K. 20 F2
Helmstedt Germany 17 M4
Helong China 44 I5
Helsingborg Sweden 15 H8
Helsingfors Fin. see Helsinki
Helsingør Denmark 15 H8
Helsinki Fin. 15 N6
Helston U.K. 19 B8
Helvécia Brazil 71 D2
Helvellyn hill U.K. 18 E4
Helwân Egypt see Ḥulwān
Hemel Hempstead U.K. 19 G7
Hemet CA U.S.A. 65 E4
Hemlock Lake U.S.A. 64 C1
Hemsby U.K. 19 I6
Hemse Sweden 15 K8
Henan prov. China 43 K6
Henares r. Spain 25 E3
Henashi-zaki pt Japan 45 E4
Hendek Turkey 34 N4
Henderson NC U.S.A. 63 K4
Henderson NV U.S.A. 65 E2
Henderson TX U.S.A. 63 I5
Henderson Island Pitcairn Is 75 L7
Henderville atoll Kiribati see Aranuka
Hendon U.K. 19 G7
Hendorābī i. Iran 35 H5
Hendy-Gwyn U.K. see Whitland
Hengduan Shan mts China 42 H7
Hengelo Neth. 17 K4
Hengnan China see Hengyang

Hengshan China 44 C3
Hengshui Hebei China 43 L5
Hengxian China 43 J8
Hengyang Hunan China 43 K7
Hengzhou China see Hengxian
Heniches'k Ukr. 13 G7
Henley N.Z. 59 C7
Henley-on-Thames U.K. 19 G7
Henlopen, Cape DE U.S.A. 64 D3
Hennenman S. Africa 51 H4
Henniker NH U.S.A. 64 F1
Henrietta Maria, Cape Canada 61 J4
Henrique de Carvalho Angola see Saurimo
Henry, Cape U.S.A. 64 C4
Henry Ice Rise Antarctica 76 A1
Henryk Arctowski research station Antarctica see Arctowski
Henry Kater, Cape Canada 61 L3
Hensall Ont. Canada 64 A1
Henshaw, Lake CA U.S.A. 65 D4
Hentiesbaai Namibia 50 B2
Henty Australia 58 C5
Henzada Myanmar see Hinthada
Heptanesus is Greece see Ionian Islands
Heraclea Turkey see Ereğli
Heraclea Pontica Turkey see Ereğli
Heraklion Greece see Iraklion
Herald Cays atolls Australia 56 E3
Herāt Afgh. 33 I3
Hérault r. France 24 F5
Herbert Downs Australia 56 B4
Herbert River Falls National Park Australia 56 D3
Herbert Wash salt flat Australia 55 D6
Hercules Dome ice feature Antarctica 76 K1
Hereford U.K. 19 E6
Hereford U.S.A. 62 G5
Héréhérétué atoll Fr. Polynesia 75 K7
Herford Germany 17 L4
Heris Iran 35 G3
Herisau Switz. 24 I3
Herkimer NY U.S.A. 64 D1
Herlen Gol r. China/Mongolia 43 L3
Herlen He r. China/Mongolia see Herlen Gol
Herm i. Channel Is 19 E9
Herma Ness hd U.K. 20 [inset]
Hermanus S. Africa 50 D8
Hermel Lebanon 39 C2
Hermes, Cape S. Africa 51 I6
Hermidale Australia 58 C3
Hermite, Islas is Chile 70 C9
Hermit Islands P.N.G. 52 E2
Hermon, Mount Lebanon/Syria 39 B3
Hermonthis Egypt see Armant
Hermopolis Magna Egypt see Al Ashmūnayn
Hermosillo Mex. 66 B3
Hernandarias Para. 70 F3
Herndon CA U.S.A. 65 C2
Herndon PA U.S.A. 64 C2
Herndon WV U.S.A. 64 A4
Herne Bay U.K. 19 I7
Herning Denmark 15 F8
Heroica Nogales Mex. see Nogales
Heroica Puebla de Zaragoza Mex. see Puebla
Hérouville-St-Clair France 19 G9
Herowābād Iran see Khalkhāl
Herrera del Duque Spain 25 D4
Hershey PA U.S.A. 64 C2
Hertford U.K. 19 G7
Hertzogville S. Africa 51 G5
Hervey Islands Cook Is 75 J7
Herzliyya Israel 39 B3
Ḥeşār Iran 35 H5
Heshan China 43 J8
Hesperia CA U.S.A. 65 D3
Hesselberg hill Germany 17 M6
Hetton U.K. 18 E4
Hevron West Bank see Hebron
Hexham U.K. 18 E4
Hexian Guangxi China see Hezhou
Ḥeydarābād Iran 35 G3
Heydebreck Poland see Kędzierzyn-Koźle
Heysham U.K. 18 E4
Heyshope Dam S. Africa 51 J4
Heywood Australia 57 C8
Heywood U.K. 18 E5
Heze China 43 K5
Hezhou China 43 K8
Hezuo China 42 I5
Hezuozhen China see Hezuo
Hialeah U.S.A. 63 K7
Hibaldstow U.K. 18 G5
Hibbing U.S.A. 63 I2
Hibbs, Point Australia 57 [inset]
Hibernia Reef Australia 54 C3
Hicks, Point Australia 58 D6
Hicks Bay N.Z. 59 G3
Hidaka-sanmyaku mts Japan 44 F4
Hidalgo Mex. 62 H7
Hidalgo del Parral Mex. 66 C3
Hidrolândia Brazil 71 A2
Hierosolyma Israel/West Bank see Jerusalem
Higashi-suidō sea chan. Japan 45 C6
Higgins Bay NY U.S.A. 64 D1
High Atlas mts Morocco see Haut Atlas
High Desert U.S.A. 62 C3
Highland Peak CA U.S.A. 65 C1
Highland Peak NV U.S.A. 65 E2
Highlands NJ U.S.A. 64 E2
Highland Springs VA U.S.A. 64 C4
High Level Canada 60 G3
High Point U.S.A. 63 L4
High Point hill NJ U.S.A. 64 D2
High Prairie Canada 60 G4
High River Canada 62 E1
Higüey Dom. Rep. 67 K5
Hiiumaa i. Estonia 15 M7
Hijānah, Buḥayrat al imp. l. Syria 39 C3
Hijaz reg. Saudi Arabia 32 E4
Ḥikmah, Ra's al pt Egypt 34 B5
Hiko NV U.S.A. 65 E2
Hila Indon. 54 D1
Hilāl, Jabal hill Egypt 39 A4
Hilāl, Ra's al pt Libya 32 D3
Hilary Coast Antarctica 76 H1
Hildale UT U.S.A. 65 F2
Hildesheim Germany 17 L4
Hillah Iraq 35 G4
Hill End Australia 58 D4
Hillerød Denmark 15 H9
Hillgrove Australia 56 D3
Hillside Australia 54 B5
Hillston Australia 58 B4
Hilo U.S.A. 62 [inset]
Hilton S. Africa 51 J5
Hilton NY U.S.A. 64 C1
Hilton Head Island U.S.A. 63 K5
Hilvan Turkey 34 E3
Hilversum Neth. 16 J4
Himachal Pradesh state India 36 D3
Himalaya mts Asia 36 D2
Himalchul mt. Nepal 37 F3
Himanka Fin. 14 M4

Ḥimār, Wādī al watercourse Syria/Turkey 39 D1
Himarë Albania 27 H4
Himatnagar India 36 C5
Himeji Japan 45 D6
Ḥimş Syria see Homs
Ḥimş, Baḥrat resr Syria see Qaţţinah, Buḥayrat
Hinchinbrook Island Australia 56 D3
Hinckley U.K. 19 F6
Hinckley Reservoir NY U.S.A. 64 D1
Hindaun India 36 D4
Hinderwell U.K. 18 G4
Hindley U.K. 18 E5
Hindmarsh, Lake dry lake Australia 57 C8
Hindu Kush mts Afgh./Pak. 33 K3
Hindupur India 38 C3
Hinesville U.S.A. 63 K5
Hinganghat India 38 C1
Hingoli India 38 C2
Hīnis Turkey 35 F3
Hinnøya i. Norway 14 I2
Hinojosa del Duque Spain 25 D4
Hinsdale NH U.S.A. 64 F1
Hinthada Myanmar 42 H9
Hinton WV U.S.A. 64 A4
Hipponium Italy see Vibo Valentia
Hippo Regius Alg. see Annaba
Hippo Zarytus Tunisia see Bizerte
Hirabit Dağ mt. Turkey 35 G3
Hirakud Dam India 37 E5
Hirakud Reservoir India 37 E5
Hirapur India 36 D4
Hiriyur India 38 C3
Hirosaki Japan 44 F4
Hiroshima Japan 45 D6
Hirschberg mt. Germany 17 M7
Hirschberg Poland see Jelenia Góra
Hirson France 24 G2
Ḥırṣova Romania see Hârşova
Hirta is U.K. see St Kilda
Hirtshals Denmark 15 F8
Hisar India 36 C3
Hisar Iran 35 H3
Honaz Turkey 27 M6
Hisarköy Turkey see Domaniç
Hisarönü Turkey 27 O4
Ḥisb, Sha'īb watercourse Iraq 35 G5
Ḥisbān Jordan 39 B4
Hisor Tajik./Uzbek. see Gissar Range
Hissar India see Hisar
Hisua India 37 F4
Ḥiṣyah Syria 39 C2
Hitachi Japan 45 F5
Hitachinaka Japan 45 F5
Hitra i. Norway 14 F5
Hiva Oa i. Fr. Polynesia 75 K6
Hixson Cay reef Australia 56 E4
Hiyon watercourse Israel 39 B4
Hizan Turkey 35 F3
Honjō Japan 45 F5
Hjälmaren l. Sweden 15 I7
Hjerkinn Norway 14 F5
Hjo Sweden 15 I7
Hjørring Denmark 15 G8
Hkakabo Razi mt. China/Myanmar 42 H7
Hlaingdet Myanmar 37 I5
Hlako Kangri mt. China see Lhagoi Kangri
Hlane Royal National Park Swaziland 51 J4
Hlatikulu Swaziland 51 J4
Hlohlowane S. Africa 51 H5
Hlotse Lesotho 51 I5
Hluhluwe-Umfolozi Park nature res. S. Africa 51 J5
Hlukhiv Ukr. 13 G6
Hlusha Belarus 13 F5
Hlybokaye Belarus 15 O9
Ho Ghana 46 D4
Hoachanas Namibia 50 D2
Hoang Sa is S. China Sea see Paracel Islands
Hobart Australia 57 [inset]
Hobart U.S.A. 62 H4
Hobbs U.S.A. 62 G5
Hobbs Coast Antarctica 76 J1
Hobiganj Bangl. see Habiganj
Hobro Denmark 15 F8
Hobyo Somalia 48 E3
Hoceima, Baie d'Al b. Morocco 25 E6
Hochfeiler mt. Austria/Italy see Gran Pilastro
Hochfeld Namibia 49 B6
Hô Chi Minh Vietnam see Ho Chi Minh City
Ho Chi Minh City Vietnam 31 J5
Hochschwab mt. Austria 17 O7
Hochschwab mts Austria 17 O7
Hôd reg. Mauritania 46 C3
Hoddesdon U.K. 19 G7
Hodgson Downs Australia 54 F3
Hódmezővásárhely Hungary 27 I1
Hodna, Chott el salt l. Alg. 25 I6
Hodo-dan pt N. Korea 45 B5
Hoeryŏng N. Korea 44 C4
Hof Germany 17 M5
Hofmeyr S. Africa 51 G6
Höfn Iceland 14 [inset]
Hofors Sweden 15 J6
Hofsjökull ice cap Iceland 14 [inset]
Hofsós Iceland 14 [inset]
Hōfu Japan 45 C6
Hofūf Saudi Arabia see Al Hufūf
Höganäs Sweden 15 H8
Hogan Group is Australia 58 C7
Hog Island U.S.A. 64 C4
Högsby Sweden 15 J8
Hohenstein Poland see Inowrocław
Hoher Dachstein mt. Austria 17 N7
Hohe Tauern mts Austria 17 N7
Hohhot China 43 K4
Hohneck mt. France 24 H2
Hoh Sai Hu l. China 37 H2
Hoh Xil Hu salt l. China 37 G2
Hoh Xil Shan mts China 37 G2
Hoima Uganda 48 D3
Hojagala Turkm. 35 J3
Hojai India 37 H4
Højryggen mts Greenland 61 M2
Hokitika N.Z. 59 C6
Hokkaidō i. Japan 44 F4
Hokksund Norway 15 F7
Hol Norway 15 F6
Holbæk Denmark 15 G9
Holbeach U.K. 19 H6
Holbrook Australia 58 C5
Holbrook U.S.A. 62 E5
Holden UT U.S.A. 65 F1
Holdrege U.S.A. 62 H3
Holguín Cuba 67 I4
Höljes Sweden 15 H6
Holland country Europe see Netherlands
Holland MI U.S.A. 64 B1
Hollandia Indon. see Jayapura
Hollick-Kenyon Peninsula Antarctica 76 L2
Hollick-Kenyon Plateau Antarctica 76 K1

Hollidaysburg PA U.S.A. 64 B2
Hollister CA U.S.A. 65 B2
Holly Springs U.S.A. 63 J5
Hollywood CA U.S.A. 65 C4
Hollywood FL U.S.A. 63 K7
Holm Norway 14 H4
Holman Canada 60 G2
Holmes Reef Australia 56 D3
Holmestrand Norway 15 G7
Holmgard Rus. Fed. see Velikiy Novgorod
Holm Ø i. Greenland see Kiatassuaq
Holmsund Sweden 14 L5
Holon Israel 39 B3
Holoog Namibia 50 C4
Holothuria Banks reef Australia 54 D3
Holroyd r. Australia 56 C2
Holstebro Denmark 15 F8
Holsteinsborg Greenland see Sisimiut
Holston r. U.S.A. 63 K4
Holsworthy U.K. 19 C8
Holt U.K. 19 I6
Holycross Ireland 21 D5
Holy Cross U.S.A. 60 C3
Holyhead U.K. 18 C5
Holyhead Bay U.K. 18 C5
Holy Island England U.K. 18 F3
Holy Island Wales U.K. 18 C5
Holyoke U.S.A. 62 G3
Holy See Europe see Vatican City
Holywell U.K. 18 E5
Holzkirchen Germany 17 M7
Homāyūnshahr Iran see Khomeynīshahr
Hombori Mali 46 C3
Home Bay Canada 61 L3
Homer NY U.S.A. 64 C1
Homestead Australia 56 D4
Homnabad India 38 C2
Homoine Moz. 51 L2
Homs Libya see Al Khums
Homs Syria 39 C2
Homyel' Belarus 13 F5
Honan prov. China see Henan
Honavar India 38 B3
Hondeklipbaai S. Africa 50 C6
Hondo U.S.A. 62 H6
Honduras country Central America 67 G6
Hønefoss Norway 15 G6
Honesdale PA U.S.A. 64 D2
Honey Lake salt l. U.S.A. 65 C1
Honeyoye Lake NY U.S.A. 64 C1
Honfleur France 24 E2
Hông, Sông r. Vietnam see Red
Hongjiang Hunan China 43 J7
Hong Kong H.K. China 43 K8
Hong Kong aut. reg. China 74 D4
Hongliuwan China see Aksay
Hongliuyuan China 42 H4
Hongshi China 44 C4
Hongwŏn N. Korea 45 B4
Hongxing China 44 A3
Hongze Hu l. China 43 L6
Honiara Solomon Is 53 F2
Honiton U.K. 19 D8
Honkajoki Fin. 15 M6
Honningsvåg Norway 14 N1
Honoka'a U.S.A. 62 [inset]
Honolulu U.S.A. 62 [inset]
Honshū i. Japan 45 D6
Honwad India 38 B2
Hood, Mount vol. U.S.A. 62 C2
Hood Point Australia 55 B8
Hood Point P.N.G. 56 D1
Hoogeveen Neth. 17 K4
Hooghly r. mouth India see Hugli
Hook Head hd Ireland 21 F5
Hook Reef Australia 56 E3
Hooper Bay U.S.A. 77 B2
Hooper Island MD U.S.A. 64 C3
Hoopstad S. Africa 51 G4
Höör Sweden 15 H9
Hoorn Neth. 16 J3
Hoorn, Îles de is Wallis and Futuna Is 53 I3
Hoosick NY U.S.A. 64 E1
Hoover Dam Arizona/Nevada U.S.A. 65 E2
Hopa Turkey 35 F2
Hope Canada 62 C2
Hope r. N.Z. 59 D5
Hope AR U.S.A. 63 I5
Hope, Lake salt flat Australia 55 C8
Hope, Point U.S.A. 60 B3
Hopedale Canada 61 L4
Hopefield S. Africa 50 D7
Hopei prov. China see Hebei
Hopetoun Australia 58 B6
Hopetown S. Africa 50 G5
Hopewell VA U.S.A. 64 C4
Hopewell Islands Canada 61 K4
Hopkins r. Australia 57 C8
Hopkins, Lake salt flat Australia 55 E6
Hopkinsville U.S.A. 63 J4
Hopland CA U.S.A. 65 A1
Horasan Turkey 35 F2
Hörby Sweden 15 H9
Horgo Mongolia 42 I3
Horizon Deep sea feature S. Pacific Ocean 74 I7
Horki Belarus 13 F5
Horlick Mountains Antarctica 76 K1
Horlivka Ukr. 13 H6
Hormuz, Strait of Iran/Oman 33 I4
Horn Austria 17 O6
Horn c. Iceland 14 [inset]
Horn, Cape Chile 70 C9
Hornavan l. Sweden 14 J3
Horncastle U.K. 18 G5
Horndal Sweden 15 J6
Horne, Îles de is Wallis and Futuna Is see Hoorn, Îles de
Hörnefors Sweden 14 K5
Hornell NY U.S.A. 64 C1
Hornepayne Canada 63 K2
Hornisgrinde mt. Germany 17 L6
Hornkranz Namibia 50 C2
Hornos, Cabo de Chile see Horn, Cape
Hornsby Australia 58 E4
Hornsea U.K. 18 G5
Hornslandet pen. Sweden 15 J6
Horodenka Ukr. 13 E6
Horodnya Ukr. 13 F6
Horodok Khmel'nyts'ka Oblast' Ukr. 13 E6
Horodok L'vivs'ka Oblast' Ukr. 13 D6
Horokanai Japan 44 F3
Horqin Youyi Qianqi China see Ulanhot
Horqin Zuoyi Houqi China see Ganjig
Horqin Zuoyi Zhongqi China see Baokang
Horrabridge U.K. 19 C8
Horrocks Australia 55 A7
Horru China 37 G3
Horsefly Canada 60 F4
Horseheads NY U.S.A. 64 C1
Horseleap Ireland 21 D4
Horsens Denmark 15 F9
Horseshoe Bend Australia 55 F5
Horseshoe Seamounts sea feature N. Atlantic Ocean 72 G3

Horsham Australia 57 C8
Horsham U.K. 19 G7
Horten Norway 15 G7
Hortobágyi nat. park Hungary 27 I1
Horton r. Canada 60 F3
Horwich U.K. 18 E5
Hoshangabad India 36 D5
Hoshiarpur India 36 C3
Hospet India 38 C3
Hospital Ireland 21 D5
Hosséré Vokre mt. Cameroon 46 E4
Hotagen r. Sweden 14 I5
Hotan China 36 E1
Hotazel S. Africa 50 F4
Hot Creek Range mts NV U.S.A. 65 D1
Hotgi India 38 C2
Hotham r. Australia 55 B8
Hoting Sweden 14 J4
Hot Springs AR U.S.A. 63 I5
Hot Springs NM U.S.A. see Truth or Consequences
Hot Springs SD U.S.A. 62 G3
Hottah Lake Canada 60 G3
Hottentots Bay Namibia 50 B4
Hottentots Point Namibia 50 B4
Houghton MI U.S.A. 63 J2
Houghton NY U.S.A. 64 B1
Houghton le Spring U.K. 18 F4
Houma China 43 K5
Houma U.S.A. 63 I6
Houston TX U.S.A. 63 H6
Hout r. S. Africa 51 I2
Houtman Abrolhos is Australia 55 A7
Houton U.K. 20 F2
Houwater S. Africa 50 F6
Hovd Hovd Mongolia 42 G3
Hovd Övörhangay Mongolia 42 I4
Hove U.K. 19 G8
Hoveton U.K. 19 I6
Hovmantorp Sweden 15 I8
Hövsgöl Nuur l. Mongolia 42 I2
Hövüün Mongolia 42 I4
Howar, Wadi watercourse Sudan 32 C6
Howard Australia 56 F5
Howard PA U.S.A. 64 C2
Howden U.K. 18 G5
Howe, Cape Australia 58 D6
Howe, Mount Antarctica 76 J1
Howick S. Africa 51 J5
Howland Island terr. N. Pacific Ocean 53 I1
Howlong Australia 58 C5
Howrah India see Haora
Howth Ireland 21 F4
Howz i-Mian i-Tak Iran 35 I4
Höxter Germany 17 L5
Hoy i. U.K. 20 F2
Høyanger Norway 15 E6
Hoyerswerda Germany 17 O5
Høylandet Norway 14 H4
Höytiäinen l. Fin. 14 P5
Hpapun Myanmar 42 I4
Hradec Králové Czech Rep. 17 O5
Hrasnica Bos.-Herz. 26 H3
Hrazdan Armenia 35 G2
Hrebinka Ukr. 13 G6
Hrodna Belarus 15 M10
Hrvatska country Europe see Croatia
Hrvatsko Grahovo Bos.-Herz. see Bosansko Grahovo
Hsiang Kang H.K. China see Hong Kong
Hsin-chia-p'o country Asia see Singapore
Hsin-chia-p'o Sing. see Singapore
Hsinchu Taiwan 43 M8
Hsinking China see Changchun
Hsipaw Myanmar 42 H8
Hsi-sha Ch'ün-tao is S. China Sea see Paracel Islands
Huab watercourse Namibia 49 B6
Huacho Peru 68 C6
Huachuan China 44 C3
Huade China 43 K4
Huai'an Jiangsu China 43 L6
Huaibei China 43 L6
Huaidezhen China 44 B4
Huaihua China 43 J7
Huaiji China 43 K8
Huaiyin Jiangsu China see Huai'an
Huajialing China 42 I5
Huajuápan de León Mex. 66 E5
Hualapai Peak AZ U.S.A. 65 F3
Hualien Taiwan see Hualien
Hualien Taiwan 43 M8
Huallaga r. Peru 68 C5
Huambo Angola 49 B5
Huanan China 44 C3
Huancane Peru 68 E7
Huancavelica Peru 68 C6
Huancayo Peru 68 C6
Huanggang China see Xingyi
Huangchuan China 43 L6
Huang Hai sea N. Pacific Ocean see Yellow Sea
Huang He r. China see Yellow
Huangshan China 43 L7
Huangshi China 43 L6
Huangtu Gaoyuan plat. China 43 J5
Huanren China 44 B4
Huánuco Peru 68 C5
Huaráz Peru 68 C5
Huarmey Peru 68 C6
Huascarán, Nevado de mt. Peru 68 C5
Huasco Chile 70 B3
Huashugou China see Jingtieshan
Huashulinzi China 44 B4
Huatabampo Mex. 66 C3
Huayxay Laos 42 I8
Huazangsi China see Tianzhu
Hubei prov. China 43 K6
Hubli India 38 B3
Hucknall U.K. 19 F5
Huddersfield U.K. 18 F5
Huder China 44 A2
Hudiksvall Sweden 15 J6
Hudson MA U.S.A. 64 F1
Hudson NY U.S.A. 64 E1
Hudson r. NY U.S.A. 64 E2
Hudson, Baie d' sea Canada see Hudson Bay
Hudson, Détroit d' strait Canada see Hudson Strait
Hudson Bay Canada 62 G1
Hudson Bay Canada see Hudson Bay
Hudson Falls NY U.S.A. 64 E1
Hudson Island Tuvalu see Nanumanga
Hudson Mountains Antarctica 76 K2
Hudson Strait Canada 61 K3
Huê Vietnam 31 J5
Huehuetenango Guat. 66 F5
Huehueto, Cerro mt. Mex. 66 C4
Huelva Spain 25 C5
Huentelauquén Chile 70 B4
Huércal-Overa Spain 25 F5
Huesca Spain 25 F2
Huéscar Spain 25 E5
Hughenden Australia 56 D4
Hughes Australia 55 E7

96

Hughson CA U.S.A. 65 B2
Hugli r. mouth India 37 F5
Hugo OK U.S.A. 63 H5
Huhehot China see Hohhot
Huhhot China see Hohhot
Huhudi S. Africa 50 G4
Hui'anpu China 42 J5
Huiarau Range mts N.Z. 59 F4
Huib-Hoch Plateau Namibia 50 C4
Huila, Nevado de vol. Col. 68 C3
Huíla, Planalto da Angola 49 B5
Huili China 42 I7
Huimanguillo Mex. 66 F5
Huiten Nur l. China 37 G2
Huittinen Fin. 15 M6
Huiyang China see Huizhou
Huize China 42 I7
Huizhou China 43 K8
Hujirt Mongolia 42 I3
Hujr Saudi Arabia 32 F4
Hukawng Valley Myanmar 37 I4
Hukuntsi Botswana 50 E2
Hulan China 44 B3
Hulan Ergi China 44 A3
Hulayfah Saudi Arabia 32 F4
Hulayhilah well Syria 39 D2
Hulin China 44 D3
Hulin Gol r. China 44 B3
Hull Canada 63 L2
Hull U.K. see Kingston upon Hull
Hull Island atoll Kiribati see Orona
Hultsfred Sweden 15 I8
Hulun China see Hulun Buir
Hulun Buir China 43 L3
Hulun Nur l. China 43 L3
Hulwān Egypt 34 C5
Huma China 44 B2
Humahuaca Arg. 70 C2
Humaitá Brazil 68 F5
Humber, Mouth of the U.K. 18 H5
Humboldt Canada 62 F1
Humboldt r. U.S.A. 60 G5
Humeburn Australia 58 B1
Hume Reservoir Australia 58 C5
Humphrey Island atoll Cook Is see Manihiki
Humphreys, Mount CA U.S.A. 65 C2
Humphreys Peak U.S.A. 62 E4
Hūn Libya 47 E2
Húnaflói b. Iceland 14 [inset]
Hunan prov. China 43 K7
Hunedoara Romania 27 J2
Hungary country Europe 23 H2
Hungerford Australia 58 B2
Hŭngnam N. Korea 45 B5
Hunjiang China see Baishan
Huns Mountains Namibia 50 C4
Hunstanton U.K. 19 H6
Hunte r. Germany 17 L4
Hunter r. Australia 58 E4
Hunter Island Australia 57 [inset]
Hunter Island S. Pacific Ocean 53 H4
Hunter Islands Australia 57 [inset]
Huntingdon U.K. 19 G6
Huntingdon PA U.S.A. 64 C2
Huntington IN U.S.A. 63 J3
Huntington WV U.S.A. 63 K4
Huntington Beach CA U.S.A. 65 C4
Huntly N.Z. 59 E3
Huntly U.K. 20 G3
Huntsville Canada 63 L2
Huntsville AL U.S.A. 63 J5
Huntsville TX U.S.A. 63 H5
Hunza reg. Jammu and Kashmir 36 C1
Huolin He r. China see Hulin Gol
Huolongmen China 44 B2
Huonville Australia 57 [inset]
Hupeh prov. China see Hubei
Hupnik r. Turkey 39 C1
Huraydīn, Wādī watercourse Egypt 39 A4
Hurd Island Kiribati see Arorae
Hurghada Egypt see Al Ghurdaqah
Hurler's Cross Ireland 21 D5
Huron CA U.S.A. 65 B2
Huron SD U.S.A. 62 H3
Huron, Lake Canada/U.S.A. 64 A1
Hurricane UT U.S.A. 65 F2
Hursley U.K. 19 F7
Hurst Green U.K. 19 H7
Husain Nika Pak. 36 B3
Húsavík Norðurland eystra Iceland 14 [inset]
Húsavík Vestfirðir Iceland 14 [inset]
Huseyinabat Turkey see Alaca
Huseyinli Turkey see Kızılırmak
Huşi Romania 27 M1
Huskvarna Sweden 15 I8
Husn Jordan see Al Ḩişn
Husn Āl 'Abr Yemen 32 G6
Husnes Norway 15 D7
Husum Germany 17 L3
Husum Sweden 14 K5
Hutag Mongolia 42 I3
Hutchinson KS U.S.A. 62 H4
Hutou China 44 D3
Huttah Kulkyne National Park Australia 57 C7
Hutton, Mount hill Australia 57 E5
Hutton Range hills Australia 55 C6
Hüvek Turkey see Bozova
Huwaytat reg. Saudi Arabia 39 C5
Huzhong China 44 A2
Huzhou China 43 M6
Hvannadalshnúkur vol. Iceland 14 [inset]
Hvar i. Croatia 26 G3
Hvide Sande Denmark 15 F8
Hvíta r. Iceland 14 [inset]
Hwange Zimbabwe 49 C5
Hwange National Park Zimbabwe 49 C5
Hwang Ho r. China see Yellow
Hwedza Zimbabwe 49 D5
Hwlffordd U.K. see Haverfordwest
Hyannis MA U.S.A. 64 F2
Hyargas Nuur salt l. Mongolia 42 G3
Hyde N.Z. 59 C7
Hyden Australia 55 B8
Hyderabad India 38 C2
Hyderabad Pak. 33 K4
Hydra i. Greece see Ydra
Hyères France 24 H5
Hyères, Îles d' is France 24 H5
Hyesan N. Korea 44 C4
Hyland, Mount Australia 58 F3
Hyland Post Canada 60 F4
Hyllestad Norway 15 D6
Hyltebruk Sweden 15 H8
Hyōno-sen mt. Japan 45 D6
Hyrcania Iran see Gorgān
Hyrynsalmi Fin. 14 P4
Hythe U.K. 19 I7
Hyūga Japan 45 C6
Hyvinkää Fin. 15 N6

I

Iaciara Brazil 71 B1
Iaco r. Brazil 68 E5
Iaçu Brazil 71 C1
Iadera Croatia see Zadar
Iakora Madag. 49 E6
Ialomiţa r. Romania 27 L2
Ianca Romania 27 L2
Iaşi Romania 27 L1
Ibadan Nigeria 46 D4
Ibagué Col. 68 C3
Ibaiti Brazil 71 A3
Ibarra Ecuador 68 C3
Ibb Yemen 32 F7
Iberá, Esteros del marsh Arg. 70 E3
Iberia Peru 68 E6
Iberian Peninsula Europe 25
Ibeto Nigeria 46 D3
iBhayi S. Africa see Port Elizabeth
Ibi Nigeria 46 D4
Ibiá Brazil 71 B2
Ibiaí Brazil 71 B2
Ibiapaba, Serra da hills Brazil 69 J4
Ibiassucê Brazil 71 C1
Ibicaraí Brazil 71 D1
Ibiquera Brazil 71 C1
Ibirama Brazil 71 A4
Ibiranhém Brazil 71 C2
Ibitinga Brazil 71 A3
Ibiza Spain 25 G4
Ibiza i. Spain 25 G4
Iblei, Monti mts Sicily Italy 26 F6
Ibn Buşayyiş well Saudi Arabia 35 G6
Ibotirama Brazil 69 J6
Iboundji, Mont hill Gabon 48 B4
Ibrā' Oman 33 I5
İbradı Turkey 34 C3
Ibrī Oman 33 I5
Ica Peru 68 C6
Ica r. Peru see Putumayo
Içana Brazil 68 E3
Içana r. Brazil 68 E3
Icaria i. Greece see Ikaria
Icatu Brazil 69 J4
Iceberg Canyon gorge NV U.S.A. 65 E2
İçel Mersin Turkey see Mersin
Iceland country Europe 14 [inset]
Iceland Basin sea feature N. Atlantic Ocean 72 G2
Icelandic Plateau sea feature N. Atlantic Ocean 77 I2
Ichalkaranji India 38 B2
Ichifusa-yama mt. Japan 45 C6
Ichinomiya Japan 45 E6
Ichinoseki Japan 45 F5
Ichinskiy, Vulkan vol. Rus. Fed. 29 Q4
Ichkeul, Parc National de l' Tunisia 26 C6
Ichnya Ukr. 13 G6
Icó Brazil 69 K5
Iconha Brazil 71 C3
Iconium Turkey see Konya
Icosium Alg. see Algiers
Iculisma France see Angoulême
Icy Cape U.S.A. 60 B2
Id Turkey see Narman
Idah Nigeria 46 D4
Idaho state U.S.A. 62 E3
Idaho Falls U.S.A. 62 E3
Idalia National Park Australia 56 D5
Idar India 36 C5
Idar-Oberstein Germany 17 K6
Ideriyn Gol r. Mongolia 42 I3
Idfū Egypt 32 D5
Idhān Awbārī des. Libya 46 E2
Idhān Murzūq des. Libya 46 E2
Idhra i. Greece see Ydra
Idi Amin Dada, Lake Dem. Rep. Congo/Uganda see Edward, Lake
Idiofa Dem. Rep. Congo 49 B4
Idivuoma Sweden 14 M2
Idkū Egypt 34 C5
Idle r. U.K. 18 G5
Idlib Syria 39 C2
Idra i. Greece see Ydra
Idre Sweden 15 H6
Idutywa S. Africa 51 I7
Idzhevan Armenia see Ijevan
Iecava Latvia 15 N8
Iepê Brazil 71 A3
Ierapetra Greece 27 K7
Ierissou, Kolpos b. Greece 27 J4
Iešjávri l. Norway 14 N2
Ifakara Tanz. 49 D4
Ifanadiana Madag. 49 E6
Ife Nigeria 46 D4
Iferlat Chad 47 E3
Iferouâne Niger 46 D3
Iffley Australia 56 C3
Ifjord Norway 14 O1
Ifôghas, Adrar des hills Mali 46 D3
Iforas, Adrar des hills Mali see Ifôghas, Adrar des
Igan Sarawak Malaysia 41 D7
Iganga Uganda 47 G4
Igarapava Brazil 71 B3
Igarka Rus. Fed. 28 J3
Igatpuri India 38 B2
Igbeti Nigeria see Igbetti
Igbetti Nigeria 46 D4
Igdir Iran 35 G3
Iğdır Turkey 35 G3
Iggesund Sweden 15 J6
Igikpak, Mount U.S.A. 60 C3
Iglesias Sardinia Italy 26 C5
Iglesiente reg. Sardinia Italy 26 C5
Igloolik Canada 61 J3
Igluligaarjuk Canada see Chesterfield Inlet
Ignace Canada 63 I2
Ignalina Lith. 15 O9
İğneada Turkey 27 L4
İğneada Burnu pt Turkey 27 M4
iGoli S. Africa see Johannesburg
Igoumenitsa Greece 27 I5
Igra Rus. Fed. 11 Q4
Igrim Rus. Fed. 11 S3
Iguaçu r. Brazil 71 A4
Iguaçu, Saltos do waterfall Arg./Brazil see Iguaçu Falls
Iguaçu Falls Arg./Brazil 70 F3
Iguaí Brazil 71 C1
Iguala Mex. 66 E5
Igualada Spain 25 G3
Iguape Brazil 71 B4
Iguaraçu Brazil 71 A3
Iguatama Brazil 71 B3
Iguatemi Brazil 70 F2
Iguatu Brazil 69 K5
Iguazú, Cataratas do waterfall Arg./Brazil see Iguaçu Falls
Iguéla Gabon 48 A4
Iguidi, Erg des. Alg./Mauritania 46 C2
Igunga Tanz. 49 D4
Iharaña Madag. 49 E5
Ihavandhippolhu Atoll Maldives 38 B5
Ihavandiffulu Atoll Maldives see Ihavandhippolhu Atoll
Ih Bogd Uul mt. Mongolia 42 I4
Ihosy Madag. 49 E6
Iide-san mt. Japan 45 E5
Iijärvi l. Fin. 14 O2
Iijoki r. Fin. 14 N4
Iisalmi Fin. 14 O5
Iizuka Japan 45 C6
Ijebu-Ode Nigeria 46 D4
Ijevan Armenia 35 G2
IJssel r. Neth. 17 J4
IJsselmeer l. Neth. 22 F1
Ikaahuk Canada see Sachs Harbour
Ikaalinen Fin. 15 M6
Ikageleng S. Africa 51 H3
Ikageng S. Africa 51 H4
iKapa S. Africa see Cape Town
Ikare Nigeria 46 D4
Ikaria i. Greece 27 L6
Ikast Denmark 15 F8
Ikeda Japan 44 F4
Ikela Dem. Rep. Congo 48 C4
Ikhtiman Bulg. 27 J3
Ikhutseng S. Africa 50 G5
Iki-Burul Rus. Fed. 13 J7
Ikom Nigeria 46 D4
Iksan S. Korea 45 B6
Ikungu Tanz. 49 D4
Ilagan Phil. 41 E6
Ilaisamis Kenya 48 D3
Īlām Iran 35 G4
Ilam Nepal 37 F4
Ilan Taiwan 43 M8
Ilave Peru 68 E7
Iława Poland 17 Q4
Ilazārān, Kūh-e mt. Iran 33 I4
Ilebo Dem. Rep. Congo 49 C4
Île Europa i. Indian Ocean see Europa, Île
Ilek Kazakh. 11 Q5
Ilen r. Ireland 21 C6
Ileret Kenya 48 D3
Ileza Rus. Fed. 12 I3
Ilfeld Germany 17 M5
Ilford U.K. 19 H7
Ilfracombe Australia 56 D4
Ilfracombe U.K. 19 C7
Ilgaz Turkey 34 D2
Ilgın Turkey 34 C3
Ilha Grande, Represa resr Brazil 70 F2
Ilha Solteíra, Represa resr Brazil 71 A3
Ílhavo Port. 25 B3
Ilhéus Brazil 71 D1
Ili Kazakh. see Kapchagay
Iliamna Lake U.S.A. 60 C4
İliç Turkey 34 E3
Il'ichevsk Azer. see Şärur
Il'ichevsk Ukr. see Illichivs'k
Ilici Spain see Elche-Elx
Ilimananngip Nunaa i. Greenland 61 P2
Il'inka Rus. Fed. 13 J7
Il'inskiy Permskaya Oblast' Rus. Fed. 11 R4
Il'inskiy Sakhalinskaya Oblast' Rus. Fed. 44 F3
Il'insko-Podomskoye Rus. Fed. 12 J3
Ilion NY U.S.A. 64 D1
Ilium tourist site Turkey see Troy
Iliysk Kazakh. see Kapchagay
Ilkal India 38 C3
Ilkeston U.K. 19 F6
Ilkley U.K. 18 F5
Illapel Chile 70 B4
Illéla Niger 46 D3
Iller r. Germany 17 L6
Illichivs'k Ukr. 27 N1
Illimani, Nevado de mt. Bol. 68 E7
Illinois r. U.S.A. 63 I4
Illinois state U.S.A. 63 J4
Illizi Alg. 46 D2
Illogwa watercourse Australia 56 A5
Ilmajoki Fin. 14 M5
Il'men', Ozero l. Rus. Fed. 12 F4
Ilminster U.K. 19 E8
Ilo Peru 68 D7
Iloilo Phil. 41 E6
Ilomantsi Fin. 14 Q5
Ilorin Nigeria 46 D4
Ilovlya Rus. Fed. 13 I6
Iluka Australia 58 F2
Ilulissat Greenland 61 M3
Iluppur India 38 C4
Ilva i. Italy see Elba, Isola d'
Imabari Japan 45 D6
Imaichi Japan 45 E5
Imala Moz. 49 D5
İmamoğlu Turkey 34 D3
Iman Rus. Fed. see Dal'nerechensk
Iman r. Rus. Fed. 44 D3
Imari Japan 45 C6
Imaruí Brazil 71 A5
Imataca, Serranía de mts Venez. 68 F2
Imatra Fin. 15 P6
Imbituva Brazil 71 A4
imeni Babushkina Rus. Fed. 12 I4
imeni 26 Bakinskikh Komissarov Azer. see Uzboy
imeni Kirova Kazakh. see Kopbirlik
imeni Petra Stuchki Latvia see Aizkraukle
imeni Poliny Osipenko Rus. Fed. 44 E1
imeni Tel'mana Rus. Fed. 44 D2
Īmī Eth. 48 E3
İmishli Azer. see İmişli
İmişli Azer. 35 H3
Imit Jammu and Kashmir 36 C1
Imja-do i. S. Korea 45 B6
Imola Italy 26 D2
iMonti S. Africa see East London
Impendle S. Africa 51 I5
Imperatriz Brazil 69 I5
Imperia Italy 26 C3
Imperial CA U.S.A. 65 E4
Imperial Beach CA U.S.A. 65 D4
Imperial Dam Arizona/California U.S.A. 65 E4
Imperial Valley plain CA U.S.A. 65 E4
Imperieuse Reef Australia 54 B4
Impfondo Congo 48 B3
Imphal India 37 H4
İmralı Adası i. Turkey 27 M4
İmroz Turkey 27 K4
İmroz i. Turkey see Gökçeada
Imtān Syria 39 C3
In r. Rus. Fed. 44 D2
Ina Japan 45 E6
Inambari r. Peru 68 E6
Inari Fin. 14 O2
Inarijärvi l. Fin. 14 O2
Inarijoki r. Fin./Norway 14 N2
Inca Spain 25 H4
İnce Burnu pt Turkey 27 L4
İnce Burun pt Turkey 34 D2
Inch Ireland 21 F5
Inchard, Loch b. U.K. 20 D2
Incheon S. Korea see Inch'ŏn
Inchicronan Lough l. Ireland 21 D5
Inch'ŏn S. Korea 45 B5
Incirli Turkey see Karasu
Indaal, Loch b. U.K. 20 C5
Indalsälven r. Sweden 14 J5
Indalstø Norway 15 D6
Inda Silasē Eth. 48 D2
Indé Mex. 66 C3
Indefatigable Island Galápagos Ecuador see Santa Cruz, Isla
Independence CA U.S.A. 65 C2
Independence MO U.S.A. 63 I4
Inder China 44 A3
Inderborskiy Kazakh. 30 E2
Indi India 38 C2
India country Asia 31 I4
Indiana PA U.S.A. 64 B2
Indiana state U.S.A. 63 J3
Indian-Antarctic Ridge sea feature Southern Ocean 74 D9
Indianapolis U.S.A. 63 J4
Indian Desert India/Pak. see Thar Desert
Indian Head Canada 62 G1
Indian Lake NY U.S.A. 64 D1
Indian Lake PA U.S.A. 64 B2
Indian Ocean 73
Indianola IA U.S.A. 63 I3
Indianola MS U.S.A. 63 I5
Indian Peak UT U.S.A. 65 F1
Indian Springs NV U.S.A. 65 E2
Indiga Rus. Fed. 12 K2
Indigirka r. Rus. Fed. 29 P2
Indigskaya Guba b. Rus. Fed. 12 K2
Inđija Serbia 27 I2
Indio CA U.S.A. 65 D4
Indira Priyadarshini Pench National Park India 36 D5
Indispensable Reefs Solomon Is 53 G3
Indjija Serbia see Inđija
Indonesia country Asia 41 D8
Indore India 36 C5
Indrapura, Gunung vol. Indon. see Kerinci, Gunung
Indravati r. India 38 D2
Indre r. France 24 E3
Indulkana Australia 55 F6
Indur India see Nizamabad
Indus r. China/Pak. 31 F4
Indus, Mouths of the Pak. 33 K5
Indus Cone sea feature Indian Ocean 73 M4
Indwe S. Africa 51 H6
İnebolu Turkey 34 D2
İnegöl Turkey 27 M4
Inevi Turkey see Cihanbeyli
Infantes Spain see Villanueva de los Infantes
Infiernillo, Presa resr Mex. 66 D5
Inga Rus. Fed. 14 S3
Ingersoll Ont. Canada 64 A1
Ingham Australia 56 D3
Ingleborough hill U.K. 18 E4
Inglefield Land reg. Greenland 61 K2
Ingleton U.K. 18 E4
Inglewood Qld Australia 58 E2
Inglewood Vic. Australia 58 A6
Inglewood CA U.S.A. 65 C4
Ingoka Pum mt. Myanmar 37 I4
Ingoldmells U.K. 18 H5
Ingolstadt Germany 17 M6
Ingomar Australia 55 F7
Ingraj Bazar India 37 G4
Ingrid Christensen Coast Antarctica 76 E2
Ingwavuma S. Africa 51 K4
Ingwavuma r. S. Africa/Swaziland see Ngwavuma
Inhaca Moz. 51 K3
Inhaca, Península pen. Moz. 51 K4
Inhambane Moz. 51 L2
Inhambane prov. Moz. 51 L2
Inhaminga Moz. 49 D5
Inharrime Moz. 51 L3
Inhassoro Moz. 49 D6
Inhaúmas Brazil 71 B1
Inhobim Brazil 71 C1
Inhumas Brazil 71 A2
Inis Ireland see Ennis
Inis Córthaidh Ireland see Enniscorthy
Inishark i. Ireland 21 B4
Inishbofin i. Ireland 21 B4
Inisheer i. Ireland 21 C4
Inishkea North i. Ireland 21 B3
Inishkea South i. Ireland 21 B3
Inishmaan i. Ireland 21 C4
Inishmore i. Ireland 21 C4
Inishmurray i. Ireland 21 D3
Inishowen pen. Ireland 21 E2
Inishowen Head hd Ireland 21 F2
Inishtrahull i. Ireland 21 E2
Inishturk i. Ireland 21 B4
Injune Australia 57 E5
Inkerman Australia 56 C3
Inland Kaikoura Range mts N.Z. 59 D6
Inland Sea Japan see Seto-naikai
Inlet NY U.S.A. 64 D1
Inn r. Europe 17 M7
Innaanganeq c. Greenland 61 L2
Innamincka Australia 57 C5
Innamincka Regional Reserve nature res. Australia 57 C5
Inndyr Norway 14 I3
Inner Sound sea chan. U.K. 20 D3
Innes National Park Australia 57 B7
Innisfail Australia 56 D3
Innokent'yevka Rus. Fed. 44 C2
Innoko r. U.S.A. 60 C3
Innsbruck Austria 17 M7
Inny r. Ireland 21 E4
Inocência Brazil 71 A2
Inongo Dem. Rep. Congo 48 B4
İnönü Turkey 27 N5
Inowrocław Poland 17 Q4
In Salah Alg. 46 D2
Insch U.K. 20 G3
Inscription, Cape Austr. 56 B3
Insterburg Rus. Fed. see Chernyakhovsk
Inta Rus. Fed. 11 S2
Interamna Italy see Teramo
Interlaken Switz. 24 H3
International Falls U.S.A. 63 I2
Intutu Peru 68 D4
Inubō-zaki pt Japan 45 F6
Inuvik Canada 60 E3
Inveraray U.K. 20 D4
Inverbervie U.K. 20 G4
Invercargill N.Z. 59 B8
Inverell Australia 58 E2
Invergordon U.K. 20 E3
Inverkeithing U.K. 20 F4
Inverleigh Australia 56 C3
Inverness U.K. 20 E3
Inverness CA U.S.A. 65 A1
Inverurie U.K. 20 G3
Investigator Group is Australia 55 F8
Investigator Ridge sea feature Indian Ocean 73 O6
Investigator Strait Australia 57 B7
Inwood WV U.S.A. 64 B3
Inya Rus. Fed. 42 F2
Inyanga Zimbabwe see Nyanga
Inyangani mt. Zimbabwe 49 D5
Inyokern CA U.S.A. 65 D3
Inyo Mountains CA U.S.A. 65 C2
Inyonga Tanz. 49 D4
Inza Rus. Fed. 13 J5
Inzhavino Rus. Fed. 13 I5
Ioannina Greece 27 I5
Iokanga r. Rus. Fed. 12 H2
Iola U.S.A. 63 H4
Iolgo, Khrebet mts Rus. Fed. 42 F2
Iolotan' Turkm. see Yolöten
Iona i. U.K. 20 C4
Iona, Parque Nacional do nat. park Angola 49 B5
Ione NV U.S.A. 65 D1
Iongo Angola 49 B4
Ionian Islands Greece 27 H5
Ionian Sea Greece/Italy 26 H5
Ionioi Nisoi is Greece see Ionian Islands
Ios i. Greece 27 K6
Iowa state U.S.A. 63 I3
Iowa City U.S.A. 63 I3
Ipameri Brazil 71 A2
Ipanema Brazil 71 C2
Ipáría Peru 68 D5
Ipatinga Brazil 71 C2
Ipatovo Rus. Fed. 13 I7
Ipelegeng S. Africa 51 G4
Ipiales Col. 68 C3
Ipiaú Brazil 71 D1
Ipirá Brazil 71 D1
Ipiranga Brazil 71 A4
iPitoli S. Africa see Pretoria
Ipixuna r. Brazil 68 F5
Ipoh Malaysia 41 C7
Iporá Brazil 71 A2
Ippy Cent. Afr. Rep. 48 C3
Ipsala Turkey 27 L4
Ipswich Australia 58 F1
Ipswich U.K. 19 I6
Ipu Brazil 69 J4
Iqaluit Canada 61 L3
Iquique Chile 70 B2
Iquiri r. Brazil see Ituxi
Iquitos Peru 68 D4
Irai Brazil 70 F3
Irakleio Greece see Iraklion
Iraklion Greece 27 K7
Iramaia Brazil 71 C1
Iran country Asia 32 I3
Īrānshahr Iran 33 J4
Irapuato Mex. 66 D4
Iraq country Asia 35 F4
Irara Brazil 71 D1
Irati Brazil 71 A4
Irayel' Rus. Fed. 12 L2
Irazú, Volcán vol. Costa Rica 67 H7
Irbid Jordan 39 B3
Irbil Iraq see Arbīl
Irbit Rus. Fed. 28 H4
Irecê Brazil 69 J6
Ireland country Europe 21 E4
Ireland i. Ireland/U.K. 21
Irema Dem. Rep. Congo 48 C4
Irgiz Kazakh. 42 A3
Irgiz r. Kazakh. 42 A3
Iri S. Korea see Iksan
Irian, Teluk b. Indon. see Cenderawasih, Teluk
Iriba Chad 47 F3
Īrī Dāgh mt. Iran 35 G3
Irîgui reg. Mali/Mauritania 46 C3
Iringa Tanz. 49 D4
Iriri r. Brazil 69 H4
Irish Sea Ireland/U.K. 21 G4
Irituia Brazil 69 I4
Irkutsk Rus. Fed. 42 I2
Irmak Turkey 34 D3
Irminger Basin sea feature N. Atlantic Ocean 72 F2
Iron Baron Australia 57 B7
Irondequoit NY U.S.A. 64 C1
Iron Mountain U.S.A. 63 J2
Iron Mountain UT U.S.A. 65 F2
Iron Range National Park Australia 56 C2
Irosin Phil. 41 E6
Irpen' Ukr. see Irpin'
Irpin' Ukr. 13 F6
Irrawaddy r. Myanmar 37 H6
Irrawaddy, Mouths of the Myanmar 31 I5
Irshad Pass Afgh./Jammu and Kashmir 36 C1
Irta Rus. Fed. 12 K3
Irthing r. U.K. 18 E4
Irtysh r. Kazakh./Rus. Fed. 31 G1
Irun Spain 25 F2
Iruña Spain see Pamplona
Iruñea Spain see Pamplona
Irvine U.K. 20 E5
Irvine CA U.S.A. 65 D4
Irvine Glacier Antarctica 76 L2
Irwin r. Australia 55 A7
Isa Nigeria 46 D3
Isaac r. Australia 56 E4
Isabela Phil. 41 E7
Isabela, Isla i. Galápagos Ecuador 68 [inset]
Isabelia, Cordillera mts Nicaragua 67 G6
Isabella Lake CA U.S.A. 65 C3
Isachsen, Cape Canada 61 H2
Ísafjarðardjúp est. Iceland 14 [inset]
Ísafjörður Iceland 14 [inset]
Isa Khel Pak. 36 B2
Isar r. Germany 17 N6
Isbister U.K. 20 [inset]
Ischia, Isola d' i. Italy 26 E4
Ise Japan 45 E6
Isère r. France 24 G4
Isère, Pointe pt Fr. Guiana 69 H2
Isernia Italy 26 F4
Ise-shima Kokuritsu-kōen Japan 45 E6
Ise-wan b. Japan 45 E6
Iseyin Nigeria 46 D4
Isfahan Iran see Eşfahān
Isheyevka Rus. Fed. 13 K5
Ishigaki Japan 43 M8
Ishikari-wan b. Japan 44 F4
Ishim r. Kazakh./Rus. Fed. 30 G1
Ishinomaki Japan 45 F5
Ishinomaki-wan b. Japan 43 Q5
Ishioka Japan 45 F5
Ishkoshim Tajik. 36 B1
Ishurdi Bangl. 37 G4
Ishwardi Bangl. see Ishurdi
Isiboro Sécure, Parque Nacional nat. park Bol. 68 E7
Isigny-sur-Mer France 19 F9
Işıklar Dağı mts Turkey 27 L4
Işıklı Turkey 27 M5
Isil'kul' Rus. Fed. 28 I4
Isipingo S. Africa 51 J5
Isiro Dem. Rep. Congo 48 C3
Isisford Australia 56 D5
Iskateley Rus. Fed. 12 L2
İskenderun Turkey 39 C1
İskenderun Körfezi b. Turkey 39 B1
İskilip Turkey 34 D2
Iskitim Rus. Fed. 28 J4
Iskŭr r. Bulg. 27 K3
Iskushuban Somalia 48 F2
Isla r. Scotland U.K. 20 F4
Isla r. Scotland U.K. 20 G3
Isla Gorge National Park Australia 56 E5
İslahiye Turkey 34 E3
Islamabad India see Anantnag
Islamabad Pak. 33 L3
Islamgarh Pak. 36 B4
Islamkot Pak. 36 B4
Island country Europe see Iceland
Island Lagoon salt flat Australia 57 B6
Island Lake Canada 63 I1
Island Magee pen. U.K. 21 G3
Islands, Bay of N.Z. 59 E2
Islay i. U.K. 20 C5
Isle of Man terr. Irish Sea 18 C4
Isle of Wight VA U.S.A. 64 C4
Ismail Ukr. see Izmayil
Ismâ'ilîya Egypt see Al Ismā'īlīyah
Ismâ'ilîya governorate Egypt see Al Ismā'īlīyah
Ismailly Azer. see İsmayıllı
İsmayıllı Azer. 35 H2
Isojoki Fin. 14 L5
Isoka Zambia 49 D5
Isokylä Fin. 14 O3
Isokyrö Fin. 14 M5
Isola di Capo Rizzuto Italy 26 G5
Ispahan Iran see Eşfahān
Isparta Turkey 27 N6
Isperikh Bulg. 27 L3
İspir Turkey 35 F2
Ispisar Tajik. see Khŭjand
Isplinji Pak. 36 A3
Israel country Asia 39 B4
Israelite Bay Australia 55 C8
Isra'il country Asia see Israel
Issia Côte d'Ivoire 46 C4
Issoire France 24 F4
Issyk-Kul' Kyrg. see Balykchy
Issyk-Kul', Ozero salt l. Kyrg. see Ysyk-Köl
İstalif Afgh. 36 B2
İstanbul Turkey 27 M4
İstanbul Boğazı strait Turkey see Bosporus
Istgāh-e Eznā Iran 35 H4
Istiaia Greece 27 J5
Istik r. Tajik. 36 C1
Istra pen. Croatia see Istria
Istres France 24 G5
Istria pen. Croatia 26 E2
Iswardi Bangl. see Ishurdi
Itabapoana r. Brazil 71 C3
Itaberá Brazil 71 A3
Itaberaba Brazil 71 C1
Itaberaí Brazil 71 A2
Itabira Brazil 71 C2
Itabirito Brazil 71 C3
Itabuna Brazil 71 D1
Itacajá Brazil 69 I5
Itacarambi Brazil 71 B1
Itacoatiara Brazil 69 G4
Itaetê Brazil 71 C1
Itagmatana Iran see Hamadān
Itaguaçu Brazil 71 C2
Itaí Brazil 71 A3
Itaiópolis Brazil 71 A4
Itäisen Suomenlahden kansallispuisto nat. park Fin. 15 O6
Itaituba Brazil 69 G4
Itajaí Brazil 71 A4
Itajubá Brazil 71 B3
Itajuipe Brazil 71 D1
Italia country Europe see Italy
Italia, Laguna l. Bol. 68 F6
Italy country Europe 26 E3
Itamarandiba Brazil 71 C2
Itambé Brazil 71 C1
Itambé, Pico de mt. Brazil 71 C2
Itampolo Madag. 49 E6
Itanagar India 37 H4
Itanguari r. Brazil 71 B1
Itanhaém Brazil 71 B4
Itanhém Brazil 71 C2
Itanhém r. Brazil 71 D2
Itaobím Brazil 71 C2
Itapaci Brazil 71 A1
Itapajipe Brazil 71 A2
Itapebi Brazil 71 D1
Itapecerica Brazil 71 B3
Itapemirim Brazil 71 C3
Itaperuna Brazil 71 C3
Itapetinga Brazil 71 C1
Itapetininga Brazil 71 A3
Itapeva Brazil 71 A3
Itapeva, Lago l. Brazil 71 A5
Itapicuru Brazil 69 J6
Itapicuru, Serra de hills Brazil 69 I5
Itapicuru Mirim Brazil 69 J4
Itapipoca Brazil 69 K4
Itapira Brazil 71 B3
Itaporanga Brazil 71 A3
Itapuã Brazil 71 A5
Itaqui Brazil 70 E3
Itararé Brazil 71 A4
Itarsi India 36 D5
Itarumã Brazil 71 A2
Itatiba Brazil 71 B3
Itatuba Brazil 68 F5
Itaúna Brazil 71 B3
Itaúnas Brazil 71 D2
Itbayat i. Phil. 43 M8
Itea Greece 27 J5
Ithaca NY U.S.A. 64 C1
iThekweni S. Africa see Durban
Ithrah Saudi Arabia 39 C4
Itilleq Greenland 61 M3
Itimbiri r. Dem. Rep. Congo 48 C3
Itinga Brazil 71 C2
Itiquira Brazil 69 H7
Itiruçu Brazil 71 C1
Itiúba, Serra de hills Brazil 69 K6
Itō Japan 45 E6
iTswane S. Africa see Pretoria
Ittiri Sardinia Italy 26 C4
Ittoqqortoormiit Greenland 61 P2
Itu Brazil 71 B3
Ituaçu Brazil 71 C1
Ituberá Brazil 71 D1
Ituí r. Brazil 68 D4
Ituiutaba Brazil 71 A2
Itumbiara Brazil 71 A2
Itumbiara, Barragem resr Brazil 71 A2
Ituni Guyana 69 G2
Itupiranga Brazil 69 I5
Ituporanga Brazil 71 A4
Iturama Brazil 71 A2
Ituri r. Dem. Rep. Congo 48 C3
Iturup, Ostrov i. Rus. Fed. 44 G3
Itutinga Brazil 71 B3
Ituxi r. Brazil 68 F5
Ityop'ia country Africa see Ethiopia
Itzehoe Germany 17 L4
Iul'tin Rus. Fed. 29 T3
Ivalo Fin. 14 O2
Ivalojoki r. Fin. 14 O2
Ivanava Belarus 15 N10
Ivanhoe Australia 58 B4
Ivankiv Ukr. 13 F6
Ivankovtsy Rus. Fed. 44 D2
Ivano-Frankivs'k Ukr. 13 E6
Ivano-Frankovsk Ukr. see Ivano-Frankivs'k
Ivanovka Rus. Fed. 44 B2
Ivanovo Belarus see Ivanava
Ivanovo tourist site Bulg. 27 K3
Ivanovo Rus. Fed. 12 I4
Ivanteyevka Rus. Fed. 13 K5
Ivantsevichi Belarus see Ivatsevichy
Ivatsevichy Belarus 15 N10
Ivaylovgrad Bulg. 27 L4
Ivdel' Rus. Fed. 11 S3
Ivittuut Greenland 61 N3
Iviza i. Spain see Ibiza
Ivory Coast country Africa see Côte d'Ivoire
Ivrea Italy 26 B2
İvrindi Turkey 27 L5
Ivris Ugheltekhili pass Georgia 35 G2
Ivugivik Canada see Ivujivik
Ivujivik Canada 61 K3
Ivyanyets Belarus 15 O10
Ivydale WV U.S.A. 64 A3
Iwaki Japan 45 F5
Iwaki-san vol. Japan 44 F4
Iwakuni Japan 45 D6

Iwamizawa Japan **44** F4
Iwo Nigeria **46** D4
Iwye Belarus **15** N10
Ixiamas Bol. **68** E6
Ixmiquilpán Mex. **66** E4
Ixopo S. Africa **51** J6
Ixtlán Mex. **66** D4
Ixworth U.K. **19** H6
İyirmi Altı Bakı Komissarı Azer. *see* **Uzboy**
Izabal, Lago de *l.* Guat. **66** G5
Izberbash Rus. Fed. **35** G2
Īzeh Iran **35** H5
Izgal Pak. **36** C2
Izhevsk Rus. Fed. **11** Q4
Izhma *Respublika Komi* Rus. Fed. **12** L2
Izhma *Respublika Komi* Rus. Fed. *see* **Sosnogorsk**
Izhma *r.* Rus. Fed. **12** L2
Izmail Ukr. *see* **Izmayil**
Izmayil Ukr. **27** M2
İzmir Turkey **27** L5
İzmir Körfezi *g.* Turkey **27** L5
İzmit Turkey **27** M4
İzmit Körfezi *b.* Turkey **27** M4
Izozog Bol. **68** F7
Izra' Syria **39** C3
Iztochni Rodopi *mts* Bulg. **27** K4
Izu-hantō *pen.* Japan **45** E6
Izuhara Japan **45** C6
Izumo Japan **45** D6
Izu-Ogasawara Trench *sea feature* N. Pacific Ocean **74** F3
Izu-shotō *is* Japan **45** E6
Izyaslav Ukr. **13** E6
Iz"yayu Rus. Fed. **12** M2
Izyum Ukr. **13** H6

J

Jabalón *r.* Spain **25** D4
Jabalpur India **36** D5
Jabbūl, Sabkhat al *salt flat* Syria **39** C2
Jabiru Australia **54** F3
Jablah Syria **39** B2
Jablanica Bos.-Herz. **26** G3
Jaboatão Brazil **69** L5
Jaboticabal Brazil **71** A3
Jacaraci Brazil **71** C1
Jacareacanga Brazil **69** G5
Jacareí Brazil **71** B3
Jacarézinho Brazil **71** A3
Jacinto Brazil **71** C2
Jack *r.* Australia **56** D2
Jackson Australia **58** D1
Jackson *AL* U.S.A. **63** J5
Jackson *CA* U.S.A. **65** B1
Jackson *MI* U.S.A. **63** K3
Jackson *MS* U.S.A. **63** I5
Jackson *TN* U.S.A. **63** J4
Jackson *WY* U.S.A. **62** E3
Jackson, Mount Antarctica **76** L2
Jackson Head *hd* N.Z. **59** B6
Jacksonville *FL* U.S.A. **63** K5
Jacksonville *IL* U.S.A. **63** I4
Jacksonville *NC* U.S.A. **63** L5
Jack Wade U.S.A. **60** D3
Jacmel Haiti **67** J5
Jacobabad Pak. **33** K4
Jacobina Brazil **69** J6
Jacobsdal S. Africa **50** G5
Jacques Cartier, Mont *mt.* Canada **63** N2
Jacuí Brazil **71** B3
Jacuípe *r.* Brazil **69** K6
Jacunda Brazil **69** I4
Jaddangi India **38** D2
J. A. D. Jensen Nunatakker *nunataks* Greenland **61** N3
Jadotville Dem. Rep. Congo *see* **Likasi**
Jādū Libya **46** E1
Jaén Spain **25** E5
Jaffa, Cape Australia **57** B8
Jaffna Sri Lanka **38** C4
Jafr, Qā' al *imp. l.* Jordan **39** C4
Jagadhri India **36** D3
Jagalur India **38** C3
Jagatsinghapur India *see* **Jagatsinghpur**
Jagatsinghpur India **37** F5
Jagdalpur India **38** D2
Jagdaqi China **44** B2
Jagersfontein S. Africa **51** G5
Jaggang China **36** D2
Jaggayyapeta India **38** D2
Jaghin Iran **33** I4
Jagok Tso *salt l.* China *see* **Urru Co**
Jagtial India **38** C2
Jaguariaíva Brazil **71** A4
Jaguaripe Brazil **71** D1
Jahanabad India *see* **Jehanabad**
Jahmah *well* Iraq **35** G5
Jahrom Iran **35** I5
Jaicós Brazil **69** J5
Jaigarh India **38** B2
Jailolo Gilolo *i.* Indon. *see* **Halmahera**
Jainpur India **37** E4
Jaintapur Bangl. *see* **Jaintiapur**
Jaintiapur Bangl. **37** H4
Jaipur India **36** C4
Jaipurhat Bangl. *see* **Joypurhat**
Jais India **37** E4
Jaisalmer India **36** B4
Jaisamand Lake India **36** C4
Jaitaran India **36** C4
Jaitgarh *hill* India **38** C1
Jajapur India *see* **Jajpur**
Jajarkot Nepal **33** N4
Jajce Bos.-Herz. **26** G2
Jajnagar *state* India *see* **Orissa**
Jajpur India **37** F5
Jakar Bhutan **37** G4
Jakarta Indon. **41** C8
Jakhan India **36** B5
Jakin *mt.* Afgh. **36** A3
Jäkkvik Sweden **14** J3
Jakliat India **36** C3
Jakobshavn Greenland *see* **Ilulissat**
Jakobstad Fin. **14** M5
Jalaid China *see* **Inder**
Jalālābād Afgh. **36** B2
Jalal-Abad Kyrg. **42** C4
Jalālah al Baḥrīyah, Jabal *plat.* Egypt **34** C5
Jalāmīd, Ḥazm al *ridge* Saudi Arabia **35** E5
Jalandhar India **36** C3
Jalapa Mex. **66** E5
Jalapa Enríquez Mex. *see* **Jalapa**
Jalapur Pirwala Pak. **36** B3
Jalasjärvi Fin. **14** M5
Jalaun India **36** D4
Jalawlā' Iraq **35** G4
Jaldak Afgh. **36** A3
Jaldrug India **38** C2
Jales Brazil **71** A3
Jalesar India **36** D4
Jalgaon India **36** C5
Jalībah Iraq **35** G5
Jalingo Nigeria **46** E4
Jalna India **38** B2
Jalón *r.* Spain **25** F3
Jalor India *see* **Jalore**
Jalore India **36** C4
Jalpa Mex. **66** D4
Jalpaiguri India **37** G4
Jālū Libya **47** F2
Jalūlā Iraq *see* **Jalawlā'**
Jamaica *country* West Indies **67** I5
Jamaica Channel Haiti/Jamaica **67** I5
Jamalpur Bangl. **37** G4
Jamalpur India **37** F4
Jamanxim *r.* Brazil **69** G4
Jambi Indon. **41** C8
Jambin Australia **56** E5
Jambo India **36** C4
Jamda India **37** F5
Jamekunte India **38** C2
James *r. N. Dakota/S. Dakota* U.S.A. **62** H3
James *r. VA* U.S.A. **64** C4
James, Baie *b.* Canada *see* **James Bay**
Jamesabad Pak. **36** B4
James Bay Canada **63** K1
James Island *Galápagos* Ecuador *see* **San Salvador, Isla**
Jameson Land *reg.* Greenland **61** P2
James Peak N.Z. **59** B7
James Ranges *mts* Australia **55** F6
James Ross Island Antarctica **76** A2
James Ross Strait Canada **61** I3
Jamestown Australia **57** B7
Jamestown S. Africa **51** H6
Jamestown St Helena **72** H7
Jamestown *ND* U.S.A. **62** H2
Jamestown *NY* U.S.A. **64** B1
Jamkhed India **38** B2
Jammu India **36** C2
Jammu and Kashmir *terr.* Asia **36** D2
Jamnagar India **36** B5
Jampur Pak. **36** B3
Jamrud Pak. **36** B2
Jämsä Fin. **15** N6
Jamsah Egypt **34** D6
Jämsänkoski Fin. **14** N6
Jamshedpur India **37** F5
Jamtari Nigeria **46** E4
Jamui India **37** F4
Jamuna *r.* Bangl. *see* **Raimangal**
Jamuna *r.* India *see* **Yamuna**
Janā *i.* Saudi Arabia **35** H6
Janāb, Wādī al *watercourse* Jordan **39** C4
Janakpur India **37** E5
Janaúba Brazil **71** C1
Jandaia Brazil **71** A2
Jandaq Iran **35** I4
Jandola Pak. **36** B2
Jandowae Australia **58** E1
Janesville *WI* U.S.A. **63** J3
Jangada Brazil **71** A4
Jangamo Moz. **51** L3
Jangaon India **38** C2
Jangipur India **37** G4
Jangnga Turkm. *see* **Jaňňa**
Jangngai Ri *mts* China **37** F2
Jan Mayen *terr.* Arctic Ocean **77** I2
Jan Mayen Fracture Zone *sea feature* Arctic Ocean **77** I2
Jaňňa Turkm. **35** I2
Jansenville S. Africa **50** G7
Januária Brazil **71** B1
Janūb Sīnā' *governorate* Egypt **39** A5
Janūb Sīnā' *governorate* Egypt *see* **Janūb Sīnā'**
Japan *country* Asia **45** D5
Japan, Sea of N. Pacific Ocean **45** D5
Japan Alps National Park Japan *see* **Chibu-Sangaku National Park**
Japan Trench *sea feature* N. Pacific Ocean **74** F3
Japiim Brazil **68** D5
Japurá *r.* Brazil **68** F4
Japvo Mount India **37** H4
Jarābulus Syria **39** D1
Jaraguá Brazil **71** A1
Jaraguá, Serra *mts* Brazil **71** A4
Jaraguá do Sul Brazil **71** A4
Jarash Jordan **39** B3
Jardine River National Park Australia **56** C1
Jardinésia Brazil **71** A2
Jardinópolis Brazil **71** B3
Jargalang China **44** A4
Jargalant *Bayanhongor* Mongolia **42** H3
Jargalant *Dornod* Mongolia **43** L3
Jargalant *Hovd* Mongolia *see* **Hovd**
Jari *r.* Brazil **69** H4
Järna Sweden **15** J7
Jarocin Poland **17** P5
Jarosław Poland **13** D6
Järpen Sweden **14** H5
Jarrettsville *MD* U.S.A. **64** C3
Jarú Brazil **68** F6
Jarud China *see* **Lubei**
Järvakandi Estonia **15** N7
Järvenpää Fin. **15** N6
Jarvis Island *terr.* S. Pacific Ocean **74** J6
Jarwa India **37** E4
Jashpurnagar India **37** F5
Jāsk Iran **33** I4
Jasliq Uzbek. **35** J2
Jasło Poland **13** D6
Jasol India **36** C4
Jason Islands Falkland Is **70** D8
Jason Peninsula Antarctica **76** L2
Jasper Canada **62** D1
Jasper *NY* U.S.A. **64** C1
Jasper *TX* U.S.A. **63** I5
Jasrasar India **36** C4
Jaşşān Iraq **35** G4
Jassy Romania *see* **Iaşi**
Jastrzębie-Zdrój Poland **17** Q6
Jaswantpura India **36** C4
Jászberény Hungary **27** H1
Jataí Brazil **71** A2
Jatapu *r.* Brazil **69** G4
Jath India **38** B2
Jati Pak. **33** K5
Játiva Spain *see* **Xátiva**
Jatoi Pak. **36** B3
Jat Poti Afgh. **36** A3
Jaú Brazil **71** A3
Jaú *r.* Brazil **68** F4
Jaú, Parque Nacional do *nat. park* Brazil **68** F4
Jaua Sarisariñama, Parque Nacional *nat. park* Venez. **68** F3
Jauja Peru **68** C6
Jaunlutriņi Latvia **15** M8
Jaunpiebalga Latvia **15** O8
Jaunpur India **37** E4
Java Georgia **35** F2
Java *i.* Indon. **41** C8
Javaés *r.* Brazil *see* **Formoso**
Javari *r.* Brazil/Peru *see* **Yavari**
Java Ridge *sea feature* Indian Ocean **73** P6
Javarthushuu Mongolia **43** K3
Java Sea Indon. *see* **Jawa, Laut**
Java Trench *sea feature* Indian Ocean **73** P6
Java Trench *sea feature* Indian Ocean **74** C6
Jävre Sweden **14** L4
Jawa *i.* Indon. *see* **Java**
Jawa, Laut *sea* Indon. **41** D8
Jawhar India **38** B2
Jawhar Somalia **48** E3
Jawor Poland **17** P5
Jaya, Puncak *mt.* Indon. **41** F8
Jayakusumu *mt.* Indon. *see* **Jaya, Puncak**
Jayakwadi Sagar *l.* India **38** B2
Jayantiapur Bangl. *see* **Jaintiapur**
Jayapura Indon. **41** G8
Jayb, Wādī al *watercourse* Israel/Jordan **39** B4
Jayfī, Wādī al *watercourse* Egypt **39** B4
Jaypur India **38** D2
Jayrūd Syria **39** C3
Jazīreh-ye Shīf Iran **35** H5
Jbail Lebanon **39** B2
Jean *NV* U.S.A. **65** E3
Jeannin, Lac *l.* Canada **61** L4
Jebel, Bahr el *r.* Sudan/Uganda *see* **White Nile**
Jebel, Bahr el *r.* Sudan/Uganda *see* **White Nile**
Jebel Abyad Plateau Sudan **32** C6
Jech Doab *lowland* Pak. **36** C3
Jedburgh U.K. **20** G5
Jeddah Saudi Arabia **32** E5
Jedeida Tunisia **26** C6
Jefferson *OH* U.S.A. **64** A2
Jefferson, Mount *NV* U.S.A. **65** D1
Jefferson City U.S.A. **63** I4
Jeffreys Bay S. Africa **50** G8
Jehanabad India **37** F4
Jeju S. Korea *see* **Cheju**
Jejuí Guazú *r.* Para. **70** E2
Jēkabpils Latvia **15** N8
Jelbart Ice Shelf Antarctica **76** B2
Jelenia Góra Poland **17** O5
Jelep La *pass* China/India **37** G4
Jelgava Latvia **15** M8
Jember Indon. **41** D8
Jena Germany **17** M5
Jendouba Tunisia **26** C6
Jengish Chokusu *mt.* China/Kyrg. *see* **Pobeda Peak**
Jenīn West Bank **39** B3
Jenne Mali *see* **Djenné**
Jennings U.S.A. **63** I5
Jenolan Caves Australia **58** E4
Jens Munk Island Canada **61** K3
Jeparit Australia **57** C8
Jequié Brazil **71** C1
Jequitaí *r.* Brazil **71** B2
Jequitinhonha Brazil **71** C2
Jequitinhonha *r.* Brazil **71** D1
Jerba, Île de *i.* Tunisia **22** G5
Jerbar Sudan **47** G4
Jereh Iran **35** H5
Jérémie Haiti **67** J5
Jerez Mex. **66** D4
Jerez de la Frontera Spain **25** C5
Jergol Norway **14** N2
Jergucat Albania **27** I5
Jericho Australia **56** D4
Jericho West Bank **39** B4
Jerid, Chott el *salt l.* Tunisia **22** F5
Jerilderie Australia **58** B5
Jerimoth Hill *RI* U.S.A. **64** F2
Jeroaquara Brazil **71** A1
Jerome U.S.A. **62** E3
Jerruck Pak. **36** B4
Jersey *terr.* Channel Is **19** E9
Jersey City *NJ* U.S.A. **64** D2
Jersey Shore *PA* U.S.A. **64** C2
Jerumenha Brazil **69** J5
Jerusalem Israel/West Bank **39** B4
Jervis Bay Australia **58** E5
Jervis Bay *b.* Australia **58** E5
Jervis Bay Territory *admin. div.* Australia **58** E5
Jesenice Slovenia **26** F1
Jesi Italy **26** E3
Jesselton *Sabah* Malaysia *see* **Kota Kinabalu**
Jessheim Norway **15** G6
Jessore Bangl. **37** G5
Jesu Maria Island P.N.G. *see* **Rambutyo Island**
Jesup U.S.A. **63** K5
Jewish Autonomous Oblast *admin. div.* Rus. Fed. *see* **Yevreyskaya Avtonomnaya Oblast'**
Jeypur India *see* **Jaypur**
Jezzine Lebanon **39** B3
Jhabua India **36** C5
Jhajhar India *see* **Jhajjar**
Jhajjar India **36** D3
Jhalawar India **36** D4
Jhal Magsi Pak. **36** A3
Jhang Pak. **33** L3
Jhansi India **36** D4
Jhapa Nepal **37** F4
Jharia India **37** F5
Jharkhand *state* India **37** F5
Jharsuguda India **37** F5
Jhawani Nepal **37** F4
Jhelum *r.* India/Pak. **36** C3
Jhelum Pak. **33** L3
Jhenaidah Bangl. **37** G5
Jhenaidaha Bangl. *see* **Jhenaidah**
Jhenida Bangl. *see* **Jhenaidah**
Jhimpir Pak. **36** B4
Jhudo Pak. **36** B4
Jhumritilaiya India **37** F4
Jhund India **36** B5
Jhunjhunun India **36** C3
Jiamusi China **44** C3
Ji'an *Jiangxi* China **43** K7
Ji'an *Jilin* China **44** B4
Jiangcheng China **42** I8
Jiangjunmiao China **42** F4
Jiangmen China **43** K8
Jiangna China *see* **Yanshan**
Jiangsi China *see* **Dejiang**
Jiangsu *prov.* China **43** L6
Jiangxi *prov.* China **43** L7
Jiangzhesongrong China **37** F3
Jianshui Hu *l.* China **37** E2
Jianyang *Fujian* China **43** L7
Jiaohe China **44** B4
Jiaojiang China *see* **Taizhou**
Jia Tsuo La *pass* China **37** F3
Jiaxing China **43** M6
Jiayi Taiwan *see* **Chiai**
Jiayin China **44** C2
Jiayuguan China **42** H5
Jībūtī *country* Africa *see* **Djibouti**
Jībūtī Djibouti *see* **Djibouti**
Jiddah Saudi Arabia *see* **Jeddah**
Jiddī, Jabal al *hill* Egypt **39** A4
Jidong China **44** C3
Jiehkkevárri *mt.* Norway **14** K2
Jiexiu China **43** K5
Jieyang China **43** L8
Jieznas Lith. **15** N9
Jigzhi China **42** I6
Jiḥār, Wādī al *watercourse* Syria **39** C2
Jihlava Czech Rep. **17** O6
Jijel Alg. **22** F4
Jijiga Eth. **48** E3
Jījīrud Iran **35** H4
Jil'ād *reg.* Jordan **39** B3
Jilf al Kabīr, Haḍabat al *plat.* Egypt **32** C5
Jilib Somalia **48** E3
Jilin China **44** B4
Jilin *prov.* China **44** B4
Jilin Hada Ling *mts* China **44** B4
Jiliu He *r.* China **44** A2
Jilo India **36** C4
Jilong Taiwan *see* **Chilung**
Jīma Eth. **48** D3
Jiménez *Chihuahua* Mex. **66** D3
Jiménez *Tamaulipas* Mex. **66** E4
Jimía, Cerro *mt.* Hond. **66** G5
Jimsar China **42** F4
Jim Thorpe *PA* U.S.A. **64** D2
Jinan China **43** L5
Jin'an China *see* **Songpan**
Jinbi China *see* **Dayao**
Jinchang China **42** I5
Jincheng *Shanxi* China **43** K5
Jinchengjiang China *see* **Hechi**
Jinchuan *Gansu* China *see* **Jinchang**
Jind India **36** D3
Jindřichův Hradec Czech Rep. **17** O6
Jingbian China **43** J5
Jingdezhen China **43** L7
Jingellic Australia **58** C5
Jinggangshan China **43** K7
Jinghong China **42** I8
Jingle China **43** K5
Jingmen China **43** K6
Jingpo China **44** C4
Jingpo Hu *resr* China **44** C4
Jingsha China *see* **Jingzhou**
Jingtai China **42** I5
Jingtieshan China **42** H5
Jingxian *Hunan* China *see* **Jingzhou**
Jingyu China **44** B4
Jingyuan China **42** I5
Jingzhou *Hubei* China **43** K6
Jingzhou *Hunan* China **43** J7
Jinhe *Nei Mongol* China **44** A2
Jinhua *Zhejiang* China **43** L7
Jining *Nei Mongol* China **43** K4
Jining *Shandong* China **43** L5
Jinja Uganda **48** D3
Jinka Eth. **48** D3
Jinotepe Nicaragua **67** G6
Jinping *Guizhou* China **43** J7
Jinsen S. Korea *see* **Inch'ŏn**
Jinsha Jiang *r.* China *see* **Yangtze**
Jinshan *Nei Mongol* China *see* **Guyang**
Jinshi *Hunan* China **43** K7
Jintur India **38** C2
Jinxi *Jiangxi* China **43** L7
Jinxi *Liaoning* China *see* **Lianshan**
Jinxian China **43** L7
Jinz, Qā' al *salt flat* Jordan **39** C4
Jinzhong China **43** K5
Jinzhou China **43** M4
Ji-Paraná Brazil **68** F6
Jipijapa Ecuador **68** B4
Ji Qu *r.* China **37** I3
Jiquiriçá Brazil **71** D1
Jiquitaia Brazil **71** D2
Jirā', Wādī *watercourse* Egypt **39** A5
Jirānīyāt, Shi'bān al *watercourse* Saudi Arabia **39** D4
Jīroft Iran **33** I4
Jirriiban Somalia **48** E3
Jishou China **43** J7
Jisr ash Shughūr Syria **39** C2
Jiu *r.* Romania **27** J3
Jiuding Shan *mt.* China **42** I6
Jiujiang *Jiangxi* China **43** L7
Jiulian China *see* **Mojiang**
Jiulong *H.K.* China *see* **Kowloon**
Jiulong *Sichuan* China **42** I7
Jiwani Pak. **33** J4
Jiwen China **44** A2
Jixi *Heilong.* China **44** C3
Jixian China **44** C3
Jīzah, Ahrāmāt al *tourist site* Egypt *see* **Pyramids of Giza**
Jīzān Saudi Arabia **32** F6
Jizzakh Uzbek. *see* **Jizzax**
Jizzax Uzbek. **33** K1
Joaçaba Brazil **71** A4
Joaíma Brazil **71** C2
João Belo Moz. *see* **Xai-Xai**
João de Almeida Angola *see* **Chibia**
João Pessoa Brazil **69** L5
João Pinheiro Brazil **71** B2
Joaquin V. González Arg. **70** D3
Joda India **37** F5
Jodhpur India **36** C4
Jodiya India **36** B5
Joensuu Fin. **14** P5
Jōetsu Japan **45** E5
Jofane Moz. **49** D6
Jogbura Nepal **36** E3
Jõgeva Estonia **15** O7
Jogjakarta Indon. *see* **Yogyakarta**
Jõgua Estonia **15** O7
Johannesburg S. Africa **51** H4
Johannesburg *CA* U.S.A. **65** D3
Johan Peninsula Canada **61** K2
Johi Pak. **36** A4
John Day U.S.A. **62** D3
John Day *r.* U.S.A. **62** C2
John F. Kennedy *airport NY* U.S.A. **64** E2
John o'Groats U.K. **20** F2
Johnsonburg *PA* U.S.A. **64** B2
Johnsondale *CA* U.S.A. **65** C3
Johnston, Lake *salt flat* Australia **55** C8
Johnston and Sand Islands *terr.* N. Pacific Ocean *see* **Johnston Atoll**
Johnston Atoll *terr.* N. Pacific Ocean **74** I4
Johnstone U.K. **20** E5
Johnstone Lake Canada *see* **Old Wives Lake**
Johnston Range *hills* Australia **55** D7
Johnstown Ireland **21** E5
Johnstown *NY* U.S.A. **64** D1
Johnstown *PA* U.S.A. **64** B2
Johor Bahru Malaysia **41** C7
Johore Bahru Malaysia *see* **Johor Bahru**
Jõhvi Estonia **15** O7
Joinville Brazil **71** A4
Joinville France **24** G2
Joinville Island Antarctica **76** A2
Jokkmokk Sweden **14** K3
Jökulsá *r.* Iceland **14** [inset]
Jökulsá á Fjöllum *r.* Iceland **14** [inset]
Jökulsá í Fljótsdal *r.* Iceland **14** [inset]
Jolfa Iran **35** G3
Joliet U.S.A. **63** J3
Jolo *i.* Phil. **41** E7
Jomda China **42** H6
Jonava Lith. **15** N9
Jonesboro *AR* U.S.A. **63** I4
Jones Sound *sea chan.* Canada **61** J2
Jonglei Canal Sudan **32** D8
Jönköping Sweden **15** I8
Jonquière Canada **63** M2
Joplin U.S.A. **63** I4
Joppa Israel *see* **Tel Aviv-Yafo**
Jora India **36** D4
Jordan *country* Asia **39** C4
Jordan *r.* Asia **39** B4
Jordan U.S.A. **62** F2
Jordânia Brazil **71** C1
Jordet Norway **15** H6
Jorhat India **37** H4
Jorm Afgh. **36** B1
Jörn Sweden **14** L4
Joroinen Fin. **14** O5
Jørpeland Norway **15** E7
Jos Nigeria **46** D4
José de San Martín Arg. **70** B6
Joseph, Lac *l.* Canada **61** L4
Joseph Bonaparte Gulf Australia **54** E3
Joshimath India **36** D3
Joshipur India **38** E1
Joshua Tree National Park *CA* U.S.A. **65** E4
Jos Plateau Nigeria **46** D4
Jostedalsbreen Nasjonalpark *nat. park* Norway **15** E6
Jotunheimen Nasjonalpark *nat. park* Norway **15** F6
Jouaiya Lebanon **39** B3
Joubertina S. Africa **50** F7
Jouberton S. Africa **51** H4
Joûnié Lebanon **39** B3
Joutsa Fin. **15** O6
Joutseno Fin. **15** P6
Jowai India **37** H4
Jowr Deh Iran **35** H3
Joyce's Country *reg.* Ireland **21** C4
Joypurhat Bangl. **37** G4
Juan Aldama Mex. **66** D4
Juan de Fuca Strait Canada/U.S.A. **62** C2
Juan Fernández, Archipiélago *is* S. Pacific Ocean **75** O8
Juan Fernández Islands S. Pacific Ocean *see* **Juan Fernández, Archipiélago**
Juanjuí Peru **68** C5
Juankoski Fin. **14** P5
Juàzeiro Brazil **69** J5
Juàzeiro do Norte Brazil **69** K5
Juba *r.* Somalia *see* **Jubba**
Juba Sudan **47** G4
Jubany *research station* Antarctica **76** A2
Jubba *r.* Somalia **48** E4
Jubbah Saudi Arabia **35** F5
Jubbulpore India *see* **Jabalpur**
Jubilee Lake *salt flat* Australia **55** D7
Juby, Cap *c.* Morocco **46** B2
Júcar *r.* Spain **25** F4
Juchitán Mex. **66** E5
Jucuruçu Brazil **71** D2
Jucuruçu *r.* Brazil **71** D2
Judaberg Norway **15** D7
Judaidat al Hamir Iraq **35** F5
Judayyidat 'Ar'ar *well* Iraq **35** F5
Judenburg Austria **17** O7
Juelsminde Denmark **15** G9
Juerana Brazil **71** D2
Jugar China *see* **Sêrxü**
Jugoslavija *country* Europe *see* **Serbia and Montenegro**
Juigalpa Nicaragua **67** G6
Juína Brazil **69** G6
Juiz de Fora Brazil **71** C3
Julaca Bol. **68** E8
Julia Brazil **68** E4
Juliaca Peru **68** D7
Julia Creek Australia **56** C4
Julian *CA* U.S.A. **65** D4
Julian Alps *mts* Slovenia *see* **Julijske Alpe**
Julianatop *mt.* Indon. *see* **Mandala, Puncak**
Juliana Top *mt.* Suriname **69** G3
Julianehåb Greenland *see* **Qaqortoq**
Julijske Alpe *mts* Slovenia **26** E1
Juliomagus France *see* **Angers**
Julius, Lake Australia **56** B4
Jullundur India *see* **Jalandhar**
Jumbilla Peru **68** C5
Jumilla Spain **25** F4
Jumla Nepal **37** E3
Jumna *r.* India *see* **Yamuna**
Junagadh India **36** B5
Junagarh India **38** D2
Junayfah Egypt **39** A4
Junction *TX* U.S.A. **62** H5
Junction City *KS* U.S.A. **63** H4
Jundiaí Brazil **71** B3
Juneau *AK* U.S.A. **60** E4
Junee Australia **58** C5
Jûn el Khudr *b.* Lebanon **39** B3
Jungar Qi China *see* **Shagedu**
Jungfrau *mt.* Switz. **24** H3
Junggar Pendi *basin* China **42** F3
Juniata *r. PA* U.S.A. **64** C2
Junín Arg. **70** D4
Junín Peru **68** C6
Junior *WV* U.S.A. **64** B3
Juniper Mountains *AZ* U.S.A. **65** F3
Junipero Serro Peak *CA* U.S.A. **65** B2
Junlian China **42** I7
Junsele Sweden **14** J5
Junxian China *see* **Danjiangkou**
Juodupė Lith. **15** N8
Jupiá Brazil **71** A3
Jupiá, Represa *resr* Brazil **71** A3
Juquiá *r.* Brazil **71** B4
Jur *r.* Sudan **32** C8
Jura *mts* France/Switz. **24** G4
Jura *i.* U.K. **20** D4
Jura, Sound of *sea chan.* U.K. **20** D5
Jurací Brazil **71** C1
Jurbarkas Lith. **15** M9
Jurf ad Darāwīsh Jordan **39** B4
Jūrmala Latvia **15** M8
Jurmu Fin. **14** O4
Juruá *r.* Brazil **68** E4
Juruena *r.* Brazil **69** G5
Juruti Brazil **69** G4
Jurva Fin. **14** L5
Jūsīyah Syria **39** C2
Jussara Brazil **71** A1
Jutaí Brazil **68** E5
Jutaí *r.* Brazil **68** E4
Jutiapa Guat. **66** G6
Juticalpa Hond. **67** G6
Jutis Sweden **14** J3
Jutland *pen.* Denmark **15** F8
Juuka Fin. **14** P5
Juva Fin. **14** O6
Jūyom Iran **35** I5
Južnoukrajinsk Ukr. *see* **Yuzhnoukrayinsk**
Jwaneng Botswana **50** G3
Jylland *pen.* Denmark *see* **Jutland**
Jyväskylä Fin. **14** N5

K

K2 *mt.* China/Jammu and Kashmir **36** D2
Ka *r.* Nigeria **46** D3
Kaafu Atoll Maldives *see* **Male Atoll**
Kaa-Iya del Gran Chaco, Parque Nacional *nat. park* Bol. **68** F7
Kaakhka Turkm. *see* **Kaka**
Kaapstad S. Africa *see* **Cape Town**
Kaarina Fin. **15** M6
Kaavi Fin. **14** P5
Kaba China *see* **Habahe**
Kabala Sierra Leone **46** B4
Kabale Uganda **48** C4
Kabalega Falls National Park Uganda *see* **Murchison Falls National Park**
Kabalo Dem. Rep. Congo **49** C4
Kabambare Dem. Rep. Congo **49** C4
Kabangu Dem. Rep. Congo **49** C5
Kabara *i.* Fiji **53** I3
Kabarega National Park Uganda *see* **Murchison Falls National Park**
Kabaw Valley Myanmar **37** H5
Kabbani *r.* India **38** C3
Kåbdalis Sweden **14** L3
Kabinakagami Lake Canada **63** K2
Kabinda Dem. Rep. Congo **49** C4
Kabīr *r.* Syria **39** B2
Kabīrkūh *mts* Iran **35** G4
Kabo Cent. Afr. Rep. **48** B3
Kābol Afgh. *see* **Kābul**
Kabompo *r.* Zambia **49** C5
Kabongo Dem. Rep. Congo **49** C4
Kabūd Rāhang Iran **35** H4
Kābul Afgh. **36** B2
Kābul *r.* Afgh. **36** C2
Kabunda Dem. Rep. Congo **49** C5
Kabunduk Indon. **54** B2
Kabwe Zambia **49** C5
Kachalinskaya Rus. Fed. **13** J6
Kachchh, Great Rann of *marsh* India *see* **Kachchh, Rann of**
Kachchh, Gulf of India **36** B5
Kachchh, Rann of *marsh* India **36** B4
Kachia Nigeria **46** D4
Kachiry Kazakh. **42** D2
Kachkanar Rus. Fed. **11** R4
Kachret'i Georgia **35** G2
Kachug Rus. Fed. **42** J2
Kaçkar Dağı *mt.* Turkey **35** F2
Kadaiyanallur India **38** C4
Kadanai *r.* Afgh./Pak. **36** A3
Kadavu *i.* Fiji **53** H3
Kadavu Passage Fiji **53** H3
Kaddam *l.* India **38** C2
Kade Ghana **46** C4
Kādhimain Iraq *see* **Al Kāẓimīyah**
Kadi India **36** C5
Kadıköy Turkey **27** M4
Kadınhanı Turkey **34** D3
Kadiolo Mali **46** C3
Kadiri India **38** C3
Kadirli Turkey **34** E3
Kadirpur Pak. **36** C3
Kadiyevka Ukr. *see* **Stakhanov**
Kadmat *atoll* India **38** B4
Ka-do *i.* N. Korea **45** B5
Kadoma Zimbabwe **49** C5
Kadu Myanmar **37** I4
Kadugli Sudan **32** C7
Kaduna Nigeria **46** D3
Kaduna *r.* Nigeria **46** D4
Kadusam *mt.* China/India **37** I3
Kaduy Rus. Fed. **12** H4
Kadyy Rus. Fed. **12** I4
Kadzherom Rus. Fed. **12** L2
Kaédi Mauritania **46** B3
Kaélé Cameroon **47** E3
Kaesŏng N. Korea **45** B5
Kāf Saudi Arabia **39** C4
Kafa Ukr. *see* **Feodosiya**
Kafakumba Dem. Rep. Congo **49** C4
Kafan Armenia *see* **Kapan**
Kafanchan Nigeria **46** D4
Kafr ash Shaykh Egypt **34** C5
Kafr el Sheikh Egypt *see* **Kafr ash Shaykh**
Kafue Zambia **49** C5
Kafue *r.* Zambia **49** C5
Kafue National Park Zambia **49** C5
Kaga Japan **45** E5
Kaga Bandoro Cent. Afr. Rep. **48** B3
Kagan Pak. **36** C2
Kaganovichabad Tajik. *see* **Kolkhozobod**
Kaganovichi Pervyye Ukr. *see* **Polis'ke**
Kagarlyk Ukr. *see* **Kaharlyk**
Kåge Sweden **14** L4
Kağızman Turkey **35** F2
Kagmar Sudan **32** D7
Kagoshima Japan **45** C7
Kagoshima *pref.* Japan **45** C7
Kagul Moldova *see* **Cahul**
Kahama Tanz. **48** D4
Kaharlyk Ukr. **13** F6
Kaherekoau Mountains N.Z. **59** A7
Kaho'olawe *i.* U.S.A. **62** [inset]
Kahperusvaarat *mts* Fin. **14** L2
Kahramanmaraş Turkey **34** E3
Kahror Pak. **36** B3
Kâhta Turkey **34** E3
Kahurangi National Park N.Z. **59** D5
Kahuku U.S.A. **62** [inset]
Kahuku Point U.S.A. **62** [inset]
Kahurangi Point N.Z. **59** D5
Kahuta Pak. **36** C2
Kahuzi-Biega, Parc National du *nat. park* Dem. Rep. Congo **48** C4
Kai, Kepulauan *is* Indon. **41** F8
Kaiapoi N.Z. **59** D6
Kaibab *AZ* U.S.A. **65** F2
Kai Besar *i.* Indon. **41** F8
Kaifeng *Henan* China **43** K6
Kaihua *Yunnan* China *see* **Wenshan**
Kaiingveld *reg.* S. Africa **50** E5
Kai Kecil *i.* Indon. **41** F8
Kaikoura N.Z. **59** D6
Kailas *mt.* China *see* **Kangrinboqê Feng**
Kailasahar India *see* **Kailashahar**
Kailashahar India **37** H4
Kailas Range *mts* China *see* **Gangdisê Shan**
Kaili China **43** J7
Kailu China **43** M4
Kailua-Kona U.S.A. **62** [inset]
Kaimana Indon. **41** F8
Kaimanawa Mountains N.Z. **59** E4
Kaimar China **37** H2
Kaimur Range *hills* India **36** E4
Käina Estonia **15** M7
Kainan Japan **45** D6
Kainji Lake National Park Nigeria **46** D4
Kaipara Harbour N.Z. **59** E3
Kairana India **36** D3
Kairouan Tunisia **26** D7
Kaiser Wilhelm II Land *reg.* Antarctica **76** E2
Kaitaia N.Z. **59** D2
Kaitangata N.Z. **59** B8
Kaitawa N.Z. **59** F4
Kaithal India **36** D3
Kaitum Sweden **14** L3
Kaiwatu Indon. **54** D2
Kaiyuan *Liaoning* China **44** B4
Kaiyuan *Yunnan* China **42** I8
Kajaani Fin. **14** O4
Kajabbi Australia **56** C4
Kajaki Afgh. **36** A2
Kajarabie, Lake Australia **58** D1
Kajrān Afgh. **36** A2
Kaka Turkm. **33** I2
Kakadu National Park Australia **54** F3
Kakamas S. Africa **50** E5
Kakamega Kenya **48** D3
Kakar Pak. **36** A4
Kakata Liberia **46** B4
Kakenge Dem. Rep. Congo **49** C4
Kakhi Azer. *see* **Qax**
Kakhovka Ukr. **27** O1
Kakhovs'ke Vodoskhovyshche *resr* Ukr. **13** G7
Kakhul Moldova *see* **Cahul**
Kākī Iran **35** H5
Kakinada India **38** D2
Kakogawa Japan **45** D6

Kakori India 36 E4
Kakshaal-Too mts China/Kyrg. 42 D4
Kaktovik U.S.A. 60 D2
Kala Pak. 36 B3
Kala Tanz. 49 D4
Kalaâ Kebira Tunisia 26 D7
Kalaallit Nunaat terr. N. America see Greenland
Kalabahi Indon. 41 E8
Kalabáka Greece see Kalampaka
Kalabgur India 38 C2
Kalabo Zambia 49 C5
Kalach Rus. Fed. 13 I6
Kalacha Dida Kenya 48 D3
Kalach-na-Donu Rus. Fed. 13 I6
Kaladan r. India/Myanmar 37 H5
Ka Lae pt U.S.A. 62 [inset]
Kalagwe Myanmar 37 I5
Kalahari Desert Africa 50 F2
Kalahari Gemsbok National Park S. Africa 50 E3
Kalajoki Fin. 14 M4
Kalalé Benin 46 D3
Kalam India 38 C1
Kalam Pak. 33 L2
Kalámai Greece see Kalamata
Kalamare Botswana 51 H2
Kalamaria Greece 27 J4
Kalamata Greece 27 J6
Kalamazoo U.S.A. 63 J3
Kalampaka Greece 27 I5
Kalanchak Ukr. 27 O1
Kalandula Angola see Calandula
Kalannie Australia 55 B7
Kalanshiyū ar Ramlī al Kabīr, Sarīr des. Libya 32 B3
Kalapana U.S.A. 62 [inset]
Kalār Iraq 35 G4
Kalāt Afgh. 36 A2
Kalāt Sīstān va Balūchestān Iran 33 I4
Kalat Balochistan Pak. 36 A3
Kalaus r. Rus. Fed. 13 J7
Kalaw Myanmar 37 I5
Kälbäcär Azer. 35 G2
Kalbarri Australia 55 A6
Kalbarri National Park Australia 55 A6
Kale Turkey 27 M6
Kalecik Turkey 34 D2
Kalemie Dem. Rep. Congo 49 C4
Kalemyo Myanmar 37 H5
Kāl-e Namak Iran 35 I4
Kalevala Rus. Fed. 12 F2
Kalewa Myanmar 37 H5
Kaleybar Iran 35 G3
Kalgan China see Zhangjiakou
Kalghatgi India 38 B3
Kalgoorlie Australia 55 C7
Kali Croatia 26 F2
Kali r. India/Nepal 36 E3
Kaliakra, Nos pt Bulg. 27 M3
Kali Gandaki r. Nepal 37 F4
Kaligiri India 38 C3
Kalikata India see Kolkata
Kalima Dem. Rep. Congo 48 C4
Kálimnos i. Greece see Kalymnos
Kalinin Rus. Fed. see Tver'
Kaliningrad Rus. Fed. 12 D5
Kalinino Armenia see Tashir
Kalinino Rus. Fed. 12 I4
Kalininsk Rus. Fed. 13 J6
Kalininskaya Rus. Fed. 13 H7
Kalinjara India 36 C5
Kalinkavichy Belarus 13 F5
Kalinkovichi Belarus see Kalinkavichy
Kalisch Poland see Kalisz
Kalispell U.S.A. 62 E2
Kalisz Poland 17 Q5
Kalitva r. Rus. Fed. 13 I6
Kaliua Tanz. 49 D4
Kaliujar India 36 E4
Kalix Sweden 14 M4
Kalkalighat India 37 H4
Kalkalpen, Nationalpark nat. park Austria 17 O7
Kalkan Turkey 27 M6
Kalkfeld Namibia 49 B6
Kalkfonteindam dam S. Africa 51 G5
Kalkudah Sri Lanka 38 D5
Kallaste Estonia 15 O7
Kallavesi l. Fin. 14 O5
Kallsedet Sweden 14 H5
Kallsjön l. Sweden 14 H5
Kallur India 38 C2
Kalmar Sweden 15 J8
Kalmarsund sea chan. Sweden 15 J8
Kalmūkh Qal'eh Iran 35 J3
Kalmunai Sri Lanka 38 D5
Kalmykia aut. rep. Rus. Fed. see Kalmykiya-Khalm'g-Tangch, Respublika
Kalmykiya-Khalm'g-Tangch, Respublika aut. rep. Rus. Fed. 35 G1
Kalmykovo Kazakh. see Taypak
Kalmytskaya Avtonomnaya Oblast' aut. rep. Rus. Fed. see Kalmykiya-Khalm'g-Tangch, Respublika
Kalnai India 37 E5
Kalodnaye Belarus 15 O11
Kalol India 36 C5
Kalomo Zambia 49 C5
Kalone Peak Canada 60 F4
Kalpa India 36 D3
Kalpeni atoll India 38 B4
Kalpetta India 38 C4
Kalpi India 36 D4
Kaltag U.S.A. 60 C3
Kaltukatjara Australia 55 E6
Kaluga Rus. Fed. 13 H5
Kalundborg Denmark 15 G9
Kalush Ukr. 13 E6
Kalvakol India 38 C2
Kälviä Fin. 14 M5
Kal'ya Rus. Fed. 11 R3
Kalyan India 38 B2
Kalyandurg India 33 M7
Kalyansingapuram India 38 D2
Kalyazin Rus. Fed. 12 H4
Kalymnos i. Greece 27 L6
Kama Dem. Rep. Congo 48 C4
Kama r. Rus. Fed. 12 L4
Kamaishi Japan 45 F5
Kamalia Pak. 36 C3
Kaman Turkey 34 D3
Kamanjab Namibia 49 B5
Kamarān i. Yemen 32 F6
Kamaran Island Yemen see Kamarān
Kamaron Sierra Leone 46 B4
Kamasin India 36 E4
Kambalda Australia 55 C7
Kambam India 38 C4
Kambara i. Fiji see Kabara
Kambia Sierra Leone 46 B4
Kambing, Pulau i. East Timor see Ataúro, Ilha de
Kambo-san mt. N. Korea see Kwanmo-bong
Kambove Dem. Rep. Congo 49 C5
Kambūt Libya 34 B5
Kamchatka, Poluostrov pen. Rus. Fed. see Kamchatka Peninsula
Kamchatka Basin sea feature Bering Sea 74 H2
Kamchatka Peninsula Rus. Fed. 29 Q4
Kamchiya r. Bulg. 27 L3
Kameia, Parque Nacional de nat. park Angola see Cameia, Parque Nacional da
Kamelik r. Rus. Fed. 13 K5
Kamen', Gory mt. Rus. Fed. 28 K3
Kamenets-Podol'skiy Ukr. see Kam"yanets'-Podil's'kyy
Kamenitsa mt. Bulg. 27 J4
Kamenjak, Rt pt Croatia 26 E2
Kamenka Kazakh. 11 Q5
Kamenka Arkhangel'skaya Oblast' Rus. Fed. 12 J2
Kamenka Penzenskaya Oblast' Rus. Fed. 13 J5
Kamenka Primorskiy Kray Rus. Fed. 44 E3
Kamenka-Bugskaya Ukr. see Kam"yanka-Buz'ka
Kamenka-Strumilovskaya Ukr. see Kam"yanka-Buz'ka
Kamen'-na-Obi Rus. Fed. 42 E2
Kamennogorsk Rus. Fed. 15 P6
Kamennomostskiy Rus. Fed. 35 F1
Kamenolomni Rus. Fed. 13 I7
Kamenongue Angola see Camanongue
Kamen'-Rybolov Rus. Fed. 44 D3
Kamenskoye Rus. Fed. 29 R3
Kamenskoye Ukr. see Dniprodzerzhyns'k
Kamensk-Shakhtinskiy Rus. Fed. 13 I6
Kamensk-Ural'skiy Rus. Fed. 28 H4
Kamet mt. China 36 D3
Kamiesberge mts S. Africa 50 D6
Kamieskroon S. Africa 50 C6
Kamileroi Australia 56 C3
Kamina Dem. Rep. Congo 49 C4
Kaminak Lake Canada 61 I3
Kaminuriak Lake Canada see Qamanirjuaq Lake
Kamishihoro Japan 44 F4
Kamloops Canada 62 C1
Kamo Armenia see Gavarr
Kamoke Pak. 36 C3
Kamonia Dem. Rep. Congo 49 C4
Kampala Uganda 48 D3
Kampara India 38 D1
Kampene Dem. Rep. Congo 48 C4
Kampinoski Park Narodowy nat. park Poland 17 R4
Kâmpóng Cham Cambodia 31 J5
Kâmpóng Saôm Cambodia see Sihanoukville
Kâmpóng Spœ Cambodia 31 J5
Kâmpóng Thum Cambodia 31 J5
Kâmpôt Cambodia 31 J5
Kampuchea country Asia see Cambodia
Kamrau, Teluk b. Indon. 41 F8
Kamsack Canada 62 G1
Kamskoye Vodokhranilishche resr Rus. Fed. 11 R4
Kamsuuma Somalia 48 E3
Kamuli Uganda 48 D3
Kam"yanets'-Podil's'kyy Ukr. 13 E6
Kam"yanka-Buz'ka Ukr. 13 E6
Kamyanyets Belarus 15 M10
Kāmyārān Iran 35 G4
Kamyshin Rus. Fed. 13 J6
Kamyzyak Rus. Fed. 13 K7
Kanab U.S.A. 62 E4
Kanab Creek r. AZ U.S.A. 65 F2
Kanak Pak. 36 A3
Kananga Dem. Rep. Congo 49 C4
Kanangra-Boyd National Park Australia 58 E4
Kanarak India see Konarka
Kanarraville UT U.S.A. 65 F2
Kanas watercourse Namibia 50 C4
Kanash Rus. Fed. 12 J5
Kanauj India see Kannauj
Kanazawa Japan 45 E5
Kanbalu Myanmar 37 H5
Kanchanjanga mt. India/Nepal see Kangchenjunga
Kanchipuram India 38 C3
Kand mt. Pak. 36 A3
Kanda Pak. 36 A3
Kandahār Afgh. 36 A3
Kandalaksha Rus. Fed. 12 G2
Kandalakshskiy Zaliv g. Rus. Fed. 12 G2
Kandar Indon. 54 E2
Kandavu i. Fiji see Kadavu
Kandavu Passage Fiji see Kadavu Passage
Kandé Togo 46 D4
Kandhkot Pak. 36 B3
Kandi Benin 46 D3
Kandi India 38 C2
Kandiaro Pak. 36 B4
Kandıra Turkey 27 N4
Kandos Australia 58 D4
Kandreho Madag. 49 E5
Kandukur India 38 C3
Kandy Sri Lanka 38 D5
Kandyagash Kazakh. 28 G5
Kane PA U.S.A. 64 B2
Kane Bassin b. Greenland 77 K1
Kaneh watercourse Iran 35 I6
Kāne'ohe U.S.A. 62 [inset]
Kaneti Pak. 36 A3
Kanevskaya Rus. Fed. 13 H7
Kang Botswana 50 F2
Kangaamiut Greenland 61 M3
Kangaarsussuaq c. Greenland 61 K2
Kangaba Mali 46 C3
Kangal Turkey 34 E3
Kangān Būshehr Iran 35 I6
Kangandala, Parque Nacional de nat. park Angola see Cangandala, Parque Nacional de
Kangar Malaysia 41 C7
Kangaroo Island Australia 57 B7
Kangaroo Point Australia 56 B3
Kangaslampi Fin. 14 P5
Kangasniemi Fin. 14 O6
Kangāvar Iran 35 G4
Kangchenjunga mt. India/Nepal 37 G4
Kangding China 42 I6
Kangean, Kepulauan is Indon. 41 D8
Kangen r. Sudan 47 G4
Kangerlussuaq Greenland 61 M3
Kangerlussuaq inlet Greenland 61 M3
Kangerlussuaq inlet Greenland 77 J2
Kangersuatsiaq Greenland 61 M2
Kangertittivaq sea chan. Greenland 61 P2
Kanggye N. Korea 44 B4
Kanghwa S. Korea 45 B5
Kangikajik c. Greenland 61 P2
Kangirsuk Canada 61 K3
Kangmar China 37 F3
Kangnŭng S. Korea 45 C5
Kango Gabon 48 B3
Kangping China 44 A4
Kangri Karpo Pass China/India 37 I3
Kangrinboqê Feng mt. China 36 E3
Kangsangdobdê China see Xainza
Kangto mt. China/India 37 H4
Kangtog China 37 F2
Kanifing Gambia 46 B3
Kanigiri India 38 C3
Kanin, Poluostrov pen. Rus. Fed. 12 J2
Kanin Nos Rus. Fed. 77 G2
Kanin Nos, Mys c. Rus. Fed. 12 I1
Kaninskiy Bereg coastal area Rus. Fed. 12 I2
Kanjiroba mt. Nepal 37 E3
Kankaanpää Fin. 15 M6
Kankakee U.S.A. 63 J3
Kankan Guinea 46 C3
Kanker India 38 D1
Kankesanturai Sri Lanka 38 D4
Kankossa Mauritania 46 B3
Kannauj India 36 D4
Kanniya Kumari c. India see Comorin, Cape
Kannonkoski Fin. 14 N5
Kannur India see Cannanore
Kannus Fin. 14 M5
Kano Nigeria 46 D3
Kanonpunt pt S. Africa 50 E8
Kanosh UT U.S.A. 65 F1
Kanovlei Namibia 49 B5
Kanoya Japan 45 C7
Kanpur Orissa India 38 E1
Kanpur Uttar Prad. India 36 E4
Kanpur Pak. 36 B3
Kansai airport Japan 45 D6
Kansas r. U.S.A. 62 I4
Kansas state U.S.A. 62 H4
Kansas City KS U.S.A. 63 I4
Kansk Rus. Fed. 29 K4
Kansu prov. China see Gansu
Kantara hill Cyprus 39 A2
Kantavu i. Fiji see Kadavu
Kantchari Burkina 46 D3
Kantemirovka Rus. Fed. 13 H6
Kanthi India 37 F5
Kantishna r. U.S.A. 60 C3
Kanton atoll Kiribati 53 I2
Kanturk Ireland 21 D5
Kanuku Mountains Guyana 69 G3
Kanur India 38 C3
Kanus Namibia 50 D4
Kanyakubja India see Kannauj
Kanyamazane S. Africa 51 J3
Kanye Botswana 51 G3
Kaohsiung Taiwan 43 M8
Kaokoveld plat. Namibia 49 B5
Kaolack Senegal 46 B3
Kaoma Zambia 49 C5
Kaouadja Cent. Afr. Rep. 48 C3
Kapa S. Africa see Cape Town
Kapa'a U.S.A. 62 [inset]
Kapan Armenia 35 G3
Kapanga Dem. Rep. Congo 49 C4
Kaparhā Iran 35 H5
Kapatu Zambia 49 D4
Kapchagay Kazakh. 42 D4
Kapchagayskoye Vodokhranilishche resr Kazakh. 42 D4
Kap Dan Greenland see Kulusuk
Kapello, Akrotirio pt Greece 27 J6
Kapellskär Sweden 15 K7
Kapelskär Sweden see Kapellskär
Kapili r. India 37 G4
Kapingamarangi atoll Micronesia 74 G5
Kapingamarangi Rise sea feature N. Pacific Ocean 74 G5
Kapıorman Dağları mts Turkey 27 N4
Kapip Pak. 36 B3
Kapiri Mposhi Zambia 49 C5
Kapisillit Greenland 61 M3
Kapiskau r. Canada 63 K1
Kapiti Island N.Z. 59 E5
Kaplankyr, Chink hills Asia 35 I2
Kaplankyr Döwlet Gorugy nature res. Turkm. 35 J2
Kapoeta Sudan 47 G4
Kaposvár Hungary 26 G1
Kappeln Germany 17 L3
Kapsukas Lith. see Marijampolė
Kaptai Bangl. 37 H5
Kapuriya India 36 C4
Kapurthala India 36 C3
Kapuskasing Canada 63 K2
Kapustin Yar Rus. Fed. 13 J6
Kaputar mt. Australia 58 E3
Kaputir Kenya 48 D3
Kapuvár Hungary 26 G1
Kapydzhik, Gora mt. Armenia/Azer. see Qazangödağ
Kapyl' Belarus 15 O10
Kara India 36 E4
Kara Togo 46 D4
Kara r. Turkey 35 F3
Kara-Balta Kyrg. 42 C4
Karabalyk Kazakh. 30 F1
Karabekaul' Turkm. see Garabekewül
Karabiga Turkey 27 L4
Kara Bogaz Gol, Proliv sea chan. Turkm. see Garabogazköl Bogazy
Kara-Bogaz-Gol'skiy Zaliv b. Turkm. see Garabogazköl Aýlagy
Karabük Turkey 34 D2
Karaburun Turkey 27 L5
Karabutak Kazakh. 28 H5
Karacabey Turkey 27 M4
Karacaköy Turkey 27 M4
Karacalı Dağ mt. Turkey 35 E3
Karaçal Tepe mt. Turkey 39 A1
Karacasu Turkey 27 M6
Karaca Yarımadası pen. Turkey 27 N6
Karachayevsk Rus. Fed. 13 I8
Karachev Rus. Fed. 13 G5
Karachi Pak. 33 K5
Karacurun Turkey see Hilvan
Karad India 38 B2
Kara Dağ hill Turkey 39 D1
Kara Dağ mt. Turkey 34 D3
Kara Deniz sea Asia/Europe see Black Sea
Karagan Rus. Fed. 44 A1
Karaganda Kazakh. 42 C3
Karagayly Kazakh. 42 D3
Karaginskiy Zaliv b. Rus. Fed. 29 R4
Karagiye, Vpadina depr. Kazakh. 35 H2
Karagola India 37 F4
Karahallı Turkey 27 M5
Karahasanlı Turkey 34 D3
Karaikal India 38 C4
Karaikkudi India 38 C4
Karaisalı Turkey 34 D3
Karaj Iran 35 H4
Karak Jordan see Al Karak
Karakalli Turkey see Özalp
Karakax China see Moyu
Karakax He r. China 36 E1
Karakax Shan mts China 36 E2
Karaki China 36 E1
Karaklis Armenia see Vanadzor
Karakoçan Turkey 35 F3
Kara-Köl Kyrg. 31 G2
Karakol Kyrg. 42 D4
Karakoram Pass China/Jammu and Kashmir 36 D2
Karakoram Range mts Asia 31 G3
Karakoram Range mts Asia 33 M2
Kara K'orē Eth. 48 D2
Karakorum Range mts Asia see Karakoram Range
Karakorum Range mts Asia see Karakoram Range
Karaköse Turkey see Ağrı
Kara Kul' Kyrg. see Kara-Köl
Karakul', Ozero l. Tajik. see Qarokŭl
Kara Kum des. Turkm. see Karakum Desert
Karakum, Peski Kazakh. see Karakum Desert
Karakum Desert Kazakh. 30 E2
Karakum Desert Turkm. 30 F3
Karakurt Turkey 35 F2
Karakuş Dağı ridge Turkey 27 N5
Karal Chad 47 E3
Karala Estonia 15 L7
Karalundi Australia 55 B6
Karaman Turkey 34 D3
Karaman prov. Turkey 39 A1
Karamanlı Turkey 27 M6
Karamay China 42 E3
Karambar Pass Afgh./Pak. 36 C1
Karamea N.Z. 59 D5
Karamea Bight b. N.Z. 59 C5
Karamiran China 37 F1
Karamiran Shankou pass China 37 F1
Karamürsel Turkey 27 M4
Karamyshevo Rus. Fed. 15 P8
Karān i. Saudi Arabia 35 H6
Karangasem Indon. 54 A2
Karanja India 38 C1
Karanjia India 36 E5
Karapınar Gaziantep Turkey 39 C1
Karapınar Konya Turkey 34 D3
Karas admin. reg. Namibia 50 C4
Karasay China 37 E1
Karasburg Namibia 50 D5
Kara Sea Rus. Fed. 28 I2
Kárášjohka Finnmark Norway see Karasjok
Karasjok Norway 14 N2
Kara Strait Rus. Fed. see Karskiye Vorota, Proliv
Karasu r. Syria/Turkey 39 C1
Karasu Bitlis Turkey see Hizan
Karasu Sakarya Turkey 27 N4
Karasu r. Turkey 35 F3
Karasubazar Ukr. see Bilohirs'k
Karasuk Rus. Fed. 28 I4
Karataş Turkey 39 B1
Karataş Burnu hd Turkey see Fener Burnu
Karatau Kazakh. 42 C4
Karatau, Khrebet mts Kazakh. 42 B4
Karatepe Turkey 39 A1
Karativu i. Sri Lanka 38 C4
Karatsu Japan 45 C6
Karaudanawa Guyana 69 G3
Karauli India 36 D4
Karavan Kyrg. see Kerben
Karavostasi Cyprus 39 A2
Karayılan Turkey 39 C1
Karayulgan China 42 E4
Karazhal Kazakh. 42 C3
Karbalā' Iraq 35 G4
Karcag Hungary 27 I1
Kardhitsa Greece see Karditsa
Karditsa Greece 27 I5
Kärdla Estonia 15 M7
Karee S. Africa 51 H5
Kareeberge mts S. Africa 50 E6
Kareima Sudan 32 D6
Kareli India 36 D5
Karelia aut. rep. Rus. Fed. see Kareliya, Respublika
Kareliya, Respublika aut. rep. Rus. Fed. 14 R5
Karel'skaya A.S.S.R. aut. rep. Rus. Fed. see Kareliya, Respublika
Karel'skiy Bereg coastal area Rus. Fed. 12 G2
Karema Tanz. 49 D4
Karera India 36 D4
Karesuando Sweden 14 M2
Kargalinskaya Rus. Fed. 35 G2
Kargalinski Rus. Fed. see Kargalinskaya
Kargapazarı Dağları mts Turkey 35 F3
Karghalik China see Yecheng
Kargı Turkey 34 D2
Kargil India 36 D2
Kargilik China see Yecheng
Kargıpınarı Turkey 39 B1
Kargopol' Rus. Fed. 12 H3
Kari Nigeria 46 E3
Kariba Zimbabwe 49 C5
Kariba, Lake resr Zambia/Zimbabwe 49 C5
Kariba Dam Zambia/Zimbabwe 49 C5
Kariba-yama vol. Japan 44 E4
Karibib Namibia 50 B1
Karigasniemi Fin. 14 N2
Karijini National Park Australia 55 B5
Karijoki Fin. 14 L5
Karikachi-tōge pass Japan 44 F4
Karikari, Cape N.Z. 59 D2
Karimata, Selat strait Indon. 41 C8
Karimganj India 37 H4
Karimnagar India 38 C2
Káristos Greece see Karystos
Karjat Mahar. India 38 B2
Karjat Mahar. India 38 B2
Karkaralinsk Kazakh. 42 D3
Karkar Island P.N.G. 52 E2
Karkh Pak. 36 A4
Karkinits'ka Zatoka g. Ukr. 27 O2
Kärkölä Fin. 15 N6
Karkonoski Park Narodowy nat. park Czech Rep./Poland see Krkonošský národní park
Karksi-Nuia Estonia 15 N7
Karkūk Iraq see Kirkūk
Karlachi Pak. 36 B2
Karlholmsbruk Sweden 15 J6
Karlik Shan mt. China 42 G4
Karlıova Turkey 35 F3
Karlivka Ukr. 13 G6
Karl Marks, Qullai mt. Tajik. 36 C1
Karl-Marx-Stadt Germany see Chemnitz
Karlovac Croatia 26 F2
Karlovka Ukr. see Karlivka
Karlovo Bulg. 27 K3
Karlovy Vary Czech Rep. 17 N5
Karlsborg Sweden 15 I7
Karlsburg Romania see Alba Iulia
Karlshamn Sweden 15 I8
Karlskoga Sweden 15 I7
Karlskrona Sweden 15 I8
Karlsruhe Germany 17 L6
Karlstad Sweden 15 H7
Karluk U.S.A. 60 C4
Karmala India 38 B2
Karmel, Har hill Israel see Carmel, Mount
Karmona Spain see Córdoba
Karmøy i. Norway 15 D7
Karmpur Pak. 36 C3
Karnafuli Reservoir Bangl. 37 H5
Karnal India 36 D3
Karnataka state India 38 B3
Karnavati India see Ahmadabad
Karnobat Bulg. 27 L3
Karodi Pak. 36 A4
Karoi Zimbabwe 49 C5
Karo La pass China 37 G3
Karong India 37 H4
Karonga Malawi 49 D4
Karonie Australia 55 C7
Karoo National Park S. Africa 50 F7
Karoo Nature Reserve S. Africa 50 G7
Karoonda Australia 57 B7
Karora Eritrea 32 E6
Káros i. Greece see Keros
Karossa, Tanjung pt Indon. 54 B2
Karpasia pen. Cyprus 39 B2
Karpas Peninsula Cyprus see Karpasia
Karpathos i. Greece 27 L7
Karpathou, Steno sea chan. Greece 27 L6
Karpaty mts Europe see Carpathian Mountains
Karpenisi Greece 27 I5
Karpilovka Belarus see Aktsyabrski
Karpinsk Rus. Fed. 11 S4
Karpogory Rus. Fed. 12 J2
Karpuz r. Turkey 39 A1
Karratha Australia 54 B5
Karroo plat. S. Africa see Great Karoo
Kars Turkey 35 F2
Kärsämäki Fin. 14 N5
Kārsava Latvia 15 O8
Karshi Qashqadaryo Uzbek. see Qarshi
Karskiye Vorota, Proliv strait Rus. Fed. 28 G3
Karskoye More sea Rus. Fed. see Kara Sea
Karstula Fin. 14 N5
Karsu Turkey 39 C1
Karsun Rus. Fed. 13 J5
Kartal Turkey 27 M4
Kartaly Rus. Fed. 28 H4
Kartayel' Rus. Fed. 12 L2
Karttula Fin. 14 O5
Karumba Australia 56 C3
Karumbhar Island India 36 B5
Kārūn, Rūd-e r. Iran 35 H5
Karuni Indon. 54 B2
Karur India 38 C4
Karvia Fin. 14 M5
Karviná Czech Rep. 17 Q6
Karwar India 38 B3
Karyagino Azer. see Füzuli
Karymskoye Rus. Fed. 43 K2
Karynzharyk, Peski des. Kazakh. 35 I2
Karystos Greece 27 K5
Kaş Turkey 27 M6
Kasa India 38 B2
Kasaba Turkey see Turgutlu
Kasaï r. Dem. Rep. Congo 48 B4
Kasaï, Plateau du Dem. Rep. Congo 49 C4
Kasaji Dem. Rep. Congo 49 C5
Kasama Zambia 49 D5
Kasane Botswana 49 C5
Kasaragod India 38 B3
Kasargod India see Kasaragod
Kasargode India see Kasaragod
Kasatkino Rus. Fed. 44 C2
Kasba Lake Canada 61 H3
Kasba Tadla Morocco 22 C5
Kasenga Dem. Rep. Congo 49 C5
Kasengu Dem. Rep. Congo 49 C4
Kasese Dem. Rep. Congo 48 C4
Kasese Uganda 48 D3
Kasevo Rus. Fed. see Neftekamsk
Kasganj India 36 D4
Kāshān Iran 35 H4
Kashary Rus. Fed. 13 I6
Kashgar China see Kashi
Kashi China 42 D5
Kashihara Japan 45 D6
Kashima-nada b. Japan 45 F5
Kashin Rus. Fed. 12 H4
Kashipur India 36 D3
Kashira Rus. Fed. 13 H5
Kashiwazaki Japan 45 E5
Kashkarantsy Rus. Fed. 12 H2
Kāshmar Iran 33 I2
Kashmir terr. Asia see Jammu and Kashmir
Kashmir, Vale of reg. India 36 C2
Kashyukulu Dem. Rep. Congo 49 C4
Kasi India see Varanasi
Kasigar Afgh. 36 B2
Kasimov Rus. Fed. 13 I5
Kaskinen Fin. 14 L5
Kaskö Fin. see Kaskinen
Kasongo Dem. Rep. Congo 49 C4
Kasongo-Lunda Dem. Rep. Congo 49 B4
Kasos i. Greece 27 L7
Kaspiy Mangy Oypaty lowland Kazakh./Rus. Fed. see Caspian Lowland
Kaspiysk Rus. Fed. 35 G2
Kaspiyskiy Rus. Fed. see Lagan'
Kaspiyskoye More l. Asia/Europe see Caspian Sea
Kassa Slovakia see Košice
Kassala Sudan 32 E6
Kassandras, Akrotirio pt Greece 27 J5
Kassandras, Kolpos b. Greece 27 J4
Kassel Germany 17 L5
Kasserine Tunisia 26 C7
Kastamonu Turkey 34 D2
Kastéllion Greece see Kissamos
Kastellorizon i. Greece see Megisti
Kastoria Greece 27 I4
Kastornoye Rus. Fed. 13 H6
Kastsyukovichy Belarus 13 G5
Kasulu Tanz. 49 D4
Kasumkent Rus. Fed. 35 H2
Kasungu Malawi 49 D5
Kasungu National Park Malawi 49 D5
Kasur Pak. 36 C3
Katāddlit Nunât terr. N. America see Greenland
Katahdin, Mount U.S.A. 63 N2
Kataklik Jammu and Kashmir 36 D2
Katako-Kombe Dem. Rep. Congo 48 C4
Katakwi Uganda 48 D3
Katana India 36 C5
Katangi India 36 D5
Katanning Australia 55 B8
Katavi National Park Tanz. 49 D4
Katea Dem. Rep. Congo 49 C4
Katerini Greece 27 J4
Katesh Tanz. 49 D4
Kate's Needle mt. Canada/U.S.A. 60 E4
Katete Zambia 49 D5
Katherîna, Gebel mt. Egypt see Kātrīnā, Jabal
Katherine Australia 54 F3
Katherine Gorge National Park Australia see Nitmiluk National Park
Kathiawar pen. India 36 B5
Kathihar India see Katihar
Kathiraveli Sri Lanka 38 D4
Kathiwara India 36 C5
Kathleen Falls Australia 54 E3
Kathmandu Nepal 37 F4
Kathu S. Africa 50 F4
Kathua India 36 C2
Kati Mali 46 C3
Katihar India 37 F4
Katikati S. Africa 51 H7
Katima Mulilo Namibia 49 C5
Katiola Côte d'Ivoire 46 C4
Kā Tiritiri o te Moana mts N.Z. see Southern Alps
Katkop Hills S. Africa 50 E6
Katlehong S. Africa 51 I4
Katmai National Park and Preserve U.S.A. 60 C4
Katmandu Nepal see Kathmandu
Kato Achaïa Greece 27 I5
Katoomba Australia 58 E4
Katowice Poland 17 Q5
Katoya India 37 G5
Katrancık Dağı mts Turkey 27 M6
Kātrīnā, Jabal mt. Egypt 34 D5
Katrine, Loch l. U.K. 20 E4
Katrineholm Sweden 15 J7
Katse Dam Lesotho 51 I5
Katsina Nigeria 46 D3
Katsina-Ala Nigeria 46 D4
Katsuura Japan 45 F6
Kattamudda Well Australia 54 D5
Kattaqo'rg'on Uzbek. 33 K2
Kattaqŭrghon Uzbek. see Kattaqo'rg'on
Kattasang Hills Afgh. 36 A2
Kattegat strait Denmark/Sweden 15 G8
Kattowitz Poland see Katowice
Katumbar India 36 D4
Katunino Rus. Fed. 12 J4
Katuri Pak. 36 B3
Katwa India see Katoya
Kaua'i i. U.S.A. [inset]
Kaua'i Channel U.S.A. 62 [inset]
Kauhajoki Fin. 14 M5
Kauhava Fin. 14 M5
Kaukkwè Hills Myanmar 37 I4
Kaukonen Fin. 14 N3
Ka'ula i. U.S.A. 62 [inset]
Kaunas Lith. 15 M9
Kaunata Latvia 15 O8
Kaundy, Vpadina depr. Kazakh. 35 I2
Kaunia Bangl. 37 G4
Kaura-Namoda Nigeria 46 D3
Kaustinen Fin. 14 M5
Kautokeino Norway 14 M2
Kavadarci Macedonia 27 J4
Kavak Turkey 34 E2
Kavaklıdere Turkey 27 M6
Kavala Greece 27 K4
Kavalas, Kolpos b. Greece 27 K4
Kavalerovo Rus. Fed. 44 D3
Kavali India 38 D3
Kavār Iran 35 I5
Kavaratti India 38 B4
Kavaratti atoll India 38 B4
Kavarna Bulg. 27 M3
Kavendou, Mont mt. Guinea 46 B3
Kaveri r. India 38 C4
Kavīr Iran 35 H4
Kavīr, Dasht-e des. Iran 35 I4
Kavkasioni mts Asia/Europe see Caucasus
Kawagoe Japan 45 E6
Kawaguchi Japan 45 E6
Kawaihae U.S.A. 62 [inset]
Kawakawa N.Z. 59 E2
Kawambwa Zambia 49 C4
Kawana Zambia 49 C5
Kawardha India 36 E5
Kawasaki Japan 45 E6
Kawau Island N.Z. 59 E3
Kawerau N.Z. 59 F4
Kawhia N.Z. 59 E4
Kawhia Harbour N.Z. 59 E4
Kawich Peak NV U.S.A. 65 D2
Kawich Range mts NV U.S.A. 65 D2
Kawlin Myanmar 37 H5
Kawm Umbū Egypt 32 D5
Kaxgar China see Kashi
Kaxgar He r. China 33 M2
Kax He r. China 42 E4
Kaxtax Shan mts China 37 E1
Kaya Burkina 46 C3
Kayadibi Turkey 34 F3
Kayankulam India 38 C4
Kayar India 38 C2
Kaydak, Sor dry lake Kazakh. 35 I1
Kaydanovo Belarus see Dzyarzhynsk
Kayembe-Mukulu Dem. Rep. Congo 49 C4
Kayenta U.S.A. 62 E4
Kayes Mali 46 B3
Kaymaz Turkey 27 N5
Kaynar Kazakh. 42 D3
Kaynar Turkey 34 E3
Kayseri Turkey 34 D3
Kayuyu Dem. Rep. Congo 48 C4
Kazach'ye Rus. Fed. 29 O2
Kazakh Azer. see Qazax
Kazakhskaya S.S.R. country Asia see Kazakhstan
Kazakhskiy Melkosopochnik plain Kazakh. 42 C2
Kazakhskiy Zaliv b. Kazakh. 35 I2
Kazakhstan country Asia 30 F2
Kazakhstan Kazakh. see Aksay
Kazakstan country Asia see Kazakhstan
Kazan' Rus. Fed. 12 K5
Kazandzhik Turkm. see Bereket
Kazanka r. Rus. Fed. 12 K5
Kazanlı Turkey 39 B1
Kazanlŭk Bulg. 27 K3
Kazan-rettō is Japan see Volcano Islands
Kazatin Ukr. see Kozyatyn
Kazbek mt. Georgia/Rus. Fed. 13 J8
Kaz Dağı mts Turkey 27 L5
Kāzerūn Iran 35 H5
Kazhim Rus. Fed. 12 K3
Kazidi Tajik. see Qozideh
Kazi Magomed Azer. see Qazımämmäd
Kazincbarcika Hungary 13 D6
Kaziranga National Park India 37 H4
Kazret'i Georgia 35 G2
Kaztalovka Kazakh. 11 P6
Kazym r. Rus. Fed. 11 T3
Kazymskiy Mys Rus. Fed. 11 T3
Keady U.K. 21 F3
Kéamu i. Vanuatu see Anatom
Kearney U.S.A. 62 H3
Keban Turkey 34 E3
Keban Barajı resr Turkey 34 E3
Kébémèr Senegal 46 B3
Kebili Tunisia 22 F5
Kebīr, Nahr al r. Lebanon/Syria 39 B2
Kebkabiya Sudan 47 F3
Kebnekaise mt. Sweden 14 K3
Kebock Head hd U.K. 20 C2
K'ebrī Dehar Eth. 48 E3
Kechika r. Canada 77 A3
Keçiborlu Turkey 27 N6
Kecskemét Hungary 27 H1
K'eda Georgia 35 F2
Kėdainiai Lith. 15 M9
Kedairu Passage Fiji see Kadavu Passage
Kedong China 44 B3
Kedva r. Rus. Fed. 12 L2
Kędzierzyn-Koźle Poland 17 Q5
Keele r. Canada 60 F3
Keele Peak Canada 60 E3
Keeler CA U.S.A. 65 D2
Keeling Islands terr. Indian Ocean see Cocos Islands
Keen, Mount hill U.K. 20 G4
Keene CA U.S.A. 65 C3
Keene NH U.S.A. 64 E1
Keepit, Lake resr Australia 58 E3
Keep River National Park Australia 54 E3
Keer-weer, Cape Australia 56 C2
Keetmanshoop Namibia 50 D4
Keewatin Canada 63 I2
Kefallinía i. Greece see Cephalonia
Kefallonia i. Greece see Cephalonia
Kefamenanu Indon. 41 E8
Kefe Ukr. see Feodosiya
Keffi Nigeria 46 D4
Keflavík Iceland 14 [inset]
Kegalla Sri Lanka 38 D5
Kegen Kazakh. 42 D4
Keg River Canada 60 G4
Kegul'ta Rus. Fed. 13 J7

Kehra Estonia 15 N7
Keighley U.K. 18 F5
Keila Estonia 15 N7
Keimoes S. Africa 50 E5
Keitele Fin. 14 O5
Keitele l. Fin. 14 O5
Keith Australia 57 C8
Keith U.K. 20 G3
Kékes mt. Hungary 17 R7
Kekri India 36 C4
K'elafo Eth. 48 E3
Kelai i. Maldives 38 B5
Kelibia Tunisia 26 D6
Kelif Uzboýy marsh Turkm. 33 J2
Kelkit Turkey 35 E2
Kelkit r. Turkey 34 E2
Kéllé Congo 48 B4
Keller Lake Canada 60 F3
Kellett, Cape Canada 60 F2
Kelloselkä Fin. 14 P3
Kells Ireland 21 F4
Kells r. U.K. 21 F3
Kelly Range hills Australia 55 C6
Kelmė Lith. 15 M9
Kélo Chad 47 E4
Kelowna Canada 62 D2
Kelseyville CA U.S.A. 65 A1
Kelso U.K. 20 G5
Kelso CA U.S.A. 65 E3
Keluang Malaysia 41 C7
Kelvington Canada 62 G1
Kem' Rus. Fed. 12 G2
Kem' r. Rus. Fed. 12 G2
Ke Macina Mali see Massina
Kemah Turkey 34 E3
Kemaliye Turkey 34 E3
Kemalpaşa Turkey 27 L5
Kemano Canada 60 F4
Kembé Cent. Afr. Rep. 48 C3
Kemeneshát hills Hungary 26 G1
Kemer Antalya Turkey 27 N6
Kemer Muğla Turkey 27 M6
Kemer Baraji resr Turkey 27 M6
Kemerovo Rus. Fed. 28 J4
Kemi Fin. 14 N4
Kemijärvi Fin. 14 O3
Kemijärvi l. Fin. 14 O3
Kemijoki r. Fin. 14 N4
Kemiö Fin. see Kimito
Kemir Turkm. see Keymir
Kemmerer U.S.A. 62 E3
Kemnay U.K. 20 G3
Kemp Coast reg. Antarctica see Kemp Land
Kempele Fin. 14 N4
Kemp Land reg. Antarctica 76 D2
Kemp Peninsula Antarctica 76 A2
Kempsey Australia 58 F3
Kempt, Lac l. Canada 63 M2
Kempten (Allgäu) Germany 17 M7
Kempton Park S. Africa 51 I4
Ken r. India 36 E4
Kenai U.S.A. 60 C3
Kenai Fiords National Park U.S.A. 60 C4
Kenai Mountains U.S.A. 60 C4
Kenâyis, Râs el pt Egypt see Ḥikmah, Ra's al
Kenbridge VA U.S.A. 64 B4
Kendal U.K. 18 E4
Kendall Australia 58 F3
Kendall, Cape Canada 61 J3
Kendari Indon. 41 E8
Kendawangan Indon. 41 D8
Kendégué Chad 47 E3
Kendrapara India 37 F5
Kendraparha India see Kendrapara
Kendujhar India see Keonjhar
Kendujhargarh India see Keonjhar
Kendyrli-Kayasanskoye, Plato plat. Kazakh. 35 I2
Kendyrlisor, Solonchak salt l. Kazakh. 35 I2
Kenebri Australia 58 D3
Kenema Sierra Leone 46 B4
Kenge Dem. Rep. Congo 49 B4
Kenhardt S. Africa 50 E5
Kéniéba Mali 46 B3
Kénitra Morocco 22 C5
Kenmare Ireland 21 C6
Kenmare River inlet Ireland 21 B6
Kenmore NY U.S.A. 64 B1
Kennebunkport ME U.S.A. 64 F1
Kennedy, Cape U.S.A. see Canaveral, Cape
Kennedy Range National Park Australia 55 A6
Kennet r. U.K. 19 G7
Kenneth Range hills Australia 55 B5
Kennewick U.S.A. 62 D2
Kenn Reef Australia 56 F4
Kenora Canada 63 I2
Kenosha U.S.A. 63 J3
Kenozero, Ozero l. Rus. Fed. 12 H3
Kent r. U.K. 18 E4
Kent OH U.S.A. 64 A2
Kent VA U.S.A. 64 A4
Kentani S. Africa 51 I7
Kent Group is Australia 57 [inset]
Kent Peninsula Canada 60 H3
Kentucky state U.S.A. 63 K4
Kenya country Africa 48 D3
Kenya, Mount Kenya 48 D4
Keokuk U.S.A. 63 I3
Keoladeo National Park India 36 D4
Keonjhar India 37 F5
Keonjhargarh India see Keonjhar
Kepina r. Rus. Fed. 12 I2
Keppel Bay Australia 56 E4
Kepsut Turkey 27 M5
Kera India 37 F5
Kerala state India 38 B4
Kerang Australia 58 A5
Kerava Fin. 15 N6
Kerba Alg. 25 G5
Kerbela Iraq see Karbalā'
Kerben Kyrg. 42 C4
Kerbi r. Rus. Fed. 44 E1
Kerch Ukr. 34 E1
Kerchem'ya Rus. Fed. 12 L3
Kerema P.N.G. 52 E2
Kerempe Burun pt Turkey 34 D2
Keren Eritrea 32 E6
Kerewan Gambia 46 B3
Kerguélen, Îles is Indian Ocean 73 M9
Kerguelen Islands Indian Ocean see Kerguélen, Îles
Kerguelen Plateau sea feature Indian Ocean 73 M9
Kericho Kenya 48 D4
Kerikeri N.Z. 59 D2
Kerimäki Fin. 14 P6
Kerinci, Gunung vol. Indon. 41 C8
Kerintji vol. Indon. see Kerinci, Gunung
Keriya He watercourse China 42 E5
Keriya Shankou pass China 37 E2
Kerkenah, Îles is Tunisia 26 D7
Kerkini, Limni l. Greece 27 J4
Kérkira i. Greece see Corfu
Kerkouane tourist site Tunisia 26 D6
Kerkyra Greece 27 H5
Kerkyra i. Greece see Corfu
Kerma Sudan 32 D6
Kermadec Islands S. Pacific Ocean 53 I5
Kermadec Trench sea feature S. Pacific Ocean 74 I8
Kermān Iran 33 I3
Kerman CA U.S.A. 65 B2
Kermānshāh Iran 35 G4
Kermānshāhān Iran 35 I5
Kermine Uzbek. see Navoiy
Kermit U.S.A. 62 G5
Kern r. CA U.S.A. 65 C3
Keros i. Greece 27 K6
Keros Rus. Fed. 12 L3
Kérouané Guinea 46 C4
Kerr, Cape Antarctica 76 H1
Kerrville U.S.A. 62 H5
Kerry Head hd Ireland 21 C5
Kerteminde Denmark 15 G9
Kerulen r. China/Mongolia see Herlen Gol
Kerur India 38 B2
Keryneia Cyprus see Kyrenia
Kerzaz Alg. 46 C2
Kerzhenets r. Rus. Fed. 12 J4
Kesagami Lake Canada 63 K1
Kesälahti Fin. 14 P6
Keşan Turkey 27 L4
Keşap Turkey 13 H8
Kesariya India 37 F4
Kesennuma Japan 45 F5
Keshan China 44 B2
Keshem Afgh. 36 B1
Keshendeh-ye Bala Afgh. 36 A1
Keshod India 36 B5
Keshvar Iran 35 H4
Keskin Turkey 34 D3
Keskozero Rus. Fed. 12 G3
Kesova Gora Rus. Fed. 12 H4
Kestell S. Africa 51 I5
Kesten'ga Rus. Fed. 14 Q4
Kestilä Fin. 14 O4
Keswick U.K. 18 D4
Keszthely Hungary 26 G1
Ketapang Indon. 41 D8
Keti Bandar Pak. 36 A4
Ketmen', Khrebet mts China/Kazakh. 42 E4
Kettering U.K. 19 G6
Kettle Creek r. PA U.S.A. 64 C2
Kettleman City CA U.S.A. 65 C2
Keuka NY U.S.A. 64 C1
Keuka Lake NY U.S.A. 64 C1
Keumgang, Mount N. Korea see Kumgang-san
Keumsang, Mount N. Korea see Kumgang-san
Keuruu Fin. 14 N5
Keweenaw Peninsula U.S.A. 63 J2
Key, Lough l. Ireland 21 D3
Keyala Sudan 47 G4
Keyihe China 44 A2
Key Largo U.S.A. 63 K6
Keymir Turkm. 35 I3
Keynsham U.K. 19 E7
Keyser WV U.S.A. 64 B3
Keysville VA U.S.A. 64 B4
Keyvy, Vozvyshennost' hills Rus. Fed. 12 H2
Key West U.S.A. 63 K7
Kez Rus. Fed. 11 Q4
Kezi Zimbabwe 49 C6
Kgalagadi admin. dist. Botswana 50 E3
Kgalazadi admin. dist. Botswana see Kgalagadi
Kgatlen admin. dist. Botswana see Kgatleng
Kgatleng admin. dist. Botswana 51 H3
Kgomofatshe Pan salt pan Botswana 50 E2
Kgoro Pan salt pan Botswana 50 G3
Kgotsong S. Africa 51 H4
Khabab Syria 39 C3
Khabar Iran 35 I5
Khabarikha Rus. Fed. 12 L2
Khabarovsk Rus. Fed. 44 D2
Khabarovskiy Kray admin. div. Rus. Fed. 44 D2
Khabarovsk Kray admin. div. Rus. Fed. see Khabarovskiy Kray
Khabary Rus. Fed. 42 D2
Khachmas Azer. see Xaçmaz
Khadro Pak. 36 B4
Khagaria India 37 F4
Khagrachari Bangl. 37 G5
Khagrachhari Bangl. see Khagrachari
Khairgarh Pak. 36 B3
Khairpur Punjab Pak. 36 C3
Khairpur Sindh Pak. 33 K4
Khāīz, Kūh-e mt. Iran 35 H5
Khaja Du Koh hill Afgh. 36 A1
Khajuha India 36 E4
Khāk-e Jabbar Afgh. 36 B2
Khakhea Botswana 50 F3
Khak-rēz Afgh. 36 A3
Khalatse Jammu and Kashmir 36 D2
Khalifat mt. Pak. 33 K3
Khalīj Surt g. Libya see Sirte, Gulf of
Khalilabad India 37 E4
Khalīlī Iran 35 I6
Khalkhāl Iran 35 H3
Khálki i. Greece see Chalki
Khalkís Greece see Chalkida
Khallikot India 38 E2
Khalturin Rus. Fed. see Orlov
Khamar-Daban, Khrebet mts Rus. Fed. 42 I2
Khamaria India 38 D1
Khambhat India 36 C5
Khambhat, Gulf of India 38 A2
Khamgaon India 38 C1
Khamir Yemen 32 F6
Khamis Mushayṭ Saudi Arabia 32 F6
Khammam India 38 D2
Khammouan Laos see Thakèk
Khamra Rus. Fed. 29 M3
Khan Afgh. 36 B2
Khānābād Afgh. 36 B1
Khān al Baghdādī Iraq 35 F4
Khān al Mashāhidah Iraq 35 G4
Khān al Muşallá Iraq 35 G4
Khanapur India 38 B2
Khān ar Raḩbah Iraq 35 G5
Khanasur Pass Iran/Turkey 35 G3
Khanbalik China see Beijing
Khānch Iran 35 G3
Khandwa India 36 D5
Khandyga Rus. Fed. 29 O3
Khanewal Pak. 33 L3
Khaniá Greece see Chania
Khānī Yek Iran 35 I5
Khanka, Lake China/Rus. Fed. 44 D3
Khanka, Ozero l. China/Rus. Fed. see Khanka, Lake
Khankendi Azer. see Xankändi
Khanna India 36 D3
Khannā, Qā' salt pan Jordan 39 C3
Khanpur Pak. 33 L4
Khān Ruḩābah Iraq see Khān ar Raḩbah
Khansar Pak. 36 B3
Khān Shaykhūn Syria 39 C2
Khantayskoye, Ozero l. Rus. Fed. 28 K3
Khanthabouli Laos see Savannakhét
Khanty-Mansiysk Rus. Fed. 28 H3
Khān Yūnis Gaza 39 B4
Khanzi admin. dist. Botswana see Ghanzi
Khapalu Jammu and Kashmir 33 M2
Khaptad National Park Nepal 36 E3
Kharabali Rus. Fed. 13 J7
Kharagpur Bihar India 37 F4
Kharagpur W. Bengal India 37 F5
Khārān r. Iran 33 I4
Kharari India see Abu Road
Kharda India 38 B2
Khardi India 36 C6
Khardong La pass Jammu and Kashmir see Khardung La
Khardung La pass Jammu and Kashmir 36 D2
Kharfiyah Iraq 35 G5
Kharga Egypt see Al Khārijah
Kharga r. Rus. Fed. 44 D1
Khârga, El Wâḥât el oasis Egypt see Khārijah, Wāḥāt al
Kharga Oasis Egypt see Khārijah, Wāḥāt al
Khārg Islands Iran 35 H5
Khargon India 36 C5
Khari r. Rajasthan India 36 C4
Khari r. Rajasthan India 36 C4
Kharian Pak. 36 C2
Khariar India 38 D1
Khārijah, Wāḥāt al oasis Egypt 32 D5
Kharīm, Gebel hill Egypt see Kharīm, Jabal
Kharīm, Jabal hill Egypt 39 A4
Kharkhara r. India 36 E5
Kharkiv Ukr. 13 H6
Khar'kov Ukr. see Kharkiv
Khār Kūh mt. Iran 35 I5
Kharlovka Rus. Fed. 12 H1
Kharlu Rus. Fed. 14 Q6
Kharmanli Bulg. 27 K4
Kharovsk Rus. Fed. 12 I4
Kharsia India 37 E5
Khartoum Sudan 32 D6
Khasavyurt Rus. Fed. 13 J8
Khāsh Iran 33 J4
Khashgort Rus. Fed. 11 T2
Khashm el Girba Sudan 32 E7
Khashm Şana' Saudi Arabia 34 E6
Khashuri Georgia 35 F2
Khasi Hills India 37 G4
Khaskovo Bulg. 27 K4
Khatanga Rus. Fed. 29 L2
Khatanga, Gulf of Rus. Fed. see Khatangskiy Zaliv
Khatangskiy Zaliv b. Rus. Fed. 29 L2
Khatayakha Rus. Fed. 12 M2
Khatinza Pass Pak. 36 B1
Khatyrka Rus. Fed. 29 S3
Khāvāk, Khowtal-e Afgh. 36 B2
Khavda India 36 B5
Khayamnandi S. Africa 51 G6
Khaybar Saudi Arabia 32 E4
Khayelitsha S. Africa 50 D8
Khayrān, Ra's al pt Oman 33 I5
Khefa Israel see Haifa
Khehuene, Ponta pt Moz. 51 L2
Khemis Miliana Alg. 25 H5
Khenchela Alg. 26 B7
Khenifra Morocco 22 C5
Kherāmeh Iran 35 I5
Kherrata Alg. 25 I5
Kherreh Iran 35 I6
Khersan r. Iran 35 H5
Kherson Ukr. 27 O1
Kheta r. Rus. Fed. 29 L2
Khezerābād Iran 35 I3
Khiching India 37 F5
Khilok Rus. Fed. 43 K2
Khilok r. Rus. Fed. 43 J2
Khinganskiy Zapovednik nature res. Rus. Fed. 44 C2
Khíos i. Greece see Chios
Khirbat Isrīyah Syria 39 C2
Khitai Dawan Aksai Chin 36 D2
Khīyāv Iran 35 G3
Khiytola Rus. Fed. 15 P6
Khlevnoye Rus. Fed. 13 H5
Khmel'nik Ukr. see Khmil'nyk
Khmel'nitskiy Ukr. see Khmel'nyts'kyy
Khmel'nyts'kyy Ukr. 13 E6
Khmer Republic country Asia see Cambodia
Khmil'nyk Ukr. 13 E6
Khobi Georgia 35 F2
Khodzha-Kala Turkm. see Hojagala
Khodzhent Tajik. see Khŭjand
Khojand Tajik. see Khŭjand
Khokhowe Pan salt pan Botswana 50 E3
Khokhropar Pak. 36 B4
Khoksar India 36 D2
Kholm Afgh. 36 A1
Kholm Poland see Chełm
Kholm Rus. Fed. 12 F4
Kholmsk Rus. Fed. 44 F3
Kholon Israel see Holon
Khomas admin. reg. Namibia 50 C2
Khomas Highland hills Namibia 50 B2
Khomeyn Iran 35 H4
Khomeynīshahr Iran 35 H4
Khong, Mae Nam r. China/Myanmar see Salween
Khong, Mae Nam r. Laos/Thai. see Mekong
Khonj Iran 35 I6
Khonj, Kūh-e mts Iran 35 I6
Khon Kaen Thai. 31 J5
Khonsa India 37 H4
Khonuu Rus. Fed. 29 P3
Khoper r. Rus. Fed. 13 I6
Khor Rus. Fed. 44 D3
Khor r. Rus. Fed. 44 D3
Khorda India see Khurda
Khordha India see Khurda
Khoreyver Rus. Fed. 12 M2
Khorinsk Rus. Fed. 43 J2
Khorixas Namibia 49 B6
Khormūj, Kūh-e mt. Iran 35 H5
Khorog Tajik. see Khorugh
Khorol Rus. Fed. 44 D3
Khorol Ukr. 13 G6
Khoroslū Dāgh hills Iran 35 G3
Khorramābād Iran 35 H4
Khorramshahr Iran 35 H5
Khorugh Tajik. 33 L2
Khosheutovo Rus. Fed. 13 J7
Khosūyeh Iran 35 I5
Khotan China see Hotan
Khouribga Morocco 22 C5
Khowrjān Iran 35 I5
Khowrnag, Kūh-e mt. Iran 35 I4
Khreum Myanmar 37 H5
Khroma r. Rus. Fed. 29 P2
Khromtau Kazakh. 28 G4
Khrushchev Ukr. see Svitlovods'k
Khrysokhou Bay Cyprus see Chrysochou Bay
Khrystynivka Ukr. 13 F6
Khudumelapye Botswana 50 G2
Khudzhand Tajik. see Khŭjand
Khuis Botswana 50 E4
Khŭjand Tajik. 33 K1
Khŭjayli Uzbek. see Xo'jayli
Khulays Saudi Arabia 32 E5
Khulkhuta Rus. Fed. 13 J7
Khulm r. Afgh. 36 A1
Khulna Bangl. 37 G5
Khulo Georgia 35 F2
Khuma S. Africa 51 H4
Khunayzīr, Jabal al mts Syria 39 C2
Khūninshahr Iran see Khorramshahr
Khunjerab Pass China/Jammu and Kashmir 36 C1
Khunsar Iran 35 H4
Khurayş Saudi Arabia 32 G4
Khurd, Koh-i- mt. Afgh. 36 A2
Khurda India 38 E1
Khurdha India see Khurda
Khurja India 36 D3
Khurmuli Rus. Fed. 44 E2
Khūrrāb Iran 35 I5
Khurz Iran 35 I4
Khushab Pak. 33 L3
Khushalgarh Pak. 36 B2
Khushshah, Wādī al watercourse Jordan/Saudi Arabia 39 C5
Khust Ukr. 13 D6
Khutse Game Reserve nature res. Botswana 50 G2
Khutsong S. Africa 51 H4
Khutu r. Rus. Fed. 44 E2
Khuzdar Pak. 33 K4
Khvāf Iran 33 J3
Khvājeh Iran 35 G3
Khvalynsk Rus. Fed. 13 K5
Khvormūj Iran 35 H5
Khvoy Iran 35 G3
Khvoynaya Rus. Fed. 12 G4
Khwaja Amran mt. Pak. 36 A3
Khwaja Muhammad Range mts Afgh. 36 B1
Khyber Pass Afgh./Pak. 33 L3
Kiama Australia 58 E5
Kiangsi prov. China see Jiangxi
Kiangsu prov. China see Jiangsu
Kiantajärvi l. Fin. 14 P4
Kīāseh Iran 35 I3
Kiatassuaq i. Greenland 61 M2
Kibaha Tanz. 49 D4
Kibali r. Dem. Rep. Congo 48 C3
Kibangou Congo 48 B4
Kibaya Tanz. 49 D4
Kiboga Uganda 48 D3
Kibombo Dem. Rep. Congo 48 C4
Kibondo Tanz. 48 D4
Kibre Mengist Eth. 47 G4
Kıbrıs country Asia see Cyprus
Kibungo Rwanda 48 D4
Kičevo Macedonia 27 I4
Kichmengskiy Gorodok Rus. Fed. 12 J4
Kiçik Qafqaz mts Asia see Lesser Caucasus
Kicking Horse Pass Canada 62 D1
Kidal Mali 46 D3
Kidderminster U.K. 19 E6
Kidepo Valley National Park Uganda 48 D3
Kidira Senegal 46 B3
Kidmang Jammu and Kashmir 36 D2
Kidnappers, Cape N.Z. 59 F4
Kidsgrove U.K. 19 E5
Kiel Germany 17 M3
Kiel Canal Germany 17 L3
Kielce Poland 17 R5
Kielder Water resr U.K. 18 E3
Kieler Bucht b. Germany 17 M3
Kienge Dem. Rep. Congo 49 C5
Kiev Ukr. 13 F6
Kiffa Mauritania 46 B3
Kifisia Greece 27 J5
Kifrī Iraq 35 G4
Kigali Rwanda 48 D4
Kiğı Turkey 35 F3
Kigoma Tanz. 49 C4
Kihlanki Fin. 14 M3
Kihniö Fin. 14 M5
Kiiminki Fin. 14 N4
Kii-sanchi mts Japan 45 D6
Kii-suidō sea chan. Japan 45 D6
Kikerino Rus. Fed. 15 P7
Kikinda Serbia 27 I2
Kikládhes is Greece see Cyclades
Kiknur Rus. Fed. 12 J4
Kikonai Japan 44 F4
Kikori P.N.G. 52 E2
Kikwit Dem. Rep. Congo 49 B4
Kilafors Sweden 15 J6
Kilar India 36 D2
Kilchu N. Korea 44 C4
Kilcoole Ireland 21 F4
Kilcormac Ireland 21 E4
Kilcoy Australia 58 F1
Kildare Ireland 21 F4
Kil'dinstroy Rus. Fed. 14 R2
Kilemary Rus. Fed. 12 J4
Kilembe Dem. Rep. Congo 49 B4
Kilfinan U.K. 20 D5
Kilham U.K. 18 E3
Kilia Ukr. see Kiliya
Kılıç Dağı mt. Syria/Turkey see Aqra', Jabal al
Kilifi Kenya 48 D4
Kilik Pass China/Jammu and Kashmir 36 C1
Kilimanjaro vol. Tanz. 48 D4
Kilimanjaro National Park Tanz. 48 D4
Kilinailau Islands P.N.G. 52 F2
Kilindoni Tanz. 49 D4
Kilingi-Nõmme Estonia 15 N7
Kilis Turkey 39 C1
Kilis prov. Turkey 39 C1
Kiliya Ukr. 27 M2
Kilkee Ireland 21 C5
Kilkeel U.K. 21 G3
Kilkenny Ireland 21 E5
Kilkhampton U.K. 19 C8
Kilkis Greece 27 J4
Killala Ireland 21 C3
Killala Bay Ireland 21 C3
Killaloe Ireland 21 D5
Killarney N.T. Australia 54 E4
Killarney Qld Australia 58 F2
Killarney Ireland 21 C5
Killarney National Park Ireland 21 C6
Killary Harbour b. Ireland 21 C4
Killeen U.S.A. 62 H5
Killenaule Ireland 21 E5
Killimor Ireland 21 D4
Killin U.K. 20 E4
Killinchy U.K. 21 G3
Killíni mt. Greece see Kyllini
Killinick Ireland 21 F5
Killorglin Ireland 21 C5
Killurin Ireland 21 F5
Killybegs Ireland 21 D3
Kilmacrenan Ireland 21 E2
Kilmaine Ireland 21 C4
Kilmallock Ireland 21 D5
Kilmaluag U.K. 20 C3
Kilmarnock U.K. 20 E5
Kilmelford U.K. 20 D4
Kil'mez' Rus. Fed. 12 K4
Kil'mez' r. Rus. Fed. 12 K4
Kilmona Ireland 21 D6
Kilmore Australia 58 B6
Kilmore Quay Ireland 21 F5
Kilosa Tanz. 49 D4
Kilpisjärvi Fin. 14 L2
Kilrea U.K. 21 F3
Kilrush Ireland 21 C5
Kilsyth U.K. 20 E5
Kiltan atoll India 38 B4
Kiltullagh Ireland 21 D4
Kilwa Masoko Tanz. 49 D4
Kilwinning U.K. 20 E5
Kimba Australia 55 G8
Kimba Congo 48 B4
Kimball U.S.A. 62 G3
Kimball, Mount U.S.A. 60 D3
Kimbe P.N.G. 52 F2
Kimberley S. Africa 50 G5
Kimberley Plateau Australia 54 D4
Kimberley Range hills Australia 55 B6
Kimch'aek N. Korea 45 C4
Kimch'ŏn S. Korea 45 C5
Kimhae S. Korea 45 C6
Kimhandu mt. Tanz. 49 D4
Kími Greece see Kymi
Kimito Fin. 15 M6
Kimmirut Canada 61 L3
Kimolos i. Greece 27 K6
Kimovsk Rus. Fed. 13 H5
Kimpese Dem. Rep. Congo 49 B4
Kimpoku-san mt. Japan see Kinpoku-san
Kimry Rus. Fed. 12 H4
Kimvula Dem. Rep. Congo 49 B4
Kinabalu, Gunung mt. Sabah Malaysia 41 D7
Kinango Kenya 49 D4
Kinbasket Lake Canada 62 D1
Kinbrace U.K. 20 F2
Kincardine U.K. 20 F4
Kinchega National Park Australia 57 C7
Kinda Dem. Rep. Congo 49 C4
Kindat Myanmar 37 H5
Kinder Scout hill U.K. 18 F5
Kindersley Canada 62 F1
Kindia Guinea 46 B3
Kindu Dem. Rep. Congo 48 C4
Kinel' Rus. Fed. 13 K5
Kineshma Rus. Fed. 12 I4
Kingaroy Australia 58 E1
King Christian Island Canada 61 H2
King City CA U.S.A. 65 B2
King Edward VII Land pen. Antarctica see Edward VII Peninsula
King George VA U.S.A. 64 C3
King George Island Antarctica 76 A2
King George Islands Canada 61 K4
King George Islands Fr. Polynesia see Roi Georges, Îles du
King Hill hill Australia 54 C5
Kingisepp Rus. Fed. 12 F4
King Island Australia 57 [inset]
Kingissepp Estonia see Kuressaare
Kinglake National Park Australia 58 B6
King Leopold and Queen Astrid Coast Antarctica 76 E2
King Leopold Range National Park Australia 54 D4
King Leopold Ranges hills Australia 54 D4
Kingman AZ U.S.A. 65 E3
Kingman Reef terr. N. Pacific Ocean 74 J5
Kingoonya Australia 57 A6
King Peak Antarctica 76 L1
King Peninsula Antarctica 76 K2
Kingri Pak. 36 B3
Kings r. Ireland 21 E5
Kings r. CA U.S.A. 65 B2
King Salmon U.S.A. 60 C4
Kingsbridge U.K. 19 D8
Kingsburg CA U.S.A. 65 C2
Kings Canyon National Park CA U.S.A. 65 C2
Kingscliff Australia 58 F2
Kingscote Australia 57 B7
Kingscourt Ireland 21 F4
King Sejong research station Antarctica 76 A2
King's Lynn U.K. 19 H6
Kingsmill Group is Kiribati 53 H2
Kingsnorth U.K. 19 H7
King Sound b. Australia 54 C4
Kings Peak U.S.A. 62 E3
Kingsport U.S.A. 63 K4
Kingston Australia 57 [inset]
Kingston Canada 63 L3
Kingston Jamaica 67 I5
Kingston Norfolk I. 53 G4
Kingston NY U.S.A. 64 D2
Kingston PA U.S.A. 64 D2
Kingston Peak CA U.S.A. 65 E3
Kingston South East Australia 57 B8
Kingston upon Hull U.K. 18 G5
Kingstown St Vincent 67 L6
Kingsville U.S.A. 62 H6
Kingswood U.K. 19 E7
Kington U.K. 19 D6
Kingungi Dem. Rep. Congo 49 B4
Kingussie U.K. 20 E3
King William VA U.S.A. 64 C4
King William Island Canada 61 I3
King William's Town S. Africa 51 H7
Kingwood WV U.S.A. 64 B3
Kinloch N.Z. 59 B7
Kinloss U.K. 20 F3
Kinna Sweden 15 H8
Kinnegad Ireland 21 E4
Kinneret, Yam l. Israel see Galilee, Sea of
Kinniyai Sri Lanka 38 D4
Kinnula Fin. 14 N5
Kinpoku-san mt. Japan 45 E5
Kinross U.K. 20 F4
Kinsale Ireland 21 D6
Kinsale VA U.S.A. 64 C3
Kinshasa Dem. Rep. Congo 49 B4
Kinston U.S.A. 63 L4
Kintore U.K. 20 G3
Kintyre pen. U.K. 20 D5
Kin-U Myanmar 37 H5
Kinyeti mt. Sudan 47 G4
Kiparissía Greece see Kyparissia
Kipawa, Lac l. Canada 63 L2
Kipnuk U.S.A. 60 B4
Kiptopeke VA U.S.A. 64 D4
Kipungo Angola see Quipungo
Kipushi Dem. Rep. Congo 49 C5
Kirakira Solomon Is 53 G3
Kirandul India 38 D2
Kircubbin U.K. 21 G3
Kirdimi Chad 47 E3
Kirenga r. Rus. Fed. 43 J1
Kirensk Rus. Fed. 29 L4
Kireyevsk Rus. Fed. 13 H5
Kirghizia country Asia see Kyrgyzstan
Kirghiz Range mts Kazakh./Kyrg. 42 C4
Kirgizskaya S.S.R. country Asia see Kyrgyzstan
Kirgizskiy Khrebet mts Kazakh./Kyrg. see Kirghiz Range
Kirgizstan country Asia see Kyrgyzstan
Kiri Dem. Rep. Congo 48 B4
Kiribati country Pacific Ocean 74 I6
Kırıkhan Turkey 39 C1
Kırıkkale Turkey 34 D3
Kirillov Rus. Fed. 12 H4
Kirillovo Rus. Fed. 44 F3
Kirin China see Jilin
Kirin prov. China see Jilin
Kirinda Sri Lanka 38 D5
Kirinyaga mt. Kenya see Kenya, Mount
Kirishi Rus. Fed. 12 G4
Kirishima-Yaku Kokuritsu-kōen Japan 45 C7
Kirishima-yama vol. Japan 45 C7
Kiritimati atoll Kiribati 75 J5
Kiriwina Islands P.N.G. see Trobriand Islands
Kırkağaç Turkey 27 L5
Kirk Bulāg Dāgi mt. Iran 35 G3
Kirkby U.K. 18 E5
Kirkby in Ashfield U.K. 19 F5
Kirkby Lonsdale U.K. 18 E4
Kirkby Stephen U.K. 18 E4
Kirkcaldy U.K. 20 F4
Kirkcolm U.K. 20 D6
Kirkcudbright U.K. 20 E6
Kirkenær Norway 15 H6
Kirkenes Norway 14 Q2
Kirkintilloch U.K. 20 E5
Kirkkonummi Fin. 15 N6
Kirkland AZ U.S.A. 65 F3
Kirkland Lake Canada 63 K2
Kırklareli Turkey 27 L4
Kirk Michael Isle of Man 18 C4
Kirkoswald U.K. 18 E4
Kirkpatrick, Mount Antarctica 76 H1
Kirksville U.S.A. 63 I3
Kirkūk Iraq 35 G4
Kirkwall U.K. 20 G2
Kirkwood S. Africa 51 G7
Kirman Iran see Kermān
Kirov Kaluzhskaya Oblast' Rus. Fed. 13 G5
Kirov Kirovskaya Oblast' Rus. Fed. 12 K4
Kirovabad Azer. see Gäncä
Kirovabad Tajik. see Panj
Kirovakan Armenia see Vanadzor
Kirovo Ukr. see Kirovohrad
Kirovo-Chepetsk Rus. Fed. 12 K4
Kirovo-Chepetskiy Rus. Fed. see Kirovo-Chepetsk
Kirovograd Ukr. see Kirovohrad
Kirovohrad Ukr. 13 G6
Kirovsk Leningradskaya Oblast' Rus. Fed. 12 F4
Kirovsk Murmanskaya Oblast' Rus. Fed. 12 G2
Kirovs'ke Ukr. 34 D1
Kirovskiy Rus. Fed. 44 D3
Kirovskoye Ukr. see Kirovs'ke
Kırpaşa pen. Cyprus see Karpasia
Kirpili Turkm. 35 J3
Kirriemuir U.K. 20 F4
Kirs Rus. Fed. 12 L4
Kirsanov Rus. Fed. 13 I5
Kırşehir Turkey 34 D3
Kirthar National Park Pak. 36 A4
Kirthar Range mts Pak. 33 K4
Kiruna Sweden 14 L3
Kirundu Dem. Rep. Congo 48 C4
Kirwan Escarpment Antarctica 76 B2
Kiryū Japan 45 E5
Kisa Sweden 15 I8
Kisama, Parque Nacional de nat. park Angola see Quiçama, Parque Nacional do
Kisandji Dem. Rep. Congo 49 B4
Kisangani Dem. Rep. Congo 48 C3
Kisantu Dem. Rep. Congo 49 B4
Kisar i. Indon. 54 D2
Kiselevsk Rus. Fed. 42 F2
Kisel'ovka Rus. Fed. 44 E2
Kishanganj India 37 F4
Kishangarh Madh. Prad. India 36 D4
Kishangarh Rajasthan India 36 B4
Kishangarh Rajasthan India 36 C4
Kishangarh Rajasthan India 36 D4
Kishi Nigeria 46 D4
Kishinev Moldova see Chişinău
Kishkenekol' Kazakh. 31 G1
Kishoreganj Bangl. 37 G4
Kishorganj Bangl. see Kishoreganj
Kisi Nigeria see Kishi
Kisii Kenya 48 D4
Kiska Island U.S.A. 29 S4
Kiskunfélegyháza Hungary 27 H1
Kiskunhalas Hungary 27 H1
Kiskunsági nat. park Hungary 27 H1
Kislovodsk Rus. Fed. 35 F2
Kismaayo Somalia 48 E4
Kismayu Somalia see Kismaayo
Kisoro Uganda 47 F5
Kissamos Greece 27 J7
Kissidougou Guinea 46 B4
Kissimmee U.S.A. 63 K6
Kissimmee, Lake U.S.A. 63 K6
Kistendey Rus. Fed. 13 I5
Kistna r. India see Krishna
Kisumu Kenya 48 D4
Kisykkamys Kazakh. see Dzhangala
Kita Mali 46 C3
Kita-Daitō-jima i. Japan 43 O7
Kitaibaraki Japan 45 F5
Kitakami Japan 45 F5
Kita-Kyūshū Japan 45 C6
Kitale Kenya 48 D3
Kitami Japan 44 F4
Kitchener Ont. Canada 64 A1
Kitee Fin. 14 Q5
Kitgum Uganda 48 D3
Kíthira i. Greece see Kythira
Kíthnos i. Greece see Kythnos
Kiti, Cape Cyprus see Kition, Cape
Kitinen r. Fin. 14 O3
Kition, Cape Cyprus 39 A2
Kitiou, Akra c. Cyprus see Kition, Cape
Kittanning PA U.S.A. 64 B2
Kittatinny Mountains hills NJ U.S.A. 64 D2
Kittery ME U.S.A. 64 F1
Kittilä Fin. 14 N3
Kittur India 38 B3
Kitui Kenya 48 D4
Kitwe Zambia 49 C5
Kitzbüheler Alpen mts Austria 17 N7
Kiuruvesi Fin. 14 O5
Kivalina U.S.A. 60 B3
Kivijärvi Fin. 14 N5
Kiviõli Estonia 15 O7
Kivu, Lake Dem. Rep. Congo/Rwanda 48 C4
Kiwaba N'zogi Angola 49 B4
Kiyev Ukr. see Kiev
Kiyevskoye Vodokhranilishche resr Ukr. see Kyyivs'ke Vodoskhovyshche
Kıyıköy Turkey 27 M4
Kizel Rus. Fed. 11 R4
Kizema Rus. Fed. 12 J3
Kızılcadağ Turkey 27 M6
Kızılca Dağ mt. Turkey 34 C3
Kızılcahamam Turkey 34 D2
Kızıldağ mt. Turkey 39 A1
Kızıldağ mt. Turkey 39 B1
Kızıl Dağı mt. Turkey 34 E3
Kızılırmak Turkey 34 D2
Kızılırmak r. Turkey 34 D2
Kızıltepe Turkey 35 F3
Kizilyurt Rus. Fed. 13 J8
Kızkalesi Turkey 39 B1
Kizlyar Rus. Fed. 13 J8
Kizlyarskiy Zaliv b. Rus. Fed. 35 G1
Kizner Rus. Fed. 12 K4
Kizyl-Arbat Turkm. see Serdar
Kizyl-Atrek Turkm. see Etrek
Kjøllefjord Norway 14 O1
Kjøpsvik Norway 14 J2
Kladno Czech Rep. 17 O5
Klagenfurt Austria 17 O7
Klaipėda Lith. 15 L9
Klaksvig Faroe Is see Klaksvík
Klaksvík Faroe Is 14 [inset]

Klamath r. U.S.A. 60 F5
Klamath Falls U.S.A. 62 C3
Klarälven r. Sweden 15 H7
Klatovy Czech Rep. 17 N6
Klawer S. Africa 50 D6
Kleides Islands Cyprus 39 B2
Kleinbegin S. Africa 50 E5
Klein Karas Namibia 50 D4
Klein Nama Land reg. S. Africa see
  Namaqualand
Klein Roggeveldberge mts S. Africa 50 E7
Kleinsee S. Africa 50 C5
Klerksdorp S. Africa 51 H4
Kletnya Rus. Fed. 13 H5
Kletsk Belarus see Klyetsk
Kletskaya Rus. Fed. 13 I6
Kletskiy Rus. Fed. see Kletskaya
Klidhes Islands Cyprus see Kleides Islands
Klimkovka Rus. Fed. 12 K4
Klimovo Rus. Fed. 13 G5
Klin Rus. Fed. 12 H4
Klínovec Czech Rep. 17 N5
Klintehamn Sweden 15 K8
Klintsy Rus. Fed. 13 G5
Ključ Bos.-Herz. 26 G2
Kłodzko Poland 16 P5
Klosterneuburg Austria 17 P6
Kluane National Park Canada 60 E3
Kluang Malaysia see Keluang
Kluczbork Poland 17 Q5
Klukhori Rus. Fed. see Karachayevsk
Klukhorskiy, Pereval Rus. Fed. 35 F2
Klukwan U.S.A. 60 E4
Klupro Pak. 33 K4
Klyetsk Belarus 15 O10
Klyuchevskaya, Sopka vol. Rus. Fed. 29 R4
Klyuchi Rus. Fed. 44 B2
Knäda Sweden 15 I6
Knaresborough U.K. 18 F4
Knighton U.K. 19 D6
Knights Landing CA U.S.A. 65 B1
Knin Croatia 26 G2
Knittelfeld Austria 17 O7
Knjaževac Serbia 27 J3
Knob Lake Canada see Schefferville
Knob Peak hill Australia 54 E3
Knock Ireland 21 D4
Knockaboy hill Ireland 21 C6
Knockalongy hill Ireland 21 D3
Knockalough Ireland 21 C5
Knockanaffrin hill Ireland 21 E5
Knock Hill hill U.K. 20 G3
Knockmealdown Mts hills Ireland 21 D5
Knocknaskagh hill Ireland 21 D5
Knowle U.K. 19 F6
Knox PA U.S.A. 65 F4
Knox Coast Antarctica 76 F2
Knoxville TN U.S.A. 63 K4
Knud Rasmussen Land reg. Greenland
  61 L2
Knysna S. Africa 50 F8
Ko, Gora mt. Rus. Fed. 44 E3
Koartac Canada see Quaqtaq
Kobbfoss Norway 14 P2
Kōbe Japan 45 D6
København Denmark see Copenhagen
Kobenni Mauritania 46 C3
Koblenz Germany 17 K5
Koboldo Rus. Fed. 44 D1
Kobrin Belarus see Kobryn
Kobroor i. Indon. 41 I8
Kobryn Belarus 15 N10
Kobuk Valley National Park U.S.A. 60 C3
K'obulet'i Georgia 35 F2
Kocaeli Kocaeli Turkey see İzmit
Kocaeli Yarımadası pen. Turkey 27 M4
Kočani Macedonia 27 J4
Kocasu r. Turkey 27 M4
Kočevje Slovenia 26 F2
Koch Bihar India 37 G4
Kuchevo Rus. Fed. 27 J2
Kōchi India see Cochin
Kōchi Japan 45 D6
Kochisar Turkey see Kızıltepe
Koch Island Canada 61 K3
Kochkor Kyrg. 42 D4
Kochkorka Kyrg. see Kochkor
Kochkurovo Rus. Fed. 13 J5
Kochubeyevskoye Rus. Fed. 35 F1
Kod India 38 B3
Kodala India 38 E2
Kodarma India 37 F4
Koderma India see Kodarma
Kodiak U.S.A. 60 C4
Kodiak Island U.S.A. 60 C4
Kodibeleng Botswana 51 H2
Kodino Rus. Fed. 12 H3
Kodiyakkarai India 38 C4
Kodok Sudan 32 D8
Kodyma Ukr. 13 F6
Kodzhaele mt. Bulg./Greece 27 K4
Koedoesberg mts S. Africa 50 E7
Koegrabie S. Africa 50 E5
Koekenaap S. Africa 50 D6
Koës Namibia 50 D3
Kofa Mountains AZ U.S.A. 65 F4
Koffiefontein S. Africa 50 G5
Koforidua Ghana 46 C4
Kōfu Japan 45 E6
Kogaluk r. Canada 61 L4
Kogan Australia 58 E1
Køge Denmark 15 H9
Kogon r. Guinea 46 B3
Kohat Pak. 33 L3
Kohestänät Afgh. 36 A2
Kohila Estonia 15 N7
Kohima India 37 H4
Kohler Range mts Antarctica 76 K2
Kohlu Pak. 36 B3
Kohtla-Järve Estonia 15 O7
Kohŭng S. Korea 45 B6
Koidu Sierra Leone see Sefadu
Koilkonda India 38 C3
Koin N. Korea 45 B4
Koin r. Rus. Fed. 12 K3
Koi Sanjaq Iraq 35 G3
Kōje-do i. S. Korea 45 C6
Kojonup Australia 55 B8
Kōkar Fin. 15 L7
Kokchetav Kazakh. see Kokshetau
Kokemäenjoki r. Fin. 15 L6
Kokerboom Namibia 50 D5
Kokkilai Sri Lanka 38 D4
Kokkola Fin. 14 M5
Koko Nigeria 46 D3
Kokomo U.S.A. 63 J3
Kokong Botswana 50 F3
Kokosi S. Africa 51 H4
Kokpekti Kazakh. 42 E3
Koksan N. Korea 45 B5
Kokshaal-Tau, Khrebet mts China/Kyrg. see
  Kakshaal-Too
Koksharka Rus. Fed. 12 J4
Kokshetau Kazakh. 31 F1
Kokstad S. Africa 51 I6
Kokterek Kazakh. 13 K6
Koktokay China see Fuyun
Kola r. Rus. Fed. 14 R2
Kolachi r. Pak. 36 A4
Kolahoi mt. Jammu and Kashmir 36 C2
Kolaka Indon. 41 E8

Kola Peninsula Rus. Fed. 12 H2
Kolar Chhattisgarh India 38 D2
Kolar Karnataka India 38 C3
Kolaras India 36 D4
Kolar Gold Fields India 38 C3
Kolari Fin. 14 M3
Kolarovgrad Bulg. see Shumen
Kolasib India 37 H4
Kolayat India 36 C4
Kolberg Poland see Kołobrzeg
Kol'chugino Rus. Fed. 12 H4
Kolda Senegal 46 B3
Kolding Denmark 15 F9
Kole Kasaï-Oriental Dem. Rep. Congo
  48 C4
Kole Orientale Dem. Rep. Congo 48 C3
Koléa Alg. 25 H5
Koler Sweden 14 L4
Kolguyev, Ostrov i. Rus. Fed. 12 K1
Kolhan reg. India 37 F5
Kolhapur India 38 B2
Kolikata India see Kolkata
Kõljala Estonia 15 M7
Kolkasrags pt Latvia 15 M8
Kolkata India 37 G5
Kolkhozabad Khatlon Tajik. see
  Kolkhozobod
Kolkhozabad Khatlon Tajik. see Vose
Kolkhozobod Tajik. 33 K2
Kollam India see Quilon
Kolleru Lake India 38 D2
Kolmanskop Namibia 50 B4
Köln Germany see Cologne
Kołobrzeg Poland 17 O3
Kologriv Rus. Fed. 12 J4
Kolokani India 46 C3
Kolombangara i. Solomon Is 53 F53
Kolomea Ukr. see Kolomyya
Kolomna Rus. Fed. 13 H5
Kolomyja Ukr. see Kolomyya
Kolomyya Ukr. 13 E6
Kolondiéba Mali 46 C3
Kolonedale Indon. 52 C2
Koloni Cyprus 39 A2
Kolonkwaneng Botswana 50 E4
Kolozsvár Romania see Cluj-Napoca
Kolpashevo Rus. Fed. 28 J4
Kolpos Messaras b. Greece 27 K7
Kol'skiy Poluostrov pen. Rus. Fed. see
  Kola Peninsula
Kölük Turkey see Kâhta
Koluli Eritrea 32 F7
Kolva r. Rus. Fed. 12 M2
Kolvan India 38 B2
Kolvereid Norway 14 G4
Kolvik Norway 14 N1
Kolvitskoye, Ozero l. Rus. Fed. 14 R3
Kolwezi Dem. Rep. Congo 49 C5
Kolyma r. Rus. Fed. 29 R3
Kolyma Lowland Rus. Fed. see
  Kolymskaya Nizmennost'
Kolyma Range mts Rus. Fed. see
  Kolymskiy, Khrebet
Kolymskaya Nizmennost' lowland
  Rus. Fed. 29 Q3
Kolymskiy, Khrebet mts Rus. Fed. 29 R3
Kolyshley Rus. Fed. 13 J5
Kom mt. Bulg. 27 J3
Komadugu-gana watercourse Nigeria 46 E3
Komaggas S. Africa 50 C5
Komaki Japan 45 E6
Komandnaya, Gora mt. Rus. Fed. 44 E2
Komandorskiye Ostrova is Rus. Fed. 29 R4
Komárno Slovakia 17 Q7
Komati r. Swaziland 51 J3
Komatipoort S. Africa 51 J3
Komatsu Japan 45 E5
Komba i. Indon. 54 C1
Komga S. Africa 51 H7
Komintern Ukr. see Marhanets'
Kominternivs'ke Ukr. 27 N1
Komiža Croatia 26 G3
Komló Hungary 26 H1
Kommunarsk Ukr. see Alchevs'k
Komodo, Taman Nasional Indon. 54 B2
Komono Congo 48 B4
Komotini Greece 27 K4
Kompong Cham Cambodia see
  Kâmpóng Cham
Kompong Som Cambodia see
  Sihanoukville
Kompong Speu Cambodia see
  Kâmpóng Spœ
Kompong Thom Cambodia see
  Kâmpóng Thum
Komrat Moldova see Comrat
Komsberg mts S. Africa 50 E7
Komsomol Kazakh. see Karabalyk
Komsomolets Kazakh. see Karabalyk
Komsomolets, Ostrov i. Rus. Fed. 28 K1
Komsomol'sk Ukr. 13 G6
Komsomol'skiy Chukotskiy Avtonomnyy
  Okrug Rus. Fed. 77 C2
Komsomol'skiy Khanty-Mansiyskiy
  Avtonomnyy Okrug Rus. Fed. see Yugorsk
Komsomol'skiy Respublika Kalmykiya -
  Khalm'g-Tangch Rus. Fed. 13 J7
Komsomol'sk-na-Amure Rus. Fed. 44 E2
Komsomol'skoye Rus. Fed. 13 J6
Kömürlü Turkey 35 F2
Kon India 37 E4
Konacık Turkey 39 B1
Konada India 38 D2
Konarak India see Konarka
Konarka India 37 F6
Konch India 36 D4
Kondagaon India 38 D2
Kondinin Australia 55 B8
Kondinskoye Rus. Fed. see Oktyabr'skoye
Kondoa Tanz. 49 D4
Kondol' Rus. Fed. 13 J5
Kondopoga Rus. Fed. 12 G3
Kondoz Afgh. see Kunduz
Kondrovo Rus. Fed. 13 G5
Kŏnëürgench Turkm. 33 I1
Köneürgench Turkm. see Kŏnëürgench
Köng, Kaôh i. Cambodia 41 C4
Kong Christian IX Land reg. Greenland
  61 O3
Kong Christian X Land reg. Greenland
  61 M3
Kongelab atoll Marshall Is see Rongelap
Kong Frederik IX Land reg. Greenland
  61 M3
Kong Frederik VI Kyst coastal area
  Greenland 61 N3
Kongolo Dem. Rep. Congo 49 C4
Kongor Sudan 47 G4
Kong Oscars Fjord inlet Greenland 61 P2
Kongoussi Burkina 46 C3
Kongsberg Norway 15 F7
Kongsvinger Norway 15 H6
Kongur Shan mt. China 42 D5
Königsberg Rus. Fed. see Kaliningrad
Konin Poland 17 Q4
Konjic Bos.-Herz. 26 G3
Konkiep watercourse Namibia 50 C5
Konnevesi Fin. 14 O5
Konosha Rus. Fed. 12 I3
Konotop Ukr. 13 G6

Konpara India 37 E5
Konqi He r. China 42 F4
Konso Eth. 48 D3
Konstantinograd Ukr. see Krasnohrad
Konstantinovka Rus. Fed. 44 B2
Konstantinovsk Rus. Fed. see Kostyantynivka
Konstanz Germany 17 L7
Kontiolahti Fin. 14 P5
Konttila Fin. 14 O4
Könugard Ukr. see Kiev
Konushin, Mys pt Rus. Fed. 12 I2
Konya Turkey 34 D3
Konzhakovskiy Kamen', Gora mt. Rus. Fed.
  11 R4
Kooch Bihar India see Koch Bihar
Kookynie Australia 55 C7
Koolyanobbing Australia 55 B7
Koondrook Australia 58 B5
Koorawatha Australia 58 D5
Koordarrie Australia 54 A5
Kootjieskolk S. Africa 50 E6
Kootenay Lake Canada 62 D1
Kopargaon India see Kopargaon
Kopbirlik Kazakh. 42 D2
Koper Slovenia 26 E2
Kopet-Dag, Khrebet mts Iran/Turkm. see
  Kopet Dag
Köpetdag Gershi mts Iran/Turkm. see
  Kopet Dag
Köping Sweden 15 J7
Köpmanholmen Sweden 14 K5
Kopong Botswana 51 G3
Koppal India 38 C3
Koppang Norway 15 G6
Kopparberg Sweden 15 I7
Koppeh Dägh mts Iran/Turkm. see
  Kopet Dag
Koppi r. Rus. Fed. 44 F2
Koppies S. Africa 51 H4
Koppieskraal Pan salt pan S. Africa 50 E4
Koprivnica Croatia 26 G1
Köprülü Turkey 39 A1
Köprülü Kanyon Milli Parkı nat. park Turkey
  27 N6
Kopyl' Belarus see Kapyl'
Kora India 36 E4
Korablino Rus. Fed. 13 I5
K'orahē Eth. 48 E3
Koramlik China 37 F1
Korangal India 38 C2
Korangi Pak. 36 A4
Korān va Monjan Afgh. 36 B1
Koraput India 38 D2
Korat Thai. see Nakhon Ratchasima
Koratla India 38 C2
Korba India 37 E5
Korçë Albania 27 I4
Korčula i. Croatia 26 G3
Korčula i. Croatia 26 G3
Korčulanski Kanal sea chan. Croatia 26 G3
Korday Kazakh. 42 C4
Kord Kūy Iran 35 I3
Korea, North country Asia 45 B5
Korea, South country Asia 45 B5
Korea Bay g. China/N. Korea 45 B5
Korea Strait Japan/S. Korea 45 C6
Koregaon India 38 B2
Korenovsk Rus. Fed. 35 E1
Korenovskaya Rus. Fed. see Korenovsk
Korenino Rus. Fed. 11 R3
Korets' Ukr. 13 E6
Körfez Turkey 27 M4
Korff Ice Rise Antarctica 76 L1
Korfovskiy Rus. Fed. 44 D2
Korgalzhyn Kazakh. 42 C2
Korgen Norway 14 H3
Korhogo Côte d'Ivoire 46 C4
Koribundu Sierra Leone 46 B4
Kori Creek inlet India 36 B5
Korinthiakos Kolpos sea chan. Greece see
  Corinth, Gulf of
Korinthos Greece see Corinth
Kőris-hegy hill Hungary 26 G1
Koritnik mt. Albania see Korçë
Köriyama Japan 45 F5
Korkuteli Turkey 27 N6
Korla China 42 F4
Kormakitis, Cape Cyprus 39 A2
Körmend Hungary 26 G1
Kornat nat. park Croatia 26 F3
Korneyevka Rus. Fed. 13 K6
Koro Côte d'Ivoire 46 C4
Koro i. Fiji 53 H3
Koro Mali 46 C3
Koroba P.N.G. 52 A4
Koröglu Dağları mts Turkey 27 O4
Köroğlu Tepesi mt. Turkey 34 D2
Korogwe Tanz. 49 D4
Koroneia, Limni l. Greece 27 J4
Koror Palau 41 F7
Koro Sea g. Fiji 53 H3
Korosten' Ukr. 13 F6
Korostyshiv Ukr. 13 F6
Koro Toro Chad 47 E3
Korpilahti Fin. 14 N5
Korpo Fin. 15 L6
Korppoo Fin. see Korpo
Korsakov Rus. Fed. 44 F3
Korsnäs Fin. 14 L5
Korsør Denmark 15 G9
Korsun'-Shevchenkivs'kyy Ukr. 13 F6
Korsun'-Shevchenkovskiy Ukr. see
  Korsun'-Shevchenkivs'kyy
Korsze Poland 17 R3
Kortesjärvi Fin. 14 M5
Korti Sudan 32 D6
Kortkeros Rus. Fed. 12 K3
Kortrijk Belgium 16 I5
Korvala Fin. 14 O3
Koryakskaya, Sopka vol. Rus. Fed. 29 Q4
Koryakskiy Khrebet mts Rus. Fed. 29 S3
Koryazhma Rus. Fed. 12 J3
Koryŏng S. Korea 45 C6
Kos i. Greece 27 L6
Kosa Rus. Fed. 12 L4
Kosam India 36 E4
Kosan N. Korea 45 B5
Kościan Poland 17 P4
Kosciusko, Mount Australia see
  Kosciuszko, Mount
Kosciuszko, Mount Australia 58 D6
Kosciuszko National Park Australia 58 D6
Köse Turkey 35 E2
Köseçobanlı Turkey 39 A1
Kosgi India 38 C2
Kosh-Agach Rus. Fed. 42 G2
Koshikijima-rettō is Japan 45 C7
Koshki Rus. Fed. 13 K5
Kosi Bay S. Africa 51 K4
Kosigi India 38 C3
Köslin Poland see Koszalin
Kosma r. Rus. Fed. 12 K2
Kosŏng N. Korea 45 C5
Kosova prov. Serbia see Kosovo
Kosovo prov. Serbia 27 I3
Kosovo-Metohija prov. Serbia see Kosovo
Kosovska Mitrovica Serbia 27 I3

Kosrae atoll Micronesia 74 G5
Kosta-Khetagurovo Rus. Fed. see Nazran'
Kostanay Kazakh. 30 F1
Kostenets Bulg. 27 J3
Kosti Sudan 32 D7
Kostinbrod Bulg. 27 J3
Kostino Rus. Fed. 28 J3
Kostomuksha Rus. Fed. 12 F2
Kostopil' Ukr. 13 E6
Kostroma Rus. Fed. 12 I4
Kostrzyn Poland 17 O4
Kostyantynivka Ukr. 13 H6
Kos'yu Rus. Fed. 11 R2
Koszalin Poland 17 P3
Kőszeg Hungary 26 G1
Kota Andhra Prad. India 38 D3
Kota Chhattisgarh India 37 E5
Kota Rajasthan India 36 C4
Kota Baharu Malaysia see Kota Bharu
Kotabaru Kalimantan Selatan Indon. 41 D8
Kota Bharu Malaysia 41 C6
Kot Addu Pak. 36 B3
Kota Kinabalu Sabah Malaysia 41 D7
Kotaparh India 38 D2
Kot Diji Pak. 36 B4
Kotel'nich Rus. Fed. 12 K4
Kotel'nikovo Rus. Fed. 13 I7
Kotel'nyy, Ostrov i. Rus. Fed. 29 O2
Kotgar India 38 D2
Kotgarh India 38 C3
Kothagudem India see Kottagudem
Kotido Uganda 47 G4
Kotikovo Rus. Fed. 44 D3
Kotka Fin. 15 O6
Kot Kapura India 36 C3
Kotkino Rus. Fed. 12 K2
Kotlas Rus. Fed. 12 J3
Kotli Pak. 36 C2
Kotlik U.S.A. 60 B3
Kotly Rus. Fed. 15 P7
Kotorkoshi Nigeria 46 D3
Kotovo Rus. Fed. 13 J6
Kotovsk Rus. Fed. 13 I5
Kotra India 36 C4
Kotra r. India 38 A3
Kotri r. India 38 D2
Kot Sarae Pak. 36 A5
Kottagudem India 38 D2
Kottarakara India 38 C4
Kottayam India 38 C4
Kotte Sri Lanka see
  Sri Jayewardenepura Kotte
Kotto r. Cent. Afr. Rep. 48 C3
Kotturu India 38 C3
Kotuy r. Rus. Fed. 29 L2
Kotzebue U.S.A. 60 B3
Kotzebue Sound sea chan. U.S.A. 60 B3
Kouango Cent. Afr. Rep. 48 C3
Koubia Guinea 46 B3
Koudougou Burkina 46 C3
Kouebokkeveld mts S. Africa 50 D7
Koufey Niger 46 E3
Koufonisi i. Greece 27 L7
Kougaberge mts S. Africa 50 F7
Koukourou r. Cent. Afr. Rep. 48 B3
Kouliikoro Mali 46 C3
Koumac New Caledonia 53 G4
Koumpentoum Senegal 46 B3
Koundâra Guinea 46 B3
Koupéla Burkina 46 C3
Kourou Fr. Guiana 69 H2
Kouroussa Guinea 46 C3
Kousséri Cameroon 47 E3
Koutiala Mali 46 C3
Kouvola Fin. 15 O6
Kovallberget Sweden 14 J4
Kovdor Rus. Fed. 14 R3
Kovdozero, Ozero l. Rus. Fed. 14 R3
Kovel' Ukr. 13 E6
Kovernino Rus. Fed. 12 I4
Kovilpatti India 38 C4
Kovno Lith. see Kaunas
Kovriga, Gora hill Rus. Fed. 12 K2
Kovrov Rus. Fed. 12 I4
Kovylkino Rus. Fed. 13 I5
Kowanyama Australia 56 C2
Kowloon H.K. China 73 H4
Kowŏn N. Korea 45 B5
Kōyama-misaki pt Japan 45 C6
Koycegiz Turkey 27 M6
Koygorodok Rus. Fed. 12 K3
Koyna Reservoir India 38 B2
Koyuk U.S.A. 60 B3
Koyukuk r. U.S.A. 60 C3
Koyulhisar Turkey 34 E2
Korong Vale Australia 58 A6
Koza Turkey 34 D3
Kozan Turkey 34 D3
Kozani Greece 27 I4
Kozara mts Bos.-Herz. 26 G2
Kozara nat. park Bos.-Herz. 26 G2
Kozarska Dubica Bos.-Herz. see
  Bosanska Dubica
Kozelets' Ukr. 13 F6
Kozel'sk Rus. Fed. 13 G5
Kozhikode India see Calicut
Kozhva Rus. Fed. 12 M2
Kozlu Turkey 27 N4
Koz'modem'yansk Rus. Fed. 12 J4
Kožuf mts Greece/Macedonia 27 J4
Kōzu-shima i. Japan 45 E6
Kozyatyn Ukr. 13 F6
Kpalimé Togo 46 D4
Kpandae Ghana 46 C4
Kpungan Pass India/Myanmar 37 I4
Krabi Thai. 38 I6
Krâchéh Cambodia 31 J5
Kragerø Norway 15 F7
Kragujevac Serbia 27 I2
Krakatau i. Indon. see Rakata
Krakau Poland see Kraków
Kraków Poland 17 Q5
Kralendijk Neth. Antilles 67 K6
Kramators'k Ukr. 13 H6
Kramfors Sweden 14 J5
Kranidi Greece 27 J6
Kranj Slovenia 26 F1
Kranskop S. Africa 51 J5
Krasavino Rus. Fed. 12 J3
Krasilov Ukr. see Krasyliv
Krasino Rus. Fed. 28 G2
Kraskino Rus. Fed. 44 C4
Krāslava Latvia 15 O9
Krasnaya Gorbatka Rus. Fed. 12 I5
Krasnaya Zarya Rus. Fed. 13 H5
Krasnoarmeysk Ukr. see Krasnoarmiys'k
Krasnoarmeysk Rus. Fed. 13 J6
Krasnoarmiys'k Ukr. 13 H6
Krasnoborsk Rus. Fed. 12 J3
Krasnodar Rus. Fed. 34 E1
Krasnodar Kray admin. div. Rus. Fed. see
  Krasnodarskiy Kray
Krasnodarskiy Kray admin. div. Rus. Fed.
  34 E1
Krasnodon Ukr. 13 H6

Krasnogorodskoye Rus. Fed. 15 P8
Krasnogorsk Rus. Fed. 44 F2
Krasnogorskoye Rus. Fed. 12 L4
Krasnogvardeysk Uzbek. see Bulung'ur
Krasnogvardeyskoye Rus. Fed. 13 I7
Krasnohrad Ukr. 13 G6
Krasnohvardiys'ke Ukr. 13 G7
Krasnokamsk Rus. Fed. 11 R4
Krasnoperekops'k Ukr. 13 G7
Krasnopol'ye Rus. Fed. 44 F2
Krasnorechenskiy Rus. Fed. 44 D3
Krasnoselkup Rus. Fed. 11 S4
Krasnoslobodsk Rus. Fed. 13 I5
Krasnotur'insk Rus. Fed. 11 S4
Krasnoufimsk Rus. Fed. 11 R4
Krasnovishersk Rus. Fed. 11 R3
Krasnovodsk Turkm. see Türkmenbaşy
Krasnovodsk, Mys pt Turkm. 35 I3
Krasnovodskoye Plato plat. Turkm. 35 I2
Krasnoyarovo Rus. Fed. 44 C2
Krasnoyarsk Rus. Fed. 28 K4
Krasnoyarskoye Vodokhranilishche resr
  Rus. Fed. 42 G2
Krasnoye Lipetskaya Oblast' Rus. Fed.
  13 H5
Krasnoye Respublika Kalmykiya - Khalm'g-
  Tangch Rus. Fed. see Ulan Erge
Krasnoznamenskiy Kazakh. see Yegindykol'
Krasnoznamenskoye Kazakh. see
  Yegindykol'
Krasnyy Rus. Fed. 13 F5
Krasnyy Chikoy Rus. Fed. 43 J2
Krasnyye Baki Rus. Fed. 12 J4
Krasnyy Kamyshanik Rus. Fed. see
  Komsomol'skiy
Krasnyy Kholm Rus. Fed. 12 H4
Krasnyy Kut Rus. Fed. 13 J6
Krasnyy Luch Ukr. 13 H6
Krasnyy Lyman Ukr. 13 H6
Krasnyy Yar Rus. Fed. 13 K6
Krasyliv Ukr. 13 E6
Kratie Cambodia see Krâchéh
Kraulshavn Greenland see Nuussuaq
Kraynovka Rus. Fed. 35 G2
Krefeld Germany 17 K5
Kremenchug Ukr. see Kremenchuk
Kremenchugskoye Vodokhranilishche resr
  Ukr. see
  Kremenchuts'ka Vodoskhovyshche
Kremenchuk Ukr. 13 G6
Kremenchuts'ka Vodoskhovyshche resr
  Ukr. 13 G6
Křemešník hill Czech Rep. 17 O6
Kremges Rus. Fed. see Svitlovods'k
Kremmydi, Akrotirio pt Greece 27 J6
Krems Austria see Krems an der Donau
Krems an der Donau Austria 17 O6
Kresta, Zaliv g. Rus. Fed. 29 T3
Krestsy Rus. Fed. 12 G4
Kretinga Lith. 15 L9
Kreva Belarus 15 O9
Kribi Cameroon 46 D4
Krichev Belarus see Krychaw
Kriel S. Africa 51 I4
Krikellos Greece 27 I5
Krishna India 38 C2
Krishna r. India 38 D2
Krishnagiri India 38 C3
Krishnanagar India 37 G5
Krishnaraja Sagara l. India 38 C3
Kristiania Norway see Oslo
Kristiansand Norway 15 E7
Kristianstad Sweden 15 I8
Kristiansund Norway 14 E5
Kristiinankaupunki Fin. see Kristinestad
Kristinehamn Sweden 15 I7
Kristinestad Fin. 14 L5
Kristinopol' Ukr. see Chervonohrad
Kriti i. Greece see Crete
Kritiko Pelagos sea Greece 27 K6
Krivoy Rog Ukr. see Kryvyy Rih
Križevci Croatia 26 G1
Krk i. Croatia 26 F2
Krkonošský národní park nat. park
  Czech Rep./Poland 17 O5
Krokom Sweden 14 I5
Krokstranda Norway 14 I3
Krokstranda Norway 14 I3
Krolevets' Ukr. 13 G6
Kronach Germany 17 M5
Kronoby Fin. 14 M5
Kronprins Christian Land reg. Greenland
  77 I1
Kronprins Frederik Bjerge nunataks
  Greenland 61 O3
Kronshtadt Romania see Braşov
Kronstadt Rus. Fed. see Kronshtadt
Kroonstad S. Africa 51 H4
Kropotkin Rus. Fed. 35 F1
Krosno Poland 13 D6
Krotoszyn Poland 17 P5
Kruger National Park S. Africa 51 J2
Kruglikovo Rus. Fed. 44 D2
Kruglyakov Rus. Fed. see Oktyabr'skiy
Krui Indon. 41 C8
Kruisfontein S. Africa 50 G8
Kruja Albania see Krujë
Krujë Albania 27 H4
Krumovgrad Bulg. 27 K4
Krungkao Thai. see Ayutthaya
Krung Thep Thai. see Bangkok
Krupa Bos.-Herz. see Bosanska Krupa
Krupa na Uni Bos.-Herz. see
  Bosanska Krupa
Krupki Belarus 13 F5
Krusenstern, Cape U.S.A. 60 B3
Kruševac Serbia 27 I3
Kruševo Macedonia 27 I4
Krychaw Belarus 13 F5
Krylov Seamount sea feature
  N. Atlantic Ocean 72 G4
Krym' pen. Ukr. see Crimea
Krymsk Rus. Fed. 13 H7
Krymskaya Rus. Fed. see Krymsk
Krym's'kyy Pivostriv pen. Ukr. see Crimea
Krystynopol' Ukr. see Chervonohrad
Kryvyy Rih Ukr. 13 G7
Ksabi Alg. 22 D5
Ksar Boukhari Alg. see Ksar el Boukhari
Ksar Chellala Alg. 25 H6
Ksar el Boukhari Alg. 25 H6
Ksar el Kebir Morocco 25 D6
Ksar-es-Souk Morocco see Er Rachidia
Ksenofontova Rus. Fed. 11 R3
Kshirpai India 37 F5
Ksour Essaf Tunisia 26 D7
Kstovo Rus. Fed. 12 J4
Ku', Jabal al Hill Saudi Arabia 32 G4
Kuaidamao China see Tonghua
Kuala Dungun Malaysia see Dungun
Kuala Kangsar Malaysia 41 C6
Kuala Lipis Malaysia 41 C6
Kuala Lumpur Malaysia 41 C7
Kuala Terengganu Malaysia 41 C7
Kuandian China 44 B4
Kuantan Malaysia 41 C7
Kuba Azer. see Quba
Kuban' r. Rus. Fed. 13 H7
Kubār Syria 35 F4
Kubaybāt Syria 39 C2
Kubaysah Iraq 35 F4
Kubenskoye, Ozero l. Rus. Fed. 12 H4

Kubrat Bulg. 27 L3
Kuchema Rus. Fed. 12 I2
Kuching Sarawak Malaysia 41 D7
Kucing Sarawak Malaysia see Kuching
Kuçovë Albania 27 H4
Kuda India 36 B5
Kudal India 38 B3
Kudat Sabah Malaysia 41 D7
Kudligi India 38 C3
Kudremukh mt. India 38 B3
Kufstein Austria 17 N7
Kugaaruk Canada 61 J3
Kugesi Rus. Fed. 12 J4
Kugk Lhai China 37 G3
Kugluktuk Canada 60 G3
Kugmallit Bay Canada 77 A2
Kuhanbokano mt. China 37 E3
Kühdasht Iran 35 G4
Kühhä-ye Zagros mts Iran see
  Zagros Mountains
Kühin Iran 35 H3
Kuhmo Fin. 14 P4
Kuhmoinen Fin. 15 N6
Kührän, Küh-e mt. Iran 33 I4
Kuis Namibia 50 C3
Kuiseb watercourse Namibia 50 B2
Kuito Angola 49 B5
Kuitun China see Kuytun
Kuivaniemi Fin. 14 N4
Kujang N. Korea 45 B5
Kuji Japan 45 F4
Kujū-san vol. Japan 45 C6
Kukan Rus. Fed. 44 D2
Kukës Albania 27 I3
Kukesi Albania see Kukës
Kukmor Rus. Fed. 12 K4
Kukshi India 36 C5
Kukunuru India 38 D3
Kula Turkey 27 M5
Kulaisila India 37 F5
Kula Kangri mt. China/Bhutan 37 G3
Kulandy Kazakh. 28 G5
Kular Rus. Fed. 29 O2
Kuldīga Latvia 15 L8
Kuldja China see Yining
Kul'dur Rus. Fed. 44 C2
Kule Botswana 50 E2
Kulebaki Rus. Fed. 13 I5
Kulgera Australia 55 F6
Kulikovo Rus. Fed. 12 J3
Kulin Australia 55 B8
Kulja Australia 55 B7
Kulkyne watercourse Australia 58 B3
Kullu India 36 D3
Kulmbach Germany 17 M5
Külob Tajik. 33 K2
Kuloy Rus. Fed. 12 I3
Kuloy r. Rus. Fed. 12 I2
Kulp Turkey 35 F3
Kul'sary Kazakh. 30 E2
Kulu India see Kullu
Kulu Turkey 34 D3
Kulunda Rus. Fed. 42 D2
Kulundinskaya Step' plain
  Kazakh./Rus. Fed. 42 D2
Kulundinskoye, Ozero salt l. Rus. Fed.
  42 D2
Kulusuk Greenland 61 O3
Kulwin Australia 57 C7
Kulyab Tajik. see Külob
Kuma r. Rus. Fed. 13 J7
Kumagaya Japan 45 E5
Kumalar Dağı mts Turkey 27 N5
Kumamoto Japan 45 C6
Kumano Japan 45 E6
Kumanovo Macedonia 27 I3
Kumara Rus. Fed. 44 B2
Kumasi Ghana 46 C4
Kumayri Armenia see Gyumri
Kumba Cameroon 46 D4
Kumbakonam India 38 C4
Kümbet Turkey 27 N5
Kumbharli Ghat mt. India 38 B2
Kumbla India 38 B3
Kumchuru Botswana 50 F2
Kum-Dag Turkm. see Gumdag
Kumdah Saudi Arabia 32 G5
Kumel well Iran 35 I4
Kumeny Rus. Fed. 12 K4
Kumertau Rus. Fed. 28 G4
Kumgang-san mt. N. Korea 45 B5
Kumguri India 37 G4
Kumhwa S. Korea 45 B5
Kumi S. Korea 45 C6
Kumi Uganda 47 G4
Kumla Sweden 15 I7
Kumlu Turkey 39 C1
Kumo Nigeria 46 E3
Kümö-do i. S. Korea 45 B6
Kums Namibia 50 D5
Kumta India 38 B3
Kumu Dem. Rep. Congo 48 C3
Kumukh Rus. Fed. 35 G2
Kumund India 38 D1
Kumylzhenskaya Rus. Fed. see
  Kumylzhenskiy
Kumylzhenskiy Rus. Fed. 13 I6
Kunar r. Afgh. 36 B2
Kunashir, Ostrov i. Rus. Fed. 44 G3
Kunashirskiy Proliv sea chan.
  Japan/Rus. Fed. see Nemuro-kaikyō
Kunchuk Tso salt l. China 37 E2
Kunda Estonia 15 O7
Kunda India 37 E4
Kundapura India 38 B3
Kundelungu, Parc National de nat. park
  Dem. Rep. Congo 49 C5
Kundelungu Ouest, Parc National de
  nat. park Dem. Rep. Congo 49 C5
Kundia India 38 B3
Kunduz Afgh. 36 B1
Kunene r. Angola see Cunene
Kuneneng admin. div. Botswana see
  Kweneng
Künes China see Xinyuan
Kungälv Sweden 15 G8
Kungsbacka Sweden 15 H8
Kungshamn Sweden 15 G7
Kungu Dem. Rep. Congo 48 B3
Kungur mt. China see Kongur Shan
Kungur Rus. Fed. 11 R4
Kuni r. India 38 C2
Kuni i. New Caledonia see Pins, Île des
Kunigai India 38 C3
Kunimi-dake mt. Japan 45 C6
Kunlavav India 36 B5
Kunlong Myanmar 36 D1
Kunlun Shan mts China 36 D1
Kunlun Shankou pass China 37 H2
Kunming China 42 I7
Kunsan S. Korea 45 B6
Kununurra Australia 54 E3
Kun'ya Rus. Fed. 12 G4
Kunya-Urgench Turkm. see Köneürgench
Kuohijärvi l. Fin. 15 N6
Kuolayarvi Rus. Fed. 14 P3
Kuopio Fin. 14 O5
Kuortane Fin. 14 M5
Kupa r. Croatia/Slovenia 26 G2

Kupang Indon. 41 E9
Kupari India 37 F5
Kupiškis Lith. 15 N9
Kupreanof Island U.S.A. 60 E4
Kupwara India 36 C2
Kup"yans'k Ukr. 13 H6
Kuqa China 42 E4
Kur r. Rus. Fed. 44 D2
Kura r. Georgia 35 G2
Kuragino Rus. Fed. 42 G2
Kurakh Rus. Fed. 13 J8
Kurama Range mts Asia 33 K1
Kuraminskiy Khrebet mts Asia see Kurama Range
Kurashiki Japan 45 D6
Kurasia India 37 E5
Kurayn i. Saudi Arabia 35 H6
Kurayoshi Japan 45 D6
Kurchatov Rus. Fed. 13 G6
Kurchum Kazakh. 42 E3
Kürdämir Azer. 35 H2
Kŭrdzhali Bulg. 27 K4
Kure Japan 45 D6
Küre Turkey 34 D2
Kure Atoll U.S.A. 74 I4
Kuressaare Estonia 15 M7
Kurgal'dzhino Kazakh. see Korgalzhyn
Kurgal'dzhinskiy Kazakh. see Korgalzhyn
Kurgan Rus. Fed. 28 H4
Kurganinsk Rus. Fed. 35 F1
Kurgannaya Rus. Fed. see Kurganinsk
Kurgantyube Tajik. see Qŭrghonteppa
Kuri India 36 B4
Kuria Muria Islands Oman see Ḥalāniyāt, Juzur al
Kuridala Australia 56 C4
Kurigram Bangl. 37 G4
Kurikka Fin. 14 M5
Kuril Basin sea feature Sea of Okhotsk 74 F2
Kuril Islands Rus. Fed. 44 H3
Kurilovka Rus. Fed. 13 K6
Kuril'sk Rus. Fed. 44 G3
Kuril'skiye Ostrova is Rus. Fed. see Kuril Islands
Kuril Trench sea feature N. Pacific Ocean 74 F3
Kurkino Rus. Fed. 13 H5
Kurmashkino Kazakh. see Kurchum
Kurmuk Sudan 32 D7
Kurnool India 38 C3
Kuroiso Japan 45 F5
Kurovskiy Rus. Fed. 44 B1
Kurow N.Z. 59 C7
Kurram Pak. 36 B2
Kurri Kurri Australia 58 E4
Kursavka Rus. Fed. 35 F1
Kürshim Kazakh. see Kurchum
Kurshskiy Zaliv b. Lith./Rus. Fed. see Courland Lagoon
Kuršių marios b. Lith./Rus. Fed. see Courland Lagoon
Kursk Rus. Fed. 13 H6
Kurskaya Rus. Fed. 35 G1
Kurskiy Zaliv b. Lith./Rus. Fed. see Courland Lagoon
Kurşunlu Turkey 34 D2
Kurtalan Turkey 35 F3
Kurtoğlu Burnu pt Turkey 27 M6
Kurtpınar Turkey 39 B1
Kurucaşile Turkey 34 D2
Kuruçay Turkey 34 E3
Kurukshetra India 36 D3
Kuruktag mts China 42 F4
Kuruman S. Africa 50 F4
Kuruman watercourse S. Africa 50 E4
Kurume Japan 45 C6
Kurumkan Rus. Fed. 43 K2
Kurunegala Sri Lanka 38 D5
Kurupam India 38 D2
Kurush, Jebel hills Sudan 32 D5
Kur'ya Rus. Fed. 11 R3
Kuryk Kazakh. 35 H2
Kuşadası Turkey 27 L6
Kuşadası Körfezi b. Turkey 27 L6
Kusaie atoll Micronesia see Kosrae
Kusary Azer. see Qusar
Kuşcenneti nature res. Turkey 39 B1
Kuschke Nature Reserve S. Africa 51 I3
Kuş Gölü l. Turkey 27 L4
Kushalgarh India 36 C5
Kushchevskaya Rus. Fed. 13 H7
Kushimoto Japan 45 D6
Kushiro Japan 44 G4
Kushka Turkm. see Serhetabat
Kushkopola Rus. Fed. 12 J3
Kushmurun Kazakh. 30 F1
Kushtagi India 38 C3
Kushtia Bangl. 37 G5
Kuskan Turkey 39 A1
Kuskokwim r. U.S.A. 60 B3
Kuskokwim Bay U.S.A. 60 B4
Kuskokwim Mountains U.S.A. 60 C3
Kuşluyan Turkey see Gölköy
Kusŏng N. Korea 45 B5
Kustanay Kazakh. see Kostanay
Küstence Romania see Constanța
Kustia Bangl. see Kushtia
Kut Iran 35 H5
Küt 'Abdollāh Iran 35 H5
Kütahya Turkey 27 M5
K'ut'aisi Georgia 35 F2
Kut-al-Imara Iraq see Al Kūt
Kutan Rus. Fed. 13 J7
Kutaraja Indon. see Banda Aceh
Kutayfat Ţurayf vol. Saudi Arabia 39 D4
Kutch, Gulf of India see Kachchh, Gulf of
Kutch, Rann of marsh India see Kachchh, Rann of
Kutchan Japan 44 F4
Kutina Croatia 26 G2
Kutjevo Croatia 26 G2
Kutno Poland 17 Q4
Kutru India 38 D2
Kutu Dem. Rep. Congo 48 B4
Kutubdia Island Bangl. 37 G5
Kutum Sudan 47 F3
Kutztown PA U.S.A. 64 D2
Kuujjua r. Canada 60 G2
Kuujjuaq Canada 61 L4
Kuujjuarapik Canada 61 K4
Kuusamo Fin. 14 P4
Kuusankoski Fin. 15 O6
Kuvango Angola 49 B5
Kuvshinovo Rus. Fed. 12 G4
Kuwait country Asia 32 G4
Kuwait Kuwait 35 G5
Kuwajleen atoll Marshall Is see Kwajalein
Kuybyshev Novosibirskaya Oblast' Rus. Fed. 28 I4
Kuybyshev Respublika Tatarstan Rus. Fed. see Bolgar
Kuybyshev Samarskaya Oblast' Rus. Fed. see Samara
Kuybysheve Ukr. 13 H7
Kuybyshevka-Vostochnaya Rus. Fed. see Belogorsk
Kuybyshevskoye Vodokhranilishche resr Rus. Fed. 13 K5
Kuyeda Rus. Fed. 11 R4
Kuygan Kazakh. 42 C3
Kuytun China 42 E4
Kuytun Rus. Fed. 42 I2
Kuyucak Turkey 27 M6
Kuzino Rus. Fed. 11 R4
Kuznechnoye Rus. Fed. 15 P6
Kuznetsk Rus. Fed. 13 J5
Kuznetsovo Rus. Fed. 44 E3
Kuznetsovs'k Ukr. 13 E6
Kuzovatovo Rus. Fed. 13 J5
Kvænangen sea chan. Norway 14 L1
Kvaløya i. Norway 14 K2
Kvalsund Norway 14 M1
Kvarnerić sea chan. Croatia 26 F2
Kvitøya ice feature Svalbard 28 E2
Kwa r. Dem. Rep. Congo see Kasaï
Kwabhaca S. Africa see Mount Frere
Kwadelen atoll Marshall Is see Kwajalein
Kwajalein atoll Marshall Is 74 H5
Kwale Nigeria 46 D4
KwaMashu S. Africa 51 J5
KwaMhlanga S. Africa 51 I3
Kwa Mtoro Tanz. 49 D4
Kwangch'ŏn S. Korea 45 B5
Kwangchow China see Guangzhou
Kwangju S. Korea 45 B6
Kwangsi Chuang Autonomous Region aut. reg. China see Guangxi Zhuangzu Zizhiqu
Kwangtung prov. China see Guangdong
Kwanmo-bong mt. N. Korea 44 C4
Kwanobuhle S. Africa 51 G7
KwaNojoli S. Africa 51 G7
Kwanonqubela S. Africa 51 H7
KwaNonzame S. Africa 50 G6
Kwanza r. Angola see Cuanza
Kwatinidubu S. Africa 51 H7
KwaZamokuhle S. Africa 51 I4
KwaZamukucinga S. Africa 50 G7
Kwazamuxolo S. Africa 50 G6
KwaZanele S. Africa 51 I4
KwaZulu-Natal prov. S. Africa 51 J5
Kweichow prov. China see Guizhou
Kweiyang China see Guiyang
Kwekwe Zimbabwe 49 C5
Kweneng admin. dist. Botswana 50 G2
Kwenge r. Dem. Rep. Congo 49 B4
Kwezi-Naledi S. Africa 51 H6
Kwidzyn Poland 17 Q4
Kwikila P.N.G. 52 E2
Kwilu r. Angola/Dem. Rep. Congo 49 B4
Kwoka mt. Indon. 41 F8
Kyabra Australia 57 C5
Kyabram Australia 58 B6
Kyakhta Rus. Fed. 42 J2
Kyalite Australia 58 A5
Kyancutta Australia 55 F8
Kyangin Myanmar 37 I6
Kyangngoin China 37 H3
Kyaukpadaung Myanmar 37 H5
Kyaukpyu Myanmar 37 H6
Kyaukse Myanmar 37 I5
Kyauktaw Myanmar 37 H5
Kybartai Lith. 15 M9
Kyêbxang Co l. China 37 G2
Kyela Tanz. 49 D4
Kyelang India 36 D2
Kyidaunggan Myanmar 37 I6
Kyiv Ukr. see Kiev
Kyklades is Greece see Cyclades
Kyle of Lochalsh U.K. 20 D3
Kyllini mt. Greece 27 J6
Kymi Greece 27 K5
Kymis, Akrotirio pt Greece 27 K5
Kyneton Australia 58 B6
Kynuna Australia 56 C4
Kyoga, Lake Uganda 48 D3
Kyōga-misaki pt Japan 45 D6
Kyogle Australia 58 F2
Kyŏngju S. Korea 45 C6
Kyōto Japan 45 D6
Kyparissia Greece 27 I6
Kypros country Asia see Cyprus
Kypshak, Ozero salt l. Kazakh. 31 F1
Kyra Rus. Fed. 43 K3
Kyra Panagia i. Greece 27 K5
Kyrenia Cyprus 39 A2
Kyrenia Mountains Cyprus see Pentadaktylos Range
Kyrgyz Ala-Too mts Kazakh./Kyrg. see Kirghiz Range
Kyrgyzstan country Asia 31 G2
Kyrksæterøra Norway 14 F5
Kyrta Rus. Fed. 11 R3
Kyssa Rus. Fed. 12 J2
Kytalyktakh Rus. Fed. 29 O3
Kythira i. Greece 27 J6
Kythnos i. Greece 27 K6
Kyunglung China 36 E3
Kyunhla Myanmar 37 H5
Kyuquot Canada 62 B1
Kyurdamir Azer. see Kürdämir
Kyūshū i. Japan 45 C7
Kyushu-Palau Ridge sea feature N. Pacific Ocean 74 F4
Kyustendil Bulg. 27 J3
Kywong Australia 58 C5
Kyyev Ukr. see Kiev
Kyyiv Ukr. see Kiev
Kyyivs'ke Vodoskhovyshche resr Ukr. 13 F6
Kyyjärvi Fin. 14 N5
Kyzyl Rus. Fed. 42 G2
Kyzyl-Burun Azer. see Siyäzän
Kyzyl-Kiya Kyrg. see Kyzyl-Kyya
Kyzylkum, Peski des. Kazakh./Uzbek. see Kyzylkum Desert
Kyzylkum Desert Kazakh./Uzbek. 30 F2
Kyzyl-Kyya Kyrg. 42 C4
Kyzyl-Mazhalyk Rus. Fed. 42 G2
Kyzylorda Kazakh. 42 B4
Kyzylrabot Tajik. see Qizilrabot
Kyzylsay Kazakh. 35 I2
Kyzylysor Kazakh. 35 H1
Kyzylzhar Kazakh. 42 B3
Kzyl-Dzhar Kazakh. see Kyzylzhar
Kzyl-Orda Kazakh. see Kyzylorda
Kzyltu Kazakh. see Kishkenekol'

L

Laagri Estonia 15 N7
La Angostura, Presa de resr Mex. 66 F5
Laanila Fin. 14 O2
Laascaanood Somalia 48 E3
La Ascensión, Bahía de b. Mex. 67 G5
Laasgoray Somalia 48 E2
Laâyoune W. Sahara 46 B2
La Bahía, Islas de is Hond. 67 G5
La Banda Arg. 70 D3
Labasa Fiji 53 H3
La Baule-Escoublac France 24 C3
Labazhskoye Rus. Fed. 12 L2
Labé Guinea 46 B3
La Bénoué, Parc National de nat. park Cameroon 47 E4
Labinsk Rus. Fed. 13 I7
La Boucle du Baoulé, Parc National de nat. park Mali 46 C3
Labouheyre France 24 D4
Laboulaye Arg. 70 D4
Labrador reg. Canada 61 L4
Labrador City Canada 61 L4
Labrador Sea Canada/Greenland 61 M3
Lábrea Brazil 68 F5
Labudalin China see Ergun
Labuhanbilik Indon. 41 C7
Labuna Indon. 41 E8
Labyrinth, Lake salt flat Australia 57 A6
Labytnangi Rus. Fed. 28 H3
Laç Albania 27 H4
La Cabrera, Sierra de mts Spain 25 C2
La Calle Alg. see El Kala
La Cañiza Spain see A Cañiza
La Capelle France 24 F2
La Carlota Arg. 70 D4
La Carolina Spain 25 E4
Lăcăuți, Vârful mt. Romania 27 L2
Laccadive, Minicoy and Amindivi Islands union terr. India see Lakshadweep
Laccadive Islands India 38 B4
Lac du Bonnet Canada 63 H1
Lacedaemon Greece see Sparti
La Ceiba Hond. 67 G5
Lacepede Bay Australia 57 B8
Lacepede Islands Australia 54 C4
Lacha, Ozero l. Rus. Fed. 12 H3
Lachlan r. Australia 58 A5
La Chorrera Panama 67 I7
Lachute Canada 63 M2
Laçın Azer. 35 G3
La Ciotat France 24 G5
Lac La Biche Canada 60 G4
Lac la Martre Canada see Whatì
Lacombe Canada 62 E1
La Comoé, Parc National de nat. park Côte d'Ivoire 46 C4
Laconi Sardinia Italy 26 C5
Laconia NH U.S.A. 64 F1
La Coruña Spain see A Coruña
La Coubre, Pointe de pt France 24 D4
La Crosse WI U.S.A. 63 I3
La Cruz Mex. 66 C4
La Cuesta Mex. 62 G6
La Culebra, Sierra de mts Spain 25 C3
Ladainha Brazil 71 C2
Ladakh reg. Jammu and Kashmir 36 D2
Ladakh Range mts India 36 D2
La Demanda, Sierra de mts Spain 25 E2
La Déroute, Passage de strait Channel Is/France 19 E9
Ladik Turkey 34 D2
Ladnun India 36 C4
Ladoga, Lake Rus. Fed. 12 F3
Ladozhskoye Ozero l. Rus. Fed. see Ladoga, Lake
Ladrones terr. N. Pacific Ocean see Northern Mariana Islands
Ladu mt. India 37 H4
Ladva-Vetka Rus. Fed. 12 G3
Ladybank U.K. 20 F4
Ladybrand S. Africa 51 H5
Lady Frere S. Africa 51 H6
Lady Grey S. Africa 51 H6
Ladysmith S. Africa 51 I5
Ladzhanurges Georgia see Lajanurpekhi
Lae P.N.G. 52 E2
Lærdalsøyri Norway 15 E6
La Esmeralda Bol. 68 F8
Læsø i. Denmark 15 G8
Lafayette Alg. see Bougaa
Lafayette IN U.S.A. 63 J3
Lafayette LA U.S.A. 63 I5
Lafia Nigeria 46 D4
Lafiagi Nigeria 46 D4
La Flèche France 24 D3
Laforge Canada 61 K4
Lāft Iran 33 I4
La Galite i. Tunisia 26 C6
La Galite, Canal de sea chan. Tunisia 26 C6
Lagan' Rus. Fed. 13 J7
Lagan r. U.K. 21 G3
La Garamba, Parc National de nat. park Dem. Rep. Congo 48 C3
Lagarto Brazil 69 K6
Lågen r. Norway 15 G7
Lagg U.K. 20 D5
Laggan U.K. 20 E3
Lagh Bor watercourse Kenya/Somalia 48 E3
Laghouat Alg. 22 E5
Lagkor Co salt l. China 37 F2
Lago Agrio Ecuador 68 C3
Lagoa Santa Brazil 71 C2
Lagoa Vermelha Brazil 71 A5
Lagodekhi Georgia 35 G2
Lagolândia Brazil 71 A1
La Gomera i. Canary Is 46 B2
La Gonâve, Île de i. Haiti 67 J5
Lagos Nigeria 46 D4
Lagos Port. 25 B5
Lagosa Tanz. 49 C4
La Grande U.S.A. 62 D2
La Grande 2, Réservoir resr Canada 61 K4
La Grande 3, Réservoir resr Canada 61 K4
La Grande 4, Réservoir resr Que. Canada 61 K4
La Grange Australia 54 C4
La Grange CA U.S.A. 65 B2
La Grange GA U.S.A. 63 J5
La Gran Sabana plat. Venez. 68 F2
La Grita Venez. 68 D2
La Guajira, Península de pen. Col. 68 D1
Laguna Brazil 71 A5
Laguna Dam Arizona/California U.S.A. 65 E4
Laguna Mountains CA U.S.A. 65 D4
Lagunas Chile 70 C2
Laguna San Rafael, Parque Nacional nat. park Chile 70 B7
Laha China 44 B2
La Habana Cuba see Havana
La Habra CA U.S.A. 65 D4
Lahad Datu Sabah Malaysia 41 D7
La Hague, Cap de c. France 24 D2
Laharpur India 36 E4
Lahat Indon. 41 C8
Lahe Myanmar 37 H4
Lahemaa rahvuspark nat. park Estonia 15 N7
La Hève, Cap de c. France 19 H9
Laḩij Yemen 32 F7
Lāhījān Iran 35 H3
Laholm Sweden 15 H8
Lahore Pak. 33 L3
Lahri Pak. 36 B3
Lahti Fin. 15 N6
Laï Chad 47 E4
Laibach Slovenia see Ljubljana
Laidley Australia 58 F1
L'Aigle France 24 E2
Laihia Fin. 14 M5
Laimakuri India 37 H4
Laimos, Akrotirio pt Greece 27 J5
Laingsburg S. Africa 50 E7
Lainioälven r. Sweden 14 M3
L'Aïr, Massif de mts Niger 46 D3
Lairg U.K. 20 E2
Laishevo Rus. Fed. 12 K5
Laitila Fin. 15 L6
Laives Italy 26 D1
Laiwu China 43 L5
Laiyang China 43 M5
Laizhou China 43 L5
Laizhou Wan b. China 43 L5
Lajamanu Australia 54 E4
Lajanurpekhi Georgia 35 F2
Lajeado Brazil 71 A5
Lajes Rio Grande do Norte Brazil 69 K5
Lajes Santa Catarina Brazil 71 A4
La Junta Mex. 62 F6
La Junta U.S.A. 62 G4
La Juventud, Isla de i. Cuba 67 H4
Lakadiya India 36 B5
L'Akagera, Parc National de nat. park Rwanda see Akagera National Park
La Kagera, Parc National de nat. park Rwanda see Akagera National Park
Lakeba i. Fiji 53 I3
Lake Bardawil Reserve nature res. Egypt 39 A4
Lake Bolac Australia 58 A6
Lake Cargelligo Australia 58 C4
Lake Cathie Australia 58 F3
Lake Charles U.S.A. 63 I5
Lake City FL U.S.A. 63 K5
Lake Clark National Park and Preserve U.S.A. 60 C3
Lake District National Park U.K. 18 D4
Lake Eyre National Park Australia 57 B6
Lakefield Australia 56 D2
Lakefield National Park Australia 56 D2
Lake Gairdner National Park Australia 57 B7
Lake George NY U.S.A. 64 E1
Lake Grace Australia 55 B8
Lake Harbour Canada see Kimmirut
Lake Havasu City AZ U.S.A. 65 E3
Lakehurst NJ U.S.A. 64 D2
Lake Isabella CA U.S.A. 65 C3
Lake King Australia 55 B8
Lakeland FL U.S.A. 63 K6
Lakemba i. Fiji see Lakeba
Lake Nash Australia 56 B4
Lake Paringa N.Z. 59 B6
Lake Pleasant NY U.S.A. 64 D1
Lakeport CA U.S.A. 65 A1
Lake Providence U.S.A. 63 I5
Lakes Entrance Australia 58 D6
Lakeside VA U.S.A. 64 C4
Lake Tabourie Australia 58 E5
Lake Tekapo N.Z. 59 C7
Lake Torrens National Park Australia 57 B6
Lakeview OR U.S.A. 62 C3
Lakewood NJ U.S.A. 64 D2
Lakewood NY U.S.A. 64 B1
Lakha India 36 B4
Lakhdenpokh'ya Rus. Fed. 14 Q6
Lakhimpur Assam India see North Lakhimpur
Lakhimpur Uttar Prad. India 36 E4
Lakhisarai India 37 F4
Lakhish r. Israel 39 B4
Lakhnadon India 36 D5
Lakhpat India 36 B5
Lakhtar India 36 B5
Lakki Pak. 33 L3
Lakonikos Kolpos b. Greece 27 J6
Lakor i. Indon. 54 E2
Lakota Côte d'Ivoire 46 C4
Laksefjorden sea chan. Norway 14 O1
Lakselv Norway 14 N1
Lakshadweep is India see Laccadive Islands
Lakshadweep union terr. India 38 B4
Lakshettipet India 38 C2
Lakshmipur Bangl. 37 G5
Laksmipur Bangl. see Lakshmipur
Lalaghat India 37 H4
La Laguna, Picacho de mt. Mex. 66 B4
Lalbara India 38 D1
L'Alcora Spain 25 F3
Lalganj India 37 F4
Lālī Iran 35 H4
La Ligua Chile 70 B4
Laliki Indon. 54 D1
Lalin China 44 B3
Lalín Spain 25 B2
La Línea de la Concepción Spain 25 D5
Lalin He r. China 44 B3
Lalitpur India 36 D4
Lalitpur Nepal see Patan
Lalmanirhat Bangl. see Lalmonirhat
Lalmonirhat Bangl. 37 G4
La Loche Canada 60 H4
La Louvière Belgium 16 J5
Lal'sk Rus. Fed. 12 J3
Lalung La pass China 37 F3
Lama Bangl. 37 H5
La Macarena, Parque Nacional nat. park Col. 68 D3
La Maddalena Sardinia Italy 26 C4
La Madeleine, Îles de is Canada 63 O2
La Madeleine, Monts de mts France 24 F3
Lamadian China 44 B3
Lamadianzi China see Lamadian
La Maiko, Parc National de nat. park Dem. Rep. Congo 48 C4
La Mancha reg. Spain 25 E4
La Manche strait France/U.K. see English Channel
Lamar CO U.S.A. 62 G4
Lamard Iran 35 I6
La Margeride, Monts de mts France 24 F4
La Marmora, Punta mt. Sardinia Italy 26 C5
La Martre, Lac l. Canada 60 G3
Lamas r. Turkey 39 B1
Lambaréné Gabon 48 B4
Lambasa Fiji see Labasa
Lambayeque Peru 68 C5
Lambay Island Ireland 21 G4
Lambert atoll Marshall Is see Ailinglaplap
Lambert Glacier Antarctica 76 E2
Lambert's Bay S. Africa 50 D7
Lambeth Ont. Canada 64 A1
Lambi India 36 C3
Lambourn Downs hills U.K. 19 F7
La Medjerda, Monts de mts Alg. 26 B6
Lamego Port. 25 C3
La Merced Arg. 70 C3
La Merced Peru 68 C6
Lameroo Australia 57 C7
La Mesa CA U.S.A. 65 D4
Lamesa U.S.A. 62 G5
Lamia Greece 27 J5
Lamington National Park Australia 58 F2
Lammerlaw Range mts N.Z. 59 B7
Lammermuir Hills U.K. 20 G5
Lammhult Sweden 15 I8
Lammi Fin. 15 N6
Lamont CA U.S.A. 65 C3
La Montagne d'Ambre, Parc National de nat. park Madag. 49 E5
La Montaña de Covadonga, Parque Nacional de nat. park Spain see Los Picos de Europa, Parque Nacional de
Lampang Thai. 31 I5
Lampazos Mex. 62 G6
Lampedusa, Isola di i. Sicily Italy 26 E7
Lampeter U.K. 19 C6
Lampsacus Turkey see Lâpseki
Lamu Kenya 48 E4
Lamu Myanmar 37 H6
Lāna'i i. U.S.A. 62 [inset]
La Nao, Cabo de c. Spain 25 G4
Lanark U.K. 20 F5
Lancang Jiang r. Xizang/Yunnan China see Mekong
Lancaster U.K. 18 E4
Lancaster CA U.S.A. 65 C3
Lancaster PA U.S.A. 64 C2
Lancaster SC U.S.A. 63 K5
Lancaster VA U.S.A. 64 C4
Lancaster Canal U.K. 18 E5
Lancaster Sound strait Canada 61 J2
Lanchow China see Lanzhou
Landana Angola see Cacongo
Landau an der Isar Germany 17 N6
Landeck Austria 17 M7
Lander watercourse Australia 54 E5
Lander U.S.A. 62 F3
Landhi Pak. 36 A4
Landor Australia 55 B6
Landsberg Poland see Gorzów Wielkopolski
Landsberg am Lech Germany 17 M6
Land's End pt U.K. 19 B8
Landshut Germany 17 N6
Landskrona Sweden 15 H9
Lanesborough Ireland 21 E4
La'nga Co l. China 36 E3
Langar Afgh. 36 B2
Langberg mts S. Africa 50 F5
Langdon U.S.A. 62 H2
Langeac France 24 F4
Langeberg mts S. Africa 50 D7
Langeland i. Denmark 15 G9
Längelmäki Fin. 15 N6
Langenthal Switz. 24 H3
Langesund Norway 15 F7
Langfang China 43 L5
Langgar China 37 H3
Langjan Nature Reserve S. Africa 51 I2
Langjökull ice cap Iceland 14 [inset]
Langklip S. Africa 50 E5
Langlo Crossing Australia 57 D5
Langøya i. Norway 14 I2
Langphu mt. China 37 F3
Langport U.K. 19 E7
Langqên Zangbo r. China 36 D3
Langres France 24 G3
Langres, Plateau de France 24 G3
Langru China 36 D1
Langsa Indon. 41 B7
Långsele Sweden 14 J5
Lang Sơn Vietnam 42 J8
Langtang National Park Nepal 37 F3
Langting India 37 H4
Langtoft U.K. 18 G4
Languedoc reg. France 24 E5
Långvattnet Sweden 14 L4
Lanigan Canada 62 F1
Lanín, Parque Nacional nat. park Arg. 70 B5
Lanín, Volcán vol. Arg./Chile 70 B5
Lanji India 36 E5
Lanka country Asia see Sri Lanka
Länkäran Azer. 35 H3
Lannion France 24 C2
Lansån Sweden 14 M3
Lansing U.S.A. 63 K3
Lanxi Heilong. China 44 B3
Lan Yü i. Taiwan 43 M8
Lanzarote i. Canary Is 46 B2
Lanzhou China 42 I5
Lanzijing China 44 A3
Laoag Phil. 41 E6
Lao Cai Vietnam 31 J4
Laodicea Syria see Latakia
Laodicea Turkey see Denizli
Laodicea ad Lycum Turkey see Denizli
Laodicea ad Mare Syria see Latakia
Laohekou China 43 K6
Laojunmiao China see Yumen
La Okapi, Parc National de nat. park Dem. Rep. Congo 48 C3
Lao Ling mts China 44 B4
Laon France 24 F2
La Oroya Peru 68 C6
Laos country Asia 41 C6
Laotougou China 44 C4
Laotuding Shan hill China 44 B4
Laowohi pass Jammu and Kashmir see Khardung La
Laoye Ling mts Heilongjiang/Jilin China 44 B4
Laoye Ling mts Heilongjiang/Jilin China 44 C4
Lapa Brazil 71 A4
La Palma i. Canary Is 46 B2
La Palma Panama 67 I7
La Palma del Condado Spain 25 C5
La Panza Range mts CA U.S.A. 65 B3
La Paragua Venez. 68 F2
La Paya, Parque Nacional nat. park Col. 68 D3
La Paz Arg. 70 E4
La Paz Bol. 68 E7
La Paz Hond. 66 G6
La Paz Mex. 66 B4
La Pedrera Col. 68 E4
La Pendjari, Parc National de nat. park Benin 46 D3
La Pérouse Strait Japan/Rus. Fed. 44 F3
La Pesca Mex. 66 E4
Lapinlahti Fin. 14 O5
Lapithos Cyprus 39 A2
La Plata Arg. 70 E4
La Plata MD U.S.A. 64 C3
La Plata, Isla i. Ecuador 68 B4
La Plata, Río de sea chan. Arg./Uruguay 70 E4
Lapmežciems Latvia 15 M8
Lapominka Rus. Fed. 12 I2
Laporte PA U.S.A. 64 C2
Lappajärvi Fin. 14 M5
Lappajärvi l. Fin. 14 M5
Lappeenranta Fin. 15 P6
Lappi Fin. 15 L6
Lappland reg. Europe 14 K3
Lâpseki Turkey 27 L4
Laptevo Rus. Fed. see Yasnogorsk
Laptev Sea Rus. Fed. 29 N2
Lapua Fin. 14 M5
Lapurdum France see Bayonne
Laqiya Arbain well Sudan 32 C5
La Quiaca Arg. 70 C2
L'Aquila Italy 26 E3
La Quinta CA U.S.A. 65 D4
Lār Iran 35 I6
Larache Morocco 25 C6
Laramie U.S.A. 62 F3
Laramie Mountains U.S.A. 62 F3
Laranda Turkey see Karaman
Laranjal Paulista Brazil 71 B3
Laranjeiras do Sul Brazil 70 F3
Laranjinha r. Brazil 71 A3
Larantuka Indon. 41 E8
Larat Indon. 41 F8
Larat i. Indon. 41 F8
Larba Alg. 25 H5
Lärbro Sweden 15 K8
L'Ardenne, Plateau de plat. Belgium see Ardennes
Laredo Spain 25 E2
Laredo U.S.A. 62 H6
La Reina Adelaida, Archipiélago de is Chile 70 B8
Largeau Chad see Faya
Largs U.K. 20 E5
Lārī Iran 35 G3
L'Ariana Tunisia 26 D6
La Rioja Arg. 70 C3
La Rioja aut. comm. Spain 25 E2
Larisa Greece 27 J5
Larissa Greece see Larisa
Larkana Pak. 33 K4
Lark Passage Australia 56 D2
L'Arli, Parc National de nat. park Burkina 46 D3
Larnaca Cyprus 39 A2
Larnaka Cyprus see Larnaca
Larnaka Bay Cyprus 39 A2
Larnakos, Kolpos b. Cyprus see Larnaka Bay
Larne U.K. 21 G3
La Robla Spain 25 D2
La Rochelle France 24 D3
La Roche-sur-Yon France 24 D3
La Roda Spain 25 E4
La Romana Dom. Rep. 67 K5
La Ronge Canada 60 H4
La Ronge, Lac l. Canada 60 H4
Larrey Point Australia 54 B4
Larrimah Australia 54 F3
Lars Christensen Coast Antarctica 76 E2
Larsen Ice Shelf Antarctica 76 L2
Larsmo Fin. 14 M5
Larvik Norway 15 G7
La Salonga Nord, Parc National de nat. park Dem. Rep. Congo 48 C4
Las Anod Somalia see Laascaanood
La Sarre Canada 63 L2
Las Cruces CA U.S.A. 65 B3
Las Cruces NM U.S.A. 62 F5
La Selle, Pic mt. Haiti 67 J5
La Serena Chile 70 B3
Las Flores Arg. 70 E5
Las Heras Arg. 70 C4
Lashio Myanmar 42 H8
Lashkar India 36 D4
Lashkar Gāh Afgh. 33 J3
Las Juntas Chile 70 C3
Las Lomitas Arg. 70 D2
Las Marismas marsh Spain 25 C5
Las Martinetas Arg. 70 C7
Las Minas, Cerro de mt. Hond. 66 G6
La Société, Archipel de is Fr. Polynesia see Society Islands
Las Palmas de Gran Canaria Canary Is 46 B2
Las Petas Bol. 69 G7
La Spezia Italy 26 C2
Las Piedras, Río de r. Peru 68 E6
Las Plumas Arg. 70 C6
Laspur Pak. 36 C1
Lassance Brazil 71 B2
Las Tablas Panama 67 H7
Las Tablas de Daimiel, Parque Nacional de nat. park Spain 25 E4
Las Termas Arg. 70 D3
Last Mountain Lake Canada 62 F1
Las Tórtolas, Cerro mt. Chile 70 C3
Lastoursville Gabon 48 B4
Lastovo i. Croatia 26 G3
Las Tres Vírgenes, Volcán vol. Mex. 66 B3
Las Tunas Cuba 67 I4
Las Varas Chihuahua Mex. 66 C3
Las Varas Nayarit Mex. 66 C4
Las Varillas Arg. 70 D4
Las Vegas NM U.S.A. 62 F4
Las Vegas NV U.S.A. 65 E2
Las Viajas, Isla de i. Peru 68 C6
Las Villuercas mt. Spain 25 D4
Latacunga Ecuador 68 C4
Latady Island Antarctica 76 L2
Latakia Syria 39 B2
La Teste-de-Buch France 24 D4
Latham Australia 55 B7
Latheron U.K. 20 F2
Lathi India 36 B4
Latho Jammu and Kashmir 36 D2
Lathrop CA U.S.A. 65 B2
Latina Italy 26 E4
La Tortuga, Isla i. Venez. 68 E1
Latrun West Bank 39 B4
Lattaquié Syria see Latakia
La Tuque Canada 63 M2
Latur India 38 C2
Latvia country Europe 15 N8
Latvija country Europe see Latvia
Latviyskaya S.S.R. country Europe see Latvia
Lauca, Parque Nacional nat. park Chile 68 E7
Lauchhammer Germany 17 N5
Lauder U.K. 20 G5
Laudio Spain see Llodio
Laufen Switz. 24 H3
Lauge Koch Kyst reg. Greenland 61 L2
Laughlen, Mount Australia 55 F5
Lauka Estonia 15 M7
Launceston Australia 57 [inset]
Launceston U.K. 19 C8
Laune r. Ireland 21 C5
La Unión Bol. 68 F7
Laura Australia 56 D2
Laurel DE U.S.A. 64 D3
Laurel MS U.S.A. 63 J5
Laureldale PA U.S.A. 64 D2
Laurel Hill hills PA U.S.A. 64 B3
Laurencekirk U.K. 20 G4
Laurieton Australia 58 F3
Laurinburg U.S.A. 63 L5
Lauru i. Solomon Is see Choiseul
Lausanne Switz. 24 H3
Laut i. Indon. 41 D8
Laut Bali sea Indon. see Bali, Laut
Lautem East Timor 54 D2
Laut Flores sea Indon. see Flores, Laut
Lautoka Fiji 53 H3
Laut Sawu sea Indon. see Sawu, Laut
Lauvuskylä Fin. 14 P5
Laval France 24 D2
La Vall d'Uixó Spain 25 F4
Lāvān i. Iran 35 I6
La Vanoise, Massif de mts France 24 H4
La Vanoise, Parc National de nat. park France 24 H4
Lavapié, Punta pt Chile 70 B5
Lāvar Iran 35 H5
Laveaga Peak CA U.S.A. 65 B2
La Vega Dom. Rep. 67 J5
Laverton Australia 55 C7
La Vila Joíosa Spain see Villajoyosa-La Vila Joíosa
La Viña Peru 68 C5
Lavongai i. P.N.G. see New Hanover
Lavras Brazil 71 B3
Lavumisa Swaziland 51 J4
Lavushi-Manda National Park Zambia 49 D5
Lawa India 36 C4
Lawa Myanmar 37 I4
Lawa Pak. 36 B2
Law Dome ice feature Antarctica 76 F2
Lawn Hill National Park Australia 56 B3
Lawra Ghana 46 C3
Lawrence KS U.S.A. 63 H4

Lawrence MA U.S.A. 64 F1
Lawrenceburg TN U.S.A. 63 J4
Lawrence Wells, Mount hill Australia 55 C6
Lawton U.S.A. 62 H5
Lawz, Jabal al mt. Saudi Arabia 34 D5
Laxá Sweden 15 I7
Laxey Isle of Man 18 C4
Laya r. Rus. Fed. 12 M2
Laydennyy, Mys c. Rus. Fed. 12 J1
Laylá Saudi Arabia 32 G5
Layla salt pan Saudi Arabia 39 D4
Laysan Island U.S.A. 74 I4
Lazarev Rus. Fed. 44 F1
Lazarevac Serbia 27 I2
Lázaro Cárdenas Mex. 66 D5
Lazcano Uruguay 70 F4
Lazdijai Lith. 15 M9
Lazo Primorskiy Kray Rus. Fed. 44 D4
Lazo Respublika Sakha (Yakutiya) Rus. Fed.
   29 O3
Lead U.S.A. 62 G3
Leader Water r. U.K. 20 G5
Leadville U.S.A. 58 D4
Leaf Bay Canada see Tasiujaq
Leamington Spa, Royal U.K. 19 F6
Leane, Lough l. Ireland 21 C5
Leap Ireland 21 C6
Leatherhead U.K. 19 G7
L'Eau Claire, Lac l. Canada 61 K4
Leavitt Peak CA U.S.A. 65 C1
Lebanon country Asia 39 B2
Lebanon MO U.S.A. 63 I4
Lebanon NH U.S.A. 64 E1
Lebanon PA U.S.A. 64 C2
Lebanon Mountains Lebanon see
   Liban, Jebel
Lebec CA U.S.A. 65 C3
Lebedyan' Rus. Fed. 13 H5
Le Blanc France 24 E3
Lębork Poland 17 P3
Lebowakgomo S. Africa 51 I3
Lebrija Spain 25 C5
Lębsko, Jezioro lag. Poland 17 P3
Lebu Chile 70 B5
Lebyazh'ye Kazakh. see Akku
Lebyazh'ye Rus. Fed. 12 K4
Le Caire Egypt see Cairo
Lecce Italy 26 H4
Lecco Italy 26 C1
Lechaina Greece 27 I6
Lech r. Austria/Germany 17 M7
Le Chasseron mt. Switz. 24 H3
Lechtaler Alpen mts Austria 17 M7
Leck Germany 17 L3
Le Creusot France 24 G3
Le Crotoy France 19 I8
Lectoure France 24 E5
Ledbury U.K. 19 E6
Ledesma Spain 25 D3
Ledmore U.K. 20 E2
Le Dorat France 24 E3
Ledmozero Rus. Fed. 14 R4
Lee r. Ireland 21 D6
Lee MA U.S.A. 64 F1
Leech Lake U.S.A. 63 I2
Leeds U.K. 18 F5
Leedstown U.K. 19 B8
Leek U.K. 19 E5
Leesburg VA U.S.A. 64 C3
Lee Steere Range hills Australia 55 C6
Leesville U.S.A. 63 I5
Leesville OH U.S.A. 64 A2
Leesville Lake U.S.A. 64 B4
Leeton Australia 58 C5
Leeu-Gamka S. Africa 50 E7
Leeuwarden Neth. 16 J4
Leeuwin, Cape Australia 55 A8
Leeuwin-Naturaliste National Park
   Australia 55 A8
Lee Vining CA U.S.A. 65 C2
Leeward Islands Caribbean Sea 67 L5
Lefka Cyprus 39 A2
Lefkada Greece 27 I5
Lefkada i. Greece 27 I5
Lefkás Greece see Lefkada
Lefkimmi Greece 27 I5
Lefkímmi Greece see Lefkimmi
Lefkoniko Cyprus see Lefkonikon
Lefkonikon Cyprus 39 A2
Lefkoşa Cyprus see Nicosia
Lefkosia Cyprus see Nicosia
Lefroy, Lake salt flat Australia 55 C7
Legges Tor mt. Australia 57 [inset]
Leghorn Italy see Livorno
Legnago Italy 26 D2
Legnica Poland 17 P5
Le Grand U.K. U.S.A. 65 B2
Legune Australia 54 E3
Leh India 36 D2
Le Havre France 24 E2
Lehighton PA U.S.A. 64 D2
Lehmo Fin. 14 P5
Lehtimäki Fin. 14 M5
Lehututu Botswana 50 E2
Leiah Pak. 33 L1
Leibnitz Austria 17 O7
Leicester U.K. 19 F6
Leichhardt r. Australia 52 B3
Leichhardt Falls Australia 56 B3
Leichhardt Range mts Australia 56 D4
Leiden Neth. 16 J4
Leifear Ireland 21 E3
Leigh N.Z. 59 E3
Leigh U.K. 18 E5
Leighton Buzzard U.K. 19 G7
Leinster Australia 55 C6
Leinster reg. Ireland 21 F4
Leinster, Mount hill Ireland 21 F5
Leipsoi i. Greece 27 L6
Leipzig Germany 17 N5
Leiranger Norway 14 I3
Leiria Port. 25 B4
Leirvik Norway 15 D7
Leisler, Mount Australia 55 E5
Leith U.K. 20 F5
Leith Hill hill U.K. 19 G7
Leiva, Cerro mt. Col. 68 D3
Leixlip Ireland 21 F4
Leiyang China 43 K7
Leizhou Bandao pen. China 43 J8
Leka Norway 14 G4
Lékana Congo 48 B4
Le Kef Tunisia 26 C6
Lekhainá Greece see Lechaina
Lekkersing S. Africa 50 C5
Lékoni Gabon 48 B4
Leksand Sweden 15 I6
Leksozero, Ozero l. Rus. Fed. 14 Q5
Lélouma Guinea 46 B3
Lelystad Neth. 16 J4
Le Maire, Estrecho de sea chan. Arg. 70 C9
Léman, Lac l. France/Switz. see
   Geneva, Lake
Le Mans France 24 E2
Le Mars U.S.A. 62 H3
Lemberg Ukr. see L'viv
Lemdiyya Alg. see Médéa
Lemesos Cyprus see Limassol
Lemi Fin. 15 O6
Lemieux Islands Canada 61 L3

Lemmenjoen kansallispuisto nat. park Fin.
   14 N2
Lemmon U.S.A. 62 G2
Lemoncove CA U.S.A. 65 C2
Lemoore CA U.S.A. 65 C2
Le Moyne, Lac l. Canada 61 L4
Lemro r. Myanmar 37 H5
Lemtybozh Rus. Fed. 11 R3
Lemvig Denmark 15 F8
Lem'yu r. Rus. Fed. 12 M3
Lena r. Rus. Fed. 42 J1
Lenadoon Point Ireland 21 C3
Lenchung Tso salt l. China 37 E2
Lençóis Brazil 71 C1
Lençóis Maranhenses, Parque Nacional
   dos nat. park Brazil 69 J4
Lendeh Iran 35 H5
Lendery Rus. Fed. 12 F3
Le Neubourg France 19 H9
Lenglong Ling mts China 42 I5
Lenham U.K. 19 H7
Lenhovda Sweden 15 I8
Lenin, Qullai mt. Kyrg./Tajik. see Lenin Peak
Lenina, Pik mt. Kyrg./Tajik. see Lenin Peak
Leninabad Tajik. see Khŭjand
Leninakan Armenia see Gyumri
Lenin Atyndagy Choku mt. Kyrg./Tajik. see
   Lenin Peak
Lenine Ukr. 34 D1
Leningrad Rus. Fed. see St Petersburg
Leningrad Oblast admin. div. Rus. Fed. see
   Leningradskaya Oblast'
Leningradskaya Rus. Fed. 13 H7
Leningradskaya Oblast' admin. div.
   Rus. Fed. 15 R7
Leningradskiy Rus. Fed. 29 S3
Lenino Ukr. see Lenine
Leninobod Tajik. see Khŭjand
Lenin Peak Kyrg./Tajik. 42 C5
Leninsk Kazakh. see Baykonyr
Leninsk Rus. Fed. 13 J6
Leninskiy Rus. Fed. 13 H5
Leninsk-Kuznetskiy Rus. Fed. 28 J3
Leninskoye Kazakh. 13 K6
Leninskoye Kirovskaya Oblast' Rus. Fed.
   12 J4
Leninskoye Yevreyskaya Avtonomnaya
   Oblast' Rus. Fed. 44 D3
Lenkoran' Azer. see Länkäran
Lenox MA U.S.A. 64 F1
Lens France 24 F1
Lensk Rus. Fed. 29 M3
Lenti Hungary 26 G1
Lentini Sicily Italy 26 F6
Léo Burkina 46 C3
Leoben Austria 17 O7
Leodhais, Eilean i. U.K. see Lewis, Isle of
Leominster U.K. 19 E6
Leominster MA U.S.A. 64 F1
León Mex. 66 D4
León Nicaragua 67 G6
León Spain 25 D3
Leonardtown MD U.S.A. 64 C3
Leonardville Namibia 50 D2
Leongatha Australia 58 B7
Leonidio Greece 27 J6
Leonidovo Rus. Fed. 44 F2
Leonora Australia 55 C7
Leopold Belgium 76 D1
Leopold and Astrid Coast Antarctica see
   King Leopold and Queen Astrid Coast
Léopold II, Lac l. Dem. Rep. Congo see
   Mai-Ndombe, Lac
Leopoldina Brazil 71 C3
Leopoldo de Bulhões Brazil 71 A2
Léopoldville Dem. Rep. Congo see
   Kinshasa
Lepale S. Africa see Lephalale
Lepaya Latvia see Liepāja
Lepel' Belarus see Lyepyel'
Lephalale r. S. Africa 51 H2
Lephalale S. Africa 51 H2
Lephepe Botswana 51 G2
Lephoi S. Africa 51 G6
Leping China 43 I7
Lepontine, Alpi mts Italy/Switz. 26 C1
Leppävirta Fin. 14 O5
Lepsa Kazakh. see Lepsy
Lepsy Kazakh. 42 D3
Le Puy France see Le Puy-en-Velay
Le Puy-en-Velay France 24 F4
Lerala Botswana 51 I2
Leratswana S. Africa 51 H5
Léré Mali 46 C3
Leribe Lesotho see Hlotse
Lérida Col. 68 D4
Lérida Spain see Lleida
Lerik Azer. 35 H3
Lerma Spain 25 E2
Lermontov Rus. Fed. 35 F1
Lermontovka Rus. Fed. 44 D3
Lermontovskiy Rus. Fed. see Lermontov
Leros i. Greece 27 L6
Le Roy NY U.S.A. 64 B1
Le Roy, Lac l. Canada 61 K4
Lerum Sweden 15 H8
Lerwick U.K. 20 [inset]
Les Amirantes is Seychelles see
   Amirante Islands
Lesbos i. Greece 27 K5
Les Cayes Haiti 67 J5
Le Seu d'Urgell Spain 25 G2
Leshan China 42 I7
Leshukonskoye Rus. Fed. 12 J2
Lesi watercourse Sudan 47 F4
Leskhimstroy Ukr. see Syeverodonets'k
Leskovac Serbia 27 I3
Lesneven France 24 B2
Lesnoy Kirovskaya Oblast' Rus. Fed. 12 L4
Lesnoy Murmanskaya Oblast' Rus. Fed. see
   Umba
Lesnoye Rus. Fed. 12 G4
Lesogorsk Rus. Fed. 44 F2
Lesopil'noye Rus. Fed. 44 D3
Lesosibirsk Rus. Fed. 28 K4
Lesotho country Africa 51 I5
Lesozavodsk Rus. Fed. 44 D3
L'Espérance Rock i. Kermadec Is 53 I5
Les Pieux France 19 F9
Les Sables-d'Olonne France 24 D3
Lesser Antarctica reg. Antarctica see
   West Antarctica
Lesser Antilles is Caribbean Sea 67 K6
Lesser Caucasus mts Asia 35 F2
Lesser Himalaya mts India/Nepal 36 D3
Lesser Khingan Mountains China see
   Xiao Hinggan Ling
Lesser Slave Lake Canada 60 H4
Lester WV U.S.A. 64 A4
Lestijärvi Fin. 14 N5
Les Vans France 24 G4
Lesvos i. Greece see Lesbos
Leszno Poland 17 P5
Letaba S. Africa 51 J2
Letea Romania 17 N7
Lienz Austria 17 N7
Liepāja Latvia 15 L8
Leteri India 36 D4
Letha Range mts Myanmar 37 H5

Liffey r. Ireland 21 F4
Lifford Ireland 21 E3
Lifi Mahuida mt. Arg. 70 C6
Lifou i. New Caledonia 53 G4
Lifou i. New Caledonia see Lifou
Lightning Ridge Australia 58 C2
Ligonha r. Moz. 49 D5
Ligure, Mar sea France/Italy see
   Ligurian Sea
Ligurian Sea France/Italy 26 C2
Ligurienne, Mer sea France/Italy see
   Ligurian Sea
Ligurta AZ U.S.A. 65 E4
Lihir Group is P.N.G. 52 F2
Lihou Reef and Cays Australia 56 E3
Lihue U.S.A. 74 I4
Liivi laht b. Estonia/Latvia see Riga, Gulf of
Lijiang Yunnan China 42 I7
Lika reg. Croatia 26 F2
Likasi Dem. Rep. Congo 49 C5
Likati Dem. Rep. Congo 48 C3
Likhachevo Ukr. see Pervomays'kyy
Likhachyovo Ukr. see Pervomays'kyy
Likhapani India 37 H4
Likhás pen. Greece see Lichas
Likhoslavl' Rus. Fed. 12 G4
Liku Indon. 41 C7
Likurga Rus. Fed. 12 I4
L'île-Rousse Corsica France 24 I5
Lilla Pak. 36 C2
Lilla Edet Sweden 15 H7
Lille France 24 F1
Lille Bælt sea chan. Denmark see Little Belt
Lillebonne France 24 E2
Lillehammer Norway 15 G6
Lillesand Norway 15 F7
Lillestrøm Norway 15 G7
Lillholmsjö Sweden 14 I5
Lillian, Point hill Australia 55 D6
Lillooet Canada 62 C1
Lilongwe Malawi 49 D5
Lilydale Australia 57 B7
Lima Peru 68 C6
Lima OH U.S.A. 63 K3
Lima Duarte Brazil 71 C3
Liman Rus. Fed. 13 J7
Limar Indon. 54 D1
Limassol Cyprus 39 A2
Limavady U.K. 21 F3
Limay r. Arg. 70 B5
Limbaži Latvia 15 N8
Limbunya Australia 54 E4
Lime Acres S. Africa 50 F5
Limeira Brazil 71 B3
Limerick Ireland 21 D5
Limfjorden sea chan. Denmark 15 F8
Limingen Norway 14 H4
Limingen l. Norway 14 H4
Liminka Fin. 14 N4
Limmen Bight b. Australia 56 B2
Limni Greece see Lefkada
Limnos i. Greece 27 K5
Limoeiro Brazil 69 K5
Limoges France 24 E4
Limón Costa Rica see Puerto Limón
Limon U.S.A. 62 G4
Limonlu Turkey 39 B1
Limonum France see Poitiers
Limousin reg. France 24 E4
Limoux France 24 F5
Limpopo prov. S. Africa 51 I2
Limpopo r. S. Africa/Zimbabwe 51 K3
Linah well Saudi Arabia 35 F5
Linakhamari Rus. Fed. 14 Q2
Linares Chile 70 B5
Linares Mex. 66 E4
Linares Spain 25 E4
Lincang China 42 I8
Linchuan China see Fuzhou
Linck Nunataks nunataks Antarctica 76 K1
Lincoln Arg. 70 D4
Lincoln U.K. 18 G5
Lincoln CA U.S.A. 65 B1
Lincoln IL U.S.A. 63 J3
Lincoln NE U.S.A. 63 H3
Lincoln National Park Australia 57 A7
Lincoln Sea Canada/Greenland 77 J1
Lincolnshire Wolds hills U.K. 18 G5
Linda, Serra hills Brazil 71 C1
Linda Creek watercourse Australia 56 B4
Lindau (Bodensee) Germany 17 L7
Lindeman Group is Australia 56 E4
Linden Guyana 69 G2
Lindesnes c. Norway 15 E7
Líndhos Greece see Lindos
Lindi r. Dem. Rep. Congo 48 C3
Lindi Tanz. 49 D4
Lindian China 44 B3
Lindisfarne i. U.K. see Holy Island
Lindley S. Africa 51 H4
Lindos Greece 23 J4
Lindsay Canada 64 C1
Lindsay CA U.S.A. 65 C2
Lindside WV U.S.A. 64 A4
Lindum U.K. see Lincoln
Line Islands Kiribati 75 J5
Linesville PA U.S.A. 64 B1
Linfen China 43 K5
Lingampet India 38 C2
Linganamakki Reservoir India 38 B3
Lingcheng Hainan China see Lingshui
Lingelethu S. Africa 51 H7
Lingen (Ems) Germany 17 K4
Lingga, Kepulauan is Indon. 41 C8
Lingomo Dem. Rep. Congo 48 C3
Lingshui China 43 J9
Lingsugur India 38 C2
Linguère Senegal 46 B3
Lingzi Tang reg. Aksai Chin 36 D2
Linhai China 43 M7
Linhares Brazil 71 C2
Linhe China 43 J4
Linhpa Myanmar 37 H4
Linjiang China 44 B4
Linköping Sweden 15 I7
Linkou China 44 C3
Linlithgow U.K. 20 F5
Linnansaaren kansallispuisto nat. park Fin.
   14 P5
Linnhe, Loch inlet U.K. 20 D4
Linosa, Isola di i. Sicily Italy 26 E7
Lins Brazil 71 A3
Lintao China 42 I5
Linton ND U.S.A. 62 G2
Linxi China 43 L4
Linxia China 42 I5
Linyi Shandong China 43 L5
Linyi Shandong China 43 L5
Linz Austria 17 O6
Lion, Golfe du g. France 24 F5
Lions, Gulf of France see Lion, Golfe du
Lioua Chad 47 E3
Lipari Sicily Italy 26 F5
Lipari, Isole is Italy 26 F5
Lipetsk Rus. Fed. 13 H5
Lipin Bor Rus. Fed. 12 H3
Lipova Romania 27 I1
Lipovtsy Rus. Fed. 44 C3
Lippe r. Germany 17 K5
Lipsoí i. Greece see Leipsoi
Lipti Lekh pass Nepal 36 E3
Liptrap, Cape Australia 58 B7
Lira Uganda 48 D3
Liranga Congo 48 B4

Llanymddyfri U.K. see Llandovery
Llay U.K. 19 D5
Lleida Spain 25 G3
Llerena Spain 25 C4
Lliria Spain 25 F4
Llodio Spain 25 E2
Lloyd George, Mount Canada 60 F4
Lloyd Lake Canada 60 H4
Lloydminster Canada 62 E1
Lluchmayor Spain see Llucmajor
Llucmajor Spain 25 H4
Llullaillaco, Volcán vol. Chile 70 C2
Loa r. Chile 70 B2
Loban' r. Rus. Fed. 12 K4
Lobatejo mt. Spain 25 D5
Lobatse Botswana 51 G3
Lobaye r. Cent. Afr. Rep. 48 B3
Loberia Arg. 70 E5
Lobito Angola 49 B5
Lobos Arg. 70 E5
Lobos de Tierra, Isla i. Peru 68 B5
Lochaline U.K. 20 D4
Loch Baghasdail U.K. see Lochboisdale
Lochboisdale U.K. 20 B3
Lochcarron U.K. 20 D3
Lochearnhead U.K. 20 E4
Lochem Neth. 16 K4
Lochern National Park Australia 56 C5
Loches France 24 E3
Loch Garman Ireland see Wexford
Lochgelly U.K. 20 F4
Lochgilphead U.K. 20 D4
Lochinver U.K. 20 D2
Loch Lomond and Trossachs National Park
   U.K. 20 E4
Lochmaddy U.K. 20 B3
Lochnagar mt. U.K. 20 F4
Loch nam Madadh U.K. see Lochmaddy
Loch Raven Reservoir MD U.S.A. 64 C3
Lochy, Loch l. U.K. 20 E4
Lock Australia 57 A7
Lockerbie U.K. 20 F5
Lockhart Australia 58 C5
Lock Haven PA U.S.A. 64 C2
Lockport NY U.S.A. 64 B1
Lod Israel 39 B4
Loddon r. Australia 58 A5
Lodève France 24 F5
Lodeynoye Pole Rus. Fed. 12 G3
Lodhikheda India 36 D5
Lodhran Pak. 36 B3
Lodi Italy 26 C2
Lodi CA U.S.A. 65 B1
Lødingen Norway 14 I2
Lodja Dem. Rep. Congo 48 C4
Lodomeria Rus. Fed. see Vladimir
Lodrani India 36 B5
Lodwar Kenya 48 D3
Łódź Poland 17 Q5
Loeriesfontein S. Africa 50 D6
Løfoten Norway 14 H2
Log Rus. Fed. 13 I6
Loga Niger 46 D3
Logan UT U.S.A. 62 E3
Logan, Mount Canada 60 D3
Logan Creek r. Australia 56 D4
Logatec Slovenia 26 F2
Logroño Spain 25 E2
Logtak Lake India 37 H4
Lohardaga India 37 F5
Loharu India 36 C3
Lohatlha S. Africa 50 F5
Lohawat India 36 B4
Lohil r. China/India see Zayü Qu
Lohiniva Fin. 14 N3
Lohjanjärvi l. Fin. 15 M6
Lohtaja Fin. 14 M4
Loi-lem Myanmar 42 H8
Loimaa Fin. 15 M6
Loipyet Hills Myanmar 37 I4
Loire r. France 24 C3
Loja Ecuador 68 C4
Loja Spain 25 D5
Lokan tekojärvi l. Fin. 14 O3
Lokchim r. Rus. Fed. 12 K3
Lokgwabe Botswana 50 E3
Lokichar Kenya 30 C6
Lokichokio Kenya 48 D3
Løkken Denmark 15 F8
Løkken Norway 14 F5
Loknya Rus. Fed. 12 F4
Lokoja Nigeria 46 D4
Lokolama Dem. Rep. Congo 48 B4
Lokossa Benin 46 D4
Lokot' Rus. Fed. 13 G5
Lol Sudan 47 F4
Lola Guinea 46 C4
Lolland i. Denmark 15 G9
Lollondo Tanz. 48 D4
Lolwane S. Africa 50 F4
Lom Bulg. 27 J3
Lom r. Dem. Rep. Congo 48 C3
Lomami r. Dem. Rep. Congo 48 C4
Lomar Pass Afgh. 36 A2
Lomas, Bahía de b. Chile 70 C8
Lomas de Zamora Arg. 70 E4
Lombarda, Serra hills Brazil 69 H3
Lomblen i. Indon. 54 C2
Lombok Indon. 54 A2
Lombok, Selat sea chan. Indon. 54 A2
Lomé Togo 46 D4
Lomela Dem. Rep. Congo 48 C4
Lomela r. Dem. Rep. Congo 47 F5
Lomond, Loch l. U.K. 20 E4
Lomonosov Rus. Fed. 15 P7
Lomonosov Ridge sea feature Arctic Ocean
   77 B1
Lomovoye Rus. Fed. 12 I2
Lompoc CA U.S.A. 65 B3
Łomża Poland 17 S4
Lonar India 38 C2
Londa Bangl. 37 G5
Londa India 38 B3
Londinières France 19 I9
Londinium U.K. see London
Londoko Rus. Fed. 44 C3
London Ont. Canada 64 A1
London U.K. 19 G7
London KY U.S.A. 63 K4
Londonderry U.K. 21 E3
Londonderry VT U.S.A. 64 E1
Londonderry, Cape Australia 54 D3
Londrina Brazil 71 A3
Lone Pine CA U.S.A. 65 C2
Longa Angola 49 B5
Longa, Proliv sea chan. Rus. Fed. 29 S2
Long Ashton U.K. 19 E7
Long Bay U.S.A. 63 L5
Long Beach CA U.S.A. 65 C4
Longbeach N.Z. 59 C7
Long Branch NJ U.S.A. 64 E2
Long Eaton U.K. 19 F6
Longford Ireland 21 E4
Longhoughton U.K. 18 F3
Longhurst, Mount Antarctica 76 H1
Long Island Bahamas 67 I4
Long Island P.N.G. 52 E2
Long Island NY U.S.A. 64 E2
Long Island Sound sea chan.
   Connecticut/New York U.S.A. 64 E2

Longjiang China 44 A3
Longlac Canada 63 J2
Longmeadow MA U.S.A. 64 E1
Long Melford U.K. 19 H6
Longmen Heilong. China 44 B2
Longmont U.S.A. 62 F3
Longnan China 42 I6
Long Point Ont. Canada 64 A1
Long Point Ont. Canada 64 A1
Long Point N.Z. 59 B8
Long Point Bay Ont. Canada 64 A1
Long Preston U.K. 18 E4
Long Range Mountains Nfld. and Lab. Canada 61 M5
Longreach Australia 56 D4
Long Stratton U.K. 19 I6
Longtown U.K. 18 E3
Longuyon France 24 G2
Longview TX U.S.A. 63 I5
Longwangmiao China 44 D3
Longwei Co l. China 37 G2
Longxi China 42 I6
Longxingchang China see Wuyuan
Long Xuyên Vietnam 31 J5
Longyan China 43 L7
Longyearbyen Svalbard 28 C2
Longzhen China 44 B2
Lönsboda Sweden 15 I8
Lons-le-Saunier France 24 G3
Lonton Myanmar 37 I4
Loochoo Islands Japan see Ryukyu Islands
Lookout, Cape U.S.A. 63 L5
Lookout, Point Australia 58 F1
Lookout Point Australia 55 B8
Loolmalasin vol. crater Tanz. 48 D4
Loongana Australia 55 D7
Loop Head hd Ireland 21 C5
Lop China 36 E1
Lopasnya Rus. Fed. see Chekhov
Lopatina, Gora mt. Rus. Fed. 44 F2
Lop Buri Thai. 31 J5
Lopez, Cap c. Gabon 48 A4
Lop Nur salt flat China 42 G4
Lopphavet b. Norway 14 L1
Loptyuga Rus. Fed. 12 K3
Lora r. Venez. 68 D2
Lora del Río Spain 25 D5
Lorain U.S.A. 61 J5
Loralai Pak. 33 K3
Loralai r. Pak. 36 B3
Lorca Spain 25 F5
Lordegān Iran 35 H5
Lord Howe Atoll Solomon Is see Ontong Java Atoll
Lord Howe Island Australia 53 F5
Lord Howe Rise sea feature S. Pacific Ocean 74 G7
Lordsburg U.S.A. 62 F5
Lore East Timor 54 D2
Lorena Brazil 71 B3
Loreto Brazil 69 I5
Loreto Mex. 62 E6
Lorient France 24 C3
Lorn, Firth of est. U.K. 20 D4
Lorne Australia 56 D5
Lorne watercourse Australia 56 B3
Lorrain, Plateau France 24 H2
Lorraine Australia 56 B3
Lorraine reg. France 24 G2
Losal India 36 C4
Los Alamos CA U.S.A. 65 B3
Los Alamos NM U.S.A. 62 F4
Los Alerces, Parque Nacional nat. park Arg. 70 B6
Los Ángeles Chile 70 B5
Los Angeles CA U.S.A. 65 C3
Los Angeles Aqueduct canal CA U.S.A. 65 C3
Los Banos CA U.S.A. 65 B2
Los Blancos Arg. 70 D2
Los Canarreos, Archipiélago de is Cuba 67 H4
Los Chonos, Archipiélago de is Chile 70 A6
Los Desventurados, Islas de is S. Pacific Ocean 75 O7
Los Estados, Isla de i. Arg. 70 D8
Los Glaciares, Parque Nacional nat. park Arg. 70 B8
Lošinj i. Croatia 26 F2
Los Jardines de la Reina, Archipiélago de is Cuba 67 I4
Los Juríes Arg. 70 D3
Los Katios, Parque Nacional nat. park Col. 67 I7
Loskop Dam S. Africa 51 I3
Los Menucos Arg. 70 C6
Los Mochis Mex. 66 C3
Los Mosquitos, Golfo de b. Panama 67 H7
Losombo Dem. Rep. Congo 48 B3
Los Picos de Europa, Parque Nacional de nat. park Spain 25 D2
Los Roques, Islas is Venez. 68 E1
Lossie r. U.K. 20 F3
Lossiemouth U.K. 20 F3
Lost Creek WV U.S.A. 64 A3
Los Teques Venez. 68 E1
Los Testigos is Venez. 68 F1
Lost Hills CA U.S.A. 65 C3
Lostwithiel U.K. 19 C8
Los Vilos Chile 70 B4
Lot r. France 24 E4
Lota Chile 70 B5
Lothringen reg. France see Lorraine
Lotikipi Plain Kenya/Sudan 48 D3
Loto Dem. Rep. Congo 48 C4
Lotsane r. Botswana 51 I2
Lot's Wife i. Japan see Sōfu-gan
Lotta r. Fin./Rus. Fed. 14 Q2
Louangnamtha Laos 40 C5
Louangphabang Laos 41 C6
Loubomo Congo 49 B4
Loudéac France 24 C2
Louga Senegal 46 B3
Loughborough U.K. 19 F6
Lougheed Island Canada 61 H2
Loughor r. U.K. 19 C7
Loughrea Ireland 21 D4
Loughton U.K. 19 H7
Louhans France 24 G3
Louisa VA U.S.A. 64 C3
Louisburgh Ireland 21 C4
Louis-Gentil Morocco see Youssoufia
Louisiade Archipelago is P.N.G. 52 F3
Louisiana state U.S.A. 63 I5
Louis Trichardt S. Africa see Makhado
Louisville KY U.S.A. 63 J4
Louisville Ridge sea feature S. Pacific Ocean 74 I8
Loukhi Rus. Fed. 12 G2
Loukoléla Congo 48 B4
Loukouo Congo 47 E5
Loulé Port. 25 B5
Loum Cameroon 46 D4
Louny Czech Rep. 17 N5
Loups Marins, Lacs des lakes Canada 61 K4
L'Our, Vallée de valley Germany/Lux. 17 K6
Lourdes France 24 D5
Lourenço Marques Moz. see Maputo
Lousã Port. 25 B3
Loushan China 44 C3
Louth Australia 58 B3
Louth U.K. 18 G5
Loutra Aidipsou Greece 27 J5
Louvain Belgium see Leuven
Louviers France 19 I9
Louwater-Suid Namibia 50 C2
Louwsburg S. Africa 51 J4
Lövånger Sweden 14 L4
Lovat' r. Rus. Fed. 12 F4
Lovech Bulg. 27 K3
Lovelock U.S.A. 62 D3
Loviisa Fin. 15 O6
Lovington U.S.A. 62 G5
Lovozero Rus. Fed. 12 G1
Lóvua Angola 49 C4
Lôvua Angola 49 C5
Low, Cape Canada 61 J3
Lowa Dem. Rep. Congo 48 C4
Lowa r. Dem. Rep. Congo 48 C4
Lowarai Pass Pak. 36 B2
Lowell MA U.S.A. 64 F1
Lower California pen. Mex. see Baja California
Lower Glenelg National Park Australia 57 C8
Lower Granite Gorge AZ U.S.A. 65 F3
Lower Hutt N.Z. 59 E5
Lower Lake CA U.S.A. 65 A1
Lower Lough Erne l. U.K. 21 E3
Lower Tunguska r. Rus. Fed. see Nizhnyaya Tunguska
Lower Zambezi National Park Zambia 49 C5
Lowestoft U.K. 19 I6
Łowicz Poland 17 Q4
Low Island Kiribati see Starbuck Island
Lowther Hills U.K. 20 F5
Lowville U.S.A. 63 L3
Loxton Australia 57 C7
Loyal, Loch l. U.K. 20 E2
Loyalsock Creek r. PA U.S.A. 64 C2
Loyalty Islands New Caledonia see Loyauté, Îles
Loyang China see Luoyang
Loyauté, Îles is New Caledonia 53 G4
Loyev Belarus see Loyew
Loyew Belarus 13 F6
Lozère, Mont mt. France 24 F4
Loznica Serbia 27 H2
Lozova Ukr. 13 H6
Lozovaya Ukr. see Lozova
Lua r. Dem. Rep. Congo 48 B3
Luacano Angola 49 C5
Lu'an China 43 L6
Luanda Angola 49 B4
Luang Namtha Laos see Louangnamtha
Luang Prabang Laos see Louangphabang
Luanhaizi China 37 H2
Luanshya Zambia 49 C5
Luanza Dem. Rep. Congo 49 C4
Luao Angola see Luau
Luarca Spain 25 C2
Luashi Dem. Rep. Congo 49 C5
Luau Angola 49 C5
Luba Equat. Guinea 46 D4
Lubaczów Poland 13 D6
Lubalo Angola 49 B4
Lubānas ezers l. Latvia 15 O8
Lubango Angola 49 B5
Lubao Dem. Rep. Congo 49 C4
Lubartów Poland 13 D6
Lubbeskolk salt pan S. Africa 50 D5
Lubbock U.S.A. 62 G5
Lübeck Germany 17 M4
Lubefu Dem. Rep. Congo 49 C4
Lubei China 43 M4
Lüben Poland see Lubin
Lubersac France 24 E4
Lubin Poland 17 P5
Lublin Poland 13 D6
Lubnān country Asia see Lebanon
Lubnān, Jabal mts Lebanon see Liban, Jebel
Lubny Ukr. 13 G6
Lubok Antu Sarawak Malaysia 41 D7
Lubudi Dem. Rep. Congo 49 C4
Lubumbashi Dem. Rep. Congo 49 C5
Lubutu Dem. Rep. Congo 48 C4
Lucala Angola 49 B4
Lucan Ont. Canada 64 A1
Lucan Ireland 21 F4
Lucapa Angola 49 C4
Lucca Italy 26 D3
Luce Bay U.K. 20 E6
Lucélia Brazil 71 A3
Lucena Phil. 41 E6
Lucena Spain 25 D5
Lučenec Slovakia 17 Q6
Lucera Italy 26 F4
Lucerne Switz. 24 I3
Lucerne Valley CA U.S.A. 65 D3
Luchegorsk Rus. Fed. 44 D3
Lucheng Sichuan China see Kangding
Łuck Ukr. see Luts'k
Luckeesarai India see Lakhisarai
Luckenwalde Germany 17 N4
Luckhoff S. Africa 50 G5
Lucknow India 36 E4
Lucrecia, Cabo c. Cuba 67 I4
Lucusse Angola 49 C5
Lucy Creek Australia 56 B4
Lüda China see Dalian
Lüdenscheid Germany 17 K5
Lüderitz Namibia 50 B4
Ludewa Tanz. 49 D5
Ludhiana India 36 C3
Ludlow U.K. 19 E6
Ludlow CA U.S.A. 65 D3
Ludogorie reg. Bulg. 27 L3
Ludvika Sweden 15 I6
Ludwigsburg Germany 17 L6
Ludwigshafen am Rhein Germany 17 L6
Ludwigslust Germany 17 M4
Ludza Latvia 15 O8
Luebo Dem. Rep. Congo 49 C4
Luena Angola 49 B5
Luena Flats plain Zambia 49 C5
Lufeng Guangdong China 43 L8
Lufkin U.S.A. 63 I5
Luga Rus. Fed. 12 F4
Luga r. Rus. Fed. 15 P7
Lugano Switz. 24 I3
Lugansk Ukr. see Luhans'k
Lugdunum France see Lyon
Lugg r. U.K. 19 E6
Luggudontsen mt. China 37 G3
Lugnaquilla hill Ireland 21 F5
Lugo Italy 26 D2
Lugo Spain 25 C2
Lugoj Romania 27 I2
Luhans'k Ukr. 13 H6
Luḩfī, Wādī watercourse Jordan 39 C3
Luhit r. China/India see Zayü Qu
Luhit r. India 37 H4
Luhuo China 42 I6
Luhyny Ukr. 13 F6
Luia Angola 49 C4
Luiana Angola 49 C5
Luichow Peninsula China see Leizhou Bandao
Luik Belgium see Liège
Luimneach Ireland see Limerick
Luiro r. Fin. 14 O3
Luis Echeverría Álvarez Baja California Mex. 65 D4
Luitpold Coast Antarctica 76 A1
Luiza Dem. Rep. Congo 49 C4
Lukachek Rus. Fed. 44 D1
Lukapa Angola see Lucapa
Lukavac Bos.-Herz. 26 H2
Lukenga, Lac l. Dem. Rep. Congo 49 C4
Lukenie r. Dem. Rep. Congo 48 B4
Lukh r. Rus. Fed. 12 I4
Lukhovitsy Rus. Fed. 13 H5
Lukovit Bulg. 27 K3
Łuków Poland 13 D6
Lukoyanov Rus. Fed. 13 J5
Lukusuzi National Park Zambia 49 D5
Luleå Sweden 14 M4
Luleälven r. Sweden 14 M4
Lüleburgaz Turkey 27 L4
Lüliang Shan mts China 43 K5
Lulimba Dem. Rep. Congo 49 C4
Lulonga r. Dem. Rep. Congo 48 B3
Luluabourg Dem. Rep. Congo see Kananga
Lülung China 37 F3
Lumachomo China 37 F3
Lumajangdong Co salt l. China 36 E2
Lumbala Moxico Angola see Lumbala Kaquengue
Lumbala Moxico Angola see Lumbala N'guimbo
Lumbala Kaquengue Angola 49 C5
Lumbala N'guimbo Angola 49 C5
Lumberton U.S.A. 63 L5
Lumbini Nepal 37 E4
Lumbrales Spain 25 C3
Lumezzane Italy 26 D2
Lumsden Canada 62 G1
Lumsden N.Z. 59 B7
Lunan Bay U.K. 20 G4
Lund Sweden 15 H9
Lund NV U.S.A. 65 E1
Lund UT U.S.A. 65 F1
Lundy U.K. 19 C7
Lune r. U.K. 18 E4
Lüneburg Germany 17 M4
Lunenburg VA U.S.A. 64 B4
Lunéville France 24 H2
Lunga r. Zambia 49 C5
Lungdo China 37 E2
Lunggar China 37 E3
Lungleh India see Lunglei
Lunglei India 37 H5
Lungmari mt. China 37 F3
Lungmu Co salt l. China 36 E2
Lungwebungu r. Zambia 49 C5
Lunh Nepal 37 E3
Luni India 36 C4
Luni r. India 36 B4
Luni r. Pak. 36 B3
Luninets Belarus see Luninyets
Luning NV U.S.A. 65 C1
Luninyets Belarus 15 O10
Lunkaransar India 36 C3
Lunkha India 36 C3
Lunsar Sierra Leone 46 B4
Lunsklip S. Africa 51 I3
Luntai China 42 E4
Luobei China 44 C3
Luobuzhuang China 42 F5
Luohe China 43 K6
Luoto Fin. see Larsmo
Luoyang Henan China 43 K6
Luozigou China 44 C4
Lupane Zimbabwe 49 C5
Lupanshui China 42 I7
L'Upemba, Parc National de nat. park Dem. Rep. Congo 49 C4
Lupeni Romania 27 J2
Lupilichi Moz. 49 D5
Luray VA U.S.A. 64 B3
Luremo Angola 49 B4
Lurgan U.K. 21 F3
Luring China see Oma
Lúrio Moz. 49 E5
Lurio r. Moz. 49 E5
Lusaka Zambia 49 C5
Lusambo Dem. Rep. Congo 49 C4
Lusancay Islands and Reefs P.N.G. 52 F2
Lusangi Dem. Rep. Congo 49 C4
Lush, Mount hill Australia 54 D4
Lushnja Albania see Lushnjë
Lushnjë Albania 27 H4
Lushuihe China 44 B4
Lusikisiki S. Africa 51 I6
Lusk U.S.A. 62 G3
Luso Angola see Luena
Lussvale Australia 58 C1
Lut, Bahrat salt l. Asia see Dead Sea
Lut, Dasht-e des. Iran 33 I3
Lutetia France see Paris
Lutherstadt Wittenberg Germany 17 N5
Luton U.K. 19 G7
Łutselk'e Canada 60 G3
Luts'k Ukr. 13 E6
Lutto r. Fin./Rus. Fed. see Lotta
Lützow-Holm Bay Antarctica 76 D2
Lutzputs S. Africa 50 E5
Lutzville S. Africa 50 D6
Luumäki Fin. 15 O6
Luuq Somalia 48 E3
Luverne MN U.S.A. 63 H3
Luvuei Angola 49 C5
Luvuvhu r. S. Africa 51 J2
Luwero Uganda 48 D3
Luwingu Zambia 49 C5
Luwuk Indon. 41 E8
Luxembourg country Europe 17 K6
Luxembourg Lux. 17 K6
Luxemburg country Europe see Luxembourg
Luxeuil-les-Bains France 24 H3
Luxi Yunnan China 42 H8
Luxolweni S. Africa 51 G6
Luxor Egypt 32 D4
Luza Rus. Fed. 12 J3
Luza r. Rus. Fed. 12 J3
Luza r. Rus. Fed. 12 M2
Luzern Switz. see Lucerne
Luzhou China 42 J7
Luziânia Brazil 71 B2
Luzon i. Phil. 41 E6
Luzon Strait Phil. 41 E5
Luzy France 24 F3
L'viv Ukr. 13 E6
L'vov Ukr. see L'viv
Lwów Ukr. see L'viv
Lyady Rus. Fed. 15 P7
Lyakhavichy Belarus 15 O10
Lyakhovichi Belarus see Lyakhavichy
Lyallpur Pak. see Faisalabad
Lyamtsa Rus. Fed. 12 H2
Lycia reg. Turkey 27 M6
Lyck Poland see Ełk
Lycksele Sweden 14 K4
Lycopolis Egypt see Asyūţ
Lydd U.K. 19 H8
Lydda Israel see Lod
Lyddan Island Antarctica 76 B2
Lydenburg S. Africa 51 J3
Lydia reg. Turkey 27 L5
Lydney U.K. 19 E7
Lyel'chytsy Belarus 13 F6
Lyell, Mount CA U.S.A. 65 C2
Lyell Brown, Mount hill Australia 55 E5
Lyepyel' Belarus 15 P9
Lykens PA U.S.A. 64 C2
Lyme Bay U.K. 19 E8
Lyme Regis U.K. 19 E8
Lymington U.K. 19 F8
Lynchburg VA U.S.A. 64 B4
Lyndhurst N.S.W. Australia 58 D4
Lyndhurst Qld Australia 56 D3
Lyndhurst S.A. Australia 57 B6
Lyndon Australia 55 A5
Lyndon r. Australia 55 A5
Lyne r. U.K. 18 D4
Lyness U.K. 20 F2
Lyngdal Norway 15 E7
Lynn U.K. see King's Lynn
Lynn MA U.S.A. 64 F1
Lynn Lake Canada 61 H4
Lynton U.K. 19 D7
Lynx Lake Canada 60 H3
Lyon France 24 G4
Lyon r. U.K. 20 F4
Lyons Australia 55 F7
Lyons France see Lyon
Lyons NY U.S.A. 64 C1
Lyons Falls NY U.S.A. 64 D1
Lyozna Belarus 13 F5
Lyra Reef P.N.G. 52 F2
Lysekil Sweden 15 G7
Lyskovo Rus. Fed. 12 J4
Lys'va Rus. Fed. 11 R4
Lysychans'k Ukr. 13 H6
Lysyye Gory Rus. Fed. 13 J6
Lytham St Anne's U.K. 18 D5
Lyuban' Belarus 15 P10
Lyubertsy Rus. Fed. 11 N4
Lyubeshiv Ukr. 13 E6
Lyubim Rus. Fed. 12 I4
Lyubytino Rus. Fed. 12 G4
Lyudinovo Rus. Fed. 13 G5
Lyunda r. Rus. Fed. 12 J4
Lyzha r. Rus. Fed. 12 M2

M

Ma'agan Israel 39 B3
Maale Maldives see Male
Maale Atholhu atoll Maldives see Male Atoll
Maalhosmadulu Atholhu Uthuruburi atoll Maldives see North Maalhosmadulu Atoll
Maalhosmadulu Atoll Maldives 38 B5
Ma'ān Jordan 39 B4
Maan Turkey see Nusratiye
Maaninka Fin. 14 O5
Maaninkavaara Fin. 14 P3
Maardu Estonia 15 N7
Maarianhamina Fin. see Mariehamn
Ma'arrat an Nu'mān Syria 39 C2
Maas-Schwalm-Nette nat. park Germany/Neth. 17 J5
Maastricht Neth. 17 J5
Maaza Plateau Egypt 34 C6
Mabalane Moz. 51 K2
Mabana Dem. Rep. Congo 48 C3
Mabaruma Guyana 68 G2
Mabein Myanmar 37 I5
Mabel Creek Australia 55 F7
Mabel Downs Australia 54 D4
Mablethorpe U.K. 18 H5
Mabopane S. Africa 51 I3
Mabote Moz. 51 L2
Mabrak, Jabal mt. Jordan 39 B4
Mabuasehube Game Reserve nature res. Botswana 50 F3
Mabule Botswana 50 G3
Mabutsane Botswana 50 F3
Macá, Monte mt. Chile 70 B7
Macadam Plains Australia 55 B6
Macaé Brazil 71 C3
Macajuba Brazil 71 C1
Macaloge Moz. 49 D5
MacAlpine Lake Canada 61 H3
Macandze Moz. 51 K2
Macao China 43 K8
Macao China see Macao
Macapá Brazil 69 H3
Macará Ecuador 68 C4
Macarani Brazil 71 C1
Macas Ecuador 68 C4
Macassar Indon. see Makassar
Macau Brazil 69 K5
Macaúba Brazil 69 H6
Macauley Island N.Z. 53 I5
Maccaretane Moz. 51 K3
Macclesfield U.K. 18 E5
Macdonald, Lake salt flat Australia 55 E5
Macdonald Range hills Australia 54 D3
Macdonnell Ranges mts Australia 55 E5
MacDowell Lake Canada 63 I1
Macduff U.K. 20 G3
Macedo de Cavaleiros Port. 25 C3
Macedon mt. Australia 58 B6
Macedon country Europe see Macedonia
Macedonia country Europe 27 I4
Maceió Brazil 69 K5
Macenta Guinea 46 C4
Macerata Italy 26 E3
Macfarlane, Lake salt flat Australia 57 B7
Macgillycuddy's Reeks mts Ireland 21 C6
Machachi Ecuador 68 C4
Machaila Moz. 51 K2
Machakos Kenya 48 D4
Machala Ecuador 68 C4
Machali China see Madoi
Machanga Moz. 49 D6
Machar Marshes Sudan 32 D8
Machattie, Lake salt flat Australia 56 B5
Machatuine Moz. 51 K3
Machaze Moz. see Chitobe
Macherla India 38 C2
Machhagan India 37 F5
Machias ME U.S.A. 63 N3
Machias NY U.S.A. 64 B1
Machilipatnam India 38 D2
Machiques Venez. 68 D1
Machrihanish U.K. 20 D5
Machu Picchu tourist site Peru 68 D6
Machynlleth U.K. 19 D6
Macia Moz. 51 K3
Macias Nguema i. Equat. Guinea see Bioco
Măcin Romania 27 M2
Macintyre r. Australia 58 E2
Macintyre Brook r. Australia 58 E2
Maçka Turkey 35 E2
Mackay Australia 56 E4
Mackay, Lake salt flat Australia 54 E5
MacKay Lake Canada 60 G3
Mackenzie r. Australia 56 E4
Mackenzie Canada 60 F4
Mackenzie r. Canada 60 E3
Mackenzie Guyana see Linden
Mackenzie atoll Micronesia see Ulithi
Mackenzie Bay Antarctica 76 E2
Mackenzie Bay Canada 60 E3
Mackenzie King Island Canada 61 G2
Mackenzie Mountains Canada 60 E3
Mackenzie-Peace-Finlay r. Can. 60 E3
Mackillop, Lake salt flat Australia see Yamma Yamma, Lake
Mackintosh Range hills Australia 55 D6
Macklin Canada 62 F1
Macksville Australia 58 F3
Maclean Australia 58 F2
Maclear S. Africa 51 I6
MacLeod Canada see Fort Macleod
MacLeod, Lake imp. l. Australia 55 A6
Macmillan Pass Canada 60 F3
Macomb U.S.A. 63 I3
Macomer Sardinia Italy 26 C4
Mâcon France 24 G3
Macon GA U.S.A. 63 K5
Macon MO U.S.A. 63 I4
Macondo Angola 49 C5
Macpherson Robertson Land reg. Antarctica see Mac. Robertson Land
Macquarie r. Australia 58 C3
Macquarie, Lake b. Australia 58 E4
Macquarie Island S. Pacific Ocean 74 G9
Macquarie Marshes Australia 58 C3
Macquarie Mountain Australia 58 D4
Macquarie Ridge sea feature S. Pacific Ocean 74 G9
Mac. Robertson Land reg. Antarctica 76 E2
Macroom Ireland 21 D6
Macumba Australia 57 A5
Macumba watercourse Australia 57 B5
Macuzari, Presa resr Mex. 66 C3
Mādabā Jordan 39 B4
Madadeni S. Africa 51 J4
Madagascar country Africa 49 E6
Madagascar Basin sea feature Indian Ocean 73 L7
Madagascar Ridge sea feature Indian Ocean 73 K8
Madagasikara country Africa see Madagascar
Madakasira India 38 C3
Madama Niger 47 E2
Madan Bulg. 27 K4
Madanapalle India 38 C3
Madang P.N.G. 52 E2
Madaoua Niger 46 D3
Madaripur Bangl. 37 G5
Madau Turkm. see Madaw
Madaw Turkm. 35 I3
Madaya Myanmar 37 I5
Madded India 38 D2
Madeira r. Brazil 68 G4
Madeira terr. N. Atlantic Ocean 46 B1
Madeira, Arquipélago da terr. N. Atlantic Ocean see Madeira
Maden Turkey 35 E3
Madera Mex. 66 C3
Madera CA U.S.A. 65 B2
Madgaon India 38 B3
Madha India 38 B2
Madhavpur India 36 B5
Madhepura India 37 F4
Madhipura India see Madhepura
Madhubani India 37 F4
Madhya Pradesh state India 36 D5
Madibogo S. Africa 51 G4
Madidi r. Bol. 68 E6
Madikeri India 38 B3
Madikwe Game Reserve nature res. S. Africa 51 H3
Madīnat ath Thawrah Syria 39 D2
Madingo-Kayes Congo 49 B4
Madingou Congo 49 B4
Madison IN U.S.A. 63 J4
Madison SD U.S.A. 63 H3
Madison VA U.S.A. 64 B3
Madison WI U.S.A. 63 J3
Madison r. U.S.A. 62 E2
Madison Heights VA U.S.A. 64 B4
Madisonville KY U.S.A. 63 J4
Madley, Mount hill Australia 55 C6
Mado Gashi Kenya 48 D3
Madoi China 37 I2
Madona Latvia 15 O8
Madpura India 36 B4
Madra Dağı mts Turkey 27 L5
Madrakah Saudi Arabia 32 E5
Madrakah, Ra's c. Oman 33 I6
Madras India see Chennai
Madras state India see Tamil Nadu
Madras U.S.A. 62 C3
Madre, Laguna lag. Mex. 66 E3
Madre de Dios r. Peru 68 E6
Madre de Dios, Isla i. Chile 70 A8
Madre del Sur, Sierra mts Mex. 66 D5
Madre Occidental, Sierra mts Mex. 66 C3
Madre Oriental, Sierra mts Mex. 66 D3
Madrid Spain 25 E3
Madridejos Spain 25 E4
Madugula India 38 D2
Madura i. Indon. 41 D8
Madurai India 38 C4
Madurantakam India 38 C3
Madvār, Kūh-e mt. Iran 35 I5
Madvezh'ya vol. Rus. Fed. 44 H3
Madwas India 37 E4
Maé i. Vanuatu see Émaé
Maebashi Japan 45 E5
Mae Hong Son Thai. 42 H9
Mae Sai Thai. 42 H8
Mae Sariang Thai. 42 H9
Maevatanana Madag. 49 E5
Maéwo i. Vanuatu 53 G3
Mafeking S. Africa see Mafikeng
Mafeteng Lesotho 51 H5
Maffra Australia 58 C6
Mafia Island Tanz. 49 D4
Mafikeng S. Africa 51 G3
Mafinga Tanz. 49 D4
Mafra Brazil 71 A4
Mafraq Jordan see Al Mafraq
Magabeni S. Africa 51 J6
Magadan Rus. Fed. 29 Q4
Magadi Kenya 48 D4
Magaiza Moz. 51 K2
Magallanes Chile see Punta Arenas
Magallanes, Estrecho de Chile see Magellan, Strait of
Magangue Col. 68 D2
Mağara Dağı mt. Turkey 39 A1
Magaramkent Rus. Fed. 35 H2
Magaria Niger 46 D3
Magarida P.N.G. 56 E1
Magas Rus. Fed. 13 J8
Magdagachi Rus. Fed. 44 B1
Magdalena Bol. 68 F6
Magdalena r. Col. 68 D1
Magdalena Sonora Mex. 66 B2
Magdalena, Bahía b. Mex. 66 B4
Magdalena, Isla i. Chile 70 B6
Magdeburg Germany 17 M4
Magdelaine Cays atoll Australia 56 E3
Magellan, Strait of Chile 70 B8
Magellan Seamounts sea feature N. Pacific Ocean 74 F4
Magenta, Lake salt flat Australia 55 B8
Magerøya i. Norway 14 N1
Maggiorasca, Monte mt. Italy 26 C2
Maggiore, Lago Italy see Maggiore, Lake
Maggiore, Lake Italy 26 C2
Maghâgha Egypt see Maghāghah
Maghāghah Egypt 34 C5
Maghama Mauritania 46 B3
Maghâra, Gebel hill Egypt see Maghārah, Jabal
Maghārah, Jabal hill Egypt 39 A4
Maghera U.K. 21 F3
Magherafelt U.K. 21 F3
Maghnia Alg. 25 F6
Maghull U.K. 18 E5
Magilligan Point U.K. 21 F2
Magna Grande mt. Sicily Italy 26 F6
Magnetic Island Australia 56 D3
Magnetic Passage Australia 56 D3
Magnetity Rus. Fed. 14 R2
Magnitogorsk Rus. Fed. 28 G4
Magnolia AR U.S.A. 63 I5
Mago Rus. Fed. 44 F1
Màgoé Moz. 49 D5
Mago National Park Eth. 48 D3
Magosa Cyprus see Famagusta
Magpie, Lac l. Canada 63 O1
Magṭa' Laḥjar Mauritania 46 B3
Magu Tanz. 48 D4
Magu, Khrebet mts Rus. Fed. 44 E1
Magude Moz. 51 K3
Magura Bangl. 37 G5
Magway Myanmar see Magwe
Magwe Myanmar 37 H5
Magyar Köztársaság country Europe see Hungary
Magyichaung Myanmar 37 H5
Mahābād Iran 35 G3
Mahabharat Range mts Nepal 37 F4
Mahaboobnagar India see Mahbubnagar
Mahad India 38 B2
Mahadeo Hills India 36 D5
Mahaffey PA U.S.A. 64 B2
Mahajan India 36 C3
Mahajanga Madag. 49 E5
Mahalapye Botswana 51 H2
Mahale Mountains National Park Tanz. 49 C4
Mahalevona Madag. 49 E5
Mahallāt Iran 35 H4
Māhān Iran 33 I3
Mahanadi r. India 38 E1
Mahanoro Madag. 49 E5
Maha Oya Sri Lanka 38 D5
Maharashtra state India 38 B2
Maha Sarakham Thai. 31 J5
Mahasham, Wâdi el watercourse Egypt see Muhashsham, Wādī al
Mahbubabad India 38 D2
Mahbubnagar India 38 C2
Mahd adh Dhahab Saudi Arabia 32 F5
Mahdia Alg. 25 G6
Mahdia Guyana 69 G2
Mahdia Tunisia 26 D7
Mahé i. Seychelles 73 L6
Mahendragiri mt. India 38 E2
Mahenge Tanz. 49 D4
Mahesana India 36 C5
Mahi r. India 36 C5
Mahia Peninsula N.Z. 59 F4
Mahilyow Belarus 13 F5
Mahim India 38 B2
Mah Jān Iran 35 I5
Mahlabatini S. Africa 51 J5
Mahmudabad Iran 35 I3
Maḩmūd-e 'Erāqī Afgh. see Maḩmūd-e Rāqī
Maḩmūd-e Rāqī Afgh. 36 B2
Maho Sri Lanka 38 D5
Mahoba India 36 D4
Maholi India 36 E4
Mahón Spain 25 I4
Mahrauni India 36 D4
Mahrès Tunisia 26 D7
Māhrūd Iran 33 J3
Mahsana India see Mahesana
Mahudaung mts Myanmar 37 H5
Mahur India 38 C2
Mahuva India 36 B5
Mahwa India 36 D4
Mahya Dağı mt. Turkey 27 L4
Mai i. Vanuatu see Émaé
Maiaia Moz. see Nacala
Maicao Col. 68 D1
Maidenhead U.K. 19 G7
Maidstone Canada 62 F1
Maidstone U.K. 19 H7
Maiduguri Nigeria 46 E3
Maiella, Parco Nazionale della nat. park Italy 26 F3
Mai Gudo mt. Eth. 48 D3
Maigue r. Ireland 21 D5
Maihar India 36 E4
Maikala Range hills India 36 E5
Maiko r. Dem. Rep. Congo 48 C3
Mailan Hill mt. India 37 E5
Mailsi Pak. 36 C3
Main r. U.K. 21 F3
Maindargi India 38 C2
Mai-Ndombe, Lac l. Dem. Rep. Congo 48 B4
Maindong Xizang China see Coqên
Maine state U.S.A. 63 N2
Maine, Gulf of Canada/U.S.A. 61 L5
Mainé Hanari, Cerro hill Col. 68 D4
Maïné-Soroa Niger 46 E3
Maingkaing Myanmar 37 H4
Maingkwan Myanmar 37 I4
Mainland i. Scotland U.K. 20 F1
Mainland i. Scotland U.K. 20 [inset]
Mainoru Australia 54 F3
Mainpat reg. India 37 E5
Mainpuri India 36 D4
Main Range National Park Australia 58 F2
Maintirano Madag. 49 E5
Mainz Germany 17 L5
Maio i. Cape Verde 46 [inset]
Maipú Arg. 70 E5
Maiskhal Island Bangl. 37 G5
Maitengwe Botswana 49 C6
Maitland N.S.W. Australia 58 E4
Maitland S.A. Australia 57 B7
Maitland r. Australia 54 B5
Maitri research station Antarctica 76 C2
Maiwo i. Vanuatu see Maéwo
Maiyu, Mount hill Australia 54 E4
Maíz, Islas del is Nicaragua 67 H6
Maizar Pak. 36 B2
Maizuru Japan 45 D6
Maja Jezercë mt. Albania 27 H3
Majdel Aanjar tourist site Lebanon 39 B3
Majene Indon. 41 D8
Majī Eth. 48 D3
Majiazi China 44 B2
Majōl country N. Pacific Ocean see Marshall Islands
Major, Puig mt. Spain 25 H4
Majorca i. Spain 25 H4
Mājro atoll Marshall Is see Majuro
Majunga Madag. see Mahajanga
Majuro atoll Marshall Is 74 H5
Majwemasweu S. Africa 51 H5
Makabana Congo 48 B4
Makale Indon. 41 D8
Makalu mt. China/Nepal 37 F4
Makalu Barun National Park Nepal 37 F4
Makanchi Kazakh. 42 E3

Makanpur India 36 E4
Makari Mountain National Park Tanz. see
   Mahale Mountains National Park
Makarov Rus. Fed. 44 F2
Makarov Basin sea feature Arctic Ocean
   77 B1
Makarska Croatia 26 G3
Makar'ye Rus. Fed. 12 K4
Makar'yev Rus. Fed. 12 I4
Makasar, Selat strait Indon. see
   Makassar, Selat
Makassar Indon. 41 D8
Makassar, Selat strait Indon. 41 D8
Makassar Strait Indon. see Makassar, Selat
Makat Kazakh. 30 E2
Makatini Flats lowland S. Africa 51 K4
Makedonija country Europe see Macedonia
Makeni Sierra Leone 46 B4
Makete Tanz. 49 D4
Makeyevka Ukr. see Makiyivka
Makgadikgadi depr. Botswana 49 C6
Makgadikgadi Pans National Park
   Botswana 49 C6
Makhachkala Rus. Fed. 13 J8
Makhad Pak. 36 B2
Makhado S. Africa 51 I2
Makhāzin, Kathib al des. Egypt 39 A4
Makhāzin, Kathib al des. Egypt 39 A4
Makhāzin, Kathib al
Makhazine, Barrage El dam Morocco
   25 D6
Makhmür Iraq 35 F4
Makhtal India 38 C2
Makin atoll Kiribati see Butaritari
Makindu Kenya 48 D4
Makinsk Kazakh. 31 G1
Makira i. Solomon Is see San Cristobal
Makiyivka Ukr. 13 H6
Makkah Saudi Arabia see Mecca
Makkovik Canada 61 M4
Makó Hungary 27 I1
Makokou Gabon 48 B3
Makopong Botswana 50 F3
Makotipoko Congo 47 E5
Makran reg. Iran/Pak. 33 J4
Makrana India 36 C4
Makran Coast Range mts Pak. 33 J4
Makri India 38 D2
Maksatikha Rus. Fed. 12 G4
Maksi India 36 D5
Maksudangarh India 36 D5
Mākū Iran 35 G3
Makunguwiro Tanz. 49 D5
Makurdi Nigeria 46 D4
Makwassie S. Africa 51 G4
Mal India 37 G4
Mala Ireland see Mallow
Mala i. Solomon Is see Malaita
Malå Sweden 14 K4
Mala, Punta pt Panama 67 H7
Malabar Coast India 38 B3
Malabo Equat. Guinea 46 D4
Malaca Spain see Málaga
Malacca Malaysia see Melaka
Malacca, Strait of Indon./Malaysia 41 B7
Malad City U.S.A. 62 E3
Maladzyechna Belarus 15 O9
Malá Fatra nat. park Slovakia 17 Q6
Málaga Spain 25 D5
Malagasy Republic country Africa see
   Madagascar
Malaita i. Solomon Is 53 G2
Malakal Sudan 32 D4
Malakanagiri India see Malkangiri
Malakheti Nepal 36 E3
Malakula i. Vanuatu 53 G3
Malang Indon. 41 D8
Malangana Nepal see Malangwa
Malange Angola see Malanje
Malangwa Nepal 37 F4
Malanje Angola 49 B4
Malappuram India 38 C4
Mälaren l. Sweden 15 J7
Malargüe Arg. 70 C5
Malatya Turkey 34 E3
Malavalli India 38 C3
Malawi country Africa 49 D5
Malawi, Lake Africa see Nyasa, Lake
Malawi National Park Zambia see
   Nyika National Park
Malaya pen. Malaysia see
   Peninsular Malaysia
Malaya Pera Rus. Fed. 12 L2
Malaya Vishera Rus. Fed. 12 G4
Malāyer Iran 35 H4
Malay Reef Australia 56 E3
Malaysia country Asia 41 C7
Malaysia, Semenanjung pen. Malaysia see
   Peninsular Malaysia
Malazgirt Turkey 35 F3
Malbon Australia 56 C4
Malbork Poland 17 Q3
Malchin Germany 17 N4
Malcolm Australia 55 C7
Malcolm, Point Australia 55 C8
Malden Island Kiribati 75 J6
Maldon Australia 58 B6
Maldon U.K. 19 H7
Maldonado Uruguay 70 F4
Male Maldives 73 M5
Male Atoll Maldives 31 G6
Malebogo S. Africa 51 G5
Malegaon Mahar. India 38 B1
Malegaon Mahar. India 38 B1
Malé Karpaty hills Slovakia 17 P6
Malele Dem. Rep. Congo 49 B4
Maler Kotla India 36 C3
Maleševske Planine mts Bulg./Macedonia
   27 J4
Malgobek Rus. Fed. 35 G2
Malgomaj l. Sweden 14 J4
Malha, Naqb al Egypt see Māliḥah, Naqb
Malhada Brazil 71 C1
Malheur Lake U.S.A. 62 D3
Mali country Africa 46 C3
Mali Dem. Rep. Congo 48 C4
Mali Guinea 46 B3
Maliana East Timor 54 D2
Malianjing China 42 H4
Māliḥah, Naqb al Egypt 39 A5
Malili Indon. 52 C2
Malin Ukr. see Malyn
Malindi Kenya 48 E4
Malines Belgium see Mechelen
Malin Head hd Ireland 21 E2
Malin More Ireland 21 D3
Mali Raginac mt. Croatia 26 F2
Malka r. Rus. Fed. 35 G2
Malkangiri India 38 D2
Malkapur India 38 B2
Malkara Turkey 27 L4
Mal'kavichy Belarus 15 O10
Malko Tŭrnovo Bulg. 27 L4
Mallacoota Australia 58 D6
Mallacoota Inlet b. Australia 58 D6
Mallaig U.K. 20 D4
Mallawi Egypt 34 C6
Mallee Cliffs National Park Australia 57 C7

Mallery Lake Canada 61 I3
Mallét Brazil 71 A4
Mallorca i. Spain see Majorca
Mallow Ireland 21 D5
Mallowa Well Australia 54 D5
Mallwyd U.K. 19 D6
Malm Norway 14 G4
Malmberget Sweden 14 L3
Malmédy Belgium 17 K5
Malmesbury S. Africa 50 D7
Malmesbury U.K. 19 E7
Malmö Sweden 15 H9
Malmyzh Rus. Fed. 12 K4
Maloca Brazil 69 G3
Malonje mt. Tanz. 49 D4
Maloshuyka Rus. Fed. 12 H3
Malosmadulu Atoll Maldives see
   Maalhosmadulu Atoll
Måløy Norway 14 D6
Maloyaroslavets Rus. Fed. 13 H5
Malozemel'skaya Tundra lowland Rus. Fed.
   12 K2
Malpelo, Isla de i. N. Pacific Ocean 67 H8
Malprabha r. India 38 C2
Malta country Europe 26 F7
Malta Latvia 15 O8
Malta MT U.S.A. 62 F2
Malta Channel Italy/Malta 26 F6
Maltahöhe Namibia 50 C3
Maltby U.K. 18 F5
Maltby le Marsh U.K. 18 H5
Malton U.K. 18 G4
Malukken is Indon. see Moluccas
Maluku is Indon. see Moluccas
Maluku, Laut sea Indon. 41 E8
Ma'lūlā, Jabal mts Syria 39 C3
Malung Sweden 15 H6
Maluti Mountains Lesotho 51 I5
Malu'u Solomon Is 53 G2
Malvan India 38 B2
Malvasia Greece see Monemvasia
Malvern U.K. see Great Malvern
Malvern U.S.A. 63 I5
Malvérnia Moz. see Chicualacuala
Malvinas, Islas terr. S. Atlantic Ocean see
   Falkland Islands
Malyn Ukr. 13 F6
Malyy Anyuy r. Rus. Fed. 29 R3
Malyy Derbety Rus. Fed. 13 J7
Malyy Kavkaz mts Asia see Lesser Caucasus
Malyy Lyakhovskiy, Ostrov i. Rus. Fed.
   29 P2
Malyy Uzen' r. Kazakh./Rus. Fed. 13 K6
Mama r. Rus. Fed. 29 P3
Mamadysh Rus. Fed. 12 K5
Mamafubedu S. Africa 51 G4
Mambai Brazil 71 B1
Mambasa Dem. Rep. Congo 48 C3
Mamelodi S. Africa 51 I3
Mamfe Cameroon 46 D4
Mamison Pass Rus. Fed. see
   Klukhorskiy, Pereval
Mamit India 37 H5
Mammoth Reservoir CA U.S.A. 65 C2
Mamonas Brazil 71 C1
Mamoré r. Bol./Brazil 68 F6
Mamou Guinea 46 B3
Mampikony Madag. 49 E5
Mampong Ghana 46 C4
Mamuju Indon. 52 B2
Mamuno Botswana 50 E2
Man Côte d'Ivoire 46 C4
Man India 38 B2
Man r. India 38 C2
Man, Isle of terr. Irish Sea 18 C4
Manacapuru Brazil 68 F4
Manacor Spain 25 H4
Manado Indon. 41 E7
Managua Nicaragua 67 G6
Manakara Madag. 49 E6
Manakau mt. N.Z. 59 D6
Manākhah Yemen 32 F6
Manama Bahrain 32 H4
Manamadurai India 38 C4
Mana Maroka National Park S. Africa
   51 H5
Manamelkudi India 38 C4
Manam Island P.N.G. 52 E2
Manananara Avaratra Madag. 49 E5
Manangoora Australia 56 B3
Mananjary Madag. 49 E6
Manantali, Lac de l. Mali 46 B3
Manantenina Madag. 49 E6
Mana Pass China/India 36 D3
Mana Pools National Park Zimbabwe
   49 C5
Manapouri, Lake N.Z. 59 A7
Manasa India 36 C4
Manas He r. China 42 F3
Manas Hu l. China 42 F3
Manaslu mt. Nepal 37 F3
Manassas VA U.S.A. 64 C4
Manastir Macedonia see Bitola
Manas Wildlife Sanctuary nature res.
   Bhutan 37 G4
Man-aung Kyun Myanmar 42 G9
Man-aung Kyun i. Myanmar see
   Man-aung Kyun
Manaus Brazil 68 F4
Manavgat Turkey 34 C3
Manbazar India 37 F5
Manbij Syria 39 C2
Manby U.K. 18 H5
Manchar India 38 B2
Manchester U.K. 18 E5
Manchester CT U.S.A. 64 E2
Manchester MD U.S.A. 64 C3
Manchester NH U.S.A. 64 F1
Manchester VT U.S.A. 64 E1
Mancılık Turkey 34 E3
Mand, Rūd-e r. Iran 35 H5
Manda Tanz. 49 D4
Manda, Jebel mt. Sudan 47 F4
Manda, Parc National de nat. park Chad
   47 E4
Mandabe Madag. 49 E6
Mandal Afgh. 33 J3
Mandal Norway 15 E7
Mandala, Puncak mt. Indon. 41 G8
Mandalay Myanmar 37 I5
Mandale Myanmar see Mandalay
Mandalgovĭ Mongolia 42 J3
Mandalī Iraq 35 G4
Mandalt China 43 K4
Mandan U.S.A. 62 G2
Mandas Sardinia Italy 26 C5
Mandasa India 38 D2
Mandasor India see Mandsaur
Mandav Hills India 36 B5
Mandera Kenya 48 E3
Manderfield UT U.S.A. 65 F1
Mandeville Jamaica 67 I5
Mandeville N.Z. 59 B7
Mandha India 36 B4
Mandhoúdhíon Greece see Mantoudi
Mandi India 36 D3
Mandiana Guinea 46 C3
Mandi Burewala Pak. 33 L3
Mandié Moz. 49 D5
Mandini S. Africa 51 J5
Mandira Dam India 37 F5

Mandla India 36 E5
Mandleshwar India 36 C5
Mandrael India 36 D4
Mandritsara Madag. 49 E5
Mandsaur India 36 C4
Mandurah Australia 55 A8
Manduria Italy 26 G4
Mandvi India 36 B5
Mandya India 38 C3
Manerbio Italy 26 D2
Manevychi Ukr. 13 E6
Manfalūṭ Egypt 34 D6
Manfredonia Italy 26 F4
Manfredonia, Golfo di g. Italy 26 G4
Manga Brazil 71 C1
Manga Burkina 46 C3
Mangabeiras, Serra das hills Brazil 69 I6
Mangai Dem. Rep. Congo 48 B4
Mangaia i. Cook Is 75 J7
Mangakino N.Z. 59 E4
Mangalagiri India 38 D2
Mangalia Romania 27 M3
Mangalmé Chad 47 E3
Mangalore India 38 B3
Mangaon India 38 B2
Mangareva Islands Fr. Polynesia see
   Gambier, Îles
Mangaung Free State S. Africa 51 H5
Mangaung Free State S. Africa see
   Bloemfontein
Mangawan India 37 E4
Mangea i. Cook Is see Mangaia
Mangghyshlaq Kazakh. see Mangystau
Mangghystaü Kazakh. see Mangystau
Mangghystaü admin. div. Kazakh. see
   Mangistauskaya Oblast'
Mangghyt Uzbek. see Mang'it
Manghit Uzbek. see Mang'it
Mangin Range mts Myanmar see
   Mingin Range
Mangistau Kazakh. see Mangystau
Mangistauskaya Oblast' admin. div.
   Kazakh. 35 I2
Mang'it Uzbek. 33 J1
Mangla Bangl. see Mongla
Mangla Pak. 33 L2
Mangnai China 42 G5
Mangnai Zhen China 42 G5
Mangochi Malawi 49 D5
Mangoky r. Madag. 49 E6
Mangole i. Indon. 41 E8
Mangoli India 44 A4
Mangotsfield U.K. 19 E7
Mangqystaü Shyghanaghy b. Kazakh. see
   Mangyshlakskiy Zaliv
Mangrol India 36 B5
Mangrul India 38 C1
Mangshi China see Luxi
Mangualde Port. 25 C3
Mangueni, Plateau du Niger 46 E2
Mangui China 44 A2
Mangula Zimbabwe see Mhangura
Mangyshlak Kazakh. see Mangystau
Mangyshlak, Poluostrov pen. Kazakh.
   35 H1
Mangystau Oblast admin. div. Kazakh. see
   Mangistauskaya Oblast'
Mangyshlakskiy Zaliv b. Kazakh. 35 H1
Mangystau Kazakh. 35 H2
Manhã Brazil 71 B1
Manhattan U.S.A. 63 H4
Manhica Moz. 51 K3
Manhoca Moz. 51 K4
Manhuaçu Brazil 71 C3
Manhuaçu r. Brazil 71 C2
Mani China 42 I6
Mania r. Madag. 49 E5
Maniago Italy 26 E1
Manicouagan r. Canada 63 N2
Manicouagan, Réservoir resr Canada 63 N1
Manifah Saudi Arabia 35 H6
Manihiki atoll Cook Is 74 J6
Maniitsoq Greenland 61 M3
Manikchhari Bangl. 37 H5
Manikgarh India see Rajura
Manila Phil. 41 E6
Manilda Australia 58 D4
Manilla Australia 58 E3
Maningrida Australia 54 F3
Manipur India see Imphal
Manipur state India 37 H4
Manisa Turkey 27 L5
Manises Turkey 27 L5
Manistee U.S.A. 63 J3
Manitoba prov. Canada 62 H1
Manitoba, Lake Canada 61 I4
Manitou Beach NY U.S.A. 64 C1
Manitou Islands U.S.A. 63 J2
Manitowoc U.S.A. 63 J3
Maniwaki Canada 63 L2
Manizales Col. 68 C2
Manja Madag. 49 E6
Manjarabad India 38 C4
Manjeri India 38 C4
Manjhand Pak. 36 B4
Manjhi India 37 F4
Manjra r. India 38 C2
Mankaiana Swaziland see Mankayane
Mankato MN U.S.A. 63 I3
Mankayane Swaziland 51 J4
Mankera Pak. 36 B3
Mankono Côte d'Ivoire 46 C4
Manley Hot Springs U.S.A. 60 C3
Manmad India 38 B1
Mann r. Australia 54 F3
Mann, Mount Australia 55 E6
Mannahill Australia 57 B7
Mannar Sri Lanka 38 C4
Mannar, Gulf of India/Sri Lanka 38 C4
Manneru r. India 38 C3
Mannheim Germany 17 L6
Mannicolo Islands Solomon Is see
   Vanikoro Islands
Manning r. Australia 58 F3
Manning Canada 60 G4
Mannington WV U.S.A. 64 A3
Manningtree U.K. 19 I7
Mann Ranges mts Australia 55 E6
Mannsville NY U.S.A. 64 C1
Mannu, Capo c. Sardinia Italy 26 C4
Man-of-War Rocks is U.S.A. see
   Gardner Pinnacles
Manohardpur India 36 D4
Manohar Thana India 36 D4
Manokotak U.S.A. 60 C4
Manokwari Indon. 41 F8
Manosque France 24 G5
Manouane, Lac l. Canada 63 M1
Manp'o N. Korea 44 B4
Manra i. Kiribati 53 I2
Manresa Spain 25 G3
Mansa Gujarat India 36 C5
Mansa Punjab India 36 C3
Mansa Konko Gambia 46 B3
Mansehra Pak. 33 L3
Mansel Island Canada 61 L3
Mansfield Australia 58 C6
Mansfield U.K. 19 F5

Mansfield LA U.S.A. 63 I5
Mansfield OH U.S.A. 63 K3
Mansfield PA U.S.A. 64 C2
Mansi Myanmar 37 H4
Manso r. Brazil see Mortes, Rio das
Manta Ecuador 68 B4
Mantaro r. Peru 68 D6
Manteca CA U.S.A. 65 B2
Mantena Brazil 71 C2
Mantes-la-Jolie France 24 E2
Manti U.S.A. 65 F1
Mantiqueira, Serra da mts Brazil 71 B3
Mantoudi Greece 27 J5
Mantova Italy see Mantua
Mäntsälä Fin. 15 N6
Mänttä Fin. 14 N5
Mantua Italy 26 D2
Mantuan Downs Australia 56 D5
Manturovo Rus. Fed. 12 J4
Mäntyharju Fin. 15 O6
Mäntyjärvi Fin. 14 O3
Manú Peru 68 D6
Manu, Parque Nacional nat. park Peru
   68 D6
Manuae atoll Fr. Polynesia 75 J7
Manu'a Islands American Samoa 53 I3
Manuel Ribas Brazil 71 A4
Manuel Vitorino Brazil 71 C1
Manuelzinho Brazil 69 H5
Manui i. Indon. 41 E8
Manukau N.Z. 59 E3
Manukau Harbour N.Z. 59 E3
Manunda watercourse Australia 57 B7
Manus Island P.N.G. 52 E2
Manvi India 38 C3
Many U.S.A. 63 I5
Manyana Botswana 51 G3
Manyas Turkey 27 L4
Manyas Gölü l. Turkey see Kuş Gölü
Manych-Gudilo, Ozero l. Rus. Fed. 13 I7
Manyoni Tanz. 49 D4
Manzai Pak. 36 B2
Manzanares Spain 25 E4
Manzanillo Cuba 67 I4
Manzanillo Mex. 66 D5
Manzhouli China 43 L3
Manzini Swaziland 51 J4
Mao Chad 47 E3
Maó Spain see Mahón
Maoke, Pegunungan mts Indon. 41 F8
Maokeng S. Africa 51 H4
Maokui Shan mt. China 44 A4
Maolin China 44 A4
Maoming China 43 K8
Maopora i. Indon. 54 D1
Mapai Moz. 51 J2
Mapam Yumco l. China 37 E3
Mapanza Zambia 49 C5
Maphodi S. Africa 51 G6
Mapimí, Bolsón de des. Mex. 66 D3
Mapinhane Moz. 51 L2
Mapiri Bol. 68 E7
Maple Creek Canada 62 F2
Mapmakers Seamounts sea feature
   N. Pacific Ocean 74 F3
Mapoon Australia 56 C1
Mapoteng Lesotho 51 H5
Mapuera r. Brazil 69 G4
Mapulanguene Moz. 51 K3
Maputo Moz. 51 K3
Maputo prov. Moz. 51 K3
Maputo r. Moz./S. Africa 51 K4
Maputo, Baía de b. Moz. 51 K4
Maputsoe Lesotho 51 H5
Maqanshy Kazakh. see Makanchi
Maqar an Na'am well Iraq 35 F5
Maqat Kazakh. see Makat
Maqên Kangri mt. China 42 H6
Maqna Saudi Arabia 34 D5
Maqteïr reg. Mauritania 46 B2
Ma Qu r. China see Yellow
Maquan He r. China 37 F3
Maquela do Zombo Angola 49 B4
Maquinchao Arg. 70 C6
Mar, Serra do mts Rio de Janeiro/São Paulo
   Brazil 71 B3
Mar, Serra do mts Rio Grande do Sul/Santa
   Catarina Brazil 71 A5
Mara r. India 37 E5
Mara S. Africa 51 I2
Maraã Brazil 68 E4
Marabá Brazil 69 I5
Maraboon, Lake resr Australia 56 D4
Maracá, Ilha de i. Brazil 69 H3
Maracaibo Venez. 68 D1
Maracaibo, Lago de Venez. see
   Maracaibo, Lake
Maracaibo, Lake Venez. 68 D2
Maracaju Brazil 70 E2
Maracaju, Serra de hills Brazil 70 E2
Maracanda Uzbek. see Samarqand
Maracás Brazil 71 C1
Maracás, Chapada de hills Brazil 71 C1
Maracay Venez. 68 E1
Marādah Libya 47 E2
Maradi Niger 46 D3
Marāgheh Iran 35 G3
Marahuaca, Cerro mt. Venez. 68 E3
Marajó, Baía de est. Brazil 69 I4
Marajó, Ilha de i. Brazil 69 H4
Marakele National Park S. Africa 51 H3
Maralal Kenya 48 D3
Maralbashi China see Bachu
Maralinga Australia 55 E7
Maralwexi China see Bachu
Maramasike i. Solomon Is 53 G2
Maramba Zambia see Livingstone
Marambio research station Antarctica 76 A2
Marand Iran 35 G3
Marandellas Zimbabwe see Marondera
Maranhão r. Brazil 71 A1
Maranoa r. Australia 58 D5
Marañón r. Peru 68 D4
Marão Moz. 51 L3
Marão mt. Port. 25 C3
Mara Rosa Brazil 71 A1
Maraş Turkey see Kahramanmaraş
Marathon NY U.S.A. 64 C1
Maraú Brazil 71 D1
Märäzä Azer. 35 H2
Marbella Spain 25 D5
Marble Bar Australia 54 B5
Marble Hall S. Africa 51 I3
Marbul Pass Jammu and Kashmir 36 C2
Marburg S. Africa 51 J6
Marburg Slovenia see Maribor
Marburg an der Lahn Germany 17 L5
Marca, Ponta do pt Angola 49 B5
Marcali Hungary 26 G1
Marcelino Ramos Brazil 71 A4
March U.K. 19 H6
Marche reg. France 24 E3
Marchena Spain 25 D5
Marchena, Isla i. Galápagos Ecuador see
   Marchinbar Island Australia 56 B1
Mar Chiquita, Laguna l. Arg. 70 D4
Marchtrenk Austria 17 O6
Marcona Peru 68 C7
Marcus Baker, Mount U.S.A. 60 D3
Marcy, Mount U.S.A. 63 M3
Mar del Plata Arg. 70 E5
Mardan Pak. 36 B2

Mardin Turkey 35 F3
Maré i. New Caledonia 53 G4
Maree, Loch l. U.K. 20 D3
Marevo Rus. Fed. 12 G4
Marfa U.S.A. 62 G5
Marganets Ukr. see Marhanets'
Margao India see Madgaon
Margaret r. Australia 54 E4
Margaret watercourse Australia 57 B6
Margaret, Mount hill Australia 54 B5
Margaret River Australia 55 A8
Margaretville NY U.S.A. 64 D1
Margaritovo Rus. Fed. 44 D4
Margate S. Africa 51 J6
Margate U.K. 19 I7
Margherita, Lake Eth. see Abaya, Lake
Margherita Peak Dem. Rep. Congo/Uganda
   48 C3
Marghilon Uzbek. see Marg'ilon
Marg'ilon Uzbek. 33 L1
Märgo, Dasht-i des. Afgh. see
   Märgow, Dasht-e
Margog Caka l. China 37 F2
Märgow, Dasht-e des. Afgh. 33 J3
Marguerite, Pic mt.
   Dem. Rep. Congo/Uganda see
   Margherita Peak
Marguerite Bay Antarctica 76 L2
Margyang China 37 G3
Marhaj Khalīl Iraq 35 G5
Marhanets' Ukr. 13 G7
Marhoum Alg. 22 D5
Maria atoll Fr. Polynesia 75 J7
María Elena Chile 70 C2
Maria Island Australia 56 A2
Maria Island National Park Australia
   57 [inset]
Mariala National Park Australia 57 D5
Mariana Brazil 71 C3
Mariana Ridge sea feature N. Pacific Ocean
   74 F4
Mariana Trench sea feature
   N. Pacific Ocean 74 F5
Mariani India 37 H4
Mariánica, Cordillera mts Spain see
   Morena, Sierra
Marianna AR U.S.A. 63 I5
Marianna FL U.S.A. 63 J5
Mariano Machado Angola see Ganda
Mariánské Lázně Czech Rep. 17 N6
Marías, Islas is Mex. 66 C4
Mariato, Punta pt Panama 67 H7
Maria van Diemen, Cape N.Z. 59 D2
Ma'rib Yemen 32 G6
Maribo Denmark 15 G9
Maribor Slovenia 26 F1
Maricopa CA U.S.A. 65 C3
Maridi Sudan 47 F4
Marie Byrd Land reg. Antarctica 76 J1
Marie-Galante i. Guadeloupe 67 L5
Mariehamn Fin. 15 K6
Marienberg r. Brazil 71 A1
Marienbad Czech Rep. see
   Mariánské Lázně
Marienburg Poland see Malbork
Mariental Namibia 50 C3
Marienwerder Poland see Kwidzyn
Mariestad Sweden 15 H7
Marietta GA U.S.A. 63 K5
Marietta OH U.S.A. 64 A3
Marignane France 24 G5
Marii, Mys pt Rus. Fed. 40 G2
Mariinsk Rus. Fed. 28 J4
Mariinskiy Posad Rus. Fed. 12 J4
Marijampolė Lith. 15 M9
Marília Brazil 71 A3
Marillana Australia 54 B5
Marimba Angola 49 B4
Marín Spain 25 B2
Marina CA U.S.A. 65 B3
Marina di Gioiosa Ionica Italy 26 G5
Mar'ina Gorka Belarus see Mar''ina Horka
Mar''ina Horka Belarus 15 P10
Marinette U.S.A. 63 J2
Maringá Brazil 71 A3
Maringa r. Dem. Rep. Congo 48 B3
Marinha Grande Port. 25 B4
Marion IN U.S.A. 63 K3
Marion OH U.S.A. 63 K3
Marion SC U.S.A. 63 L5
Marion VA U.S.A. 63 K4
Marion, Lake U.S.A. 63 K5
Marion Reef Australia 56 E3
Maripa Venez. 68 E2
Mariposa CA U.S.A. 65 C2
Mariscal José Félix Estigarribia Para. 70 D2
Maritime Alps mts France/Italy 24 H4
Maritime Kray admin. div. Rus. Fed. see
   Primorskiy Kray
Maritimes, Alpes mts France/Italy see
   Maritime Alps
Maritsa r. Bulg. 27 L4
Maritime, Alpi mts France/Italy see
   Maritime Alps
Mariupol' Ukr. 13 H7
Mariusa nat. park Venez. 68 F2
Marīvān Iran 35 G3
Marjan Afgh. see Wazi Khwa
Marjayoûn Lebanon 39 B3
Marka Somalia 48 E3
Markala Mali 46 C3
Markam China see Bachu
Markaryd Sweden 15 H8
Marken S. Africa 51 I2
Markermeer l. Neth. 16 J4
Market Deeping U.K. 19 G6
Market Drayton U.K. 19 E6
Market Harborough U.K. 19 G6
Markethill U.K. 21 F3
Market Weighton U.K. 18 G5
Markha r. Rus. Fed. 29 M3
Markit China 33 M2
Markleeville CA U.S.A. 65 C2
Markounda Cent. Afr. Rep. 48 B3
Markovo Rus. Fed. 29 S3
Marks Rus. Fed. 13 J6
Marla Australia 55 F6
Marlborough Downs hills U.K. 19 F7
Marlinton WV U.S.A. 64 A4
Marlo Australia 58 D6
Marmagao India 38 B3
Marmande France 24 E4
Marmara, Sea of g. Turkey see
   Marmara, Sea of
Marmara Denizi g. Turkey see
   Marmara, Sea of
Marmara Gölü l. Turkey 27 M5
Marmaricea Alg. China see Bachu
Marmaris Turkey 27 M6
Marmion, Lake salt l. Australia 55 C7
Marmolada mt. Italy 26 D1
Marne r. France 24 F2
Marne-la-Vallée France 24 F2
Maroantsetra Madag. 49 E5
Maroc country Africa see Morocco
Marol Jammu and Kashmir 36 D2
Marol Pak. 36 C3
Maromokotro mt. Madag. 49 E5
Marondera Zimbabwe 49 D5
Maroochydore Australia 57 F5
Maroonah Australia 55 A5
Marosvásárhely Romania see
   Târgu Mureş

Maroua Cameroon 47 E3
Marovoay Madag. 49 E5
Marqādah Syria 35 F4
Marquard S. Africa 51 H5
Marquesas Islands Fr. Polynesia 75 K6
Marquês de Valença Brazil 71 C3
Marquette U.S.A. 63 J2
Marquise France 19 I8
Marquises, Îles is Fr. Polynesia see
   Marquesas Islands
Marra Australia 58 A3
Marra r. Australia 58 C2
Marra, Jebel mt. Sudan 47 F3
Marra, Jebel Sudan 47 F3
Marracuene Moz. 51 K3
Marrakech Morocco 22 C5
Marrakesh Morocco see Marrakech
Marrangua, Lagoa l. Moz. 51 L3
Marrar Australia 58 C5
Marrawah Australia 57 [inset]
Marree Australia 57 B6
Marruecos country Africa see Morocco
Marrupa Moz. 49 D5
Marryat Australia 55 F6
Marsá 'Alam Egypt 32 D4
Marsá 'Alam Egypt see Marsá al 'Alam
Marsa al Burayqah Libya 47 E1
Marsabit Kenya 48 D3
Marsala Sicily Italy 26 E6
Marsá Maṭrūḥ Egypt 34 B5
Marsciano Italy 26 E3
Marsden Australia 58 C4
Marseille France 24 G5
Marseilles France see Marseille
Marsfjället mt. Sweden 14 I4
Marshall watercourse Australia 56 B4
Marshall MN U.S.A. 63 H3
Marshall MO U.S.A. 63 I4
Marshall TX U.S.A. 63 I5
Marshall Islands country N. Pacific Ocean
   74 H5
Marshalltown U.S.A. 63 I3
Marsh Harbour Bahamas 67 I3
Marsh Island U.S.A. 63 I6
Märsta Sweden 15 J7
Marsyaty Rus. Fed. 11 S3
Martapura Indon. 41 D8
Martha's Vineyard i. MA U.S.A. 64 F2
Martigny Switz. 24 H3
Martim Vaz, Ilhas is S. Atlantic Ocean see
   Martin Vas, Ilhas
Martin Slovakia 17 Q6
Martin SD U.S.A. 62 G3
Martinez Lake AZ U.S.A. 65 E4
Martinho Campos Brazil 71 B2
Martinique terr. West Indies 67 L6
Martinique Passage Dominica/Martinique
   67 L5
Martin Peninsula Antarctica 76 K2
Martinsburg WV U.S.A. 64 C3
Martins Ferry OH U.S.A. 64 A2
Martinsville VA U.S.A. 63 L4
Martin Vas, Ilhas is S. Atlantic Ocean 72 G7
Martin Vaz Islands S. Atlantic Ocean see
   Martin Vas, Ilhas
Martök Kazakh. see Martuk
Marton N.Z. 59 E5
Martorell Spain 25 G3
Martos Spain 25 E5
Martuk Kazakh. 30 E1
Martuni Armenia 35 G2
Marufgh Afgh. 36 A3
Maruim Brazil 69 K6
Marukhis Ugheltekhili pass
   Georgia/Rus. Fed. 35 F2
Marulan Australia 58 D5
Marvast Iran 35 I4
Marv Dasht Iran 35 I5
Marvejols France 24 F4
Mary r. Australia 54 F3
Mary Turkm. 30 F3
Maryborough Qld Australia 57 F5
Maryborough Vic. Australia 58 A6
Marydale S. Africa 50 F5
Maryland state U.S.A. 64 C4
Maryport U.K. 18 D4
Marysville CA U.S.A. 65 B1
Marysville KS U.S.A. 63 I14
Maryvale N.T. Australia 55 F6
Maryvale Qld Australia 56 D3
Maryville MO U.S.A. 63 I3
Maryville TN U.S.A. 63 K4
Marzagão Brazil 71 A2
Masada tourist site Israel 39 B4
Masai Steppe plain Tanz. 49 D4
Masaka Uganda 48 D4
Masakhane S. Africa 51 H6
Masallı Azer. 35 H3
Masan S. Korea 45 C6
Masasi Tanz. 49 D5
Masavi Bol. 68 F7
Masbate Phil. 41 E6
Mascara Alg. 25 G6
Mascarene Basin sea feature Indian Ocean
   73 L7
Mascarene Plain sea feature Indian Ocean
   73 L7
Mascarene Ridge sea feature Indian Ocean
   73 L6
Mascote Brazil 71 D1
Masela Indon. 54 E2
Masela i. Indon. 54 E2
Maseru Lesotho 51 H5
Mashai Lesotho 51 I5
Masherbrum mt. Jammu and Kashmir
   36 D2
Mashhad Iran 33 I2
Masi Norway 14 M2
Masibambane S. Africa 51 H6
Masilah, Wādī al watercourse Yemen 32 H6
Masilo S. Africa 51 H5
Masi-Manimba Dem. Rep. Congo 49 B4
Masindi Uganda 48 D3
Masinyusane S. Africa 50 F6
Masira, Gulf of Oman see Maşīrah, Khalīj
Maşīrah, Jazīrat i. Oman 33 I6
Maşīrah, Khalīj b. Oman 33 I6
Masira Island Oman see Maşīrah, Jazīrat
Masjed Soleymān Iran 35 H5
Mask, Lough l. Ireland 21 C4
Maslovo Rus. Fed. 11 S3
Masoala, Tanjona c. Madag. 49 F5
Mason, Lake salt flat Australia 55 B6
Mason Bay N.Z. 59 A8
Mason City U.S.A. 63 I3
Masontown PA U.S.A. 64 B3
Masqaṭ Oman see Muscat
Massa Italy 26 D2
Massachusetts state U.S.A. 64 E1
Massachusetts Bay MA U.S.A. 64 F1
Massafra Italy 26 G4
Massakory Chad 47 E3
Massa Marittimo Italy 26 D3
Massangena Moz. 49 D6
Massango Angola 49 B4
Massawa Eritrea 32 E6
Massenya Chad 47 E3
Masset Canada 60 E4
Massif Central mts France 24 F4
Massilia France see Marseille
Massillon OH U.S.A. 64 A2

Massina Mali 46 C3
Massinga Moz. 51 L2
Massingir Moz. 51 K2
Massingir, Barragem de resr Moz. 51 K2
Masson Island Antarctica 76 F2
Masterton N.Z. 59 E5
Mastung Pak. 30 F4
Mastūrah Saudi Arabia 32 E5
Masty Belarus 15 N10
Masuda Japan 45 C6
Masuku Gabon see Franceville
Masulipatam India see Machilipatnam
Masulipatnam India see Machilipatnam
Masuna i. American Samoa see Tutuila
Masvingo Zimbabwe 51 J1
Masvingo prov. Zimbabwe 51 J1
Maswa Tanz. 48 D4
Maşyāf Syria 39 C2
Matabeleland South prov. Zimbabwe 51 I1
Matadi Dem. Rep. Congo 49 B4
Matagalpa Nicaragua 67 G6
Matagami Canada 63 L2
Matagami, Lac l. Canada 63 L2
Matagorda Island U.S.A. 63 H6
Matakana Island N.Z. 59 F3
Matala Angola 49 B5
Maţāli', Jabal hill Saudi Arabia 35 F6
Matam Senegal 46 B3
Matamey Niger 46 D3
Matamoras PA U.S.A. 64 D2
Matamoros Coahuila Mex. 66 D3
Matamoros Tamaulipas Mex. 66 E3
Matandu r. Tanz. 49 D4
Matane Canada 63 N2
Matanzas Cuba 67 H4
Matapan, Cape pt Greece see
  Tainaron, Akrotirio
Matara Sri Lanka 38 D5
Mataram Indon. 41 D8
Matarani Peru 68 D7
Mataranka Australia 54 F3
Mataripe Brazil 71 D1
Mataró Spain 25 H3
Matatiele S. Africa 51 I6
Mataura N.Z. 59 B8
Matā'utu Wallis and Futuna Is 53 I3
Mata-Utu Wallis and Futuna Is see
  Matā'utu
Matawai N.Z. 59 F4
Matay Kazakh. 42 D3
Mategua Bol. 68 F6
Matehuala Mex. 66 D4
Matemanga Tanz. 49 D5
Matera Italy 26 G4
Mateur Tunisia 26 C6
Mathaji India 36 B4
Mathews VA U.S.A. 64 C4
Mathis U.S.A. 62 H6
Mathoura Australia 58 B5
Mathura India 36 D4
Mati Phil. 41 E7
Matiali India 37 G4
Matias Cardoso Brazil 71 C1
Matías Romero Mex. 66 E5
Matin India 37 G5
Matla r. India 37 G5
Matlabas r. S. Africa 51 H2
Matli Pak. 36 B4
Matlock U.K. 19 F5
Mato, Cerro mt. Venez. 68 E2
Matobo Hills Zimbabwe see Matobo Hills
Matos Costa Brazil 71 A4
Matosinhos Port. 25 B3
Mato Verde Brazil 71 C1
Matsesta Rus. Fed. 35 E2
Matsue Japan 45 D6
Matsumoto Japan 45 E5
Matsu Tao i. Taiwan 43 M7
Matsuyama Japan 45 D6
Mattagami r. Canada 63 K1
Matterhorn mt. Italy/Switz. 26 B2
Matterhorn mt. U.S.A. 62 D3
Matthew Town Bahamas 67 J4
Matturai Sri Lanka see Matara
Matuku i. Fiji 53 H3
Matumbo Angola 49 B5
Maturín Venez. 68 F2
Matusadona National Park Zimbabwe
  49 C5
Matwabeng S. Africa 51 H5
Maty Island P.N.G. see Wuvulu Island
Mau India see Maunath Bhanjan
Maúa Moz. 49 D5
Maubourguet France 24 E5
Mauchline U.K. 20 E5
Maudaha India 36 E4
Maude Australia 57 D7
Maud Seamount sea feature
  S. Atlantic Ocean 72 I10
Mau-é-ele Moz. see Marão
Maués Brazil 69 G4
Maughold Head hd Isle of Man 18 C4
Maui i. U.S.A. 62 [inset]
Maukkadaw Myanmar 37 H5
Maule r. Chile 70 B5
Maulvi Bazar Bangl. see Moulvibazar
Maumere Indon. 54 C2
Maumturk Mts hills Ireland 21 C4
Maun Botswana 49 C5
Maunath Bhanjan India 37 E4
Maunatlala Botswana 51 H2
Maungaturoto N.Z. 59 E3
Maungdaw Myanmar 37 H5
Mauriac France 24 F4
Maurice country Indian Ocean see
  Mauritius
Maurice, Lake salt flat Australia 55 E7
Mauritania country Africa 46 B3
Mauritanie country Africa see Mauritania
Mauritius country Indian Ocean 73 L7
Maurs France 24 F4
Mava Dem. Rep. Congo 48 C3
Mavago Moz. 49 D5
Mavanza Moz. 51 L2
Mavinga Angola 49 C5
Mavrovo i. nat. park Macedonia 27 I4
Mavume Moz. 51 L2
Mavuya S. Africa 51 H6
Mawana India 36 D3
Mawanga Dem. Rep. Congo 49 B4
Mawjib, Wādī al r. Jordan 39 B4
Mawkmai Myanmar 42 H3
Mawlaik Myanmar 37 H5
Mawlamyaing Myanmar 31 I5
Mawlamyine Myanmar see Mawlamyaing
Mawqaq Saudi Arabia 35 F6
Mawson research station Antarctica 76 E2
Mawson Coast Antarctica 76 E2
Mawson Escarpment Antarctica 76 E2
Mawson Peninsula Antarctica 76 H2
Mawza Yemen 32 F7
Maxán Arg. 70 C3
Maxia, Punta mt. Sardinia Italy 26 C5

Maxixe Moz. 51 L2
Maxmo Fin. 14 M5
Maya, Isle of i. U.K. 20 G4
Maya r. Rus. Fed. 29 O3
Mayaguana i. Bahamas 67 J4
Mayagüez Puerto Rico 67 K5
Mayahi Niger 46 D3
Mayak Rus. Fed. 44 E2
Mayakovskiy, Qullai mt. Tajik. 36 B1
Mayakovskogo, Pik mt. Tajik. see
  Mayakovskiy, Qullai
Mayama Congo 48 B4
Maya Mountains Belize/Guat. 66 G5
Mayar hill U.K. 20 F4
Maybeury WV U.S.A. 64 A4
Maybole U.K. 20 E5
Mayci̇hen U.K. 18 G5
Maydān Shahr Afgh. see Meydān Shahr
Maydh Somalia 32 G7
Maydos Turkey see Eceabat
Mayenne France 24 D2
Mayenne r. France 24 D3
Mayêr Kangri mt. China 37 F2
Mayfield N.Z. 59 C6
Mayi He r. China 44 C3
Maykop Rus. Fed. 13 I7
Mayna Respublika Khakasiya Rus. Fed.
  28 K4
Mayna Ul'yanovskaya Oblast' Rus. Fed.
  13 J5
Mayni India 38 B2
Mayo Alim Cameroon 46 E4
Mayoko Congo 48 B4
Mayor, Puig mt. Spain see Major, Puig
Mayor Island N.Z. 59 F3
Mayor Pablo Lagerenza Para. 70 D1
Mayotte terr. Africa 49 E5
Mayskiy Amurskaya Oblast' Rus. Fed. 44 C1
Mayskiy Kabardino-Balkarskaya Respublika
  Rus. Fed. 35 G2
Mays Landing NJ U.S.A. 64 D3
Mayumba Gabon 48 B4
Mayum La pass China 37 E3
Mayuram India 38 C4
Mayville NY U.S.A. 64 B1
Mazabuka Zambia 49 C5
Mazaca Turkey see Kayseri
Mazagan Morocco see El Jadida
Mazar China 36 D1
Mazar, Koh-i- mt. Afgh. 36 A2
Mazara, Val di valley Sicily Italy 26 E6
Mazara del Vallo Sicily Italy 26 E6
Mazār-e Sharif Afgh. 36 A1
Mazatán Mex. 66 B2
Mazatenango Guat. 66 F6
Mazatlán Mex. 66 C4
Mazdaj Iran 35 H4
Mažeikiai Lith. 15 M8
Mazocruz Peru 68 E7
Mazu Dao i. Taiwan see Matsu Tao
Mazunga Zimbabwe 49 C6
Mazyr Belarus 13 F5
Mazzouna Tunisia 26 C7
Mbabane Swaziland 51 J4
Mbahiakro Côte d'Ivoire 46 C4
Mbaïki Cent. Afr. Rep. 48 B3
Mbakaou, Lac de l. Cameroon 46 E4
Mbala Zambia 49 D4
Mbale Uganda 48 D3
Mbalmayo Cameroon 46 E4
Mbam r. Cameroon 46 E4
Mbandaka Dem. Rep. Congo 48 B4
M'banza Congo Angola 49 B4
Mbarara Uganda 47 D3
Mbari r. Cent. Afr. Rep. 48 C3
Mbaswana S. Africa 51 K4
Mbemkuru r. Tanz. 49 D4
Mbeya Tanz. 49 D4
Mbinga Tanz. 49 D5
Mbini Equat. Guinea 46 D4
Mbizi Zimbabwe 49 D6
Mboki Cent. Afr. Rep. 48 C3
Mbomo Congo 48 B3
Mbouda Cameroon 46 E4
Mbour Senegal 46 B3
Mbout Mauritania 46 B3
Mbozi Tanz. 49 D4
Mbrès Cent. Afr. Rep. 48 B3
Mbuji-Mayi Dem. Rep. Congo 49 C4
Mbulu Tanz. 49 D4
Mburucuyá Arg. 70 E3
McAlester U.S.A. 63 H5
McAlister mt. Australia 58 D5
McAllen U.S.A. 62 H6
McArthur r. Australia 56 B2
McCall U.S.A. 62 D3
McClintock, Mount Antarctica 76 H1
McClintock Channel Canada 61 H2
McClintock Range hills Australia 54 D4
McClure, Lake l. U.S.A. 65 B2
McClure Strait Canada 60 G2
McComb U.S.A. 63 I6
McConaughy, Lake U.S.A. 62 G3
McConnellsburg PA U.S.A. 64 C3
McCook U.S.A. 62 G3
McDermitt U.S.A. 62 D3
McDonald Islands Indian Ocean 73 M9
McDonald Peak U.S.A. 62 D2
McDougall's Bay S. Africa 50 C5
McFarland CA U.S.A. 65 C3
McGrath AK U.S.A. 60 C3
McGraw NY U.S.A. 64 C1
McGregor S. Africa 50 D7
McGregor Range hills Australia 57 C5
McGuire, Mount Australia 55 F5
Mchinga Tanz. 49 D4
Mchinji Malawi 49 D5
McIlwraith Range hills Australia 56 C2
McInnes Lake Canada 63 I1
McKay Range hills Australia 54 C5
McKean i. Kiribati 53 I2
McKinlay r. Australia 56 C4
McKinley, Mount U.S.A. 60 C3
McKittrick U.S.A. 65 C3
McLennan Canada 60 G4
McMinnville OR U.S.A. 62 C2
McMurdo research station Antarctica 76 H1
McMurdo Sound b. Antarctica 76 H1
McNaughton Lake Canada see
  Kinbasket Lake
McPherson U.S.A. 62 H4
McVeytown PA U.S.A. 64 C2
Mdantsane S. Africa 51 H7
M'Daourouch Alg. 26 B6
Mead, Lake resr NV U.S.A. 65 E2
Meade r. U.S.A. 60 C2
Meadow Australia 55 A6
Meadow UT U.S.A. 65 F1
Meadville PA U.S.A. 64 A2
Meaken-dake vol. Japan 44 G4
Mealhada Port. 25 B3
Mealy Mountains Canada 61 M4
Meandarra Australia 58 D1
Meaux France 24 F2
Mecca Saudi Arabia 32 E5
Mecca CA U.S.A. 65 D3
Mechanicsville VA U.S.A. 64 C4
Mechelen Belgium 16 J5
Mecheria Alg. 22 D5
Mecitözü Turkey 34 D2
Meda r. Australia 54 C4

Meda Port. 25 C3
Medak India 38 C2
Medan Indon. 41 B7
Medanosa, Punta pt Arg. 70 C7
Médanos de Coro, Parque Nacional
  nat. park Venez. 68 E1
Medawachchiya Sri Lanka 38 D4
Médéa Alg. 25 H5
Medellín Col. 68 C2
Medenine Tunisia 22 G5
Mederdra Mauritania 46 B3
Medford OR U.S.A. 62 C3
Medgidia Romania 27 M2
Mediaş Romania 27 K1
Medicine Bow Mountains U.S.A. 62 F3
Medicine Bow Peak U.S.A. 62 F3
Medicine Hat Canada 62 E1
Medicine Lodge U.S.A. 62 H4
Medina Brazil 71 C2
Medina Saudi Arabia 32 E5
Medina NY U.S.A. 64 B1
Medinaceli Spain 25 E3
Medina del Campo Spain 25 D3
Medina de Rioseco Spain 25 D3
Medinipur India 37 F5
Mediolanum Italy see Milan
Mediterranean Sea 22 K5
Mednyy, Ostrov i. Rus. Fed. 74 H2
Médoc reg. France 24 D4
Medog China 42 H7
Meduro atoll Marshall Is see Majuro
Medvedevo Rus. Fed. 12 J4
Medveditsa r. Rus. Fed. 13 I6
Medvednica mts Croatia 26 G2
Medvezh'i, Ostrova is Rus. Fed. 29 R2
Medvezh'ya, Gora mt. Rus. Fed. 44 E3
Medvezh'yegorsk Rus. Fed. 12 G3
Medway r. U.K. 19 H7
Meekatharra Australia 55 B6
Meeker CO U.S.A. 62 F3
Meerut India 36 D3
Mega Escarpment Eth./Kenya 48 D3
Megalopoli Greece 27 J6
Megara Greece 27 J5
Megezez mt. Eth. 48 D3
Meghalaya state India 37 G4
Meghasani mt. India 37 F5
Meghri Armenia see Meghri
Megisti i. Greece 27 M6
Mehamn Norway 14 O1
Meharry, Mount Australia 55 B5
Mehdia Tunisia see Mahdia
Meherpur Bangl. 37 G5
Meherrin VA U.S.A. 64 C4
Meherrin r. U.S.A. 64 C4
Mehrabad Iran see Mahesana
Mehtar Lām Afgh. 36 B2
Mehrān Hormozgan Iran 35 I6
Mehrān r. Iran 35 G4
Mehriz Iran 35 I5
Mehsana India see Mahesana
Mehtar Lām Afgh. 36 B2
Meia Ponte r. Brazil 71 A2
Meiganga Cameroon 47 E4
Meighen Island Canada 61 I2
Meihekou China 44 B4
Meikle Says Law hill U.K. 20 G5
Meiktila Myanmar 37 H5
Meiningen Germany 17 M5
Meißen Germany 17 N5
Meixi China 44 C3
Meixian China see Meizhou
Meizhou China 43 L8
Mej r. India 36 D4
Mejicana mt. Arg. 70 C3
Mejillones Chile 70 B2
Mékambo Gabon 48 B3
Mek'elē Eth. 48 D2
Mekelle Eth. see Mek'elē
Mékhé Senegal 46 B3
Mekhtar Pak. 36 B3
Meknassy Tunisia 26 C7
Meknès Morocco 22 C5
Mekong r. Xizang/Yunnan China 42 I8
Mekong r. Laos/Thai. 31 J5
Mekong, Mouths of the Vietnam 31 J6
Mekoryuk U.S.A. 60 B3
Melaka Malaysia 41 C7
Melanesia is Pacific Ocean 74 G6
Melanesian Basin sea feature Pacific Ocean
  74 G5
Melbourne Australia 58 B6
Melbourne U.S.A. 63 K6
Melby U.K. 20 [inset]
Meldorf Germany 17 L3
Melekeok Palau 41 I7
Melekess Rus. Fed. see Dimitrovgrad
Melenki Rus. Fed. 13 I5
Melet Turkey see Mesudiye
Mélèzes, Rivière aux r. Canada 61 K4
Melfa VA U.S.A. 64 D4
Melfi Chad 47 E3
Melfi Italy 26 F4
Melfort Canada 62 G1
Melhus Norway 14 G5
Melide Spain 25 C2
Melilla N. Africa 25 E6
Melilli Sicily Italy 26 F6
Melimoyu, Monte mt. Chile 70 B6
Melitene Turkey see Malatya
Melitopol' Ukr. 13 G7
Melk Austria 17 O6
Melka Guba Eth. 48 D3
Melksham U.K. 19 E7
Mellakoski Fin. 14 N3
Mellansel Sweden 14 K5
Mellerud Sweden 15 H7
Mellid Spain see Melide
Mellilla N. Africa see Melilla
Mellor Glacier Antarctica 76 E2
Mel'nichnoye Rus. Fed. 44 D3
Melo Uruguay 70 F4
Meloco Moz. 49 D5
Melolo Indon. 54 C2
Melozitna r. U.S.A. 60 C3
Melrhir, Chott salt l. Alg. 22 F5
Melrose Australia 55 C6
Melrose U.K. 20 G5
Melton Australia 58 B6
Melton Mowbray U.K. 19 G6
Melun France 24 F2
Melville Canada 62 G1
Melville, Cape Australia 56 D2
Melville, Lake Canada 61 M4
Melville Bugt b. Greenland see
  Qimusseriarsuaq
Melville Island Australia 54 E2
Melville Island Canada 61 H2
Melville Peninsula Canada 61 J3
Melvin, Lough l. Ireland/U.K. 21 D3
Mêmar Co salt l. China 37 E2
Memba Moz. 49 E5
Memberamo r. Indon. 52 D2
Memel Lith. see Klaipėda
Memel S. Africa 51 I4
Memmingen Germany 17 M7
Memphis tourist site Egypt 34 C5

Mempawah Indon. 41 C7
Memphis tourist site Egypt 34 C5
Memphis TN U.S.A. 63 I4
Memphis TX U.S.A. 62 G5
Mena Ukr. 13 G6
Mena U.S.A. 63 I5
Menado Indon. see Manado
Ménaka Mali 46 D3
Mendanha Brazil 71 C2
Mende France 24 F4
Mendefera Eritrea 32 E7
Mendeleyev Ridge sea feature Arctic Ocean
  77 B1
Mendeleyevsk Rus. Fed. 12 L5
Mendenhall, Cape U.S.A. 60 B4
Mendi Eth. 48 D3
Mendi P.N.G. 52 E2
Mendip Hills U.K. 19 E7
Mendooran Australia 58 D3
Mendota CA U.S.A. 65 B2
Mendoza Arg. 70 C4
Menemen Turkey 27 L5
Ménerville Alg. see Thenia
Menglie China see Jiangcheng
Menindee Australia 57 C7
Menindee, Lake Australia 57 C7
Menkere Rus. Fed. 29 N3
Mennecy France 24 F2
Menongue Angola 49 B5
Menorca i. Spain see Minorca
Mentawai, Kepulauan is Indon. 41 B8
Menton France 24 H5
Menuf Egypt see Minūf
Menzel Bourguiba Tunisia 26 C6
Menzel Bouzelfa resr Turkey 34 E3
Menzelinsk Rus. Fed. 11 Q4
Menzel Temime Tunisia 26 D6
Menzies Australia 55 C7
Menzies, Mount Antarctica 76 E2
Meobbaai b. Namibia 50 A3
Meppel Neth. 16 K3
Meppen Germany 17 K4
Mepuze Moz. 51 L2
Meqheleng S. Africa 51 H5
Meråker Norway 14 G5
Merano Italy 26 D1
Meratswe r. Botswana 50 G2
Merauke Indon. 41 K8
Merca Somalia see Marka
Mercantour, Parc National du nat. park
  France 24 H4
Merced CA U.S.A. 65 B2
Merced r. CA U.S.A. 65 B2
Mercedes Arg. 70 E4
Mercedes Uruguay 70 E4
Mercês Brazil 71 C3
Mercury Islands N.Z. 59 E3
Mercy, Cape Canada 61 L3
Merdenik Turkey see Göle
Mere U.K. 19 E7
Meredith NH U.S.A. 64 F1
Merefa Ukr. 13 H6
Merga Oasis Sudan 32 C6
Mergui Archipelago is Myanmar 31 I5
Meriç r. Turkey 27 L4
Mérida Mex. 66 G4
Mérida Spain 25 C4
Mérida Venez. 68 D2
Mérida, Cordillera de mts Venez. 68 D2
Meriden CT U.S.A. 64 E2
Meridian MS U.S.A. 63 J5
Mérignac France 24 D4
Merijärvi Fin. 14 N4
Merikarvia Fin. 15 L6
Merimbula Australia 58 D6
Merín, Laguna l. Brazil/Uruguay see
  Mirim, Lagoa
Meringur Australia 57 C7
Merjayoun Lebanon see Marjayoûn
Merluna Australia 56 C2
Mermaid Reef Australia 54 B4
Meron, Har mt. Israel 39 B3
Merowe Sudan 32 D6
Mêrqung Co l. China 37 F3
Merredin Australia 55 B7
Merrick hill U.K. 20 E5
Merrill WI U.S.A. 63 J2
Merriwa Australia 58 E4
Merrygoen Australia 58 D3
Mersa Fatma Eritrea 32 F7
Mersa Matrûh Egypt see Marsá Maţrūḩ
Mersey est. U.K. 18 E5
Mersin Turkey 39 B1
Mersin prov. Turkey 39 A1
Mērsrags Latvia 15 M8
Merta India 36 C4
Merthyr Tydfil U.K. 19 D7
Mértola Port. 25 C5
Mertz Glacier Antarctica 76 G2
Mertz Glacier Tongue Antarctica 76 G2
Meru Tanz. 48 D4
Merv Turkm. see Mary
Merweville S. Africa 50 E7
Merzifon Turkey 34 D2
Merzig Germany 17 K6
Merz Peninsula Antarctica 76 L2
Mesa AZ U.S.A. 65 H5
Mesagne Italy 26 G4
Meselefors Sweden 14 J4
Meshed Iran see Mashhad
Meshra'er Req Sudan 32 C8
Mesimeri Greece 27 J4
Mesolongi Greece 27 I5
Mesolóngion Greece see Mesolongi
Mesopotamia reg. Iraq 35 F4
Mesquita Brazil 71 C2
Mesquite NV U.S.A. 65 E2
Mesquite Lake CA U.S.A. 65 E3
Messaad Alg. 25 G5
Messana Sicily Italy see Messina
Messina Sicily Italy 26 F5
Messina, Strait of Italy 26 F5
Messina, Stretta di Italy see
  Messina, Strait of
Messini Greece 27 I6
Messiniakos Kolpos b. Greece 27 I6
Mesta r. Bulg. 27 K4
Mesta r. Greece see Nestos
Mesta, Akrotirio pt Greece 27 K5
Mestghanem Alg. see Mostaganem
Mestre Italy 26 E2
Meta r. Col./Venez. 68 E2
Meta Incognita Peninsula Canada 61 L3
Metallifere, Colline mts Italy 26 D3
Metán Arg. 70 C3
Meteor Depth sea feature S. Atlantic Ocean
  72 G9
Methoni Greece 27 I6
Methuen MA U.S.A. 64 F1
Methven N.Z. 59 C6
Metković Croatia 26 G3
Metlaoui Tunisia 22 F5
Metoro Moz. 49 D5
Metsada tourist site Israel see Masada
Mettler CA U.S.A. 65 C3
Mettur India 38 C4
Metu Eth. 48 D3
Metz France 24 H2
Meuse r. Belgium/France 16 J5
Mevagissey U.K. 19 C8

Mexia U.S.A. 63 H5
Mexiana, Ilha i. Brazil 69 I3
Mexicali Mex. 66 A2
México country Central America 66 D4
Mexico NY U.S.A. 64 C1
Mexico, Gulf of Mex./U.S.A. 63 H6
Mexico City Mex. 66 E5
Meybod Iran 35 I4
Meydān Shahr Afgh. 36 B2
Meyersdale PA U.S.A. 64 B3
Meymaneh Afgh. 36 A2
Meymeh Iran 35 H4
Meynypil'gyno Rus. Fed. 77 C2
Mezada tourist site Israel see Masada
Mezdra Bulg. 27 J3
Mezen' Rus. Fed. 12 J2
Mezen' r. Rus. Fed. 12 J2
Mézenc, Mont mt. France 24 G4
Mezhdurechensk Kemerovskaya Oblast'
  Rus. Fed. 42 F2
Mezhdurechensk Respublika Komi Rus. Fed.
  12 K3
Mezhdusharskiy, Ostrov i. Rus. Fed. 28 G2
Meziti Turkey 39 B1
Mezőtúr Hungary 27 I1
Mézvidi Latvia 15 O8
Mhail, Rubh' a' pt U.K. 20 C5
Mhangura Zimbabwe 49 D5
Mhlume Swaziland 51 J4
Mhow India 36 D5
Mi r. Myanmar 37 H5
Miahuatlán Mex. 66 E5
Miajadas Spain 25 D3
Miaméré Cent. Afr. Rep. 48 B3
Miami FL U.S.A. 63 K6
Miami OK U.S.A. 63 H4
Miami Beach U.S.A. 63 K6
Mïándowāb Iran 35 G3
Miandrivazo Madag. 49 E5
Mīāneh Iran 35 G3
Miani Hor b. Pak. 36 A4
Mianwali Pak. 33 I3
Mianyang Hubei China see Xiantao
Mianyang Sichuan China 42 I6
Miarinarivo Madag. 49 E5
Miass Rus. Fed. 28 H4
Mica Creek Canada 62 D1
Michalovce Slovakia 13 R6
Michelson, Mount U.S.A. 60 D3
Michigan state U.S.A. 63 J3
Michigan, Lake U.S.A. 63 J3
Michinberi India 38 D2
Michipicoten Island Canada 63 J2
Michipicoten River Canada 63 K2
Michurin Bulg. see Tsarevo
Michurinsk Rus. Fed. 13 I5
Micronesia country N. Pacific Ocean see
  Micronesia, Federated States of
Micronesia is Pacific Ocean 74 F5
Micronesia, Federated States of country
  N. Pacific Ocean 74 G5
Mid-Atlantic Ridge sea feature
  Atlantic Ocean 72 F4
Mid-Atlantic Ridge sea feature
  Atlantic Ocean 72 G8
Middelburg E. Cape S. Africa 51 G6
Middelburg Mpumalanga S. Africa 51 I3
Middelfart Denmark 15 F9
Middelwit S. Africa 51 H3
Middle America Trench sea feature
  N. Pacific Ocean 75 N5
Middlebourne WV U.S.A. 64 A3
Middleburg PA U.S.A. 64 C2
Middleburg NY U.S.A. 64 E1
Middle Congo country Africa see Congo
Middlemarch N.Z. 59 C7
Middlemount Australia 56 E4
Middle River MD U.S.A. 64 C3
Middlesbrough U.K. 18 F4
Middleton Australia 56 C4
Middleton Island atoll American Samoa see
  Rose Island
Middletown CA U.S.A. 65 A1
Middletown CT U.S.A. 64 E2
Middletown NY U.S.A. 64 D2
Midelt Morocco 22 D5
Midhurst U.K. 19 G8
Midi, Canal du France 24 F5
Mid-Indian Basin sea feature Indian Ocean
  73 N6
Mid-Indian Ridge sea feature Indian Ocean
  73 N7
Midland Canada 63 L3
Midland MI U.S.A. 63 K3
Midland TX U.S.A. 62 G5
Midleton Ireland 21 D6
Midnapore India see Medinipur
Midnapur India see Medinipur
Midongy Atsimo Madag. 49 E6
Mid-Pacific Mountains sea feature
  N. Pacific Ocean 74 G4
Miðvágur Faroe Is 14 [inset]
Midway Oman see Thamarīt
Midway Islands terr. N. Pacific Ocean 74 I4
Midway Well Australia 55 C5
Midyat Turkey 35 F3
Midye Turkey see Kıyıköy
Mid Yell U.K. 20 [inset]
Miehikkälä Fin. 15 O6
Miekojärvi l. Fin. 14 N3
Mielec Poland 13 R5
Mieraslompolo Fin. 14 O2
Mierasluoppal Fin. see Mieraslompolo
Miercurea-Ciuc Romania 27 K1
Mieres Spain 25 D2
Mieres del Camín Spain see Mieres
Mi'ēso Eth. 48 E3
Mifflinburg PA U.S.A. 64 C2
Mifflintown PA U.S.A. 64 C2
Migdol S. Africa 51 G4
Migriggyangzham Co l. China 37 G2
Miguel Auza Mex. 62 G7
Mihaïlçcik Turkey 39 N5
Mihara Japan 45 D6
Mihintale Sri Lanka 38 D4
Mihmandar Turkey 39 B1
Mijares r. Spain see Millárs
Mikhaylov Rus. Fed. 13 H5
Mikhaylov Island Antarctica 76 E2
Mikhaylovgrad Bulg. see Montana
Mikhaylovka Amurskaya Oblast' Rus. Fed.
  44 C2
Mikhaylovka Primorskiy Kray Rus. Fed.
  44 D4
Mikhaylovka Tul'skaya Oblast' Rus. Fed. see
  Kimovsk
Mikhaylovka Volgogradskaya Oblast'
  Rus. Fed. 13 I6
Mikhaylovskiy Rus. Fed. 42 F2
Mikhaylovskoye Rus. Fed. see
  Shpakovskoye
Mikhaytov Island Antarctica 76 E2
Mikhrot Timna Israel 39 B5
Mikir Hills India 37 H4

Mikkeli Fin. 15 O6
Mikkeli mlk Fin. 15 O6
Mikonos i. Greece see Mykonos
Mikoyan Armenia see Yeghegnadzor
Mikulkin, Mys c. Rus. Fed. 12 J2
Mikumi National Park Tanz. 49 D4
Mikun' Rus. Fed. 12 K3
Mikuni-sanmyaku mts Japan 45 E5
Mikura-jima i. Japan 45 E6
Miladhunmadulu Atoll Maldives 38 B5
Miladummadulu Atoll Maldives see
  Miladhunmadulu Atoll
Milan Italy 26 C2
Milange Moz. 49 D5
Milano Italy see Milan
Milas Turkey 27 L6
Milazzo Sicily Italy 26 F5
Milazzo, Capo di c. Sicily Italy 26 F5
Mildenhall U.K. 19 H6
Mildura Australia 57 C7
Mile China 42 I8
Mileiz, Wādī el watercourse Egypt see
  Mulayz, Wādī al
Miles Australia 58 E1
Miles City U.S.A. 62 F2
Milestone Ireland 21 D5
Miletto, Monte mt. Italy 26 F4
Mileura Australia 55 B6
Milford Ireland 21 E2
Milford DE U.S.A. 64 D3
Milford MA U.S.A. 64 F1
Milford NH U.S.A. 64 F1
Milford PA U.S.A. 64 D2
Milford UT U.S.A. 65 G2
Milford VA U.S.A. 64 C3
Milford Haven U.K. 19 B7
Milford Sound N.Z. 59 A7
Milford Sound inlet N.Z. 59 A7
Milgarra Australia 56 C3
Milh, Bahr al l. Iraq see
  Razāzah, Buḩayrat ar
Miliana Alg. 25 H5
Milid Turkey see Malatya
Milikapiti Australia 54 E2
Miling Australia 55 B7
Milk r. U.S.A. 62 F2
Milk, Wadi el watercourse Sudan 32 D6
Milkovo Rus. Fed. 29 Q4
Millaa Millaa Australia 56 D3
Millárs r. Spain 25 F4
Millau France 24 F4
Milledgeville U.S.A. 63 K5
Mille Lacs lakes U.S.A. 63 I1
Mille Lacs, Lac des l. Canada 61 I5
Millennium Island atoll Kiribati see
  Caroline Island
Miller U.S.A. 62 H3
Millerovo Rus. Fed. 13 I6
Millersburg PA U.S.A. 64 C2
Millerton Lake CA U.S.A. 65 C2
Milleur Point U.K. 20 D5
Mill Hall PA U.S.A. 64 C2
Millicent Australia 57 C8
Mill Island Canada 61 K3
Millmerran Australia 58 E1
Millom U.K. 18 D4
Millport U.K. 20 E5
Millsboro DE U.S.A. 64 D3
Mills Creek watercourse Australia 56 C4
Mills Lake Canada 60 G3
Millstone WV U.S.A. 64 A3
Millstream-Chichester National Park
  Australia 54 B5
Millthorpe Australia 58 D4
Milltown Malbay Ireland 21 C5
Millungera Australia 56 C3
Millville NJ U.S.A. 64 D3
Milly Milly Australia 55 B6
Milne Land i. Greenland see
  Ilimananngip Nunaa
Milo r. Guinea 46 C3
Milogradovo Rus. Fed. 44 D4
Miloli'i i. U.S.A. 62 [inset]
Milos i. Greece 27 K6
Milparinka Australia 57 C6
Milpitas CA U.S.A. 65 B2
Milroy PA U.S.A. 64 C2
Milton N.Z. 59 B8
Milton DE U.S.A. 64 D3
Milton NH U.S.A. 64 F1
Milton Keynes U.K. 19 G6
Milverton Ont. Canada 64 A1
Milwaukee U.S.A. 63 J3
Milwaukee Deep sea feature Caribbean Sea
  72 D4
Mimili Australia 55 F6
Mimisal India 38 C4
Mimizan France 24 D4
Mimongo Gabon 48 B4
Mimosa Rocks National Park Australia
  58 E6
Mina NV U.S.A. 65 C1
Mināb Iran 33 I4
Minaçu Brazil 71 A1
Minahasa, Semenanjung pen. Indon. 41 F7
Minahassa Peninsula Indon. see
  Minahasa, Semenanjung
Minaker Canada see Prophet River
Mīnākh Syria 39 C1
Minamia Australia 54 F3
Minami-Daitō-jima i. Japan 43 O7
Minas Uruguay 70 E4
Minas Gerais state Brazil 71 B2
Minas Novas Brazil 71 C2
Minatitlán Mex. 66 F5
Minbu Myanmar 37 H5
Minbya Myanmar 37 H5
Minchinmávida vol. Chile 70 B6
Mindanao i. Phil. 41 E7
Mindanao Trench sea feature
  N. Pacific Ocean see Philippine Trench
Mindelo Cape Verde 46 [inset]
Minden Germany 17 L4
Minden LA U.S.A. 63 I5
Minden NE U.S.A. 62 H3
Minden NV U.S.A. 65 C1
Mindon Myanmar 37 H6
Mindoro i. Phil. 41 E6
Mindouli Congo 48 B4
Mine Head hd Ireland 21 E6
Minehead U.K. 19 D7
Mineola NY U.S.A. 64 E2
Mineral U.S.A. 64 C3
Mineral'nyye Vody Rus. Fed. 35 F1
Mineral Wells U.S.A. 62 H5
Mineralwells WV U.S.A. 64 A3
Minerva OH U.S.A. 64 A2
Minerva Reefs Fiji 53 I4
Minfeng China 37 E1
Minga Dem. Rep. Congo 49 C5
Mingāçevir Azer. 35 G2
Mingala Cent. Afr. Rep. 48 C3
Mingbuloq Uzbek. 33 I1
Mingechaur Azer. see Mingāçevir
Mingechaurskoye Vodokhranilishche resr
  Azer. see Mingāçevir Su Anbarı
Mingenew Australia 55 A7
Mingin Range mts Myanmar 37 H5

Minglanilla Spain 25 F4
Mingoyo Tanz. 49 D5
Mingshui Gansu China 42 H4
Mingshui Heilong. China 44 B3
Mingteke China 36 C1
Mingulay i. U.K. 20 B4
Mingzhou China see Suide
Minhe China see Jinxian
Minhla Magwe Myanmar 37 H6
Minho r. Port./Spain see Miño
Minicoy atoll India 38 B4
Minigwal, Lake salt flat Australia 55 C7
Minilya Australia 55 A5
Minilya r. Australia 55 A5
Minipi Lake Canada 61 L4
Minna Nigeria 46 D4
Minna Bluff pt Antarctica 76 H1
Minne Sweden 14 I5
Minneapolis MN U.S.A. 63 I3
Minnedosa Canada 62 H1
Minnehaha Springs WV U.S.A. 64 B3
Minnesota r. U.S.A. 63 I3
Minnesota state U.S.A. 63 I2
Minnitaki Lake Canada 63 I1
Miño r. Port./Spain 25 B3
Minorca i. Spain 25 H3
Minot U.S.A. 62 G2
Minqār, Ghadīr imp. l. Syria 39 C3
Minsin Myanmar 37 H4
Minsk Belarus 15 O10
Mińsk Mazowiecki Poland 17 R4
Minsterley U.K. 19 E6
Mintaka Pass China/Jammu and Kashmir 36 C1
Minto, Lac l. Canada 61 K4
Minto, Mount Antarctica 76 H2
Minto Inlet Canada 60 G2
Mīnudasht Iran 35 I3
Minūf Egypt 34 C5
Minusinsk Rus. Fed. 42 G2
Minvoul Gabon 48 B3
Minxian China 42 I6
Minya Konka mt. China see Gongga Shan
Minywa Myanmar 37 H5
Minzong India 37 I4
Mirabela Brazil 71 B2
Mirador, Parque Nacional de nat. park Brazil 69 I5
Mirah, Wādī al watercourse Iraq/Saudi Arabia 35 F4
Miraí Brazil 71 C3
Miraj India 38 B2
Miramar Arg. 70 E5
Miramichi Canada 63 N2
Miramichi Bay Canada 63 N2
Mirampellou, Kolpos b. Greece 27 K7
Miranda Brazil 70 E2
Miranda Moz. see Macaloge
Miranda, Lake salt flat Australia 55 C6
Miranda de Ebro Spain 25 E2
Mirandela Port. 25 C3
Mirandola Italy 26 D2
Mirante Brazil 71 C1
Mirante, Serra do hills Brazil 71 A3
Mirassol Brazil 71 A3
Mir-Bashir Azer. see Tärtär
Mirbāţ Oman 33 H6
Mirboo North Australia 58 C7
Mirepoix France 24 E5
Mirgorod Ukr. see Myrhorod
Miri Sarawak Malaysia 41 D7
Mirialguda India 38 C2
Miri Hills India 37 H4
Mirim, Lagoa l. Brazil/Uruguay 70 F4
Mirim, Lagoa do l. Brazil 71 A5
Mirintu watercourse Australia 58 A2
Mirjan India 38 B3
Mirny research station Antarctica 76 F2
Mirnyy Arkhangel'skaya Oblast' Rus. Fed. 12 I3
Mirnyy Respublika Sakha (Yakutiya) Rus. Fed. 29 M3
Mironovka Ukr. see Myronivka
Mirpur Khas Pak. 33 K4
Mirpur Sakro Pak. 36 A4
Mirtoan Sea Greece see Myrtoo Pelagos
Miryalaguda India see Mirialguda
Miryang S. Korea 45 C6
Mirzachul Uzbek. see Guliston
Mirzapur India 37 E4
Mirzawal India 36 C3
Mi-shima i. Japan 45 C6
Mishmi Hills India 37 H3
Mishvan' Rus. Fed. 12 L2
Misima Island P.N.G. 56 F1
Misis Dağ hills Turkey 39 B1
Miskitos, Cayos is Nicaragua 67 H6
Miskolc Hungary 13 D6
Mismā, Tall al hill Jordan 39 C3
Misoöl i. Indon. 41 F8
Misr country Africa see Egypt
Misraç Turkey see Kurtalan
Mişrātah Libya 47 E1
Missinaibi r. Canada 63 K1
Mission Beach Australia 56 D3
Mission Viejo CA U.S.A. 65 D4
Missisa Lake Canada 63 J1
Mississauga Ont. Canada 64 B1
Mississippi r. U.S.A. 63 J6
Mississippi state U.S.A. 63 J5
Mississippi Delta U.S.A. 63 J6
Mississippi-Missouri r. U.S.A. 63 I4
Missolonghi Greece see Mesolongi
Missoula U.S.A. 62 E2
Missouri r. U.S.A. 63 I4
Missouri state U.S.A. 63 I4
Mistassibi r. Canada 61 K5
Mistassini, Lac l. Canada 63 M1
Mistelbach Austria 17 P6
Mistinibi, Lac l. Canada 61 L4
Mistissini Canada 63 M1
Misty Fiords National Monument Wilderness nat. park U.S.A. 60 E4
Misumba Dem. Rep. Congo 49 C4
Misuratah Libya see Mişrātah
Mitchell Australia 57 D5
Mitchell r. N.S.W. Australia 58 F2
Mitchell r. Qld Australia 56 C2
Mitchell r. Vic. Australia 58 C6
Mitchell Ont. Canada 64 A1
Mitchell SD U.S.A. 62 H3
Mitchell, Lake Australia 56 D3
Mitchell, Mount U.S.A. 63 K4
Mitchell and Alice Rivers National Park Australia 56 C2
Mitchell Island Cook Is see Nassau
Mitchell Island atoll Tuvalu see Nukulaelae
Mitchell Point Australia 54 E2
Mitchelstown Ireland 21 D5
Mīt Ghamr Egypt 34 C5
Mit Ghamr Egypt see Mīt Ghamr
Mithi Pak. 36 B4
Mitilíni Greece see Mytilini
Mito Japan 45 F5
Mitole Tanz. 49 D4
Mitre mt. N.Z. 59 E5
Mitre Island Solomon Is 53 H3
Mitrofanovka Rus. Fed. 13 H6
Mitrovica Serbia see Kosovska Mitrovica
Mitrovicë Serbia see Kosovska Mitrovica
Mitsinjo Madag. 49 E5
Mits'iwa Eritrea see Massawa
Mitta Mitta Australia 58 C6
Mittellandkanal canal Germany 17 L4
Mittimatalik Canada see Pond Inlet
Mitú Col. 68 D3
Mitumba, Chaîne des mts Dem. Rep. Congo 49 C5
Mitzic Gabon 48 B3
Miughalaigh i. U.K. see Mingulay
Miura Japan 45 E6
Miyake-jima i. Japan 45 E6
Miyako Japan 45 F5
Miyakonojō Japan 45 C7
Miyang China see Mile
Miyani India 36 B5
Miyazaki Japan 45 C7
Miyazu Japan 45 D6
Miyoshi Japan 45 D6
Mīzāni Afgh. 36 A2
Mīzan Teferī Eth. 48 D3
Mizdah Libya 47 E1
Mizen Head hd Ireland 21 C6
Mizhhir"ya Ukr. 13 D6
Mizo Hills state India see Mizoram
Mizoram state India 37 H5
Mizpe Ramon Israel 39 B4
Mizusawa Japan 45 F5
Mjölby Sweden 15 I7
Mkata Tanz. 49 D4
Mkushi Zambia 49 C5
Mladá Boleslav Czech Rep. 17 O5
Mladenovac Serbia 27 I2
Mława Poland 17 R4
Mlilwane Nature Reserve Swaziland 51 J4
Mljet i. Croatia 26 G3
Mlungisi S. Africa 51 H6
Mmabatho S. Africa 51 G3
Mmamabula Botswana 51 H2
Mmathethe Botswana 51 G3
Mo Norway 15 D6
Moa i. Indon. 54 E2
Moab reg. Jordan 39 B4
Moab U.S.A. 62 F4
Moa Island Australia 56 C1
Moala i. Fiji 53 H3
Mo'alla Iran 35 I4
Moamba Moz. 51 K3
Moanda Gabon 48 B4
Moapa NV U.S.A. 65 E2
Moate Ireland 21 E4
Mobārakeh Iran 35 H4
Mobayembongo Dem. Rep. Congo see Mobayi-Mbongo
Mobayi-Mbongo Dem. Rep. Congo 48 C3
Moberly U.S.A. 63 I4
Mobha India 36 C5
Mobile AL U.S.A. 63 J5
Mobile Bay U.S.A. 63 J5
Moble watercourse Australia 58 B1
Mobridge U.S.A. 62 G2
Mobutu, Lake Dem. Rep. Congo/Uganda see Albert, Lake
Mobutu Sese Seko, Lake Dem. Rep. Congo/Uganda see Albert, Lake
Moca Geçidi pass Turkey 39 A1
Moçambique country Africa see Mozambique
Moçambique Moz. 49 E5
Moçâmedes Angola see Namibe
Mocha Yemen 32 F7
Mocha, Isla i. Chile 70 B5
Mochirma, Parque Nacional nat. park Venez. 68 F1
Mochudi Botswana 51 H3
Mochudi admin. dist. Botswana see Kgatleng
Mocimboa da Praia Moz. 49 E5
Mockträsk Sweden 14 L4
Mocoa Col. 68 C3
Mococa Brazil 71 B3
Mocoduene Moz. 51 L2
Moctezuma Chihuahua Mex. 66 C2
Moctezuma San Luis Potosí Mex. 66 D4
Mocuba Moz. 49 D5
Modane France 24 H4
Modder r. S. Africa 51 G5
Modena Italy 26 D2
Modena UT U.S.A. 65 F2
Modesto CA U.S.A. 65 B2
Modesto Lake CA U.S.A. 65 B2
Modimolle S. Africa 51 I3
Modot Mongolia 43 J3
Modung China 37 I3
Moe Australia 58 C7
Moel Sych hill U.K. 19 D6
Moelv Norway 15 G6
Moen Norway 14 K2
Moeraki Point N.Z. 59 C7
Moero, Lake Dem. Rep. Congo/Zambia see Mweru, Lake
Moffat U.K. 20 F5
Moga India 36 C3
Mogadishu Somalia 48 E3
Mogador Morocco see Essaouira
Mogadore Reservoir OH U.S.A. 64 A2
Moganyaka S. Africa 51 I3
Mogaung Myanmar 42 H7
Mogdy Rus. Fed. 44 D2
Mogilev Belarus see Mahilyow
Mogilev Podol'skiy Ukr. see Mohyliv Podil's'kyy
Mogi-Mirim Brazil 71 B3
Mogiquiçaba Brazil 71 D2
Mogocha Rus. Fed. 43 L2
Mogod mts Tunisia 26 C6
Mogoditshane Botswana 51 G3
Mogontiacum Germany see Mainz
Mogroum Chad 47 E3
Moguqi China 44 A3
Mogwadi S. Africa 51 I2
Mogwase S. Africa 51 H3
Mogzon Rus. Fed. 43 K2
Mohács Hungary 26 H2
Mohaka r. N.Z. 59 F4
Mohala India 38 D1
Mohale Dam Lesotho 51 I5
Mohale's Hoek Lesotho 51 H6
Mohammadia Alg. 25 G6
Mohan r. India/Nepal 36 E3
Mohana India 36 D4
Mohave, Lake NV U.S.A. 65 E3
Mohawk r. NY U.S.A. 64 E1
Mohawk Mountains AZ U.S.A. 65 F4
Mohenjo Daro tourist site Pak. 36 B4
Moher, Cliffs of Ireland 21 C5
Mohill Ireland 21 E4
Mohon Peak AZ U.S.A. 65 F3
Mohoro Tanz. 49 D4
Mohyliv Podil's'kyy Ukr. 13 E6
Moi Norway 15 E7
Moijabana Botswana 51 H2
Moincêr China 36 E3
Moinda China 37 G3
Moine Moz. 51 K3
Moinești Romania 27 L1
Mointy Kazakh. see Moyynty
Mo i Rana Norway 14 I3
Mõisaküla Estonia 15 N7
Moissac France 24 E4
Mojave CA U.S.A. 65 C3
Mojave r. CA U.S.A. 65 D3
Mojave Desert CA U.S.A. 65 D3
Mojiang China 42 I8
Moji das Cruzes Brazil 71 B3
Mojos, Llanos de plain Bol. 68 E6
Moju r. Brazil 69 I4
Mokama India 37 F4
Mokau N.Z. 59 E4
Mokau r. N.Z. 59 E4
Mokelumne r. CA U.S.A. 65 B1
Mokelumne Aqueduct canal CA U.S.A. 65 B1
Mokhoabong Pass Lesotho 51 I5
Mokhotlong Lesotho 51 I5
Moknine Tunisia 26 D7
Mokohinau Islands N.Z. 59 E2
Mokokchung India 37 H4
Mokolo Cameroon 47 E3
Mokolo r. S. Africa 51 H2
Mokopane S. Africa 51 I3
Mokp'o S. Korea 45 B6
Mokrous Rus. Fed. 13 J6
Moksha r. Rus. Fed. 13 I5
Mokshan Rus. Fed. 13 J5
Möksy Fin. 14 N5
Mōktama, Gulf of Myanmar see Mottama, Gulf of
Mokundurra India see Mukandwara
Mokwa Nigeria 46 D4
Molatón mt. Spain 25 F4
Moldavia country Europe see Moldova
Moldavskaya S.S.R. country Europe see Moldova
Molde Norway 14 E5
Moldjord Norway 14 I3
Moldova country Europe 13 F7
Moldoveanu, Vârful mt. Romania 27 K2
Moldovei de Sud, Câmpia plain Moldova 27 M1
Molen r. S. Africa 51 I4
Mole National Park Ghana 46 C4
Molepolole Botswana 51 G3
Molėtai Lith. 15 N9
Molfetta Italy 26 G4
Molière Alg. see Bordj Bounaama
Molihong Shan mt. China see Morihong Shan
Molina de Aragón Spain 25 F3
Molkom Sweden 15 H7
Mollagara Turkm. 35 I3
Mollakara Turkm. see Mollagara
Mol Len mt. India 37 H4
Mollendo Peru 68 D7
Mölnlycke Sweden 15 H8
Molochnyy Rus. Fed. 14 R2
Molodechno Belarus see Maladzyechna
Molodezhnaya research station Antarctica 76 D2
Moloka'i i. U.S.A. 62 [inset]
Moloma r. Rus. Fed. 12 K4
Molong Australia 58 D4
Molopo watercourse Botswana/S. Africa 50 E5
Molotov Rus. Fed. see Perm'
Molotovsk Arkhangel'skaya Oblast' Rus. Fed. see Severodvinsk
Molotovsk Kirovskaya Oblast' Rus. Fed. see Nolinsk
Moloundou Cameroon 47 E4
Molson Lake Canada 63 H1
Moluccas is Indon. 41 E8
Molucca Sea sea Indon. see Maluku, Laut
Moma Moz. 49 D5
Momba Australia 58 A3
Mombaça Brazil 69 K5
Mombasa Kenya 48 D4
Mombetsu Hokkaidō Japan see Monbetsu
Mombetsu Hokkaidō Japan see Monbetsu
Mombi New India 37 H4
Momchilgrad Bulg. 27 K4
Momi, Ra's pt Yemen 33 H7
Mompós Col. 68 D2
Møn i. Denmark 15 H9
Mon India 37 H4
Mona terr. Irish Sea see Isle of Man
Monach, Sound of sea chan. U.K. 20 B3
Monach Islands U.K. 20 B3
Monaco country Europe 24 H5
Monaco Basin sea feature N. Atlantic Ocean 72 G4
Monadhliath Mountains U.K. 20 E3
Monaghan Ireland 21 F3
Mona Passage Dom. Rep./Puerto Rico 67 K5
Monapo Moz. 49 E5
Monar, Loch l. U.K. 20 D3
Monarch Pass U.S.A. 62 F4
Monastir Macedonia see Bitola
Monastir Tunisia 26 D7
Monastyrishche Ukr. see Monastyryshche
Monastyryshche Ukr. 13 F6
Monbetsu Hokkaidō Japan 44 F3
Monbetsu Hokkaidō Japan 44 F4
Moncalieri Italy 26 B2
Monchegorsk Rus. Fed. 12 G2
Mönchengladbach Germany 17 K5
Monchique Port. 25 B5
Monclova Mex. 66 D3
Moncton Canada 63 O2
Mondego r. Port. 25 B3
Mondlo S. Africa 51 J4
Mondo Chad 47 E3
Mondovi Italy 26 B2
Mondragone Italy 26 E4
Mondy Rus. Fed. 42 I2
Monemvasia Greece 27 J6
Monessen PA U.S.A. 64 B2
Moneygall Ireland 21 E5
Moneymore U.K. 21 F3
Monfalcone Italy 26 E2
Monfalut Egypt see Manfalūţ
Monforte de Lemos Spain 25 C2
Monga Dem. Rep. Congo 48 C3
Mongala r. Dem. Rep. Congo 48 B3
Mongar Bhutan 37 G4
Mongbwalu Dem. Rep. Congo 48 D3
Mông Cai Vietnam 31 J4
Mongers Lake salt flat Australia 55 B7
Monghyr India see Munger
Mongla Bangl. 37 G5
Mong Loi Myanmar 42 I8
Mong Long Myanmar 37 I5
Mongo Chad 47 E3
Mongolia country Asia 42 I3
Mongol Uls country Asia see Mongolia
Mongonu Nigeria 46 E3
Mongora Pak. 33 L3
Mongour hill U.K. 20 G4
Mongu Zambia 49 C5
Mönh Hayrhan Uul mt. Mongolia 42 G3
Moniaive U.K. 20 F5
Monitor Mountain NV U.S.A. 65 D1
Monitor Range mts NV U.S.A. 65 D1
Monivea Ireland 21 D4
Monkey Bay Malawi 49 D5
Monkira Australia 56 C5
Monkton Ont. Canada 64 A1
Monmouth U.K. 19 E7
Monnow r. U.K. 19 E7
Mono, Punta del pt Nicaragua 67 H6
Mono Lake CA U.S.A. 65 C1
Monolithos Greece 27 L6
Monomoy Point MA U.S.A. 64 F2
Monopoli Italy 26 G4
Monreal del Campo Spain 25 F3
Monreale Sicily Italy 26 E5
Monroe LA U.S.A. 63 I5
Monroeton PA U.S.A. 64 C2
Monrovia Liberia 46 B4
Mons Belgium 16 I5
Monselice Italy 26 D2
Montagu S. Africa 50 E7
Montague Range hills Australia 55 B6
Montalto mt. Italy 26 F5
Montalto Uffugo Italy 26 G5
Montana Bulg. 27 J3
Montana state U.S.A. 62 F2
Montanhas do Tumucumaque, Parque Nacional 69 H3
Montargis France 24 F3
Montauban France 24 E4
Montauk NY U.S.A. 64 F2
Montauk Point NY U.S.A. 64 F2
Mont-aux-Sources mt. Lesotho 51 I5
Montbard France 24 G3
Montblanc Spain 25 G3
Montblanch Spain see Montblanc
Montbrison France 24 G4
Montceau-les-Mines France 24 G3
Mont-de-Marsan France 24 D5
Montdidier France 24 F2
Monte Alegre Brazil 69 H4
Monte Alegre de Goiás Brazil 71 B1
Monte Alegre de Minas Brazil 71 A2
Monte Azul Brazil 71 C1
Monte Azul Paulista Brazil 71 A3
Montebello Islands Australia 54 A5
Montebelluna Italy 26 E2
Monte-Carlo Monaco 24 H5
Monte Cristi Dom. Rep. 67 J5
Monte Cristo S. Africa 51 H2
Monte Dourado Brazil 69 H4
Monte Falterona, Campigna e delle Foreste Casentinesi, Parco Nazionale del nat. park Italy 26 D3
Montego Bay Jamaica 67 I5
Montélimar France 24 G4
Monte Lindo r. Para. 70 E2
Montemorelos Mex. 66 E3
Montemor-o-Novo Port. 25 B4
Montenegro country Europe 26 H3
Montepulciano Italy 26 D3
Monte Quemado Arg. 70 D3
Montereau-fault-Yonne France 24 F2
Monterey Mex. see Monterrey
Monterey CA U.S.A. 65 B2
Monterey VA U.S.A. 64 B3
Monterey Bay CA U.S.A. 65 A2
Montería Col. 68 C2
Monteros Arg. 70 C3
Monterrey Baja California Mex. 65 E4
Monterrey Nuevo León Mex. 66 D3
Montervary hd Ireland 21 C6
Montesano sulla Marcellana Italy 26 F4
Monte Santo Brazil 69 K6
Monte Santu, Capo di c. Sardinia Italy 26 C4
Montes Claros Brazil 71 C2
Montesilvano Italy 26 F3
Montevarchi Italy 26 D3
Montevideo Uruguay 70 E4
Montezuma Peak NV U.S.A. 65 D2
Montgomery U.K. 19 D6
Montgomery AL U.S.A. 63 J5
Montgomery WV U.S.A. 64 A3
Montgomery Islands Australia 54 C3
Monthey Switz. 24 H3
Monticello NY U.S.A. 64 D2
Monticello UT U.S.A. 62 F4
Montignac France 24 E4
Montilla Spain 25 D5
Monti Sibillini, Parco Nazionale dei nat. park Italy 26 E3
Montividiu Brazil 71 A2
Montivilliers France 19 H9
Mont-Laurier Canada 63 L2
Montluçon France 24 F3
Montmagny Canada 63 M2
Montmorillon France 24 E3
Monto Australia 56 E5
Montour Falls NY U.S.A. 64 C1
Montpelier VT U.S.A. 63 M3
Montpellier France 24 F5
Montréal Canada 61 K5
Montreal Lake Canada 62 F1
Montreuil France 19 I8
Montreux Switz. 24 H3
Montrose well S. Africa 50 E4
Montrose U.K. 20 G4
Montrose CO U.S.A. 62 F4
Montrose PA U.S.A. 64 D2
Montross VA U.S.A. 64 C3
Montserrat terr. West Indies 67 L5
Mont-St-Aignan France 19 I9
Monywa Myanmar 37 H5
Monza Italy 26 C2
Monze, Cape pt Pak. see Muari, Ras
Monzón Spain 25 G3
Mooi r. S. Africa 51 J5
Mooifontein Namibia 50 C4
Mookane Botswana 51 H2
Mookgopong S. Africa see Naboomspruit
Moolawatana Australia 57 B6
Moomba Australia 57 C6
Moomin Creek r. Australia 58 D2
Moonaree Australia 57 A6
Moonbi Range mts Australia 58 E3
Moonda Lake salt flat Australia 57 C5
Moonie Australia 58 E1
Moonie r. Australia 58 D2
Moora Australia 55 B7
Mooraberree Australia 56 C5
Moore r. Australia 55 A7
Moore, Lake salt flat Australia 55 B7
Moore Embayment b. Antarctica 76 H1
Moorefield WV U.S.A. 64 B3
Moore Reef Australia 56 E3
Moore River National Park Australia 55 A7
Moorfoot Hills U.K. 20 F5
Moorhead U.S.A. 63 H2
Moornanyah Lake imp. l. Australia 58 A4
Mooroopna Australia 58 B6
Moorreesburg S. Africa 50 D7
Moorrinya National Park Australia 56 D4
Moose r. Canada 63 K1
Moose Factory Canada 63 K1
Moosehead Lake U.S.A. 63 N2
Moose Jaw Canada 62 F1
Moosomin Canada 62 G1
Moosonee Canada 63 K1
Mootwingee National Park Australia 57 C6
Mopane S. Africa 51 I2
Mopeia Moz. 49 D5
Mopipi Botswana 49 C6
Mopti Mali 46 C3
Moqor Afgh. 36 A2
Moquegua Peru 68 D7
Mora Cameroon 47 E3
Mora Spain 25 E4
Mora Sweden 15 I6
Moradabad India 36 D3
Morada Nova Brazil 69 K5
Moraleda, Canal sea chan. Chile 70 B6
Moram India 38 C2
Moramanga Madag. 49 E5
Moranbah Australia 56 E4
Morang Nepal see Biratnagar
Morar, Loch l. U.K. 20 D4
Morari, Tso l. Jammu and Kashmir 36 D2
Moratuwa Sri Lanka 38 C5
Moravia reg. Czech Rep. 17 P6
Moravia NY U.S.A. 64 C1
Morawa Australia 55 A7
Moray Firth b. U.K. 20 E3
Moray Range hills Australia 54 E3
Morbeng S. Africa see Soekmekaar
Morbi India 36 B5
Morcenx France 24 D4
Mordaga China 43 M2
Mor Dağı mt. Turkey 35 G3
Morden Canada 62 H2
Mordovo Rus. Fed. 13 I5
Morecambe U.K. 18 E4
Morecambe Bay U.K. 18 D4
Moree Australia 58 D2
Morehead P.N.G. 52 E2
Morehead City U.S.A. 67 I2
More Laptevykh sea Rus. Fed. see Laptev Sea
Morelia Mex. 66 D5
Morella Australia 56 C4
Morella Spain 25 F3
Morena India 36 D4
Morena, Sierra mts Spain 25 C5
Moreni Romania 27 K2
Moreno Valley CA U.S.A. 65 D4
Moresby, Mount Canada 60 E4
Moresby Island Canada 60 E4
Moreswe Pan salt pan Botswana 50 G2
Moreton Bay Australia 58 F1
Moreton-in-Marsh U.K. 19 F7
Moreton Island Australia 58 F1
Moreton Island National Park Australia 58 F1
Morez France 24 H3
Morfou Cyprus 39 A2
Morfou Bay Cyprus 39 A2
Morgan Hill CA U.S.A. 65 B2
Morganton U.S.A. 63 K4
Morgantown WV U.S.A. 64 B3
Morgenzon S. Africa 51 I4
Morges Switz. 24 H3
Morgh, Kowtal-e Afgh. 36 B2
Morhar r. India 37 F4
Mori China 42 G4
Mori Japan 44 F4
Moriah, Mount NV U.S.A. 65 E1
Moriarty's Range hills Australia 58 B2
Morice Lake Canada 60 F4
Morichal Col. 68 D3
Morihong Shan mt. China 44 B4
Morija Lesotho 51 H5
Morin Dawa China see Nirji
Morioka Japan 45 F5
Morisset Australia 58 E4
Moriyoshi-zan vol. Japan 45 F5
Morjärv Sweden 14 M3
Morki Rus. Fed. 12 K4
Morlaix France 24 C2
Morley U.K. 18 F5
Mormugao India see Marmagao
Morne Diablotins vol. Dominica 67 L5
Morney watercourse Australia 56 C5
Mornington, Isla i. Chile 70 A7
Mornington Abyssal Plain sea feature S. Atlantic Ocean 72 C9
Mornington Island Australia 56 B3
Mornington Peninsula National Park Australia 58 B7
Moro Pak. 36 A4
Morobe P.N.G. 52 E2
Morocco country Africa 46 C1
Morococala mt. Bol. 68 E7
Morogoro Tanz. 49 D4
Moro Gulf Phil. 41 E7
Morojaneng S. Africa 51 H5
Morokweng S. Africa 50 F4
Morombe Madag. 49 E6
Mörön Mongolia 42 I3
Morondava Madag. 49 E6
Morón de la Frontera Spain 25 D5
Moroni Comoros 49 E5
Moron Us He r. China see Tongtian He
Morotai i. Indon. 41 E7
Moroto Uganda 48 D3
Morozovsk Rus. Fed. 13 I6
Morpeth Ont. Canada 64 A1
Morpeth U.K. 18 F3
Morphou Cyprus see Morfou
Morrinhos Brazil 71 A2
Morris Canada 63 H2
Morris PA U.S.A. 64 C2
Morris Jesup, Kap c. Greenland 77 I1
Morristown AZ U.S.A. 65 F4
Morristown NJ U.S.A. 64 D2
Morristown TN U.S.A. 63 K4
Morrisville NY U.S.A. 64 D1
Morro Brazil 71 B2
Morro Bay CA U.S.A. 65 B3
Morro d'Anta Brazil 71 D2
Morro do Chapéu Brazil 69 J6
Morro Grande hill Brazil 69 H4
Morrosquillo, Golfo de b. Col. 68 C2
Morrumbene Moz. 51 L2
Morse, Cape Antarctica 76 G2
Morshanka Rus. Fed. 13 I5
Morshansk Rus. Fed. see Morshanka
Morsott Alg. 26 C7
Mort watercourse Australia 56 C4
Mortagne-au-Perche France 24 E2
Mortagne-sur-Sèvre France 24 D3
Mortara Italy 26 C2
Mortehoe U.K. 19 C7
Morteros Arg. 70 D4
Mortes, Rio das r. Brazil 71 A1
Mortlake Australia 58 A7
Mortlock Islands Micronesia 74 G5
Mortlock Islands P.N.G. see Takuu Islands
Morton U.K. 19 G6
Morton National Park Australia 58 E5
Morundah Australia 58 C5
Morupule Botswana 51 H2
Moruroa atoll Fr. Polynesia see Mururoa
Moruya Australia 58 E5
Morven Australia 57 D5
Morven hill U.K. 20 F2
Morvern reg. U.K. 20 D4
Morvi India see Morbi
Morwara India 36 B4
Morwell Australia 58 C7
Morzhovets, Ostrov i. Rus. Fed. 12 I2
Mosbach Germany 17 L6
Mosborough U.K. 18 F5
Moscow Rus. Fed. 12 H5
Moscow ID U.S.A. 62 D2
Moscow PA U.S.A. 64 D2
Moscow University Ice Shelf Antarctica 76 G2
Moselebe watercourse Botswana 50 F3
Moselle r. France 24 H2
Moses Lake U.S.A. 62 D2
Mosgiel N.Z. 59 C7
Moshaweng watercourse S. Africa 50 F4
Moshchnyy, Ostrov i. Rus. Fed. 15 O7
Moshi Tanz. 48 D4
Mosh'yuga Rus. Fed. 12 L2
Mosi-oa-Tunya waterfall Zambia/Zimbabwe see Victoria Falls
Mosjøen Norway 14 H4
Moskal'vo Rus. Fed. 44 F1
Moskenesøy i. Norway 14 H3
Moskva Rus. Fed. see Moscow
Mosonmagyaróvár Hungary 17 P7
Mosquera Col. 68 C3
Mosquito r. Brazil 71 C1
Mosquito Creek Lake OH U.S.A. 64 A2
Moss Norway 15 G7
Mossâmedes Angola see Namibe
Mossat U.K. 20 G3
Mossburn N.Z. 59 B7
Mosselbaai S. Africa see Mossel Bay
Mossel Bay S. Africa 50 F8
Mossel Bay b. S. Africa 50 F8
Mossgiel Australia 58 B4
Mossman Australia 56 D3
Mossoró Brazil 69 K5
Moss Vale Australia 58 E5
Most Czech Rep. 17 N5
Mostaganem Alg. 25 G6
Mostar Bos.-Herz. 26 G3
Mostovskoy Rus. Fed. 35 F1
Mosty Belarus see Masty
Mosul Iraq 35 F3
Møsvatnet l. Norway 15 F7
Motala Sweden 15 I7
Motaze Moz. 51 K3
Motetema S. Africa 51 I3
Moth India 36 D4
Motherwell U.K. 20 F5
Motian Ling hill China 44 A4
Motihari India 37 F4
Motilla del Palancar Spain 25 F4
Motiti Island N.Z. 59 F3
Motokwe Botswana 50 F3
Motril Spain 25 E5
Motru Romania 27 J2
Mottama, Gulf of Myanmar 31 I5
Motu Ihupuku i. N.Z. see Campbell Island
Motul Mex. 66 G4
Mouaskar Alg. see Mascara
Moudjéria Mauritania 46 B3
Moudros Greece 27 K5
Mouhijärvi Fin. 15 M6
Mouila Gabon 48 B4
Moulamein Australia 58 B5
Moulamein Creek r. Australia 58 A5
Moulavibazar Bangl. see Moulvibazar
Mould Bay Canada 60 G2
Moulèngui Binza Gabon 48 B4
Moulins France 24 F3
Moulouya, Oued r. Morocco 22 D4
Moultrie U.S.A. 63 K5
Moultrie, Lake U.S.A. 63 L5
Moulvibazar Bangl. 37 G4
Moundou Chad 47 E4
Moundsville WV U.S.A. 64 A3
Mount Abu India 36 C4
Mountain Home AR U.S.A. 63 I4
Mountain Home ID U.S.A. 62 D3
Mountain Lake Park MD U.S.A. 64 B3
Mountain Zebra National Park S. Africa 51 G7
Mount Aspiring National Park N.Z. 59 B7
Mount Ayliff S. Africa 51 I6
Mount Bellew Ireland 21 D4
Mount Buffalo National Park Australia 58 C6
Mount Carmel Junction UT U.S.A. 65 F2
Mount Coolon Australia 56 D4
Mount Darwin Zimbabwe 49 D5
Mount Denison Australia 54 F5
Mount Dutton Australia 57 A5
Mount Eba Australia 57 A6
Mount Elgon National Park Uganda 48 D3
Mount Fletcher S. Africa 51 I6
Mount Frankland National Park Australia 55 B8
Mount Frere S. Africa 51 I6
Mount Gambier Australia 57 C8
Mount Hagen P.N.G. 52 E2
Mount Holly NJ U.S.A. 64 D3
Mount Hope Australia 58 B4
Mount Hope WV U.S.A. 64 A4
Mount Howitt Australia 57 C5
Mount Isa Australia 56 B4
Mount Jackson VA U.S.A. 64 B3
Mount Jewett PA U.S.A. 64 B2
Mount Joy PA U.S.A. 64 C2
Mount Kaputar National Park Australia 58 E3
Mount Keith Australia 55 C6
Mount Lofty Range mts Australia 57 B7
Mount Magnet Australia 55 B7
Mount Manara Australia 58 A4
Mount McKinley National Park U.S.A. see Denali National Park and Preserve
Mountmellick Ireland 21 E4
Mount Moorosi Lesotho 51 H6
Mount Morgan Australia 56 E4
Mount Morris NY U.S.A. 64 C1
Mount Murchison Australia 58 A3
Mount Nebo WV U.S.A. 64 A3
Mount Pleasant IA U.S.A. 63 I3
Mount Pleasant MI U.S.A. 63 K3
Mount Pleasant TX U.S.A. 63 I5
Mount Remarkable National Park Australia 57 B7
Mount Rogers National Recreation Area park VA U.S.A. 64 A4
Mount Sanford Australia 54 E4
Mount's Bay U.K. 19 B8
Mount Shasta U.S.A. 62 C3
Mountsorrel U.K. 19 F6
Mount Swan Australia 56 A4
Mount Union PA U.S.A. 64 C2
Mount Vernon Australia 55 B6
Mount Vernon IL U.S.A. 63 J4
Mount Vernon WA U.S.A. 62 C2
Mount William National Park Australia 57 [inset]
Mount Willoughby Australia 55 F6
Moura Australia 56 E5
Moura Brazil 68 F4
Moura Port. 25 C4
Mourdi, Dépression du depr. Chad 47 F3
Mourdiah Mali 46 C3
Mourne r. U.K. 21 E3
Mourne Mountains hills U.K. 21 F3
Mousa i. U.K. 20 [inset]
Mouscron Belgium 16 I5
Mousgougou Chad 48 B2
Moussafoyo Chad 47 E4
Moussoro Chad 47 E3
Moutamba Congo 48 B4
Moutong Indon. 41 E7
Mouydir, Monts du plat. Alg. 46 D2
Mowbullan, Mount Australia 58 E1
Moy r. Ireland 21 C3
Moyale Eth. 48 D3
Moyen Atlas mts Morocco 22 C5
Moyen Congo country Africa see Congo
Moyeni Lesotho 51 H6
Moynalyk Rus. Fed. 42 H2

Moyo *i.* Indon. **54** B2
Moyobamba Peru **68** C5
Moyola *r.* U.K. **21** F3
Moyu China **36** D1
Moyynkum Kazakh. **42** C4
Moyynkum, Peski *des.* Kazakh. **42** B4
Moyynty Kazakh. **28** I5
Mozambique *country* Africa **49** D6
Mozambique Channel Africa **49** E6
Mozambique Ridge *sea feature* Indian Ocean **73** K7
Mozdok Rus. Fed. **13** J8
Mozhaysk Rus. Fed. **13** H5
Mozhga Rus. Fed. **12** L4
Mozyr' Belarus *see* **Mazyr**
Mpaathutlwa Pan *salt pan* Botswana **50** E3
Mpanda Tanz. **49** D4
Mpen India **37** I4
Mpika Zambia **49** D5
Mpolweni S. Africa **51** J5
Mporokoso Zambia **49** D4
Mpulungu Zambia **49** D4
Mpumalanga *prov.* S. Africa **51** I4
Mpunde *mt.* Tanz. **49** D4
Mpwapwa Tanz. **49** D4
Mqanduli S. Africa **51** I6
Mqinvartsveri *mt.* Georgia/Rus. Fed. *see* **Kazbek**
Mrauk-U Myanmar **37** H5
Mrewa Zimbabwe *see* **Murehwa**
Mrkonjić-Grad Bos.-Herz. **26** G2
M'Saken Tunisia **26** D7
Mshinskaya Rus. Fed. **15** P7
M'Sila Alg. **25** I6
Msta *r.* Rus. Fed. **12** F4
Mstislavl' Belarus *see* **Mstsislaw**
Mstsislaw Belarus **13** F5
Mtelo Kenya **48** D3
Mtoko Zimbabwe *see* **Mutoko**
Mtorwi Tanz. **49** D4
Mtsensk Rus. Fed. **13** H5
Mts'ire Kavkasioni Asia *see* **Lesser Caucasus**
Mtubatuba S. Africa **51** K5
Mtunzini S. Africa **51** J5
Mtwara Tanz. **49** E5
Mu *r.* Myanmar **37** H5
Mu'āb, Jibāl *reg.* Jordan *see* **Moab**
Muanda Dem. Rep. Congo **49** B4
Muang Khoua Laos **42** I8
Muang Pakxan Laos *see* **Pakxan**
Muang Phôn-Hông Laos **42** I9
Muang Sing Laos **42** I8
Muang Thai *country* Asia *see* **Thailand**
Muari, Ras *pt* Pak. **36** A4
Mu'ayqil, Khashm al *hill* Saudi Arabia **35** H6
Mubarek Uzbek. *see* **Muborak**
Mubarraz *well* Saudi Arabia **35** F5
Mubende Uganda **48** D3
Mubi Nigeria **46** E3
Muborak Uzbek. **33** K2
Mucajaí, Serra do *mts* Brazil **68** F3
Muccan Australia **54** C5
Muchinga Escarpment Zambia **49** D5
Muck *i.* U.K. **20** C4
Mucojo Moz. **49** E5
Muconda Angola **49** C5
Mucubela Moz. **49** D5
Mucugê Brazil **71** C1
Mucur Turkey **34** D3
Mucuri Brazil **71** D2
Mucuri *r.* Brazil **71** D2
Mudabidri India **38** B3
Mudan China *see* **Heze**
Mudanjiang China **44** C3
Mudan Jiang *r.* China **44** C3
Mudan Ling *mts* China **44** B4
Mudanya Turkey **27** M4
Mudaysīsāt, Jabal al *hill* Jordan **39** C4
Muddus nationalpark *nat. park* Sweden **14** K3
Muddy *r. NV* U.S.A. **65** E2
Muddy Peak *NV* U.S.A. **65** E2
Mudgal India **38** C3
Mudgee Australia **58** D4
Mudhol India **38** B2
Mudigere India **38** B3
Mud Lake *NV* U.S.A. **65** D2
Mudraya *country* Africa *see* **Egypt**
Mudurnu Turkey **27** N4
Mud'yuga Rus. Fed. **12** H3
Mueda Moz. **49** D5
Mueller Range *hills* Australia **54** D4
Muftyuga Rus. Fed. **12** J2
Mufulira Zambia **49** C5
Mufumbwe Zambia **49** C5
Muğan Düzü *lowland* Azer. **35** H3
Mugarripug China **37** F2
Mughalbhin Pak. *see* **Jati**
Mughal Kot Pak. **36** B3
Mughal Sarai India **37** E4
Mūghār Iran **35** I5
Mughayrā' Saudi Arabia **39** C5
Muğla Turkey **27** M6
Mugxung China **37** H2
Muḩ, Sabkhat *imp. l.* Syria **39** D2
Muhammad Ashraf Pak. **36** B4
Muhammad Qol Sudan **32** E5
Muhammarah Iran *see* **Khorramshahr**
Muhashsham, Wādī al *watercourse* Egypt **39** B4
Muḩaysh, Wādī al *watercourse* Jordan **39** C5
Muḩaysin Syria **39** D1
Mühlhausen (Thüringen) Germany **17** M5
Mühlig-Hofmann Mountains Antarctica **76** C2
Muhos Fin. **14** N4
Muḩradah Syria **39** C2
Muhri Pak. **36** A3
Mui Bai Bung *c.* Vietnam *see* **Mui Ca Mau**
Mui Ca Mau *c.* Vietnam **31** J6
Muié Angola **49** C5
Muineachán Ireland *see* **Monaghan**
Muine Bheag Ireland **21** F5
Muirkirk U.K. **20** E5
Muir of Ord U.K. **20** E3
Muite Moz. **49** D5
Muji China **36** D1
Muju S. Korea **45** B5
Mukacheve Ukr. **13** D6
Mukachevo Ukr. *see* **Mukacheve**
Mukalla Yemen **32** G7
Mukandwara India **36** D4
Mukden China *see* **Shenyang**
Mukhen Rus. Fed. **44** E2
Mukhino Rus. Fed. **44** B1
Mukhtuya Rus. Fed. *see* **Lensk**
Mukinbudin Australia **55** B7
Mukojima-rettō *is* Japan **45** F8
Muktsar India **36** C3
Mula *r.* India **38** B2
Mulan China **44** C3
Mulanje, Mount Malawi **49** D5
Mulapula, Lake *salt flat* Australia **57** B6
Mulayz, Wādī al *watercourse* Egypt **39** A4
Mulchatna *r.* U.S.A. **60** C3
Mulde *r.* Germany **17** N5
Mulegé Mex. **66** B3
Mules *i.* Indon. **54** C2
Muleshoe U.S.A. **62** G5
Mulga Park Australia **55** E6
Mulgathing Australia **55** F7
Mulhacén *mt.* Spain **25** E5
Mülhausen France *see* **Mulhouse**
Mulhouse France **24** H3
Muli China **42** I7
Muli Rus. Fed. *see* **Vysokogorniy**
Muling *Heilong.* China **44** C3
Muling *Heilong.* China **44** C3
Muling He *r.* China **44** D3
Mull *i.* U.K. **20** D4
Mull, Sound of *sea chan.* U.K. **20** C4
Mullaghcleevaun *hill* Ireland **21** F4
Mullaittivu Sri Lanka **38** D4
Mullaley Australia **58** D3
Mullengudgery Australia **58** C3
Mullens *WV* U.S.A. **64** A4
Muller *watercourse* Australia **54** F5
Mullewa Australia **55** A7
Mullica *r. NJ* U.S.A. **64** D3
Mullingar Ireland **21** E4
Mullion Creek Australia **58** D4
Mull of Galloway *c.* U.K. **20** E6
Mull of Kintyre *hd* U.K. **20** D5
Mull of Oa *hd* U.K. **20** C5
Mullumbimby Australia **58** F2
Mulobezi Zambia **49** C5
Mulshi Lake India **38** B2
Multai India **36** D5
Multan Pak. **33** L3
Multia Fin. **14** N5
Mulug India **38** C2
Mumbai India **38** B2
Mumbil Australia **58** D4
Mumbwa Zambia **49** C5
Muna Mex. **66** G4
Muna *r.* Rus. Fed. **29** N3
Munabao Pak. **36** B4
Munaðarnes Iceland **14** [inset]
München Germany *see* **Munich**
München-Gladbach Germany *see* **Mönchengladbach**
Muncoonie West, Lake *salt flat* Australia **56** B5
Muncy *PA* U.S.A. **64** C2
Munda Pak. **36** B3
Mundel Lake Sri Lanka **38** C5
Mundesley U.K. **19** I6
Mundford U.K. **19** H6
Mundiwindi Australia **55** C5
Mundra India **36** B5
Mundrabilla Australia **52** C5
Mundubbera Australia **57** E5
Mundwa India **36** C4
Mungallala Australia **57** D5
Mungana Australia **56** D3
Mungári Moz. **49** D5
Mungbere Dem. Rep. Congo **48** C3
Mungeli India **37** E5
Munger India **37** F4
Mu Nggava *i.* Solomon Is *see* **Rennell**
Mungindi Australia **58** D2
Mungla Bangl. *see* **Mongla**
Mungo Angola **49** B5
Mungo, Lake Australia **58** A4
Mungo National Park Australia **58** A4
Munich Germany **17** M6
Munjpur India **36** B5
Munkács Ukr. *see* **Mukacheve**
Munkebakken Norway **14** P2
Munkedal Sweden **15** G7
Munkfors Sweden **15** H7
Munkhafaḑ al Qaţţārah *depr.* Egypt *see* **Qattara Depression**
Munku-Sardyk, Gora *mt.* Mongolia/Rus. Fed. **42** I2
Munnik S. Africa **51** I2
Munsan S. Korea **45** B5
Münster *Niedersachsen* Germany **17** M4
Münster *Nordrhein-Westfalen* Germany **17** K5
Munster *reg.* Ireland **21** D5
Muntadgin Australia **55** B7
Munyal-Par *sea feature* India *see* **Bassas de Pedro Padua Bank**
Munzur Vadisi Milli Parkı *nat. park* Turkey **23** L4
Muojärvi *l.* Fin. **14** P4
Muonio Fin. **14** M3
Muonioälven *r.* Fin./Sweden **14** M3
Muonionjoki *r.* Fin./Sweden *see* **Muonioälven**
Mupa, Parque Nacional da *nat. park* Angola **49** B5
Muqdisho Somalia *see* **Mogadishu**
Muquem Brazil **71** A1
Muqui Brazil **71** C3
Mur *r.* Austria **17** P7
Mura *r.* Croatia/Slovenia *see* **Mur**
Murakami Japan **45** E5
Murallón, Cerro *mt.* Chile **70** B7
Muramvya Burundi **48** C4
Murashi Rus. Fed. **12** K4
Murat *r.* Turkey **35** E3
Muratlı Turkey **27** L4
Muraysah, Ra's al *pt* Libya **34** B5
Murchison *watercourse* Australia **55** A6
Murchison, Mount Antarctica **76** H2
Murchison, Mount *hill* Australia **55** B6
Murchison Falls National Park Uganda **48** D3
Murcia Spain **25** F5
Murcia *aut. comm.* Spain **25** F5
Murehwa Zimbabwe **49** D5
Mureșul *r.* Romania **27** I1
Muret France **24** E5
Murewa Zimbabwe *see* **Murehwa**
Murfreesboro *TN* U.S.A. **63** J4
Murgab Tajik. *see* **Murghob**
Murgab *r.* Turkm. *see* **Murgap**
Murgap *r.* Turkm. **33** J2
Murghab *r.* Afgh. **36** A2
Murgha Kibzai Pak. **36** B3
Murghob Tajik. **33** L2
Murgon Australia **57** E5
Murgoo Australia **55** B6
Muri India **37** F5
Muriaé Brazil **71** C3
Muriege Angola **49** C4
Müritz *l.* Germany **17** N4
Müritz, Nationalpark *nat. park* Germany **17** N4
Murmansk Rus. Fed. **12** G1
Murmanskaya Oblast' *admin. div.* Rus. Fed. **14** S2
Murmanskiy Bereg *coastal area* Rus. Fed. **12** G1
Murmansk Oblast *admin. div.* Rus. Fed. *see* **Murmanskaya Oblast'**
Muro, Capo di *c. Corsica* France **24** I6
Murom Rus. Fed. **12** I5
Muroran Japan **44** F4
Muros Spain **25** B2
Muroto Japan **45** D6
Muroto-zaki *pt* Japan **45** D6
Murrah al Kubrá, Al Buḩayrah al *l.* Egypt *see* **Great Bitter Lake**
Murrah aş Şughrá, Al Buḩayrah al *l.* Egypt *see* **Little Bitter Lake**
Murra Murra Australia **58** C2
Murrat el Kubra, Buheirat *l.* Egypt *see* **Great Bitter Lake**
Murrat el Sughra, Buheirat *l.* Egypt *see* **Little Bitter Lake**
Murray *r. S.A.* Australia **57** B7
Murray *r. W.A.* Australia **55** A8
Murray *KY* U.S.A. **63** J4
Murray, Lake P.N.G. **52** E2
Murray Bridge Australia **57** B7
Murray-Darling *r.* Austr. **52** E5
Murray Downs Australia **54** F5
Murray Range *hills* Australia **55** E6
Murraysburg S. Africa **50** F6
Murray Sunset National Park Australia **57** C7
Murrieta *CA* U.S.A. **65** D4
Murringo Australia **58** D5
Murrisk *reg.* Ireland **21** C4
Murroogh Ireland **21** C4
Murrumbidgee *r.* Australia **58** A5
Murrumburrah Australia **58** D5
Murrurundi Australia **58** E3
Mursan India **36** D4
Murshidabad India **37** G4
Murska Sobota Slovenia **26** G1
Murtoa Australia **57** C8
Murua *i.* P.N.G. *see* **Woodlark Island**
Murud India **38** B2
Murunkan Sri Lanka **38** D4
Murupara N.Z. **59** F4
Mururoa *atoll* Fr. Polynesia **75** K7
Murviedro Spain *see* **Sagunto**
Murwara India **36** E5
Murwillumbah Australia **58** F2
Murzūq Libya **47** E2
Mürzzuschlag Austria **17** O7
Muş Turkey **35** F3
Mūsā, Khowr-e *b.* Iran **35** H5
Musa Khel Bazar Pak. **36** B3
Musala *mt.* Bulg. **27** J3
Musan N. Korea **44** C4
Muscat Oman **33** I5
Muscat and Oman *country* Asia *see* **Oman**
Muscatine U.S.A. **63** I3
Musgrave Australia **56** C2
Musgrave Ranges *mts* Australia **55** E6
Mushāsh al Kabid *well* Jordan **39** C5
Mushayyish, Wādī al *watercourse* Jordan **39** C4
Mushie Dem. Rep. Congo **48** B4
Music Mountain *AZ* U.S.A. **65** F3
Musina S. Africa **51** J2
Muskeget Channel *MA* U.S.A. **64** F2
Muskogee U.S.A. **63** H4
Musmar Sudan **32** E6
Musoma Tanz. **48** D4
Mussau Island P.N.G. **52** E2
Musselburgh U.K. **20** F5
Mussende Angola **49** B5
Mustafakemalpaşa Turkey **27** M4
Mustjala Estonia **15** M7
Mustvee Estonia **15** O7
Musu-dan *pt* N. Korea **44** C4
Muswellbrook Australia **58** E4
Mūţ Egypt **32** C4
Mut Turkey **39** A1
Mutá, Ponta do *pt* Brazil **71** D1
Mutare Zimbabwe **49** D5
Mutina Italy *see* **Modena**
Mutis Col. **68** C2
Mutnyy Materik Rus. Fed. **12** L2
Mutoko Zimbabwe **49** D5
Mutsamudu Comoros **49** E5
Mutsu Japan **44** F4
Muttaburra Australia **56** D4
Mutton Island Ireland **21** C5
Muttukuru India **38** D3
Muttupet India **38** C4
Mutum Brazil **71** C2
Mutunópolis Brazil **71** A1
Mutur Sri Lanka **38** D4
Mutusjärvi *r.* Fin. **14** O2
Muurola Fin. **14** N3
Mu Us Shamo *des.* China **43** J5
Muxaluando Angola **49** B4
Muxima Angola **49** B4
Muyezerskiy Rus. Fed. **12** G3
Muyinga Burundi **48** D4
Muyumba Dem. Rep. Congo **49** C4
Muyunkum, Peski *des.* Kazakh. *see* **Moyynkum, Peski**
Muzaffarabad Pak. **36** C2
Muzaffargarh Pak. **33** L3
Muzaffarnagar India **36** D3
Muzaffarpur India **37** F4
Muzamane Moz. **51** K2
Muzhi Rus. Fed. **11** S2
Múzquiz Mex. **66** D3
Muztag *mt.* China **36** E2
Muz Tag *mt.* China **37** F1
Muztor Kyrg. *see* **Toktogul**
Mvadi Gabon **48** B3
Mvolo Sudan **47** F4
Mvuma Zimbabwe **49** D5
Mwanza Malawi **49** D5
Mwanza Tanz. **48** D4
Mweelrea *hill* Ireland **21** C4
Mweka Dem. Rep. Congo **49** C4
Mwene-Ditu Dem. Rep. Congo **49** C4
Mwenezi Zimbabwe **49** D6
Mwenga Dem. Rep. Congo **48** C4
Mweru, Lake Dem. Rep. Congo/Zambia **49** C4
Mweru Wantipa National Park Zambia **49** C4
Mwimba Dem. Rep. Congo **49** C4
Mwinilunga Zambia **49** C5
Myadaung Myanmar **37** I5
Myadzyel Belarus **15** O9
Myajlar India **36** B4
Myall Lakes National Park Australia **58** F4
Myanmar *country* Asia **31** I4
Myauk-U Myanmar *see* **Mrauk-U**
Mybster U.K. **20** F2
Myeik Myanmar **31** I5
Myeik Myanmar *see* **Myeik**
Myingyan Myanmar **37** H5
Myitkyina Myanmar **42** H7
Myitson Myanmar **37** I5
Myittha Myanmar **37** I5
Mykolayiv Ukr. **27** O1
Mykonos *i.* Greece **27** K6
Myla Rus. Fed. **12** K2
Myla *r.* Rus. Fed. **12** K2
Mylae *Sicily* Italy *see* **Milazzo**
Mylasa Turkey *see* **Milas**
Mymensing Bangl. *see* **Mymensingh**
Mymensingh Bangl. **37** G4
Mynämäki Fin. **15** M6
Myŏnggan N. Korea **44** C4
Myory Belarus **15** O9
Mýrdalsjökull *ice cap* Iceland **14** [inset]
Myre Norway **14** I2
Myrheden Sweden **14** L4
Myrhorod Ukr. **13** G6
Myronivka Ukr. **13** F6
Myrtle Beach U.S.A. **63** L5
Myrtleford Australia **58** C6
Myrtoo Pelagos *sea* Greece **27** J6
Mys Articheskiy *c.* Rus. Fed. **77** E1
Mysia *reg.* Turkey **27** L5
Mys Lazareva Rus. Fed. *see* **Lazarev**
Myślibórz Poland **17** O4
Mysore India **38** C3
Mysore *state* India *see* **Karnataka**
Mys Shmidta Rus. Fed. **29** T3
Mysy Rus. Fed. **12** L3
My Tho Vietnam **31** J5
Mytilene *i.* Greece *see* **Lesbos**
Mytilini Greece **27** L5
Mytilini Strait Greece/Turkey **27** L5
Mytishchi Rus. Fed. **12** H5
Myyeldino Rus. Fed. **12** L3
Mzamomhle S. Africa **51** H6
Mzimba Malawi **49** D5
Mzuzu Malawi **49** D5

N

Naantali Fin. **15** M6
Naas Ireland **21** F4
Nā'ālehu U.S.A. **62** [inset]
Naba Myanmar **37** I4
Nababeep S. Africa **50** C5
Nababganj Bangl. *see* **Nawabganj**
Nabadwip India *see* **Navadwip**
Nabarangapur India **38** D2
Nabarangpur India *see* **Nabarangapur**
Nabari Japan **45** E6
Nabatîyé et Tahta Lebanon **39** B3
Nabatiyet et Tahta Lebanon *see* **Nabatîyé et Tahta**
Nabberu, Lake *salt flat* Australia **55** C6
Naberera Tanz. **49** D4
Naberezhnyye Chelny Rus. Fed. **11** Q4
Nabeul Tunisia **26** D6
Nabha India **36** D3
Nabil'skiy Zaliv *lag.* Rus. Fed. **44** F2
Nabire Indon. **41** F8
Nabi Younés, Ras en *pt* Lebanon **39** B3
Nāblus West Bank **39** B3
Naboomspruit S. Africa **51** I3
Nabq Reserve *nature res.* Egypt **34** D5
Nābulus West Bank *see* **Nāblus**
Nacala Moz. **49** E5
Nachalovo Rus. Fed. **13** K7
Nachingwea Tanz. **49** D5
Nachna India **36** B4
Nacimiento Reservoir *CA* U.S.A. **65** B3
Nacogdoches U.S.A. **63** I5
Nådendal Fin. *see* **Naantali**
Nadezhdinskoye Rus. Fed. **44** D2
Nadiad India **36** C5
Nadol India **36** C4
Nador Morocco **25** E6
Nadūshan Iran **35** I4
Nadvirna Ukr. **13** E6
Nadvoitsy Rus. Fed. **12** G3
Nadvornaya Ukr. *see* **Nadvirna**
Nadym Rus. Fed. **28** I3
Næstved Denmark **15** G9
Nafarroa *aut. comm.* Spain *see* **Navarra**
Nafas, Ra's an *mt.* Egypt **39** B5
Nafha, Har *hill* Israel **39** B4
Nafpaktos Greece **27** I5
Nafplio Greece **27** J6
Naftalan Azer. **35** G2
Naft-e Safīd Iran **35** H5
Naft-e Shāh Iran *see* **Naft Shahr**
Naft Shahr Iran **35** G4
Nafūd al Ghuwayţah *des.* Saudi Arabia **39** D5
Nafūd al Jur'ā *des.* Saudi Arabia **35** G6
Nafūsah, Jabal *hills* Libya **46** E1
Nafy Saudi Arabia **32** F4
Nag, Co *l.* China **37** G2
Naga Phil. **41** E6
Nagahama Japan **45** D6
Naga Hills India **37** H4
Naga Hills *state* India *see* **Nagaland**
Nagaland *state* India **37** H4
Nagamangala India **38** C3
Nagambie Australia **58** B6
Nagano Japan **45** E5
Nagaoka Japan **45** E5
Nagaon India **37** H4
Nagapatam India *see* **Nagapattinam**
Nagapattinam India **38** C4
Nagar *Hima. Prad.* India **33** M3
Nagar *Karnataka* India **38** B3
Nagaram India **38** D2
Nagari Hills India **38** C3
Nagarjuna Sagar Reservoir India **38** C2
Nagar Parkar Pak. **33** L5
Nagasaki Japan **45** C6
Nagato Japan **45** C6
Nagaur India **36** C4
Nagbhir India **38** C1
Nagda India **36** C5
Nagercoil India **38** C4
Nag' Ḩammâdî Egypt *see* **Naj' Ḩammādī**
Nagina India **36** D3
Nagong Chu *r.* China *see* **Parlung Zangbo**
Nagorno-Karabakh *aut. reg.* Azer. *see* **Dağlıq Qarabağ**
Nagornyy Karabakh *aut. reg.* Azer. *see* **Dağlıq Qarabağ**
Nagorsk Rus. Fed. **12** K4
Nagoya Japan **45** E6
Nagpur India **36** D5
Nagqu China **42** G6
Nag Qu *r.* China **37** H3
Nagurskoye Rus. Fed. **28** F1
Nagyatád Hungary **26** G1
Nagybecskerek Serbia *see* **Zrenjanin**
Nagyenyed Romania *see* **Aiud**
Nagykanizsa Hungary **26** G1
Nagyvárad Romania *see* **Oradea**
Naha Japan **43** N7
Nahan India **36** D3
Nahanni Butte Canada **60** F3
Nahanni National Park Reserve Canada **60** F3
Naharāyim Jordan **39** B3
Nahariyya Israel **39** B3
Nahāvand Iran **35** H4
Nahr Dijlah *r.* Iraq/Syria **35** G5 *see* **Tigris**
Nahuel Huapi, Parque Nacional *nat. park* Arg. **70** B6
Naij Tal China **37** H2
Naikliu Indon. **54** C2
Nain Canada **61** L4
Nā'īn Iran **35** I4
Nainital India **36** D3
Naini Tal India *see* **Nainital**
Nairn U.K. **20** F3
Nairn *r.* U.K. **20** F3
Nairobi Kenya **48** D4
Naissus Serbia *see* **Niš**
Naivasha Kenya **48** D4
Najafābād Iran **35** H4
Najd *reg.* Saudi Arabia **32** F4
Nájera Spain **25** E2
Naj' Ḩammādī Egypt **32** D4
Naji China **44** A2
Najibabad India **36** D3
Najin N. Korea **44** C4
Najitun China *see* **Naji**
Najrān Saudi Arabia **32** F6
Nakadōri-shima *i.* Japan **45** C6
Nakambé *r.* Burkina/Ghana *see* **White Volta**
Nakanbe *r.* Burkina/Ghana *see* **White Volta**
Nakanno Rus. Fed. **29** L3
Nakano-shima *i.* Japan **45** D5
Nakasongola Uganda **47** G4
Nakatsu Japan **45** C6
Nakatsugawa Japan **45** E6
Nakfa Eritrea **32** E6
Nakhichevan' Azer. *see* **Naxçıvan**
Nakhl Egypt **39** A5
Nakhodka Rus. Fed. **44** D4
Nakhola India **37** H4
Nakhon Pathom Thai. **31** J5
Nakhon Ratchasima Thai. **31** J5
Nakhon Sawan Thai. **31** J5
Nakhon Si Thammarat Thai. **31** I6
Nakhtarana India **36** B5
Nakina Canada **63** J1
Naknek U.S.A. **60** C4
Nakonde Zambia **49** D4
Nakskov Denmark **15** G9
Naktong-gang *r.* S. Korea **45** C6
Nakuru Kenya **48** D4
Nal Pak. **36** A4
Nalázi Moz. **51** K3
Nalbari India **37** G4
Nal'chik Rus. Fed. **13** I8
Naldurg India **38** C2
Nalgonda India **38** C2
Naliya India **36** B5
Nallamala Hills India **38** C3
Nallıhan Turkey **27** N4
Nālūt Libya **46** E1
Namaacha Moz. **51** K3
Namacurra Moz. **49** D5
Namadgi National Park Australia **58** D5
Namahadi S. Africa **51** I4
Namak, Daryācheh-ye *salt flat* Iran **35** H4
Namakkal India **38** C4
Namakwaland *reg.* Namibia *see* **Great Namaqualand**
Namakzar-e Shadad *salt flat* Iran **33** I3
Namaland *reg.* Namibia *see* **Great Namaqualand**
Namangan Uzbek. **33** L1
Namaqualand *reg.* Namibia *see* **Great Namaqualand**
Namaqualand *reg.* S. Africa **50** C5
Namaqua National Park S. Africa **50** C6
Namatanai P.N.G. **52** F2
Nambour Australia **58** F1
Nambucca Heads Australia **58** F3
Nambung National Park Australia **55** A7
Namcha Barwa *mt.* China *see* **Namjagbarwa Feng**
Namche Bazar Nepal **37** F4
Nam Co *salt l.* China **37** G3
Namdalen *valley* Norway **14** H4
Namdalseid Norway **14** G4
Nam Đinh Vietnam **31** J4
Namen Belgium *see* **Namur**
Nam-gang *r.* N. Korea **45** B5
Namhae-do *i.* S. Korea **45** B6
Namib Desert Namibia **50** B3
Namibe Angola **49** B5
Namibia *country* Africa **49** B6
Namibia Abyssal Plain *sea feature* N. Atlantic Ocean **72** I8
Namib-Naukluft Game Park *nature res.* Namibia **50** B3
Namie Japan **45** F5
Namīn Iran **35** H3
Namjagbarwa Feng *mt.* China **42** G7
Namoi *r.* Australia **58** D3
Nampa *mt.* Nepal **36** E3
Nampa U.S.A. **62** D3
Nampala Mali **46** C3
Namp'o N. Korea **45** B5
Nampula Moz. **49** D5
Namsen *r.* Norway **14** G4
Namsos Norway **14** G4
Namti Myanmar **37** I4
Namtsy Rus. Fed. **29** N3
Namtu Myanmar **42** H8
Namuli, Monte *mt.* Moz. **49** D5
Namuno Moz. **49** D5
Namur Belgium **16** J5
Namutoni Namibia **49** B5
Namwŏn S. Korea **45** B6
Namya Ra Myanmar **37** I4
Nan Thai. **31** J5
Nana Bakassa Cent. Afr. Rep. **48** B3
Nanaimo Canada **62** C2
Nanam N. Korea **44** C4
Nan'an China **43** L8
Nanango Australia **58** F1
Nananib Plateau Namibia **50** C3
Nanao Japan **45** E5
Nanatsu-shima *i.* Japan **45** E5
Nancha China **44** C3
Nanchang *Jiangxi* China **43** L7
Nanchong China **42** J6
Nancy France **24** H2
Nanda Devi *mt.* India **36** E3
Nanda Kot *mt.* India **36** E3
Nandapur India **38** D2
Nanded India **38** C2
Nander India *see* **Nanded**
Nandewar Range *mts* Australia **58** E3
Nandod India **38** B1
Nandurbar India **36** C5
Nandyal India **38** C3
Nang China **42** G7
Nanga Eboko Cameroon **46** E4
Nanga Parbat *mt.* Jammu and Kashmir **36** C2
Nangar National Park Australia **58** D4
Nangnim-sanmaek *mts* N. Korea **45** B4
Nangqên China **42** H6
Nangulangwa Tanz. **49** D4
Nanguneri India **38** C4
Nanjing China **43** L6
Nanking China *see* **Nanjing**
Nankova Angola **49** B5
Nan Ling *mts* China **43** K8
Nannilam India **38** C4
Nannine Australia **55** B6
Nanning China **43** J8
Nannup Australia **55** A8
Nanortalik Greenland **61** N3
Nanouki *atoll* Kiribati *see* **Nonouti**
Nanouti *atoll* Kiribati *see* **Nonouti**
Nanping China **43** L7
Nansei-shotō *is* Japan *see* **Ryukyu Islands**
Nansen Basin *sea feature* Arctic Ocean **77** H1
Nansen Sound *sea chan.* Canada **61** I1
Nan-sha Ch'ün-tao *is* S. China Sea *see* **Spratly Islands**
Nansha Qundao *is* S. China Sea *see* **Spratly Islands**
Nansio Tanz. **48** D4
Nantes France **24** D3
Nantes à Brest, Canal de France **24** C3
Nanthi Kadal *lag.* Sri Lanka **38** D4
Nanticoke *Ont.* Canada **64** A1
Nanticoke *MD* U.S.A. **64** D3
Nanticoke *PA* U.S.A. **64** D2
Nantong China **43** M6
Nantucket *MA* U.S.A. **64** F2
Nantucket Island *MA* U.S.A. **64** G2
Nantucket Sound *g. MA* U.S.A. **64** F2
Nantwich U.K. **19** E5
Nanumaga *i.* Tuvalu *see* **Nanumanga**
Nanumanga *i.* Tuvalu **53** H2
Nanumea *atoll* Tuvalu **53** H2
Nanuque Brazil **71** C2
Nanxiong China **43** K7
Nanyang China **43** K6
Nanyuki Kenya **48** D4
Naococane, Lac *l.* Canada **61** K4
Naoero *country* S. Pacific Ocean *see* **Nauru**
Naogaon Bangl. **37** G4
Naokot Pak. **33** K5
Naoli He *r.* China **44** D3
Naomid, Dasht-e *des.* Afgh./Iran **33** J3
Naoshera Jammu and Kashmir **36** C2
Napa *CA* U.S.A. **65** A1
Napaktulik Lake Canada **60** G3
Napasoq Greenland **61** M3
Napier N.Z. **59** F4
Napier Range *hills* Australia **54** D4
Naples Italy **26** F4
Naples *FL* U.S.A. **63** K6
Napoli Italy *see* **Naples**
Naqadeh Iran **35** G3
Nara India **36** B5
Nara Japan **45** D6
Nara Mali **46** C3
Narach Belarus **15** O9
Naracoorte Australia **57** C8
Naradhan Australia **58** C4
Narainpur India **38** D2
Naralua India **37** F4
Naranjal Ecuador **68** C4
Narasapur India **38** D2
Narasaraopet India **38** D2
Narasinghapur India **38** E1
Narayanganj Bangl. **37** G5
Narayanganj India **36** E5
Narayangarh India **36** C4
Narbada *r.* India *see* **Narmada**
Narberth U.K. **19** C7
Narbo France *see* **Narbonne**
Narbonne France **24** F5
Narborough Island *Galápagos* Ecuador *see* **Fernandina, Isla**
Narcea *r.* Spain **25** C2
Nardò Italy **26** H4
Narechi *r.* Pak. **36** B3
Narembeen Australia **55** B8
Nares Abyssal Plain *sea feature* S. Atlantic Ocean **72** D4
Nares Deep *sea feature* N. Atlantic Ocean **72** D4
Nares Strait Canada/Greenland **61** K2
Naretha Australia **55** D7
Narew *r.* Poland **17** R4
Narib Namibia **50** C3
Narimanov Rus. Fed. **13** J7
Narimskiy Khrebet *mts* Kazakh. *see* **Narymskiy Khrebet**
Narin Afgh. **36** B1
Narince Turkey **34** E3
Narin Gol *watercourse* China **37** H1
Narkher India **36** D5
Narmada *r.* India **36** C5
Narman Turkey **35** F2
Narnaul India **36** D3
Narni Italy **26** E3
Narnia Italy *see* **Narni**
Narodnaya, Gora *mt.* Rus. Fed. **11** S3
Naro-Fominsk Rus. Fed. **13** H5
Narok Kenya **48** D4
Narooma Australia **58** E6
Narovchat Rus. Fed. **13** I5
Narowlya Belarus **13** F6
Närpes Fin. **14** L5
Narrabri Australia **58** D3
Narragansett Bay *RI* U.S.A. **64** F2
Narran *r.* Australia **58** C2
Narrandera Australia **58** C5
Narran Lake Australia **58** C2
Narrogin Australia **55** B8
Narromine Australia **58** D4
Narrows *VA* U.S.A. **64** A4
Narrowsburg *NY* U.S.A. **64** D2
Narsapur India **38** C2
Narsaq Greenland **61** N3
Narshingdi Bangl. *see* **Narsingdi**
Narsimhapur India *see* **Narsinghpur**
Narsingdi Bangl. **37** G5
Narsinghpur India **36** D5
Narsipatnam India **38** D2
Nartkala Rus. Fed. **35** F2
Naruto Japan **45** D6
Narva Estonia **15** P7
Narva Bay Estonia/Rus. Fed. **15** O7
Narva laht *b.* Estonia/Rus. Fed. *see* **Narva Bay**
Narva Reservoir *resr* Estonia/Rus. Fed. *see* **Narvskoye Vodokhranilishche**
Narva veehoidla *resr* Estonia/Rus. Fed. *see* **Narvskoye Vodokhranilishche**
Narvik Norway **14** J2
Narvskiy Zaliv *b.* Estonia/Rus. Fed. *see* **Narva Bay**
Narvskoye Vodokhranilishche *resr* Estonia/Rus. Fed. **15** P7
Narwana India **36** D3
Nar'yan-Mar Rus. Fed. **12** L2
Narymskiy Khrebet *mts* Kazakh. **42** E3
Naryn Kyrg. **42** D4
Näsåker Sweden **14** J5
Nashik India **38** B1
Nashua *NH* U.S.A. **64** F1
Nashville *TN* U.S.A. **63** J4
Naşīb Syria **39** C3
Näsijärvi *l.* Fin. **15** M6
Nasik India *see* **Nashik**
Nasir Pak. **36** B3
Nasir Sudan **32** D8
Nasirabad Bangl. *see* **Mymensingh**
Nasirabad India **36** C4
Naşr Egypt **34** C5
Nasratabad Iran *see* **Zābol**
Naşrīān-e Pā'īn Iran **35** G4
Nassau *r.* Australia **56** C2
Nassau Bahamas **67** I3
Nassau *i.* Cook Is **53** J3
Nassau *NY* U.S.A. **64** E1
Nassawadox *VA* U.S.A. **64** D4
Nasser, Lake *resr* Egypt **32** D5
Nässjö Sweden **15** I8
Nassuttooq *inlet* Greenland **61** M3
Nasva Rus. Fed. **12** F4
Nata Botswana **49** C6
Natal Brazil **69** K5
Natal *prov.* S. Africa *see* **KwaZulu-Natal**
Natal Basin *sea feature* Indian Ocean **73** K8
Naţanz Iran **35** H4
Natashquan *r.* Canada **61** L4
Natchez U.S.A. **63** I5
Natchitoches U.S.A. **63** I5
Nathalia Australia **58** B6
Nathia Gali Pak. **36** C2
Nati, Punta *pt* Spain **25** H3
National City *CA* U.S.A. **65** D4
National West Coast Tourist Recreation Area *park* Namibia **50** B2
Natitingou Benin **46** D3
Natividade Brazil **69** I6
Natmauk Myanmar **37** H5

Nator Bangl. see Natore
Natore Bangl. 37 G4
Natori Japan 45 F5
Natron, Lake salt l. Tanz. 48 D4
Nattai National Park Australia 58 E5
Natuna, Kepulauan is Indon. 41 C7
Natuna Besar i. Indon. 41 C7
Naturaliste, Cape Australia 55 A8
Naturaliste Plateau sea feature
  Indian Ocean 73 P8
Nauchas Namibia 50 C2
Naujoji Akmenė Lith. 15 M8
Naukh India 38 C4
Naupada India 38 E2
Na'ūr Jordan 39 B4
Nauroz Kalat Pak. 36 A3
Naurskaya Rus. Fed. 13 J8
Nauru i. Nauru 53 G2
Nauru country S. Pacific Ocean 53 G2
Naustdal Norway 14 D5
Nauta Peru 68 D4
Nautaca Uzbek. see Qarshi
Navadwip India 37 G5
Navahrudak Belarus 15 N10
Navalmoral de la Mata Spain 25 D4
Navalvillar de Pela Spain 25 D4
Navan Ireland 21 E3
Navangar India see Jamnagar
Navapolatsk Belarus 15 P9
Năvăvăr, Dasht-e depr. Afgh. 36 A2
Navarin, Mys c. Rus. Fed. 29 S3
Navarra aut. comm. Spain 25 F2
Navarra, Comunidad Foral de aut. comm.
  Spain see Navarra
Navarre Australia 58 A6
Navarre aut. comm. Spain see Navarra
Navarro r. CA U.S.A. 65 B3
Navashino Rus. Fed. 12 I5
Navassa Island terr. West Indies 67 I5
Naver r. U.K. 20 E2
Näverede Sweden 14 I5
Navi 38 B2
Navlakhi India 36 B5
Navlya Rus. Fed. 13 G5
Năvodari Romania 27 M2
Navoiy Uzbek. 33 K1
Navoiy Uzbek. see Navoiy
Navojoa Mex. 66 C3
Navolato Mex. 66 C4
Navpaktos Greece see Nafpaktos
Návplion Greece see Nafplio
Navşar Turkey see Şemdinli
Navsari India 36 B5
Nawá Syria 39 C3
Nawabganj India 37 G4
Nawabshah Pak. 33 K4
Nawada India 37 F4
Nāwah Afgh. 36 A2
Nawalgarh India 36 C4
Nawanshahr India 36 D3
Nawan Shehar India see Nawanshahr
Nawar, Dasht-i depr. Afgh. see
  Năvăr, Dasht-e
Nawarangpur India see Nabarangapur
Nawngleng Myanmar 32 H8
Nawoiy Uzbek. see Navoiy
Naxçıvan Azer. 35 G3
Naxos i. Greece 27 K6
Nayagarh India 38 E1
Nayak Afgh. 36 A2
Nayar Mex. 66 D4
Nāy Band, Küh-e mt. Iran 33 I3
Nayoro Japan 44 F3
Naypyidaw Myanmar 31 I5
Nazaré Brazil 71 D1
Nazareth Israel 39 B3
Nazário Brazil 71 A2
Nazas r. Mex. 62 G6
Nazca Peru 68 D6
Nazca Ridge sea feature S. Pacific Ocean
  75 O7
Nazilli Turkey 27 M6
Nazimabad Pak. 36 A4
Nazımiye Turkey 35 E3
Nazir Hat Bangl. 37 G5
Nazran' Rus. Fed. 35 G2
Nazrēt Eth. 48 D3
Nazwá Oman 33 I5
Nazyvayevsk Rus. Fed. 28 I4
Ncojane Botswana 50 E2
N'dalatando Angola 49 B4
Ndélé Cent. Afr. Rep. 48 C3
Ndendé Gabon 48 B4
Ndende i. Solomon Is see Ndeni
Ndeni i. Solomon Is 53 G3
Ndindi i. Fiji see Doi
Ndjamena Chad see Ndjamena
N'Djamena Chad 47 E3
Ndjouani i. Comoros see Nzwani
Ndoi i. Fiji see Doi
Ndola Zambia 49 C5
2nd Three Mile Opening sea chan.
  Australia 56 C2
Nduke i. Solomon Is see Kolombangara
Ndwedwe S. Africa 51 J5
Neabul Creek r. Australia 58 C1
Neagh, Lough l. U.K. 21 F3
Neale, Lake salt flat Australia 55 E6
Néa Liosia Greece 27 J5
Neapoli Greece 27 J6
Neapolis Italy see Naples
Néa Roda Greece 27 J4
Neath r. U.K. 19 D7
Neath U.K. 19 D7
Nebbi Uganda 48 D3
Nebine Creek r. Australia 58 C2
Neblina, Pico da mt. Brazil 68 E3
Nebo Australia 56 E4
Nebolchi Rus. Fed. 12 G4
Nebraska state U.S.A. 62 G3
Nebraska City U.S.A. 63 H3
Nebrodi, Monti mts Sicily Italy 26 F6
Nechisar National Park Eth. 48 D3
Necker Island U.S.A. 74 J4
Necochea Arg. 70 E5
Nederland country Europe see Netherlands
Nederlandse Antillen terr. West Indies see
  Netherlands Antilles
Nedlouc, Lac l. Canada 61 K4
Nedluk Lake Canada see Nedlouc, Lac
Nêdong China see Zêtang
Nedre Soppero Sweden 14 L2
Needles U.S.A. 65 E3
Neemach India see Neemuch
Neemuch India 36 C4
Neepawa Canada 62 H1
Neergaard Lake Canada 61 J2
Neftçala Azer. 35 H3
Neftechala Azer. see Uzboy
Neftechala Azer. see Neftçala
Neftegorsk Sakhalinskaya Oblast' Rus. Fed.
  44 F1
Neftegorsk Samarskaya Oblast' Rus. Fed.
  13 K5
Neftekamsk Rus. Fed. 11 Q4
Neftekumsk Rus. Fed. 35 G1
Nefteyugansk Rus. Fed. 28 I3
Neftezavodsk Turkm. see Seýdi
Neftezawodsk Turkm. see Seýdi

Nefyn U.K. 19 C6
Nefza Tunisia 26 C6
Negage Angola 49 B4
Negara Indon. 54 A2
Negēlē Eth. 48 D3
Negomane Moz. 49 D5
Negombo Sri Lanka 38 C5
Negotino Macedonia 27 J4
Negra, Cordillera mts Peru 68 C5
Negra, Punta pt Peru 68 B5
Negra, Serra mts Brazil 71 C2
Négrine Alg. 26 B7
Negro r. Arg. 70 D6
Negro r. Brazil 71 A4
Negro r. S. America 68 G4
Negro, Cabo c. Morocco 25 D6
Negroponte i. Greece see Evvoia
Negros i. Phil. 41 E7
Negru Vodă, Podişul plat. Romania 27 M3
Nehbandān Iran 33 J3
Nehe China 44 A2
Neijiang China 42 J7
Neimenggu aut. reg. China see
  Nei Mongol Zizhiqu
Nei Mongol Zizhiqu aut. reg. China 44 A2
Neiva Col. 68 C3
Nejanilini Lake Canada 61 I4
Nejd reg. Saudi Arabia see Najd
Neka Iran 35 I3
Nek'emtē Eth. 48 D3
Nekrasovskoye Rus. Fed. 12 I4
Nekso Denmark 15 I9
Nelang India 36 D3
Nelia Australia 56 C4
Nel'kan Rus. Fed. 29 P3
Nellore India 38 C3
Nelluz watercourse Turkey 39 D1
Nel'ma Rus. Fed. 44 E3
Nelson Canada 62 D2
Nelson r. Canada 61 I4
Nelson N.Z. 59 D5
Nelson U.K. 18 E5
Nelson AZ U.S.A. 65 F3
Nelson, Cape Australia 57 C8
Nelson, Estrecho strait Chile 70 A8
Nelsonia U.S.A. 64 D4
Nelson Bay Australia 58 F4
Nelson Lakes National Park N.Z. 59 D6
Nelspruit S. Africa 51 J3
Néma Mauritania 46 C3
Nema Rus. Fed. 12 K4
Neman r. Belarus/Lith. see Nyoman
Neman Rus. Fed. 15 M9
Nemausus France see Nîmes
Nemawar India 36 D5
Nemed Rus. Fed. 12 L3
Nementcha, Monts des mts Alg. 26 B7
New England National Park Australia 58 F3
New England Range mts Australia 58 E3
New England Seamounts sea feature
  N. Atlantic Ocean 72 E3
Nemetocenna France see Arras
Nemetskiy, Mys c. Rus. Fed. 14 Q2
Nemirov Ukr. see Nemyriv
Nemor He r. China 44 B2
Nemours France see Ghazaouet
Nemours France 24 F2
Nemrut Dağı mt. Turkey 35 F3
Nemunas r. Lith. see Nyoman
Nemuro Japan 44 G4
Nemuro-kaikyō sea chan. Japan/Rus. Fed.
  44 G4
Nemyriv Ukr. 13 F6
Nenagh Ireland 21 D5
Nenana U.S.A. 60 D3
Nene r. U.K. 19 H6
Nenjiang China 44 B2
Nen Jiang r. China 44 B3
Neosho U.S.A. 63 I4
Nepal country Asia 37 E3
Nepalganj Nepal 37 E3
Nepean, Point Australia 58 B7
Nephi U.S.A. 62 E4
Nephin h. Ireland 21 C3
Nephin Beg Range hills Ireland 21 C3
Nepisiguit r. Canada 63 N2
Nepoko r. Dem. Rep. Congo 48 C3
Nérac France 24 E4
Nerang Australia 58 F1
Nera Tso l. China 37 H3
Nerchinsk Rus. Fed. 43 L2
Nerekhta Rus. Fed. 12 I4
Neretva r. Bos.-Herz./Croatia 26 G3
Néri Púnco l. China 37 G3
Neriquinha Angola 49 C5
Neris r. Lith. 15 M9
Nerl' r. Rus. Fed. 12 H4
Nerópolis Brazil 71 A2
Neryungri Rus. Fed. 29 N4
Nes Norway 15 F6
Nes' Rus. Fed. 12 J2
Nesbyen Norway 15 F6
Neskaupstaður Iceland 14 [inset]
Nesna Norway 14 H3
Nesri India 38 B2
Ness r. U.K. 20 E3
Ness, Loch l. U.K. 20 E3
Nestos r. Greece 27 K4
Nesvizh Belarus see Nyasvizh
Netanya Israel 39 B3
Netherlands country Europe 16 J4
Netherlands Antilles terr. West Indies
  67 K6
Netrakonda Bangl. 37 G4
Netrakona Bangl. see Netrakona
Nettilling Lake Canada 61 K3
Neubrandenburg Germany 17 N4
Neuchâtel Switz. 24 H3
Neuchâtel, Lac de l. Switz. 24 H3
Neufchâteau France 24 G2
Neufchâtel-en-Bray France 24 E2
Neufchâtel-Hardelot France 19 I8
Neuhausen Rus. Fed. see Gur'yevsk
Neukuhren Rus. Fed. see Pionerskiy
Neumayer research station Antarctica 76 B2
Neumünster Germany 17 L3
Neunkirchen Austria 17 P7
Neunkirchen Germany 17 K6
Neuquén Arg. 70 C5
Neuruppin Germany 17 N4
Neu Sandez Poland see Nowy Sącz
Neusiedler See l. Austria/Hungary 17 P7
Neusiedler See Seewinkel, Nationalpark
  nat. park Austria 17 P7
Neustrelitz Germany 17 N4
Neuville-lès-Dieppe France 19 I9
Neuwied Germany 17 K5
Nevada MO U.S.A. 63 I4
Nevada IA U.S.A. 63 I3
Nevada state U.S.A. 62 D4
Nevada, Sierra Spain 25 E5
Nevada, Sierra mts U.S.A. 62 C3
Nevado, Cerro mt. Arg. 70 C5
Nevado, Sierra del mts Arg. 70 C5
Nevasa India 38 B2
Nevatim Israel 39 B4
Nevdubstroy Rus. Fed. see Kirovsk
Nevel' Rus. Fed. 12 F4
Nevel'sk Rus. Fed. 44 F3
Never Rus. Fed. 44 B1
Nevers France 24 F3
Nevertire Australia 58 C3
Nevesinje Bos.-Herz. 26 H3

Nevinnomyssk Rus. Fed. 13 I7
Nevşehir Turkey 34 D3
Nevskoye Rus. Fed. 44 D3
New r. CA U.S.A. 65 E4
New r. WV U.S.A. 64 E4
Newala Tanz. 49 D5
New Albany IN U.S.A. 63 J4
New Amsterdam Guyana 69 G2
New Angledool Australia 58 C2
Newark DE U.S.A. 64 D3
Newark NJ U.S.A. 64 E2
Newark NY U.S.A. 64 C1
Newark-on-Trent U.K. 19 G5
New Bedford U.S.A. 64 F2
New Berlin NY U.S.A. 64 D1
New Bern U.S.A. 64 E4
Newberry SC U.S.A. 63 K5
Newberry Springs CA U.S.A. 65 D3
New Bethlehem PA U.S.A. 64 B2
Newbiggin-by-the-Sea U.K. 18 F3
New Bloomfield PA U.S.A. 64 C2
New Boston U.S.A. 64 B3
New Braunfels U.S.A. 62 H6
Newbridge Ireland 21 E4
New Britain i. P.N.G. 52 E2
New Britain i. P.N.G. 52 E2
New Britain Trench sea feature
  S. Pacific Ocean 52 F2
New Brunswick prov. Canada 63 N2
New Brunswick NJ U.S.A. 64 D2
Newburgh U.K. 20 G3
Newburgh NY U.S.A. 64 D2
Newbury U.K. 19 F7
Newburyport MA U.S.A. 64 F1
Newby Bridge U.K. 18 E4
New Caledonia terr. S. Pacific Ocean 53 G4
New Caledonia Trough sea feature
  Tasman Sea 53 G4
Newcastle Australia 58 E4
Newcastle Ireland 21 F4
Newcastle S. Africa 51 I4
Newcastle U.K. 21 G3
New Castle PA U.S.A. 64 A2
New Castle UT U.S.A. 65 F2
New Castle VA U.S.A. 64 A4
Newcastle WY U.S.A. 62 G3
Newcastle Emlyn U.K. 19 C6
Newcastle-under-Lyme U.K. 19 E5
Newcastle upon Tyne U.K. 18 F4
Newcastle Waters Australia 54 F4
Newcastle West Ireland 21 C5
Newchwang China see Yingkou
New City NY U.S.A. 64 E2
New Cumberland WV U.S.A. 64 A2
New Cumnock U.K. 20 E5
New Deer U.K. 20 G3
New Delhi India 36 D3
New Don Pedro Reservoir CA U.S.A. 65 B2
Newell, Lake salt flat Australia 55 D6
Newenham, Cape U.S.A. 60 B4
Newent U.K. 19 E7
Newfane NY U.S.A. 64 B1
Newfane VT U.S.A. 64 E1
Newfoundland i. Canada 61 M5
Newfoundland prov. Canada see
  Newfoundland and Labrador
Newfoundland and Labrador prov. Canada
  61 M4
New Galloway U.K. 20 E5
New Georgia i. Solomon Is 53 F2
New Georgia Islands Solomon Is 53 F2
New Georgia Sound sea chan. Solomon Is
  53 F2
New Guinea i. Indon./P.N.G. 41 G8
New Halfa Sudan 32 E6
New Hampshire state U.S.A. 64 F1
New Hanover i. P.N.G. 52 F2
New Haven CT U.S.A. 64 E2
New Hebrides country S. Pacific Ocean see
  Vanuatu
New Hebrides Trench sea feature
  S. Pacific Ocean 74 H7
New Iberia U.S.A. 63 I5
New Ireland i. P.N.G. 52 F2
New Jersey state U.S.A. 64 D3
New Kensington PA U.S.A. 64 B2
New Kent VA U.S.A. 64 F5
New Lanark U.K. 20 F5
New Liskeard Canada 63 L2
New London CT U.S.A. 64 E2
Newman Australia 55 B5
Newmarket Ireland 21 C5
Newmarket U.K. 19 H6
New Market VA U.S.A. 64 B3
Newmarket-on-Fergus Ireland 21 D5
New Martinsville WV U.S.A. 64 A3
New Mexico state U.S.A. 62 F5
New Milford PA U.S.A. 64 D2
New Orleans U.S.A. 63 I6
New Philadelphia OH U.S.A. 64 A2
New Pitsligo U.K. 20 G3
New Plymouth N.Z. 59 E4
Newport Mayo Ireland 21 C4
Newport Tipperary Ireland 21 D5
Newport England U.K. 19 E6
Newport England U.K. 19 F8
Newport Wales U.K. 19 D7
Newport AR U.S.A. 63 I4
Newport NH U.S.A. 64 F1
Newport NJ U.S.A. 64 D3
Newport OR U.S.A. 62 C3
Newport RI U.S.A. 64 F2
Newport VT U.S.A. 64 F1
Newport WA U.S.A. 62 D2
Newport Beach CA U.S.A. 65 D4
Newport News VA U.S.A. 64 C4
Newquay U.K. 19 B8
New Roads U.S.A. 63 I5
New Rochelle NY U.S.A. 64 E2
New Romney U.K. 19 H8
New Ross Ireland 21 E5
Newry U.K. 21 F3
New Siberia Islands Rus. Fed. 29 P2
New South Wales state Australia 58 C4
New Stanton PA U.S.A. 64 B2
Newton U.K. 18 E5
Newton IA U.S.A. 63 I3
Newton KS U.S.A. 63 H4
Newton MA U.S.A. 64 F1
Newton NJ U.S.A. 64 D2
Newton Abbot U.K. 19 D8
Newton Mearns U.K. 20 E5
Newton Stewart U.K. 20 E6
Newtown Ireland 21 D5
Newtown England U.K. 19 E6
Newtown Wales U.K. 19 D6
New Town U.S.A. 62 G2
Newtownabbey U.K. 21 G3
Newtownards U.K. 21 G3
Newtownbarry Ireland see Bunclody
Newtownbutler U.K. 21 E3

Newtownmountkennedy Ireland 21 F4
Newtown St Boswells U.K. 20 G5
Newtownstewart U.K. 21 E3
New Ulm U.S.A. 63 I3
Newville PA U.S.A. 64 C2
New York NY U.S.A. 64 E2
New York state U.S.A. 64 D1
New Zealand country Oceania 59 D5
Neya Rus. Fed. 12 I4
Neyriz Iran 35 I5
Neyshābūr Iran 33 I2
Nezhin Ukr. see Nizhyn
Ngabé Congo 48 B4
Ngagahtawng Myanmar 37 I4
Ngagau mt. Tanz. 49 D4
Ngalu Indon. 54 C2
Ngamring China 37 F3
Ngangla Ringco salt l. China 37 E3
Nganglong Kangri mt. China 36 E2
Nganglong Kangri mts China 36 E2
Ngangzê Co salt l. China 37 F3
Ngangzê Shan mts China 37 F3
Ngaoundal Cameroon 46 E4
Ngaoundéré Cameroon 47 E4
Ngape Myanmar 37 H5
Ngarrab China see Gyaca
Ngau i. Fiji see Gau
Ngawa China see Aba
Ngga Pulu mt. Indon. see Jaya, Puncak
Ngilmina Indon. 54 D2
Ngiva Angola see Ondjiva
Ngoako Ramalepe S. Africa see
  Duiwelskloof
Ngoin, Co salt l. China 37 G3
Ngoko r. Cameroon/Congo 47 E4
Ngom Qu r. China see Ji Qu
Ngoqumaima China 37 F2
Ngoring China 37 I2
Ngoring Hu l. China 37 I2
Ngourti Niger 46 E3
Nguigmi Niger 46 E3
Nguiu Australia 54 E2
Ngukurr Australia 54 F3
Ngulu atoll Micronesia 41 F7
Ngunza Angola see Sumbe
Ngunza-Kabolu Angola see Sumbe
Nguru Nigeria 46 E3
Ngwaketse admin. dist. Botswana see
  Southern
Ngwane country Africa see Swaziland
Ngwathe S. Africa 51 H4
Ngwavuma r. S. Africa/Swaziland 51 K4
Ngwelezana S. Africa 51 J5
Nhachengue Moz. 51 L2
Nhamalabué Moz. 51 L2
Nha Trang Vietnam 31 J5
Nhecolândia Brazil 69 G7
Nhill Australia 57 C8
Nhlangano Swaziland 51 J4
Nhow i. Fiji see Gau
Nhulunbuy Australia 56 B2
Niafounké Mali 46 C3
Niagara Falls Ont. Canada 64 B1
Niagara Falls NY U.S.A. 64 B1
Niagara-on-the-Lake Ont. Canada 64 B1
Niagzu Aksai Chin 36 D2
Niakaramandougou Côte d'Ivoire 46 C4
Niamey Niger 46 D3
Niangara Dem. Rep. Congo 48 C3
Niangay, Lac l. Mali 46 C3
Nianzishan China 44 A3
Nias i. Indon. 41 B7
Niassa, Lago l. Africa see Nyasa, Lake
Nibil Well Australia 54 D5
Nīca Latvia 15 L8
Nicaragua country Central America 67 G6
Nicaragua, Lago de Nicaragua see
  Nicaragua, Lake
Nicastro Italy see Lamezia
Nice France 24 H5
Nice CA U.S.A. 65 A1
Nicephorium Syria see Ar Raqqah
Nicholson r. Australia 56 B3
Nicholson Range hills Australia 55 B6
Nicobar Islands India 31 I6
Nicolaus CA U.S.A. 65 B2
Nicomedia Kocaeli Turkey see İzmit
Nicosia Cyprus 39 A2
Nicoya, Península de pen. Costa Rica 67 G7
Nida Lith. 15 L9
Nidagunda India 38 C2
Nidd r. U.K. 18 F4
Nidzica Poland 17 R4
Niebüll Germany 17 L3
Niedere Tauern mts Austria 17 N7
Niederösterreich state Austria see
  Lower Austria
Niedersächsisches Wattenmeer,
  Nationalpark nat. park Germany 16 K4
Niefang Equat. Guinea 46 E4
Niellé Côte d'Ivoire 46 C3
Nienburg (Weser) Germany 17 L4
Nieuw Nickerie Suriname 69 G2
Nieuwoudtville S. Africa 50 D6
Niğde Turkey 34 D3
Niger country Africa 46 D3
Niger r. Africa 46 D4
Niger, Mouths of the Nigeria 46 D4
Niger Cone sea feature S. Atlantic Ocean
  72 I5
Nigeria country Africa 46 D4
Nighthawk Lake Canada 63 K2
Nigrita Greece 27 J4
Nihing Pak. 36 A3
Nihon country Asia see Japan
Niigata Japan 45 E5
Niihama Japan 45 D6
Ni'ihau i. U.S.A. 62 [inset]
Nii-jima i. Japan 45 E6
Niimi Japan 45 D6
Niitsu Japan 45 E5
Nijil, Wādī watercourse Jordan 39 B4
Nijmegen Neth. 17 J5
Nikel' Rus. Fed. 12 F1
Nikki Benin 46 D4
Nikkō Kokuritsu-kōen Japan 45 E5
Nikolayev Ukr. see Mykolayiv
Nikolayevka Rus. Fed. 13 J5
Nikolayev-na-Amure Rus. Fed. 44 F1
Nikol'sk Kazakh. see Satpayev
Nikol'skiy Kazakh. see Satpayev
Nikol'skoye Kamchatskaya Oblast' Rus. Fed.
  29 R4
Nikol'skoye Vologod. Obl. Rus. Fed. see
  Sheksna
Nikopol' Ukr. 13 G7
Niksar Turkey 34 E2
Nikshahr Iran 33 J4
Nikšić Montenegro 27 H3
Nikumaroro atoll Kiribati 53 I2
Nikunau i. Kiribati 53 H2
Nīl, Bahr el r. Africa see Nile
Nilagiri India 37 F5
Niland U.S.A. 65 E4
Nilang India see Nelang
Nilanga India 38 C2
Nilaveli Sri Lanka 38 D4
Nile r. Africa 34 C5
Niles OH U.S.A. 64 A2

Nilgiri Hills India 38 C4
Nīl Kowtal Afgh. 36 A2
Nilphamari Bangl. 37 G4
Nilsiä Fin. 14 P5
Nimach India see Neemuch
Niman r. Rus. Fed. 44 D2
Nimba, Monts mts Africa see
  Nimba, Mount
Nimba, Mount Africa 46 C4
Nimbal India 38 B3
Nimberra Well Australia 55 C5
Nimelen r. Rus. Fed. 44 E1
Nîmes France 24 G5
Nimmitabel Australia 57 E8
Nimrod Glacier Antarctica 76 H1
Nimu Jammu and Kashmir 36 D2
Nimule Sudan 47 G4
Nindiguly Australia 58 D2
Nine Degree Channel India 38 B4
Nine Islands P.N.G. see Kilinailau Islands
Ninetyeast Ridge sea feature Indian Ocean
  73 N8
Ninety Mile Beach Australia 58 C7
Ninety Mile Beach N.Z. 59 D2
Nineveh NY U.S.A. 64 D1
Ning 'an China 44 C3
Ningbo China 43 M7
Ningde China 43 L7
Ningguo China 43 L6
Ninghsia Hui Autonomous Region aut. reg.
  China see Ningxia Huizu Zizhiqu
Ningjing China 37 H3
Ningjiang China see Songyuan
Ningjing Shan mts China 42 H6
Ningnan China 42 I8
Ningwu China 43 K5
Ningxia aut. reg. China see
  Ningxia Huizu Zizhiqu
Ningxia Huizu Zizhiqu aut. reg. China 42 J5
Ningxian China 43 J5
Ninh Binh Vietnam 42 J8
Ninnis Glacier Antarctica 76 G2
Ninnis Glacier Antarctica 76 H2
Ninohe Japan 45 F4
Niobrara r. U.S.A. 62 H3
Niokolo Koba, Parc National du nat. park
  Senegal 46 B3
Niono Mali 46 C3
Nioro Mali 46 C3
Niort France 24 D3
Nipani India 38 B3
Niphad India 38 B1
Nipigon Canada 61 J5
Nipigon, Lake Canada 61 J5
Nipissing, Lake Canada 63 L2
Nippon country Asia see Japan
Nippon Hai sea N. Pacific Ocean see
  Japan, Sea of
Nipton CA U.S.A. 65 E3
Niquelândia Brazil 71 A1
Nir Ardabīl Iran 35 G3
Nir Yazd Iran 35 I3
Nira r. India 38 B2
Nirji China 44 B2
Nirmal India 38 C2
Nirmali India 37 F4
Nirmal Range hills India 38 C2
Niš Serbia 27 I3
Nisa Port. 25 C4
Niscemi Sicily Italy 26 F6
Nishapur Iran see Neyshabur
Nishino-shima i. Japan 45 C5
Nishi-Sonogi-hantō pen. Japan 45 C6
Nisibis Turkey see Nusaybin
Nísiros i. Greece see Nisyros
Nissan r. Sweden 15 H8
Nistru r. Moldova see Dniester
Nistru r. Moldova 27 N1 see Dniester
Nísyros i. Greece 27 L6
Nīţā Saudi Arabia 35 H6
Nitendi i. Solomon Is see Ndeni
Niterói Brazil 71 C3
Nith r. U.K. 20 F5
Niti Pass China/India 36 D3
Niti Shankou pass China/India see Niti Pass
Nitmiluk National Park Australia 54 F3
Nitra Slovakia 17 Q6
Niuafo'ou i. Tonga 53 I3
Niuatoputapu i. Tonga 53 I3
Niue terr. S. Pacific Ocean 53 J3
Niulakita i. Tuvalu 53 H3
Niutao i. Tuvalu 53 H2
Nivala Fin. 14 N5
Nive watercourse Australia 56 D5
Niwai India 36 C4
Niwas India 36 E5
Nixia China see Sêrxü
Niya China see Minfeng
Niya He r. China 37 E1
Nizamabad India 38 C2
Nizam Sagar l. India 38 C2
Nizh Aydere Turkm. 35 J3
Nizhnedevitsk Rus. Fed. 13 H6
Nizhnekamsk Rus. Fed. 12 K5
Nizhnekamskoye Vodokhranilishche resr
  Rus. Fed. 11 Q4
Nizhnekolymsk Rus. Fed. 29 R3
Nizhnetambovskoye Rus. Fed. 44 E2
Nizhneudinsk Rus. Fed. 42 H2
Nizhnevartovsk Rus. Fed. 28 I3
Nizhnevolzhsk Rus. Fed. see Narimanov
Nizhneyansk Rus. Fed. 29 P2
Nizhniy Baskunchak Rus. Fed. 13 J6
Nizhniye Kresty Rus. Fed. see Cherskiy
Nizhniy Lomov Rus. Fed. 13 I5
Nizhniy Novgorod Rus. Fed. 12 I4
Nizhniy Odes Rus. Fed. 12 L3
Nizhniy Tagil Rus. Fed. 11 R4
Nizhnyaya Mola Rus. Fed. 12 I2
Nizhnyaya Omra Rus. Fed. 12 L3
Nizhnyaya Pirenga, Ozero l. Rus. Fed.
  14 R3
Nizhnyaya Tunguska r. Rus. Fed. 28 J3
Nizhnyaya Tura Rus. Fed. 11 R4
Nizhyn Ukr. 13 F6
Nizina Mazowiecka reg. Poland 17 R4
Nizip Turkey 39 C1
Nízke Tatry nat. park Slovakia 17 Q6
Nizwá Oman see Nazwá
Nizza France see Nice
Njallavarri mt. Norway 14 L2
Njavve Sweden 14 K3
Njazidja i. Comoros 49 E5
Njombe Tanz. 49 D4
Njurundabommen Sweden 14 J5
Nkambe Cameroon 46 E4
Nkandla S. Africa 51 J5
Nkawkaw Ghana 46 C4
Nkhata Bay Malawi 49 D4
Nkhotakota Malawi 49 D5
Nkondwe Tanz. 49 D4
Nkongsamba Cameroon 46 D4
Nkululeko S. Africa 51 H6
Nkwenkwezi S. Africa 51 H7
Noakhali Bangl. 37 G5
Noatak r. U.S.A. 60 B3
Nobber Ireland 21 F4
Nobeoka Japan 45 C6

Noboribetsu Japan 44 F4
Noccundra Australia 57 C5
Nockatunga Australia 57 C5
Noel Kempff Mercado, Parque Nacional
  nat. park Bol. 68 F6
Nogales Mex. 66 B2
Nogales U.S.A. 62 E5
Nōgata Japan 45 C6
Nogent-le-Rotrou France 24 E2
Noginsk Rus. Fed. 12 H5
Nogliki Rus. Fed. 44 F2
Nogoa r. Australia 56 E4
Nohar India 36 C3
Nohèji Japan 44 F4
Noida India 36 D3
Noirmoutier, Île de i. France 24 C3
Noirmoutier-en-l'Île France 24 C3
Nokis Uzbek. see Nukus
Nok Kundi Pak. 33 J4
Nokou Chad 47 E3
Nokrek Peak India 37 G4
Nola Cent. Afr. Rep. 46 E4
Nolinsk Rus. Fed. 12 K4
No Mans Land i. MA U.S.A. 64 F2
Nome U.S.A. 60 B3
Nomgon Mongolia 44 J4
Nomhon China 37 I1
Nomoi Islands Micronesia see
  Mortlock Islands
Nomonde S. Africa 51 H6
Nomzha Rus. Fed. 12 I4
Nondweni S. Africa 51 J5
Nong'an China 44 B3
Nongoma S. Africa 51 J4
Nongstoin India 37 G4
Nonidas Namibia 50 B2
Nonni r. China see Nen Jiang
Nonning Australia 57 B7
Nonouti atoll Kiribati 53 H2
Nonzwakazi S. Africa 50 G6
Noolyeanna Lake salt flat Australia 57 B5
Noondie, Lake salt flat Australia 55 B7
Noonthorangee Range hills Australia 57 C6
Noorama Creek watercourse Australia
  58 B1
Nora r. Rus. Fed. 44 C2
Noranda Canada 63 L2
Nor-Bayazet Armenia see Gavarr
Norberg Sweden 15 I6
Nord Greenland see Station Nord
Nordaustlandet i. Svalbard 28 D2
Norden Germany 17 K4
Nordenshel'da, Arkhipelag is Rus. Fed.
  28 K2
Nordenskjold Archipelago is Rus. Fed. see
  Nordenshel'da, Arkhipelag
Norderstedt Germany 17 M4
Nordfjordeid Norway 14 D6
Nordfold Norway 14 I3
Nordfriesische Inseln Germany see
  North Frisian Islands
Nordhausen Germany 17 M5
Nordkapp c. Norway see North Cape
Nordkinnhalvøya i. Norway 14 O1
Nordkjosbotn Norway 14 K2
Nordli Norway 14 H4
Nordmaling Sweden 14 K5
Nord- og Østgrønland, Nationalparken i
  nat. park Greenland 61 O2
Nordøstrundingen c. Greenland 77 I1
Nord-Ostsee-Kanal Germany see
  Kiel Canal
Nordøyar i. Faroe Is 10 E3
Nordre Strømfjord inlet Greenland see
  Nassuttooq
Nordvik Rus. Fed. 29 M2
Nore r. Ireland 21 E5
Nore, Pic de mt. France 24 F5
Noreg country Europe see Norway
Norfolk NE U.S.A. 63 H3
Norfolk VA U.S.A. 64 C4
Norfolk Island terr. S. Pacific Ocean 53 G4
Norfolk Island Ridge sea feature
  Tasman Sea 74 H7
Norge country Europe see Norway
Norheimsund Norway 15 E6
Noril'sk Rus. Fed. 28 J3
Norma Co l. China 37 G2
Norman r. Australia 56 C3
Normanby Island P.N.G. 56 E1
Normandes, Îles is English Chan. see
  Channel Islands
Normandia Brazil 69 G3
Normandie reg. France see Normandy
Normandie, Collines de hills France 24 D2
Normandy reg. France see Normandy
Normanton Australia 56 C3
Norman Wells Canada 60 F3
Norquinco Arg. 70 B6
Norra Kvarken strait Fin./Sweden 14 L5
Norra Storfjället mts Sweden 14 I4
Norristown PA U.S.A. 64 D2
Norrköping Sweden 15 J7
Norrtälje Sweden 15 K7
Norseman Australia 55 C8
Norsjö Sweden 14 K4
Norsk Rus. Fed. 44 C2
Norsup Vanuatu 53 G3
Norte, Punta pt Arg. 70 E5
Norte, Serra do hills Brazil 69 G6
Nortelândia Brazil 69 G6
North, Cape Antarctica 76 H2
Northallerton U.K. 18 F4
Northam Australia 55 B7
Northampton Australia 55 A6
Northampton U.K. 19 G6
Northampton MA U.S.A. 64 E1
Northampton PA U.S.A. 64 D2
North Anna r. VA U.S.A. 64 C4
North Atlantic Ocean Atlantic Ocean 63 O4
North Australian Basin sea feature
  Indian Ocean 73 N6
North Battleford Canada 62 F1
North Bay Canada 63 L2
North Berwick U.K. 20 G4
North Berwick ME U.S.A. 64 F1
North Bourke Australia 58 B3
North Canton OH U.S.A. 64 A2
North Cape Norway 14 N1
North Cape N.Z. 59 D2
North Cape U.S.A. 60 A4
North Caribou Lake Canada 61 J4
North Carolina state U.S.A. 63 L4
North Channel lake channel Canada
  63 K2
North Channel U.K. 21 G2
Northcliffe Glacier Antarctica 76 F2
North Collins NY U.S.A. 64 B1
North Dakota state U.S.A. 62 G2
North Downs hills U.K. 19 G7
North East PA U.S.A. 64 B1
Northeast Foreland c. Greenland see
  Nordøstrundingen
North-East Frontier Agency state India see
  Arunachal Pradesh
Northeast Pacific Basin sea feature
  N. Pacific Ocean 75 J4
North Edwards CA U.S.A. 65 D3
Northern prov. S. Africa see Limpopo
Northern Areas admin. div. Pak. 36 C1

Northern Cape *prov.* S. Africa 50 D5
Northern Donets *r.* Rus. Fed./Ukr. *see* Severskiy Donets
Northern Dvina *r.* Rus. Fed. *see* Severnaya Dvina
Northern Ireland *prov.* U.K. 21 F3
Northern Lau Group *is* Fiji 53 I3
Northern Mariana Islands *terr.* N. Pacific Ocean 41 G6
Northern Rhodesia *country* Africa *see* Zambia
Northern Sporades *is* Greece *see* Voreies Sporades
Northern Territory *admin. div.* Australia 52 D3
Northern Transvaal *prov.* S. Africa *see* Limpopo
North Esk *r.* U.K. 20 G4
North Foreland *c.* U.K. 19 I7
North Fork *r.* CA U.S.A. 65 C2
North Fork Pass Canada 60 E3
North Frisian Islands Germany 17 L3
North Geomagnetic Pole Arctic Ocean 61 K2
North Grimston U.K. 18 G4
North Haven CT U.S.A. 64 E2
North Head *hd* N.Z. 59 E3
North Horr Kenya 48 D3
North Island N.Z. 38 B4
North Island N.Z. 59 D4
North Kingsville OH U.S.A. 64 E2
North Korea *country* Asia 45 B5
North Lakhimpur India 37 H4
North Las Vegas NV U.S.A. 65 C3
North Luangwa National Park Zambia 49 D5
North Maalhosmadulu Atoll Maldives 38 B5
North Magnetic Pole Canada 77 A1
North Malosmadulu Atoll Maldives *see* North Maalhosmadulu Atoll
North Palisade *mt.* CA U.S.A. 65 C2
North Perry OH U.S.A. 64 E2
North Platte U.S.A. 62 G3
North Platte *r.* U.S.A. 62 G3
North Pole Arctic Ocean 77 I1
North Rona *i.* U.K. *see* Rona
North Ronaldsay *i.* U.K. 20 G1
North Ronaldsay Firth *sea chan.* U.K. 20 G1
North Saskatchewan *r.* Canada 62 F1
North Sea Europe 16 H2
North Shields U.K. 18 F3
North Shoshone Peak NV U.S.A. 65 D1
North Siberian Lowland Rus. Fed. 28 L2
North Siberian Lowland Rus. Fed. 77 E2
North Simlipal National Park India 37 F5
North Sinai *governorate* Egypt *see* Shamāl Sīnā'
North Slope *plain* U.S.A. 60 D3
North Somercotes U.K. 18 H5
North Spirit Lake Canada 63 I1
North Stradbroke Island Australia 58 F1
North Sunderland U.K. 18 F3
North Syracuse NY U.S.A. 64 C1
North Taranaki Bight *b.* N.Z. 59 E4
Northton U.K. 20 B3
North Tonawanda NY U.S.A. 64 B1
North Trap *reef* N.Z. 59 A8
North Tyne *r.* U.K. 18 E4
North Uist *i.* U.K. 20 B3
Northumberland National Park U.K. 18 E3
Northumberland Strait Canada 63 O2
Northville NY U.S.A. 64 D1
North Walsham U.K. 19 I6
North West *prov.* S. Africa 50 D4
Northwest Atlantic Mid-Ocean Channel N. Atlantic Ocean 72 E1
North West Cape Australia 54 A5
North West Frontier *prov.* Pak. 36 B2
North West Nelson Forest Park *nat. park* N.Z. *see* Kahurangi National Park
Northwest Pacific Basin *sea feature* N. Pacific Ocean 74 G3
Northwest Territories *admin. div.* Canada 60 H3
Northwich U.K. 18 E5
North Wildwood NJ U.S.A. 64 D3
Northwind Ridge *sea feature* Arctic Ocean 77 B1
Northwood NH U.S.A. 64 F1
North York Moors *moorland* U.K. 18 G4
North York Moors National Park U.K. 18 G4
Norton U.K. 18 G4
Norton de Matos Angola *see* Balombo
Norton Sound *sea chan.* U.S.A. 60 B3
Norvegia, Cape Antarctica 76 B2
Norwalk CT U.S.A. 64 E2
Norwalk OH U.S.A. 63 K3
Norway *country* Europe 14 E6
Norway House Canada 62 H1
Norwegian Basin *sea feature* N. Atlantic Ocean 72 H1
Norwegian Sea N. Atlantic Ocean 77 H2
Norwich Ont. Canada 64 A1
Norwich U.K. 19 I6
Norwich CT U.S.A. 64 E2
Norwich NY U.S.A. 64 D1
Noshiro Japan 45 F4
Nosovaya Rus. Fed. 12 L1
Noṣraṭābād Iran 33 I4
Noss, Isle of *i.* U.K. 20 [inset]
Nossebro Sweden 15 H7
Nossob *watercourse* Africa 50 D2
Nossob *watercourse* Africa *see* Nosop
Notch Peak UT U.S.A. 65 F1
Noteć *r.* Poland 17 P4
Noto, Golfo di *g.* Sicily Italy 26 F6
Notodden Norway 15 F7
Noto-hantō *pen.* Japan 45 E5
Notre Dame, Monts *mts* Canada 63 N2
Notre Dame Bay Canada 61 M5
Notre-Dame-de-Koartac Canada *see* Quaqtaq
Nottaway *r.* Canada 63 L1
Nottingham U.K. 19 F6
Nottingham Island Canada 61 K3
Nottoway *r.* VA U.S.A. 64 C4
Nouabalé-Ndoki, Parc National *nat. park* Congo 48 B3
Nouâdhibou Mauritania 46 B2
Nouâdhibou, Râs *c.* Mauritania 46 B2
Nouâmghâr Mauritania 46 B3
Nouméa New Caledonia 53 G4
Nouna Burkina 46 C3
Noupoort S. Africa 50 G6
Nousu Fin. 14 P3
Nouveau-Brunswick *prov.* Canada *see* New Brunswick
Nouveau-Comptoir Canada *see* Wemindji
Nouvelle Calédonie *i.* S. Pacific Ocean *see* New Caledonia
Nouvelle Calédonie *terr.* S. Pacific Ocean *see* New Caledonia
Nouvelle-France, Cap de *c.* Canada 61 K3
Nouvelles Hébrides *country* S. Pacific Ocean *see* Vanuatu
Nova América Brazil 71 A1

Nova Chaves Angola *see* Muconda
Nova Freixa Moz. *see* Cuamba
Nova Friburgo Brazil 71 C3
Nova Gaia Angola *see* Cambundi-Catembo
Nova Goa India *see* Panaji
Nova Gradiška Croatia 26 G2
Nova Iguaçu Brazil 71 C3
Nova Lima Brazil 71 C2
Nova Lisboa Angola *see* Huambo
Nova Mambone Moz. 49 D6
Nova Nabúri Moz. 49 D5
Nova Odesa Ukr. 13 F7
Nova Paraiso Brazil 68 F3
Nova Ponte Brazil 71 B2
Nova Pilão Arcado Brazil 69 J5
Nova Ponte, Represa *resr* Brazil 71 B2
Novara Italy 26 C2
Nova Roma Brazil 71 B1
Nova Scotia *prov.* Canada 63 N3
Nova Sento Sé Brazil 69 J5
Novato CA U.S.A. 65 A1
Nova Trento Brazil 71 A4
Nova Venécia Brazil 71 C2
Nova Xavantina Brazil 69 H6
Novaya Kakhovka Ukr. *see* Nova Kakhovka
Novaya Kazanka Kazakh. 11 P6
Novaya Ladoga Rus. Fed. 12 G3
Novaya Lyalya Rus. Fed. 11 S4
Novaya Odesa Ukr. *see* Nova Odesa
Novaya Sibir', Ostrov *i.* Rus. Fed. 29 P2
Novaya Ussura Rus. Fed. 44 D3
Novaya Zemlya *is* Rus. Fed. 28 G2
Nova Zagora Bulg. 27 L3
Novelda Spain 25 F4
Nové Zámky Slovakia 17 Q7
Novgorod Rus. Fed. *see* Velikiy Novgorod
Novgorod-Severskiy Ukr. *see* Novhorod-Sivers'kyy
Novgorod-Volynskiy Ukr. *see* Novohrad-Volyns'kyy
Novhorod-Sivers'kyy Ukr. 13 G6
Novi Grad Bos.-Herz. *see* Bosanski Novi
Novi Iskŭr Bulg. 27 J3
Novikovo Rus. Fed. 44 F3
Novi Kritsim Bulg. *see* Stamboliyski
Novi Ligure Italy 26 C2
Novi Pazar Bulg. 27 L3
Novi Pazar Serbia 27 I3
Novo Acre Brazil 71 C1
Novoaltaysk Rus. Fed. 42 E2
Novoanninskiy Rus. Fed. 13 I6
Novo Aripuanã Brazil 68 F5
Novoazovs'k Ukr. 13 H7
Novocheboksarsk Rus. Fed. 12 J4
Novocherkassk Rus. Fed. 13 I7
Novodugino Rus. Fed. 12 G5
Novodvinsk Rus. Fed. 12 I2
Novoekonomicheskoye Ukr. *see* Dymytrov
Novogeorgiyevka Rus. Fed. 44 B2
Novogrudok Belarus *see* Navahrudak
Novo Hamburgo Brazil 71 A5
Novohradské hory *mts* Czech Rep. 17 O6
Novohrad-Volyns'kyy Ukr. 13 E6
Novokhopersk Rus. Fed. 13 I6
Novokiyevskiy Uval Rus. Fed. 44 C2
Novokubansk Rus. Fed. 35 F1
Novokubanskiy Rus. Fed. *see* Novokubansk
Novokuybyshevsk Rus. Fed. 13 K5
Novokuznetsk Rus. Fed. 42 F2
Novolazarevskaya *research station* Antarctica 76 C2
Novolukoml' Belarus *see* Novalukoml'
Novo Mesto Slovenia 26 F2
Novomikhaylovskiy Rus. Fed. 34 E1
Novomoskovsk Rus. Fed. 13 H5
Novomoskovs'k Ukr. 13 G6
Novonikolayevka Ukr. *see* Novosibirsk
Novonikolayevskiy Rus. Fed. 13 I6
Novooleksiyivka Ukr. 13 G7
Novopashiyskiy Rus. Fed. *see* Gornozavodsk
Novopokrovka Rus. Fed. 44 D3
Novopokrovskaya Rus. Fed. 13 I7
Novopolotsk Belarus *see* Navapolatsk
Novopskov Ukr. 13 H6
Novo Redondo Angola *see* Sumbe
Novorossiyka Rus. Fed. 44 C1
Novorossiysk Rus. Fed. 13 H7
Novorybnaya Rus. Fed. 29 L2
Novorzhev Rus. Fed. 12 F4
Novoselovo Rus. Fed. 42 G1
Novoselskoye Rus. Fed. *see* Achkhoy-Martan
Novosel'ye Rus. Fed. 15 P7
Novosergiyevka Rus. Fed. 13 J6
Novoshakhtinsk Rus. Fed. 13 H7
Novosheshminsk Rus. Fed. 12 K5
Novosibirsk Rus. Fed. 28 J4
Novosibirskiye Ostrova *is* Rus. Fed. *see* New Siberia Islands
Novosil' Rus. Fed. 13 H5
Novosokol'niki Rus. Fed. 12 F4
Novospasskoye Rus. Fed. 13 J5
Novotroyits'ke Ukr. 13 G7
Novoukrainka Ukr. *see* Novoukrayinka
Novoukrayinka Ukr. 13 F6
Novouzensk Rus. Fed. 13 K6
Novovolyns'k Ukr. 13 E6
Novovoronezh Rus. Fed. 13 H6
Novovoronezhskiy Rus. Fed. *see* Novovoronezh
Novo-Voskresenovka Rus. Fed. 44 B1
Novozybkov Rus. Fed. 13 G5
Nový Jičín Czech Rep. 17 P6
Novyy Afon Georgia *see* Akhali Ap'oni
Novyy Bor Rus. Fed. 12 L2
Novyy Donbass Ukr. *see* Dymytrov
Novyye Petushki Rus. Fed. *see* Petushki
Novyy Kholmogory Rus. Fed. *see* Archangel
Novyy Margelan Uzbek. *see* Farg'ona
Novyy Nekouz Rus. Fed. 12 H4
Novyy Oskol Rus. Fed. 13 H6
Novyy Port Rus. Fed. 28 I3
Novyy Urengoy Rus. Fed. 28 I3
Novyy Urgal Rus. Fed. 44 D2
Novyy Uzen' Kazakh. *see* Zhanaozen
Novyy Zay Rus. Fed. 12 L5
Now Iran 35 I5
Nowabganj Bangl. *see* Nawabganj
Nowdī Iran 35 H3
Nowgong India *see* Nagaon
Nowogard Poland 17 O4
Nowogrodiec Poland *see* Radomsko
Nowra Australia 58 E5
Nowrangapur India *see* Nabarangapur
Nowshera Pak. 33 I3
Nowy Sącz Poland 17 R6
Nowy Targ Poland 17 R6
Noxen PA U.S.A. 64 C2
Noyabr'sk Rus. Fed. 28 I3
Nozizwe S. Africa 51 G6
Nqamakwe S. Africa 51 H7
Nqutu S. Africa 51 J5
Nsanje Malawi 49 D5
Nsombo Zambia 49 C5
Nsukka Nigeria 46 D4

Nsumbu National Park Zambia *see* Sumbu National Park
Ntambu Zambia 49 C5
Ntha S. Africa 51 H4
Ntoro, Kavo *pt* Greece 27 K5
Ntoum Gabon 48 A3
Ntungamo Uganda 48 D4
Nuanetsi Zimbabwe *see* Mwenezi
Nuba Mountains Sudan 32 D7
Nubian Desert Sudan 32 D5
Nudo Coropuna *mt.* Peru 68 D7
Nueltin Lake Canada 61 I3
Nueva Gerona Cuba 67 H4
Nueva Harberton Arg. 70 C8
Nueva Imperial Chile 70 B5
Nueva Loja Ecuador *see* Lago Agrio
Nueva Rosita Mex. 62 G6
Nueva San Salvador El Salvador 66 G6
Nueve de Julio Arg. *see* 9 de Julio
Nuevitas Cuba 67 I4
Nuevo, Golfo *g.* Arg. 70 C6
Nuevo Casas Grandes Mex. 66 C2
Nuevo Ideal Mex. 66 D3
Nuevo Laredo Mex. 66 E3
Nuevo Rocafuerte Ecuador 68 C4
Nugaal *watercourse* Somalia 48 E3
Nugget Point N.Z. 59 B8
Nugur India 38 D2
Nuguria Islands P.N.G. 52 F2
Nuhaka N.Z. 59 F4
Nui *atoll* Tuvalu 53 H2
Nui Con Voi *r.* Vietnam *see* Red
Nuiqsut U.S.A. 60 C2
Nujiang China 37 I3
Nukey Bluff *hill* Australia 57 A7
Nukha Azer. *see* Şäki
Nuku'alofa Tonga 53 I4
Nuku'alofa Tonga *see* 'Ahau
Nukufetau *atoll* Tuvalu 53 H2
Nukuhu *i.* Fr. Polynesia *see* Nuku Hiva
Nuku Hiva *i.* Fr. Polynesia 75 K6
Nukulaelae *atoll* Tuvalu 53 H2
Nukulailai *atoll* Tuvalu *see* Nukulaelae
Nukumanu Islands P.N.G. 53 F2
Nukunau *i.* Kiribati *see* Nikunau
Nukunono *atoll* Tokelau *see* Nukunonu
Nukunonu *atoll* Tokelau 53 I2
Nukus Uzbek. 33 I1
Nulato U.S.A. 60 C3
Nullagine Australia 54 C5
Nullarbor Australia 55 E7
Nullarbor National Park Australia 55 E7
Nullarbor Plain Australia 55 D7
Nullarbor Regional Reserve *park* Australia 55 F7
Nulu'erhu Shan *mts* China 43 L4
Numalla, Lake *salt flat* Australia 58 B2
Numan Nigeria 48 B3
Numanuma P.N.G. 56 I1
Numazu Japan 45 E6
Numbulwar Australia 56 A2
Numedal *valley* Norway 15 F6
Numfoor *i.* Indon. 41 F8
Numin He *r.* China 43 M3
Numurkah Australia 58 C6
Nunap Isua *c.* Greenland *see* Farewell, Cape
Nunarsuit *i.* Greenland *see* Nunakuluut
Nunavut *admin. div.* Canada 61 J2
Nunda NY U.S.A. 64 C1
Nundle Australia 58 E3
Nuneaton U.K. 19 F6
Nungba India 37 H4
Nungnain Sum China 43 L3
Nunivak Island U.S.A. 60 B4
Nunkapasi India 38 E1
Nunkun *mt.* Jammu and Kashmir 36 D2
Nunligran Rus. Fed. 29 T3
Nuñomoral Spain 25 C3
Nuoro Sardinia Italy 26 C4
Nupani *i.* Solomon Is 53 G3
Nuqrah Saudi Arabia 32 F4
Nūrābād Iran 35 H4
Nurakita *i.* Tuvalu *see* Niulakita
Nur Dağları *mts* Turkey 39 B1
Nuremberg Germany 17 M6
Nurla Jammu and Kashmir 36 D2
Nurlat Rus. Fed. 13 K5
Nurmes Fin. 14 P5
Nurmo Fin. 14 M5
Nürnberg Germany *see* Nuremberg
Nurota Uzbek. 33 K1
Nurota Uzbek. *see* Nurota
Nurri, Mount *hill* Australia 58 C3
Nusaybin Turkey 35 F3
Nu Shan *mts* China 42 H7
Nushki Pak. 36 A3
Nusratiye Turkey 39 D1
Nuttal Pak. 36 B3
Nutwood Downs Australia 54 F3
Nuuk Greenland 61 M3
Nuupas Fin. 14 O3
Nuussuaq Greenland 61 M2
Nuussuaq *pen.* Greenland 61 M2
Nuwaybi' al Muzayyinah Egypt 34 D5
Nuweiba el Muzeina Egypt *see* Nuwaybi' al Muzayyinah
Nuwerus S. Africa 50 D6
Nuweveldberge *mts* S. Africa 50 E7
Nuyts, Point Australia 55 B8
Nuyts Archipelago *is* Australia 55 F8
Nuzvid India 38 D2
Nwanedi Nature Reserve S. Africa 51 J2
Nxai Pan National Park Botswana 49 C5
Nyagan' Rus. Fed. 11 S3
Nyahururu Kenya 48 D3
Nyah West Australia 58 A5
Nyaingêntanglha Feng *mt.* China 37 G3
Nyainqêntanglha Shan *mts* China 37 G3
Nyainrong China 42 G6
Nyainrongluong China *see* Nyainrong
Nyåker Sweden 14 K5
Nyakh Rus. Fed. *see* Nyagan'
Nyaksimvol' Rus. Fed. 11 S3
Nyala Sudan 47 F3
Nyalam China *see* Congdü
Nyalikungu Tanz. *see* Maswa
Nyamandhlovu Zimbabwe 49 C5
Nyamtumbo Tanz. 49 D5
Nyande Zimbabwe *see* Masvingo
Nyandoma Rus. Fed. 12 I3
Nyandomskiy Vozvyshennost' *hills* Rus. Fed. 12 H3
Nyanga Congo 48 B4
Nyanga Zimbabwe 49 D5
Nyasa, Lake Africa 49 D4
Nyasaland *country* Africa *see* Malawi
Nyashabozh Rus. Fed. 12 L2
Nyasvizh Belarus 15 O10
Nyaunglebin Myanmar *see* Nyaunglebin
Nyborg Denmark 15 G9
Nyborg Norway 14 P1
Nybro Sweden 15 I8
Nyeboe Land *reg.* Greenland 61 M1
Nyêmo China 37 F3

Nyima China 37 F3
Nyimba Zambia 49 D5
Nyíngchi China 37 H3
Nyiru, Mount Kenya 48 D3
Nykarleby Fin. 14 M5
Nykøbing Denmark 15 G9
Nykøbing Sjælland Denmark 15 G9
Nyköping Sweden 15 J7
Nyland Sweden 14 J5
Nylsvley *nature res.* S. Africa 51 I3
Nymagee Australia 58 C4
Nymboida National Park Australia 58 F2
Nynäshamn Sweden 15 J7
Nyngan Australia 58 C4
Nyogzê China 37 E3
Nyoman *r.* Belarus/Lith. 15 M10
Nyon Switz. 24 H3
Nyons France 24 G4
Nyrob Rus. Fed. 11 R3
Nysa Poland 17 P5
Nysh Rus. Fed. 44 F2
Nystad Fin. *see* Uusikaupunki
Nytva Rus. Fed. 11 R4
Nyukesitsa Rus. Fed. 44 F2
Nyunzu Dem. Rep. Congo 49 C4
Nyurba Rus. Fed. 29 M3
Nzambi Congo 48 B4
Nzega Tanz. 49 D4
Nzérékoré Guinea 46 C4
N'zeto Angola 49 B4
Nzwani *i.* Comoros 49 E5

O

Oahe, Lake U.S.A. 62 G3
O'ahu *i.* U.S.A. 60 [inset]
Oaitupu *i.* Tuvalu *see* Vaitupu
Oak Bluffs MA U.S.A. 64 F2
Oakey Australia 58 E1
Oakham U.K. 19 G6
Oak Hill WV U.S.A. 64 A4
Oakhurst CA U.S.A. 65 C2
Oakland CA U.S.A. 65 A2
Oakland MD U.S.A. 64 B3
Oakland *airport* CA U.S.A. 65 A2
Oaklands Australia 58 C5
Oakover *r.* Australia 54 C5
Oakridge U.S.A. 62 C3
Oakvale Australia 57 C7
Oak View CA U.S.A. 65 C3
Oamaru N.Z. 59 C7
Oaro N.Z. 59 D6
Oasis CA U.S.A. 65 D2
Oates Coast Antarctica *see* Oates Land
Oates Land *reg.* Antarctica 76 H2
Oaxaca Mex. 66 E5
Oaxaca de Juárez Mex. *see* Oaxaca
Ob' *r.* Rus. Fed. 42 I2
Ob, Gulf of *sea chan.* Rus. Fed. *see* Obskaya Guba
Oba *i.* Vanuatu *see* Aoba
Obala Cameroon 46 E4
Obama Japan 45 D6
Oban U.K. 20 D4
O Barco Spain 25 C2
Obbia Somalia *see* Hobyo
Obdorsk Rus. Fed. *see* Salekhard
Obecse Serbia *see* Bečej
Oberon Australia 58 D4
Oberpfälzer Wald *mts* Germany 17 N6
Obi *i.* Indon. 41 E8
Óbidos Brazil 69 G4
Obihiro Japan 44 F4
Obil'noye Rus. Fed. 13 J7
Ob'-Irtysh *r.* Rus. Fed. 28 H3
Obluch'ye Rus. Fed. 44 D2
Obninsk Rus. Fed. 13 H5
Obo Cent. Afr. Rep. 48 C3
Obock Djibouti 32 F7
Öbök N. Korea 44 C4
Obokote Dem. Rep. Congo 48 C4
Obo Liang China 42 G5
Obouya Congo 48 B4
Oboyan' Rus. Fed. 13 H6
Obozerskiy Rus. Fed. 12 I3
Obrenovac Serbia 27 I2
Obruk Turkey 34 D3
Observatory Hill *hill* Australia 55 F7
Obshchiy Syrt *hills* Rus. Fed. 11 Q5
Obskaya Guba *sea chan.* Rus. Fed. 28 I3
Obuasi Ghana 46 C4
Ob''yachevo Rus. Fed. 12 K3
Ocala U.S.A. 63 K6
Ocaña Col. 68 D2
Ocaña Spain 25 E4
Occidental, Cordillera *mts* Chile 68 E7
Occidental, Cordillera *mts* Col. 68 C2
Occidental, Cordillera *mts* Peru 68 D7
Ocean City MD U.S.A. 64 D3
Ocean City NJ U.S.A. 64 D3
Ocean Falls Canada 60 E4
Ocean Island *atoll* Kiribati *see* Banaba
Ocean Island *atoll* U.S.A. *see* Kure Atoll
Oceanside CA U.S.A. 65 D4
Ochakiv Ukr. 27 N1
Och'amch'ire Georgia 35 F2
Ocher Rus. Fed. 11 Q4
Ochiishi-misaki *pt* Japan 44 G4
Ochil Hills U.K. 20 F4
Ochrida, Lake Albania/Macedonia *see* Ohrid, Lake
Ochsenfurt Germany 17 M6
Ockelbo Sweden 15 J6
Ocolaşul Mare, Vârful *mt.* Romania 27 K1
Octeville-sur-Mer France 19 H9
October Revolution Island Rus. Fed. *see* Oktyabr'skoy Revolyutsii, Ostrov
Ocussi *enclave* East Timor 54 C2
Ocussi-Ambeno *enclave* East Timor *see* Ocussi
Oda, Jebel *mt.* Sudan 32 E5
Ódáðahraun *lava field* Iceland 14 [inset]
Ōdate Japan 44 F4
Odawara Japan 45 E6
Odda Norway 15 E6
Odemira Port. 25 B5
Ödemiş Turkey 27 L5
Ödenburg Hungary *see* Sopron
Odense Denmark 15 G9
Odenwald *reg.* Germany 17 L6
Oderbucht *b.* Germany 17 O3
Odesa Ukr. 27 N1
Ödeshog Sweden 15 I7
Odessa Ukr. *see* Odesa
Odessa TX U.S.A. 62 G5
Odessus Bulg. *see* Varna
Odiel *r.* Spain 25 C5
Odienné Côte d'Ivoire 46 C4
Odintsovo Rus. Fed. 12 H5
Odra *r.* Germany/Pol. 17 Q6
Odzala, Parc National d' *nat. park* Congo 48 B3
Oea Libya *see* Tripoli

Oé-Cusse *enclave* East Timor *see* Ocussi
Oecussi *enclave* East Timor *see* Ocussi
Oeiras Brazil 69 J5
Oekussi *enclave* East Timor *see* Ocussi
Oenpelli Australia 54 F3
Oeno *atoll* Pitcairn Is *see* Oeno Island
Of Turkey 35 F2
Ofanto *r.* Italy 26 G4
Offa Nigeria 46 D4
Offenbach am Main Germany 17 L5
Offenburg Germany 17 K6
Oga Japan 45 E5
Oga-hantō *pen.* Japan 45 E5
Ōgaki Japan 45 E6
Ogallala U.S.A. 62 G3
Ogasawara-shotō *is* Japan *see* Bonin Islands
Ogbomosho Nigeria 46 D4
Ogbomosho Nigeria *see* Ogbomosho
Ogden UT U.S.A. 62 E3
Ogilvie Canada 60 E3
Ogilvie Mountains Canada 60 D3
Oglio *r.* Italy 26 D2
Oglongi Rus. Fed. 44 E1
Ogmore Australia 56 E4
Ogodzha Rus. Fed. 44 D1
Ogoja Nigeria 46 D4
Ogoki Reservoir Canada 63 J1
Ogoron Rus. Fed. 44 C1
Ogosta *r.* Bulg. 27 J3
Ogre Latvia 15 N8
Ogulin Croatia 26 F2
Ogurchinskiy, Ostrov *i.* Turkm. *see* Ogurjaly Adasy
Ogurjaly Adasy *i.* Turkm. 35 I3
Ohai N.Z. 59 A7
Ohakune N.Z. 59 E4
Ohanet Alg. 46 D2
Ōhata Japan 44 F4
Ohcejohka Fin. *see* Utsjoki
Ohio *r.* Ohio/West Virginia U.S.A. 64 A3
Ohio *state* U.S.A. 64 A2
Ohrid Macedonia 27 I4
Ohrid, Lake Albania/Macedonia 27 I4
Ohridsko Ezero *l.* Albania/Macedonia *see* Ohrid, Lake
Ohrigstad S. Africa 51 J3
Ohrit, Liqeni i *l.* Albania/Macedonia *see* Ohrid, Lake
Ohura N.Z. 59 E4
Oich *r.* U.K. 20 E3
Oiga China 37 H3
Oil City PA U.S.A. 64 B2
Oise *r.* France 24 F2
Ōita Japan 45 C6
Oiti *mt.* Greece 27 J5
Ojai CA U.S.A. 65 C3
Ojalava *i.* Samoa *see* 'Upolu
Ojinaga Mex. 66 D3
Ojiya Japan 45 E5
Ojos del Salado, Nevado *mt.* Arg./Chile 70 C3
Oka *r.* Rus. Fed. 13 I4
Oka *r.* Rus. Fed. 42 I1
Okahandja Namibia 50 C1
Okahukura N.Z. 59 E4
Okakarara Namibia 49 B6
Okanagan Lake Canada 62 D2
Okanda Sri Lanka 38 D5
Okano *r.* Gabon 48 B4
Okanogan U.S.A. 62 D2
Okanogan *r.* U.S.A. 62 D2
Okara Pak. 33 L3
Okarem Turkm. *see* Ekerem
Okataina *vol.* N.Z. *see* Tarawera, Mount
Okaukuejo Namibia 49 B5
Okavango *r.* Africa 49 C5
Okavango Delta *swamp* Botswana 49 C5
Okavango Swamps Botswana *see* Okavango Delta
Okaya Japan 45 E5
Okayama Japan 45 D6
Okazaki Japan 45 E6
Okeechobee, Lake U.S.A. 63 K6
Okefenokee Swamp U.S.A. 63 K5
Okehampton U.K. 19 C8
Okha India 36 B5
Okha Rus. Fed. 44 F1
Okha Rann *marsh* India 36 B5
Okhotsk Rus. Fed. 29 P4
Okhotsk, Sea of Japan/Rus. Fed. 44 G3
Okhotskoye More *sea* Japan/Rus. Fed. *see* Okhotsk, Sea of
Okhtyrka Ukr. 13 G6
Okinawa *i.* Japan 45 B8
Okinawa-guntō *is* Japan *see* Okinawa-shotō
Okinawa-shotō *is* Japan 43 O5
Okino-Daitō-jima *i.* Japan 43 O8
Okino-Tori-shima *i.* Japan 43 P8
Oki-shotō *is* Japan 43 O5
Oki-shotō *is* Japan 45 D5
Oklahoma *state* U.S.A. 62 H4
Oklahoma City U.S.A. 62 H4
Okmulgee U.S.A. 63 H4
Okondja Gabon 48 B4
Okovskiy Les *for.* Rus. Fed. 12 G5
Okoyo Congo 48 B4
Okstindan *mts* Norway 14 H3
Øksfjord Norway 14 M1
Oktemberyan Armenia *see* Armavir
Oktyabr' Kazakh. *see* Kandyagash
Oktyabr'skiy Kazakh. *see* Kandyagash
Oktyabr'skiy Amurskaya Oblast' Rus. Fed. 44 C1
Oktyabr'skiy Arkhangel'skaya Oblast' Rus. Fed. 12 I3
Oktyabr'skiy Kamchatskaya Oblast' Rus. Fed. 29 Q4
Oktyabr'skiy Respublika Bashkortostan Rus. Fed. 11 Q5
Oktyabr'skiy Volgogradskaya Oblast' Rus. Fed. 13 I7
Oktyabr'skoye Rus. Fed. 11 T3
Oktyabr'skoy Revolyutsii, Ostrov *i.* Rus. Fed. 29 K2
Okulovka Rus. Fed. 12 G4
Okushiri-tō *i.* Japan 44 E4
Okusi *enclave* East Timor *see* Ocussi
Okuta Nigeria 46 D4
Okwa *watercourse* Botswana 50 G1
Ólafsvík Iceland 14 [inset]
Olakkur India 38 C3
Olancha CA U.S.A. 65 C2
Olancha Peak CA U.S.A. 65 C2
Öland *i.* Sweden 15 J8
Olary Australia 57 C7
Olavarría Arg. 70 D5
Oława Poland 17 P5
Olbia Sardinia Italy 26 C4
Oldcastle Ireland 21 E4
Old Bastar India 38 D2
Old Cork Australia 56 C4
Old Crow Canada 60 E3
Oldenburg Germany 17 L4
Oldenburg in Holstein Germany 17 M3
Olderdalen Norway 14 L2

Oldham U.K. 18 E5
Old Harbor U.S.A. 60 C4
Old Head of Kinsale *hd* Ireland 21 D6
Oldmeldrum U.K. 20 G3
Old River CA U.S.A. 65 C3
Olds Canada 62 E1
Old Wives Lake Canada 62 F1
Olean NY U.S.A. 64 B1
Olecko Poland 17 S3
Olekma *r.* Rus. Fed. 29 N3
Olekminsk Rus. Fed. 29 N3
Olekminsky-Stanovik *mts* Rus. Fed. 43 M2
Oleksandriia Ukr. *see* Zaporizhzhya
Oleksandriya Ukr. 13 G6
Ølen Norway 15 D7
Olenegorsk Rus. Fed. 12 G1
Olenek Rus. Fed. 29 M3
Olenek *r.* Rus. Fed. 29 M2
Olenek Bay Rus. Fed. *see* Olenekskiy Zaliv
Olenekskiy Zaliv *b.* Rus. Fed. 29 N2
Olenino Rus. Fed. 12 G4
Olenitsa Rus. Fed. 12 G2
Olenivs'ki Kar"yery Ukr. *see* Dokuchayevs'k
Olenya Rus. Fed. *see* Olenegorsk
Oleshky Ukr. *see* Tsyurupyns'k
Olevs'k Ukr. 13 E6
Ol'ga Rus. Fed. 44 D4
Olga, Mount Australia 55 E6
Ol'ginsk Rus. Fed. 44 D1
Ol'ginskoye Rus. Fed. *see* Kochubeyevskoye
Ölgiy Mongolia 42 F3
Olhão Port. 25 C5
Olia Chain *mts* Australia 55 E6
Olifants *r.* Moz./S. Africa 51 J3
Olifants *watercourse* Namibia 50 D3
Olifants S. Africa 51 J2
Olifants *r.* W. Cape S. Africa 50 D6
Olifants *r.* W. Cape S. Africa 50 D6
Olifantshoek S. Africa 50 F5
Olifantsrivierberge *mts* S. Africa 50 D6
Olimbos *hill* Cyprus *see* Olympos
Olimbos *mt.* Greece *see* Olympus, Mount
Olimpos Beydağları Milli Parkı *nat. park* Turkey 27 N6
Olinda Brazil 69 L5
Olinga Moz. 49 D5
Olio Australia 56 C4
Oliphants Drift S. Africa 51 H3
Olisipo Port. *see* Lisbon
Oliva Spain 25 F4
Oliva, Cordillera de *mts* Arg./Chile 70 C3
Olivares, Cerro de *mt.* Arg./Chile 70 C4
Olivehurst CA U.S.A. 65 B1
Oliveira dos Brejinhos Brazil 71 C1
Olivença Moz. *see* Lupilichi
Olivenza Spain 25 C4
Ol'khovka Rus. Fed. 13 J6
Ollague Chile 70 C2
Ollombo Congo 48 B4
Olmaliq Uzbek. 42 B4
Olmaliq Uzbek. *see* Olmaliq
Olmos Peru 68 C5
Olmütz Czech Rep. *see* Olomouc
Olney U.K. 19 G6
Olney MD U.S.A. 64 C3
Olofström Sweden 15 I8
Olomouc Czech Rep. 17 P6
Olonets Rus. Fed. 12 G3
Oloron-Ste-Marie France 24 D5
Olosenga *atoll* American Samoa *see* Swains Island
Olot Spain 25 H2
Olovyannaya Rus. Fed. 43 L2
Oloy, Qatorkŭhi *mts* Asia *see* Alai Range
Olsztyn Poland 17 R4
Olt *r.* Romania 27 K3
Olten Switz. 24 H3
Olteniţa Romania 27 L2
Oltu Turkey 35 F2
Ol'viopol' Ukr. *see* Pervomays'k
Olymbos *hill* Cyprus *see* Olympos
Olympia U.S.A. 62 C2
Olympos *hill* Cyprus 39 A2
Olympos Greece *see* Olympus, Mount
Olympou, Ethnikos Drymos *nat. park* Greece 27 J4
Olympus, Mount Greece 27 J4
Olympus, Mount U.S.A. 62 C2
Olyutorskiy Rus. Fed. 29 R3
Olyutorskiy, Mys *c.* Rus. Fed. 29 S4
Olyutorskiy Zaliv *b.* Rus. Fed. 29 R4
Olzheras Rus. Fed. *see* Mezhdurechensk
Oma China 37 E2
Oma *r.* Rus. Fed. 12 J2
Omagh U.K. 21 E3
Omaha U.S.A. 63 H3
Omaheke *admin. reg.* Namibia 50 D2
Omal'skiy Khrebet *mts* Rus. Fed. 44 E1
Oman *country* Asia 33 I6
Oman, Gulf of Asia 33 I4
Omarkot Pak. 36 B3
Omaruru Namibia 49 B6
Omate Peru 68 D7
Omawenino Botswana 50 F2
Omba *i.* Vanuatu *see* Aoba
Ombai, Selat *sea chan.* East Timor/Indon. 54 D2
Ombalantu Namibia *see* Uutapi
Omboué Gabon 48 A4
Ombu China 37 F3
Omdraaisvlei S. Africa 50 F6
Omdurman Sudan 32 D6
Omeo Australia 58 C6
Ometepec Mex. 66 E5
Om Hajér Eritrea 32 E7
Omidīyeh Iran 35 I15
Omineca Mountains Canada 60 F4
Omitara Namibia 50 C2
Ōmiya Japan 45 E6
Omolon Rus. Fed. 29 R3
Omo National Park Eth. 48 D3
Omsk Rus. Fed. 28 H4
Omsukchan Rus. Fed. 29 Q3
Ōmū Japan 44 F3
Omu, Vârful *mt.* Romania 27 K2
Ōmura Japan 45 C6
Omutninsk Rus. Fed. 12 L4
Onancock VA U.S.A. 64 D4
Onangué, Lac *l.* Gabon 48 B4
Onaping Lake Canada 63 K2
Oncativo Arg. 70 D4
Onchan Isle of Man 18 C4
Oncócua Angola 49 B5
Öncül Turkey 39 D1
Ondal India *see* Andal
Ondangwa Namibia 49 B5
Onderstedorings S. Africa 50 E6
Ondjiva Angola 49 B5
Ondo Nigeria 46 D4
Öndörhaan Mongolia 43 K3
Ondozero Rus. Fed. 12 G3
One Botswana 50 E2
Onega Rus. Fed. 12 H3
Onega *r.* Rus. Fed. 12 H3
Onega, Lake *l.* Rus. Fed. *see* Onezhskoye Ozero
Onega Bay *g.* Rus. Fed. *see* Onezhskaya Guba
One Hundred Mile House Canada *see* 100 Mile House

Oneida NY U.S.A. 64 D1
Oneida Lake NY U.S.A. 64 D1
O'Neill U.S.A. 62 H3
Onekotan, Ostrov i. Rus. Fed. 29 Q5
Oneonta NY U.S.A. 64 D1
Onești Romania 27 L1
Onezhskaya Guba g. Rus. Fed. 12 G2
Onezhskoye Ozero Rus. Fed. 11 N3
Onezhskoye Ozero l. Rus. Fed. see Onega, Lake
Ong r. India 38 D1
Onga Gabon 48 B4
Ongers watercourse S. Africa 50 F5
Ongi Mongolia 42 I3
Ongjin N. Korea 45 B5
Ongole India 38 D3
Onilahy r. Madag. 49 E6
Onitsha Nigeria 46 D4
Onjati Mountain Namibia 50 C2
Onjiva Angola see Ondjiva
Ono-i-Lau i. Fiji 53 I4
Onomichi Japan 45 D6
Onor, Gora mt. Rus. Fed. 44 F2
Onotoa atoll Kiribati 53 H2
Onseepkans S. Africa 50 D5
Onslow Australia 54 A5
Ontake-san vol. Japan 45 E6
Ontario prov. Canada 64 A1
Ontario CA U.S.A. 65 D3
Ontario, Lake Canada/U.S.A. 64 C1
Ontong Java Atoll Solomon Is 53 F2
Onutu atoll Kiribati see Onotoa
Onverwacht Suriname 69 G2
Onyx CA U.S.A. 65 C3
Oodnadatta Australia 57 A5
Oodweyne Somalia 48 E3
Ooldea Australia 55 E7
Ooldea Range hills Australia 55 E7
Ooratippra r. Australia 56 B4
Oos-Londen S. Africa see East London
Oostende Belgium see Ostend
Ootacamund India see Udagamandalam
Ootsa Lake Canada 60 F4
Opala Dem. Rep. Congo 48 C4
Oparino Rus. Fed. 12 K4
Oparo i. Fr. Polynesia see Rapa
Opataca, Lac l. Canada 63 M1
Opava Czech Rep. 17 P6
Opelika U.S.A. 63 J5
Opelousas U.S.A. 63 I5
Opienge Dem. Rep. Congo 48 C3
Opinaca, Réservoir resr Canada 63 L1
Opiscotéo, Lac l. Canada 61 L4
Opochka Rus. Fed. 12 F4
Opodepe Mex. 66 B3
Opole Poland 17 P5
Oporto Port. 25 B3
Opotiki N.Z. 59 F4
Oppdal Norway 14 F5
Oppeln Poland see Opole
Opunake N.Z. 59 D4
Opuwo Namibia 49 B5
Oradea Romania 27 I1
Orahovac Serbia 27 I3
Orai India 36 D4
Oral Kazakh. see Ural'sk
Oran Alg. 25 F6
Orán Arg. 70 D2
Orang India 37 H4
Ŏrang N. Korea 44 C4
Orange Australia 58 D4
Orange France 24 G4
Orange r. Namibia/S. Africa 50 C5
Orange CA U.S.A. 65 D4
Orange MA U.S.A. 64 E1
Orange TX U.S.A. 63 I5
Orange VA U.S.A. 64 B3
Orange, Cabo c. Brazil 69 H3
Orangeburg U.S.A. 63 K5
Orange Cone sea feature S. Atlantic Ocean 72 I8
Orange Free State prov. S. Africa see Free State
Orange Walk Belize 66 G5
Oranje r. Namibia/S. Africa see Orange
Oranje Gebergte hills Suriname 69 G3
Oranjemund Namibia 50 C5
Oranjestad Aruba 67 J6
Oranmore Ireland 21 D4
Orapa Botswana 49 C6
Orăştie Romania 27 J2
Oraşul Stalin Romania see Braşov
Oravais Fin. 14 M5
Orba Co l. China 36 E2
Orbetello Italy 26 D3
Orbost Australia 58 D6
Orcadas research station S. Atlantic Ocean 76 A2
Orchha India 36 D4
Orchila, Isla i. Venez. 68 E1
Orchy r. U.K. 20 D4
Orcutt CA U.S.A. 65 B3
Ord r. Australia 54 E3
Ord, Mount hill Australia 54 D4
Ordenes Spain see Ordes
Orderville UT U.S.A. 65 F2
Ordes Spain 25 B2
Ordesa-Monte Perdido, Parque Nacional nat. park Spain 25 G2
Ord Mountain CA U.S.A. 65 D3
Ordos Nei Mongol China 43 K5
Ord River Dam Australia 54 E4
Ordu Hatay Turkey see Yayladağı
Ordu Ordu Turkey 34 E2
Ordubad Azer. 35 G3
Ordzhonikidze Rus. Fed. see Vladikavkaz
Ore Nigeria 46 D4
Örebro Sweden 15 I7
Oregon state U.S.A. 62 C3
Oregon City U.S.A. 62 C2
Orekhov Ukr. see Orikhiv
Orekhovo-Zuyevo Rus. Fed. 12 H5
Orel Rus. Fed. 13 H5
Orel, Gora mt. Rus. Fed. 44 E1
Orel', Ozero l. Rus. Fed. 44 E1
Ore Mountains Czech Rep./Germany see Erzgebirge
Orenburg Rus. Fed. 28 G4
Orense Spain see Ourense
Oreor Palau see Koror
Orepuki N.Z. 59 A8
Öresund strait Denmark/Sweden 15 H9
Oretana, Cordillera mts Spain see Toledo, Montes de
Orewa N.Z. 59 E3
Orfanou, Kolpos b. Greece 27 J4
Orford Australia 57 [inset]
Orford U.K. 19 I6
Orford Ness hd U.K. 19 I6
Organabo Fr. Guiana 69 H2
Orgūn Afgh. 36 B2
Orhaneli Turkey 27 M5
Orhangazi Turkey 27 M4
Orhon Gol r. Mongolia 42 J2
Orichi Rus. Fed. 12 K4
Oriental, Cordillera mts Bol. 68 E7
Oriental, Cordillera mts Col. 68 D2
Oriental, Cordillera mts Peru 68 E6
Orihuela Spain 25 F4
Orikhiv Ukr. 13 G7
Orimattila Fin. 15 N6
Orinoco r. Col./Venez. 68 F2
Orinoco Delta Venez. 68 F2
Orissa state India 38 E1
Orissaare Estonia 15 M7
Oristano Sardinia Italy 26 C5
Orivesi Fin. 15 N6
Orivesi l. Fin. 14 P5
Oriximiná Brazil 69 G4
Orizaba Mex. 66 E5
Orizaba, Pico de vol. Mex. 66 E5
Orizona Brazil 71 A2
Orkanger Norway 14 F5
Örkelljunga Sweden 15 H8
Orkla r. Norway 14 F5
Orkney S. Africa 51 H4
Orkney Islands is U.K. 20 F1
Orlândia Brazil 71 B3
Orlando U.S.A. 63 K6
Orleaes Brazil 71 A5
Orléans France 24 E3
Orléansville Alg. see Chlef
Orlik Rus. Fed. 42 H2
Orlov Rus. Fed. 12 K4
Orlov Gay Rus. Fed. 13 K6
Orlovskiy Rus. Fed. 13 I7
Ormara Pak. 33 J4
Ormskirk U.K. 18 E5
Orne r. France 24 D2
Ørnes Norway 14 H3
Örnsköldsvik Sweden 14 K5
Orobie, Alpi mts Italy 26 C1
Orobo, Serra do hills Brazil 71 C1
Orodara Burkina 46 C3
Orofino U.S.A. 62 D2
Oro Grande CA U.S.A. 65 D3
Orol Dengizi salt l. Kazakh./Uzbek. see Aral Sea
Oron Israel 39 B4
Orona atoll Kiribati 53 I2
Orontes r. Asia 34 E3 see 'Āṣī, Nahr al
Orontes r. Lebanon/Syria 39 C2
Oroqen Zizhiqi China see Alihe
Oroquieta Phil. 41 E7
Orós, Açude resr Brazil 69 K5
Orosei, Golfo di b. Sardinia Italy 26 C4
Orosháza Hungary 27 I1
Oroville U.S.A. 62 C4
Orqohan China 44 A2
Orsa Sweden 15 I6
Orsha Belarus 13 F5
Orshanka Rus. Fed. 12 J4
Orsk Rus. Fed. 28 G4
Ørsta Norway 14 E5
Orta Toroslar plat. Turkey 39 A1
Ortegal, Cabo c. Spain 25 C2
Orthez France 24 D5
Ortigueira Spain 25 C2
Ortles mt. Italy 26 D1
Orton U.K. 18 E4
Ortona Italy 26 F3
Ortonville U.S.A. 63 H2
Ortospana Afgh. see Kābul
Orulgan, Khrebet mts Rus. Fed. 29 N3
Orumbo Namibia 50 C2
Orūmīyeh Iran see Urmia
Oruro Bol. 68 E7
Orūzgān Afgh. 36 A2
Orvieto Italy 26 E3
Orville Coast Antarctica 76 L1
Orwell OH U.S.A. 64 A2
Oryol Rus. Fed. see Orel
Os Norway 14 G5
Osa Rus. Fed. 11 R4
Osa, Península de pen. Costa Rica 67 H7
Ōsaka Japan 45 D6
Osakarovka Kazakh. 42 C2
Osby Sweden 15 H8
Oschiri Sardinia Italy 26 C4
Ösel i. Estonia see Hiiumaa
Osetr r. Rus. Fed. 13 H5
Ōse-zaki pt Japan 45 C6
Osh Kyrg. 42 C4
Oshakati Namibia 49 B5
Oshawa Canada 63 L3
Oshika-hantō pen. Japan 45 F5
Ō-shima i. Japan 44 E4
Ō-shima i. Japan 45 E6
Oshkosh WI U.S.A. 63 J3
Oshmyany Belarus see Ashmyany
Oshnovīyeh Iran 35 G3
Oshogbo Nigeria 46 D4
Oshtorān Kūh mt. Iran 35 H4
Oshwe Dem. Rep. Congo 48 B4
Osijek Croatia 26 H2
Osimo Italy 26 E3
Osipenko Ukr. see Berdyans'k
Osipovichi Belarus see Asipovichy
Osiyan India 36 C4
Osizweni S. Africa 51 J4
Osječenica mts Bos.-Herz. 26 G2
Ösjön l. Sweden 14 I5
Oskarshamn Sweden 15 J8
Öskemen Kazakh. see Ust'-Kamenogorsk
Oslo Norway 15 G7
Oslofjorden sea chan. Norway 15 G7
Osmanabad India 38 C2
Osmancık Turkey 34 D2
Osmaneli Turkey 27 M4
Osmaniye Turkey 34 E3
Osmannagar India 38 C2
Os'mino Rus. Fed. 15 P7
Osnabrück Germany 17 L4
Osnaburg atoll Fr. Polynesia see Mururoa
Osogbo Nigeria see Oshogbo
Osogovska Planina mts Bulg./Macedonia 27 J3
Osogovske Planine mts Bulg./Macedonia see Osogovska Planina
Osogovski Planini mts Bulg./Macedonia see Osogovska Planina
Osorno Chile 70 B6
Osorno Spain 25 D2
Osoyoos Canada 62 D2
Osøyri Norway 15 D6
Osprey Reef Australia 56 D2
Oss Neth. 17 J5
Ossa, Mount Australia 57 [inset]
Ossining NY U.S.A. 64 E2
Ossora Rus. Fed. 29 R4
Ostashkov Rus. Fed. 12 G4
Ostend Belgium 16 I5
Ostende Belgium see Ostend
Österbymo Sweden 15 I8
Österdalälven l. Sweden 15 H6
Østerdalen valley Norway 15 G5
Österreich country Europe see Austria
Östersund Sweden 14 I5
Ostfriesische Inseln Germany see East Frisian Islands
Östhammar Sweden 15 K6
Ostrava Czech Rep. 17 Q6
Ostróda Poland 17 Q4
Ostrogozhsk Rus. Fed. 13 H6
Ostrov Rus. Fed. 12 F4
Ostrovets Poland see Ostrowiec Świętokrzyski
Ostrovskoye Rus. Fed. 12 I4
Ostrov Vrangelya i. Rus. Fed. see Wrangel Island
Ostrów Poland see Ostrów Wielkopolski
Ostrowiec Poland see Ostrowiec Świętokrzyski
Ostrowiec Świętokrzyski Poland 13 D6
Ostrów Mazowiecka Poland 17 R4
Ostrowo Poland see Ostrów Wielkopolski
Ostrów Wielkopolski Poland 17 P5
Osŭm r. Bulg. 27 K3
Ōsumi-shotō is Japan 45 C7
Osuna Spain 25 D5
Oswego NY U.S.A. 64 C1
Oswestry U.K. 19 D6
Otago Peninsula N.Z. 59 C7
Otahiti i. Fr. Polynesia see Tahiti
Otaki N.Z. 59 E5
Otanmäki Fin. 14 O4
Otaru Japan 44 F4
Otavi Namibia 49 B5
Ōtawara Japan 45 F5
Otdia atoll Marshall Is see Wotje
Otematata N.Z. 59 C7
Otepää Estonia 15 O7
Otgon Tenger Uul mt. Mongolia 42 H3
Otira N.Z. 59 C6
Otjinene Namibia 49 B6
Otjiwarongo Namibia 49 B6
Otjozondjupa admin. reg. Namibia 50 C1
Otley U.K. 18 F5
Otorohanga N.Z. 59 E4
Otpan, Gora hill Kazakh. 35 H1
Otpor Rus. Fed. see Zabaykal'sk
Otradnoye Rus. Fed. see Otradnyy
Otradnyy Rus. Fed. 13 K5
Otranto Italy 26 H4
Otranto, Strait of Albania/Italy 26 H4
Otrogovo Rus. Fed. see Stepnoye
Otrozhnyy Rus. Fed. 29 S3
Otsego Lake NY U.S.A. 64 D1
Ōtsu Japan 45 D6
Otta Norway 15 F6
Ottawa Canada 61 K5
Ottawa r. Canada 63 M2
Ottawa IL U.S.A. 63 J3
Ottawa KS U.S.A. 63 H4
Ottawa Islands Canada 61 J4
Otter r. U.K. 19 D8
Otterburn U.K. 18 E3
Otter Rapids Canada 63 K1
Ottumwa U.S.A. 63 I3
Otukpo Nigeria 46 D4
Oturkpo Nigeria see Otukpo
Otuzco Peru 68 C5
Otway, Cape Australia 58 A7
Otway National Park Australia 58 A7
Ouachita Mountains Arkansas/Oklahoma U.S.A. 63 I5
Ouadda Cent. Afr. Rep. 48 C3
Ouaddaï reg. Chad 47 F3
Ouagadougou Burkina 46 C3
Ouahigouya Burkina 46 C3
Ouahran Alg. see Oran
Ouaka r. Cent. Afr. Rep. 48 B3
Oualâta Mauritania 46 C3
Ouallam Niger 46 D3
Ouanda-Djallé Cent. Afr. Rep. 48 C3
Ouando Cent. Afr. Rep. 48 C3
Ouango Cent. Afr. Rep. 48 C3
Ouara r. Cent. Afr. Rep. 48 C3
Ouarâne reg. Mauritania 46 C2
Ouargaye Burkina 46 D3
Ouargla Alg. 22 F5
Ouarogou Burkina see Ouargaye
Ouarzazate Morocco 22 C5
Oubangui r. Cent. Afr. Rep./Dem. Rep. Congo see Ubangi
Oubergpas pass S. Africa 50 G7
Oudtshoorn S. Africa 50 F7
Oued Tlélat Alg. 25 F6
Oued Zem Morocco 22 C5
Oued Zénati Alg. 26 B6
Ouessant, Île d' i. France 24 B2
Ouesso Congo 48 B3
Ouezzane Morocco 25 D6
Oughter, Lough l. Ireland 21 E3
Ouguati Namibia 50 B1
Ouistreham France 19 G9
Oujda Morocco 25 F6
Oujeft Mauritania 46 B3
Oulainen Fin. 14 N4
Oulangan kansallispuisto nat. park Fin. 14 P3
Ouled Djellal Alg. 25 I6
Ouled Farès Alg. 25 G5
Ouled Naïl, Monts des mts Alg. 25 H6
Oulu Fin. 14 N4
Oulujärvi l. Fin. 14 O4
Oulujoki r. Fin. 14 N4
Oulunsalo Fin. 14 N4
Oulx Italy 26 B2
Oum-Chalouba Chad 47 F3
Oum el Bouaghi Alg. 26 B7
Oum-Hadjer Chad 47 E3
Ounasjoki r. Fin. 14 N3
Oundle U.K. 19 G6
Ounianga Kébir Chad 47 F3
Oura, Akrotirio pt Greece 27 L5
Ourense Spain 25 C2
Ouricuri Brazil 69 J5
Ourinhos Brazil 71 A3
Ouro r. Brazil 71 A1
Ouro Preto Brazil 71 C3
Ous Rus. Fed. 11 S3
Ouse r. England U.K. 18 G5
Ouse r. England U.K. 19 H8
Outaouais, Rivière des r. Canada see Ottawa
Outardes Quatre, Réservoir resr Canada 63 N1
Outer Hebrides is U.K. 20 B3
Outer Mongolia country Asia see Mongolia
Outer Santa Barbara Channel CA U.S.A. 65 C4
Outjo Namibia 49 B6
Outlook Canada 62 F1
Outokumpu Fin. 14 P5
Out Skerries is U.K. 20 [inset]
Ouvéa atoll New Caledonia 53 G4
Ouyen Australia 57 C7
Ouzel r. U.K. 19 G6
Ovace, Punta d' mt. Corsica France 24 I6
Ovacık Turkey 39 A1
Ovada Italy 26 C2
Ovalle Chile 70 B4
Ovamboland reg. Namibia 49 B5
Ovan Gabon 48 B3
Ovar Port. 25 B3
Överkalix Sweden 14 M3
Overlander Roadhouse Australia 55 A6
Overton NV U.S.A. 65 E2
Övertorneå Sweden 14 M3
Överum Sweden 15 J8
Ovid NY U.S.A. 64 C1
Oviedo Spain 25 D2
Ovoot Mongolia 43 K3
Øvre Anárjohka Nasjonalpark nat. park Norway 14 N2
Øvre Dividal Nasjonalpark nat. park Norway 14 K2
Øvre Rendal Norway 15 G6
Ovruch Ukr. 13 F6
Ovsyanka Rus. Fed. 44 B1
Owando Congo 48 B4
Owa Rafa i. Solomon Is see Santa Ana
Owasco Lake NY U.S.A. 64 C1
Owase Japan 45 E6
Owatonna U.S.A. 63 I3
Owbeh Afgh. 33 J3
Owego NY U.S.A. 64 C1
Owel, Lough l. Ireland 21 E4
Owenmore r. Ireland 21 C3
Owenmore r. Ireland 21 D3
Owenreagh r. U.K. 21 E3
Owen River N.Z. 59 D5
Owens r. CA U.S.A. 65 D2
Owensboro U.S.A. 63 J4
Owens Lake CA U.S.A. 65 D2
Owen Sound Canada 63 K3
Owen Stanley Range mts P.N.G. 52 E2
Owerri Nigeria 46 D4
Owo Nigeria 46 D4
Owyhee U.S.A. 62 D3
Owyhee r. U.S.A. 62 D3
Öxarfjörður b. Iceland 14 [inset]
Oxelösund Sweden 15 J7
Oxford N.Z. 59 D6
Oxford U.K. 19 F7
Oxford MD U.S.A. 64 C3
Oxford MS U.S.A. 63 J5
Oxford NY U.S.A. 64 D1
Oxford Lake Canada 63 H1
Oxley Australia 58 B5
Oxleys Peak Australia 58 E3
Oxley Wild Rivers National Park Australia 58 F3
Ox Mountains hills Ireland see Slieve Gamph
Oxnard CA U.S.A. 65 C3
Oxus r. Asia see Amudar'ya
Øya Norway 14 H3
Oyama Japan 45 E5
Oyapock r. Brazil/Fr. Guiana 69 H3
Oyem Gabon 48 B3
Oyen Canada 62 E1
Oygon Mongolia 42 H3
Oykel r. U.K. 20 E3
Oyo Nigeria 46 D4
Oyonnax France 24 G3
Oyster Rocks is India 38 B3
Oytograk China 37 E1
Oyukludağı mt. Turkey 39 A1
Özalp Turkey 35 G3
Ozark AL U.S.A. 63 J5
Ozark Plateau U.S.A. 63 I4
Ozarks, Lake of the U.S.A. 63 I4
O'zbekiston country Asia see Uzbekistan
Özen Kazakh. see Kyzylsay
Ozernovskiy Rus. Fed. 29 Q4
Ozernyy Rus. Fed. 13 G5
Ozerpakh Rus. Fed. 44 F1
Ozersk Rus. Fed. 15 M9
Ozerskiy Rus. Fed. 44 F3
Ozery Rus. Fed. 13 H5
Ozeryane Rus. Fed. 44 C2
Ozieri Sardinia Italy 26 C4
Ozinki Rus. Fed. 13 K6
Oznachennoye Rus. Fed. see Sayanogorsk
Ozuki Japan 45 C6

P

Paamiut Greenland 61 N3
Paanopa i. Kiribati see Banaba
Paarl S. Africa 50 D7
Paatsjoki r. Europe see Patsoyoki
Paballelo S. Africa 50 E5
P'abal-li N. Korea 44 C4
Pabbay i. U.K. 20 B3
Pabianice Poland 17 Q5
Pabianitz Poland see Pabianice
Pabna Bangl. 37 G4
Pabradė Lith. 15 N9
Pab Range mts Pak. 33 K4
Pacaás Novos, Parque Nacional nat. park Brazil 68 F6
Pacaraimã, Serra mts S. America see Pakaraima Mountains
Pacasmayo Peru 68 C5
Pachagarh Bangl. see Panchagarh
Pachikha Rus. Fed. 12 J3
Pachino Sicily Italy 26 F6
Pachmarhi India 36 D5
Pachor India 36 D5
Pachora India 38 B1
Pachpadra India 36 C4
Pachuca Mex. 66 E4
Pachuca de Soto Mex. see Pachuca
Pacific-Antarctic Ridge sea feature S. Pacific Ocean 75 J9
Pacific Grove CA U.S.A. 65 B2
Pacific Ocean 74
Packsaddle Australia 57 C6
Pacoval Brazil 69 H4
Pacuí r. Brazil 71 B2
Paczków Poland 17 P5
Padali Rus. Fed. see Amursk
Padampur India 36 C3
Padang Indon. 41 C8
Padany Rus. Fed. 12 G3
Padatha, Kūh-e mt. Iran 35 H4
Padcaya Bol. 68 F8
Paddington Australia 58 B4
Paden City WV U.S.A. 64 A3
Paderborn Germany 17 L5
Padeşu, Vârful mt. Romania 27 J2
Padibyu Myanmar 37 I5
Padilla Bol. 68 F7
Padjelanta nationalpark nat. park Sweden 14 J3
Padova Italy see Padua
Padrão, Ponta pt Angola 49 B4
Padrauna India 37 F4
Padre Island U.S.A. 63 H6
Padstow U.K. 19 C8
Padsvillye Belarus 15 O9
Padua India 38 D2
Padua Italy 26 D2
Paducah KY U.S.A. 63 J4
Paducah TX U.S.A. 62 G5
Padum Jammu and Kashmir 36 D2
Paegam N. Korea 44 C4
Paektu-san mt. China/N. Korea see Baotou Shan
Paengnyŏng-do i. S. Korea 45 B5
Pafos Cyprus see Paphos
Pafuri Moz. 51 J2
Pag Croatia 26 F2
Pag i. Croatia 26 F2
Paga Indon. 54 C2
Pagadian Phil. 41 E7
Pagai Selatan i. Indon. 41 C8
Pagalu i. Equat. Guinea see Annobón
Pagan i. N. Mariana Is 41 G6
Pagasitikos Kolpos b. Greece 27 J5
Paget, Mount S. Georgia 70 I8
Paget Cay reef Australia 56 F3
Pagon i. N. Mariana Is see Pagan
Pagosa Springs U.S.A. 62 F4
Pāhala U.S.A. 62 [inset]
Pahlgam Jammu and Kashmir 36 C2
Pāhoa U.S.A. 62 [inset]
Pahranagat Range mts NV U.S.A. 65 E2
Pahrump NV U.S.A. 65 E2
Pahuj r. India 36 D4
Pahute Mesa plat. NV U.S.A. 65 D2
Paicines CA U.S.A. 65 B2
Paide Estonia 15 N7
Paignton U.K. 19 D8
Päijänne l. Fin. 15 N6
Paikü Co l. China 37 F3
Paimio Fin. 15 M6
Painel Brazil 71 A4
Painesville OH U.S.A. 64 A2
Pains Brazil 71 B3
Painted Rock Dam AZ U.S.A. 65 F4
Paint Hills Canada see Wemindji
Paisley U.K. 20 E5
Paita Peru 68 B5
Paiva Couceiro Angola see Quipungo
Pajala Sweden 14 M3
Pakala India 38 C3
Pakangyi Myanmar 37 H5
Pakaraima Mountains Guyana 67 M8
Pakaraima Mountains S. America 68 F3
Pakaur India 37 F4
Pakhachi Rus. Fed. 29 R3
Pakhoi China see Beihai
Paki Nigeria 46 D3
Pakistan country Asia 33 J4
Paknampho Thai. see Nakhon Sawan
Pakokku Myanmar 37 H5
Pakpattan Pak. 36 C3
Pakruojis Lith. 15 M9
Paks Hungary 26 H1
Pakse Laos see Pakxé
Pakur India see Pakaur
Pakxan Laos 42 I9
Pakxé Laos 41 C6
Pala Chad 47 E4
Palaestinia reg. Asia see Palestine
Palaiochora Greece 27 J7
Palaiseau France 24 F2
Palakkad India see Palghat
Palakkat India see Palghat
Palamakoloi Botswana 50 F2
Palamau India see Palamu
Palamós Spain 25 H3
Palamu India 37 F5
Palana Rus. Fed. 29 Q4
Palandur India 38 D1
Palani India 38 C4
Palanpur India 36 C4
Palapye Botswana 51 H2
Palatka Rus. Fed. 29 Q3
Palatka U.S.A. 63 K6
Palau country N. Pacific Ocean 41 F7
Palau Islands Palau 41 F7
Palawan i. Phil. 41 D7
Palawan Trough sea feature N. Pacific Ocean 74 D5
Palayankottai India 38 C4
Palchal Lake India 38 D2
Paldiski Estonia 15 N7
Palekh Rus. Fed. 12 I4
Palembang Indon. 41 C8
Palena Chile 70 B6
Palencia Spain 25 D2
Palermo Sicily Italy 26 E5
Palestine reg. Asia 39 B3
Palestine U.S.A. 63 H5
Paletwa Myanmar 37 H5
Palezgir Chauki Pak. 36 B3
Palghat India 38 C4
Palgrave, Mount hill Australia 55 A5
Palhoca Brazil 71 A4
Pali Chhattisgarh India 38 D1
Pali Mahar. India 38 B2
Pali Rajasthan India 36 C4
Palikir Micronesia 74 G5
Palinuro, Capo c. Italy 26 F4
Paliouri, Akrotirio pt Greece 27 J5
Palitana India 36 B5
Palivere Estonia 15 M7
Palk Bay Sri Lanka 38 C4
Palkino Rus. Fed. 15 P8
Palkonda Range mts India 38 C3
Palk Strait India/Sri Lanka 38 C4
Palla Bianca mt. Austria/Italy see Weißkugel
Pallamallawa Australia 58 E2
Pallas Green Ireland 21 D5
Pallas ja Ounastunturin kansallispuisto nat. park Fin. 14 M2
Pallasovka Rus. Fed. 13 J6
Pallavaram India 38 D3
Palliser, Cape N.Z. 59 E5
Palliser, Îles is Fr. Polynesia 75 K7
Palliser Bay N.Z. 59 E5
Pallu India 36 C3
Palma r. Brazil 71 B1
Palma del Río Spain 25 D5
Palma de Mallorca Spain 25 H4
Palmaner India 38 C3
Palmares Brazil 69 K5
Palmares do Sul Brazil 71 A5
Palmas Brazil 71 A4
Palmas 68 I6
Palmas, Cape Liberia 46 C4
Palmdale CA U.S.A. 65 C3
Palmeira Brazil 71 A4
Palmeira das Missões Brazil 70 F3
Palmeira dos Índios Brazil 69 K5
Palmeirais Brazil 69 J5
Palmeiras Brazil 71 C1
Palmeirinhas, Ponta das pt Angola 49 B4
Palmer research station Antarctica 76 L2
Palmer r. Australia 56 C3
Palmer watercourse Australia 55 F6
Palmer U.S.A. 60 D3
Palmer Land reg. Antarctica 76 L2
Palmerston N.T. Australia 54 E3
Palmerston N.T. Australia see Darwin
Palmerston atoll Cook Is 53 J3
Palmerston N.Z. 59 C7
Palmerston North N.Z. 59 E5
Palmerton PA U.S.A. 64 D2
Palmerville Australia 56 D2
Palmi Italy 26 F5
Palmira Col. 68 C3
Palm Springs CA U.S.A. 65 D4
Palmyra Syria see Tadmur
Palmyra VA U.S.A. 64 B4
Palmyra Atoll terr. N. Pacific Ocean 74 J5
Palmyras Point India 37 F5
Palni Hills India 38 C4
Palo Alto CA U.S.A. 65 A2
Paloich Sudan 32 D7
Palojärvi Fin. 14 M2
Palojoensuu Fin. 14 M2
Palomaa Fin. 14 O2
Palomar Mountain CA U.S.A. 65 D4
Paloncha India 38 D2
Palopo Indon. 41 E8
Palos, Cabo de c. Spain 25 F5
Palo Verde CA U.S.A. 65 E4
Paltamo Fin. 14 O4
Palu Indon. 41 D8
Palu i. Indon. 54 C2
Palu Turkey 35 E3
Palwal India 36 D3
Palwancha India see Paloncha
Palyeskaya Nizina marsh Belarus/Ukr. see Pripet Marshes
Pamana i. Indon. 54 C2
Pambarra Moz. 51 L1
Pambula Australia 58 D6
Pamidi India 38 C3
Pamiers France 24 E5
Pamir mts Asia 33 L2
Pamlico Sound sea chan. U.S.A. 63 L4
Pampa de Infierno Arg. 70 D3
Pampas reg. Arg. 70 D5
Pampeluna Spain see Pamplona
Pamphylia reg. Turkey 27 N6
Pamplin VA U.S.A. 64 B4
Pamplona Col. 68 D2
Pamplona Spain 25 F2
Pamukova Turkey 27 N4
Pamzal Jammu and Kashmir 36 D2
Panaca NV U.S.A. 65 E2
Panagyurishte Bulg. 27 K3
Panaji India 38 B3
Panama country Central America 67 H7
Panamá Panama see Panama City
Panamá, Canal de Panama 67 I7
Panamá, Golfo de Panama see Panama, Gulf of
Panama, Gulf of Panama 67 I7
Panama, Isthmus of Panama 67 I7
Panamá, Istmo de Panama see Panama, Isthmus of
Panama City Panama 67 I7
Panama City U.S.A. 63 J5
Panamint Range mts CA U.S.A. 65 D2
Panamint Valley valley CA U.S.A. 65 D2
Panao Peru 68 C5
Panarea, Isola i. Italy 26 F5
Panay i. Phil. 41 E6
Panayarvi Natsional'nyy Park nat. park Rus. Fed. 14 Q3
Pancake Range mts NV U.S.A. 65 E1
Pančevo Serbia 27 I2
Panchagarh Bangl. 37 G4
Pancsova Serbia see Pančevo
Panda Moz. 51 L3
Pandeiros r. Brazil 71 B1
Pandharpur India 38 B2
Pandy U.K. 19 E7
Paneas Syria see Bāniyās
Panevėžys Lith. 15 N9
Panfilov Kazakh. see Zharkent
Pangi Range mts Pak. 36 C2
Pangkalanbuun Indon. 41 D8
Pangkalpinang Indon. 41 C8
Pangnirtung Canada 61 L3
Pangody Rus. Fed. 28 I3
Pangong Tso salt l. China/Jammu and Kashmir see Bangong Co
Pangu He r. China 44 B1
Panguitch UT U.S.A. 65 F2
Panipat India 36 D3
Panir Pak. 36 A3
Panj Tajik. 36 B1
Panjāb Afgh. 36 A2
Panjim India see Panaji
Panjnad r. Pak. 36 B3
Pankakoski Fin. 14 Q5
Panna India 36 E4
Panna reg. India 36 D4
Pannawonica Australia 54 B5
Pano Lefkara Cyprus 39 A2
Panorama Brazil 71 A3
Panormus Sicily Italy see Palermo
Panshi China 44 B4
Pantanal marsh Brazil 69 G7
Pantanal Matogrossense, Parque Nacional do nat. park Brazil 69 G7
Pantar i. Indon. 54 D2
Pantelaria Sicily Italy see Pantelleria
Pantelleria Sicily Italy 26 D6
Pantelleria, Isola di i. Sicily Italy 26 E6
Panth Piploda India 36 C5
Panticapaeum Ukr. see Kerch
Pánuco Veracruz Mex. 66 E4
Panwari India 36 D4
Panzhihua China 42 I7
Panzi Dem. Rep. Congo 49 B4
Paola Italy 26 G5
Paoua Cent. Afr. Rep. 48 B3
Pápa Hungary 26 G1
Papa, Monte del mt. Italy 26 F4
Papagni r. India 38 C3
Papakura N.Z. 59 E3
Papanasam India 38 C4
Papantla Mex. 66 E4
Paparoa National Park N.Z. 59 C6
Papa Stour i. U.K. 20 [inset]
Papa Westray i. U.K. 20 G1
Papay i. U.K. see Papa Westray
Papeete Fr. Polynesia 75 K7
Papenburg Germany 17 K4
Paphos Cyprus 39 A2
Paphus Cyprus see Paphos
Papoose Lake NV U.S.A. 65 E2
Papua, Gulf of P.N.G. 52 E2
Papua New Guinea country Oceania 52 E2
Par U.K. 19 C8
Pará r. Brazil 71 B2
Pará, Rio do r. Brazil 69 I4
Paraburdoo Australia 55 B5
Paracatu Brazil 71 B2
Paracatu r. Brazil 71 B2
Paracel Islands S. China Sea 41 D6
Parachilna Australia 57 B6
Paraćin Serbia 27 I3
Paracuru Brazil 69 K4
Pará de Minas Brazil 71 B2
Paradise U.S.A. 62 C4
Paradise Peak NV U.S.A. 65 D1
Paradwip India 37 F5
Paraetonium Egypt see Marsá Maṭrūḥ
Paragominas Brazil 69 I4
Paragould U.S.A. 63 I4
Paragua i. Phil. see Palawan
Paraguaçu Paulista Brazil 71 A3
Paraguay r. Arg./Para. 70 E3
Paraguay country S. America 70 E2
Paraíba do Sul r. Brazil 71 C3
Parainen Fin. see Pargas
Paraíso do Norte Brazil 69 I6
Paraisópolis Brazil 71 B3
Parak Iran 35 I6
Parakou Benin 46 D4
Paralakhemundi India 38 E2
Paralkot India 38 D2
Paramagudi India see Paramakkudi
Paramakkudi India 38 C4
Paramaribo Suriname 69 G2
Paramillo, Parque Nacional nat. park Col. 68 C2
Paramirim Brazil 71 C1
Paramo Frontino mt. Col. 68 C2
Paramus NJ U.S.A. 64 D2
Paramushir, Ostrov i. Rus. Fed. 29 Q4
Paran watercourse Israel 39 B4
Paraná Arg. 70 D4
Paranã Brazil 71 B1
Paraná r. Brazil 71 A1
Paraná state Brazil 71 A4
Paraná r. S. America 70 E4
Paraná, Serra do hills Brazil 71 B1
Paranaguá Brazil 71 A4
Paranaíba Brazil 71 A2

Paranaíba r. Brazil 71 A3
Paranapiacaba, Serra mts Brazil 71 A4
Paranavaí Brazil 70 F2
Parang Aru r. Sri Lanka 38 D4
Parang Pass India 36 D2
Parângul Mare, Vârful mt. Romania 27 J2
Paranthan Sri Lanka 38 D4
Paraopeba Brazil 71 B2
Pārapāra Iraq 35 G4
Paraparaumu N.Z. 59 E5
Paras Pak. 36 C2
Paraspori, Akrotirio pt Greece 27 L7
Parateca Brazil 71 C1
Paratinga Brazil 71 C1
Parāū, Kūh-e mt. Iraq 35 G4
Paraúna Brazil 71 A2
Parbhani India 38 C2
Parchim Germany 17 M4
Parding China 37 G2
Pardo r. Bahia Brazil 71 D1
Pardo r. Mato Grosso do Sul Brazil 70 F2
Pardo r. São Paulo Brazil 71 A3
Pardoo Australia 54 B5
Pardubice Czech Rep. 17 O5
Parece Vela i. Japan see Okino-Tori-shima
Parecis, Serra dos hills Brazil 68 F6
Pareh Iran 35 G3
Parenda India 38 B2
Parent, Lac l. Canada 63 L2
Pareora N.Z. 59 C7
Parepare Indon. 41 D8
Parga Greece 27 I5
Pargas Fin. 15 M6
Parghelia Italy 26 F5
Pargi India 38 C2
Paria, Gulf of Trin. and Tob./Venez. 67 L6
Paria, Península de pen. Venez. 68 F1
Parikkala Fin. 15 P6
Parikud Islands India 38 E2
Parima, Serra mts Brazil 68 F3
Parima-Tapirapecó, Parque Nacional
   nat. park Venez. 68 F3
Parintins Brazil 69 G4
Paris Ont. Canada 64 A1
Paris France 24 F2
Paris TX U.S.A. 63 H5
Park U.K. 21 E3
Parkano Fin. 15 M5
Parker AZ U.S.A. 65 E5
Parker Dam CA U.S.A. 65 E3
Parker Range hills Australia 55 B8
Parkersburg WV U.S.A. 64 A3
Parkes Australia 58 D4
Park Falls U.S.A. 63 I2
Parkhill Ont. Canada 64 A1
Parkutta Jammu and Kashmir 36 D2
Parla Kimedi India see Paralakhemundi
Parlakimidi India see Paralakhemundi
Parli Vaijnath India 38 C2
Parlung Zangbo r. China 37 H3
Parma Italy 26 D2
Parma OH U.S.A. 64 A2
Parnaíba Brazil 69 J4
Parnaíba r. Brazil 69 J4
Parnassus N.Z. 59 D6
Parnassus, Mount mt. Greece 27 J5
Parner India 38 B2
Parnonas mts Greece 27 J6
Pärnu Estonia 15 N7
Pärnu-Jaagupi Estonia 15 N7
Paroikia Greece 27 K6
Paroo watercourse Australia 58 A3
Paroo Channel watercourse Australia 58 A3
Paropamisus mts Afgh. 33 J2
Paros i. Greece 27 K6
Parowan UT U.S.A. 65 F2
Parral Chile 70 B5
Parramatta Australia 58 E4
Parramore Island VA U.S.A. 64 D4
Parras Mex. 66 E3
Parrett r. U.K. 19 D7
Parry, Cape Canada 77 A2
Parry, Kap c. Greenland see
   Kangaarsussuaq
Parry Bay Canada 61 J3
Parry Channel Canada 61 G2
Parry Islands Canada 61 G2
Parry Range hills Australia 54 A5
Parry Sound Canada 63 K2
Parsnip Peak NV U.S.A. 65 E1
Parsons KS U.S.A. 63 H4
Parsons WV U.S.A. 64 B3
Parsons Range hills Australia 54 F3
Partabgarh India 38 B2
Parthenay France 24 D3
Partizansk Rus. Fed. 44 D4
Partney U.K. 18 H5
Partry Ireland 21 C4
Partry Mts hills Ireland 21 C4
Paru r. Brazil 69 H4
Paryang China 37 E3
Parys S. Africa 51 H4
Pasa Dağı mt. Turkey 34 D3
Pasadena U.S.A. 63 C3
Pasado, Cabo c. Ecuador 68 B4
Pascagoula U.S.A. 63 J5
Paşcani Romania 27 L1
Pascoal, Monte hill Brazil 71 D2
Pascua, Isla de i. S. Pacific Ocean see
   Easter Island
Pas de Calais strait France/U.K. see
   Dover, Strait of
Pasewalk Germany 17 O4
Pasha Rus. Fed. 12 G3
Pashih Haihsia sea chan. Phil./Taiwan see
   Bashi Channel
Pashkovo Rus. Fed. 44 C2
Pashkovskiy Rus. Fed. 13 H7
Pasighat India 37 H3
Pasinler Turkey 35 F3
Pasni Pak. 33 M4
Paso de los Toros Uruguay 70 E4
Pasok Myanmar 37 H5
Paso Robles CA U.S.A. 65 B3
Passaic NJ U.S.A. 64 D3
Passa Tempo Brazil 71 B3
Passau Germany 17 N6
Passo del San Gottardo Switz. see
   St Gotthard Pass
Passo Fundo Brazil 70 F3
Passos Brazil 71 B3
Passur r. Bangl. see Pusur
Passuri Nadi r. Bangl. see Pusur
Pastavy Belarus 15 O9
Pastaza r. Peru 68 C4
Pasto Col. 68 C3
Pastos Bons Brazil 69 J5
Pasu Jammu and Kashmir 36 C1
Pasur Turkey see Kulp
Pasvalys Lith. 15 N8
Pasvikelva r. Europe see Patsoyoki
Patache, Punta pt Chile 70 B4
Patagonia reg. Arg. 70 B8
Pataliputra India see Patna
Patan Gujarat India see Somnath
Patan Gujarat India 36 C5
Patan Mahar. India 38 B2
Patan Nepal 37 F4
Patan Pak. 36 C2

Patavium Italy see Padua
Patea N.Z. 59 E4
Patea inlet N.Z. see Doubtful Sound
Pate Island Kenya 48 E4
Pateley Bridge U.K. 18 F4
Patensie S. Africa 50 G7
Patera India 38 E2
Paterson Australia 58 E4
Paterson r. Australia 58 C2
Paterson NJ U.S.A. 64 D3
Paterson Range hills Australia 54 C5
Pathanamthitta India 38 C4
Pathankot India 36 C2
Pathari India 36 D5
Pathein Myanmar see Bassein
Patía r. Col. 68 C3
Patiala India 36 D3
Patkai Bum mts India/Myanmar 37 H4
Patkaklik China 37 G1
Patmos i. Greece 27 L6
Patna India 37 F4
Patna Orissa India 37 F5
Patnagarh India 37 E5
Pato Branco Brazil 70 F3
Patoda India 38 B2
Patos Albania 27 H4
Patos Brazil 69 K5
Patos, Lagoa dos l. Brazil 70 F4
Patos de Minas Brazil 71 B2
Patquía Arg. 70 C4
Patra Greece see Patras
Patrae Greece see Patras
Pátrai Greece see Patras
Patreksfjörður Iceland 14 [inset]
Patricio Lynch, Isla i. Chile 70 A7
Patrick Creek watercourse Australia 56 D4
Patrimônio Brazil 71 B2
Patrocínio Brazil 71 B2
Patsoyoki r. Europe 14 Q2
Pattadakal tourist site India 38 B3
Patterson CA U.S.A. 65 B2
Patti India 37 E4
Pattijoki Fin. 14 N4
Pättikkä Fin. 14 L2
Patton PA U.S.A. 64 B2
Pattullo, Mount Canada 60 F4
Patu Brazil 69 K5
Patuakhali Bangl. 37 G5
Patuca, Punta pt Hond. 67 H5
Patur India 38 C1
Patuxent r. MD U.S.A. 64 C4
Patuxent Range mts Antarctica 76 L1
Patvinsuon kansallispuisto nat. park Fin.
   14 Q5
Pau France 24 D5
Pauhunri mt. China/India 37 G4
Pauillac France 24 D4
Pauini Brazil 68 E5
Pauini r. Brazil 68 E5
Pauk Myanmar 37 H5
Paulatuk Canada 77 A2
Paulicéia Brazil 71 A3
Paulis Dem. Rep. Congo see Isiro
Paulo Afonso Brazil 69 K5
Paulo de Faria Brazil 71 A3
Paulpietersburg S. Africa 51 J4
Paumotu, Îles is Fr. Polynesia see
   Tuamotu Islands
Paungbyin Myanmar 37 H4
Pauni India 38 C1
Pauri India 36 D3
Pavagada India 38 C3
Pavão Brazil 71 C2
Pavia Italy 26 C2
Pāvilosta Latvia 15 L8
Pavino Rus. Fed. 12 J4
Pavlikeni Bulg. 27 K3
Pavlodar Kazakh. 42 D2
Pavlof Volcano U.S.A. 60 B4
Pavlograd Ukr. see Pavlohrad
Pavlohrad Ukr. 13 G6
Pavlovka Rus. Fed. 13 J5
Pavlovo Rus. Fed. 12 I5
Pavlovsk Altayskiy Kray Rus. Fed. 42 E2
Pavlovsk Voronezhskaya Oblast' Rus. Fed.
   13 I6
Pavlovskaya Rus. Fed. 13 H7
Pawai India 36 E4
Paw Paw U.S.A. 64 B3
Pawtucket RI U.S.A. 64 F2
Paxson U.S.A. 60 D3
Payakumbuh Indon. 41 C8
Payette U.S.A. 62 D3
Pay-Khoy, Khrebet hills Rus. Fed. 28 H3
Payne Canada see Kangirsuk
Payne, Lac l. Canada 61 K4
Payne's Find Australia 55 B7
Paysandú Uruguay 70 E4
Pazar Turkey 35 F2
Pazarcık Turkey 34 E3
Pazardzhik Bulg. 27 K3
Pazin Croatia 26 E2
Peabody MA U.S.A. 64 F1
Peace r. Canada 60 G4
Peace River Canada 77 L3
Peach Springs AZ U.S.A. 65 F3
Peak Charles hill Australia 55 C8
Peak Charles National Park Australia 55 C8
Peak District National Park U.K. 18 F5
Peake watercourse Australia 57 A6
Peak Hill N.S.W. Australia 58 D4
Peak Hill W.A. Australia 55 B6
Peale, Mount U.S.A. 62 J2
Pearce Point Australia 54 E3
Pearisburg VA U.S.A. 64 A4
Pearl r. U.S.A. 62 J5
Pearl Harbor U.S.A. 62 [inset]
Pearsall U.S.A. 62 H6
Pearston S. Africa 50 G7
Peary Channel Canada 61 I2
Peary Land reg. Greenland 77 J1
Pebane Moz. 49 D5
Pebas Peru 68 D4
Peć Serbia 27 I3
Peçanha Brazil 71 C2
Peças, Ilha das i. Brazil 71 A4
Pechenga Rus. Fed. 14 Q2
Pechora Rus. Fed. 12 M2
Pechora r. Rus. Fed. 12 L1
Pechora Sea Rus. Fed. see
   Pechorskoye More
Pechorskaya G. b. Rus. Fed. 12 L1
Pechorskoye More sea Rus. Fed. 77 G2
Pechory Rus. Fed. 15 O8
Pecos U.S.A. 62 G6
Pecos r. U.S.A. 62 G6
Pécs Hungary 26 H1
Pedda Vagu r. India 38 C2
Peddapalli India see Kulp
Pedder, Lake Australia 57 [inset]
Peddie S. Africa 51 H7
Pedernales Dom. Rep. 67 J5
Pediaios r. Cyprus 39 A2
Pediva Angola 49 B5
Pedra Azul Brazil 71 C2
Pedra Preta, Serra da mts Brazil 71 A1
Pedras de Maria da Cruz Brazil 71 B1

Pedregulho Brazil 71 B3
Pedreiras Brazil 69 J4
Pedro Sri Lanka 38 D4
Pedro II, Ilha reg. Brazil/Venez. 68 E3
Pedro Juan Caballero Para. 70 E2
Peebles U.K. 20 F5
Pee Dee r. U.S.A. 63 L5
Peekskill NY U.S.A. 64 E2
Peel r. Australia 58 C2
Peel r. Canada 60 E3
Peel Isle of Man 18 C4
Peera Peera Poolanna Lake salt flat
   Australia 57 B5
Peery Lake salt flat Australia 58 A3
Pegasus Bay N.Z. 59 D6
Pegu Myanmar 42 H9
Pegu Yoma mts Myanmar 37 H6
Pehuajó Arg. 70 D5
Peine Chile 70 C2
Peipsi järv l. Estonia/Rus. Fed. see
   Peipus, Lake
Peipus, Lake Estonia/Rus. Fed. 15 O7
Peiraias Greece see Piraeus
Pei Shan mts China see Bei Shan
Peixe Brazil 69 I6
Peixe r. Brazil 71 A1
Peixoto de Azevedo Brazil 69 H6
Pejë Serbia see Peć
Pek Laos see Xiangkhoang
Peka Lesotho 51 H5
Peking China see Beijing
Pekinga Benin 46 D3
Pelagie, Isole is Sicily Italy 26 E7
Peleaga, Vârful mt. Romania 27 J2
Peles Rus. Fed. 12 K3
Pelkosenniemi Fin. 14 O3
Pella S. Africa 50 D5
Pello Fin. 14 M3
Pelly Crossing Canada 60 E3
Pelly r. Canada 60 C2
Pelly Mountains Canada 60 E3
Peloponnese admin. reg. Greece see
   Peloponnese
Peloponnesos admin. reg. Greece see
   Peloponnese
Pelopónnesos admin. reg. Greece see
   Peloponnese
Pelotas Brazil 70 F4
Pelotas, Rio das r. Brazil 71 A4
Pelusium tourist site Egypt 39 A4
Pelusium, Bay of Egypt see Ṭīnah, Khalīj aṭ
Pemba Moz. 49 E5
Pemba Island Tanz. 49 D4
Pemberton Canada 62 C1
Pemberton Australia 55 A8
Pembina r. Canada 63 L2
Pembroke Canada 63 L3
Pembroke U.K. 19 C7
Pembroke Coast National Park U.K.
   19 B7
Pen India 38 B2
Peña Cerredo mt. Spain see Torrecerredo
Peñalara mt. Spain 25 E3
Penamar Brazil 71 C1
Peña Nevada, Cerro mt. Mex. 66 E4
Penang Malaysia see George Town
Penápolis Brazil 71 A3
Peñaranda de Bracamonte Spain 25 D3
Penarie Australia 58 A5
Penarlâg U.K. see Hawarden
Peñarroya mt. Spain 25 F3
Peñarroya-Pueblonuevo Spain 25 D4
Penarth U.K. 19 D7
Peñas, Cabo c. Spain 25 D2
Penas, Golfo de g. Chile 70 A7
Peña Ubiña mt. Spain 25 D2
Pendik r. India 38 C2
Pendle Hill hill U.K. 18 E5
Pendleton U.S.A. 62 D2
Pend Oreille Lake U.S.A. 62 D2
Pendra India 37 E5
Penduv India 38 B2
Peneda Gerês, Parque Nacional da
   nat. park Port. 25 B3
Penedo Brazil 69 K6
Penenome Panama 67 H7
Penfro U.K. see Pembroke
Penganga r. India 38 C2
Penge Dem. Rep. Congo 49 C4
Penge S. Africa 51 J3
P'enghu Ch'üntao is Taiwan 43 L8
P'enghu Liehtao is Taiwan see
   P'enghu Ch'üntao
Penha Brazil 71 A4
Penhoek Pass S. Africa 51 H6
Penhook VA U.S.A. 64 B4
Peniche Port. 25 B4
Penicuik U.K. 20 F5
Peninga Rus. Fed. 14 R5
Peninsular Malaysia Malaysia 41 C7
Penitente, Serra do hills Brazil 69 I5
Pennell Coast Antarctica 76 H2
Penn Hills PA U.S.A. 64 B2
Pennine, Alpi mts Italy/Switz. 26 B2
Pennine Alps mts Italy/Switz. see
   Pennine, Alpi
Pennines hills U.K. 18 E4
Pennsburg PA U.S.A. 64 D2
Penns Grove NJ U.S.A. 64 D3
Pennsville NJ U.S.A. 64 D3
Pennsylvania state U.S.A. 64 B2
Penn Yan NY U.S.A. 64 C1
Penny Icecap Canada 61 L3
Penny Point Antarctica 76 H1
Penong Australia 55 F7
Penonome Panama 67 H7
Penrhyn atoll Cook Is 75 J6
Penrhyn Basin sea feature S. Pacific Ocean
   73 J6
Penrith Australia 58 E4
Penrith U.K. 18 E4
Pensacola U.S.A. 63 J5
Pensacola Mountains Antarctica 76 L1
Pensi La pass Jammu and Kashmir 36 D2
Pentadaktylos Range mts Cyprus 39 A2
Pentakota India 38 D2
Pentecost Island Vanuatu 53 G3
Pentecôte, Île i. Vanuatu see
   Pentecost Island
Penticton Canada 62 G1
Pentire Point U.K. 19 B8
Pentland Australia 56 D4
Pentland Firth sea chan. U.K. 20 F2
Pentland Hills U.K. 20 F5
Pen-y-Bont ar Ogwr U.K. see Bridgend
Penygadair hill U.K. 19 D6
Penza Rus. Fed. 13 J5
Penzance U.S. 19 B8
Penzhinskaya Guba b. Rus. Fed. 29 R3
Peoria IL U.S.A. 63 J3
Peradeniya Sri Lanka 38 D5
Pera Head hd India 56 C1
Perales del Alfambra Spain 25 F3
Perambalur India 38 C4
Perāmeren kansallispuisto nat. park Fin.
   14 N4
Perandapur India see Anandapur
Percival Lakes salt flat Australia 54 D5
Percy Isles Australia 56 E4
Perdizes Brazil 71 B2
Pereira Col. 68 C3
Pereira Barreto Brazil 71 A3
Pereira de Eça Angola see Ondjiva

Peremul Par reef India 38 B4
Perenjori Australia 55 B7
Pereslavl'-Zalesskiy Rus. Fed. 12 H4
Pereslavskiy Natsional'nyy Park nat. park
   Rus. Fed. 12 H4
Pereyaslavka Rus. Fed. 44 D3
Pereyaslav-Khmel'nitskiy Ukr. see
   Pereyaslav-Khmel'nyts'kyy
Pereyaslav-Khmel'nyts'kyy Ukr. 13 F6
Pergamino Arg. 70 D4
Perho Fin. 14 N5
Perico Arg. 70 C2
Pericos Mex. 66 C3
Périgueux France 24 E4
Perijá, Parque Nacional nat. park Venez.
   68 D2
Perijá, Sierra de mts Venez. 68 D2
Periyar India see Erode
Perlas, Punta de pt Nicaragua 67 H6
Perleberg Germany 17 M4
Perm' Rus. Fed. 11 R4
Permas Rus. Fed. 12 J3
Pernambuco Brazil see Recife
Pernambuco Plain sea feature
   S. Atlantic Ocean 72 G6
Pernatty Lagoon salt flat Australia 57 B6
Pernem India 38 B3
Pernik Bulg. 27 J3
Pernov Estonia see Pärnu
Perojpur India see Pirojpur
Péronne France 24 F2
Perpignan France 24 F5
Perranporth U.K. 19 B8
Perrégaux Alg. see Mohammadia
Perris CA U.S.A. 65 E5
Perros-Guirec France 24 C2
Perry FL U.S.A. 63 K6
Perryton U.S.A. 62 G4
Perryville AK U.S.A. 60 C4
Perryville MO U.S.A. 63 J4
Perseverancia Bol. 68 F6
Pershore U.K. 19 E6
Persia country Asia see Iran
Persian Gulf Asia see The Gulf
Pertek Turkey 35 E3
Perth Australia 55 A7
Perth Canada 63 L3
Perth U.K. 20 F4
Perth Amboy NJ U.S.A. 64 D2
Perth Basin sea feature Indian Ocean 73 P7
Pertominsk Rus. Fed. 12 H2
Pertunmaa Fin. 15 O6
Pertusato, Capo c. Corsica France 24 I6
Peru atoll Kiribati see Beru
Peru country S. America 68 D6
Peru-Chile Trench sea feature
   S. Pacific Ocean 75 O6
Perugia Italy 26 E3
Peruru India 38 C3
Perusia Italy see Perugia
Pervomaysk Rus. Fed. 13 I5
Pervomays'k Ukr. 13 F6
Pervomayskiy Arkhangel'skaya Oblast'
   Rus. Fed. see Novodvinsk
Pervomayskiy Tambovskaya Oblast'
   Rus. Fed. 13 I5
Pervomays'kyy Ukr. 13 H6
Pervorechenskiy Rus. Fed. 29 R3
Pesaro Italy 26 E3
Pescadores is Taiwan see P'enghu Ch'üntao
Pescara Italy 26 F3
Pescara r. Italy 26 F3
Peschanokopskoye Rus. Fed. 13 I7
Peschanoye Rus. Fed. see Yashkul'
Peschanyy, Mys pt Kazakh. 35 H2
Pesha r. Rus. Fed. 12 J2
Peshawar Pak. 33 I3
Peshkopi Albania 27 I4
Peshtera Bulg. 27 K3
Peski Karakumy des. Turkm. see
   Karakum Desert
Peskovka Rus. Fed. 12 L4
Pesnica Slovenia 26 F1
Pessac France 24 D4
Pestovo Rus. Fed. 12 G4
Pestravka Rus. Fed. 13 K5
Petah Tiqwa Israel 39 B3
Petäjävesi Fin. 14 N5
Petalion, Kolpos sea chan. Greece 27 K5
Petaluma CA U.S.A. 65 A1
Petatlán Mex. 66 D5
Petauke Zambia 49 D5
Peterborough Australia 57 B7
Peterborough Canada 63 L3
Peterborough U.K. 19 G6
Peterborough NH U.S.A. 64 F2
Peterculter U.K. 20 G3
Peterhead U.K. 20 H3
Peter I Øy i. Antarctica see Peter I Island
Peter I Island Antarctica 76 K2
Peterlee U.K. 18 F4
Petermann Bjerg nunatak Greenland 61 P2
Petermann Ranges mts Australia 55 E6
Peter Pond Lake Canada 60 H4
Petersburg NY U.S.A. 64 E1
Petersburg VA U.S.A. 64 C4
Petersburg WV U.S.A. 64 B3
Petersfield U.S.A. 19 G7
Petersville U.S.A. 60 C3
Peter the Great Bay Rus. Fed. see
   Petra Velikogo, Zaliv
Peth India 38 B2
Petilia Policastro Italy 26 G5
Petit Atlas mts Morocco see Anti Atlas
Petitjean Morocco see Sidi Kacem
Petit Lac Manicouagan l. Canada 61 L4
Petit Mécatina r. Nfld. and Lab./Que.
   Canada 61 M4
Petit Saut, Barrage de resr Fr. Guiana
   69 H3
Petit St-Bernard, Col du pass France 24 H4
Peto Mex. 66 G4
Petoskey U.S.A. 63 K2
Petra tourist site Jordan 39 B4
Petra Velikogo, Zaliv b. Rus. Fed. 44 C4
Petre, Point Ont. Canada 64 C2
Petrich Bulg. 27 J4
Petrikau Poland see Piotrków Trybunalski
Petrikov Belarus see Pyetrykaw
Petrinja Croatia 26 G2
Petroaleksandrovsk Uzbek. see To'rtko'l
Petrograd Rus. Fed. see St Petersburg
Petrokhanski Prokhod pass Bulg. 27 J3
Petrokov Poland see Piotrków Trybunalski
Petrolina Brazil 69 J5
Petrolina de Goiás Brazil 71 A2
Petropavl Kazakh. see Petropavlovsk
Petropavlovsk Kazakh. 31 F1
Petropavlovsk-Kamchatskiy Rus. Fed.
   29 Q4
Petrópolis Brazil 71 C3
Petroşani Romania 27 J2
Petrovac Serbia 27 J2
Petrovka Rus. Fed. 13 J5
Petrovskoye Rus. Fed. see Svetlograd
Petrovsk-Zabaykal'skiy Rus. Fed. 43 J2
Petrozavodsk Rus. Fed. 12 G3

Piler India 38 C3
Pili, Cerro mt. Chile 70 C2
Pilibangan India 36 C3
Pilibhit India 36 D3
Pilipinas country Asia see Philippines
Pillau Rus. Fed. see Baltiysk
Pillcopata Peru 68 D6
Pilliga Australia 58 D3
Pil'na Rus. Fed. 12 J5
Pil'nya, Ozero l. Rus. Fed. 12 M1
Pilões, Serra dos mts Brazil 71 B2
Pílos Greece see Pylos
Pilot Peak NV U.S.A. 65 D1
Pilot Station U.S.A. 60 B3
Pilsen Czech Rep. see Plzeň
Piltene Latvia 15 L8
Pil'tun, Zaliv lag. Rus. Fed. 44 F1
Pilu Pak. 36 A4
Pimenta Bueno Brazil 68 F6
Pimpalner India 38 B1
Pin r. India 36 D2
Pin r. Myanmar 37 H5
Pinahat India 36 D4
Pinamar Arg. 70 E5
Pinang Malaysia see George Town
Pınarbaşı Turkey 34 E3
Pinar del Río Cuba 67 H4
Pınarhisar Turkey 27 L4
Piñas Ecuador 68 C4
Pinchang Brazil 71 B3
Pindar Australia 55 A7
Pindaré r. Brazil 69 J4
Píndhos Óros mts Greece see
   Pindus Mountains
Pindos mts Greece see
   Pindus Mountains
Pindrei India 38 E5
Pindus Mountains Greece 27 I5
Pine watercourse Australia 57 C7
Pine Bluff U.S.A. 63 I5
Pine Creek Australia 54 E3
Pine Creek r. PA U.S.A. 64 C2
Pinecrest CA U.S.A. 65 B1
Pinedale WY U.S.A. 62 F3
Pine Flat Lake CA U.S.A. 65 C3
Pinega Rus. Fed. 12 I2
Pinega r. Rus. Fed. 12 I2
Pinegrove Australia 55 A6
Pine Grove PA U.S.A. 64 C2
Pineios r. Greece 27 J5
Pine Island Bay Antarctica 75 N10
Pine Island Glacier Antarctica 76 K1
Pine Mountain CA U.S.A. 65 B3
Pine Peak AZ U.S.A. 65 F3
Pine Point Canada 60 G3
Pineridge CA U.S.A. 65 C2
Pine Ridge U.S.A. 62 G3
Pinerolo Italy 26 B2
Pines, Akrotirio pt Greece 27 K4
Pines, Isle of i. Cuba see
   La Juventud, Isla de
Pines, Île of i. New Caledonia see
   Pins, Île des
Pinetown S. Africa 51 J5
Pine Valley NY U.S.A. 64 C1
Ping'an China 42 I5
Ping'anyi China see Ping'an
Pingdingbu China see Guyuan
Pingdingshan China 43 K6
Pingdong Taiwan see P'ingtung
Pingdu Shandong China 43 L5
Pinggang China 44 B4
Pingliang China 42 J5
Pingtan Dao i. China see Haitan Dao
P'ingtung Taiwan 43 M8
Pingxiang Guangxi China 42 J8
Pingxiang Jiangxi China 43 K3
Pingyang Heilong. China 44 B2
Pinhal Brazil 71 B3
Pinheiro Brazil 69 I4
Pinhoe U.K. 19 D8
Piniós r. Greece see Pineios
Pinjin Australia 55 C7
Pinlebu Myanmar 37 H4
Pinnacle hill Virginia/West Virginia U.S.A.
   64 B3
Pinnacles National Monument nat. park
   CA U.S.A. 65 B3
Pinon Hills CA U.S.A. 65 D3
Pinos, Isla de i. Cuba see
   La Juventud, Isla de
Pinos, Mount CA U.S.A. 65 C3
Pinotepa Nacional Mex. 66 E5
Pins, Île des i. New Caledonia 53 G4
Pins, Pointe aux pt Ont. Canada 64 A1
Pinsk Belarus 15 O10
Pintados Chile 70 C2
Pintura UT U.S.A. 65 F2
Pioche NV U.S.A. 65 E2
Piodi Dem. Rep. Congo 49 C4
Pioner, Ostrov i. Rus. Fed. 28 K2
Pionerskiy Kaliningradskaya Oblast'
   Rus. Fed. 15 L9
Pionerskiy Khanty-Mansiyskiy Avtonomnyy
   Okrug Rus. Fed. 11 S3
Pionki Poland 17 R5
Piopio N.Z. 59 E4
Piopiotahi inlet N.Z. see Milford Sound
Piorini, Lago l. Brazil 68 F4
Piotrków Trybunalski Poland 17 Q5
Pipa Dingzi mt. China 44 C4
Pipar India 36 C4
Pipar Road India 36 C4
Niperi i. Greece 27 K5
Piper Peak NV U.S.A. 65 D2
Pipli India 36 C3
Pipmuacan, Réservoir resr Canada 63 M2
Piquiri r. Brazil 71 A4
Pira Benin 46 D4
Piracanjuba Brazil 71 A2
Piracicaba Brazil 71 B3
Piracicaba r. Brazil 71 B3
Piraçununga Brazil 71 B3
Piracuruca Brazil 69 J4
Piraeus Greece 27 J6
Piraí do Sul Brazil 71 A4
Piráievs Greece see Piraeus
Piraju Brazil 71 A3
Pirajuí Brazil 71 A3
Pirallahı Adası Azer. 35 H2
Piranhas Bahia Brazil 71 C1
Piranhas Goiás Brazil 71 A2
Piranhas r. Rio Grande do Norte Brazil 69 K5
Piranhas r. Brazil 71 A2
Pirapora Brazil 71 B2
Pirawa India 36 D4
Pirenópolis Brazil 71 A1
Pires do Rio Brazil 71 A2
Pírgos Greece see Pyrgos
Pirin nat. park Bulg. 27 J4
Pirineos mts Europe see Pyrenees
Piripiri Brazil 69 J4
Pirlerkondu Turkey see Taşkent
Pirojpur Bangl. 37 G5
Pir Panjal Pass Jammu and Kashmir 36 C2
Pir Panjal Range mts India/Pak. 36 C2
Piryatin Ukr. see Pyryatyn
Pisa Italy 26 D3
Pisae Italy see Pisa

Pisagua Chile 68 D7
Pisaurum Italy see Pesaro
Pisco Peru 68 C6
Písek Czech Rep. 17 O6
Pisha China see Ningnan
Pishan China 36 D1
Pīshīn Iran 33 J4
Pishin Pak. 36 A3
Pishpek Kyrg. see Bishkek
Pisidia reg. Turkey 34 C3
Pissis, Cerro Arg. 70 C3
Pisté Mex. 66 G4
Pisticci Italy 26 G4
Pistoia Italy 26 D3
Pistoriae Italy see Pistoia
Pisuerga r. Spain 25 D3
Pita Guinea 46 B3
Pitanga Brazil 71 A4
Pitangui Brazil 71 B2
Pitar India 36 B5
Pitarpunga Lake imp. l. Australia 58 A5
Pitcairn, Henderson, Ducie and Oeno Islands terr. S. Pacific Ocean see Pitcairn Islands
Pitcairn Island Pitcairn Is 75 L7
Pitcairn Islands terr. S. Pacific Ocean 75 L7
Piteå Sweden 14 L4
Piteälven r. Sweden 14 L4
Pitelino Rus. Fed. 13 I5
Piterka Rus. Fed. 13 J6
Pitești Romania 27 K2
Pithoragarh India 36 E3
Pitihra India 36 D5
Pitkyaranta Rus. Fed. 12 F3
Pitlochry U.K. 20 F4
Pitsane Siding Botswana 51 G3
Pitti i. India 38 B4
Pitt Island N.Z. 53 I6
Pitt Islands Solomon Is see Vanikoro Islands
Pittsburgh PA U.S.A. 64 B2
Pittsfield MA U.S.A. 64 E1
Pittsworth Australia 58 E1
Piumhí Brazil 71 B3
Piura Peru 68 B5
Piute Mountains CA U.S.A. 65 E3
Piute Peak CA U.S.A. 65 C3
Piuthan Nepal 37 E3
Pivka Slovenia 26 F2
Pixariá mt. Greece see Pyxaria
Pixley CA U.S.A. 65 C3
Piz Bernina mt. Italy/Switz. 26 C1
Piz Buin mt. Austria/Switz. 17 M7
Pizhanka Rus. Fed. 12 K4
Pizhi Nigeria 46 D4
Pizhma Rus. Fed. 12 J4
Pizhma r. Rus. Fed. 12 K4
Pizhma r. Rus. Fed. 12 L2
Placentia Italy see Piacenza
Placerville CA U.S.A. 65 B1
Plácido de Castro Brazil 68 E6
Plainfield CT U.S.A. 64 F2
Plainview U.S.A. 62 G5
Plaka, Akrotirio pt Greece 27 L7
Plakoti, Cape Cyprus 39 B2
Planada CA U.S.A. 65 B2
Planaltina Brazil 71 B1
Planura Brazil 71 A3
Plaquemine U.S.A. 63 I5
Plasencia Spain 25 C3
Plaster City CA U.S.A. 65 E4
Plastun Rus. Fed. 44 E3
Platani r. Sicily Italy 26 E6
Platberg mt. S. Africa 51 I5
Platinum U.S.A. 77 B3
Plato Col. 68 D2
Platte r. U.S.A. 62 H3
Plattsburgh U.S.A. 63 M3
Plauen Germany 17 N5
Plavsk Rus. Fed. 13 H5
Playas Ecuador 68 B4
Pleasant Bay MA U.S.A. 64 G2
Pleasanton U.S.A. 66 E3
Pleasant Point N.Z. 59 C7
Pleasantville NJ U.S.A. 64 D3
Pleaux France 24 F4
Pledger Lake Canada 63 K1
Plenty watercourse Australia 56 B5
Plenty, Bay of g. N.Z. 59 F3
Plentywood U.S.A. 62 G2
Plesetsk Rus. Fed. 12 I3
Pleshchentsy Belarus see Plyeshchanitsy
Plétipi, Lac l. Canada 63 M1
Plettenberg Bay S. Africa 50 F8
Pleven Bulg. 27 K3
Plevna Bulg. see Pleven
Pljevlja Montenegro 27 H3
Płock Poland 17 Q4
Pločno mt. Bos.-Herz. 26 G3
Plodovoye Rus. Fed. 12 F3
Ploemeur France 24 C3
Ploești Romania see Ploiești
Ploiești Romania 27 L2
Plomb du Cantal mt. France 24 F4
Ploskoye Rus. Fed. see Stanovoye
Płoty Poland 17 O4
Ploudalmézeau France 24 B2
Plouzané France 24 B2
Plovdiv Bulg. 27 K3
Plozk Poland see Płock
Plumridge Lakes salt flat Australia 55 D7
Plungė Lith. 15 L9
Plyeshchanitsy Belarus 15 O9
Plymouth Montserrat 67 L5
Plymouth U.K. 19 C8
Plymouth CA U.S.A. 65 B1
Plymouth IN U.S.A. 63 J3
Plymouth MA U.S.A. 64 F2
Plymouth Bay MA U.S.A. 64 F2
Plynlimon hill U.K. 19 D6
Plyussa Rus. Fed. 15 P7
Plzeň Czech Rep. 17 N6
Pô Burkina 46 C3
Po r. Italy 26 E2
Pô, Parc National de nat. park Burkina 46 C3
Pobeda Peak China/Kyrg. 31 H2
Pobedy, Pik mt. China/Kyrg. see Pobeda Peak
Pocatello U.S.A. 62 E3
Pochala Sudan 47 G4
Pochayiv Ukr. 13 E6
Pochep Rus. Fed. 13 G5
Pochinki Rus. Fed. 13 J5
Pochinok Rus. Fed. 13 G5
Pochutla Mex. 66 E5
Pocking Germany 17 N6
Pocklington U.K. 18 G5
Poções Brazil 71 C1
Pocomoke City MD U.S.A. 64 D3
Pocomoke Sound b. Maryland/Virginia U.S.A. 64 D4
Poconé Brazil 69 G7
Pocono Mountains hills PA U.S.A. 64 D2
Poços de Caldas Brazil 71 B3
Podanur India 38 C4
Poddor'ye Rus. Fed. 12 F4
Podgorenskiy Rus. Fed. 13 H6
Podgorica Montenegro 27 H3
Podgornoye Rus. Fed. 28 J4
Podile India 38 C3
Podișul Transilvaniei plat. Romania see Transylvanian Basin
Podkamennaya Tunguska r. Rus. Fed. 29 K3
Podocarpus, Parque Nacional nat. park Ecuador 68 C4
Podol'sk Rus. Fed. 13 H5
Podporozh'ye Rus. Fed. 12 G3
Podujevë Serbia see Podujevo
Podujevo Serbia 27 I3
Podz' Rus. Fed. 12 K3
Poelela, Lagoa l. Moz. 51 L3
Poeppel Corner salt flat Australia 57 B5
Poetovio Slovenia see Ptuj
Pofadder S. Africa 50 D5
Pogar Rus. Fed. 13 G5
Poggibonsi Italy 26 D3
Poggio di Montieri mt. Italy 26 D3
Pogradec Albania 27 I4
Pogranichnyy Rus. Fed. 44 C3
Po Hai g. China see Bo Hai
P'ohang S. Korea 45 C5
Pohnpei atoll Micronesia 74 G5
Pohri India 36 D4
Poi India 37 H4
Poiana Mare Romania 27 J3
Poinsett, Cape Antarctica 76 F2
Point Arena CA U.S.A. 65 A1
Pointe-à-Pitre Guadeloupe 67 L5
Pointe-Noire Congo 49 B4
Point Hope U.S.A. 60 B3
Point Lake Canada 60 G3
Point Pleasant NJ U.S.A. 64 D2
Poitiers France 24 E3
Poitou reg. France 24 E3
Pojuca r. Brazil 71 D1
Pokaran India 36 B4
Pokataroo Australia 58 D2
Pokcha Rus. Fed. 11 R3
Pokhara Nepal 37 E3
Pokhvistnevo Rus. Fed. 11 Q5
Poko Dem. Rep. Congo 48 C3
Pokosnoye Rus. Fed. 42 I1
Pokran Pak. 36 A4
P'ok'r Kovkas mts Asia see Lesser Caucasus
Pokrovka Chitinskaya Oblast' Rus. Fed. 44 A1
Pokrovka Primorskiy Kray Rus. Fed. 44 C4
Pokrovsk Respublika Sakha (Yakutiya) Rus. Fed. 29 N3
Pokrovsk Saratovskaya Oblast' Rus. Fed. see Engel's
Pokrovskoye Rus. Fed. 13 H7
Pokshen'ga r. Rus. Fed. 12 J3
Pol India 36 C5
Pola Croatia see Pula
Pola de Lena Spain 25 D2
Pola de Siero Spain 25 D2
Poland country Europe 10 J5
Poland NY U.S.A. 64 D1
Polar Plateau Antarctica 76 A1
Polatlı Turkey 34 D3
Polatsk Belarus 15 P9
Polavaram India 38 D2
Polcirkeln Sweden 14 L3
Pol-e Fāsā Iran 35 I5
Pol-e Khomrī Afgh. 36 B2
Polessk Rus. Fed. 15 L9
Poles'ye marsh Belarus/Ukr. see Pripet Marshes
Polgahawela Sri Lanka 38 D5
Poli Cyprus see Polis
Políaigos i. Greece see Polyaigos
Police Poland 17 O4
Policoro Italy 26 G4
Poligny France 24 G3
Políkastron Greece see Polykastro
Polillo Islands Phil. 41 E6
Polis Cyprus 39 A2
Polis'ke Ukr. 13 F6
Polis'kyy Zapovidnyk nature res. Ukr. 13 F6
Politovo Rus. Fed. 12 K2
Políyiros Greece see Polygyros
Polkowice Poland 17 P5
Pollachi India 38 C4
Pollard Islands U.S.A. see Gardner Pinnacles
Pollino, Monte mt. Italy 26 G5
Pollino, Parco Nazionale del nat. park Italy 26 G5
Pollock Pines CA U.S.A. 65 B1
Pollock Reef Australia 55 C8
Polmak Norway 14 O1
Polnovat Rus. Fed. 11 T3
Polo Fin. 14 P4
Pologi Ukr. see Polohy
Polohy Ukr. 13 H7
Polokwane S. Africa 51 I2
Polonne Ukr. 13 E6
Polonnoye Ukr. see Polonne
Polotsk Belarus see Polatsk
Polperro U.K. 19 C8
Polska country Europe see Poland
Polson U.S.A. 62 E2
Polta r. Rus. Fed. 12 I2
Poltava Ukr. 13 G6
Poltoratsk Turkm. see Aşgabat
Põltsamaa Estonia 15 N7
Polunochnoye Rus. Fed. 11 S3
Põlva Estonia 15 O7
Polvijärvi Fin. 14 P5
Polyaigos i. Greece 27 K6
Polyanovgrad Bulg. see Karnobat
Polyarnyy Chukotskiy Avtonomnyy Okrug Rus. Fed. 29 S3
Polyarnyy Murmanskaya Oblast' Rus. Fed. 12 G1
Polyarnyye Zori Rus. Fed. 12 G2
Polyarnyy Ural mts Rus. Fed. 11 S2
Polygyros Greece 27 J4
Polykastro Greece 27 J4
Polynesia is Pacific Ocean 74 I6
Polynésie Française terr. S. Pacific Ocean see French Polynesia
Pomarkku Fin. 15 M6
Pombal Pará Brazil 69 H4
Pombal Paraíba Brazil 69 K5
Pombal Port. 25 B4
Pomene Moz. 51 L2
Pomeranian Bay Poland 17 O3
Pomeroy S. Africa 51 J5
Pomeroy U.K. 21 F3
Pomezia Italy 26 E4
Pomfret S. Africa 50 F3
Pomona Namibia 50 B4
Pomona CA U.S.A. 65 D3
Pomorie Bulg. 27 L3
Pomorskie, Pojezierze reg. Poland 17 O4
Pomorskiy Bereg coastal area Rus. Fed. 12 G2
Pomorskiy Proliv sea chan. Rus. Fed. 12 K1
Pomos Point Cyprus 39 A2
Pomo Tso l. China see Puma Yumco
Pomou, Akra pt Cyprus see Pomos Point
Pomozdino Rus. Fed. 12 L3
Pompain China 37 H3
Pompei Italy 26 F4
Pompéia Brazil 71 A3
Pompeyevka Rus. Fed. 44 C2
Ponape atoll Micronesia see Pohnpei
Ponazyrevo Rus. Fed. 12 J4
Ponca City U.S.A. 63 H4
Ponce Puerto Rico 67 K5
Pondicherry India see Puducherry
Pondicherry union terr. India 38 C4
Pond Inlet Canada 77 K2
Ponds Bay Canada see Pond Inlet
Ponente, Riviera di coastal area Italy 26 B3
Ponferrada Spain 25 C2
Pongara, Pointe pt Gabon 48 A3
Pongaroa N.Z. 59 F5
Pongo watercourse Sudan 47 F4
Pongola r. S. Africa 51 K4
Pongolapoort Dam l. S. Africa 51 J4
Ponnagyun Myanmar 37 H5
Ponnaivar r. India 38 C4
Ponnampet India 38 B3
Ponnani India 38 B4
Ponnyadaung Range mts Myanmar 37 H5
Ponoka Canada 62 E1
Ponoy r. Rus. Fed. 12 I2
Ponta Delgada Arquipélago dos Açores 72 G3
Ponta Grossa Brazil 71 A4
Pontal Brazil 71 A3
Pontalina Brazil 71 A2
Pont-à-Mousson France 24 H2
Ponta Porã Brazil 70 E2
Pontarfynach U.K. see Devil's Bridge
Pont-Audemer France 19 H9
Ponte Alta do Norte Brazil 69 I6
Ponte de Sor Port. 25 B4
Ponte Firme Brazil 71 B2
Pontefract U.K. 18 F5
Ponteix Canada 62 F2
Ponteland U.K. 18 F3
Ponte Nova Brazil 71 C3
Pontes-e-Lacerda Brazil 69 G7
Pontevedra Spain 25 B2
Ponthierville Dem. Rep. Congo see Ubundu
Pontiac IL U.S.A. 63 J3
Pontiac MI U.S.A. 63 K3
Pontiae is Italy see Ponziane, Isole
Pontianak Indon. 41 C8
Pontine Islands is Italy see Ponziane, Isole
Pont-l'Abbé France 24 B3
Pontoise France 24 F2
Ponton watercourse Australia 55 C7
Ponton Canada 62 H1
Pontypool U.K. 19 D7
Pontypridd U.K. 19 D7
Ponza, Isola di i. Italy 26 E4
Ponziane, Isole is Italy 26 E4
Poochera Australia 55 F8
Poole U.K. 19 F8
Poolowanna Lake salt flat Australia 57 B5
Poona India see Pune
Pooncarie Australia 57 C7
Poonch India see Punch
Poopelloe Lake salt l. Australia 58 B3
Poopó, Lago de l. Bol. 68 E7
Poor Knights Islands N.Z. 59 E2
Popayán Col. 68 C3
Popigay r. Rus. Fed. 29 L2
Popiltah Australia 57 C7
Popilta Lake imp. l. Australia 57 C7
Poplar r. Canada 63 H1
Poplar Bluff U.S.A. 63 I4
Poplar Camp VA U.S.A. 64 A4
Popocatépetl, Volcán vol. Mex. 66 E5
Popokabaka Dem. Rep. Congo 49 B4
Popovichskaya Rus. Fed. see Kalininskaya
Popovo Bulg. 27 L3
Popovo Polje plain Bos.-Herz. 26 G3
Poprad Slovakia 17 R6
Poquoson VA U.S.A. 64 C4
Porangahau N.Z. 59 F5
Porangatu Brazil 71 A1
Porbandar India 36 B5
Porcos r. Brazil 71 B1
Porcupine Abyssal Plain sea feature N. Atlantic Ocean 72 G2
Porcupine Gorge National Park Australia 56 D4
Poreč Croatia 26 E2
Porecatu Brazil 71 A3
Poretskoye Rus. Fed. 13 J5
Pori Fin. 15 L6
Porirua N.Z. 59 E5
Porkhov Rus. Fed. 12 F4
Porlamar Venez. 68 F1
Pormpuraaw Australia 56 C2
Pornic France 24 C3
Poronaysk Rus. Fed. 44 F2
Porong China 37 G3
Poros Greece 27 J6
Porosozero Rus. Fed. 12 G3
Porpoise Bay Antarctica 76 G2
Porsangerfjorden sea chan. Norway 14 N1
Porsangerhalvøya pen. Norway 14 N1
Porsgrunn Norway 15 F7
Porsuk r. Turkey 27 N5
Portadown U.K. 21 F3
Portaferry U.K. 21 G3
Portage PA U.S.A. 64 B2
Portage WI U.S.A. 63 J3
Portage la Prairie Canada 62 H2
Port Alberni Canada 62 C2
Port Albert Australia 58 C7
Portalegre Port. 25 C4
Portales U.S.A. 62 G5
Port Alfred S. Africa 51 H7
Port Allegany PA U.S.A. 64 B2
Port Alma Australia 56 E4
Port Angeles U.S.A. 62 C2
Port Antonio Jamaica 67 I5
Portarlington Ireland 21 E4
Port Arthur Australia 57 [inset]
Port Arthur U.S.A. 63 I6
Port Askaig U.K. 20 C5
Port Augusta Australia 57 B7
Port-au-Prince Haiti 67 J5
Portavogie U.K. 21 G3
Port Beaufort S. Africa 50 E8
Port Blair India 31 I5
Portbou Spain 25 H2
Port Burwell Ont. Canada 64 A1
Port Campbell Australia 58 A7
Port Campbell National Park Australia 58 A7
Port Chalmers N.Z. 59 C7
Port Charlotte U.S.A. 63 K6
Port-de-Paix Haiti 67 J5
Port Douglas Australia 56 D3
Port Edward S. Africa 51 J6
Porteira Brazil 69 G4
Porteirinha Brazil 71 C1
Portel Brazil 69 H4
Port Elizabeth S. Africa 51 G7
Port Ellen U.K. 20 C5
Port Erin Isle of Man 18 C4
Porterville S. Africa 50 D7
Porterville CA U.S.A. 65 C2
Port Étienne Mauritania see Nouâdhibou
Port Everglades U.S.A. see Fort Lauderdale
Port Fitzroy N.Z. 59 E3
Port Francqui Dem. Rep. Congo see Ilebo
Port-Gentil Gabon 48 A4
Port Glasgow U.K. 20 E5
Port Harcourt Nigeria 46 D4
Porthcawl U.K. 19 D7
Port Hedland Australia 54 B5
Port Herald Malawi see Nsanje
Porthleven U.K. 19 B8
Porthmadog U.K. 19 C6
Port Hope Simpson Canada 61 M4
Port Hueneme CA U.S.A. 65 C3
Port Huron U.S.A. 63 K3
Portimão Port. 25 B5
Port Jackson Australia see Sydney
Port Jackson inlet Australia 58 E4
Port Keats Australia see Wadeye
Port Láirge Ireland see Waterford
Portland N.S.W. Australia 58 D4
Portland Vic. Australia 57 C8
Portland ME U.S.A. 63 M3
Portland OR U.S.A. 62 C2
Portland, Isle of pen. U.K. 19 E8
Portland Bill hd U.K. see Bill of Portland
Portland Roads Australia 56 C2
Port-la-Nouvelle France 24 F5
Portlaoise Ireland 21 E4
Port Lavaca U.S.A. 63 H6
Portlaw Ireland 21 E5
Portlethen U.K. 20 G3
Port Lincoln Australia 57 A7
Port Loko Sierra Leone 46 B4
Port Louis Mauritius 73 L7
Port-Lyautrey Morocco see Kénitra
Port Macquarie Australia 58 F3
Portmadoc U.K. see Porthmadog
Port McNeill Canada 62 B1
Port-Menier Canada 63 O2
Port Moresby P.N.G. 52 E2
Portnaguran U.K. 20 C2
Portnahaven U.K. 20 C5
Port nan Giúran U.K. see Portnaguran
Port Neill Australia 57 B7
Port Nis U.K. see Port of Ness
Port Noarlunga Australia 57 B7
Port Nolloth S. Africa 50 C5
Port Norris NJ U.S.A. 64 D3
Porto Port. see Oporto
Porto Acre Brazil 68 E5
Porto Alegre Brazil 71 A5
Porto Alexandre Angola see Tombua
Porto Amboim Angola 49 B5
Porto Amélia Moz. see Pemba
Porto Artur Brazil 69 G6
Porto Belo Brazil 71 A4
Porto de Moz Brazil 69 H4
Porto de Santa Cruz Brazil 71 C1
Porto dos Gaúchos Óbidos Brazil 69 G6
Porto Esperança Brazil 69 G7
Porto Esperidião Brazil 69 G7
Portoferraio Italy 26 D3
Port of Ness U.K. 20 C2
Porto Franco Brazil 69 I5
Port of Spain Trin. and Tob. 67 L6
Porto Grande Brazil 69 H3
Portogruaro Italy 26 E2
Porto Jofre Brazil 69 G7
Portomaggiore Italy 26 D2
Porto Mendes Brazil 70 F2
Porto Murtinho Brazil 70 E2
Porto Nacional Brazil 69 I6
Porto-Novo Benin 46 D4
Porto Novo Cape Verde 46 [inset]
Porto Primavera, Represa resr Brazil 70 F2
Porto Rico Angola 49 B4
Porto Santo, Ilha de i. Madeira 46 B1
Porto Seguro Brazil 71 D2
Porto Tolle Italy 26 E2
Porto Torres Sardinia Italy 26 C4
Porto União Brazil 71 A4
Porto-Vecchio Corsica France 24 I6
Porto Velho Brazil 68 F5
Portoviejo Ecuador 68 B4
Porto Wálter Brazil 68 D5
Portpatrick U.K. 20 D6
Port Phillip Bay Australia 58 B7
Port Pirie Australia 57 B7
Portreath U.K. 19 B8
Portree U.K. 20 C3
Port Royal VA U.S.A. 64 C3
Portrush U.K. 21 F2
Port Safaga Egypt see Būr Safājah
Port Said Egypt 39 A4
Portsalon Ireland 21 E2
Port Shepstone S. Africa 51 J6
Portsmouth U.K. 19 F8
Portsmouth NH U.S.A. 64 F1
Portsmouth OH U.S.A. 63 K4
Portsmouth VA U.S.A. 64 C4
Portsoy U.K. 20 G3
Port Stanley Falkland Is see Stanley
Port Stephens b. Australia 58 F4
Portstewart U.K. 21 F2
Port St Joe U.S.A. 63 J6
Port St Mary Isle of Man 18 C4
Port Sudan Sudan 32 E6
Port Talbot U.K. 19 D7
Porttipahdan tekojärvi l. Fin. 14 O2
Portugal country Europe 25 C4
Portugália Angola see Chitato
Portuguese East Africa country Africa see Mozambique
Portuguese Guinea country Africa see Guinea-Bissau
Portuguese Timor country Asia see East Timor
Portuguese West Africa country Africa see Angola
Portumna Ireland 21 D4
Portus Herculis Monoeci country Europe see Monaco
Port-Vendres France 24 F5
Port Vila Vanuatu 53 G3
Portville NY U.S.A. 64 B1
Port Vladimir Rus. Fed. 14 R2
Port Waikato N.Z. 59 E3
Port William U.K. 20 E6
Porvenir Bol. 68 E6
Porvenir Chile 70 B8
Porvoo Fin. 15 N6
Posada Spain 25 D2
Posada de Llanera Spain see Posada
Posadas Arg. 70 E3
Posen Poland see Poznań
Poshekhon'ye Rus. Fed. 12 H4
Poshekon'ye-Volodarsk Rus. Fed. see Poshekhon'ye
Posht-e Badam Iran 35 I4
Posht-e Kūh mts Iran 35 G4
Posht Kūh hill Iran 35 H3
Posio Fin. 14 P3
Poso Indon. 41 E8
Posof Turkey 35 F2
Posŏng S. Korea 45 B6
Possession Island Namibia 50 B4
Post U.S.A. 62 G5
Postavy Belarus see Pastavy
Poste-de-la-Baleine Canada see Kuujjuarapik
Postmasburg S. Africa 50 F5
Poston AZ U.S.A. 65 E3
Post Weygand Alg. 46 D2
Postysheve Ukr. see Krasnoarmiys'k
Pota Indon. 54 C2
Poté Brazil 71 C2
Potegaon India 38 D2
Potentia Italy see Potenza
Potenza Italy 26 F4
P'ot'i Georgia 35 F2
Potikal India 38 D2
Potiraguá Brazil 71 D1
Potiskum Nigeria 46 E3
Potomac r. Maryland/Virginia U.S.A. 64 C3
Potosí Bol. 68 E7
Potosi Mountain NV U.S.A. 65 E3
Potrerillos Chile 70 C3
Potsdam Germany 17 N4
Potterne U.K. 19 E7
Potters Bar U.K. 19 G7
Pottstown PA U.S.A. 64 D2
Pottsville PA U.S.A. 64 C2
Pottuvil Sri Lanka 38 D5
Poughkeepsie NY U.S.A. 64 E2
Poulton-le-Fylde U.K. 18 E5
Pouso Alegre Brazil 71 B3
Poŭthĭsăt Cambodia 31 J5
Považská Bystrica Slovakia 17 Q6
Povenets Rus. Fed. 12 G3
Poverty Bay N.Z. 59 F4
Povlen mt. Serbia 27 H2
Póvoa de Varzim Port. 25 B3
Povorino Rus. Fed. 13 I6
Povorotnyy, Mys hd Rus. Fed. 44 D4
Poway CA U.S.A. 65 D4
Powell, Lake resr U.S.A. 62 E4
Powell Mountain NV U.S.A. 65 C1
Powell River Canada 62 C2
Powhatan VA U.S.A. 64 C4
Poxoréu Brazil 69 H7
Poyang Hu l. China 43 L7
Poyarkovo Rus. Fed. 44 C2
Pozantı Turkey 34 D3
Požarevac Serbia 27 I2
Poza Rica Mex. 66 E4
Pozdeyevka Rus. Fed. 44 C2
Požega Croatia 26 F2
Požega Serbia 27 I3
Pozharskoye Rus. Fed. 44 D3
Poznań Poland 17 P4
Pozoblanco Spain 25 D4
Pozo Colorado Para. 70 E2
Pozsony Slovakia see Bratislava
Pozzuoli Italy 26 F4
Prachatice Czech Rep. 17 O6
Prachi r. India 37 F6
Prachuap Khiri Khan Thai. 31 I5
Prades France 24 F5
Prado Brazil 71 D2
Prague Czech Rep. 17 O5
Praha Czech Rep. see Prague
Praia Cape Verde 46 [inset]
Praia do Bilene Moz. 51 K3
Prainha Brazil 69 H4
Prairie Australia 56 D4
Prairie du Chien U.S.A. 63 I3
Prasonisi, Akrotirio pt Greece 27 L7
Prata Brazil 71 A2
Prata r. Brazil 71 A2
Prat de Llobregat Spain see El Prat de Llobregat
Prathes Thai country Asia see Thailand
Prato Italy 26 D3
Pratt U.S.A. 62 H4
Pravdinsk Rus. Fed. 15 L9
Praya Indon. 54 B2
Preble NY U.S.A. 64 C1
Prechistoye Smolenskaya Oblast' Rus. Fed. 13 G5
Prechistoye Yaroslavskaya Oblast' Rus. Fed. 12 I4
Precipice National Park Australia 56 E5
Preeceville Canada 62 G1
Pregolya r. Rus. Fed. 15 L9
Preiļi Latvia 15 O8
Premer Australia 58 D3
Prémery France 24 F3
Prenzlau Germany 17 N4
Přerov Czech Rep. 17 P6
Prescelly Mts hills U.K. see Preseli, Mynydd
Prescott AZ U.S.A. 62 E5
Preseli, Mynydd hills U.K. 19 C7
Preševo Serbia 27 I3
Presidencia Roque Sáenz Peña Arg. 70 D3
Presidente Dutra Brazil 69 J5
Presidente Eduardo Frei research station Antarctica 76 A2
Presidente Hermes Brazil 68 F6
Presidente Olegário Brazil 71 B2
Presidente Prudente Brazil 71 A3
Presidente Venceslau Brazil 71 A3
Presidio U.S.A. 62 G6
Preslav Bulg. see Veliki Preslav
Prešov Slovakia 13 D6
Prespa, Lake Europe 27 I4
Prespansko Ezero l. Europe see Prespa, Lake
Prespes nat. park Greece 27 I4
Prespës, Liqeni i l. Europe see Prespa, Lake
Presque Isle ME U.S.A. 63 N2
Pressburg Slovakia see Bratislava
Presteigne U.K. 19 D6
Preston U.K. 18 E5
Preston ID U.S.A. 62 E3
Preston, Cape Australia 54 B5
Prestonpans U.K. 20 G5
Prestwick U.K. 20 E5
Preto r. Bahia Brazil 69 J6
Preto r. Minas Gerais Brazil 71 B2
Preto r. Brazil 71 D1
Pretoria S. Africa 51 I3
Pretoria-Witwatersrand-Vereeniging prov. S. Africa see Gauteng
Preussisch-Eylau Rus. Fed. see Bagrationovsk
Preußisch Stargard Poland see Starogard Gdański
Preveza Greece 27 I5
Priargunsk Rus. Fed. 43 L2
Pribilof Islands U.S.A. 60 A4
Priboj Serbia 27 H3
Price r. Australia 54 E3
Price UT U.S.A. 62 E4
Pridorozhnoye Rus. Fed. see Khulkhuta
Priekule Latvia 15 L8
Priekuļi Latvia 15 N8
Prienai Lith. 15 M9
Prieska S. Africa 50 F5
Prievidza Slovakia 17 Q6
Prijedor Bos.-Herz. 26 G2
Prijepolje Serbia 27 H3
Prikaspiyskaya Nizmennost' lowland Kazakh./Rus. Fed. see Caspian Lowland
Prilep Macedonia 27 I4
Priluki Ukr. see Pryluky
Primorsk Rus. Fed. 15 P6
Primorsk Ukr. see Prymors'k
Primorskiy Kray admin. div. Rus. Fed. 44 D3
Primorsko-Akhtarsk Rus. Fed. 13 H7
Prince Albert Canada 60 H4
Prince Albert S. Africa 50 F7
Prince Albert Mountains Antarctica 76 H1
Prince Albert Peninsula Canada 60 G2
Prince Albert Road S. Africa 50 E7
Prince Alfred, Cape Canada 60 F2
Prince Alfred Hamlet S. Africa 50 D7
Prince Charles Island Canada 61 K3
Prince Charles Mountains Antarctica 76 E2
Prince Edward Island prov. Canada 63 O2
Prince Edward Islands Indian Ocean 73 K9
Prince Frederick MD U.S.A. 64 C3
Prince George Canada 60 F4
Prince Harald Coast Antarctica 76 D2
Prince of Wales, Cape U.S.A. 60 B3
Prince of Wales Island Australia 56 C1
Prince of Wales Island Canada 61 I2
Prince of Wales Island U.S.A. 60 E4
Prince of Wales Strait Canada 60 G2
Prince Patrick Island Canada 60 G2
Prince Regent Inlet sea chan. Canada 61 I2
Prince Rupert Canada 60 E4
Princess Anne MD U.S.A. 64 D3
Princess Astrid Coast Antarctica 76 C2
Princess Charlotte Bay Australia 56 C2
Princess Elizabeth Land reg. Antarctica 76 E2
Princess Ragnhild Coast Antarctica 76 C2
Princess Royal Island Canada 60 F4
Princeton Canada 62 C2
Princeton NJ U.S.A. 64 D2
Princeton WV U.S.A. 64 A4
Prince William Sound b. U.S.A. 60 D3
Príncipe i. São Tomé and Príncipe 46 D4
Prins Harald Kyst coastal area Antarctica see Prince Harald Coast
Prinzapolca Nicaragua 67 H6
Priozersk Rus. Fed. 12 F3
Priozyorsk Rus. Fed. see Priozersk
Pripet r. Belarus 23 J1
Pripet r. Belarus/Ukr. 13 F6
Pripet Marshes Belarus/Ukr. 13 E6
Pirechnyy Rus. Fed. 14 Q2
Prishtinë Serbia see Priština
Priština Serbia 27 I3
Pritzwalk Germany 17 N4
Privas France 24 G4
Privlaka Croatia 26 F2
Privolzhsk Rus. Fed. 12 I4
Privolzhskaya Vozvyshennost' hills Rus. Fed. 13 J6
Privolzhskiy Rus. Fed. 13 J6
Privolzh'ye Rus. Fed. 13 K5
Priyutnoye Rus. Fed. 13 I7
Prizren Serbia 27 I3
Probus U.K. 19 C8
Proddatur India 38 C3
Professor van Blommestein Meer resr Suriname 69 G3
Progreso Hond. see El Progreso
Progress Rus. Fed. 44 C2
Prokhladnyy Rus. Fed. 13 J8
Prokop'yevsk Rus. Fed. 42 F2
Prokuplje Serbia 27 I3
Proletarsk Rus. Fed. 13 I7
Proletarskaya Rus. Fed. see Proletarsk
Prome Myanmar see Pyè
Promissão Brazil 71 A3
Promissão, Represa resr Brazil 71 A3
Prophet r. Canada 77 A3
Prophet River Canada 60 F4
Propriá Brazil 69 K6
Proskurov Ukr. see Khmel'nyts'kyy
Protem S. Africa 50 E8
Provadiya Bulg. 27 L3
Prøven Greenland see Kangersuatsiaq
Provence reg. France 24 G5
Providence RI U.S.A. 64 F2
Providence, Cape N.Z. 59 A8
Providencia, Isla de i. Caribbean Sea 67 H6
Provideniya Rus. Fed. 29 T3
Provincetown MA U.S.A. 64 F1
Provo U.S.A. 62 E3
Prudentópolis Brazil 71 A4
Prudhoe Bay U.S.A. 60 D2
Prunelli-di-Fiumorbo Corsica France 24 I5
Prusa Turkey see Bursa
Prushkov Poland see Pruszków
Pruszków Poland 17 R4
Prut r. Europe 13 F7
Prydz Bay Antarctica 76 E2
Pryelbrussky Natsional'nyy Park nat. park Rus. Fed. 13 I8
Pryluky Ukr. 13 G6
Prymors'k Ukr. 13 H7
Prymors'ke Ukr. see Sartana
Pryp"yat' r. Ukr. 13 F6 see Pripet
Prypyats' r. Belarus 11 L5 see Pripet
Prypyats' r. Belarus see Pripet
Przemyśl Poland 13 D6
Przheval'sk Kyrg. see Karakol
Psara i. Greece 27 K5
Pskov Rus. Fed. 12 F4
Pskov, Lake Estonia/Rus. Fed. 15 O7
Pskov Oblast admin. div. Rus. Fed. see Pskovskaya Oblast'
Pskovskaya Oblast' admin. div. Rus. Fed. 15 P8
Pskovskoye Ozero l. Estonia/Rus. Fed. see Pskov, Lake
Ptolemaïda Greece 27 I4
Ptolemais Israel see 'Akko
Ptuj Slovenia 26 F1
Puan S. Korea 45 B6
Pucallpa Peru 68 D5
Puchezh Rus. Fed. 12 I4
Puch'ŏn S. Korea 45 B5
Puck Poland 17 Q3
Pudasjärvi Fin. 14 O4
Pudimoe S. Africa 50 G4
Pudozh Rus. Fed. 12 H3
Pudsey U.K. 18 F5
Pudu China see Suizhou
Puduchcheri India see Puducherry
Puducherry India 38 C4
Pudukkottai India 38 C4
Puebla Baja California Mex. 65 E4
Puebla Puebla Mex. 66 E5
Puebla de Sanabria Spain 25 C2
Puebla de Zaragoza Mex. see Puebla
Pueblo U.S.A. 62 G4
Puelches Arg. 70 C5
Puelén Arg. 70 C5
Puente-Genil Spain 25 D5
Puerto Acosta Bol. 68 E7
Puerto Alegre Bol. 68 F6
Puerto Ángel Mex. 66 E5
Puerto Armuelles Panama 67 H7
Puerto Ayacucho Venez. 68 E2
Puerto Bahía Negra Para. see Bahía Negra
Puerto Baquerizo Moreno Galápagos Ecuador 68 [inset]
Puerto Barrios Guat. 66 G5
Puerto Cabello Venez. 68 E1
Puerto Cabezas Nicaragua 67 H6
Puerto Carreño Col. 68 E2
Puerto Casado Para. 70 E2
Puerto Cavinas Bol. 68 E6
Puerto Coig Arg. 70 C8
Puerto Cortés Mex. 66 B4
Puerto Escondido Mex. 66 E5
Puerto Francisco de Orellana Ecuador see Coca
Puerto Frey Bol. 68 F6
Puerto Génova Bol. 68 E6
Puerto Guarani Para. 70 E2
Puerto Heath Bol. 68 E6
Puerto Huitoto Col. 68 D3
Puerto Inírida Col. 68 E3
Puerto Isabel Bol. 69 G7
Puerto Leguízamo Col. 68 D4

Puerto Lempira Hond. 67 H5
Puerto Libertad Mex. 66 B3
Puerto Limón Costa Rica 67 H6
Puertollano Spain 25 D4
Puerto Lobos Arg. 70 C6
Puerto Madryn Arg. 70 C6
Puerto Maldonado Peru 68 E6
Puerto Máncora Peru 68 B4
Puerto México Mex. see Coatzacoalcos
Puerto Montt Chile 70 B6
Puerto Natales Chile 70 B8
Puerto Nuevo Col. 68 E2
Puerto Peñasco Mex. 66 B2
Puerto Pirámides Arg. 70 D6
Puerto Plata Dom. Rep. 67 J5
Puerto Portillo Peru 68 D5
Puerto Prado Peru 68 D6
Puerto Princesa Phil. 41 D7
Puerto Rico Arg. 70 E3
Puerto Rico Bol. 68 E6
Puerto Rico terr. West Indies 67 K5
Puerto Rico Trench sea feature Caribbean Sea 72 D4
Puerto Santa Cruz Arg. 70 C8
Puerto Sastre Para. 70 E2
Puerto Saucedo Bol. 68 F6
Puerto Suárez Bol. 69 G7
Puerto Supe Peru 68 C6
Puerto Vallarta Mex. 66 C4
Puerto Victoria Peru 68 D5
Puerto Visser Arg. 70 C7
Puerto Yartou Chile 70 B8
Puerto Ybapobó Para. 70 E2
Pugachev Rus. Fed. 13 K5
Pugal India 36 C3
Puhiwaero c. N.Z. see South West Cape
Puigmal mt. France/Spain 24 F5
Pukaki, Lake N.Z. 59 C7
Pukapuka atoll Cook Is 53 J3
Pukchin N. Korea 45 B4
Pukch'ŏng N. Korea 45 C4
Pukekohe N.Z. 59 E3
Puketeraki Range mts N.Z. 59 D6
Pukeuri Junction N.Z. 59 C7
Puksubaek-san mt. N. Korea 44 B4
Pula China see Nyingchi
Pula Croatia 26 E2
Pula Sardinia Italy 26 C5
Pulaski NY U.S.A. 64 C1
Pulaski VA U.S.A. 64 A4
Pulicat Lake inlet India 38 D3
Pulivendla India 38 C3
Pulkkila Fin. 14 N4
Pullman U.S.A. 62 D2
Pulozero Rus. Fed. 14 R2
Pulu China 36 E1
Pülümür Turkey 35 E3
Pumasillo, Cerro mt. Peru 68 D6
Puma Yumco l. China 37 G3
Puná, Isla i. Ecuador 68 B4
Punakha Bhutan 37 G4
Punch India 36 C2
Punda Maria S. Africa 51 J2
Pundri India 36 D3
Pune India 38 B2
P'ungsan N. Korea 44 C4
Punjab state India 36 C3
Punjab prov. Pak. 36 B3
Punmah Glacier China/Jammu and Kashmir 36 D2
Puno Peru 68 D7
Punta, Cerro de mt. Puerto Rico 67 K5
Punta Alta Arg. 70 D5
Punta Arenas Chile 70 B8
Punta Balestrieri mt. Italy 26 C4
Punta del Este Uruguay 70 F5
Punta Delgada Arg. 70 D6
Punta Gorda Belize 66 G5
Punta Norte Arg. 70 D6
Puntarenas Costa Rica 67 H6
Punxsutawney PA U.S.A. 64 B2
Puokio Fin. 14 O4
Puolanka Fin. 14 O4
Puqi China see Chibi
Pur r. Rus. Fed. 28 I3
Puracé, Volcán de vol. Col. 68 C3
Puri India 38 E2
Purna r. Mahar. India 36 D5
Purna r. Mahar. India 38 C2
Purnea India see Purnia
Purnia India 37 F4
Purnululu National Park Australia 54 E4
Pursat Cambodia see Poŭthĭsăt
Puruliya India 37 F5
Purus r. Peru 68 F4
Puruvesi l. Fin. 14 P6
Puryŏng N. Korea 44 C4
Pusad India 38 C2
Pusan S. Korea 45 C6
Pusatlı Dağı mt. Turkey 39 A1
Pushchino Rus. Fed. 13 H5
Pushemskiy Rus. Fed. 12 J3
Pushkin Rus. Fed. 12 F4
Pushkino Azer. see Biläsuvar
Pushkinskaya, Gora mt. Rus. Fed. 44 F3
Pushkinskiye Gory Rus. Fed. 15 P8
Pustoshka Rus. Fed. 12 F4
Pusur r. Bangl. 37 G5
Putain Indon. 54 D2
Putao Myanmar 42 H7
Puteoli Italy see Pozzuoli
Puthein Myanmar see Bassein
Putian China 43 L7
Putna r. Romania 27 L2
Putney VT U.S.A. 64 E1
Putorana, Gory mts Rus. Fed. 77 E2
Putrajaya Malaysia 41 C7
Putre Chile 68 E7
Putsonderwater S. Africa 50 E5
Puttalam Sri Lanka 38 C4
Puttalam Lagoon Sri Lanka 38 C4
Puttgarden Germany 17 M3
Putumayo r. Col. 68 D4
Puumala Fin. 15 P6
Pu'uwai U.S.A. 62 [inset]
Puvirnituq Canada 61 K3
Puyang China 43 L5
Puy de Sancy mt. France 24 F4
Puyehue, Parque Nacional nat. park Chile 70 B6
Puysegur Point N.Z. 59 A8
Puzla Rus. Fed. 12 L3
Pweto Dem. Rep. Congo 49 C4
Pwinbyu Myanmar 37 H5
Pwllheli U.K. 19 C6
Pyal'ma Rus. Fed. 12 G3
Pyalo Myanmar 37 H6
Pyandzh Tajik. see Panj
Pyaozero, Ozero l. Rus. Fed. 14 Q3
Pyaozerskiy Rus. Fed. 14 Q4
Pyapali India 38 C3
Pyasina r. Rus. Fed. 28 J2
Pyatigorsk Rus. Fed. 13 I7
Pyatikhatki Ukr. see P"yatykhatky
P"yatykhatky Ukr. 13 G6
Pyay Myanmar see Pyè
Pychas Rus. Fed. 12 L4
Pyè Myanmar 42 H9
Pye, Mount hill N.Z. 59 B8
Pyetrykaw Belarus 13 F5
Pyhäjoki Fin. 14 N4
Pyhäjoki r. Fin. 14 N4
Pyhäntä Fin. 14 O4
Pyhäsalmi Fin. 14 N5
Pyhäselkä l. Fin. 14 P5
Pyi Myanmar see Pyè
Pyin Myanmar see Pyè
Pyingaing Myanmar 37 H5
Pyinmana Myanmar 37 I6
Pyin-U-Lwin Myanmar 37 I5
Pyle U.K. 19 D7
Pyl'karamo Rus. Fed. 28 J3
Pylos Greece 27 I6
Pymatuning Reservoir PA U.S.A. 64 A2
Pyŏktong N. Korea 44 B4
P'yŏnggang N. Korea 45 B5
P'yŏnghae S. Korea 45 C5
P'yŏngsong N. Korea 45 B5
P'yŏngt'aek S. Korea 45 B5
P'yŏngyang N. Korea 45 B5
Pyramid Hill Australia 58 B6
Pyramid Lake U.S.A. 62 D3
Pyramids of Giza tourist site Egypt 34 C5
Pyrénées mts Europe see Pyrenees
Pyrenees mts Europe 25 H2
Pyrénées Occidentales, Parc National des nat. park France/Spain 24 D5
Pyrgos Greece 27 I6
Pyryatyn Ukr. 13 G6
Pyrzyce Poland 17 O4
Pyshchug Rus. Fed. 12 J4
Pytalovo Rus. Fed. 15 O8
Pyxaria mt. Greece 27 J5

Q

Qaa Lebanon 39 C2
Qaanaaq Greenland see Thule
Qabātiya West Bank 39 B3
Qabnag China 37 H3
Qabqa China see Gonghe
Qacentina Alg. see Constantine
Qacha's Nek Lesotho 51 I6
Qādisīyah, Sadd dam Iraq 35 F4
Qadisiyah Dam Iraq see Qādisīyah, Sadd
Qagan China 43 L3
Qagan Nur China 43 K4
Qagan Nur l. China 44 B3
Qagan Us Nei Mongol China 43 K4
Qagan Us Qinghai China see Dulan
Qagbasêrag China 37 H3
Qagcaka China 37 E2
Qahremānshahr Iran see Kermānshāh
Qaidam He r. China 37 H1
Qaidam Pendi basin China 42 G5
Qainaqangma China 37 G2
Qaisar, Koh-i- mt. Afgh. see Qeyṣār, Kūh-e
Qakar China 36 E1
Qal'a Beni Hammad tourist site Alg. 25 I6
Qalā Diza Iraq 35 G3
Qalagai Afgh. 36 B2
Qalansīyah Yemen 33 H7
Qala Shinia Takht Afgh. 36 A2
Qalāt Afgh. see Kalāt
Qal'at al Ḥiṣn Syria 39 C2
Qal'at al Mu'aẓẓam Saudi Arabia 34 E6
Qal'at Bīshah Saudi Arabia 32 F5
Qal'at Muqaybirah, Jabal mt. Syria 39 D2
Qal'eh Dāgh mt. Iran 35 G3
Qal'eh-ye Now Afgh. 33 J3
Qalīb Bāqūr well Iraq 35 G5
Qalyūb Egypt 34 C5
Qalyûb Egypt see Qalyūb
Qamanirjuaq Lake Canada 61 I3
Qamanittuaq Canada see Baker Lake
Qamashi Uzbek. 33 K2
Qamashi Uzbek. see Qamashi
Qamata S. Africa 51 H6
Qamdo China 42 H6
Qandahar Afgh. see Kandahār
Qandarānbāshī, Kūh-e mt. Iran 35 G3
Qandyaghash Kazakh. see Kandyagash
Qangzê China 36 D3
Qapan Iran 35 I3
Qapshagay Kazakh. see Kapchagay
Qapshagay Bögeni resr Kazakh. see Kapchagayskoye Vodokhranilishche
Qapugtang China see Zadoi
Qaqortoq Greenland 61 N3
Qara Āghach r. Iran see Mand, Rūd-e
Qarabutaq Kazakh. see Karabutak
Qara Ertis r. China/Kazakh. see Ertix He
Qaraghandy Kazakh. see Karaganda
Qaraghayly Kazakh. see Karagayly
Qārah Egypt 34 B5
Qārah Saudi Arabia 35 F5
Qarah Bāgh Afgh. 36 B2
Qaraqum des. Turkm. see Karakum Desert
Qara Quzi Iran 35 I3
Qarasu Azer. 35 H2
Qara Şū Chāy r. Syria/Turkey see Karasu
Qara Tarai mt. Afgh. 36 A2
Qarataū Kazakh. see Karatau
Qarataū Zhotasy mts Kazakh. see Karatau, Khrebet
Qara Tikan Iran 35 H3
Qarazhal Kazakh. see Karazhal
Qardho Somalia 48 E3
Qareh Chāy r. Iran 35 H4
Qareh Sū r. Iran 35 G3
Qarhan China 37 H1
Qarkilik China see Ruoqiang
Qarn al Kabsh, Jabal mt. Egypt 34 D5
Qarn el Kabsh, Gebel mt. Egypt see Qarn al Kabsh, Jabal
Qarokŭl l. Tajik. 33 L2
Qarqan China see Qiemo
Qarqan He r. China 42 F5
Qarqaraly Kazakh. see Karkaralinsk
Qarshi Uzbek. 33 K2
Qarshi Uzbek. see Qarshi
Qartaba Lebanon 39 B2
Qārūh, Jazīrat i. Kuwait 35 H5
Qārūn, Birkat l. Egypt 34 C5
Qârûn, Birket l. Egypt see Qārūn, Birkat
Qaryat al Gharab Iraq 35 G5
Qaryat al Ulyā Saudi Arabia 35 G6
Qasigiannguit Greenland 61 M3
Qaşr al Azraq Jordan 39 C4
Qaşr al Farāfirah Egypt 34 B6
Qaşr al Kharānah Jordan 39 C4
Qaşr al Khubbāz Iraq 35 F4
Qaşr 'Amrah tourist site Jordan 39 C4
Qaşr Burqu' tourist site Jordan 39 C3
Qaşr-e Shīrīn Iran 35 G4
Qaşr Farâfra Egypt see Qaşr al Farāfirah
Qassimiut Greenland 61 N3
Qaṭanā Syria 39 C3
Qatar country Asia 32 H4
Qaṭmah Syria 39 C1
Qaṭrūyeh Iran 35 I5
Qaṭṭāfī, Wādī al watercourse Jordan 39 C4
Qaṭṭāra, Rās esc. Egypt see Qaṭṭārah, Ra's
Qattara Depression Egypt 34 B5
Qaṭṭārah, Ra's esc. Egypt 34 B5
Qaṭṭīnah, Buḥayrat resr Syria 39 C2
Qax Azer. 35 G2
Qāyen Iran 33 I3
Qaynar Kazakh. see Kaynar
Qaysīyah, Qā' al imp. l. Jordan 39 C4
Qaysūm, Juzur is Egypt 34 D6
Qayyārah Iraq 35 F4
Qazangödağ mt. Armenia/Azer. 35 G3
Qazaq Shyghanaghy b. Kazakh. see Kazakhskiy Zaliv
Qazaqstan country Asia see Kazakhstan
Qazax Azer. 32 G1
Qazi Ahmad Pak. 36 B4
Qazımämmäd Azer. 35 H2
Qazvīn Iran 35 H3
Qeisûm, Gezâ'ir is Egypt see Qaysūm, Juzur
Qeisum Islands Egypt see Qaysūm, Juzur
Qena Egypt see Qinā
Qeqertarsuaq Greenland 61 M3
Qeqertarsuaq i. Greenland 61 M3
Qeqertarsuatsiaat Greenland 61 M3
Qeqertarsuup Tunua b. Greenland 61 M3
Qeshm Iran 33 I4
Qeydār Iran 35 H3
Qeydū Iran 35 H4
Qeyṣār, Kūh-e mt. Afgh. 33 J3
Qezel Owzan, Rūdkhāneh-ye r. Iran 35 H3
Qeẓi'ot Israel 39 B4
Qian'an China 44 B3
Qian Gorlos China see Qianguozhen
Qianguozhen China 44 B3
Qianjiang Chongqing China 43 J7
Qianjin Heilong. China 44 D3
Qianjin Jilin China 44 C3
Qianqihao China 44 A3
Qian Shan mts China 44 A4
Qiaowa China see Muli
Qiaowan China 42 H4
Qibā' Saudi Arabia 35 G6
Qibing S. Africa 51 H5
Qidukou China 37 H2
Qiemo China 42 F5
Qijiaojing China 42 G4
Qikiqtarjuaq Canada 61 L3
Qila Ladgasht Pak. 33 J4
Qila Saifullah Pak. 33 K3
Qilian Shan mts China 42 H5
Qillak i. Greenland 61 O3
Qiman Tag mts China 37 G1
Qimusseriarsuaq b. Greenland 61 L2
Qinā Egypt 32 D4
Qing'an China 44 B3
Qingdao China 43 M5
Qinggang China 44 B3
Qinggil China see Qinghe
Qinghai prov. China 42 H5
Qinghai Hu salt l. China 42 I5
Qinghai Nanshan mts China 31 I3
Qinghe Heilong. China 44 C3
Qinghe Xinjiang China 42 G3
Qinghecheng China 44 B4
Qingjiang Jiangsu China see Huai'an
Qingjiang Jiangxi China see Zhangshu
Qinglung China 37 G3
Qingshan China see Wudalianchi
Qingshuihe Nei Mongol China 43 K5
Qingshuihe Qinghai China 42 H6
Qingyuan Guangdong China 43 K8
Qingyuan Guangxi China see Yizhou
Qingyuan Liaoning China 44 B4
Qingzang Gaoyuan plat. China see Tibet, Plateau of
Qinhuangdao China 43 L5
Qin Ling mts China 43 J6
Qinzhou China 43 J8
Qionghai China 43 K9
Qiongjiexue China see Qonggyai
Qionglai China 42 I6
Qionglai Shan mts China 42 I6
Qiongzhou Haixia strait China see Hainan Strait
Qiqian China 44 A1
Qiqihar China 44 A3
Qīr Iran 35 I5
Qira China 36 E1
Qîraîya, Wâdi watercourse Egypt see Qurayyah, Wādī
Qiryat Israel 39 B3
Qiryat Shemona Israel 39 B3
Qishon r. Israel 39 B3
Qitab ash Shāmah vol. crater Saudi Arabia 39 C4
Qitaihe China 44 C3
Qixing He r. China 44 D3
Qizilqum des. Kazakh./Uzbek. see Kyzylkum Desert
Qizilrabot Tajik. 36 C1
Qogir Feng mt. China/Jammu and Kashmir see K2
Qog Qi China see Sain Us
Qom Iran 35 H4
Qomdo China see Qumdo
Qomīsheh Iran see Shahrezā
Qomolangma Feng mt. China/Nepal see Everest, Mount
Qomsheh Iran see Shahrezā
Qonāq, Kūh-e hill Iran 35 H4
Qondūz Afgh. see Kunduz
Qonggyai China 37 G3
Qo'ng'irot Uzbek. 33 I1
Qong Muztag mt. China 37 E2
Qongrat Uzbek. see Qo'ng'irot
Qoornoq Greenland 61 M3
Qoqek China see Tacheng
Qo'qon Uzbek. 33 L1
Qorako'l Uzbek. 33 J2
Qorghalzhyn Kazakh. see Korgalzhyn
Qornet es Saouda mt. Lebanon 39 C2
Qorveh Iran 35 G4
Qosh Tepe Iraq 35 F3
Qostanay Kazakh. see Kostanay
Qoubaiyat Lebanon 39 C2
Qowowuyag mt. China/Nepal see Cho Oyu
Qozideh Tajik. 36 B1
Quabbin Reservoir MA U.S.A. 64 E1
Quadros, Lago dos l. Brazil 71 A5
Quaidabad Pak. 36 B2
Quail Mountains CA U.S.A. 65 D3
Quairading Australia 55 B8
Quambatook Australia 58 A5
Quambone Australia 58 C3
Quamby Australia 56 C4
Quan Dao Hoang Sa is S. China Sea see Paracel Islands
Quan Dao Truong Sa is S. China Sea see Spratly Islands
Quang Ngai Vietnam 31 J5
Quan Long Vietnam see Ca Mau
Quantock Hills U.K. 19 D7
Quanzhou Fujian China 43 L8
Quanzhou Guangxi China 43 K7
Qu'Appelle r. Canada 62 G1
Quaqtaq Canada 61 L3
Quartu Sant'Elena Sardinia Italy 26 C5
Quartzite Mountain NV U.S.A. 65 D2
Quartzsite AZ U.S.A. 65 E4
Quba Azer. 35 H2
Quchan Iran 33 I2
Qudaym Syria 39 D2
Queanbeyan Australia 58 D5
Québec Canada 61 K5
Québec prov. Canada 63 L2
Quebra Anzol r. Brazil 71 B2
Queen Adelaide Islands Chile see La Reina Adelaida, Archipiélago de
Queen Anne MD U.S.A. 64 D3
Queen Charlotte Islands Canada 60 E4
Queen Charlotte Sound sea chan. Canada 60 F4
Queen Charlotte Strait Canada 62 B1
Queen Elizabeth Islands Canada 61 H2
Queen Elizabeth National Park Uganda 48 C4
Queen Mary Land reg. Antarctica 76 F2
Queen Maud Gulf Canada 61 H3
Queen Maud Land reg. Antarctica 72 G10
Queen Maud Land reg. Antarctica 76 C2
Queen Maud Mountains Antarctica 76 J1
Queenscliff Australia 58 B7
Queensland state Australia 58 B1
Queenstown Australia 57 [inset]
Queenstown Ireland see Cobh
Queenstown N.Z. 59 B7
Queenstown S. Africa 51 H6
Queimada, Ilha i. Brazil 69 H4
Quelimane Moz. 49 D5
Quellón Chile 70 B6
Quelpart Island S. Korea see Cheju-do
Que Que Zimbabwe see Kwekwe
Querétaro Mex. 66 D4
Querétaro de Arteaga Mex. see Querétaro
Quesnel Lake Canada 62 C1
Quetta Pak. 33 K3
Quetzaltenango Guat. 66 F6
Queuco Chile 70 B5
Quezaltenango Guat. see Quetzaltenango
Quezon City Phil. 41 E6
Quibala Angola 49 B5
Quibaxe Angola 49 B4
Quibdó Col. 68 C2
Quiberon France 24 C3
Quiçama, Parque Nacional do nat. park Angola 49 B4
Quilengues Angola 49 B5
Quillabamba Peru 68 D6
Quillacollo Bol. 68 E7
Quillan France 24 F5
Quill Lakes Canada 62 G1
Quilmes Arg. 70 E4
Quilon India 38 C4
Quilpie Australia 58 B1
Quilpué Chile 70 B4
Quimbele Angola 49 B4
Quimilí Arg. 70 D3
Quimper France 24 B3
Quimperlé France 24 C3
Quinag hill U.K. 20 D2
Quincy IL U.S.A. 63 I4
Quincy MA U.S.A. 64 F1
Quines Arg. 70 C4
Quinga Moz. 49 E5
Quinn Canyon Range mts NV U.S.A. 65 E2
Quinto Spain 25 F3
Quionga Moz. 49 E5
Quipungo Angola 49 B5
Quirima Angola 49 B5
Quirindi Australia 58 E3
Quirinópolis Brazil 71 A2
Quissanga Moz. 49 E5
Quissico Moz. 51 L3
Quitapa Angola 49 B5
Quitilipi Arg. 70 D3
Quito Ecuador 68 C4
Quixadá Brazil 69 K4
Quixeramobim Brazil 69 K5
Qujing China 42 I7
Qulandy Kazakh. see Kulandy
Qulin Gol r. China 44 A3
Qulsary Kazakh. see Kul'sary
Qulyndy Zhazyghy plain Kazakh./Rus. Fed. see Kulundinskaya Step'
Qulzum, Baḥr al Egypt see Suez Bay
Qumar He r. China 42 G6
Qumarheyan China 37 H2
Qumarlêb China see Sêrwolungwa
Qumarrabdün China 37 H2
Qumbu S. Africa 51 I6
Qumdo China 37 H3
Qumrha S. Africa 51 H7
Qumulangma mt. China/Nepal see Everest, Mount
Qundūz Afgh. see Kunduz
Qŭnghirot Uzbek. see Qo'ng'irot
Quntamari China 37 G2
Quoich, Loch l. U.K. 20 D3
Quoile r. U.K. 21 G3
Quoin Point S. Africa 50 D8
Quoxo r. Botswana 50 G2
Qŭqon Uzbek. see Qo'qon
Qurama, Qatorkŭhi mts Asia see Kurama Range
Qurama Tizmasi mts Asia see Kurama Range
Qurayyah, Wādī watercourse Egypt 39 B4
Qurayyat al Milḥ l. Jordan 39 C4
Qŭrghonteppa Tajik. 33 K2
Qusar Azer. 35 H2
Qusmuryn Kazakh. see Kushmurun
Qusum China 36 D2
Quthing Lesotho see Moyeni
Quttinirpaaq National Park Canada 61 K1
Quwayq, Nahr r. Syria/Turkey 39 C2
Quxar China see Lhazê
Quxian Zhejiang China see Quzhou
Quyang China see Jingzhou
Quyghan Kazakh. see Kuygan
Quy Nhơn Vietnam 31 J5
Qūyūn Eshek i. Iran 35 G3
Quzhou China 43 L7
Qypshaq Kōli salt l. Kazakh. see Kypshak, Ozero
Qyrghyz Zhotasy mts Kazakh./Kyrg. see Kirghiz Range
Qyteti Stalin Albania see Kuçovë
Qyzylorda Kazakh. see Kyzylorda
Qyzylqum des. Kazakh./Uzbek. see Kyzylkum Desert
Qyzyltū Kazakh. see Kishkenekol'
Qyzylzhar Kazakh. see Kyzylzhar

R

Raa Atoll Maldives see North Maalhosmadulu Atoll
Raab r. Austria 17 P7
Raab Hungary see Győr
Raahe Fin. 14 N4
Rääkkylä Fin. 14 P5
Raanujärvi Fin. 14 N3
Raasay i. U.K. 20 C3
Raasay, Sound of sea chan. U.K. 20 C3
Raba Indon. 41 D8
Rabang China 36 E2
Rabat Gozo Malta see Victoria
Rabat Malta 26 F7
Rabat Morocco 22 C5
Rabaul P.N.G. 52 F2
Rabbath Ammon Jordan see 'Ammān
Rabbit Flat Australia 54 E5
Rābigh Saudi Arabia 32 E5
Rabnabad Islands Bangl. 37 G5
Râbniţa Moldova see Rîbniţa
Rabocheostrovsk Rus. Fed. 12 G2
Racaka China 37 I3
Race, Cape Canada 72 E2
Race Point MA U.S.A. 64 F1
Rachaïya Lebanon 39 B3
Rachaya Lebanon see Rachaïya
Rachel NV U.S.A. 65 E2
Rach Gia Vietnam 31 J6
Racibórz Poland 17 Q5
Racine WI U.S.A. 63 J3
Rădăuţi Romania 13 E7
Radcliff U.S.A. 63 J4
Radde Rus. Fed. 44 C2
Radford VA U.S.A. 64 A4
Radisson Que. Canada 61 K4
Radlinski, Mount Antarctica 76 K1
Radnevo Bulg. 27 K3
Radom Poland 17 R5
Radom Sudan 47 F4
Radomir Bulg. 27 J3
Radom National Park Sudan 47 F4
Radomsko Poland 17 Q5
Radoviš Macedonia 34 A2
Radstock U.K. 19 E7
Radstock, Cape Australia 55 F8
Radun' Belarus 15 N9
Radviliškis Lith. 15 M9
Radyvyliv Ukr. 13 E6
Rae Bareli India 36 E4
Rae-Edzo Canada 60 G3
Rae Lakes Canada 60 G3
Raeside, Lake salt flat Australia 55 C7
Raetihi N.Z. 59 E4
Rāf hill Saudi Arabia 35 E5
Rafaela Arg. 70 D4
Rafaḥ Gaza see Rafiah
Rafaï Cent. Afr. Rep. 48 C3
Rafḥā' Saudi Arabia 35 F5
Rafiah Gaza 39 B4
Rafsanjān Iran 33 I3
Raga Sudan 47 F4
Ragged, Mount hill Australia 55 C8
Rago Nasjonalpark nat. park Norway 14 J3
Ragusa Croatia see Dubrovnik
Ragusa Sicily Italy 26 F6
Raha Indon. 41 E8
Rahachow Belarus 13 F5
Rahad r. Sudan 32 D7
Rahaeng Thai. see Tak
Rahimyar Khan Pak. 33 L4
Rahovec Serbia see Orahovac
Rahuri India 38 B2
Raiatea i. Fr. Polynesia 75 J7
Raichur India 38 C2
Raiganj India 37 G4
Raigarh Chhattisgarh India 37 E5
Raigarh Orissa India 38 D2
Raijua i. Indon. 54 C2
Railroad Valley valley NV U.S.A. 65 E1
Raimangal r. Bangl. 37 G5
Rainbow Lake Canada 60 G4
Raine Island Australia 56 D1
Rainelle WV U.S.A. 64 A4
Raini r. Pak. 36 B3
Rainier, Mount vol. U.S.A. 62 C2
Rainy Lake Canada/U.S.A. 63 I2
Rainy River Canada 63 I2
Raipur Chhattisgarh India 37 E5
Raipur W. Bengal India 37 F5
Raisen India 36 D5
Raisio Fin. 15 M6
Raitalai India 36 D5
Raivavae i. Fr. Polynesia 75 K7
Raiwind Pak. 36 C3
Rajahmundry India 38 D2
Raja-Jooseppi Fin. 14 P2
Rajanpur Pak. 36 B3
Rajapalaiyam India 38 C4
Rajapur India 38 B2
Rajasthan state India 36 C4
Rajasthan Canal India 36 C3
Rajauri India see Rajouri
Rajevadi India 38 B2
Rajgarh India 36 D4
Rājījovsset Fin. see Raja-Jooseppi
Rajkot India 36 B5
Raj Mahal India 36 C4
Rajmahal Hills India 37 F4
Raj Nandgaon India 36 E5
Rajouri India 36 C2
Rajpipla India 36 C5
Rajpur India 36 C5
Rajpura India 36 D3
Rajputana Agency state India see Rajasthan
Rajsamand India 36 C4
Rajshahi Bangl. 37 G4
Rājū Syria 39 C1
Rajula India 38 A1
Rajur India 38 C1
Rajura India 38 C2
Raka China 37 F3
Rakaposhi mt. Jammu and Kashmir 36 C1
Raka Zangbo r. China see Dogxung Zangbo
Rakhiv Ukr. 13 E6
Rakhni Pak. 33 K3
Rakitnoye Belgorodskaya Oblast' Rus. Fed. 13 G6
Rakitnoye Primorskiy Kray Rus. Fed. 44 D3
Rakiura i. N.Z. see Stewart Island
Rakke Estonia 15 O7
Rakkestad Norway 15 G7
Rakni r. Pak. 36 B3
Rakovski Bulg. 27 K3
Rakushechnyy, Mys pt Kazakh. 35 H2
Rakvere Estonia 15 O7
Raleigh U.S.A. 63 L4
Ralston PA U.S.A. 64 C2
Ramagiri India 38 E2
Ramalho, Serra do hills Brazil 71 B1
Ramallah West Bank 39 B4
Ramanagaram India 38 C3
Ramanathapuram India 38 C4
Ramapo Deep sea feature N. Pacific Ocean 74 F3
Ramapur India 38 D1
Ramas, Cape India 38 B3
Ramatlabama S. Africa 51 G3
Rambhapur India 36 C5
Rambutyo Island P.N.G. 52 E2
Rame Head hd Australia 58 D6
Rame Head hd U.K. 19 C8
Rameshki Rus. Fed. 12 H4
Ramgarh Jharkhand India 37 F5
Ramgarh Rajasthan India 36 B4
Ramgarh Rajasthan India 36 C3
Rāmhormoz Iran 35 H5
Ramingining Australia 54 F3
Ramla Israel 39 B4
Ramlat Rabyānah des. Libya see Rebiana Sand Sea
Ramm, Jabal mts Jordan 39 B5
Ramnad India see Ramanathapuram
Râmnicu Sărat Romania 27 L2
Râmnicu Vâlcea Romania 27 K2
Ramon' Rus. Fed. 13 H6
Ramona CA U.S.A. 65 D4
Ramotswa Botswana 51 G3
Rampart of Genghis Khan tourist site Asia 43 K3
Rampur India 36 D3
Rampur Boalia Bangl. see Rajshahi
Ramree Island Myanmar 37 H6
Rāmsar Iran 35 H3
Ramsele Sweden 14 J5
Ramsey Isle of Man 18 C4
Ramsey U.K. 19 G6
Ramsey NJ U.S.A. 64 D2
Ramsey Bay Isle of Man 18 C4
Ramsey Island U.K. 19 B7
Ramsgate U.K. 19 I7
Rāmshir Iran 35 H5
Ramsing mt. India 37 H3
Ramu Bangl. 37 H5
Ramygala Lith. 15 N9
Ranaghat India 37 G5
Rana Pratap Sagar resr India 36 C4
Ranapur India 36 C5
Ranasar India 36 B4
Rancagua Chile 70 B4
Rancharia Brazil 71 A3
Ranchi India 37 F5
Ranco, Lago l. Chile 70 B6
Rand Australia 58 C5
Randalstown U.K. 21 F3
Randers Denmark 15 G8
Randijaure l. Sweden 14 K3
Randsjö Sweden 14 H5
Råneå Sweden 14 M4
Ranérou Senegal 46 B3
Ranfurly N.Z. 59 C7
Rangamati Bangl. 37 H5
Rangapara India 37 H4
Rangiora N.Z. 59 D6
Rangitata r. N.Z. 59 C7
Rangitikei r. N.Z. 59 E5
Rangke China see Zamtang
Rangôn Myanmar see Rangoon
Rangoon Myanmar 31 I5
Rangpur Bangl. 37 G4
Rangse Myanmar 37 H4
Ranibennur India 38 B3
Raniganj India 37 F5
Ranipur Pak. 36 B4
Raniwara India 36 C4
Rankin's Springs Australia 58 C4
Ranna Estonia 15 O7
Rannes Australia 56 E5
Rannoch, Loch U.K. 20 E4
Ranong Thai. 31 I6
Ranpur India 36 B5
Ranrkan Pak. 36 B3
Rānsa Iran 35 H4
Ransby Sweden 15 H6
Rantasalmi Fin. 14 P5
Rantauprapat Indon. 41 B7
Rantsila Fin. 14 N4
Ranua Fin. 14 O4
Rānya Iraq 35 G3
Ranyah, Wādī watercourse Saudi Arabia 32 F5
Rao Go mt. Laos/Vietnam 42 J9
Raohe China 44 D3
Raoul Island Kermadec Is 53 I4
Rapa i. Fr. Polynesia 75 K7
Rapa-iti i. Fr. Polynesia see Rapa
Rapallo Italy 26 C2
Rapar India 36 B5
Raphoe Ireland 21 E3
Rapidan r. VA U.S.A. 64 C3
Rapid City U.S.A. 62 G3
Rapla Estonia 15 N7
Rapur Andhra Prad. India 38 C3
Rapur Gujarat India 36 B5
Raqqa Syria see Ar Raqqah
Rara National Park Nepal 37 E3
Raritan Bay NJ U.S.A. 64 D2
Raroia atoll Fr. Polynesia 75 K7
Rarotonga i. Cook Is 75 J7
Ras India 36 C4
Rasa, Punta pt Arg. 70 D6
Ra's ad Daqm Oman 33 I6
Ra's al Ḥikmah Egypt 34 B5
Ras al Khaimah U.A.E. see Ra's al Khaymah
Ra's al Khaymah U.A.E. 33 I4
Ra's an Naqb Jordan 39 B4
Ras Dashen mt. Eth. see Ras Dejen
Ras Dejen mt. Eth. 48 D2
Raseiniai Lith. 15 M9
Râs el Hikma Egypt see Ra's al Ḥikmah
Ra's Ghārib Egypt 34 D5
Rashad Sudan 32 D7
Rashīd Egypt 34 C5
Rashîd Egypt see Rashīd
Rashid Qala Afgh. 36 A3
Rashm Iran 35 I4
Rasht Iran 35 H3
Raskam mts China 36 C1
Raskoh mts Pak. 33 K4
Raso, Cabo c. Arg. 70 C6
Raso da Catarina hills Brazil 69 K5
Rason Lake salt flat Australia 55 D7
Rasony Belarus 15 P9
Rasra India 37 E4
Rasshua, Ostrov i. Rus. Fed. 43 S3
Rass Jebel Tunisia 26 D6
Rasskazovo Rus. Fed. 13 I5
Rasul Pak. 36 C2
Ratae U.K. see Leicester
Rätan Sweden 14 I5
Ratanda S. Africa 51 I4
Ratangarh India 36 C3
Rätansbyn Sweden 14 I5
Rat Buri Thai. 31 I5
Rathangan Ireland 21 F4
Rathdowney Ireland 21 E5
Rathdrum Ireland 21 F5
Rathedaung Myanmar 37 H5
Rathenow Germany 17 N4
Rathfriland U.K. 21 F3
Rathkeale Ireland 21 D5
Rathlin Island U.K. 21 F2
Rathluirc Ireland 21 D5
Ratibor Poland see Racibórz
Ratisbon Germany see Regensburg
Ratiya India 36 C3
Ratlam India 36 C5
Ratnagiri India 38 B2
Ratnapura Sri Lanka 38 D5
Ratne Ukr. 13 E6
Ratno Ukr. see Ratne
Raton U.S.A. 62 G4
Rattray Head hd U.K. 20 H3
Rättvik Sweden 15 I6
Rauðamýri Iceland 14 [inset]
Raudhatain Kuwait 35 G5
Raufarhöfn Iceland 14 [inset]
Raukumara Range mts N.Z. 59 F4
Raul Soares Brazil 71 C3
Rauma Fin. 15 L6
Raurkela India 37 F5
Rauschen Rus. Fed. see Svetlogorsk
Rausu Japan 44 G3
Rautavaara Fin. 14 P5
Rautjärvi Fin. 15 P6
Ravānsar Iran 35 G4
Rāvar Iran 33 I3
Ravena NY U.S.A. 64 E1
Ravenglass U.K. 18 D4
Ravenna Italy 26 E2
Ravenna OH U.S.A. 64 A2
Ravensburg Germany 17 L7

Ravenshoe Australia 56 D3
Ravenswood Australia 56 D4
Ravi r. Pak. 36 B3
Rāwah Iraq 35 F4
Rawaki i. Kiribati 53 I2
Rawalpindi Pak. 33 L3
Rawāndiz Iraq 35 G3
Rawicz Poland 17 P5
Rawlinna Australia 55 D7
Rawlins U.S.A. 62 F3
Rawlinson Range hills Australia 55 E6
Rawson Arg. 70 C6
Rawu China 42 H7
Raxón, Cerro mt. Guat. 66 G5
Rayachoti India 38 C3
Rayadurg India 38 C3
Rayagada India 38 D2
Rayagarha India see Rayagada
Rayak Lebanon 39 C3
Raychikhinsk Rus. Fed. 44 C2
Raydah Yemen 32 F6
Rayes Peak CA U.S.A. 65 C3
Rayevskiy Rus. Fed. 11 Q5
Rayleigh U.K. 19 H7
Raymond NH U.S.A. 64 F1
Raymond Terrace Australia 58 E4
Raymondville U.S.A. 62 H6
Rayner Glacier Antarctica 76 D2
Raystown Lake PA U.S.A. 64 B2
Raz, Pointe du pt France 24 B2
Razan Iran 35 H4
Rāzān Iran 35 H4
Razani Pak. 36 B2
Razāzah, Buḩayrat ar l. Iraq 35 F4
Razdan Armenia see Hrazdan
Razdel'naya Ukr. see Rozdil'na
Razdol'noye Rus. Fed. 44 C4
Razeh Iran 35 H4
Razgrad Bulg. 27 L3
Razim, Lacul lag. Romania 27 M2
Razlog Bulg. 27 J4
Razmak Pak. 36 B2
Raz"yezd 3km Rus. Fed. see Novyy Urgal
Ré, Île de i. France 24 D3
Reading U.K. 19 G7
Reading PA U.S.A. 64 D2
Reagile S. Africa 51 H3
Realicó Arg. 70 D5
Réalmont France 24 F5
Reate Italy see Rieti
Rebecca, Lake salt flat Australia 55 C7
Rebiana Sand Sea des. Libya 47 F2
Reboly Rus. Fed. 14 Q5
Rebrikha Rus. Fed. 42 E2
Rebun-tō i. Japan 44 F3
Recherche, Archipelago of the is Australia 55 C8
Rechitsa Belarus see Rechytsa
Rechna Doab lowland Pak. 36 C3
Rechytsa Belarus 13 F5
Recife Brazil 69 L5
Recife, Cape S. Africa 51 G8
Recklinghausen Germany 17 K5
Reconquista Arg. 70 E3
Recreo Arg. 70 C3
Red r. Australia 56 C3
Red r. U.S.A. 63 I5
Red r. Vietnam 42 J8
Red Bank NJ U.S.A. 64 D2
Red Basin China see Sichuan Pendi
Red Bluff U.S.A. 62 C3
Redcar U.K. 18 F4
Redcliffe, Mount hill Australia 55 C7
Red Cliffs Australia 57 C7
Red Deer Canada 62 E1
Red Deer r. Alberta/Saskatchewan Canada 62 E1
Red Deer Lake Canada 62 G1
Reddersburg S. Africa 51 H5
Redding U.S.A. 62 C3
Redditch U.K. 19 F6
Rede r. U.K. 18 E3
Redenção Brazil 69 H5
Redeyef Tunisia 26 C7
Redfield U.S.A. 62 H3
Red Hook NY U.S.A. 64 E2
Redkino Rus. Fed. 12 H4
Red Lake Canada 63 I1
Red Lakes U.S.A. 63 I2
Redlands CA U.S.A. 65 D3
Red Lion PA U.S.A. 64 C3
Red Oak U.S.A. 63 H3
Redondo Port. 25 C4
Redondo Beach CA U.S.A. 65 C4
Red Rock PA U.S.A. 64 C2
Red Sea Africa/Asia 32 D4
Red Wing U.S.A. 63 I3
Redwood City CA U.S.A. 65 A2
Redwood Falls U.S.A. 63 H3
Ree, Lough l. Ireland 21 E4
Reedley CA U.S.A. 65 C2
Reedville VA U.S.A. 64 C4
Reedy WV U.S.A. 64 A3
Reedy Glacier Antarctica 76 J1
Reefton N.Z. 59 C6
Refahiye Turkey 34 E3
Regen Germany 17 N6
Regência Brazil 71 D2
Regensburg Germany 17 N6
Reggane Alg. 46 D2
Reggio Calabria Italy see Reggio di Calabria
Reggio Emilia-Romagna Italy see Reggio nell'Emilia
Reggio di Calabria Italy 26 F5
Reggio Emilia Italy see Reggio nell'Emilia
Reggio nell'Emilia Italy 26 D2
Reghin Romania 27 K1
Regina Canada 62 G1
Régina Fr. Guiana 69 H3
Registro Brazil 70 G2
Registro do Araguaia Brazil 71 A1
Regium Lepidum Italy see Reggio nell'Emilia
Regozero Rus. Fed. 14 Q4
Rehli India 36 D5
Rehoboth Namibia 50 C2
Rehoboth Bay DE U.S.A. 64 D3
Rehovot Israel 39 B4
Reibell Alg. see Ksar Chellala
Reichshoffen France 24 H2
Reid Australia 55 E7
Reidh, Rubha pt U.K. 20 D3
Reigate U.K. 19 G7
Reims France 24 G2
Reinbek Germany 17 M4
Reindeer r. Canada 60 H4
Reindeer Island Canada 62 H1
Reindeer Lake Canada 61 H4
Reine Norway 14 H3
Reinosa Spain 25 D2
Reipholsfjöll hill Iceland 14 [inset]
Reisaelva r. Norway 14 L2
Reisa Nasjonalpark nat. park Norway 14 M2
Reisjärvi Fin. 14 N5
Reitz S. Africa 51 I4
Rekapalle India 38 D2
Relizane Alg. 25 G6
Remarkable, Mount hill Australia 57 B7
Remeshk Iran 33 I4
Remhoogte Pass Namibia 50 C2
Remi France see Reims
Rena Norway 15 G6
Renapur India 38 C2
Rendsburg Germany 17 L3
Renfrew U.K. 20 E5
Rengali Reservoir India 37 F5
Rengo Chile 70 B4
Reni Ukr. 27 M2
Renick WV U.S.A. 64 A4
Renland reg. Greenland see Tuttut Nunaat
Rennell i. Solomon Is 53 G3
Rennes France 24 D2
Rennick Glacier Antarctica 76 H2
Reno r. Italy 26 E2
Reno U.S.A. 62 D4
Renovo PA U.S.A. 64 C2
Réo Burkina 46 C3
Reo Indon. 54 C2
Repalle India 38 D2
Repolka Rus. Fed. 15 P7
Republican r. U.S.A. 62 H4
Republic of South Africa country Africa 50 F5
Repulse Bay b. Australia 56 E4
Repulse Bay Canada 61 J3
Requena Peru 68 D5
Requena Spain 25 F4
Reşadiye Turkey 34 E2
Reserva Brazil 71 A4
Reshteh-ye Alborz mts Iran see Elburz Mountains
Resistencia Arg. 70 E3
Reşiţa Romania 27 I2
Resolute Canada 61 I2
Resolution Island Canada 61 L3
Resolution Island N.Z. 59 A7
Resplendor Brazil 71 C2
Resülayn Turkey see Ceylanpınar
Retalhuleu Guat. 66 F6
Retezat, Parcul Naţional nat. park Romania 27 J2
Retford U.K. 18 G5
Rethel France 24 G2
Réthimnon Greece see Rethymno
Rethymno Greece 27 K7
Retreat Australia 56 C5
Réunion terr. Indian Ocean 73 L7
Reus Spain 25 G3
Reutlingen Germany 17 L6
Reval Estonia see Tallinn
Revda Rus. Fed. 12 G2
Revel Estonia see Tallinn
Revel France 24 F5
Revillagigedo, Islas is Mex. 66 B5
Revillagigedo Island U.S.A. 60 E4
Revivim Israel 39 B4
Rewa India 36 E4
Rewari India 36 D3
Rexburg U.S.A. 62 E3
Reyes, Point CA U.S.A. 65 A1
Reyhanlı Turkey 39 C1
Reykir Iceland 14 [inset]
Reykjanes Ridge sea feature N. Atlantic Ocean 72 F2
Reykjanestá pt Iceland 14 [inset]
Reykjavík Iceland 14 [inset]
Reyneke, Ostrov i. Rus. Fed. 44 E1
Reynolds Range mts Australia 54 F5
Reynosa Mex. 66 E3
Rezā Iran 35 I4
Rezā'īyeh Iran see Urmia
Rezā'īyeh, Daryācheh-ye salt l. Iran see Urmia, Lake
Rēzekne Latvia 15 O8
Rezvāndeh Iran see Rezvānshahr
Rezvānshahr Iran 35 H3
Rhaeader Gwy U.K. see Rhayader
Rhayader U.K. 19 D6
Rhegium Italy see Reggio di Calabria
Rheims France see Reims
Rhein r. Germany see Rhine
Rheine Germany 17 K4
Rhemilès well Alg. 46 C2
Rhin r. France see Rhine
Rhine r. France 24 I2
Rhine r. Germany 17 K5
Rhinebeck NY U.S.A. 64 E2
Rhinelander U.S.A. 63 J2
Rhiwabon U.K. see Ruabon
Rho Italy 26 C2
Rhode Island state U.S.A. 64 F2
Rhodes Greece 27 M6
Rhodes i. Greece 27 M6
Rhodesia country Africa see Zimbabwe
Rhodope Mountains Bulg./Greece 27 J4
Rhodus i. Greece see Rhodes
Rhône r. France/Switz. 24 G5
Rhum i. U.K. see Rum
Rhuthun U.K. see Ruthin
Rhydaman U.K. see Ammanford
Rhyl U.K. 18 D5
Riachão Brazil 69 I5
Riacho Brazil 71 C2
Riacho de Santana Brazil 71 C1
Riacho dos Machados Brazil 71 C1
Rialma Brazil 71 A1
Rialto CA U.S.A. 65 D3
Riasi Jammu and Kashmir 36 C2
Riau, Kepulauan is Indon. 41 C7
Ribadeo Spain 25 C2
Ribadesella Spain 25 D2
Ribas do Rio Pardo Brazil 70 F2
Ribat Afgh. 36 B1
Ribáuè Moz. 49 D5
Ribble r. U.K. 18 E5
Ribblesdale valley U.K. 18 E4
Ribe Denmark 15 F9
Ribeira r. Brazil 71 B4
Ribeirão Preto Brazil 71 B3
Ribérac France 24 E4
Riberalta Bol. 68 E6
Rîbniţa Moldova 13 F7
Ribnitz-Damgarten Germany 17 N3
Říčany Czech Rep. 17 O6
Rice VA U.S.A. 64 B4
Richards Bay S. Africa 51 K5
Richards Inlet Antarctica 76 H1
Richards Island Canada 60 E3
Richardson Mountains Canada 60 E3
Richardson Mountains N.Z. 59 B7
Richfield U.S.A. 62 E4
Richfield Springs NY U.S.A. 64 D1
Richford NY U.S.A. 64 C1
Richgrove CA U.S.A. 65 C3
Richland U.S.A. 62 D2
Richmond N.S.W. Australia 58 E4
Richmond Qld Australia 56 C4
Richmond N.Z. 59 D5
Richmond Kwazulu-Natal S. Africa 51 J5
Richmond N. Cape S. Africa 50 F6
Richmond U.K. 18 F4
Richmond CA U.S.A. 65 A2
Richmond IN U.S.A. 63 K4
Richmond KY U.S.A. 63 K4
Richmond VA U.S.A. 64 C4
Richmond Range hills Australia 58 F2
Richtersveld National Park S. Africa 50 C5
Richwood WV U.S.A. 64 A3
Ricomagus France see Riom
Riddell Nunataks Antarctica 76 E2
Rideau Lakes Canada 63 L3
Ridgecrest CA U.S.A. 65 D3
Ridgway PA U.S.A. 64 B2
Riecito Venez. 68 E1
Riesa Germany 17 N5
Riesco, Isla i. Chile 70 B8
Riet watercourse S. Africa 50 E6
Rietavas Lith. 15 L9
Rietfontein S. Africa 50 E4
Rieti Italy 26 E3
Rifā'ī, Tall mt. Jordan/Syria 39 C3
Rifstangi pt Iceland 14 [inset]
Rift Valley Lakes National Park Eth. see Abijatta-Shalla National Park
Rīga Latvia 15 N8
Riga, Gulf of Estonia/Latvia 15 M8
Rigain Pünco l. China 37 F2
Rīgān Iran 33 I4
Rigas jūras līcis b. Estonia/Latvia see Riga, Gulf of
Rigby U.S.A. 62 E3
Rigside U.K. 20 F5
Riia laht b. Estonia/Latvia see Riga, Gulf of
Riihimäki Fin. 15 N6
Riiser-Larsen Ice Shelf Antarctica 76 B2
Rijau Nigeria 46 D3
Rijeka Croatia 26 F2
Rikuchū-kaigan Kokuritsu-kōen Japan 45 F5
Rikuzen-takata Japan 45 F5
Rila mts Bulg. 27 J3
Rila China 37 F3
Rileyville VA U.S.A. 64 B3
Rillieux-la-Pape France 24 G4
Rimah, Wādī al watercourse Saudi Arabia 32 F4
Rimavská Sobota Slovakia 17 R6
Rimini Italy 26 E2
Rîmnicu Sărat Romania see Râmnicu Sărat
Rîmnicu Vîlcea Romania see Râmnicu Vâlcea
Rimouski Canada 63 N2
Rimsdale, Loch l. U.K. 20 E2
Rinbung China 37 G3
Rincão Brazil 71 A3
Rindal Norway 14 F5
Ringarooma Bay Australia 57 [inset]
Ringas India 36 C4
Ringebu Norway 15 G6
Ringkøbing Denmark 15 F8
Ringsend U.K. 21 F2
Ringsted Denmark 15 G9
Ringtor China 37 E3
Ringvassøya i. Norway 14 K2
Ringwood Australia 58 B6
Ringwood U.K. 19 F8
Rinns Point U.K. 20 C5
Rinqênzê China 37 G3
Río Abiseo, Parque Nacional nat. park Peru 68 C5
Rio Azul Brazil 71 A4
Riobamba Ecuador 68 C4
Rio Bonito Brazil 71 C3
Rio Branco Brazil 68 E6
Rio Branco, Parque Nacional do nat. park Brazil 68 F3
Rio Brilhante Brazil 70 F2
Rio Casca Brazil 71 C3
Rio Claro Brazil 71 B3
Río Colorado Arg. 70 D5
Río Cuarto Arg. 70 D4
Rio das Pedras Moz. 51 L2
Rio de Contas Brazil 71 C1
Rio de Janeiro Brazil 71 C3
Rio de Janeiro state Brazil 71 C3
Río de la Plata-Paraná r. S. America 70 E4
Rio do Sul Brazil 71 A4
Río Gallegos Arg. 70 C8
Río Grande Arg. 70 C8
Rio Grande Brazil 70 F4
Río Grande Mex. 66 D4
Rio Grande r. Mex./U.S.A. 62 H6
Rio Grande City U.S.A. 62 H6
Rio Grande do Sul state Brazil 71 A5
Rio Grande Rise sea feature S. Atlantic Ocean 72 F8
Ríohacha Col. 68 D1
Río Hondo, Embalse resr Arg. 70 C3
Rioja Peru 68 C5
Río Lagartos Mex. 66 G4
Rio Largo Brazil 69 K5
Riom France 24 F4
Río Mansó, Represa do resr Brazil 69 G6
Río Mulatos Bol. 68 E7
Río Muni reg. Equat. Guinea 46 E4
Río Negro, Embalse del resr Uruguay 70 E4
Rioni r. Georgia 35 F2
Rio Novo Brazil 71 C3
Rio Pardo de Minas Brazil 71 C1
Rio Preto Brazil 71 C3
Rio Preto, Serra do hills Brazil 71 B2
Rio Rancho U.S.A. 62 F4
Río Tigre Ecuador 68 C4
Rio Verde Brazil 71 A2
Rio Verde de Mato Grosso Brazil 69 H7
Rio Vista CA U.S.A. 65 B1
Ripky Ukr. 13 F6
Ripley England U.K. 18 F4
Ripley England U.K. 19 F5
Ripley NY U.S.A. 64 B1
Ripoll Spain 25 H2
Ripon U.K. 18 F4
Ripon CA U.S.A. 65 B2
Ripu India 37 G4
Risca U.K. 19 D7
Rishiri-tō i. Japan 44 F3
Rishon Le Ẕiyyon Israel 39 B4
Rising Sun MD U.S.A. 64 C3
Risle r. France 19 H9
Risør Norway 15 F7
Rissa Norway 14 F5
Ristiina Fin. 15 O6
Ristijärvi Fin. 14 P4
Ristikent Rus. Fed. 12 F1
Risum China 36 D2
Ritchie S. Africa 50 G5
Ritscher Upland mts Antarctica 76 B2
Ritsem Sweden 14 J3
Ritter, Mount CA U.S.A. 65 C2
Ritzville U.S.A. 62 D2
Riva del Garda Italy 26 D2
Rivas Nicaragua 67 G6
Rivera Arg. 70 D5
Rivera Uruguay 70 E4
River Cess Liberia 46 C4
Riverhead NY U.S.A. 64 E2
Riverhurst Canada 62 F1
Riverina Australia 55 C7
Riverina reg. Australia 58 B5
Riversdale S. Africa 50 E8
Riverside S. Africa 51 I6
Riverside CA U.S.A. 65 D4
Riversleigh Australia 56 B3
Riverton N.Z. 59 B8
Riverton VA U.S.A. 64 B3
Riverton WY U.S.A. 62 F3
Riverview Canada 63 O2
Rivesaltes France 24 F5
Rivière-du-Loup Canada 63 N2
Rivne Ukr. 13 E6
Rivungo Angola 49 C5
Riwaka N.Z. 59 D5
Riwoqê China see Racaka
Riyadh Saudi Arabia 32 G5
Riza well Iran 35 I4
Rize Turkey 35 F2
Rizokarpaso Cyprus see Rizokarpason
Rizokarpason Cyprus 39 B2
Rjukan Norway 15 F7
Rjuvbrokkene mt. Norway 15 E7
Rkîz Mauritania 46 B3
Roa Norway 15 G6
Roach Lake NV U.S.A. 65 E3
Roade U.K. 19 G6
Road Town Virgin Is (U.K.) 67 L5
Roan Norway 14 G4
Roan Fell hill U.K. 20 G5
Roanne France 24 G3
Roanoke VA U.S.A. 64 B4
Roanoke Rapids U.S.A. 63 L4
Roaring Spring PA U.S.A. 64 B2
Roaringwater Bay Ireland 21 C6
Roatán Hond. 67 G5
Röbäck Sweden 14 L5
Robāţe Tork Iran 35 H4
Robāţ Karīm Iran 35 H4
Robbins Island Australia 57 [inset]
Robe Australia 57 B8
Robe r. Australia 54 A5
Robe r. Ireland 21 C4
Robert Glacier Antarctica 76 D2
Roberts, Mount Australia 58 F2
Roberts Butte mt. Antarctica 76 H2
Robertsfors Sweden 14 L4
Robertsganj India 37 E4
Robertson S. Africa 50 D7
Robertson Bay Antarctica 76 H2
Robertson Island Antarctica 76 A2
Robertson Range hills Australia 55 C5
Robertsport Liberia 46 B4
Roberval Canada 63 M2
Robhanais, Rubha hd U.K. see Butt of Lewis
Robin Hood's Bay U.K. 18 G4
Robinson Range hills Australia 55 B6
Robinson River Australia 56 B3
Robson, Mount Canada 62 D1
Roçadas Angola see Xangongo
Rocca Busambra mt. Sicily Italy 26 E6
Rocha Uruguay 70 F4
Rochdale U.K. 18 E5
Rochechouart France 24 E4
Rochefort France 24 D4
Rochegda Rus. Fed. 12 I3
Rochester Australia 58 B6
Rochester U.K. 19 H7
Rochester MN U.S.A. 63 I3
Rochester NH U.S.A. 64 F1
Rochester NY U.S.A. 64 C1
Rochford U.K. 19 H7
Roc'h Trévezel hill France 24 C2
Rockall i. N. Atlantic Ocean 10 D4
Rockall Bank sea feature N. Atlantic Ocean 72 G2
Rock Creek OH U.S.A. 64 A2
Rockefeller Plateau Antarctica 76 J1
Rockford IL U.S.A. 63 J3
Rockhampton Australia 56 E4
Rockhampton Downs Australia 54 F4
Rockingham Australia 55 A8
Rockingham Bay Australia 56 D3
Rock Island U.S.A. 63 I3
Rockland MA U.S.A. 64 F1
Rocksprings U.S.A. 62 G6
Rockstone Guyana 69 G2
Rockville CT U.S.A. 64 E2
Rockville MD U.S.A. 64 C3
Rockwood PA U.S.A. 64 B3
Rocky Mount VA U.S.A. 64 B4
Rocky Mountains Canada/U.S.A. 62 F3
Rodberg Norway 15 F6
Rødbyhavn Denmark 15 G9
Rodeio Brazil 71 A4
Rodel U.K. 20 C3
Rodeo Arg. 70 C4
Rodez France 24 F4
Ródhos i. Greece see Rhodes
Rodi i. Greece see Rhodes
Rodney, Cape U.S.A. 60 B3
Rodniki Rus. Fed. 12 I4
Rodopi Planina mts Bulg./Greece see Rhodope Mountains
Rodos Greece see Rhodes
Rodos i. Greece see Rhodes
Rodosto Turkey see Tekirdağ
Rodrigues Island Mauritius 73 M7
Roe r. U.K. 21 F2
Roebourne Australia 54 B5
Roebuck Bay Australia 54 C4
Roedtan S. Africa 51 I3
Roe Plains Australia 55 D7
Roeselare Belgium 16 I5
Roes Welcome Sound sea chan. Canada 61 J3
Rogachev Belarus see Rahachow
Rogers Lake CA U.S.A. 65 D3
Roggeveen Basin sea feature S. Pacific Ocean 75 O8
Roggeveld plat. S. Africa 50 E7
Roggeveldberge esc. S. Africa 50 E7
Roghadal U.K. see Rodel
Rognan Norway 14 I3
Roha India 38 B2
Rohnert Park CA U.S.A. 65 A1
Rohrbach in Oberösterreich Austria 17 N6
Rohri Sangar Pak. 36 B4
Rohtak India 36 D3
Roi Georges, Îles du is Fr. Polynesia 75 K6
Rois-Bheinn hill U.K. 20 D4
Roja Latvia 15 M8
Rojas Arg. 70 D4
Rokeby Australia 56 C2
Rokeby National Park Australia 56 C2
Rokiškis Lith. 15 N9
Roknäs Sweden 14 L4
Rokytne Ukr. 13 E6
Rolagang China 37 G2
Rola Kangri mt. China 37 G2
Rolândia Brazil 71 A3
Rolim de Moura Brazil 68 F6
Roll AZ U.S.A. 65 F4
Rolla MO U.S.A. 63 I4
Rollag Norway 15 F6
Rolleston Australia 56 E5
Roma Australia 57 E5
Roma Italy see Rome
Roma Lesotho 51 H5
Roma Sweden 15 K8
Romain, Cape U.S.A. 63 L5
Roman Romania 27 L1
Română, Câmpia plain Romania 27 J2
Romanche Gap sea feature S. Atlantic Ocean 72 G6
Romang, Pulau i. Indon. 41 E8
Romania country Europe 27 K2
Roman-Kosh mt. Ukr. 34 D1
Romanovka Rus. Fed. 43 K2
Romans-sur-Isère France 24 G4
Romanzof, Cape U.S.A. 60 B3
Rombas France 24 H2
Romblon Phil. 41 E6
Rome Italy 26 E4
Rome GA U.S.A. 63 J5
Rome NY U.S.A. 64 D1
Romford U.K. 19 H7
Romilly-sur-Seine France 24 F2
Romney WV U.S.A. 64 B3
Romney Marsh reg. U.K. 19 H7
Romny Ukr. 13 G6
Rømø i. Denmark 15 F9
Romodanovo Rus. Fed. 13 J5
Romorantin-Lanthenay France 24 E3
Romsey U.K. 19 F8
Ron India 38 B3
Rona i. U.K. 20 D1
Ronas Hill U.K. 20 [inset]
Roncador, Serra do hills Brazil 69 H6
Roncador Reef Solomon Is 53 F2
Ronda Spain 25 D5
Ronda, Serranía de mts Spain 25 D5
Rondane Nasjonalpark nat. park Norway 15 F6
Rondon Brazil 70 F2
Rondonópolis Brazil 69 H7
Rondout Reservoir NY U.S.A. 64 D2
Rong Chu r. China 37 G3
Rongelap atoll Marshall Is 74 H5
Rongklang Range mts Myanmar 37 H5
Rongwo China see Tongren
Rongyul China 37 I3
Rönlap atoll Marshall Is see Rongelap
Rønne Denmark 15 I9
Ronneby Sweden 15 I8
Ronne Entrance strait Antarctica 76 L2
Ronne Ice Shelf Antarctica 76 L1
Rooke Island P.N.G. see Umboi
Roorkee India 36 D3
Roosendaal Neth. 16 J5
Roosevelt, Mount Canada 60 F4
Roosevelt Island Antarctica 76 I1
Ropar India see Rupnagar
Roper r. Australia 56 A2
Roper Bar Australia 54 F3
Roquefort France 24 D4
Roraima, Mount Guyana 68 F2
Rori India 36 C3
Røros Norway 14 G5
Rørvik Norway 14 G4
Rosamond CA U.S.A. 65 C3
Rosamond Lake CA U.S.A. 65 C3
Rosario Arg. 70 D4
Rosário Brazil 69 J4
Rosario Baja California Mex. 66 A2
Rosario Sinaloa Mex. 66 C4
Rosario Sonora Mex. 62 F6
Rosario Venez. 68 D1
Rosário do Sul Brazil 70 F4
Rosário Oeste Brazil 69 G6
Rosarito Baja California Mex. 62 E6
Rosarno Italy 26 F5
Roscoff France 24 C2
Roscommon Ireland 21 D4
Roscrea Ireland 21 E5
Rose r. Australia 56 A2
Rose Atoll American Samoa see Rose Island
Roseau Dominica 67 L5
Roseberth Australia 57 B5
Roseburg U.S.A. 62 C3
Rosedale Abbey U.K. 18 G4
Roseires Reservoir Sudan 32 D7
Rose Island atoll American Samoa 53 J3
Rosenberg U.S.A. 63 H6
Rosendal Norway 15 E7
Rosendal S. Africa 51 H5
Rosenheim Germany 17 N7
Roseto degli Abruzzi Italy 26 F3
Rosetown Canada 62 F1
Rosetta Egypt see Rashīd
Roseville CA U.S.A. 65 B1
Rosewood Australia 58 F1
Roshchino Rus. Fed. 15 P6
Rosh Pinah Namibia 50 C4
Roshtkala Tajik. see Roshtqal'a
Roshtqal'a Tajik. 36 B1
Rosignano Marittimo Italy 26 D3
Roşiori de Vede Romania 27 K2
Roskilde Denmark 15 H9
Roslavl' Rus. Fed. 13 G5
Roslyakovo Rus. Fed. 14 R2
Roslyatino Rus. Fed. 12 J4
Ross N.Z. 59 C6
Ross, Mount hill N.Z. 59 E5
Rossano Italy 26 G5
Rossan Point Ireland 21 D3
Ross Carbery Ireland 21 C6
Ross Dependency reg. Antarctica 76 I2
Rossel Island P.N.G. 56 F1
Ross Ice Shelf Antarctica 76 I1
Rössing Namibia 50 B2
Ross Island Antarctica 76 H1
Rossiyskaya Sovetskaya Federativnaya Sotsialisticheskaya Respublika country Asia/Europe see Russian Federation
Rosslare Ireland 21 F5
Rosslare Harbour Ireland 21 F5
Rosso Mauritania 46 B3
Ross-on-Wye U.K. 19 E7
Rossony Belarus see Rasony
Rossosh' Rus. Fed. 13 H6
Ross River Canada 60 E3
Ross Sea Antarctica 76 H1
Røssvatnet l. Norway 14 I4
Rostāq Afgh. 36 B1
Rostāq Iran 35 I6
Rosthern Canada 62 F1
Rostock Germany 17 N3
Rostov Rus. Fed. 12 H4
Rostov-na-Donu Rus. Fed. 13 H7
Rostov-on-Don Rus. Fed. see Rostov-na-Donu
Rosvik Sweden 14 L4
Roswell U.S.A. 62 G5
Rota i. N. Mariana Is 41 G6
Rotch Island Kiribati see Tamana
Rote i. Indon. 41 E9
Roth Germany 17 M6
Rothbury U.K. 18 F3
Rothenburg ob der Tauber Germany 17 M6
Rother r. U.K. 19 G8
Rothera research station Antarctica 76 L2
Rotherham U.K. 18 F5
Rothes U.K. 20 F3
Rothesay U.K. 20 D5
Rothwell U.K. 19 G6
Roti Indon. 54 C2
Roti i. Indon. see Rote
Roto Australia 58 B4
Rotomagus France see Rouen
Rotomanu N.Z. 59 C6
Rotondo, Monte mt. Corsica France 24 I5
Rotorua N.Z. 59 F4
Rotorua, Lake N.Z. 59 F4
Rottenmann Austria 17 O7
Rotterdam Neth. 16 J5
Rottnest Island Australia 55 A8
Rottweil Germany 17 L6
Rotuma i. Fiji 53 H3
Rötviken Sweden 14 I5
Roubaix France 24 F1
Rouen France 24 E2
Roulers Belgium see Roeselare
Roumania country Europe see Romania
Round Hill hill U.K. 18 F4
Round Mountain Australia 58 F3
Roundup U.S.A. 62 F2
Rousay i. U.K. 20 F1
Rouxville S. Africa 51 H6
Rouyn-Noranda Canada 63 L2
Rovaniemi Fin. 14 N3
Roven'ki Rus. Fed. 13 H6
Rovereto Italy 26 D2
Rovigo Italy 26 D2
Rovinj Croatia 26 E2
Rovno Ukr. see Rivne
Rovnoye Rus. Fed. 13 J6
Rovuma r. Moz./Tanz. see Ruvuma
Rowena Australia 58 D2
Rowley Island Canada 61 K3
Rowley Shoals sea feature Australia 54 B4
Równe Ukr. see Rivne
Roxburgh N.Z. 59 B7
Roxburgh Island Cook Is see Rarotonga
Roxby Downs Australia 57 B6
Roxo, Cabo c. Senegal 46 B3
Royal Canal Ireland 21 E4
Royal Chitwan National Park Nepal 37 F4
Royale, Île i. Canada see Cape Breton Island
Royale, Isle i. U.S.A. 63 J2
Royal Natal National Park S. Africa 51 I5
Royal National Park Australia 58 E5
Royal Sukla Phanta Wildlife Reserve Nepal 36 E3
Royan France 24 D4
Roy Hill Australia 54 B5
Royston U.K. 19 G6
Rozdil'na Ukr. 27 N1
Rozivka Ukr. 13 H7
Rtishchevo Rus. Fed. 13 I5
Ruabon U.K. 19 D6
Ruaha National Park Tanz. 49 D4
Ruahine Range mts N.Z. 59 F5
Ruanda country Africa see Rwanda
Ruapehu, Mount vol. N.Z. 59 E4
Ruapuke Island N.Z. 59 B8
Ruatoria N.Z. 59 G3
Ruba Belarus 13 F5
Rub' al Khālī des. Saudi Arabia 32 G6
Rubtsovsk Rus. Fed. 42 E2
Ruby U.S.A. 60 C3
Ruckersville VA U.S.A. 64 B3
Rudall River National Park Australia 54 C5
Rudarpur India 37 E4
Ruda Śląska Poland 17 Q5
Rudauli India 37 E4
Rūdbār Iran 35 H3
Rudkøbing Denmark 15 G9
Rudnaya Pristan' Rus. Fed. 44 D3
Rudnichnyy Rus. Fed. 12 L4
Rudnya Smolenskaya Oblast' Rus. Fed. 13 F5
Rudnya Volgogradskaya Oblast' Rus. Fed. 13 J6
Rudnyy Kazakh. 30 F1
Rudolf, Lake salt l. Eth./Kenya see Turkana, Lake
Rudol'fa, Ostrov i. Rus. Fed. 28 G1
Rudolph Island Rus. Fed. see Rudol'fa, Ostrov
Rūdsar Iran 35 H3
Rue France 19 I8
Rufiji r. Tanz. 49 D4
Rufino Arg. 70 D4
Rufisque Senegal 46 B3
Rufunsa Zambia 49 C5
Rugao China 43 M6
Rugby U.K. 19 F6
Rugby U.S.A. 62 G2
Rugeley U.K. 19 F6
Rügen i. Germany 17 N3
Ruhengeri Rwanda 48 C4
Ruhnu i. Estonia 15 M8
Ruhuna National Park Sri Lanka 38 D5
Rui Barbosa Brazil 71 C1
Ruijin China 43 L7
Ruipa Tanz. 49 D4
Ruiz Mex. 66 C4
Ruiz, Nevado del vol. Col. 68 C3
Rujaylah, Ḩarrat ar lava field Jordan 39 C3
Rūjiena Latvia 15 N8
Ruk is Micronesia see Chuuk
Rukumkot Nepal 37 E3
Rukwa, Lake Tanz. 49 D4
Rum i. U.K. 20 C4
Rum, Jebel mts Jordan see Ramm, Jabal
Ruma Serbia 27 H2
Rumāh Saudi Arabia 32 G4
Rumania country Europe see Romania
Rumbek Sudan 47 F4
Rum Cay i. Bahamas 67 J4
Rum Jungle Australia 54 E3
Rummānā hill Syria 39 D3
Rumphi Malawi 49 D5
Runaway, Cape N.Z. 59 F3
Runcorn U.K. 18 E5
Rundu Namibia 49 B5
Rundvik Sweden 14 K5
Rungwa Tanz. 49 D4
Rungwa r. Tanz. 49 D4
Runton Range hills Australia 55 C5
Ruokolahti Fin. 15 P6
Ruoqiang China 42 F5
Rupa India 37 H4
Rupert r. Canada 63 L1
Rupert WV U.S.A. 64 A4
Rupert Bay Canada 63 L1
Rupert Coast Antarctica 76 J1
Rupert House Canada see Waskaganish
Rupnagar India 36 D3
Rupshu reg. Jammu and Kashmir 36 D2
Ruqqād, Wādī ar watercourse Israel 39 B3
Rural Retreat VA U.S.A. 64 A4
Rusaddir N. Africa see Melilla
Rusape Zimbabwe 49 D5
Ruschuk Bulg. see Ruse
Ruse Bulg. 27 K3
Rusera India 37 F4
Rushden U.K. 19 G6
Rushinga Zimbabwe 49 D5
Rushville NE U.S.A. 62 G3
Rushworth Australia 58 B6
Russell N.Z. 59 E2
Russell PA U.S.A. 64 B2
Russell Bay Antarctica 76 J2
Russell Range hills Australia 55 C8
Russellville AR U.S.A. 63 I4
Rüsselsheim Germany 17 L5
Russia country Asia/Europe see Russian Federation
Russian r. CA U.S.A. 65 A1
Russian Federation country Asia/Europe 28 I3
Russian Soviet Federal Socialist Republic country Asia/Europe see Russian Federation
Russkiy, Ostrov i. Rus. Fed. 44 C4
Russkiy Kameshkir Rus. Fed. 13 J5
Rust'avi Georgia 35 G2
Rustburg VA U.S.A. 64 B4
Rustenburg S. Africa 51 H3
Ruston U.S.A. 63 I5
Rutanzige, Lake Dem. Rep. Congo/Uganda see Edward, Lake
Ruteng Indon. 41 E8
Rutherglen Australia 58 C6

Ruther Glen VA U.S.A. 64 C4
Ruthin U.K. 18 D5
Ruthiyai India 36 D4
Rutka r. Rus. Fed. 12 J4
Rutland VT U.S.A. 64 E1
Rutland Water resr U.K. 19 G6
Rutög China see Dêrub
Rutog Xizang China 37 F3
Rutog Xizang China 42 G7
Rutul Rus. Fed. 35 G2
Ruukki Fin. 14 N4
Ruvuma r. Moz./Tanz. 49 E5
Ruwayshid, Wādī watercourse Jordan 39 C4
Ruwaytah, Wādī watercourse Jordan 39 C5
Ruwenzori National Park Uganda see
  Queen Elizabeth National Park
Ruza Rus. Fed. 12 H5
Ruzayevka Kazakh. 30 F1
Ruzayevka Rus. Fed. 12 J4
Ružomberok Slovakia 17 Q6
Rwanda country Africa 48 C4
Ryābād Iran 35 I3
Ryan, Loch b. U.K. 20 D5
Ryazan' Rus. Fed. 13 H5
Ryazhsk Rus. Fed. 13 I5
Rybachiy, Poluostrov pen. Rus. Fed. 12 G1
Rybach'ye Kyrg. see Balykchy
Rybinsk Rus. Fed. 12 H4
Rybinskoye Vodokhranilishche resr
  Rus. Fed. 12 H4
Rybnik Poland 17 Q5
Rybnitsa Moldova see Rîbniţa
Rybnoye Rus. Fed. 13 H5
Rybreka Rus. Fed. 12 G3
Ryd Sweden 15 I8
Rydberg Peninsula Antarctica 76 L2
Ryde U.K. 19 F8
Rye U.K. 19 H8
Rye r. U.K. 18 G4
Rye Bay U.K. 19 H8
Rykovo Ukr. see Yenakiyeve
Ryl'sk Rus. Fed. 13 G6
Rylstone Australia 58 D4
Ryn-Peski des. Kazakh. 11 P6
Ryukyu Islands Japan 45 B8
Ryūkyū-rettō is Japan see Ryukyu Islands
Ryukyu Trench sea feature N. Pacific Ocean
  74 E4
Rzeszów Poland 13 D6
Rzhaksa Rus. Fed. 13 I5
Rzhev Rus. Fed. 12 G4

S

Sa'ādah al Barşa' pass Saudi Arabia 39 C5
Sa'ādatābād Iran 35 I5
Saale r. Germany 17 M5
Saalfeld Germany 17 M5
Saarbrücken Germany 17 L5
Saaremaa i. Estonia 15 M7
Saarenkylä Fin. 14 N3
Saarijärvi Fin. 14 N5
Saari-Kämä Fin. 14 O3
Saarikoski Fin. 14 L2
Saaristomeren kansallispuisto nat. park
  Fin. see Skärgårdshavets nationalpark
Saarlouis Germany 17 K6
Saatlı Azer. 35 H3
Saatly Azer. see Saatlı
Saba i. Neth. Antilles 67 L5
Sab'a Egypt see Saba'ah
Saba'ah Egypt 39 A4
Sab' Ābār Syria 39 C3
Šabac Serbia 27 H2
Sabadell Spain 25 H3
Sabae Japan 45 E6
Sabana, Archipiélago de is Cuba 67 H4
Şabanözü Turkey 34 D2
Sabará Brazil 71 C2
Sabastiya West Bank 39 B3
Sab'atayn, Ramlat as des. Yemen 32 G6
Sabaudia Italy 26 E4
Sabaya Bol. 68 E7
Sabelo S. Africa 50 F6
Sāberī, Hāmūūn-e marsh Afgh./Iran 33 J3
Şabḩā Jordan 39 C3
Sabhā Libya 47 E2
Sabhrai India 36 B5
Sabi r. India 36 D3
Sabi r. Moz./Zimbabwe see Save
Sabie Moz. 51 K3
Sabie r. Moz./S. Africa 51 K3
Sabie S. Africa 51 J3
Sabinas Mex. 66 D3
Sabinas Hidalgo Mex. 66 D3
Sabini, Monti mts Italy 26 E3
Sabirabad Azer. 35 H2
Sabkhat al Bardawīl Reserve nature res.
  Egypt see Lake Bardawil Reserve
Sable, Cape Canada 61 I5
Sable, Cape U.S.A. 63 K6
Sable Island Canada 61 M5
Sabon Kafi Niger 46 D3
Sabrina Coast Antarctica 76 F2
Sabugal Port. 25 C3
Sabzawar Afgh. see Shindand
Sabzevār Iran 33 I2
Sabzvārān Iran see Jiroft
Sacalinul Mare, Insula i. Romania 27 M2
Săcele Romania 27 K2
Sachigo Lake Canada 63 I1
Sachin India 36 C5
Sachin'ton S. Korea 45 C6
Sach Pass India 36 D2
Sachs Harbour Canada 60 F2
Sacirsuyu r. Syria/Turkey see Säjür, Nahr
Saco ME U.S.A. 64 F1
Sacramento Brazil 71 B2
Sacramento CA U.S.A. 65 B1
Sacramento r. CA U.S.A. 65 B1
Sacramento Mountains U.S.A. 62 F5
Sada S. Africa 51 H7
Sádaba Spain 25 F2
Sá da Bandeira Angola see Lubango
Şadad Syria 39 C2
Şa'dah Yemen 32 F6
Saddat al Hindīyah Iraq 35 G4
Saddle Hill hill Australia 56 D2
Sadêng China 37 H3
Sadiola Mali 46 B3
Sadiqabad Pak. 36 B3
Sad Istragh mt. Afgh./Pak. 36 C1
Sa'dīyah, Hawr as imp. l. Iraq 35 G4
Sado r. Port. 25 B4
Sadoga-shima i. Japan 45 E5
Sadot Egypt see Sadūt
Sadovoye Rus. Fed. 13 J7
Sa Dragonera i. Spain 25 H4
Sadras India 38 C4
Sadūt Egypt 39 B4
Sadut Egypt see Sadūt
Saeby Denmark 15 G8
Saena Julia Italy see Siena
Safad Israel see Zefat
Safāshahr Iran 35 I5
Safed Koh mts Afgh. 35 I3
Safed Koh mts Afgh./Pak. 36 B2
Saffānīyah, Ra's as pt Saudi Arabia 35 H5

Säffle Sweden 15 H7
Safford U.S.A. 62 F5
Saffron Walden U.K. 19 H6
Safi Morocco 22 C5
Safīdār, Küh-e mt. Iran 35 I5
Safīd Küh mts Afgh. see Paropamisus
Safiras, Serra das mts Brazil 71 C2
Şāfītā Syria 39 C2
Safonovo Arkhangel'skaya Oblast' Rus. Fed.
  12 K2
Safonovo Smolenskaya Oblast' Rus. Fed.
  13 G5
Safrā' as Sark esc. Saudi Arabia 32 F4
Safranbolu Turkey 34 D2
Saga China 37 F3
Saga Japan 45 C6
Sagaing Myanmar 37 H5
Sagami-nada g. Japan 45 E6
Sagamore PA U.S.A. 64 F3
Sagar Karnataka India 38 B3
Sagar Karnataka India 38 B3
Sagar Madh. Prad. India 36 D5
Sagaredzho Georgia see Sagarejo
Sagarejo Georgia 35 G2
Sagar Island India 37 G5
Sagarmatha mt. Nepal see Everest, Mount
Sagarmatha National Park Nepal 37 F4
Sagastyr Rus. Fed. 29 N2
Sagavanirktok r. U.S.A. 60 D2
Saggi, Har mt. Israel 39 B4
Saghand Iran 35 I4
Saginaw U.S.A. 63 K3
Saginaw Bay U.S.A. 63 K3
Saglouc Canada see Salluit
Sagone, Golfe de b. Corsica France 24 I5
Sagres Port. 25 B5
Sagthale India 36 C5
Sagua la Grande Cuba 67 H4
Saguenay r. Canada 63 N2
Sagunt Spain see Sagunto
Sagunto Spain 25 F4
Saguntum Spain see Sagunto
Sahagún Spain 25 D2
Sahand, Kūh-e mt. Iran 35 G3
Sahara des. Africa 46 D3
Şaḩarā el Gharbîya des. Egypt see
  Western Desert
Şaḩarā el Sharqîya des. Egypt see
  Eastern Desert
Saharan Atlas mts Alg. see Atlas Saharien
Saharanpur India 36 D3
Sahara Well Australia 54 C5
Saharsa India 37 F4
Sahaswan India 36 D3
Sahat, Kūh-e hill Iran 35 I4
Sahatwar India 37 F4
Sahdol India see Shahdol
Sahebganj India see Sahibganj
Sahebgunj India see Sahibganj
Saheira, Wādī el watercourse Egypt see
  Suhaymī, Wādī as
Sahel reg. Africa 46 C3
Sahibganj India 37 F4
Sahiwal Pak. 36 C3
Sahlābād Iran 33 I3
Şaḩneh Iran 35 G3
Sahuayo Mex. 66 D4
Sahuteng China see Zadoi
Sahyadri mts India see Western Ghats
Sahyadriparvat Range hills India 38 B1
Sai r. India 37 E4
Saïda Alg. 25 G6
Saida Lebanon see Sidon
Saidia Morocco 25 E6
Sa'īdīyeh Iran see Solţānīyeh
Saidpur Bangl. 37 G4
Saiha India 37 H5
Saihan Tal China 43 K4
Saijō Japan 45 D6
Saikai National Park Japan 45 C6
Saiki India 36 C5
Sailana India 36 C5
Saimaa l. Fin. 15 P6
Saimbeyli Turkey 34 E3
Sa'in Qal'eh Iran see Sa'indezh
Sa'indezh Iran 35 G3
St Abb's Head hd U.K. 20 G5
St Agnes U.K. 19 B8
St Agnes i. U.K. 19 B8
St Albans U.K. 19 G7
St Aldhelm's Head hd U.K. 19 E8
St-Amand-Montrond France 24 F3
St-Amour France 24 G3
St-André, Cap c. Madag. see
  Vilanandro, Tanjona
St Andrews U.K. 20 G4
St Ann's Bay Jamaica 67 I5
St Anthony Canada 61 M4
St Anthony U.S.A. 62 E3
St-Arnaud Alg. see El Eulma
St Arnaud Australia 58 B6
St Arnaud Range mts N.Z. 59 D6
St Augustin r. Canada 61 M4
St Augustine U.S.A. 63 K6
St Austell U.K. 19 C8
St-Avertin France 24 E3
St-Barthélemy i. West Indies 67 L5
St Bees U.K. 18 D4
St Bees Head hd U.K. 18 D4
St Bride's Bay U.K. 19 B7
St-Brieuc France 24 C2
St Catharines Ont. Canada 64 F1
St Catherine's Point U.K. 19 F8
St-Céré France 24 E4
St-Chamond France 24 G4
St Charles MD U.S.A. 64 C3
St Charles MO U.S.A. 63 I4
St-Chély-d'Apcher France 24 F4
St Christopher and Nevis country
  West Indies see St Kitts and Nevis
St Clair, Lake Canada/U.S.A. 63 K3
St-Claude France 24 G3
St Clears U.K. 19 C7
St Cloud U.S.A. 63 I2
St Croix i. U.S.A. 63 I2
St David's Head hd U.K. 19 B7
St-Denis Réunion 73 L7
St-Denis-du-Sig Alg. see Sig
St-Dié France 24 H2
St-Dizier France 24 G2
St-Domingue country West Indies see Haiti
St Elias, Cape U.S.A. 60 D4
St Elias Mountains Canada 60 D3
Ste-Marie, Cap c. Madag. see
  Vohimena, Tanjona
Sainte-Marie, Île i. Madag. see
  Boraha, Nosy
Ste-Maxime France 24 H5
Sainte Rose du Lac Canada 62 H1
Saintes France 24 D4
St-Étienne France 24 G4
St-Étienne-du-Rouvray France 19 I9
Saintfield U.K. 21 G3
St-Florent Corsica France 24 I5
St-Florent-sur-Cher France 24 F3
St Floris, Parc National nat. park
  Cent. Afr. Rep. 48 C3
St-Flour France 24 F4
St Francis U.S.A. 62 C4
St Francis Isles Australia 55 F8

St-Gaudens France 24 E5
St George Australia 58 D2
St George r. Australia 56 D3
Sakar mts Bulg. 27 L4
Sakaraha Madag. 49 E6
Sak'art'velo country Asia see Georgia
Sakarya r. Turkey 27 N4
Sakassou Côte d'Ivoire 46 C4
Sakata Japan 45 E5
Sakchu N. Korea 45 B4
Sakhalin i. Rus. Fed. 44 F2
Sakhalin Oblast' admin. div. Rus. Fed. see
  Sakhalinskaya Oblast'
Sakhalinskaya Oblast' admin. div. Rus. Fed.
  44 F2
Sakhalinskiy Zaliv b. Rus. Fed. 44 F1
Sakhi India 36 C3
Sakhile S. Africa 51 I4
Šāki Azer. 35 G2
Saki Nigeria see Shaki
Saki Ukr. see Saky
Šakiai Lith. 15 M9
Sakir mt. Pak. 36 A3
Sakishima-shotō is Japan 43 M8
Sakoli India 36 D5
Sakon Nakhon Thai. 31 J5
Sakrivier S. Africa 50 E6
Sakura Japan 45 F6
Saky Ukr. 34 D1
Säkylä Fin. 15 M6
Sal i. Cape Verde 46 [inset]
Sal r. Rus. Fed. 13 I7
Sala Sweden 15 J7
Sala Consilina Italy 26 F4
Saladas Arg. 70 E3
Salado r. Buenos Aires Arg. 70 E5
Salado r. Santa Fé Arg. 70 D4
Salado r. Arg. 70 C5
Salaga Ghana 46 C4
Salairskiy Kryazh ridge Rus. Fed. 42 E2
Salajwe Botswana 50 G2
Şalālah Oman 33 H6
Salamanca Mex. see Samarskoye
Salamanca Spain 25 D3
Salamanga Moz. 51 K4
Salamantica Spain see Salamanca
Salamat, Bahr r. Chad 47 E4
Salamina i. Greece 27 J6
Salamis tourist site Cyprus 39 A2
Salamís i. Greece see Salamina
Salamīyah Syria 39 C2
Salang Tunnel Afgh. 36 B2
Salantai Lith. 15 L8
Salar de Pocitos Arg. 70 C2
Salas Spain 25 C2
Salaspils Latvia 15 N8
Salawati i. Indon. 41 I7
Salaya Indon. 41 E8
Salayar i. Indon. 41 E8
Sala y Gómez, Isla i. S. Pacific Ocean
  75 N7
Salazar Angola see N'dalatando
Salbris France 24 F3
Šalčininkai Lith. 15 N9
Salcombe U.K. 19 D8
Saldae Alg. see Bejaïa
Saldaña Spain 25 D2
Saldanha S. Africa 50 C7
Saldanha Bay S. Africa 50 C7
Saldus Latvia 15 M8
Sale Australia 58 C7
Salé Morocco 22 C5
Salehard Rus. Fed. 28 H3
Salem India 38 C4
Salem MA U.S.A. 64 F1
Salem NJ U.S.A. 64 D3
Salem NY U.S.A. 64 E1
Salem OH U.S.A. 64 A2
Salem OR U.S.A. 62 C3
Salem VA U.S.A. 64 A4
Salen Scotland U.K. 20 D4
Salen Scotland U.K. 20 D4
Salerno Italy 26 F4
Salerno, Golfo di g. Italy 26 F4
Salernum Italy see Salerno
Salford U.K. 18 E5
Salgótarján Hungary 17 Q6
Salgueiro Brazil 69 K5
Salida U.S.A. 62 F4
Salies-de-Béarn France 24 D5
Salihli Turkey 27 M5
Salihorsk Belarus 15 O10
Salima Malawi 49 D5
Salina i. Isole Lipari Italy 26 F5
Salina KS U.S.A. 62 H4
Salina UT U.S.A. 62 E4
Salina Cruz Mex. 66 E5
Salinas Ecuador 68 B4
Salinas Mex. 66 D4
Salinas r. Mex. 67 G5
Salinas CA U.S.A. 65 B2
Salinas r. CA U.S.A. 65 B2
Salinas, Cabo de c. Spain see
  Ses Salines, Cap de
Salinas, Ponta das pt Angola 49 B5
Saline Valley depr. CA U.S.A. 65 D2
Salinópolis Brazil 69 I4
Salinosó Lachay, Punta pt Peru 68 C6
Salisbury U.K. 19 F7
Salisbury MD U.S.A. 64 D4
Salisbury Zimbabwe see Harare
Salisbury Plain U.K. 19 E7
Salkhad Syria 39 C3
Salla Fin. 14 P3
Salluit Canada 77 K2
Sallum, Khalīj as b. Egypt see
  Sallum, Khalīj el
Sallyana Nepal 37 E3
Salmās Iran 35 G3
Salmi Rus. Fed. 12 G3
Salmo Canada 62 D2
Salmon U.S.A. 62 E2
Salmon r. U.S.A. 62 D2
Salmon Arm Canada 62 C5
Salmon Gums Australia 55 C8
Salmon Reservoir NY U.S.A. 64 D1
Salmon River Mountains U.S.A. 62 D3
Salo Fin. 15 M6
Salome AZ U.S.A. 65 D4
Salon India 36 E4
Salon-de-Provence France 24 G5
Salonica Greece see Thessaloniki
Salonika Greece see Thessaloniki
Salpausselkä reg. Fin. 15 N6
Salqin Syria 39 C1
Salses, Étang de l. France see
  Leucate, Étang de
Sal'sk Rus. Fed. 13 I7
Salt Jordan see As Salţ
Salt r. S. Africa 51 J2
Salt r. AZ U.S.A. 62 E5
Salta Arg. 70 C2
Saltaire U.K. 18 F5
Saltash U.K. 19 C8
Saltcoats U.K. 20 E5
Saltee Islands Ireland 21 F5
Saltfjellet Svartisen Nasjonalpark nat. park
  Norway 14 I3
Saltfjorden sea chan. Norway 14 H3
Salt Fork Lake OH U.S.A. 64 A2

Saltillo Mex. 66 D3
Salt Lake City U.S.A. 62 E3
Salto Brazil 71 B3
Salto Uruguay 70 E4
Salto da Divisa Brazil 71 D2
Salto Grande Brazil 71 A3
Salton Sea salt l. CA U.S.A. 65 E4
Salto Santiago, Represa de resr Brazil 70 F3
Salt Range hills Pak. 36 C2
Saluda VA U.S.A. 64 C4
Şalūm Egypt see As Sallūm
Salūm, Khalīg el b. Egypt see
  Sallum, Khalīj as
Salur India 38 D2
Saluzzo Italy 26 B2
Salvador Brazil 71 D1
Salvador country Central America see
  El Salvador
Salvaleón de Higüey Dom. Rep. see Higüey
Salwah Saudi Arabia 48 F1
Salween r. China/Myanmar 31 I4
Salween r. China/Myanmar 42 H9
Salyan Azer. 35 H3
Salyan Nepal see Sallyana
Sal'yany Azer. see Salyan
Salzbrunn Namibia 50 C3
Salzburg Austria 17 N7
Salzgitter Germany 17 M4
Sam India 36 B4
Samagaltay Rus. Fed. 42 G2
Samāh well Saudi Arabia 35 G5
Samaida Iran see Someydeh
Samaixung China 37 E2
Samalayuca Mex. 62 F5
Samalkot India 38 D2
Samālūţ Egypt 34 C5
Samālūţ Egypt see Samālūţ
Samanala mt. Sri Lanka see Adam's Peak
Samandağ Turkey 39 B1
Samangān Afgh. see Aybak
Samani Japan 44 F4
Samanlı Dağları mts Turkey 27 M4
Samar i. Phil. 41 H4
Samar Rus. Fed. 13 K5
Samara r. Rus. Fed. 11 Q5
Samarga Rus. Fed. 44 E3
Samarinda Indon. 41 D8
Samarka Rus. Fed. 44 D3
Samarobriva France see Amiens
Samarqand Uzbek. 33 K2
Samarqand Uzbek. see Samarqand
Sāmarrā' Iraq 35 F4
Samarskoye Kazakh. 42 E3
Samasata Pak. 36 B3
Samastipur India 37 F4
Şamaxı Azer. 35 H2
Samba Jammu and Kashmir 36 C2
Sambalung mts Indon. 41 D7
Sambalpur India 37 E5
Sambar, Tanjung pt Indon. 41 D8
Sambat Ukr. see Kiev
Sambava Madag. 49 F5
Sambhajinagar India see Aurangabad
Sambhal India 36 D3
Sambhar Lake India 36 C4
Sambir Ukr. 13 D6
Sambito r. Brazil 69 J5
Sambor Ukr. see Sambir
Samborombón, Bahía b. Arg. 70 E5
Samch'ŏk S. Korea 45 C5
Samch'ŏnp'o S. Korea see Sach'on
Same Tanz. 48 D4
Samer France 19 I8
Sami India 36 B5
Samīrah Saudi Arabia 32 F4
Samirum Iran see Yazd-e Khvāst
Samjiyŏn N. Korea 45 C4
Şämkir Azer. 35 G2
Sam Neua Laos see Xam Nua
Samoa country S. Pacific Ocean 53 I3
Samoa Basin sea feature S. Pacific Ocean
  74 I7
Samoa i Sisifo country S. Pacific Ocean see
  Samoa
Samobor Croatia 26 F2
Samoded Rus. Fed. 12 I3
Šamorín Slovakia 17 P6
Samos i. Greece 27 L6
Samothrace i. Greece see Samothraki
Samothraki i. Greece 27 K4
Samoylovka Rus. Fed. 13 I6
Sampit Indon. 41 D8
Sam Rayburn Reservoir U.S.A. 63 I5
Samsang China 37 F3
Samsun Turkey 34 E2
Samyai China 37 G3
Sama Mali 46 C3
Şan'ā' Yemen 32 F6
Sanaa Malawi see Şan'ā'
SANAE research station Antarctica 76 B2
San Agostín U.S.A. see St Augustine
Sanak Island U.S.A. 60 B4
Sanandaj Iran 35 G3
San Andreas CA U.S.A. 65 B1
San Andrés, Isla de i. Caribbean Sea 67 H6
San Angelo U.S.A. 62 G5
San Antonio Chile 70 B4
San Antonio TX U.S.A. 62 H6
San Antonio, Cabo c. Cuba 67 H4
San Antonio Oeste Arg. 70 D6
San Antonio Reservoir CA U.S.A. 65 B3
San Augustín de Valle Fértil Arg. 70 C4
San Benedetto del Tronto Italy 26 E3
San Benedicto, Isla i. Mex. 66 B5
San Benito r. CA U.S.A. 65 B2
San Benito Mountain CA U.S.A. 65 B2
San Bernardino CA U.S.A. 65 D3
San Bernardino Mountains CA U.S.A.
  65 D3
San Bernardo Chile 70 B4
San Blas, Cape U.S.A. 63 J6
San Borja Bol. 68 E6
Sanbornville NH U.S.A. 64 F1
San Buenaventura Mex. 66 D3
San Carlos Chile 70 B5
San Carlos Equat. Guinea see Luba
San Carlos Venez. 68 E2
San Carlos de Bariloche Arg. 70 B6
San Carlos de Bolívar Arg. 70 D5
Sanchahe China see Fuyu
Sanchi India 36 D5
Sanchor India 36 B4
San Clemente CA U.S.A. 65 D4
San Clemente Island CA U.S.A. 65 C5
San Cristóbal Arg. 70 D4
San Cristóbal i. Solomon Is 53 I3
San Cristóbal Venez. 68 D2
San Cristóbal, Isla i. Galápagos Ecuador
  68 [inset]
San Cristóbal de las Casas Mex. 66 F5
Sancti Spíritus Cuba 67 I4
Sand r. S. Africa 51 J2
Sandagou Rus. Fed. 44 D4
Sanda Island U.K. 20 D5
Sandakan Sabah Malaysia 41 D7
Sandane Norway 14 E6
Sandanski Bulg. 27 J4

Sandaré Mali 46 B3
Sanday i. U.K. 20 G1
Sandbach U.K. 19 E5
Sand Cay reef India 38 B4
Sandefjord Norway 15 G7
Sandercock Nunataks Antarctica 76 D2
Sanderson U.S.A. 62 G6
Sandfire Roadhouse Australia 54 C4
Sand Fork WV U.S.A. 64 A3
Sandgate Australia 58 F1
Sandhead U.K. 20 E6
Sandia Peru 68 E6
San Diego CA U.S.A. 65 D4
Sandıklı Turkey 27 N5
Sandila India 36 E4
Sandnes Norway 15 D7
Sandnessjøen Norway 14 H3
Sando i. Faroe Is see Sandoy
Sandoa Dem. Rep. Congo 49 C4
Sandomierz Poland 13 D6
San Donà di Piave Italy 26 E2
Sandover watercourse Australia 56 B4
Sandovo Rus. Fed. 12 H4
Sandown U.K. 19 F8
Sandoy i. Faroe Is 14 [inset]
Sand Point U.S.A. 60 B4
Sandpoint U.S.A. 62 D2
Sandray i. U.K. 20 B4
Sandringham Australia 56 B5
Şandrul Mare, Vârful mt. Romania 27 L1
Šandsjö Sweden 15 I6
Sandstone Australia 55 B6
Sandur Faroe Is 14 [inset]
Sandusky OH U.S.A. 63 K3
Sandveld mts S. Africa 50 D6
Sandverhaar Namibia 50 C4
Sandvika Akershus Norway 15 G7
Sandvika Nord-Trøndelag Norway 14 H5
Sandviken Sweden 15 J6
Sandwich Island Vanuatu see Éfaté
Sandwich Islands N. Pacific Ocean see
  Hawai'ian Islands
Sandwick U.K. 20 [inset]
Sandwip Bangl. 37 G5
Sandy Cape Qld Australia 56 F5
Sandy Cape Tas. Australia 57 [inset]
Sandy Hook pt NJ U.S.A. 64 D2
Sandy Island Australia 54 C3
Sandy Lake Ont. Canada 63 I1
Sandy Lake Ont. Canada 63 I1
San Estanislao Para. 70 E2
San Felipe Chile 70 B4
San Felipe Baja California Mex. 66 B2
San Felipe Venez. 68 E1
San Felipe de Puerto Plata Dom. Rep. see
  Puerto Plata
San Fernando Chile 70 B4
San Fernando Mex. 66 E4
San Fernando Phil. 41 E6
San Fernando Spain 25 C5
San Fernando Trin. and Tob. 67 L6
San Fernando CA U.S.A. 65 D3
San Fernando de Apure Venez. 68 E2
San Fernando de Atabapo Venez. 68 E2
San Fernando de Monte Cristi Dom. Rep.
  see Monte Cristi
Sanford FL U.S.A. 63 K6
Sanford ME U.S.A. 64 F1
Sanford NC U.S.A. 63 L4
Sanford, Mount U.S.A. 60 D3
San Francisco Arg. 70 D4
San Francisco CA U.S.A. 65 A2
San Francisco, Cabo de c. Ecuador 68 B3
San Francisco, Passo de pass Arg./Chile
  70 C3
San Francisco Bay inlet CA U.S.A. 65 A2
San Francisco de Paula, Cabo c. Arg. 70 C7
San Francisco Javier Spain 25 G4
San Gabriel Mountains CA U.S.A. 65 C3
Sangachaly Azer. see Sanqaçal
Sangameshwar India 38 B2
Sangan, Koh-i- mt. Afgh. see Sangān, Kūh-e
Sangān, Kūh-e mt. Afgh. 36 A2
Sangar Rus. Fed. 29 N3
Sangareddi India 38 C2
Sangareddy India see Sangareddi
San Gavino Monreale Sardinia Italy 26 C4
Sangay, Parque Nacional nat. park Ecuador
  68 C4
Sangeang i. Indon. 54 B2
Sanger CA U.S.A. 65 C2
Sang-e Surakh Iran 35 I3
Sangilen, Nagor'ye mts Rus. Fed. 42 H2
San Giovanni in Fiore Italy 26 G5
Sangir i. Indon. 41 H6
Sangir, Kepulauan is Indon. 41 I7
Sangiyn Dalay Mongolia 42 I3
Sangkulirang Indon. 41 D7
Sangli India 38 B2
Sangmai China see Dêrong
Sangmélima Cameroon 46 E4
Sango Zimbabwe 49 D6
Sangole India 38 B2
San Gorgonio Mountain CA U.S.A. 65 D3
Sangre de Cristo Range mts U.S.A. 62 F4
Sangrur India 36 C3
Sanguem India 38 B3
Sangutane r. Moz. 51 K3
San Hipólito, Punta pt Mex. 66 B3
Sanhür Egypt 34 C5
Sanhür Egypt see Sanhür
San Ignacio Santa Cruz Bol. 68 F7
San Ignacio Beni Bol. 68 E6
San Ignacio Para. 70 E3
Sanikiluaq Canada 61 K4
Sanin-kaigan Kokuritsu-köen Japan 45 D6
San Jacinto CA U.S.A. 65 D4
San Jacinto Peak CA U.S.A. 65 D4
San Javier Bol. 68 F7
Sanjeli India 36 C5
San Joaquin r. CA U.S.A. 65 B1
San Joaquin Valley valley CA U.S.A. 65 B2
San Jorge, Golfo de g. Arg. 70 C7
San Jorge, Golfo de g. Spain see
  Sant Jordi, Golf de
Sanjō Japan 45 E5
San Joaquín r. CA U.S.A. 65 B1
San José Costa Rica 67 H7
San José Phil. 41 E6
San José, Isla i. Mex. 66 B4
San José de Amacuro Venez. 68 F2
San José de Bavicora Mex. 62 F6
San José de Buenavista Phil. 41 E6
San José de Chiquitos Bol. 68 F7
San José de Comondú Mex. 66 B3
San José del Cabo Mex. 66 C4
San José del Guaviare Col. 68 D3
San José de Mayo Uruguay 70 E4
San Juan r. Costa Rica/Nicaragua 67 H6
San Juan Arg. 70 C4
San Juan Puerto Rico 67 K5
San Juan r. U.S.A. 62 E4
San Juan, Cabo c. Arg. 70 D8
San Juan, Cabo c. Equat. Guinea 46 D4
San Juan Bautista Para. 70 E3
San Juan Bautista de las Misiones Para. see
  San Juan Bautista

San Juan de los Morros Venez. 68 E2
San Juan Mountains U.S.A. 62 F4
San Julián Arg. 70 C7
San Justo Arg. 70 D4
Sankari Drug India 38 C4
Sankhu India 36 C3
Sankra Chhattisgarh India 38 D1
Sankra Rajasthan India 36 B4
Sankt Gallen Switz. 24 I3
Sankt-Peterburg Rus. Fed. see
   St Petersburg
Sankt Pölten Austria 17 O6
Sankt Veit an der Glan Austria 17 O7
Sanku Jammu and Kashmir 36 D2
Şanlıurfa Turkey 34 E3
Şanlıurfa prov. Turkey 39 D1
San Lorenzo Arg. 70 D4
San Lorenzo Beni Bol. 68 E7
San Lorenzo Tarija Bol. 68 F8
San Lorenzo Ecuador 68 C3
San Lorenzo mt. Spain 25 E2
San Lorenzo, Cerro mt. Arg./Chile 70 B7
Sanlúcar de Barrameda Spain 25 C5
San Lucas Baja California Sur Mex. 66 C4
San Lucas, Serranía de mts Col. 68 D2
San Luis Arg. 70 C4
San Luis AZ U.S.A. 65 E4
San Luis Obispo CA U.S.A. 65 B3
San Luis Obispo Bay CA U.S.A. 65 B3
San Luis Potosí Mex. 66 D4
San Luis Reservoir CA U.S.A. 65 B2
San Luis Río Colorado Mex. 62 E5
San Marcos U.S.A. 62 H6
San Marino country Europe 26 E3
San Marino San Marino 26 E3
San Martín research station Antarctica 76 L2
San Martín Catamarca Arg. 70 C3
San Martín Mendoza Arg. 70 C4
San Martín, Lago l. Arg./Chile 70 B7
San Martín de los Andes Arg. 70 B6
San Mateo CA U.S.A. 65 B3
San Matías Bol. 69 G7
San Matías, Golfo g. Arg. 70 D6
Sanmenxia China 43 K6
San Miguel El Salvador 66 G6
San Miguel CA U.S.A. 65 B3
San Miguel de Huachi Bol. 68 E7
San Miguel de Tucumán Arg. 70 C3
San Miguel do Araguaia Brazil 71 A1
San Miguel Island CA U.S.A. 65 B3
Sanming China 43 L7
Sanndatti India 38 B3
Sanndraigh i. U.K. see Sandray
Sannicandro Garganico Italy 26 F4
San Nicolas Island CA U.S.A. 65 C4
Sannieshof S. Africa 51 G4
Sanniquellie Liberia 46 C4
Sanok Poland 13 D6
San Pablo Bol. 68 E8
San Pablo de Manta Ecuador see Manta
San Pedro Arg. 70 D2
San Pedro Bol. 68 F7
San Pedro Chile 70 C2
San-Pédro Côte d'Ivoire 46 C4
San Pedro Baja California Sur Mex. 62 E7
San Pedro Para. see
   San Pedro de Ycuamandyyú
San Pedro watercourse 2 62 E5
San Pedro, Sierra de mts Spain 25 C4
San Pedro Channel CA U.S.A. 65 C4
San Pedro de Arimena Col. 68 D3
San Pedro de Atacama Chile 70 C2
San Pedro de las Colonias Mex. 66 D3
San Pedro de Macorís Dom. Rep. 67 K5
San Pedro de Ycuamandyyú Para. 70 E2
San Pedro Sula Hond. 66 G5
San Pietro, Isola di i. Sardinia Italy 26 C5
Sanqaçal Azer. 35 H2
Sanquhar U.K. 20 F5
Sanquianga, Parque Nacional nat. park Col.
   68 C3
San Quintín, Cabo c. Mex. 66 A2
San Rafael Arg. 70 C4
San Rafael CA U.S.A. 65 A2
San Rafael Mountains CA U.S.A. 65 B3
San Ramón Bol. 68 F6
San Remo Italy 26 B3
San Roque Spain 25 B2
San Salvador i. Bahamas 67 J4
San Salvador El Salvador 66 G6
San Salvador, Isla i. Galápagos Ecuador
   68 [inset]
San Salvador de Jujuy Arg. 70 C2
Sansanné-Mango Togo 46 D3
San Sebastián Arg. 70 C8
San Sebastián Spain see
   Donostia-San Sebastián
San Sebastián de los Reyes Spain 25 E3
Sansepolcro Italy 26 E3
San Severo Italy 26 F4
Sanski Most Bos.-Herz. 26 G2
Santa r. Peru 68 C5
Santa Ana Bol. 68 E7
Santa Ana El Salvador 66 G6
Santa Ana Mex. 66 B2
Santa Ana i. Solomon Is 53 G4
Santa Ana de Yacuma Bol. 68 E6
Santa Bárbara Brazil 71 C2
Santa Bárbara Mex. 66 C3
Santa Barbara CA U.S.A. 65 C3
Santa Bárbara, Ilha i. Brazil 71 D2
Santa Barbara Channel CA U.S.A. 65 B3
Santa Bárbara d'Oeste Brazil 71 B3
Santa Barbara Island CA U.S.A. 65 C4
Santa Catalina, Gulf of CA U.S.A. 65 D4
Santa Catalina de Armada Spain 25 B2
Santa Catalina Island CA U.S.A. 65 C4
Santa Catarina state Brazil 71 A4
Santa Catarina, Ilha de i. Brazil 71 A4
Santa Clara Col. 68 E4
Santa Clara Cuba 67 I4
Santa Clara CA U.S.A. 65 B2
Santa Clara UT U.S.A. 65 F2
Santa Clarita CA U.S.A. 65 C3
Santa Clotilde Peru 68 D4
Santa Comba Angola see Waku-Kungo
Santa Croce, Capo c. Sicily Italy 26 F6
Santa Cruz Bol. 69 F7
Santa Cruz Brazil 69 K5
Santa Cruz Costa Rica 68 A1
Santa Cruz CA U.S.A. 65 A2
Santa Cruz i. Galápagos Ecuador
   68 [inset]
Santa Cruz Cabrália Brazil 71 D2
Santa Cruz de Goiás Brazil 71 A1
Santa Cruz de la Palma Canary Is 46 B2
Santa Cruz del Sur Cuba 67 I4
Santa Cruz de Moya Spain 25 F3
Santa Cruz de Tenerife Canary Is 46 B2
Santa Cruz do Sul Brazil 70 F3
Santa Cruz Island CA U.S.A. 65 C3
Santa Cruz Islands Solomon Is 53 G3
Santa Elena, Bahía de b. Ecuador 68 B4
Santa Elena, Punta pt Ecuador 68 B4
Santa Eudóxia Brazil 71 B3
Santa Eufemia, Golfo di g. Italy 26 G5
Santa Fé Arg. 70 D4
Santa Fe U.S.A. 62 F4
Santa Fé de Bogotá Col. see Bogotá

Santa Fé de Minas Brazil 71 B2
Santa Fé do Sul Brazil 71 A3
Santa Helena Brazil 69 I4
Santa Helena de Goiás Brazil 71 A2
Santa Inês Brazil 69 I4
Santa Inés, Isla i. Chile 76 L3
Santa Isabel Arg. 70 C5
Santa Isabel Equat. Guinea see Malabo
Santa Isabel i. Solomon Is 53 F2
Santa Juliana Brazil 71 B2
Santalpur India 36 B5
Santa Lucia Range mts CA U.S.A. 65 B2
Santa Margarita CA U.S.A. 65 B3
Santa Margarita, Isla i. Mex. 66 B4
Santa María Arg. 70 C3
Santa María Amazonas Brazil 69 G4
Santa María Rio Grande do Sul Brazil 70 F3
Santa María Cape Verde 46 [inset]
Santa María r. Mex. 66 C2
Santa María Peru 68 D4
Santa María CA U.S.A. 65 B3
Santa María, Cabo de c. Moz. 51 K4
Santa María, Cabo de c. Port. 25 C5
Santa María, Chapadão de hills Brazil
   71 B1
Santa María, Isla i. Galápagos Ecuador
   68 [inset]
Santa María, Serra de hills Brazil 71 B1
Santa María da Vitória Brazil 71 B1
Santa María do Suaçuí Brazil 71 C2
Santa María Island Vanuatu 53 G3
Santa María Madalena Brazil 71 C3
Santa María Mountains AZ U.S.A. 65 F3
Santa Marta Col. 68 D1
Santa Marta, Cabo de c. Angola 49 B5
Santa Marta Grande, Cabo de c. Brazil
   71 A5
Santa Maura i. Greece see Lefkada
Santa Monica CA U.S.A. 65 C3
Santa Monica Bay CA U.S.A. 65 C4
Santana Brazil 71 C1
Santana r. Brazil 71 A2
Santana do Araguaia Brazil 69 H5
Santander Spain 25 E2
Santa Nella CA U.S.A. 65 B2
Santanilla, Islas is Caribbean Sea see
   Swan Islands
Sant'Antioco Sardinia Italy 26 C5
Sant'Antioco, Isola di i. Sardinia Italy 26 C5
Sant Antoni de Portmany Spain 25 G4
Santapilly India 38 D2
Santa Quitéria Brazil 69 J4
Santarém Brazil 69 H4
Santarém Port. 25 B4
Santa Rosa Arg. 70 D5
Santa Rosa Acre Brazil 68 D5
Santa Rosa Rio Grande do Sul Brazil 70 F3
Santa Rosa CA U.S.A. 65 A1
Santa Rosa NM U.S.A. 62 G5
Santa Rosa de Copán Hond. 66 G6
Santa Rosa de la Roca Bol. 68 F7
Santa Rosa Island CA U.S.A. 65 B4
Santa Rosalía Mex. 66 B3
Santa Sylvina Arg. 70 D3
Santa Teresa r. Brazil 71 A1
Santa Vitória Brazil 71 A2
Santa Ynez r. CA U.S.A. 65 B3
Santa Ysabel i. Solomon Is see Santa Isabel
Santee CA U.S.A. 65 D4
Santiago Brazil 70 F3
Santiago i. Cape Verde 46 [inset]
Santiago Chile 70 B4
Santiago Dom. Rep. 67 J5
Santiago Panama 67 I7
Santiago de Compostela Spain 25 B2
Santiago de Cuba Cuba 67 I4
Santiago del Estero Arg. 70 D3
Santiago de los Caballeros Dom. Rep. see
   Santiago
Santiago de Veraguas Panama see Santiago
Santipur India see Shantipur
Sant Jordi, Golf de g. Spain 25 G3
Santo Amaro Brazil 71 D1
Santo Amaro de Campos Brazil 71 C3
Santo Anastácio Brazil 71 A3
Santo André Brazil 71 B3
Santo Ângelo Brazil 70 F3
Santo Antão i. Cape Verde 46 [inset]
Santo Antônio Brazil 68 F4
Santo Antônio r. Brazil 71 C2
Santo Antônio São Tomé and Príncipe
   46 D4
Santo Antônio, Cabo c. Brazil 71 D1
Santo Antônio da Platina Brazil 71 A3
Santo Antônio de Jesus Brazil 71 D1
Santo Antônio do Içá Brazil 68 E4
Santo Corazón Bol. 69 G7
Santo Domingo Dom. Rep. 67 K5
Santo Domingo country West Indies see
   Dominican Republic
Santo Domingo de Guzmán Dom. Rep. see
   Santo Domingo
Santo Hipólito Brazil 71 B2
Santorini i. Greece 27 K6
Santos Brazil 71 B3
Santos Dumont Brazil 71 C3
Santos Plateau sea feature S. Atlantic Ocean
   72 F7
Santo Tomás Peru 68 D6
Santo Tomé Arg. 70 E3
Sanup Plateau AZ U.S.A. 65 F2
San Valentín, Cerro mt. Chile 70 B7
San Vicente El Salvador 66 G6
San Vicente Mex. 66 A2
San Vicente de Baracaldo Spain see
   Barakaldo
San Vicente de Cañete Peru 68 C6
San Vincenzo Italy 26 D3
San Vito, Capo c. Sicily Italy 26 E5
Sanwer India 36 C5
Sanya China 43 J9
Sanza Pombo Angola 49 B4
São Bernardo do Campo Brazil 71 B3
São Borja Brazil 70 E3
São Carlos Brazil 71 B3
São Domingos Brazil 71 B1
São Felipe, Serra de hills Brazil 71 B1
São Félix Bahia Brazil 71 D1
São Félix Mato Grosso Brazil 69 H6
São Fidélis Brazil 71 C3
São Francisco Brazil 71 B1
São Francisco r. Brazil 71 C1
São Francisco, Ilha de i. Brazil 71 A5
São Francisco de Paula Brazil 71 A5
São Francisco de Sales Brazil 71 A2
São Francisco do Sul Brazil 71 A4
São Gabriel Brazil 70 F4
São Gonçalo Brazil 71 C3
São Gonçalo do Abaeté Brazil 71 B2
São Gonçalo do Sapucaí Brazil 71 B3
São Gotardo Brazil 71 B2
São João, Ilhas de is Brazil 69 J4
São João da Barra Brazil 71 C3
São João da Boa Vista Brazil 71 B3
São João da Madeira Port. 25 B3
São João da Ponte Brazil 71 B1
São João del Rei Brazil 71 B3
São João do Paraíso Brazil 71 C1

São Joaquim Brazil 71 A5
São Joaquim da Barra Brazil 71 B3
São José Amazonas Brazil 68 E4
São José Santa Catarina Brazil 71 A4
São José do Rio Preto Brazil 71 A3
São José dos Campos Brazil 71 B3
São José dos Pinhais Brazil 71 A4
São Leopoldo Brazil 71 A5
São Lourenço Brazil 71 B3
São Lourenço r. Brazil 69 G7
São Luís Brazil 69 J4
São Luís Brazil 69 G4
São Luís de Montes Belos Brazil 71 A2
São Manuel Brazil 71 A3
São Marcos r. Brazil 71 B2
São Mateus Brazil 71 D2
São Mateus do Sul Brazil 71 A4
São Miguel i. Arquipélago dos Açores
   72 G3
São Miguel r. Brazil 71 B2
São Miguel do Tapuio Brazil 69 J5
Saône r. France 24 G4
Saoner India 36 D5
São Nicolau i. Cape Verde 46 [inset]
São Paulo Brazil 71 B3
São Paulo state Brazil 71 A3
São Paulo de Olivença Brazil 68 E4
São Pedro da Aldeia Brazil 71 C3
São Pedro e São Paulo is N. Atlantic Ocean
   72 G5
São Pires r. Brazil see Teles Pires
São Raimundo Nonato Brazil 69 J5
São Romão Amazonas Brazil 68 E5
São Romão Minas Gerais Brazil 71 B2
São Roque Brazil 71 B3
São Roque, Cabo de c. Brazil 69 K5
São Salvador Angola see M'banza Congo
São Salvador do Congo Angola see
   M'banza Congo
São Sebastião Brazil 71 B3
São Sebastião, Ilha do i. Brazil 71 B3
São Sebastião do Paraíso Brazil 71 B3
São Sebastião dos Poções Brazil 71 B1
São Simão Minas Gerais Brazil 69 H7
São Simão São Paulo Brazil 71 B3
São Simão, Barragem de resr Brazil 71 A2
São Tiago i. Cape Verde see Santiago
São Tomé São Tomé and Príncipe 46 D4
São Tomé i. São Tomé and Príncipe 46 D4
São Tomé, Cabo de c. Brazil 71 C3
São Tomé, Pico de mt.
   São Tomé and Príncipe 46 D4
São Tomé and Príncipe country Africa
   46 D4
Saoura, Oued watercourse Alg. 22 D6
São Vicente Brazil 71 B3
São Vicente i. Cape Verde 46 [inset]
São Vicente, Cabo de c. Port. 25 B5
Sapanca Turkey 27 N4
Şaphane Dağı mt. Turkey 27 N5
Sapo National Park Liberia 46 C4
Sapouy Burkina 46 C3
Sapozhok Rus. Fed. 13 I5
Sapporo Japan 44 F4
Saputing China see Zadoi
Saqqez Iran 35 G3
Sarāb Iran 35 G3
Sara Buri Thai. 31 J5
Saradiya India 36 B5
Saragossa Spain see Zaragoza
Saragt Turkm. 33 J2
Saragt Akhal'skaya Oblast' Turkm. see
   Saragt
Saraguro Ecuador 68 C4
Sarahs Turkm. see Saragt
Sarai Afgh. 36 A2
Sarai Sidhu Pak. 36 C3
Sarajevo Bos.-Herz. 26 H3
Saraktash Rus. Fed. 28 G4
Saramati mt. India/Myanmar 37 H4
Saran' Kazakh. 42 C3
Saranda Albania see Sarandë
Sarandë Albania 27 I5
Sarandib country Asia see Sri Lanka
Sarangpur India 36 D5
Saransk Rus. Fed. 13 J5
Sara Peak Nigeria 46 D4
Sarapul Rus. Fed. 11 Q4
Sarāqib Syria 39 C2
Sarasota U.S.A. 63 J6
Sarata Ukr. 27 M1
Saratoga CA U.S.A. 65 A2
Saratoga WY U.S.A. 62 F3
Saratok Sarawak Malaysia 41 D7
Saratov Rus. Fed. 13 J6
Saratovskoye Vodokhranilishche resr
   Rus. Fed. 13 J5
Saratsina, Akrotirio pt Greece 27 K5
Saravan Iran 33 J4
Saray Turkey 27 L4
Sarayköy Turkey 27 M6
Sarayönü Turkey 34 D3
Sarbāz Iran 33 J4
Sarbhang Bhutan 37 G4
Sarbīsheh Iran 33 I3
Sarda r. Nepal 37 E3
Sardarshahr India 36 C3
Sar Dasht Iran 35 G3
Sardegna i. Sardinia Italy see Sardinia
Sardica Bulg. see Sofia
Sardinia i. Sardinia Italy 26 C4
Sardis WV U.S.A. 64 A3
Sar-e Būm Afgh. 36 A2
Sareks nationalpark nat. park Sweden 14 J3
Sarektjåkkå mt. Sweden 14 J3
Sar-e Pol Afgh. 36 A1
Sar-e Pol-e Zahāb Iran 35 G3
Sar Eskandar Iran see Hashtrud
Sare Yazd Iran 35 I5
Sargasso Sea N. Atlantic Ocean 75 P4
Sargodha Pak. 33 L3
Sarh Chad 47 E4
Sārī Iran 35 I3
Saria i. Greece 27 L7
Sar-i-Bum Afgh. see Sar-e Būm
Sarigh Jilganang Kol salt l. Aksai Chin
   36 D2
Sarıgöl Turkey 27 M5
Sarıkamış Turkey 35 F2
Sarila India 36 D4
Sarina Australia 56 E4
Sarıoğlan Kayseri Turkey 34 D3
Sarıoğlan Konya Turkey see Belören
Sariqamish Kuli salt l. Turkm./Uzbek. see
   Sarykamyshskoye Ozero
Sarir Tibesti des. Libya 47 E2
Sariwŏn N. Korea 45 B5
Sarıyar Barajı resr Turkey 27 N5
Sarıyer Turkey 39 M4
Sarız Turkey 34 E3
Sark i. Channel Is 19 E9
Sarkand Kazakh. 42 D3
Şarkikaraağaç Turkey 27 N5
Şarkışla Turkey 34 E3
Şarköy Turkey 27 L4
Sarlath Range mts Afgh./Pak. 36 A3
Sarmi Indon. 41 F8

Särna Sweden 15 H6
Sarneh Iran 35 G4
Sarnen Switz. 24 I3
Sarni India see Amla
Sarnia Canada 63 K3
Sarny Ukr. 13 E6
Saroma-ko l. Japan 44 F3
Saronikos Kolpos g. Greece 27 J6
Saros Körfezi b. Turkey 27 L4
Sarova Rus. Fed. 13 I5
Sarowbī Afgh. 36 B2
Sarpa, Ozero l. Rus. Fed. 13 J6
Sarpan i. N. Mariana Is see Rota
Sarpsborg Norway 15 G7
Sarqant Kazakh. see Sarkand
Sarrebourg France 24 H2
Sarria Spain 25 C2
Sartana Ukr. 13 H7
Sartène Corsica France 24 I6
Sarthe r. France 24 D3
Sartu China see Daqing
Saruna Pak. 36 A4
Sarupsar India 36 C3
Şärur Azer. 35 G3
Sarv Iran 35 I4
Sarvābād Iran 35 G4
Sárvár Hungary 26 G1
Sarwar India 36 C4
Sarygamysh Köli salt l. Turkm./Uzbek. see
   Sarykamyshskoye Ozero
Sary-Ishikotrau, Peski des. Kazakh. see
   Saryyesik-Atyrau, Peski
Sarykamyshskoye Ozero salt l.
   Turkm./Uzbek. 35 J2
Saryozek Kazakh. 42 D4
Saryshagan Kazakh. 42 C3
Sarysu watercourse Kazakh. 42 B3
Sarytash Kazakh. 35 H1
Saryyesik-Atyrau, Peski des. Kazakh. 42 D3
Sarzha Kazakh. 35 H2
Sasar, Tanjung pt Indon. 54 B2
Sasaram India 37 F4
Sasebo Japan 45 C6
Saskatchewan prov. Canada 62 F1
Saskatchewan r. Canada 60 H4
Saskatoon Canada 60 H4
Saskylakh Rus. Fed. 29 M2
Saslaya, Nicaragua 67 H6
Sasoi r. India 36 B5
Sasolburg S. Africa 51 H4
Sasovo Rus. Fed. 13 I5
Sassandra Côte d'Ivoire 46 C4
Sassari Sardinia Italy 26 C4
Sassnitz Germany 17 N3
Sass Town Liberia 46 C4
Sasykkol', Ozero l. Kazakh. 42 E3
Sasykoli Rus. Fed. 13 J7
Sasyqköl l. Kazakh. see Sasykkol', Ozero
Sata-misaki c. Japan 45 C7
Satana India 38 B1
Satara India 38 B2
Satara S. Africa 51 J3
Sätbaev Kazakh. see Satpayev
Satırlar Turkey see Yeşilova
Satkania Bangl. 37 H5
Satkhira Bangl. 37 G5
Satluj r. India/Pak. see Sutlej
Satmala Range hills India 38 C2
Satna India 36 E4
Satpayev Kazakh. 42 B3
Satpura Range hills India 36 C5
Satsuma-hantō pen. Japan 45 C7
Satthwa Myanmar 37 H4
Satu Mare Romania 13 D7
Satwas India 36 D5
Sauce Norway 15 E7
Saudárkrókur Iceland 14 [inset]
Saudi Arabia country Asia 32 F4
Saujbolagh Iran see Mahābād
Saulieu France 24 G3
Sault Sainte Marie Canada 63 K2
Sault Sainte Marie U.S.A. 63 K2
Saumalkol' Kazakh. 30 F1
Saumarez Reef Australia 56 F4
Saumlakki Indon. 54 E2
Saumur France 24 D3
Saunders, Mount hill Australia 54 E3
Saunders Coast Antarctica 76 J1
Saurimo Angola 49 C4
Sautar Angola 49 B5
Sava r. Europe 26 I2
Savage River Australia 57 [inset]
Savai'i i. Samoa 53 I3
Savala r. Rus. Fed. 13 I6
Savalou Benin 46 D4
Savannah GA U.S.A. 63 K5
Savannah r. U.S.A. 63 K5
Savannakhét Laos 41 C7
Savanna-la-Mar Jamaica 67 I5
Savant Lake Canada 63 I1
Savanur India 38 B3
Savastepe Turkey 27 L5
Save Benin 46 D4
Save r. Moz./Zimbabwe 49 D6
Sāveh Iran 35 H4
Saviaho Fin. 14 P4
Savinskiy Rus. Fed. 12 I3
Savitri r. India 38 B2
Savli India 36 C5
Savoie reg. France see Savoy
Savona Italy 26 C2
Savonlinna Fin. 14 P6
Savonranta Fin. 14 P5
Savoy reg. France 24 H3
Şavşat Turkey 35 F2
Sävsjö Sweden 15 I8
Savu i. Indon. 54 C2
Savukoski Fin. 14 P3
Savur Turkey 35 F3
Saw Myanmar 37 H4
Sawai Madhopur India 36 D4
Sawangan Indon. 54 C3
Sawara Japan 45 F6
Sawatch Range mts NV U.S.A. 65 E3
Sawel Mountain hill U.K. 21 E3
Sawhāj Egypt 32 D4
Sawtell Australia 58 F3
Sawu i. Indon. see Savu
Sawu, Laut sea Indon. 41 E8
Sawye Myanmar 37 I5
Saxilby U.K. 18 G5
Saxmundham U.K. 19 I6
Saxnäs Sweden 14 I4
Saxton PA U.S.A. 64 E3
Say Niger 46 D3
Sayabouri Laos see Xaignabouli
Sayak Kazakh. 42 D3
Sayanogorsk Rus. Fed. 42 G2
Sayano-Shushenskoye Vodokhranilishche
   resr Rus. Fed. 42 G2
Sayansk Rus. Fed. 42 I2
Sayaq Kazakh. see Sayak
Şaydā Lebanon see Sidon
Şäyen Iran 35 I5
Sayghān Afgh. 36 A2
Sayhūt Yemen 32 H6
Saykhin Kazakh. 11 C7
Saylac Somalia 47 H3

Saylan country Asia see Sri Lanka
Saynshand Mongolia 43 K4
Sayn-Ust Mongolia 42 G3
Sayoa mt. Spain see Saioa
Şayqal, Bahr Imp. l. Syria 39 C3
Sayqyn Kazakh. see Saykhin
Sayre PA U.S.A. 64 D2
Sayreville NJ U.S.A. 64 D2
Sayula Mex. 66 F5
Sazin Pak. 36 C2
Sazdy Rus. Fed. 13 K7
Sazin Pak. 36 C2
Sbaa Alg. 22 D6
Sbeitla Tunisia 26 C7
Scaddan Australia 55 C8
Scafell Pike hill U.K. 18 D4
Scalasaig U.K. 20 C4
Scalea Italy 26 F5
Scalloway U.K. 20 [inset]
Scalpaigh, Eilean i. U.K. see Scalpay
Scalpay i. U.K. 20 C3
Scapa Flow inlet U.K. 20 F2
Scarba i. U.K. 20 D4
Scarborough Canada 63 L3
Scarborough Trin. and Tob. 67 L6
Scarborough U.K. 18 G4
Scariff Island Ireland 21 B6
Scarp i. U.K. 20 B2
Scarpanto i. Greece see Karpathos
Schaffhausen Switz. 24 I3
Schakalskuppe Namibia 50 C4
Schärding Austria 17 N6
Schefferville Canada 61 L4
Scheibbs Austria 17 O6
Schellville CA U.S.A. 65 A1
Schenectady NY U.S.A. 64 E1
Schio Italy 26 D2
Schleswig Germany 17 L3
Schleswig-Holsteinisches Wattenmeer,
   Nationalpark nat. park Germany 17 L3
Schmidt Island Rus. Fed. see
   Shmidta, Ostrov
Schmidt Peninsula Rus. Fed. see
   Shmidta, Poluostrov
Schneidemühl Poland see Piła
Schneverdingen Germany 17 L4
Schoharie NY U.S.A. 64 D1
Schönebeck (Elbe) Germany 17 M4
Schouten Island Australia 57 [inset]
Schouten Islands P.N.G. 52 E2
Schrankogel mt. Austria 17 M7
Schröttersburg Poland see Płock
Schull Ireland 21 C6
Schuyler Lake NY U.S.A. 64 D1
Schwäbische Alb mts Germany 17 L7
Schwäbisch Hall Germany 17 L6
Schwandorf Germany 17 N6
Schwarzenberg Germany 17 N5
Schwarzrand mts Namibia 50 C4
Schwarzwald mts Germany see
   Black Forest
Schwatka Mountains U.S.A. 60 C3
Schwaz Austria 17 M7
Schwedt an der Oder Germany 17 O4
Schweinfurt Germany 17 M5
Schweiz country Europe see Switzerland
Schweizer-Reneke S. Africa 51 G4
Schwerin Germany 17 M4
Schwyz Switz. 24 I3
Sciacca Sicily Italy 26 E6
Scicli Sicily Italy 26 F6
Scilly, Île atoll Fr. Polynesia see Manuae
Scilly, Isles of U.K. 19 A9
Scodra Albania see Shkodër
Scole U.K. 19 I6
Scone Australia 58 E4
Scone U.K. 20 F4
Scoresby Land reg. Greenland 61 P2
Scoresbysund Greenland see
   Ittoqqortoormiit
Scoresby Sund sea chan. Greenland see
   Kangertittivaq
Scorno, Punta dello pt Sardinia Italy see
   Caprara, Punta
Scorpion Bight b. Australia 55 D8
Scotia Ridge sea feature S. Atlantic Ocean
   72 E9
Scotia Ridge sea feature S. Atlantic Ocean
   76 A2
Scotia Sea S. Atlantic Ocean 72 F9
Scotland Ont. Canada 63 L3
Scotland admin. div. U.K. 20 F3
Scotland MD U.S.A. 64 D3
Scott, Cape Australia 54 E3
Scott, Cape Canada 62 E1
Scott Base research station Antarctica
   76 H1
Scottburgh S. Africa 51 J6
Scott City U.S.A. 62 L4
Scott Coast Antarctica 76 H1
Scott Glacier Antarctica 76 I1
Scott Island Antarctica 76 H2
Scott Mountains Antarctica 76 D2
Scott Reef Australia 54 C3
Scottsbluff U.S.A. 62 G3
Scottsboro U.S.A. 63 J5
Scottsville U.S.A. 64 B4
Scourie U.K. 20 D2
Scousburgh U.K. 20 [inset]
Scrabster U.K. 20 F2
Scranton PA U.S.A. 64 D2
Scunthorpe U.K. 18 G5
Scuol Switz. 24 I3
Scupi Macedonia see Skopje
Scutari Albania see Shkodër
Scutari, Lake Albania/Montenegro 27 H3
Seabrook, Lake salt flat Australia 55 B7
Seaford U.K. 19 H8
Seaforth Ont. Canada 64 A1
Seal r. Canada 61 I4
Seal, Cape S. Africa 50 F8
Sea Lake Australia 57 C7
Sealy U.S.A. 63 H6
Seaman Range mts NV U.S.A. 65 E2
Seamer U.K. 18 G4
Searchlight NV U.S.A. 65 E3
Searcy U.S.A. 63 I4
Searles Lake CA U.S.A. 65 D3
Seaside Park NJ U.S.A. 64 E3
Seattle U.S.A. 62 C3
Seaview Range mts Australia 56 D3
Seba Indon. 54 C2
Sebastea Turkey see Sivas
Sebastián Vizcaíno, Bahía b. Mex. 62 D5
Sebastopol CA U.S.A. 65 A1
Sebastopol Ukr. see Sevastopol'
Sebba Burkina 46 D3
Sebes Turkey 27 N4
Sebenico Croatia see Šibenik
Sebeş Romania 27 J2
Sebezh Rus. Fed. 15 P8
Şebinkarahisar Turkey 34 E2
Sebring U.S.A. 63 K6
Sebrovo Rus. Fed. 13 I6
Sebta N. Africa see Ceuta
Sebuku i. Indon. 54 C3
Sechelt Canada 62 C2
Sechenovo Rus. Fed. 13 J5
Sechura Peru 68 B5
Sechura, Bahía de b. Peru 68 B5
Secretary Island N.Z. 59 A7
Secunda S. Africa 51 I4
Secunderabad India 38 C2

Sedalia U.S.A. 63 I4
Sedam India 38 C2
Sedan France 24 G2
Sedan Dip Australia 56 C3
Seddon N.Z. 59 E5
Seddonville N.Z. 59 C5
Sedeh Iran 33 I3
Sederot Israel 39 B4
Sedlčany Czech Rep. 17 O6
Sedlets Poland see Siedlce
Sedom Israel 39 B4
Sédrata Alg. 26 B6
Seduva Lith. 15 M9
Seeheim Namibia 50 C4
Seelig, Mount Antarctica 76 K1
Sées France 24 E2
Sefadu Sierra Leone 46 B4
Sefare Botswana 51 H2
Seferihisar Turkey 27 L5
Sefophe Botswana 51 H2
Segalstad Norway 15 G6
Segamat Malaysia 31 J6
Ségbana Benin 46 D3
Segezha Rus. Fed. 12 G3
Seghnān Afgh. 36 B1
Segontia U.K. see Caernarfon
Segontium U.K. see Caernarfon
Segorbe Spain 25 F4
Ségou Mali 46 C3
Segovia r. Hond./Nicaragua see Coco
Segovia Spain 25 D3
Segozerskoye, Ozero resr Rus. Fed. 12 G3
Seguam Island U.S.A. 60 A4
Séguédine Niger 46 E2
Séguéla Côte d'Ivoire 46 C4
Seguin U.S.A. 62 H6
Segura r. Spain 25 F4
Segura, Sierra de mts Spain 25 E5
Sehithwa Botswana 49 C5
Sehlabathebe National Park Lesotho 51 I5
Sehore India 36 D5
Sehwan Pak. 36 A4
Seikphyu Myanmar 37 H5
Seiland i. Norway 14 M1
Seinäjoki Fin. 14 M5
Seine r. France 24 F2
Seine, Baie de b. France 24 D2
Seine, Val de valley France 24 F2
Sejny Poland 15 M9
Sekayu Indon. 41 C8
Sekoma Botswana 50 F3
Sekondi Ghana 46 C4
Sek'ot'a Eth. 48 D2
Sela i. U.K. see Shali
Šelaru i. Indon. 41 F8
Selat, Tanjung pt Indon. 54 C3
Selatan, Tanjung pt Indon. 54 C3
Selat Makassar strait Indon. see
   Makassar, Selat
Selawik U.S.A. 60 B3
Selbekken Norway 14 F5
Selbu Norway 14 G5
Selby U.K. 18 F5
Selbyville DE U.S.A. 64 D3
Selçuk Turkey 27 L6
Selcbi-Phikwe Botswana see Selebi-Phikwe
Selebi-Pikwe Botswana see Selebi-Phikwe
Selemdzha r. Rus. Fed. 44 C1
Selemdzhinsk Rus. Fed. 44 C1
Selemdzhinskiy Khrebet mts Rus. Fed.
   44 D1
Selendi Turkey 27 M5
Selenga r. Mongolia/Rus. Fed. 42 J2
Selenga Mörön r. Mongolia see Selenga
Selety r. Kazakh. see Sileti
Seletyteniz, Ozero salt l. Kazakh. see
   Siletiteniz, Ozero
Seleucia Turkey see Silifke
Seleucia Pieria Turkey see Samandağı
Sel'gon Stantsiya Rus. Fed. 44 D2
Selib Rus. Fed. 12 K3
Sélibabi Mauritania 46 B3
Selibe-Phikwe Botswana see Selebi-Phikwe
Seliger, Ozero l. Rus. Fed. 12 G4
Seligman AZ U.S.A. 65 F3
Seliklinio Rus. Fed. 14 M2
Selma CA U.S.A. 65 C3
Selma AL U.S.A. 63 J5
Selma CA U.S.A. 65 C2
Selsey Bill hd U.K. 19 G8
Selty Rus. Fed. 12 L4
Selu i. Indon. 54 E1
Selvas reg. Brazil 68 D5
Selway r. U.S.A. 62 D3
Selwyn Lake Canada 60 H3
Selwyn Mountains Canada 60 E3
Selwyn Range hills Australia 56 B4
Semarang Indon. 41 D8
Semau i. Indon. 54 C2
Sembé Congo 48 B3
Şemdinli Turkey 35 G3
Semendire Serbia see Smederevo
Semenivka Ukr. 13 G5
Semenov Rus. Fed. 12 J4
Semenovka Ukr. see Semenivka
Semey Kazakh. see Semipalatinsk
Semidi Islands U.S.A. 60 C4
Semikarakorsk Rus. Fed. 13 I7
Semiluki Rus. Fed. 13 I6
Seminole U.S.A. 62 G5
Semipalatinsk Kazakh. 42 F2
Semirom Iran 35 H5
Sem Kolodezey Ukr. see Lenine
Semnän Iran 35 I4
Semyonovskoye Arkhangel'skaya Oblast'
   Rus. Fed. see Bereznik
Semyonovskoye Kostromskaya Oblast'
   Rus. Fed. see Ostrovskoye
Sena Bol. 68 E6
Sena Madureira Brazil 68 E5
Senanga Zambia 49 C5
Sendai Kagoshima Japan 45 C7
Sendai Miyagi Japan 45 F5
Sêndo China 37 H3
Seneca Lake NY U.S.A. 64 C1
Seneca Rocks WV U.S.A. 64 B3
Senecaville Lake OH U.S.A. 64 A3
Senegal country Africa 46 B3
Sénégal r. Mauritania/Senegal 46 B3
Senftenberg Germany 17 O5
Senga Hill Zambia 49 D4
Sengerema Tanz. 48 D4
Sengeyskiy, Ostrov i. Rus. Fed. 12 K1
Sengiley Rus. Fed. 13 K5
Séngiri, Mys pt Kazakh. see Syngyrli, Mys
Senhor do Bonfim Brazil 69 J6
Senigallia Italy 26 E3
Senj Croatia 26 F2
Senja i. Norway 14 J2
Sen'kina Rus. Fed. 12 L2
Şenkaya Turkey 39 C1
Senlac S. Africa 50 F3
Senlin Shan mt. China 44 C4
Senlis France 24 F2

Sennar Sudan 32 D7
Sennen U.K. 19 B8
Senneterre Canada 63 L2
Senqu r. Lesotho 51 H6
Sens France 24 F2
Sensuntepeque El Salvador 66 G6
Senta Serbia 27 I2
Senthal India 36 D3
Sentinel AZ U.S.A. 65 F4
Sentinel Peak Canada 60 F4
Senwabarwana S. Africa see Bochum
Şenyurt Turkey 35 F3
Seo de Urgell Spain see Le Seu d'Urgell
Seonath r. India 38 D1
Seoni India 36 D5
Seorinarayan India 37 E5
Seoul S. Korea 45 B5
Separation Well Australia 54 C5
Sepik r. P.N.G. 52 E2
Sep'o N. Korea 45 B5
Sepon India 37 H4
Seppa India 37 H4
Sept-Îles Canada 63 N1
Sequoia National Park CA U.S.A. 65 C2
Serafimovich Rus. Fed. 13 I6
Sêraitang China see Baima
Serakhs Akhal'skaya Oblast' Turkm. see Saragt
Seram i. Indon. 41 E8
Seram, Laut sea Indon. 41 F8
Serbâl, Gebel mt. Egypt see Sirbâl, Jabal
Serbia country Europe 27 I2
Sêrbug Co l. China 37 G2
Sêrca China 37 H3
Serchhip India 37 H5
Serdar Turkm. 35 J3
Serdar Turkm. see Serdar
Serder Turkm. see Serdar
Serdica Bulg. see Sofia
Serdo Eth. 48 E2
Serdoba r. Rus. Fed. 13 J5
Serdobsk Rus. Fed. 13 J5
Seredka Rus. Fed. 15 P7
Şereflikoçhisar Turkey 34 D3
Seremban Malaysia 41 C7
Serengeti National Park Tanz. 48 D4
Serenje Zambia 49 D5
Serezha r. Rus. Fed. 12 I5
Sergach Rus. Fed. 12 J5
Sergeyevka Rus. Fed. 44 B2
Sergiyev Posad Rus. Fed. 12 H4
Sergo Ukr. see Stakhanov
Serh China 37 I1
Serhetabat Turkm. 33 J2
Serhetabat Turkm. see Serhetabat
Serifos i. Greece 27 K6
Serik Turkey 34 C3
Seringapatam Reef Australia 54 C3
Sêrkang China see Nyainrong
Sermata, Kepulauan is Indon. 54 E2
Sermersuaq glacier Greenland 61 M2
Sermilik inlet Greenland 61 O3
Sernur Rus. Fed. 12 K4
Seronga Botswana 49 C5
Serov Rus. Fed. 11 S4
Serowe Botswana 51 H2
Serpa Port. 25 C5
Serpa Pinto Angola see Menongue
Serpentine Lakes salt flat Australia 55 E7
Serpukhov Rus. Fed. 13 H5
Serra Brazil 71 C3
Serra Alta Brazil 71 A4
Serrachis r. Cyprus 39 A2
Serra da Bocaina, Parque Nacional da nat. park Brazil 71 B3
Serra da Canastra, Parque Nacional da nat. park Brazil 71 B2
Serra da Mesa, Represa resr Brazil 71 A1
Serra das Araras Brazil 71 B1
Serra do Divisor, Parque Nacional da nat. park Brazil 68 D5
Sérrai Greece see Serres
Serranía de la Neblina, Parque Nacional nat. park Venez. 68 E3
Serraria, Ilha i. Brazil see Queimada, Ilha
Serra Talhada Brazil 69 K5
Serres Greece 27 J4
Serrinha Brazil 69 K6
Sêrro Brazil 71 C2
Sers Tunisia 26 C6
Sertanópolis Brazil 71 A3
Sertãozinho Brazil 71 B3
Sertavul Geçidi pass Turkey 39 A1
Sertolovo Rus. Fed. 15 Q6
Serule Botswana 49 C6
Seruna India 36 C3
Sêrwolungwa China 37 H2
Sêrxü China 42 H6
Sese Islands Uganda 48 D4
Sesel country Indian Ocean see Seychelles
Sesfontein Namibia 49 B5
Seshachalam Hills India 38 C3
Sesheke Zambia 49 C5
Sesostris Bank sea feature India 38 A3
Ses Salines, Cap de c. Spain 25 H4
Sestri Levante Italy 26 C2
Sestroretsk Rus. Fed. 15 P6
Sète France 24 F5
Sete Lagoas Brazil 71 B2
Setermoen Norway 14 K2
Setesdal valley Norway 15 E7
Seti r. Nepal 36 E3
Sétif Alg. 22 F1
Seto Japan 45 E6
Seto-naikai sea Japan 43 O6
Seto-naikai Kokuritsu-kōen Japan 45 D6
Settat Morocco 22 C5
Settepani, Monte mt. Italy 26 C2
Settle U.K. 18 E4
Setúbal Port. 25 B4
Setúbal, Baía de b. Port. 25 B4
Seul, Lac l. Canada 63 I1
Sevan Armenia 35 G2
Sevan, Lake Armenia 35 G2
Sevan, Ozero l. Armenia see Sevan, Lake
Sevana Lich l. Armenia see Sevan, Lake
Sevastopol' Ukr. 34 D1
Seven Islands Canada see Sept-Îles
Sevenoaks U.K. 19 H7
Sévérac-le-Château France 24 F4
Severn r. Australia 58 E2
Severn r. Canada 63 J3
Severn r. S. Africa 50 F4
Severn r. U.K. 19 E6
Severnaya Dvina r. Rus. Fed. 12 I2
Severnaya Sos'va r. Rus. Fed. 11 T3
Severnaya Zemlya is Rus. Fed. 29 L1
Severnoye Rus. Fed. 12 K5
Severnyy Nenetskiy Avtonomnyy Okrug Rus. Fed. 12 K1
Severnyy Respublika Komi Rus. Fed. 28 H3
Severo-Baykal'skoye Nagor'ye mts Rus. Fed. 29 M4
Severobaykal'sk Rus. Fed. 29 M4
Severodonetsk Ukr. see Syeverodonets'k
Severodvinsk Rus. Fed. 12 H2
Severo-Kuril'sk Rus. Fed. 29 Q4
Severomorsk Rus. Fed. 12 G1

Severoonezhsk Rus. Fed. 12 H3
Severo-Sibirskaya Nizmennost' lowland Rus. Fed. see North Siberian Lowland
Severoural'sk Rus. Fed. 11 R3
Severo-Yeniseyskiy Rus. Fed. 28 K3
Severskiy Donets r. Rus. Fed./Ukr. 13 I7
Sevier Lake UT U.S.A. 65 F1
Sevilla Col. 68 C3
Sevilla Spain see Seville
Seville Spain 25 D5
Sevlyush Ukr. see Vynohradiv
Sewani India 36 C3
Seward AK U.S.A. 60 D3
Seward Mountains Antarctica 76 L2
Seward Peninsula U.S.A. 60 B3
Sexi Spain see Almuñécar
Seyakha Rus. Fed. 77 F2
Seychelles country Indian Ocean 73 L6
Seydi Turkm. 33 J2
Seydişehir Turkey 34 C3
Seyðisfjörður Iceland 14 [inset]
Seyhan Turkey see Adana
Seyhan r. Turkey 39 B1
Seyitgazi Turkey 27 N5
Seymchan Rus. Fed. 29 Q3
Seymour Australia 58 B6
Seymour S. Africa 51 H7
Seymour IN U.S.A. 63 J4
Seymour TX U.S.A. 61 D5
Seymour Range mts Australia 55 F6
Seypan i. N. Mariana Is see Saipan
Seyyedâbâd Afgh. 36 B2
Sézanne France 24 F2
Sfântu Gheorghe Romania 27 K2
Sfax Tunisia 26 D7
Sfikias, Limni resr Greece 27 J4
Sfîntu Gheorghe Romania see Sfântu Gheorghe
Sgiersch Poland see Zgierz
's-Gravenhage Neth. see The Hague
Sgurr Alasdair hill U.K. 20 C5
Sgurr Dhomhnuill hill U.K. 20 D4
Sgurr Mòr mt. U.K. 20 D3
Sgurr na Ciche mt. U.K. 20 D3
Shaanxi prov. China 43 J5
Shaartuz Tajik. see Shahrtuz
Shaban Pak. 36 A3
Shabani Zimbabwe see Zvishavane
Shabestar Iran 35 G3
Shabībī, Jabal ash mt. Jordan 39 B5
Shabla, Nos pt Bulg. 27 M3
Shabunda Dem. Rep. Congo 48 C4
Shache China 42 D5
Shackleton Coast Antarctica 76 H1
Shackleton Glacier Antarctica 76 I1
Shackleton Ice Shelf Antarctica 76 F2
Shackleton Range mts Antarctica 76 A1
Shādegān Iran 35 H4
Shady Spring WV U.S.A. 64 A4
Shafer, Lake Antarctica 76 H2
Shafter CA U.S.A. 65 C4
Shaftesbury U.K. 19 E7
Shagedu China 43 K5
Shageluk U.S.A. 60 C3
Shagonar Rus. Fed. 42 G2
Shag Point N.Z. 59 C7
Shag Rocks is S. Georgia 70 H8
Shahabad Karnataka India 38 C2
Shahabad Rajasthan India 36 D4
Shahabad Uttar Prad. India 36 D4
Shāhābād Iran see Eslāmābād-e Gharb
Shahbandar Pak. 36 A5
Shahdol India 36 E5
Shah Fuladi mt. Afgh. 36 A2
Shāhīn Dezh Iran see Sā'indezh
Shahjahanpur India 36 D4
Shāh Jūy Afgh. 36 A2
Shāhpūr Iran see Salmās
Shahrak Afgh. 33 J3
Shahr-e Bābak Iran 35 I4
Shahr-e Kord Iran 35 H4
Shahr-e Şafā Afgh. 36 A3
Shahreẕā Iran 35 H4
Shahrig Pak. 36 A4
Shahrisabz Uzbek. 33 K2
Shahr Rey Iran 35 H3
Shahr Sultan Pak. 36 B3
Shahrtuz Tajik. 36 B1
Shāhrūd Iran see Emāmrūd
Shāhrūd, Rūdkhāneh-ye r. Iran 35 H3
Shaikh Husain mt. Pak. 36 A3
Shaikhpura India see Sheikhpura
Sha'ir, Jabal mts Syria 39 C2
Sha'ira, Gebel mt. Egypt see Sha'irah, Jabal
Sha'irah, Jabal mt. Egypt 39 D5
Shajapur India 36 D5
Shajianzi China 44 B4
Shakaville S. Africa 51 J5
Shakhbuz Azer. see Şahbuz
Shakhovskaya Rus. Fed. 12 G4
Shakhrisabz Uzbek. see Shahrisabz
Shakhtinsk Kazakh. 42 D3
Shakhty Respublika Buryatiya Rus. Fed. see Gusinoozersk
Shakhty Rostovskaya Oblast' Rus. Fed. 13 I7
Shakhun'ya Rus. Fed. 12 J4
Shaki Nigeria 46 D4
Shakotan-hantō pen. Japan 44 F4
Shalakusha Rus. Fed. 12 I3
Shali Rus. Fed. 35 G2
Shaliuhe China see Gangca
Shalkar India 36 D3
Shalkar Kazakh. 20 G5
Shalqar Kazakh. see Shalkar
Shaluli Shan mts China 42 H6
Shaluni mt. India 37 I3
Shama r. Tanz. 49 D4
Shamāl Sīnā' governorate Egypt see Shamāl Sīnā'
Shamāl Sīnā' governorate Egypt see Shamāl Sīnā'
Shamalzā'ī Afgh. 36 A3
Shāmat al Akbād des. Saudi Arabia 35 F5
Shamattawa Canada 61 I4
Shambar Iran 35 H4
Shamgong Bhutan see Shemgang
Shāmīyah des. Iraq/Syria 39 D2
Shamkhor Azer. see Şämkir
Shamrock Ireland 21 C6
Shandong prov. China 43 L5
Shandong Bandao pen. China 43 M5
Shandur Pass India 36 C1
Shangdu China 43 K4
Shangganling China 44 C3
Shanghai China 43 M6
Shanghai municipality China 43 M6
Shangluo China 43 J6
Shangnan China 43 J6
Shangrao China 43 L7
Shangyou Shuiku resr China 42 H4
Shangzhi China 44 B3
Shanhetun China 44 B3
Shannon airport Ireland 21 D5
Shannon est. Ireland 21 C5
Shannon r. Ireland 21 D5
Shannon N. Ireland 21 C5
Shannon National Park Australia 55 B8
Shannon Ø i. Greenland 77 I1

Shansi prov. China see Shanxi
Shantipur India 37 G5
Shantou China 43 L8
Shantung prov. China see Shandong
Shanxi prov. China 43 K5
Shaoguan China 43 K8
Shaowu China 43 L7
Shaoxing China 43 M6
Shaoyang China 43 K7
Shap U.K. 18 E4
Shapinsay i. U.K. 20 G1
Shapkina r. Rus. Fed. 12 L2
Shapsha'l skiy Khrebet mts Rus. Fed. 42 F2
Shaqrā' Saudi Arabia 32 G4
Shār, Jabal mt. Saudi Arabia 34 D6
Sharaf well Iraq 35 F5
Sharan Jogizai Pak. 36 B3
Sharbulag Mongolia 42 G3
Shardara Kazakh. 33 I4
Shardara, Step' plain Kazakh. see Chardara, Step'
Sharga Mongolia 42 I4
Sharhulsan Mongolia 42 J4
Shari r. Cameroon/Chad see Chari
Shārī, Buḩayrat imp. l. Iraq 35 G4
Sharifah Syria 39 C2
Sharjah U.A.E. 33 I4
Sharka-leb La pass China 37 G3
Sharkawshchyna Belarus 15 O9
Shark Bay Australia 55 A6
Shark Reef Australia 56 D2
Sharlyk Rus. Fed. 11 Q5
Sharm ash Shaykh Egypt 34 D6
Sharm el Sheikh Egypt see Sharm ash Shaykh
Sharon PA U.S.A. 64 A2
Sharqat Iraq see Ash Sharqāt
Sharqī, Jabal ash mts Lebanon/Syria 39 B3
Sharur Azer. see Şärur
Shar'ya Rus. Fed. 12 J4
Shashe r. Botswana/Zimbabwe 49 C6
Shashemenē Eth. 48 D3
Shashi China see Jingzhou
Shasta, Mount vol. U.S.A. 62 C3
Shatilki Belarus see Svyetlahorsk
Shatki Rus. Fed. 12 J5
Shaṭnat as Salmās, Wādī watercourse Syria 39 D2
Shatoy Rus. Fed. 35 G2
Shatsk Rus. Fed. 13 I5
Shatt al 'Arab r. Iran/Iraq 35 H5
Shatura Rus. Fed. 13 H5
Shaubak Jordan see Ash Shawbak
Shaunavon Canada 62 F2
Shaver Lake CA U.S.A. 65 C2
Shaw r. Australia 54 B5
Shawangunk Mountains hills NY U.S.A. 64 D2
Shawano U.S.A. 63 J3
Shawnee OK U.S.A. 63 H4
Shay Gap Australia 54 C5
Shaykh, Jabal ash mt. Lebanon/Syria see Hermon, Mount
Shaykh Miskīn Syria 39 C3
Shāzand Iran 35 H4
Shazāz, Jabal mt. Saudi Arabia 35 F6
Shchekino Rus. Fed. 13 H5
Shchel'yayur Rus. Fed. 12 L2
Shcherbakov Rus. Fed. see Rybinsk
Shchigry Rus. Fed. 13 H6
Shchors Ukr. 13 G6
Shchuchin Belarus see Shchuchyn
Shchuchyn Belarus 15 N10
Shebalino Rus. Fed. 42 F2
Shebekino Rus. Fed. 13 H6
Sheberghan Afgh. 36 A1
Sheboygan U.S.A. 63 J3
Shebshi Mountains Nigeria 46 E4
Shebunino Rus. Fed. 44 F3
Shedok Rus. Fed. 35 F1
Sheelin, Lough l. Ireland 21 E4
Sheep Haven b. Ireland 21 E2
Sheepmoor S. Africa 51 J4
Sheep Peak NV U.S.A. 65 E3
Sheep's Head hd Ireland see Montervary
Sheerness U.K. 19 H7
Shefar'am Israel 39 B3
Sheffield N.Z. 59 D6
Sheffield U.K. 18 F5
Sheffield PA U.S.A. 64 B2
Shegmas Rus. Fed. 12 K2
Sheikh, Jebel esh mt. Lebanon/Syria see Hermon, Mount
Sheikhpura India 37 F4
Sheikhupura Pak. 33 L3
Shekār Āb Iran 35 I4
Shekhem West Bank see Nāblus
Shekhpura India see Sheikhpura
Sheki Azer. see Şäki
Sheksna Rus. Fed. 12 H4
Sheksninskoye Vodokhranilishche resr Rus. Fed. 12 H4
Shela China 37 H3
Shelagskiy, Mys pt Rus. Fed. 29 S2
Shelburne N.S. Canada 63 N3
Shelburne Bay Australia 56 C1
Shelby MT U.S.A. 62 E2
Shelbyville TN U.S.A. 63 J4
Shelikhova, Zaliv g. Rus. Fed. 29 Q3
Shelikof Strait U.S.A. 60 C4
Shellbrook Canada 62 F1
Shellharbour Australia 58 E5
Shelter Island NY U.S.A. 64 E2
Shelter Point N.Z. 59 B8
Shemakha Azer. see Şamaxı
Shemgang Bhutan 37 G4
Shemordan Rus. Fed. 12 K4
Shenandoah U.S.A. 64 C4
Shenandoah Mountains Virginia/West Virginia U.S.A. 64 B4
Shenandoah National Park VA U.S.A. 64 B3
Shendam Nigeria 46 D4
Shending Shan hill China 44 D3
Shengena mt. Tanz. 49 D4
Shengli Feng mt. China/Kyrg. see Pobeda Peak
Shengping China 44 B3
Shen Khan Bandar Afgh. 36 B1
Shenkursk Rus. Fed. 12 I3
Shenmu China 43 K5
Shenshu China 44 C3
Shensi prov. China see Shaanxi
Shentala Rus. Fed. 13 K5
Shenton, Mount hill Australia 55 C7
Shenyang China 44 A4
Shenzhen China 43 K8
Sheopur India 36 D4
Shepetivka Ukr. 13 E6
Shepetovka Ukr. see Shepetivka
Shepherd Islands Vanuatu 53 G3
Shepparton Australia 58 B6
Sheppey, Isle of i. U.K. 19 H7
Sherabad Uzbek. see Sherobod
Shorkozakhly, Solonchak salt flat Turkm. 35 J2
Sherborne U.K. 19 E7
Sherbro Island Sierra Leone 46 B4
Sherbrooke Canada 63 M2
Sherburne NY U.S.A. 64 C1
Shercock Ireland 21 F4
Shereiq Sudan 32 D6
Shergaon India 37 H4

Shergarh India 36 C4
Sheridan WY U.S.A. 62 F3
Sheringham U.K. 19 I6
Sherman U.S.A. 63 H5
Sherobod Uzbek. 33 K3
Sherpur Dhaka Bangl. 37 G4
Sherpur Rajshahi Bangl. 37 G4
's-Hertogenbosch Neth. 16 J5
Sherwood Forest reg. U.K. 19 F5
Sheryshevo Rus. Fed. 44 C2
Shetland Islands is U.K. 20 [inset]
Shetpe Kazakh. 30 E2
Shevchenko Kazakh. see Aktau
Shevli r. Rus. Fed. 44 D1
Sheyenne r. U.S.A. 62 G2
Shey Phoksundo National Park Nepal 37 E3
Shiant Islands U.K. 20 C3
Shiashkotan, Ostrov i. Rus. Fed. 29 Q5
Shibām Yemen 32 G6
Shibar, Kowtal-e Afgh. 36 B2
Shibata Japan 45 E5
Shibazhan China 44 B1
Shibh Jazīrat Sīnā' pen. Egypt see Sinai
Shibīn al Kawm Egypt 34 C5
Shibīn el Kôm Egypt see Shibīn al Kawm
Shibotsu-jima i. Rus. Fed. see Zelenyy, Ostrov
Shidād al Mismā' hill Saudi Arabia 39 D4
Shidao China 43 M5
Shiel, Loch l. U.K. 20 D4
Shiela, Loch l. U.K. see Shiel, Loch
Shield, Cape Australia 56 B2
Shieli Kazakh. see Chiili
Shifa, Jabal ash mts Saudi Arabia 34 D5
Shigatse China see Xigazê
Shiḩān mt. Jordan 39 B4
Shihezi China 42 F3
Shihkiachwang China see Shijiazhuang
Shijiazhuang China 43 K5
Shikarpur Pak. 33 K4
Shikhany Rus. Fed. 13 J5
Shikohabad India 36 D4
Shikoku i. Japan 45 D6
Shikoku-sanchi mts Japan 45 D6
Shikotan, Ostrov i. Rus. Fed. 44 G4
Shikotan-tō i. Rus. Fed. see Shikotan, Ostrov
Shikotsu-Tōya Kokuritsu-kōen Japan 44 F4
Shildon U.K. 18 F4
Shilega Rus. Fed. 12 I2
Shiliguri India 37 G4
Shilka r. Jammu and Kashmir 36 C2
Shillelagh Ireland 21 F5
Shillo r. Israel 39 B3
Shillong India 37 G4
Shilovo Rus. Fed. 13 I5
Shimada Japan 45 E6
Shimanovsk Rus. Fed. 44 B1
Shimbiris mt. Somalia 48 E2
Shimen Hunan China 43 K7
Shimla India 36 D3
Shimoga India 38 B3
Shimokita-hantō pen. Japan 44 F4
Shimoni Kenya 49 D4
Shimonoseki Japan 45 C6
Shin, Loch l. U.K. 20 E2
Shinafiyah Iraq see Ash Shanāfiyah
Shindand Afgh. 33 J3
Shingbwiyang Myanmar 37 I4
Shinghshal Pass China 36 C1
Shingū China 36 C2
Shingwedzi S. Africa 51 J2
Shingwedzi r. S. Africa 51 J2
Shinkay Afgh. 36 A3
Shinkay Ghar Afgh. 36 B3
Shinnston WV U.S.A. 64 A3
Shinshār Syria 39 C2
Shinyanga Tanz. 48 D4
Shiogama Japan 45 F5
Shiono-misaki c. Japan 45 D6
Shipki Pass China/India 36 D3
Shipman VA U.S.A. 64 B4
Shippensburg PA U.S.A. 64 C3
Shipunovo Rus. Fed. 42 F2
Shiquanhe Xizang China see Ali
Shiquanhe Xizang China see Gar
Shira r. Rus. Fed. 42 F2
Shirābād Iran 35 H3
Shirakawa-Go and Gokayama tourist site Japan 45 E5
Shirane-san vol. Japan 45 E5
Shirase Coast Antarctica 76 J1
Shirase Glacier Antarctica 76 D2
Shīrāz Iran 35 I5
Shire r. Malawi 49 D5
Shirīn Tagāb Afgh. 36 A1
Shiriya-zaki c. Japan 44 F4
Shīr Kūh mt. Iran 35 I5
Shiroro Reservoir Nigeria 46 D3
Shirpur India 36 C5
Shirten Holoy Gobi des. China 42 H4
Shirvān Iran 33 J2
Shisanzhan China 44 B2
Shishaldin Volcano U.S.A. 60 B4
Shisha Pangma mt. China see Xixabangma Feng
Shithāthah Iraq 35 F4
Shiv India 36 B4
Shiveluch, Sopka vol. Rus. Fed. 29 R4
Shivpuri India 36 D4
Shivwits UT U.S.A. 65 F2
Shivwits Plateau AZ U.S.A. 65 F2
Shiwa Ngandu Zambia 49 D5
Shiyan China 43 K6
Shizuoka Japan 45 E6
Shkhara mt. Georgia/Rus. Fed. 35 F2
Shklov Belarus see Shklow
Shklow Belarus 13 F5
Shkodër Albania 27 H3
Shkodra Albania see Shkodër
Shkodrës, Liqeni i l. Albania/Montenegro see Scutari, Lake
Shmidta, Ostrov i. Rus. Fed. 28 K1
Shmidta, Poluostrov pen. Rus. Fed. 44 F1
Shōbara Japan 45 D6
Shoh Tajik. 36 B1
Shohi Pass Pak. see Tal Pass
Shokanbetsu-dake mt. Japan 44 F4
Sholakkorgan Kazakh. 42 B4
Sholapur India see Solapur
Sholaqorghan Kazakh. see Sholakkorgan
Shomba r. Rus. Fed. 14 R4
Shomvukva Rus. Fed. 12 K3
Shona Ridge sea feature S. Atlantic Ocean 72 I9
Shonzha Kazakh. see Chundzha
Shor India 36 D2
Sho'rchi Uzbek. 42 B5
Shorkot Pak. 36 B3
Shorkozakhly, Solonchak salt flat Turkm. 35 J2
Shoshone CA U.S.A. 65 D3
Shoshone Peak NV U.S.A. 65 D2
Shoshong Botswana 51 H2
Shostka Ukr. 13 G6
Shotor Khūn Afgh. 36 A2
Showak Sudan 32 E7
Show Low U.S.A. 62 E5

Shoyna Rus. Fed. 12 J2
Shpakovskoye Rus. Fed. 35 F1
Shpola Ukr. 13 F6
Shqipëria country Europe see Albania
Shreveport U.S.A. 63 H5
Shrewsbury U.K. 19 E6
Shri Lanka country Asia see Sri Lanka
Shri Mohangarh India 36 B4
Shrirampur India 37 G5
Shu Kazakh. 42 C4
Shū r. Kazakh./Kyrg. see Chu
Shu'ab, Ra's pt Yemen 33 H7
Shuangcheng Heilong. China 44 B3
Shuanghedagang China 44 C2
Shuangjiao China 44 A4
Shuangliao China 44 A4
Shuangshipu China see Fengxian
Shuangyang China 44 B4
Shuangyashan China 44 C3
Shubarkuduk Kazakh. 28 G5
Shubayh well Saudi Arabia 39 D4
Shugozero Rus. Fed. 12 G4
Shuicheng China see Lupanshui
Shulan China 44 B3
Shumagin Islands U.S.A. 60 B4
Shumba Zimbabwe 49 C5
Shumen Bulg. 27 L3
Shumerlya Rus. Fed. 12 J5
Shumilina Belarus 13 F5
Shumyachi Rus. Fed. 13 G5
Shuncheng China 44 A4
Shuoxian China see Shuozhou
Shuozhou China 43 K5
Shuqrah Yemen 32 G7
Shūr r. Iran 35 I5
Shūr r. Iran 35 I5
Shūrjestān Iran 35 I5
Shuryshkarskiy Sor, Ozero l. Rus. Fed. 11 T2
Shūsh Iran 35 H4
Shusha Azer. see Şuşa
Shushtar Iran 35 H4
Shuwaysh, Tall ash hill Jordan 39 C4
Shuya Ivanovskaya Oblast' Rus. Fed. 12 I4
Shuya Respublika Kareliya Rus. Fed. 12 G3
Shuyskoye Rus. Fed. 12 I4
Shwebo Myanmar 37 H5
Shwedwin Myanmar 37 H4
Shweudaung mt. Myanmar 37 I5
Shyghanaq Kazakh. see Chiganak
Shymkent Kazakh. 42 B4
Shyok Jammu and Kashmir 36 D2
Shypuvate Ukr. 13 H6
Shyroke Ukr. 13 G7
Sia Indon. 41 F8
Siahan Range mts Pak. 33 J4
Siah Chashmeh Iran 35 G3
Siahgird Afgh. 36 A1
Sialkot Pak. 33 L3
Siam country Asia see Thailand
Sian China see Xi'an
Sian Rus. Fed. 44 B2
Siang r. India see Brahmaputra
Siantan i. Indon. 41 D7
Siargao i. Phil. 41 D7
Siazan' Azer. see Siyäzän
Sibasa S. Africa 51 J2
Šibenik Croatia 26 F3
Siberia reg. Rus. Fed. 29 M3
Siberut i. Indon. 41 B8
Sibi Pak. 33 K4
Sibiloi National Park Kenya 48 D3
Sibir' reg. Rus. Fed. see Siberia
Sibiti Congo 48 B4
Sibiu Romania 27 K2
Sibolga Indon. 41 B7
Sibsagar India 37 H4
Sibu Sarawak Malaysia 41 D7
Sibut Cent. Afr. Rep. 48 B3
Sicca Veneria Tunisia see Le Kef
Sicheng Anhui China see Sixian
Sichuan prov. China 42 I6
Sichuan Pendi basin China 42 I7
Sicié, Cap c. France 24 G5
Sicilia i. Italy see Sicily
Sicilian Channel Italy/Tunisia 26 E6
Sicily i. Italy 26 F6
Sicuani Peru 68 D6
Siddhapur India 36 C5
Siddipet India 38 C2
Sideros, Akrotirio pt Greece 27 L7
Sidesaviwa S. Africa 50 F7
Sidhauli India 36 E4
Sidhi India 37 E4
Sidhpur India see Siddhapur
Sidi Aïssa Alg. 25 H6
Sidi Ali Alg. 25 G5
Sidi Barrāni Egypt 34 B5
Sidi Bel Abbès Alg. 25 F6
Sidi Bennour Morocco 22 C5
Sidi Bou Sa'id Tunisia see Sidi Bouzid
Sidi Bouzid Tunisia 26 C7
Sidi el Barrâni Egypt see Sīdī Barrāni
Sidi El Hani, Sebkhet de salt pan Tunisia 26 D7
Sidi Ifni Morocco 46 B2
Sidi Kacem Morocco 22 C5
Sidi Khaled Alg. 25 F6
Sidlaw Hills U.K. 20 F4
Sidley, Mount Antarctica 76 J1
Sidli India 37 E4
Sidmouth U.K. 19 D8
Sidney MT U.S.A. 62 G2
Sidney NE U.S.A. 62 G3
Sidney OH U.S.A. 63 K3
Sidoktaya Myanmar 37 H5
Sidon Lebanon 39 B3
Sidr Egypt see Sudr
Siedlce Poland 13 D5
Siegen Germany 17 L5
Siena Italy 26 D3
Sieradz Poland 17 Q5
Si'erdingka China 37 H3
Sierra Colorada Arg. 70 C6
Sierra Grande Arg. 70 C6
Sierra Leone country Africa 46 B4
Sierra Leone Basin sea feature N. Atlantic Ocean 72 G5
Sierra Leone Rise sea feature N. Atlantic Ocean 72 G5
Sierra Madre Mountains CA U.S.A. 65 B3
Sierra Nevada, Parque Nacional nat. park Venez. 68 D2
Sierra Nevada de Santa Marta, Parque Nacional nat. park Col. 68 D1
Sierra Vista U.S.A. 62 E5
Sierre Switz. 24 H3
Sievi Fin. 14 N5
Sifangtai China 44 B3
Sifeni Eth. 48 E2
Sifnos i. Greece 27 K6
Sig Alg. 25 F6
Sigguup Nunaa pen. Greenland 61 M2
Sighetu Marmaţiei Romania 13 D7
Sighişoara Romania 27 K1
Sigli Indon. 41 B6
Siglufjörður Iceland 14 [inset]
Signal de la Ste-Baume mt. France 24 G5
Signal Peak AZ U.S.A. 65 F4
Signy research station Antarctica 76 A2
Sigsbee Deep sea feature G. of Mexico 75 N4
Sigüenza Spain 25 E3

Siguiri Guinea 46 C3
Sigulda Latvia 15 N8
Sihanoukville Cambodia 31 J5
Sihaung Myauk Myanmar 37 H5
Sihawa India 38 D1
Sihora India 36 E5
Siikajoki Fin. 14 N4
Siilinjärvi Fin. 14 O5
Siirt Turkey 35 F3
Sijawal Pak. 36 B4
Sika India 36 B5
Sikaka Saudi Arabia see Sakākah
Sikandra Rao India 36 D4
Sikar India 36 C4
Sikaram mt. Afgh. 36 B2
Sikasso Mali 46 C3
Sikeston U.S.A. 63 J4
Sikhote-Alin' mts Rus. Fed. 44 D4
Sikhote-Alinskiy Zapovednik nature res. Rus. Fed. 44 D4
Sikinos i. Greece 27 K6
Sikkim state India 37 G4
Siksjö Sweden 14 J4
Sil r. Spain 25 C2
Şila'i Iran see Selseleh-ye Pīr Shūrān
Šilalė Lith. 15 M9
Silavatturai Sri Lanka 38 C4
Silchar India 37 H4
Şile Turkey 27 M4
Sileru r. India 38 D2
Silesia reg. Czech Rep./Poland 17 P5
Sileti r. Kazakh. 42 D2
Siletiteniz, Ozero salt l. Kazakh. 31 G1
Silghat India 37 H4
Siliana Tunisia 26 C6
Silifke Turkey 39 A1
Siliguri India see Shiliguri
Siling Co salt l. China 37 G3
Silipur India 36 D4
Silistra Bulg. 27 L2
Silistria Bulg. see Silistra
Silivri Turkey 27 M4
Siljan l. Sweden 15 I6
Silkeborg Denmark 15 F8
Sillajhuay mt. Chile 68 E7
Sillamäe Estonia 15 O7
Sille Turkey 34 D3
Silli India 37 F5
Sillod India 38 B1
Silobela S. Africa 51 J4
Siltaharju Fin. 14 O3
Silvan Turkey 35 F3
Silvânia Brazil 71 A2
Silvassa India 38 B1
Silver Bank Passage Turks and Caicos Is 67 J4
Silver City NM U.S.A. 62 F5
Silver City NV U.S.A. 65 C1
Silver Lake CA U.S.A. 65 D3
Silvermine Mts hills Ireland 21 D5
Silver Peak Range mts NV U.S.A. 65 D2
Silver Spring MD U.S.A. 64 C3
Silverton U.K. 19 D8
Silverton CO U.S.A. 62 F4
Sima China 37 I3
Simanggang Sarawak Malaysia see Sri Aman
Simao China 42 I8
Simärd, Lac l. Canada 63 L2
Simaria India 37 F4
Simav Turkey 27 M5
Simav Dağları mts Turkey 27 M5
Simba Dem. Rep. Congo 48 C3
Simbirsk Rus. Fed. see Ul'yanovsk
Simcoe Ont. Canada 64 A2
Simcoe, Lake Canada 63 L3
Simdega India 38 I1
Simën mts Eth. 48 D2
Simën Mountains Eth. see Simën
Simeulue i. Indon. 41 B7
Simferopol' Ukr. 34 D1
Simi i. Greece see Symi
Simikot Nepal 37 E3
Simi Valley CA U.S.A. 65 C3
Simla India see Shimla
Şimleu Silvaniei Romania 27 J1
Şimojärvi l. Fin. 14 O3
Simplício Mendes Brazil 69 J5
Simplon Pass Switz. 24 I3
Simpson Desert Australia 56 B5
Simpson Desert National Park Australia 56 B5
Simpson Desert Regional Reserve nature res. Australia 57 B5
Simpson Peninsula Canada 61 J3
Simrishamn Sweden 15 I9
Simushir, Ostrov i. Rus. Fed. 43 S3
Sina r. India 38 B2
Sinai pen. Egypt 39 A5
Sinai al Janūbīya governorate Egypt see Janūb Sīnā'
Sinai ash Shamālīya governorate Egypt see Shamāl Sīnā'
Sinalunga Italy 26 D3
Sinancha Rus. Fed. see Cheremshany
Sinbyugyun Myanmar 37 H5
Sincan Turkey 34 D3
Sincelejo Col. 68 C2
Sincora, Serra do hills Brazil 71 C1
Sind r. India 36 D4
Sind Pak. see Thul
Sind prov. Pak. see Sindh
Sinda Rus. Fed. 44 D2
Sinda India 36 B4
Sindelfingen Germany 17 L6
Sindh prov. Pak. 36 B4
Sindhuli Garhi Nepal 37 F4
Sindhulimadi Nepal see Sindhuli Garhi
Sındırgı Turkey 27 M5
Sindor Rus. Fed. 12 K3
Sindou Burkina 46 C3
Sindri India 37 F5
Sind Sagar Doab lowland Pak. 36 B3
Sinel'nikovo Ukr. see Synel'nykove
Sines Port. 25 B5
Sines, Cabo de c. Port. 25 B5
Sinettä Fin. 14 N3
Sinfra Côte d'Ivoire 46 C4
Singa Sudan 32 D7
Singanallur India 38 C4
Singapore country Asia 41 C7
Singapore Sing. 41 [inset]
Singapura country Asia see Singapore
Singapura Sing. see Singapore
Singaraja Indon. 54 A2
Singhana India 36 C3
Singida Tanz. 49 D4
Singidunum Serbia see Belgrade
Singkaling Hkamti Myanmar 37 H4
Singkawang Indon. 41 C7
Singleton N.S.W. Australia 58 E4
Singleton, Mount hill N.T. Australia 54 E5
Singleton, Mount hill W.A. Australia 55 B7
Singora Thai. see Songkhla
Sin'gosan N. Korea see Kosan
Singra India 37 G4
Singri India 37 H4
Singwara India 38 D1
Sin'gye N. Korea 45 B5

Sinhala country Asia see Sri Lanka
Sining China see Xining
Siniscola Sardinia Italy 26 C4
Sinj Croatia 26 G3
Sinjai Indon. 41 E8
Sinjār, Jabal mt. Iraq 35 F3
Sinkat Sudan 32 E6
Sinkiang aut. reg. China see Xinjiang Uygur Zizhiqu
Sinkiang Uighur Autonomous Region aut. reg. China see Xinjiang Uygur Zizhiqu
Sinmi-do i. N. Korea 45 B5
Sinnamary Fr. Guiana 69 H2
Sinn Bishr, Gebel hill Egypt see Sinn Bishr, Jabal
Sinn Bishr, Jabal hill Egypt 39 A5
Sinneh Iran see Sanandaj
Sinoia Zimbabwe see Chinhoyi
Sinop Brazil 69 G6
Sinop Turkey 34 D2
Sinope Turkey see Sinop
Sinp'a N. Korea 44 B4
Sinp'o N. Korea 45 C4
Sinsang N. Korea 45 B5
Sint Eustatius i. Neth. Antilles 67 L5
Sint Maarten i. Neth. Antilles 67 L5
Sint-Niklaas Belgium 16 J5
Sintra Port. 25 B4
Sinŭiju N. Korea 45 B4
Siófok Hungary 26 H1
Sioma Ngwezi National Park Zambia 49 C5
Sion Switz. 24 H3
Sion Mills U.K. 21 E3
Siorapaluk Greenland 61 K2
Sioux Center U.S.A. 63 H3
Sioux City U.S.A. 63 H3
Sioux Falls U.S.A. 63 H3
Sioux Lookout Canada 63 I1
Siphaqeni S. Africa see Flagstaff
Siping China 44 B4
Siple, Mount Antarctica 76 J2
Siple Coast Antarctica 76 I1
Siple Island Antarctica 76 J2
Sipura i. Indon. 41 B8
Sīq, Wādī as watercourse Egypt 39 A5
Sir r. Pak. 36 B5
Sir, Dar"yoi r. Asia see Syrdar'ya
Sira India 38 C3
Sira r. Norway 15 E7
Siracusa Sicily Italy see Syracuse
Siraha Nepal see Sirha
Sirajganj Bangl. 37 G4
Şiran Turkey 35 E2
Sirbāl, Jabal mt. Egypt 34 D5
Sircilla India see Sirsilla
Sirdaryo r. Asia see Syrdar'ya
Sirdaryo Uzbek. 42 B4
Sirdaryo Uzbek. see Sirdaryo
Sirdingka China see Si'erdingka
Sir Edward Pellew Group is Australia 56 B2
Sirha Nepal 37 F4
Sirḩān, Wādī as watercourse Jordan/Saudi Arabia 39 C4
Sirína i. Greece see Syrna
Sir James MacBrien, Mount Canada 60 F3
Sīrjān Iran 33 I4
Sirkazhi India 38 C4
Sirmilik National Park Canada 61 K2
Şırnak Turkey 35 F3
Sirohi India 36 C4
Sironj India 36 D4
Siros i. Greece see Syros
Sirpur India 38 C2
Sirretta Peak CA U.S.A. 65 C3
Sirsa India 36 C3
Sirsi Karnataka India 38 B3
Sirsi Madh. Prad. India 36 D4
Sirsi Uttar Prad. India 36 D3
Sirsilla India 38 C2
Sirte Libya 47 E1
Sirte, Gulf of Libya 47 E1
Sir Thomas, Mount hill Australia 55 E6
Siruguppa India 38 C3
Sirur India 38 B2
Şirvan Turkey 35 F3
Şirvel India 38 C3
Širvintai Lith. see Širvintos
Širvintos Lith. 15 N9
Sīrwān r. Iraq 35 G4
Sis Turkey see Kozan
Sisak Croatia 26 G2
Siscia Croatia see Sisak
Sishen S. Africa 50 F4
Sisian Armenia 35 G3
Sisimiut Greenland 61 M3
Sisteron France 24 G4
Sitamarhi India 37 F4
Sitapur India 36 E4
Siteia Greece 27 L7
Siteki Swaziland 51 J4
Sithonias, Chersonisos pen. Greece 27 J4
Sitia Greece see Siteia
Sitidgi Lake Canada 60 E3
Sitila Moz. 51 L2
Sítio do Mato Brazil 71 C1
Sitka U.S.A. 60 E4
Sitra oasis Egypt see Sitrah
Sitrah oasis Egypt 34 B5
Sittaung Myanmar 37 H4
Sittingbourne U.K. 19 H7
Sittwe Myanmar 37 H5
Siuri India 37 F5
Sivaganga India 38 C4
Sivakasi India 38 C4
Sivaki Rus. Fed. 44 B1
Sivan India see Siwan
Sivas Turkey 34 E3
Sivaslı Turkey 27 M5
Siverek Turkey 35 E3
Siverskiy Rus. Fed. 15 Q7
Sivers'kyy Donets' r. Rus. Fed./Ukr. see Severskiy Donets
Sivomaskinskiy Rus. Fed. 11 S2
Sivrice Turkey 35 E3
Sivrihisar Turkey 27 N5
Sivukile S. Africa 51 I4
Sīwa Egypt see Sīwah
Sīwah Egypt 34 B5
Sīwah, Wāḩāt oasis Egypt 34 B5
Siwalik Range mts India/Nepal 36 D3
Siwan India 37 F4
Siwana India 36 C4
Siwa Oasis oasis Egypt see Sīwah, Wāḩāt
Sixian China 43 L6
Sixmilecross U.K. 21 E3
Siyabuswa S. Africa 51 I3
Siyäzän Azer. 35 H2
Sīyunī Iran 35 I4
Siziwang Qi China see Ulan Hua
Sjælland i. Denmark see Zealand
Sjenica Serbia 27 I3
Sjöbo Sweden 15 H9
Sjøvegan Norway 14 J2
Skadarsko Jezero nat. park Montenegro 27 H3
Skadovs'k Ukr. 27 O1
Skaftafell nat. park Iceland 14 [inset]
Skaftárós r. mouth Iceland 14 [inset]
Skagafjörður inlet Iceland 14 [inset]
Skagen Denmark 15 G8
Skagerrak strait Denmark/Norway 15 F8
Skagit r. U.S.A. 62 C2
Skagway U.S.A. 77 A3
Skaidi Norway 14 N1
Skaland Norway 14 J2
Skalmodal Sweden 14 I4
Skanderborg Denmark 15 F8
Skaneateles Lake NY U.S.A. 64 C1
Skara Sweden 15 H7
Skardarsko Jezero l. Albania/Montenegro see Scutari, Lake
Skardu Jammu and Kashmir 36 C2
Skärgårdshavets nationalpark nat. park Fin. 15 L7
Skarnes Norway 15 G6
Skarżysko-Kamienna Poland 17 R5
Skaulo Sweden 14 L3
Skawina Poland 17 Q6
Skeena Mountains Canada 60 F4
Skegness U.K. 18 H5
Skellefteå Sweden 14 L4
Skellefteälven r. Sweden 14 L4
Skelleftehamn Sweden 14 L4
Skellig Rocks is Ireland 21 B6
Skelmersdale U.K. 18 E5
Skerries Ireland 21 F4
Ski Norway 15 G7
Skiathos i. Greece 27 J5
Skibbereen Ireland 21 C6
Skibotn Norway 14 L2
Skiddaw hill U.K. 18 D4
Skien Norway 15 F7
Skierniewice Poland 17 R5
Skikda Alg. 26 B6
Skipsea U.K. 18 G5
Skipton Australia 58 A6
Skipton U.K. 18 E5
Skirlaugh U.K. 18 G5
Skíros i. Greece see Skyros
Skive Denmark 15 F8
Skjern Denmark 15 F9
Skjolden Norway 15 E6
Skobelev Uzbek. see Farg'ona
Skodje Norway 14 E5
Skoganvarri Norway 14 N2
Skomer Island U.K. 19 B7
Skopelos i. Greece 27 J5
Skopin Rus. Fed. 13 H5
Skopje Macedonia 27 I4
Skoplje Macedonia see Skopje
Skövde Sweden 15 H7
Skovorodino Rus. Fed. 44 A1
Skowhegan U.S.A. 63 N3
Skrunda Latvia 15 M8
Skukum, Mount Canada 60 E3
Skukuza S. Africa 51 J3
Skull Valley AZ U.S.A. 65 F3
Skuodas Lith. 15 L8
Skurup Sweden 15 H9
Skutskär Sweden 15 J6
Skvyra Ukr. 13 F6
Skye i. U.K. 20 C3
Skyring, Seno b. Chile 70 B8
Skyros Greece 27 K5
Skyros i. Greece 27 K5
Skytrain Ice Rise Antarctica 76 L1
Slættaratindur hill Faroe Is 14 [inset]
Slagelse Denmark 15 G9
Slagnäs Sweden 14 K4
Slane Ireland 21 F4
Slaney r. Ireland 21 F5
Slantsy Rus. Fed. 15 P7
Slapovi Krke nat. park Croatia 26 F3
Slashers Reefs Australia 56 D3
Slatina Croatia 26 G2
Slatina Romania 27 K2
Slaty Fork WV U.S.A. 64 A3
Slava Rus. Fed. 44 C1
Slave r. Canada 77 L2
Slave Coast Africa 46 D4
Slave Lake Canada 77 L3
Slavgorod Belarus see Slawharad
Slavgorod Rus. Fed. 42 D2
Slavkovichi Rus. Fed. 15 P8
Slavonska Požega Croatia see Požega
Slavonski Brod Croatia 26 H2
Slavuta Ukr. 13 E6
Slavutych Ukr. 13 F6
Slavyanka Rus. Fed. 44 C4
Slavyansk Ukr. see Slov"yans'k
Slavyanskaya Rus. Fed. see Slavyansk-na-Kubani
Slavyansk-na-Kubani Rus. Fed. 34 E1
Slawharad Belarus 13 F5
Sławno Poland 17 P3
Sleaford U.K. 19 G5
Slea Head hd Ireland 21 B5
Sleat, Sound of sea chan. U.K. 20 D3
Sleeper Islands Canada 61 K4
Slessor Glacier Antarctica 76 B1
Slide Mountain NY U.S.A. 64 D2
Slieve Bloom Mts hills Ireland 21 E5
Slieve Car hill Ireland 21 C3
Slieve Donard hill U.K. 21 G3
Slieve Gamph hills Ireland 21 C4
Slievekimalta hill Ireland 21 D5
Slieve Mish Mts hills Ireland 21 B5
Slieve Snaght hill Ireland 21 E2
Sligachan U.K. 20 C3
Sligeach Ireland see Sligo
Sligo Ireland 21 D3
Sligo PA U.S.A. 64 B2
Sligo Bay Ireland 21 D3
Slippery Rock PA U.S.A. 64 A2
Slite Sweden 15 K8
Sliven Bulg. 27 L3
Sloan NV U.S.A. 65 E3
Sloboda Rus. Fed. see Ezhva
Slobodchikovo Rus. Fed. 12 K3
Slobodskoy Rus. Fed. 12 K4
Slobozia Romania 27 L2
Slonim Belarus 15 N10
Slough U.K. 19 G7
Slovakia country Europe 10 J6
Slovenia country Europe 26 F2
Slovenija country Europe see Slovenia
Slovenj Gradec Slovenia 26 F1
Slovensko country Europe see Slovakia
Slovenský raj nat. park Slovakia 17 R6
Slov"yans'k Ukr. 13 H6
Słowiński Park Narodowy nat. park Poland 17 P3
Sluch r. Ukr. 13 E6
Słupsk Poland 17 P3
Slussfors Sweden 14 J4
Slutsk Belarus 15 O10
Slyne Head hd Ireland 21 B4
Slyudyanka Rus. Fed. 42 I2
Smallwood Reservoir Canada 61 L4
Smalyavichy Belarus 15 P9
Smalyenskaya Wzwyshsha hills Belarus/Rus. Fed. see Smolensko-Moskovskaya Vozvyshennost'
Smarhon' Belarus 15 O9
Smeaton Canada 62 G1
Smederevo Serbia 27 I2
Smederevska Palanka Serbia 27 I2
Smela Ukr. see Smila
Smethport PA U.S.A. 64 B2
Smidovich Rus. Fed. 44 D2
Smila Ukr. 13 F6
Smiltene Latvia 15 N8
Smirnykh Rus. Fed. 44 F2
Smithfield S. Africa 51 H6
Smith Glacier Antarctica 76 K1
Smith Island MD U.S.A. 64 C3
Smith Island VA U.S.A. 64 D4
Smith Mountain Lake VA U.S.A. 64 B4
Smiths Falls Canada 63 L3
Smithton Australia 57 [inset]
Smithtown Australia 58 F3
Smithville WV U.S.A. 64 A3
Smoky Bay Australia 55 F8
Smoky Cape Australia 58 F3
Smoky Hills KS U.S.A. 62 H4
Smøla i. Norway 14 E5
Smolenka Rus. Fed. 13 K6
Smolensk Rus. Fed. 13 G5
Smolensk-Moscow Upland hills Belarus/Rus. Fed. see Smolensko-Moskovskaya Vozvyshennost'
Smolensko-Moskovskaya Vozvyshennost' hills Belarus/Rus. Fed. 13 G5
Smolevichi Belarus see Smalyavichy
Smolyan Bulg. 27 K4
Smørfjord Norway 14 N1
Smorgon' Belarus see Smarhon'
Smyley Island Antarctica 76 L2
Smyrna Turkey see İzmir
Smyrna DE U.S.A. 64 D3
Smyth Island atoll Marshall Is see Taongi
Snæfell mt. Iceland 14 [inset]
Snaefell hill Isle of Man 18 C4
Snake r. U.S.A. 62 D2
Snake Island Australia 58 C7
Snake River Plain U.S.A. 62 E3
Snare Lakes Canada see Wekweti
Snares Islands N.Z. 53 G6
Snåsa Norway 14 H4
Sneek Neth. 17 J4
Sneem Ireland 21 C6
Sneeuberge mts S. Africa 50 G6
Snegurovka Ukr. see Tetiyiv
Snelling CA U.S.A. 65 B2
Snettisham U.K. 19 H6
Snezhnogorsk Rus. Fed. 28 J3
Snežnik mt. Slovenia 26 F2
Sniečkus Lith. see Visaginas
Snihurivka Ukr. 13 G7
Snits Neth. see Sneek
Snizort, Loch b. U.K. 20 C3
Snøtinden mt. Norway 14 H3
Snovsk Ukr. see Shchors
Snowbird Lake Canada 61 H3
Snowdon mt. U.K. 19 C5
Snowdonia National Park U.K. 19 D6
Snowdrift Canada see Łutselk'e
Snowdrift r. Canada 60 G3
Snow Hill MD U.S.A. 64 D3
Snow Lake Canada 61 H4
Snowy r. Australia 58 D6
Snowy Mountain NY U.S.A. 64 D1
Snowy Mountains Australia 58 C6
Snowy River National Park Australia 58 D6
Snyder U.S.A. 62 G5
Soalala Madag. 49 E5
Soalara Madag. 49 E6
Soanierana-Ivongo Madag. 49 E5
Soan-kundo is S. Korea 45 B6
Soavinandriana Madag. 49 E5
Sobat r. Sudan 32 D8
Sobinka Rus. Fed. 12 I5
Sobradinho, Barragem de resr Brazil 69 J6
Sobral Brazil 69 J4
Sochi Rus. Fed. 13 H8
Soch'on S. Korea 45 B5
Society Islands Fr. Polynesia 75 J7
Socorro Brazil 71 B3
Socorro Col. 68 D2
Socorro U.S.A. 62 F5
Socorro, Isla i. Mex. 66 B5
Socotra i. Yemen 33 H7
Socuéllamos Spain 25 E4
Soda Lake CA U.S.A. 65 C3
Soda Lake CA U.S.A. 65 D3
Sodankylä Fin. 14 O3
Soda Plains Aksai Chin 36 D2
Soda Springs U.S.A. 62 E3
Söderhamn Sweden 15 J6
Söderköping Sweden 15 J7
Södertälje Sweden 15 J7
Sodiri Sudan 32 C7
Sodo Eth. 48 D3
Södra Kvarken strait Fin./Sweden 15 K6
Sodus NY U.S.A. 64 C1
Soekarno, Puntjak mt. Indon. see Jaya, Puncak
Soekmekaar S. Africa 51 I2
Soerabaia Indon. see Surabaya
Sofala Australia 58 D4
Sofia Bulg. 27 J3
Sofiya Bulg. see Sofia
Sofiyevka Ukr. see Vil'nyans'k
Sofiysk Khabarovskiy Kray Rus. Fed. 44 D1
Sofiysk Khabarovskiy Kray Rus. Fed. 44 E2
Sofporog Rus. Fed. 12 F2
Sofrana i. Greece 27 L6
Sofra Kalesi tourist site Turkey 39 A1
Sōfu-gan i. Japan 45 F7
Sog China 42 G6
Soğanlı Dağları mts Turkey 35 E2
Sogda Rus. Fed. 44 D2
Sogma China 36 E2
Søgne Norway 15 E7
Sognefjorden inlet Norway 15 D6
Söğüt Turkey 27 N4
Söğüt Dağı mts Turkey 27 M6
Soh Iran 35 H4
Sohâg Egypt see Sawhāj
Sohagpur India 36 D5
Soham U.K. 19 H6
Sohan r. Pak. 36 B2
Sohano P.N.G. 52 F2
Sohar Oman see Şuḩār
Sohawal India 36 E4
Sohela India 37 E5
Sŏho-ri N. Korea 45 C4
Sohŭksan-do i. S. Korea 45 B6
Soila China 37 I3
Soini Fin. 14 N5
Soissons France 24 F2
Sojat India 36 C4
Sojat Road India 36 C4
Sok r. Rus. Fed. 13 K5
Sokal' Ukr. 13 E6
Sokch'o S. Korea 45 C5
Söke Turkey 27 L6
Sokhor, Gora mt. Rus. Fed. 42 J2
Sokhumi Georgia 35 F2
Sokiryany Ukr. see Sokyryany
Sokodé Togo 46 D4
Sokol Rus. Fed. 12 I4
Sokolo Mali 46 C3
Sokoto Nigeria 46 D3
Sokoto r. Nigeria 46 D3
Sokyryany Ukr. 13 E6
Sola i. Tonga see Ata
Solan India 36 D3
Solana Beach CA U.S.A. 65 D4
Solander Island N.Z. 59 A8
Solapur India 38 B2
Soldotna U.S.A. 60 C3
Soledad CA U.S.A. 65 B2
Soledade Brazil 70 F3
Solenoye Rus. Fed. 13 I7
Solfjellsjøen Norway 14 H3
Solginskiy Rus. Fed. 12 I3
Solhan Turkey 35 F3
Soligalich Rus. Fed. 12 I4
Soligorsk Belarus see Salihorsk
Solihull U.K. 19 F6
Solikamsk Rus. Fed. 11 R4
Sol'-Iletsk Rus. Fed. 28 G4
Solimões r. S. America see Amazon
Solitaire Namibia 50 B2
Sol-Karmala Rus. Fed. see Severnoye
Şollar Azer. 35 H2
Sollefteå Sweden 14 J5
Sollum, Gulf of Egypt see Sallum, Khalīj as
Solnechnogorsk Rus. Fed. 12 H4
Solnechnyy Amurskaya Oblast' Rus. Fed. 44 A1
Solnechnyy Khabarovskiy Kray Rus. Fed. 44 E2
Solomon Islands country S. Pacific Ocean 53 G2
Solomon Sea S. Pacific Ocean 52 F2
Solor i. Indon. 54 C2
Solor, Kepulauan is Indon. 54 C2
Solothurn Switz. 24 H3
Solovetskiye Ostrova is Rus. Fed. 12 G2
Solov'yevsk Rus. Fed. 44 B1
Šolta i. Croatia 26 G3
Soltānābād Iran 35 H4
Solţānīyeh Iran 35 H3
Sol'tsy Rus. Fed. 12 F4
Solvay NY U.S.A. 64 C1
Sölvesborg Sweden 15 I8
Solway Firth est. U.K. 20 F6
Solwezi Zambia 49 C5
Soma Turkey 27 L5
Somalia country Africa 48 E3
Somali Basin sea feature Indian Ocean 73 L6
Somali Republic country Africa see Somalia
Sombo Angola 49 C4
Sombor Serbia 27 H2
Sombrio, Lago do l. Brazil 71 A5
Somero Fin. 15 M6
Somerset KY U.S.A. 63 K4
Somerset PA U.S.A. 64 B3
Somerset, Lake Australia 58 F1
Somerset East S. Africa 51 G7
Somerset Island Canada 61 I2
Somerset Reservoir VT U.S.A. 64 E1
Somerset West S. Africa 50 D8
Somersworth NH U.S.A. 64 F1
Somerton AZ U.S.A. 65 E4
Somerville NJ U.S.A. 64 D2
Someydeh Iran 35 G4
Somme r. France 19 I8
Sommen l. Sweden 15 I7
Somnath India 36 B5
Son r. India 37 F4
Sonapur India 38 D1
Sonar r. India 36 D4
Sŏnch'ŏn N. Korea 45 B5
Sønderborg Denmark 15 F9
Sondershausen Germany 17 M5
Søndre Strømfjord Greenland see Kangerlussuaq
Søndre Strømfjord inlet Greenland see Kangerlussuaq
Sondrio Italy 26 C1
Sonepat India see Sonipat
Sonepur India see Sonapur
Songea Tanz. 49 D5
Songhua Hu resr China 44 B4
Songhua Jiang r. Heilongjiang/Jilin China 44 D3
Songhua Jiang r. Jilin China see Di'er Songhua Jiang
Songjianghe China 44 B4
Sŏngjin N. Korea see Kimch'aek
Songkhla Thai. 31 J6
Songling China see Ta'erqi
Sŏngnam S. Korea 45 B5
Songnim N. Korea 45 B5
Songo Angola 49 B4
Songo Moz. 49 D5
Songpan China 42 I6
Songxi China 43 L7
Songyuan Fujian China see Songxi
Songyuan Jilin China 44 B3
Sonid Youqi China see Saihan Tal
Sonid Zuoqi China see Mandalt
Sonipat India 36 D3
Sonkajärvi Fin. 14 O5
Sonkovo Rus. Fed. 12 H4
Sơn La Vietnam 31 J4
Sonmiani Pak. 33 K4
Sonmiani Bay Pak. 36 A4
Sono r. Minas Gerais Brazil 71 B2
Sono r. Tocantins Brazil 69 I5
Sonoma CA U.S.A. 65 A1
Sonora r. Mex. 66 B3
Sonora CA U.S.A. 65 B2
Sonora TX U.S.A. 62 G5
Sonoran Desert AZ U.S.A. 65 F4
Sonqor Iran 35 G4
Sonsonate El Salvador 66 G6
Sonwabile S. Africa 51 I6
Soochow China see Suzhou
Soomaaliya country Africa see Somalia
Sopo watercourse Sudan 47 F4
Sopot Bulg. 27 K3
Sopot Poland 17 Q3
Sopron Hungary 26 G1
Sopur Jammu and Kashmir 36 C2
Sora Italy 26 E4
Sorab India 38 B3
Sorada India 38 E2
Söråker Sweden 14 J5
Sŏrak-san mt. S. Korea 45 C5
Sorak-san National Park S. Korea 45 C5
Sorel Canada 63 M2
Soreq r. Israel 39 B4
Sorgun Turkey 34 D3
Sorgun r. Turkey 39 B1
Soria Spain 25 E3
Sorkh, Kūh-e mts Iran 35 I4
Sorkheh Iran 35 I4
Sørli Norway 14 H4
Soro India 37 F5
Soroca Moldova 13 F6
Sorocaba Brazil 71 B3
Soroki Moldova see Soroca
Sorol atoll Micronesia 41 G7
Sorong Indon. 41 F8
Soroti Uganda 48 D3
Sørøya i. Norway 14 M1
Sorraia r. Port. 25 B4
Sørreisa Norway 14 K2
Sorrento Italy 26 F4
Sorsele Sweden 14 J4
Sorsogon Phil. 41 E6
Sortavala Rus. Fed. 12 F3
Sortland Norway 14 I2
Sortopolovskaya Rus. Fed. 12 K3
Sorvizhi Rus. Fed. 12 K4
Sŏsan S. Korea 45 B5
Sosenskiy Rus. Fed. 13 G5
Soshanguve S. Africa 51 I3
Sosna r. Rus. Fed. 13 H5
Sosneado mt. Arg. 70 C4
Sosnogorsk Rus. Fed. 12 L3
Sosnovka Arkhangel'skaya Oblast' Rus. Fed. 12 J3
Sosnovka Kaliningradskaya Oblast' Rus. Fed. 11 K5
Sosnovka Murmanskaya Oblast' Rus. Fed. 12 I2
Sosnovka Tambovskaya Oblast' Rus. Fed. 13 I5
Sosnovo Rus. Fed. 15 Q6
Sosnovo-Ozerskoye Rus. Fed. 43 K2
Sosnovyy Rus. Fed. 14 R4
Sosnovyy Bor Rus. Fed. 12 F4
Sosnowiec Poland 17 Q5
Sosnowitz Poland see Sosnowiec
Sos'va Khanty-Mansiyskiy Avtonomnyy Okrug Rus. Fed. 11 S3
Sos'va Sverdlovskaya Oblast' Rus. Fed. 11 S4
Sotang China 37 H3
Sotara, Volcán vol. Col. 68 C3
Sotkamo Fin. 14 P4
Sotteville-lès-Rouen France 19 I9
Souanké Congo 48 B3
Soubré Côte d'Ivoire 46 C4
Souderton PA U.S.A. 64 D2
Soufli Greece 27 L4
Soufrière St Lucia 67 L6
Soufrière vol. St Vincent 67 L6
Sougueur Alg. 25 G6
Souillac France 24 E4
Souk Ahras Alg. 26 B6
Souk el Arbaâ du Rharb Morocco 22 C5
Sŏul S. Korea see Seoul
Soulac-sur-Mer France 24 D4
Soulom France 24 D5
Souni Cyprus 39 A2
Soûr Lebanon see Tyre
Soure Brazil 69 I4
Sour el Ghozlane Alg. 25 H5
Souris Canada 62 G2
Souris r. Canada 62 G2
Souriya country Asia see Syria
Sousa Brazil 69 K5
Sousa Lara Angola see Bocoio
Sousse Tunisia 26 D7
Soustons France 24 D5
South Africa, Republic of country Africa 50 F5
Southampton Canada 63 K3
Southampton U.K. 19 F8
Southampton NY U.S.A. 64 E2
Southampton, Cape Canada 61 J3
Southampton Island Canada 61 J3
South Anna r. VA U.S.A. 64 C4
South Anston U.K. 18 F5
South Australia state Australia 52 D5
South Australian Basin sea feature Indian Ocean 73 P8
South Bank U.K. 18 F4
South Bend IN U.S.A. 63 J3
South Carolina state U.S.A. 63 K5
South China Sea N. Pacific Ocean 41 D6
South Coast Town Australia see Gold Coast
South Dakota state U.S.A. 62 G3
South Downs hills U.K. 19 G8
South-East admin. dist. Botswana 51 G3
South East Cape Australia 57 [inset]
Southeast Cape U.S.A. 60 B3
Southeast Indian Ridge sea feature Indian Ocean 73 N8
South East Isles Australia 55 C8
Southeast Pacific Basin sea feature S. Pacific Ocean 75 M10
South East Point Australia 58 C7
Southend U.K. 20 D5
Southend-on-Sea U.K. 19 H7
Southern admin. dist. Botswana 50 G3
Southern Alps mts N.Z. 59 C6
Southern Cross Australia 55 B7
Southern Indian Lake Canada 61 I4
Southern Lau Group is Fiji 53 I3
Southern National Park Sudan 47 F4
Southern Ocean 76 C2
Southern Rhodesia country Africa see Zimbabwe
Southern Uplands hills U.K. 20 E5
South Esk r. U.K. 20 F4
South Esk Tableland reg. Australia 54 D4
South Fiji Basin sea feature S. Pacific Ocean 74 H7
South Geomagnetic Pole Antarctica 76 F1
South Georgia i. S. Atlantic Ocean 70 I8
South Georgia and the South Sandwich Islands terr. S. Atlantic Ocean 70 I8
South Harris pen. U.K. 20 B3
South Henik Lake Canada 61 I3
South Honshu Ridge sea feature N. Pacific Ocean 74 F3
South Island India 38 B4
South Island N.Z. 59 D7
South Korea country Asia 45 B5
South Lake Tahoe CA U.S.A. 65 B1
South Luangwa National Park Zambia 49 D5
South Magnetic Pole Antarctica 76 G2
Southminster U.K. 19 H7
South Mountains hills PA U.S.A. 64 C3
South New Berlin NY U.S.A. 64 D1
South Orkney Islands S. Atlantic Ocean 72 F10
South Platte r. U.S.A. 62 G3
South Pole Antarctica 76 C1
Southport Qld Australia 58 F1
Southport Tas. Australia 57 [inset]
Southport U.K. 18 D5
South Ronaldsay i. U.K. 20 G2
South Sand Bluff pt S. Africa 51 J6
South Sandwich Islands S. Atlantic Ocean 72 G9
South Sandwich Trench sea feature S. Atlantic Ocean 72 G9
South San Francisco CA U.S.A. 65 A2
South Saskatchewan r. Canada 62 F1
South Shetland Islands Antarctica 76 A2
South Shetland Trough sea feature S. Atlantic Ocean 76 L2
South Shields U.K. 18 F3
South Sinai governorate Egypt see Janūb Sīnā'
South Solomon Trench sea feature S. Pacific Ocean 74 G6
South Taranaki Bight b. N.Z. 59 E4
South Tasman Rise sea feature Southern Ocean 74 F9
South Tons r. India 37 E4
South Tyne r. U.K. 18 E4
South Uist i. U.K. 20 B3
South Wellesley Islands Australia 56 B3
South-West Africa country Africa see Namibia
South West Cape N.Z. 59 A8
South West Entrance sea chan. P.N.G. 56 E1
Southwest Indian Ridge sea feature Indian Ocean 73 K8
South West National Park Australia 57 [inset]
Southwest Pacific Basin sea feature S. Pacific Ocean 74 I8
Southwest Peru Ridge sea feature S. Pacific Ocean see Nazca Ridge
South West Rocks Australia 58 F3
Southwold U.K. 19 I6
Southwood National Park Australia 58 E1
Soutpansberg mts S. Africa 51 I2
Souttouf, Adrar mts W. Sahara 46 B2
Soverato Italy 26 G5
Sovetsk Kaliningradskaya Oblast' Rus. Fed. 12 D5
Sovetsk Kirovskaya Oblast' Rus. Fed. 12 K4
Sovetskaya Gavan' Rus. Fed. 44 F2
Sovetskiy Khanty-Mansiyskiy Avtonomnyy Okrug Rus. Fed. 11 S3
Sovetskiy Leningradskaya Oblast' Rus. Fed. 15 P6
Sovetskiy Respublika Mariy El Rus. Fed. 12 K4
Sovetskoye Chechenskaya Respublika Rus. Fed. see Shatoy
Sovetskoye Stavropol'skiy Kray Rus. Fed. see Zelenokumsk
Sovyets'kyy Ukr. 34 D1
Soweto S. Africa 51 H4
Sōya-kaikyō strait Japan/Rus. Fed. see La Pérouse Strait
Sōya-misaki c. Japan 44 F3
Soyana r. Rus. Fed. 12 I2
Soyma r. Rus. Fed. 12 K2
Sozh r. Europe 13 F6
Sozopol Bulg. 27 L3
Spain country Europe 25 E3
Spalato Croatia see Split
Spalatum Croatia see Split
Spalding U.K. 19 G6
Spanish Guinea country Africa see Equatorial Guinea
Spanish Netherlands country Europe see Belgium
Spanish Sahara terr. Africa see Western Sahara
Spanish Town Jamaica 67 I5
Sparks U.S.A. 62 D4
Sparta Greece see Sparti
Spartanburg U.S.A. 63 K5
Sparti Greece 27 J6
Spartivento, Capo c. Italy 26 G6
Spas-Demensk Rus. Fed. 13 G5
Spas-Klepiki Rus. Fed. 13 I5
Spassk-Dal'niy Rus. Fed. 44 D3
Spassk-Ryazanskiy Rus. Fed. 13 I5
Spata (Eleftherios Venezielos) airport Greece 27 J6
Spatha, Akrotirio pt Greece 27 J7
Spence Bay Canada see Taloyoak
Spencer IA U.S.A. 63 H3
Spencer WV U.S.A. 64 A3
Spencer Bay Namibia 50 B3
Spencer Gulf est. Australia 57 B7
Spencer Range hills Australia 54 E3
Spennymoor U.K. 18 F4
Sperrin Mountains hills U.K. 21 E3
Sperryville VA U.S.A. 64 B3
Spessart reg. Germany 17 L6
Spétsai i. Greece see Spetses
Spetses i. Greece 27 J6
Spey r. U.K. 20 F3
Speyer Germany 17 L6
Spezand Pak. 36 A3
Spice Islands Indon. see Moluccas
Spijkenisse Neth. 16 J5
Spilimbergo Italy 26 E1
Spilsby U.K. 18 H5
Spīn Būldak Afgh. 36 A3
Spintangi Pak. 36 B3
Spirovo Rus. Fed. 12 G4
Spišská Nová Ves Slovakia 13 D6
Spiti r. India 36 D3
Spitsbergen i. Svalbard 28 C2
Spittal an der Drau Austria 17 N7
Spitzbergen i. Svalbard see Spitsbergen
Split Croatia 26 G3
Spokane U.S.A. 62 D2
Spoletium Italy see Spoleto
Spoleto Italy 26 E3
Spooner U.S.A. 63 I2
Spotsylvania VA U.S.A. 64 C3
Spratly Islands S. China Sea 41 D6
Spree r. Germany 17 N4
Springbok S. Africa 50 C5
Springdale Canada 61 M5
Springer U.S.A. 62 G4
Springfield CO U.S.A. 62 G4
Springfield IL U.S.A. 63 J4
Springfield MA U.S.A. 64 E1
Springfield MO U.S.A. 63 I4
Springfield OH U.S.A. 63 K4
Springfield WV U.S.A. 64 B3
Springfontein S. Africa 51 G6
Spring Hill U.S.A. 63 K6
Spring Mountains NV U.S.A. 65 E2
Springs Junction N.Z. 59 D6
Springsure Australia 56 E5
Spring Valley NY U.S.A. 64 D2
Springville CA U.S.A. 65 C2
Springville NY U.S.A. 64 B1
Springville PA U.S.A. 64 D2
Sprowston U.K. 19 I6
Spurn Head hd U.K. 18 H5
Squillace, Golfo di g. Italy 26 G5
Squires, Mount hill Australia 55 D6
Srbinje Bos.-Herz. see Foča
Srebrenica 27 H2
Sredets Burgas Bulg. 27 L3
Sredets Sofiya-Grad Bulg. see Sofia
Sredinnyy Khrebet mts Rus. Fed. 29 Q4
Sredna Gora mts Bulg. 27 J3
Srednekolymsk Rus. Fed. 29 Q3
Sredne-Russkaya Vozvyshennost' hills Rus. Fed. see Central Russian Upland
Sredne-Sibirskoye Ploskogor'ye plat. Rus. Fed. see Central Siberian Plateau
Sredneye Kuyto, Ozero l. Rus. Fed. 14 Q4
Sredniy Ural mts Rus. Fed. 11 R4
Srednogorie Bulg. 27 K3
Srednyaya Akhtuba Rus. Fed. 13 J6
Sreepur Bangl. see Sripur
Sretensk Rus. Fed. 43 L2
Sri Aman Sarawak Malaysia 41 D7
Sriharikota Island India 38 D3
Sri Jayewardenepura Kotte Sri Lanka 38 C5
Srikakulam India 38 E2
Sri Kalahasti India 38 C3
Sri Lanka country Asia 38 D5
Srinagar India 36 C2
Sri Pada mt. Sri Lanka see Adam's Peak
Sripur Bangl. 37 G4
Srirangam India 38 C4
Srivardhan India 38 B2
Staaten r. Australia 56 C3
Staaten River National Park Australia 56 C3
Stabroek Guyana see Georgetown
Stade Germany 17 L4
Stadskanaal Neth. 17 K4
Staffa i. U.K. 20 C4
Stafford U.K. 19 E6
Stafford VA U.S.A. 64 C3
Stafford Springs CT U.S.A. 64 E2

Staicele Latvia 15 N8
Staines U.K. 19 G7
Stakhanov Ukr. 13 H6
Stakhanovo Rus. Fed. see Zhukovskiy
Stalbridge U.K. 19 E8
Stalham U.K. 19 I6
Stalin Bulg. see Varna
Stalinabad Tajik. see Dushanbe
Stalingrad Rus. Fed. see Volgograd
Staliniri Georgia see Ts'khinvali
Stalino Ukr. see Donets'k
Stalinogorsk Rus. Fed. see Novomoskovsk
Stalinogród Poland see Katowice
Stalinsk Rus. Fed. see Novokuznetsk
Stalowa Wola Poland 13 D6
Stamboliyski Bulg. 27 K3
Stamford Australia 56 C4
Stamford U.K. 19 G6
Stamford CT U.S.A. 64 E2
Stamford NY U.S.A. 64 D1
Stampalia i. Greece see Astypalaia
Stampriet Namibia 50 D3
Stamsund Norway 14 H2
Stanardsville VA U.S.A. 64 B3
Stancomb-Wills Glacier Antarctica 76 B1
Standerton S. Africa 51 I4
Standish U.S.A. 63 K3
Stanger S. Africa 51 J5
Stanislaus r. CA U.S.A. 65 B2
Stanislav Ukr. see Ivano-Frankivs'k
Stanke Dimitrov Bulg. see Dupnitsa
Stanley Australia 57 [inset]
Stanley Falkland Is 70 E8
Stanley U.K. 18 F4
Stanley ND U.S.A. 62 G2
Stanley VA U.S.A. 64 B3
Stanley, Mount hill N.T. Australia 54 E5
Stanley, Mount hill Tas. Australia 57 [inset]
Stanley, Mount Dem. Rep. Congo/Uganda see Margherita Peak
Stanleyville Dem. Rep. Congo see Kisangani
Stann Creek Belize see Dangriga
Stannington U.K. 18 F3
Stanovoye Rus. Fed. 13 H5
Stanovoye Nagor'ye mts Rus. Fed. 43 L1
Stanovoy Khrebet mts Rus. Fed. 29 N4
Stansmore Range hills Australia 54 E5
Stanthorpe Australia 58 E2
Stanton U.K. 19 H6
Starachowice Poland 17 R5
Stara Planina mts Bulg./Serbia see Balkan Mountains
Staraya Russa Rus. Fed. 12 F4
Stara Zagora Bulg. 27 K3
Starbuck Island Kiribati 75 J6
Starcke National Park Australia 56 D2
Stargard in Pommern Poland see Stargard Szczeciński
Stargard Szczeciński Poland 17 O4
Staritsa Rus. Fed. 12 G4
Starkville U.S.A. 63 J5
Starnberger See l. Germany 17 M7
Starobel'sk Ukr. see Starobil's'k
Starobil's'k Ukr. 13 H6
Starogard Gdański Poland 17 Q4
Starokonstantinov Ukr. see Starokostyantyniv
Starokostyantyniv Ukr. 13 E6
Starominskaya Rus. Fed. 13 H7
Staroshcherbinovskaya Rus. Fed. 13 H7
Start Point U.K. 19 D8
Starve Island Kiribati see Starbuck Island
Staryya Darohi Belarus 13 F5
Staryye Dorogi Belarus see Staryya Darohi
Staryy Kayak Rus. Fed. 29 L2
Staryy Oskol Rus. Fed. 13 H6
State College PA U.S.A. 64 C2
Staten Island Arg. see Los Estados, Isla de
Statesboro U.S.A. 63 K5
Statia i. Neth. Antilles see Sint Eustatius
Station Nord Greenland 77 I1
Staunton VA U.S.A. 64 B3
Stavanger Norway 15 D7
Staveley U.K. 18 F5
Stavropol' Rus. Fed. 13 I7
Stavropol Kray admin. div. Rus. Fed. see Stavropol'skiy Kray
Stavropol'-na-Volge Rus. Fed. see Tol'yatti
Stavropol'skaya Vozvyshennost' hills Rus. Fed. 13 I7
Stavropol'skiy Kray admin. div. Rus. Fed. 35 F1
Steadville S. Africa 51 I5
Steamboat Springs U.S.A. 62 F3
Stebbins U.S.A. 60 B3
Steele Island Antarctica 76 L2
Steenkampsberge mts S. Africa 51 J3
Steen River Canada 60 G4
Steens Mountain U.S.A. 62 D3
Steenstrup Gletscher glacier Greenland see Sermersuaq
Stefansson Island Canada 61 H2
Stegi Swaziland see Siteki
Steigerwald mts Germany 17 M6
Steinhausen Namibia 49 B6
Steinkjer Norway 14 G4
Steinkopf S. Africa 50 C5
Steinsdalen Norway 14 G4
Stella S. Africa 50 G4
Stellenbosch S. Africa 50 D7
Stello, Monte mt. Corsica France 24 I5
Stelvio, Parco Nazionale dello nat. park Italy 26 D1
Stendal Germany 17 M4
Stenhousemuir U.K. 20 F4
Stenungsund Sweden 15 G7
Steornabhagh U.K. see Stornoway
Stepanakert Azer. see Xankändi
Stephens, Cape N.Z. 59 D5
Stephens City VA U.S.A. 64 B3
Stephenville U.S.A. 62 H5
Stepnoy Rus. Fed. see Elista
Stepnoye Rus. Fed. 13 J6
Sterkfontein Dam resr S. Africa 51 I5
Sterkstroom S. Africa 51 H6
Sterlibashevo Rus. Fed. 11 R5
Sterling S. Africa 50 E6
Sterling CO U.S.A. 62 G3
Sterlitamak Rus. Fed. 28 G4
Stettin Poland see Szczecin
Steubenville OH U.S.A. 64 A2
Stevenage U.K. 19 G7
Stevenson Lake Canada 63 H1
Stevens Village U.S.A. 60 D3
Stevensville PA U.S.A. 64 C2
Stewart Canada 60 F4
Stewart r. Canada 60 E3
Stewart, Isla i. Chile 70 B8
Stewart Island N.Z. 59 A8
Stewart Islands Solomon Is 53 G2
Stewart Lake Canada 61 J3
Stewarton U.K. 20 E5
Stewarts Point CA U.S.A. 65 A1
Steynsburg S. Africa 51 G6
Steyr Austria 17 O6
Steytlerville S. Africa 50 G7
Stif Alg. see Sétif
Stikine r. Canada 60 E4
Stikine Plateau Canada 60 E4
Stilbaai S. Africa 50 E8
Stillwater OK U.S.A. 63 H4
Stilton U.K. 19 G6
Štip Macedonia 27 J4
Stirling Australia 54 F5
Stirling U.K. 20 F4
Stirling Creek r. Australia 54 E4
Stirling Range National Park Australia 55 B8
Stjørdalshalsen Norway 14 G5
Stockerau Austria 17 P6
Stockholm Sweden 15 K7
Stockinbingal Australia 58 C5
Stockport U.K. 18 E5
Stockton CA U.S.A. 65 B2
Stockton-on-Tees U.K. 18 F4
Stoer, Point of U.K. 20 D2
Stoke-on-Trent U.K. 19 E5
Stokesley U.K. 18 F4
Stokes Point Australia 57 [inset]
Stokes Range hills Australia 54 E4
Stokkseyri Iceland 14 [inset]
Stokkvågen Norway 14 H3
Stokmarknes Norway 14 I2
Stolac Bos.-Herz. 26 G3
Stolbovoy Rus. Fed. 77 G2
Stolbtsy Belarus see Stowbtsy
Stolin Belarus 15 O11
Stolp Poland see Słupsk
Stone U.K. 19 E6
Stoneboro PA U.S.A. 64 A2
Stonehaven U.K. 20 G4
Stonehenge Australia 56 C5
Stonehenge tourist site U.K. 19 F7
Stonewall Jackson Lake WV U.S.A. 64 A3
Stony Creek VA U.S.A. 64 C4
Stony Rapids Canada 60 H4
Stony River U.S.A. 60 C3
Stora Lulevatten l. Sweden 14 K3
Stora Sjöfallets nationalpark nat. park Sweden 14 J3
Storavan l. Sweden 14 K4
Store Bælt sea chan. Denmark see Great Belt
Støren Norway 14 G5
Storfjordbotn Norway 14 O1
Storforshei Norway 14 I3
Storjord Norway 14 I3
Storkerson Peninsula Canada 61 H2
Storm Bay Australia 57 [inset]
Stormberg S. Africa 51 H6
Storm Lake U.S.A. 63 H3
Stornosa mt. Norway 14 E6
Stornoway U.K. 20 C2
Storozhevsk Rus. Fed. 12 L3
Storozhynets' Ukr. 13 E6
Storrs CT U.S.A. 64 E2
Storseleby Sweden 14 J4
Storsjön l. Sweden 14 I5
Storskrymten mt. Norway 14 F5
Storslett Norway 14 L2
Storuman Sweden 14 J4
Storuman l. Sweden 14 J4
Storvik Sweden 15 J6
Storvorde Denmark 15 G8
Storvreta Sweden 15 J7
Stotfold U.K. 19 G6
Stour r. England U.K. 19 F6
Stour r. England U.K. 19 F8
Stour r. England U.K. 19 I7
Stour r. England U.K. 19 I7
Stourbridge U.K. 19 E6
Stourport-on-Severn U.K. 19 E6
Stout Lake Canada 63 I1
Stowbtsy Belarus 15 O10
Stowmarket U.K. 19 H6
Stoyba Rus. Fed. 44 C1
Strabane U.K. 21 E3
Stradbally Ireland 21 E4
Stradbroke U.K. 19 I6
Stradella Italy 26 C2
Strakonice Czech Rep. 17 N6
Stralsund Germany 17 N3
Strand S. Africa 50 D8
Stranda Norway 14 E5
Strangford U.K. 21 G3
Strangford Lough inlet U.K. 21 G3
Strangways r. Australia 54 F3
Stranraer U.K. 20 D6
Strasbourg France 24 H2
Strasburg VA U.S.A. 64 B3
Strassburg France see Strasbourg
Stratford Australia 58 C6
Stratford Ont. Canada 64 A1
Stratford CA U.S.A. 65 C2
Stratford TX U.S.A. 62 G4
Stratford-upon-Avon U.K. 19 F6
Strathaven U.K. 20 E5
Strathmore r. U.K. 20 E2
Strathroy Ont. Canada 64 A1
Strathspey valley U.K. 20 F3
Strathy U.K. 20 F2
Stratton U.K. 19 C8
Stratton Mountain VT U.S.A. 64 E1
Straubing Germany 17 N6
Straumnes pt Iceland 14 [inset]
Streaky Bay Australia 55 F8
Streaky Bay b. Australia 55 F8
Street U.K. 19 E7
Streetsboro OH U.S.A. 64 A2
Strehaia Romania 27 J2
Streich Mound hill Australia 55 C7
Strelka Rus. Fed. 29 Q3
Strel'na r. Rus. Fed. 12 H2
Strenči Latvia 15 N8
Streymoy i. Faroe Is 14 [inset]
Strichen U.K. 20 G3
Stroeder Arg. 70 D6
Strokestown Ireland 21 D4
Stroma, Island of U.K. 20 F2
Stromboli, Isola i. Italy 26 F5
Stromness S. Georgia 70 I8
Stromness U.K. 20 F2
Strömstad Sweden 15 G7
Strömsund Sweden 14 I5
Stronsay i. U.K. 20 G1
Stroud Australia 58 E4
Stroud U.K. 19 E7
Stroud Road Australia 58 E4
Stroudsburg PA U.S.A. 64 D2
Struer Denmark 15 F8
Struga Macedonia 27 I4
Strugi-Krasnyye Rus. Fed. 15 P7
Struis Bay S. Africa 50 E8
Struma r. Bulg. 27 J4
Strumble Head hd U.K. 19 B6
Strumica Macedonia 27 J4
Struthers OH U.S.A. 64 A2
Stryama r. Bulg. 27 K3
Strydenburg S. Africa 50 F5
Strymonas r. Greece 27 J4
Stryn Norway 14 E6
Stryy Ukr. 13 D6
Strzelecki, Mount hill Australia 54 F5
Strzelecki Regional Reserve nature res. Australia 57 B6
Stuart Lake Canada 60 F4
Stuart Range hills Australia 57 A6
Stuarts Draft VA U.S.A. 64 B3
Stuart Town Australia 58 D4
Stuchka Latvia see Aizkraukle
Stučka Latvia see Aizkraukle
Studholme Junction N.Z. 59 C7
Studsviken Sweden 14 K5
Stupino Rus. Fed. 13 H5
Sturge Island Antarctica 76 H2
Sturgis SD U.S.A. 62 G3
Sturt, Mount hill Australia 57 C6
Sturt Creek watercourse Australia 54 D4
Sturt National Park Australia 57 C6
Sturt Stony Desert Australia 57 C6
Stutterheim S. Africa 51 H7
Stuttgart Germany 17 L6
Stuttgart U.S.A. 63 I5
Stykkishólmur Iceland 14 [inset]
Styr r. Belarus/Ukr. 13 E5
Suaçuí Grande r. Brazil 71 C2
Suai East Timor 54 D2
Suakin Sudan 32 E6
Suau P.N.G. 56 E1
Subačius Lith. 15 N9
Subankhata India 37 G4
Subarnapur India see Sonapur
Sūbāshī Iran 35 H4
Şubayḩah Saudi Arabia 39 D4
Subei China 42 G5
Subotica Serbia 27 H1
Success, Lake CA U.S.A. 65 C2
Succiso, Alpi di mts Italy 26 D2
Suceava Romania 13 E7
Suchan Rus. Fed. see Partizansk
Suck r. Ireland 21 D4
Suckling, Mount P.N.G. 56 E1
Sucre Bol. 68 E7
Suczawa Romania see Suceava
Sud, Grand Récif du reef New Caledonia 53 G4
Suda Rus. Fed. 12 H4
Sudak Ukr. 34 D1
Sudan country Africa 47 F3
Suday Rus. Fed. 12 I4
Sudbury Canada 63 K2
Sudbury U.K. 19 H6
Sudd swamp Sudan 32 C8
Sudest Island P.N.G. see Tagula Island
Sudetenland mts Czech Rep./Poland see Sudety
Sudety mts Czech Rep./Poland 17 O5
Sudislavl' Rus. Fed. 12 I4
Sudlersville MD U.S.A. 64 D3
Sudogda Rus. Fed. 12 I5
Sudr Egypt 39 A5
Suðuroy i. Faroe Is 14 [inset]
Sue watercourse Sudan 47 F4
Sueca Spain 25 F4
Suez Egypt 39 A5
Suez, Gulf of Egypt 39 A5
Suez Bay Egypt 39 A5
Suez Canal Egypt 39 A4
Suffolk U.S.A. 63 L4
Sugarloaf Point Australia 58 F4
Sugun China 42 D5
Sūhāj Egypt see Sawhāj
Şuḩār Oman 33 I5
Suhaymī, Wādī as watercourse Egypt 39 A4
Sühbaatar Mongolia 42 J2
Suheli Par i. India 38 B4
Suhl Germany 17 M5
Şuhut Turkey 27 N5
Sui Pak. 36 B3
Suibin China 44 C3
Suid-Afrika country Africa see Republic of South Africa
Suide China 43 K5
Suidzhikurmsy Turkm. see Madaw
Suifenhe China 44 C3
Suihua China 44 B3
Suileng China 44 B3
Suining Sichuan China 42 J6
Suir r. Ireland 21 E5
Suisse country Europe see Switzerland
Sui Vehar Pak. 36 B3
Suixian Hubei China see Suizhou
Suiza country Europe see Switzerland
Suizhong China 43 M4
Suizhou China 43 K6
Sujangarh India 36 C4
Sujawal Pak. 36 B4
Sukabumi Indon. 41 C8
Sukagawa Japan 45 F5
Sukarnapura Indon. see Jayapura
Sukarno, Puncak mt. Indon. see Jaya, Puncak
Sukchŏn N. Korea 45 B5
Sukhinichi Rus. Fed. 13 G5
Sukhona r. Rus. Fed. 12 J3
Sukhumi Georgia see Sokhumi
Sukhum-Kale Georgia see Sokhumi
Sukkertoppen Greenland see Maniitsoq
Sukkozero Rus. Fed. 12 G3
Sukkur Pak. 33 K4
Sukma India 38 D2
Sukpay Rus. Fed. 44 E3
Sukpay r. Rus. Fed. 44 E3
Sukri r. India 36 C4
Sukri r. India 36 C4
Suktel r. India 38 D1
Sukun i. Indon. 54 C2
Sula i. Norway 15 D6
Sula r. Rus. Fed. 12 K2
Sula, Kepulauan is Indon. 41 E8
Sulaiman Range mts Pak. 33 K3
Sulak Rus. Fed. 35 G2
Sülär Iran 35 H5
Sula Sgeir i. U.K. 20 C1
Sulawesi i. Indon. see Celebes
Sulaymān Beg Iraq 35 G4
Sulci Sardinia Italy see Sant'Antioco
Sulcis Sardinia Italy see Sant'Antioco
Suledeh Iran 35 H3
Sule Skerry i. U.K. 20 E1
Sule Stack i. U.K. 20 E1
Sulitjelma Norway 14 J3
Sulkava Fin. 14 P6
Sullana Peru 68 B4
Sulmo Italy see Sulmona
Sulmona Italy 26 E3
Sulphur Springs U.S.A. 63 H5
Sultanabad India see Osmannagar
Sultanabad Iran see Arāk
Sultan Dağları mts Turkey 27 N5
Sultanıye Turkey see Karapınar
Sultanpur India 37 E4
Sulu Archipelago is Phil. 41 E7
Sulu Basin sea feature N. Pacific Ocean 74 E5
Sülüklü Turkey 34 D3
Sulusaray Turkey 34 E3
Sulu Sea N. Pacific Ocean 41 D7
Sulzberger Bay Antarctica 76 I1
Sumāil Oman 33 I5
Sumampa Arg. 70 D3
Sumapaz, Parque Nacional nat. park Col. 68 D3
Sūmār Iran 35 G4
Sumatera i. Indon. see Sumatra
Sumatra i. Indon. 41 B7
Šumava nat. park Czech Rep. 17 N6
Sumba i. Indon. 41 D8
Sumba, Selat sea chan. Indon. 41 D8
Sumbar r. Turkm. 35 I3
Sumbawa i. Indon. 41 D8
Sumbawabesar Indon. 54 B2
Sumbawanga Tanz. 49 D4
Sumbe Angola 49 B5
Sumbu National Park Zambia 49 D4
Sumburgh U.K. 20 [inset]
Sumburgh Head hd U.K. 20 [inset]
Sume'eh Sarā Iran 35 H3
Sumeih Sudan 32 C8
Sumgait Azer. see Sumqayıt
Sumisu-jima i. Japan 43 Q6
Summēl Iraq 35 F3
Summer Isles U.K. 20 D2
Summersville WV U.S.A. 64 A3
Summit Lake Canada 60 F4
Sumnal Aksai Chin 36 D2
Sumner N.Z. 59 D6
Sumner, Lake N.Z. 59 D6
Sumon-dake mt. Japan 45 E5
Šumperk Czech Rep. 17 P6
Sumpu Japan see Shizuoka
Sumqayıt Azer. 35 H2
Sumskiy Posad Rus. Fed. 12 G2
Sumter U.S.A. 63 K5
Sumur Jammu and Kashmir 36 D2
Sumy Ukr. 13 G6
Sumzom China 37 I3
Suna Rus. Fed. 12 K4
Sunaj India 36 D4
Sunam India 36 C3
Sunamganj Bangl. 37 G4
Sunart, Loch inlet U.K. 20 D4
Sunbury Australia 58 B6
Sunbury PA U.S.A. 64 C2
Sunch'ŏn S. Korea 45 B6
Sun City S. Africa 51 H3
Sun City CA U.S.A. 65 D4
Sunda, Selat strait Indon. 41 C8
Sunda Kalapa Indon. see Jakarta
Sundance U.S.A. 62 G3
Sundarbans coastal area Bangl./India 37 G5
Sundarbans National Park Bangl./India 37 G5
Sundargarh India 37 F5
Sunda Shelf sea feature Indian Ocean 73 P5
Sunda Strait Indon. see Sunda, Selat
Sunda Trench sea feature Indian Ocean see Java Trench
Sunda Trench sea feature Indian Ocean see Java Trench
Sunderland U.K. 18 F4
Sündiken Dağları mts Turkey 27 N5
Sundown National Park Australia 58 E2
Sundsvall Sweden 14 J5
Sundumbili S. Africa 51 J5
Sungari r. China see Songhua Jiang
Sungqu China see Songpan
Sungurlu Turkey 34 D2
Sun Kosi r. Nepal 37 F4
Sunndal Norway 15 E6
Sunndalsøra Norway 14 F5
Sunne Sweden 15 H7
Sunnyside U.S.A. 62 D2
Sunnyvale CA U.S.A. 65 A2
Suntar Rus. Fed. 29 M3
Suntsar Pak. 33 J4
Sunwi-do i. N. Korea 45 B5
Sunwu China 44 B2
Sunyani Ghana 46 C4
Suolijärvet l. Fin. 14 P3
Suomi country Europe see Finland
Suomussalmi Fin. 14 P4
Suō-nada b. Japan 45 C6
Suonenjoki Fin. 14 O5
Suoyarvi Rus. Fed. 12 G3
Supa India 38 B3
Supaul India 37 F4
Superior NE U.S.A. 62 H3
Superior WI U.S.A. 63 I2
Superior, Lake Canada/U.S.A. 63 J2
Süphan Dağı mt. Turkey 35 F3
Suponevo Rus. Fed. 13 G5
Support Force Glacier Antarctica 76 A1
Sūq ash Shuyūkh Iraq 35 G5
Suqian China 43 L6
Suquţrá i. Yemen see Socotra
Şūr Oman 33 I5
Sur, Point CA U.S.A. 65 B2
Sur, Punta pt Arg. 70 E5
Sura r. Rus. Fed. 13 J4
Şuraabad Azer. 35 H2
Surabaya Indon. 41 D8
Surakarta Indon. 41 D8
Şūrān Syria 39 C2
Surat Australia 58 D1
Surat India 36 C5
Suratgarh India 36 C3
Surat Thani Thai. 31 I6
Surazh Rus. Fed. 13 G5
Surbiton Australia 56 D4
Surdulica Serbia 27 J3
Surendranagar India 36 B5
Surf CA U.S.A. 65 B3
Surgut Rus. Fed. 28 I3
Suri India see Siuri
Suriapet India 38 C2
Surigao Phil. 41 E7
Surin Thai. 31 J5
Surinam country S. America see Suriname
Suriname country S. America 69 G3
Surkhet Nepal 37 E3
Sürmene Turkey 35 F2
Surovikino Rus. Fed. 13 I6
Surpura India 36 C4
Surry VA U.S.A. 64 C4
Surskoye Rus. Fed. 13 J5
Surt Libya see Sirte
Surtsey i. Iceland 14 [inset]
Suruç Turkey 39 D1
Surud, Raas pt Somalia 48 E2
Surud Ad mt. Somalia see Shimbiris
Suruga-wan b. Japan 45 E6
Suryapet India see Suriapet
Şuşa Azer. 35 G3
Susah Tunisia see Sousse
Susaki Japan 45 D6
Susan VA U.S.A. 64 C4
Süsangerd Iran 35 H5
Susanino Rus. Fed. 44 F1
Susanville U.S.A. 62 C3
Suşehri Turkey 34 E2
Susquehanna PA U.S.A. 64 D2
Susquehanna r. PA U.S.A. 64 C3
Susquehanna, West Branch r. PA U.S.A. 64 C2
Susques Arg. 70 C2
Sussex VA U.S.A. 64 C4
Susuman Rus. Fed. 29 P3
Susurluk Turkey 27 M5
Sutak Jammu and Kashmir 36 D2
Sutherland Australia 58 E5
Sutherland S. Africa 50 E7
Sutherland Range hills Australia 55 D6
Sutjeska nat. park Bos.-Herz. 26 H3
Sutlej r. India/Pak. 36 B3
Sütlüce Turkey 39 A1
Sutter CA U.S.A. 65 B1
Sutterton U.K. 19 G6
Sutton U.K. 19 H6
Sutton WV U.S.A. 64 A3
Sutton Coldfield U.K. 19 F6
Sutton in Ashfield U.K. 19 F5
Sutton Lake WV U.S.A. 64 A3
Suttor r. Australia 56 D4
Suttsu Japan 44 F4
Sutwik Island U.S.A. 60 C4
Sutyr' r. Rus. Fed. 44 D2
Suva Fiji 53 H3
Suvalki Poland see Suwałki
Suvorov atoll Cook Is see Suwarrow
Suvorov Rus. Fed. 13 H5
Suwa Japan 45 E5
Suwałki Poland 13 D5
Suwanose-jima i. Japan 45 C7
Suwarrow atoll Cook Is 53 J3
Suwaylih Jordan 39 B3
Suwayqiyah, Hawr as imp. l. Iraq 35 G4
Suways, Khalīj as g. Egypt see Suez, Gulf of
Suways, Qanāt as canal Egypt see Suez Canal
Suweilih Jordan see Suwaylih
Suweis, Khalîg el g. Egypt see Suez, Gulf of
Suweis, Qanâ el canal Egypt see Suez Canal
Suwŏn S. Korea 45 B5
Suyūl Ḩanīsh i. Yemen 32 F7
Suz, Mys pt Kazakh. 35 I2
Suzaka Japan 45 E5
Suzdal' Rus. Fed. 12 I4
Suzhou Anhui China 43 L6
Suzhou Jiangsu China 43 M6
Suzi He r. China 44 B4
Suzuka Japan 45 E6
Suzu-misaki pt Japan 45 E5
Sværholthalvøya pen. Norway 14 O1
Svalbard terr. Arctic Ocean 28 C2
Svappavaara Sweden 14 L3
Svartenhuk Halvø pen. Greenland see Sigguup Nunaa
Svatove Ukr. 13 H6
Svecha Rus. Fed. 12 J4
Sveg Sweden 15 I5
Sveķi Latvia 15 O8
Svelgen Norway 14 D6
Svellingen Norway 14 F5
Švenčionėliai Lith. 15 N9
Švenčionys Lith. 15 O9
Svendborg Denmark 15 G9
Svensbu Norway 14 K2
Svenstavik Sweden 14 I5
Sverdlovsk Rus. Fed. see Yekaterinburg
Sverdlovs'k Ukr. 13 H6
Sverdrup Islands Canada 61 I2
Sverige country Europe see Sweden
Sveti Nikole Macedonia 27 I4
Svetlaya Rus. Fed. 44 E3
Svetlogorsk Belarus see Svyetlahorsk
Svetlogorsk Kaliningradskaya Oblast' Rus. Fed. 15 L9
Svetlogorsk Krasnoyarskiy Kray Rus. Fed. 28 J3
Svetlograd Rus. Fed. 13 I7
Svetlovodsk Ukr. see Svitlovods'k
Svetlyy Kaliningradskaya Oblast' Rus. Fed. 15 L9
Svetlyy Yar Rus. Fed. 13 J6
Svetogorsk Rus. Fed. 12 F3
Svíahnúkar vol. Iceland 14 [inset]
Svilaja mts Croatia 26 G3
Svilengrad Bulg. 27 L4
Svinecea Mare, Vârful mt. Romania 27 J2
Svir Belarus 15 O9
Svir' r. Rus. Fed. 12 G3
Svishtov Bulg. 27 K3
Svitava r. Czech Rep. 17 P6
Svitavy Czech Rep. 17 P6
Svitlovods'k Ukr. 13 G6
Sviyaga r. Rus. Fed. 12 K5
Svizzer, Parc Naziunal Switz. 26 D1
Svizzera country Europe see Switzerland
Svobodnyy Rus. Fed. 44 C2
Svolvær Norway 14 I2
Svrljiške Planine mts Serbia 27 J3
Svyatoy Nos, Mys c. Rus. Fed. 12 K2
Svyetlahorsk Belarus 13 F5
Swadlincote U.K. 19 F6
Swaffham U.K. 19 H6
Swain Reefs Australia 56 F4
Swains Island atoll American Samoa 53 I3
Swakop watercourse Namibia 50 B2
Swakopmund Namibia 50 B2
Swale r. U.K. 18 F4
Swallow Islands Solomon Is 53 G3
Swamihalli India 38 C3
Swan r. Australia 55 A7
Swanage U.K. 19 F8
Swandale WV U.S.A. 64 A3
Swan Hill Australia 58 A5
Swan Islands is Caribbean Sea 67 H5
Swan Lake Man. Canada 62 G1
Swanley U.K. 19 H7
Swan Reach Australia 57 B7
Swan River Canada 62 G1
Swansea U.K. 19 D7
Swansea Bay U.K. 19 D7
Swanton CA U.S.A. 65 A2
Swartbergpas pass S. Africa 50 F7
Swart Nossob watercourse Namibia see Black Nossob
Swartruggens S. Africa 51 H3
Swatow China see Shantou
Swaziland country Africa 51 J4
Sweden country Europe 14 I5
Sweet Springs WV U.S.A. 64 A4
Sweetwater U.S.A. 62 G5
Sweetwater r. U.S.A. 62 F3
Swellendam S. Africa 50 E8
Świdnica Poland 17 P5
Świdwin Poland 17 O4
Świebodzin Poland 17 O4
Świecie Poland 17 Q4
Swift Current Canada 62 F1
Swilly r. Ireland 21 E3
Swilly, Lough inlet Ireland 21 E2
Swindon U.K. 19 F7
Swinford Ireland 21 D4
Świnoujście Poland 17 O4
Swinton U.K. 20 G5
Swiss Confederation country Europe see Switzerland
Switzerland country Europe 24 I3
Swords Ireland 21 F4
Swords Range hills Australia 56 C4
Syamozero, Ozero l. Rus. Fed. 12 G3
Syamzha Rus. Fed. 12 I3
Syang Nepal 37 E3
Syas'troy Rus. Fed. 12 G3
Sychevka Rus. Fed. 12 G5
Sydenham atoll Kiribati see Nonouti
Sydney Australia 58 E4
Sydney Island Kiribati see Manra
Syedra tourist site Turkey 39 A1
Syeverodonets'k Ukr. 13 H6
Sykesville PA U.S.A. 64 B2
Syktyvkar Rus. Fed. 12 K3
Sylarna mt. Norway/Sweden 14 H5
Sylhet Bangl. 37 G4
Syloga Rus. Fed. 12 I3
Sylt i. Germany 17 L3
Sylvester, Lake salt flat Australia 56 A3
Symi i. Greece 27 L6
Synel'nykove Ukr. 13 G6
Syngyrli, Mys pt Kazakh. 35 I2
Synya Rus. Fed. 11 R2
Syowa research station Antarctica 76 D2
Syracusae Sicily Italy see Syracuse
Syracuse Sicily Italy 26 F6
Syracuse KS U.S.A. 62 G4
Syracuse NY U.S.A. 64 C1
Syrdar'ya r. Asia 30 F2
Syrdaryinskiy Uzbek. see Sirdaryo
Syria country Asia 34 E4
Syrian Desert Asia 34 E4
Syrna i. Greece 27 L6
Syros i. Greece 27 K6
Syrskiy Rus. Fed. 13 H5
Sysmä Fin. 15 N6
Sysola r. Rus. Fed. 12 K3
Syumsi Rus. Fed. 12 K4
Syurkum Rus. Fed. 44 F2
Syurkum, Mys pt Rus. Fed. 44 F2
Syzran' Rus. Fed. 13 K5
Szabadka Serbia see Subotica
Szczecin Poland 17 O4
Szczecinek Poland 17 P4
Szczytno Poland 17 R4
Szechwan prov. China see Sichuan
Szeged Hungary 27 I1
Székesfehérvár Hungary 26 H1
Szekszárd Hungary 26 H1
Szentes Hungary 27 I1
Szentgotthárd Hungary 26 G1
Szigetvár Hungary 26 G1
Szolnok Hungary 27 I1
Szombathely Hungary 26 G1
Sztálinváros Hungary see Dunaújváros

T

Taagga Duudka reg. Somalia 48 E3
Tābah Saudi Arabia 32 F4
Tabajara Brazil 68 F5
Tabakhmela Georgia see Kazret'i
Tabanan Indon. 54 A2
Tabankulu S. Africa 51 I6
Ţabaqah Ar Raqqah Syria 39 D2
Ţabaqah Ar Raqqah Syria see Madīnat ath Thawrah
Tabar Islands P.N.G. 52 F2
Tabarka Tunisia 26 C6
Tabāsin Iran 33 I3
Tābask, Kūh-e mt. Iran 35 H5
Tabatinga Amazonas Brazil 68 E4
Tabatinga São Paulo Brazil 71 A3
Tabatinga, Serra da hills Brazil 69 J6
Tabatsquri, Tba l. Georgia 35 F2
Tabayin Myanmar 37 H5
Tabbita Australia 58 B5
Tabelbala Alg. 22 D6
Tabia Tsaka salt l. China 37 F3
Tabiteuea atoll Kiribati 53 H2
Tabivere Estonia 15 O7
Table Cape N.Z. 59 F4
Tabligbo Togo 46 D4
Tábor Czech Rep. 17 O6
Tabora Tanz. 49 D4
Tabou Côte d'Ivoire 46 C4
Tabrīz Iran 35 G3
Tabuaeran atoll Kiribati 75 J5
Tabūk Saudi Arabia 34 E5
Tabulam Australia 58 F2
Tabwémasana, Mount Vanuatu 53 G3
Täby Sweden 15 K7
Tacalé Brazil 69 H3
Tacheng China 42 E3
Tachov Czech Rep. 17 N6
Tacloban Phil. 41 E6
Tacna Peru 68 D7
Tacoma U.S.A. 62 C2
Taco Pozo Arg. 70 D3
Tacuarembó Uruguay 70 E4
Tadcaster U.K. 18 F5
Tademaït, Plateau du Alg. 22 E6
Tadin New Caledonia 53 G4
Tadjikistan country Asia see Tajikistan
Tadjourah Djibouti 32 F7
Tadmur Syria 39 D2
Tadohae Haesang National Park S. Korea 45 B6
Tadoule Lake Canada 61 I4
Tadpatri India 38 C3
Tadwale India 38 C2
Tadzhikskaya S.S.R. country Asia see Tajikistan
T'aean Haean National Park S. Korea 45 B5
Taech'ŏng-do i. S. Korea 45 B5
Taedasa-do N. Korea 45 B5
Taedong-man b. N. Korea 45 B5
Taegu S. Korea 45 C6
Taehan-min'guk country Asia see South Korea
Taehŭksan-kundo is S. Korea 45 B6
Taejŏn S. Korea 45 B5
Taejŏng S. Korea 45 B6
T'aepaek S. Korea 45 C5
Ta'erqi China 43 M3
Taf r. U.K. 19 C7
Tafahi i. Tonga 53 I3
Tafalla Spain 25 F2
Tafila Jordan see Aţ Ţafīlah
Tafí Viejo Arg. 70 C3
Tafresh Iran 35 H4
Taft Iran 35 I5
Taft CA U.S.A. 65 C3
Taftān, Kūh-e mt. Iran 33 J4
Taftanāz Syria 39 C2
Taganrog Rus. Fed. 13 H7
Taganrog, Gulf of Rus. Fed./Ukr. 13 H7
Taganrogskiy Zaliv b. Rus. Fed./Ukr. see Taganrog, Gulf of
Tagaung Myanmar 37 I5
Tagchagpu Ri mt. China 37 E2
Tagdempt Alg. see Tiaret
Taghmon Ireland 21 F5
Tagtabazar Turkm. 33 J2
Tagula P.N.G. 56 F1
Tagula Island P.N.G. 56 F1
Tagus r. Port. 25 B4
Tagus r. Spain 22 C4
Taha China 44 B3
Tahanroz'ka Zatoka b. Rus. Fed./Ukr. see Taganrog, Gulf of
Tahat, Mont mt. Alg. 46 D2
Tahe China 44 B1
Taheke N.Z. 59 D2
Tahiti i. Fr. Polynesia 75 K7
Tahlequah U.S.A. 63 I4
Tahoe, Lake CA U.S.A. 65 B1
Tahoe Lake Canada 61 H3
Tahoe Vista CA U.S.A. 65 B1
Tahoua Niger 46 D3
Tahrūd Iran 33 I4
Taï, Parc National de nat. park Côte d'Ivoire 46 C4
Tai'an China 43 L5
Taibei Taiwan see T'aipei
Taibus Qi China see Baochang
Taidong Taiwan see T'aitung
Taihang Shan mts Hebei China 43 K5
Taihang Shan mts China 43 K5
Taihape N.Z. 59 E4
Taihe Jiangxi China 43 K7
Tai Hu l. China 40 E4
Taikang China 44 B3

Tailai China 44 A3
Tailem Bend Australia 57 B7
Tain U.K. 20 F2
T'ainan Taiwan 43 M8
Tainaro, Akrotirio pt Greece 27 J6
Taiobeiras Brazil 71 C1
T'aipei Taiwan 43 M7
Taiping Malaysia 41 C7
Taipingchuan China 44 A3
Tai Poutini National Park N.Z. see Westland National Park
Tairbeart U.K. see Tarbert
Tairuq Iran 35 G4
Taishan China 43 K8
Taitanu N.Z. 59 D6
Taitao, Península de pen. Chile 70 B7
T'aitung Taiwan 43 M8
Taivalkoski Fin. 14 P4
Taivaskero hill Fin. 14 N2
Taiwan country Asia 43 M8
T'aiwan Haihsia strait China/Taiwan see Taiwan Strait
Taiwan Haixia strait China/Taiwan see Taiwan Strait
Taiwan Strait China/Taiwan 40 D5
Taiyuan China 43 K5
Taizhao China 37 H3
Taizhong Taiwan see Fengyüan
Taizhong Taiwan see Fengyüan
Taizhou Jiangsu China 43 L6
Taizhou Zhejiang China 43 M7
Taizi He r. China 44 B4
Ta'izz Yemen 32 F7
Tajal Pak. 36 B4
Tajamulco, Volcán de vol. Guat. 66 F5
Tajerouine Tunisia 26 C7
Tajikistan country Asia 33 L2
Tajo r. Spain see Tagus
Tajo r. Spain 25 C4 see Tagus
Tajrīsh Iran 35 H4
Tak Thai. 31 I5
Takāb Iran 35 G3
Takabba Kenya 48 E3
Takahashi Japan 45 D6
Takamatsu Japan 45 D6
Takaoka Japan 45 E5
Takapuna N.Z. 59 E3
Ta karpo China 37 G4
Takatokwane Botswana 50 G3
Takatshwaane Botswana 50 E2
Takatsuki-yama mt. Japan 45 D6
Takayama Japan 45 E5
Takefu Japan 45 E6
Take-shima i. N. Pacific Ocean see Liancourt Rocks
Takestān Iran 35 H3
Takhemaret Alg. 25 G6
Takhta-Bazar Turkm. see Tagtabazar
Takhteh Iran 35 I5
Takhteh Pol Afgh. 36 A3
Takht-e Soleymān mt. Iran 35 H3
Takht-i-Bahi tourist site Pak. 36 B2
Takht-i-Sulaiman mt. Pak. 36 B3
Takijuq Lake Canada see Napaktulik Lake
Takinoue Japan 44 F3
Takla Lake Canada 60 F4
Takla Makan des. China see Taklimakan Desert
Taklimakan Desert China 36 E1
Taklimakan Shamo des. China see Taklimakan Desert
Takpa Shiri mt. China 37 H3
Takum Nigeria 46 D4
Takuu Islands P.N.G. 53 F2
Talachyn Belarus 13 F5
Talaja India 36 C5
Talakan Amurskaya Oblast' Rus. Fed. 44 C2
Talakan Khabarovskiy Kray Rus. Fed. 44 D2
Talandzha Rus. Fed. 44 C2
Talara Peru 68 B4
Talar-i-Band mts Pak. see Makran Coast Range
Talas Kyrg. 42 C4
Tal'at Musá mt. Lebanon/Syria 39 C2
Talaud, Kepulauan is Indon. 41 E7
Talavera de la Reina Spain 25 D4
Talaya Rus. Fed. 29 Q3
Talbehat India 36 D4
Talbīsah Syria 39 C2
Talbot, Mount hill Australia 55 D6
Talbragar r. Australia 58 D4
Talca Chile 70 B5
Talcahuano Chile 70 B5
Taldan Rus. Fed. 44 B1
Taldom Rus. Fed. 12 H4
Taldykorgan Kazakh. 42 D4
Taldy-Kurgan Kazakh. see Taldykorgan
Taldyqorghan Kazakh. see Taldykorgan
Tālesh Iran see Hashtpar
Talgarth U.K. 19 D7
Talguppa India 38 B3
Talia Australia 57 A7
Taliabu i. Indon. 41 E8
Talikota India 38 C2
Talin Hiag China 44 B3
Taliparamba India 38 B3
Taliş Dağları mts Azer./Iran 35 H3
Talitsa Rus. Fed. 12 J4
Taliwang Indon. 54 B2
Talkeetna U.S.A. 60 C3
Talkeetna Mountains U.S.A. 60 D3
Tallacootra, Lake salt flat Australia 55 F7
Tallahassee U.S.A. 63 K5
Tall al Aḥmar Syria 39 D1
Tall Baydar Syria 35 F3
Tall-e Ḥalāl Iran 35 I5
Tallinn Estonia 15 N7
Tall Kalakh Syria 39 C2
Tall Kayf Iraq 35 F3
Tall Kūjik Syria 35 F3
Tallow Ireland 21 D5
Tallulah U.S.A. 63 I5
Tall 'Uwaynāt Iraq 35 F3
Talmont-St-Hilaire France 24 D3
Tal'ne Ukr. 13 F6
Tal'noye Ukr. see Tal'ne
Taloda India 36 C5
Talodi Sudan 32 D7
Tāloqān Afgh. 36 B1
Talos Dome ice feature Antarctica 76 H2
Talovaya Rus. Fed. 13 I6
Taloyoak Canada 61 I3
Tal Pass Pak. 36 C2
Talsi Latvia 15 M8
Taltal Chile 70 B3
Taltson r. Canada 60 G3
Talu China 37 H3
Talvik Norway 14 M1
Talwood Australia 58 D2
Talyshskiye Gory mts Azer./Iran see Taliş Dağları
Talyy Rus. Fed. 12 L2
Tamala Australia 55 A6
Tamala Rus. Fed. 13 I5
Tamale Ghana 46 C4
Tamana i. Kiribati 53 H2
Tamano Japan 45 D6
Tamanrasset Alg. 46 D2
Tamanthi Myanmar 37 H4
Tamaqua PA U.S.A. 64 D2
Tamar India 37 F5
Tamar Syria see Tadmur
Tamar r. U.K. 19 C8
Tamarugal, Pampa de plain Chile 68 E7
Tamasane Botswana 51 H2
Tamatave Madag. see Toamasina
Tambacounda Senegal 46 B3
Tambaqui Brazil 68 F5
Tambar Springs Australia 58 D3
Tambelan, Kepulauan is Indon. 41 C7
Tambo r. Australia 58 C6
Tambohorano Madag. 49 E5
Tambora, Gunung vol. Indon. 54 B2
Tamboritha mt. Australia 58 C6
Tambov Rus. Fed. 13 I5
Tambovka Rus. Fed. 44 C2
Tambura Sudan 47 F4
Tamburi Brazil 71 C1
Tâmchekket Mauritania 46 B3
Tamdybulak Uzbek. see Tomdibuloq
Tâmega r. Port. 25 B3
Tamenghest Alg. see Tamanrasset
Tamenglong India 37 H4
Tamerza Tunisia 26 B7
Tamgak, Adrar mt. Niger 46 D3
Tamgué, Massif du mt. Guinea 46 B3
Tamiahua, Laguna de lag. Mex. 66 E4
Tamil Nadu state India 38 C4
Tamitsa Rus. Fed. 12 H2
Ṭāmīya Egypt see Ṭāmīyah
Ṭāmīyah Egypt 34 C5
Tamkuhi India 37 F4
Tammerfors Fin. see Tampere
Tammisaari Fin. see Ekenäs
Tampa U.S.A. 63 K6
Tampa Bay U.S.A. 63 K6
Tampere Fin. 15 M6
Tampico Mex. 66 E4
Tamsagbulag Mongolia 43 L3
Tamsweg Austria 17 N7
Tamu Myanmar 37 H4
Tamworth Australia 58 E3
Tamworth U.K. 19 F6
Tana r. Fin./Norway see Tenojoki
Tana r. Kenya 48 E4
Tana Madag. see Antananarivo
Tana i. Vanuatu see Tanna
Tana, Lake Eth. 48 D2
Tanabe Japan 45 D6
Tanabi Brazil 71 A3
Tana Bru Norway 14 P1
Tanafjorden inlet Norway 14 P1
T'ana Hāyk' l. Eth. see Tana, Lake
Tanami Australia 54 E4
Tanami Desert Australia 54 E4
Tananarive Madag. see Antananarivo
Tanandava Madag. 49 E6
Tanch'ŏn N. Korea 45 C4
Tanda Côte d'Ivoire 46 C4
Tanda Uttar Prad. India 36 D3
Tanda Uttar Prad. India 37 E4
Țăndărei Romania 27 L2
Tandaué Angola 49 B5
Tandi India 36 D2
Tandil Arg. 70 E5
Tando Adam Pak. 33 K4
Tando Alahyar Pak. 36 B4
Tando Bago Pak. 36 B4
Tandou Lake imp. l. Australia 57 C7
Tandragee U.K. 21 F3
Tandur India 38 C2
Tanduri Pak. 36 A3
Tanega-shima i. Japan 45 C7
Tanezrouft reg. Alg./Mali 46 C2
Ṭanf, Jabal aṭ hill Syria 39 D3
Tanga Tanz. 49 D4
Tangail Bangl. 37 G4
Tanga Islands P.N.G. 52 F2
Tanganyika country Africa see Tanzania
Tanganyika, Lake Africa 49 C4
Tangará Brazil 71 A4
Tangasseri India 38 C4
Tangeli Iran 35 I3
Tanger Morocco see Tangier
Tanggulashan China 42 G6
Tanggula Shan mt. China 37 G2
Tanggula Shan mts China 37 G2
Tanggula Shankou pass China 37 G2
Tangguo China 37 F3
Tanghe China 43 K6
Tangier Morocco 25 D6
Tangiers Morocco see Tangier
Tang La pass China 37 G4
Tangla India 37 G4
Tangmai China 37 H3
Tangorin Australia 56 D4
Tangra Yumco salt l. China 37 F3
Tangshan Hebei China 43 L5
Tangtse Jammu and Kashmir see Tanktse
Tangwanghe China 44 C2
Tangyuan China 44 C3
Tangyung Tso salt l. China 37 F3
Tanhaçu Brazil 71 C1
Tanhua Fin. 14 O3
Taniantaweng Shan mts China 42 H6
Tanimbar, Kepulauan is Indon. 41 F8
Tanjah Morocco see Tangier
Tanjay Phil. 41 E7
Tanjore India see Thanjavur
Tanjungkarang-Telukbetung Indon. see Bandar Lampung
Tanjungredeb Indon. 41 D7
Tanjungselor Indon. 41 D7
Tankse Jammu and Kashmir see Tanktse
Tanktse Jammu and Kashmir 36 D2
Tankwa-Karoo National Park S. Africa 50 D7
Tanna i. Vanuatu 53 G3
Tannadice U.K. 20 G4
Tännäs Sweden 14 H5
Tannu-Ola, Khrebet mts Rus. Fed. 42 G2
Tanot India 36 B4
Tanout Niger 46 D3
Tansen Nepal 37 E4
Ṭanṭā Egypt 34 C5
Tanta Egypt see Ṭanṭā
Tan-Tan Morocco 46 B2
Tantu China 44 A3
Tanuku India 38 D2
Tanumbirini Australia 54 F4
Tanumshede Sweden 15 G7
Tanzania country Africa 49 D4
Tao'an China see Taonan
Taobh Tuath U.K. see Northton
Taolanaro Madag. see Tôlañaro
Taonan China 44 A3
Taongi atoll Marshall Is 74 H5
Taos U.S.A. 62 F4
Taounate Morocco 22 D5
Taourirt Morocco 22 D5
Taoyang China see Lintao
Tapa Estonia 15 N7
Tapachula Mex. 66 F6
Tapajós r. Brazil 69 H4
Tapauá Brazil 68 F5
Tapauá r. Brazil 68 F5
Taperoá Brazil 71 D1
Tapi r. India 36 C5
Tapiau Rus. Fed. see Gvardeysk
Taplejung Nepal 37 F4
Tappahannock VA U.S.A. 64 C4
Tappeh, Küh-e hill Iran 35 H4
Taprobane country Asia see Sri Lanka
Tapuaenuku mt. N.Z. 59 D5
Tapurucuara Brazil 68 E4
Taputeouea atoll Kiribati see Tabiteuea
Ṭaqṭaq Iraq 35 G4
Taquara Brazil 71 A5
Taquari Rio Grande do Sul Brazil 71 A5
Taquari r. Brazil 69 G7
Taquaritinga Brazil 71 A3
Tar r. Ireland 21 E5
Tara Australia 58 E1
Ṭarābulus Lebanon see Tripoli
Ṭarābulus Libya see Tripoli
Tarahuwan India 36 E4
Tarai reg. India 37 G4
Tarakan Indon. 41 D7
Taraklı Turkey 27 N4
Taran, Mys pt Rus. Fed. 15 K9
Tarana Australia 58 D4
Taranagar India 36 C3
Taranaki, Mount vol. N.Z. 59 E4
Tarancón Spain 25 E3
Tarangambadi India 38 C4
Tarangire National Park Tanz. 48 D4
Taranto Italy 26 G4
Taranto, Golfo di g. Italy 26 G4
Taranto, Gulf of Italy see Taranto, Golfo di
Tarapoto Peru 68 C5
Tarapur India 38 B2
Tararua Range mts N.Z. 59 E5
Tarascon-sur-Ariège France 24 E5
Tarasovskiy Rus. Fed. 13 I6
Tarauacá Brazil 68 D5
Tarauacá r. Brazil 68 E5
Tarawera N.Z. 59 F4
Tarawera, Mount vol. N.Z. 59 F4
Taraz Kazakh. 42 C4
Tarazona Spain 25 F3
Tarazona de la Mancha Spain 25 F4
Tarbagatay, Khrebet mts Kazakh. 42 E3
Tarbat Ness pt U.K. 20 F3
Tarbert Ireland 21 C5
Tarbert Scotland U.K. 20 C3
Tarbert Scotland U.K. 20 D5
Tarbes France 24 E5
Tarcoola Australia 55 F7
Tarcoon Australia 58 C3
Tarcoonyinna watercourse Australia 55 F6
Tarcutta Australia 58 C5
Tardoki-Yani, Gora mt. Rus. Fed. 44 E2
Taree Australia 58 F3
Tarella Australia 57 C6
Tarentum Italy see Taranto
Tarfaya Morocco 46 B2
Targa well Niger 46 D3
Targan China see Talin Hiag
Targhee Pass U.S.A. 62 E3
Târgovişte Romania 27 K2
Targuist Morocco 25 D6
Târgu Jiu Romania 27 J2
Târgu Mureş Romania 27 K1
Târgu Neamţ Romania 27 L1
Târgu Secuiesc Romania 27 L1
Targyailing China 37 F3
Tarif U.A.E. 48 F1
Tarifa Spain 25 D5
Tarifa, Punta de pt Spain 25 D5
Tarija Bol. 68 F8
Tarikere India 38 B3
Tariku r. Indon. 41 F8
Tarīm Yemen 32 G6
Tarim Basin China 42 E5
Tarime Tanz. 48 D4
Tarim He r. China 42 F4
Tarim Pendi basin China see Tarim Basin
Tarīn Kowt Afgh. 36 A2
Taritatu r. Indon. 41 F8
Tarka r. S. Africa 51 G7
Tarkastad S. Africa 51 H7
Tarko-Sale Rus. Fed. 28 I3
Tarkwa Ghana 46 C4
Tarlac Phil. 41 E6
Tarlo River National Park Australia 58 D5
Tarma Peru 68 C6
Tarn r. France 24 E4
Tärnaby Sweden 14 I4
Tarnak r. Afgh. 36 A3
Târnăveni Romania 27 K1
Tarnobrzeg Poland 13 D6
Tarnogskiy Gorodok Rus. Fed. 12 I3
Tarnopol Ukr. see Ternopil'
Tarnów Poland 13 D6
Tarnowitz Poland see Tarnowskie Góry
Tarnowskie Góry Poland 17 Q5
Taro Co salt l. China 37 E3
Taroom Australia 57 E5
Taroudannt Morocco 22 C5
Tarpaulin Swamp Australia 56 B3
Tarq Iran 35 H4
Tarquinia Italy 26 D3
Tarquinii Italy see Tarquinia
Tarrabool Lake salt flat Australia 56 A3
Tarraco Spain see Tarragona
Tarrafal Cape Verde 46 [inset]
Tarragona Spain 25 G3
Tårrajaur Sweden 14 K3
Tarran Hills hill Australia 58 C4
Tarrant Point Australia 56 B3
Tàrrega Spain 25 G3
Tarrong China see Nyêmo
Tarso Emissi mt. Chad 47 E2
Tarsus Turkey 39 B1
Tart China 37 H1
Tärtär Azer. 35 G2
Tartu Estonia 15 O7
Ṭarṭūs Syria 39 B2
Tarumovka Rus. Fed. 35 G1
Tarung Hka r. Myanmar 37 I4
Tarvisium Italy see Treviso
Tashauz Turkm. see Daşoguz
Tashi Chho Bhutan see Thimphu
Tashigang Bhutan 37 G4
Tashino Rus. Fed. see Pervomaysk
Tashir Armenia 35 G2
Tashk, Daryācheh-ye l. Iran 35 I5
Tashkent Toshkent Uzbek. see Toshkent
Tāshqurghān Afgh. see Kholm
Tashtagol Rus. Fed. 42 F2
Tashtyp Rus. Fed. 42 F2
Tasiat, Lac l. Canada 61 K4
Tasiilap Karra c. Greenland 61 O3
Tasiilaq Greenland see Ammassalik
Tasīl Syria 39 B3
Tasiujaq Canada 61 L4
Tasiusaq Greenland 61 M2
Taşkent Turkey 39 A1
Tasker Niger 46 E3
Taskesken Kazakh. 42 E3
Taşköprü Turkey 34 D2
Tasman Abyssal Plain sea feature Tasman Sea 74 G8
Tasman Basin sea feature Tasman Sea 74 G8
Tasman Bay N.Z. 59 D5
Tasmania state Australia 57 [inset]
Tasman Islands P.N.G. see Nukumanu Islands
Tasman Mountains N.Z. 59 D5
Tasman Peninsula Australia 57 [inset]
Tasman Sea S. Pacific Ocean 52 H6
Taşova Turkey 34 E2
Tassara Niger 46 D3
Tassili du Hoggar plat. Alg. 46 D2
Tassili n'Ajjer plat. Alg. 46 D2
Tasty Kazakh. 42 B4
Taşucu Turkey 39 A1
Tas-Yuryakh Rus. Fed. 29 M3
Tata Morocco 22 C6
Tatabánya Hungary 26 H1
Tatamailau, Foho mt. East Timor 54 D2
Tataouine Tunisia 22 G5
Tatarbunary Ukr. 27 M2
Tatarsk Rus. Fed. 28 I4
Tatarskiy Proliv strait Rus. Fed. 44 F2
Tatar Strait Rus. Fed. see Tatarskiy Proliv
Tate r. Australia 56 C3
Tateyama Japan 45 E6
Tathlina Lake Canada 60 G3
Tathlīth Saudi Arabia 32 F6
Tathlīth, Wādī watercourse Saudi Arabia 32 F5
Tathra Australia 58 D6
Tatishchevo Rus. Fed. 13 J6
Tatkon Myanmar 37 I5
Tatra Mountains Poland/Slovakia 17 Q6
Tatry mts Poland/Slovakia see Tatra Mountains
Tatrzański Park Narodowy nat. park Poland 17 Q6
Tatsinskiy Rus. Fed. 13 I6
Tatta Pak. 33 K5
Tatuí Brazil 71 B3
Tatvan Turkey 35 F3
Tau Norway 15 D7
Taua Brazil 69 J5
Tauapeçaçu Brazil 68 F4
Taubaté Brazil 71 B3
Taukum, Peski des. Kazakh. 42 C4
Taumarunui N.Z. 59 E4
Taumaturgo Brazil 68 D5
Taung S. Africa 50 G4
Taungdwingyi Myanmar 37 H5
Taunggyi Myanmar 42 H8
Taung-ngu Myanmar 42 H9
Taungtha Myanmar 37 H5
Taungup Myanmar 42 G9
Taunton U.K. 19 D7
Taunton MA U.S.A. 64 F2
Taupo N.Z. 59 F4
Taupo, Lake N.Z. 59 E4
Tauragė Lith. 15 M9
Tauranga N.Z. 59 F3
Taurasia Italy see Turin
Taurianova Italy 26 G5
Tauroa Point N.Z. 59 D2
Taurus Mountains Turkey 39 A1
Taute r. France 19 F9
Tauz Azer. see Tovuz
Tavas Turkey 27 M6
Tavastehus Fin. see Hämeenlinna
Taverham U.K. 19 I6
Taveuni i. Fiji 53 I3
Tavira Port. 25 C5
Tavistock U.K. 19 C8
Tavoy Myanmar 31 I5
Tavşanlı Turkey 27 M5
Taw r. U.K. 19 C7
Tawang India 37 G4
Tawas City U.S.A. 63 K3
Tawau Sabah Malaysia 41 D7
Tawè Myanmar see Tavoy
Tawe r. U.K. 19 D7
Tawmaw Myanmar 37 I4
Taxkorgan China 42 D5
Tay r. U.K. 20 F4
Tay, Firth of est. U.K. 20 F4
Tay, Lake salt flat Australia 55 C8
Tay, Loch l. U.K. 20 E4
Taybola Rus. Fed. 14 R2
Tayinloan U.K. 20 D5
Taylor AK U.S.A. 60 B3
Taylor TX U.S.A. 63 H5
Taymā' Saudi Arabia 34 E6
Taymura r. Rus. Fed. 29 K3
Taymyr, Ozero l. Rus. Fed. 29 L2
Taymyr, Poluostrov pen. Rus. Fed. see Taymyr Peninsula
Taymyr Peninsula Rus. Fed. 28 J2
Tây Ninh Vietnam 31 J5
Taypak Kazakh. 11 Q6
Taypaq Kazakh. see Taypak
Tayshet Rus. Fed. 42 H1
Taytay Phil. 41 D6
Tayuan China 44 B2
Tayyebād Iran 33 J3
Taz r. Rus. Fed. 28 I3
Taza Morocco 22 D5
Tāza Khurmātū Iraq 35 G4
Taze Myanmar 37 H5
Tāzirbū Libya 47 F2
Tazmalt Alg. 25 I5
Tazovskaya Guba sea chan. Rus. Fed. 28 I3
Tbessa Alg. see Tébessa
T'bilisi Georgia 35 G2
Tbilisskaya Rus. Fed. 13 I7
Tchabal Mbabo mt. Cameroon 46 E4
Tchad country Africa see Chad
Tchamba Togo 46 D4
Tchibanga Gabon 48 B4
Tchigaï, Plateau du Niger 47 E2
Tchin-Tabaradene Niger 46 D3
Tcholliré Cameroon 47 E4
Tczew Poland 17 Q3
Teague, Lake salt flat Australia 55 C6
Te Anau N.Z. 59 A7
Te Anau, Lake N.Z. 59 A7
Teapa Mex. 66 F5
Te Araroa N.Z. 59 G3
Teate Italy see Chieti
Te Awamutu N.Z. 59 E4
Tébarat Niger 46 D3
Tebay U.K. 18 E4
Tébessa Alg. 26 C7
Tébessa, Monts de mts Alg. 26 C7
Tébourba Tunisia 26 C6
Téboursouk Tunisia 26 C6
Tebulos Mt'a Georgia/Rus. Fed. 35 G2
Tecate Baja California Mex. 65 D4
Tece Turkey 39 B1
Techiman Ghana 46 C4
Tecka Arg. 70 B6
Tecoripa Mex. 66 C3
Técpan Mex. 66 D5
Tecuala Mex. 66 C4
Tecuci Romania 27 L2
Tedzhen Turkm. see Tejen
Tees r. U.K. 18 F4
Tefé r. Brazil 68 F4
Tefenni Turkey 27 M6
Tegucigalpa Hond. 67 G6
Teguidda-n-Tessoumt Niger 46 D3
Tehachapi CA U.S.A. 65 C3
Tehachapi Mountains CA U.S.A. 65 C3
Tehachapi Pass CA U.S.A. 65 C3
Tehek Lake Canada 61 I3
Teheran Iran see Tehrān
Téhini Côte d'Ivoire 46 C4
Tehrān Iran 35 H4
Tehri India see Tikamgarh
Tehuacán Mex. 66 E5
Tehuantepec, Golfo de Mex. see Tehuantepec, Gulf of
Tehuantepec, Gulf of Mex. 66 F5
Tehuantepec, Istmo de isthmus Mex. 66 F5
Teide, Pico del vol. Canary Is 46 B2
Teifi r. U.K. 19 C6
Teignmouth U.K. 19 D8
Teixeira de Sousa Angola see Luau
Teixeiras Brazil 71 C3
Teixeira Soares Brazil 71 A4
Tejakula Indon. 54 A2
Tejen Turkm. 30 F3
Tejo r. Port. 25 B4 see Tagus
Tejon Pass CA U.S.A. 65 C3
Tekapo, Lake N.Z. 59 C6
Tekax Mex. 66 G4
Tekeli Kazakh. 42 D4
Tekes China 42 E4
Tekiliktag mt. China 36 E1
Tekin Rus. Fed. 44 D2
Tekirdağ Turkey 27 L4
Tekka India 38 D2
Tekkali India 38 E2
Teknaf Bangl. 37 H5
Te Kuiti N.Z. 59 E4
Tel r. India 38 D1
Télagh Alg. 25 F6
Telanaipura Indon. see Jambi
Tel Ashqelon tourist site Israel 39 B4
Télataï Mali 46 D3
Tel Aviv-Yafo Israel 39 B3
Telč Czech Rep. 17 O6
Telchac Puerto Mex. 66 G4
Telekhany Belarus see Tsyelyakhany
Telêmaco Borba Brazil 71 A4
Teleorman r. Romania 27 K3
Telertheba, Djebel mt. Alg. 46 D2
Telescope Peak CA U.S.A. 65 D2
Teles Pires r. Brazil 69 G5
Telford U.K. 19 E6
Télimélé Guinea 46 B3
Teljo, Jebel mt. Sudan 32 C7
Tell Atlas mts Alg. see Atlas Tellien
Teller U.S.A. 60 B3
Tell es Sultan West Bank see Jericho
Tellicherry India 38 B4
Telloh Iraq 35 G5
Tel'novskiy Rus. Fed. 44 F2
Telo Martius France see Toulon
Tel'pos-Iz, Gora mt. Rus. Fed. 11 R3
Telsen Arg. 70 C6
Telšiai Lith. 15 M9
Telukbetung Indon. see Bandar Lampung
Temagami Lake Canada 63 L2
Têmarxung China 37 G2
Temba S. Africa 51 I3
Tembagapura Indon. 52 D2
Tembenchi r. Rus. Fed. 29 K3
Tembisa S. Africa 51 I4
Tembo Aluma Angola 49 B4
Teme r. U.K. 19 E6
Temecula CA U.S.A. 65 D4
Teminabuan Indon. 52 D2
Temirtau Kazakh. 42 C2
Temmes Fin. 14 N4
Temnikov Rus. Fed. 13 I5
Temora Australia 58 C5
Tempe Downs Australia 55 F6
Temple TX U.S.A. 63 H5
Temple Bar U.K. 19 C6
Temple Dera Pak. 36 B3
Templemore Ireland 21 E5
Temple Sowerby U.K. 18 E4
Templeton watercourse Australia 56 B4
Tempué Angola 49 B5
Temryuk Rus. Fed. 13 H7
Temryukskiy Zaliv b. Rus. Fed. 13 H7
Temuco Chile 70 B5
Temuka N.Z. 59 C7
Tena Ecuador 68 C4
Tenabo Mex. 66 F4
Tenali India 38 D2
Tenbury Wells U.K. 19 E6
Tenby U.K. 19 C7
Tendaho Eth. 48 E2
Tende, Col de pass France/Italy 24 H4
Ten Degree Channel India 31 I6
Tendo Japan 45 F5
Tenedos i. Turkey see Bozcaada
Ténenkou Mali 46 C3
Ténéré reg. Niger 46 D2
Ténéré du Tafassâsset des. Niger 46 E2
Tenerife i. Canary Is 46 B2
Ténès Alg. 25 G5
Tengah, Kepulauan is Indon. 41 D8
Tengger Shamo des. China 42 I5
Tengréla Côte d'Ivoire 46 C3
Ten'gushevo Rus. Fed. 13 I5
Teni India see Theni
Teniente Jubany research station Antarctica see Jubany
Tenke Dem. Rep. Congo 49 C5
Tenkeli Rus. Fed. 29 P2
Tenkodogo Burkina 46 C3
Ten Mile Lake salt flat Australia 55 C6
Tennant Creek Australia 54 F4
Tennessee r. U.S.A. 63 J4
Tennessee state U.S.A. 63 J4
Tennevoll Norway 14 J2
Tenojoki r. Fin./Norway 14 P1
Tenosique Mex. 66 F5
Tenterden U.K. 19 H7
Tenterfield Australia 58 F2
Tentudia mt. Spain 25 C4
Tentulia Bangl. see Tetulia
Teodoro Sampaio Brazil 70 F2
Teófilo Otôni Brazil 71 C2
Tepa Indon. 54 E1
Tepache Mex. 66 C3
Te Paki N.Z. 59 D2
Tepatitlán Mex. 66 D4
Tepehuanes Mex. 62 F6
Tepeköy Turkey see Karakoçan
Tepelenë Albania 27 I4
Tepequem, Serra mts Brazil 67 L8
Tepic Mex. 66 D4
Te Pirita N.Z. 59 C6
Teplice Czech Rep. 17 N5
Teplogorka Rus. Fed. 12 L3
Teploozersk Rus. Fed. 44 C2
Teploye Rus. Fed. 13 H5
Teploye Ozero Rus. Fed. see Teploozersk
Tequila Mex. 66 D4
Téra Niger 46 D3
Teramo Italy 26 E3
Terang Australia 58 A7
Teratani r. Pak. 36 B3
Tercan Turkey 35 F3
Terebovlya Ukr. 13 E6
Terekty Kazakh. 42 F3
Teresa Cristina Brazil 71 A4
Tereshka r. Rus. Fed. 13 J6
Teresina Brazil 69 J5
Teresina de Goias Brazil 71 B1
Teresita Col. 68 E3
Teresópolis Brazil 71 C3
Terezinha Brazil 69 H3
Tergeste Italy see Trieste
Teriberka Rus. Fed. 14 S2
Termez Uzbek. see Termiz
Termini Imerese Sicily Italy 26 E6
Términos, Laguna de lag. Mex. 66 F5
Termit-Kaoboul Niger 46 E3
Termiz Uzbek. 33 K2
Termoli Italy 26 F4
Tern r. U.K. 19 E6
Ternate Indon. 41 E7
Terney Rus. Fed. 44 E3
Terni Italy 26 E3
Ternopil' Ukr. 13 E6
Ternopol' Ukr. see Ternopil'
Terpeniya, Mys c. Rus. Fed. 44 G2
Terpeniya, Zaliv g. Rus. Fed. 44 F2
Terra Alta WV U.S.A. 64 B3
Terra Bella CA U.S.A. 65 C3
Terrace Canada 60 F4
Terrace Bay Canada 63 J2
Terra Firma S. Africa 50 F3
Terråk Norway 14 H4
Terralba Sardinia Italy 26 C5
Terra Nova Bay Antarctica 76 H1
Terre Haute U.S.A. 63 J4
Terre-Neuve prov. Canada see Newfoundland and Labrador
Terre-Neuve-et-Labrador prov. Canada see Newfoundland and Labrador
Terres Australes et Antarctiques Françaises terr. Indian Ocean see French Southern and Antarctic Lands
Terskiy Bereg coastal area Rus. Fed. 12 H2
Tertenia Sardinia Italy 26 C5
Terter Azer. see Tärtär
Teruel Spain 25 F3
Tervola Fin. 14 N3
Tešanj Bos.-Herz. 26 G2
Teseney Eritrea 32 E6
Tesha r. Rus. Fed. 13 I5
Teshekpuk Lake U.S.A. 60 C2
Teshio Japan 44 F3
Teshio-gawa r. Japan 44 F3
Teslin Canada 60 E3
Teslin Lake Canada 60 E3
Tesouras r. Brazil 71 A1
Tessalit Mali 46 D2
Tessaoua Niger 46 D3
Tessolo Moz. 51 L1
Test r. U.K. 19 F8
Testour Tunisia 26 C6
Tetas, Punta pt Chile 70 B2
Tete Moz. 49 D5
Te Teko N.Z. 59 F4
Teteriv r. Ukr. 13 F6
Teterow Germany 17 N4
Tetiyev Ukr. see Tetiyiv
Tetiyiv Ukr. 13 F6
Tetney U.K. 18 G5
Tétouan Morocco 25 D6
Tetovo Macedonia 27 I3
Tetpur India 36 B5
Tetuán Morocco see Tétouan
Tetulia Bangl. 37 G4
Tetulia sea chan. Bangl. 37 G5
Tetyukhe Rus. Fed. see Dal'negorsk
Tetyukhe-Pristan' Rus. Fed. see Rudnaya Pristan'
Tetyushi Rus. Fed. 13 K5
Teuco r. Arg. 70 D2
Teufelsbach Namibia 50 C2
Teuva Fin. 14 L5
Tevere r. Italy see Tiber
Teverya Israel see Tiberias
Teviot r. U.K. 20 G5
Te Waewae Bay N.Z. 59 A8
Te Waipounamu i. N.Z. see South Island
Tewane Botswana 51 H2
Tewantin Australia 57 F5
Tewkesbury U.K. 19 E7
Têwo China 42 I6
Texarkana TX U.S.A. 63 I5
Texas Australia 58 E2
Texas state U.S.A. 62 H5
Texoma, Lake U.S.A. 63 H5
Teyateyaneng Lesotho 51 H5
Teykovo Rus. Fed. 12 I4
Teza r. Rus. Fed. 12 I4
Tezpur India 37 H4
Tezu India 37 I4
Tha-anne r. Canada 61 I3
Thabana-Ntlenyana mt. Lesotho 51 I5
Thaba Nchu S. Africa 51 H5
Thaba Putsoa mt. Lesotho 51 H5
Thaba-Tseka Lesotho 51 I5
Thabazimbi S. Africa 51 H3
Thabong S. Africa 51 H4
Thabyedaung Myanmar 37 I5
Tha Hin Thai. see Lop Buri
Thai Binh Vietnam 31 J4
Thailand country Asia 31 J5
Thailand, Gulf of Asia 41 C6
Thai Nguyên Vietnam 31 J4
Thakèk Laos 41 C6
Thakurgaon Bangl. 37 G4
Thakurtola India 36 E5
Thala Tunisia 26 C7
Thalassery India see Tellicherry
Thal Desert Pak. 33 L3
Thaliparamba India see Taliparamba
Thallon Australia 58 D2
Thamaga Botswana 51 G3
Thamar, Jabal mt. Yemen 32 G7
Thamarīt Oman 33 H6
Thame r. U.K. 19 F7
Thames r. Ont. Canada 63 K3
Thames N.Z. 59 E3
Thames est. U.K. 19 H7
Thames r. U.K. 19 H7
Thamesford Ont. Canada 64 A1
Thana India see Thane
Thandwè Myanmar 42 G9
Thandwè Myanmar see Thandwè
Thane India 38 B2
Thanet, Isle of pen. U.K. 19 I7
Thangoo Australia 54 C4
Thangra Jammu and Kashmir 36 D2
Thanh Hoa Vietnam 31 J5
Thanjavur India 38 C4
Thanlwin r. China/Myanmar see Salween
Thapsacus Syria see Dibsī
Tharad India 36 B4
Thar Desert India/Pak. 33 K4
Thargomindah Australia 58 A1
Tharthār, Buḥayrat ath l. Iraq 35 F4
Thasos i. Greece 27 K4
Thaton Myanmar 31 I5
Thaungdut Myanmar 37 H4
Thayetmyo Myanmar 37 H6
Thazi Mandalay Myanmar 37 I5
The Aldermen Islands N.Z. 59 F3
Theba AZ U.S.A. 65 F4
The Bahamas country West Indies 67 I4
Thebes Greece see Thiva
The Broads nat. park U.K. 19 I6
The Calvados Chain is P.N.G. 56 F1
The Cheviot hill U.K. 18 E3
The Dalles U.S.A. 62 C2
Thedford U.S.A. 62 G3
The Entrance Australia 58 E4
The Faither stack U.K. 20 [inset]
The Fens reg. U.K. 19 G6
The Gambia country Africa 46 B3
The Grampians mts Australia 57 C8
The Great Oasis oasis Egypt see Khārijah, Wāḥāt al
The Grenadines is St Vincent 67 L6

The Gulf Asia 32 H4
The Hague Neth. 16 J4
The Hunters Hills N.Z. 59 C7
The Lakes National Park Australia 58 C6
Thelon r. Canada 61 I3
The Lynd Junction Australia 56 D3
Thembalihle S. Africa 51 I4
The Minch sea chan. U.K. 20 C2
The Naze c. Norway see Lindesnes
The Needles stack U.K. 19 F8
Theni India 38 C4
Thenia Alg. 25 H5
Theniet El Had Alg. 25 H6
The North Sound sea chan. U.K. 20 G1
Theodore Australia 56 E5
Theodosia Ukr. see Feodosiya
The Old Man of Coniston hill U.K. 18 D4
The Paps hill Ireland 21 C5
The Pas Canada 62 G1
The Pilot mt. Australia 58 D6
Thera i. Greece see Santorini
Thermaïkos Kolpos g. Greece 27 J4
Thermopolis U.S.A. 62 F3
The Rock Australia 58 C5
The Salt Lake salt flat Australia 57 C6
The Settlement Christmas I. 74 D4
The Skaw spit Denmark see Grenen
The Slot sea chan. Solomon Is see New Georgia Sound
The Solent strait U.K. 19 F8
Thessalon Canada 63 K2
Thessalonica Greece see Thessaloniki
Thessaloniki Greece 27 J4
The Storr hill U.K. 20 C3
Thet r. U.K. 19 H6
The Terraces hills Australia 55 C7
Thetford U.K. 19 H6
Thetford Mines Canada 63 M2
The Triangle mts Myanmar 42 H7
The Trossachs hills U.K. 20 E4
The Twins Australia 57 A6
Theva-i-Ra reef Fiji see Ceva-i-Ra
The Valley Anguilla 67 L5
Thevenard Island Australia 54 A5
Thévenet, Lac l. Canada 61 L4
Theveste Alg. see Tébessa
The Wash b. U.K. 19 H6
The Weald reg. U.K. 19 H7
The Woodlands U.S.A. 63 H5
Thibodaux U.S.A. 63 I6
Thief River Falls U.S.A. 63 H2
Thiel Mountains Antarctica 76 K1
Thiers France 24 F4
Thiès Senegal 46 B3
Thika Kenya 48 D4
Thiladhunmathi Atoll Maldives 38 B5
Thiladunmathi Atoll Maldives see Thiladhunmathi Atoll
Thimbu Bhutan see Thimphu
Thimphu Bhutan 37 G4
Thionville France 24 H2
Thira i. Greece see Santorini
Thirsk U.K. 18 F4
Thiruvananthapuram India see Trivandrum
Thiruvannamalai India see Tiruvannamalai
Thiruvarur India 38 C4
Thiruvattiyur India see Tiruvottiyur
Thisted Denmark 15 F8
Thityabin Myanmar 37 H5
Thiva Greece 27 J5
Thívai Greece see Thiva
Thoen Thai. 42 H9
Thoeng Thai. 42 I9
Thohoyandou S. Africa 51 J2
Thomas Hubbard, Cape Canada 61 I1
Thomaston CT U.S.A. 64 E2
Thomastown Ireland 21 E5
Thomasville GA U.S.A. 63 K5
Thompson Canada 61 I4
Thompson r. U.S.A. 62 I4
Thompson Falls U.S.A. 62 D2
Thompson's Falls Kenya see Nyahururu
Thompson Sound Canada 62 B1
Thoothukudi India see Tuticorin
Thorn Poland see Toruń
Thornaby-on-Tees U.K. 18 F4
Thornbury U.K. 19 E7
Thorne U.K. 18 G5
Thorne NV U.S.A. 65 C1
Thornton r. Australia 56 B3
Thorshavnfjella reg. Antarctica see Thorshavnheiane
Thorshavnheiane reg. Antarctica 76 C2
Thota-ea-Moli Lesotho 51 H5
Thouars France 24 D3
Thoubal India 37 H4
Thousand Oaks CA U.S.A. 65 C3
Thrace reg. Europe 27 L4
Thraki reg. Europe see Thrace
Thrakiko Pelagos sea Greece 27 K4
Three Gorges Dam Project resr China 43 J6
Three Hummock Island Australia 57 [inset]
Three Kings Islands N.Z. 59 D2
Three Points, Cape Ghana 46 C4
Three Springs Australia 55 A7
Thrissur India see Trichur
Throssell, Lake salt flat Australia 55 D6
Throssel Range hills Australia 54 C5
Thrushton National Park Australia 58 C1
Thuddungra Australia 58 D5
Thul Pak. 36 B3
Thulaythawāt Gharbī, Jabal hill Syria 39 D2
Thule Greenland 61 L2
Thun Switz. 24 H3
Thunder Bay Canada 61 J5
Thurles Ireland 21 E5
Thurn, Pass Austria 17 N7
Thursday Island Australia 56 C1
Thurso U.K. 20 F2
Thurso r. U.K. 20 F2
Thurston Island Antarctica 76 K2
Thurston Peninsula i. Antarctica see Thurston Island
Thuthukudi India see Tuticorin
Thwaite U.K. 18 E4
Thwaites Glacier Tongue Antarctica 76 K1
Thyatira Turkey see Akhisar
Thyborøn Denmark 15 F8
T'ianet'i Georgia 35 G2
Tianjin China 43 L5
Tianjin municipality China 43 L5
Tianjun China 42 H5
Tianqiaoling China 44 C4
Tianshan China 43 M4
Tian Shan mts China/Kyrg. see Tien Shan
Tianshui China 42 J6
Tianshuihai Aksai Chin 36 D2
Tiantang China see Yuexi
Tianzhu Gansu China 42 I5
Tiaret Alg. 25 G6
Tiassalé Côte d'Ivoire 46 C4
Tibagi Brazil 71 A4
Tibal, Wādī watercourse Iraq 35 F4
Tibati Cameroon 46 E4
Tibba Pak. 36 B3
Tibé, Pic de mt. Guinea 46 C4
Tiber r. Italy 26 E4
Tiberias Israel 39 B3
Tiberias, Lake Israel see Galilee, Sea of
Tibesti mts Chad 47 E2
Tibet aut. reg. China see Xizang Zizhiqu
Tibet, Plateau of China 37 F2
Tibooburra Australia 57 C6
Tibrikot Nepal 37 E3
Tibro Sweden 15 I7
Tibur Italy see Tivoli
Tiburón, Isla i. Mex. 66 B3
Ticehurst U.K. 19 H7
Tīchīt Mauritania 46 C3
Tichla W. Sahara 46 B2
Ticinum Italy see Pavia
Ticul Mex. 66 G4
Tidaholm Sweden 15 H7
Tiddim Myanmar 37 H5
Tidjikja Mauritania 46 B3
Tieli China 44 B3
Tieling China 44 A4
Tielongtan Aksai Chin 36 D2
Tien Shan mts China/Kyrg. 42 D4
Tientsin municipality China see Tianjin
Tierp Sweden 15 J6
Tierra del Fuego, Isla Grande de i. Arg./Chile 70 C8
Tierra del Fuego, Parque Nacional nat. park Arg. 70 C8
Tiétar r. Spain 25 D4
Tiétar, Valle de valley Spain 25 D3
Tietê r. Brazil 71 A3
Tieyon Australia 55 F6
Tiflis Georgia see T'bilisi
Tifton U.S.A. 63 K5
Tiga Reservoir Nigeria 46 D3
Tigen Kazakh. 35 H1
Tigheciului, Dealurile hills Moldova 27 M2
Tighina Moldova 27 M1
Tigiria India 38 E1
Tignère Cameroon 46 E4
Tignish Canada 63 O2
Tigranocerta Turkey see Siirt
Tigre r. Venez. 68 F2
Tigris r. Asia 35 G5
Tigris r. Turkey 32 F2
Tigrovaya Balka Zapovednik nature res. Tajik. 36 B1
Tiguidit, Falaise de esc. Niger 46 D3
Tīh, Gebel el plat. Egypt see Tīh, Jabal at
Tīh, Jabal at plat. Egypt 39 A5
Tijuana Mex. 66 A2
Tikamgarh India 36 D4
Tikanlik China 42 F4
Tikhoretsk Rus. Fed. 13 I7
Tikhvin Rus. Fed. 12 G4
Tikhvinskaya Gryada ridge Rus. Fed. 12 G4
Tiki Basin sea feature S. Pacific Ocean 75 L7
Tikokino N.Z. 59 F4
Tikopia i. Solomon Is 53 G3
Tikrīt Iraq 35 F4
Tikse Jammu and Kashmir 36 D2
Tiksheozero, Ozero l. Rus. Fed. 14 R3
Tiksi Rus. Fed. 29 N2
Tiladummati Atoll Maldives see Thiladhunmathi Atoll
Tilaiya Reservoir India 37 F4
Tilbeşar Ovasi plain Turkey 39 C1
Tilbooroo Australia 58 B1
Tilburg Neth. 16 J5
Tilbury U.K. 19 H7
Tilcara Arg. 70 C2
Tilemsès Niger 46 D3
Tilemsi, Vallée du watercourse Mali 46 D3
Tilhar India 36 D4
Tilimsen Alg. see Tlemcen
Tilin Myanmar 37 H5
Tillabéri Niger 46 D3
Tillia Niger 46 D3
Tillicoultry U.K. 20 F4
Tillsonburg Ont. Canada 64 A1
Tillyfourie U.K. 20 G3
Tilos i. Greece 27 L6
Tilothu India 37 F4
Tilpa Australia 58 B3
Tilsit Rus. Fed. see Sovetsk
Tilt r. U.K. 20 F4
Tilton NH U.S.A. 64 F1
Tim Rus. Fed. 13 H6
Ţimā Egypt 32 D4
Timakara i. India 38 B4
Timanskiy Kryazh ridge Rus. Fed. 12 K2
Timar Turkey 35 F3
Timaru N.Z. 59 C7
Timashevsk Rus. Fed. 13 H7
Timashevskaya Rus. Fed. see Timashevsk
Timbedgha Mauritania 46 C3
Timber Creek Australia 52 D3
Timber Mountain NV U.S.A. 65 D2
Timberville VA U.S.A. 64 B3
Timbuktu Mali 46 C3
Timétrine reg. Mali 46 C3
Timiaouine Alg. 46 D2
Timimoun Alg. 22 E6
Timirist, Râs pt Mauritania 46 B3
Timişoara Romania 27 I2
Timmins Canada 61 J5
Timon Brazil 69 J5
Timor i. East Timor/Indon. 54 D2
Timor-Leste country Asia see East Timor
Timor Loro Sae country Asia see East Timor
Timor Sea Australia/Indon. 52 C3
Timor Timur country Asia see East Timor
Timperley Range hills Australia 55 C6
Timrå Sweden 14 J5
Tīn, Ra's at pt Libya 34 A4
Ţīna, Khalīg el b. Egypt see Ţīnah, Khalīj aţ
Tīnah Syria 39 D1
Ţīnah, Khalīj aţ b. Egypt 39 A4
Tin Can Bay Australia 57 F5
Tindivanam India 38 C3
Tindouf Alg. 22 C6
Ti-n-Essako Mali 46 D3
Tingha Australia 58 E2
Tingis Morocco see Tangier
Tingo María Peru 68 C5
Tingréla Côte d'Ivoire see Tengréla
Tingsryd Sweden 15 I8
Tingvoll Norway 14 F5
Tingwall U.K. 20 F1
Tinharé, Ilha de i. Brazil 71 D1
Tinian i. N. Mariana Is 41 G6
Tini Heke is N.Z. see Snares Islands
Tinnelvelly India see Tirunelveli
Tinogasta Arg. 70 C3
Tinos Greece 27 K6
Tinos i. Greece 27 K6
Tinrhert, Plateau du Alg. 46 D2
Tinsukia India 37 H4
Tintagel U.K. 19 C8
Tîntâne Mauritania 46 B3
Tintina Arg. 70 D3
Tintinara Australia 57 C7
Tionesta PA U.S.A. 64 B2
Tionesta Lake PA U.S.A. 64 B2
Tipasa Alg. 25 H5
Tiphsah Syria see Dibsī
Tipperary Ireland 21 D5
Tipton CA U.S.A. 65 C2
Tipton, Mount AZ U.S.A. 65 E3
Tiptree U.K. 19 H7
Tiptur India 38 C3
Tipturi India see Tiptur
Tiracambu, Serra do hills Brazil 69 I4
Tirana Albania 27 H4
Tiranë Albania see Tirana
Tirano Italy 26 D1
Tirari Desert Australia 57 B5
Tiraspol Moldova 27 M1
Tiraz Mountains Namibia 50 C4
Tire Turkey 27 L5
Tirebolu Turkey 35 E2
Tiree i. U.K. 20 C4
Tîrgovişte Romania see Târgovişte
Tîrgu Jiu Romania see Târgu Jiu
Tîrgu Mureş Romania see Târgu Mureş
Tîrgu Neamţ Romania see Târgu Neamţ
Tîrgu Secuiesc Romania see Târgu Secuiesc
Tiri Pak. 36 A3
Tirich Mir mt. Pak. 33 L2
Tirna r. India 38 C2
Tîrnăveni Romania see Târnăveni
Tírnavos Greece see Tyrnavos
Tiros Brazil 71 B2
Tirourda, Col de pass Alg. 25 I5
Tirreno, Mare sea France/Italy see Tyrrhenian Sea
Tirso r. Sardinia Italy 26 C5
Tirthahalli India 38 B3
Tiruchchendur India 38 C4
Tiruchchirappalli India 38 C4
Tiruchengodu India 38 C4
Tirunelveli India 38 C4
Tirupati India 38 C3
Tiruppattur Tamil Nadu India 38 C3
Tiruppattur Tamil Nadu India 38 C4
Tiruppur India 38 C4
Tiruttani India 38 C3
Tirutturaippundi India 38 C4
Tiruvallur India 38 C3
Tiruvannamalai India 38 C3
Tiruvottiyur India 38 D3
Tiru Well Australia 54 D5
Tisa r. Serbia 27 I2
Tisdale Canada 62 G1
Ţīsīyah Syria 39 C3
Tissemsilt Alg. 25 G6
Tisza r. Hungary see Tisa
Titalya Bangl. see Tetulia
Titan Dome ice feature Antarctica 76 H1
Titao Burkina 46 C3
Tit-Ary Rus. Fed. 29 N2
Titawin Morocco see Tétouan
Titicaca, Lago Bol./Peru see Titicaca, Lake
Titicaca, Lake Bol./Peru 68 E7
Titi Islands N.Z. 59 A8
Titiea mt. N.Z. see Aspiring, Mount
Titlagarh India 38 D1
Titograd Montenegro see Podgorica
Titova Mitrovica Serbia see Kosovska Mitrovica
Titov Drvar Bos.-Herz. 26 G2
Titovo Užice Serbia see Užice
Titovo Velenje Slovenia see Velenje
Titov Veles Macedonia see Veles
Titov Vrbas Serbia see Vrbas
Ti Tree Australia 54 F5
Titu Romania 27 K2
Titusville FL U.S.A. 63 K6
Titusville PA U.S.A. 64 B2
Tiumpain, Rubha an hd U.K. see Tiumpan Head
Tiumpan Head hd U.K. 20 C2
Tiva watercourse Kenya 48 D4
Tivari India 36 C4
Tiverton U.K. 19 D8
Tivoli Italy 26 E4
Ţīwī Oman 33 I5
Tizi El Arba hill Alg. 25 H5
Tizimín Mex. 66 G4
Tizi N'Kouilal pass Alg. 25 I5
Tizi Ouzou Alg. 25 I5
Tiznap He r. China 36 D1
Tiznit Morocco 46 C2
Tiztoutine Morocco 25 E6
Tjaneni Swaziland 51 J3
Tjappsåive Sweden 14 K4
Tjirebon Indon. see Cirebon
Tjolotjo Zimbabwe see Tsholotsho
Tjorhom Norway 15 E7
Tkibuli Georgia see Tqibuli
Tlahualilo Mex. 62 G6
Tlaxcala Mex. 66 E5
Tlemcen Alg. 25 F6
Tlhakalatlou S. Africa 50 F5
Tlholong S. Africa 51 I5
Tlokweng Botswana 51 G3
Tlyarata Rus. Fed. 35 G2
Toamasina Madag. 49 E5
Toano VA U.S.A. 64 C4
Toba China 37 I3
Toba and Kakar Ranges mts Pak. 33 K3
Tobago i. Trin. and Tob. 67 L6
Tobelo Indon. 41 E7
Tobermorey Australia 56 B4
Tobermory Australia 58 A1
Tobermory Canada 63 K2
Tobermory U.K. 20 C4
Tobin, Lake salt flat Australia 54 D5
Tobin Lake Canada 62 G1
Tobi-shima i. Japan 45 E5
Tobol r. Kazakh./Rus. Fed. 30 F1
Tobol'sk Rus. Fed. 28 H4
Tobruk Libya see Tubruq
Tobseda Rus. Fed. 12 L1
Tobyl r. Kazakh./Rus. Fed. see Tobol
Tobysh r. Rus. Fed. 12 K2
Tocache Nuevo Peru 68 C5
Tocantinópolis Brazil 69 I5
Tocantins r. Brazil 71 A1
Tocantins state Brazil 71 A1
Tocantinzinha r. Brazil 71 A1
Toccoa U.S.A. 63 K5
Tochi r. Pak. 36 B2
Töcksfors Sweden 15 G7
Tocopilla Chile 70 B2
Tocumwal Australia 58 B5
Todd watercourse Australia 56 A5
Todi Italy 26 E3
Todoga-saki pt Japan 45 F5
Todos Santos Mex. 66 B4
Toe Head hd U.K. 20 B3
Tofino Canada 62 B2
Toft U.K. 20 [inset]
Tofua i. Tonga 53 I3
Togatax China 36 E2
Togian, Kepulauan is Indon. 41 E8
Togliatti Rus. Fed. see Tol'yatti
Togo country Africa 46 D4
Togtoh China 43 K4
Togton He r. China 37 H2
Togton Heyan China see Tanggulashan
Toholampi Fin. 14 N5
Toiba China 37 G3
Toijala Fin. 15 M6
Toi-misaki pt Japan 45 C7
Toivakka Fin. 14 O5
Toiyabe Range mts NV U.S.A. 65 D1
Tojikiston country Asia see Tajikistan
Tok U.S.A. 60 D3
Tokar Sudan 32 E6
Tokara-rettō is Japan 45 C7
Tokarevka Rus. Fed. 13 I6
Tokat Turkey 34 E2
Tŏkchok-to i. S. Korea 45 B5
Tokdo i. N. Pacific Ocean see Liancourt Rocks
Tokelau terr. S. Pacific Ocean 53 I2
Tokmak Kyrg. see Tokmok
Tokmak Ukr. 13 G7
Tokmok Kyrg. 42 D4
Tokomaru Bay N.Z. 59 G4
Tokoroa N.Z. 59 E4
Tokoza S. Africa 51 I4
Toksun China 42 F4
Tok-tō i. N. Pacific Ocean see Liancourt Rocks
Toktogul Kyrg. 42 C4
Tokto-ri i. N. Pacific Ocean see Liancourt Rocks
Tokur Rus. Fed. 44 D1
Tokushima Japan 45 D6
Tokuyama Japan 45 C6
Tōkyō Japan 45 E6
Tokzār Afgh. 36 A2
Tolaga Bay N.Z. 59 G4
Tôlañaro Madag. 49 E6
Tolbo Mongolia 42 G3
Tolbukhin Bulg. see Dobrich
Tolbuzino Rus. Fed. 44 B1
Toledo Brazil 70 F2
Toledo Spain 25 D4
Toledo OH U.S.A. 63 K3
Toledo, Montes de mts Spain 25 D4
Toletum Spain see Toledo
Toliara Madag. 49 E6
Tolitoli Indon. 41 E7
Tol'ka Rus. Fed. 28 J3
Tolmachevo Rus. Fed. 15 P7
Tolo Dem. Rep. Congo 48 B4
Tolochin Belarus see Talachyn
Tolosa France see Toulouse
Tolosa Spain 25 E2
Toluca Mex. 66 E5
Toluca de Lerdo Mex. see Toluca
To-lun Nei Mongol China see Dolonnur
Tol'yatti Rus. Fed. 13 K5
Tom' r. Rus. Fed. 44 B2
Tomah U.S.A. 63 I3
Tomakomai Japan 44 F4
Tomales CA U.S.A. 65 A1
Tomamae Japan 44 F3
Tomanivi mt. Fiji 53 H3
Tomar Brazil 68 F4
Tomar Port. 25 B4
Tomari Rus. Fed. 44 F3
Tomarza Turkey 34 D3
Tomaszów Lubelski Poland 13 D6
Tomaszów Mazowiecki Poland 17 R5
Tomatin U.K. 20 F3
Tomatlán Mex. 66 C5
Tomazina Brazil 71 A3
Tombador, Serra do hills Brazil 69 G6
Tombigbee r. U.S.A. 63 J5
Tomboco Angola 49 B4
Tombouctou Mali see Timbuktu
Tombua Angola 49 B5
Tom Burke S. Africa 51 H2
Tomdibuloq Uzbek. 33 J1
Tome Moz. 51 L2
Tomelilla Sweden 15 H9
Tomelloso Spain 25 E4
Tomi Romania see Constanţa
Tomingley Australia 58 D4
Tomini, Teluk g. Indon. 41 E8
Tominian Mali 46 C3
Tomintoul U.K. 20 F3
Tomislavgrad Bos.-Herz. 26 G3
Tomkinson Ranges mts Australia 55 E6
Tømmerneset Norway 14 I3
Tommot Rus. Fed. 29 N4
Tomo r. Col. 68 E2
Tomortei China 43 K4
Tom Price Australia 54 B5
Tomra China 37 F3
Tomsk Rus. Fed. 28 J4
Toms River NJ U.S.A. 64 D3
Tomtabacken hill Sweden 15 I8
Tomtor Rus. Fed. 29 P3
Tomur Feng mt. China/Kyrg. see Pobeda Peak
Tomuzlovka r. Rus. Fed. 13 J7
Tom White, Mount U.S.A. 60 D3
Tonalá Mex. 66 F5
Tonantins Brazil 68 E4
Tonbridge U.K. 19 H7
Tønder Denmark 15 F9
Tondi India 38 C4
Tone r. U.K. 19 E7
Toney Mountain Antarctica 76 K1
Tonga country S. Pacific Ocean 53 I4
Tongaat S. Africa 51 J5
Tongariro National Park N.Z. 59 E4
Tongatapu Group is Tonga 53 I4
Tonga Trench sea feature S. Pacific Ocean 74 I7
T'ongch'ŏn N. Korea 45 B5
Tongchuan Shaanxi China 43 J5
Tongduch'ŏn S. Korea 45 B5
Tonghae S. Korea 45 C5
Tonghe China 44 C3
Tonghua Jilin China 44 B4
Tonghua Jilin China 44 B4
Tongi Bangl. see Tungi
Tongjiang Heilong. China 44 D3
Tongking, Gulf of China/Vietnam 31 J4
Tongliao China 43 M4
Tongling China 43 L6
Tonglu China 43 L7
Tongo Australia 58 A3
Tongo Lake salt flat Australia 58 A3
Tongren Guizhou China 43 J7
Tongren Qinghai China 42 I5
Tongsa Bhutan 37 G4
Tongtian He r. Qinghai China 37 H2
Tongtian He r. Qinghai China see Yangtze
Tongue U.K. 20 E2
Tongxin China 42 J5
T'ongyŏng S. Korea 45 C6
Tonk India 36 C4
Tonkābon Iran 35 H3
Tônlé Sab l. Cambodia see Tonle Sap
Tonle Sap l. Cambodia 31 J5
Tonopah AZ U.S.A. 65 F4
Tonopah NV U.S.A. 65 D1
Tønsberg Norway 15 G7
Tonstad Norway 15 E7
Tonzang Myanmar 37 H5
Toobeah Australia 58 D2
Toobli Liberia 46 C4
Tooele U.S.A. 62 E3
Toogoolawah Australia 58 F1
Tooma r. Australia 58 D6
Toompine Australia 58 B1
Toora Australia 58 C7
Tooraweenah Australia 58 D3
Toorberg mt. S. Africa 50 G7
Toowoomba Australia 58 E1
Tooxin Somalia 48 F2
Top Afgh. 36 B2
Top Boğazı Geçidi pass Turkey 39 C1
Topeka U.S.A. 63 H4
Topia Mex. 66 C3
Topoľčany Slovakia 17 Q6
Topolovgrad Bulg. 27 L3
Topozero, Ozero l. Rus. Fed. 12 G2
Tor Eth. 47 G4
Tor Baldak mt. Afgh. 36 A3
Torbalı Turkey 27 L5
Torbat-e Heydarīyeh Iran 33 I2
Torbat-e Jām Iran 33 J2
Torbay Bay Australia 55 B8
Torbert, Mount U.S.A. 60 C3
Torbeyevo Rus. Fed. 13 I5
Tordesillas Spain 25 D3
Tordesilos Spain 25 F3
Töre Sweden 14 M4
Torelló Spain 25 H2
Toretam Kazakh. see Baykonyr
Torgau Germany 17 N5
Torghay Kazakh. see Turgay
Torgun r. Rus. Fed. 13 J6
Torino Italy see Turin
Tori-shima i. Japan 45 F7
Torit Sudan 47 G4
Torkamān Iran 35 G3
Torkovichi Rus. Fed. 12 F4
Torneå Fin. see Tornio
Torneälven r. Sweden 14 N4
Torneträsk l. Sweden 14 K2
Torngat, Monts mts Canada see Torngat Mountains
Torngat Mountains Canada 61 L4
Tornio Fin. 14 N4
Toro Spain 25 D3
Torom Rus. Fed. 44 D1
Toronto Canada 61 K5
Toro Peak CA U.S.A. 65 D4
Toropets Rus. Fed. 12 F4
Tororo Uganda 48 D3
Toros Dağları mts Turkey see Taurus Mountains
Torphins U.K. 20 G3
Torquay Australia 58 B7
Torquay U.K. 19 D8
Torrance CA U.S.A. 65 C4
Torrão Port. 25 B4
Torre mt. Port. 25 C3
Torreblanca Spain 25 G3
Torrecerredo mt. Spain 25 D2
Torre del Greco Italy 26 F4
Torre de Moncorvo Port. 25 C3
Torrelavega Spain 25 D2
Torremolinos Spain 25 D5
Torrens, Lake imp. l. Australia 57 B6
Torrens Creek Australia 56 D4
Torrent Spain 25 F4
Torrente Spain see Torrent
Torreón Mex. 66 D3
Torres Brazil 71 A5
Torres del Paine, Parque Nacional nat. park Chile 70 B8
Torres Islands Vanuatu 53 G3
Torres Novas Port. 25 B4
Torres Strait Australia 52 E2
Torres Vedras Port. 25 B4
Torrevieja Spain 25 F5
Torridge r. U.K. 19 C8
Torridon, Loch b. U.K. 20 D3
Torrijos Spain 25 D4
Torrington Australia 58 E2
Torsby Sweden 15 H6
Tórshavn Faroe Is 14 [inset]
To'rtko'l Uzbek. 33 J1
Törtköl Uzbek. see To'rtko'l
Tortolì Sardinia Italy 26 C5
Tortona Italy 26 C2
Tortosa Spain 25 G3
Tortum Turkey 35 F2
Ţorūd Iran 35 I4
Torugart, Pereval pass China/Kyrg. see Turugart Pass
Torul Turkey 35 E2
Toruń Poland 17 Q4
Tory Island Ireland 21 D2
Tory Sound sea chan. Ireland 21 D2
Torzhok Rus. Fed. 12 G4
Tosa Japan 45 D6
Tosbotn Norway 14 H4
Tosca S. Africa 50 F3
Toscano, Arcipelago is Italy 26 C3
Tosham India 36 C3
Tōshima-yama mt. Japan 45 F4
Toshkent Uzbek. 33 K1
Toshkent Uzbek. see Toshkent
Tosno Rus. Fed. 15 Q6
Toson Hu l. China 37 I1
Tostado Arg. 70 D3
Tosya Turkey 34 D2
Totapola mt. Sri Lanka 38 D5
Tôtes France 19 I9
Tot'ma Rus. Fed. 12 I4
Totness Suriname 69 G2
Tottenham Australia 58 C4
Totton U.K. 19 F8
Tottori Japan 45 D6
Touba Côte d'Ivoire 46 C4
Touba Senegal 46 B3
Toubkal, Jbel mt. Morocco 22 C5
Toubkal, Parc National nat. park Morocco 22 C5
Touboro Cameroon 47 E4
Tougan Burkina 46 C3
Touggourt Alg. 22 F5
Tougué Guinea 46 B3
Touil Mauritania 46 B3
Toul France 24 G2
Toulon France 24 G5
Toulouse France 24 E5
Toumodi Côte d'Ivoire 46 C4
Tourane Vietnam see Đa Nẵng
Tourlaville France 19 F9
Tournai Belgium 16 I5
Tournon-sur-Rhône France 24 G4
Tournus France 24 G3
Touros Brazil 69 K5
Tours France 24 E3
Tousside, Pic mt. Chad 47 E2
Toussoro, Mont mt. Cent. Afr. Rep. 48 C3
Toutai China 44 B3
Touwsrivier S. Africa 50 E7
Tovarkovo Rus. Fed. 13 G5
Tovuz Azer. 35 G2
Towada Japan 44 F4
Towak Mountain hill U.S.A. 60 B3
Towanda PA U.S.A. 64 C2
Towcester U.K. 19 G6
Tower Ireland 21 D6
Townes Pass CA U.S.A. 65 D2
Townsend U.S.A. 62 E2
Townsend, Mount Australia 58 D6
Townshend Island Australia 56 E4
Townsville Australia 56 D3
Towot Sudan 47 G4
Towr Kham Afgh. 36 B2
Towson MD U.S.A. 64 C3
Towyn U.K. see Tywyn
Toyama Japan 45 E5
Toyama-wan b. Japan 45 E5
Toyohashi Japan 45 E6
Toyokawa Japan 45 E6
Toyonaka Japan 45 D6
Toyooka Japan 45 D6
Toyota Japan 45 E6
Tozanlı Turkey see Almus
Tozê Kangri mt. China 37 E2
Tozeur Tunisia 22 F5
Tozi, Mount U.S.A. 60 C3
Tqibuli Georgia 35 F2
Trâblous Lebanon see Tripoli
Trabotivište Macedonia 27 J4
Trabzon Turkey 35 E2
Tracy CA U.S.A. 65 B2
Trafalgar, Cabo c. Spain 25 C5
Tràille, Rubha na pt U.K. 20 D5
Traill Island Greenland see Traill Ø
Traill Ø i. Greenland 61 P2
Trajectum Neth. see Utrecht
Trakai Lith. 15 N9
Trakiya reg. Europe see Thrace
Trakt Rus. Fed. 12 K3
Trakya reg. Europe see Thrace
Tralee Ireland 21 C5
Tralee Bay Ireland 21 C5
Trá Li Ireland see Tralee
Tramandaí Brazil 71 A5
Tramán Tepuí mt. Venez. 68 F2
Trá Mhór Ireland see Tramore
Tramore Ireland 21 E5
Tranås Sweden 15 I7
Trancas Arg. 70 C3
Trancoso Brazil 71 D2
Tranemo Sweden 15 H8
Tranent U.K. 20 G5
Trangan i. Indon. 41 F8
Trangie Australia 58 C4
Transantarctic Mountains Antarctica 76 H2
Transylvanian Alps mts Romania 27 J2
Transylvanian Basin plat. Romania 27 K1
Trapani Sicily Italy 26 E5
Trapezus Turkey see Trabzon
Traralgon Australia 58 C7
Trashigang Bhutan see Tashigang
Trasimeno, Lago l. Italy 26 E3
Trasvase, Canal de Spain 25 E4
Traunsee l. Austria 17 N7
Traunstein Germany 17 N7
Travellers Lake imp. l. Australia 57 C7
Travers, Mount N.Z. 59 D6
Traverse City U.S.A. 63 J3
Travnik Bos.-Herz. 26 G2
Trbovlje Slovenia 26 F1
Treasury Islands Solomon Is 52 F2
Trebebvić nat. park Bos.-Herz. 26 H3
Třebíč Czech Rep. 17 O6
Trebinje Bos.-Herz. 26 H3
Trebišov Slovakia 13 D6
Trebizond Turkey see Trabzon
Trebnje Slovenia 26 F2
Tree Island India 38 B4
Trefaldwyn U.K. see Montgomery
Treffynnon U.K. see Holywell
Trefyclawdd U.K. see Knighton
Trefynwy U.K. see Monmouth
Tregosse Islets and Reefs Australia 56 E3
Treinta y Tres Uruguay 70 F4
Trelew Arg. 70 C6
Trelleborg Sweden 15 H9
Tremblant, Mont hill Canada 63 M2
Tremiti, Isole is Italy 26 F3
Tremont PA U.S.A. 64 C2
Tremonton U.S.A. 62 E3
Tremp Spain 25 G2
Trenance U.K. 19 B8
Trenčín Slovakia 17 Q6
Trenque Lauquén Arg. 70 D5
Trent Italy see Trento
Trent r. U.K. 19 G5
Trento Italy 26 D1
Trenton Canada 63 L3
Trenton MO U.S.A. 63 I3
Trenton NJ U.S.A. 64 D2
Treorchy U.K. 19 D7
Trepassey Canada 61 M5
Tres Arroyos Arg. 70 D5
Tresco i. U.K. 19 A9
Três Corações Brazil 71 B3
Tres Esquinas Col. 68 C3
Tres Forcas, Cabo c. Morocco see Trois Fourches, Cap des
Três Lagoas Brazil 71 A3
Três Marias, Represa resr Brazil 71 B2
Tres Picos, Cerro mt. Arg. 70 D5
Três Pontas Brazil 71 B3
Tres Puntas, Cabo c. Arg. 70 C7
Três Rios Brazil 71 C3
Tretten Norway 15 G6
Tretyy Severnyy Rus. Fed. see 3-y Severnyy
Treungen Norway 15 F7
Treves Germany see Trier
Treviglio Italy 26 C2
Treviso Italy 26 E2
Trevose Head hd U.K. 19 B8
Triánda Greece see Trianta
Triangle VA U.S.A. 64 C3
Trianta Greece 27 M6
Tribal Areas admin. div. Pak. 36 B2
Tri Brata, Gora hill Rus. Fed. 44 F1
Tricase Italy 26 H5
Trichinopoly India see Tiruchchirappalli
Trichur India 38 C4
Trida Australia 58 B4
Tridentum Italy see Trento
Trier Germany 17 K6
Trieste Italy 26 E2
Trieste, Golfo di g. Europe see Trieste, Gulf of
Trieste, Gulf of Europe 26 E2
Triglav mt. Slovenia 26 E1
Triglavski narodni park nat. park Slovenia 26 E1
Trikala Greece 27 I5
Tríkkala Greece see Trikala
Trikora, Puncak mt. Indon. 41 F8
Trim Ireland 21 F4
Trincomalee Sri Lanka 38 D4
Trindade Brazil 71 A2
Trindade, Ilha da i. S. Atlantic Ocean 72 G7
Trinidad Bol. 68 F6
Trinidad Cuba 67 I4
Trinidad i. Trin. and Tob. 67 L6
Trinidad Uruguay 70 E4
Trinidad U.S.A. 62 G4
Trinidad country West Indies see Trinidad and Tobago
Trinidad and Tobago country West Indies 67 L6
Trinity Bay Canada 61 M5
Trinity Islands U.S.A. 60 C4
Trionto, Capo c. Italy 26 G5
Tripoli Greece 27 J6
Tripoli Lebanon 39 B2
Tripoli Libya 47 E1
Trípolis Greece see Tripoli
Tripolis Lebanon see Tripoli
Tripunittura India 38 C4
Tripura state India 37 G5
Tristan da Cunha i. S. Atlantic Ocean 72 H8
Trisul mt. India 36 D3
Trivandrum India 38 C4
Trivento Italy 26 F4
Trnava Slovakia 17 P6
Trobriand Islands P.N.G. 52 F2
Trofors Norway 14 H4
Trogir Croatia 26 G3
Troia Italy 26 F4
Troisdorf Germany 17 K5
Trois Fourches, Cap des c. Morocco 25 E6
Trois-Rivières Canada 63 M2

Troitsko-Pechorsk Rus. Fed. 11 R3
Troitskoye Altayskiy Kray Rus. Fed. 42 E2
Troitskoye Khabarovskiy Kray Rus. Fed. 44 E2
Troitskoye Respublika Kalmykiya - Khalm'g-Tangch Rus. Fed. 13 J7
Troll 76 B2
Trollhättan Sweden 15 H7
Trombetas r. Brazil 69 G4
Tromelin, Île i. Indian Ocean 73 L7
Tromen, Volcán vol. Arg. 70 B5
Tromie r. U.K. 20 E3
Trompsburg S. Africa 51 G6
Tromsø Norway 14 K2
Trona CA U.S.A. 65 D3
Tronador, Monte mt. Arg. 70 B6
Trondheim Norway 14 G5
Trondheimsfjorden sea chan. Norway 14 F5
Trongsa Bhutan see Tongsa
Troödos, Mount Cyprus 39 A2
Troödos Mountains Cyprus 39 A2
Troon U.K. 20 E5
Tropeiros, Serra dos hills Brazil 71 B1
Tropic of Capricorn 56 G4
Trosh Rus. Fed. 12 L2
Trostan hill U.K. 21 F2
Trout Lake Alta Canada 60 G4
Trout Lake N.W.T. Canada 60 F3
Trout Lake Ont. Canada 63 I1
Trout Run PA U.S.A. 64 C2
Trouville-sur-Mer France 19 H9
Trowbridge U.K. 19 E7
Troy tourist site Turkey 27 L5
Troy AL U.S.A. 63 J5
Troy NH U.S.A. 64 E1
Troy NY U.S.A. 64 E1
Troy PA U.S.A. 64 C2
Troyan Bulg. 27 K3
Troyes France 24 G2
Troy Lake CA U.S.A. 65 D3
Troy Peak NV U.S.A. 65 E1
Trstenik Serbia 27 I3
Trucial Coast country Asia see United Arab Emirates
Trucial States country Asia see United Arab Emirates
Trud Rus. Fed. 12 G4
Trufanovo Rus. Fed. 12 J2
Trujillo Hond. 67 G5
Trujillo Peru 68 C5
Trujillo Spain 25 D4
Trujillo Venez. 68 D2
Trujillo, Monte mt. Dom. Rep. see Duarte, Pico
Truk is Micronesia see Chuuk
Trumbull, Mount AZ U.S.A. 65 F2
Trundle Australia 58 C4
Truong Sa is S. China Sea see Spratly Islands
Truro Canada 63 O2
Truro U.K. 19 B8
Truskmore hill Ireland 21 D3
Truth or Consequences U.S.A. 62 F5
Trutnov Czech Rep. 17 O5
Truuli Peak U.S.A. 60 C4
Truva tourist site Turkey see Troy
Trypiti, Akrotirio pt Greece 27 K7
Trysil Norway 15 H6
Trzebiatów Poland 17 O3
Tsagaan-Uul Mongolia see Sharga
Tsagan Aman Rus. Fed. 13 J7
Tsagan-Nur Rus. Fed. 13 J7
Tsaidam Basin China see Qaidam Pendi
Tsaka La pass China/Jammu and Kashmir 36 D2
Tsalenjikha Georgia 35 F2
Tsangbo r. China see Brahmaputra
Tsangpo r. China see Brahmaputra
Tsaratanana, Massif du mts Madag. 49 E5
Tsarevo Bulg. 27 L3
Tsaris Mountains Namibia 50 C3
Tsaritsyn Rus. Fed. see Volgograd
Tsaukaib Namibia 50 B4
Tsavo East National Park Kenya 48 D4
Tsavo West National Park Africa 48 D3
Tsefat Israel see Zefat
Tselinograd Kazakh. see Astana
Tsenogora Rus. Fed. 12 J2
Tses Namibia 50 D3
Tsetsegnuur Mongolia 42 G3
Tsetseng Botswana 50 F2
Tsetserleg Arhangay Mongolia 42 I3
Tsetserleg Hövsgöl Mongolia see Halban
Tshabong Botswana 50 F4
Tshad country Africa see Chad
Tshane Botswana 50 E3
Tshela Dem. Rep. Congo 49 B4
Tshibala Dem. Rep. Congo 49 C4
Tshikapa Dem. Rep. Congo 49 C4
Tshing S. Africa 51 H4
Tshipise S. Africa 51 J2
Tshitanzu Dem. Rep. Congo 49 C4
Tshofa Dem. Rep. Congo 49 C4
Tshokwane S. Africa 51 J3
Tsholotsho Zimbabwe 49 C5
Tshootsha Botswana 50 E2
Tshuapa r. Dem. Rep. Congo 47 F5
Tshwane S. Africa see Pretoria
Tsil'ma r. Rus. Fed. 12 K2
Tsimlyansk Rus. Fed. 13 I7
Tsimlyanskoye Vodokhranilishche resr Rus. Fed. 13 I7
Tsimmermanovka Rus. Fed. 44 E2
Tsinan China see Jinan
Tsineng S. Africa 50 F4
Tsinghai prov. China see Qinghai
Tsingtao China see Qingdao
Tsining China see Jining
Tsiombe Madag. 49 E6
Tsiroanomandidy Madag. 49 E5
Tsitsihar China see Qiqihar
Tsitsikamma Forest and Coastal National Park S. Africa 50 F8
Tsivil'sk Rus. Fed. 12 J5
Tskhaltubo Georgia see Tsqaltubo
Ts'khinvali Georgia 35 F2
Tsna r. Rus. Fed. 13 I5
Tsnori Georgia 35 G2
Tsokar Chumo l. Jammu and Kashmir 36 D2
Tsolo S. Africa 51 I6
Tsomo S. Africa 51 H7
Tsona China see Cona
Tsqaltubo Georgia 35 F2
Tsu Japan 45 E6
Tsuchiura Japan 45 F5
Tsugarū-kaikyō strait Japan 44 F4
Tsugaru Strait Japan see Tsugarū-kaikyō
Tsumeb Namibia 49 B5
Tsumis Park Namibia 50 C2
Tsumkwe Namibia 49 C5
Tsuruga Japan 45 E6
Tsurugi-san mt. Japan 45 D6
Tsurukhaytuy Rus. Fed. see Priargunsk
Tsuruoka Japan 45 E5
Tsushima is Japan 45 C6
Tsushima-kaikyō strait Japan/S. Korea see Korea Strait
Tsuyama Japan 45 D6
Tswaane Botswana 50 E2
Tswaraganang S. Africa 51 G5
Tswelelang S. Africa 51 G4
Tsyelyakhany Belarus 15 N10
Tsyp-Navolok Rus. Fed. 14 R2
Tsyurupyns'k Ukr. 27 O1
Tthenaagoo Canada see Nahanni Butte
Tua Dem. Rep. Congo 48 B4
Tual Indon. 41 F8
Tuam Ireland 21 D4
Tuamotu, Archipel des is Fr. Polynesia see Tuamotu Islands
Tuamotu Islands Fr. Polynesia 75 K6
Tuapse Rus. Fed. 13 H7
Tuath, Loch a' b. U.K. 20 C2
Tuba City U.S.A. 62 E4
Tubarão Brazil 71 A5
Tubarjal Saudi Arabia 39 D4
Tubbercurry Ireland 21 D3
Tübingen Germany 17 L6
Tubmanburg Liberia 46 B4
Tubruq Libya 34 A4
Tubuai i. Fr. Polynesia 75 K7
Tubuai Islands Fr. Polynesia 75 J7
Tucano Brazil 69 K6
Tucavaca Bol. 69 G7
Tuchitua Canada 60 F3
Tuckerton NJ U.S.A. 64 D3
Tucopia i. Solomon Is see Tikopia
Tucson U.S.A. 62 E5
Tucumán Arg. see San Miguel de Tucumán
Tucumcari U.S.A. 62 G4
Tucupita Venez. 68 F2
Tucuruí Brazil 69 I4
Tucuruí, Represa resr Brazil 69 I4
Tudela Spain 25 F2
Tuder Italy see Todi
Tuela r. Port. 25 C3
Tuensang India 37 H4
Tufts Abyssal Plain sea feature N. Pacific Ocean 75 K2
Tugela r. S. Africa 51 J5
Tuglung China 37 H3
Tuguegarao Phil. 41 E6
Tugur Rus. Fed. 44 E1
Tujiabu China see Yongxiu
Tukangbesi, Kepulauan is Indon. 41 E8
Tukituki r. N.Z. 59 F4
Tuktoyaktuk Canada 60 E3
Tuktut Nogait National Park Canada 60 F3
Tukums Latvia 15 M8
Tukuringra, Khrebet mts Rus. Fed. 44 B1
Tukuyu Tanz. 49 D4
Tula Rus. Fed. 13 H5
Tulach Mhór Ireland see Tullamore
Tulagt Ar Gol r. China 37 H1
Tula Mountains Antarctica 76 D2
Tulancingo Mex. 66 E4
Tulare CA U.S.A. 65 C2
Tulare Lake Bed CA U.S.A. 65 C3
Tulasi mt. India 38 D2
Tulbagh S. Africa 50 D7
Tulcán Ecuador 68 C3
Tulcea Romania 27 M2
Tuléar Madag. see Toliara
Tulemalu Lake Canada 61 I3
Tulia U.S.A. 62 G5
Tulihe China 44 A2
Tulkarem West Bank see Ṭūlkarm
Ṭūlkarm West Bank 39 B3
Tulla Ireland 21 D5
Tullamore Australia 58 C4
Tullamore Ireland 21 E4
Tulle France 24 E4
Tulleråsen Sweden 14 I5
Tullibigeal Australia 58 C4
Tullow Ireland 21 F5
Tully Australia 56 D3
Tully r. Australia 56 D3
Tully U.K. 21 E3
Tulos Rus. Fed. 14 Q5
Tulqarem West Bank see Ṭūlkarm
Tulsa U.S.A. 63 H4
Tulsipur Nepal 37 E3
Tuluá Col. 68 C3
Tuluksak U.S.A. 77 B2
Tulūl al Ashāqif hills Jordan 39 C3
Tulun Rus. Fed. 42 I2
Tulu-Tuloi, Serra hills Brazil 68 F3
Tulu Welel mt. Eth. 48 D3
Tuma Rus. Fed. 13 I5
Tumaco Col. 68 C3
Tumahole S. Africa 51 H4
Tumain China 37 G2
Tumannyy Rus. Fed. 14 S2
Tumasik Sing. see Singapore
Tumba Dem. Rep. Congo 48 C4
Tumba Sweden 15 J7
Tumba, Lac l. Dem. Rep. Congo 48 B4
Tumbarumba Australia 58 D5
Tumbes Peru 68 B4
Tumby Bay Australia 57 B7
Tumcha r. Fin./Rus. Fed. 14 Q3
Tumen Jilin China 44 C4
Tumereng Guyana 68 F2
Tumiritinga Brazil 71 C2
Tumkur India 38 C3
Tummel r. U.K. 20 F4
Tummel, Loch l. U.K. 20 F4
Tumnin r. Rus. Fed. 44 F2
Tump Pak. 33 J4
Tumu Ghana 46 C3
Tumucumaque, Serra hills Brazil 69 G3
Tumudibandh India 38 D2
Tumut Australia 58 D5
Tuna India 36 B5
Tunbridge Wells, Royal U.K. 19 H7
Tunceli Turkey 35 E3
Tuncurry Australia 58 F4
Tundun-Wada Nigeria 46 D3
Tunduru Tanz. 49 D5
Tunes Tunisia see Tunis
Tunga Nigeria 46 D4
Tungabhadra Reservoir India 38 C3
Tungi Bangl. 37 G5
Tungnaá r. Iceland 14 [inset]
Tungor Rus. Fed. 44 F1
Tungsten Canada 60 F3
Tuni India 38 D2
Tūnis country Africa see Tunisia
Tunis Tunisia 26 D6
Tunis, Golfe de g. Tunisia 26 D6
Tunisia country Africa 22 F5
Tunja Col. 68 D2
Tunkhannock PA U.S.A. 64 D2
Tunnsjøen l. Norway 14 H4
Tunstall U.K. 19 I6
Tuntsa Fin. 14 P3
Tuntsajoki r. Fin./Rus. Fed. see Tumcha
Tununak U.S.A. 60 B3
Tunxi China see Huangshan
Tuotuo He r. China see Togton He
Tuotuoheyan China see Tanggulashan
Tüp Kyrg. 42 D4
Tupã Brazil 71 A3
Tupelo U.S.A. 63 J5
Tupik Rus. Fed. 43 L2
Tupinambarana, Ilha i. Brazil 69 G4
Tupiraçaba Brazil 71 A1
Tupiza Bol. 68 E8
Tüpqaraghan Tübegi pen. Kazakh. see Mangyshlak, Poluostrov
Tupungato, Cerro mt. Arg./Chile 70 C4
Tuquan China 43 M3
Tura China 37 F1
Tura India 37 G4
Tura Rus. Fed. 29 L3
Turabah Saudi Arabia 32 F5
Turakina N.Z. 59 E5
Turan Rus. Fed. 42 G2
Turana, Khrebet mts Rus. Fed. 44 C2
Turan Lowland Asia 33 I2
Turan Oypaty lowland Asia see Turan Lowland
Turan Pasttekisligi lowland Asia see Turan Lowland
Turan Peslīgi lowland Asia see Turan Lowland
Turanskaya Nizmennost' lowland Asia see Turan Lowland
Ṭurāq al 'Ilab hills Syria 39 D3
Turar Ryskulov Kazakh. 33 L1
Tura-Ryskulova Kazakh. see Turar Ryskulov
Ṭurayf Saudi Arabia 39 D4
Turba Estonia 15 N7
Turbat Pak. 33 J4
Turbo Col. 68 C2
Turda Romania 27 J1
Tūreh Iran 35 H4
Turfan China see Turpan
Turfan Basin depr. China see Turpan Pendi
Turfan Depression China see Turpan Pendi
Turgay Kazakh. 42 A3
Türgovishte Bulg. 27 L3
Turgutlu Turkey 27 L5
Turhal Turkey 34 E2
Türi Estonia 15 N7
Turia r. Spain 25 F4
Turin Italy 26 B2
Turiy Rog Rus. Fed. 44 C3
Turkana, Lake salt l. Eth./Kenya 48 D3
Turkestan Kazakh. 42 B4
Turkey country Asia/Europe 34 D3
Turki Rus. Fed. 13 I6
Türkistan Kazakh. see Turkestan
Türkiye country Asia/Europe see Turkey
Türkmenabat Turkm. 30 F3
Türkmen Adasy i. Turkm. see Ogurjaly Adasy
Türkmen Aýlagy b. Turkm. 35 I3
Türkmen Aylagy b. Turkm. see Türkmen Aýlagy
Türkmenbaşy Turkm. 35 I2
Türkmenbaşy Turkm. see Türkmenbaşy
Türkmenbaşy Aýlagy b. Turkm. 35 I3
Türkmenbaşy Aylagy b. Turkm. see Türkmenbaşy Aýlagy
Türkmenbaşy Döwlet Gorugy nature res. Turkm. 35 I3
Türkmen Dağı mt. Turkey 27 N5
Turkmenistan country Asia 33 I2
Turkmeniya country Asia see Turkmenistan
Türkmenostan country Asia see Turkmenistan
Turkmenskaya S.S.R. country Asia see Turkmenistan
Türkoğlu Turkey 34 E3
Turks and Caicos Islands terr. West Indies 67 J4
Turks Islands Turks and Caicos Is 67 J4
Turku Fin. 15 M6
Turkwel watercourse Kenya 48 D3
Turlock CA U.S.A. 65 B2
Turlock Lake CA U.S.A. 65 B2
Turmalina Brazil 71 C2
Turnagain, Cape N.Z. 59 F5
Turnberry U.K. 20 E5
Turneffe Islands atoll Belize 66 G5
Turnor Lake Canada 60 H4
Türnovo Bulg. see Veliko Türnovo
Turnu Măgurele Romania 27 K3
Turnu Severin Romania see Drobeta-Turnu Severin
Turon r. Australia 58 D4
Turones France see Tours
Turovets Rus. Fed. 12 I4
Turpan China 42 F4
Turpan Pendi depr. China 42 F4
Turquino, Pico mt. Cuba 67 I4
Turriff U.K. 20 G3
Turris Libisonis Sardinia Italy see Porto Torres
Tursāq Iraq 35 G4
Turtle Island Fiji see Vatoa
Turugart Pass China/Kyrg. 31 G2
Turugart Shankou pass China/Kyrg. see Turugart Pass
Turuvanur India 38 C3
Turvo r. Brazil 71 A2
Turvo r. Brazil 71 A2
Tuscaloosa U.S.A. 63 J5
Tuscarawas r. OH U.S.A. 64 A2
Tuscarora Mountains hills PA U.S.A. 64 C2
Tuskegee U.S.A. 63 J5
Tussey Mountains hills PA U.S.A. 64 B2
Tutak Turkey 35 F3
Tutayev Rus. Fed. 12 H4
Tutera Spain see Tudela
Tuticorin India 38 C4
Tuttlingen Germany 17 L7
Tuttut Nunaat reg. Greenland 61 P2
Tutuala East Timor 54 D2
Tutubu P.N.G. 56 E1
Tutubu Tanz. 49 D4
Tutuila i. American Samoa 53 I3
Tutume Botswana 49 C6
Tuun-bong mt. N. Korea 44 B4
Tuupovaara Fin. 14 Q5
Tuusniemi Fin. 14 P5
Tuvalu country S. Pacific Ocean 53 H2
Tuwayq, Jabal hills Saudi Arabia 32 G4
Tuwayq, Jabal mts Saudi Arabia 32 G5
Ṭuwayyil ash Shihāq mt. Jordan 39 C4
Tuwwal Saudi Arabia 32 E5
Tuxpan Mex. 66 E4
Tuxtla Gutiérrez Mex. 66 F5
Tuy Hoa Vietnam 31 J5
Tuz, Lake salt l. Turkey 34 D3
Tuz Gölü salt l. Turkey see Tuz, Lake
Tuzha Rus. Fed. 12 J4
Tuz Khurmātū Iraq 35 G4
Tuzla Bos.-Herz. 26 H2
Tuzla Turkey 39 B1
Tuzla Gölü lag. Turkey 27 L4
Tuzlov r. Rus. Fed. 13 I7
Tuzu r. Myanmar 37 H4
Tvedestrand Norway 15 F7
Tver' Rus. Fed. 12 G4
Twain Harte CA U.S.A. 65 B1
Tweed r. U.K. 20 G5
Tweed Heads Australia 58 F2
Tweefontein S. Africa 50 D7
Twee Rivier Namibia 50 D3
Twentynine Palms CA U.S.A. 65 D3
Twin Bridges CA U.S.A. 65 B1
Twin Falls U.S.A. 62 E3
Twin Heads hill Australia 54 D5
Twin Peak CA U.S.A. 65 B1
Twitchen Reservoir CA U.S.A. 65 B3
Twofold Bay Australia 58 D6
Two Harbors U.S.A. 63 I2
Tyan' Shan' mts China/Kyrg. see Tien Shan
Tyatya, Vulkan vol. Rus. Fed. 44 G3
Tydal Norway 14 G5
Tygart Valley valley WV U.S.A. 64 B3
Tygda Rus. Fed. 44 B1
Tygda r. Rus. Fed. 44 B1
Tyler U.S.A. 63 H5
Tym' r. Rus. Fed. 44 F2
Tymovskoye Rus. Fed. 44 F2
Tynda Rus. Fed. 43 M1
Tyndinskiy Rus. Fed. see Tynda
Tyne r. U.K. 20 G4
Tynemouth U.K. 18 F3
Tynset Norway 14 G5
Tyoploozyorsk Rus. Fed. see Teploozersk
Tyoploye Ozero Rus. Fed. see Teploozersk
Tyr Lebanon see Tyre
Tyras Ukr. see Bilhorod-Dnistrovs'kyy
Tyre Lebanon 39 B3
Tyree, Mount Antarctica 76 L1
Tyrma Rus. Fed. 44 D2
Tyrma r. Rus. Fed. 44 C2
Tyrnävä Fin. 14 N4
Tyrnavos Greece 27 J5
Tyrnyauz Rus. Fed. 35 F2
Tyrone PA U.S.A. 64 B2
Tyrrell r. Australia 58 A5
Tyrrell, Lake dry lake Australia 57 C7
Tyrrhenian Sea France/Italy 26 D4
Tyrus Lebanon see Tyre
Tysa r. Ukr. see Tisa
Tyukalinsk Rus. Fed. 28 I4
Tyulen'i Ostrova is Kazakh. 35 H1
Tyumen' Rus. Fed. 28 H4
Tyup Kyrg. see Tüp
Tyuratam Kazakh. see Baykonyr
Tywi r. U.K. 19 C7
Tywyn U.K. 19 C6
Tzaneen S. Africa 51 J2
Tzia i. Greece 27 K6

U

Uaco Congo Angola see Waku-Kungo
Ualan atoll Micronesia see Kosrae
Uamanda Angola 49 C5
Uarc, Ras c. Morocco see Trois Fourches, Cap des
Uaroo Australia 55 A5
Uatumã r. Brazil 69 G4
Uauá Brazil 69 K5
Uaupés r. Brazil 68 E3
U'aylī, Wādī al watercourse Saudi Arabia 39 D4
U'aywij well Saudi Arabia 35 G5
U'aywij, Wādī al watercourse Saudi Arabia 35 F5
Ubá Brazil 71 C3
Ubaí Brazil 71 B2
Ubaitaba Brazil 71 D1
Ubangi r. Cent. Afr. Rep./Dem. Rep. Congo 48 B4
Ubangi-Shari country Africa see Central African Republic
Ubauro Pak. 36 B3
Ubayyiḍ, Wādī al watercourse Iraq/Saudi Arabia 35 F4
Ube Japan 45 C6
Úbeda Spain 25 E4
Uberaba Brazil 71 B2
Uberlândia Brazil 71 A2
Ubombo S. Africa 51 K4
Ubon Ratchathani Thai. 31 J5
Ubundu Dem. Rep. Congo 47 F5
Üçajy Turkm. 33 J2
Ucar Azer. 35 G2
Uçarı Turkey 39 A1
Ucayali r. Peru 68 D4
Uch Pak. 36 B3
Üchajy Turkm. see Üçajy
Üchān Iran 35 H3
Ucharal Kazakh. 42 E3
Uchiura-wan b. Japan 44 F4
Uchkeken Rus. Fed. 35 F2
Uchkuduk Uzbek. see Uchquduq
Uchquduq Uzbek. 33 J1
Uchte r. Pak. 36 A4
Uchur r. Rus. Fed. 29 O4
Uckfield U.K. 19 H8
Uda r. Rus. Fed. 43 J2
Uda r. Rus. Fed. 44 D1
Udachnoye Rus. Fed. 13 J7
Udachnyy Rus. Fed. 77 E2
Udagamandalam India 38 C4
Udaipur Rajasthan India 36 C4
Udaipur Tripura India 37 G5
Udanti r. India/Myanmar 37 E5
Uday r. Ukr. 13 G6
Uddevalla Sweden 15 G7
Uddingston U.K. 20 E5
Uddjaure l. Sweden 14 J4
Udgir India 38 C2
Udhagamandalam India see Udagamandalam
Udhampur India 36 C2
Udia-Milai atoll Marshall Is see Bikini
Udimskiy Rus. Fed. 12 J3
Udine Italy 26 E1
Udmalaippettai India see Udumalaippettai
Udomlya Rus. Fed. 12 G4
Udon Thani Thai. 31 J5
Udskaya Guba b. Rus. Fed. 29 O4
Udskoye Rus. Fed. 44 D1
Udumalaippettai India 38 C4
Udupi India 38 B3
Udyl', Ozero l. Rus. Fed. 44 E1
Udzhary Azer. see Ucar
Udzungwa Mountains National Park Tanz. 49 D4
Uéa atoll New Caledonia see Ouvéa
Ueckermünde Germany 17 O4
Ueda Japan 45 E5
Uele r. Dem. Rep. Congo 48 C3
Uelen Rus. Fed. 29 U3
Uelzen Germany 17 M4
Ufa Rus. Fed. 11 R5
Ufa r. Rus. Fed. 11 R5
Uftyuga r. Rus. Fed. 12 J3
Ugab watercourse Namibia 49 B6
Ugalla r. Tanz. 49 D4
Uganda country Africa 48 D3
Ugie S. Africa 51 I6
Uglegorsk Rus. Fed. 44 F2
Uglich Rus. Fed. 12 H4
Ugljan i. Croatia 26 F2
Uglovoye Rus. Fed. 44 C2
Ugol'noye Rus. Fed. 29 P3
Ugolnyy Rus. Fed. see Beringovskiy
Ugol'nyye Kopi Rus. Fed. 29 S3
Ugra Rus. Fed. 13 G5
Uherské Hradiště Czech Rep. 17 P6
Uhrichsville OH U.S.A. 64 A2
Uibhist a' Deas i. U.K. see South Uist
Uibhist a' Tuath i. U.K. see North Uist
Uig U.K. 20 C3
Uíge Angola 49 B4
Ŭijŏngbu S. Korea 45 B5
Ŭiju N. Korea 44 B4
Uimaharju Fin. 14 Q5
Uinta Mountains U.S.A. 62 E3
Uis Mine Namibia 49 B6
Uitenhage S. Africa 51 G7
Ujhani India 36 D4
Uji Japan 45 D6
Uji-guntō is Japan 45 C7
Ujiyamada Japan see Ise
Ujjain India 36 C5
Ujung Pandang Indon. see Makassar
Újvidék Serbia see Novi Sad
Ukal Sagar l. India 36 C5
Ukata Nigeria 46 D3
'Ukayrishah well Saudi Arabia 35 G6
uKhahlamba-Drakensberg Park nat. park S. Africa 51 I5
Ukholovo Rus. Fed. 13 I5
Ukhrul India 37 H4
Ukhta Respublika Kareliya Rus. Fed. see Kalevala
Ukhta Respublika Komi Rus. Fed. 12 L3
Ukiah CA U.S.A. 65 A1
Ukkusissat Greenland 61 M2
Ukmergė Lith. 15 N9
Ukraine country Europe 13 F6
Ukrainskaya S.S.R. country Europe see Ukraine
Ukrayina country Europe see Ukraine
Uku-jima i. Japan 45 C6
Ukwi Botswana 50 E2
Ukwi Pan salt pan Botswana 50 E2
Ulaanbaatar Mongolia see Ulan Bator
Ulaangom Mongolia 42 G3
Ulan Australia 58 D4
Ulan Bator Mongolia 42 J3
Ulanbel' Kazakh. 42 C4
Ulan Erge Rus. Fed. 13 J7
Ulanhad China see Chifeng
Ulanhot China 44 A3
Ulan Hua China 43 K4
Ulan-Khol Rus. Fed. 13 J7
Ulan-Ude Rus. Fed. 43 J2
Ulan Ul Hu l. China 37 G2
Ulaş Turkey 34 E3
Ulawa Island Solomon Is 53 G2
Ul'banskiy Zaliv b. Rus. Fed. 44 E1
Ulchin S. Korea 45 C5
Uldz r. Mongolia 43 L3
Uleåborg Fin. see Oulu
Ulefoss Norway 15 F7
Ülenurme Estonia 15 O7
Ulety Rus. Fed. 43 K2
Ulhasnagar India 38 B2
Uliastai China 43 L3
Uliastay Mongolia 42 H3
Uliatea i. Fr. Polynesia see Raiatea
Ulita r. Rus. Fed. 14 R2
Ulithi atoll Micronesia 41 F6
Ulladulla Australia 58 E5
Ullapool U.K. 20 D3
Ulla Ulla, Parque Nacional nat. park Bol. 68 E6
Ullava Fin. 14 M5
Ullersuaq c. Greenland 61 K2
Ullswater l. U.K. 18 E4
Ullŭng-do i. S. Korea 45 C5
Ulm Germany 17 L6
Ulmarra Australia 58 F2
Uloowaranie, Lake salt flat Australia 57 B5
Ulricehamn Sweden 15 H8
Ulsan S. Korea 45 C6
Ulsberg Norway 14 F5
Ulster reg. Ireland/U.K. 21 E3
Ulster PA U.S.A. 64 C2
Ulster Canal Ireland/U.K. 21 E3
Ultima Australia 58 A5
Ulubat Gölü l. Turkey 27 M4
Ulubey Turkey 27 M5
Uluborlu Turkey 27 N5
Uludağ mt. Turkey 27 M4
Uludağ Milli Parkı nat. park Turkey 27 M4
Ulugqat China see Wuqia
Ulukışla Turkey 34 D3
Ulundi S. Africa 51 J5
Ulungur Hu l. China 42 F3
Ulunkhan Rus. Fed. 43 K2
Uluqsaqtuuq Canada see Holman
Uluru hill Australia 55 E6
Uluru-Kata Tjuta National Park Australia 55 E6
Uluru National Park Australia see Uluru-Kata Tjuta National Park
Ulutau Kazakh. see Ulytau
Ulutau, Gory mts Kazakh. see Ulytau, Gory
Uluyatır Turkey 39 C1
Ulva i. U.K. 20 C4
Ulverston U.K. 18 D4
Ulvsjön Sweden 15 I6
Ül'yanov Kazakh. see Ul'yanovskiy
Ul'yanovsk Rus. Fed. 13 K5
Ul'yanovskiy Kazakh. 42 C2
Ul'yanovskoye Kazakh. see Ul'yanovskiy
Ulysses KS U.S.A. 62 G4
Ulytau Kazakh. 42 B3
Ulytau, Gory mts Kazakh. 42 B3
Uma Rus. Fed. 44 A1
Umaltinskiy Rus. Fed. 44 D2
'Umān country Asia see Oman
Uman' Ukr. 13 F6
'Umarī, Qā' al salt pan Jordan 39 C4
Umaria India 36 E5
Umarkhed India 38 C2
Umarkot India 38 D2
Umarkot Pak. 33 K4
Umaroona, Lake salt flat Australia 57 B5
Umarpada India 36 C5
Umba Rus. Fed. 12 G2
Umbeara Australia 55 F6
Umboi i. P.N.G. 52 E2
Umeå Sweden 14 L5
Umeälven r. Sweden 14 L5
Umfolozi r. S. Africa 51 K5
Umhlanga Rocks S. Africa 51 J5
Umiiviip Kangertiva inlet Greenland 61 N3
Umingmaktok Canada 77 L2
Umirzak Kazakh. 35 H2
Umkomaas S. Africa 51 J6
Umlaiteng India 37 H4
Umlazi S. Africa 51 J5
Umm ad Daraj, Jabal mt. Jordan 39 B3
Umm al 'Amad Syria 39 C2
Umm ar Raqabah, Khabrat imp. l. Saudi Arabia 39 C5
Umm at Qalbān Saudi Arabia 35 F6
Umm Bel Sudan 32 C7
Umm Keddada Sudan 32 C7
Umm Lajj Saudi Arabia 32 E4
Umm Nukhaylah hill Saudi Arabia 39 D5
Umm Qaṣr Iraq 35 G5
Umm Quṣūr i. Saudi Arabia 34 D6
Umm Ruwaba Sudan 32 D7
Umm Sa'ad Libya 34 B5
Umm Shugeira Sudan 32 C7
Umm Wa'āl hill Saudi Arabia 39 D4
Umnak Island U.S.A. 60 B4
Umpulo Angola 49 B5
Umraniye Turkey 27 N5
Umred India 38 C1
Umri India 36 D4
Umtali Zimbabwe see Mutare
Umtata S. Africa 51 I6
Umtentweni S. Africa 51 J6
Umuahia Nigeria 46 D4
Umuarama Brazil 70 F2
Umvuma Zimbabwe see Mvuma
Umzimkulu S. Africa 51 I6
Una r. Bos.-Herz./Croatia 26 G2
Una Brazil 71 D1
Una India 36 D3
'Unāb, Jabal al hill Jordan 39 C5
'Unāb, Wādī al watercourse Jordan 39 C4
Unaí Brazil 71 B2
Unalaska Island U.S.A. 60 B4
Unapool U.K. 20 D2
'Unayzah Saudi Arabia 32 F4
'Unayzah, Jabal hill Iraq 35 E4
Uncia Bol. 68 E7
Undara National Park Australia 56 D3
Underberg S. Africa 51 I5
Underbool Australia 57 C7
Unecha Rus. Fed. 13 G5
Ungama Bay Kenya see Ungwana Bay
Ungarie Australia 58 C4
Ungava, Baie d' b. Canada see Ungava Bay
Ungava, Péninsule d' pen. Canada 61 K3
Ungava Bay Canada 61 L4
Ungava Peninsula Canada see Ungava, Péninsule d'
Ungeny Moldova see Ungheni
Unggi N. Korea 44 C4
Ungheni Moldova 27 L1
Unguana Moz. 51 L2
Unguja i. Tanz. see Zanzibar Island
Unguz, Solonchakovyye Vpadiny salt flat Turkm. 33 I2
Üngüz Angyrsyndaky Garagum des. Turkm. 33 I1
Üngüz Angyrsyndaky Garagum des. Turkm. see Üngüz Angyrsyndaky Garagum
Ungvár Ukr. see Uzhhorod
Ungwana Bay Kenya 48 E4
Uni Rus. Fed. 12 K4
União Brazil 69 J4
União da Vitória Brazil 71 A4
União dos Palmares Brazil 69 K5
Unimak Island U.S.A. 60 B4
Unini r. Brazil 68 F4
Union WV U.S.A. 64 A4
Union City PA U.S.A. 64 B2
Union City TN U.S.A. 63 J4
Uniondale S. Africa 50 F7
Uniontown PA U.S.A. 64 B3
Unionville PA U.S.A. 64 C2
United Arab Emirates country Asia 33 H5
United Arab Republic country Africa see Egypt
United Kingdom country Europe 16 G3
United Provinces state India see Uttar Pradesh
United States of America country N. America 62 F3
United States Range mts Canada 61 L1
Unity Canada 62 F1
Unjha India 36 C5
Unnao India 36 E4
Ŭnp'a N. Korea 45 B5
Unsan N. Korea 45 B4
Ŭnsan N. Korea 45 B5
Unst i. U.K. 20 [inset]
Untari India 37 E4
Untor, Ozero l. Rus. Fed. 11 T3
Unuli Horog China 37 G2
Unzen-dake vol. Japan 45 C6
Unzha Rus. Fed. 12 J4
Upar Ghat reg. India 37 F5
Upemba, Lac l. Dem. Rep. Congo 49 C4
Uperbada India 37 F5
Upernavik Greenland 61 M2
Upington S. Africa 50 E5
Upland CA U.S.A. 65 D3
Upleta India 36 B5
Upoloksha Rus. Fed. 14 Q3
'Upolu i. Samoa 53 I3
Upper Chindwin Myanmar see Mawlaik
Upper Hutt N.Z. 59 E5
Upper Klamath Lake U.S.A. 62 C3
Upper Lough Erne l. U.K. 21 E3
Upper Marlboro MD U.S.A. 64 C3
Upper Tunguska r. Rus. Fed. see Angara
Upper Volta country Africa see Burkina
Upper Yarra Reservoir Australia 58 B6
Uppinangadi India 38 B3
Uppsala Sweden 15 J7
Upshi Jammu and Kashmir 36 D2
Upton MA U.S.A. 64 F1
'Uqayqah, Wādī watercourse Jordan 39 B4
'Uqayribāt Syria 39 C2
'Uqlat al 'Udhaybah well Iraq 35 G5
Urad Houqi China see Sain Us
Urakawa Japan 44 F4
Ural hill Australia 58 C4
Ural r. Kazakh./Rus. Fed. 30 E2
Uralla Australia 58 E3
Ural Mountains Rus. Fed. 11 S2
Ural'sk Kazakh. 30 E1
Ural'skaya Oblast' admin. div. Kazakh. see Zapadnyy Kazakhstan
Ural'skiye Gory mts Rus. Fed. see Ural Mountains
Ural'skiy Khrebet mts Rus. Fed. see Ural Mountains
Urambo Tanz. 49 D4
Uran India 38 B2
Urana Australia 58 C5
Urana, Lake Australia 58 C5
Urandangi Australia 56 B4
Urandi Brazil 71 C1
Uranium City Canada 60 H4
Uranquinty Australia 58 C5
Uraricoera r. Brazil 68 F3
Urartu country Asia see Armenia
Uravakonda India 38 C3
Urawa Japan 45 E6
'Urayf an Nāqah, Jabal hill Egypt 39 B4
Urbino Italy 26 E3
Urbinum Italy see Urbino
Urbs Vetus Italy see Orvieto
Urdoma Rus. Fed. 12 K3
Urdyuzhskoye, Ozero l. Rus. Fed. 12 K2
Ure r. U.K. 18 F4
Ureki Georgia 35 F2
Uren' Rus. Fed. 12 J4
Urengoy Rus. Fed. 28 I3
Uréparapara i. Vanuatu 53 G3
Urewera National Park N.Z. 59 F4
Urfa Turkey see Şanlıurfa
Urfa prov. Turkey see Şanlıurfa
Urga Mongolia see Ulan Bator
Urgal r. Rus. Fed. 44 D2
Urganch Uzbek. 33 J1
Urgench Uzbek. see Urganch
Ürgüp Turkey 34 D3
Urho China 42 F3
Urho Kekkosen kansallispuisto nat. park Fin. 14 O2
Urie r. U.K. 20 G3
Uril Rus. Fed. 44 C2
Urisino Australia 58 A2
Urjala Fin. 15 M6
Urkan Rus. Fed. 44 B1
Urkan r. Rus. Fed. 44 B1
Urla Turkey 27 L5
Urlingford Ireland 21 E5
Urluk Rus. Fed. 43 J2

Urmā aş Şughrá Syria 39 C1
Urmai China 37 F3
Urmia Iran 35 G3
Urmia, Lake salt l. Iran 35 G3
Uromi Nigeria 46 D4
Uroševac Serbia 27 I3
Urosozero Rus. Fed. 12 G3
Urru Co salt l. China 37 F3
Urt Moron China 42 G5
Uruáchic Mex. 62 F6
Uruaçu Brazil 71 A1
Uruana Brazil 71 A1
Uruapan Michoacán Mex. 66 D5
Urubamba r. Peru 68 D6
Urucara Brazil 69 G4
Urucu r. Brazil 68 F4
Uruçuca Brazil 71 D1
Uruçuí Brazil 69 J5
Uruçuí, Serra do hills Brazil 69 I5
Urucuia Brazil 71 B2
Urucurituba Brazil 69 G4
Uruguai r. Arg./Uruguay see Uruguay
Uruguaiana Brazil 70 E3
Uruguay r. Arg./Uruguay 70 E4
Uruguay country S. America 70 E4
Uruhe China 44 B2
Urumchi China see Ürümqi
Ürümqi China 42 F4
Urundi country Africa see Burundi
Urup, Ostrov i. Rus. Fed. 43 S3
Urusha Rus. Fed. 44 A1
Urutaí Brazil 71 A2
Uryupino Rus. Fed. 43 M2
Uryupinsk Rus. Fed. 13 I6
Urzhum Rus. Fed. 12 K4
Urziceni Romania 27 L2
Usa Japan 45 C6
Usa r. Rus. Fed. 12 M2
Uşak Turkey 27 M5
Usakos Namibia 50 B1
Usarp Mountains Antarctica 76 H2
Usborne, Mount hill Falkland Is 70 E8
Ushakova, Ostrov i. Rus. Fed. 28 I1
Ushant i. France see Ouessant, Île d'
Usharal Kazakh. see Ucharal
Ush-Bel'dyr Rus. Fed. 42 H2
Ushtobe Kazakh. 42 D3
Ush-Tyube Kazakh. see Ushtobe
Ushuaia Arg. 70 C8
Ushumun Rus. Fed. 44 B1
Usinsk Rus. Fed. 11 R2
Usk U.K. 19 E7
Usk r. U.K. 19 E7
Uskhodni Belarus 15 O10
Uskoplje Bos.-Herz. see Gornji Vakuf
Üsküdar Turkey 27 M4
Usman' Rus. Fed. 13 H5
Usmanabad India see Osmanabad
Usmas ezers l. Latvia 15 M8
Usogorsk Rus. Fed. 12 K3
Usol'ye-Sibirskoye Rus. Fed. 42 I2
Uspenovka Rus. Fed. 44 B1
Ussel France 24 F4
Ussuri r. China/Rus. Fed. 44 D2
Ussuriysk Rus. Fed. 44 C4
Ust'-Abakanskoye Rus. Fed. see Abakan
Usta Muhammad Pak. 36 B3
Ust'-Balyk Rus. Fed. see Nefteyugansk
Ust'-Donetskiy Rus. Fed. 13 I7
Ust'-Dzheguta Rus. Fed. 35 F1
Ust'-Dzhegutinskaya Rus. Fed. see Ust'-Dzheguta
Ustica, Isola di i. Sicily Italy 26 E5
Ust'-Ilimsk Rus. Fed. 29 L4
Ust'-Ilimskiy Vodokhranilishche resr Rus. Fed. 29 L4
Ust'-Ilych Rus. Fed. 11 R3
Ústí nad Labem Czech Rep. 17 O5
Ustinov Rus. Fed. see Izhevsk
Üstirt plat. Kazakh./Uzbek. see Ustyurt Plateau
Ustka Poland 17 P3
Ust'-Kamchatsk Rus. Fed. 29 R4
Ust'-Kamenogorsk Kazakh. 42 E3
Ust'-Kan Rus. Fed. 42 E2
Ust'-Koksa Rus. Fed. 42 F2
Ust'-Kulom Rus. Fed. 12 L3
Ust'-Kut Rus. Fed. 29 L4
Ust'-Kuyga Rus. Fed. 29 O2
Ust'-Labinsk Rus. Fed. 35 E1
Ust'-Labinskaya Rus. Fed. see Ust'-Labinsk
Ust'-Lyzha Rus. Fed. 12 M2
Ust'-Maya Rus. Fed. 29 O3
Ust'-Nera Rus. Fed. 29 P3
Ust'-Ocheya Rus. Fed. 12 K3
Ust'-Olenek Rus. Fed. 29 M2
Ust'-Omchug Rus. Fed. 29 P3
Ust'-Ordynskiy Rus. Fed. 42 I2
Ust'-Penzhino Rus. Fed. see Kamenskoye
Ust'-Port Rus. Fed. 28 J3
Ustrem Rus. Fed. 11 T3
Ust'-Tsil'ma Rus. Fed. 12 L2
Ust'-Uda Rus. Fed. 42 I2
Ust'-Umalta Rus. Fed. 44 D2
Ust'-Undurga Rus. Fed. 43 L2
Ust'-Ura Rus. Fed. 12 J3
Ust'-Urgal Rus. Fed. 44 D2
Ust'-Usa Rus. Fed. 12 M2
Ust'-Vayen'ga Rus. Fed. 12 I3
Ust'-Voya Rus. Fed. 11 R3
Ust'-Vyyskaya Rus. Fed. 12 J3
Ust'ya r. Rus. Fed. 12 I3
Ust'ye Rus. Fed. 12 H4
Ustyurt, Plato plat. Kazakh./Uzbek. see Ustyurt Plateau
Ustyurt Plateau Kazakh./Uzbek. 30 E2
Ustyurt Platosi plat. Kazakh./Uzbek. see Ustyurt Plateau
Ustyuzhna Rus. Fed. 12 H4
Usulután El Salvador 66 G6
Usumbura Burundi see Bujumbura
Usvyaty Rus. Fed. 12 F5
Utah state U.S.A. 62 E4
Utah Lake U.S.A. 62 E3
Utajärvi Fin. 14 O4
Utashinai Rus. Fed. see Yuzhno-Kuril'sk
'Utaybah, Buḩayrat al imp. l. Syria 39 C3
Utena Lith. 15 N9
Uterlai India 36 B4
Uthal Pak. 36 A4
'Uthmānīyah Syria 39 C2
Utiariti Brazil 69 G6
Utica NY U.S.A. 64 D1
Utiel Spain 25 F4
Utlwanang S. Africa 51 G4
Utrecht Neth. 16 J4
Utrecht S. Africa 51 J4
Utrera Spain 25 D5
Utsjoki Fin. 14 O2
Utsunomiya Japan 45 E5
Utta Rus. Fed. 13 J7
Uttaradit Thai. 31 J5
Uttarakhand state India see Uttaranchal
Uttaranchal state India 36 D3
Uttarkashi India 36 D3
Uttar Kashi India see Uttarkashi
Uttar Pradesh state India 36 D4
Uttoxeter U.K. 19 F6
Uttranchal state India see Uttaranchal
Utubulak China 42 F3
Utupua i. Solomon Is 53 G3
Uummannaq Greenland see Dundas
Uummannaq Fjord inlet Greenland 77 J2
Uummannarsuaq c. Greenland see Farewell, Cape
Uurainen Fin. 14 N5
Uusikaarlepyy Fin. see Nykarleby
Uusikaupunki Fin. 15 L6
Uutapi Namibia 49 B5
Uva Rus. Fed. 12 L4
Uvalde U.S.A. 62 H6
Uval Karabaur hills Kazakh./Uzbek. 35 I2
Uval Muzbel' hills Kazakh. 35 I2
Uvarovo Rus. Fed. 13 I6
Uvéa atoll New Caledonia see Ouvéa
Uvinza Tanz. 49 D4
Uvs Nuur salt l. Mongolia 42 G2
Uwajima Japan 45 D6
'Uwayriḍ, Ḩarrat al lava field Saudi Arabia 32 E4
Uwaysiţ well Saudi Arabia 39 D4
Uweinat, Jebel mt. Sudan 32 C5
Uxbridge U.K. 19 G7
Uxin Qi China see Dabqig
Uyar Rus. Fed. 42 G1
Üydzin Mongolia 42 J4
Uyo Nigeria 46 D4
Uyu Chaung r. Myanmar 37 H4
Uyuni Bol. 68 E8
Uyuni, Salar de salt flat Bol. 68 E8
Uza r. Rus. Fed. 13 J5
Uzbekistan country Asia 30 F2
Ŭzbekiston country Asia see Uzbekistan
Uzbekskaya S.S.R. country Asia see Uzbekistan
Uzbek S.S.R. country Asia see Uzbekistan
Uzboy Azer. 35 H3
Uzboý Turkm. 35 I3
Uzen' Kazakh. see Kyzylsay
Uzhgorod Ukr. see Uzhhorod
Uzhhorod Ukr. 13 D6
Užhorod Ukr. see Uzhhorod
Užice Serbia 27 H3
Uzlovaya Rus. Fed. 13 H5
Üzümlü Turkey 27 M6
Uzunköprü Turkey 27 L4

V

Vaajakoski Fin. 14 N5
Vaal r. S. Africa 51 F5
Vaala Fin. 14 O4
Vaalbos National Park S. Africa 50 G5
Vaal Dam S. Africa 51 I4
Vaalwater S. Africa 51 I3
Vaasa Fin. 14 L5
Vác Hungary 17 Q7
Vacaria Brazil 71 A5
Vacaria, Campo da plain Brazil 71 A5
Vacaville CA U.S.A. 65 B1
Vad Rus. Fed. 12 J5
Vad r. Rus. Fed. 13 I5
Vada India 38 B2
Vadla Norway 15 E7
Vadodara India 36 C5
Vadsø Norway 14 P1
Vaduz Liechtenstein 24 I3
Værøy i. Norway 14 H3
Vaga r. Rus. Fed. 12 I3
Vågåmo Norway 15 F6
Vaganski Vrh mt. Croatia 26 F2
Vágar i. Faroe Is 14 [inset]
Vägsele Sweden 14 K4
Vágur Faroe Is 14 [inset]
Váh r. Slovakia 17 Q7
Vähäkyrö Fin. 14 M5
Vaiaku Tuvalu 53 H2
Vaida Estonia 15 N7
Vail U.S.A. 62 F4
Vaitupu i. Tuvalu 53 H2
Vajrakarur India see Kanur
Vakīlābād Iran 33 I4
Valbo Sweden 15 J6
Valcheta Arg. 70 C6
Valdai Hills Rus. Fed. see Valdayskaya Vozvyshennost'
Valday Rus. Fed. 12 G4
Valdayskaya Vozvyshennost' hills Rus. Fed. 12 G4
Valdecañas, Embalse de resr Spain 25 D4
Valdemārpils Latvia 15 M8
Valdemarsvik Sweden 15 J7
Valdepeñas Spain 25 E4
Val-de-Reuil France 24 E2
Valdés, Península pen. Arg. 70 D6
Valdez U.S.A. 60 D3
Valdivia Chile 70 B5
Val-d'Or Canada 63 L2
Valdosta U.S.A. 63 K5
Valdres valley Norway 15 F6
Vale Georgia 35 F2
Valemount Canada 62 D1
Valença Brazil 71 D1
Valence France 24 G4
Valencia Spain 25 F4
València Spain see Valencia
Valencia reg. Spain 25 F4
Valencia Venez. 68 E1
Valencia, Golfo de g. Spain 25 G4
Valencia de Don Juan Spain 25 D2
Valencia Island Ireland 21 B6
Valenciennes France 24 F1
Valensole, Plateau de France 24 H5
Valentia Spain see Valencia
Valentin Rus. Fed. 44 D4
Valentine U.S.A. 62 G3
Valer Norway 15 G6
Valera Venez. 68 D2
Vale Verde Brazil 71 D2
Val Grande, Parco Nazionale della nat. park Italy 26 C1
Valjevo Serbia 27 H2
Valka Latvia 15 O8
Valkeakoski Fin. 15 N6
Valky Ukr. 13 G6
Valkyrie Dome ice feature Antarctica 76 D1
Valladolid Mex. 66 G4
Valladolid Spain 25 D3
Valle Norway 15 E7
Valle de la Pascua Venez. 68 E2
Valledupar Col. 68 D1
Valle Fértil, Sierra de mts Arg. 70 C4
Valle Grande Bol. 68 F7
Vallejo CA U.S.A. 65 A1
Vallenar Chile 70 B3
Valletta Malta 26 F7
Valley U.K. 18 C5
Valley City U.S.A. 62 H2
Valls Spain 25 G3
Val Marie Canada 62 F2
Valmiera Latvia 15 N8
Valnera mt. Spain 25 E2
Valognes France 19 F9
Valona Albania see Vlorë
Valozhyn Belarus 15 O9
Valparai India 38 C4
Valparaíso Chile 70 B4
Valpoi India 38 B3
Valréas France 24 G4
Vals, Tanjung c. Indon. 41 F8
Valsad India 38 B1
Valspan S. Africa 50 G4
Val'tevo Rus. Fed. 12 J2
Valtimo Fin. 14 P5
Valuyevka Rus. Fed. 13 I7
Valuyki Rus. Fed. 13 H6
Vammala Fin. 15 M6
Van Turkey 35 F3
Van, Lake salt l. Turkey 35 F3
Vanadzor Armenia 35 G2
Vancouver Canada 62 C2
Vancouver U.S.A. 62 C2
Vancouver Island Canada 62 B2
Vanda Fin. see Vantaa
Vandalia IL U.S.A. 63 J4
Vanderbijlpark S. Africa 51 H4
Vandergrift PA U.S.A. 64 B2
Vanderkloof Dam resr S. Africa 50 G6
Vanderlin Island Australia 56 B2
Van Diemen, Cape N.T. Australia 54 E2
Van Diemen, Cape Qld Australia 56 B3
Van Diemen Gulf Australia 54 F2
Van Diemen's Land state Australia see Tasmania
Vändra Estonia 15 N7
Väner, Lake Sweden see Vänern
Vänern l. Sweden 15 H7
Vänersborg Sweden 15 H7
Vangaindrano Madag. 49 E6
Van Gölü salt l. Turkey see Van, Lake
Van Horn U.S.A. 62 G5
Vanikoro Islands Solomon Is 53 G3
Vanimo P.N.G. 52 E2
Vanino Rus. Fed. 44 F2
Vanivilasa Sagara resr India 38 C3
Vaniyambadi India 38 C3
Vännäs Sweden 14 K5
Vannes France 24 C3
Vannovka Kazakh. see Turar Ryskulov
Vannøya i. Norway 14 K1
Van Rees, Pegunungan mts Indon. 41 F8
Vanrhynsdorp S. Africa 50 D6
Vansbro Sweden 15 I6
Vansittart Island Canada 61 J3
Vantaa Fin. 15 N6
Van Truer Tableland reg. Australia 55 C6
Vanua Lava i. Vanuatu 53 G3
Vanua Levu i. Fiji 53 H3
Vanuatu country S. Pacific Ocean 53 G3
Vanwyksvlei S. Africa 50 E6
Vanwyksvlei l. S. Africa 50 E6
Van Zylsrus S. Africa 50 F4
Varahi India 36 B5
Varakļāni Latvia 15 O8
Varalé Côte d'Ivoire 46 C4
Varāmīn Iran 35 H4
Varanasi India 37 E4
Varandey Rus. Fed. 12 M1
Varangerfjorden sea chan. Norway 14 P1
Varangerhalvøya pen. Norway 11 L1
Varangerhalvøya pen. Norway 14 P1
Varaždin Croatia 26 G1
Varberg Sweden 15 H8
Vardar r. Macedonia 27 J4
Varde Denmark 15 F9
Vardenis Armenia 35 G2
Vardø Norway 14 Q1
Varėna Lith. 15 N9
Varese Italy 26 C2
Varfolomeyevka Rus. Fed. 44 D3
Vårgårda Sweden 15 H7
Varginha Brazil 71 B3
Varillas Chile 70 B2
Varkana Iran see Gorgān
Varkaus Fin. 14 O5
Varna Bulg. 27 L3
Värnamo Sweden 15 I8
Värnäs Sweden 15 H6
Varnavino Rus. Fed. 12 J4
Várnjárg pen. Norway see Varangerhalvøya
Varpaisjärvi Fin. 14 O5
Várpalota Hungary 26 H1
Varsaj Afgh. 36 B1
Varsh, Ozero l. Rus. Fed. 12 J2
Varto Turkey 35 F3
Várzea da Palma Brazil 71 B2
Vasa Fin. see Vaasa
Vasai India 38 B2
Vashka r. Rus. Fed. 12 J2
Vasht Iran see Khāsh
Vasilkov Ukr. see Vasyl'kiv
Vasknarva Estonia 15 O7
Vaslui Romania 27 L1
Vas-Soproni-síkság hills Hungary 26 G1
Vastan Turkey see Gevaş
Västerås Sweden 15 J7
Västerdalälven r. Sweden 15 I6
Västerfjäll Sweden 14 J3
Västerhaninge Sweden 15 K7
Västervik Sweden 15 J8
Vasto Italy 26 F3
Vasyl'kiv Ukr. 13 F6
Vatan France 24 E3
Vaté i. Vanuatu see Éfaté
Vatersay i. U.K. 20 B4
Vathar India 38 B2
Vathí Greece see Vathy
Vathy Greece 27 L6
Vatican City Europe 26 E4
Vaticano, Città del Europe see Vatican City
Vatnajökull ice cap Iceland 14 [inset]
Vatoa i. Fiji 53 I3
Vatra Dornei Romania 27 K1
Vätter, Lake Sweden see Vättern
Vättern l. Sweden 15 I7
Vaughn U.S.A. 62 F5
Vaupés r. Col. 68 E3
Vauvert France 24 G5
Vavatenina Madag. 49 E5
Vava'u Group is Tonga 53 I3
Vavitao i. Fr. Polynesia see Raivavae
Vavoua Côte d'Ivoire 46 C4
Vavozh Rus. Fed. 12 K4
Vavuniya Sri Lanka 38 D4
Vawkavysk Belarus 15 N10
Växjö Sweden 15 I8
Vayenga Rus. Fed. see Severomorsk
Vazante Brazil 71 B2
Vazáš Sweden see Vittangi
Veaikevárri Sweden see Svappavaara
Vedaranniyam India 38 C4
Vedasandur India 38 C4
Veddige Sweden 15 H8
Vedea r. Romania 27 K3
Veendam Neth. 17 K4
Vega i. Norway 14 G4
Vehkalahti Fin. 15 O6
Vehoa Pak. 36 B3
Veinticinco de Mayo Buenos Aires Arg. see 25 de Mayo
Veinticinco de Mayo La Pampa Arg. see 25 de Mayo
Veirwaro Pak. 36 B4
Vejle Denmark 15 F9
Velbŭzhdki Prokhod pass Bulg./Macedonia 27 J3
Velddrif S. Africa 50 D7
Velebit mts Croatia 26 F2
Velenje Slovenia 26 F1
Veles Macedonia 27 I4
Vélez-Málaga Spain 25 D5
Vélez-Rubio Spain 25 E5
Velhas r. Brazil 71 B2
Velibaba Turkey see Aras
Velika Gorica Croatia 26 G2
Velika Plana Serbia 27 I2
Velikaya r. Rus. Fed. 12 K4
Velikaya r. Rus. Fed. 15 P8
Velikaya r. Rus. Fed. 29 S3
Velikaya Kema Rus. Fed. 44 E3
Veliki Preslav Bulg. 27 L3
Velikiye Luki Rus. Fed. 12 F4
Velikiy Novgorod Rus. Fed. 12 F4
Velikiy Ustyug Rus. Fed. 12 J3
Velikonda Range hills India 38 C3
Veliko Tŭrnovo Bulg. 27 K3
Velikoye Rus. Fed. 12 H4
Velikoye, Ozero l. Rus. Fed. 13 I5
Veli Lošinj Croatia 26 F2
Velizh Rus. Fed. 12 F5
Vella Lavella i. Solomon Is 53 F2
Vellar r. India 38 C4
Vellore India 38 C3
Vel'sk Rus. Fed. 12 I3
Velsuna Italy see Orvieto
Velten Germany 17 N4
Velykyy Tokmak Ukr. see Tokmak
Vel'yu r. Rus. Fed. 12 L3
Vemalwada India 38 C2
Vema Seamount sea feature S. Atlantic Ocean 72 I8
Vema Trench sea feature Indian Ocean 73 M6
Vempalle India 38 C3
Venado Tuerto Arg. 70 D4
Venafro Italy 26 F4
Venceslau Bráz Brazil 71 A3
Vendinga Rus. Fed. 12 J3
Vendôme France 24 E3
Venetia Italy see Venice
Venetie Landing U.S.A. 60 D3
Venev Rus. Fed. 13 H5
Venezia Italy see Venice
Venezia, Golfo di g. Europe see Venice, Gulf of
Venezuela country S. America 68 E2
Venezuela, Golfo de g. Venez. 68 D1
Venezuelan Basin sea feature S. Atlantic Ocean 72 D4
Vengurla India 38 B3
Veniaminof Volcano U.S.A. 60 C4
Venice Italy 26 E2
Venice U.S.A. 63 K6
Venice, Gulf of Europe 26 E2
Vénissieux France 24 G4
Venkatapalem India 38 D2
Venkatapuram India 38 D2
Vennesla Norway 15 E7
Venta r. Latvia/Lith. 15 M8
Venta Lith. 15 M8
Ventersburg S. Africa 51 H5
Ventersdorp S. Africa 51 H4
Venterstad S. Africa 51 G6
Ventnor U.K. 19 F8
Ventotene, Isola i. Italy 26 E4
Ventoux, Mont mt. France 24 G4
Ventspils Latvia 15 L8
Ventura CA U.S.A. 65 C3
Venus Bay Australia 58 B7
Vera Arg. 70 D3
Vera Spain 25 F5
Vera Cruz Brazil 71 A3
Veracruz Mex. 66 E5
Vera Cruz Mex. see Veracruz
Veraval India 36 B5
Verbania Italy 26 C2
Vercelli Italy 26 C2
Vercors reg. France 24 G4
Verdalsøra Norway 14 G5
Verde r. Goiás Brazil 71 A2
Verde r. Goiás Brazil 71 A2
Verde r. Goiás Brazil 71 B2
Verde r. Minas Gerais Brazil 71 A2
Verde r. Mex. 66 C3
Verden (Aller) Germany 17 L4
Verde Pequeno r. Brazil 71 C1
Verdon r. France 24 G5
Verdun France 24 G2
Vereeniging S. Africa 51 H4
Vereshchagino Rus. Fed. 11 Q4
Véria Greece see Veroia
Verín Spain 25 C3
Veríssimo Brazil 71 A2
Verkhneimbatsk Rus. Fed. 28 J3
Verkhnekolvinsk Rus. Fed. 12 M2
Verkhnespasskoye Rus. Fed. 12 J4
Verkhnetulomskiy Rus. Fed. 14 Q2
Verkhnetulomskoye Vodokhranilishche resr Rus. Fed. 14 Q2
Verkhnevilyuysk Rus. Fed. 29 N3
Verkhneye Kuyto, Ozero l. Rus. Fed. 14 Q4
Verkhnezeysk Rus. Fed. 43 N2
Verkhniy Vyalozerskiy Rus. Fed. 12 G2
Verkhnyaya Khava Rus. Fed. 13 H6
Verkhnyaya Salda Rus. Fed. 11 S4
Verkhnyaya Tunguska r. Rus. Fed. see Angara
Verkhnyaya Tura Rus. Fed. 11 R4
Verkhoshizhem'ye Rus. Fed. 12 K4
Verkhovazh'ye Rus. Fed. 12 I3
Verkhov'ye Rus. Fed. 13 H5
Verkhoyansk Rus. Fed. 29 O3
Verkhoyanskiy Khrebet mts Rus. Fed. 29 N2
Vermelho r. Brazil 71 A1
Vermilion Canada 62 E1
Vermillion U.S.A. 63 H3
Vermont state U.S.A. 64 E1
Vernadsky research station Antarctica 76 L2
Vernal U.S.A. 62 F3
Verneuk Pan salt pan S. Africa 50 E5
Vernon Canada 62 D1
Vernon TX U.S.A. 62 H5
Vernon Islands Australia 54 E3
Vernoye Rus. Fed. 44 C2
Vernyy Kazakh. see Almaty
Vero Beach U.S.A. 63 K6
Veroia Greece 27 J4
Verona Italy 26 D2
Verona VA U.S.A. 64 B3
Versailles France 24 F2
Versec Serbia see Vršac
Vertou France 24 D3
Verulam S. Africa 51 J5
Verulamium U.K. see St Albans
Verviers Belgium 17 J5
Vescovato Corsica France 24 I5
Vesele Ukr. 13 G7
Veselyy Rus. Fed. 13 I7
Veshenskaya Rus. Fed. 13 I6
Veslyana r. Rus. Fed. 12 L3
Vesontio France see Besançon
Vesoul France 24 H3
Vesselyy Yar Rus. Fed. 44 D4
Vesterålen is Norway 14 H2
Vesterålsfjorden sea chan. Norway 14 H2
Vestertana Norway 14 O1
Vestfjorddalen valley Norway 15 F7
Vestfjorden sea chan. Norway 14 H3
Véstia Brazil 71 A3
Vestmanna Faroe Is 14 [inset]
Vestmannaeyjar Iceland 14 [inset]
Vestmannaeyjar is Iceland 14 [inset]
Vestnes Norway 14 E5
Vesturhorn hd Iceland 14 [inset]
Vesuvio vol. Italy see Vesuvius
Vesuvius vol. Italy 26 F4
Ves'yegonsk Rus. Fed. 12 H4
Veszprém Hungary 26 G1
Veteli Fin. 14 M5
Vetlanda Sweden 15 I8
Vetluga Rus. Fed. 12 J4
Vetluga r. Rus. Fed. 12 J4
Vetluzhskiy Kostromskaya Oblast' Rus. Fed. 12 J4
Vetluzhskiy Nizhegorodskaya Oblast' Rus. Fed. 12 J4
Vettore, Monte mt. Italy 26 E3
Vevey Switz. 24 H3
Veyo UT U.S.A. 65 F2
Vézère r. France 24 E4
Vezirköprü Turkey 34 D2
Vhembe Dongola National Park S. Africa 51 I2
Vialar Alg. see Tissemsilt
Viamao Brazil 71 A5
Viana Espírito Santo Brazil 71 C3
Viana Maranhão Brazil 69 J4
Viana do Castelo Port. 25 B3
Viangchan Laos see Vientiane
Viannos Greece 27 K7
Vianópolis Brazil 71 A2
Viareggio Italy 26 D3
Viborg Denmark 15 F8
Viborg Rus. Fed. see Vyborg
Vibo Valentia Italy 26 G5
Vic Spain 25 H3
Vicecomodoro Marambio research station Antarctica see Marambio
Vicente, Point CA U.S.A. 65 C4
Vicente Guerrero Mex. 66 A2
Vicenza Italy 26 D2
Vich Spain see Vic
Vichada r. Col. 68 E3
Vichadero Uruguay 70 F4
Vichy France 24 F3
Vicksburg AZ U.S.A. 65 F4
Vicksburg MS U.S.A. 63 I5
Viçosa Brazil 71 C3
Victor, Mount Antarctica 76 D2
Victor Harbor Australia 57 B7
Victoria Arg. 70 D4
Victoria r. Australia 54 E3
Victoria state Australia 58 B6
Victoria Canada 62 C2
Victoria Chile 70 B5
Victoria Malta 26 F6
Victoria Seychelles 73 L6
Victoria TX U.S.A. 63 H6
Victoria VA U.S.A. 64 B4
Victoria prov. Zimbabwe see Masvingo
Victoria, Lake Africa 48 D4
Victoria, Lake Australia 57 C7
Victoria, Mount Fiji see Tomanivi
Victoria, Mount Myanmar 37 H5
Victoria, Mount P.N.G. 52 E2
Victoria and Albert Mountains Canada 61 K2
Victoria Falls Zambia/Zimbabwe 49 C5
Victoria Island Canada 60 H2
Victoria Land coastal area Antarctica 76 H2
Victoria Peak Belize 66 G5
Victoria Range mts N.Z. 59 D6
Victoria River Downs Australia 54 E4
Victoria West S. Africa 50 F6
Victorica Arg. 70 C5
Victorville CA U.S.A. 65 D3
Victory Downs Australia 55 F6
Vidal Junction CA U.S.A. 65 E3
Videle Romania 27 K2
Vidisha India 36 D5
Vidlin U.K. 20 [inset]
Vidlitsa Rus. Fed. 12 G3
Viedma Arg. 70 D6
Viedma, Lago l. Arg. 70 B7
Vienna Austria 17 P6
Vienne France 24 G4
Vienne r. France 24 E3
Vientiane Laos 41 C4
Vieques i. Puerto Rico 67 K5
Vieremä Fin. 14 O5
Vierzon France 24 F3
Viesīte Latvia 15 N8
Vieste Italy 26 G4
Vietas Sweden 14 K3
Vietnam country Asia 31 J5
Việt Nam country Asia see Vietnam
Việt Tri Vietnam 42 J8
Vigan Phil. 41 E6
Vigevano Italy 26 C2
Vigia Brazil 69 I4
Vignemale mt. France 22 D3
Vignola Italy 26 D2
Vigo Spain 25 B2
Vihanti Fin. 14 N4
Vihari Pak. 36 C3
Vihti Fin. 15 N6
Viipuri Rus. Fed. see Vyborg
Viitasaari Fin. 14 N5
Vijayadurg India 38 B2
Vijayanagaram India see Vizianagaram
Vijayapati India 38 C4
Vijayawada India 38 D2
Vík Iceland 14 [inset]
Vikajärvi Fin. 14 O3
Vikeke East Timor see Viqueque
Vikna i. Norway 14 G4
Vikøyri Norway 15 E6
Vila Vanuatu see Port Vila
Vila Alferes Chamusca Moz. see Guija
Vila Bittencourt Brazil 68 E4
Vila Bugaço Angola see Camanongue
Vila Cabral Moz. see Lichinga
Vila da Ponte Angola see Kuvango
Vila de Aljustrel Angola see Cangamba
Vila de Almoster Angola see Chiange
Vila de João Belo Moz. see Xai-Xai
Vila de María Arg. 70 D3
Vila de Trego Morais Moz. see Chókwé
Vila do Tarrafal Cape Verde see Tarrafal
Vila Fontes Moz. see Caia
Vila Franca de Xira Port. 25 B4
Vilagarcía de Arousa Spain 25 B2
Vila Gomes da Costa Moz. 51 K3
Vilalba Spain 25 C2
Vila Luísa Moz. see Marracuene
Vila Marechal Carmona Angola see Uíge
Vila Miranda Moz. see Macaloge
Vilanandro, Tanjona pt Madag. 49 E5
Vilanculos Moz. 51 L1
Vila Nova de Gaia Port. 25 B3
Vilanova i la Geltrú Spain 25 G3
Vila Pery Moz. see Chimoio
Vila Real Port. 25 C3
Vilar Formoso Port. 25 C3
Vila Salazar Angola see N'dalatando
Vila Salazar Zimbabwe see Sango
Vila Teixeira de Sousa Angola see Luau
Vila Velha Brazil 71 C3
Vilcabamba, Cordillera mts Peru 68 D6
Vil'cheka, Zemlya i. Rus. Fed. 28 H1
Viled' r. Rus. Fed. 12 J3
Vileyka Belarus see Vilyeyka
Vil'gort Rus. Fed. 12 K3
Vilhelmina Sweden 14 J4
Vilhena Brazil 68 F6
Viliya r. Belarus/Lith. see Neris
Viljandi Estonia 15 N7
Viljoenskroon S. Africa 51 H4
Vilkaviškis Lith. 15 M9
Vilkija Lith. 15 M9
Vil'kitskogo, Proliv strait Rus. Fed. 29 K2
Vilkovo Ukr. see Vylkove
Villa Abecia Bol. 68 E8
Villa Ahumada Mex. 66 C2
Villa Ángela Arg. 70 D3
Villa Bella Bol. 68 E6
Villa Bens Morocco see Tarfaya
Villablino Spain 25 C2
Villacañas Spain 25 E4
Villach Austria 17 N7
Villacidro Sardinia Italy 26 C5
Villa Cisneros W. Sahara see Ad Dakhla
Villa Constitución Mex. see Ciudad Constitución
Villa Dolores Arg. 70 C4
Villagarcía de Arosa Spain see Vilagarcía de Arousa
Villagrán Mex. 62 H7
Villaguay Arg. 70 E4
Villahermosa Mex. 66 F5
Villa Insurgentes Mex. 66 B3
Villajoyosa Spain see Villajoyosa-La Vila Joíosa
Villajoyosa-La Vila Joíosa Spain 25 F4
Villa María Arg. 70 D4
Villa Montes Bol. 68 F8
Villa Nora S. Africa 51 I2
Villanueva de la Serena Spain 25 D4
Villanueva de los Infantes Spain 25 E4
Villanueva-y-Geltrú Spain see Vilanova i la Geltrú
Villa Ocampo Arg. 70 E3
Villa Ojo de Agua Arg. 70 D3
Villaputzu Sardinia Italy 26 C5
Villa Regina Arg. 70 C5
Villarrica Para. 70 E3
Villarrica, Lago l. Chile 70 B5
Villarrica, Parque Nacional nat. park Chile 70 B5
Villarrobledo Spain 25 E4
Villas NJ U.S.A. 64 D3
Villasalazar Zimbabwe see Sango
Villa San Giovanni Italy 26 F5
Villa Sanjurjo Morocco see Al Hoceima
Villa San Martín Arg. 70 D3
Villa Unión Arg. 70 C3
Villa Unión Durango Mex. 66 D4
Villa Unión Sinaloa Mex. 66 C4
Villa Valeria Arg. 70 D4
Villavicencio Col. 68 D3
Villazon Bol. 68 E8
Villefranche-sur-Saône France 24 G4
Ville-Marie Canada see Montréal
Villena Spain 25 F4
Villeneuve-sur-Lot France 24 E4
Villeneuve-sur-Yonne France 24 F2
Villers-sur-Mer France 19 G9
Villeurbanne France 24 G4
Villiers S. Africa 51 I4
Villingen Germany 17 L6
Villuppuram India see Villupuram
Villupuram India 38 C4
Vilna Lith. see Vilnius
Vilnius Lith. 15 N9
Vil'nyans'k Ukr. 13 G7
Vilppula Fin. 14 N5
Vilyeyka Belarus 15 O9
Vilyuy r. Rus. Fed. 29 N3
Vilyuyskoye Vodokhranilishche resr Rus. Fed. 29 M3
Vimmerby Sweden 15 I8
Vina r. Cameroon 47 E4
Viña del Mar Chile 70 B4
Vinaròs Spain 25 G3
Vinaroz Spain see Vinaròs
Vincennes U.S.A. 63 J4
Vincennes Bay Antarctica 76 F2
Vinchina Arg. 70 C3
Vindelälven r. Sweden 14 K5
Vindeln Sweden 14 K4
Vindhya Range hills India 36 C5
Vindobona Austria see Vienna
Vineland NJ U.S.A. 64 D3
Vinh Vietnam 31 J5
Vinita U.S.A. 63 H4
Vinjhan India 36 B5
Vinland i. Canada see Newfoundland
Vinnitsa Ukr. see Vinnytsya
Vinnytsya Ukr. 13 F6
Vinogradov Ukr. see Vynohradiv
Vinson Massif mt. Antarctica 76 L1
Vinstra Norway 15 F6
Vinukonda India 38 C2
Viqueque East Timor 54 D2
Viramgam India 36 C5
Viranşehir Turkey 35 E3
Virawah Pak. 36 B4
Virchow, Mount hill Australia 54 B5
Virdel India 36 C5
Virden Canada 62 G2
Vire France 24 D2
Virei Angola 49 B5
Virgem da Lapa Brazil 71 C2
Virgin r. AZ U.S.A. 65 E2
Virginia Ireland 21 E4
Virginia S. Africa 51 H5
Virginia state U.S.A. 64 B4
Virginia Beach VA U.S.A. 64 D4
Virginia City NV U.S.A. 65 C1
Virgin Islands (U.K.) terr. West Indies 67 L5
Virgin Islands (U.S.A.) terr. West Indies 67 L5
Virgin Mountains AZ U.S.A. 65 E2
Virginópolis Brazil 71 C2
Virkkala Fin. 15 N6
Virovitica Croatia 26 G2
Virrat Fin. 14 M5
Virtsu Estonia 15 M7
Virudhunagar India 38 C4
Virudunagar India see Virudhunagar
Virunga, Parc National des nat. park Dem. Rep. Congo 48 C4
Vis i. Croatia 26 G3
Visaginas Lith. 15 O9
Visakhapatnam India see Vishakhapatnam
Visalia CA U.S.A. 65 C2
Visapur India 38 B2
Visby Sweden 15 K8
Viscount Melville Sound sea chan. Canada 61 G2
Vise, Ostrov i. Rus. Fed. 28 I2
Viseu Brazil 69 I4
Viseu Port. 25 C3
Vishakhapatnam India 38 D2
Vishera r. Rus. Fed. 11 R4
Vishera r. Rus. Fed. 12 L3
Višķi Latvia 15 O8
Visnagar India 36 C5
Viso, Monte mt. Italy 26 B2
Visoko Bos.-Herz. 26 H3
Visp Switz. 24 H3

Vista CA U.S.A. 65 D4
Vista Lake CA U.S.A. 65 C3
Vistonida, Limni lag. Greece 27 K4
Vistula r. Poland 17 Q3
Vitebsk Belarus see Vitsyebsk
Viterbo Italy 26 E3
Vitichi Bol. 68 E8
Vitigudino Spain 25 C3
Viti Levu i. Fiji 53 H3
Vitimskoye Ploskogor'ye plat. Rus. Fed. 43 K2
Vitória Brazil 71 C3
Vitória da Conquista Brazil 71 C1
Vitoria-Gasteiz Spain 25 E2
Vitória Seamount sea feature S. Atlantic Ocean 72 F7
Vitré France 24 D2
Vitry-le-François France 24 G2
Vitsyebsk Belarus 15 F3
Vittangi Sweden 14 L3
Vittel France 24 G2
Vittoria Sicily Italy 26 F6
Vittorio Veneto Italy 26 E2
Viveiro Spain 25 C2
Vivero Spain see Viveiro
Vivo S. Africa 51 I2
Vizagapatam India see Vishakhapatnam
Vizcaíno, Sierra mts Mex. 66 B3
Vize Turkey 27 L4
Vizhas r. Rus. Fed. 12 J2
Vizianagaram India 38 D2
Vizinga Rus. Fed. 12 K3
Vlaardingen Neth. 16 J5
Vlădeasa, Vârful mt. Romania 27 J1
Vladikavkaz Rus. Fed. 35 G2
Vladimir Primorskiy Kray Rus. Fed. 44 D4
Vladimir Vladimirskaya Oblast' Rus. Fed. 12 I4
Vladimiro-Aleksandrovskoye Rus. Fed. 44 D4
Vladimir-Volynskiy Ukr. see Volodymyr-Volyns'kyy
Vladivostok Rus. Fed. 44 C4
Vlakte S. Africa 51 I3
Vlasotince Serbia 27 J3
Vlas'yevo Rus. Fed. 44 F1
Vlissingen Neth. 16 I5
Vlora Albania see Vlorë
Vlorë Albania 27 H4
Vlotslavsk Poland see Włocławek
Vltava r. Czech Rep. 17 O5
Vöcklabruck Austria 17 N6
Vodlozero, Ozero l. Rus. Fed. 12 H3
Voe U.K. 20 [inset]
Vogelkop Peninsula Indon. see Doberai, Jazirah
Voghera Italy 26 C2
Vohémar Madag. see Iharaña
Vohibinany Madag. see Ampasimanolotra
Vohimarina Madag. see Iharaña
Vohimena, Tanjona c. Madag. 49 E6
Vohipeno Madag. 49 E6
Võhma Estonia 15 N7
Voinjama Liberia 46 C4
Vojens Denmark 15 F9
Vojvodina prov. Serbia 27 H2
Vokhma Rus. Fed. 12 J4
Voknavolok Rus. Fed. 14 Q4
Vol' r. Rus. Fed. 12 L3
Volcano Bay Japan see Uchiura-wan
Volcano Islands Japan 43 Q8
Volda Norway 14 E5
Vol'dino Rus. Fed. 12 L3
Volga Rus. Fed. 12 H4
Volga r. Rus. Fed. 13 J5
Volga Upland hills Rus. Fed. see Privolzhskaya Vozvyshennost'
Volgodonsk Rus. Fed. 13 I7
Volgograd Rus. Fed. 13 J6
Volgogradskoye Vodokhranilishche resr Rus. Fed. 13 J6
Völkermarkt Austria 17 O7
Volkhov Rus. Fed. 12 G4
Volkhov r. Rus. Fed. 12 G3
Volkovysk Belarus see Vawkavysk
Volksrust S. Africa 51 I4
Vol'no-Nadezhdinskoye Rus. Fed. 44 C4
Volnovakha Ukr. 13 H7
Vol'nyansk Ukr. see Vil'nyans'k
Volochanka Rus. Fed. 28 K2
Volochisk Ukr. see Volochys'k
Volochys'k Ukr. 13 E6
Volodars'ke Ukr. 13 H7
Volodarskoye Kazakh. see Saumalkol'
Volodymyr-Volyns'kyy Ukr. 13 E6
Vologda Rus. Fed. 12 H4
Volokolamsk Rus. Fed. 12 G4
Volokovaya Rus. Fed. 12 K2
Volos Greece 27 J5
Volosovo Rus. Fed. 15 P7
Volot Rus. Fed. 12 F4
Volovo Rus. Fed. 13 H5
Volozhin Belarus see Valozhyn
Volsinii Italy see Orvieto
Vol'sk Rus. Fed. 13 J5
Volta, Lake resr Ghana 46 D4
Volta Blanche r. Burkina/Ghana see White Volta
Voltaire, Cape Australia 54 D3
Volta Redonda Brazil 71 B3
Volturno r. Italy 26 E4
Volubilis tourist site Morocco 22 C5
Volvi, Limni l. Greece 27 J4
Volzhsk Rus. Fed. 12 K5
Volzhskiy Samarskaya Oblast' Rus. Fed. 13 K5
Volzhskiy Volgogradskaya Oblast' Rus. Fed. 13 J6
Vondanka Rus. Fed. 12 J4
Vontimitta India 38 C3
Vopnafjörður Iceland 14 [inset]
Vopnafjörður b. Iceland 14 [inset]
Vörå Fin. 14 M5
Voranava Belarus 15 N9
Voreies Sporades is Greece 27 J5
Voriai Sporádhes is Greece see Voreies Sporades
Voring Plateau sea feature N. Atlantic Ocean 72 I1
Vorjing mt. India 37 H3
Vorkuta Rus. Fed. 28 H3
Vormsi i. Estonia 15 M7
Vorona r. Rus. Fed. 13 I6
Voronezh Rus. Fed. 13 H6
Voronezh r. Rus. Fed. 13 H6
Voronov, Mys pt Rus. Fed. 12 I2
Vorontsovo-Aleksandrovskoye Rus. Fed. see Zelenokumsk
Voroshilov Rus. Fed. see Ussuriysk
Voroshilovgrad Ukr. see Luhans'k
Voroshilovsk Rus. Fed. see Stavropol'
Voroshilovsk Ukr. see Alchevs'k
Vorotynets Rus. Fed. 12 J4
Vorozhba Ukr. 13 G6
Vorpommersche Boddenlandschaft, Nationalpark nat. park Germany 17 N3
Vorskla r. Rus. Fed. 13 G6
Võrtsjärv l. Estonia 15 N7
Võru Estonia 15 O8
Vosburg S. Africa 50 F6
Vose Tajik. 33 K2
Vosges mts France 24 H3
Voskresensk Rus. Fed. 13 H5
Voskresenskoye Rus. Fed. 12 H4
Voss Norway 15 E6
Vostochno-Sakhalinskiy Gory mts Rus. Fed. 44 F2
Vostochno-Sibirskoye More sea Rus. Fed. see East Siberian Sea
Vostochnyy Kirovskaya Oblast' Rus. Fed. 12 L4
Vostochnyy Sakhalinskaya Oblast' Rus. Fed. 44 F2
Vostochnyy Sayan mts Rus. Fed. 42 G2
Vostok research station Antarctica 76 F1
Vostok Primorskiy Kray Rus. Fed. 44 D3
Vostok Sakhalinskaya Oblast' Rus. Fed. see Neftegorsk
Vostok Island Kiribati 75 J6
Vostroye Rus. Fed. 12 J3
Votkinsk Rus. Fed. 11 Q4
Votkinskoye Vodokhranilishche resr Rus. Fed. 11 R4
Votuporanga Brazil 71 A3
Voves France 24 E2
Voynitsa Rus. Fed. 12 F2
Vöyri Fin. see Vörå
Voyvozh Rus. Fed. 12 L3
Vozhayel' Rus. Fed. 12 K3
Vozhe, Ozero l. Rus. Fed. 12 H3
Vozhega Rus. Fed. 12 I3
Vozhgaly Rus. Fed. 12 K4
Voznesens'k Ukr. 13 F7
Vozonin Trough sea feature Arctic Ocean 77 F1
Vozzhayevka Rus. Fed. 44 C2
Vrangel' Rus. Fed. 44 D4
Vrangelya, Mys pt Rus. Fed. 44 E1
Vranje Serbia 27 I3
Vratnik pass Bulg. 27 L3
Vratsa Bulg. 27 J3
Vrbas Serbia 27 H2
Vrede S. Africa 51 I4
Vredefort S. Africa 51 H4
Vredenburg S. Africa 50 C7
Vredendal S. Africa 50 D6
Vriddhachalam India 38 C4
Vrigstad Sweden 15 I8
Vršac Serbia 27 I2
Vryburg S. Africa 50 G4
Vryheid S. Africa 51 J4
Vsevidof, Mount vol. U.S.A. 60 B4
Vsevolozhsk Rus. Fed. 12 F3
Vučitrn Serbia 27 I3
Vukovar Croatia 27 H2
Vuktyl' Rus. Fed. 11 R3
Vukuzakhe S. Africa 51 I4
Vulcan Island P.N.G. see Manam Island
Vulcano, Isola i. Italy 26 F5
Vulture Mountains AZ U.S.A. 65 F4
Vuohijärvi Fin. 15 O6
Vuolijoki Fin. 14 O4
Vuollerim Sweden 14 L3
Vuostimo Fin. 14 O3
Vurnary Rus. Fed. 12 J5
Vushtri Serbia see Vučitrn
Vvedenovka Rus. Fed. 44 C2
Vyara India 36 C5
Vyarkhowye Belarus see Ruba
Vyatka Rus. Fed. see Kirov
Vyatka r. Rus. Fed. 12 K5
Vyatskiye Polyany Rus. Fed. 12 K4
Vyazemskiy Rus. Fed. 44 D3
Vyaz'ma Rus. Fed. 13 G5
Vyazniki Rus. Fed. 12 I4
Vyazovka Rus. Fed. 13 J5
Vyborg Rus. Fed. 12 F3
Vychegda r. Rus. Fed. 12 J3
Vychegodskiy Rus. Fed. 12 J3
Vyerkhnyadzvinsk Belarus 15 O9
Vyetryna Belarus 15 P9
Vygozero, Ozero l. Rus. Fed. 12 G3
Vyksa Rus. Fed. 13 I5
Vylkove Ukr. 27 M2
Vym' r. Rus. Fed. 12 K3
Vynohradiv Ukr. 13 D6
Vypin Island India 38 C4
Vypolzovo Rus. Fed. 12 G4
Vyritsa Rus. Fed. 15 Q7
Vyrnwy, Lake U.K. 19 D6
Vyselki Rus. Fed. 13 H7
Vysha Rus. Fed. 13 I5
Vyshhorod Ukr. 13 F6
Vyshnevolotskaya Gryada ridge Rus. Fed. 12 G4
Vyshniy-Volochek Rus. Fed. 12 G4
Vyškov Czech Rep. 17 P6
Vysokaya Gora Rus. Fed. 12 K5
Vysokogorniy Rus. Fed. 44 E2
Vystupovychi Ukr. 13 F6
Vytegra Rus. Fed. 12 H3
Vyya r. Rus. Fed. 12 J3
Vyžuona r. Lith. 15 N9

W

Wa Ghana 46 C3
Waal r. Neth. 10 G5
Waat Sudan 32 D8
Wabē Gestro r. Eth. 30 D6
Wabē Shebelē Wenz r. Eth. 48 E3
Wabowden Canada 62 H1
Wabrah well Saudi Arabia 35 G6
Waccasassa Bay U.S.A. 63 K6
Waco U.S.A. 63 H5
Wad Pak. 36 A4
Wadbilliga National Park Australia 58 D6
Waddān Libya 23 H6
Waddeneilanden Neth. 16 J4
Waddenzee sea chan. Neth. 16 J4
Waddington, Mount Canada 62 B1
Wadebridge U.K. 19 C8
Wadena Canada 62 G1
Wadena U.S.A. 63 H2
Wadeye Australia 54 E3
Wadhwan India see Surendranagar
Wadi India 38 C2
Wādī as Sīr Jordan 39 B4
Wadi Halfa Sudan 32 D5
Wad Medani Sudan 32 D7
Wad Rawa Sudan 32 D6
Waenhuiskrans S. Africa 50 E8
Wafangdian China 43 M5
Wafra Kuwait see Al Wafrah
Wagga Wagga Australia 58 C5
Wah Pak. 36 C2
Wahai Indon. 52 C2
Wāḥāt Jālū Libya 47 F2
Wahpeton U.S.A. 63 H2
Wahran Alg. see Oran
Wah Wah Mountains UT U.S.A. 65 F1
Wai India 38 B2
Waiau N.Z. see Franz Josef Glacier
Waiau r. N.Z. 59 D6
Waidhofen an der Ybbs Austria 17 O7
Waigeo i. Indon. 41 F8
Waiheke Island N.Z. 59 E3
Waikabubak Indon. 41 D8
Waikaia r. N.Z. 59 B7
Waikari N.Z. 59 D6
Waikerie Australia 57 B7
Waikouaiti N.Z. 59 C7
Waimangaroa N.Z. 59 C5
Waimarama N.Z. 59 F4
Waimate N.Z. 59 C7
Wainganga r. India 38 C2
Waingapu Indon. 41 E8
Wainhouse Corner U.K. 19 C8
Waini Point Guyana 69 G2
Wainwright Canada 62 E1
Wainwright U.S.A. 60 C2
Waiouru N.Z. 59 E4
Waipahi N.Z. 59 B8
Waipaoa r. N.Z. 59 F4
Waipara N.Z. 59 D6
Waipawa N.Z. 59 F4
Waipukurau N.Z. 59 F4
Wairarapa, Lake N.Z. 59 E5
Wairau r. N.Z. 59 E5
Wairoa N.Z. 59 F4
Wairoa r. N.Z. 59 F4
Waitahanui N.Z. 59 F4
Waitahuna N.Z. 59 B7
Waitakaruru N.Z. 59 E3
Waitaki r. N.Z. 59 C7
Waitangi N.Z. 53 I6
Waite River Australia 54 F5
Waiuku N.Z. 59 E3
Waiwera South N.Z. 59 B8
Wajima Japan 45 E5
Wajir Kenya 48 E3
Waka Indon. 54 C2
Wakasa-wan b. Japan 45 D6
Wakatipu, Lake N.Z. 59 B7
Wakayama Japan 45 D6
Wake Atoll terr. N. Pacific Ocean see Wake Island
WaKeeney U.S.A. 62 H4
Wakefield N.Z. 59 D5
Wakefield U.K. 18 F5
Wakefield RI U.S.A. 64 F2
Wakefield VA U.S.A. 64 C4
Wake Island terr. N. Pacific Ocean 74 H4
Wakkanai Japan 44 F3
Wakkerstroom S. Africa 51 J4
Wakool Australia 58 B5
Wakool r. Australia 58 A5
Waku-Kungo Angola 49 B5
Wałbrzych Poland 17 P5
Walcha Australia 58 E3
Wałcz Poland 17 P4
Waldburg Range mts Australia 55 B6
Walden NY U.S.A. 64 D2
Waldenburg Poland see Wałbrzych
Waldkraiburg Germany 17 N6
Waldorf MD U.S.A. 64 C3
Waldron, Cape Antarctica 76 F2
Walebing Australia 55 B7
Wales admin. div. U.K. 19 D6
Walgaon India 36 D5
Walgett Australia 58 D3
Walgreen Coast Antarctica 76 K1
Walikale Dem. Rep. Congo 47 F5
Walker r. Australia 56 A2
Walker watercourse Australia 55 F6
Walker r. NV U.S.A. 65 C1
Walker Bay S. Africa 50 D8
Walker Creek r. Australia 56 C3
Walker Lake NV U.S.A. 65 C1
Walker Pass CA U.S.A. 65 C3
Walkersville MD U.S.A. 64 C3
Wall, Mount hill Australia 54 B5
Wallaby Island Australia 56 C2
Wallal Downs Australia 54 C4
Wallangarra Australia 58 E2
Wallaroo Australia 57 B7
Wallasey U.K. 18 D5
Walla Walla Australia 58 C5
Walla Walla U.S.A. 62 D2
Wallekraal S. Africa 50 C6
Wallendbeen Australia 58 D5
Wallingford U.K. 19 F7
Wallis, Îles is Wallis and Futuna Is 53 I3
Wallis and Futuna Islands terr. S. Pacific Ocean 53 I3
Wallis et Futuna, Îles terr. S. Pacific Ocean see Wallis and Futuna Islands
Wallis Islands Wallis and Futuna Is see Wallis, Îles
Wallis Lake inlet Australia 58 F4
Wallops Island VA U.S.A. 64 D4
Walls U.K. 20 [inset]
Walls of Jerusalem National Park Australia 57 [inset]
Wallumbilla Australia 57 E5
Walney, Isle of i. U.K. 18 D4
Walnut Creek CA U.S.A. 65 A2
Walnut Grove CA U.S.A. 65 B1
Walong India 37 I3
Walpole NH U.S.A. 64 E1
Walsall U.K. 19 F6
Walsenburg U.S.A. 62 G4
Waltair India 38 D2
Walterboro U.S.A. 63 K5
Walter's Range hills Australia 58 B2
Waltham MA U.S.A. 64 F1
Walton WV U.S.A. 64 A3
Walvisbaai Namibia see Walvis Bay
Walvisbaai b. Namibia see Walvis Bay
Walvis Bay Namibia 50 B2
Walvis Bay b. Namibia 50 B2
Walvis Ridge sea feature S. Atlantic Ocean 72 H8
Wama Afgh. 36 B2
Wamba Équateur Dem. Rep. Congo 47 F5
Wamba Orientale Dem. Rep. Congo 48 C3
Wamba Nigeria 46 D4
Wampusirpi Hond. 67 H5
Wana Pak. 33 K3
Wanaaring Australia 58 B2
Wanaka N.Z. 59 B7
Wanaka, Lake N.Z. 59 B7
Wanapitei Lake Canada 63 K2
Wanbi Australia 57 C7
Wanbrow, Cape N.Z. 59 C7
Wanda Shan mts China 44 D3
Wando S. Korea 45 B6
Wandoan Australia 57 E5
Wanganui N.Z. 59 E4
Wanganui r. N.Z. 59 E4
Wangaratta Australia 58 C6
Wangda China see Zogang
Wangdain China 37 G3
Wangdi Phodrang Bhutan 37 G4
Wanggamet, Gunung mt. Indon. 54 C2
Wang Gaxun China 37 I1
Wangkui China 44 B3
Wangmo China 42 J7
Wangqing China 44 C4
Wan Hsa-la Myanmar 42 H8
Wanie-Rukula Dem. Rep. Congo 48 C3
Wankaner India 36 B5
Wankie Zimbabwe see Hwange
Wanlaweyn Somalia 48 E3
Wanna Lakes salt flat Australia 55 E7
Wantage U.K. 19 F7
Wanxian Chongqing China 43 J6
Wanyuan China 43 J6
Wapusk National Park Canada 61 I4
Waqf aş Şawwān, Jibāl hills Jordan 39 C4
Warab Sudan 32 C8
Warangal India 38 C2
Waranga Reservoir Australia 58 B6
Waratah Bay Australia 58 B7
Warbreccan Australia 56 C5
Warburton Australia 55 D6
Warburton watercourse Australia 57 B5
Ward, Mount N.Z. 59 B6
Warden S. Africa 51 I4
Wardha India 38 C1
Wardha r. India 38 C2
Ward Hill hill U.K. 20 F2
Ware Canada 60 F4
Ware MA U.S.A. 64 E1
Wareham U.K. 19 E8
Waren Germany 17 N4
Warendorf Germany 17 K5
Warginburra Peninsula Australia 56 E4
Wargla Alg. see Ouargla
Warialda Australia 58 E2
Warkworth U.K. 18 F3
Warmbad Namibia 50 D5
Warmbad S. Africa 51 I3
Warmbaths S. Africa see Warmbad
Warminster U.K. 19 E7
Warminster PA U.S.A. 64 D2
Warm Springs NV U.S.A. 65 D1
Warm Springs VA U.S.A. 64 B3
Warmwaterberg mts S. Africa 50 E7
Warnes Bol. 68 F7
Warning, Mount Australia 58 F2
Waronda India 38 C2
Warora India 38 C1
Warra Australia 58 E1
Warragamba Reservoir Australia 58 E5
Warragul Australia 58 B7
Warrambool r. Australia 58 C3
Warrandirinna, Lake salt flat Australia 57 B5
Warrandyte Australia 58 B6
Warrawagine Australia 54 C5
Warrego r. Australia 58 B3
Warrego Range hills Australia 56 D5
Warren Australia 58 C3
Warren OH U.S.A. 64 A2
Warren PA U.S.A. 64 B2
Warrenpoint U.K. 21 F3
Warrensburg MO U.S.A. 63 I4
Warrensburg NY U.S.A. 64 E1
Warrenton S. Africa 50 G5
Warrenton VA U.S.A. 64 C3
Warri Nigeria 46 D4
Warriners Creek watercourse Australia 57 B6
Warrington N.Z. 59 C7
Warrington U.K. 18 E5
Warrnambool Australia 57 C8
Warrumbungle National Park Australia 58 D3
Warsaw Poland 17 R4
Warsaw NY U.S.A. 64 B1
Warsaw VA U.S.A. 64 C4
Warshiikh Somalia 48 E3
Warszawa Poland see Warsaw
Warta r. Poland 17 O4
Warwick Australia 58 F2
Warwick U.K. 19 F6
Warwick RI U.S.A. 64 F2
Wasbank S. Africa 51 J5
Wasco CA U.S.A. 65 C3
Washburn ND U.S.A. 62 G2
Washim India 38 C1
Washington DC U.S.A. 64 C3
Washington NC U.S.A. 63 L4
Washington NJ U.S.A. 64 D2
Washington PA U.S.A. 64 A2
Washington UT U.S.A. 65 F2
Washington state U.S.A. 62 C2
Washington, Cape Antarctica 76 H2
Washington, Mount U.S.A. 63 M3
Washington Land reg. Greenland 61 L2
Washpool National Park Australia 58 F2
Wasi India 38 B2
Waskaganish Canada 63 L1
Waskaghegamish Canada see Waskaganish
Waskey, Mount U.S.A. 60 C4
Wasser Namibia 50 D4
Wassuk Range mts NV U.S.A. 65 C1
Waswanipi, Lac l. Canada 63 L2
Watampone Indon. 41 E8
Watarrka National Park Australia 55 E6
Watenstadt-Salzgitter Germany see Salzgitter
Waterbury CT U.S.A. 64 E2
Waterford Ireland 21 E5
Waterford Harbour Ireland 21 F5
Watergrasshill Ireland 21 D5
Waterloo Australia 54 E4
Waterloo Ont. Canada 64 A1
Waterloo IA U.S.A. 63 I3
Waterloo NY U.S.A. 64 C1
Waterlooville U.K. 19 F8
Watertown NY U.S.A. 63 L3
Watertown SD U.S.A. 63 H3
Waterval Boven S. Africa 51 J3
Watford U.K. 19 G7
Watford City U.S.A. 62 G2
Watheroo National Park Australia 55 A7
Watīr, Wādī watercourse Egypt 39 B5
Watkins Glen NY U.S.A. 64 C1
Watling Island Bahamas see San Salvador
Watmuri Indon. 54 E1
Watrous Canada 62 F1
Watsi Kengo Dem. Rep. Congo 47 F5
Watson r. Australia 56 C2
Watson Lake Canada 60 F3
Watsonville CA U.S.A. 65 B2
Watten U.K. 20 F2
Watton U.K. 19 H6
Wattsburg PA U.S.A. 64 B1
Watubela, Kepulauan is Indon. 41 F8
Wau P.N.G. 52 E2
Wau Sudan 32 C8
Wauchope N.S.W. Australia 58 F3
Wauchope N.T. Australia 54 F5
Waukaringa Australia 57 B7
Waukarlycarly, Lake salt flat Australia 54 C5
Waukegan U.S.A. 63 J3
Wausau U.S.A. 63 J3
Wave Hill Australia 54 E4
Waveney r. U.K. 19 I6
Waverly NY U.S.A. 64 C1
Waverly VA U.S.A. 64 C4
Wāw al Kabīr Libya 47 E2
Waxxari China 42 F4
Way, Lake salt flat Australia 55 C6
Waycross U.S.A. 63 K5
Waynesboro VA U.S.A. 64 B3
Waynesburg PA U.S.A. 64 A3
Waza, Parc National de nat. park Cameroon 47 E3
Wāzah Khwāh Afgh. see Wazi Khwa
Wazi Khwa Afgh. 36 B2
Wazirabad Pak. 36 C2
W du Niger, Parcs Nationaux du nat. park Niger 46 D3
Wear r. U.K. 18 F4
Weatherford U.S.A. 62 H5
Weaverville U.S.A. 62 C3
Webb, Mount hill Australia 54 E5
Webequie Canada 63 J1
Weber Basin sea feature Laut Banda 74 E6
Webi Shabeelle r. Somalia 48 E3
Webster MA U.S.A. 64 F1
Webster SD U.S.A. 63 H2
Webster Springs WV U.S.A. 64 A3
Wedau P.N.G. 56 E1
Weddell Abyssal Plain sea feature Southern Ocean 76 A2
Weddell Island Falkland Is 70 D8
Weddell Sea Antarctica 76 A2
Wedderburn Australia 58 A6
Weddin Mountains National Park Australia 58 D4
Weedville PA U.S.A. 64 B2
Weenen S. Africa 51 J5
Weethalle Australia 58 C4
Wee Waa Australia 58 D3
Węgorzewo Poland 17 R3
Weichang China 43 L4
Weidongmen China see Qianjin
Weifang China 43 L5
Weihai China 43 M5
Weilmoringle Australia 58 C2
Weimar Germany 17 M5
Weinan China 43 J6
Weipa Australia 56 C2
Weir r. Australia 58 D2
Weirton WV U.S.A. 64 A2
Weißkugel mt. Austria/Italy 17 M7
Weissrand Mountains Namibia 50 D3
Weiya China 42 G4
Weiz Austria 17 O7
Wejherowo Poland 17 Q3
Wekweti Canada 60 G3
Welbourn Hill Australia 55 F6
Weldiya Eth. 48 D2
Welford National Park Australia 56 C5
Welk'īt'ē Eth. 48 D3
Welkom S. Africa 51 H4
Welland Ont. Canada 64 B1
Welland r. U.K. 19 G6
Welland Canal Ont. Canada 64 B1
Wellesley Ont. Canada 64 A1
Wellesley Islands Australia 56 B3
Wellfleet MA U.S.A. 64 F2
Wellingborough U.K. 19 G6
Wellington Australia 58 D4
Wellington N.Z. 59 E5
Wellington S. Africa 50 D7
Wellington England U.K. 19 D8
Wellington England U.K. 19 E6
Wellington NV U.S.A. 65 C1
Wellington, Isla i. Chile 70 B7
Wellington Range hills N.T. Australia 54 F3
Wellington Range hills W.A. Australia 55 C6
Wells U.K. 19 E7
Wells, Lake salt flat Australia 55 C6
Wellsboro PA U.S.A. 64 C2
Wellsburg WV U.S.A. 64 A2
Wellsford N.Z. 59 E3
Wells-next-the-Sea U.K. 19 H6
Wellsville NY U.S.A. 64 C1
Wellton AZ U.S.A. 65 E4
Wels Austria 17 O6
Welshpool U.K. 19 D6
Welwitschia Namibia see Khorixas
Welwyn Garden City U.K. 19 G7
Wem U.K. 19 E6
Wembesi S. Africa 51 I5
Wemindji Canada 63 L1
Wenatchee U.S.A. 62 C2
Wenbu China see Nyima
Wenchang Hainan China 43 K9
Wenchow China see Wenzhou
Wenden Latvia see Cēsis
Wenden AZ U.S.A. 65 F4
Wendover U.S.A. 62 E3
Wenlock r. Australia 56 C2
Wenquan Qinghai China 37 G2
Wenquan Xinjiang China 42 E4
Wenshan China 42 I8
Wensum r. U.K. 19 I6
Wentworth Australia 57 C7
Wenzhou China 43 M7
Wepener S. Africa 51 H5
Wer India 36 D4
Werda Botswana 50 F3
Werder Eth. 48 E3
Werder Germany 17 N4
Werra r. Germany 17 L5
Werris Creek Australia 58 E3
Wesel Germany 17 K5
Weser r. Germany 17 L4
Wessel, Cape Australia 56 B1
Wessel Islands Australia 56 B1
Wesselsbron S. Africa 51 H4
Wesselton S. Africa 51 I4
Westall, Point Australia 55 F8
West Antarctica reg. Antarctica 76 J1
West Australian Basin sea feature Indian Ocean 73 O7
West Bank terr. Asia 39 B3
West Bend U.S.A. 63 J3
West Bengal state India 37 F5
West Bromwich U.K. 19 F6
West Burra i. U.K. see Burra
Westbury U.K. 19 E7
West Cape Howe Australia 55 B8
West Caroline Basin sea feature N. Pacific Ocean 74 F5
West Chester PA U.S.A. 64 D3
West Coast National Park S. Africa 50 D7
Westerland Germany 17 L3
Westerly RI U.S.A. 64 F2
Western Australia state Australia 55 C6
Western Cape prov. S. Africa 50 E7
Western Desert Egypt 34 C6
Western Dvina r. Europe see Zapadnaya Dvina
Western Ghats mts India 38 B3
Western Port b. Australia 58 B7
Western Sahara terr. Africa 46 B2
Western Samoa country S. Pacific Ocean see Samoa
Western Sayan Mountains reg. Rus. Fed. see Zapadnyy Sayan
West Falkland i. Falkland Is 70 D8
Westfield MA U.S.A. 64 E1
Westfield NY U.S.A. 64 B1
Westfield PA U.S.A. 64 C2
West Frisian Islands Neth. see Waddeneilanden
Westgate Australia 58 C1
West Hartford CT U.S.A. 64 E2
West Haven CT U.S.A. 64 E2
Westhill U.K. 20 G3
Westhope U.S.A. 62 G2
West Ice Shelf Antarctica 76 E2
West Indies is Caribbean Sea 67 J4
West Kazakhstan Oblast admin. div. Kazakh. see Zapadnyy Kazakhstan
West Kingston RI U.S.A. 64 F2
Westland Australia 56 C4
Westland National Park N.Z. 59 C6
Westleigh S. Africa 51 H4
Westleton U.K. 19 I6
West Linton U.K. 20 F5
West Loch Roag b. U.K. 20 C2
West Lorne Ont. Canada 64 A1
West Lunga National Park Zambia 49 C5
West MacDonnell National Park Australia 55 F5
West Malaysia pen. Malaysia see Peninsular Malaysia
Westmar Australia 58 D1
West Mariana Basin sea feature N. Pacific Ocean 74 F4
Westminster MD U.S.A. 64 C3
Westmoreland Australia 56 B3
Westmorland CA U.S.A. 65 E4
Weston WV U.S.A. 64 A3
Weston-super-Mare U.K. 19 E7
West Palm Beach U.S.A. 63 K6
West Plains U.S.A. 63 I4
West Point pt Australia 57 [inset]
West Point CA U.S.A. 65 B1
West Point VA U.S.A. 64 C4
Westport Ireland 21 C4
Westport N.Z. 59 C5
Westray Canada 62 G1
Westray i. U.K. 20 F1
Westray Firth sea chan. U.K. 20 F1
West Rutland VT U.S.A. 64 E1
West Siberian Plain Rus. Fed. 28 J3
West Union WV U.S.A. 64 A3
West Virginia state U.S.A. 64 A3
West Wyalong Australia 58 C4
West York PA U.S.A. 64 C3
Wetar i. Indon. 41 E8
Wetar, Selat sea chan. East Timor/Indon. 54 D2
Wetaskiwin Canada 62 E1
Wete Tanz. 49 D4
Wetzlar Germany 17 L5
Wewak P.N.G. 52 E2
Wexford Ireland 21 F5
Wexford Harbour b. Ireland 21 F5
Weyakwin Canada 62 F1
Weybridge U.K. 19 G7
Weyburn Canada 62 G2
Weymouth U.K. 19 E8
Weymouth MA U.S.A. 64 F1
Whakaari i. N.Z. 59 F3
Whakatane N.Z. 59 F3
Whalan Creek r. Australia 58 D2
Whalsay i. U.K. 20 [inset]
Whangamata N.Z. 59 E3
Whanganui National Park N.Z. 59 E4
Whangarei N.Z. 59 E2
Wharfe r. U.K. 18 F5
Wharfedale valley U.K. 18 F4
Wharton U.S.A. 63 H6
Wharton Lake Canada 61 I3
Wha Ti Canada 60 G3
Wheatland WY U.S.A. 62 F3
Wheaton-Glenmont MD U.S.A. 64 C3
Wheeler Peak NM U.S.A. 62 F4
Wheeler Peak NV U.S.A. 65 E1
Wheeling WV U.S.A. 64 A2
Whernside hill U.K. 18 E4
Whinham, Mount Australia 55 E6
Whitburn U.K. 20 F5
Whitby U.K. 18 G4
Whitchurch U.K. 19 E6
White r. Canada/U.S.A. 60 E3
White r. AR U.S.A. 63 I5
White r. NV U.S.A. 65 E2
White, Lake salt flat Australia 54 E5
White Bay Canada 61 M5
White Butte mt. U.S.A. 62 G2
Whitecourt Canada 60 G4
Whitehall Ireland 21 E5
Whitehall U.K. 20 G1
Whitehall NY U.S.A. 64 E1
Whitehaven U.K. 18 D4
Whitehead U.K. 21 G3
Whitehill U.K. 19 G7
Whitehorse Canada 60 E3
White Horse, Vale of valley U.K. 19 F7
White Island Antarctica 76 D2
White Island N.Z. see Whakaari
White Lake LA U.S.A. 63 I6
Whitemark Australia 57 [inset]
White Mountain Peak CA U.S.A. 65 C2
White Mountains National Park Australia 56 D4
White Nile r. Sudan/Uganda 32 D6
White Nile r. Sudan/Uganda 47 G3
White Nossob watercourse Namibia 50 D2
White Pine Range mts NV U.S.A. 65 E1
White Plains NY U.S.A. 64 E2
White River Valley valley NV U.S.A. 65 E1
White Rock Peak NV U.S.A. 65 E1
White Russia country Europe see Belarus
White Sea Rus. Fed. 12 H2
White Stone VA U.S.A. 64 C4
White Sulphur Springs WV U.S.A. 64 A4
Whiteville U.S.A. 63 L5
White Volta r. Burkina/Ghana 46 C4
Whitewater Baldy mt. U.S.A. 62 F5
Whitewood Australia 56 C4
Whitewood Canada 62 G1
Whitfield U.K. 19 I7
Whithorn U.K. 20 E6
Whitianga N.Z. 59 E3
Whitland U.K. 19 C7
Whitley Bay U.K. 18 F3
Whitmore Mountains Antarctica 76 K1
Whitney, Mount CA U.S.A. 65 C2
Whitstable U.K. 19 I7
Whitsunday Group is Australia 56 E4
Whitsunday Island National Park Australia 56 E4
Whitsun Island Vanuatu see Pentecost Island
Whittlesea Australia 58 B6
Whittlesey U.K. 19 G6
Whitton Australia 58 C5
Wholdaia Lake Canada 60 H3
Whyalla Australia 57 B7
Wichita U.S.A. 63 H4
Wichita Falls U.S.A. 62 H5
Wick U.K. 20 F2
Wick r. U.K. 20 F2
Wickenburg AZ U.S.A. 65 F4
Wickford U.K. 19 H7
Wickham r. Australia 54 E4
Wickham, Cape Australia 57 [inset]
Wickham, Mount hill Australia 54 E4
Wicklow Ireland 21 F5
Wicklow Head hd Ireland 21 G5
Wicklow Mountains Ireland 21 F5
Wicklow Mountains National Park Ireland 21 F4
Widerøe, Mount Antarctica 76 C2
Widerøefjellet mt. Antarctica see Widerøe, Mount
Widgeegoara watercourse Australia 58 B1
Widgiemooltha Australia 55 C7
Widnes U.K. 18 E5
Wi-do i. S. Korea 45 B6
Wielkopolskie, Pojezierze reg. Poland 17 O4
Wielkopolski Park Narodowy nat. park Poland 17 P4
Wieluń Poland 17 Q5
Wien Austria see Vienna
Wiener Neustadt Austria 17 P7
Wiesbaden Germany 17 L5
Wieżyca hill Poland 17 Q3
Wigan U.K. 18 E5
Wight, Isle of i. England U.K. 19 F8

Wigierski Park Narodowy nat. park Poland 15 M9
Wigton U.K. 19 F6
Wigton U.K. 18 D4
Wigtown U.K. 20 E6
Wigtown Bay U.K. 20 E6
Wilberforce, Cape Australia 56 B1
Wilcannia Australia 58 A3
Wilcox PA U.S.A. 64 D2
Wilczek Land i. Rus. Fed. see Vil'cheka, Zemlya
Wildcat Peak NV U.S.A. 65 D1
Wild Coast S. Africa 51 I6
Wilderness National Park S. Africa 50 F8
Wildspitze mt. Austria 17 M7
Wildwood NJ U.S.A. 64 D3
Wilge r. S. Africa 51 I4
Wilge r. S. Africa 51 I3
Wilgena Australia 55 F7
Wilhelm, Mount P.N.G. 52 E2
Wilhelm II Land reg. Antarctica see Kaiser Wilhelm II Land
Wilhelmina Gebergte mts Suriname 69 G3
Wilhelmshaven Germany 17 L4
Wilhelmstal Namibia 50 C1
Wilkes-Barre PA U.S.A. 64 D2
Wilkes Coast Antarctica 76 G2
Wilkes Land reg. Antarctica 76 G2
Wilkie Canada 62 F5
Wilkins Coast Antarctica 76 L2
Wilkins Ice Shelf Antarctica 76 L2
Wilkinson Lakes salt flat Australia 55 F7
Willand U.K. 19 D8
Willandra Billabong watercourse Australia 58 B4
Willandra National Park Australia 58 B4
Willcox AZ U.S.A. 62 F5
Willemstad Neth. Antilles 67 K6
Willeroo Australia 54 E3
William, Mount Australia 57 C8
William Creek Australia 57 B6
Williams AZ U.S.A. 62 E4
Williams CA U.S.A. 65 A1
Williams Lake Canada 62 C1
Williamsburg VA U.S.A. 64 C4
Williamson NY U.S.A. 64 C1
Williamson WV U.S.A. 63 K4
Williamsport PA U.S.A. 64 C2
Williamstown NJ U.S.A. 64 D3
Williamstown NY U.S.A. 64 D1
Willimantic CT U.S.A. 64 E2
Willis Group atolls Australia 56 E3
Williston S. Africa 50 E6
Williston ND U.S.A. 62 G2
Williston Lake Canada 60 F4
Williton U.K. 19 D7
Willmar U.S.A. 63 H2
Willow Beach AZ U.S.A. 65 E3
Willow Hill PA U.S.A. 64 C2
Willowmore S. Africa 50 F7
Willowra Australia 54 F5
Willowvale S. Africa 51 I7
Wills, Lake salt flat Australia 54 E5
Wilmington DE U.S.A. 64 D3
Wilmington NC U.S.A. 63 L5
Wilmslow U.K. 18 E5
Wilno Lith. see Vilnius
Wilpattu National Park Sri Lanka 38 D5
Wilson watercourse Australia 57 C5
Wilson NC U.S.A. 63 L4
Wilson NY U.S.A. 64 B1
Wilson, Mount NV U.S.A. 65 E1
Wilsonia CA U.S.A. 65 C2
Wilson's Promontory pen. Australia 58 C7
Wilson's Promontory National Park Australia 58 C7
Wilton r. Australia 54 F3
Wiluna Australia 55 C6
Wimereux France 19 I8
Wina r. Cameroon see Vina
Winbin watercourse Australia 57 D5
Winburg S. Africa 51 H5
Wincanton U.K. 19 E7
Winchester U.K. 19 F7
Winchester KY U.S.A. 63 K4
Winchester NH U.S.A. 64 E1
Winchester VA U.S.A. 64 B3
Windau Latvia see Ventspils
Windber PA U.S.A. 64 B2
Windermere l. U.K. 18 E4
Windermere l. U.K. 18 E4
Windhoek Namibia 50 C2
Windlestraw Law hill U.K. 20 G5
Windom U.S.A. 63 H3
Windorah Australia 56 C5
Wind River Range mts U.S.A. 62 F3
Windrush r. U.K. 19 F7
Windsor Australia 58 E4
Windsor Ont. Canada 63 K3
Windsor U.K. 19 G7
Windsor NY U.S.A. 64 D1
Windsor VT U.S.A. 64 E1
Windsor Locks CT U.S.A. 64 E2
Windward Islands Caribbean Sea 67 L5
Windward Passage Cuba/Haiti 67 J5
Windy U.S.A. 60 D3
Winfield KS U.S.A. 63 H4
Wingate U.K. 18 F4
Wingen Australia 58 E3
Wingham Australia 58 F3
Winisk Canada 61 J4
Winisk r. Canada 61 J4
Winisk Lake Canada 61 J1
Winneba Ghana 46 C4
Winnecke Creek watercourse Australia 54 F4
Winnemucca U.S.A. 62 D3
Winner U.S.A. 62 G3
Winfield U.S.A. 63 I5
Winning Australia 55 A5
Winnipeg Canada 61 I5
Winnipeg, Lake Canada 61 I4
Winnipegosis, Lake Canada 61 H4
Winnipesaukee, Lake NH U.S.A. 64 F1
Winona MN U.S.A. 63 I3
Winona MS U.S.A. 63 J5
Winsford U.K. 18 E5
Winslow AZ U.S.A. 62 E4
Winsted CT U.S.A. 64 E2
Winston-Salem U.S.A. 63 K4
Winters CA U.S.A. 65 B2
Winterton S. Africa 51 I5
Winterthur Switz. 24 I3
Winton Australia 56 C4
Winton N.Z. 59 B8
Winwick U.K. 19 G6
Wirral pen. U.K. 18 D5
Wirrulla Australia 57 A7
Wisbech U.K. 19 H6
Wisconsin state U.S.A. 63 J3
Wisconsin Rapids U.S.A. 63 J3
Wiseman U.S.A. 60 C3
Wishaw U.K. 20 F5
Wisil Dabarow Somalia 48 E3
Wisła r. Poland see Vistula
Wismar Germany 17 M4
Witbank S. Africa 51 I3
Witbooisvlei Namibia 50 D3
Witham U.K. 19 H7
Witham r. U.K. 19 H6
Withernsea U.K. 18 H5

Witjira National Park Australia 57 A5
Witney U.K. 19 F7
Witrivier S. Africa 51 J3
Witteberg mts S. Africa 51 H6
Wittenberg Germany see Lutherstadt Wittenberg
Wittenberge Germany 17 M4
Wittenburg Germany 17 M4
Wittlich Germany 17 K6
Wittstock Germany 17 N4
Witu Islands P.N.G. 52 F2
Witvlei Namibia 50 D2
Wivenhoe, Lake Australia 58 F1
Władysławowo Poland 17 Q3
Włocławek Poland 17 Q4
Wodonga Australia 58 C6
Wohlthat Mountains Antarctica 76 D2
Wöjjä atoll Marshall Is see Wotje
Wokam i. Indon. 41 F8
Woken He r. China 44 C3
Wokha India 37 H4
Woking U.K. 19 G7
Wokingham watercourse Australia 56 C4
Wokingham U.K. 19 G7
Woko National Park Australia 58 E3
Wolcott NY U.S.A. 64 C1
Wolfenbüttel Germany 17 M4
Wolf Point U.S.A. 62 F2
Wolfsberg Austria 17 O7
Wolfsburg Germany 17 M4
Wolfville Canada 63 O2
Wolgast Germany 17 N3
Wolin Poland 17 O4
Wollaston Lake Canada 60 H4
Wollaston Lake l. Canada 60 H4
Wollaston Peninsula Canada 60 G3
Wollemi National Park Australia 58 E4
Wollongong Australia 58 E5
Wolmaransstad S. Africa 51 G4
Wolseley Australia 57 C8
Wolseley S. Africa 50 D7
Wolsingham U.K. 18 F4
Wolverhampton U.K. 19 E6
Wonarah Australia 56 B3
Wonay, Kowtal-e Afgh. 36 B2
Wondai Australia 57 E5
Wongalarroo Lake salt l. Australia 58 B3
Wongarbon Australia 58 D4
Wŏnju S. Korea 45 B5
Wonowon Canada 60 F4
Wŏnsan N. Korea 45 B5
Wonthaggi Australia 58 B7
Wonyulgunna, Mount hill Australia 55 B6
Woocalla Australia 57 B6
Woodbine NJ U.S.A. 64 D3
Woodbridge U.K. 19 I6
Woodbridge VA U.S.A. 64 C3
Woodbury NJ U.S.A. 64 D3
Wooded Bluff hd Australia 58 F2
Woodlake CA U.S.A. 65 C2
Woodland CA U.S.A. 65 B1
Woodland PA U.S.A. 64 B2
Woodlark Island P.N.G. 52 F2
Woodroffe watercourse Australia 56 B4
Woodroffe, Mount Australia 55 E6
Woods, Lake of the Canada/U.S.A. 63 I2
Woodsfield OH U.S.A. 64 A3
Woodside Australia 58 C7
Woodstock Ont. Canada 64 A1
Woodstock U.K. 19 F7
Woodstock VT U.S.A. 64 E1
Woodward U.S.A. 62 H4
Woody CA U.S.A. 65 C3
Wooler U.K. 18 E3
Woolgoolga Australia 58 F3
Wooli Australia 58 F3
Woollard, Mount Antarctica 76 K1
Woolyeenyer Hill hill Australia 55 C8
Woomera Australia 57 B6
Woomera Prohibited Area Australia 55 F7
Woorabinda Australia 56 E5
Wooramel r. Australia 55 A6
Wooster U.S.A. 64 K3
Worbody Point Australia 56 C2
Worcester S. Africa 50 D7
Worcester U.K. 19 E6
Worcester MA U.S.A. 64 F1
Worcester NY U.S.A. 64 D1
Wörgl Austria 17 N7
Workington U.K. 18 D4
Worksop U.K. 18 F5
Worland U.S.A. 62 F3
Worms Head hd U.K. 19 C7
Worthing U.K. 19 G8
Wotje atoll Marshall Is 74 H5
Wotu Indon. 52 C2
Wowoni i. Indon. 41 E8
Wrangel Island Rus. Fed. 29 T2
Wrangell Mountains U.S.A. 77 B3
Wrangell-St Elias National Park and Preserve U.S.A. 77 B3
Wrath, Cape U.K. 20 D2
Wray U.S.A. 62 G3
Wreake r. U.K. 19 F6
Wreck Point S. Africa 50 C5
Wreck Reef Australia 56 F4
Wrecsam U.K. see Wrexham
Wrexham U.K. 19 E5
Wrightwood CA U.S.A. 65 D3
Wrigley Canada 60 F3
Wrigley Gulf Antarctica 76 J2
Wrocław Poland 17 P5
Września Poland 17 P4
Wubin Australia 55 B7
Wuchang Heilong. China 44 B3
Wuchow China see Wuzhou
Wudalianchi China 44 B2
Wudinna Australia 55 F8
Wuhai China 42 J5
Wuhan China 43 K6
Wuhu China 43 K6
Wüjang China 36 D2
Wujin Jiangsu China see Changzhou
Wukari Nigeria 46 D4
Wuli China 42 G6
Wuliang Shan mts China 42 I8
Wuliaru i. Indon. 54 E1
Wulur Indon. 54 E1
Wunnummin Lake Canada 61 J4
Wunstorf Germany 17 M5
Wuntho Myanmar 37 I5
Wuppertal Germany 17 K5
Wuppertal S. Africa 50 D7
Wuqi China 43 J5
Wuqia China 42 C5
Wuranga Australia 55 B7
Wurno Nigeria 46 D3
Würzburg Germany 17 L6
Wusuli Jiang r. China/Rus. Fed. see Ussuri
Wuvulu Island P.N.G. 52 E2
Wuwei China 42 I5
Wuxi Jiangsu China 43 M6
Wuxian China see Suzhou
Wuxing China see Huzhou
Wuyang Guizhou China see Zhenyuan
Wuyiling China 44 C2
Wuyishan China 43 L7
Wuyi Shan mts China 43 L7
Wuyuan Nei Mongol China 43 J4

Wuzhong China 42 J5
Wuzhou China 43 K8
Wyalkatchem Australia 55 B7
Wyalong Australia 58 C4
Wyandra Australia 58 B1
Wyangala Reservoir Australia 58 D4
Wyara, Lake salt flat Australia 58 B2
Wycheproof Australia 58 A6
Wylliesburg VA U.S.A. 64 B4
Wyloo Australia 54 B5
Wylye r. U.K. 19 F7
Wymondham U.K. 19 I6
Wynbring Australia 55 F7
Wyndham Australia 54 E3
Wyndham-Werribee Australia 58 B6
Wynyard Canada 62 G1
Wyola Lake salt flat Australia 55 E7
Wyoming state U.S.A. 62 F3
Wyong Australia 58 E4
Wyperfeld National Park Australia 57 C7
Wysox PA U.S.A. 64 C2
Wythall U.K. 19 F6
Wytheville VA U.S.A. 64 A4

Xaafuun Somalia 48 F2
Xaafuun, Raas pt Somalia 32 H7
Xabyaisamba China 37 I3
Xaçmaz Azer. 35 H3
Xago China 37 G3
Xaguka China 37 H3
Xaidulla China 36 D1
Xaignabouli Laos 42 I9
Xaignabouri Laos see Xaignabouli
Xainza China 37 G3
Xai-Xai Moz. 51 K3
Xalapa Mex. see Jalapa
Xambioá Brazil 69 I5
Xam Nua Laos 40 C5
Xá-Muteba Angola 49 B4
Xanagas Botswana 50 E2
Xangda China see Nangqên
Xangdin Hural China 43 L4
Xangdong China 37 E2
Xangongo Angola 49 B5
Xankändi Azer. 35 G3
Xanlar Azer. 35 G2
Xanthi Greece 27 K4
Xarag China 37 I1
Xarardheere Somalia 48 E3
Xàtiva Spain 25 F4
Xavantes, Serra dos hills Brazil 69 I6
Xaxa China 37 G2
Xayar China 42 E4
Xela Guat. see Quetzaltenango
Xelva Spain see Chelva
Xero Potamos r. Cyprus see Xeros
Xeros r. Cyprus 39 A2
Xhora S. Africa see Elliotdale
Xiabole Shan mt. China 44 B2
Xiaguan China see Dali
Xiamen China 43 L8
Xi'an China 43 J5
Xianfeng China 43 J7
Xiangfan China 43 K6
Xianggang H.K. China see Hong Kong
Xianggang Tebie Xingzhengqu aut. reg. China see Hong Kong
Xianggelila China 42 H7
Xiangkhoang Laos 41 C6
Xiangning China 43 K5
Xiangquan He r. China see Langqên Zangbo
Xiangride China 37 I2
Xiangtan China 43 K7
Xiangyang China see Xiangfan
Xiangyang Hu l. China 37 G2
Xianning China 43 K7
Xiantao China 43 K6
Xianxia Ling mts China 43 L7
Xianyang China 43 J6
Xiaocaohu China 42 F4
Xiao'ergou China 44 A2
Xiaogan China 43 K6
Xiao Hinggan Ling mts China 44 B2
Xiaonanchuan China 37 H2
Xiaoshi China see Benxi
Xiao Surmang China 37 I2
Xiashan China see Zhanjiang
Xiayingpan Guizhou China see Lupanshui
Xichang China 42 I7
Xieng Khouang Laos see Xiangkhoang
Xifeng Liaoning China 44 B4
Xigazê China 37 G3
Xi Jiang r. China 43 K8
Xijir China 37 G2
Xijir Ulan Hu salt l. China 37 G2
Xiliao He r. China 43 M4
Xilinhot China 43 L4
Ximiao China 42 I4
Xinavane Moz. 51 K3
Xin Barag Zuoqi China see Amgalang
Xincun China see Dongchuan
Xindian China 44 B3
Xindu Sichuan China see Luhuo
Xing'an Shaanxi China see Ankang
Xingba China 42 G7
Xingba China see Xingba
Xingguo Jiangxi China 43 L7
Xinghai China 42 H5
Xingkai China 44 D3
Xingkai Hu l. China/Rus. Fed. see Khanka, Lake
Xinglong China 44 A2
Xinglongzhen Heilong. China 44 B3
Xingning Guangdong China 43 L8
Xingtai China 43 K5
Xingu r. Brazil 69 H4
Xingu, Parque Indígena do res. Brazil 69 H6
Xinguara Brazil 69 H5
Xingyi China 43 J7
Xinhua Yunnan China see Funing
Xinhuang China 43 J7
Xining China 42 I5
Xinjiang aut. reg. China see Xinjiang Uygur Zizhiqu
Xinjiang Uygur Zizhiqu aut. reg. China 36 E1
Xinkai He r. China 44 A4
Xinlitun China 44 B2
Xinmin China 44 B2
Xinning Gansu China see Ningxian
Xinqing China 44 C2
Xintai China 43 L5
Xinxiang China 43 K5
Xinyang Henan China 43 K6
Xinyi Jiangsu China 43 L5
Xinyu China 43 K7
Xinyuan Qinghai China see Tianjun
Xinyuan Xinjiang China 42 E4
Xinzhangfang China 44 A2
Xinzhou Shanxi China 43 K5
Xinzhu Taiwan see Hsinchu
Xinzo de Limia Spain 25 C2
Xiongzhou China see Nanxiong

Xiqing Shan mts China 42 I6
Xique Xique Brazil 69 J6
Xisha Qundao is S. China Sea see Paracel Islands
Xiugu China see Jinxi
Xi Ujimqin Qi China see Bayan Ul Hot
Xiwu China 37 I2
Xixabangma Feng mt. China 37 F3
Xixiang China 43 J6
Xixiu China see Anshun
Xixón Spain see Gijón-Xixón
Xizang aut. reg. China see Xizang Zizhiqu
Xizang Gaoyuan plat. China see Tibet, Plateau of
Xizang Zizhiqu aut. reg. China 37 G3
Xo'jayli Uzbek. 33 I1
Xorkol China 42 G5
Xuanhua China 43 L4
Xuanwei China 42 I7
Xucheng China see Xuwen
Xuddur Somalia 48 E3
Xugui China 42 H5
Xuguit Qi China see Yakeshi
Xümatang China 37 I2
Xungba China see Xangdoring
Xungmai China 37 G3
Xunhe China 44 C2
Xun He r. China 44 C2
Xun Jiang r. China 40 D5
Xuru Co salt l. China 37 G3
Xuwen China 31 K4
Xuyong China 42 J7
Xuzhou China see Xuzhou
Xuzhou China 43 L6

Ya'an China 42 I6
Yabanabat Turkey see Kızılcahamam
Yabêlo Eth. 48 D3
Yablonovyy Khrebet mts Rus. Fed. 43 J2
Yabuli China 44 C3
Yacuma r. Bol. 68 E6
Yadgir India 38 C2
Yadrin Rus. Fed. 12 J5
Yaeyama-rettō is Japan 43 M8
Yafa Israel see Tel Aviv-Yafo
Yagaba Ghana 46 C3
Yagan China 42 I4
Yağda Turkey see Erdemli
Yaghan Basin sea feature S. Atlantic Ocean 72 D9
Yagman Turkm. 35 I3
Yagodnoye Rus. Fed. 29 P3
Yagodnyy Rus. Fed. 44 E2
Yagoua Cameroon 47 E3
Yagra China 37 F3
Yagradagzê Shan mt. China 37 H2
Yahualica Mex. 66 D4
Yahyalı Turkey 23 L4
Yaizu Japan 45 E6
Yakacık Turkey 39 C1
Yakeshi China 43 M3
Yakima U.S.A. 62 C2
Yako Burkina 46 C3
Yakovlevka Rus. Fed. 44 D3
Yaku-shima i. Japan 45 C7
Yakutat U.S.A. 60 E4
Yakutat Bay U.S.A. 60 D4
Yakutsk Rus. Fed. 29 N3
Yakymivka Ukr. 13 G7
Yala Thai. 31 C5
Yalai China 37 F3
Yala National Park Sri Lanka see Ruhuna National Park
Yalan Dünya Mağarası tourist site Turkey 39 U4
Yalgoo Australia 55 B7
Yalleroi Australia 56 D5
Yaloké Cent. Afr. Rep. 48 B3
Yalova Turkey 27 M4
Yalta Ukr. 34 D1
Yalu r. China/N. Korea 44 B4
Yalujiang Kou r. mouth China/N. Korea 45 B5
Yalvaç Turkey 27 N5
Yamagata Japan 45 F5
Yamaguchi Japan 45 C6
Yamal, Poluostrov pen. Rus. Fed. see Yamal Peninsula
Yam Alin', Khrebet mts Rus. Fed. 44 D1
Yamal Peninsula Rus. Fed. 28 H2
Yamanie Falls National Park Australia 56 D3
Yamba Australia 58 F2
Yambarran Range hills Australia 54 E3
Yambi, Mesa de hills Col. 68 D3
Yambio Sudan 47 F4
Yambol Bulg. 27 L3
Yamdena i. Indon. 54 E1
Yamethin Myanmar 37 I5
Yamkanmardi India 38 B2
Yamkhad Syria see Aleppo
Yamm Rus. Fed. 15 P7
Yamma Yamma, Lake salt flat Australia 57 C5
Yamoussoukro Côte d'Ivoire 46 C4
Yampil' Ukr. see Yampil'
Yamuna r. India 36 E4
Yamunanagar India 36 D3
Yamzho Yumco l. China 37 G3
Yana r. Rus. Fed. 29 O2
Yanam India 38 D2
Yan'an China 43 J5
Yanaoca Peru 68 D6
Yanaon India see Yanam
Yanaul Rus. Fed. 11 Q4
Yanbu' al Baḥr Saudi Arabia 32 E5
Yancheng Jiangsu China 43 M6
Yanchep Australia 55 A7
Yanco Australia 58 C5
Yanco Creek r. Australia 58 B5
Yanco Glen Australia 57 C4
Yanda watercourse Australia 58 B3
Yandama Creek watercourse Australia 57 C6
Yandun China 42 G4
Yanfolila Mali 46 C3
Ya'ngamdo China 37 H3
Yangdok N. Korea 45 B5
Yang Hu l. China 37 F2
Yangiqishloq Uzbek. 33 K1
Yangirabot Uzbek. 33 K1
Yangi'ol Uzbek. 42 B4
Yangôn Myanmar see Rangoon
Yangquan China 43 K5
Yangtze r. Qinghai China 42 H6
Yangtze r. China 43 M6
Yangtze Kiang r. Qinghai China see Yangtze
Yangtze Kiang r. China see Yangtze
Yangudi Rassa National Park Eth. 48 E2
Yangyang S. Korea 45 C5
Yangzhou Jiangsu China 43 L6
Yanhuqu China 37 E2

Yanishpole Rus. Fed. 12 G3
Yanis"yarvi, Ozero l. Rus. Fed. 14 Q5
Yanji China 44 C4
Yanjiang China see Ziyang
Yanjing Sichuan China see Yanyuan
Yankara National Park Nigeria 46 E4
Yankton U.S.A. 62 H3
Yannina Greece see Ioannina
Yano-Indigirskaya Nizmennost' lowland Rus. Fed. 29 P2
Yanrey r. Australia 55 A5
Yanshan Yunnan China 42 I8
Yanshiping China 37 H2
Yanskiy Zaliv g. Rus. Fed. 29 O2
Yantabulla Australia 58 B2
Yantai China 43 M5
Yantongshan China 44 B4
Yany-Kurgan Kazakh. see Zhanakorgan
Yanyuan China 42 I7
Yao Chad 47 E3
Yaoundé Cameroon 46 E4
Yaoxiaoling China 44 B2
Yap i. Micronesia 41 F7
Yapen i. Indon. 41 F8
Yappar r. Australia 56 C3
Yap Trench sea feature N. Pacific Ocean 74 F5
Yaqui r. Mex. 66 B3
Yar Rus. Fed. 12 L4
Yaraka Australia 56 D5
Yarangüme Turkey see Tavas
Yaransk Rus. Fed. 12 J4
Yardea Australia 57 B7
Yardımcı Burnu pt Turkey 27 N6
Yardımlı Azer. 35 H3
Yardymly Azer. see Yardımlı
Yare r. U.K. 19 I6
Yarega Rus. Fed. 12 L3
Yaren Nauru 53 G2
Yarensk Rus. Fed. 12 K3
Yariga-take mt. Japan 45 E5
Yarim Yemen 32 F7
Yarımca Turkey see Körfez
Yarkand China see Shache
Yarkant China see Shache
Yarkant He r. China 33 M2
Yarkhun r. Pak. 36 C1
Yarlung Zangbo r. China see Brahmaputra
Yarmouth Canada 63 N3
Yarmouth England U.K. 19 F8
Yarmouth England U.K. see Great Yarmouth
Yarmuk r. Asia 39 B3
Yarnell AZ U.S.A. 65 F3
Yaroslavl' Rus. Fed. 12 H4
Yaroslavskiy Rus. Fed. 44 D3
Yarra r. Australia 58 B6
Yarram Australia 58 C7
Yarraman Australia 58 E1
Yarrawonga Australia 58 B6
Yarronvale Australia 58 B1
Yarra Junction Australia 58 B6
Yarra Yarra Lakes salt flat Australia 55 A7
Yarrowmere Australia 56 D4
Yartö Tra La pass China 37 H3
Yartsevo Krasnoyarskiy Kray Rus. Fed. 28 J3
Yartsevo Smolenskaya Oblast' Rus. Fed. 13 G5
Yarumal Col. 68 C2
Yaş Romania see Iaşi
Yasawa Group is Fiji 53 H3
Yashkul' Rus. Fed. 13 J7
Yasin Jammu and Kashmir 36 C1
Yasnogorsk Rus. Fed. 13 H5
Yasnyy Rus. Fed. 11 Q2
Yass Australia 58 D5
Yass r. Australia 58 D5
Yassı Burnu c. Cyprus see Plakoti, Cape
Yāsūj Iran 35 H5
Yasuní, Parque Nacional nat. park Ecuador 68 C4
Yatağan Turkey 27 M6
Yaté New Caledonia 53 G4
Yathkyed Lake Canada 61 I3
Yatsushiro Japan 45 C6
Yatta West Bank 39 B4
Yatton U.K. 19 E7
Yauca Peru 68 D7
Yavari r. Brazil/Peru 68 E4
Yavatmal India 38 C1
Yavi Turkey 35 F3
Yaví, Cerro mt. Venez. 68 E2
Yavoriv Ukr. 33 D6
Yavuzlu Turkey 39 C1
Yawatongguzlangar China 37 E1
Yaw Chaung r. Myanmar 37 H5
Yaxian China see Sanya
Yayladağı Turkey 39 C2
Yazd Iran 35 I5
Yazd-e Khvāst Iran 35 I5
Yazıhan Turkey 34 E3
Yazoo City U.S.A. 63 I5
Y Bala U.K. see Bala
Yding Skovhøj hill Denmark 17 L3
Ydra i. Greece 27 J6
Y Drenewydd U.K. see Newtown
Yea Australia 58 B6
Yealmpton U.K. 19 D8
Yebawmi Myanmar 37 H4
Yebbi-Bou Chad 47 E2
Yecheng China 42 C5
Yécora Mex. 66 C3
Yedatore India 38 C3
Yedi Burun Başı pt Turkey 27 M6
Yeeda River Australia 54 C4
Yefremov Rus. Fed. 13 H5
Yeghegnadzor Armenia 35 G3
Yegindykol' Kazakh. 42 D2
Yegorlykskaya Rus. Fed. 13 I7
Yegorova, Mys pt Rus. Fed. 44 E3
Yegor'yevsk Rus. Fed. 13 H5
Yei Sudan 47 G4
Yei r. Sudan 47 G4
Yejiji China 43 L6
Yejiaji China see Yeji
Yekaterinburg Rus. Fed. 28 I4
Yekaterinodar Rus. Fed. see Krasnodar
Yekaterinoslav Ukr. see Dnipropetrovs'k
Yekaterinoslavka Rus. Fed. 44 C2
Yekaterinovka Rus. Fed. see Yeghegnadzor
Yelabuga Khabarovskiy Kray Rus. Fed. 44 D2
Yelabuga Respublika Tatarstan Rus. Fed. 12 K5
Yelan' Rus. Fed. 13 I6
Yelan' r. Rus. Fed. 13 I6
Yelandur India 38 C3
Yelantsy Rus. Fed. 42 I2
Yelarbon Australia 58 E2
Yelenovskiye Kar'yery Ukr. see Dokuchayevs'k
Yelets Rus. Fed. 13 H5
Yélimané Mali 46 B3
Yelizavetgrad Ukr. see Kirovohrad
Yelkhovka Rus. Fed. 13 K5
Yell i. U.K. 20 [inset]
Yellabina Regional Reserve nature res. Australia 55 F7
Yellandu India 38 D2
Yellapur India 38 B3
Yellow r. China 43 L5
Yellowknife Canada 60 G3

Yellow Mountain hill Australia 58 C4
Yellow Sea N. Pacific Ocean 43 N5
Yellowstone r. U.S.A. 62 G2
Yellowstone Lake U.S.A. 62 E3
Yell Sound strait U.K. 20 [inset]
Yelovo Rus. Fed. 11 Q4
Yel'sk Belarus 13 F6
Yelva r. Rus. Fed. 12 K3
Yematan China 37 I2
Yemen country Asia 32 G6
Yemetsk Rus. Fed. 12 I3
Yemişenbükü Turkey see Taşova
Yemmiganur India see Emmiganuru
Yemtsa Rus. Fed. 12 I3
Yemva Rus. Fed. 12 K3
Yena Rus. Fed. 14 Q3
Yenagoa Nigeria 46 D4
Yenakiyeve Ukr. 13 H6
Yenakiyevo Ukr. see Yenakiyeve
Yenangyat Myanmar 37 H5
Yenangyaung Myanmar 37 H5
Yenanma Myanmar 37 H6
Yenda Australia 58 C5
Yengo National Park Australia 58 E4
Yenice Turkey 27 L5
Yenidamlar Turkey see Demirtaş
Yenihan Turkey see Yıldızeli
Yenije-i-Vardar Greece see Giannitsa
Yenişehir Greece see Larisa
Yenişehir Turkey 27 M4
Yenisey r. Rus. Fed. 28 J2
Yenisey-Angara-Selenga r. Rus. Fed. 28 J2
Yeniseysk Rus. Fed. 28 K4
Yeniseyskiy Kryazh ridge Rus. Fed. 28 K4
Yeniseyskiy Zaliv inlet Rus. Fed. 77 F2
Yeniyol Turkey see Borçka
Yenotayevka Rus. Fed. 13 J7
Yeola India 38 B1
Yeo Lake salt flat Australia 55 D6
Yeotmal India see Yavatmal
Yeoval Australia 58 D4
Yeovil U.K. 19 E8
Yeo Yeo r. Australia see Bland
Yeppoon Australia 56 E4
Yerakhtur Rus. Fed. see Kuryk
Yeraliyev Kazakh. see Kuryk
Yerbogachen Rus. Fed. 29 L3
Yercaud India 38 C4
Yerevan Armenia 35 G2
Yereymentau Kazakh. 42 C2
Yergara India 38 C2
Yergeni hills Rus. Fed. 13 J7
Yergoğu Romania see Giurgiu
Yeriho West Bank see Jericho
Yerilla Australia 55 C7
Yerington NV U.S.A. 65 C1
Yerköy Turkey 34 D3
Yerla r. India 38 B2
Yermak Kazakh. see Aksu
Yermakovo Rus. Fed. 44 B1
Yermak Plateau sea feature Arctic Ocean 77 H1
Yermentau Kazakh. see Yereymentau
Yermo CA U.S.A. 65 D3
Yerofey Pavlovich Rus. Fed. 44 A1
Yeroham Israel 39 B4
Yersa r. Rus. Fed. 12 L2
Yershov Rus. Fed. 13 K6
Yertsevo Rus. Fed. 12 I3
Yerupaja mt. Peru 68 C6
Yerushalayim Israel/West Bank see Jerusalem
Yeruslan r. Rus. Fed. 13 J6
Yesagyo Myanmar 37 H5
Yesan S. Korea 45 B5
Yesil' Kazakh. 30 F1
Yeşilhisar Turkey 34 D3
Yeşilırmak r. Turkey 34 E2
Yeşilova Burdur Turkey 27 M6
Yeşilova Yozgat Turkey see Sorgun
Yessentuki Rus. Fed. 35 F1
Yessey Rus. Fed. 29 L3
Yes Tor hill U.K. 19 C8
Yêtatang China see Baqên
Yetman Australia 58 E2
Ye-U Myanmar 37 H5
Yeu, Île d' i. France 24 C3
Yevdokimovskoye Rus. Fed. see Krasnogvardeyskoye
Yevlakh Azer. see Yevlax
Yevlax Azer. 35 G2
Yevpatoriya Ukr. 34 D1
Yevreyskaya Avtonomnaya Oblast' admin. div. Rus. Fed. 44 D2
Yexian China see Laizhou
Yeyik China 37 E1
Yeysk Rus. Fed. 13 H7
Yeyungou China 42 F4
Yezhuga r. Rus. Fed. 12 J2
Yezo i. Japan see Hokkaidō
Yezyaryshcha Belarus 12 F5
Y Fenni U.K. see Abergavenny
Y Fflint U.K. see Flint
Y Gelli Gandryll U.K. see Hay-on-Wye
Yiali i. Greece see Gyali
Yi'allaq, Gebel mt. Egypt see Yu'alliq, Jabal
Yialousa Cyprus see Aigialousa
Yi'an China 44 B3
Yianisádha i. Greece see Gianisada
Yiannitsá Greece see Giannitsa
Yibin China 42 I7
Yibug Caka salt l. China 37 F2
Yichang Hubei China 43 K6
Yicheng Henan China see Zhumadian
Yichun Heilong. China 44 B3
Yichun Jiangxi China 43 K7
Yilaha China 44 A2
Yilan China 44 C3
Yilan Taiwan see Ilan
Yıldız Dağları mts Turkey 27 L4
Yıldızeli Turkey 34 E3
Yilong Heilong. China 44 B3
Yimianpo China 44 C3
Yinchuan China 42 J5
Yindarlgooda, Lake salt flat Australia 55 C7
Yinggehai China 43 J5
Yingkou China 43 M4
Yingtan China 43 L7
Yining Xinjiang China 42 E4
Yinmabin Myanmar 37 H5
Yin Shan mts China 43 J4
Yinxian China see Ningbo
Yirga Alem Eth. 48 D3
Yirol Sudan 47 G4
Yishan Guangxi China see Yizhou
Yishui China 43 L5
Yíthion Greece see Gytheio
Yitiaoshan China see Jingtai
Yitong He r. China 44 B3
Yitulihe China 44 A2
Yixing China 43 L6
Yiyang China 43 K7
Yizhou China 43 J8
Yizre'el Israel see Jezreel
Yläne Fin. 15 M6
Ylihärmä Fin. 14 M5
Yli-Ii Fin. 14 N4
Yli-Kärppä Fin. 14 N4
Ylikiiminki Fin. 14 O4
Yli-Kitka l. Fin. 14 P3

Ylistaro Fin. 14 M5
Ylitornio Fin. 14 M3
Ylivieska Fin. 14 N4
Ylöjärvi Fin. 15 M6
Ymer Ø i. Greenland 61 P2
Ynys Enlli i. U.K. see Bardsey Island
Ynys Môn i. U.K. see Anglesey
Yogan, Cerro mt. Chile 70 B8
Yogyakarta Indon. 41 D8
Yokadouma Cameroon 47 E4
Yokkaichi Japan 45 E6
Yoko Cameroon 46 E4
Yokohama Japan 45 E6
Yokosuka Japan 45 E6
Yokote Japan 45 F5
Yola Nigeria 46 E4
Yolo CA U.S.A. 65 B1
Yolombo Dem. Rep. Congo 48 C4
Yoloten Turkm. 33 J2
Yolöten Turkm. see Yoloten
Yomou Guinea 46 C4
Yonezawa Japan 45 F5
Yong'an Fujian China 43 L7
Yonghung N. Korea 45 B5
Yonghung-man b. N. Korea 45 B5
Yongil-man b. S. Korea 45 C6
Yongjing Liaoning China see Xifeng
Yongju S. Korea 45 C5
Yongkang Yunnan China 42 H8
Yongning Sichuan China see Xuyong
Yongxiu China 43 L7
Yongzhou China 43 K7
Yonkers NY U.S.A. 64 E2
Yopal Col. 68 D2
Yopurga China 42 D5
Yordu Jammu and Kashmir 36 C2
York Australia 55 B7
York Ont. Canada 64 B1
York U.K. 18 F5
York PA U.S.A. 64 C3
York, Cape Australia 56 C1
York, Kap c. Greenland see Innaanganeq
York, Vale of valley U.K. 18 F4
Yorke Peninsula Australia 57 B7
Yorkshire Dales National Park U.K. 18 E4
Yorkshire Wolds hills U.K. 18 G5
Yorkton Canada 62 G1
Yorktown VA U.S.A. 64 C4
Yorosso Mali 46 C3
Yosemite National Park CA U.S.A. 65 C2
Yoshkar-Ola Rus. Fed. 12 J4
Yos Sudarso i. Indon. see Dolok, Pulau
Yôsu S. Korea 45 B6
Yotvata Israel 39 B5
Youghal Ireland 21 E6
Young Australia 58 D5
Younghusband, Lake salt flat Australia 57 B6
Younghusband Peninsula Australia 57 B7
Young Island Antarctica 76 H2
Youngstown OH U.S.A. 64 E2
Youssoufia Morocco 22 C5
Youvarou Mali 46 C3
Youyang China 43 J7
Youyi China 44 C3
Youyi Feng mt. China/Rus. Fed. 42 F3
Yowah watercourse Australia 58 B2
Yozgat Turkey 34 D3
Ypres Belgium see Ieper
Yreka U.S.A. 62 C3
Yrghyz Kazakh. see Irgiz
Yr Wyddfa mt. U.K. see Snowdon
Ystad Sweden 15 H9
Ystwyth r. U.K. 19 C6
Ysyk-Köl Kyrg. see Balykchy
Ysyk-Köl salt l. Kyrg. 42 D4
Ythan r. U.K. 20 G3
Y Trallwng U.K. see Welshpool
Ytyk-Kyuyel' Rus. Fed. 29 O3
Yu'alliq, Jabal mt. Egypt 39 A4
Yuanlin China 44 A2
Yuanquan China see Anxi
Yub'a i. Saudi Arabia 34 D6
Yuba City CA U.S.A. 65 B1
Yucatán pen. Mex. 66 F5
Yucatan Channel Cuba/Mex. 67 G4
Yucca AZ U.S.A. 65 F3
Yucca Lake NV U.S.A. 65 D2
Yucca Valley CA U.S.A. 65 D3
Yucheng Sichuan China see Ya'an
Yuci China see Jinzhong
Yudi Shan mt. China 44 A1
Yuelai China see Huachuan
Yueliang Pao l. China 44 A3
Yuendumu Australia 54 E5
Yuexi China 43 L6
Yueyang Hunan China 43 K7
Yug r. Rus. Fed. 12 J3
Yugorsk Rus. Fed. 11 S3
Yuhu China see Eryuan
Yuin Australia 55 B6
Yukagirskoye Ploskogor'ye plat. Rus. Fed. 29 Q3
Yukamenskoye Rus. Fed. 12 L4
Yukarı Sakarya Ovaları plain Turkey 27 N5
Yukarısarıkaya Turkey 34 D3
Yukon r. Canada/U.S.A. 60 B3
Yukon Territory admin. div. Canada 60 E3
Yüksekova Turkey 35 G3
Yulara Australia 55 E6

Yule r. Australia 54 B5
Yuleba Australia 58 D1
Yulin Guangxi China 43 K8
Yulin Shaanxi China 43 J5
Yulong Xueshan mt. China 42 I7
Yuma AZ U.S.A. 65 E4
Yumen China 42 H5
Yumenguan China 42 G4
Yumurtalık Turkey 39 B1
Yuna Australia 55 A7
Yunak Turkey 34 C3
Yunaska Island U.S.A. 60 A4
Yuncheng China 43 K6
Yundamindera Australia 55 C7
Yungas reg. Bol. 68 E7
Yungui Gaoyuan plat. China 42 I7
Yunjinghong China see Jinghong
Yunkai Dashan mts China 43 K8
Yunling China see Yunxiao
Yunnan prov. China 42 I8
Yunta Australia 57 B7
Yunt Dağı mt. Turkey 39 A1
Yunxiao China 43 L8
Yuraygir National Park Australia 58 F2
Yurba Co l. China 37 F2
Yürekli Turkey 39 B1
Yurga Rus. Fed. 28 J4
Yuriria Mex. 66 D4
Yurungkax He r. China 36 E1
Yur'ya Rus. Fed. 12 K4
Yur'yakha r. Rus. Fed. 12 L2
Yuryev Estonia see Tartu
Yur'yevets Rus. Fed. 12 I4
Yur'yev-Pol'skiy Rus. Fed. 12 H4
Yü Shan mt. Taiwan 43 M8
Yushino Rus. Fed. 12 L1
Yushkozero Rus. Fed. 12 G2
Yushu Jilin China 44 B3
Yushu Qinghai China 42 H6
Yushuwan China see Huaihua
Yusufeli Turkey 35 F2
Yus'va Rus. Fed. 11 Q4
Yuta West Bank see Yatta
Yuxi Yunnan China 42 I8
Yuzawa Japan 45 F5
Yuzha Rus. Fed. 12 I4
Yuzhno-Kamyshovyy Khrebet ridge Rus. Fed. 44 F3
Yuzhno-Kuril'sk Rus. Fed. 44 G3
Yuzhno-Muyskiy Khrebet mts Rus. Fed. 43 K1
Yuzhno-Sakhalinsk Rus. Fed. 44 F3
Yuzhno-Sukhokumsk Rus. Fed. 13 J7
Yuzhnoukrayinsk Ukr. 13 F7
Yuzhnyy Rus. Fed. see Adyk
Yuzhou Chongqing China see Chongqing
Yuzhou Henan China 43 K6
Yuzovka Ukr. see Donets'k
Yverdon Switz. 24 H3
Yvetot France 24 E2
Ywamun Myanmar 37 H5

Zaandam Neth. 16 J4
Zab, Monts du mts Alg. 25 I6
Zabaykal'sk Rus. Fed. 43 L3
Zabīd Yemen 32 F7
Zābol Iran 33 J3
Zacapa Guat. 66 G5
Zacatecas Mex. 66 D4
Zacharo Greece 27 I6
Zacoalco Mex. 66 D4
Zacynthus i. Greece see Zakynthos
Zadar Croatia 26 F2
Zadoi China 42 H6
Zadonsk Rus. Fed. 13 H5
Za'farāna Egypt see Za'faranah
Za'farānah Egypt 39 A4
Zafer Adalan is Cyprus see Kleides Islands
Zafer Burnu c. Cyprus see Apostolos Andreas, Cape
Zafra Spain 25 C4
Zagazig Egypt see Az Zaqāzīq
Zaghouan Tunisia 26 D6
Zagorsk Rus. Fed. see Sergiyev Posad
Zagreb Croatia 26 F2
Zagros Mountains Iran 35 G4
Za'gya Zangbo r. China 37 G3
Zāhedān Iran 33 J4
Zahir Pir Pak. 36 B3
Zahlah Lebanon see Zahlé
Zahlé Lebanon 39 B3
Zahrān Saudi Arabia 32 F6
Zahrez Chergui salt pan Alg. 25 H6
Zahrez Rharbi salt pan Alg. 25 H6
Zainsk Rus. Fed. see Novyy Zay
Zaire country Africa see Congo, Democratic Republic of the
Zaïre r. Congo/Dem. Rep. Congo see Congo
Zaječar Serbia 27 J3
Zaka Zimbabwe 49 D6
Zakamensk Rus. Fed. 42 I2
Zakataly Azer. see Zaqatala
Zakháro Greece see Zacharo
Zākhō Iraq 35 F3

Zakhodnyaya Dzvina r. Europe see Zapadnaya Dvina
Zákinthos i. Greece see Zakynthos
Zakopane Poland 17 Q6
Zakouma, Parc National de nat. park Chad 47 E3
Zakynthos Greece 27 I6
Zakynthos i. Greece 27 I6
Zalaegerszeg Hungary 26 G1
Zalai-domsag hills Hungary 26 G1
Zalamea de la Serena Spain 25 D4
Zalantun China 44 A3
Zalari Rus. Fed. 42 I2
Zalău Romania 27 J1
Zalim Saudi Arabia 32 F5
Zalingei Sudan 47 F3
Zalmā, Jabal az mt. Saudi Arabia 32 E4
Zambeze r. Africa 49 C5 see Zambezi
Zambezi r. Africa 49 C5
Zambezi Zambia 49 C5
Zambia country Africa 49 C5
Zamboanga Phil. 41 E7
Zamfara watercourse Nigeria 46 D3
Zamkog China see Zamtang
Zamora Ecuador 68 C4
Zamora Spain 25 D3
Zamora de Hidalgo Mex. 66 D5
Zamość Poland 13 D6
Zamost'ye Poland see Zamość
Zamtang China 42 I6
Zamuro, Sierra del mts Venez. 68 F3
Zanaga Congo 48 B4
Zancle Sicily Italy see Messina
Zandamela Moz. 51 L3
Zanesville U.S.A. 64 D3
Zangguy China 36 D1
Zangsêr Kangri mt. China 37 F2
Zangskar reg. Jammu and Kashmir see Zanskar
Zangskar Mountains India see Zanskar Mountains
Zanjān Iran 35 H3
Zanjān Rūd r. Iran 35 G3
Zanskar reg. Jammu and Kashmir 36 D2
Zanskar Mountains India 36 D2
Zante i. Greece see Zakynthos
Zanthus Australia 55 C7
Zanzibar Tanz. 49 D4
Zanzibar Island Tanz. 49 D4
Zaouatallaz Alg. 46 D2
Zaouet el Kahla Alg. see Bordj Omer Driss
Zaozernyy Rus. Fed. 29 K4
Zaozhuang China 43 L6
Zapadnaya Dvina r. Europe 12 F5
Zapadnaya Dvina Rus. Fed. 12 G4
Zapadni Rodopi mts Bulg. 27 J4
Zapado-Kazakhstanskaya Oblast' admin. div. Kazakh. see Zapadnyy Kazakhstan
Zapadno-Sakhalinskiy Khrebet mts Rus. Fed. 44 F2
Zapadno-Sibirskaya Nizmennost' plain Rus. Fed. see West Siberian Plain
Zapadno-Sibirskaya Ravnina plain Rus. Fed. see West Siberian Plain
Zapadnyy Chink Ustyurta esc. Kazakh. 35 I2
Zapadnyy Kazakhstan admin. div. Kazakh. 11 Q6
Zapadnyy Kil'din Rus. Fed. 14 S2
Zapadnyy Sayan reg. Rus. Fed. 42 F2
Zapata U.S.A. 62 H6
Zapiga Chile 68 E7
Zapolyarnyy Rus. Fed. 12 F1
Zapol'ye Rus. Fed. 12 H4
Zaporizhzhia Ukr. 13 G7
Zaporozh'ye Ukr. see Zaporizhzhya
Zapug China 36 E2
Zaqatala Azer. 35 G2
Za Qu r. China 42 H6
Zaqungngomar mt. China 37 G2
Zara China see Moinda
Zara Croatia see Zadar
Zara Turkey 34 E3
Zarafshan Uzbek. see Zarafshon
Zarafshon Uzbek. 33 J1
Zaragoza Spain 25 F3
Zarand Iran 33 I3
Zarang China 36 D3
Zaranikh Reserve nature res. Egypt 39 B4
Zaranj Afgh. 33 J3
Zarasai Lith. 15 O9
Zárate Arg. 70 E4
Zaraysk Rus. Fed. 13 H5
Zaraza Venez. 68 E2
Zärdab Azer. 13 J8
Zarechensk Rus. Fed. 14 Q3
Zāreh Iran 35 H4
Zargun mt. Pak. 36 A3
Zari Afgh. 36 A2
Zaria Nigeria 46 D3
Zarichne Ukr. 13 E6
Zarifète, Col des pass Alg. 25 F6
Zaring China see Liangdaohe
Zarinsk Rus. Fed. 42 E2
Zarneh Iran 35 G4
Zărneşti Romania 27 K2

Zarqā' Jordan see Az Zarqā'
Zarqā', Nahr az r. Jordan 39 B3
Zarubino Rus. Fed. 44 C4
Żary Poland 17 O5
Zarzis Tunisia 22 G5
Zasheyek Rus. Fed. 14 Q3
Zaskar reg. Jammu and Kashmir see Zanskar
Zaskar Range mts India see Zanskar Mountains
Zaslawye Belarus 15 O9
Zastron S. Africa 51 H6
Za'tarī, Wādī az watercourse Jordan 39 C3
Zaterechnyy Rus. Fed. 13 J7
Zavetnoye Rus. Fed. 13 I7
Zavety Il'icha Rus. Fed. 44 F2
Zavidovići Bos.-Herz. 26 H2
Zavitaya Rus. Fed. see Zavitinsk
Zavitinsk Rus. Fed. 44 C2
Zavolzhsk Rus. Fed. 12 I4
Zavolzh'ye Rus. Fed. see Zavolzhsk
Závora, Ponta pt Moz. 51 L3
Zawiercie Poland 17 Q5
Zawīlah Libya 47 E2
Zäwiyah, Jabal az hills Syria 39 C2
Zaydī, Wādī az watercourse Syria 39 C3
Zaysan Kazakh. 42 F3
Zaysan, Lake Kazakh. see Zaysan, Lake
Zaysan, Ozero l. Kazakh. 42 F3
Zayü China see Gyigang
Zayü Qu r. China/India 37 I3
Žd'ar nad Sázavou Czech Rep. 17 O6
Zdolbuniv Ukr. 13 E6
Zdolbunov Ukr. see Zdolbuniv
Zealand i. Denmark 15 G9
Zêbâk Afgh. 36 B1
Zeerust S. Africa 51 H3
Zefat Israel 39 B3
Zeil, Mount Australia 55 F5
Zela Turkey see Zile
Zelenik Rus. Fed. 12 J3
Zelenoborsk Rus. Fed. 11 S3
Zelenoborskiy Rus. Fed. 14 R3
Zelenodol'sk Rus. Fed. 12 K5
Zelenogorsk Rus. Fed. 12 F3
Zelenograd Rus. Fed. 12 H4
Zelenogradsk Rus. Fed. 15 L9
Zelenokumsk Rus. Fed. 35 F1
Zelentsovo Rus. Fed. 12 J3
Zelenyy, Ostrov i. Rus. Fed. 44 G4
Zell am See Austria 17 N7
Žemaitijos nacionalinis parkas nat. park Lith. 15 L8
Zemetchino Rus. Fed. 13 I5
Zémio Cent. Afr. Rep. 48 C3
Zemmora Alg. 25 G6
Zempoaltépetl, Nudo de mt. Mex. 66 E5
Zenica Bos.-Herz. 26 G2
Zenifim watercourse Israel 39 B4
Zennor U.K. 19 B8
Zenta Serbia see Senta
Zenzach Alg. 25 H6
Zerenike Reserve nature res. Egypt see Zaranikh Reserve
Zernograd Rus. Fed. 13 I7
Zernovoy Rus. Fed. see Zernograd
Zêtang China 37 G3
Zeven Germany 17 L4
Zevgari, Cape Cyprus 39 A2
Zeya Rus. Fed. 44 B1
Zeya r. Rus. Fed. 44 B2
Zeyskiy Zapovednik nature res. Rus. Fed. 44 B1
Zeysko-Bureinskaya Vpadina depr. Rus. Fed. 44 C2
Zeyskoye Vodokhranilishche resr Rus. Fed. 44 B1
Zeytin Burnu c. Cyprus see Elaia, Cape
Zêzere r. Port. 25 B4
Zgharta Lebanon 39 B2
Zghorta Lebanon see Zgharta
Zgierz Poland 17 Q5
Zhabdün China see Zhongba
Zhabinka Belarus 15 N10
Zhaggo China see Luhuo
Zhaksy Sarysu watercourse Kazakh. see Sarysu
Zhalpaktal Kazakh. 11 P6
Zhalpaqtal Kazakh. see Zhalpaktal
Zhaltyr Kazakh. 38 H4
Zhambyl Karagandinskaya Oblast' Kazakh. 42 C3
Zhambyl Zhambylskaya Oblast' Kazakh. see Taraz
Zhamo China see Bomi
Zhanaozen Kazakh. 42 B4
Zhanaozen Kazakh. see Zhanaozen
Zhanatas Kazakh. 42 B4
Zhanbei China 44 B2
Zhangaözen Kazakh. see Zhanaozen
Zhanga Qazan Kazakh. see Novaya Kazanka
Zhangaqorghan Kazakh. see Zhanakorgan
Zhangatas Kazakh. see Zhanatas
Zhangbei China 43 K4
Zhangde China see Anyang
Zhangdian China see Zibo
Zhangguangcai Ling mts China 44 C3
Zhanghua Taiwan see Changhua
Zhangjiajie China 43 K7
Zhangjiakou China 43 K4

Zhangjiapan China see Jingbian
Zhangling China 44 A1
Zhangqiangzhen China 44 A4
Zhangshu China 43 L7
Zhangye China 42 I5
Zhangzhou China 43 L8
Zhanhe China see Zhanbei
Zhanibek Kazakh. 11 P6
Zhanjiang China 43 K8
Zhaodong China 44 B3
Zhaoqing China 43 K8
Zhaotong China 42 I7
Zhaoyuan China 44 B3
Zhaozhou China 44 B3
Zhari Namco salt l. China 37 F3
Zharkent Kazakh. 42 E4
Zharkovskiy Rus. Fed. 12 G5
Zharma Kazakh. 42 E3
Zhashkiv Ukr. 13 F6
Zhashkov Ukr. see Zhashkiv
Zhaslyk Uzbek. see Jasliq
Zhaxi Co salt l. China 37 F2
Zhaxigang China 36 D2
Zhaxizê China 37 I3
Zhaxizong China 37 F3
Zhayyq r. Kazakh./Rus. Fed. see Ural
Zhdanov Ukr. see Mariupol'
Zhdanovsk Azer. see Beyläqan
Zhejiang prov. China 43 M7
Zhelaniya, Mys c. Rus. Fed. 28 H2
Zheleznodorozhnyy Rus. Fed. see Yemva
Zheleznodorozhnyy Uzbek. see Qo'ng'irot
Zheleznogorsk Rus. Fed. 13 G5
Zheltyye Vody Ukr. see Zhovti Vody
Zhem Kazakh. see Emba
Zhengjiatun China see Shuangliao
Zhengzhou China 43 K6
Zhenlai China 44 A3
Zhenxi China 44 A3
Zhenyuan China 43 J7
Zherdevka Rus. Fed. 13 I6
Zheshart Rus. Fed. 12 K3
Zhêxam China 37 F3
Zhezkazgan Kazakh. see Zhezkazgan
Zhezqazghan Kazakh. see Zhezkazgan
Zhidoi China 42 H6
Zhigalovo Rus. Fed. 42 J2
Zhigansk Rus. Fed. 29 N3
Zhigung China 37 G3
Zhi Qu r. China see Yangtze
Zhitikara Kazakh. 30 I1
Zhitkovichi Belarus see Zhytkavichy
Zhitomir Ukr. see Zhytomyr
Zhïvär Iran 35 G4
Zhlobin Belarus 13 F5
Zhmerinka Ukr. see Zhmerynka
Zhmerynka Ukr. 13 F6
Zhob Pak. 33 K3
Zhob r. Pak. 36 B2
Zhongba Xizang China 37 F3
Zhongduo China see Youyang
Zhongguo country China see China
Zhongguo Renmin Gongheguo country Asia see China
Zhongping China see Huize
Zhongshan research station Antarctica 76 E2
Zhongwei China 42 J5
Zhongxin Yunnan China see Xianggelila
Zhongyaozhan China 44 B2
Zhosaly Kazakh. see Dzhusaly
Zhoujiajing China 42 I5
Zhoukou Henan China 43 K6
Zhoushan Dao i. China 43 M6
Zhovti Vody Ukr. 13 G6
Zhuanghe China 45 A5
Zhubgyügoin China 37 I2
Zhukovka Rus. Fed. 13 G5
Zhukovskiy Rus. Fed. 13 H5
Zhumadian China 43 K6
Zhuxi China 13 J6
Zhuzhou Hunan China 43 K7
Zhydachiv Ukr. 13 D6
Zhympity Kazakh. 11 Q5
Zhytkavichy Belarus 15 O10
Zhytomyr Ukr. 13 F6
Ziä'äbäd Iran 35 H4
Zibā salt pan Saudi Arabia 39 D4
Zibo China 43 L5
Zicheng China see Zijin
Zidi Pak. 36 A1
Ziel, Mount Australia see Zeil, Mount
Zielona Góra Poland 17 O5
Ziemelkursas augstiene hills Latvia 15 M8
Ziftá Egypt 34 C5
Zighan Libya 47 F2
Zigong China 42 I7
Ziguey Chad 47 E3
Ziguinchor Senegal 46 B3
Žiguri Latvia 15 O8
Zihuatanejo Mex. 66 D5
Zijin China 43 L8
Ziketan China see Xinghai
Zile Turkey 34 D2
Žilina Slovakia 17 Q6
Zillah Libya 47 E2

Zima Rus. Fed. 42 I2
Zimba Zambia 49 C5
Zimbabwe country Africa 49 C5
Zimi Sierra Leone see Zimmi
Zimmerbude Rus. Fed. see Svetlyy
Zimmi Sierra Leone 46 B4
Zimnicea Romania 27 K3
Zimniy Bereg coastal area Rus. Fed. 12 H2
Zimovniki Rus. Fed. 13 I7
Zimrīn Syria 39 B2
Zin watercourse Israel 39 B4
Zinave, Parque Nacional de nat. park Moz. 49 D6
Zinder Niger 46 D3
Ziniaré Burkina 46 C3
Zinjibār Yemen 32 G7
Zinoyevsk Ukr. see Kirovohrad
Zion National Park UT U.S.A. 65 F2
Zippori Israel 39 B3
Ziqudukou China 37 H2
Zirc Hungary 26 G1
Ziro India 37 H4
Zīr Rūd Iran 32 H4
Zi Shui r. China 43 K7
Zistersdorf Austria 17 P6
Zitácuaro Mex. 66 D5
Zito China see Lhorong
Zittau Germany 17 O6
Ziyang Sichuan China 42 I6
Ziyaret Dağı hill Turkey 39 B1
Ziz, Oued watercourse Morocco 22 D5
Zlatoustovsk Rus. Fed. 44 D1
Zlín Czech Rep. 17 P6
Zmeinogorsk Rus. Fed. 42 E2
Zmiyevka Rus. Fed. 13 H5
Znamenka Ukr. see Znam"yanka
Znam"yanka Ukr. 13 G6
Znojmo Czech Rep. 17 P6
Zoar S. Africa 50 E7
Zogang China 42 H7
Zoigê China 42 I6
Zoji La pass Jammu and Kashmir 36 C2
Zola S. Africa 51 H7
Zolochev Kharkiv's'ka Oblast' Ukr. see Zolochiv
Zolochev L'vivs'ka Oblast' Ukr. see Zolochiv
Zolochiv Kharkivs'ka Oblast' Ukr. 13 G6
Zolochiv L'vivs'ka Oblast' Ukr. 13 E6
Zolotonosha Ukr. 13 G6
Zolotoye Rus. Fed. 13 J6
Zolotukhino Rus. Fed. 13 H5
Zomba Malawi 49 D5
Zombor Serbia see Sombor
Zongga China see Gyirong
Zonguldak Turkey 27 N4
Zungoi China 37 G3
Zorgho Burkina 46 C3
Zorgo Burkina see Zorgho
Zory Poland 17 Q5
Zouar Chad 47 E2
Zouérat Mauritania 46 B2
Zousfana, Oued watercourse Alg. 22 D5
Zrenjanin Serbia 27 I2
Zubālah, Birkat waterhole Saudi Arabia 35 F5
Zubillaga Arg. 70 D5
Zubova Polyana Rus. Fed. 13 I5
Zubtsov Rus. Fed. 12 G4
Zuénoula Côte d'Ivoire 46 C4
Zug Switz. 24 I3
Zugdidi Georgia 35 F2
Zugspitze mt. Austria/Germany 17 M7
Zugu Nigeria 46 D3
Zuider Zee l. Neth. see IJsselmeer
Zújar r. Spain 25 D4
Zumba Ecuador 68 C4
Zunheboto India 37 H4
Zuni Mountains U.S.A. 62 F4
Zunyi Guizhou China 42 J7
Županja Croatia 26 H2
Züräbäd Āżarbāyjān-e Gharbī Iran 35 G3
Zürhen Ul Shan mts China 37 G2
Zürich Switz. 24 I3
Zuru Nigeria 46 D3
Zurzuna Turkey see Çıldır
Zuwārah Libya 46 E1
Zuyevka Rus. Fed. 12 K4
Zvishavane Zimbabwe 49 D6
Zvolen Slovakia 17 Q6
Zvornik Bos.-Herz. 27 H2
Zwedru Liberia 46 C4
Zweletemba S. Africa 50 D7
Zwelitsha S. Africa 51 H7
Zwettl Austria 17 O6
Zwickau Germany 17 N5
Zwolle Neth. 17 K4
Zygi Cyprus 39 A2
Zyryan Kazakh. see Zyryanovsk
Zyryanka Rus. Fed. 29 Q3
Zyryanovsk Kazakh. 42 E3
Zyyi Cyprus see Zygi